LITERATURE

LITERATURE

LITERATURE

An Introduction to Fiction,
Poetry, Drama, and Writing

TWELFTH EDITION

X. J. Kennedy

Dana Gioia
University of Southern California

PEARSON

Boston   Columbus   Indianapolis   New York   San Francisco   Upper Saddle River
Amsterdam   Cape Town   Dubai   London   Madrid   Milan   Munich   Paris   Montreal   Toronto
Delhi   Mexico City   São Paulo   Sydney   Hong Kong   Seoul   Singapore   Taipei   Tokyo

Vice President and Editor in Chief: Joe Terry
Senior Director of Development: Mary Ellen Curley
Senior Development Editor: Katharine Glynn
Executive Marketing Manager: Joyce Nilsen
Senior Supplements Editor: Donna Campion
Production Manager: Savoula Amanatidis
Project Coordination, Text Design, and Electronic Page Makeup: Cenveo Publisher Services,
   Nesbitt Graphics, Inc.
Cover Designer/Manager: John Callahan
Cover Image: Sailing at Argenteuil, c.1874 (oil on canvas), Monet, Claude (1840–1926)/Private
   Collection/The Bridgeman Art Library International
Photo Research: PreMedia Global USA
Senior Manufacturing Buyer: Roy L. Pickering, Jr.
Printer and Binder: RR Donnelley
Cover Printer: Lehigh-Phoenix Color Corporation–Hagerstown

Credits and acknowledgments borrowed from other sources and reproduced, with permission, in
this textbook appear on pages 2082–2099.

Library of Congress Cataloging-in-Publication Data

Literature : an introduction to fiction, poetry, drama, and writing / [compiled by] X.J. Kennedy,
Dana Gioia. – 12th ed.
   p. cm.
Includes index.
ISBN 978-0-205-23038-9 – ISBN 978-0-205-23039-6 (interactive)
1. Literature–Collections. I. Kennedy, X. J. II. Gioia, Dana.
PN6014.L58 2011
808–dc23

                    2011047149

Copyright © 2013, 2010, 2007, and 2005 by X. J. Kennedy and Dana Gioia.

10 9 8 7 6 5 4 —DOC—15 14

www.pearsonhighered.com

(Literature)
ISBN-10: 0-205-23038-5; ISBN-13: 978-0-205-23038-9
(Literature Interactive)
ISBN-10: 0-205-23039-3; ISBN-13: 978-0-205-23039-6
(Literature Portable)
ISBN-10: 0-205-22956-5; ISBN-13: 978-0-205-22956-7

CONTENTS

DRAMA

TALKING WITH *David Ives*   1148

36 CRITICAL CASEBOOK
Sophocles 1199

37 CRITICAL CASEBOOK
Shakespeare 1284

38 THE MODERN THEATER 1595

PREFACE

*L*iterature, Twelfth Edition—the book in your hands—is really four interlocking volumes sharing one cover. Each of the first three sections is devoted to one of the major literary forms—fiction, poetry, and drama. The fourth section is a comprehensive introduction to critical writing. All together, the book is an attempt to provide the college student with a reasonably compact introduction to the study and appreciation of stories, poems, and plays—as well as practical advice on the sort of writing expected in a college English course.

We assume that appreciation begins in delighted attention to words on a page. Speed reading has its uses; but at times, as Robert Frost said, the person who reads for speed "misses the best part of what a good writer puts into it." Close reading, then, is essential. Still, we do not believe that close reading tells us everything, that it is wrong to read a literary work by any light except that of the work itself. At times we suggest different approaches such as referring to the facts of an author's life, looking for myth, or seeing the conventions that typify a kind of writing—noticing, for instance, that an old mansion, cobwebbed and creaking, is the setting for a Gothic horror story.

Although we cannot help having a few convictions about the meanings of stories, poems, and plays, we have tried to step back and give you room to make up your own mind. Here and there, in the wording of a question, our opinions may occasionally stick out. If you should notice any, please feel free to ignore them. Be assured that no one interpretation, laid down by authority, is the only right one for any work of literature. Trust your own interpretation—provided that in making it you have looked clearly and carefully at the evidence.

Reading literature often will provide you with a reason to write. Following the fiction, poetry, and drama sections, there are several chapters that give the student writer some practical advice. It will guide you, step by step, in finding a topic, planning an essay, writing, revising, and putting your paper into finished form. Further, you will find there specific help in writing about fiction, poetry, and drama. There are also short features at the end of most chapters that provide help and perspective on writing about literature. In a few places we have even offered some suggestions about writing your own stories or poems—in case reading the selections in this book inspires you to try your hand at imaginative writing.

A WORD ABOUT CAREERS

Most students agree that to read celebrated writers such as William Faulkner, Emily Dickinson, and William Shakespeare is probably good for the spirit. Most students even take some pleasure in the experience. But many, not planning to teach English and impatient to begin some other career, wonder if the study of literature, however enjoyable, isn't a waste of time—or at least, an annoying obstacle.

This objection may seem reasonable at first glance, but it rests on a shaky assumption. Success in a career does not depend merely on learning the specialized information and skills required to join a profession. In most careers, according to one senior business executive, people often fail not because they don't understand their jobs, but because they don't understand their co-workers, their clients, or their customers. They don't ever see the world from another person's point of view. Their problem is a failure of imagination.

To leap over the wall of self and to look through another's eyes is valuable experience that literature offers. If you are lucky, you may never meet (or have to do business with) anyone exactly like Mrs. Turpin in the story "Revelation," and yet you will learn much about the kind of person she is from Flannery O'Connor's fictional portrait of her. What is it like to be black, a white may wonder? James Baldwin, Gwendolyn Brooks, Rita Dove, Langston Hughes, Zora Neale Hurston, Alice Walker, August Wilson, and others have knowledge to impart. What is it like to be a woman? If a man would like to learn, let him read (for a start) Sandra Cisneros, Kate Chopin, Susan Glaspell, Alice Munro, Sylvia Plath, Katherine Anne Porter, Flannery O'Connor, Adrienne Rich, and Amy Tan, and perhaps, too, Henrik Ibsen's A Doll's House and John Steinbeck's "The Chrysanthemums."

Plodding single-mindedly toward careers, some people are like horses wearing blinders. For many, the goals look fixed and predictable. Competent nurses, accountants, and dental technicians seem always in demand. Others may find that in our society some careers, like waves in the sea, will rise or fall unexpectedly. Think how many professions we now take for granted, which a few years ago didn't even exist: genetic engineering, energy conservation, digital editing, and website design. Others that once looked like lifetime meal tickets have been cut back and nearly ruined: shoe repairing, commercial fishing, railroading.

In a perpetually changing society, it may be risky to lock yourself on one track to a career, refusing to consider any other. "We are moving," writes John Naisbitt in Megatrends, a study of our changing society, "from the specialist, soon obsolete, to the generalist who can adapt." Perhaps the greatest opportunity in your whole life lies in a career that has yet to be invented. If you do change your career as you go along, you will be like most people. According to a U.S. Bureau of Labor Statistics survey conducted in September 2010, the average American holds over eleven jobs between the ages of 18 and 44—often completely changing his or her basic occupation. When for some unforeseen reason you have to make such a change, basic skills—and a knowledge of humanity—may be your most valuable credentials.

Literature has much practical knowledge to offer you. An art of words, it can help you become more sensitive to language—both your own and other people's. It can make you aware of the difference between the word that is exactly right and the word that is merely good enough—Mark Twain calls it "the difference between the lightning and the lightning-bug." Read a fine work of literature alertly, and some of its writer's sensitivity to words may grow on you. A Supreme Court Justice, John Paul Stevens, once remarked that the best preparation for law school is to study poetry. Why? George D. Gopen, an English professor with a law degree, says it may be because "no other discipline so closely replicates the central question asked in the study of legal thinking: Here is a text; in how many ways can it have meaning?"

Many careers today, besides law, call for close reading and clear writing—as well as careful listening and thoughtful speech. Lately, college placement directors have reported more demand for graduates who are good readers and writers. The reason is evident: Employers need people who can handle words. In a survey conducted by Cornell University, business executives were asked to rank in importance the traits they look for when hiring. Leadership was first, but skill in writing and speaking came in fourth, ahead of both managerial and analytical skills. Times change, but to think cogently and to express yourself well will always be the abilities the world needs.

KEY LITERARY TERMS

Every discipline has its own terminology. This book introduces a large range of critical terms that may help you in both your reading and writing. When these important words and phrases are first defined, they are printed in **boldface**. If you find a critical term anywhere in this book you don't know or don't recall (for example, what is a *carpe diem* poem or a *dramatic question?*), just check the Index of Literary Terms in the back of the book, and you'll see the page where the term is discussed; or look it up in the Glossary of Literary Terms, also at the back of the book.

TEXTS AND DATES

Every effort has been made to supply each selection in its most accurate text and (where necessary) in a lively, faithful translation. For the reader who wishes to know when a work was written, at the right of each title appears the date of its first publication in book form. Parentheses around a date indicate the work's date of composition or first magazine publication, given when it was composed much earlier than when it was first published in book form.

But enough housekeeping—let's enjoy ourselves and read some unforgettable stories, poems, and plays.

X. J. K. AND D. G.

TO THE INSTRUCTOR

*L*iterature is a book with two major goals. First, it introduces college students to the appreciation and experience of literature in its major forms. Second, the book tries to develop the student's ability to think critically and communicate effectively through writing.

Both editors of this volume are writers. We believe that textbooks should be not only informative and accurate but also lively, accessible, and engaging. In education, it never hurts to have a little fun. Our intent has always been to write a book that students will read eagerly and enjoy.

WHAT'S NEW TO THIS EDITION?

- **Eleven new stories**—including Isabel Allende's "The Judge's Wife," David Leavitt's "A Place I've Never Been," Eudora Welty's "A Worn Path," Daniel Orozco's "Orientation," Anne Tyler's "Teenage Wasteland," Ray Bradbury's now-classic "A Sound of Thunder," and ZZ Packer's "Brownies," as well as new fables by Aesop and Bidpai.
- **New casebook on Edgar Allan Poe's fiction**—featuring three of Poe's most popular stories ("The Tell-Tale Heart," "The Cask of Amontillado," and "The Fall of the House of Usher"), excerpts from his critical writing, interesting illustrations, plus insightful and accessible prose excerpts by Poe scholars.
- **Sixty-five new poems**—ranging from classic selections by John Keats, Emily Dickinson, Gwendolyn Brooks, Jorge Luis Borges, Robert Hayden, Antonio Machado, H.D., Robinson Jeffers, and William Shakespeare to fresh contemporary works by Kay Ryan, Rafael Campo, Harryette Mullen, Derek Walcott, Lorna Dee Cervantes, Carolyn Kizer, Amit Majmudar, Katha Pollitt, Brian Turner, and Julie Sheehan.
- **Four new one-act plays**—providing greater flexibility in studying diverse contemporary trends in a crowded curriculum. The new works include two short comedies, David Ives's *Sure Thing* and Jane Martin's *Beauty*, as well as Milcha Sanchez-Scott's *The Cuban Swimmer* and Edward Bok Lee's experimental *El Santo Americano*.
- **New audio version of *Trifles***—specially created for this edition by the celebrated L.A. Theatre Works. To help students less familiar with the experience of live theater, we offer this new audio production of Susan Glaspell's *Trifles* (featured in our introductory "Reading a Play" chapter). This play is introduced with commentary by Dana Gioia and is available for students to download in *MyLiteratureLab*.
- **New writing assignments**—new writing ideas have been introduced in many chapters.
- **Updated MLA coverage**—our concise Reference Guide for MLA Citations has been updated and expanded to reflect the latest MLA guidelines and illustrate a greater variety of online sources.

Overall, we have tried to create a book to help readers develop sensitivity to language, culture, and identity, to lead them beyond the boundaries of their own selves, and to see the world through the eyes of others. This book is built on the assumption that great literature can enrich and enlarge the lives it touches.

KEY FEATURES

We have revised this edition of *Literature* with the simple aim of introducing useful new features and selections without losing the best-liked material. We have been guided in this effort by scores of instructors and students who use the book in their classrooms. Teaching is a kind of conversation between instructor and student and between reader and text. By revising *Literature*, we try to help keep this conversation fresh by mixing the classic with the new and the familiar with the unexpected.

- **Wide variety of popular and provocative stories, poems, plays, and critical prose**—offers traditional favorites with exciting and sometimes surprising contemporary selections.
  - **67 stories, 11 new selections**—diverse and exciting stories from authors new and old from around the globe.
  - **452 poems, 65 new selections**—great poems, familiar and less well known, mixing classic favorites with engaging contemporary work from a wonderful range of poets.
  - **17 plays, 4 new selections**—a rich array of drama from classical Greek tragedy to Shakespeare to contemporary work by August Wilson and Anna Deavere Smith.
  - **149 critical prose pieces, 19 new selections**—extensive selections help students think about different approaches to reading, interpreting, and writing about literature.
- **"Talking with Writers"**—Exclusive conversations between Dana Gioia and celebrated fiction writer Amy Tan, former U.S. Poet Laureate Kay Ryan, and contemporary playwright David Ives offer students an insider's look into the importance of literature and reading in the lives of three modern masters.
- **Nine casebooks on major authors and literary masterpieces**—provide students with a variety of material, including biographies, photographs, critical commentaries, and author statements, to begin an in-depth study of writers and works frequently used for critical analyses or research papers.
  - Edgar Allan Poe
  - Flannery O'Connor
  - Emily Dickinson
  - Langston Hughes
  - Sophocles
  - William Shakespeare
  - Charlotte Perkins Gilman's "The Yellow Wallpaper"
  - Alice Walker's "Everyday Use"
  - T. S. Eliot's "The Love Song of J. Alfred Prufrock"
- **Chapters on Latin American Fiction and Poetry in Spanish**—present some of the finest authors of the region, including Sor Juana, Jorge Luis Borges, Octavio Paz, Gabriel García Márquez, and Isabel Allende. These important and unique chapters will not only broaden most students' knowledge of world literature but

will also recognize the richness of Spanish language fiction and poetry in the literature of the Americas—a very relevant subject in today's multicultural classrooms. The bilingual selections in poetry will also allow your Spanish-speaking students a chance to bring their native language into their coursework.

■ **Shakespeare, richly illustrated**—production photos of every major scene and character make Shakespeare more accessible to students who have never seen a live production, helping them to visualize the play's action (as well as break up the long blocks of print to make the play's text less intimidating).

- **Three plays by Shakespeare—Othello, Hamlet, and A Midsummer Night's Dream**—in an illustrated format featuring dozens of production photos.
- **"Picturing Shakespeare" photo montages**—offer students a pictorial introduction to each Shakespeare play with a visual preview of the key scenes and characters.

■ **Audio version of Susan Glaspell's Trifles**—specially created for this book.

■ **Terms for Review at the end of every major chapter**—provides students a simple study guide to go over key concepts and terms in each chapter.

■ **Writing Effectively feature in every major chapter** of Fiction, Poetry, and Drama has four elements designed to make the writing process easier, clearer, and less intimidating:

- **Writers on Writing** personalizes the composition process
- **Thinking About _____** discusses the specific topic of the chapter
- **Checklist** provides a step-by-step approach to composition and critical thinking
- **Writing Assignment** plus **More Topics for Writing** provide a rich source of ideas for writing a paper.

■ **Writing About Literature**—eight full writing chapters provide comprehensive coverage of the composition and research process, in general and by genre. All chapters have been edited for increased clarity and accessibility. Our chief aim has been to make the information and structure of the writing chapters more visual for today's Internet-oriented students. (We strive to simplify the text but not to dumb it down. Clarity and concision are never out of place in a textbook, but condescension is fatal.)

■ **Student writing**—sixteen sample papers by students with annotations, prewriting exercises and rough drafts, plus a journal entry, provide credible examples of how to write about literature. Includes many samples of student work-in-progress that illustrate the writing process, including a step-by-step presentation of the development of a topic, idea generation, and the formulation of a strong thesis and argument. Samples include several types of papers:

- Argument papers
- Explication papers
- Analysis papers
- Comparison and contrast papers
- Response paper
- Research paper

■ **Updated MLA guidelines**—provide students source citation requirements from the seventh edition of the *MLA Handbook* and incorporates them in all sample student papers.

■ **Accessible, easy-to-use format**—section titles and subtitles help web-oriented students navigate easily from topic to topic in every chapter. Additionally, all chapters have been reviewed and updated to include relevant cultural references.

- **Critical Approaches to Literature, a chapter with 30 prose selections**—provides depth and flexibility for instructors who prefer to incorporate literary theory and criticism into their introductory courses. Includes three pieces for every major critical school, carefully chosen both to illustrate the major theoretical approaches and to be accessible to beginning students, focusing on literary works found in the present edition (including examinations of work by Zora Neale Hurston and Franz Kafka, a piece by Camille Paglia on William Blake as well as a piece in gender theory by Richard Bozorth that provides a gay reading of Auden's "Funeral Blues").
- **Glossary of Literary Terms**—Over 350 terms defined, including those highlighted in boldface throughout the text as well as other important terms. Provides clear and accurate definitions, usually with cross references to related terms.

OTHER EDITIONS AVAILABLE

Compact Edition

There is also the Seventh Compact Edition of *Literature: An Introduction to Fiction, Poetry, Drama, and Writing* in paperback, for instructors who find the full edition "too much book." Although this compact version offers a slightly abridged table of contents, it still covers the complete range of topics presented in the full edition. Both the full text and the compact edition are available in interactive editions.

Backpack Edition

There is an even more compact edition of this book, which we have titled *Backpack Literature*, Fourth Edition, in honor of the heavy textbook loads many students must carry from class to class. This much briefer anthology contains only the most essential selections and writing apparatus, and it is published in a smaller format to create a more travel-friendly book.

Interactive Editions

Both *Compact*, Seventh Edition, and *Literature*, Twelfth Edition, are published as interactive editions and come with access to *MyLiteratureLab.com* (as described in the following section) for instructors who want to incorporate media into their class.

Portable Edition

This edition provides all the content of the hardcover text in four lightweight paperback volumes—*Fiction*, *Poetry*, *Drama*, and *Writing*—packed in a slipcase.

Fiction and Poetry Available Separately

Instructors who wish to use only the fiction section or only the poetry section of this book are directed to *An Introduction to Fiction*, Eleventh Edition, and *An Introduction to Poetry*, Thirteenth Edition. Each book has writing chapters applicable to its subject, as well as the chapters "Writing a Research Paper" and "Critical Approaches to Literature."

RESOURCES FOR STUDENTS AND INSTRUCTORS

For Students

MyLiteratureLab.com

MyLiteratureLab is a state-of-the-art, web-based, interactive learning system for use in literature courses, either as a media supplement, or as a management system to completely administer a course online. It provides a wealth of resources geared to meet the diverse teaching and learning needs of today's instructors and students. *MyLiteratureLab* adds a new dimension to the study of literature with Longman Lectures—evocative, richly illustrated audio readings along with advice on how to read, interpret, and write about literary works from our roster of Longman authors (including X. J. Kennedy). This powerful program also features an eAnthology with 200 additional selections, feature-length films from Films for the Humanities and Sciences, a composing space with a "Writer's Toolkit," Interactive Readings with clickable prompts, "Writers on Writing" (video interviews with distinguished authors that inspire students to explore their creativity), grammar diagnostics, which produce personalized study plans, sample student papers, Literature Timelines, Avoiding Plagiarism, and more.

Audio Production of Trifles

So many students today have limited experience attending live theater that we felt it would be useful to offer a complete audio version of our opening play, Susan Glaspell's *Trifles*, which we use to teach the elements of drama. The audio version was produced especially for this edition by the celebrated L.A. Theatre Works for students to download in *MyLiteratureLab*. It includes an introduction and commentary by Dana Gioia.

Handbook of Literary Terms

Handbook of Literary Terms by X. J. Kennedy, Dana Gioia, and Mark Bauerlein is a user-friendly primer of over 350 critical terms brought to life with literary examples, pronunciation guides, and scholarly yet accessible explanations. Aimed at undergraduates getting their first taste of serious literary study, the volume will help students engage with the humanities canon and become critical readers and writers ready to experience the insights and joys of great fiction, poetry, and drama.

Responding to Literature: A Writer's Journal

This journal provides students with their own personal space for writing and is available at no additional cost when packaged with this anthology. Helpful writing prompts for responding to fiction, poetry, and drama are also included.

Evaluating Plays on Film and Video

This guide walks students through the process of analyzing and writing about plays on film, whether in a short review or a longer essay. It covers each stage of the process, from preparing and analyzing material through writing the piece. The four appendixes include writing and editing tips and a glossary of film terms. The final section of the guide offers worksheets to help students organize their notes and thoughts before they begin writing.

Evaluating a Performance

Perfect for the student assigned to review a local production, this supplement offers students a convenient place to record their evaluations and is available at no additional cost when packaged with this anthology. Useful tips and suggestions of things to consider when evaluating a production are included.

For Instructors

Instructor's Manual

A separate *Instructor's Manual* is available to instructors. If you have never seen our *Instructor's Manual* before, don't prejudge it. We actually write much of the manual ourselves, and we work hard to make it as interesting, lively, and informed as is the parent text. It offers commentary and teaching ideas for every selection in the book. It also contains additional commentary, debate, qualifications and information—including scores of classroom ideas—from over 100 teachers and authors. As you will see, our *Instructor's Manual* is no ordinary supplement.

Penguin Discount Paperback Program

In cooperation with Penguin Group USA, Pearson is proud to offer a variety of Penguin paperbacks, such as Tennessee Williams's *A Streetcar Named Desire*, George Orwell's *Animal Farm*, and Charlotte Brontë's *Jane Eyre*, at a significant discount—almost sixty percent off the retail price—when packaged with any Pearson title. To review the list of titles available, visit the Pearson Penguin Group USA website at *www.pearsonhighered.com/penguin*.

Video Program

For qualified adopters, an impressive selection of videos is available to enrich students' experience of literature. The videos include selections from William Shakespeare, Sylvia Plath, Ezra Pound, and Alice Walker. Contact your Pearson sales representative to see if you qualify.

Teaching Literature Online

Concise and practical, *Teaching Literature Online* provides instructors with strategies and advice for incorporating elements of computer technology into the literature classroom. Offering a range of information and examples, this manual provides ideas and activities for enhancing literature courses with the help of technology.

The Longman Electronic Testbank for Literature

This electronic testbank features various objective questions on major works of fiction, short fiction, poetry, and drama. It's available as a download from the Instructor Resource Center located at *www.pearsonhighered.com*.

CONTACT US

For examination copies of any of these books, videos, and programs, contact your Pearson sales representative, or write to Literature Marketing Manager, Pearson Higher Education, 51 Madison Avenue, New York, NY 10010. For examination copies only, call (800) 922-0579.

To order an examination copy online, go to *http://www.pearsonhighered.com* or send an e-mail to *exam.copies@pearsonhighered.com*.

THANKS

The collaboration necessary to create this new edition goes far beyond the partnership of its two editors. *Literature: An Introduction to Fiction, Poetry, Drama, and Writing* has once again been revised, corrected, and shaped by wisdom and advice from instructors who actually put it to the test—and also from a number who, in teaching literature, preferred other textbooks to it, but who generously criticized this book anyway and made suggestions for it. (Some responded to the book in part, focusing their comments on the previous editions of *An Introduction to Poetry* and *An Introduction to Fiction*.) Deep thanks to the following individuals:

Alvaro Aleman, University of Florida

Jonathan Alexander, University of Southern Colorado

Ann P. Allen, Salisbury State University

Karla Alwes, SUNY Cortland

Brian Anderson, Central Piedmont Community College

Kimberly Green Angel, Georgia State University

Carmela A. Arnoldt, Glendale Community College

Herman Asarnow, University of Portland

Beverly Bailey, Seminole Community College

Carolyn Baker, San Antonio College

Rosemary Baker, SUNY Morrisville

Lee Barnes, Community College of Southern Nevada, Las Vegas

Sandra Barnhill, South Plains College

Bob Baron, Mesa Community College

Melinda Barth, El Camino Community College

Robin Barrow, University of Iowa

Joseph Bathanti, Mitchell Community College

Judith Baumel, Adelphi University

Anis Bawarski, University of Kansas

Bruce Beckum, Colorado Mountain College

Elaine Bender, El Camino Community College

Pamela Benson, Tarrant County Junior College

Jennifer Black, McLennan Community College

Brian Blackley, North Carolina State University

Debbie Borchers, Pueblo Community College

Alan Braden, Tacoma Community College

Glenda Bryant, South Plains College

Paul Buchanan, Biola University

Andrew Burke, University of Georgia

Jolayne Call, Utah Valley State College

Stasia Callan, Monroe Community College

Uzzie T. Cannon, University of North Carolina at Greensboro

Al Capovilla, Folsom Lake Community College

Eleanor Carducci, Sussex County Community College

Thomas Carper, University of Southern Maine

Jean W. Cash, James Madison University

Michael Cass, Mercer University

Patricia Cearley, South Plains College

Fred Chancey, Chemeketa Community College

Kitty Chen, Nassau Community College

Edward M. Cifelli, County College of Morris

Marc Cirigliano, Empire State College

Bruce Clary, McPherson College

Maria Clayton, Middle Tennessee State University

Cheryl Clements, Blinn College

Jerry Coats, Tarrant County Community College

Peggy Cole, Arapahoe Community College

Doris Colter, Henry Ford Community College

Dean Cooledge, University of Maryland Eastern Shore

Patricia Connors, University of Memphis

Steve Cooper, California State University, Long Beach

Cynthia Cornell, DePauw University

Ruth Corson, Norwalk Community Technical College, Norwalk

James Finn Cotter, Mount St. Mary College

Dessa Crawford, Delaware Community College

Janis Adams Crowe, Furman University

Allison M. Cummings, University of Wisconsin, Madison

Elizabeth Curtin, Salisbury State University

Robert Darling, Keuka College

Denise David, Niagara County Community College

Alan Davis, Moorhead State University

Michael Degen, Jesuit College Preparatory School, Dallas

Kathleen De Grave, Pittsburgh State University

Apryl Denny, Viterbo University

Fred Dings, University of South Carolina

Leo Doobad, Stetson University

Stephanie Dowdle, Salt Lake Community College

Dennis Driewald, Laredo Community College

David Driscoll, Benedictine College

John Drury, University of Cincinnati

Tony D'Souza, Shasta College

Victoria Duckworth, Santa Rosa Junior College

Ellen Dugan-Barrette, Brescia University

Dixie Durman, Chapman University

Bill Dynes, University of Indianapolis

Janet Eber, County College of Morris

Terry Ehret, Santa Rosa Junior College

George Ellenbogen, Bentley College

Peggy Ellsberg, Barnard College

Toni Empringham, El Camino Community College

Lin Enger, Moorhead State University

Alexina Fagan, Virginia Commonwealth University

Lynn Fauth, Oxnard College

Annie Finch, University of Southern Maine

Katie Fischer, Clarke College

Susan Fitzgerald, University of Memphis

Juliann Fleenor, Harper College

Richard Flynn, Georgia Southern University

Billy Fontenot, Louisiana State University at Eunice

Deborah Ford, University of Southern Mississippi

Doug Ford, Manatee Community College

James E. Ford, University of Nebraska, Lincoln

Peter Fortunato, Ithaca College

Ray Foster, Scottsdale Community College

Maryanne Garbowsky, County College of Morris

John Gery, University of New Orleans

Mary Frances Gibbons, Richland College

Maggie Gordon, University of Mississippi

Joseph Green, Lower Columbia College

William E. Gruber, Emory University

Huey Guagliardo, Louisiana State University

R. S. Gwynn, Lamar University

Steven K. Hale, DeKalb College

Renée Harlow, Southern Connecticut State University

David Harper, Chesapeake College

John Harper, Seminole Community College

Iris Rose Hart, Santa Fe Community College

Karen Hatch, California State University, Chico

Jim Hauser, William Patterson College

Kevin Hayes, Essex County College

Jennifer Heller, Johnson County Community College

Hal Hellwig, Idaho State University

Gillian Hettinger, William Paterson University

Mary Piering Hiltbrand, University of Southern Colorado

Martha Hixon, Middle Tennessee State University

Jan Hodge, Morningside College

David E. Hoffman, Averett University

Mary Huffer, Lake-Sumter Community College

Patricia Hymson, Delaware County Community College

Carol Ireland, Joliet Junior College

Alan Jacobs, Wheaton College

Ann Jagoe, North Central Texas College

Kimberlie Johnson, Seminole Community College

Peter Johnson, Providence College

Ted E. Johnston, El Paso Community College

Cris Karmas, Graceland University

Howard Kerner, Polk Community College

Lynn Kerr, Baltimore City Community College

D. S. Koelling, Northwest College

Dennis Kriewald, Laredo Community College

Paul Lake, Arkansas Technical University

Susan Lang, Southern Illinois University

Greg LaPointe, Elmira College

Tracy Lassiter, Eastern Arizona College

Sherry Little, San Diego State University

Alfred Guy Litton, Texas Woman's University

Heather Lobban-Viravong, Grinnell College

Karen Locke, Lane Community College

Eric Loring, Scottsdale Community College

Deborah Louvar, Seminole State College

Gerald Luboff, County College of Morris

Susan Popkin Mach, UCLA

Samuel Maio, California State University, San Jose

Jim Martin, Mount Ida College

Paul Marx, University of New Haven

David Mason, Colorado College

Mike Matthews, Tarrant County Junior College

Beth Maxfield, Henderson State University

Janet McCann, Texas A&M University

Susan McClure, Indiana University of Pennsylvania

Kim McCollum-Clark, Millersville University

David McCracken, Texas A&M University

Nellie McCrory, Gaston College

William McGee, Jr., Joliet Junior College

Kerri McKeand, Joliet Junior College

Robert McPhillips, Iona College

Jim McWilliams, Dickinson State University

Elizabeth Meador, Wayne Community College

Bruce Meyer, Laurentian University

Tom Miller, University of Arizona

Joseph Mills, University of California at Davis

Cindy Milwe, Santa Monica High School

Dorothy Minor, Tulsa Community College

Mary Alice Morgan, Mercer University

Samantha Morgan, University of Tennessee

Bernard Morris, Modesto Junior College

Brian T. Murphy, Burlington Community College

William Myers, University of Colorado at Colorado Springs

Madeleine Mysko, Johns Hopkins University

Kevin Nebergall, Kirkwood Community College

Eric Nelson, Georgia Southern University

Jeff Newberry, University of West Florida

Marsha Nourse, Dean College

Hillary Nunn, University of Akron

James Obertino, Central Missouri State University

Julia O'Brien, Meredith College

Sally O'Friel, John Carroll University

Elizabeth Oness, Viterbo College

Regina B. Oost, Wesleyan College

Mike Osborne, Central Piedmont Community College

Jim Owen, Columbus State University

Jeannette Palmer, Motlow State Community College

Mark Palmer, Tacoma Community College

Dianne Peich, Delaware County Community College

Betty Jo Peters, Morehead State University

Timothy Peters, Boston University

Norm Peterson, County College of Morris

Susan Petit, College of San Mateo

Louis Phillips, School of Visual Arts

Robert Phillips, University of Houston
Jason Pickavance, Salt Lake Community College
Teresa Point, Emory University
Deborah Prickett, Jacksonville State University
William Provost, University of Georgia
Wyatt Prunty, University of the South, Sewanee
Allen Ramsey, Central Missouri State University
Ron Rash, Tri-County Technical College
Michael W. Raymond, Stetson University
Mary Anne Reiss, Elizabethtown Community College
Barbara Rhodes, Central Missouri State University
Diane Richard-Alludya, Lynn University
Gary Richardson, Mercer University
Fred Robbins, Southern Illinois University
Douglas Robillard Jr., University of Arkansas at Pine Bluff
Daniel Robinson, Colorado State University
Dawn Rodrigues, University of Texas, Brownsville
Linda C. Rollins, Motlow State Community College
Mark Rollins, Ohio University
Laura Ross, Seminole Community College
Jude Roy, Madisonville Community College
M. Runyon, Saddleback College
Mark Sanders, College of the Mainland
Kay Satre, Carroll College
Ben Sattersfield, Mercer University
SueAnn Schatz, University of New Mexico
Roy Scheele, Doane College
Bill Schmidt, Seminole Community College
Beverly Schneller, Millersville University
Meg Schoerke, San Francisco State University
Janet Schwarzkopf, Western Kentucky University
William Scurrah, Pima Community College
Susan Semrow, Northeastern State University
Tom Sexton, University of Alaska, Anchorage

Chenliang Sheng, Northern Kentucky University
Roger Silver, University of Maryland–Asian Division
Phillip Skaar, Texas A&M University
Michael Slaughter, Illinois Central College
Martha K. Smith, University of Southern Indiana
Richard Spiese, California State, Long Beach
Lisa S. Starks, Texas A&M University
John R. Stephenson, Lake Superior State University
Jack Stewart, East Georgia College
Dabney Stuart, Washington and Lee University
David Sudol, Arizona State University
Stan Sulkes, Raymond Walters College
Gerald Sullivan, Savio Preparatory School
Henry Taylor, American University
Jean Tobin, University of Wisconsin Center, Sheboygan County
Linda Travers, University of Massachusetts, Amherst
Tom Treffinger, Greenville Technical College
Peter Ulisse, Housatonia Community College
Lee Upton, Lafayette College
Rex Veeder, St. Cloud University
Deborah Viles, University of Colorado, Boulder
Joyce Walker, Southern Illinois University–Carbondale
Sue Walker, University of South Alabama
Irene Ward, Kansas State University
Penelope Warren, Laredo Community College
Barbara Wenner, University of Cincinnati
Terry Witek, Stetson University
Sallie Wolf, Arapahoe Community College
Beth Rapp Young, University of Alabama
William Zander, Fairleigh Dickinson University
Tom Zaniello, Northern Kentucky University
Guanping Zeng, Pensacola Junior College
John Zheng, Mississippi Valley State University

Ongoing thanks go to our friends and colleagues who helped with earlier editions: Michael Palma, who scrupulously examined and updated every chapter of the previous edition; Diane Thiel of the University of New Mexico, who originally helped develop the Latin American poetry chapter; Susan Balée of Temple University, who contributed to the chapter on writing a research paper; April Lindner of Saint Joseph's University in Philadelphia, Pennsylvania, who served as associate editor for the writing sections; Mark Bernier of Blinn College in Brenham, Texas, who helped improve the writing material; Joseph Aimone of Santa Clara University, who helped integrate web-based materials and research techniques; and John Swensson of De Anza College, who provided excellent practical suggestions from the classroom.

On the publisher's staff, Joseph Terry, Katharine Glynn, and Joyce Nilsen made many contributions to the development and revision of the new edition. Savoula

Amanatidis and Lois Lombardo directed the complex job of managing the production of the book in all of its many versions from the manuscript to the final printed form. Beth Keister handled the difficult job of permissions. Rona Tuccillo and Jennifer Nonenmacher supervised the expansion of photographs in the new edition.

Mary Gioia was involved in every stage of planning, editing, and execution. Not only could the book not have been done without her capable hand and careful eye, but her expert guidance made every chapter better.

Past debts that will never be repaid are outstanding to hundreds of instructors named in prefaces past and to Dorothy M. Kennedy.

X. J. K. AND D. G.

Playwright David Ives.

DRAMA

TALKING WITH *David Ives*

"Comedy is just tragedy without the sentimentality."
Dana Gioia Interviews David Ives

Q: When did you first become interested in theater?

DAVID IVES: I played The Wolf opposite drop-dead-sexy Amy Skeehan in our third-grade production of "Little Red Riding Hood" at St. Mary Magdalene School in South Chicago. Basically it was all over after that. The show was so successful Amy and I took it on tour to the fourth and fifth grades. By then I had learned the Great Lesson of Theater, which is: *theater is a great way to hang out with girls*. It may be why Shakespeare became both an actor and a playwright: *more girls*.

Q: When did you discover that you could make people laugh?

DAVID IVES: There's some debate about this. An aunt of mine, a few years ago, said to me, "You're just like you were as a boy. Such a happy, funny child." I reported this to my mother, who said without a pause: "I wouldn't say that." She didn't seem to want to explain. One of my old high-school classmates recently mentioned that I was funny in high school. I only remember reading Russian novels about suicide in high school. Maybe I was funny between novels, but they were pretty thick.

Q: Tell us about your first play.

DAVID IVES: I wrote my first play when I was nine. It was about gangsters and had lots of gunfire and a girl I based on Amy Skeehan. I wrote my second play in high school. It was about Russian-like people talking about suicide a lot. My third play was at college and was The Worst Play Ever Written. From there, I had nowhere to go but up. My next play got produced, and suddenly I was a real live playwright. I've been faking it ever since.

Q: When you see one of your plays onstage, how different is it from what you imagined while writing it?

DAVID IVES: It's always better than I imagined it, unless it's worse.

Q: You are the master of the short comic play. What drew you to this unconventional form?

DAVID IVES: Probably a shorter and shorter attention span, like everybody else. Also, my wife Martha is on the short side and I am very drawn to her, so it is only a short (so to speak) way to short plays. I'm fond in general of the concise, the compact, the jeweled, the specific, and perfect as opposed to the verbose, the bloated, the baggy, and general. A good rock-and-roll song can be three or four minutes long and when it's over, if it's been made right and played right, you feel like you've gotten into a barfight, had a love affair, and ridden a convertible down Pacific Coast One on the most beautiful day of the year, all in three minutes. Imagine what you can do with a ten- or fifteen-minute play. You can make an audience feel like they've done all those things, plus they've gotten married, had kids, died, and went to heaven.

There they are, breathless just inside the pearly gates with their heads still spinning, and only ten minutes have passed. As far as I'm concerned, all plays, short or long, should aspire to the conditions of rock-and-roll, whose purpose is to make us aware of our mortality and the fact that we had better get with it before the song ends. Not a bad rule of thumb for art as a whole.

Q: Who are your favorite comic writers and comedians?

DAVID IVES: Nothing depresses me like comedians. Maybe it's because people who try to make me laugh instantly put me in a really bad mood. I once shot a man in Tucson and spent 38 years in the penitentiary because he tried to tell me a joke that started "A priest, a minister, and a rabbi walk into a bar. . . ." As for funny playwrights, Joe Orton and Noel Coward and Chris Durang do it for me because they're not just trying to be funny. They have a vision of life that happens to be comic. They've also got *style*, which is the outward and visible sign of having a vision of life.

Q: Why do people need comedy?

DAVID IVES: Comedy is important for three reasons. First, it's funny. Second, it makes us laugh. Third, it's easier to get a girl to go see a comedy than, let's say, *Hamlet*. Fourth, it shows us what frigging idiots we can be under the right circumstances. As Wendell Berry once said, "It is not from ourselves that we will learn to be better." Watching idiots cavort around onstage is one possible way to do that. First, of course, you have to be interested in being better.

Q: Comedy seems to get less critical respect than tragedy. Does that seem fair to you?

DAVID IVES: Nothing seems fair to me. That's why I write comedy. If you've ever met a critic you'll understand why they give more respect to sadder plays: because critics are the saddest dogs you'll ever meet. The fact is, comedy is much harder to do—to write, to act—than drama, the same way it's harder to look at life and say, *Okay*, than it is to mope around thinking about Russian roulette all the time. But let's get one thing clear: Comedy is not jokes. It certainly isn't sitcoms, which to me are about as funny as a sack of dead kittens. I'm talking about real comedy—human comedy, which is to say comedy that thinks and feels. I'm talking about *Twelfth Night*, or *The Marriage of Bette and Boo*, or *The Importance of Being Earnest*, where there's truth and sadness mixed in with the joy, just as there is in life. Theater *is* life, and fails when it settles for merely being funny, the same way life is not enough when it settles for just being funny. In the end, comedy is just tragedy without the sentimentality. Dostoyevsky, anyone?

Drama is life with the dull bits left out.

—ALFRED HITCHCOCK

Unlike a short story or a novel, a **play** is a work of storytelling in which actors represent the characters. A play also differs from a work of fiction in another essential way: it is addressed not to readers but to spectators.

To be part of an audience in a theater is an experience far different from reading a story in solitude. As the house lights dim and the curtain rises, we become members of a community. The responses of people around us affect our own responses. We, too, contribute to the community's response whenever we laugh, sigh, applaud, murmur in surprise, or catch our breath in excitement. In contrast, when we watch a movie by ourselves in our living room—say, a slapstick comedy—we probably laugh less often than if we were watching the same film in a theater, surrounded by a roaring crowd. On the other hand, no one is spilling popcorn down the backs of our necks. Each kind of theatrical experience, to be sure, has its advantages.

A theater of live actors has another advantage: a sensitive give-and-take between actors and audience. (Such rapport, of course, depends on the skill of the actors and the perceptiveness of the audience.) Although professional actors may try to give a first-rate performance on all occasions, it is natural for them to feel more keenly inspired by a lively, appreciative audience than by a lethargic one. As veteran playgoers well know, something unique and wonderful can happen when good actors and a good audience respond to each other.

In another sense, a play is more than actors and audience. Like a short story or a poem, a play is a work of art made of words. Watching a play, of course, we don't notice the playwright standing between us and the characters. If the play is absorbing, it flows before our eyes. In a silent reading, the usual play consists mainly of **dialogue**, exchanges of speech, punctuated by stage directions. In performance, though, stage directions vanish. And although the thoughtful efforts of perhaps a hundred people—actors, director, producer, stage designer, costumer, makeup artist, technicians—may have gone into a production, a successful play makes us forget its artifice. We may even forget that the play is literature, for its gestures, facial expressions, bodily stances, lighting, and special effects are as much a part of it as the playwright's written words. Even though words are not all there is to a living play, they are its bones. And the whole play, the finished production, is the total of whatever takes place on stage.

There is an aspect of theater related to both religious ritual and civic festival—a mixture of church service and rock concert. These are occasions when people gather for the special communal experiences of being reawakened emotionally and spiritually and celebrating their complex identities. Twice in the history of Europe, drama has sprung forth as a part of worship. In ancient Greece, plays were performed on feast days of Dionysus; and in the Christian Middle Ages, a play was introduced as an adjunct to the Easter mass with the enactment of the meeting between the three Marys and the angel at Jesus's empty tomb. Evidently, something in drama remains constant over the years—something as old, perhaps, as the deepest desires and highest aspirations of humanity.

34

READING A PLAY

I regard the theatre as the greatest of all art forms,
the most immediate way in which a human being can share
with another the sense of what it is to be a human being.

—OSCAR WILDE

Most plays are written not to be read in books but to be performed. Finding plays in a literature anthology, the student may well ask: Isn't there something wrong with the idea of reading plays on the printed page? Isn't that a perversion of their nature?

True, plays are meant to be seen on stage, but equally true, reading a play may afford advantages. One is that it is better to know some masterpieces by reading them than never to know them at all. Even if you live in a large city with many theaters, even if you attend a college with many theatrical productions, to succeed in your life-time in witnessing, say, all the plays of Shakespeare might well be impossible. In print, they are as near to hand as a book on a shelf, ready to be enacted (if you like) on the stage of the mind.

After all, a play is literature before it comes alive in a theater, and it might be ar-gued that when we read an unfamiliar play, we meet it in the same form in which it first appears to its actors and its director. If a play is rich and complex or if it dates from the remote past and contains difficulties of language and allusion, to read it on the page enables us to study it at our leisure and return to the parts that demand greater scrutiny.

But even if a play may be seen in a theater, sometimes to read it in print may be our way of knowing it as the author wrote it in its entirety. Far from regarding Shakespeare's words as holy writ, producers of *Hamlet, King Lear, Othello,* and other masterpieces often shorten or even leave out whole speeches and scenes. Besides, the nature of the play, as far as you can tell from a stage production, may depend on decisions of the director. In one production Othello may dress as a Renaissance Moor, in another as a modern general. Every actor who plays Iago in *Othello* makes his own interpretation of this knotty character. Some see Iago as a figure of pure evil; others, as a madman; still others, as a suffering human being consumed by hatred, jealousy, and pride. What do you think Shakespeare meant? You can always read the play and decide for yourself. If every stage production of a play is a fresh interpretation, so, too, is every reader's reading of it. Some readers, when silently reading a play to themselves, try to visualize a stage, imagining the characters in costume and under lights. If such a reader is an actor or a director and is reading the play with an eye toward staging it, then he or she may try to imagine every detail of a possible production, even shades of makeup and the loudness of sound effects. But the nonprofessional reader, who regards the play as literature, need not attempt such exhaustive imagining. Although some readers find it enjoyable to imagine the play taking place on a stage, others prefer to imagine the people and events that the play brings vividly to mind. Sympathetically following the tangled life of Nora in *A Doll's House* by Henrik Ibsen, we forget that we are reading printed stage directions and instead feel ourselves in the presence of human conflict. Thus regarded, a play becomes a form of storytelling, and the playwright's instructions to the actors and the director become a conventional mode of narrative that we accept much as we accept the methods of a novel or short story.

THEATRICAL CONVENTIONS

Most plays, whether seen in a theater or in print, employ some **conventions**: customary methods of presenting an action, usual and recognizable devices that an audience is willing to accept. In reading a great play from the past, such as *Oedipus the King* or *Othello*, it will help if we know some of the conventions of the classical Greek theater or the Elizabethan theater. When in *Oedipus the King* we encounter a character called the Chorus, it may be useful to be aware that this is a group of citizens who stand to one side of the action, conversing with the principal character and commenting. In *Othello*, when the sinister Iago, left on stage alone, begins to speak (at the end of Act I, Scene iii), we recognize the conventional device of a **soliloquy,** a monologue in which we seem to overhear the character's inmost thoughts uttered aloud. Another such device is the **aside,** in which a character addresses the audience directly, unheard by the other characters on stage, as when the villain in a melodrama chortles, "Heh! Heh! Now she's in my power!" Like conventions in poetry, such familiar methods of staging a narrative afford us a happy shock of recognition. Often, as in these examples, they are ways of making clear to us exactly what the playwright would have us know.

ELEMENTS OF A PLAY

When we read a play on the printed page and find ourselves swept forward by the motion of its story, we need not wonder how—and from what ingredients—the playwright put it together. Still, to analyze the structure of a play is one way to understand and appreciate a playwright's art. Analysis is complicated, however, because in an excellent play the elements (including plot, theme, and characters) do not stand in isolation. Often, deeds clearly follow from the kinds of people the characters are, and from those deeds it is left to the reader to infer the **theme** of the play—the general point or truth about human beings that may be drawn from it. Perhaps the most meaningful way to study the elements of a play (and certainly the most enjoyable) is to consider a play in its entirety.

Here is a short, famous one-act play worth reading for the boldness of its elements—and for its own sake. *Trifles* tells the story of a murder. As you will discover, the "trifles" mentioned in its title are not of trifling stature. In reading the play, you will probably find yourself imagining what you might see on stage if you were in a theater. You may also want to imagine what took place in the lives of the characters before the curtain rose. All this imagining may sound like a tall order, but don't worry. Just read the play for enjoyment the first time through, and then we will consider what makes it effective.

Susan Glaspell

Trifles   1916

Susan Glaspell (1876–1948) grew up in her native Davenport, Iowa, daughter of a grain dealer. After four years at Drake University and a job as a reporter in Des Moines, she settled in New York's Greenwich Village. In 1915, with her husband, George Cram Cook, a theatrical director, she founded the Provincetown Players, the first influential noncommercial theater troupe in America. During the summers of 1915 and 1916, in a makeshift playhouse on a Cape Cod pier, the Players staged the earliest plays of Eugene O'Neill and works by John Reed, Edna St. Vincent Millay, and Glaspell herself. Transplanting the company to New York in the fall of 1916, Glaspell and Cook renamed it the Playwrights' Theater. Glaspell wrote several still-remembered plays, among them a pioneering work of feminist drama, The Verge *(1921), and the Pulitzer Prize-winning* Alison's House *(1930), about the family of a reclusive poet like Emily Dickinson who, after her death, squabble over the right to publish her poems. First widely known for her fiction with an Iowa background, Glaspell wrote ten novels, including* Fidelity *(1915) and* The Morning Is Near Us *(1939). Shortly after writing the play* Trifles, *she rewrote it as a short story, "A Jury of Her Peers."*

CHARACTERS

George Henderson, county attorney
Henry Peters, sheriff
Lewis Hale, a neighboring farmer
Mrs. Peters
Mrs. Hale

SCENE. *The kitchen in the now abandoned farmhouse of John Wright, a gloomy kitchen, and left without having been put in order—unwashed pans under the sink, a loaf of bread outside the breadbox, a dish towel on the table—other signs of incompleted work. At the rear the outer door opens and the Sheriff comes in followed by the County Attorney and Hale. The Sheriff and Hale are men in middle life, the County Attorney is a young man; all are much bundled up and go at once to the stove. They are followed by two women—the Sheriff's wife first; she is a slight wiry woman, a thin nervous face. Mrs. Hale is larger and would ordinarily be called more comfortable looking, but she is disturbed now and looks fearfully about as she enters. The women have come in slowly, and stand close together near the door.*

County Attorney (*rubbing his hands*): This feels good. Come up to the fire, ladies.
Mrs. Peters (*after taking a step forward*): I'm not—cold.
Sheriff (*unbuttoning his overcoat and stepping away from the stove as if to mark the beginning of official business*): Now, Mr. Hale, before we move things about, you explain to Mr. Henderson just what you saw when you came here yesterday morning.
County Attorney: By the way, has anything been moved? Are things just as you left them yesterday?
Sheriff (*looking about*): It's just the same. When it dropped below zero last night I thought I'd better send Frank out this morning to make a fire for us—no use

getting pneumonia with a big case on, but I told him not to touch anything except the stove—and you know Frank.

County Attorney: Somebody should have been left here yesterday.

Sheriff: Oh—yesterday. When I had to send Frank to Morris Center for that man who went crazy—I want you to know I had my hands full yesterday, I knew you could get back from Omaha by today and as long as I went over everything here myself—

County Attorney: Well, Mr. Hale, tell just what happened when you came here yesterday morning.

Hale: Harry and I had started to town with a load of potatoes. We came along the road from my place and as I got here I said, "I'm going to see if I can't get John Wright to go in with me on a party telephone." I spoke to Wright about it once before and he put me off, saying folks talked too much anyway, and all he asked was peace and quiet—I guess you know about how much he talked himself; but I thought maybe if I went to the house and talked about it before his wife, though I said to Harry that I didn't know as what his wife wanted made much difference to John—

County Attorney: Let's talk about that later, Mr. Hale. I do want to talk about that, but tell now just what happened when you got to the house.

Hale: I didn't hear or see anything; I knocked at the door, and still it was all quiet inside. I knew they must be up, it was past eight o'clock. So I knocked again, and I thought I heard somebody say, "Come in." I wasn't sure, I'm not sure yet, but I opened the door—this door (*indicating the door by which the two women are still standing*) and there in that rocker—(*pointing to it*) sat Mrs. Wright.

(*They all look at the rocker.*)

County Attorney: What—was she doing?

Hale: She was rockin' back and forth. She had her apron in her hand and was kind of—pleating it.

County Attorney: And how did she—look?

Hale: Well, she looked queer.

County Attorney: How do you mean—queer?

Hale: Well, as if she didn't know what she was going to do next. And kind of done up.

County Attorney: How did she seem to feel about your coming?

Hale: Why, I don't think she minded—one way or other. She didn't pay much attention. I said, "How do, Mrs. Wright, it's cold, ain't it?" And she said, "Is it?"—and went on kind of pleating at her apron. Well, I was surprised; she didn't ask me to come up to the stove, or to set down, but just sat there, not even looking at me, so I said, "I want to see John." And then she—laughed. I guess you would call it a laugh. I thought of Harry and the team outside, so I said a little sharp: "Can't I see John?" "No," she says, kind o' dull like. "Ain't he home?" says I. "Yes," says she, "he's home." "Then why can't I see him?" I asked her, out of patience. "'Cause he's dead," says she. "*Dead?*" says I. She just nodded her head, not getting a bit excited, but rockin' back and forth. "Why—where is he?" says I, not knowing what to say. She just pointed upstairs—like that. (*Himself pointing to the room above.*) I got up, with the idea of going up there. I walked from there to here—then I says, "Why, what did he die of?" "He died of a rope round his neck," says she, and just went on pleatin' at her apron. Well, I went out and called Harry. I thought I might—need help. We went upstairs and there he was lyin'—

County Attorney: I think I'd rather have you go into that upstairs, where you can point it all out. Just go on now with the rest of the story.

Hale: Well, my first thought was to get that rope off. It looked . . . (*stops, his face twitches*) . . . but Harry, he went up to him, and he said, "No, he's dead all right, and we'd better not touch anything." So we went back down stairs. She was still sitting that same way. "Has anybody been notified?" I asked. "No," says she, unconcerned. "Who did this, Mrs. Wright?" said Harry. He said it businesslike—and she stopped pleatin' of her apron. "I don't know," she says. "You don't *know?*" says Harry. "No," says she. "Weren't you sleepin' in the bed with him?" says Harry. "Yes," says she, "but I was on the inside." "Somebody slipped a rope round his neck and strangled him and you didn't wake up?" says Harry. "I didn't wake up," she said after him. We must 'a looked as if we didn't see how that could be, for after a minute she said, "I sleep sound." Harry was going to ask her more questions but I said maybe we ought to let her tell her story first to the coroner, or the sheriff, so Harry went fast as he could to Rivers' place, where there's a telephone.

County Attorney: And what did Mrs. Wright do when she knew that you had gone for the coroner?

Hale: She moved from that chair to this one over here (*pointing to a small chair in the corner*) and just sat there with her hands held together and looking down. I got a feeling that I ought to make some conversation, so I said I had come in to see if John wanted to put in a telephone, and at that she started to laugh, and then she stopped and looked at me—scared. (*The County Attorney, who has had his notebook out, makes a note.*) I dunno, maybe it wasn't scared. I wouldn't like to say it was. Soon Harry got back, and then Dr. Lloyd came, and you, Mr. Peters, and so I guess that's all I know that you don't.

County Attorney (*looking around*): I guess we'll go upstairs first—and then out to the barn and around there. (*To the Sheriff*) You're convinced that there was nothing important here—nothing that would point to any motive.

Sheriff: Nothing here but kitchen things.

(*The County Attorney, after again looking around the kitchen, opens the door of a cupboard closet. He gets up on a chair and looks on a shelf. Pulls his hand away, sticky.*)

County Attorney: Here's a nice mess.

(*The women draw nearer.*)

Mrs. Peters (*to the other woman*): Oh, her fruit; it did freeze. (*To the County Attorney*) She worried about that when it turned so cold. She said the fire'd go out and her jars would break.

Sheriff: Well, can you beat the women! Held for murder and worryin' about her preserves.

County Attorney: I guess before we're through she may have something more serious than preserves to worry about.

Hale: Well, women are used to worrying over trifles.

(*The two women move a little closer together.*)

County Attorney (*with the gallantry of a young politician*): And yet, for all their worries, what would we do without the ladies? (*The women do not unbend. He goes to the sink, takes a dipperful of water from the pail and pouring it into a basin, washes his hands. Starts to wipe them on the roller towel, turns it for a cleaner place.*) Dirty towels! (*Kicks his foot against the pans under the sink.*) Not much of a housekeeper, would you say, ladies?

Mrs. Hale (*stiffly*): There's a great deal of work to be done on a farm.

County Attorney: To be sure. And yet (*with a little bow to her*) I know there are some Dickson County farmhouses which do not have such roller towels.

(*He gives it a pull to expose its full length again.*)

Mrs. Hale: Those towels get dirty awful quick. Men's hands aren't always as clean as they might be.

County Attorney: Ah, loyal to your sex, I see. But you and Mrs. Wright were neighbors. I suppose you were friends, too.

Mrs. Hale (*shaking her head*): I've not seen much of her of late years. I've not been in this house—it's more than a year.

County Attorney: And why was that? You didn't like her?

Mrs. Hale: I liked her all well enough. Farmers' wives have their hands full, Mr. Henderson. And then——

County Attorney: Yes—?

Mrs. Hale (*looking about*): It never seemed a very cheerful place.

County Attorney: No—it's not cheerful. I shouldn't say she had the home-making instinct.

Mrs. Hale: Well, I don't know as Wright had, either.

County Attorney: You mean that they didn't get on very well?

Mrs. Hale: No, I don't mean anything. But I don't think a place'd be any cheerfuller for John Wright's being in it.

County Attorney: I'd like to talk more of that a little later. I want to get the lay of things upstairs now.

(*He goes to the left, where three steps lead to a stair door.*)

Sheriff: I suppose anything Mrs. Peters does'll be all right. She was to take in some clothes for her, you know, and a few little things. We left in such a hurry yesterday.

County Attorney: Yes, but I would like to see what you take, Mrs. Peters, and keep an eye out for anything that might be of use to us.

Mrs. Peters: Yes, Mr. Henderson.

(*The women listen to the men's steps on the stairs, then look about the kitchen.*)

Mrs. Hale: I'd hate to have men coming into my kitchen, snooping around and criticizing.

(*She arranges the pans under sink which the County Attorney had shoved out of place.*)

Mrs. Peters: Of course it's no more than their duty.

Mrs. Hale: Duty's all right, but I guess that deputy sheriff that came out to make the fire might have got a little of this on. (*Gives the roller towel a pull.*) Wish I'd thought of that sooner. Seems mean to talk about her for not having things slicked up when she had to come away in such a hurry.

Mrs. Peters (*who has gone to a small table in the left rear corner of the room, and lifted one end of a towel that covers a pan*): She had bread set.

(*Stands still.*)

Mrs. Hale (*eyes fixed on a loaf of bread beside the breadbox, which is on a low shelf at the other side of the room; moves slowly toward it*): She was going to put this in there. (*Picks up loaf, then abruptly drops it. In a manner of returning to familiar things.*) It's a shame about her fruit. I wonder if it's all gone. (*Gets up on the chair and looks.*) I think there's some here that's all right, Mrs. Peters. Yes—here; (*holding it toward the window*) this is cherries, too. (*Looking again.*) I declare I believe that's the only one. (*Gets down, bottle in her hand. Goes to the sink and wipes it off on the outside.*) She'll feel awful bad after all her hard work in the hot weather. I remember the afternoon I put up my cherries last summer.

(*She puts the bottle on the big kitchen table, center of the room. With a sigh, is about to sit down in the rocking-chair. Before she is seated realizes what chair it is; with a slow look at it, steps back. The chair which she has touched rocks back and forth.*)

Mrs. Peters: Well, I must get those things from the front room closet. (*She goes to the door at the right, but after looking into the other room, steps back.*) You coming with me, Mrs. Hale? You could help me carry them.

(*They go in the other room; reappear, Mrs. Peters carrying a dress and skirt, Mrs. Hale following with a pair of shoes.*)

Mrs. Peters: My, it's cold in there.

(*She puts the clothes on the big table, and hurries to the stove.*)

Mrs. Hale (*examining her skirt*): Wright was close. I think maybe that's why she kept so much to herself. She didn't even belong to the Ladies Aid. I suppose she felt she couldn't do her part, and then you don't enjoy things when you feel shabby. She used to wear pretty clothes and be lively, when she was Minnie Foster, one of the town girls singing in the choir. But that—oh, that was thirty years ago. This all you was to take in?

Mrs. Peters: She said she wanted an apron. Funny thing to want, for there isn't much to get you dirty in jail, goodness knows. But I suppose just to make her feel more natural. She said they was in the top drawer in this cupboard. Yes, here. And then her little shawl that always hung behind the door. (*Opens stair door and looks.*) Yes, here it is.

(*Quickly shuts door leading upstairs.*)

Mrs. Hale (*abruptly moving toward her*): Mrs. Peters?

Mrs. Peters: Yes, Mrs. Hale?

Mrs. Hale: Do you think she did it?

Mrs. Peters (*in a frightened voice*): Oh, I don't know.

Mrs. Hale: Well, I don't think she did. Asking for an apron and her little shawl. Worrying about her fruit.

Mrs. Peters (*starts to speak, glances up, where footsteps are heard in the room above; in a low voice*): Mr. Peters says it looks bad for her. Mr. Henderson is awful sarcastic in a speech and he'll make fun of her sayin' she didn't wake up.

Mrs. Hale: Well, I guess John Wright didn't wake when they was slipping that rope under his neck.

Mrs. Peters: No, it's strange. It must have been done awful crafty and still. They say it was such a—funny way to kill a man, rigging it all up like that.

Mrs. Hale: That's just what Mr. Hale said. There was a gun in the house. He says that's what he can't understand.

Mrs. Peters: Mr. Henderson said coming out that what was needed for the case was a motive; something to show anger, or—sudden feeling.

Mrs. Hale (*who is standing by the table*): Well, I don't see any signs of anger around here. (*She puts her hand on the dish towel which lies on the table, stands looking down at table, one half of which is clean, the other half messy.*) It's wiped to here. (*Makes a move as if to finish work, then turns and looks at loaf of bread outside the breadbox. Drops towel. In that voice of coming back to familiar things.*) Wonder how they are finding things upstairs. I hope she had it a little more red-up° there. You know, it seems kind of sneaking. Locking her up in town and then coming out here and trying to get her own house to turn against her!

Mrs. Peters: But Mrs. Hale, the law is the law.

Mrs. Hale: I s'pose 'tis. (*Unbuttoning her coat.*) Better loosen up your things, Mrs. Peters. You won't feel them when you go out.

(*Mrs. Peters takes off her fur tippet, goes to hang it on hook at back of room, stands looking at the under part of the small corner table.*)

Mrs. Peters: She was piecing a quilt.

(*She brings the large sewing basket and they look at the bright pieces.*)

Mrs. Hale: It's a log cabin pattern. Pretty, isn't it? I wonder if she was goin' to quilt it or just knot it?

(*Footsteps have been heard coming down the stairs. The Sheriff enters followed by Hale and the County Attorney.*)

Sheriff: They wonder if she was going to quilt it or just knot it!

(*The men laugh; the women look abashed.*)

County Attorney (*rubbing his hands over the stove*): Frank's fire didn't do much up there, did it? Well, let's go out to the barn and get that cleared up.

(*The men go outside.*)

Mrs. Hale (*resentfully*): I don't know as there's anything so strange, our takin' up our time with little things while we're waiting for them to get the evidence. (*She sits*

---

red-up: (slang) readied up, ready to be seen.

down at the big table smoothing out a block with decision.) I don't see as it's anything to laugh about.

Mrs. Peters (*apologetically*): Of course they've got awful important things on their minds.

(*Pulls up a chair and joins Mrs. Hale at the table.*)

Mrs. Hale (*examining another block*): Mrs. Peters, look at this one. Here, this is the one she was working on, and look at the sewing! All the rest of it has been so nice and even. And look at this! It's all over the place! Why, it looks as if she didn't know what she was about!

(*After she has said this they look at each, then start to glance back at the door. After an instant Mrs. Hale has pulled at a knot and ripped the sewing.*)

Mrs. Peters: Oh, what are you doing, Mrs. Hale?

Mrs. Hale (*mildly*): Just pulling out a stitch or two that's not sewed very good. (*Threading a needle.*) Bad sewing always made me fidgety.

Mrs. Peters (*nervously*): I don't think we ought to touch things.

Mrs. Hale: I'll just finish up this end. (*Suddenly stopping and leaning forward.*) Mrs. Peters?

Mrs. Peters: Yes, Mrs. Hale?

Mrs. Hale: What do you suppose she was so nervous about?

Mrs. Peters: Oh—I don't know. I don't know as she was nervous. I sometimes sew awful queer when I'm just tired. (*Mrs. Hale starts to say something, looks at Mrs. Peters, then goes on sewing.*) Well, I must get these things wrapped up. They may be through sooner than we think. (*Putting apron and other things together.*) I wonder where I can find a piece of paper, and string.

Mrs. Hale: In that cupboard, maybe.

Mrs. Peters (*looking in cupboard*): Why, here's a birdcage. (*Holds it up.*) Did she have a bird, Mrs. Hale?

Mrs. Hale: Why, I don't know whether she did or not—I've not been here for so long. There was a man around last year selling canaries cheap, but I don't know as she took one; maybe she did. She used to sing real pretty herself.

Mrs. Peters (*glancing around*): Seems funny to think of a bird here. But she must have had one, or why would she have a cage? I wonder what happened to it.

Mrs. Hale: I s'pose maybe the cat got it.

Mrs. Peters: No, she didn't have a cat. She's got that feeling some people have about cats—being afraid of them. My cat got in her room and she was real upset and asked me to take it out.

Mrs. Hale: My sister Bessie was like that. Queer, ain't it?

Mrs. Peters (*examining the cage*): Why, look at this door. It's broke. One hinge is pulled apart.

Mrs. Hale (*looking too*): Looks as if someone must have been rough with it.

Mrs. Peters: Why, yes.

(*She brings the cage forward and puts it on the table.*)

Mrs. Hale: I wish if they're going to find any evidence they'd be about it. I don't like this place.

Mrs. Peters: But I'm awful glad you came with me, Mrs. Hale. It would be lonesome for me sitting here alone.

Mrs. Hale: It would, wouldn't it? (*Dropping her sewing.*) But I tell you what I do wish, Mrs. Peters. I wish I had come over sometimes when *she* was here. I—(*looking around the room*)—wish I had.

Mrs. Peters: But of course you were awful busy, Mrs. Hale—your house and your children.

Mrs. Hale: I could've come. I stayed away because it weren't cheerful—and that's why I ought to have come. I—I've never liked this place. Maybe because it's down in a hollow and you don't see the road. I dunno what it is but it's a lonesome place and always was. I wish I had come over to see Minnie Foster sometimes. I can see now—

(*Shakes her head.*)

Mrs. Peters: Well, you mustn't reproach yourself, Mrs. Hale. Somehow we just don't see how it is with other folks until—something comes up.

Mrs. Hale: Not having children makes less work—but it makes a quiet house, and Wright out to work all day, and no company when he did come in. Did you know John Wright, Mrs. Peters?

Mrs. Peters: Not to know him; I've seen him in town. They say he was a good man.

Mrs. Hale: Yes—good; he didn't drink, and kept his word as well as most, I guess, and paid his debts. But he was a hard man, Mrs. Peters. Just to pass the time of day with him—(*shivers*). Like a raw wind that gets to the bone. (*Pauses, her eye falling on the cage.*) I should think she would'a wanted a bird. But what do you suppose went with it?

Mrs. Peters: I don't know, unless it got sick and died.

(*She reaches over and swings the broken door, swings it again. Both women watch it.*)

Mrs. Hale: You weren't raised round here, were you? (*Mrs. Peters shakes her head.*) You didn't know—her?

Mrs. Peters: Not till they brought her yesterday.

Mrs. Hale: She—come to think of it, she was kind of like a bird herself—real sweet and pretty, but kind of timid and—fluttery. How—she—did—change. (*Silence; then as if struck by a happy thought and relieved to get back to everyday things.*) Tell you what, Mrs. Peters, why don't you take the quilt in with you? It might take up her mind.

Mrs. Peters: Why, I think that's a real nice idea, Mrs. Hale. There couldn't possibly be any objection to it, could there? Now, just what would I take? I wonder if her patches are in here—and her things.

(*They look in the sewing basket.*)

Mrs. Hale: Here's some red. I expect this has got sewing things in it. (*Brings out a fancy box.*) What a pretty box. Looks like something somebody would give you. Maybe her scissors are in here. (*Opens box. Suddenly puts her hand to her nose.*) Why—(*Mrs. Peters bends nearer, then turns her face away.*) There's something wrapped up in this piece of silk.

Mrs. Peters: Why, this isn't her scissors.

Mrs. Hale (*lifting the silk*): Oh, Mrs. Peters—it's—

(*Mrs. Peters bends closer.*)

Mrs. Peters: It's the bird.

2000 production of *Trifles*, by Echo Theatre of Dallas.

Mrs. Hale (*jumping up*): But, Mrs. Peters—look at it! Its neck! Look at its neck! It's all—other side *to*.

Mrs. Peters: Somebody—wrung—its—neck.

(*Their eyes meet. A look of growing comprehension, of horror. Steps are heard outside. Mrs. Hale slips box under quilt pieces, and sinks into her chair. Enter Sheriff and County Attorney. Mrs. Peters rises.*)

County Attorney (*as one turning from serious things to little pleasantries*): Well, ladies, have you decided whether she was going to quilt it or knot it?

Mrs. Peters: We think she was going to—knot it.

County Attorney: Well, that's interesting, I'm sure. (*Seeing the birdcage.*) Has the bird flown?

Mrs. Hale (*putting more quilt pieces over the box*): We think the—cat got it.

County Attorney (*preoccupied*): Is there a cat?

(*Mrs. Hale glances in a quick covert way at Mrs. Peters.*)

Mrs. Peters: Well, not *now*. They're superstitious, you know. They leave.

County Attorney (*to Sheriff Peters, continuing an interrupted conversation*): No sign at all of anyone having come from the outside. Their own rope. Now let's go up again and go over it piece by piece. (*They start upstairs.*) It would have to have been someone who knew just the—

(*Mrs. Peters sits down. The two women sit there not looking at one another, but as if peering into something and at the same time holding back. When they talk now it is in the manner of feeling their way over strange ground, as if afraid of what they are saying, but as if they cannot help saying it.*)

Mrs. Hale: She liked the bird. She was going to bury it in that pretty box.

Mrs. Peters (*in a whisper*): When I was a girl—my kitten—there was a boy took a hatchet, and before my eyes—and before I could get there—(*covers her face an instant*). If they hadn't held me back I would have—(*catches herself, looks upstairs where steps are heard, falters weakly*)—hurt him.

Mrs. Hale (*with a slow look around her*): I wonder how it would seem never to have had any children around. (*Pause.*) No, Wright wouldn't like the bird—a thing that sang. She used to sing. He killed that, too.

Mrs. Peters (*moving uneasily*): We don't know who killed the bird.

Mrs. Hale: I knew John Wright.

Mrs. Peters: It was an awful thing was done in this house that night, Mrs. Hale. Killing a man while he slept, slipping a rope around his neck that choked the life out of him.

Mrs. Hale: His neck. Choked the life out of him.

(*Her hand goes out and rests on the birdcage.*)

Mrs. Peters (*with rising voice*): We don't know who killed him. We don't *know*.

Mrs. Hale (*her own feeling not interrupted*): If there'd been years and years of nothing, then a bird to sing to you, it would be awful—still, after the bird was still.

Mrs. Peters (*something within her speaking*): I know what stillness is. When we homesteaded in Dakota, and my first baby died—after he was two years old, and me with no other then—

Mrs. Hale (*moving*): How soon do you suppose they'll be through looking for the evidence?

Mrs. Peters: I know what stillness is. (*Pulling herself back.*) The law has got to punish crime, Mrs. Hale.

Mrs. Hale (*not as if answering that*): I wish you'd seen Minnie Foster when she wore a white dress with blue ribbons and stood up there in the choir and sang. (*A look around the room.*) Oh, I *wish* I'd come over here once in a while! That was a crime! That was a crime! Who's going to punish that?

Mrs. Peters (*looking upstairs*): We mustn't—take on.

Mrs. Hale: I might have known she needed help! I know how things can be—for women. I tell you, it's queer, Mrs. Peters. We live close together and we live far apart. We all go through the same things—it's all just a different kind of the same thing. (*Brushes her eyes; noticing the bottle of fruit, reaches out for it.*) If I was you I wouldn't tell her her fruit was gone. Tell her it *ain't*. Tell her it's all right. Take this in to prove it to her. She—she may never know whether it was broke or not.

Mrs. Peters (*takes the bottle, looks about for something to wrap it in; takes petticoat from the clothes brought from the other room, very nervously begins winding this around the bottle; in a false voice*): My, it's a good thing the men couldn't hear us. Wouldn't they just laugh! Getting all stirred up over a little thing like a—dead canary. As if that could have anything to do with—with—wouldn't they *laugh!*

(*The men are heard coming down stairs.*)

Mrs. Hale (*under her breath*): Maybe they would—maybe they wouldn't.

County Attorney: No, Peters, it's all perfectly clear except a reason for doing it. But you know juries when it comes to women. If there was some definite thing. Something to show—something to make a story about—a thing that would connect up with this strange way of doing it—

(*The women's eyes meet for an instant. Enter Hale from outer door.*)

Hale: Well, I've got the team around. Pretty cold out there.

County Attorney: I'm going to stay here a while by myself. (*To the Sheriff*) You can send Frank out for me, can't you? I want to go over everything. I'm not satisfied that we can't do better.

Sheriff: Do you want to see what Mrs. Peters is going to take in?

(*The County Attorney goes to the table, picks up the apron, laughs.*)

County Attorney: Oh, I guess they're not very dangerous things the ladies have picked out. (*Moves a few things about, disturbing the quilt pieces which cover the box. Steps back.*) No, Mrs. Peters doesn't need supervising. For that matter, a sheriff's wife is married to the law. Ever think of it that way, Mrs. Peters?

Mrs. Peters: Not—just that way.

Sheriff (*chuckling*): Married to the law. (*Moves toward the other room.*) I just want you to come in here a minute, George. We ought to take a look at these windows.

County Attorney (*scoffingly*): Oh, windows!

Sheriff: We'll be right out, Mr. Hale.

(*Hale goes outside. The Sheriff follows the County Attorney into the other room. Then Mrs. Hale rises, hands tight together, looking intensely at Mrs. Peters, whose eyes make a slow turn, finally meeting Mrs. Hale's. A moment Mrs. Hale holds her, then her own eyes point the way to where the box is concealed. Suddenly Mrs. Peters throws back quilt pieces and tries to put the box in the bag she is wearing. It is too big. She opens box, starts to take bird out, cannot touch it, goes to pieces, stands there helpless. Sound of a knob turning in the other room. Mrs. Hale snatches the box and puts it in the pocket of her big coat. Enter County Attorney and Sheriff.*)

County Attorney (*facetiously*): Well, Henry, at least we found out that she was not going to quilt it. She was going to—what is it you call it, ladies?

Mrs. Hale (*her hand against her pocket*): We call it—knot it, Mr. Henderson.

CURTAIN

Questions

1. What attitudes toward women do the Sheriff and the County Attorney express? How do Mrs. Hale and Mrs. Peters react to these sentiments?

2. Why does the County Attorney care so much about discovering a motive for the killing?

3. What does Glaspell show us about the position of women in this early twentieth-century community?

4. What do we learn about the married life of the Wrights? By what means is this knowledge revealed to us?

5. What is the setting of this play, and how does it help us to understand Mrs. Wright's deed?

6. What do you infer from the wildly stitched block in Minnie's quilt? Why does Mrs. Hale rip out the crazy stitches?

7. What is so suggestive in the ruined birdcage and the dead canary wrapped in silk? What do these objects have to do with Minnie Foster Wright? What similarity do you notice between the way the canary died and John Wright's own death?

8. What thoughts and memories confirm Mrs. Peters and Mrs. Hale in their decision to help Minnie beat the murder rap?

9. In what places does Mrs. Peters show that she is trying to be a loyal, law-abiding sheriff's wife? How do she and Mrs. Hale differ in background and temperament?

10. What ironies does the play contain? Comment on Mrs. Hale's closing speech: "We call it—knot it, Mr. Henderson." Why is that little hesitation before "knot it" such a meaningful pause?

11. Point out some moments in the play when the playwright conveys much to the audience without needing dialogue.

12. How would you sum up the play's major theme?

13. How does this play, first produced in 1916, show its age? In what ways does it seem still remarkably new?

14. "*Trifles* is a lousy mystery. All the action took place before the curtain went up. Almost in the beginning, on the third page, we find out 'who done it.' So there isn't really much reason for us to sit through the rest of the play." Discuss this view.

ANALYZING *TRIFLES*

Some plays endure, perhaps because (among other reasons) actors take pleasure in performing them. *Trifles* is such a play, a showcase for the skills of its two principals. While the men importantly bumble about, trying to discover a motive, Mrs. Peters and Mrs. Hale solve the case right under their dull noses. The two players in these leading roles face a challenging task: to show both characters growing onstage before us. Discovering a secret that binds them, the two women must realize painful truths in their own lives, become aware of all they have in common with Minnie Wright, and gradually resolve to side with the accused against the men. That *Trifles* has enjoyed a revival of attention may reflect its evident feminist views, its convincing portrait of two women forced reluctantly to arrive at a moral judgment and to make a defiant move.

Conflict

Some critics say that the essence of drama is **conflict,** the central struggle between two or more forces in a play. Evidently, Glaspell's play is rich in this essential, even though its most violent conflict—the war between John and Minnie Wright—takes place before the play begins. Right away, when the menfolk barge through the door into the warm room, letting the women trail in after them; right away, when the sheriff makes fun of Minnie for worrying about "trifles" and the county attorney (that slick politician) starts crudely trying to flatter the "ladies," we sense a conflict between officious, self-important men and the women they expect to wait on them. What is the play's *theme*? Surely the title points to it: women, who men say worry over trifles, can find large meanings in those little things.

Plot

Like a carefully constructed traditional short story, *Trifles* has a **plot,** a term sometimes taken to mean whatever happens in a story, but more exactly referring to the unique arrangement of events that the author has made. (For more about plot in a story, see Chapter 1.) If Glaspell had elected to tell the story of John and Minnie Wright in chronological order, the sequence in which events took place in time, she might have written a much longer play, opening perhaps with a scene of Minnie's buying her canary and John's cold complaint, "That damned bird keeps twittering all day long!" She might have included scenes showing John strangling the canary and swearing when it beaks him; the Wrights in their loveless bed while Minnie knots her noose; and farmer Hale's entrance after the murder, with Minnie rocking. Only at the end would she have shown us what happened after the crime. That arrangement of events would have made for a quite different play than the short, tight one Glaspell wrote. By telling of events in retrospect, by having the women detectives piece together what happened, Glaspell leads us to focus not only on the murder but, more importantly, on the developing bond between the two women and their growing compassion for the accused.

Subplot

Tightly packed, the one-act *Trifles* contains but one plot: the story of how two women discover evidence that might hang another woman and then hide it. Some plays, usually longer ones, may be more complicated. They may contain a **double plot** (or **subplot**), a secondary arrangement of incidents, involving not the protagonist but someone less important. In Henrik Ibsen's *A Doll's House*, the main plot involves a woman and her husband; they are joined by a second couple, whose fortunes we also follow with interest and whose futures pose different questions.

Protagonist

If *Trifles* may be said to have a **protagonist,** a leading character—a word we usually save for the primary figure of a larger and more eventful play such as *Othello* or *Death of a Salesman*—then you would call the two women dual protagonists. They act in unison to make the plot unfold. Or you could argue that Mrs. Hale—because she destroys the wild stitching in the quilt, because she finds the dead canary, because she invents a cat to catch the bird (thus deceiving the county attorney), and because in the end when Mrs. Peters helplessly "goes to pieces" it is she who takes the initiative and seizes the evidence—deserves to be called the protagonist. More than anyone else in the play, you could claim, the more decisive Mrs. Hale makes things happen.

Exposition

A vital part of most plays is an **exposition,** the part in which we first meet the characters, learn what happened before the curtain rose, and find out what is happening now. For a one-act play, *Trifles* has a fairly long exposition, extending from the opening of the kitchen door through the end of farmer Hale's story. Clearly, this substantial exposition is necessary to set the situation and to fill in the facts of the crime. By comparison, Shakespeare's far longer *Tragedy of Richard III* begins almost abruptly, with its protagonist, a duke who yearns to be king, summing up history in an opening speech and revealing his evil character: "And therefore, since I cannot prove a lover . . . I am determinèd to prove a villain." But Glaspell, too, knows her craft. In the exposition, we are given a **foreshadowing** (or hint of what is to come) in Hale's dry remark, "I didn't know as what his wife wanted made much difference to John." The remark announces the play's theme that men often ignore women's feelings, and it hints at Minnie Wright's motive, later to be revealed. The county attorney, failing to pick up a valuable clue, tables the discussion. (Still another foreshadowing occurs in Mrs. Hale's ripping out the wild, panicky stitches in Minnie's quilt. In the end, Mrs. Hale will make a similar final move to conceal the evidence.)

Dramatic Question

With the county attorney's speech to the sheriff, "You're convinced that there was nothing important here—nothing that would point to any motive," we begin to understand what he seeks. As he will make even clearer later, the attorney needs a motive in order to convict the accused wife of murder in the first degree. Will Minnie's motive in killing her husband be discovered? Through the first two-thirds of *Trifles*, this is the play's **dramatic question**. Whether or not we state such a question in our minds (and it is doubtful that we do), our interest quickens as we sense that here is a problem to be solved, an uncertainty to be cleared up. When Mrs. Hale and Mrs. Peters find the dead canary with the twisted neck, the question is answered. We know that Minnie killed John to repay him for his act of gross cruelty. The playwright, however, now raises a *new* dramatic question. Having discovered Minnie's motive, will the women reveal it to the lawmen? Alternatively (if you care to phrase the new question differently), what will they do with the incriminating evidence? We keep reading, or stay clamped to our theater seats, because we want that question answered. We share the women's secret now, and we want to see what they will do with it.

Climax

Step by step, *Trifles* builds to a **climax**: a moment, usually coming late in a play, when tension reaches its greatest height. At such a moment, we sense that the play's dramatic question (or its final dramatic question, if the writer has posed more than one) is about to be answered. In *Trifles* this climax occurs when Mrs. Peters finds herself torn between her desire to save Minnie and her duty to the law. "It was an awful thing was done in this house that night," she reminds herself in one speech, suggesting that Minnie deserves to be punished; then in the next speech she insists, "We don't know who killed him. We don't *know*." Shortly after that, in one speech she voices two warring attitudes. Remembering the loss of her first child, she sympathizes with Minnie: "I know what stillness is." But in her next breath she recalls once more her duty to be a loyal sheriff's wife: "The law has got to punish crime, Mrs. Hale." For a moment, she is placed in conflict with Mrs. Hale, who knew Minnie personally. The two now stand on the edge of a fateful brink. Which way will they decide?

You will sometimes hear *climax* used in a different sense to mean any **crisis**—that is, a moment of tension when one or another outcome is possible. What *crisis* means will be easy to remember if you think of a crisis in medicine: the turning point in an illness when it becomes clear that a patient will either die or recover. In talking about plays, you will probably find both *crisis* and *climax* useful. You can say that a play has more than one crisis, perhaps several. In such a play, the last and most decisive crisis is the climax. A play has only one climax.

Resolution and Dénouement

From this moment of climax, the play, like its protagonist (or if you like, protagonists), will make a final move. Mrs. Peters takes her stand. Mrs. Hale, too, decides.

She owes Minnie something to make up for her own "crime"—her failure to visit the desperate woman. The plot now charges ahead to its outcome or **resolution,** also called the **conclusion** or **dénouement** (French for "untying of a knot"). The two women act: they scoop up the damaging evidence. Seconds before the very end, Glaspell heightens the **suspense,** our enjoyable anxiety, by making Mrs. Peters fumble with the incriminating box as the sheriff and the county attorney draw near. Mrs. Hale's swift grab for the evidence saves the day and presumably saves Minnie's life. The sound of the doorknob turning in the next room, as the lawmen return, is a small but effective bit of **stage business**—any nonverbal action that engages the attention of an audience. Earlier, when Mrs. Hale almost sits down in Minnie's place, the empty chair that ominously starts rocking is another brilliant piece of stage business. Not only does it give us something interesting to watch, but it also gives us something to think about.

Rising and Falling Action

The German critic Gustav Freytag maintained that events in a plot can be arranged in the outline of a pyramid. In his influential view, a play begins with a **rising action,** that part of the narrative (including the exposition) in which events start moving toward a climax. After the climax, the story tapers off in a **falling action**—that is, the subsequent events, including a resolution. In a tragedy, this falling action usually is recognizable: the protagonist's fortunes proceed downhill to an inevitable end.

Some plays indeed have demonstrable pyramids. In *Trifles*, we might claim that in the first two-thirds of the play a rising action builds in intensity. It proceeds through each main incident: the finding of the crazily stitched quilt, Mrs. Hale's ripping out the evidence, the discovery of the birdcage, then of the bird itself, and Mrs. Hale's concealing it. At the climax, the peak of the pyramid, the two women seem about to clash as Mrs. Peters wavers uncertainly. The action then falls to a swift resolution. If you outlined that pyramid on paper, however, it would look lopsided—a long rise and a short, steep fall. The pyramid metaphor seems more meaningfully to fit longer plays, among them some classic tragedies, such as *Oedipus the King*. Nevertheless, in most other plays, it is hard to find a symmetrical pyramid. (For a demonstration of another, quite different way to outline *Trifles*, see "Writing a Card Report" on pages 1957.)

Unity of Time, Place, and Action

Because its action occurs all at one time and in one place, *Trifles* happens to observe the **unities,** certain principles of good drama laid down by Italian literary critics in the sixteenth century. Interpreting the theories of Aristotle as binding laws, these critics set down three basic principles: a good play, they maintained, should display unity of *action*, unity of *time*, and unity of *place*. In practical terms, this theory maintained that a play must represent a single series of interrelated actions that take place within twenty-four hours in a single location. Furthermore, they insisted, to have true unity of action, a play had to be entirely serious or entirely funny. Mixing tragic and comic elements was not allowed. That Glaspell consciously strove to obey those critics is doubtful, and certainly many great plays, such as Shakespeare's *Othello*, defy such arbitrary rules. Still, it is at least arguable that some of the power of *Trifles* (or Sophocles's *Oedipus the King*) comes from the intensity of the playwright's concentration on what happens in one place, in one short expanse of time.

Symbols in Drama

Brief though it is, *Trifles* has main elements you will find in much longer, more complicated plays. It even has **symbols,** things that hint at large meanings—for example, the broken birdcage and the dead canary, both suggesting the music and the joy that John Wright stifled in Minnie and the terrible stillness that followed his killing the one thing she loved. Perhaps the lone remaining jar of cherries, too, radiates suggestions: it is the one bright, cheerful thing poor Minnie has to show for a whole summer of toil. Plays can also contain symbolic characters (generally flat ones such as a prophet who croaks, "Beware the ides of March"), symbolic settings, and symbolic gestures. Symbols in drama may be as big as a house—the home in Ibsen's *A Doll's House,* for instance—or they may appear to be trifles. In Glaspell's rich art, such trifles aren't trifling at all.

WRITING *effectively*

Susan Glaspell on Writing

Creating *Trifles*   1927

We went to the theater, and for the most part we came away wishing we had gone somewhere else. Those were the days when Broadway flourished almost unchallenged. Plays, like magazine stories, were patterned. They might be pretty good within themselves, seldom did they open out to— where it surprised or thrilled your spirit to follow. They didn't ask much of *you*, those plays. Having paid for your seat, the thing was all done for you, and your mind came out where it went in, only tireder. An audience, Jig° said, had imagination. What was this "Broadway," which could make a thing as interesting as life into a thing as dull as a Broadway play?

Susan Glaspell

There was a meeting at the Liberal Club—Eddie Goodman, Phil Moeller, Ida Rauh, the Boni brothers, exciting talk about starting a theater.

• • •

He [Jig] wrote a letter to the people who had seen the plays, asking if they cared to become associate members of the Provincetown Players. The purpose was to give American playwrights of sincere purpose a chance to work out their ideas in freedom, to give all who worked with the plays their opportunity as artists. Were they interested in this? One dollar for the three remaining bills.

Jig: the nickname of George Cram Cook (1873–1924), Glaspell's husband, who was the central founder and director of the Provincetown Players, perhaps the most influential theater company in the history of American drama.

The response paid for seats and stage, and for sets. A production need not cost a lot of money, Jig would say. The most expensive set at the Wharf Theater° cost thirteen dollars. There were sets at the Provincetown Playhouse which cost little more. . . .

"Now, Susan," he [Jig] said to me, briskly, "I have announced a play of yours for the next bill."

"But I have no play!"

"Then you will have to sit down to-morrow and begin one."

I protested. I did not know how to write a play. I had never "studied it."

"Nonsense," said Jig. "You've got a stage, haven't you?"

So I went out on the wharf, sat alone on one of our wooden benches without a back, and looked a long time at that bare little stage. After a time the stage became a kitchen—a kitchen there all by itself. I saw just where the stove was, the table, and the steps going upstairs. Then the door at the back opened, and people all bundled up came in—two or three men, I wasn't sure which, but sure enough about the two women, who hung back, reluctant to enter that kitchen. When I was a newspaper reporter out in Iowa, I was sent down-state to do a murder trial, and I never forgot going into the kitchen of a woman locked up in town. I had meant to do it as a short story, but the stage took it for its own, so I hurried in from the wharf to write down what I had seen. Whenever I got stuck, I would run across the street to the old wharf, sit in that leaning little theater under which the sea sounded, until the play was ready to continue. Sometimes things written in my room would not form on the stage, and I must go home and cross them out. "What playwrights need is a stage," said Jig, "their own stage."

Ten days after the director said he had announced my play, there was a reading at Mary Heaton Vorse's. I was late to the meeting, home revising the play. But when I got there the crowd liked "Trifles," and voted to put it in rehearsal next day.

From *The Road to the Temple*

THINKING ABOUT A PLAY

A good play almost always presents a conflict. Conflict creates suspense and keeps an audience from meandering out to the lobby water fountain. Without it, a play would be static and, most likely, dull. When a character intensely desires something but some obstacle—perhaps another character—stands in the way, the result is dramatic tension. To understand a play, it is essential to understand the basic conflicts motivating the plot.

- **Identify the play's protagonist.** Who is the central character of the play? What motivates this character? What does this character want most to achieve or avoid? Is this goal reasonable or does it reflect some delusion on the part of the protagonist?
- **Identify the antagonist.** Who prevents the main character from achieving his or her goal? Is the opposition conscious or accidental? What motivates this character to oppose the protagonist?
- **Identify the central dramatic conflict.** What does the struggle between the protagonist and antagonist focus on? Is it another person, a possession, an action, some sort of recognition, or honor?

Wharf Theater: the makeshift theater that Cook created from an old fish-house at the end of a Provincetown wharf.

▪ **How does the conflict influence the action of the play?** The central conflict usually fuels the plot, causing characters to do and say all sorts of things they might not otherwise undertake. What series of later events does the central conflict set in motion?

CHECKLIST: Writing About a Play

☐ List the play's three or four main characters. Jot down what each character wants most at the play's beginning.

☐ Which of these characters is the protagonist?

☐ What stands in the way of the protagonist achieving his or her goal?

☐ How do the other characters' motivations fit into the central conflict? Identify any double plots or subplots.

☐ What are the play's main events? How does each relate to the protagonist's struggle?

☐ Where do you find the play's climax?

☐ How is the conflict resolved? What qualities in the protagonist's character bring about the play's outcome?

☐ Does the protagonist achieve his or her goal? How does success or failure affect the protagonist?

WRITING ASSIGNMENT ON CONFLICT

Select any short play, and write a brief essay identifying the protagonist, central conflict, and dramatic question.

Here is a paper by Tara Mazzucca, a student of Beverly Schneller at Millersville University, that examines and compares the protagonists and dramatic questions of two short plays by Susan Glaspell.

SAMPLE STUDENT PAPER

Mazzucca 1

Tara Mazzucca

Professor Schneller

English 102

29 January 2012

Outside *Trifles*

Susan Glaspell was one of America's first feminist playwrights. A founder of the non-commercial Provincetown Players, she used this experimental company

Useful background

to present plays that realistically explored the lives of women. I would like to examine and compare two of Glaspell's early one-act plays, *Trifles* (1916) and *The Outside* (1917). I will discuss how they present women who are forced to survive in a world where men make most of the rules.

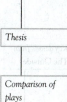

Thesis

Both plays focus on female protagonists, and both realistically present the emotional hardships these women endure in their daily lives. Both plays have contemporary settings; they take place in the early twentieth century. Both plays present women who are isolated from society—Mrs. Wright in *Trifles* and the two protagonists of *The Outside*. And in both plays a pair of female characters work together to solve the central dramatic question.

Comparison of plays

In *Trifles* Glaspell ironically places two wives, one married to a farmer and the other to the sheriff, at the scene of a mysterious murder case. The play takes place entirely in familiar territory for women in the early 1900s—a kitchen. The kitchen becomes a symbol for the game of hot and cold that the characters unwittingly play. In the kitchen where it is hot, the women find all the clues necessary to solve the case. Meanwhile the men search the rest of the cold house and find nothing to suggest a motive for the crime.

Key details from Trifles

Significance of setting

The two wives soon recognize the story behind the murder by observing small details in the house. They see clues in what the men pass over as mere trifles. When the women mention the ruined fruit preserves in the kitchen, Mr. Hale dismisses the potential importance of housekeeping details and comments, "Well, women are used to worrying over trifles" (1156). The two women, however, understand that small things can affect a person deeply.

Significance of details

The two women also recognize the importance of singing in Mrs. Wright's life. Singing was something she was known for when she was younger, only to have it taken away from her when she married John Wright. Doing housework alone all day in silence, Mrs. Wright became a different person. The stress of loneliness and depression finally got to Mrs. Wright. She bought a canary for company and enjoyment. She loved the singing bird, but her husband killed it. In desperation the woman decided to live without her husband.

More details

Mrs. Hale and Mrs. Peters instinctively understand Mrs. Wright's worries. Their perspective gives them an advantage over their male counterparts. The women must work together, because if they did not, each would break under the pressure of the cold treatment they receive from their husbands—break like the glass jars of canned fruit Mrs. Wright stores away in her cabinet.

Examination of thesis from first play

Mazzucca 3

The plot of *The Outside* is relatively simple. The widowed Mrs. Patrick lives in a remote building that was once a life-saving station. Mrs. Patrick employs another widow, Allie Mayo, to help her with housekeeping. They lead lives of almost total isolation. One day three life-savers bring in the body of a drowned sailor and attempt unsuccessfully to revive him. Mrs. Patrick is furious that they have used her house as a rescue station and demands that they leave. Her behavior so upsets the usually silent Allie that the servant confronts Mrs. Patrick with a passionate speech about the futility of renouncing life.

Key details from The Outside

Allie also keeps to herself from grief. As a girl, she was talkative, but after her young husband vanished at sea, she resolved never to say an unnecessary word. Now twenty years later, she is notorious for her silence. The two women share a common grief of having lost the husbands they loved. Losing a husband changed each woman. Allie chose silence. Mrs. Patrick left society.

When the men bring the drowned young man into the former life-saving station, the incident upsets Mrs. Patrick, and she explodes with anger. This incident disturbs Allie in a different way. She realizes how isolated they have become. She knows that if they do not change, they will die without anyone caring. Deeply disturbed, Allie breaks her silence and argues with her employer. Mrs. Patrick initially resists Allie's remarks because she still has not come to terms with life without her husband. Allie resembles Mrs. Wright in *Trifles*. Both women keep quiet for years and do what they're told, until they reach a breaking point. A critical event forces each of them to take dramatic action. Allie violently argues with her employer; Mrs. Wright decides to murder her husband.

Comparison between two plays

Comparison continued

Mrs. Hale and Mrs. Peters resemble Mrs. Patrick from *The Outside*. Throughout the play Mrs. Hale and Mrs. Peters try to understand why Mrs. Wright killed her husband. In the end, they recognize that their lives have much in common with that of the murderer. Their actions show their confusion about their own values. They do things that hinder the sheriff's investigation to protect an oppressed woman. First, Mrs. Hale rips out Mrs. Wright's erratic stitching so the men will not notice her nervous condition. Second, Mrs. Peters, who is—ironically—the sheriff's wife, hides the strangled bird from her husband and the other man. The women see a new side of Mrs. Wright's marriage and sympathize with her pathetic situation. By the end of *The Outside* Mrs. Patrick also sees a new side of Allie. Allie's outburst forces Mrs. Patrick to consider changing her life and reconsider her ideas.

Mazzucca 4

Mrs. Patrick of *The Outside* and Mrs. Wright of *Trifles* are also alike because they are now isolated from the world they used to enjoy. One stopped living because of a harsh husband, the other because of a dead husband. Mrs. Hale and Allie also resemble one another because they both waited too late to understand the depression of their neighbor or living companion. In *Trifles*, Mrs. Hale decides to help her neighbor even though it means protecting a criminal. Allie speaks truthfully even though it might jeopardize her job. In the end, the actions Allie and Mrs. Hale take are helpful. The men never find a motive for the murder. Mrs. Patrick finally considers changing her way of life in *The Outside*. In the end each woman has found something new inside of her.

Topic sentence— comparison

Mrs. Hale and Mrs. Peters both realize the secret they must keep to protect Mrs. Wright. They also realize the injustices women go through to be accepted in society. Mrs. Hale says:

Topic sentence/textual analysis

> I might have known she needed help! I know how things can be—
> for women. I tell you, it's queer, Mrs. Peters. We live close
> together and we live far apart. We all go through the same
> things—it's all just a different kind of the same thing. (1162)

In *The Outside*, the women don't feel socially oppressed by men, but they cannot define their lives except in relation to their husbands. When they become widows, they lose their reason to live. Allie realizes that their grief has gone too far. She finds her voice to say that life must be lived. Mrs. Patrick listens enough to feel uncertainty about her life of loneliness and isolation. Each play deals with death and its effects on the survivors.

Topic sentence/textual analysis

A major difference between the two plays is found in the way the central female characters treat one another. In *Trifles* the women work together to solve the mystery, but in *The Outside* the women clash and refuse to help one another. Glaspell did not have only one idealized image of female behavior. She realized that different women behave differently. Each play presents different ways women in the early twentieth century used to survive in a man's world. Trapped in the trifles of everyday life, many women felt as if they were living on the outside of the world.

Contrast

Conclusion

Restatement of thesis

Mazzucca 5

Works Cited

Glaspell, Susan. *The Outside. A Century of Plays by American Women*. Ed. Rachel France. New York: Rosen, 1979. 48–54. Print.

Glaspell, Susan. *Trifles. Literature: An Introduction to Fiction, Poetry, Drama, and Writing*. Ed. X. J. Kennedy and Dana Gioia. 12th ed. New York: Pearson, 2013. 1153–63. Print.

MORE TOPICS FOR WRITING

1. Write a brief essay on the role gender differences play in Susan Glaspell's *Trifles*.
2. Write an analysis of the exposition—how the scene is set, characters introduced, and background information communicated—in *Trifles*.
3. Describe the significance of setting in *Trifles*.
4. Imagine you are a lawyer hired to defend Minnie Wright. Present your closing argument to the jury.
5. Watch any hour-long television drama. Write about the main conflict that drives the story. What motivates the protagonist? What stands in his or her way? How do each of the drama's main events relate to the protagonist's struggle? How is the conflict resolved? Is the show's outcome connected to the protagonist's character, or do events just happen to him or her? Do you believe the script is well written? Why or why not?

TERMS FOR *review*

Plot Elements

Exposition ▶ The opening portion of a narrative or drama in which the scene is set, the protagonist is introduced, and the author discloses any other background information necessary for the audience to understand the events that are to follow.

Foreshadowing ▶ The technique of arranging events and information in such a way that later events are prepared for beforehand, whether through specific words, images, or actions.

Double plot ▶ Also called **subplot**. A second story or plotline that is complete and interesting in its own right, often doubling or inverting the main plot.

Conflict ▶ The central struggle between two or more forces. Conflict generally occurs when some person or thing prevents the protagonist from achieving his or her goal.

Crisis ▶ A point when a crucial action, decision, or realization must be made, often marking a turning point or reversal of the protagonist's fortunes.

Climax ▶ The moment of greatest intensity, which almost inevitably occurs toward the end of the work. The climax often takes the form of a decisive confrontation between the protagonist and antagonist.

Resolution ▶ The final part of a narrative, the concluding action or actions that follow the climax.

Theatrical Conventions

Unities ▶ Unity of time, place, and action, the three formal qualities recommended by Renaissance critics to give a theatrical plot cohesion and integrity. According to this theory, a play should depict the causes and effects of a single action unfolding in one day in one place.

Soliloquy ▶ In drama, a speech by a character alone onstage in which he or she utters his or her thoughts aloud.

Aside ▶ A speech that a character addresses directly to the audience, unheard by the other characters on stage, as when the villain in a melodrama chortles: "Heh! Heh! Now she's in my power!"

Stage business ▶ Nonverbal action that engages the attention of an audience.

35 MODES OF DRAMA
Tragedy and Comedy

Show me a hero and I will write you a tragedy.

— F. SCOTT FITZGERALD

In 1770, Horace Walpole wrote, "the world is a comedy to those that think, a tragedy to those that feel." All of us, of course, both think and feel, and all of us have moments when we stand back and laugh, whether ruefully or with glee, at life's absurdities, just as we all have times when our hearts are broken by its pains and losses. Thus, the modes of tragedy and comedy, diametrically opposed to one another though they are, do not demand that we choose between them: both of them speak to something deep and real within us, and each of them has its own truth to tell about the infinitely complex experience of living in this world.

TRAGEDY

By **tragedy** we mean a play that portrays a serious conflict between human beings and some superior, overwhelming force. It ends sorrowfully and disastrously, and this outcome seems inevitable. Few spectators of *Oedipus the King* wonder how the play will turn out or wish for a happy ending. "In a tragedy," French playwright Jean Anouilh has remarked, "nothing is in doubt and everyone's destiny is known. . . . Tragedy is restful, and the reason is that hope, that foul, deceitful thing, has no part in it. There isn't any hope. You're trapped. The whole sky has fallen on you, and all you can do about it is shout."[1]

Many of our ideas of tragedy (from the Greek *tragoidia*, "goat song," referring to the goatskin dress of the performers), go back to ancient Athens; the plays of the Greek dramatists Sophocles, Aeschylus, and Euripides exemplify the art of tragedy. In the fourth century B.C., the philosopher Aristotle described Sophocles's *Oedipus the King* and other tragedies he had seen, analyzing their elements and trying to account for their power over our emotions. Aristotle's observations will make more sense after you read *Oedipus the King*, so we will save our principal discussion of them for the next chapter. But for now, to understand something of the nature of tragedy, let us take a brief overview of the subject.

---

[1]*Preface to Antigone*, translated by Louis Galantière (New York: Random, 1946).

One of the oldest and most durable of literary genres, tragedy is also one of the simplest—the protagonist undergoes a reversal of fortune, from good to bad, ending in catastrophe. However simple, though, tragedy can be one of the most complex genres to explain satisfactorily, with almost every principal point of its definition open to differing and often hotly debated interpretations. It is a fluid and adaptive genre, and for every one of its defining points, we can cite a tragic masterpiece that fails to observe that particular convention. Its fluidity and adaptability can also be shown by the way in which the classical tragic pattern is played out in pure form in such unlikely places as Orson Welles's film *Citizen Kane* (1941) and Chinua Achebe's great novel *Things Fall Apart* (1958): in each of these works, a man of high position and character—one a multimillionaire newspaper publisher, the other a late nineteenth-century African warrior—moves inexorably to destruction, impelled by his rigidity and self-righteousness. Even a movie such as *King Kong*—despite its oversized and hirsute protagonist—exemplifies some of the principles of tragedy.

To gain a clearer understanding of what tragedy is, let us first take a moment to talk about what it is not. Consider the kinds of events that customarily bring the term "tragedy" to mind: the death of a child, a fire that destroys a family's home and possessions, the killing of a bystander caught in the crossfire of a shootout between criminals, and so on. What all of these unfortunate instances have in common, obviously, is that they involve the infliction of great and irreversible suffering. But what they also share is the sense that the sufferers are innocent, that they have done nothing to cause or to deserve their fate. This is what we usually describe as a tragedy in real life, but tragedy in a literary or dramatic context has a different meaning: most theorists take their lead from Aristotle (see the next chapter for a fuller discussion of several of the points raised here) in maintaining that the protagonist's reversal of fortune is brought about through some error or weakness on his part, generally referred to as his **tragic flaw**.

Despite this weakness, the hero is traditionally a person of nobility, of both social rank and personality. Just as the suffering of totally innocent people stirs us to sympathetic sorrow rather than a tragic response, so too the destruction of a purely evil figure, a tyrant or a murderer with no redeeming qualities, would inspire only feelings of relief and satisfaction—hardly the emotions that tragedy seeks to stimulate. In most tragedies, the catastrophe entails not only the loss of outward fortune—things such as reputation, power, and life itself, which even the basest villain may possess and then be deprived of—but also the erosion of the protagonist's moral character and greatness of spirit.

Tragic Style

In keeping with this emphasis on nobility of spirit, tragedies are customarily written in an elevated style, one characterized by dignity and seriousness. In the Middle Ages, just as *tragedy* meant a work written in a high style in which the central character went from good fortune to bad, *comedy* indicated just the opposite, a work written in a low or common style, in which the protagonist moved from adverse circumstances to happy ones—hence Dante's great triptych of hell, purgatory, and heaven, written in everyday Italian rather than scholarly Latin, is known as *The Divine Comedy*, despite the relative absence of humor, let alone hilarity, in its pages. The tragic view of life, clearly, presupposes that in the end we will prove unequal to the challenges we must face, while the comic outlook asserts a view of human possibility in which our common sense and resilience—or pure dumb luck—will enable us to win out.

Tragedy's complexity can be seen also in the response that, according to Aristotle, it seeks to arouse in the viewer: pity and fear. By its very nature, pity distances the one who pities from the object of that pity, since we can feel sorry only for those whom we perceive to be worse off than ourselves. When we watch or read a tragedy, moved as we may be, we observe the downfall of the protagonist with a certain detachment; "better him than me" may be a rather crude way of putting it, but perhaps not an entirely incorrect one. Fear, on the other hand, usually involves an immediate anxiety about our own well-being. Even as we regard the hero's destruction from the safety of a better place, we are made to feel our own vulnerability in the face of life's dangers and instability, because we see that neither position nor virtue can protect even the great from ruin.

The following is a scene from Christopher Marlowe's classic Elizabethan tragedy *Doctor Faustus*. Based on an anonymous pamphlet published in Germany in 1587 and translated into English shortly thereafter, this celebrated play tells the story of an elderly professor who feels that he has wasted his life in fruitless inquiry. Chafing at the limits of human understanding, he makes a pact with the devil to gain forbidden knowledge and power. The scene presented here is the decisive turning point of the play, in which Faustus seals the satanic bargain that will damn him. Stimulated by his thirst for knowledge and experience, spurred on by his pride to assume that the divinely ordained limits of human experience no longer apply to him, he rushes to embrace his own undoing. Marlowe dramatizes Faustus's situation by bringing a good angel and a fallen angel (i.e., a demon) to whisper conflicting advice in this pivotal scene. (This good angel versus bad angel device has proved popular for centuries. We still see it today in everything from TV commercials to cartoons such as *The Simpsons*.) Notice the dignified and often gorgeous language Marlowe employs to create the serious mood necessary for tragedy.

Christopher Marlowe

Scene from Doctor Faustus[2]   (about 1588)

Edited by Sylvan Barnet

Christopher Marlowe was born in Canterbury, England, in February 1564, about ten weeks before William Shakespeare. Marlowe, the son of a prosperous shoemaker, received a B.A. from Cambridge University in 1584 and an M.A. in 1587, after which he settled in London. The rest of his short life was marked by rumor, secrecy, and violence, including suspicions that he was a secret agent for Queen Elizabeth's government and allegations against him of blasphemy and atheism—no small matter in light of the political instability and religious controversies of the times. Peripherally implicated in several violent deaths, he met his own end in May 1593 when he was stabbed above the right eye during a tavern brawl, under circumstances that have never been fully explained. Brief and crowded as his life was, he wrote a number of intense, powerful, and highly influential tragedies—Tamburlaine the Great, Parts 1 and 2 (1587), Doctor Faustus (1588), The Jew of Malta (1589), Edward the Second (c. 1592), The Massacre at Paris (1593), and Dido, Queen of Carthage (c. 1593, with Thomas Nashe). He is also the author of the lyric poem "The Passionate Shepherd to His Love," with its universally known first line: "Come live with me and be my love."

[2]This scene is from the 1616 text, or "B-Text," published as *The Tragicall History of the Life and Death of Doctor Faustus*. Modernizations have been made in spelling and punctuation.

Doctor Faustus with the Bad Angel and the Good Angel, from the Utah Shakespearean Festival's 2005 production.

DRAMATIS PERSONAE

Doctor Faustus
Good Angel
Bad Angel
Mephistophilis, a devil

ACT II

SCENE I

(*Enter Faustus in his study.*)

Faustus: Now, Faustus, must thou needs be damned;
    Canst thou not be saved!
    What boots° it then to think on God or heaven?
    Away with such vain fancies, and despair—
    Despair in God and trust in Belzebub!
    Now go not backward Faustus; be resolute!   5
    Why waver'st thou? O something soundeth in mine ear,
    "Abjure this magic, turn to God again."
    Ay, and Faustus will turn to God again.
    To God? He loves thee not.   10

3 *boots*: avails

The god thou serv'st is thine own appetite
Wherein is fixed the love of Belzebub!
To him I'll build an altar and a church,
And offer lukewarm blood of newborn babes!

(*Enter the two Angels.*)

Bad Angel: Go forward, Faustus, in that famous art.   15
Good Angel: Sweet Faustus, leave that execrable art.
Faustus: Contrition, prayer, repentance? What of these?
Good Angel: O, they are means to bring thee unto heaven.
Bad Angel: Rather illusions, fruits of lunacy,
    That make men foolish that do use them most.   20
Good Angel: Sweet Faustus, think of heaven and heavenly things.
Bad Angel: No, Faustus, think of honor and of wealth.

                                                                                (*Exeunt Angels.*)

Faustus: Wealth!
    Why, the signory of Emden° shall be mine!
    When Mephistophilis shall stand by me   25
    What power can hurt me? Faustus, thou art safe.
    Cast no more doubts! Mephistophilis, come,
    And bring glad tidings from great Lucifer.
    Is't not midnight? Come Mephistophilis,
    Veni, veni, Mephostophile!°   30

(*Enter Mephistophilis.*)

    Now tell me, what saith Lucifer thy lord?
Mephistophilis: That I shall wait on Faustus whilst he lives,
    So he will buy my service with his soul.
Faustus: Already Faustus hath hazarded that for thee.
Mephistophilis: But now thou must bequeath it solemnly   35
    And write a deed of gift with thine own blood,
    For that security craves Lucifer.
    If thou deny it I must back to hell.
Faustus: Stay Mephistophilis and tell me,
    What good will my soul do thy lord?   40
Mephistophilis: Enlarge his kingdom.
Faustus: Is that the reason why he tempts us thus?
Mephistophilis: *Solamen miseris socios habuisse doloris.*°
Faustus: Why, have you any pain that torture other?°
Mephistophilis: As great as have the human souls of men.   45
    But tell me, Faustus, shall I have thy soul—
    And I will be thy slave and wait on thee
    And give thee more than thou hast wit to ask?
Faustus: Ay Mephistophilis, I'll give it him.°

---

24 *signory of Emden:* lordship of the rich German port at the mouth of the Ems   30 *Veni, veni,*
Mephostophile!: Come, come, Mephistophilis (Latin)   43 *Solamen . . . doloris:* Misery loves company
(Latin)   44 *other:* others   49 *him:* i.e., to Lucifer

Mephistophilis: Then, Faustus, stab thy arm courageously, 50
    And bind thy soul, that at some certain day
    Great Lucifer may claim it as his own.
    And then be thou as great as Lucifer!
Faustus: Lo, Mephistophilis: for love of thee
    Faustus hath cut his arm, and with his proper° blood 55
    Assures° his soul to be great Lucifer's,
    Chief Lord and Regent of perpetual night.
    View here this blood that trickles from mine arm,
    And let it be propitious for my wish.
Mephistophilis: But, Faustus, 60
    Write it in manner of a deed of gift.
Faustus: Ay, so I do—But Mephistophilis,
    My blood congeals and I can write no more.
Mephistophilis: I'll fetch thee fire to dissolve it straight.

                                     (Exit.)

Faustus: What might the staying of my blood portend? 65
    Is it unwilling I should write this bill?°
    Why streams it not that I may write afresh:
    "Faustus gives to thee his soul"? O there it stayed.
    Why should'st thou not? Is not thy soul thine own?
    Then write again: "Faustus gives to thee his soul." 70

    (Enter Mephistophilis, with the chafer° of fire.)

Mephistophilis: See, Faustus, here is fire. Set it° on.
Faustus: So, now the blood begins to clear again.
    Now will I make an end immediately.
Mephistophilis (aside): What will not I do to obtain his soul!
Faustus: Consummatum est!° This bill is ended: 75
    And Faustus hath bequeathed his soul to Lucifer.
    —But what is this inscription on mine arm?
    Homo fuge!° Whither should I fly?
    If unto God, He'll throw me down to hell.
    My senses are deceived; here's nothing writ. 80
    O yes, I see it plain! Even here is writ
    Homo fuge! Yet shall not Faustus fly!
Mephistophilis (aside): I'll fetch him somewhat° to delight his mind.

                                    (Exit Mephistophilis.)

    (Enter Devils, giving crowns and rich apparel to Faustus. They dance and then depart.)

    (Enter Mephistophilis.)

Faustus: What means this show? Speak, Mephistophilis.
Mephistophilis: Nothing, Faustus, but to delight thy mind, 85
    And let thee see what magic can perform.
Faustus: But may I raise such spirits when I please?

55 *proper:* own   56 *Assures:* conveys by contract   66 *bill:* contract   70 *s.d. chafer:* portable grate
71 *it:* i.e., the receptacle containing the congealed blood   75 *Consummatum est:* It is finished. (Latin: a
blasphemous repetition of Christ's words on the Cross; see John 19:30.)   78 *Homo fuge:* fly, man
(Latin)   83 *somewhat:* something

Mephistophilis: Ay, Faustus, and do greater things than these.
Faustus: Then, Mephistophilis, receive this scroll,
    A deed of gift of body and of soul: 90
    But yet conditionally that thou perform
    All covenants and articles between us both.
Mephistophilis: Faustus, I swear by hell and Lucifer
    To effect all promises between us both.
Faustus: Then hear me read it, Mephistophilis: 95

"On these conditions following:

First, that Faustus may be a spirit° in form and substance.

Secondly, that Mephistophilis shall be his servant, and be by him commanded.

Thirdly, that Mephistophilis shall do for him and bring him whatsoever.   100

Fourthly, that he shall be in his chamber or house invisible.

Lastly, that he shall appear to the said John Faustus, at all times, in what shape and form soever he please.

I, John Faustus of Wittenberg, Doctor, by these presents, do give both body and soul to Lucifer, Prince of the East, and his minister Mephistophilis, and further-   105
more grant unto them that, four and twenty years being expired, and these articles written being inviolate,° full power to fetch or carry the said John Faustus, body and soul, flesh, blood, into their habitation wheresoever.

                                           By me John Faustus."

Mephistophilis: Speak, Faustus, do you deliver this as your deed?   110
Faustus: Ay, take it, and the devil give thee good of it!
Mephistophilis: So, now Faustus, ask me what thou wilt.
Faustus: First, I will question with thee about hell.
    Tell me, where is the place that men call hell?
Mephistophilis: Under the heavens.   115
Faustus: Ay, so are all things else, but whereabouts?
Mephistophilis: Within the bowels of these elements,
    Where we are tortured, and remain forever.
    Hell hath no limits, nor is circumscribed,
    In one self place, but where we are is hell,   120
    And where hell is there must we ever be.
    And to be short, when all the world dissolves,
    And every creature shall be purified,
    All places shall be hell that is not heaven!
Faustus: I think hell's a fable.   125
Mephistophilis: Ay, think so still—till experience change thy mind.
Faustus: Why, dost thou think that Faustus shall be damned?
Mephistophilis: Ay, of necessity, for here's the scroll
    In which thou hast given thy soul to Lucifer.

---

97 *spirit:* evil spirit, devil. (But to see Faustus as transformed now into a devil deprived of freedom to repent is to deprive the remainder of the play of much of its meaning.)   107 *inviolate:* unviolated

Faustus: Ay, and body too; but what of that?   130
    Think'st thou that Faustus is so fond° to imagine,
    That after this life there is any pain?
    No, these are trifles, and mere old wives' tales.
Mephistophilis: But I am an instance to prove the contrary,
    For I tell thee I am damned, and now in hell!   135
Faustus: Nay, and this be hell, I'll willingly be damned—
    What, sleeping, eating, walking, and disputing?
    But leaving this, let me have a wife,
    The fairest maid in Germany,
    For I am wanton and lascivious,   140
    And cannot live without a wife.
Mephistophilis: Well, Faustus, thou shalt have a wife.

    (*He fetches in a woman devil.*)

Faustus: What sight is this?
Mephistophilis: Now, Faustus, wilt thou have a wife?
Faustus: Here's a hot whore indeed! No, I'll no wife.   145
Mephistophilis: Marriage is but a ceremonial toy,°

                                                    (*Exit she-devil.*)
    And if thou lov'st me, think no more of it.
    I'll cull thee out° the fairest courtesans
    And bring them every morning to thy bed.
    She whom thine eye shall like, thy heart shall have,   150
    Were she as chaste as was Penelope,°
    As wise as Saba,° or as beautiful
    As was bright Lucifer before his fall.
    Here, take this book and peruse it well.
    The iterating° of these lines brings gold;   155
    The framing° of this circle on the ground
    Brings thunder, whirlwinds, storm, and lightning;
    Pronounce this thrice devoutly to thyself,
    And men in harness° shall appear to thee,
    Ready to execute what thou command'st.   160
Faustus: Thanks, Mephistophilis, for this sweet book.
    This will I keep as chary as my life.

                                                    (*Exeunt.*)

Questions

1. What specifically motivates Faustus to make his satanic compact? Cite the text to back up your response.
2. How does his behavior constitute a compromise of his nobility?
3. "Is not thy soul thine own?" Faustus asks rhetorically (line 69). Discuss the implications of this statement in terms of the larger thematic concerns of the work.
4. Does Faustus inspire your pity and fear in this scene? Why or why not?

131 *fond:* foolish   146 *toy:* trifle   148 *cull thee out:* select for you   151 *Penelope:* wife of Ulysses, famed for her fidelity   152 *Saba:* the Queen of Sheba   155 *iterating:* repetition   156 *framing:* drawing   159 *harness:* armor

Traditional masks of Comedy and Tragedy.

COMEDY

The best-known traditional emblem of drama—a pair of masks, one sorrowful (representing tragedy) and one smiling (representing comedy)—suggests that tragedy and comedy, although opposites, are close relatives. Often, comedy shows people getting into trouble through error or weakness; in this respect it is akin to tragedy. An important difference between comedy and tragedy lies in the attitude toward human failing that is expected of us. When a main character in a comedy suffers from overweening pride, as does Oedipus, or if he fails to recognize that his bride-to-be is actually his mother, we laugh—something we would never do in watching a competent performance of *Oedipus the King*.

Comedy, from the Greek *komos*, "a revel," is thought to have originated in festivities to celebrate spring, ritual performances in praise of Dionysus, god of fertility and wine. In drama, comedy may be broadly defined as whatever makes us laugh. A comedy may be a name for one entire play, or we may say that there is comedy in only part of a play—as in a comic character or a comic situation.

Theories of Comedy

Many theories have been propounded to explain why we laugh; most of these notions fall into a few familiar types. One school, exemplified by French philosopher Henri Bergson, sees laughter as a form of ridicule, implying a feeling of disinterested superiority; all jokes are *on* somebody. Bergson suggests that laughter springs from situations in which we sense a conflict between some mechanical or rigid pattern of behavior and our sense of a more natural or "organic" kind of behavior that is possible. An example occurs in Buster Keaton's comic film *The Boat*. Having launched a little boat that springs a leak, Keaton rigidly goes down with it, with frozen face. (The more natural and organic thing to do would be to swim for shore.)

Other thinkers view laughter as our response to expectations fulfilled or to expectations set up but then suddenly frustrated. Some hold it to be the expression of our delight in seeing our suppressed urges acted out (as when a comedian hurls an egg at a pompous stuffed shirt); some, to be our defensive reaction to a painful and disturbing truth.

Satiric Comedy

Derisive humor is basic to **satiric comedy**, in which human weakness or folly is ridiculed from a vantage point of supposedly enlightened superiority. Satiric comedy may be coolly malicious and gently biting, but it tends to be critical of people, their manners, and their morals. It is at least as old as the comedies of Aristophanes, who thrived in the fifth century B.C. In *Lysistrata,* the satirist shows how the women of two warring cities speedily halt a war by agreeing to deny themselves to their husbands. (The satirist's target is men so proud that they go to war rather than make the slightest concession.)

High Comedy

Comedy is often divided into two varieties—"high" and "low." **High comedy** relies more on wit and wordplay than on physical action for its humor. It tries to address the audience's intelligence by pointing out the pretension and hypocrisy of human behavior. High comedy also generally avoids derisive humor. Jokes about physical appearance would, for example, be avoided. One technique it employs to appeal to a sophisticated, verbal audience is use of the **epigram**, a brief and witty statement that memorably expresses some truth, large or small. Oscar Wilde's plays such as *The Importance of Being Earnest* (1895) and *Lady Windermere's Fan* (1892) sparkle with such brilliant epigrams as: "I can resist everything except temptation"; "Experience is simply the name we give our mistakes"; "There is only one thing in the world worse than being talked about, and that is not being talked about."

A type of high comedy is the **comedy of manners,** a witty satire set in elite or fashionable society. Popular since the seventeenth-century Restoration period, splendid comedies of manners continue to be written to this day. Bernard Shaw's *Pygmalion* (1913), which eventually became the musical *My Fair Lady,* contrasts life in the streets of London with that in aristocratic drawing rooms. Contemporary playwrights such as Tom Stoppard, Michael Frayn, Tina Howe, and John Guare have all created memorable comedies of manners.

Low Comedy

Low comedy explores the opposite extreme of humor. It places greater emphasis on physical action and visual gags, and its verbal jokes do not require much intellect to appreciate (as in Groucho Marx's pithy put-down to his brother Chico, "You have the brain of a five-year-old, and I bet he was glad to get rid of it!"). Low comedy does not avoid derisive humor; rather, it revels in making fun of whatever will get a good laugh. Drunkenness, stupidity, lust, senility, trickery, insult, and clumsiness are inexhaustible staples of this style of comedy. Although it is all too easy for critics to dismiss low comedy, like high comedy it serves a valuable purpose in satirizing human failings. Shakespeare indulged in coarse humor in some of his noblest plays. Low comedy is usually the preferred style of popular culture, and it has inspired many incisive satires on modern life—from the classic films of W. C. Fields and the Marx Brothers to the weekly TV antics of Matt Groening's *The Simpsons* or Tina Fey's *30 Rock.*

Low comedy includes several distinct types. One is the **burlesque,** a broadly humorous parody or travesty of another play or kind of play. (In the United States, *burlesque* is something else: a once-popular form of show business featuring stripteases interspersed with bits of ribald low comedy.) Another valuable type of low comedy is the **farce,** a broadly humorous play whose action is usually fast-moving and improbable. The farce is a descendant of the Italian *commedia dell'arte* ("artistic comedy") of the late Renaissance, a kind of theater developed by comedians who traveled from town to town, regaling crowds at country fairs and in marketplaces. This popular art featured familiar stock characters in masks or whiteface: Harlequin, a clown; Columbine, his peppery sweetheart; and Pantaloon, a doddering duffer. Lately making a comeback, the more modern farces of French playwright Georges Feydeau (1862–1921) are practically all plot, with only the flattest of characters, mindless ninnies who play frantic games of hide-and-seek in order to deceive their spouses. **Slapstick comedy** (such as that of the Three Stooges) is a kind of farce. Featuring pratfalls, pie-throwing, fisticuffs, and other violent action, it takes its name from a circus clown's prop—a bat with two boards that loudly clap together when one clown swats another.

Romantic Comedy

Romantic comedy, another traditional sort of comedy, is subtler. Its main characters are generally lovers, and its plot unfolds their ultimately successful strivings to be united. Unlike satiric comedy, romantic comedy portrays its characters not with withering contempt but with kindly indulgence. It may take place in the everyday world, or perhaps in some never-never land, such as the forest of Arden in Shakespeare's *As You Like It*. Romantic comedy is also a popular staple of Hollywood, which depicts two people undergoing humorous mishaps on their way to falling in love. The characters often suffer humiliation and discomfort along the way, but these moments are funny rather than sad, and the characters are rewarded in the end by true love.

Here is a short contemporary comedy by one of America's most ingenious playwrights.

David Ives

Sure Thing   1988

David Ives (b. 1950) grew up on the South Side of Chicago. He attended Catholic schools before entering Northwestern University. Later Ives studied at the Yale Drama School—"a blissful time for me," he recalls, "in spite of the fact that there is slush on the ground in New Haven 238 days a year." Ives received his first professional production in Los Angeles at the age of twenty-one "at America's smallest, and possibly worst theater, in a storefront that had a pillar dead center in the middle of the stage." He continued writing for the theater while working as an editor at Foreign Affairs, and gradually achieved a reputation in theatrical circles for his wildly original and brilliantly written short comic plays. His public breakthrough came in 1993 with the New York staging of All in the Timing, which presented six short comedies, including Sure Thing. This production earned ecstatic reviews and a busy box office, and in the 1995–1996 season, All in the Timing was the most widely performed play in America (except for the works of Shakespeare). His second group of one-act comedies, Mere Mortals (1997), was produced with great success in New York City, followed by Lives of the Saints, a third group of one-act plays. Ives's full-length plays Don Juan in Chicago (1995), Ancient History (1996), The Red Address (1997), and Polish Joke (2000) are collected in the volume Polish Joke and Other Plays (2004). A talented adapter, Ives was chosen to rework a newly discovered play by Mark Twain, Is He Dead?, which had a successful run on Broadway in 2007. His most recent plays are Venus in Fur (2010) and a number of translations and adaptations of French theater, including Pierre Corneille's comedy The Liar (2010) and Molière's The Misanthrope, which Ives titled The School For Lies (2011). He also writes short stories and screenplays for both motion pictures and television. Ives lives in New York City.

Original 1993 Off-Broadway production of *Sure Thing* by Primary Stages.

CHARACTERS

Betty
Bill

SCENE. *A café. Betty, a woman in her late twenties, is reading at a café table. An empty chair is opposite her. Bill, same age, enters.*

Bill: Excuse me. Is this chair taken?
Betty: Excuse me?
Bill: Is this taken?
Betty: Yes it is.
Bill: Oh. Sorry.
Betty: Sure thing.

   (*A bell rings softly.*)

Bill: Excuse me. Is this chair taken?
Betty: Excuse me?
Bill: Is this taken?
Betty: No, but I'm expecting somebody in a minute.
Bill: Oh. Thanks anyway.
Betty: Sure thing.

   (*A bell rings softly.*)

Bill: Excuse me. Is this chair taken?
Betty: No, but I'm expecting somebody very shortly.
Bill: Would you mind if I sit here till he or she or it comes?
Betty (glances at her watch): They do seem to be pretty late. . . .
Bill: You never know who you might be turning down.

Betty: Sorry. Nice try, though.
Bill: Sure thing.

 (*Bell.*)

 Is this seat taken?
Betty: No it's not.
Bill: Would you mind if I sit here?
Betty: Yes I would.
Bill: Oh.

 (*Bell.*)

 Is this chair taken?
Betty: No it's not.
Bill: Would you mind if I sit here?
Betty: No. Go ahead.
Bill: Thanks. (*He sits. She continues reading.*) Everyplace else seems to be taken.
Betty: Mm-hm.
Bill: Great place.
Betty: Mm-hm.
Bill: What's the book?
Betty: I just wanted to read in quiet, if you don't mind.
Bill: No. Sure thing.

 (*Bell.*)

 Everyplace else seems to be taken.
Betty: Mm-hm.
Bill: Great place for reading.
Betty: Yes, I like it.
Bill: What's the book?
Betty: *The Sound and the Fury.*
Bill: Oh. Hemingway.

 (*Bell.*)

 What's the book?
Betty: *The Sound and the Fury.*
Bill: Oh. Faulkner.
Betty: Have you read it?
Bill: Not . . . actually. I've sure read *about* it, though. It's supposed to be great.
Betty: It is great.
Bill: I hear it's great. (*Small pause.*) Waiter?

 (*Bell.*)

 What's the book?
Betty: *The Sound and the Fury.*
Bill: Oh. Faulkner.
Betty: Have you read it?
Bill: I'm a Mets fan, myself.

 (*Bell.*)

Betty: Have you read it?
Bill: Yeah, I read it in college.
Betty: Where was college?
Bill: I went to Oral Roberts University.

(*Bell.*)

Betty: Where was college?
Bill: I was lying. I never really went to college. I just like to party.

(*Bell.*)

Betty: Where was college?
Bill: Harvard.
Betty: Do you like Faulkner?
Bill: I love Faulkner. I spent a whole winter reading him once.
Betty: I've just started.
Bill: I was so excited after ten pages that I went out and bought everything else he wrote. One of the greatest reading experiences of my life. I mean, all that incredible psychological understanding. Page after page of gorgeous prose. His profound grasp of the mystery of time and human existence. The smells of the earth . . . What do you think?
Betty: I think it's pretty boring.

(*Bell.*)

Bill: What's the book?
Betty: *The Sound and the Fury.*
Bill: Oh! Faulkner!
Betty: Do you like Faulkner?
Bill: I love Faulkner.
Betty: He's incredible.
Bill: I spent a whole winter reading him once.
Betty: I was so excited after ten pages that I went out and bought everything else he wrote.
Bill: All that incredible psychological understanding.
Betty: And the prose is so gorgeous.
Bill: And the way he's grasped the mystery of time—
Betty: —and human existence. I can't believe I've waited this long to read him.
Bill: You never know. You might not have liked him before.
Betty: That's true.
Bill: You might not have been ready for him. You have to hit these things at the right moment or it's no good.
Betty: That's happened to me.
Bill: It's all in the timing. (*Small pause.*) My name's Bill, by the way.
Betty: I'm Betty.
Bill: Hi.
Betty: Hi. (*Small pause.*)
Bill: Yes I thought reading Faulkner was . . . a great experience.
Betty: Yes. (*Small pause.*)
Bill: *The Sound and the Fury.* . . . (*Another small pause.*)

Betty: Well. Onwards and upwards. (*She goes back to her book.*)
Bill: Waiter—?

(*Bell.*)

You have to hit these things at the right moment or it's no good.
Betty: That's happened to me.
Bill: It's all in the timing. My name's Bill, by the way.
Betty: I'm Betty.
Bill: Hi.
Betty: Hi.
Bill: Do you come in here a lot?
Betty: Actually I'm just in town for two days from Pakistan.
Bill: Oh. Pakistan.

(*Bell.*)

My name's Bill, by the way.
Betty: I'm Betty.
Bill: Hi.
Betty: Hi.
Bill: Do you come in here a lot?
Betty: Every once in a while. Do you?
Bill: Not so much anymore. Not as much as I used to. Before my nervous breakdown.

(*Bell.*)

Do you come in here a lot?
Betty: Why are you asking?
Bill: Just interested.
Betty: Are you really interested, or do you just want to pick me up?
Bill: No, I'm really interested.
Betty: Why would you be interested in whether I come in here a lot?
Bill: I'm just . . . getting acquainted.
Betty: Maybe you're only interested for the sake of making small talk long enough
to ask me back to your place to listen to some music, or because you've just
rented this great tape for your VCR, or because you've got some terrific
unknown Django Reinhardt record, only all you really want to do is fuck—
which you won't do very well—after which you'll go into the bathroom and
pee very loudly, then pad into the kitchen and get yourself a beer from the
refrigerator without asking me whether I'd like anything, and then you'll proceed to lie back down beside me and confess that you've got a girlfriend named
Stephanie who's away at medical school in Belgium for a year, and that you've
been involved with her—*off and on*—in what you'll call a very "intricate" relationship, for the past *seven* YEARS. None of which *interests* me, mister!
Bill: Okay.

(*Bell.*)

Do you come in here a lot?
Betty: Every other day, I think.

Bill: I come in here quite a lot and I don't remember seeing you.

Betty: I guess we must be on different schedules.

Bill: Missed connections.

Betty: Yes. Different time zones.

Bill: Amazing how you can live right next door to somebody in this town and never even know it.

Betty: I know.

Bill: City life.

Betty: It's crazy.

Bill: We probably pass each other in the street every day. Right in front of this place, probably.

Betty: Yep.

Bill (looks around): Well the waiters here sure seem to be in some different time zone. I can't seem to locate one anywhere. . . . Waiter! (*He looks back.*) So what do you—(*He sees that she's gone back to her book.*)

Betty: I beg pardon?

Bill: Nothing. Sorry.

    (*Bell.*)

Betty: I guess we must be on different schedules.

Bill: Missed connections.

Betty: Yes. Different time zones.

Bill: Amazing how you can live right next door to somebody in this town and never even know it.

Betty: I know.

Bill: City life.

Betty: It's crazy.

Bill: You weren't waiting for somebody when I came in, were you?

Betty: Actually I was.

Bill: Oh. Boyfriend?

Betty: Sort of.

Bill: What's a sort-of boyfriend?

Betty: My husband.

Bill: Ah-ha.

    (*Bell.*)

    You weren't waiting for somebody when I came in, were you?

Betty: Actually I was.

Bill: Oh. Boyfriend?

Betty: Sort of.

Bill: What's a sort-of boyfriend?

Betty: We were meeting here to break up.

Bill: Mm-hm . . .

    (*Bell.*)

    What's a sort-of boyfriend?

Betty: My lover. Here she comes right now!

(*Bell.*)

Bill: You weren't waiting for somebody when I came in, were you?

Betty: No, just reading.

Bill: Sort of a sad occupation for a Friday night, isn't it? Reading here, all by yourself?

Betty: Do you think so?

Bill: Well sure. I mean, what's a good-looking woman like you doing out alone on a Friday night?

Betty: Trying to keep away from lines like that.

Bill: No, listen—

(*Bell.*)

You weren't waiting for somebody when I came in, were you?

Betty: No, just reading.

Bill: Sort of a sad occupation for a Friday night, isn't it? Reading here all by yourself?

Betty: I guess it is, in a way.

Bill: What's a good-looking woman like you doing out alone on a Friday night anyway? No offense, but . . .

Betty: I'm out alone on a Friday night for the first time in a very long time.

Bill: Oh.

Betty: You see, I just recently ended a relationship.

Bill: Oh.

Betty: Of rather long standing.

Bill: I'm sorry. (*Small pause.*) Well listen, since reading by yourself *is* such a sad occupation for a Friday night, would you like to go elsewhere?

Betty: No . . .

Bill: Do something else?

Betty: No thanks.

Bill: I was headed out to the movies in a while anyway.

Betty: I don't think so.

Bill: Big chance to let Faulkner catch his breath. All those long sentences get him pretty tired.

Betty: Thanks anyway.

Bill: Okay.

Betty: I appreciate the invitation.

Bill: Sure thing.

(*Bell.*)

You weren't waiting for somebody when I came in, were you?

Betty: No, just reading.

Bill: Sort of a sad occupation for a Friday night, isn't it? Reading here all by yourself?

Betty: I guess I was trying to think of it as existentially romantic. You know—cappuccino, great literature, rainy night . . .

Bill: That only works in Paris. We *could* hop the late plane to Paris. Get on a Concorde. Find a café . . .

Betty: I'm a little short on plane fare tonight.

Bill: Darn it, so am I.

Betty: To tell you the truth, I was headed to the movies after I finished this section. Would you like to come along? Since you can't locate a waiter?

Bill: That's a very nice offer, but . . .

Betty: Uh-huh. Girlfriend?

Bill: Two, actually. One of them's pregnant, and Stephanie—

(*Bell.*)

Betty: Girlfriend?

Bill: No, I don't have a girlfriend. Not if you mean the castrating bitch I dumped last night.

(*Bell.*)

Betty: Girlfriend?

Bill: Sort of. Sort of.

Betty: What's a sort-of girlfriend?

Bill: My mother.

(*Bell.*)

I just ended a relationship, actually.

Betty: Oh.

Bill: Of rather long standing.

Betty: I'm sorry to hear it.

Bill: This is my first night out alone in a long time. I feel a little bit at sea, to tell you the truth.

Betty: So you didn't stop to talk because you're a Moonie, or you have some weird political affiliation—?

Bill: Nope. Straight-down-the-ticket Republican.

(*Bell.*)

Straight-down-the-ticket Democrat.

(*Bell.*)

Can I tell you something about politics?

(*Bell.*)

I like to think of myself as a citizen of the universe.

(*Bell.*)

I'm unaffiliated.

Betty: That's a relief. So am I.

Bill: I vote my beliefs.

Betty: Labels are not important.

Bill: Labels are not important, exactly. Take me, for example. I mean, what does it matter if I had a two-point at—

(*Bell.*)

three-point at—

(*Bell.*)

four-point at college? Or if I did come from Pittsburgh—

(*Bell.*)

Cleveland—

(*Bell.*)

Westchester County?

Betty: Sure.

Bill: I believe that a man is what he is.

(*Bell.*)

A person is what he is.

(*Bell.*)

A person is . . . what they are.

Betty: I think so too.

Bill: So what if I admire Trotsky?

(*Bell.*)

So what if I once had a total-body liposuction?

(*Bell.*)

So what if I don't have a penis?

(*Bell.*)

So what if I spent a year in the Peace Corps? I was acting on my convictions.

Betty: Sure.

Bill: You just can't hang a sign on a person.

Betty: Absolutely. I'll bet you're a Scorpio.

(*Many bells ring.*)

Listen, I was headed to the movies after I finished this section. Would you like to come along?

Bill: That sounds like fun. What's playing?

Betty: A couple of the really early Woody Allen movies.

Bill: Oh.

Betty: You don't like Woody Allen?

Bill: Sure. I like Woody Allen.

Betty: But you're not crazy about Woody Allen.

Bill: Those early ones kind of get on my nerves.

Betty: Uh-huh.

(*Bell.*)

Bill: Y'know I was headed to the—

Betty (*simultaneously*): I was thinking about—

Bill: I'm sorry.

Betty: No, go ahead.

Bill: I was going to say that I was headed to the movies in a little while, and . . .

Betty: So was I.

Bill: The Woody Allen festival?

Betty: Just up the street.

Bill: Do you like the early ones?

Betty: I think anybody who doesn't ought to be run off the planet.

Bill: How many times have you seen *Bananas?*

Betty: Eight times.

Bill: Twelve. So are you still interested? (*Long pause.*)

Betty: Do you like Entenmann's crumb cake . . . ?

Bill: Last night I went out at two in the morning to get one. Did you have an Etch-a-Sketch as a child?

Betty: Yes! And do you like Brussels sprouts? (*Pause.*)

Bill: No, I think they're disgusting.

Betty: They *are* disgusting!

Bill: Do you still believe in marriage in spite of current sentiments against it?

Betty: Yes.

Bill: And children?

Betty: Three of them.

Bill: Two girls and a boy.

Betty: Harvard, Vassar, and Brown.

Bill: And will you love me?

Betty: Yes.

Bill: And cherish me forever?

Betty: Yes.

Bill: Do you still want to go to the movies?

Betty: Sure thing.

Bill and Betty (*together*): Waiter!

BLACKOUT

Questions

1. Ives originally planned to set *Sure Thing* at a bus stop. What does its current setting in a café suggest about the characters?

2. What happens on stage when the bell rings?

3. Who is the protagonist? What does the protagonist want?

4. Does the play have a dramatic question?

5. When does the climax of the play occur?

6. Is *Sure Thing* a romantic comedy or a farce? (See pages 1185–86 for a discussion of these types of comedy.)

7. "*Sure Thing* was not a funny play because it isn't realistic. Conversations just don't happen this way." Discuss that opinion. Do you agree or disagree?

WRITING *effectively*

David Ives on Writing

On the One-Act Play

2006

David Ives

Moss Hart said that you never really learn how to write a play, you only learn how to write *this* play. That is as true of one-acts as of two-, three-, four- or five-acts. To my mind the challenge of the one-act may be even greater than the challenge of larger and necessarily messier plays, in the same way that the sonnet with only fourteen lines remains the ever-attempted Everest of poetry. For what the one-act demands is a kind of concentrated perfection. "A play," said Lorca, "is a poem standing up," and I can't think of a better description of a one-act.

The long play, like the symphony, luxuriates in development and recapitulation. The one-act has no time for them. Develop the story and you start to look overly melodramatic, forcing too much event into too little time. Develop the characters and you look like you're not doing them justice. (In fact you start to look like you want to write a larger play.) Develop your theme and you start to sound like one of those guys at a party trying to explain all of particle theory between two grabs at the canapés. Recapitulate and you're dead.

A one-act masterpiece like Pinter's *The Dumb Waiter* would be tedious and attenuated if stretched over two hours. It says all it needs to say—and that's volumes—in a quarter of that, then stops. *Death of a Salesman* as a one-act would look either like a character study or a short story transcribed for the stage. A full-length is a four-ton, cast-steel, Richard Serra ellipse that you can walk around in; a one-act, a piece of string draped by Richard Tuttle on a gallery wall. Not a ride on the *Titanic*, but a single suitcase left floating in the middle of a theatrical sea.

So what does a one-act like, if not development and recapitulation?

Compression, obviously. Think of a one-act and chances are good you're thinking of something short and sharp, a punch in the nose, the rug pulled out from under you, over before you know it—as if an actor had turned a camera on the audience and flashed a picture. A good one-act should leave you blinking. Think of a one-act and chances are also good you're picturing something like a small, bare, black-box stage with just a park bench, or a table and chair, or a bus-stop sign. One or two people. Minimal props. There is something necessarily stripped-down about the mere staging of one-acts, and this goes to the heart of the nature of one-acts themselves. They are *elemental*.

From *The Dramatist*

THINKING ABOUT COMEDY

If you have ever tried to explain a punch line to an uncomprehending friend, you know how hard it can be to convey the essence of humor. Too much explanation makes any joke fizzle out fast. We don't often stop to analyze why a joke strikes us as funny. It simply makes us laugh. For this reason, writing about comedy can be challenging.

- **What makes the play amusing?** Is there a central gag or situation (such as mistaken identity) that creates comic potential in every scene? Note that the central gag is often visual (such as a disguise), something that the audience constantly sees but is not equally apparent in the written text.
- **What is the flavor of the humor?** Is the comedy high or low? Is it verbal or visual, or both? Is there mostly slapstick action or clever wordplay? Is it a romantic comedy in which love plays a central role? A play often mixes types of comedy, but usually one style predominates. A farce may have a few moments of intellectual wit, but it will mostly keep silly jokes and pratfalls coming fast and furiously.
- **How do the personalities of the main characters intensify the humor?** Even when comedy arises out of a situation, character is likely to play an important role. In *A Midsummer Night's Dream,* for example, the fairy queen Titania is bewitched into falling in love with the weaver Bottom, whose head has been transformed into that of an ass. The situation is funny in its own right, but the humor is intensified by the personalities involved, the proud fairy queen pursuing the lowly and foolish tradesman. Humor often may be found in the unexpected, a twist on the normal and the logical.

CHECKLIST: Writing About Comedy

- ☐ What kind of comedy is the play? Romantic? Slapstick? Satire? How can you tell?
- ☐ Which style of comedy prevails? Is there more emphasis on high comedy or low? More emphasis on verbal humor or physical comedy?
- ☐ Focus on a key comic moment. Does the comedy grow out of situation? Character? A mix of both?
- ☐ How does the play end? In a wedding or romance? A reconciliation? Mutual understanding?

WRITING ASSIGNMENT ON COMEDY

Read *Sure Thing* and write a brief analysis of what makes the play amusing or humorous. Provide details to back up your argument. See pages 1184–86 for more information on specific types of humor.

TOPICS FOR WRITING ABOUT TRAGEDY

1. According to Oscar Wilde, "In this world there are only two tragedies: one is not getting what one wants, and the other is getting it." Write an essay in which you discuss this statement in its application to the scene from *Doctor Faustus*.

2. Imagine that Faustus, after his death, has sought forgiveness and salvation with the claim, "The Devil tricked me. I didn't know what I was doing." Write a "judicial opinion" setting forth the grounds for the denial of his plea.

TOPICS FOR WRITING ABOUT COMEDY

1. What or who is being satirized in *Sure Thing*? How true or incisive do you find this satire? Why?

2. "*Sure Thing* isn't good drama because it doesn't have a plot or conflict." Write a two-page response to that complaint.

3. Write about a recent romantic comedy film. How does its plot fulfill the notion of comedy?

4. Write about a movie you've seen lately that was meant to be funny but fell short. What was lacking?

▶ TERMS FOR *review*

Dramatic Genres

Tragedy ▶ A play that portrays a serious conflict between human beings and some superior, overwhelming force. It ends sorrowfully and disastrously, an outcome that seems inevitable.

Comedy ▶ A literary work aimed at amusing an audience. In traditional comedy, the protagonist often faces obstacles and complications that threaten disaster but are overturned at the last moment to produce a happy ending.

Kinds of Comedy

High comedy ▶ A comic genre evoking thoughtful laughter from an audience in response to the play's depiction of the folly, pretense, and hypocrisy of human behavior.

Satiric comedy ▶ A genre using derisive humor to ridicule human weakness and folly or attack political injustices and incompetence. Satiric comedy often focuses on ridiculing overly serious characters who resist the festive mood of comedy.

Comedy of manners ▶ A realistic form of high comic drama. It deals with the social relations and romantic intrigues of sophisticated upper-class men and women, whose verbal fencing and witty repartee produce the principal comic effects.

Romantic comedy ▶ A form of comic drama in which the plot focuses on one or more pairs of young lovers who overcome difficulties to achieve a happy ending (usually marriage).

Low comedy ▶ A comic style arousing laughter through jokes, slapstick antics, sight gags, boisterous clowning, and vulgar humor.

Burlesque ▶ A broadly humorous parody or travesty of another play or kind of play.

Farce ▶ A broadly humorous play whose action is usually fast-moving and improbable.

Slapstick comedy ▶ A kind of farce. Featuring pratfalls, pie-throwing, fisticuffs, and other violent action, it takes its name from a circus clown's prop—a bat with two boards that loudly clap together when one clown swats another.

36

CRITICAL CASEBOOK
Sophocles

Oedipus with chorus in Tyrone Guthrie's 1957 film
Oedipus Rex.

None but a poet can write a tragedy.

—EDITH HAMILTON

THE THEATER OF SOPHOCLES

For the citizens of Athens in the fifth century B.C., theater was both a religious and a civic occasion. Plays were presented only twice a year at religious festivals, both associated with Dionysus, the god of wine and crops. In January there was the Lenaea, the festival of the winepress, when plays, especially comedies, were performed. But the major theatrical event of the year came in March at the Great Dionysia, a citywide celebration that included sacrifices, prize ceremonies, and spectacular processions as well as three days of drama.

Each day at dawn a different author presented a trilogy of tragic plays—three interrelated dramas that portrayed an important mythic or legendary event. Each intense tragic trilogy was followed by a **satyr play**, an obscene parody of a mythic story, performed with the chorus dressed as satyrs, unruly mythic attendants of Dionysus who were half goat or horse and half human.

The Greeks loved competition and believed it fostered excellence. Even theater was a competitive event—not unlike the Olympic games. A panel of five judges voted each year at the Great Dionysia for the best dramatic presentation, and a substantial cash prize was given to the winning poet-playwright (all plays were written in verse). Any aspiring writer who has ever lost a literary contest may be comforted to learn that Sophocles, who triumphed in the competition twenty-four times, seems not to have won the annual prize for *Oedipus the King*. Although this play ultimately proved to be the most celebrated Greek tragedy ever written, it lost the award to a revival of a popular trilogy by Aeschylus, who had recently died.

Staging

Seated in the open air in a hillside amphitheater, as many as 17,000 spectators could watch a performance that must have somewhat resembled an opera or musical. The audience was arranged in rows, with the Athenian governing council and young military cadets seated in the middle sections. Priests, priestesses, and foreign dignitaries were given special places of honor in the front rows. The performance space they watched was divided into two parts—the **orchestra**, a level circular "dancing space" (at the base of the amphitheater), and a slightly raised stage built in front of the *skene* or stage house, originally a canvas or wooden hut for costume changes.

The actors spoke and performed primarily on the stage, and the chorus sang and danced in the orchestra. The *skene* served as a general set or backdrop—the exterior of a palace, a temple, a cave, or a military tent, depending on the action of the play. The *skene* had a large door at its center that served as the major entrance for principal characters. When opened wide, the door could be used to frame a striking tableau, as when the body of Eurydicê is displayed at the end of Sophocles's play *Antigonê*. The *skene* supported a hook and pulley by which actors who played gods could be lowered or lifted—hence the Latin phrase **deus ex machina** ("god out of the machine") for any means of bringing a play quickly to a resolution.

What did the actors look like? They wore **masks** (*personae*, the source of our word *person*, "a thing through which sound comes"): some of these masks had exaggerated mouthpieces, possibly designed to project speech across the open air. Certainly, the masks, each of which covered an actor's entire head, helped spectators far away recognize the chief characters. The masks often represented certain

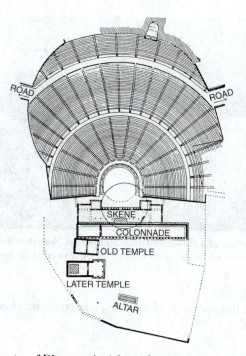

**The Theater of Dionysus in Athens during the time of Sophocles;
a modern drawing based on scholarly guesswork.
From R. C. Flickinger, *The Greek Theater and Its Drama* (1918).**

conventional types of characters: the old king, the young soldier, the shepherd, the beautiful girl (women's parts were played by male actors). Perhaps in order to gain in both increased dignity and visibility, actors in the Greek theater eventually came to wear **cothurni**, high, thick-soled elevator shoes that made them appear taller than ordinary men. All this equipment must have given the actors a slightly inhuman yet very imposing appearance, but we may infer that the spectators accepted such conventions as easily as opera lovers accept an opera's special artifice or today's football fans hardly notice the elaborate helmets, shoulderpads, kneepads, and garishly colored uniforms worn by their favorite teams.

Dramatic Structure

By Sophocles's time, the tragedy had a conventional structure understood by most of the citizens sitting in the audience. No more than three actors were allowed on stage at any one time, along with a chorus of fifteen (the number was fixed by Sophocles himself). The actors' spoken monologue and dialogue alternated with the chorus's singing and dancing. Each tragedy began with a **prologue**, a preparatory scene. In *Oedipus the King,* for example, the play begins with Oedipus asking the suppliants why they have come and the priest telling him about the plague ravaging Thebes. Next came the *párodos*, the song for the entrance of the chorus. Then the action was enacted in **episodes**, like the acts or scenes in modern plays; the episodes were separated by danced choral songs or **odes**. Finally, there was a

A modern reconstruction of a classical Athenian theater. Note that the chorus performs in the circular orchestra while the actors stand on the raised stage behind.

closing *éxodos*, the last scene, in which the characters and chorus concluded the action and departed.

THE CIVIC ROLE OF GREEK DRAMA

Athenian drama was supported and financed by the state. Administration of the Great Dionysia fell to the head civil magistrate. He annually appointed three wealthy citizens to serve as *choregoi*, or producers, for the competing plays. Each producer had to equip the chorus and rent the rehearsal space in which the poet-playwright would prepare the new work for the festival. The state covered the expenses of the theater, actors, and prizes (which went to author, actors, and *choregos* alike). Theater tickets were distributed free to citizens, which meant that every registered Athenian, even the poorest, could participate. The playwrights therefore addressed themselves to every element of the Athenian democracy. Only the size of the amphitheater limited the attendance. Holding between 14,000 and 17,000 spectators, it could accommodate slightly less than half of Athens's 40,000 citizens.

Greek theater was directed at the moral and political education of the community. The poet's role was the improvement of the *polis* or city-state (made up of a town and its surrounding countryside). Greek city-states traditionally sponsored public contests between *rhapsodes* (professional poetry performers) reciting stories from Homer's epics, the *Iliad* and *Odyssey*. As Greek society developed and urbanized, however, the competitive and individualized heroism of the Homeric epics had to be tempered with the values of cooperation and compromise necessary to a democracy. Civic theater provided the ideal medium to address these cultural needs.

Tragedy and Empathy

As a public art form, tragedy was not simply a stage for political propaganda to promote the status quo. Nor was it exclusively a celebration of idealized heroes nobly enduring the blows of harsh circumstance and misfortune. Tragedy often enabled its audience to reflect on personal values that might be in conflict with civic ideals, on the claims of minorities that it neglected or excluded from public life, on its own irrational prejudices toward the foreign or the unknown. Frequently a play challenged its audience to feel sympathy for a vanquished enemy (as in Euripides's *Trojan Women*, the greatest antiwar play of the period, which dramatizes the horrible fate of captured women). Some plays explored the problems facing members of the politically powerless groups that made up nearly three-fourths of the Athenian population—women, children, resident aliens, and slaves. A largely male audience also frequently watched male performers enact stories of the power and anger of women, such as Euripides's *Medea*, which made their tragic violence understandable (if not entirely pardonable) to an audience not particularly disposed to treat them sympathetically. Other plays such as Sophocles's *Oedipus the King* or Euripides's *Herakles* depicted powerful men undone by misfortune, their own bad judgment, or hubris, and thrown into defeat and exile.

Such tragic stories required performers and audience to put themselves in the places of persons quite unlike themselves, in situations that might engulf any unlucky citizen—war, political upheaval, betrayal, domestic crisis. The release of the powerful emotions of pity and fear through a carefully crafted plot in the orderly context of highly conventionalized performance accounts for the paradox of tragic drama—how a viewer takes aesthetic pleasure in witnessing the sufferings of others.

ARISTOTLE'S CONCEPT OF TRAGEDY

> *Tragedy is an imitation of an action of high importance, complete and of some amplitude; in language enhanced by distinct and varying beauties; acted not narrated; by means of pity and fear effecting its purgation of these emotions.*
>
> —ARISTOTLE, POETICS, CHAPTER VI

Aristotle's famous definition of tragedy, constructed in the fourth century B.C., is the testimony of one who probably saw many classical tragedies performed. In making his observations, Aristotle does not seem to be laying down laws for what a tragedy ought to be. More likely, he is drawing—from tragedies he has seen or read—a general description of them.

Tragic Hero

Aristotle observes that the protagonist, the hero or chief character of a tragedy, is a person of "high estate," apparently a king or queen or other member of a royal family. In thus being as keenly interested as are contemporary dramatists in the private lives of the powerful, Greek dramatists need not be accused of snobbery. It is the nature of tragedy that the protagonist must fall from power and from happiness; his high estate gives him a place of dignity to fall from and perhaps makes his fall seem all the more a calamity in that it involves an entire nation or people. Nor is the protagonist extraordinary merely by his position in society. Oedipus is not only a king but also a noble soul who suffers profoundly and who employs splendid eloquence to express his suffering.

The tragic hero, however, is not a superman; he is fallible. The hero's downfall is the result, as Aristotle said, of his **hamartia**: his error or transgression or (as some translators would have it) his flaw or weakness of character. The notion that a tragic hero has such a **tragic flaw** has often been attributed to Aristotle, but it is by no means clear that Aristotle meant just that. According to this interpretation, every tragic hero has some fatal weakness, some moral Achilles's heel, that brings him to a bad end. In some classical tragedies, his transgression is a weakness the Greeks called **hubris**—extreme pride, leading to overconfidence.

Whatever Aristotle had in mind, however, many later critics find value in the idea of the tragic flaw. In this view, the downfall of a hero follows from his very nature. Whatever view we take—whether we find the hero's sufferings due to a flaw of character or to an error of judgment—we will probably find that his downfall results from acts for which he himself is responsible. In a Greek tragedy, the hero is a character amply capable of making choices—capable, too, of accepting the consequences.

Katharsis

It may be useful to take another look at Aristotle's definition of *tragedy*, with which we began. By **purgation** (or *katharsis*), did the ancient theorist mean that after witnessing a tragedy we feel relief, having released our pent-up emotions? Or did he mean that our feelings are purified, refined into something more ennobling? Scholars continue to argue. Whatever his exact meaning, clearly Aristotle implies that after witnessing a tragedy we feel better, not worse—not depressed, but somehow elated. We take a kind of pleasure in the spectacle of a noble man being brought down, but surely this pleasure is a legitimate one. Part of that catharsis may also be based in our feeling of the "rightness" or accuracy of what we have just witnessed. The terrible but undeniable truth of the tragic vision of life is that blind overreaching and the destruction of hopes and dreams are very much a part of what really happens in the world.

Recognition and Reversal

Aristotle, in describing the workings of this inexorable force in *Oedipus the King*, uses terms that later critics have found valuable. One is **recognition**, or discovery (*anagnorisis*): the revelation of some fact not known before or some person's true identity. Oedipus makes such a discovery: he recognizes that he himself was the child whom his mother had given over to be destroyed. Such a recognition also occurs in Shakespeare's *Macbeth* when Macduff reveals himself to have been "from his mother's womb / Untimely ripped," thus disclosing a double meaning in the witches' prophecy that Macbeth could be harmed by "none of woman born," and sweeping aside Macbeth's last shred of belief that he is infallible. Modern critics have taken the term to mean also the terrible enlightenment that accompanies such a recognition with the protagonist's consequent awareness of his role in his own undoing. "To see things plain—that is *anagnorisis*," Clifford Leech observes, "It is what tragedy ultimately is about: the realization of the unthinkable."

Having made his discovery, Oedipus suffers a reversal in his fortunes; he goes off into exile, blinded and dethroned. Such a fall from happiness seems intrinsic to tragedy, but we should know that Aristotle has a more particular meaning for his term **reversal** (*peripeteia*, anglicized as **peripety**). He means an action that turns out to have the opposite effect from the one its doer had intended. One of his illustrations of such an ironic reversal is from *Oedipus the King*. The first messenger intends to cheer Oedipus with the partially good news that, contrary to the prophecy that Oedipus would kill his father, his father has died of old age. The reversal is in the fact that, when the messenger further reveals that old Polybus was Oedipus's father only by adoption, the king, instead of having his fears allayed, is stirred to new dread.

We are not altogether sorry, perhaps, to see an arrogant man such as Oedipus humbled, and yet it is difficult not to feel that the punishment of Oedipus is greater than he deserves. Possibly this feeling is what Aristotle meant in his observation that a tragedy arouses our pity and our fear—our compassion for Oedipus and our terror as we sense the remorselessness of a universe in which a man is doomed. Notice, however, that at the end of the play Oedipus does not curse God and die. Although such a complex play is open to many interpretations, it is probably safe to say that the play is not a bitter complaint against the universe. At last, Oedipus accepts the divine will, prays for blessings upon his children, and prepares to endure his exile—fallen from high estate but uplifted, through his newfound humility and piety, in moral dignity.

SOPHOCLES

Sophocles

Sophocles (496?–406 B.C.) tragic dramatist, priest, for a time one of ten Athenian generals, was one of the three great ancient Greek writers of tragedy whose work has survived. (The other two were his contemporaries: Aeschylus, his senior, and Euripides, his junior.) Sophocles won his first victory in the Athenian spring drama competition in 468 B.C., when a tragedy he had written defeated one by Aeschylus. He went on to win many prizes, writing more than 120 plays, of which only seven have survived in their entirety—Ajax, Antigonê, Oedipus the King, Electra, Philoctetes, The Trachinian Women, and Oedipus at Colonus. (Of the lost plays, about a thousand fragments remain.) In his long life, Sophocles saw Greece rise to supremacy over the Persian Empire. He enjoyed the favor of the statesman Pericles, who, making peace with enemy Sparta, ruled Athens during a Golden Age (461–429 B.C.), during which the Parthenon was built and music, art, drama, and philosophy flourished. The playwright lived on to see his native city-state in decline, its strength drained by the disastrous Peloponnesian War. His last play, Oedipus at Colonus, set twenty years after the events of Oedipus the King, shows the former king in old age, ragged and blind, cast into exile by his sons, but still accompanied by his faithful daughter Antigonê. It was written when Sophocles was nearly ninety. Oedipus the King is believed to have been first produced in 425 B.C., five years after the plague had broken out in Athens.

THE ORIGINS OF *OEDIPUS THE KING*

On a Great Dionysia feast day several years after Athens had survived a devastating plague, the audience turned out to watch a tragedy by Sophocles, set in the city of Thebes at the moment of another terrible plague. This timely play was *Oedipus*, later given the name (in Greek) *Oedipus Tyrannos* to distinguish it from Sophocles's last Oedipus play, *Oedipus at Colonus*, written many years later when the author was nearly ninety.

A folktale figure, Oedipus gets his name through a complex pun. *Oida* means "to know" (from the root *vid-*, "see"), pointing to the tale's contrasting themes of sight and blindness, wisdom and ignorance. *Oedipus* also means "swollen foot" or "clubfoot," pointing to the injury sustained in the title character's infancy, when his ankles were pinioned together like a goat's. Oedipus is the man who comes to knowledge of his true parentage through the evidence of his feet and his old injury. The term *tyrannos,* in the context of the play, simply means a man who comes to rule through his own intelligence and merit, though not related to the ruling family. The traditional Greek title might be translated, therefore, as *Clubfoot the Ruler.* (*Oedipus Rex,* which means "Oedipus the King," is the conventional Latin title for the play.)

Presumably the audience already knew the story portrayed in the play. They would have known that because a prophecy had foretold that Oedipus would grow up to slay his father, he had been taken out as a newborn to perish in the wilderness of Mount Cithaeron outside Thebes. (Exposure was the common fate of unwanted children in ancient Greece, though only in the most extraordinary circumstances would a royal heir be exposed.) The audience would also have known that before he was left to die, the baby's feet had been pinned together. And they would have known that later, adopted by King Polybus and Queen Merope of Corinth and grown to maturity, Oedipus won both the throne and the recently widowed queen of Thebes as a reward for ridding the city of the Sphinx, a winged, woman-headed lion. All who approached the Sphinx were asked a riddle, and failure to solve it meant death. Her lethal riddle was: "What goes on four legs in the morning, two at noon, and three at evening?" Oedipus correctly answered, "Man." (As a baby he crawls on all fours, as a man he walks erect, then as an old man he uses a cane.) Chagrined and outwitted, the Sphinx leaped from her rocky perch and dashed herself to death. Familiarity with all these events is necessary to understand *Oedipus the King,* which begins years later, after the title character has long been established as ruler of Thebes.

Laurence Olivier in *Oedipus Rex.*

Oedipus the King

425 B.C.?

Translated by Dudley Fitts and Robert Fitzgerald

CHARACTERS°

Oedipus	Messenger
A Priest	Shepherd of Laïos
Creon	Second Messenger
Teiresias	Chorus of Theban Elders
Iocastê	

SCENE. *Before the palace of Oedipus, King of Thebes. A central door and two lateral doors open onto a platform which runs the length of the façade. On the platform, right and left, are altars; and three steps lead down into the "orchestra," or chorus-ground. At the beginning of the action these steps are crowded by suppliants° who have brought branches and chaplets of olive leaves and who lie in various attitudes of despair. Oedipus enters.*

PROLOGUE°

Oedipus: My children, generations of the living
   In the line of Kadmos,° nursed at his ancient hearth:
   Why have you strewn yourself before these altars
   In supplication, with your boughs and garlands?
   The breath of incense rises from the city   5
   With a sound of prayer and lamentation.
                        Children,
   I would not have you speak through messengers,
   And therefore I have come myself to hear you—
   I, Oedipus, who bear the famous name.
   (To a Priest.) You, there, since you are eldest in the company,   10
   Speak for them all, tell me what preys upon you,
   Whether you come in dread, or crave some blessing:
   Tell me, and never doubt that I will help you
   In every way I can; I should be heartless
   Were I not moved to find you suppliant here.   15
Priest: Great Oedipus, O powerful King of Thebes!
   You see how all the ages of our people
   Cling to your altar steps: here are boys
   Who can barely stand alone, and here are priests
   By weight of age, as I am a priest of God,   20
   And young men chosen from those yet unmarried;
   As for the others, all that multitude,
   They wait with olive chaplets in the squares,

Characters: Some of these names are usually anglicized: Jocasta, Laius. In this version, the translators prefer spelling names more like the Greek originals.   *suppliants:* persons who come to ask some favor of the king.   *Prologue:* portion of the play containing the exposition.   *2 line of Kadmos:* according to legend the city of Thebes, where the play takes place, had been founded by the hero Cadmus.

At the two shrines of Pallas,° and where Apollo°
Speaks in the glowing embers.
                          Your own eyes   25
Must tell you: Thebes is tossed on a murdering sea
And can not lift her head from the death surge.
A rust consumes the buds and fruits of the earth;
The herds are sick; children die unborn,
And labor is vain. The god of plague and pyre   30
Raids like detestable lightning through the city,
And all the house of Kadmos is laid waste,
All emptied, and all darkened: Death alone
Battens upon the misery of Thebes.

You are not one of the immortal gods, we know;   35
Yet we have come to you to make our prayer
As to the man surest in mortal ways
And wisest in the ways of God. You saved us
From the Sphinx, that flinty singer, and the tribute
We paid to her so long; yet you were never   40
Better informed than we, nor could we teach you:
It was some god breathed in you to set us free.

Therefore, O mighty King, we turn to you:
Find us our safety, find us a remedy,
Whether by counsel of the gods or men.   45
A king of wisdom tested in the past
Can act in a time of troubles, and act well.
Noblest of men, restore
Life to your city! Think how all men call you
Liberator for your triumph long ago;   50
Ah, when your years of kingship are remembered,
Let them not say *We rose, but later fell*—
Keep the State from going down in the storm!
Once, years ago, with happy augury,
You brought us fortune; be the same again!   55
No man questions your power to rule the land:
But rule over men, not over a dead city!
Ships are only hulls, citadels are nothing,
When no life moves in the empty passageways.
Oedipus: Poor children! You may be sure I know   60
All that you longed for in your coming here.
I know that you are deathly sick; and yet,
Sick as you are, not one is as sick as I.
Each of you suffers in himself alone
His anguish, not another's; but my spirit   65
Groans for the city, for myself, for you.

---

24 *Pallas:* title for Athena, goddess of wisdom. *Apollo:* god of music, poetry, and prophecy. At his shrine near Thebes, the ashes of fires were used to divine the future.

I was not sleeping, you are not waking me.
No, I have been in tears for a long while
And in my restless thought walked many ways.
In all my search, I found one helpful course,   70
And that I have taken: I have sent Creon,
Son of Menoikeus, brother of the Queen,
To Delphi, Apollo's place of revelation,°
To learn there, if he can,
What act or pledge of mine may save the city.   75
I have counted the days, and now, this very day,
I am troubled, for he has overstayed his time.
What is he doing? He has been gone too long.
Yet whenever he comes back, I should do ill
To scant whatever duty God reveals.   80
Priest: It is a timely promise. At this instant
    They tell me Creon is here.
Oedipus: O Lord Apollo!
    May his news be fair as his face is radiant!
Priest: It could not be otherwise: he is crowned with bay,
    The chaplet is thick with berries.
Oedipus: We shall soon know;   85
    He is near enough to hear us now.

    Enter Creon.

                    O Prince:
    Brother: son of Menoikeus:
    What answer do you bring us from the god?
Creon: A strong one. I can tell you, great afflictions
    Will turn out well, if they are taken well.   90
Oedipus: What was the oracle? These vague words
    Leave me still hanging between hope and fear.
Creon: Is it your pleasure to hear me with all these
    Gathered around us? I am prepared to speak,
    But should we not go in?
Oedipus: Let them all hear it   95
    It is for them I suffer, more than for myself.
Creon: Then I will tell you what I heard at Delphi.

    In plain words
    The god commands us to expel from the land of Thebes
    An old defilement we are sheltering.   100
    It is a deathly thing, beyond cure.
    We must not let it feed upon us longer.
Oedipus: What defilement? How shall we rid ourselves of it?

---

73 *Delphi . . . revelation:* In the temple of Delphi at the foot of Mount Parnassus, a priestess of Dionysos, while in an ecstatic trance, would speak the wine god's words. Such a priestess was called an *oracle;* the word can also mean "a message from the god."

Creon: By exile or death, blood for blood. It was
    Murder that brought the plague-wind on the city.   105

Oedipus: Murder of whom? Surely the god has named him?

Creon: My lord: long ago Laïos was our king,
    Before you came to govern us.

Oedipus: I know;
    I learned of him from others; I never saw him.

Creon: He was murdered; and Apollo commands us now   110
    To take revenge upon whoever killed him.

Oedipus: Upon whom? Where are they? Where shall we find a clue
    To solve that crime, after so many years?

Creon: Here in this land, he said.
                 If we make enquiry,
    We may touch things that otherwise escape us.   115

Oedipus: Tell me: Was Laïos murdered in his house,
    Or in the fields, or in some foreign country?

Creon: He said he planned to make a pilgrimage.
    He did not come home again.

Oedipus: And was there no one,
    No witness, no companion, to tell what happened?   120

Creon: They were all killed but one, and he got away
    So frightened that he could remember one thing only.

Oedipus: What was that one thing? One may be the key
    To everything, if we resolve to use it.

Creon: He said that a band of highwaymen attacked them,   125
    Outnumbered them, and overwhelmed the King.

Oedipus: Strange, that a highwayman should be so daring—
    Unless some faction here bribed him to do it.

Creon: We thought of that. But after Laïos' death
    New troubles arose and we had no avenger.   130

Oedipus: What troubles could prevent your hunting down the killers?

Creon: The riddling Sphinx's song
    Made us deaf to all mysteries but her own.

Oedipus: Then once more I must bring what is dark to light.
    It is most fitting that Apollo shows,   135
    As you do, this compunction for the dead.
    You shall see how I stand by you, as I should,
    To avenge the city and the city's god,
    And not as though it were for some distant friend,
    But for my own sake, to be rid of evil.   140
    Whoever killed King Laïos might—who knows?—
    Decide at any moment to kill me as well.
    By avenging the murdered king I protect myself.

    Come, then, my children: leave the altar steps,
    Lift up your olive boughs!
                One of you go   145
    And summon the people of Kadmos to gather here.
    I will do all that I can; you may tell them that.

Exit a Page.

So, with the help of God,
We shall be saved—or else indeed we are lost.
Priest: Let us rise, children. It was for this we came,   150
And now the King has promised it himself.
Phoibos° has sent us an oracle; may he descend
Himself to save us and drive out the plague.

Exeunt Oedipus and Creon into the palace by the central door. The Priest and the Suppliants disperse right and left. After a short pause the Chorus enters the orchestra.

PÁRODOS°

Strophe° 1

Chorus: What is God singing in his profound
Delphi of gold and shadow?
What oracle for Thebes, the sunwhipped city?

Fear unjoints me, the roots of my heart tremble.

Now I remember, O Healer, your power, and wonder: 5
Will you send doom like a sudden cloud, or weave it
Like nightfall of the past?

Speak, speak to us, issue of holy sound:
Dearest to our expectancy: be tender!

Antistrophe° 1

Let me pray to Athenê, the immortal daughter of Zeus,   10
And to Artemis her sister
Who keeps her famous throne in the market ring,
And to Apollo, bowman at the far butts of heaven—

O gods, descend! Like three streams leap against
The fires of our grief, the fires of darkness;   15
Be swift to bring us rest!

As in the old time from the brilliant house
Of air you stepped to save us, come again!

Strophe 2

Now our afflictions have no end,
Now all our stricken host lies down   20
And no man fights off death with his mind;

The noble plowland bears no grain,
And groaning mothers can not bear—

---

152 *Phoibos:* the sun god Phoebus Apollo. *Párodos:* part to be sung by the chorus on first entering.
Strophe: a *strophe* (according to theory) was sung while the chorus danced from stage right to stage
left. *Antistrophe:* part sung while the chorus danced back again across the stage, from left to right.

See, how our lives like birds take wing,
Like sparks that fly when a fire soars,   25
To the shore of the god of evening.

Antistrophe 2

The plague burns on, it is pitiless,
Though pallid children laden with death
Lie unwept in the stony ways,

And old gray women by every path   30
Flock to the strand about the altars

There to strike their breasts and cry
Worship of Phoibos in wailing prayers:
Be kind, God's golden child!

Strophe 3

There are no swords in this attack by fire,   35
No shields, but we are ringed with cries.

Send the besieger plunging from our homes
Into the vast sea-room of the Atlantic
Or into the waves that foam eastward of Thrace—

For the day ravages what the night spares—   40

Destroy our enemy, lord of the thunder!
Let him be riven by lightning from heaven!

Antistrophe 3

Phoibos Apollo, stretch the sun's bowstring,
That golden cord, until it sing for us,
Flashing arrows in heaven!
                    Artemis, Huntress,   45
Race with flaring lights upon our mountains!

O scarlet god, O golden-banded brow,
O Theban Bacchos in a storm of Maenads,°

Enter Oedipus, center.

Whirl upon Death, that all the Undying hate!
Come with blinding torches, come in joy!   50

SCENE I

Oedipus: Is this your prayer? It may be answered. Come,
    Listen to me, act as the crisis demands,
    And you shall have relief from all these evils.

    Until now I was a stranger to this tale,
    As I had been a stranger to the crime.   5
    Could I track down the murderer without a clue?
    But now, friends,

48 *Bacchos . . . Maenads:* god of wine with his attendant girl revelers.

As one who became a citizen after the murder,
I make this proclamation to all Thebans:

If any man knows by whose hand Laïos, son of Labdakos,   10
Met his death, I direct that man to tell me everything,
No matter what he fears for having so long withheld it.
Let it stand as promised that no further trouble
Will come to him, but he may leave the land in safety.

Moreover: If anyone knows the murderer to be foreign,   15
Let him not keep silent: he shall have his reward from me.
However, if he does conceal it; if any man
Fearing for his friend or for himself disobeys this edict,
Hear what I propose to do:

I solemnly forbid the people of this country,   20
Where power and throne are mine, ever to receive that man
Or speak to him, no matter who he is, or let him
Join in sacrifice, lustration,° or in prayer.
I decree that he be driven from every house,
Being, as he is, corruption itself to us: the Delphic   25
Voice of Zeus has pronounced this revelation.
Thus I associate myself with the oracle
And take the side of the murdered king.

As for the criminal, I pray to God—
Whether it be a lurking thief, or one of a number—   30
I pray that that man's life be consumed in evil and wretchedness.
And as for me, this curse applies no less
If it should turn out that the culprit is my guest here,
Sharing my hearth.
                    You have heard the penalty.
I lay it on you now to attend to this   35
For my sake, for Apollo's, for the sick
Sterile city that heaven has abandoned.
Suppose the oracle had given you no command:
Should this defilement go uncleansed for ever?
You should have found the murderer: your king,   40
A noble king, had been destroyed!
                    Now I,
Having the power that he held before me,
Having his bed, begetting children there
Upon his wife, as he would have, had he lived—
Their son would have been my children's brother,   45
If Laïos had had luck in fatherhood!
(But surely ill luck rushed upon his reign)—
I say I take the son's part, just as though
I were his son, to press the fight for him

---

23 *lustration:* propitiatory sacrifice.

And see it won! I'll find the hand that brought   50
Death to Labdakos' and Polydoros' child,
Heir of Kadmos' and Agenor's line.
And as for those who fail me,
May the gods deny them the fruit of the earth,
Fruit of the womb, and may they rot utterly!   55
Let them be wretched as we are wretched, and worse!

For you, for loyal Thebans, and for all
Who find my actions right, I pray the favor
Of justice, and of all the immortal gods.

Choragos:° Since I am under oath, my lord, I swear   60
I did not do the murder, I can not name
The murderer. Might not the oracle
That has ordained the search tell where to find him?

Oedipus: An honest question. But no man in the world
Can make the gods do more than the gods will.   65

Choragos: There is one last expedient—

Oedipus: Tell me what it is.
Though it seem slight, you must not hold it back.

Choragos: A lord clairvoyant to the lord Apollo,
As we all know, is the skilled Teiresias.
One might learn much about this from him, Oedipus.   70

Oedipus: I am not wasting time:
Creon spoke of this, and I have sent for him—
Twice, in fact; it is strange that he is not here.

Choragos: The other matter—that old report—seems useless.

Oedipus: Tell me. I am interested in all reports.   75

Choragos: The King was said to have been killed by highwaymen.

Oedipus: I know. But we have no witnesses to that.

Choragos: If the killer can feel a particle of dread,
Your curse will bring him out of hiding!

Oedipus: No.
The man who dared that act will fear no curse.   80

Enter the blind seer Teiresias, led by a Page.

Choragos: But there is one man who may detect the criminal.
This is Teiresias, this is the holy prophet
In whom, alone of all men, truth was born.

Oedipus: Teiresias: seer: student of mysteries,
Of all that's taught and all that no man tells,   85
Secrets of Heaven and secrets of the earth:
Blind though you are, you know the city lies
Sick with plague; and from this plague, my lord,
We find that you alone can guard or save us.

Possibly you did not hear the messengers?   90
Apollo, when we sent to him,

60 *Choragos:* spokesperson for the chorus.

Sent us back word that this great pestilence
Would lift, but only if we established clearly
The identity of those who murdered Laïos.
They must be killed or exiled.

                                 Can you use   95
Birdflight or any art of divination
To purify yourself, and Thebes, and me
From this contagion? We are in your hands.
There is no fairer duty
Than that of helping others in distress.   100

Teiresias: How dreadful knowledge of the truth can be
When there's no help in truth! I knew this well,
But made myself forget. I should not have come.

Oedipus: What is troubling you? Why are your eyes so cold?

Teiresias: Let me go home. Bear your own fate, and I'll   105
Bear mine. It is better so: trust what I say.

Oedipus: What you say is ungracious and unhelpful
To your native country. Do not refuse to speak.

Teiresias: When it comes to speech, your own is neither temperate
Nor opportune. I wish to be more prudent.   110

Oedipus: In God's name, we all beg you—

Teiresias: You are all ignorant.
No; I will never tell you what I know.
Now it is my misery; then, it would be yours.

Oedipus: What! You do know something, and will not tell us?
You would betray us all and wreck the State?   115

Teiresias: I do not intend to torture myself, or you.
Why persist in asking? You will not persuade me.

Oedipus: What a wicked old man you are! You'd try a stone's
Patience! Out with it! Have you no feeling at all?

Teiresias: You call me unfeeling. If you could only see   120
The nature of your own feelings . . .

Oedipus: Why,
Who would not feel as I do? Who could endure
Your arrogance toward the city?

Teiresias: What does it matter!
Whether I speak or not; it is bound to come.

Oedipus: Then, if "it" is bound to come, you are bound to tell me.   125

Teiresias: No, I will not go on. Rage as you please.

Oedipus: Rage? Why not!
                  And I'll tell you what I think:
You planned it, you had it done, you all but
Killed him with your own hands: if you had eyes,
I'd say the crime was yours, and yours alone.   130

Teiresias: So? I charge you, then,
Abide by the proclamation you have made:
From this day forth
Never speak again to these men or to me;
You yourself are the pollution of this country.   135

Oedipus: You dare say that! Can you possibly think you have
    Some way of going free, after such insolence?
Teiresias: I have gone free. It is the truth sustains me.
Oedipus: Who taught you shamelessness? It was not your craft.
Teiresias: You did. You made me speak. I did not want to.   140
Oedipus: Speak what? Let me hear it again more clearly.
Teiresias: Was it not clear before? Are you tempting me?
Oedipus: I did not understand it. Say it again.
Teiresias: I say that you are the murderer whom you seek.
Oedipus: Now twice you have spat out infamy. You'll pay for it!   145
Teiresias: Would you care for more? Do you wish to be really angry?
Oedipus: Say what you will. Whatever you say is worthless.
Teiresias: I say you live in hideous shame with those
    Most dear to you. You can not see the evil.
Oedipus: It seems you can go on mouthing like this for ever.   150
Teiresias: I can, if there is power in truth.
Oedipus: There is:
    But not for you, not for you,
    You sightless, witless, senseless, mad old man!
Teiresias: You are the madman. There is no one here
    Who will not curse you soon, as you curse me.   155
Oedipus: You child of endless night! You can not hurt me
    Or any other man who sees the sun.
Teiresias: True: it is not from me your fate will come.
    That lies within Apollo's competence,
    As it is his concern.
Oedipus: Tell me: 160
    Are you speaking for Creon, or for yourself?
Teiresias: Creon is no threat. You weave your own doom.
Oedipus: Wealth, power, craft of statesmanship!
    Kingly position, everywhere admired!
    What savage envy is stored up against these,   165
    If Creon, whom I trusted, Creon my friend,
    For this great office which the city once
    Put in my hands unsought—if for this power
    Creon desires in secret to destroy me!

    He has brought this decrepit fortune-teller, this   170
    Collector of dirty pennies, this prophet fraud—
    Why, he is no more clairvoyant than I am!
                           Tell us:
    Has your mystic mummery ever approached the truth?
    When that hellcat the Sphinx was performing here,
    What help were you to these people?   175
    Her magic was not for the first man who came along:
    It demanded a real exorcist. Your birds—
    What good were they? or the gods, for the matter of that?
    But I came by,
    Oedipus, the simple man, who knows nothing—   180

I thought it out for myself, no birds helped me!
And this is the man you think you can destroy,
That you may be close to Creon when he's king!
Well, you and your friend Creon, it seems to me,
Will suffer most. If you were not an old man,   185
You would have paid already for your plot.
Choragos: We can not see that his words or yours
    Have been spoken except in anger, Oedipus,
    And of anger we have no need. How can God's will
    Be accomplished best? That is what most concerns us.   190
Teiresias: You are a king. But where argument's concerned
    I am your man, as much a king as you.
    I am not your servant, but Apollo's.
    I have no need of Creon to speak for me.

    Listen to me. You mock my blindness, do you?   195
    But I say that you, with both your eyes, are blind:
    You can not see the wretchedness of your life,
    Nor in whose house you live, no, nor with whom.
    Who are your father and mother? Can you tell me?
    You do not even know the blind wrongs   200
    That you have done them, on earth and in the world below.
    But the double lash of your parents' curse will whip you
    Out of this land some day, with only night
    Upon your precious eyes.
    Your cries then—where will they not be heard?   205
    What fastness of Kithairon will not echo them?
    And that bridal-descant of yours—you'll know it then,
    The song they sang when you came here to Thebes
    And found your misguided berthing.
    All this, and more, that you can not guess at now,   210
    Will bring you to yourself among your children.

    Be angry, then. Curse Creon. Curse my words.
    I tell you, no man that walks upon the earth
    Shall be rooted out more horribly than you.
Oedipus: Am I to bear this from him?—Damnation   215
    Take you! Out of this place! Out of my sight!
Teiresias: I would not have come at all if you had not asked me.
Oedipus: Could I have told that you'd talk nonsense, that
    You'd come here to make a fool of yourself, and of me?
Teiresias: A fool? Your parents thought me sane enough.   220
Oedipus: My parents again!—Wait: who were my parents?
Teiresias: This day will give you a father, and break your heart.
Oedipus: Your infantile riddles! Your damned abracadabra!
Teiresias: You were a great man once at solving riddles.
Oedipus: Mock me with that if you like; you will find it true.   225
Teiresias: It was true enough. It brought about your ruin.
Oedipus: But if it saved this town?
Teiresias (to the Page):   Boy, give me your hand.

Oedipus: Yes, boy; lead him away.
                              —While you are here
    We can do nothing. Go; leave us in peace.
Teiresias: I will go when I have said what I have to say.   230
    How can you hurt me? And I tell you again:
    The man you have been looking for all this time,
    The damned man, the murderer of Laïos,
    That man is in Thebes. To your mind he is foreign-born,
    But it will soon be shown that he is a Theban,   235
    A revelation that will fail to please.
                              A blind man,
    Who has his eyes now; a penniless man, who is rich now;
    And he will go tapping the strange earth with his staff;
    To the children with whom he lives now he will be
    Brother and father—the very same; to her   240
    Who bore him, son and husband—the very same
    Who came to his father's bed, wet with his father's blood.

    Enough. Go think that over.
    If later you find error in what I have said,
    You may say that I have no skill in prophecy.   245

Exit Teiresias, led by his Page. Oedipus goes into the palace.

ODE°I

                                                                    Strophe 1

Chorus: The Delphic stone of prophecies
    Remembers ancient regicide
    And a still bloody hand.
    That killer's hour of flight has come.
    He must be stronger than riderless   5
    Coursers of untiring wind,
    For the son of Zeus° armed with his father's thunder
    Leaps in lightning after him;
    And the Furies° follow him, the sad Furies.

                                                                Antistrophe 1

    Holy Parnassos' peak of snow   10
    Flashes and blinds that secret man,
    That all shall hunt him down:
    Though he may roam the forest shade
    Like a bull gone wild from pasture
    To rage through glooms of stone.   15
    Doom comes down on him; flight will not avail him;

Ode: a choral song. Here again (as in the *párodos*), *strophe* and *antistrophe* probably indicate the movements of a dance.   7 *son of Zeus:* Apollo.   9 *Furies:* three horrific female spirits whose task was to seek out and punish evildoers.

For the world's heart calls him desolate,
And the immortal Furies follow, for ever follow.

Strophe 2

But now a wilder thing is heard
From the old man skilled at hearing Fate in the wingbeat of a bird.   20
Bewildered as a blown bird, my soul hovers and can not find
Foothold in this debate, or any reason or rest of mind.
But no man ever brought—none can bring
Proof of strife between Thebes' royal house,
Labdakos' line,° and the son of Polybos;°   25
And never until now has any man brought word
Of Laïos' dark death staining Oedipus the King.

Antistrophe 2

Divine Zeus and Apollo hold
Perfect intelligence alone of all tales ever told;
And well though this diviner works, he works in his own night;   30
No man can judge that rough unknown or trust in second sight,
For wisdom changes hands among the wise.
Shall I believe my great lord criminal
At a raging word that a blind old man let fall?
I saw him, when the carrion woman faced him of old,   35
Prove his heroic mind! These evil words are lies.

SCENE II

Creon: Men of Thebes:
  I am told that heavy accusations
  Have been brought against me by King Oedipus.

  I am not the kind of man to bear this tamely.

  If in these present difficulties   5
  He holds me accountable for any harm to him
  Through anything I have said or done—why, then,
  I do not value life in this dishonor.

  It is not as though this rumor touched upon
  Some private indiscretion. The matter is grave.   10
  The fact is that I am being called disloyal
  To the State, to my fellow citizens, to my friends.
Choragos: He may have spoken in anger, not from his mind.
Creon: But did you not hear him say I was the one
  Who seduced the old prophet into lying?   15
Choragos: The thing was said; I do not know how seriously.
Creon: But you were watching him! Were his eyes steady?
  Did he look like a man in his right mind?

---

25 *Labdakos' line:* descendants of Laïos (true father of Oedipus, although the chorus does not know it).
Polybos: king who adopted the child Oedipus.

Choragos: I do not know.
    I can not judge the behavior of great men.
    But here is the King himself.

        Enter Oedipus.

Oedipus: So you dared come back.   20
    Why? How brazen of you to come to my house,
    You murderer!
                Do you think I do not know
    That you plotted to kill me, plotted to steal my throne?
    Tell me, in God's name: am I coward, a fool,
    That you should dream you could accomplish this?   25
    A fool who could not see your slippery game?
    A coward, not to fight back when I saw it?
    You are the fool, Creon, are you not? hoping
    Without support or friends to get a throne?
    Thrones may be won or bought: you could do neither.   30
Creon: Now listen to me. You have talked; let me talk, too.
    You can not judge unless you know the facts.
Oedipus: You speak well: there is one fact; but I find it hard
    To learn from the deadliest enemy I have.
Creon: That above all I must dispute with you.   35
Oedipus: That above all I will not hear you deny.
Creon: If you think there is anything good in being stubborn
    Against all reason, then I say you are wrong.
Oedipus: If you think a man can sin against his own kind
    And not be punished for it, I say you are mad.   40
Creon: I agree. But tell me: what have I done to you?
Oedipus: You advised me to send for that wizard, did you not?
Creon: I did. I should do it again.
Oedipus: Very well. Now tell me:
    How long has it been since Laïos—
Creon: What of Laïos?
Oedipus: Since he vanished in that onset by the road?   45
Creon: It was long ago, a long time.
Oedipus: And this prophet,
    Was he practicing here then?
Creon: He was; and with honor, as now.
Oedipus: Did he speak of me at that time?
Creon: He never did;
    At least, not when I was present.
Oedipus: But . . . . the enquiry?
    I suppose you held one?
Creon: We did, but we learned nothing.   50
Oedipus: Why did the prophet not speak against me then?
Creon: I do not know; and I am the kind of man
    Who holds his tongue when he has no facts to go on.
Oedipus: There's one fact that you know, and you could tell it.
Creon: What fact is that? If I know it, you shall have it.   55

Oedipus: If he were not involved with you, he could not say
    That it was I who murdered Laïos.
Creon: If he says that, you are the one that knows it!—
    But now it is my turn to question you.
Oedipus: Put your questions. I am no murderer.   60
Creon: First then: You married my sister?
Oedipus: I married your sister.
Creon: And you rule the kingdom equally with her?
Oedipus: Everything that she wants she has from me.
Creon: And I am the third, equal to both of you?
Oedipus: That is why I call you a bad friend.   65
Creon: No. Reason it out, as I have done.
    Think of this first: Would any sane man prefer
    Power, with all a king's anxieties,
    To that same power and the grace of sleep?
    Certainly not I.   70
    I have never longed for the king's power—only his rights.
    Would any wise man differ from me in this?
    As matters stand, I have my way in everything
    With your consent, and no responsibilities.
    If I were king, I should be a slave to policy.   75

    How could I desire a scepter more
    Than what is now mine—untroubled influence?
    No, I have not gone mad; I need no honors,
    Except those with the perquisites I have now.
    I am welcome everywhere; every man salutes me,   80
    And those who want your favor seek my ear,
    Since I know how to manage what they ask.
    Should I exchange this ease for that anxiety?
    Besides, no sober mind is treasonable.
    I hate anarchy   85
    And never would deal with any man who likes it.

    Test what I have said. Go to the priestess
    At Delphi, ask if I quoted her correctly.
    And as for this other thing: if I am found
    Guilty of treason with Teiresias,   90
    Then sentence me to death! You have my word
    It is a sentence I should cast my vote for—
    But not without evidence!
                      You do wrong
    When you take good men for bad, bad men for good.
    A true friend thrown aside—why, life itself   95
    Is not more precious!
                  In time you will know this well:
    For time, and time alone, will show the just man,
    Though scoundrels are discovered in a day.
Choragos: This is well said, and a prudent man would ponder it.
    Judgments too quickly formed are dangerous.   100

Oedipus: But is he not quick in his duplicity?
     And shall I not be quick to parry him?
     Would you have me stand still, hold my peace, and let
     This man win everything, through my inaction?
Creon: And you want—what is it, then? To banish me?   105
Oedipus: No, not exile. It is your death I want,
     So that all the world may see what treason means.
Creon: You will persist, then? You will not believe me?
Oedipus: How can I believe you?
Creon: Then you are a fool.
Oedipus: To save myself?
Creon: In justice, think of me.   110
Oedipus: You are evil incarnate.
Creon: But suppose that you are wrong?
Oedipus: Still I must rule.
Creon: But not if you rule badly.
Oedipus: O city, city!
Creon: It is my city, too!
Choragos: Now, my lords, be still. I see the Queen,
     Iocastê, coming from her palace chambers;   115
     And it is time she came, for the sake of you both.
     This dreadful quarrel can be resolved through her.

     Enter Iocastê.

Iocastê: Poor foolish men, what wicked din is this?
     With Thebes sick to death, is it not shameful
     That you should rake some private quarrel up?   120
     (*To Oedipus.*) Come into the house.
                              —And you, Creon, go now:
     Let us have no more of this tumult over nothing.
Creon: Nothing? No, sister: what your husband plans for me
     Is one of two great evils: exile or death.
Oedipus: He is right.
                    Why, woman, I have caught him squarely   125
     Plotting against my life.
Creon: No! Let me die
     Accurst if ever I have wished you harm!
Iocastê: Ah, believe it, Oedipus!
     In the name of the gods, respect this oath of his
     For my sake, for the sake of these people here!   130

                                        Strophe 1

Choragos: Open your mind to her, my lord. Be ruled by her, I beg you!
Oedipus: What would you have me do?
Choragos: Respect Creon's word. He has never spoken like a fool,
     And now he has sworn an oath.
Oedipus: You know what you ask?
Choragos: I do.
Oedipus: Speak on, then.

Choragos: A friend so sworn should not be baited so,   135
    In blind malice, and without final proof.
Oedipus: You are aware, I hope, that what you say
    Means death for me, or exile at the least.

Strophe 2

Choragos: No, I swear by Helios, first in Heaven!
    May I die friendless and accurst,   140
    The worst of deaths, if ever I meant that!
        It is the withering fields
            That hurt my sick heart:
        Must we bear all these ills,
            And now your bad blood as well?   145
Oedipus: Then let him go. And let me die, if I must,
    Or be driven by him in shame from the land of Thebes.
    It is your unhappiness, and not his talk,
    That touches me.
            As for him—
    Wherever he goes, hatred will follow him.   150
Creon: Ugly in yielding, as you were ugly in rage!
    Natures like yours chiefly torment themselves.
Oedipus: Can you not go? Can you not leave me?
Creon: I can.
    You do not know me; but the city knows me,
    And in its eyes I am just, if not in yours.   155

    Exit Creon.

Antistrophe 1

Choragos: Lady Iocastê, did you not ask the King to go to his chambers?
Iocastê: First tell me what has happened.
Choragos: There was suspicion without evidence; yet it rankled
    As even false charges will.
Iocastê: On both sides?
Choragos: On both.
Iocastê: But what was said?
Choragos: Oh let it rest, let it be done with!   160
    Have we not suffered enough?
Oedipus: You see to what your decency has brought you:
    You have made difficulties where my heart saw none.

Antistrophe 2

Choragos: Oedipus, it is not once only I have told you—
    You must know I should count myself unwise   165
    To the point of madness, should I now forsake you—
        You, under whose hand,
            In the storm of another time,
        Our dear land sailed out free.
            But now stand fast at the helm!   170
Iocastê: In God's name, Oedipus, inform your wife as well:
    Why are you so set in this hard anger?

Oedipus: I will tell you, for none of these men deserves
    My confidence as you do. It is Creon's work,
    His treachery, his plotting against me. 175
Iocastê: Go on, if you can make this clear to me.
Oedipus: He charges me with the murder of Laïos.
Iocastê: Has he some knowledge? Or does he speak from hearsay?
Oedipus: He would not commit himself to such a charge,
    But he has brought in that damnable soothsayer 180
    To tell his story.
Iocastê: Set your mind at rest.
    If it is a question of soothsayers, I tell you
    That you will find no man whose craft gives knowledge
    Of the unknowable.

                      Here is my proof:

An oracle was reported to Laïos once 185
(I will not say from Phoibos himself, but from
His appointed ministers, at any rate)
That his doom would be death at the hands of his own son—
His son, born of his flesh and of mine!

Now, you remember the story: Laïos was killed 190
By marauding strangers where three highways meet;
But his child had not been three days in this world
Before the King had pierced the baby's ankles
And left him to die on a lonely mountainside.

Thus, Apollo never caused that child 195
To kill his father, and it was not Laïos' fate
To die at the hands of his son, as he had feared.
This is what prophets and prophecies are worth!
Have no dread of them.
               It is God himself
Who can show us what he wills, in his own way. 200
Oedipus: How strange a shadowy memory crossed my mind,
    Just now while you were speaking; it chilled my heart.
Iocastê: What do you mean? What memory do you speak of?
Oedipus: If I understand you, Laïos was killed
    At a place where three roads meet.
Iocastê: So it was said; 205
    We have no later story.
Oedipus: Where did it happen?
Iocastê: Phokis, it is called: at a place where the Theban Way
    Divides into the roads toward Delphi and Daulia.
Oedipus: When?
Iocastê: We had the news not long before you came
    And proved the right to your succession here. 210
Oedipus: Ah, what net has God been weaving for me?
Iocastê: Oedipus! Why does this trouble you?

Oedipus: Do not ask me yet.
   First, tell me how Laïos looked, and tell me
   How old he was.
Iocastê: He was tall, his hair just touched
   With white; his form was not unlike your own.   215
Oedipus: I think that I myself may be accurst
   By my own ignorant edict.
Iocastê: You speak strangely.
   It makes me tremble to look at you, my King.
Oedipus: I am not sure that the blind man can not see.
   But I should know better if you were to tell me—   220
Iocastê: Anything—though I dread to hear you ask it.
Oedipus: Was the King lightly escorted, or did he ride
   With a large company, as a ruler should?
Iocastê: There were five men with him in all: one was a herald,
   And a single chariot, which he was driving.   225
Oedipus: Alas, that makes it plain enough!
                          But who—
   Who told you how it happened?
Iocastê: A household servant,
   The only one to escape.
Oedipus: And is he still
   A servant of ours?
Iocastê: No; for when he came back at last
   And found you enthroned in the place of the dead king,   230
   He came to me, touched my hand with his, and begged
   That I would send him away to the frontier district
   Where only the shepherds go—
   As far away from the city as I could send him.
   I granted his prayer; for although the man was a slave,   235
   He had earned more than this favor at my hands.
Oedipus: Can he be called back quickly?
Iocastê: Easily.
   But why?
Oedipus: I have taken too much upon myself
   Without enquiry; therefore I wish to consult him.
Iocastê: Then he shall come.
                 But am I not one also   240
   To whom you might confide these fears of yours?
Oedipus: That is your right; it will not be denied you,
   Now least of all; for I have reached a pitch
   Of wild foreboding. Is there anyone
   To whom I should sooner speak?   245

   Polybos of Corinth is my father.
   My mother is a Dorian: Meropê.
   I grew up chief among the men of Corinth
   Until a strange thing happened—
   Not worth my passion, it may be, but strange.   250

At a feast, a drunken man maundering in his cups
Cries out that I am not my father's son!

I contained myself that night, though I felt anger
And a sinking heart. The next day I visited
My father and mother, and questioned them. They stormed,   255
Calling it all the slanderous rant of a fool;
And this relieved me. Yet the suspicion
Remained always aching in my mind;
I knew there was talk; I could not rest;
And finally, saying nothing to my parents,   260
I went to the shrine at Delphi.
The god dismissed my question without reply;
He spoke of other things.
                              Some were clear,
Full of wretchedness, dreadful, unbearable:
As, that I should lie with my own mother, breed   265
Children from whom all men would turn their eyes;
And that I should be my father's murderer.

I heard all this, and fled. And from that day
Corinth to me was only in the stars
Descending in that quarter of the sky,   270
As I wandered farther and farther on my way
To a land where I should never see the evil
Sung by the oracle. And I came to this country
Where, so you say, King Laïos was killed.

I will tell you all that happened there, my lady.   275

There were three highways
Coming together at a place I passed;
And there a herald came towards me, and a chariot
Drawn by horses, with a man such as you describe
Seated in it. The groom leading the horses   280
Forced me off the road at his lord's command;
But as this charioteer lurched over towards me
I struck him in my rage. The old man saw me
And brought his double goad down upon my head
As I came abreast.
                   He was paid back, and more!   285
Swinging my club in this right hand I knocked him
Out of his car, and he rolled on the ground.
                                I killed him.

I killed them all.
Now if that stranger and Laïos were—kin,
Where is a man more miserable than I?   290
More hated by the gods? Citizen and alien alike
Must never shelter me or speak to me—

I must be shunned by all.
And I myself

Pronounced this malediction upon myself!

Think of it: I have touched you with these hands,   295
These hands that killed your husband. What defilement!

Am I all evil, then? It must be so,
Since I must flee from Thebes, yet never again
See my own countrymen, my own country,
For fear of joining my mother in marriage   300
And killing Polybos, my father.
Ah,

If I was created so, born to this fate,
Who could deny the savagery of God?

O holy majesty of heavenly powers!
May I never see that day! Never!   305
Rather let me vanish from the race of men
Than know the abomination destined me!
Choragos: We too, my lord, have felt dismay at this.
But there is hope: you have yet to hear the shepherd.
Oedipus: Indeed, I fear no other hope is left me.   310
Iocastê: What do you hope from him when he comes?
Oedipus: This much:
If his account of the murder tallies with yours,
Then I am cleared.
Iocastê: What was it that I said
Of such importance?
Oedipus: Why, "marauders," you said,
Killed the King, according to this man's story.   315
If he maintains that still, if there were several,
Clearly the guilt is not mine: I was alone.
But if he says one man, singlehanded, did it,
Then the evidence all points to me.
Iocastê: You may be sure that he said there were several;   320
And can he call back that story now? He can not.
The whole city heard it as plainly as I.
But suppose he alters some detail of it:
He can not ever show that Laïos' death
Fulfilled the oracle: for Apollo said   325
My child was doomed to kill him; and my child—
Poor baby!—it was my child that died first.

No. From now on, where oracles are concerned,
I would not waste a second thought on any.
Oedipus: You may be right.
But come: let someone go   330

For the shepherd at once. This matter must be settled.
Iocastê: I will send for him.

I would not wish to cross you in anything,
And surely not in this.—Let us go in.

Exeunt into the palace.

ODE II

Chorus: Let me be reverent in the ways of right,   *Strophe 1*
Lowly the paths I journey on;
Let all my words and actions keep
The laws of the pure universe
From highest Heaven handed down.   5
For Heaven is their bright nurse,
Those generations of the realms of light;
Ah, never of mortal kind were they begot,
Nor are they slaves of memory, lost in sleep:
Their Father is greater than Time, and ages not.   10

The tyrant is a child of Pride   *Antistrophe 1*
Who drinks from his great sickening cup
Recklessness and vanity,
Until from his high crest headlong
He plummets to the dust of hope.   15
That strong man is not strong.
But let no fair ambition be denied;
May God protect the wrestler for the State
In government, in comely policy,
Who will fear God, and on His ordinance wait.   20

Haughtiness and the high hand of disdain   *Strophe 2*
Tempt and outrage God's holy law;
And any mortal who dares hold
No immortal Power in awe
Will be caught up in a net of pain: 25
The price for which his levity is sold.
Let each man take due earnings, then,
And keep his hands from holy things,
And from blasphemy stand apart—
Else the crackling blast of heaven   30
Blows on his head, and on his desperate heart;
Though fools will honor impious men,
In their cities no tragic poet sings.

Shall we lose faith in Delphi's obscurities,   *Antistrophe 2*
We who have heard the world's core   35
Discredited, and the sacred wood
Of Zeus at Elis praised no more?
The deeds and the strange prophecies
Must make a pattern yet to be understood.
Zeus, if indeed you are lord of all,   40

Throned in light over night and day,
Mirror this in your endless mind:
Our masters call the oracle
Words on the wind, and the Delphic vision blind!
Their hearts no longer know Apollo,   45
And reverence for the gods has died away.

SCENE III

Enter Iocastê.

Iocastê: Princes of Thebes, it has occurred to me
To visit the altars of the gods, bearing
These branches as a suppliant, and this incense.
Our King is not himself: his noble soul
Is overwrought with fantasies of dread,   5
Else he would consider
The new prophecies in the light of the old.
He will listen to any voice that speaks disaster,
And my advice goes for nothing.

She approaches the altar, right.

                        To you, then, Apollo,
Lycean lord, since you are nearest, I turn in prayer.   10
Receive these offerings, and grant us deliverance
From defilement. Our hearts are heavy with fear
When we see our leader distracted, as helpless sailors
Are terrified by the confusion of their helmsman.

Enter Messenger.

Messenger: Friends, no doubt you can direct me: 15
Where shall I find the house of Oedipus,
Or, better still, where is the King himself?
Choragos: It is this very place, stranger; he is inside.
This is his wife and mother of his children.
Messenger: I wish her happiness in a happy house,   20
Blest in all the fulfillment of her marriage.
Iocastê: I wish as much for you: your courtesy
Deserves a like good fortune. But now, tell me:
Why have you come? What have you to say to us?
Messenger: Good news, my lady, for your house and your husband.   25
Iocastê: What news? Who sent you here?
Messenger: I am from Corinth.
The news I bring ought to mean joy for you,
Though it may be you will find some grief in it.
Iocastê: What is it? How can it touch us in both ways?
Messenger: The word is that the people of the Isthmus   30
Intend to call Oedipus to be their king.
Iocastê: But old King Polybos—is he not reigning still?

Messenger: No. Death holds him in his sepulchre.
Iocastê: What are you saying? Polybos is dead?
Messenger: If I am not telling the truth, may I die myself.   35
Iocastê (to a Maidservant): Go in, go quickly; tell this to your master.

> O riddlers of God's will, where are you now!
> This was the man whom Oedipus, long ago,
> Feared so, fled so, in dread of destroying him—
> But it was another fate by which he died.   40

> *Enter Oedipus, center.*

Oedipus: Dearest Iocastê, why have you sent for me?
Iocastê: Listen to what this man says, and then tell me
> What has become of the solemn prophecies.
Oedipus: Who is this man? What is his news for me?
Iocastê: He has come from Corinth to announce your father's death!   45
Oedipus: Is it true, stranger? Tell me in your own words.
Messenger: I can not say it more clearly: the King is dead.
Oedipus: Was it by treason? Or by an attack of illness?
Messenger: A little thing brings old men to their rest.
Oedipus: It was sickness, then?
Messenger: Yes, and his many years.   50
Oedipus: Ah!
> Why should a man respect the Pythian hearth,° or
> Give heed to the birds that jangle above his head?
> They prophesied that I should kill Polybos,
> Kill my own father; but he is dead and buried,   55
> And I am here—I never touched him, never,
> Unless he died of grief for my departure,
> And thus, in a sense, through me. No. Polybos
> Has packed the oracles off with him underground.
> They are empty words.
Iocastê: Had I not told you so?   60
Oedipus: You had; it was my faint heart that betrayed me.
Iocastê: From now on never think of those things again.
Oedipus: And yet—must I not fear my mother's bed?
Iocastê: Why should anyone in this world be afraid,
> Since Fate rules us and nothing can be foreseen?   65
> A man should live only for the present day.

> Have no more fear of sleeping with your mother:
> How many men, in dreams, have lain with their mothers!
> No reasonable man is troubled by such things.
Oedipus: That is true; only—   70
> If only my mother were not still alive!
> But she is alive. I can not help my dread.
Iocastê: Yet this news of your father's death is wonderful.

---

52 *Pythian hearth:* the shrine at Delphi, whose priestess was famous for her prophecies.

Oedipus: Wonderful. But I fear the living woman.

Messenger: Tell me, who is this woman that you fear? 75

Oedipus: It is Meropê, man; the wife of King Polybos.

Messenger: Meropê? Why should you be afraid of her?

Oedipus: An oracle of the gods, a dreadful saying.

Messenger: Can you tell me about it or are you sworn to silence?

Oedipus: I can tell you, and I will. 80
   Apollo said through his prophet that I was the man
   Who should marry his own mother, shed his father's blood
   With his own hands. And so, for all these years
   I have kept clear of Corinth, and no harm has come—
   Though it would have been sweet to see my parents again. 85

Messenger: And is this the fear that drove you out of Corinth?

Oedipus: Would you have me kill my father?

Messenger: As for that
   You must be reassured by the news I gave you.

Oedipus: If you could reassure me, I would reward you.

Messenger: I had that in mind, I will confess: I thought 90
   I could count on you when you returned to Corinth.

Oedipus: No: I will never go near my parents again.

Messenger: Ah, son, you still do not know what you are doing—

Oedipus: What do you mean? In the name of God tell me!

Messenger: —If these are your reasons for not going home. 95

Oedipus: I tell you, I fear the oracle may come true.

Messenger: And guilt may come upon you through your parents?

Oedipus: That is the dread that is always in my heart.

Messenger: Can you not see that all your fears are groundless?

Oedipus: How can you say that? They are my parents, surely? 100

Messenger: Polybos was not your father.

Oedipus: Not my father?

Messenger: No more your father than the man speaking to you.

Oedipus: But you are nothing to me!

Messenger: Neither was he.

Oedipus: Then why did he call me son?

Messenger: I will tell you:
   Long ago he had you from my hands, as a gift. 105

Oedipus: Then how could he love me so, if I was not his?

Messenger: He had no children, and his heart turned to you.

Oedipus: What of you? Did you buy me? Did you find me by chance?

Messenger: I came upon you in the crooked pass of Kithairon.

Oedipus: And what were you doing there?

Messenger: Tending my flocks. 110

Oedipus: A wandering shepherd?

Messenger: But your savior, son, that day.

Oedipus: From what did you save me?

Messenger: Your ankles should tell you that.

Oedipus: Ah, stranger, why do you speak of that childhood pain?

Messenger: I cut the bonds that tied your ankles together.

Oedipus: I have had the mark as long as I can remember. 115

Messenger: That was why you were given the name you bear.
Oedipus: God! Was it my father or my mother who did it?
    Tell me!
Messenger: I do not know. The man who gave you to me
    Can tell you better than I.
Oedipus: It was not you that found me, but another?   120
Messenger: It was another shepherd gave you to me.
Oedipus: Who was he? Can you tell me who he was?
Messenger: I think he was said to be one of Laïos' people.
Oedipus: You mean the Laïos who was king here years ago?
Messenger: Yes; King Laïos; and the man was one of his herdsmen.   125
Oedipus: Is he still alive? Can I see him?
Messenger: These men here
    Know best about such things.
Oedipus: Does anyone here
    Know this shepherd that he is talking about?
    Have you seen him in the fields, or in the town?
    If you have, tell me. It is time things were made plain.   130
Choragos: I think the man he means is that same shepherd
    You have already asked to see. Iocastê perhaps
    Could tell you something.
Oedipus: Do you know anything
    About him, Lady? Is he the man we have summoned?
    Is that the man this shepherd means?
Iocastê: Why think of him?   135
    Forget this herdsman. Forget it all.
    This talk is a waste of time.
Oedipus: How can you say that,
    When the clues to my true birth are in my hands?
Iocastê: For God's love, let us have no more questioning!
    Is your life nothing to you?   140
    My own is pain enough for me to bear.
Oedipus: You need not worry. Suppose my mother a slave,
    And born of slaves: no baseness can touch you.
Iocastê: Listen to me, I beg you: do not do this thing!
Oedipus: I will not listen; the truth must be made known.   145
Iocastê: Everything that I say is for your own good!
Oedipus: My own good
    Snaps my patience, then; I want none of it.
Iocastê: You are fatally wrong! May you never learn who you are!
Oedipus: Go, one of you, and bring the shepherd here.
    Let us leave this woman to brag of her royal name.   150
Iocastê: Ah, miserable!
    That is the only word I have for you now.
    That is the only word I can ever have.

    Exit into the palace.

Choragos: Why has she left us, Oedipus? Why has she gone
    In such a passion of sorrow? I fear this silence: 155
    Something dreadful may come of it.

Oedipus: Let it come!
    However base my birth, I must know about it.
    The Queen, like a woman, is perhaps ashamed
    To think of my low origin. But I
    Am a child of Luck; I can not be dishonored.   160
    Luck is my mother; the passing months, my brothers,
    Have seen me rich and poor.
              If this is so,
    How could I wish that I were someone else?
    How could I not be glad to know my birth?

ODE III

Strophe

Chorus: If ever the coming time were known
    To my heart's pondering,
    Kithairon, now by Heaven I see the torches
    At the festival of the next full moon,
    And see the dance, and hear the choir sing   5
    A grace to your gentle shade:
    Mountain where Oedipus was found,
    O mountain guard of a noble race!
    May the god who heals us lend his aid,
    And let that glory come to pass   10
    For our king's cradling-ground.

Antistrophe

    Of the nymphs that flower beyond the years,
    Who bore you, royal child,
    To Pan of the hills or the timberline Apollo,
    Cold in delight where the upland clears,   15
    Or Hermês for whom Kyllenê's° heights are piled?
    Or flushed as evening cloud,
    Great Dionysos, roamer of mountains,
    He—was it he who found you there,
    And caught you up in his own proud   20
    Arms from the sweet god-ravisher
    Who laughed by the Muses' fountains?

SCENE IV

Oedipus: Sirs: though I do not know the man,
    I think I see him coming, this shepherd we want:
    He is old, like our friend here, and the men
    Bringing him seem to be servants of my house.
    But you can tell, if you have ever seen him.   5

    Enter Shepherd escorted by servants.

---

16 *Kyllenê:* a sacred mountain, birthplace of Hermês, the deities' messenger. The chorus assumes
that the mountain was created in order to afford him birth.

Choragos: I know him, he was Laïos' man. You can trust him.

Oedipus: Tell me first, you from Corinth: is this the shepherd
    We were discussing?

Messenger: This is the very man.

Oedipus (to Shepherd): Come here. No, look at me. You must answer
    Everything I ask.—You belonged to Laïos?   10

Shepherd: Yes: born his slave, brought up in his house.

Oedipus: Tell me: what kind of work did you do for him?

Shepherd: I was a shepherd of his, most of my life.

Oedipus: Where mainly did you go for pasturage?

Shepherd: Sometimes Kithairon, sometimes the hills near-by.   15

Oedipus: Do you remember ever seeing this man out there?

Shepherd: What would he be doing there? This man?

Oedipus: This man standing here. Have you ever seen him before?

Shepherd: No. At least, not to my recollection.

Messenger: And that is not strange, my lord. But I'll refresh   20
    His memory: he must remember when we two
    Spent three whole seasons together, March to September,
    On Kithairon or thereabouts. He had two flocks;
    I had one. Each autumn I'd drive mine home
    And he would go back with his to Laïos' sheepfold.—   25
    Is this not true, just as I have described it?

Shepherd: True, yes; but it was all so long ago.

Messenger: Well, then: do you remember, back in those days
    That you gave me a baby boy to bring up as my own?

Shepherd: What if I did? What are you trying to say?   30

Messenger: King Oedipus was once that little child.

Shepherd: Damn you, hold your tongue!

Oedipus: No more of that!
    It is your tongue needs watching, not this man's.

Shepherd: My King, my Master, what is it I have done wrong?

Oedipus: You have not answered his question about the boy.   35

Shepherd: He does not know . . . He is only making trouble . . .

Oedipus: Come, speak plainly, or it will go hard with you.

Shepherd: In God's name, do not torture an old man!

Oedipus: Come here, one of you; bind his arms behind him.

Shepherd: Unhappy king! What more do you wish to learn?   40

Oedipus: Did you give this man the child he speaks of?

Shepherd: I did.
    And I would to God I had died that very day.

Oedipus: You will die now unless you speak the truth.

Shepherd: Yet if I speak the truth, I am worse than dead.

Oedipus: Very well; since you insist upon delaying—   45

Shepherd: No! I have told you already that I gave him the boy.

Oedipus: Where did you get him? From your house? From somewhere else?

Shepherd: Not from mine, no. A man gave him to me.

Oedipus: Is that man here? Do you know whose slave he was?

Shepherd: For God's love, my King, do not ask me any more!   50

Oedipus: You are a dead man if I have to ask you again.

Shepherd: Then . . . Then the child was from the palace of Laïos.
Oedipus: A slave child? or a child of his own line?
Shepherd: Ah, I am on the brink of dreadful speech!
Oedipus: And I of dreadful hearing. Yet I must hear.   55
Shepherd: If you must be told, then . . .

                                  They said it was Laïos' child;
But it is your wife who can tell you about that.
Oedipus: My wife!—Did she give it to you?
Shepherd: My lord, she did.
Oedipus: Do you know why?
Shepherd: I was told to get rid of it.
Oedipus: An unspeakable mother!
Shepherd: There had been prophecies . . .   60
Oedipus: Tell me.
Shepherd: It was said that the boy would kill his own father.
Oedipus: Then why did you give him over to this old man?
Shepherd: I pitied the baby, my King,
    And I thought that this man would take him far away   65
    To his own country.

                    He saved him—but for what a fate!
For if you are what this man says you are,
No man living is more wretched than Oedipus.
Oedipus: Ah God!
    It was true!
           All the prophecies!
                    —Now,   70
O Light, may I look on you for the last time!
I, Oedipus,
Oedipus, damned in his birth, in his marriage damned,
Damned in the blood he shed with his own hand!

He rushes into the palace.

ODE IV

                                              Strophe 1

Chorus: Alas for the seed of men.

    What measure shall I give these generations
    That breathe on the void and are void
    And exist and do not exist?

    Who bears more weight of joy   5
    Than mass of sunlight shifting in images,
    Or who shall make his thought stay on
    That down time drifts away?

    Your splendor is all fallen.

    O naked brow of wrath and tears,   10
    O change of Oedipus!

I who saw your days call no man blest—
Your great days like ghosts gone.

Antistrophe 1

That mind was a strong bow.

Deep, how deep you drew it then, hard archer,   15
At a dim fearful range,
And brought dear glory down!

You overcame the stranger—
The virgin with her hooking lion claws—
And though death sang, stood like a tower   20
To make pale Thebes take heart.

Fortress against our sorrow!

True king, giver of laws,
Majestic Oedipus!
No prince in Thebes had ever such renown,   25
No prince won such grace of power.

Strophe 2

And now of all men ever known
Most pitiful is this man's story:
His fortunes are most changed, his state
Fallen to a low slave's   30
Ground under bitter fate.

O Oedipus, most royal one!
The great door that expelled you to the light
Gave at night—ah, gave night to your glory:
As to the father, to the fathering son.   35

All understood too late.

How could that queen whom Laïos won,
The garden that he harrowed at his height,
Be silent when that act was done?

Antistrophe 2

But all eyes fail before time's eye,   40
All actions come to justice there.
Though never willed, though far down the deep past,
Your bed, your dread sirings,
Are brought to book at last.

Child by Laïos doomed to die,   45
Then doomed to lose that fortunate little death,
Would God you never took breath in this air
That with my wailing lips I take to cry:

For I weep the world's outcast.

I was blind, and now I can tell why: 50
Asleep, for you had given ease of breath
To Thebes, while the false years went by.

ÉXODOS°

Enter, from the palace, Second Messenger.

Second Messenger: Elders of Thebes, most honored in this land,
What horrors are yours to see and hear, what weight
Of sorrow to be endured, if, true to your birth,
You venerate the line of Labdakos!
I think neither Istros nor Phasis, those great rivers,   5
Could purify this place of the corruption
It shelters now, or soon must bring to light—
Evil not done unconsciously, but willed.

The greatest griefs are those we cause ourselves.
Choragos: Surely, friend, we have grief enough already;   10
What new sorrow do you mean?
Second Messenger: The Queen is dead.
Choragos: Iocastê? Dead? But at whose hand?
Second Messenger: Her own.
The full horror of what happened, you can not know,
For you did not see it; but I, who did, will tell you
As clearly as I can how she met her death.   15

When she had left us,
In passionate silence, passing through the court,
She ran to her apartment in the house,
Her hair clutched by the fingers of both hands.
She closed the doors behind her; then, by that bed   20
Where long ago the fatal son was conceived—
That son who should bring about his father's death—
We heard her call upon Laïos, dead so many years,
And heard her wail for the double fruit of her marriage,
A husband by her husband, children by her child.   25

Exactly how she died I do not know:
For Oedipus burst in moaning and would not let us
Keep vigil to the end: it was by him
As he stormed about the room that our eyes were caught.
From one to another of us he went, begging a sword,   30
Cursing the wife who was not his wife, the mother
Whose womb had carried his own children and himself.
I do not know: it was none of us aided him,
But surely one of the gods was in control!
For with a dreadful cry   35
He hurled his weight, as though wrenched out of himself,
At the twin doors: the bolts gave, and he rushed in.
And there we saw her hanging, her body swaying
From the cruel cord she had noosed about her neck.
A great sob broke from him, heartbreaking to hear,   40
As he loosed the rope and lowered her to the ground.

Éxodos: final scene, containing the resolution.

I would blot out from my mind what happened next!
For the King ripped from her gown the golden brooches
That were her ornament, and raised them, and plunged them down
Straight into his own eyeballs, crying, "No more,   45
No more shall you look on the misery about me,
The horrors of my own doing! Too long you have known
The faces of those whom I should never have seen,
Too long been blind to those for whom I was searching!
From this hour, go in darkness!" And as he spoke,   50
He struck at his eyes—not once, but many times;
And the blood spattered his beard,
Bursting from his ruined sockets like red hail.

So from the unhappiness of two this evil has sprung,
A curse on the man and woman alike. The old   55
Happiness of the house of Labdakos
Was happiness enough: where is it today?
It is all wailing and ruin, disgrace, death—all
The misery of mankind that has a name—
And it is wholly and for ever theirs.   60
Choragos: Is he in agony still? Is there no rest for him?
Second Messenger: He is calling for someone to lead him to the gates
So that all the children of Kadmos may look upon
His father's murderer, his mother's—no,
I can not say it!
                    And then he will leave Thebes,   65
Self-exiled, in order that the curse
Which he himself pronounced may depart from the house.
He is weak, and there is none to lead him,
So terrible is his suffering.
                    But you will see:
Look, the doors are opening; in a moment   70
You will see a thing that would crush a heart of stone.

The central door is opened; Oedipus, blinded, is led in.

Choragos: Dreadful indeed for men to see.
     Never have my own eyes
     Looked on a sight so full of fear.

     Oedipus!   75
     What madness came upon you, what daemon
     Leaped on your life with heavier
     Punishment than a mortal man can bear?
     No: I can not even
     Look at you, poor ruined one.   80
     And I would speak, question, ponder,
     If I were able. No.
     You make me shudder.
Oedipus: God. God.

Is there a sorrow greater? 85
Where shall I find harbor in this world?
My voice is hurled far on a dark wind.
What has God done to me?
Choragos: Too terrible to think of, or to see.

Strophe 1

Oedipus: O cloud of night, 90
Never to be turned away: night coming on,
I can not tell how: night like a shroud!

My fair winds brought me here.
　　　　　　　　　　Oh God. Again
The pain of the spikes where I had sight,
The flooding pain 95
Of memory, never to be gouged out.
Choragos: This is not strange.
You suffer it all twice over, remorse in pain,
Pain in remorse.

Antistrophe 1

Oedipus: Ah dear friend 100
Are you faithful even yet, you alone?
Are you still standing near me, will you stay here,
Patient, to care for the blind?
　　　　　　　　　　The blind man!
Yet even blind I know who it is attends me,
By the voice's tone— 105
Though my new darkness hide the comforter.
Choragos: Oh fearful act!
What god was it drove you to rake black
Night across your eyes?

Strophe 2

Oedipus: Apollo. Apollo. Dear 110
Children, the god was Apollo.
He brought my sick, sick fate upon me.
But the blinding hand was my own!
How could I bear to see
When all my sight was horror everywhere? 115
Choragos: Everywhere; that is true.
Oedipus: And now what is left?
Images? Love? A greeting even,
Sweet to the senses? Is there anything?
Ah, no, friends: lead me away. 120
Lead me away from Thebes.
　　　　　　　　　Lead the great wreck
And hell of Oedipus, whom the gods hate.
Choragos: Your fate is clear, you are not blind to that.
Would God you had never found it out!

Antistrophe 2

Oedipus: Death take the man who unbound   125
       My feet on that hillside
       And delivered me from death to life! What life?
       If only I had died,
       This weight of monstrous doom
       Could not have dragged me and my darlings down.   130
Choragos: I would have wished the same.
Oedipus: Oh never to have come here
       With my father's blood upon me! Never
       To have been the man they call his mother's husband!
       Oh accurst! Oh child of evil,   135
       To have entered that wretched bed—
                                        the selfsame one!
       More primal than sin itself, this fell to me.
Choragos: I do not know how I can answer you.
       You were better dead than alive and blind.
Oedipus: Do not counsel me any more. This punishment   140
       That I have laid upon myself is just.
       If I had eyes,
       I do not know how I could bear the sight
       Of my father, when I came to the house of Death,
       Or my mother: for I have sinned against them both   145
       So vilely that I could not make my peace
       By strangling my own life.
                             Or do you think my children,
       Born as they were born, would be sweet to my eyes?
       Ah never, never! Nor this town with its high walls,
       Nor the holy images of the gods.
                             For I,   150
       Thrice miserable!—Oedipus, noblest of all the line
       Of Kadmos, have condemned myself to enjoy
       These things no more, by my own malediction
       Expelling that man whom the gods declared
       To be a defilement in the house of Laïos.   155
       After exposing the rankness of my own guilt,
       How could I look men frankly in the eyes?
       No, I swear it,
       If I could have stifled my hearing at its source,
       I would have done it and made all this body   160
       A tight cell of misery, blank to light and sound:
       So I should have been safe in a dark agony
       Beyond all recollection.
                             Ah Kithairon!
       Why did you shelter me? When I was cast upon you,
       Why did I not die? Then I should never   165
       Have shown the world my execrable birth.

       Ah Polybos! Corinth, city that I believed
       The ancient seat of my ancestors: how fair
       I seemed, your child! And all the while this evil

Was cancerous within me!
       For I am sick   170
In my daily life, sick in my origin.

O three roads, dark ravine, woodland and way
Where three roads met: you, drinking my father's blood,
My own blood, spilled by my own hand: can you remember
The unspeakable things I did there, and the things 175
I went on from there to do?
      O marriage, marriage!
The act that engendered me, and again the act
Performed by the son in the same bed—
         Ah, the net
Of incest, mingling fathers, brothers, sons,
With brides, wives, mothers: the last evil   180
That can be known by men: no tongue can say
How evil!
   No. For the love of God, conceal me
Somewhere far from Thebes; or kill me; or hurl me
Into the sea, away from men's eyes for ever.

              185
Come, lead me. You need not fear to touch me.
Of all men, I alone can bear this guilt.

Enter Creon.

Choragos: We are not the ones to decide; but Creon here
 May fitly judge of what you ask. He only
 Is left to protect the city in your place.
Oedipus: Alas, how can I speak to him? What right have I 190
 To beg his courtesy whom I have deeply wronged?
Creon: I have not come to mock you, Oedipus,
 Or to reproach you, either.
 (*To Attendants.*)   —You, standing there:
 If you have lost all respect for man's dignity,
 At least respect the flame of Lord Helios: 195
 Do not allow this pollution to show itself
 Openly here, an affront to the earth
 And Heaven's rain and the light of day. No, take him
 Into the house as quickly as you can.
 For it is proper   200
 That only the close kindred see his grief.
Oedipus: I pray you in God's name, since your courtesy
 Ignores my dark expectation, visiting
 With mercy this man of all men most execrable:
 Give me what I ask—for your good, not for mine. 205
Creon: And what is it that you would have me do?
Oedipus: Drive me out of this country as quickly as may be
 To a place where no human voice can ever greet me.
Creon: I should have done that before now—only,
 God's will had not been wholly revealed to me.   210

Oedipus: But his command is plain: the parricide
    Must be destroyed. I am that evil man.
Creon: That is the sense of it, yes; but as things are,
    We had best discover clearly what is to be done.
Oedipus: You would learn more about a man like me?   215
Creon: You are ready now to listen to the god.
Oedipus: I will listen. But it is to you
    That I must turn for help. I beg you, hear me.

    The woman in there—
    Give her whatever funeral you think proper: 220
    She is your sister.
                 —But let me go, Creon!
    Let me purge my father's Thebes of the pollution
    Of my living here, and go out to the wild hills,
    To Kithairon, that has won such fame with me,
    The tomb my mother and father appointed for me,   225
    And let me die there, as they willed I should.
    And yet I know
    Death will not ever come to me through sickness
    Or in any natural way: I have been preserved
    For some unthinkable fate. But let that be.   230

    As for my sons, you need not care for them.
    They are men, they will find some way to live.
    But my poor daughters, who have shared my table,
    Who never before have been parted from their father—
    Take care of them, Creon; do this for me.   235
    And will you let me touch them with my hands
    A last time, and let us weep together?
    Be kind, my lord,
    Great prince, be kind!
                Could I but touch them,
    They would be mine again, as when I had my eyes.   240

Enter Antigonê and Ismene, attended.

    Ah, God!
    Is it my dearest children I hear weeping?
    Has Creon pitied me and sent my daughters?
Creon: Yes, Oedipus: I knew that they were dear to you
    In the old days, and know you must love them still.   245
Oedipus: May God bless you for this—and be a friendlier
    Guardian to you than he has been to me!

    Children, where are you?
    Come quickly to my hands: they are your brother's—
    Hands that have brought your father's once clear eyes   250
    To this way of seeing—
              Ah dearest ones,
    I had neither sight nor knowledge then, your father

By the woman who was the source of his own life!
And I weep for you—having no strength to see you—,
I weep for you when I think of the bitterness   255
That men will visit upon you all your lives.
What homes, what festivals can you attend
Without being forced to depart again in tears?
And when you come to marriageable age,
Where is the man, my daughters, who would dare   260
Risk the bane that lies on all my children?
Is there any evil wanting? Your father killed
His father; sowed the womb of her who bore him;
Engendered you at the fount of his own existence!
That is what they will say of you.

                                  Then, whom   265
Can you ever marry? There are no bridegrooms for you,
And your lives must wither away in sterile dreaming.

O Creon, son of Menoikeus!
You are the only father my daughters have,
Since we, their parents, are both of us gone for ever.   270
They are your own blood: you will not let them
Fall into beggary and loneliness;
You will keep them from the miseries that are mine!
Take pity on them; see, they are only children,
Friendless except for you. Promise me this,   275
Great Prince, and give me your hand in token of it.

Creon clasps his right hand.

Children:
I could say much, if you could understand me,
But as it is, I have only this prayer for you:
Live where you can, be as happy as you can—   280
Happier, please God, than God has made your father!
Creon: Enough. You have wept enough. Now go within.
Oedipus: I must; but it is hard.
Creon: Time eases all things.
Oedipus: But you must promise—
Creon: Say what you desire.
Oedipus: Send me from Thebes!
Creon: God grant that I may!   285
Oedipus: But since God hates me . . .
Creon: No, he will grant your wish.
Oedipus: You promise?
Creon: I can not speak beyond my knowledge.
Oedipus: Then lead me in.
Creon: Come now, and leave your children.
Oedipus: No! Do not take them from me!
Creon: Think no longer
That you are in command here, but rather think   290
How, when you were, you served your own destruction.

Exeunt into the house all but the Chorus; the Choragos chants directly to the audience.

Choragos: Men of Thebes: look upon Oedipus.

This is the king who solved the famous riddle
And towered up, most powerful of men.   295
No mortal eyes but looked on him with envy,
Yet in the end ruin swept over him.

Let every man in mankind's frailty
Consider his last day; and let none
Presume on his good fortune until he find   300
Life, at his death, a memory without pain.

Questions

1. How explicitly does the prophet Teiresias reveal the guilt of Oedipus? Does it seem to you stupidity on the part of Oedipus or a defect in Sophocles's play that the king takes so long to recognize his guilt and to admit to it?

2. How does Oedipus exhibit weakness of character? Point to lines that reveal him as imperfectly noble in his words, deeds, or treatment of others.

3. "Oedipus is punished not for any fault in himself, but for his ignorance. Not knowing his family history, unable to recognize his parents on sight, he is blameless; and in slaying his father and marrying his mother, he behaves as any sensible person might behave in the same circumstances." Do you agree with this interpretation?

4. Besides the predictions of Teiresias, what other foreshadowings of the shepherd's revelation does the play contain?

5. Consider the character of Iocastê. Is she a "flat" character—a generalized queen figure— or an individual with distinctive traits of personality? Point to speeches or details in the play to back up your opinion.

6. What is dramatic irony? Besides the example given on page 182, what other instances of dramatic irony do you find in *Oedipus the King*? What do they contribute to the effectiveness of the play?

7. In the drama of Sophocles, violence and bloodshed take place offstage; thus, the suicide of Iocastê is only reported to us. Nor do we witness Oedipus's removal of his eyes; this horror is only given in the report by the second messenger. Of what advantage or disadvantage to the play is this limitation?

8. For what reason does Oedipus blind himself? What meaning, if any, do you find in his choice of a surgical instrument?

9. What are your feelings toward him as the play ends?

10. Read the famous interpretation of this play offered by Sigmund Freud (page 1275). How well does Freud explain why the play moves you?

11. With what attitude toward the gods does the play leave you? By inflicting a plague on Thebes, by causing barrenness, by cursing both the people and their king, do the gods seem cruel, unjust, or tyrannical? Does the play show any reverence toward them?

12. Does this play end in total gloom?

THE BACKGROUND OF *ANTIGONÊ*

Although *Antigonê* tells a later part of the Oedipus story, it was not part of the trilogy that originally contained *Oedipus the King* (the other plays in that trilogy have been lost). *Antigonê* was written in 441 B.C., over twenty years before the author took up the tale of Oedipus himself. In *Antigonê* duties to family and duties to the state are pitted against one another in a story that has Creon, now king of Thebes many years

Martha Henry in the 1971 Lincoln Center Repertory production of *Antigonê*.

after Oedipus's exile and death, refusing burial to the body of Oedipus's son (and brother) Polyneicês, who has led an army against the city to claim the throne from his brother. His sister Antigonê (Oedipus's daughter and sister) resists Creon's unjust edict in the name of family loyalty, a defiance both noble and potentially threatening to political stability in a time of crisis. Though the gods approve of her action, she dies a victim of Creon's hubris. (Or perhaps, as Patricia Lines suggests on page 1278, Antigonê's own hubris is her downfall.) Creon suffers the death (by suicide) of his son and his wife as a result. Antigonê's claim is especially compelling when we imagine her played by a mature male actor who in his public life, as a citizen, must know both how to rule and how to be ruled, to submit to legitimate authority when he steps down from office.

Antigonê
441 B.C.

Translated by Dudley Fitts and Robert Fitzgerald

CHARACTERS

Antigonê	Teiresias
Ismenê	A Sentry
Eurydicê	A Messenger
Creon	Chorus
Haimon	

SCENE. *Before the palace of Creon, King of Thebes. A central double door, and two lateral doors. A platform extends the length of the façade, and from this platform three steps lead down into the "orchestra," or chorus-ground.*

TIME. *Dawn of the day after the repulse of the Argive army from the assault on Thebes.*

PROLOGUE°

Antigonê and Ismenê enter from the central door of the palace.

Antigonê: Ismenê, dear sister,
    You would think that we had already suffered enough
    For the curse on Oedipus:°
    I cannot imagine any grief
    That you and I have not gone through. And now—   5
    Have they told you of the new decree of our King Creon?
Ismenê: I have heard nothing: I know
    That two sisters lost two brothers, a double death
    In a single hour; and I know that the Argive army
    Fled in the night; but beyond this, nothing.   10
Antigonê: I thought so. And that is why I wanted you
    To come out here with me. There is something we must do.
Ismenê: Why do you speak so strangely?
Antigonê: Listen, Ismenê:
    Creon buried our brother Eteoclês
    With military honors, gave him a soldier's funeral,   15
    And it was right that he should; but Polyneicês,
    Who fought as bravely and died as miserably,—
    They say that Creon has sworn
    No one shall bury him, no one mourn for him,
    But his body must lie in the fields, a sweet treasure   20
    For carrion birds to find as they search for food.
    That is what they say, and our good Creon is coming here
    To announce it publicly; and the penalty—
    Stoning to death in the public square!
                    There it is,   25

Prologue: portion of the play containing the exposition, or explanation of what has gone before and what is now happening. *3 the curse on Oedipus:* As Sophocles tells in *Oedipus the King*, the King of Thebes discovered that he had lived his life under a curse. Unknowingly, he had slain his father and married his mother. On realizing this terrible truth, Oedipus put out his own eyes and departed into exile. Now, years later, as *Antigonê* opens, Antigonê and Ismenê, daughters of Oedipus, are recalling how their two brothers died. After the abdication of their father, the brothers had ruled Thebes together. But they fell to quarreling. When Eteoclês expelled Polyneicês, the latter returned with an army and attacked the city. The two brothers killed each other in combat, leaving the throne to Creon. The new king of Thebes has buried Eteoclês with full honors, but, calling Polyneicês a traitor, has decreed that his body shall be left to the crows—an especially terrible decree, for a rotting corpse might offend Zeus; bring down plague, blight, and barrenness upon Thebes; and prevent the soul of a dead hero from entering the Elysian Fields, abode of those favored by the gods.

And now you can prove what you are:
A true sister, or a traitor to your family.
Ismenê: Antigonê, you are mad! What could I possibly do?
Antigonê: You must decide whether you will help me or not.
Ismenê: I do not understand you. Help you in what?   30
Antigonê: Ismenê, I am going to bury him. Will you come?
Ismenê: Bury him! You have just said the new law forbids it.
Antigonê: He is my brother. And he is your brother, too.
Ismenê: But think of the danger! Think what Creon will do!
Antigonê: Creon is not strong enough to stand in my way.   35
Ismenê: Ah sister!
    Oedipus died, everyone hating him
    For what his own search brought to light, his eyes
    Ripped out by his own hand; and Iocastê died,
    His mother and wife at once: she twisted the cords   40
    That strangled her life; and our two brothers died,
    Each killed by the other's sword. And we are left:
    But oh, Antigonê,
    Think how much more terrible than these
    Our own death would be if we should go against Creon   45
    And do what he has forbidden! We are only women,
    We cannot fight with men, Antigonê!
    The law is strong, we must give in to the law
    In this thing, and in worse. I beg the Dead
    To forgive me, but I am helpless: I must yield   50
    To those in authority. And I think it is dangerous business
    To be always meddling.
Antigonê: If that is what you think,
    I should not want you, even if you asked to come.
    You have made your choice, you can be what you want to be.
    But I will bury him; and if I must die,   55
    I say that this crime is holy: I shall lie down
    With him in death, and I shall be as dear
    To him as he to me.
                    It is the dead,
    Not the living, who make the longest demands:
    We die for ever . . .
                    You may do as you like,   60
    Since apparently the laws of the gods mean nothing to you.
Ismenê: They mean a great deal to me; but I have no strength
    To break laws that were made for the public good.
Antigonê: That must be your excuse, I suppose. But as for me,
    I will bury the brother I love.
Ismenê: Antigonê,   65
    I am so afraid for you!
Antigonê: You need not be:
    You have yourself to consider, after all.
Ismenê: But no one must hear of this, you must tell no one!
    I will keep it a secret, I promise!

Antigonê: O tell it! Tell everyone!
    Think how they'll hate you when it all comes out   70
    If they learn that you knew about it all the time!
Ismenê: So fiery! You should be cold with fear.
Antigonê: Perhaps. But I am doing only what I must.
Ismenê: But you can do it? I say that you cannot.
Antigonê: Very well: when my strength gives out, I shall do no more.   75
Ismenê: Impossible things should not be tried at all.
Antigonê: Go away, Ismenê:
    I shall be hating you soon, and the dead will too,
    For your words are hateful. Leave me my foolish plan:
    I am not afraid of the danger; if it means death,   80
    It will not be the worst of deaths—death without honor.
Ismenê: Go then, if you feel that you must.
    You are unwise,
    But a loyal friend indeed to those who love you.

Exit into the palace. Antigonê goes off, left. Enter the Chorus.

PARODOS°

Strophe° 1

Chorus: Now the long blade of the sun, lying
    Level east to west, touches with glory
    Thebes of the Seven Gates. Open, unlidded
    Eye of golden day! O marching light
    Across the eddy and rush of Dircê's stream,°   5
    Striking the white shields of the enemy
    Thrown headlong backward from the blaze of morning!
Choragos:° Polyneicês their commander
    Roused them with windy phrases,
    He the wild eagle screaming   10
    Insults above our land,
    His wings their shields of snow,
    His crest their marshalled helms.

Antistrophe° 1

Chorus: Against our seven gates in a yawning ring
    The famished spears came onward in the night;   15
    But before his jaws were sated with our blood,
    Or pinefire took the garland of our towers,
    He was thrown back; and as he turned, great Thebes—
    No tender victim for his noisy power—
    Rose like a dragon behind him, shouting war.   20
Choragos: For God hates utterly
    The bray of bragging tongues;

Párodos: a song sung by the chorus on first entering. Its *strophe* (according to scholarly theory) was sung while the chorus danced from stage right to stage left; its *antistrophe*, while it danced back again. Another *párodos* follows the prologue of *Oedipus the King*.   5 *Dircê's stream:* river near Thebes.   8 *Choragos:* leader of the Chorus and principal commentator on the play's action.

And when he beheld their smiling,
Their swagger of golden helms,
The frown of his thunder blasted   25
Their first man from our walls.

Strophe 2

Chorus: We heard his shout of triumph high in the air
Turn to a scream; far out in a flaming arc
He fell with his windy torch, and the earth struck him.
And others storming in fury no less than his   30
Found shock of death in the dusty joy of battle.

Choragos: Seven captains at seven gates
Yielded their clanging arms to the god
That bends the battle-line and breaks it.
These two only, brothers in blood,   35
Face to face in matchless rage,
Mirroring each the other's death,
Clashed in long combat.

Antistrophe 2

Chorus: But now in the beautiful morning of victory
Let Thebes of the many chariots sing for joy!   40
With hearts for dancing we'll take leave of war:
Our temples shall be sweet with hymns of praise,
And the long night shall echo with our chorus.

SCENE I

Choragos: But now at last our new King is coming:
Creon of Thebes, Menoikeus' son.
In this auspicious dawn of his reign
What are the new complexities
That shifting Fate has woven for him?   5
What is his counsel? Why has he summoned
The old men to hear him?

Enter Creon from the palace, center. He addresses the Chorus from the top step.

Creon: Gentlemen: I have the honor to inform you that our Ship of State, which recent storms have threatened to destroy, has come safely to harbor at last, guided
by the merciful wisdom of Heaven. I have summoned you here this morning   10
because I know that I can depend upon you: your devotion to King Laïos was absolute; you never hesitated in your duty to our late ruler Oedipus; and when
Oedipus died, your loyalty was transferred to his children. Unfortunately, as you
know, his two sons, the princes Eteoclês and Polyneicês, have killed each other
in battle; and I, as the next in blood, have succeeded to the full power of the   15
throne.

I am aware, of course, that no Ruler can expect complete loyalty from his
subjects until he has been tested in office. Nevertheless, I say to you at the very
outset that I have nothing but contempt for the kind of Governor who is afraid,
for whatever reason, to follow the course that he knows is best for the State; and   20
as for the man who sets private friendship above the public welfare,—I have no

use for him, either. I call God to witness that if I saw my country headed for ruin,
I should not be afraid to speak out plainly; and I need hardly remind you that I
would never have any dealings with an enemy of the people. No one values
friendship more highly than I; but we must remember that friends made at the   25
risk of wrecking our Ship are not real friends at all.

These are my principles, at any rate, and that is why I have made the following decision concerning the sons of Oedipus: Eteoclês, who died as a man
should die, fighting for his country, is to be buried with full military honors,
with all the ceremony that is usual when the greatest heroes die; but his brother   30
Polyneicês, who broke his exile to come back with fire and sword against his native city and the shrines of his fathers' gods, whose one idea was to spill the
blood of his blood and sell his own people into slavery—Polyneicês, I say, is to
have no burial: no man is to touch him or say the least prayer for him; he shall
lie on the plain, unburied; and the birds and the scavenging dogs can do with   35
him whatever they like.

This is my command, and you can see the wisdom behind it. As long as I am
King, no traitor is going to be honored with the loyal man. But whoever shows
by word and deed that he is on the side of the State,—he shall have my respect
while he is living, and my reverence when he is dead.   40

Choragos: If that is your will, Creon son of Menoikeus,
You have the right to enforce it: we are yours.

Creon: That is my will. Take care that you do your part.

Choragos: We are old men: let the younger ones carry it out.

Creon: I do not mean that: the sentries have been appointed.   45

Choragos: Then what is it that you would have us do?

Creon: You will give no support to whoever breaks this law.

Choragos: Only a crazy man is in love with death!

Creon: And death it is, yet money talks, and the wisest
Have sometimes been known to count a few coins too many.   50

Enter Sentry from left.

Sentry: I'll not say that I'm out of breath from running, King, because every time I
stopped to think about what I have to tell you, I felt like going back. And all the
time a voice kept saying, "You fool, don't you know you're walking straight into
trouble?"; and then another voice: "Yes, but if you let somebody else get the
news to Creon first, it will be even worse than that for you!" But good sense won   55
out, at least I hope it was good sense, and here I am with a story that makes no
sense at all; but I'll tell it anyhow, because, as they say, what's going to happen's
going to happen and—

Creon: Come to the point. What have you to say?

Sentry: I did not do it. I did not see who did it. You must not punish me for what   60
someone else has done.

Creon: A comprehensive defense! More effective, perhaps,
If I knew its purpose. Come: what is it?

Sentry: A dreadful thing . . . I don't know how to put it—

Creon: Out with it!

Sentry: Well, then;   65

The dead man—
      Polyneicês—

Pause. The Sentry is overcome, fumbles for words. Creon waits impassively.

                out there—
                      someone,—
New dust on the slimy flesh!

Pause. No sign from Creon.

Someone has given it burial that way, and
Gone . . .

Long pause. Creon finally speaks with deadly control.

Creon: And the man who dared do this?
Sentry: I swear I   70
Do not know! You must believe me!
                      Listen:
The ground was dry, not a sign of digging, no,
Not a wheeltrack in the dust, no trace of anyone.
It was when they relieved us this morning: and one of them,
The corporal, pointed to it.
                    There it was,   75
The strangest—
         Look:
The body, just mounded over with light dust: you see?
Not buried really, but as if they'd covered it
Just enough for the ghost's peace. And no sign
Of dogs or any wild animal that had been there.   80

And then what a scene there was! Every man of us
Accusing the other: we all proved the other man did it,
We all had proof that we could not have done it.
We were ready to take hot iron in our hands,
Walk through fire, swear by all the gods,   85
It was not I!
I do not know who it was, but it was not I!

Creon's rage has been mounting steadily, but the Sentry is too intent upon his story to notice it.

And then, when this came to nothing, someone said
A thing that silenced us and made us stare
Down at the ground: you had to be told the news,   90
And one of us had to do it! We threw the dice,
And the bad luck fell to me. So here I am,
No happier to be here than you are to have me:
Nobody likes the man who brings bad news.
Choragos: I have been wondering, King: can it be that the gods have done this?   95
Creon (*furiously*): Stop!

Must you doddering wrecks
Go out of your heads entirely? "The gods"!
Intolerable!
The gods favor this corpse? Why? How had he served them?   100
Tried to loot their temples, burn their images,
Yes, and the whole State, and its laws with it!
Is it your senile opinion that the gods love to honor bad men?
A pious thought!—
                No, from the very beginning
There have been those who have whispered together,   105
Stiff-necked anarchists, putting their heads together,
Scheming against me in alleys. These are the men,
And they have bribed my own guard to do this thing.

(*Sententiously.*) Money!
There's nothing in the world so demoralizing as money.   110
Down go your cities,
Homes gone, men gone, honest hearts corrupted,
Crookedness of all kinds, and all for money!
(*To Sentry.*)   But you—!
I swear by God and by the throne of God,
The man who has done this thing shall pay for it!   115
Find that man, bring him here to me, or your death
Will be the least of your problems: I'll string you up
Alive, and there will be certain ways to make you
Discover your employer before you die;
And the process may teach you a lesson you seem to have missed: 120
The dearest profit is sometimes all too dear:
That depends on the source. Do you understand me?
A fortune won is often misfortune.

Sentry: King, may I speak?
Creon: Your very voice distresses me.
Sentry: Are you sure that it is my voice, and not your conscience?   125
Creon: By God, he wants to analyze me now!
Sentry: It is not what I say, but what has been done, that hurts you.
Creon: You talk too much.
Sentry: Maybe; but I've done nothing.
Creon: Sold your soul for some silver: that's all you've done.
Sentry: How dreadful it is when the right judge judges wrong!   130
Creon: Your figures of speech
May entertain you now; but unless you bring me the man,
You will get little profit from them in the end.

Exit Creon into the palace.

Sentry: "Bring me the man"—!
I'd like nothing better than bringing him the man!   135
But bring him or not, you have seen the last of me here.
At any rate, I am safe!

Exit Sentry.

ODE I°

Strophe 1

Chorus: Numberless are the world's wonders, but none
More wonderful than man; the stormgray sea
Yields to his prows, the huge crests bear him high;
Earth, holy and inexhaustible, is graven
With shining furrows where his plows have gone   5
Year after year, the timeless labor of stallions.

Antistrophe 1

The lightboned birds and beasts that cling to cover,
The lithe fish lighting their reaches of dim water,
All are taken, tamed in the net of his mind;
The lion on the hill, the wild horse windy-maned,   10
Resign to him; and his blunt yoke has broken
The sultry shoulders of the mountain bull.

Strophe 2

Words also, and thought as rapid as air,
He fashions to his good use; statecraft is his,
And his the skill that deflects the arrows of snow,   15
The spears of winter rain: from every wind
He has made himself secure—from all but one:
In the late wind of death he cannot stand.

Antistrophe 2

O clear intelligence, force beyond all measure!
O fate of man, working both good and evil!   20
When the laws are kept, how proudly his city stands!
When the laws are broken, what of his city then?
Never may the anárchic man find rest at my hearth,
Never be it said that my thoughts are his thoughts.

SCENE II

Re-enter Sentry leading Antigonê.

Choragos: What does this mean? Surely this captive woman
Is the Princess, Antigonê. Why should she be taken?
Sentry: Here is the one who did it! We caught her
In the very act of burying him.—Where is Creon?
Choragos: Just coming from the house.

Enter Creon, center.

Creon: What has happened?   5
Why have you come back so soon?
Sentry (*expansively*):   O King,

Ode I: first song sung by the Chorus, who at the same time danced. Here again, as in the
párodos, *strophe* and *antistrophe* probably divide the song into two movements of the dance:
right to left, then left to right.

A man should never be too sure of anything:
I would have sworn
That you'd not see me here again: your anger
Frightened me so, and the things you threatened me with;   10
But how could I tell then
That I'd be able to solve the case so soon?

No dice-throwing this time: I was only too glad to come!

Here is this woman. She is the guilty one:
We found her trying to bury him.   15
Take her, then; question her; judge her as you will.
I am through with the whole thing now, and glad of it.
Creon: But this is Antigonê! Why have you brought her here?
Sentry: She was burying him, I tell you!
Creon (severely):   Is this the truth?
Sentry: I saw her with my own eyes. Can I say more?   20
Creon: The details: come, tell me quickly!
Sentry: It was like this:
After those terrible threats of yours, King,
We went back and brushed the dust away from the body.
The flesh was soft by now, and stinking,
So we sat on a hill to windward and kept guard.   25
No napping this time! We kept each other awake.
But nothing happened until the white round sun
Whirled in the center of the round sky over us:
Then, suddenly,
A storm of dust roared up from the earth, and the sky   30
Went out, the plain vanished with all its trees
In the stinging dark. We closed our eyes and endured it.
The whirlwind lasted a long time, but it passed;
And then we looked, and there was Antigonê!

I have seen   35
A mother bird come back to a stripped nest, heard
Her crying bitterly a broken note or two
For the young ones stolen. Just so, when this girl
Found the bare corpse, and all her love's work wasted,
She wept, and cried on heaven to damn the hands   40
That had done this thing.
                             And then she brought more dust
And sprinkled wine three times for her brother's ghost.

We ran and took her at once. She was not afraid,
Not even when we charged her with what she had done.
She denied nothing.
                       And this was a comfort to me,   45
And some uneasiness: for it is a good thing
To escape from death, but it is no great pleasure
To bring death to a friend.
                             Yet I always say
There is nothing so comfortable as your own safe skin!

Creon (*slowly, dangerously*): And you, Antigonê,   50
  You with your head hanging,—do you confess this thing?
Antigonê: I do. I deny nothing.
Creon (*to Sentry*):   You may go.

  Exit Sentry.

  (*To Antigonê.*) Tell me, tell me briefly:
  Had you heard my proclamation touching this matter?
Antigonê: It was public. Could I help hearing it?   55
Creon: And yet you dared defy the law.
Antigonê: I dared.
    It was not God's proclamation. That final Justice
    That rules the world below makes no such laws.

    Your edict, King, was strong,
    But all your strength is weakness itself against   60
    The immortal unrecorded laws of God.
    They are not merely now: they were, and shall be,
    Operative for ever, beyond man utterly.

    I knew I must die, even without your decree:
    I am only mortal. And if I must die   65
    Now, before it is my time to die,
    Surely this is no hardship: can anyone
    Living, as I live, with evil all about me,
    Think Death less than a friend? This death of mine
    Is of no importance; but if I had left my brother   70
    Lying in death unburied, I should have suffered.
    Now I do not.
              You smile at me. Ah Creon,
    Think me a fool, if you like; but it may well be
    That a fool convicts me of folly.
Choragos: Like father, like daughter: both headstrong, deaf to reason!   75
  She has never learned to yield.
Creon: She has much to learn.
    The inflexible heart breaks first, the toughest iron
    Cracks first, and the wildest horses bend their necks
    At the pull of the smallest curb.
                          Pride? In a slave?
    This girl is guilty of a double insolence,   80
    Breaking the given laws and boasting of it.
    Who is the man here,
    She or I, if this crime goes unpunished?
    Sister's child, or more than sister's child,
    Or closer yet in blood—she and her sister   85
    Win bitter death for this!
  (*To Servants.*)   Go, some of you,
    Arrest Ismenê. I accuse her equally.
    Bring her: you will find her sniffling in the house there.

    Her mind's a traitor: crimes kept in the dark

Cry for light, and the guardian brain shudders;   90
But how much worse than this
Is brazen boasting of barefaced anarchy!

Antigonê: Creon, what more do you want than my death?

Creon: Nothing.
That gives me everything.

Antigonê: Then I beg you: kill me.
This talking is a great weariness: your words   95
Are distasteful to me, and I am sure that mine
Seem so to you. And yet they should not seem so:
I should have praise and honor for what I have done.
All these men here would praise me
Were their lips not frozen shut with fear of you.   100
(*Bitterly.*) Ah the good fortune of kings,
Licensed to say and do whatever they please!

Creon: You are alone here in that opinion.

Antigonê: No, they are with me. But they keep their tongues in leash.

Creon: Maybe. But you are guilty, and they are not.   105

Antigonê: There is no guilt in reverence for the dead.

Creon: But Eteoclês—was he not your brother too?

Antigonê: My brother too.

Creon: And you insult his memory?

Antigonê (*softly*): The dead man would not say that I insult it.

Creon: He would: for you honor a traitor as much as him.   110

Antigonê: His own brother, traitor or not, and equal in blood.

Creon: He made war on his country. Eteoclês defended it.

Antigonê: Nevertheless, there are honors due all the dead.

Creon: But not the same for the wicked as for the just.

Antigonê: Ah Creon, Creon,   115
Which of us can say what the gods hold wicked?

Creon: An enemy is an enemy, even dead.

Antigonê: It is my nature to join in love, not hate.

Creon (*finally losing patience*): Go join them, then; if you must have your love,
Find it in hell!   120

Choragos: But see, Ismenê comes:

Enter Ismenê, guarded.

Those tears are sisterly, the cloud
That shadows her eyes rains down gentle sorrow.

Creon: You too, Ismenê,
Snake in my ordered house, sucking my blood   125
Stealthily—and all the time I never knew
That these two sisters were aiming at my throne!
                                                        Ismenê,
Do you confess your share in this crime, or deny it?
Answer me.

Ismenê: Yes, if she will let me say so. I am guilty.   130

Antigonê (*coldly*): No, Ismenê. You have no right to say so.
You would not help me, and I will not have you help me.

Ismenê: But now I know what you meant; and I am here
    To join you, to take my share of punishment.
Antigonê: The dead man and the gods who rule the dead   135
    Know whose act this was. Words are not friends.
Ismenê: Do you refuse me, Antigonê? I want to die with you:
    I too have a duty that I must discharge to the dead.
Antigonê: You shall not lessen my death by sharing it.
Ismenê: What do I care for life when you are dead?   140
Antigonê: Ask Creon. You're always hanging on his opinions.
Ismenê: You are laughing at me. Why, Antigonê?
Antigonê: It's a joyless laughter, Ismenê.
Ismenê: But can I do nothing?
Antigonê: Yes. Save yourself. I shall not envy you.
    There are those who will praise you; I shall have honor, too.   145
Ismenê: But we are equally guilty!
Antigonê: No more, Ismenê.
    You are alive, but I belong to Death.
Creon (to the Chorus): Gentlemen, I beg you to observe these girls:
    One has just now lost her mind; the other,
    It seems, has never had a mind at all.   150
Ismenê: Grief teaches the steadiest minds to waver, King.
Creon: Yours certainly did, when you assumed guilt with the guilty!
Ismenê: But how could I go on living without her?
Creon: You are.
    She is already dead.
Ismenê: But your own son's bride!
Creon: There are places enough for him to push his plow.   155
    I want no wicked women for my sons!
Ismenê: O dearest Haimon, how your father wrongs you!
Creon: I've had enough of your childish talk of marriage!
Choragos: Do you really intend to steal this girl from your son?
Creon: No; Death will do that for me.
Choragos: Then she must die?   160
Creon (ironically): You dazzle me.
                —But enough of this talk!
    (*To Guards.*) You, there, take them away and guard them well:
    For they are but women, and even brave men run
    When they see Death coming.

    Exeunt Ismenê, Antigonê, and Guards.

ODE II

Strophe 1

Chorus: Fortunate is the man who has never tasted God's vengeance!
    Where once the anger of heaven has struck, that house is shaken
    For ever: damnation rises behind each child
    Like a wave cresting out of the black northeast,
    When the long darkness under sea roars up   5
    And bursts drumming death upon the windwhipped sand.

Antistrophe 1

I have seen this gathering sorrow from time long past
Loom upon Oedipus' children: generation from generation
Takes the compulsive rage of the enemy god.
So lately this last flower of Oedipus' line   10
Drank the sunlight! but now a passionate word
And a handful of dust have closed up all its beauty.

Strophe 2

    What mortal arrogance
    Transcends the wrath of Zeus?
Sleep cannot lull him nor the effortless long months   15
Of the timeless gods: but he is young for ever,
And his house is the shining day of high Olympos.
      All that is and shall be,
      And all the past, is his.
No pride on earth is free of the curse of heaven.   20

Antistrophe 2

    The straying dreams of men
    May bring them ghosts of joy:
But as they drowse, the waking embers burn them;
Or they walk with fixed eyes, as blind men walk.
But the ancient wisdom speaks for our own time: 25
    Fate works most for woe
    With Folly's fairest show.
Man's little pleasure is the spring of sorrow.

SCENE III

Choragos: But here is Haimon, King, the last of all your sons.
    Is it grief for Antigonê that brings him here,
    And bitterness at being robbed of his bride?

Enter Haimon.

Creon: We shall soon see, and no need of diviners.
—Son,
    You have heard my final judgment on that girl: 5
    Have you come here hating me, or have you come
    With deference and with love, whatever I do?
Haimon: I am your son, father. You are my guide.
    You make things clear for me, and I obey you.
    No marriage means more to me than your continuing wisdom.   10
Creon: Good. That is the way to behave: subordinate
    Everything else, my son, to your father's will.
    This is what a man prays for, that he may get
    Sons attentive and dutiful in his house,
    Each one hating his father's enemies,   15
    Honoring his father's friends. But if his sons
    Fail him, if they turn out unprofitably,
    What has he fathered but trouble for himself

And amusement for the malicious?

                           So you are right

Not to lose your head over this woman.   20

Your pleasure with her would soon grow cold, Haimon,

And then you'd have a hellcat in bed and elsewhere.

Let her find her husband in Hell!

Of all the people in this city, only she

Has had contempt for my law and broken it.   25

Do you want me to show myself weak before the people?

Or to break my sworn word? No, and I will not.

The woman dies.

I suppose she'll plead "family ties." Well, let her.

If I permit my own family to rebel,   30

How shall I earn the world's obedience?

Show me the man who keeps his house in hand,

He's fit for public authority.

                       I'll have no dealings

With law-breakers, critics of the government:

Whoever is chosen to govern should be obeyed—   35

Must be obeyed, in all things, great and small,

Just and unjust! O Haimon,

The man who knows how to obey, and that man only,

Knows how to give commands when the time comes.

You can depend on him, no matter how fast   40

The spears come: he's a good soldier, he'll stick it out.

Anarchy, anarchy! Show me a greater evil!

This is why cities tumble and the great houses rain down,

This is what scatters armies!

No, no: good lives are made so by discipline.   45

We keep the laws then, and the lawmakers,

And no woman shall seduce us. If we must lose,

Let's lose to a man, at least! Is a woman stronger than we?

Choragos: Unless time has rusted my wits,

    What you say, King, is said with point and dignity.   50

Haimon (*boyishly earnest*): Father:

    Reason is God's crowning gift to man, and you are right

    To warn me against losing mine. I cannot say—

    I hope that I shall never want to say!—that you

    Have reasoned badly. Yet there are other men   55

    Who can reason, too; and their opinions might be helpful.

    You are not in a position to know everything

    That people say or do, or what they feel:

    Your temper terrifies them—everyone

    Will tell you only what you like to hear.   60

    But I, at any rate, can listen; and I have heard them

    Muttering and whispering in the dark about this girl.

    They say no woman has ever, so unreasonably,

Died so shameful a death for a generous act:
"She covered her brother's body. Is this indecent?   65
She kept him from dogs and vultures. Is this a crime?
Death?—She should have all the honor that we can give her!"

This is the way they talk out there in the city.

You must believe me:
Nothing is closer to me than your happiness.   70
What could be closer? Must not any son
Value his father's fortune as his father does his?
I beg you, do not be unchangeable:
Do not believe that you alone can be right.
The man who thinks that,   75
The man who maintains that only he has the power
To reason correctly, the gift to speak, the soul—
A man like that, when you know him, turns out empty.

It is not reason never to yield to reason!

In flood time you can see how some trees bend,   80
And because they bend, even their twigs are safe,
While stubborn trees are torn up, roots and all.
And the same thing happens in sailing:
Make your sheet fast, never slacken,—and over you go,
Head over heels and under: and there's your voyage.   85
Forget you are angry! Let yourself be moved!
I know I am young; but please let me say this:
The ideal condition
Would be, I admit, that men should be right by instinct;
But since we are all too likely to go astray,   90
The reasonable thing is to learn from those who can teach.
Choragos: You will do well to listen to him, King,
    If what he says is sensible. And you, Haimon,
    Must listen to your father.—Both speak well.
Creon: You consider it right for a man of my years and experience   95
    To go to school to a boy?
Haimon: It is not right,
    If I am wrong. But if I am young, and right,
    What does my age matter?
Creon: You think it right to stand up for an anarchist?
Haimon: Not at all. I pay no respect to criminals.   100
Creon: Then she is not a criminal?
Haimon: The City would deny it, to a man.
Creon: And the City proposes to teach me how to rule?
Haimon: Ah. Who is it that's talking like a boy now?
Creon: My voice is the one voice giving orders in this City!   105
Haimon: It is no City if it takes orders from one voice.
Creon: The State is the King!
Haimon: Yes, if the State is a desert.

    Pause.

Creon: This boy, it seems, has sold out to a woman.

Haimon: If you are a woman: my concern is only for you.

Creon: So? Your "concern"! In a public brawl with your father! 110

Haimon: How about you, in a public brawl with justice?

Creon: With justice, when all that I do is within my rights?

Haimon: You have no right to trample on God's right.

Creon (completely out of control): Fool, adolescent fool! Taken in by a woman!

Haimon: You'll never see me taken in by anything vile. 115

Creon: Every word you say is for her!

Haimon (quietly, darkly):   And for you.
    And for me. And for the gods under the earth.

Creon: You'll never marry her while she lives.

Haimon: Then she must die.—But her death will cause another.

Creon: Another? 120
    Have you lost your senses? Is this an open threat?

Haimon: There is no threat in speaking to emptiness.

Creon: I swear you'll regret this superior tone of yours!
    You are the empty one!

Haimon: If you were not my father,
    I'd say you were perverse. 125

Creon: You girl-struck fool, don't play at words with me!

Haimon: I am sorry. You prefer silence.

Creon: Now, by God—!
    I swear, by all the gods in heaven above us,
    You'll watch it, I swear you shall!
    (*To the Servants.*)   Bring her out!
    Bring the woman out! Let her die before his eyes! 130
    Here, this instant, with her bridegroom beside her!

Haimon: Not here, no; she will not die here, King.
    And you will never see my face again.
    Go on raving as long as you've a friend to endure you.

    Exit Haimon.

Choragos: Gone, gone. 135
    Creon, a young man in a rage is dangerous!

Creon: Let him do, or dream to do, more than a man can.
    He shall not save these girls from death.

Choragos: These girls?
    You have sentenced them both?

Creon: No, you are right.
    I will not kill the one whose hands are clean. 140

Choragos: But Antigonê?

Creon (somberly):   I will carry her far away
    Out there in the wilderness, and lock her
    Living in a vault of stone. She shall have food,
    As the custom is, to absolve the State of her death.
    And there let her pray to the gods of hell: 145
    They are her only gods:
    Perhaps they will show her an escape from death,

Or she may learn,

                though late,
That piety shown the dead is pity in vain.

Exit Creon.

ODE III

Strophe

Chorus: Love, unconquerable
        Waster of rich men, keeper
        Of warm lights and all-night vigil
        In the soft face of a girl:
        Sea-wanderer, forest-visitor!   5
        Even the pure Immortals cannot escape you,
        And mortal man, in his one day's dusk,
        Trembles before your glory.

Antistrophe

        Surely you swerve upon ruin
        The just man's consenting heart,   10
        As here you have made bright anger
        Strike between father and son—
        And none has conquered but Love!
        A girl's glánce wórking the will of heaven:
        Pleasure to her alone who mocks us,   15
        Merciless Aphroditê.°

SCENE IV

Choragos (*as Antigonê enters guarded*):
        But I can no longer stand in awe of this,
        Nor, seeing what I see, keep back my tears.
        Here is Antigonê, passing to that chamber
        Where all find sleep at last.

Strophe 1

Antigonê: Look upon me, friends, and pity me   5
        Turning back at the night's edge to say
        Good-by to the sun that shines for me no longer;
        Now sleepy Death
        Summons me down to Acheron,° that cold shore:
        There is no bridesong there, nor any music.   10
Chorus: Yet not unpraised, not without a kind of honor,
        You walk at last into the underworld;
        Untouched by sickness, broken by no sword.
        What woman has ever found your way to death?

Antistrophe 1

16 *Aphroditê:* goddess of love and beauty.   9 *Acheron:* river in Hades, domain of the dead.

Antigonê: How often I have heard the story of Niobê,° 15
    Tantalos' wretched daughter, how the stone
    Clung fast about her, ivy-close: and they say
    The rain falls endlessly
    And sifting soft snow; her tears are never done.
    I feel the loneliness of her death in mine. 20
Chorus: But she was born of heaven, and you
    Are woman, woman-born. If her death is yours,
    A mortal woman's, is this not for you
    Glory in our world and in the world beyond?

Strophe 2

Antigonê: You laugh at me. Ah, friends, friends, 25
    Can you not wait until I am dead? O Thebes,
    O men many-charioted, in love with Fortune,
    Dear springs of Dircê, sacred Theban grove,
    Be witnesses for me, denied all pity,
    Unjustly judged! and think a word of love 30
    For her whose path turns
    Under dark earth, where there are no more tears.
Chorus: You have passed beyond human daring and come at last
    Into a place of stone where Justice sits.
    I cannot tell 35
    What shape of your father's guilt appears in this.

Antistrophe 2

Antigonê: You have touched it at last: that bridal bed
    Unspeakable, horror of son and mother mingling:
    Their crime, infection of all our family!
    O Oedipus, father and brother! 40
    Your marriage strikes from the grave to murder mine.
    I have been a stranger here in my own land:
    All my life
    The blasphemy of my birth has followed me.
Chorus: Reverence is a virtue, but strength 45
    Lives in established law: that must prevail.
    You have made your choice,
    Your death is the doing of your conscious hand.

Epode°

Antigonê: Then let me go, since all your words are bitter,
    And the very light of the sun is cold to me. 50
    Lead me to my vigil, where I must have
    Neither love nor lamentation; no song, but silence.

    Creon interrupts impatiently.

---

15 *story of Niobê:* a Theban queen whose fourteen children were slain. She wept so copiously she was
transformed to a stone on Mount Sipylos, and her tears became the mountain's streams.   48 *Epode:*
the final section (after the *strophe* and *antistrophe*) of a lyric passage; whereas the earlier sections are
symmetrical, it takes a different metrical form.

Creon: If dirges and planned lamentations could put off death,
   Men would be singing for ever.
   (*To the Servants.*)   Take her, go!
   You know your orders: take her to the vault   55
   And leave her alone there. And if she lives or dies,
   That's her affair, not ours: our hands are clean.
Antigonê: O tomb, vaulted bride-bed in eternal rock,
   Soon I shall be with my own again
   Where Persephonê° welcomes the thin ghosts underground: 60
   And I shall see my father again, and you, mother,
   And dearest Polyneicês—
                          dearest indeed
   To me, since it was my hand
   That washed him clean and poured the ritual wine:
   And my reward is death before my time!   65

   And yet, as men's hearts know, I have done no wrong,
   I have not sinned before God. Or if I have,
   I shall know the truth in death. But if the guilt
   Lies upon Creon who judged me, then, I pray,
   May his punishment equal my own.
Choragos: O passionate heart,   70
   Unyielding, tormented still by the same winds!
Creon: Her guards shall have good cause to regret their delaying.
Antigonê: Ah! That voice is like the voice of death!
Creon: I can give you no reason to think you are mistaken.
Antigonê: Thebes, and you my fathers' gods,   75
   And rulers of Thebes, you see me now, the last
   Unhappy daughter of a line of kings,
   Your kings, led away to death. You will remember
   What things I suffer, and at what men's hands,
   Because I would not transgress the laws of heaven.   80
   (*To the Guards, simply.*) Come: let us wait no longer.

   Exit Antigonê, left, guarded.

ODE IV

Strophe 1

Chorus: All Danaê's beauty was locked away
   In a brazen cell where the sunlight could not come:
   A small room still as any grave, enclosed her.°
   Yet she was a princess too,
   And Zeus in a rain of gold poured love upon her.°   5

---

60 *Persephonê:* daughter of Zeus and Demeter whom Pluto, god of the underworld, abducted to be his queen. 1–5 *All Danaê's beauty . . . poured love upon her:* In legend, when an oracle told Acrisius, king of Argos, that his daughter Danaê would bear a son who would grow up to slay him, he locked the princess into a chamber made of bronze, lest any man impregnate her. But Zeus, father of the gods, entered Danaê's prison in a shower of gold. The resultant child, the hero Perseus, was accidentally to fulfill the prophecy by killing Acrisius with an ill-aimed discus throw.

O child, child,
No power in wealth or war
Or tough sea-blackened ships
Can prevail against untiring Destiny!

Antistrophe 1

And Dryas' son° also, that furious king,   10
Bore the god's prisoning anger for his pride:
Sealed up by Dionysos in deaf stone,
His madness died among echoes.
So at the last he learned what dreadful power
His tongue had mocked: 15
For he had profaned the revels,
And fired the wrath of the nine
Implacable Sisters° that love the sound of the flute.

Strophe 2

And old men tell a half-remembered tale
Of horror° where a dark ledge splits the sea   20
And a double surf beats on the gráy shóres:
How a king's new woman, sick
With hatred for the queen he had imprisoned,
Ripped out his two sons' eyes with her bloody hands
While grinning Arês° watched the shuttle plunge   25
Four times: four blind wounds crying for revenge,

Antistrophe 2

Crying, tears and blood mingled.—Piteously born,
Those sons whose mother was of heavenly birth!
Her father was the god of the North Wind
And she was cradled by gales,   30
She raced with young colts on the glittering hills
And walked untrammeled in the open light:
But in her marriage deathless Fate found means
To build a tomb like yours for all her joy.

SCENE V

Enter blind Teiresias, led by a boy. The opening speeches of Teiresias should be in singsong contrast to the realistic lines of Creon.

Teiresias: This is the way the blind man comes, Princes, Princes,
     Lockstep, two heads lit by the eyes of one.
Creon: What new thing have you to tell us, old Teiresias?
Teiresias: I have much to tell you: listen to the prophet, Creon.

10 *Dryas' son:* King Lycurgus of Thrace, whom Dionysos, god of wine, caused to be stricken with madness.   18 *Sisters:* the Muses, nine sister goddesses who presided over poetry and music, arts and sciences.   19–20 *a half-remembered tale of horror:* As the Chorus recalls in the rest of this song, the point of this tale is that being nobly born will not save one from disaster. King Phineas cast off his first wife, Cleopatra (not the later Egyptian queen, but the daughter of Boreas, god of the north wind) and imprisoned her in a cave. Out of hatred for Cleopatra, the cruel Eidothea, second wife of the king, blinded her stepsons.   25 *Arês:* god of war, said to gloat over bloodshed.

Creon: I am not aware that I have ever failed to listen.   5
Teiresias: Then you have done wisely, King, and ruled well.
Creon: I admit my debt to you. But what have you to say?
Teiresias: This, Creon: you stand once more on the edge of fate.
Creon: What do you mean? Your words are a kind of dread.
Teiresias: Listen Creon: 10
    I was sitting in my chair of augury, at the place
    Where the birds gather about me. They were all a-chatter,
    As is their habit, when suddenly I heard
    A strange note in their jangling, a scream, a
    Whirring fury; I knew that they were fighting,   15
    Tearing each other, dying
    In a whirlwind of wings clashing. And I was afraid.
    I began the rites of burnt-offering at the altar,
    But Hephaistos° failed me: instead of bright flame,
    There was only the sputtering slime of the fat thigh-flesh   20
    Melting: the entrails dissolved in gray smoke,
    The bare bone burst from the welter. And no blaze!

    This was a sign from heaven. My boy described it,
    Seeing for me as I see for others.

    I tell you, Creon, you yourself have brought   25
    This new calamity upon us. Our hearths and altars
    Are stained with the corruption of dogs and carrion birds
    That glut themselves on the corpse of Oedipus' son.
    The gods are deaf when we pray to them, their fire
    Recoils from our offering, their birds of omen   30
    Have no cry of comfort, for they are gorged
    With the thick blood of the dead.
                    O my son,
    These are no trifles! Think: all men make mistakes,
    But a good man yields when he knows his course is wrong,
    And repairs the evil. The only crime is pride.   35

    Give in to the dead man, then: do not fight with a corpse—
    What glory is it to kill a man who is dead?
    Think, I beg you:
    It is for your own good that I speak as I do.
    You should be able to yield for your own good.   40
Creon: It seems that prophets have made me their especial province.
    All my life long
    I have been a kind of butt for the dull arrows
    Of doddering fortune-tellers!
               No, Teiresias:
    If your birds—if the great eagles of God himself   45
    Should carry him stinking bit by bit to heaven,
    I would not yield. I am not afraid of pollution:

19 Hephaistos: god of fire.

No man can defile the gods.
                          Do what you will,
Go into business, make money, speculate
In India gold or that synthetic gold from Sardis,   50
Get rich otherwise than by my consent to bury him.
Teiresias, it is a sorry thing when a wise man
Sells his wisdom, lets out his words for hire!

Teiresias: Ah Creon! Is there no man left in the world—
Creon: To do what?—Come, let's have the aphorism!   55
Teiresias: No man who knows that wisdom outweighs any wealth?
Creon: As surely as bribes are baser than any baseness.
Teiresias: You are sick, Creon! You are deathly sick!
Creon: As you say: it is not my place to challenge a prophet.
Teiresias: Yet you have said my prophecy is for sale.   60
Creon: The generation of prophets has always loved gold.
Teiresias: The generation of kings has always loved brass.
Creon: You forget yourself! You are speaking to your King.
Teiresias: I know it. You are a king because of me.
Creon: You have a certain skill; but you have sold out.   65
Teiresias: King, you will drive me to words that—
Creon: Say them, say them!
     Only remember: I will not pay you for them.
Teiresias: No, you will find them too costly.
Creon: No doubt. Speak:
     Whatever you say, you will not change my will.
Teiresias: Then take this, and take it to heart!   70
The time is not far off when you shall pay back
Corpse for corpse, flesh of your own flesh.
You have thrust the child of this world into living night,
You have kept from the gods below the child that is theirs:
The one in a grave before her death, the other,   75
Dead, denied the grave. This is your crime:
And the Furies and the dark gods of Hell
Are swift with terrible punishment for you.

Do you want to buy me now, Creon?

                        Not many days,
And your house will be full of men and women weeping,   80
And curses will be hurled at you from far
Cities grieving for sons unburied, left to rot
Before the walls of Thebes.

These are my arrows, Creon: they are all for you.

(*To Boy.*) But come, child: lead me home.   85
Let him waste his fine anger upon younger men.
Maybe he will learn at last
To control a wiser tongue in a better head.

Exit Teiresias.

Choragos: The old man has gone, King, but his words
       Remain to plague us. I am old, too,   90
       But I cannot remember that he was ever false.
Creon: That is true. . . . It troubles me.
       Oh it is hard to give in! but it is worse
       To risk everything for stubborn pride.
Choragos: Creon: take my advice.
Creon: What shall I do?   95
Choragos: Go quickly: free Antigonê from her vault
       And build a tomb for the body of Polyneicês.
Creon: You would have me do this!
Choragos: Creon, yes!
       And it must be done at once: God moves
       Swiftly to cancel the folly of stubborn men.   100
Creon: It is hard to deny the heart! But I
       Will do it: I will not fight with destiny.
Choragos: You must go yourself, you cannot leave it to others.
Creon: I will go.
              —Bring axes, servants:
       Come with me to the tomb. I buried her, I   105
       Will set her free.
                    Oh quickly!
       My mind misgives—
       The laws of the gods are mighty, and a man must serve them
       To the last day of his life!

Exit Creon.

PAEAN°

                                                                    Strophe 1

Choragos: God of many names
Chorus: O Iacchos
                          son
       of Kadmeian Sémelê
                    O born of the Thunder!
       Guardian of the West
                    Regent
       of Eleusis' plain
                    O Prince of maenad Thebes
       and the Dragon Field by rippling Ismenós:°   5

Paean: a song of praise or prayer, here to Dionysos, god of wine.   *1–5 God of many names . . .
Dragon Field by rippling Ismenós:* Dionysos was also called Iacchos (or, by the Romans, Bacchus). He
was the son of Zeus ("the Thunderer") and of Sémelê, daughter of Kadmos (or Cadmus), legendary
founder of Thebes. "Regent of Eleusis' plain" is another name for Dionysos, honored in secret rites at
Eleusis, a town northwest of Athens. "Prince of maenad Thebes" is yet another: the Maenads were
women of Thebes said to worship Dionysos with wild orgiastic rites. Kadmos, so the story goes,
sowed dragon's teeth in a field beside the river Ismenós. Up sprang a crop of fierce warriors who
fought among themselves until only five remained. These victors became the first Thebans.

Antistrophe 1

Choragos: God of many names
Chorus: the flame of torches
      flares on our hills
                    the nymphs of Iacchos
      dance at the spring of Castalia:°

      from the vine-close mountain
                              come ah come in ivy:
      Evohé evohé!° sings through the streets of Thebes   10

Strophe 2

Choragos: God of many names
Chorus: Iacchos of Thebes
      heavenly Child
                    of Sémelê bride of the Thunderer!
      The shadow of plague is upon us:
                              come
      with clement feet
                    oh come from Parnasos
      down the long slopes
                              across the lamenting water   15

Antistrophe 2

Choragos: Iô° Fire! Chorister of the throbbing stars!
      O purest among the voices of the night!
      Thou son of God, blaze for us!
Chorus: Come with choric rapture of circling Maenads
      Who cry *Iô Iacche!*
                    God of many names!   20

EXODOS°

Enter Messenger from left.

Messenger: Men of the line of Kadmos, you who live
      Near Amphion's citadel:°
                    I cannot say
      Of any condition of human life "This is fixed,
      This is clearly good, or bad." Fate raises up,
      And Fate casts down the happy and unhappy alike: 5
      No man can foretell his Fate.
                    Take the case of Creon:

---

8 *Castalia:* a spring on Mount Parnassus, named for a maiden who drowned herself in it to avoid rape by the god Apollo. She became a nymph, or nature spirit, dwelling in its waters. In the temple of Delphi, at the mountain's foot, priestesses of Dionysos (the "nymphs of Iacchos") used the spring's waters in rites of purification.   10 *Evohé evohé!:* cry of the Maenads in supplicating Dionysos: "Come forth, come forth!"   16 *Iô:* "Hail" or "Praise be to . . ."   *Éxodos:* the final scene, containing the play's resolution.   2 *Amphion's citadel:* a name for Thebes. Amphion, son of Zeus, had built a wall around the city by playing so beautifully on his lyre that the charmed stones leaped into their slots.

Creon was happy once, as I count happiness:
Victorious in battle, sole governor of the land,
Fortunate father of children nobly born.
And now it has all gone from him! Who can say   10
That a man is still alive when his life's joy fails?
He is a walking dead man. Grant him rich,
Let him live like a king in his great house:
If his pleasure is gone, I would not give
So much as the shadow of smoke for all he owns.   15

Choragos: Your words hint at sorrow: what is your news for us?
Messenger: They are dead. The living are guilty of their death.
Choragos: Who is guilty? Who is dead? Speak!
Messenger: Haimon.
  Haimon is dead; and the hand that killed him
  Is his own hand.
Choragos: His father's? or his own?   20
Messenger: His own, driven mad by the murder his father had done.
Choragos: Teiresias, Teiresias, how clearly you saw it all!
Messenger: This is my news: you must draw what conclusions you can from it.
Choragos: But look: Eurydicê, our Queen:
  Has she overheard us?   25

  Enter Eurydicê from the palace, center.

Eurydicê: I have heard something, friends:
  As I was unlocking the gate of Pallas'° shrine,
  For I needed her help today, I heard a voice
  Telling of some new sorrow. And I fainted
  There at the temple with all my maidens about me.   30
  But speak again: whatever it is, I can bear it:
  Grief and I are no strangers.
Messenger: Dearest Lady.
  I will tell you plainly all that I have seen.
  I shall not try to comfort you: what is the use,
  Since comfort could lie only in what is not true?   35
  The truth is always best.
                        I went with Creon
  To the outer plain where Polyneicês was lying,
  No friend to pity him, his body shredded by dogs.
  We made our prayers in that place to Hecatê
  And Pluto,° that they would be merciful. And we bathed   40
  The corpse with holy water, and we brought
  Fresh-broken branches to burn what was left of it,
  And upon the urn we heaped up a towering barrow
  Of the earth of his own land.
                        When we were done, we ran

27 *Pallas:* Pallas Athene, goddess of wisdom, and hence an excellent source of advice. 39–40
Hecatê and Pluto: two fearful divinities—the goddess of witchcraft and sorcery and the king of
Hades, underworld of the dead.

To the vault where Antigonê lay on her couch of stone.   45
One of the servants had gone ahead,
And while he was yet far off he heard a voice
Grieving within the chamber, and he came back
And told Creon. And as the King went closer,
The air was full of wailing, the words lost,   50
And he begged us to make all haste. "Am I a prophet?"
He said, weeping, "And must I walk this road,
The saddest of all that I have gone before?
My son's voice calls me on. Oh quickly, quickly!
Look through the crevice there, and tell me   55
If it is Haimon, or some deception of the gods!"

We obeyed; and in the cavern's farthest corner
We saw her lying:
She had made a noose of her fine linen veil
And hanged herself. Haimon lay beside her,   60
His arms about her waist, lamenting her,
His love lost under ground, crying out
That his father had stolen her away from him.

When Creon saw him the tears rushed to his eyes
And he called to him: "What have you done, child? Speak to me.   65
What are you thinking that makes your eyes so strange?
O my son, my son, I come to you on my knees!"
But Haimon spat in his face. He said not a word,
Staring—
      And suddenly drew his sword
And lunged. Creon shrank back, the blade missed; and the boy,   70
Desperate against himself, drove it half its length
Into his own side, and fell. And as he died
He gathered Antigonê close in his arms again,
Choking, his blood bright red on her white cheek.
And now he lies dead with the dead, and she is his   75
At last, his bride in the houses of the dead.

Exit Eurydicê into the palace.

Choragos: She has left us without a word. What can this mean?
Messenger: It troubles me, too; yet she knows what is best,
    Her grief is too great for public lamentation,
    And doubtless she has gone to her chamber to weep   80
    For her dead son, leading her maidens in his dirge.
Choragos: It may be so: but I fear this deep silence.

    Pause.

Messenger: I will see what she is doing. I will go in.

    Exit Messenger into the palace.

    Enter Creon with attendants, bearing Haimon's body.

Choragos: But here is the king himself: oh look at him,
　　Bearing his own damnation in his arms.　　　　　　　　　　　　　　85
Creon: Nothing you say can touch me any more.
　　My own blind heart has brought me
　　From darkness to final darkness. Here you see
　　The father murdering, the murdered son—
　　And all my civic wisdom!　　　　　　　　　　　　　　　　　　90

　　Haimon my son, so young, so young to die,
　　I was the fool, not you; and you died for me.
Choragos: That is the truth; but you were late in learning it.
Creon: This truth is hard to bear. Surely a god
　　Has crushed me beneath the hugest weight of heaven,　　　　　　95
　　And driven me headlong a barbaric way
　　To trample out the thing I held most dear.

　　The pains that men will take to come to pain!

Enter Messenger from the palace.

Messenger: The burden you carry in your hands is heavy,
　　But it is not all: you will find more in your house.　　　　　　　100
Creon: What burden worse than this shall I find there?
Messenger: The Queen is dead.
Creon: O port of death, deaf world,
　　Is there no pity for me? And you, Angel of evil,
　　I was dead, and your words are death again.　　　　　　　　　105
　　Is it true, boy? Can it be true?
　　Is my wife dead? Has death bred death?
Messenger: You can see for yourself.

The doors are opened and the body of Eurydicê is disclosed within.

Creon: Oh pity!
　　All true, all true, and more than I can bear!　　　　　　　　　110
　　O my wife, my son!
Messenger: She stood before the altar, and her heart
　　Welcomed the knife her own hand guided,
　　And a great cry burst from her lips for Megareus° dead,
　　And for Haimon dead, her sons; and her last breath　　　　　115
　　Was a curse for their father, the murderer of her sons.
　　And she fell, and the dark flowed in through her closing eyes.
Creon: O God, I am sick with fear.
　　Are there no swords here? Has no one a blow for me?
Messenger: Her curse is upon you for the deaths of both.　　　　120
Creon: It is right that it should be. I alone am guilty.
　　I know it, and I say it. Lead me in,
　　Quickly, friends.
　　I have neither life nor substance. Lead me in.

114 Megareus: Son of Creon and brother of Haimon, Megareus was slain in the unsuccessful
attack upon Thebes.

Choragos: You are right, if there can be right in so much wrong. 125
 The briefest way is best in a world of sorrow.
Creon: Let it come,
 Let death come quickly, and be kind to me.
 I would not ever see the sun again.
Choragos: All that will come when it will; but we, meanwhile, 130
 Have much to do. Leave the future to itself.
Creon: All my heart was in that prayer!
Choragos: Then do not pray any more: the sky is deaf.
Creon: Lead me away. I have been rash and foolish.
 I have killed my son and my wife. 135
 I look for comfort; my comfort lies here dead.
 Whatever my hands have touched has come to nothing.
 Fate has brought all my pride to a thought of dust.

As Creon is being led into the house, the Choragos advances and speaks directly to the audience.

Choragos: There is no happiness where there is no wisdom;
 No wisdom but in submission to the gods. 140
 Big words are always punished,
 And proud men in old age learn to be wise.

Questions

1. What is Creon's motivation for forbidding the burial of his own nephew Polyneicês? Why would he issue an edict that runs so contrary to his family obligations?
2. What are Antigonê's reasons for performing funeral rites on her brother's corpse in direct violation of Creon's edict?
3. What are the larger issues behind the conflicting positions of both Creon and Antigonê? Is either person or position clearly wrong?
4. Does the chorus take a position in the argument between Creon and Antigonê?
5. If Antigonê is a tragic heroine, what is her tragic flaw? Does she have any particular hubris or excess of virtue that dooms her?
6. Can a modern reader discern Sophocles's own position on the debate between civic responsibility (Creon's edict) and family duty (Antigonê's defiance)? Are his authorial sympathies anywhere evident in the play?
7. What is the role of Eurydicê? Is her presence essential to the story? What would be the effect of removing her from the drama?
8. Can you imagine a modern setting in which a new production of *Antigonê* might be staged? Describe your idea in terms of sets, costumes, and staging.

CRITICS ON SOPHOCLES

Aristotle (384–322 B.C.)

Defining Tragedy   330 B.C.?

Translated by L. J. Potts

Tragedy is an imitation of an action of high importance, complete and of some amplitude; in language enhanced by distinct and varying beauties; acted not narrated; by means of pity and fear effecting its purgation of these emotions. By the beauties enhancing the language I mean rhythm and melody; by "distinct and varying" I mean that some are produced by meter alone, and others at another time by melody.

• • •

What will produce the tragic effect? Since, then, tragedy, to be at its finest, requires a complex, not a simple, structure, and its structure should also imitate fearful and pitiful events (for that is the peculiarity of this sort of imitation), it is clear: first, that decent people must not be shown passing from good fortune to misfortune (for that is not fearful or pitiful but disgusting); again, vicious people must not be shown passing from misfortune to good fortune (for that is the most untragic situation possible—it has none of the requisites, it is neither humane, nor pitiful, nor fearful); nor again should an utterly evil man fall from good fortune into misfortune (for though a plot of that kind would be humane, it would not induce pity or fear—pity is induced by undeserved misfortune, and fear by the misfortunes of normal people, so that this situation will be neither pitiful nor fearful). So we are left with the man between these extremes: that is to say, the kind of man who neither is distinguished for excellence and virtue, nor comes to grief on account of baseness and vice, but on account of some error; a man of great reputation and prosperity, like Oedipus and Thyestes and conspicuous people of such families as theirs. So, to be well formed, a fable must be single rather than (as some say) double—there must be no change from misfortune to good fortune, but only the opposite, from good fortune to misfortune; the cause must not be vice, but a great error; and the man must be either of the type specified or better, rather than worse. This is borne out by the practice of poets; at first they picked a fable at random and made an inventory of its contents, but now the finest tragedies are plotted, and concern a few families—for example, the tragedies about Alcmeon, Oedipus, Orestes, Meleager, Thyestes, Telephus, and any others whose lives were attended by terrible experiences or doings.

This is the plot that will produce the technically finest tragedy. Those critics are therefore wrong who censure Euripides on this very ground—because he does this in his tragedies, and many of them end in misfortune; for it is, as I have said, the right thing to do. This is clearly demonstrated on the stage in the competitions, where such plays, if they succeed, are the most tragic, and Euripides, even if he is inefficient in every other respect, still shows himself the most tragic of our poets. The next best plot, which is said by some people to be the best, is the tragedy with a double plot, like the *Odyssey*, ending in one way for the better people and in the opposite way for the worse. But it is the weakness of theatrical performances that gives priority to this kind; when poets write what the audience would like to happen, they are in leading strings.° This is not the pleasure proper to tragedy, but rather to comedy, where the

---

in leading strings: each is led, by a string, wherever the audience wills.

greatest enemies in the fable, say Orestes and Aegisthus, make friends and go off at the end, and nobody is killed by anybody.

• • •

The pity and fear can be brought about by the *mise en scène;*° but they can also come from the mere plotting of the incidents, which is preferable, and better poetry. For, without seeing anything, the fable ought to have been so plotted that if one heard the bare facts, the chain of circumstances would make one shudder and pity. That would happen to any one who heard the fable of the *Oedipus.* To produce this effect by the *mise en scène* is less artistic and puts one at the mercy of the technician; and those who use it not to frighten but merely to startle have lost touch with tragedy altogether. We should not try to get all sorts of pleasure from tragedy, but the particular tragic pleasure. And clearly, since this pleasure coming from pity and fear has to be produced by imitation, it is by his handling of the incidents that the poet must create it.

From Poetics, VI, XIII, XIV

Sigmund Freud (1856–1939)

The Destiny of Oedipus   1900

Translated by James Strachey

If *Oedipus the King* moves a modern audience no less than it did the contemporary Greek one, the explanation can only be that its effect does not lie in the contrast between destiny and human will, but is to be looked for in the particular nature of the material on which that contrast is exemplified. There must be something which makes a voice within us ready to recognize the compelling force of destiny in the *Oedipus,* while we can dismiss as merely arbitrary such dispositions as are laid down in *Die Ahnfrau°* or other modern tragedies of destiny. And a factor of this kind is in fact involved in the story of King Oedipus. His destiny moves us only because it might have been ours—because the oracle laid the same curse upon us before our birth as upon him. It is the fate of all of us, perhaps, to direct our first sexual impulse towards our mother and our first hatred and our first murderous wish against our father. Our dreams convince us that that is so. King Oedipus, who slew his father Laius and married his mother Jocasta, merely shows us the fulfillment of our own childhood wishes. But, more fortunate than he, we have meanwhile succeeded, insofar as we have not become psychoneurotics, in detaching our sexual impulses from our mothers and in forgetting our jealousy of our fathers. Here is one in whom these primeval wishes of our childhood have been fulfilled, and we shrink back from him with the whole force of the repression by which those wishes have since that time been held down within us. While the poet, as he unravels the past, brings to light the guilt of Oedipus, he is at the same time compelling us to recognize our own inner minds, in which those same impulses, though suppressed, are still to be found. The contrast with which the closing Chorus leaves us confronted—

look upon Oedipus.

This is the king who solved the famous riddle
And towered up, most powerful of men.
No mortal eyes but looked on him with envy,
Yet in the end ruin swept over him.

---

mise en scène: arrangement of actors and scenery. *Die Ahnfrau: The Foremother,* a play by Franz Grillparzer (1791–1872), Austrian dramatist and poet.

—strikes as a warning at ourselves and our pride, at us who since our childhood have grown so wise and so mighty in our own eyes. Like Oedipus, we live in ignorance of these wishes, repugnant to morality, which have been forced upon us by Nature, and after their revelation we may all of us well seek to close our eyes to the scenes of our childhood.

From The Interpretation of Dreams

E. R. Dodds (1893–1979)

On Misunderstanding Oedipus   1966

Some readers of the *Oedipus Rex* have told me that they find its atmosphere stifling and oppressive: they miss the tragic exaltation that one gets from the *Antigonê* or the *Prometheus Vinctus*. And I fear that what I have said here has done nothing to remove that feeling. Yet it is not a feeling which I share myself. Certainly the *Oedipus Rex* is a play about the blindness of man and the desperate insecurity of the human condition: in a sense every man must grope in the dark as Oedipus gropes, not knowing who he is or what he has to suffer; we all live in a world of appearance which hides from us who-knows-what dreadful reality. But surely the *Oedipus Rex* is also a play about human greatness. Oedipus is great, not in virtue of a great worldly position—for his worldly position is an illusion which will vanish like a dream—but in virtue of his inner strength: strength to pursue the truth at whatever personal cost, and strength to accept and endure it when found. "This horror is mine," he cries, "and none but I is *strong* enough to bear it." Oedipus is great because he accepts the responsibility for *all* his acts, including those which are objectively most horrible, though subjectively innocent.

To me personally Oedipus is a kind of symbol of the human intelligence which cannot rest until it has solved all the riddles—even the last riddle, to which the answer is that human happiness is built on an illusion. I do not know how far Sophocles intended that. But certainly in the last lines of the play (which I firmly believe to be genuine) he does generalize the case, does appear to suggest that in some sense Oedipus is every man and every man is potentially Oedipus. Freud felt this (he was not insensitive to poetry), but as we all know he understood it in a specific psychological sense. "Oedipus' fate," he says, "moves us only because it might have been our own, because the oracle laid upon us before birth is the very curse which rested upon him. It may be that we were all destined to direct our first sexual impulses towards our mothers, and our first impulses of hatred and violence towards our fathers; our dreams convince us that we were." Perhaps they do; but Freud did not ascribe his interpretation of the myth to Sophocles, and it is not the interpretation I have in mind. Is there not in the poet's view a much wider sense in which every man is Oedipus? If every man could tear away the last veils of illusion, if he could see human life as time and the gods see it, would he not see that against that tremendous background all the generations of men are as if they had not been, *isa kai to mēden zōsas*? That was how Odysseus saw it when he had conversed with Athena, the embodiment of divine wisdom. "In Ajax' condition," he says, "I recognize my own: I perceive that all men living are but appearance or unsubstantial shadow."

From "On Misunderstanding the Oedipus Rex"

A. E. Haigh (1855–1905)

The Irony of Sophocles   1896

The use of "tragic irony," as it has been called, is a favorite device in all dramatic literature. It is mostly employed when some catastrophe is about to happen, which is known and foreseen by the spectators, but concealed either from all, or from some, of the actors in the drama. In such cases the dialogue may be couched in terms which, though perfectly harmless upon the surface, carry an ominous significance to the initiated, and point suggestively to what is about to happen; and the contrast between the outer and the inner meaning of the language produces a deep effect upon the stage. Examples of this "irony" are to be found in most tragic writers, but especially in those of Greece, who use it with far greater frequency than the moderns; the reason being that, as the subjects of Greek tragedy were taken from the old legends with which everyone was familiar, it was far easier for the ancient dramatist to indulge in those ambiguous allusions which presuppose a certain knowledge on the part of the spectators. Sophocles, however, is distinguished even among the Greek poets for his predilection for this form of speech, and his "irony" has become proverbial. It figures so prominently in his dramas, and goes so far to determine their general tone, that a detailed consideration of the matter will not be out of place.

Tragic irony may be divided into two kinds, the conscious and the unconscious. Conscious irony occurs in those cases where the speaker is not himself the victim of any illusion, but foresees the calamity that is about to fall on others, and exults in the prospect. His language, though equivocal, is easily intelligible to the audience, and to those actors who are acquainted with the facts; and its dark humor adds to the horror of the situation. This kind of irony is the one more commonly met with in the modern drama.

• • •

The other kind of irony, the unconscious, is perhaps the more impressive of the two. Here the sufferer is himself the spokesman. Utterly blind as to the doom which overhangs him, he uses words which, to the mind of the audience, have an ominous suggestiveness, and without knowing it, probes his own wounds to the bottom. Such irony is not confined merely to the language, but runs through the whole situation; and the contrast between the cheerful heedlessness of the victim, and the dark shadows which surround him, produces an impression more terrible than that which any form of speech could convey. Scenes of this kind had a peculiar fascination for the ancients. The fear of a sudden reverse of fortune, and of some fatal Nemesis which waits upon pride and boastfulness, was of all ideas the one most deeply impressed upon the mind of antiquity. Hence the popularity upon the stage of those thrilling spectacles, in which confidence and presumption were seen advancing blindfold to destruction, and the bitterness of the doom was intensified by the unconscious utterances of the victim.

•••

The greatest example of all is the *Oedipus Rex,* the masterpiece of Sophocles, and the most typical of all Greek tragedies. The irony of destiny is here exhibited with un-exampled force. In the opening scene Oedipus is depicted in the height of his prosperity, renowned and venerated, and surrounded by his suppliant countrymen; and the priest addresses him as the "wisest of men in dealing with life's chances and with the visitations of heaven." To the audience who know that within a few short hours the wrath of heaven will have crushed and shattered him, the pathetic meaning of these words is indescribable. From this first scene until the final catastrophe the speeches of Oedipus are all full of the same tragic allusiveness. He can scarcely open his lips without touching unconsciously on his own approaching fate. When he insists upon the fact that his search for the assassin is "not on behalf of strangers, but in his own cause," and when he cautiously warns Jocasta that, as his mother still lives, the guilt of incest is not yet an impossibility, every word that he utters has a concealed barb. Perhaps the most tragic passage of all is that in which, while cursing the murderer of Laius, he pronounces his own doom. "As for the man who did the deed of guilt, whether alone he lurks, or in league with others, I pray that he may waste his life away in suffering, perishing vilely for his vile actions. And if he should become a dweller in my house, I knowing it, may every curse I utter fall on my own head."

From The Tragic Drama of the Greeks

David Wiles

The Chorus as Democrat   2000

Oedipus becomes a political play when we focus on the interaction of actor and chorus, and see how the chorus forms a democratic mass jury. Each sequence of dialogue takes the form of a contest for the chorus' sympathy, with Oedipus sliding from the role of prosecutor to that of defendant, and each choral dance offers a provisional verdict. After Oedipus' set-to with Teiresias the soothsayer, the chorus decides to trust Oedipus on the basis of his past record; after his argument with his brother-in-law Creon, the chorus shows their distress and urges compromise. Once Oedipus has confessed to a killing and Iocastê has declared that oracles have no force, the chorus is forced to think about political tyranny, torn between respect for divine law and trust in their rulers. In the next dance they assume that the contradiction is resolved and Oedipus has turned out to be the son of a god. Finally a slave's evidence reveals that the man most honored by society is in fact the least to be envied. The political implications are clear: there is no space in democratic society for such as Oedipus. Athenians, like the chorus of the play, must reject the temptation to believe one man can calculate the future.

From Greek Theatre Performance: An Introduction

Patricia M. Lines (b. 1938)

What Is Antigonê's Tragic Flaw?   1999

Antigonê does not seem to fit the Aristotelian formula. Aristotle himself did not seem to know what to make of it. In the *Poetica*'s sole reference to the play Aristotle offers *Antigonê* as an example of a poor plot for a tragedy. The least tragic plot, he avers, involves a character who resolves to do a fearful deed and does not do it. His example is Haimon who seems ready to slay his father, Creon, and does not. This may be one of those rare cases where Aristotle misses the point. First, after more than two millennia of experience with drama, one can imagine a situation where delay in doing the dread deed makes the tragedy. Nor is it clear that Haimon had resolved to kill his father; his veiled threat may have been to kill himself, an action which he finally takes. Most important, the conflict between Haimon and his father does not stir our emotions as much as the conflict swirling around Antigonê.

The play strikes us as a fine one—Hegel thought it was the supreme example of tragedy, prompting him to pose a different theory for the form. Hegel sees a dialectical clash between two ideals of justice. A noble and wise Antigonê fights for the justice of traditional belief, while a tyrannical Creon fights for a right based on might. Irving Babbitt has suggested a more subtle variation of dialectic theory, hailing Antigonê as the "perfect example of the ethical imagination" in contrast to her sister, Ismenê, who knows merely "the law of the community." Both Antigonê and Ismenê are ethical, but Ismenê lacks ethical imagination. As Babbitt sees it:

> This law, the convention of a particular place and time, is always but a very imperfect image, a mere shadow indeed of the unwritten law which being above the ordinary rational level is . . . infinite and incapable of final formulation.

While such interpretations no doubt are true—with each uncovering layers of meaning—alone they reduce *Antigonê* to a morality play. Such interpretations fail to explain the play's more complex and turbulent moods.

• • •

The suggestion that Sophocles intended to present a flawed Antigonê rubs against the grain. She is the paragon. The religion of the Greeks, like virtually all religions, required burial of the dead—even the enemy dead. The ancient tales in the *Iliad*, the bible to the Greeks, warn of the anger of the gods upon a failure to honor the dead. Besides, the restless shades of the unburied could cause trouble. Antigonê stands for all that is right and for the opposition to tyranny. Thus, we have only a play about Creon's excessive harshness and his tragically delayed conversion. Yet, Sophocles provides a fair amount of evidence that he intended to create something more complex than a morality play.

Consider first the parallels between *Antigonê* and *Oedipus Rex*. Both stories begin with a problem facing family and polis, and with the central character resolving to make things right. Antigonê proceeds with unswerving resolution in her judgment of the situation. She possesses complete confidence in her ability to choose and execute a just action. She does not see the full situation; she is blind to key elements of the problem. She is like her father in most respects. Both Antigonê and Oedipus claim to know justice with the certainty of a god. Oedipus believes most in his cunning and strength, Antigonê in her goodness.

The flaw of hubris is easy to spot in Oedipus, but Antigonê's brilliance is so dazzling that we overlook her flaw. After all, she has formulated a great and noble truth and maintains it with courage. She asserts God's law over man's law. Especially in our own time, where we formally recognize the superiority, within specified spheres, of individual right over the demands of overly broad laws, Antigonê seems a genius beyond her time.

Creon, by contrast, understands the needs of the polis. Following a civil war, he has placed a premium on order. He will do whatever is necessary, including the stern enforcement of harsh rules. He faces another dilemma in his role as leader: he forbade the burial of Polyneicês and decreed this harsh punishment before he was aware of Antigonê's guilt. To pardon his future daughter-in-law as his first serious act as ruler of Thebes would compromise all future claims to fairness in his rule. Yet Creon listens to the chorus of old men; he listens to the blind seer. After struggling with the issue, he reconsiders his judgment; he determines to bury the body of Polyneicês and to unbury Antigonê with his own hands.

Antigonê, on the other hand, recognizes the demands of true justice and champions it. She spurns Ismenê, who initially hesitated to assist her but soon after wished to share in her sister's punishment and death. Antigonê refuses the offer. When Ismenê asks whether her sister has cast her aside, Antigonê's answer ignores Ismenê's change of heart: "Yes. For you chose to live when I chose death." Antigonê seems to speak not to spare Ismenê, but to wound her to the quick. Antigonê leaves Haimon, her betrothed, in the cold, as she left Ismenê. She never seeks him out, nor even mentions his name. Yet Haimon is ready to defy his father for Antigonê's sake, and he refuses to live without her. Ironically, this may be what he must do to win her affection, for Antigonê reveals no tenderness for anyone except those already dead.

• • •

The chorus, often the truth-sayer for Sophocles, provides more clues. Of Antigonê, they tell us:

> The girl is bitter. She's her father's child.
> She cannot yield to trouble; nor could he.

In perhaps the most revealing exchange, the chorus turns to Antigonê and tells her, plainly:

> You showed respect for the dead.
> So we for you: but power
> is not to be thwarted so.
> Your self-sufficiency has brought you down.

The last line is key: "δ' αὐτόγνωτος ὤλεσ' ὀργά." The above quotation is from Wyckoff's translation. But all translations seem to head in the same direction: "A self-determined impulse hath undone thee" (Campbell). "You were self-willed. That has been your undoing" (Townsend). "And thee, thy stubborne mood, self-chosen, layeth low" (students of the University of Notre Dame, 1983).[1] In any translation, it seems the chorus has identified Antigonê's flaw. She follows a truth that springs only from her self: It is αὐτόγνωτος, or autognotos. She will not consult with others. We could call it self-certainty or, perhaps even better, self-righteousness. It is a form of hubris.

At another point, the chorus tells Antigonê she is autonomous. Literally, this means "a law unto yourself." The English word autonomy does not convey quite the right meaning, as individual autonomy was a condition the Greeks viewed with discomfort and suspicion. The autonomous being is either beast or god, living only within the horizons of its own laws.

"Antigonê's Flaw"

---

[1]Scene IV, lines 47–48 in the Fitts and Fitzgerald translation: "You have made your choice, / Your death is the doing of your conscious hand."

■ WRITING *effectively*

Robert Fitzgerald on Writing

Translating Sophocles into English   1941

The style of Sophocles was smooth. It has been likened by a modern critic to a molten flow of language, fitting and revealing every contour of the meaning, with no words wasted and no words poured on for effect. To approximate such purity I have sought a spare but felicitous manner of speech, not common and not "elevated" either, except by force of natural eloquence. The Greek writer did not disdain plainness when plainness was appropriate—appropriate, that is, both dramatically and within a context of verse very brilliant, mellifluous and powerful. As in every highly inflected language, the Greek order of words was controlled, by its masters, for special purposes of emphasis and even of meaning; and such of these as I have been acute enough to grasp I have tried to bring out by a comparable phrasing or rhythm in English. This I hold to be part of the business of "literal" rendering.

The difficulties involved in translating Greek dialogue are easily tripled when it comes to translating a chorus. Here the ellipses and compressions possible to the inflected idiom are particularly in evidence; and in the chorus, too, the poet concentrates his allusive power. For the modern reader, who has very little "literature" in the sense in which Samuel Johnson° used the term, two out of three allusions in the Greek odes will be meaningless. This is neither surprising nor deplorable. The Roman writer Ennius,° translating Euripides for a Latin audience two centuries after the Periclean period, found it advisable to omit many place names and to omit or explain many mythological references; and his public had greater reason to be familiar with such things than we have. My handling of this problem has been governed by the general wish to leave nothing in the English that would drive the literate reader to a library.

"Commentary" on Sophocles's The Oedipus Cycle

THINKING ABOUT GREEK TRAGEDY

Reading an ancient work of literature, such as Sophocles's *Oedipus the King* or *Antigonê*, you might have two contradictory reactions. On the one hand, you are likely to note how differently people thought, spoke, and conducted themselves in the ancient world from the way they do now. On the other hand, you might notice how many facets of human nature remain constant across the ages. Though Sophocles's characters are mythic, they also are recognizably human.

- ■ **Stay alert to both impulses.** Be open to the play's universal appeal, but never forget its foreignness. Take note of the basic beliefs and values that the characters hold that are different from your own. How do those elements influence their actions and motivations?

Samuel Johnson: Johnson (1709–1784) was the great eighteenth-century critic, lexicographer, poet, and conversationalist. His definition of *literature* would have referred mostly to the Greek and Latin classics. *Ennius:* Quintus Ennius (239–169 B.C.) was an early Latin epic poet and tragedian. He created Latin versions of the Greek tragic plays, especially those of Euripides.

- **Jot down something about each major character that seems odd or exotic to you.** Don't worry about being too basic; these notes are just a starting place. You might observe, for example, that Oedipus and Iocastê both believe in the power of prophecy. They also believe that Apollo and the other gods would punish the city with a plague because of an unsolved crime committed twenty years earlier. These are certainly not mainstream modern beliefs.
- **Focus on the differences themselves.** You do not need to understand the historical origins or cultural context of the differences you note. You can safely leave those things to scholars. But observing these differences—at least a few important ones—will keep you from making inappropriate modern assumptions about the characters, and keeping the differences in mind will give you greater insight into their behavior.

CHECKLIST: Writing About Greek Drama

- ☐ Identify the play's major characters.
- ☐ In what ways do they seem alien to you?
- ☐ What do you notice about a character's beliefs? About his or her values? How do these differ from your own?
- ☐ In what ways are the play's characters like the people you know?
- ☐ How do these qualities—both the alien and the familiar—influence the characters' motivations and actions?

WRITING ASSIGNMENT ON SOPHOCLES

Write a brief personality profile (two or three pages) of any major character in *Oedipus the King* or *Antigonê*. Describe the character's age, social position, family background, personality, and beliefs. What is his or her major motivation in the play? In what ways does the character resemble his or her modern equivalent? In what ways do they differ?

MORE TOPICS FOR WRITING

1. Suppose you were to direct and produce a new stage production of *Oedipus the King*. How would you go about it? Would you use masks? How would you render the chorus? Would you set the play in contemporary North America? Justify your decisions by referring to the play itself.

2. Write a brief comment on the play under the title "Does Sophocles's Oedipus Have an Oedipus Complex?" Consider Sigmund Freud's famous observations (quoted on page 1275). Your comment can be either serious or light.

3. Compare *Oedipus the King* to *Antigonê* in terms of their characterizations of their protagonists. In what ways does Antigonê resemble Oedipus, and in what ways does she differ?

4. Taking the protagonist of either play by Sophocles, write an essay explaining how he or she exemplifies or refutes Aristotle's definition of a tragic hero.

▶ TERMS FOR *review*

Stagecraft in Ancient Greece

Skene ▶ The canvas or wooden stage building in which actors changed masks and costumes when changing roles. Its façade, with double center doors and possibly two side doors, served as the setting for action taking place before a palace, temple, cave, or other interior space.

Orchestra ▶ "The place for dancing"; a circular, level performance space at the base of a horseshoe-shaped amphitheater, where twelve, then later (in Sophocles's plays) fifteen masked young male chorus members sang and danced the odes interspersed between dramatic episodes in a play. (Today the term *orchestra* refers to the ground-floor seats in a theater or concert hall.)

Deus ex machina ▶ (Latin for "god out of the machine.") Originally, the phrase referred to the Greek playwrights' frequent use of a god, mechanically lowered to the stage from the *skene* roof to resolve the human conflict. Today, *deus ex machina* refers to any forced or improbable device used to resolve a plot.

Masks ▶ (In Latin, *personae*.) Classical Greek theater masks covered an actor's entire head. Large, recognizable masks allowed far-away spectators to distinguish the conventional characters of tragedy and comedy.

Cothurni ▶ High, thick-soled elevator boots worn by tragic actors in late classical times to make them appear taller than ordinary men. (Earlier, in the fifth-century classical Athenian theater, actors wore soft shoes or boots or went barefoot.)

Elements of Classical Tragedy

Hamartia ▶ (Greek for "error.") An offense committed in ignorance of some material fact; a great mistake made as a result of an error by a morally good person.

Tragic flaw ▶ A fatal weakness or moral flaw in the protagonist that brings him or her to a bad end. Sometimes offered as an alternative understanding of *hamartia*, in contrast to the idea that the tragic hero's catastrophe is caused by an error in judgment.

Hubris ▶ Overweening pride, outrageous behavior, or the insolence that leads to ruin, the antithesis of moderation or rectitude.

Peripeteia ▶ (Anglicized as *peripety*; Greek for "sudden change.") A reversal of fortune, a sudden change of circumstance affecting the protagonist. According to Aristotle, the play's peripety occurs when a certain result is expected and instead its *opposite* effect is produced. In a tragedy, the reversal takes the protagonist from good fortune to catastrophe.

Recognition ▶ In tragic plotting, the moment of recognition occurs when ignorance gives way to knowledge, illusion to disillusion.

Katharsis, catharsis ▶ (Often translated from Greek as *purgation* or *purification*.) The feeling of emotional release or calm the spectator feels at the end of tragedy. The term is drawn from Aristotle's definition of tragedy, relating to the final cause or purpose of tragic art. Some feel that through *katharsis*, drama taught the audience compassion for the vulnerabilities of others and schooled it in justice and other civic virtues.

Principum *amicitias!*

"*To be or not to be . . .*" *Is it Shakespeare?* **In 2009 the Shakespeare Birthplace Trust unveiled this newly discovered portrait they believe is William Shakespeare. If authentic—and many scholars disagree—it is the only surviving portrait of the author painted during his lifetime.**

All the world's a stage

—WILLIAM SHAKESPEARE, *AS YOU LIKE IT* (II, vii, 139)

The reconstructed Globe Theatre in today's London—built in 1997 as an exact replica of the original.

THE THEATER OF SHAKESPEARE

Compared with the technical resources of a theater of today, those of a London public theater in the time of Queen Elizabeth I seem hopelessly limited. Plays had to be performed by daylight, and scenery had to be kept simple: a table, a chair, a throne, perhaps an artificial tree or two to suggest a forest. But these limitations were, in a sense, advantages. What the theater of today can spell out for us realistically, with massive scenery and electric lighting, Elizabethan playgoers had to imagine and the playwright had to make vivid for them by means of language. Not having a lighting technician to work a panel, Shakespeare had to indicate the dawn by having Horatio, in *Hamlet,* say in a speech rich in metaphor and descriptive detail:

> But look, the morn in russet mantle clad
> Walks o'er the dew of yon high eastward hill.

And yet the theater of Shakespeare was not bare, for the playwright did have *some* valuable technical resources. Costumes could be elaborate, and apparently some costumes conveyed recognized meanings: one theater manager's inventory included "a robe for to go invisible in." There could be musical accompaniment and sound effects such as gunpowder explosions and the beating of a pan to simulate thunder.

    The stage itself was remarkably versatile. At its back were doors for exits and entrances and a curtained booth or alcove useful for hiding inside. Above the stage was a higher acting area—perhaps a porch or balcony—useful for a Juliet to stand upon and for a Romeo to raise his eyes to. In the stage floor was a trapdoor leading to a "hell" or cellar, especially useful for ghosts or devils who had to appear or disappear. The stage itself was a rectangular platform that projected into a yard enclosed by three-storied galleries.

    The building was round or octagonal. In *Henry V,* Shakespeare calls it a "wooden O." The audience sat in these galleries or else stood in the yard in front of the stage and at its sides. A roof or awning protected the stage and the high-priced gallery seats, but in a sudden rain, the *groundlings,* who paid a penny to stand in the yard, must have been dampened.

Built by the theatrical company to which Shakespeare belonged, the Globe, most celebrated of Elizabethan theaters, was not in the city of London itself but on the south bank of the Thames River. This location had been chosen because earlier, in 1574, public plays had been banished from the city by an ordinance that blamed them for "corruptions of youth and other enormities" (such as providing opportunities for prostitutes and pickpockets).

A playwright had to please all members of the audience, not only the mannered and educated. This obligation may help to explain the wide range of subject matter and tone in an Elizabethan play: passages of subtle poetry, of deep philosophy, of coarse bawdry; scenes of sensational violence and of quiet psychological conflict (not that most members of the audience did not enjoy all these elements). Because he was an actor as well as a playwright, Shakespeare well knew what his company could do and what his audience wanted. In devising a play, he could write a part to take advantage of some actor's specific skills, or he could avoid straining the company's resources (some of his plays have few female parts, perhaps because of a shortage of competent boy actors). The company might offer as many as thirty plays in a season, customarily changing the program daily. The actors thus had to hold many parts in their heads, which may account for Elizabethan playwrights' fondness for blank verse. Lines of fixed length were easier for actors to commit to memory.

WILLIAM SHAKESPEARE

William Shakespeare (1564–1616), the supreme writer of English, was born, baptized, and buried in the market town of Stratford-on-Avon, eighty miles from London. Son of a glove maker and merchant who was high bailiff (or mayor) of the town, he probably attended grammar school and learned to read Latin authors in the original. At eighteen, he married Anne Hathaway, twenty-six, by whom he had three children, including twins. By 1592 he had become well known and envied as an actor and playwright in London. From 1594 until he retired, he belonged to the same theatrical company, the Lord Chamberlain's Men (later renamed the King's Men in honor of their patron, James I), for whom he wrote thirty-six plays—some of them, such as Hamlet *and*

William Shakespeare

King Lear, *profound reworkings of old plays. As an actor, Shakespeare is believed to have played supporting roles, such as the ghost of Hamlet's father. The company prospered, moved into the Globe in 1599, and in 1608 bought the fashionable Blackfriars as well; Shakespeare owned an interest in both theaters. When plagues shut down the theaters from 1592 to 1594, Shakespeare turned to story poems; his great Sonnets (published only in 1609) probably also date from the 1590s. Plays were regarded as entertainments of little literary merit, like comic books today, and Shakespeare did not bother to supervise their publication. After writing* The Tempest *(1611), the last play entirely from his hand, he retired to Stratford, where since 1597 he had owned the second-largest house in town. Most critics agree that when he wrote* Othello, *about 1604, Shakespeare was at the height of his powers.*

James Earl Jones as Othello.

A NOTE ON *OTHELLO*

Othello, the Moor of Venice, here offered for study, may be (if you are fortunate) new to you. It is seldom taught in high school, for it is ablaze with passion and violence. Even if you already know the play, we trust that you (like your instructor and your editors) still have much more to learn from it. Following his usual practice, Shakespeare based the play on a story he had appropriated—from a tale, "Of the Unfaithfulness of Husbands and Wives," by a sixteenth-century Italian writer, Giraldi Cinthio. As he could not help but do, Shakespeare freely transformed his source material. In the original tale, the heroine Disdemona (whose name Shakespeare so hugely improved) is beaten to death with a stocking full of sand—a shoddier death than the bard imagined for her.

Surely no character in literature can touch us more than Desdemona; no character can shock and disgust us more than Iago. Between these two extremes stands Othello, a black man of courage and dignity—and yet insecure, capable of being fooled, a pushover for bad advice. Besides breathing life into these characters and a host of others, Shakespeare—as brilliant a writer as any the world has known—enables them to speak poetry. Sometimes this poetry seems splendid and rich in imagery; at other times quiet and understated. Always, it seems to grow naturally from the nature of Shakespeare's characters and from their situations. *Othello, the Moor of Venice* has never ceased to grip readers and beholders alike. It is a safe bet that it will triumphantly live as long as fathers dislike whomever their daughters marry, as long as husbands suspect their wives of cheating, as long as blacks remember slavery, and as long as the ambitious court favor and the jealous practice deceit. The play may well make sense as long as public officials connive behind smiling faces, and it may even endure as long as the world makes room for the kind, the true, the beautiful—the blessed pure in heart.

PICTURING *Othello*

▲ Desdemona's father,
Brabantio, *page 1295*

▼ Othello and Desdemona,
page 1308

▲ Desdemona arrives in Cyprus, *page
1317*

▲ Desdemona offers the
wrong handkerchief,
page 1349

▲ Iago's machinations, *page 1356*

▶ Iago with the fateful
handkerchief,
page 1343

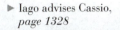
► Iago advises Cassio, *page 1328*

▲ Iago plants doubts about Desdemona, *page 1338*

▲ Drunken Cassio fights, *page 1324*

▼ Othello despairs, *page 1364*

▲ Othello smothers Desdemona, *page 1381*

► Enter Othello, *page 1378*

Othello, the Moor of Venice

1604?

Edited by David Bevington

THE NAMES OF THE ACTORS

Othello, the Moor
Brabantio, [a senator,] father to Desdemona
Cassio, an honorable lieutenant [to Othello]
Iago, [Othello's ancient,] a villain
Roderigo, a gulled gentleman
Duke of Venice
Senators [of Venice]
Montano, governor of Cyprus
Gentlemen of Cyprus
Lodovico and Gratiano, [kinsmen to Brabantio,] two noble Venetians
Sailors
Clown
Desdemona, [daughter to Brabantio and] wife to Othello
Emilia, wife to Iago
Bianca, a courtesan [and mistress to Cassio]
[*A Messenger*
A Herald
A Musician
Servants, Attendants, Officers, Senators, Musicians, Gentlemen

SCENE. *Venice; a seaport in Cyprus*]

ACT I

SCENE I [VENICE. A STREET.]

Enter Roderigo and Iago.

Roderigo: Tush, never tell me!° I take it much unkindly
   That thou, Iago, who hast had my purse
   As if the strings were thine, shouldst know of this.°

NOTE ON THE TEXT: This text of *Othello* is based on that of the First Folio, or large collection, of Shakespeare's plays (1623). But there are many differences between the Folio text and that of the play's first printing in the Quarto, or small volume, of 1621 (eighteen or nineteen years after the play's first performance). Some readings from the Quarto are included. For the reader's convenience, some material has been added by the editor, David Bevington (some indications of scene, some stage directions). Such additions are enclosed in brackets. Mr. Bevington's text and notes were prepared for his book *The Complete Works of Shakespeare*, updated 4th ed. (New York: Longman, 1997).

PRODUCTION PHOTOS: The photos included are from the 2003 production of *Othello* by the Guthrie Theater of Minneapolis, with Lester Purry (Othello), Bill McCallum (Iago), Cheyenne Casebier (Desdemona), Robert O. Berdahl (Cassio), Virginia S. Burke (Emilia), Nathaniel Fuller (Brabantio), and Shawn Hamilton (Montano).

1 *never tell me* (An expression of incredulity, like "tell me another one.")   3 *this* i.e., Desdemona's elopement

Iago: 'Sblood,° but you'll not hear me.
    If ever I did dream of such a matter,   5
    Abhor me.
Roderigo: Thou toldst me thou didst hold him in thy hate.
Iago: Despise me
    If I do not. Three great ones of the city,
    In personal suit to make me his lieutenant,   10
    Off-capped to him;° and by the faith of man,
    I know my price, I am worth no worse a place.
    But he, as loving his own pride and purposes,
    Evades them with a bombast circumstance°
    Horribly stuffed with epithets of war,°   15
    And, in conclusion,
    Nonsuits° my mediators. For, "Certes,"° says he,
    "I have already chose my officer."
    And what was he?
    Forsooth, a great arithmetician,°   20
    One Michael Cassio, a Florentine,
    A fellow almost damned in a fair wife,°
    That never set a squadron in the field
    Nor the division of a battle° knows
    More than a spinster°—unless the bookish theoric,°   25
    Wherein the togaed° consuls° can propose°
    As masterly as he. Mere prattle without practice
    Is all his soldiership. But he, sir, had th' election;
    And I, of whom his° eyes had seen the proof
    At Rhodes, at Cyprus, and on other grounds   30
    Christened° and heathen, must be beleed and calmed°
    By debitor and creditor.° This countercaster,°
    He, in good time,° must his lieutenant be,
    And I—God bless the mark!°—his Moorship's ancient.°
Roderigo: By heaven, I rather would have been his hangman.°   35
Iago: Why, there's no remedy. 'Tis the curse of service;
    Preferment° goes by letter and affection,°

---

4 *'Sblood* by His (Christ's) blood   11 *him* i.e., Othello   14 *bombast circumstance* wordy evasion. (Bombast is cotton padding.)   15 *epithets of war* military expressions   17 *Nonsuits* rejects the petition of. *Certes* certainly   20 *arithmetician* i.e., a man whose military knowledge is merely theoretical, based on books of tactics   22 *A . . . wife* (Cassio does not seem to be married, but his counterpart in Shakespeare's source does have a woman in his house. See also IV, i, 127.)   24 *division of a battle* disposition of a military unit 25 *a spinster* i.e., a housewife, one whose regular occupation is spinning. *theoric* theory   26 *togaed* wearing the toga. *consuls* counselors, senators. *propose* discuss   29 *his* i.e., Othello's   31 *Christened* Christian. *beleed and calmed* left to leeward without wind, becalmed. (A sailing metaphor.)   32 *debitor and creditor* (A name for a system of bookkeeping, here used as a contemptuous nickname for Cassio.) *countercaster* i.e., bookkeeper, one who tallies with *counters*, or "metal disks." (Said contemptuously.)   33 *in good time* opportunely, i.e., forsooth   34 *God bless the mark* (Perhaps originally a formula to ward off evil; here an expression of impatience.) *ancient* standard-bearer, ensign   35 *his hangman* his executioner   37 *Preferment* promotion. *letter and affection* personal influence and favoritism

And not by old gradation,° where each second
Stood heir to th' first. Now, sir, be judge yourself
Whether I in any just term° am affined°   40
To love the Moor.
Roderigo: I would not follow him then.
Iago: O sir, content you.°
I follow him to serve my turn upon him.
We cannot all be masters, nor all masters   45
Cannot be truly° followed. You shall mark
Many a duteous and knee-crooking knave
That, doting on his own obsequious bondage,
Wears out his time, much like his master's ass,
For naught but provender, and when he's old, cashiered.°   50
Whip me° such honest knaves. Others there are
Who, trimmed in forms and visages of duty,°
Keep yet their hearts attending on themselves,
And, throwing but shows of service on their lords,
Do well thrive by them, and when they have lined their coats,°   55
Do themselves homage.° These fellows have some soul,
And such a one do I profess myself. For, sir,
It is as sure as you are Roderigo,
Were I the Moor I would not be Iago.°
In following him, I follow but myself—   60
Heaven is my judge, not I for love and duty,
But seeming so for my peculiar° end.
For when my outward action doth demonstrate
The native° act and figure° of my heart
In compliment extern,° 'tis not long after   65
But I will wear my heart upon my sleeve
For daws° to peck at. I am not what I am.°
Roderigo: What a full° fortune does the thick-lips° owe°
If he can carry 't thus!°
Iago: Call up her father.
Rouse him, make after him, poison his delight,   70
Proclaim him in the streets; incense her kinsmen,
And, though he in a fertile climate dwell,
Plague him with flies.° Though that his joy be joy,°

---

38 *old gradation* step-by-step seniority, the traditional way   40 *term* respect.   *affined* bound   43 *content you* don't you worry about that   46 *truly* faithfully   50 *cashiered* dismissed from service   51 *Whip me* whip, as far as I'm concerned   52 *trimmed . . . duty* dressed up in the mere form and show of dutifulness   55 *lined their coats* i.e., stuffed their purses   56 *Do themselves homage* i.e., attend to self-interest solely   59 *Were . . . Iago* i.e., if I were able to assume command, I certainly would not choose to remain a subordinate, or, I would keep a suspicious eye on a flattering subordinate   62 *peculiar* particular, personal   64 *native* innate.   *figure* shape, intent   65 *compliment extern* outward show. (Conforming in this case to the inner workings and intention of the heart.)   67 *daws* small crowlike birds, proverbially stupid and avaricious.   *I am not what I am* i.e., I am not one who wears his heart on his sleeve   68 *full* swelling.   *thick-lips* (Elizabethans often applied the term "Moor" to blacks.)   *owe* own   69 *carry 't thus* carry this off   72–73 *though . . . flies* though he seems prosperous and happy now, vex him with misery   73 *Though . . . be joy* although he seems fortunate and happy. (Repeats the idea of line 72.)

Yet throw such changes of vexation° on 't
   As it may° lose some color.° 75
Roderigo: Here is her father's house. I'll call aloud.
Iago: Do, with like timorous° accent and dire yell
   As when, by night and negligence,° the fire
   Is spied in populous cities.
Roderigo: What ho, Brabantio! Signor Brabantio, ho! 80
Iago: Awake! What ho, Brabantio! Thieves, thieves, thieves!
   Look to your house, your daughter, and your bags!
   Thieves, thieves!

   Brabantio [enters] above [at a window].°

Brabantio: What is the reason of this terrible summons?
   What is the matter° there? 85
Roderigo: Signor, is all your family within?
Iago: Are your doors locked?
Brabantio: Why, wherefore ask you this?
Iago: Zounds,° sir, you're robbed. For shame, put on your gown!
   Your heart is burst; you have lost half your soul.
   Even now, now, very now, an old black ram 90
   Is tupping° your white ewe. Arise, arise!
   Awake the snorting° citizens with the bell,
   Or else the devil° will make a grandsire of you.
   Arise, I say!
Brabantio: What, have you lost your wits?
Roderigo: Most reverend signor, do you know my voice? 95
Brabantio: Not I. What are you?
Roderigo: My name is Roderigo.
Brabantio: The worser welcome.
   I have charged thee not to haunt about my doors.
   In honest plainness thou hast heard me say 100
   My daughter is not for thee; and now, in madness,
   Being full of supper and distempering° drafts,
   Upon malicious bravery° dost thou come
   To start° my quiet.
Roderigo: Sir, sir, sir—
Brabantio: But thou must needs be sure 105
   My spirits and my place° have in° their power
   To make this bitter to thee.
Roderigo: Patience, good sir.
Brabantio: What tell'st thou me of robbing? This is Venice;

---

74 *changes of vexation* vexing changes   75 *As it may* that may cause it to.   *some color* some of its fresh gloss
77 *timorous* frightening   78 *and negligence* i.e., by negligence   83 s.d. *at a window* (This stage direction,
from the Quarto, probably calls for an appearance on the gallery above and rearstage.)   85 *the matter* your
business   88 *Zounds* by His (Christ's) wounds   91 *tupping* covering, copulating with. (Said of sheep.)
92 *snorting* snoring   93 *the devil* (The devil was conventionally pictured as black.)   102 *distempering*
intoxicating   103 *Upon malicious bravery* with hostile intent to defy me   104 *start* startle, disrupt   106
My spirits and my place my temperament and my authority of office.   *have in* have it in

My house is not a grange.°

Roderigo: Most grave Brabantio,
In simple° and pure soul I come to you.   110

Iago: Zounds, sir, you are one of those that will not serve God if the devil bid you.
Because we come to do you service and you think we are ruffians, you'll have your
daughter covered with a Barbary° horse; you'll have your nephews° neigh to you;
you'll have coursers° for cousins° and jennets° for germans.°

Brabantio: What profane wretch art thou?   115

Iago: I am one, sir, that comes to tell you your daughter and the Moor are now
making the beast with two backs.

Brabantio: Thou art a villain.

Iago: You are—a senator.°

Brabantio: This thou shalt answer.° I know thee, Roderigo.

Roderigo: Sir, I will answer anything. But I beseech you,   120
If't be your pleasure and most wise° consent—
As partly I find it is—that your fair daughter,
At this odd-even° and dull watch o' the night,
Transported with° no worse nor better guard
But with a knave° of common hire, a gondolier,   125
To the gross clasps of a lascivious Moor—
If this be known to you and your allowance°
We then have done you bold and saucy° wrongs.
But if you know not this, my manners tell me
We have your wrong rebuke. Do not believe   130
That, from° the sense of all civility,°
I thus would play and trifle with your reverence.°
Your daughter, if you have not given her leave,
I say again, hath made a gross revolt,
Tying her duty, beauty, wit,° and fortunes   135
In an extravagant° and wheeling° stranger°
Of here and everywhere. Straight° satisfy yourself.
If she be in her chamber or your house,
Let loose on me the justice of the state
For thus deluding you.

Brabantio: Strike on the tinder,° ho!   140
Give me a taper! Call up all my people!
This accident° is not unlike my dream.
Belief of it oppresses me already.
Light, I say, light!   *Exit [above].*

---

109 *grange* isolated country house   110 *simple* sincere   113 *Barbary* from northern Africa (and hence
associated with Othello).   *nephews* i.e., grandsons   114 *coursers* powerful horses.   *cousins* kinsmen.
jennets small Spanish horses.   *germans* near relatives   118 *a senator* (Said with mock politeness, as though
the word itself were an insult.)   119 *answer* be held accountable for   121 *wise* well-informed   123 *odd-
even* between one day and the next, i.e., about midnight   124 *with* by   125 *But with a knave* than by a low
fellow, a servant   127 *allowance* permission   128 *saucy* insolent   131 *from* contrary to.   *civility* good
manners, decency   132 *your reverence* the respect due to you   135 *wit* intelligence   136 *extravagant*
expatriate, wandering far from home.   *wheeling* roving about, vagabond.   *stranger* foreigner   137 *Straight*
straightway   140 *tinder* charred linen ignited by a spark from flint and steel, used to light torches or *tapers*
(lines 141, 166)   142 *accident* occurrence, event

Roused from sleep, Desdemona's father, Brabantio, rushes to the street to search out his daughter (I, i, 160–180).

Iago:	Farewell, for I must leave you.	
	It seems not meet° nor wholesome to my place°	145
	To be produced°—as, if I stay, I shall—	
	Against the Moor. For I do know the state,	
	However this may gall° him with some check,°	
	Cannot with safety cast° him, for he's embarked°	
	With such loud reason° to the Cyprus wars,	150
	Which even now stands in act,° that, for their souls,°	
	Another of his fathom° they have none	

145 *meet* fitting. *place* position (as ensign) 146 *produced* produced (as a witness) 148 *gall* rub; oppress.
check rebuke 149 *cast* dismiss. *embarked* engaged 150 *loud reason* unanimous shout of confirmation (in
the Senate) 151 *stands in act* are going on. *for their souls* to save themselves 152 *fathom* i.e., ability,
depth of experience

To lead their business; in which regard,°
Though I do hate him as I do hell pains,
Yet for necessity of present life°   155
I must show out a flag and sign of love,
Which is indeed but sign. That you shall surely find him,
Lead to the Sagittary° the raisèd search,°
And there will I be with him. So farewell.

                                                                                     Exit.

    Enter [below] Brabantio [in his nightgown°] with servants and torches.

Brabantio: It is too true an evil. Gone she is;   160
   And what's to come of my despisèd time°
   Is naught but bitterness. Now, Roderigo,
   Where didst thou see her?—O unhappy girl!—
   With the Moor, sayst thou?—Who would be a father!—
   How didst thou know 'twas she?—O, she deceives me   165
   Past thought!—What said she to you?—Get more tapers.
   Raise all my kindred.—Are they married, think you?
Roderigo: Truly, I think they are.
Brabantio: O heaven! How got she out? O treason of the blood!
   Fathers, from hence trust not your daughters' minds   170
   By what you see them act. Is there not charms°
   By which the property° of youth and maidhood
   May be abused?° Have you not read, Roderigo,
   Of some such thing?
Roderigo: Yes, sir, I have indeed.
Brabantio: Call up my brother.—O, would you had had her!—   175
   Some one way, some another.—Do you know
   Where we may apprehend her and the Moor?
Roderigo: I think I can discover° him, if you please
   To get good guard and go along with me.
Brabantio: Pray you, lead on. At every house I'll call;   180
   I may command° at most.—Get weapons, ho!
   And raise some special officers of night.—
   On, good Roderigo. I will deserve° your pains.

    Exeunt.

SCENE II [VENICE. ANOTHER STREET, BEFORE OTHELLO'S LODGINGS.]

    Enter Othello, Iago, attendants with torches.

Iago: Though in the trade of war I have slain men,
   Yet do I hold it very stuff° o' the conscience

---

153 *in which regard* out of regard for which   155 *life* livelihood   158 *Sagittary* (An inn or house where Othello and Desdemona are staying, named for its sign of Sagittarius, or Centaur.)   *raisèd search* search party roused out of sleep   159 s.d. *nightgown* dressing gown. (This costuming is specified in the Quarto text.)   161 *time* i.e., remainder of life   171 *charms* spells   172 *property* special quality, nature   173 *abused* deceived   178 *discover* reveal, uncover   181 *command* demand assistance   183 *deserve* show gratitude for   2 *very stuff* essence, basic material (continuing the metaphor of *trade* from line 1)

To do no contrived° murder. I lack iniquity
Sometimes to do me service. Nine or ten times
I had thought t' have yerked° him° here under the ribs. 5
Othello: 'Tis better as it is.
Iago: Nay, but he prated,
And spoke such scurvy and provoking terms
Against your honor
That, with the little godliness I have,
I did full hard forbear him.° But, I pray you, sir, 10
Are you fast married? Be assured of this,
That the magnifico° is much beloved,
And hath in his effect° a voice potential°
As double as the Duke's. He will divorce you,
Or put upon you what restraint or grievance 15
The law, with all his might to enforce it on,
Will give him cable.°
Othello: Let him do his spite.
My services which I have done the seigniory°
Shall out-tongue his complaints. 'Tis yet to know°—
Which, when I know that boasting is an honor, 20
I shall promulgate—I fetch my life and being
From men of royal siege,° and my demerits°
May speak unbonneted° to as proud a fortune
As this that I have reached. For know, Iago,
But that I love the gentle Desdemona, 25
I would not my unhousèd° free condition
Put into circumscription and confine°
For the sea's worth.° But look, what lights come yond?

Enter Cassio [and certain officers°] with torches.

Iago: Those are the raisèd father and his friends.
You were best go in.
Othello: Not I. I must be found. 30
My parts, my title, and my perfect soul°
Shall manifest me rightly. Is it they?
Iago: By Janus,° I think no.
Othello: The servants of the Duke? And my lieutenant?
The goodness of the night upon you, friends! 35
What is the news?

---

3 *contrived* premeditated 5 *yerked* stabbed. *him* i.e., Roderigo 10 *I . . . him* I restrained myself with great difficulty from assaulting him 12 *magnifico* Venetian grandee, i.e., Brabantio 13 *in his effect* at his command. *potential* powerful 17 *cable* i.e., scope 18 *seigniory* Venetian government 19 *yet to know* not yet widely known 22 *siege* i.e., rank. (Literally, a seat used by a person of distinction.) *demerits* deserts 23 *unbonneted* without removing the hat, i.e., on equal terms (?) (Or "with hat off," "in all due modesty.") 26 *unhousèd* unconfined, undomesticated 27 *circumscription and confine* restriction and confinement 28 *the sea's worth* all the riches at the bottom of the sea. s.d. *officers* (The Quarto text calls for "Cassio with lights, officers with torches.") 31 *My . . . soul* my natural gifts, my position or reputation, and my unflawed conscience 33 *Janus* Roman two-faced god of beginnings

Cassio: The Duke does greet you, General,
    And he requires your haste-post-haste appearance
    Even on the instant.
Othello: What is the matter,° think you?
Cassio: Something from Cyprus, as I may divine.°
    It is a business of some heat.° The galleys   40
    Have sent a dozen sequent° messengers
    This very night at one another's heels,
    And many of the consuls,° raised and met,
    Are at the Duke's already. You have been hotly called for;
    When, being not at your lodging to be found,   45
    The Senate hath sent about° three several° quests
    To search you out.
Othello: 'Tis well I am found by you.
    I will but spend a word here in the house
    And go with you.
                                                     [Exit.]
Cassio: Ancient, what makes° he here?
Iago: Faith, he tonight hath boarded° a land carrack.°   50
    If it prove lawful prize,° he's made forever.
Cassio: I do not understand.
Iago: He's married.
Cassio: To who?

    [Enter Othello.]

Iago: Marry,° to—Come, Captain, will you go?
Othello: Have with you.°
Cassio: Here comes another troop to seek for you.   55

    Enter Brabantio, Roderigo, with officers and torches. °

Iago: It is Brabantio. General, be advised.°
    He comes to bad intent.
Othello: Holla! Stand there!
Roderigo: Signor, it is the Moor.
Brabantio: Down with him, thief!

    [They draw on both sides.]

Iago: You, Roderigo! Come, sir, I am for you.
Othello: Keep up° your bright swords, for the dew will rust them.   60
    Good signor, you shall more command with years
    Than with your weapons.

---

38 *matter* business   39 *divine* guess   40 *heat* urgency   41 *sequent* successive   43 *consuls* senators
46 *about* all over the city.   *several* separate   49 *makes* does   50 *boarded* gone aboard and seized as an act
of piracy (with sexual suggestion).   *carrack* large merchant ship   51 *prize* booty   53 *Marry* (An oath,
originally "by the Virgin Mary"; here used with wordplay on *married*.)   54 *Have with you* i.e., let's go
55 s.d. *officers and torches* (The Quarto text calls for "others with lights and weapons.")   56 *be advised* be
on your guard   60 *Keep up* keep in the sheath

Brabantio: O thou foul thief, where hast thou stowed my daughter?
    Damned as thou art, thou hast enchanted her!
    For I'll refer me° to all things of sense,°   65
    If she in chains of magic were not bound
    Whether a maid so tender, fair, and happy,
    So opposite to marriage that she shunned
    The wealthy curlèd darlings of our nation,
    Would ever have, t' incur a general mock,   70
    Run from her guardage° to the sooty bosom
    Of such a thing as thou—to fear, not to delight.
    Judge me the world if 'tis not gross in sense°
    That thou hast practiced on her with foul charms,
    Abused her delicate youth with drugs or minerals°   75
    That weaken motion.° I'll have 't disputed on;°
    'Tis probable and palpable to thinking.
    I therefore apprehend and do attach° thee
    For an abuser of the world, a practicer
    Of arts inhibited° and out of warrant.°—   80
    Lay hold upon him! If he do resist,
    Subdue him at his peril.
Othello: Hold your hands,
    Both you of my inclining° and the rest.
    Were it my cue to fight, I should have known it
    Without a prompter.—Whither will you that I go   85
    To answer this your charge?
Brabantio: To prison, till fit time
    Of law and course of direct session°
    Call thee to answer.
Othello: What if I do obey?
    How may the Duke be therewith satisfied,   90
    Whose messengers are here about my side
    Upon some present business of the state
    To bring me to him?
Officer: 'Tis true, most worthy signor.
    The Duke's in council, and your noble self,
    I am sure, is sent for.
Brabantio: How? The Duke in council?   95
    In this time of the night? Bring him away.°
    Mine's not an idle° cause. The Duke himself,
    Or any of my brothers of the state,
    Cannot but feel this wrong as 'twere their own;

---

65 *refer me* submit my case. *things of sense* commonsense understandings, or, creatures possessing common sense   71 *her guardage* my guardianship of her   73 *gross in sense* obvious   75 *minerals* i.e., poisons 76 *weaken motion* impair the vital faculties.   *disputed on* argued in court by professional counsel, debated by experts   78 *attach* arrest   80 *arts inhibited* prohibited arts, black magic.   *out of warrant* illegal   83 *inclining* following, party   88 *course of direct session* regular or specially convened legal proceedings   96 *away* right along   97 *idle* trifling

For if such actions may have passage free,°   100
Bondslaves and pagans shall our statesmen be.

Exeunt.

SCENE III [VENICE. A COUNCIL CHAMBER.]

Enter Duke [and] Senators [and sit at a table, with lights], and Officers.° [The Duke
and Senators are reading dispatches.]

Duke: There is no composition° in these news
   That gives them credit.
First Senator: Indeed, they are disproportioned.°
   My letters say a hundred and seven galleys.
Duke: And mine, a hundred forty.
Second Senator: And mine, two hundred.   5
   But though they jump° not on a just° account—
   As in these cases, where the aim° reports
   'Tis oft with difference—yet do they all confirm
   A Turkish fleet, and bearing up to Cyprus.
Duke: Nay, it is possible enough to judgment.   10
   I do not so secure me in the error
   But the main article I do approve°
   In fearful sense.
Sailor (within):   What ho, what ho, what ho!

   Enter Sailor.

Officer: A messenger from the galleys.
Duke: Now, what's the business?   15
Sailor: The Turkish preparation° makes for Rhodes.
   So was I bid report here to the state
   By Signor Angelo.
Duke: How say you by° this change?
First Senator: This cannot be
   By no assay° of reason. 'Tis a pageant°   20
   To keep us in false gaze.° When we consider
   Th' importancy of Cyprus to the Turk,
   And let ourselves again but understand
   That, as it more concerns the Turk than Rhodes,
   So may he with more facile question bear it,°   25
   For that° it stands not in such warlike brace,°
   But altogether lacks th' abilities°

---

100 *have passage free* are allowed to go unchecked   s.d. *Enter . . . Officers* (The Quarto text calls for the
Duke and senators to "sit at a table with lights and attendants.")   1 *composition* consistency   3 *disproportioned*
inconsistent   6 *jump* agree.   *just* exact   7 *the aim* conjecture   11–12 *I do not . . . approve* I do not take
such (false) comfort in the discrepancies that I fail to perceive the main point, i.e., that the Turkish fleet is
threatening   16 *preparation* fleet prepared for battle   19 *by* about   20 *assay* test.   *pageant* mere show
21 *in false gaze* looking the wrong way   25 *So may . . . it* so also he (the Turk) can more easily capture it
(Cyprus)   26 *For that* since.   *brace* state of defense   27 *abilities* means of self-defense

That Rhodes is dressed in°—if we make thought of this,
We must not think the Turk is so unskillful°
To leave that latest° which concerns him first,   30
Neglecting an attempt of ease and gain
To wake° and wage° a danger profitless.
Duke: Nay, in all confidence, he's not for Rhodes.
Officer: Here is more news.

   Enter a Messenger.

Messenger: The Ottomites, reverend and gracious,   35
   Steering with due course toward the isle of Rhodes,
   Have there injointed them° with an after° fleet.
First Senator: Ay, so I thought. How many, as you guess?
Messenger: Of thirty sail; and now they do restem
   Their backward course,° bearing with frank appearance°   40
   Their purposes toward Cyprus. Signor Montano,
   Your trusty and most valiant servitor,°
   With his free duty° recommends° you thus,
   And prays you to believe him.
Duke: 'Tis certain then for Cyprus.   45
   Marcus Luccicos, is not he in town?
First Senator: He's now in Florence.
Duke: Write from us to him, post-post-haste. Dispatch.
First Senator: Here comes Brabantio and the valiant Moor.

   Enter Brabantio, Othello, Cassio, Iago, Roderigo, and officers.

Duke: Valiant Othello, we must straight° employ you   50
   Against the general enemy° Ottoman.
   [*To Brabantio.*] I did not see you; welcome, gentle° signor.
   We lacked your counsel and your help tonight.
Brabantio: So did I yours. Good Your Grace, pardon me;
   Neither my place° nor aught I heard of business   55
   Hath raised me from my bed, nor doth the general care
   Take hold on me, for my particular° grief
   Is of so floodgate° and o'erbearing nature
   That it engluts° and swallows other sorrows
   And it is still itself.°   60
Duke: Why, what's the matter?
Brabantio: My daughter! O, my daughter!
Duke and Senators: Dead?
Brabantio: Ay, to me.
   She is abused,° stol'n from me, and corrupted

---

28 *dressed in* equipped with   29 *unskillful* deficient in judgment   30 *latest* last   32 *wake* stir up. *wage* risk   37 *injointed them* joined themselves. *after* second, following   39–40 *restem . . . course* retrace their original course   40 *frank appearance* undisguised intent   42 *servitor* officer under your command   43 *free duty* freely given and loyal service. *recommends* commends himself and reports to   50 *straight* straightway   51 *general enemy* universal enemy to all Christendom   52 *gentle* noble   55 *place* official position   57 *particular* personal   58 *floodgate* i.e., overwhelming (as when floodgates are opened)   59 *engluts* engulfs   60 *is still itself* remains undiminished   62 *abused* deceived

Othello answers Brabantio's charges before the Duke (I, iii, 78–172).

By spells and medicines bought of mountebanks;
For nature so preposterously to err,
Being not deficient,° blind, or lame of sense,°   65
Sans° witchcraft could not.
Duke: Whoe'er he be that in this foul proceeding
Hath thus beguiled your daughter of herself,
And you of her, the bloody book of law
You shall yourself read in the bitter letter   70
After your own sense°—yea, though our proper° son
Stood in your action.°
Brabantio: Humbly I thank Your Grace.
Here is the man, this Moor, whom now it seems
Your special mandate for the state affairs
Hath hither brought.
All: We are very sorry for 't.   75
Duke [to Othello]: What, in your own part, can you say to this?
Brabantio: Nothing, but this is so.
Othello: Most potent, grave, and reverend signors,
My very noble and approved° good masters:
That I have ta'en away this old man's daughter,   80

---

65 *deficient* defective. *lame of sense* deficient in sensory perception 66 *Sans* without 71 *After . . . sense*
according to your own interpretation. *our proper* my own 72 *Stood . . . action* were under your accusation 79 *approved* proved, esteemed

It is most true; true, I have married her.
The very head and front° of my offending
Hath this extent, no more. Rude° am I in my speech,
And little blessed with the soft phrase of peace;
For since these arms of mine had seven years' pith,°   85
Till now some nine moons wasted,° they have used
Their dearest° action in the tented field;
And little of this great world can I speak
More than pertains to feats of broils and battle,
And therefore little shall I grace my cause   90
In speaking for myself. Yet, by your gracious patience,
I will a round° unvarnished tale deliver
Of my whole course of love—what drugs, what charms,
What conjuration, and what mighty magic,
For such proceeding I am charged withal,°   95
I won his daughter.
Brabantio: A maiden never bold;
Of spirit so still and quiet that her motion
Blushed at herself;° and she, in spite of nature,
Of years,° of country, credit,° everything,
To fall in love with what she feared to look on!   100
It is a judgment maimed and most imperfect
That will confess° perfection so could err
Against all rules of nature, and must be driven
To find out practices° of cunning hell
Why this should be. I therefore vouch° again   105
That with some mixtures powerful o'er the blood,°
Or with some dram conjured to this effect,°
He wrought upon her.
Duke: To vouch this is no proof,
Without more wider° and more overt test°
Than these thin habits° and poor likelihoods°   110
Of modern seeming° do prefer° against him.
First Senator: But Othello, speak.
Did you by indirect and forcèd courses°
Subdue and poison this young maid's affections?
Or came it by request and such fair question°   115
As soul to soul affordeth?
Othello: I do beseech you,
Send for the lady to the Sagittary

---

82 *head and front* height and breadth, entire extent   83 *Rude* unpolished   85 *since . . . pith* i.e., since I was seven. *pith* strength, vigor   86 *Till . . . wasted* until some nine months ago (since when Othello has evidently not been on active duty, but in Venice)   87 *dearest* most valuable   92 *round* plain   95 *withal* with   97–98 *her . . . herself* i.e., she blushed easily at herself. (*Motion* can suggest the impulse of the soul or of the emotions, or physical movement.)   99 *years* i.e., difference in age.   *credit* virtuous reputation   102 *confess* concede (that)   104 *practices* plots   105 *vouch* assert   106 *blood* passions   107 *dram . . . effect* dose made by magical spells to have this effect   109 *more wider* fuller.   *test* testimony   110 *habits* garments, i.e., appearances.   *poor likelihoods* weak inferences   111 *modern seeming* commonplace assumption.   *prefer* bring forth   113 *forcèd courses* means used against her will   115 *question* conversation

And let her speak of me before her father.
If you do find me foul in her report,
The trust, the office I do hold of you   120
Not only take away, but let your sentence
Even fall upon my life.
Duke: Fetch Desdemona hither.
Othello: Ancient, conduct them. You best know the place.

[*Exeunt Iago and attendants.*]

And, till she come, as truly as to heaven
I do confess the vices of my blood,°   125
So justly° to your grave ears I'll present
How I did thrive in this fair lady's love,
And she in mine.
Duke: Say it, Othello.
Othello: Her father loved me, oft invited me,   130
Still° questioned me the story of my life
From year to year—the battles, sieges, fortunes
That I have passed.
I ran it through, even from my boyish days
To th' very moment that he bade me tell it,   135
Wherein I spoke of most disastrous chances,
Of moving accidents° by flood and field,
Of hairbreadth scapes i' th' imminent deadly breach,°
Of being taken by the insolent foe
And sold to slavery, of my redemption thence,   140
And portance° in my travels' history,
Wherein of antres° vast and deserts idle,°
Rough quarries,° rocks, and hills whose heads touch heaven,
It was my hint° to speak—such was my process—
And of the Cannibals that each other eat,   145
The Anthropophagi,° and men whose heads
Do grow beneath their shoulders. These things to hear
Would Desdemona seriously incline;
But still the house affairs would draw her thence,
Which ever as she could with haste dispatch   150
She'd come again, and with a greedy ear
Devour up my discourse. Which I, observing,
Took once a pliant° hour, and found good means
To draw from her a prayer of earnest heart
That I would all my pilgrimage dilate,°   155
Whereof by parcels° she had something heard,

---

125 *blood* passions, human nature   126 *justly* truthfully, accurately   131 *Still* continually   137 *moving accident* stirring happenings   138 *imminent . . . breach* death-threatening gaps made in a fortification   141 *portance* conduct   142 *antres* caverns.   *idle* barren, desolate   143 *Rough quarries* rugged rock formations   144 *hint* occasion, opportunity   146 *Anthropophagi* man-eaters. (A term from Pliny's *Natural History*.)   153 *pliant* well-suiting   155 *dilate* relate in detail   156 *by parcels* piecemeal

But not intentively.° I did consent,
And often did beguile her of her tears,
When I did speak of some distressful stroke
That my youth suffered. My story being done,   160
She gave me for my pains a world of sighs.
She swore, in faith, 'twas strange, 'twas passing° strange,
'Twas pitiful, 'twas wondrous pitiful.
She wished she had not heard it, yet she wished
That heaven had made her° such a man. She thanked me, 165
And bade me, if I had a friend that loved her,
I should but teach him how to tell my story,
And that would woo her. Upon this hint° I spake.
She loved me for the dangers I had passed,
And I loved her that she did pity them.   170
This only is the witchcraft I have used.
Here comes the lady. Let her witness it.

Enter Desdemona, Iago, [and] attendants.

Duke: I think this tale would win my daughter too.
    Good Brabantio,
    Take up this mangled matter at the best.°   175
    Men do their broken weapons rather use
    Than their bare hands.
Brabantio: I pray you, hear her speak.
    If she confess that she was half the wooer,
    Destruction on my head if my bad blame
    Light on the man!—Come hither, gentle mistress.   180
    Do you perceive in all this noble company
    Where most you owe obedience?
Desdemona: My noble Father,
    I do perceive here a divided duty.
    To you I am bound for life and education;°
    My life and education both do learn° me   185
    How to respect you. You are the lord of duty;°
    I am hitherto your daughter. But here's my husband,
    And so much duty as my mother showed
    To you, preferring you before her father,
    So much I challenge° that I may profess   190
    Due to the Moor my lord.
Brabantio: God be with you! I have done.
    Please it Your Grace, on to the state affairs.
    I had rather to adopt a child than get° it.
    Come hither, Moor.   [*He joins the hands of Othello and Desdemona.*] 195

---

157 *intentively* with full attention, continuously   162 *passing* exceedingly   165 *made her* created her to be
168 *hint* opportunity. (Othello does not mean that she was dropping hints.)   175 *Take . . . best* make the
best of a bad bargain   184 *education* upbringing   185 *learn* teach   186 *of duty* to whom duty is due   190
challenge claim   194 *get* beget

     I here do give thee that with all my heart°
     Which, but thou hast already, with all my heart°
     I would keep from thee.—For your sake,° jewel,
     I am glad at soul I have no other child,
     For thy escape° would teach me tyranny,   200
     To hang clogs° on them.—I have done, my lord.
Duke: Let me speak like yourself,° and lay a sentence°
     Which, as a grece° or step, may help these lovers
     Into your favor.
     When remedies° are past, the griefs are ended   205
     By seeing the worst, which late on hopes depended.°
     To mourn a mischief° that is past and gone
     Is the next° way to draw new mischief on.
     What° cannot be preserved when fortune takes,
     Patience her injury a mockery makes.°   210
     The robbed that smiles steals something from the thief;
     He robs himself that spends a bootless grief.°
Brabantio: So let the Turk of Cyprus us beguile,
     We lose it not, so long as we can smile.
     He bears the sentence well that nothing bears   215
     But the free comfort which from thence he hears,
     But he bears both the sentence and the sorrow
     That, to pay grief, must of poor patience borrow.°
     These sentences, to sugar or to gall,
     Being strong on both sides, are equivocal.°   220
     But words are words. I never yet did hear
     That the bruisèd heart was piercèd through the ear.°
     I humbly beseech you, proceed to th' affairs of state.
Duke: The Turk with a most mighty preparation makes for Cyprus. Othello, the
     fortitude° of the place is best known to you; and though we have there a 225
     substitute° of most allowed° sufficiency, yet opinion, a sovereign mistress
     of effects, throws a more safer voice on you.° You must therefore be content
     to slubber° the gloss of your new fortunes with this more stubborn° and boister-
     ous expedition.
Othello: The tyrant custom, most grave senators,   230
     Hath made the flinty and steel couch of war

---

196 *with all my heart* wherein my whole affection has been engaged   197 *with all my heart* willingly, gladly
198 *For your sake* on your account   200 *escape* elopement   201 *clogs* (Literally, blocks of wood fastened to
the legs of criminals or convicts to inhibit escape.)   202 *like yourself* i.e., as you would, in your proper temper.
lay a sentence apply a maxim   203 *grece* step   205 *remedies* hopes of remedy   206 *which . . . depended*
which griefs were sustained until recently by hopeful anticipation   207 *mischief* misfortune, injury   208
next nearest   209 *What* whatever   210 *Patience . . . makes* patience laughs at the injury inflicted by fortune (and thus eases the pain)   212 *spends a bootless grief* indulges in unavailing grief   215–218 *He bears . . .
borrow* a person well bears out your maxim who can enjoy its platitudinous comfort, free of all genuine
sorrow, but anyone whose grief bankrupts his poor patience is left with your saying and his sorrow, too.
(*Bears the sentence* also plays on the meaning, "receives judicial sentence.")   219–220 *These . . . equivocal*
these fine maxims are equivocal, either sweet or bitter in their application   222 *piercèd . . . ear* i.e., surgi-
cally lanced and cured by mere words of advice   225 *fortitude* strength   226 *substitute* deputy. *allowed*
acknowledged   226–227 *opinion . . . on you* general opinion, an important determiner of affairs, chooses
you as the best man   228 *slubber* soil, sully. *stubborn* harsh, rough

My thrice-driven° bed of down. I do agnize°
A natural and prompt alacrity
I find in hardness,° and do undertake
These present wars against the Ottomites.   235
Most humbly therefore bending to your state,°
I crave fit disposition for my wife,
Due reference of place and exhibition,°
With such accommodation° and besort°
As levels° with her breeding.°   240
Duke: Why, at her father's.
Brabantio: I will not have it so.
Othello: Nor I.
Desdemona: Nor I. I would not there reside,
To put my father in impatient thoughts
By being in his eye. Most gracious Duke,
To my unfolding° lend your prosperous° ear,   245
And let me find a charter° in your voice,
T' assist my simpleness.
Duke: What would you, Desdemona?
Desdemona: That I did love the Moor to live with him,
My downright violence and storm of fortunes°   250
May trumpet to the world. My heart's subdued
Even to the very quality of my lord.°
I saw Othello's visage in his mind,
And to his honors and his valiant parts°
Did I my soul and fortunes consecrate.   255
So that, dear lords, if I be left behind
A moth° of peace, and he go to the war,
The rites° for why I love him are bereft me,
And I a heavy interim shall support
By his dear° absence. Let me go with him.   260
Othello: Let her have your voice.°
Vouch with me, heaven, I therefore beg it not
To please the palate of my appetite,
Nor to comply with heat°—the young affects°
In me defunct—and proper° satisfaction,   265
But to be free° and bounteous to her mind.
And heaven defend° your good souls that you think°

---

232 *thrice-driven* thrice sifted, winnowed. *agnize* know in myself, acknowledge   234 *hardness* hardship
236 *bending . . . state* bowing or kneeling to your authority   238 *reference . . . exhibition* provision of appropriate place to live and allowance of money   239 *accommodation* suitable provision. *besort* attendance   240 *levels* equals, suits. *breeding* social position, upbringing   245 *unfolding* explanation, proposal.
prosperous propitious   246 *charter* privilege, authorization   250 *My . . . fortunes* my plain and total
breach of social custom, taking my future by storm and disrupting my whole life   251–252 *My heart's . . .
lord* my heart is brought wholly into accord with Othello's virtues; I love him for his virtues   254 *parts*
qualities   257 *moth* i.e., one who consumes merely   258 *rites* rites of love (with a suggestion, too, of
"rights," sharing)   260 *dear* (1) heartfelt (2) costly   261 *voice* consent   264 *heat* sexual passion. *young
affects* passions of youth, desires   265 *proper* personal   266 *free* generous   267 *defend* forbid. *think*
should think

Desdemona declares her loyalty to her husband Othello (I, iii, 182–301).

I will your serious and great business scant
When she is with me. No, when light-winged toys
Of feathered Cupid seel° with wanton dullness   270
My speculative and officed instruments,°
That° my disports° corrupt and taint° my business,
Let huswives make a skillet of my helm,
And all indign° and base adversities
Make head° against my estimation!°   275

Duke: Be it as you shall privately determine,
Either for her stay or going. Th' affair cries haste,
And speed must answer it.

A Senator: You must away tonight.

Desdemona: Tonight, my lord?

Duke: This night.

Othello: With all my heart.

270 *seel* i.e., make blind (as in falconry, by sewing up the eyes of the hawk during training) 271 *speculative . . . instruments* eyes and other faculties used in the performance of duty 272 *That* so that. *disports* sexual pastimes. *taint* impair 274 *indign* unworthy, shameful 275 *Make head* raise an army. *estimation* reputation

Duke: At nine i' the morning here we'll meet again.   280
    Othello, leave some officer behind,
    And he shall our commission bring to you,
    With such things else of quality and respect°
    As doth import° you.
Othello: So please Your Grace, my ancient;
    A man he is of honesty and trust.   285
    To his conveyance I assign my wife,
    With what else needful Your Good Grace shall think
    To be sent after me.
Duke: Let it be so.
    Good night to everyone. [*To Brabantio.*] And, noble signor,
    If virtue no delighted° beauty lack,   290
    Your son-in-law is far more fair than black.
First Senator: Adieu, brave Moor. Use Desdemona well.
Brabantio: Look to her, Moor, if thou hast eyes to see.
    She has deceived her father, and may thee.

> *Exeunt* [*Duke, Brabantio, Cassio, Senators, and officers*].

Othello: My life upon her faith! Honest Iago,   295
    My Desdemona must I leave to thee.
    I prithee, let thy wife attend on her,
    And bring them after in the best advantage.°
    Come, Desdemona. I have but an hour
    Of love, of worldly matters and direction,°   300
    To spend with thee. We must obey the time.°

> *Exit* [*with Desdemona*].

Roderigo: Iago—
Iago: What sayst thou, noble heart?
Roderigo: What will I do, think'st thou?
Iago: Why, go to bed and sleep.   305
Roderigo: I will incontinently° drown myself.
Iago: If thou dost, I shall never love thee after. Why, thou silly gentleman?
Roderigo: It is silliness to live when to live is torment; and then have we a prescrip-
    tion° to die when death is our physician.
Iago: O villainous!° I have looked upon the world for four times seven years, and,   310
    since I could distinguish betwixt a benefit and an injury, I never found man that
    knew how to love himself. Ere I would say I would drown myself for the love of a
    guinea hen,° I would change my humanity with a baboon.
Roderigo: What should I do? I confess it is my shame to be so fond,° but it is not
    in my virtue° to amend it.   315

---

283 *of quality and respect* of importance and relevance   284 *import* concern   290 *delighted* capable of delighting   298 *in . . . advantage* at the most favorable opportunity   300 *direction* instructions   301 *the time* the urgency of the present crisis   306 *incontinently* immediately, without self-restraint   308–309 *prescription* (1) right based on long-established custom (2) doctor's prescription   310 *villainous* i.e., what perfect nonsense   313 *guinea hen* (A slang term for a prostitute.)   314 *fond* infatuated   315 *virtue* strength, nature

Iago: Virtue? A fig!° 'Tis in ourselves that we are thus or thus. Our bodies are our gardens, to the which our wills are gardeners; so that if we will plant nettles or sow lettuce, set hyssop° and weed up thyme, supply it with one gender° of herbs or distract it with° many, either to have it sterile with idleness° or manured with industry—why, the power and corrigible authority° of this lies in our wills. If the 320
beam° of our lives had not one scale of reason to poise° another of sensuality, the blood° and baseness of our natures would conduct us to most preposterous conclusions. But we have reason to cool our raging motions,° our carnal stings, our unbitted° lusts, whereof I take this that you call love to be a sect or scion.°

Roderigo: It cannot be. 325

Iago: It is merely a lust of the blood and a permission of the will. Come, be a man. Drown thyself? Drown cats and blind puppies. I have professed me thy friend, and I confess me knit to thy deserving with cables of perdurable° toughness. I could never better stead° thee than now. Put money in thy purse. Follow thou the wars; defeat thy favor° with an usurped° beard. I say, put money in thy purse. 330
It cannot be long that Desdemona should continue her love to the Moor—put money in thy purse—nor he his to her. It was a violent commencement in her, and thou shalt see an answerable sequestration° —put but money in thy purse. These Moors are changeable in their wills°—fill thy purse with money. The food that to him now is as luscious as locusts° shall be to him shortly as bitter as 335
coloquintida.° She must change for youth; when she is sated with his body, she will find the error of her choice. She must have change, she must. Therefore put money in thy purse. If thou wilt needs damn thyself, do it a more delicate way than drowning. Make° all the money thou canst. If sanctimony° and a frail vow betwixt an erring° barbarian and a supersubtle Venetian be not too hard for my 340
wits and all the tribe of hell, thou shalt enjoy her. Therefore make money. A pox of drowning thyself! It is clean out of the way.° Seek thou rather to be hanged in compassing° thy joy than to be drowned and go without her.

Roderigo: Wilt thou be fast° to my hopes if I depend on the issue?°

Iago: Thou art sure of me. Go, make money. I have told thee often, and I retell thee 345
again and again, I hate the Moor. My cause is hearted;° thine hath no less reason. Let us be conjunctive° in our revenge against him. If thou canst cuckold him, thou dost thyself a pleasure, me a sport. There are many events in the womb of time which will be delivered. Traverse,° go, provide thy money. We will have more of this tomorrow. Adieu. 350

Roderigo: Where shall we meet i' the morning?

Iago: At my lodging.

---

316 *fig* (To give a fig is to thrust the thumb between the first and second fingers in a vulgar and insulting gesture.) 318 *hyssop* an herb of the mint family. *gender* kind 319 *distract it with* divide it among. *idleness* want of cultivation 320 *corrigible authority* power to correct 321 *beam* balance. *poise* counterbalance 322 *blood* natural passions 323 *motions* appetites 324 *unbitted* unbridled, uncontrolled. *sect or scion* cutting or offshoot 328 *perdurable* very durable 329 *stead* assist 330 *defeat thy favor* disguise your face. *usurped* (The suggestion is that Roderigo is not man enough to have a beard of his own.) 333 *an answerable sequestration* a corresponding separation or estrangement 334 *wills* carnal appetites 335 *locusts* fruit of the carob tree (see Matthew 3:4), or perhaps honeysuckle. 336 *coloquintida* colocynth or bitter apple, a purgative 339 *Make* raise, collect. *sanctimony* sacred ceremony 340 *erring* wandering, vagabond, unsteady 342 *clean . . . way* entirely unsuitable as a course of action 343 *compassing* encompassing, embracing 344 *fast* true. *issue* (successful) outcome 346 *hearted* fixed in the heart, heartfelt 347 *conjunctive* united 349 *Traverse* (A military marching term.)

Roderigo: I'll be with thee betimes.°   [*He starts to leave.*]
Iago: Go to, farewell.—Do you hear, Roderigo?
Roderigo: What say you?   355
Iago: No more of drowning, do you hear?
Roderigo: I am changed.
Iago: Go to, farewell. Put money enough in your purse.
Roderigo: I'll sell all my land.   *Exit.*
Iago: Thus do I ever make my fool my purse;   360
    For I mine own gained knowledge should profane
    If I would time expend with such a snipe°
    But for my sport and profit. I hate the Moor;
    And it is thought abroad° that twixt my sheets
    He's done my office.° I know not if 't be true;   365
    But I, for mere suspicion in that kind,
    Will do as if for surety.° He holds me well;°
    The better shall my purpose work on him.
    Cassio's a proper° man. Let me see now:
    To get his place and to plume up° my will   370
    In double knavery—How, how?—Let's see:
    After some time, to abuse° Othello's ear
    That he° is too familiar with his wife.
    He hath a person and a smooth dispose°
    To be suspected, framed to make women false.   375
    The Moor is of a free° and open° nature,
    That thinks men honest that but seem to be so,
    And will as tenderly° be led by the nose
    As asses are.
    I have 't. It is engendered. Hell and night   380
    Must bring this monstrous birth to the world's light.

    [*Exit.*]

ACT II

SCENE I [A SEAPORT IN CYPRUS. AN OPEN PLACE NEAR THE QUAY.]

    Enter Montano and two Gentlemen.

Montano: What from the cape can you discern at sea?
First Gentleman: Nothing at all. It is a high-wrought flood.°
    I cannot, twixt the heaven and the main,°
    Descry a sail.
Montano: Methinks the wind hath spoke aloud at land;   5
    A fuller blast ne'er shook our battlements.

---

353 *betimes* early   362 *snipe* woodcock, i.e., fool   364 *it is thought abroad* it is rumored   365 *my office* i.e., my
sexual function as husband   367 *do . . . surety* act as if on certain knowledge.   *holds me well* regards me favorably
369 *proper* handsome   370 *plume up* put a feather in the cap of, i.e., glorify, gratify   372 *abuse* deceive   373 *he*
i.e., Cassio   374 *dispose* disposition   376 *free* frank, generous. *open* unsuspicious   378 *tenderly* readily   2
high-wrought flood very agitated sea   3 *main* ocean (also at line 41)

If it hath ruffianed° so upon the sea,
What ribs of oak, when mountains° melt on them,
Can hold the mortise?° What shall we hear of this?
Second Gentleman: A segregation° of the Turkish fleet.   10
For do but stand upon the foaming shore,
The chidden° billow seems to pelt the clouds;
The wind-shaked surge, with high and monstrous mane,°
Seems to cast water on the burning Bear°
And quench the guards of th' ever-fixèd pole.   15
I never did like molestation° view
On the enchafèd° flood.
Montano: If that° the Turkish fleet
Be not ensheltered and embayed,° they are drowned;
It is impossible to bear it out.°   20

Enter a [Third] Gentleman.

Third Gentleman: News, lads! Our wars are done.
The desperate tempest hath so banged the Turks
That their designment° halts.° A noble ship of Venice
Hath seen a grievous wreck° and sufferance°
On most part of their fleet.   25
Montano: How? Is this true?
Third Gentleman: The ship is here put in,
A Veronesa;° Michael Cassio,
Lieutenant to the warlike Moor Othello,
Is come on shore; the Moor himself at sea,   30
And is in full commission here for Cyprus.
Montano: I am glad on 't. 'Tis a worthy governor.
Third Gentleman: But this same Cassio, though he speak of comfort
Touching the Turkish loss, yet he looks sadly°
And prays the Moor be safe, for they were parted   35
With foul and violent tempest.
Montano: Pray heaven he be,
For I have served him, and the man commands
Like a full° soldier. Let's to the seaside, ho!
As well to see the vessel that's come in
As to throw out our eyes for brave Othello,   40
Even till we make the main and th' aerial blue°
An indistinct regard.°

---

7 _ruffianed_ raged   8 _mountains_ i.e., of water   9 _hold the mortise_ hold their joints together. (A _mortise_ is the socket hollowed out in fitting timbers.)   10 _segregation_ dispersal   12 _chidden_ i.e., rebuked, repelled (by the shore), and thus shot into the air   13 _monstrous mane_ (The surf is like the mane of a wild beast.)   14 _the burning Bear_ i.e., the constellation Ursa Minor or the Little Bear, which includes the polestar (and hence regarded as the _guards of th' ever-fixèd pole_ in the next line; sometimes the term _guards_ is applied to the two "pointers" of the Big Bear or Dipper, which may be intended here).   16 _like molestation_ comparable disturbance   17 _enchafèd_ angry   18 _If that_ if   19 _embayed_ sheltered by a bay   20 _bear it out_ survive, weather the storm   23 _designment_ design, enterprise. _halts_ is lame   24 _wreck_ shipwreck. _sufferance_ damage, disaster   28 _Veronesa_ i.e., fitted out in Verona for Venetian service, or possibly _Verennessa_ (the Folio spelling), i.e., _verrinessa_, a cutter (from _verrinare_, "to cut through")   34 _sadly_ gravely   38 _full_ perfect   41 _the main . . . blue_ the sea and the sky   42 _An indistinct regard_ indistinguishable in our view

Third Gentleman: Come, let's do so,
   For every minute is expectancy°
   Of more arrivance.°

   Enter Cassio.

Cassio: Thanks, you the valiant of this warlike isle,   45
   That so approve° the Moor! O, let the heavens
   Give him defense against the elements,
   For I have lost him on a dangerous sea.
Montano: Is he well shipped?
Cassio: His bark is stoutly timbered, and his pilot   50
   Of very expert and approved allowance;°
   Therefore my hopes, not surfeited to death,°
   Stand in bold cure.°

   [A cry] within: "A sail, a sail, a sail!"

Cassio: What noise?
A Gentleman: The town is empty. On the brow o' the sea°   55
   Stand ranks of people, and they cry "A sail!"
Cassio: My hopes do shape him for° the governor.

   [A shot within.]

Second Gentleman: They do discharge their shot of courtesy;°
   Our friends at least.
Cassio: I pray you, sir, go forth,
   And give us truth who 'tis that is arrived.   60
Second Gentleman: I shall.   *Exit.*
Montano: But, good Lieutenant, is your general wived?
Cassio: Most fortunately. He hath achieved a maid
   That paragons° description and wild fame,°
   One that excels the quirks° of blazoning° pens,   65
   And in th' essential vesture of creation
   Does tire the enginer.°

   Enter [Second] Gentleman.°

          How now? Who has put in?°
Second Gentleman: 'Tis one Iago, ancient to the General.
Cassio: He's had most favorable and happy speed.
   Tempests themselves, high seas, and howling winds,   70
   The guttered° rocks and congregated sands—

---

43 *is expectancy* gives expectation   44 *arrivance* arrival   46 *approve* admire, honor   51 *approved allowance*
tested reputation   52 *surfeited to death* i.e., overextended, worn thin through repeated application or delayed fulfillment   53 *in bold cure* in strong hopes of fulfillment   55 *brow o' the sea* cliff-edge   57 *My . . .
for* I hope it is   58 *discharge . . . courtesy* fire a salute in token of respect and courtesy   64 *paragons* sur-
passes. *wild fame* extravagant report   65 *quirks* witty conceits. *blazoning* setting forth as though in
heraldic language   66–67 *in . . . enginer* in her real, God-given, beauty, (she) defeats any attempt to
praise her. *enginer* engineer, i.e., poet, one who devises. s.d. *[Second] Gentleman* (So identified in the
Quarto text here and in lines 58, 61, 68, and 96; the Folio calls him a gentleman.)   67 *put in* i.e., to harbor
71 *guttered* jagged, trenched

Traitors ensteeped° to clog the guiltless keel—
As° having sense of beauty, do omit°
Their mortal° natures, letting go safely by
The divine Desdemona.

Montano: What is she?   75
Cassio: She that I spake of, our great captain's captain,
    Left in the conduct of the bold Iago,
    Whose footing° here anticipates our thoughts
    A sennight's° speed. Great Jove, Othello guard,
    And swell his sail with thine own powerful breath,   80
    That he may bless this bay with his tall° ship,
    Make love's quick pants in Desdemona's arms,
    Give renewed fire to our extincted spirits,
    And bring all Cyprus comfort!

Enter Desdemona, Iago, Roderigo, and Emilia.

                              O, behold,
    The riches of the ship is come on shore!   85
    You men of Cyprus, let her have your knees.

[*The gentlemen make curtsy to Desdemona.*]

    Hail to thee, lady! And the grace of heaven
    Before, behind thee, and on every hand
    Enwheel thee round!
Desdemona: I thank you, valiant Cassio.
    What tidings can you tell me of my lord?   90
Cassio: He is not yet arrived, nor know I aught
    But that he's well and will be shortly here.
Desdemona: O, but I fear—How lost you company?
Cassio: The great contention of the sea and skies
    Parted our fellowship.

(Within)   "A sail, a sail!" [*A shot.*]

                              But hark. A sail!   95
Second Gentleman: They give their greeting to the citadel.
    This likewise is a friend.
Cassio: See for the news.

[*Exit Second Gentleman.*]

    Good Ancient, you are welcome. [*Kissing Emilia.*] Welcome, mistress.
    Let it not gall your patience, good Iago,
    That I extend° my manners; 'tis my breeding°   100
    That gives me this bold show of courtesy.
Iago: Sir, would she give you so much of her lips
    As of her tongue she oft bestows on me,
    You would have enough.

---

72 *ensteeped* lying under water   73 *As* as if.   *omit* forbear to exercise   74 *mortal* deadly   78 *footing* landing
79 *sennight's* week's   81 *tall* splendid, gallant   100 *extend* give scope to.   *breeding* training in the
niceties of etiquette

Desdemona: Alas, she has no speech!° 105
Iago: In faith, too much.
    I find it still,° when I have list° to sleep.
    Marry, before your ladyship, I grant,
    She puts her tongue a little in her heart
    And chides with thinking.°
Emilia: You have little cause to say so. 110
Iago: Come on, come on. You are pictures out of doors,°
    Bells° in your parlors, wildcats in your kitchens,°
    Saints° in your injuries, devils being offended,
    Players° in your huswifery,° and huswives° in your beds.
Desdemona: O, fie upon thee, slanderer! 115
Iago: Nay, it is true, or else I am a Turk.°
    You rise to play, and go to bed to work.
Emilia: You shall not write my praise.
Iago: No, let me not.
Desdemona: What wouldst write of me, if thou shouldst praise me?
Iago: O gentle lady, do not put me to 't, 120
    For I am nothing if not critical.°
Desdemona: Come on, essay.°—There's one gone to the harbor?
Iago: Ay, madam.
Desdemona: I am not merry, but I do beguile
    The thing I am° by seeming otherwise. 125
    Come, how wouldst thou praise me?
Iago: I am about it, but indeed my invention
    Comes from my pate as birdlime° does from frieze°—
    It plucks out brains and all. But my Muse labors,°
    And thus she is delivered: 130
    If she be fair and wise, fairness and wit,
    The one's for use, the other useth it.°
Desdemona: Well praised! How if she be black° and witty?
Iago: If she be black, and thereto have a wit,
    She'll find a white° that shall her blackness fit.° 135
Desdemona: Worse and worse.
Emilia: How if fair and foolish?
Iago: She never yet was foolish that was fair,
    For even her folly° helped her to an heir.°
Desdemona: These are old fond° paradoxes to make fools laugh i' th' alehouse.
    What miserable praise hast thou for her that's foul and foolish? 140

---

105 *she has no speech* i.e., she's not a chatterbox, as you allege   107 *still* always. *list* desire   110 *with thinking* i.e., in her thoughts only   111 *pictures out of doors* i.e., silent and well-behaved in public   112 *Bells* i.e., jangling, noisy, and brazen. *in your kitchens* i.e., in domestic affairs. (Ladies would not do the cooking.)   113 *Saints* martyrs   114 *Players* idlers, triflers, or deceivers. *huswifery* housekeeping. *huswives* hussies (i.e., women are "busy" in bed, or unduly thrifty in dispensing sexual favors)   116 *a Turk* an infidel, not to be believed   121 *critical* censorious   122 *essay* try   125 *The thing I am* i.e., my anxious self   128 *birdlime* sticky substance used to catch small birds. *frieze* coarse woolen cloth   129 *labors* (1) exerts herself (2) prepares to deliver a child (with a following pun on *delivered* in line 130)   132 *The one's . . . it* i.e., her cleverness will make use of her beauty   133 *black* dark-complexioned, brunette   135 *a white* a fair person (with word-play on "wight," a person). *fit* (with sexual suggestion of mating)   138 *folly* (with added meaning of "lechery, wantonness"). *to an heir* i.e., to bear a child   139 *fond* foolish

Iago: There's none so foul° and foolish thereunto,°
But does foul° pranks which fair and wise ones do.
Desdemona: O heavy ignorance! Thou praisest the worst best. But what praise
couldst thou bestow on a deserving woman indeed, one that, in the authority of
her merit, did justly put on the vouch° of very malice itself?   145
Iago: She that was ever fair, and never proud,
Had tongue at will, and yet was never loud,
Never lacked gold and yet went never gay,°
Fled from her wish, and yet said, "Now I may,"°
She that being angered, her revenge being nigh,   150
Bade her wrong stay° and her displeasure fly,
She that in wisdom never was so frail
To change the cod's head for the salmon's tail,°
She that could think and ne'er disclose her mind,
See suitors following and not look behind,   155
She was a wight, if ever such wight were—
Desdemona: To do what?
Iago: To suckle fools° and chronicle small beer.°
Desdemona: O most lame and impotent conclusion! Do not learn of him, Emilia, though
he be thy husband. How say you, Cassio? Is he not a most profane° and liberal°   160
counselor?
Cassio: He speaks home,° madam. You may relish° him more in° the soldier than in
the scholar.

[*Cassio and Desdemona stand together, conversing intimately.*]

Iago [aside]: He takes her by the palm. Ay, well said,° whisper. With as little a
web as this will I ensnare as great a fly as Cassio. Ay, smile upon her, do; I will 165
gyve° thee in thine own courtship.° You say true;° 'tis so, indeed. If such tricks as
these strip you out of your lieutenantry, it had been better you had not kissed
your three fingers so oft, which now again you are most apt to play the sir° in.
Very good; well kissed! An excellent courtesy! 'Tis so, indeed. Yet again your
fingers to your lips? Would they were clyster pipes° for your sake! [*Trumpet*   170
within.] The Moor! I know his trumpet.
Cassio: 'Tis truly so.
Desdemona: Let's meet him and receive him.
Cassio: Lo, where he comes!

Enter Othello and attendants.

Othello: O my fair warrior!
Desdemona: My dear Othello!   175

---

141 *foul* ugly. *thereunto* in addition 142 *foul* sluttish 145 *put . . . vouch* compel the approval 148 *gay*
extravagantly clothed 149 *Fled . . . may* avoided temptation where the choice was hers 151 *Bade . . .*
stay i.e., resolved to put up with her injury patiently 153 *To . . . tail* i.e., to exchange a lackluster husband for a sexy lover (?) (*Cod's head* is slang for "penis," and *tail,* for "pudendum.") 158 *suckle fools*
breastfeed babies. *chronicle small beer* i.e., keep petty household accounts, keep track of trivial matters
160 *profane* irreverent, ribald. *liberal* licentious, free-spoken 162 *home* right to the target. (A term from
fencing.) *relish* appreciate *in* in the character of 164 *well said* well done 166 *gyve* fetter, shackle.
courtship courtesy, show of courtly manners. *You say true* i.e., that's right, go ahead 168 *the sir* i.e., the
fine gentleman 170 *clyster pipes* tubes used for enemas and douches

Desdemona arrives in Cyprus and reunites with Othello as Cassio looks on (II, i, 175–208).

Othello: It gives me wonder great as my content
   To see you here before me. O my soul's joy,
   If after every tempest come such calms,
   May the winds blow till they have wakened death,
   And let the laboring bark climb hills of seas   180
   Olympus-high, and duck again as low
   As hell's from heaven! If it were now to die,
   'Twere now to be most happy, for I fear
   My soul hath her content so absolute
   That not another comfort like to this   185
   Succeeds in unknown fate.°
Desdemona: The heavens forbid
   But that our loves and comforts should increase
   Even as our days do grow!
Othello: Amen to that, sweet powers!
   I cannot speak enough of this content.   190
   It stops me here; it is too much of joy.
   And this, and this, the greatest discords be

   [They kiss.]°

   That e'er our hearts shall make!

---

186 *Succeeds . . . fate* i.e., can follow in the unknown future   192 s.d. *They kiss* (The direction is from the Quarto.)

Iago [*aside*]: O, you are well tuned now!
But I'll set down° the pegs that make this music,   195
As honest as I am.°
Othello: Come, let us to the castle.
News, friends! Our wars are done, the Turks are drowned.
How does my old acquaintance of this isle?—
Honey, you shall be well desired° in Cyprus;   200
I have found great love amongst them. O my sweet,
I prattle out of fashion,° and I dote
In mine own comforts.—I prithee, good Iago,
Go to the bay and disembark my coffers.°
Bring thou the master° to the citadel;   205
He is a good one, and his worthiness
Does challenge° much respect.—Come, Desdemona.—
Once more, well met at Cyprus!

Exeunt Othello and Desdemona [and all but Iago and Roderigo].

Iago [*to an attendant*]: Do thou meet me presently at the harbor. [*To Roderigo.*]
Come hither. If thou be'st valiant—as, they say, base men° being in love have   210
then a nobility in their natures more than is native to them—list° me. The Lieutenant tonight watches on the court of guard.° First, I must tell thee this: Desdemona is directly in love with him.
Roderigo: With him? Why, 'tis not possible.
Iago: Lay thy finger thus,° and let thy soul be instructed. Mark me with what violence   215
she first loved the Moor, but° for bragging and telling her fantastical lies. To love
him still for prating? Let not thy discreet heart think it. Her eye must be fed; and
what delight shall she have to look on the devil? When the blood is made dull
with the act of sport,° there should be, again to inflame it and to give satiety
a fresh appetite, loveliness in favor,° sympathy° in years, manners, and beauties—   220
all which the Moor is defective in. Now, for want of these required conveniences,° her delicate tenderness will find itself abused,° begin to heave the
gorge,° disrelish and abhor the Moor. Very nature° will instruct her in it and compel her to some second choice. Now, sir, this granted—as it is a most pregnant° and
 unforced position—who stands so eminent in the degree of° this fortune as Cassio   225
does? A knave very voluble,° no further conscionable° than in putting on the
mere form of civil and humane° seeming for the better compassing of his salt°
and most hidden loose affection.° Why, none, why, none. A slipper° and subtle
knave, a finder out of occasions, that has an eye can stamp° and counterfeit

195 *set down* loosen (and hence untune the instrument)   196 *As . . . I am* for all my supposed honesty
200 *desired* welcomed   202 *out of fashion* irrelevantly, incoherently (?)   204 *coffers* chests, baggage   205
master ship's captain   207 *challenge* lay claim to, deserve   210 *base men* even lowly born men   211 *list* listen to   212 *court of guard* guardhouse. (Cassio is in charge of the watch.)   215 *thus* i.e., on your lips   216 *but*
only   219 *the act of sport* sex   220 *favor* appearance. *sympathy* correspondence, similarity
221–222 *required conveniences* things conducive to sexual compatibility   222 *abused* cheated, revolted
222–223 *heave the gorge* experience nausea   223 *Very nature* her very instincts   224 *pregnant* evident,
cogent   225 *in the degree of* as next in line for   226 *voluble* facile, glib. *conscionable* conscientious,
conscience-bound   227 *humane* polite, courteous. *salt* licentious   228 *affection* passion. *slipper* slippery
229 *an eye can stamp* an eye that can coin, create

advantages,° though true advantage never present itself; a devilish knave. Besides, 230
the knave is handsome, young, and hath all those requisites in him that folly°
and green° minds look after. A pestilent complete knave, and the woman hath
found him° already.

Roderigo: I cannot believe that in her. She's full of most blessed condition.°

Iago: Blessed fig's end!° The wine she drinks is made of grapes. If she had been 235
blessed, she would never have loved the Moor. Blessed pudding!° Didst thou not
see her paddle with the palm of his hand? Didst not mark that?

Roderigo: Yes, that I did; but that was but courtesy.

Iago: Lechery, by this hand. An index° and obscure° prologue to the history of lust
and foul thoughts. They met so near with their lips that their breaths embraced 240
together. Villainous thoughts, Roderigo! When these mutualities° so marshal
the way, hard at hand° comes the master and main exercise, th' incorporate°
conclusion. Pish! But, sir, be you ruled by me. I have brought you from Venice.
Watch you° tonight; for the command, I'll lay 't upon you.° Cassio knows you
not. I'll not be far from you. Do you find some occasion to anger Cassio, either by 245
speaking too loud, or tainting° his discipline, or from what other course you
please, which the time shall more favorably minister.°

Roderigo: Well.

Iago: Sir, he's rash and very sudden in choler,° and haply° may strike at you. Provoke
him that he may, for even out of that will I cause these of Cyprus to mutiny,° 250
whose qualification° shall come into no true taste° again but by the displanting
of Cassio. So shall you have a shorter journey to your desires by the means I shall
then have to prefer° them, and the impediment most profitably removed, without the which there were no expectation of our prosperity.

Roderigo: I will do this, if you can bring it to any opportunity. 255

Iago: I warrant° thee. Meet me by and by° at the citadel. I must fetch his necessaries
ashore. Farewell.

Roderigo: Adieu.   *Exit.*

Iago: That Cassio loves her, I do well believe 't;
That she loves him, 'tis apt° and of great credit.° 260
The Moor, howbeit that I endure him not,
Is of a constant, loving, noble nature,
And I dare think he'll prove to Desdemona
A most dear husband. Now, I do love her too,
Not out of absolute lust—though peradventure 265
I stand accountant° for as great a sin—
But partly led to diet° my revenge
For that I do suspect the lusty Moor

---

230 *advantages* favorable opportunities   231 *folly* wantonness   232 *green* immature   233 *found him* sized
him up, perceived his intent   234 *condition* disposition   235 *fig's end* (See Act I, Scene iii, line 316 for the
vulgar gesture of the fig.)   236 *pudding* sausage   239 *index* table of contents.   *obscure* (i.e., the *lust and foul
thoughts* in lines 239–240 are secret, hidden from view)   241 *mutualities* exchanges, intimacies   242 *hard at
hand* closely following.   *incorporate* carnal   244 *Watch you* stand watch.   *for the command . . . you* I'll
arrange for you to be appointed, given orders   246 *tainting* disparaging   247 *minister* provide   249 *choler*
wrath.   *haply* perhaps   250 *mutiny* riot   251 *qualification* appeasement.   *true taste* i.e., acceptable state
253 *prefer* advance   256 *warrant* assure.   *by and by* immediately   260 *apt* probable.   *credit* credibility
266 *accountant* accountable   267 *diet* feed

Hath leaped into my seat, the thought whereof
Doth, like a poisonous mineral, gnaw my innards; 270
And nothing can or shall content my soul
Till I am evened with him, wife for wife,
Or failing so, yet that I put the Moor
At least into a jealousy so strong
That judgment cannot cure. Which thing to do, 275
If this poor trash of Venice, whom I trace°
For° his quick hunting, stand the putting on,°
I'll have our Michael Cassio on the hip,°
Abuse° him to the Moor in the rank garb°—
For I fear Cassio with my nightcap° too— 280
Make the Moor thank me, love me, and reward me
For making him egregiously an ass
And practicing upon° his peace and quiet
Even to madness. 'Tis here, but yet confused.
Knavery's plain face is never seen till used.   *Exit.* 285

SCENE II [CYPRUS. A STREET.]

Enter Othello's Herald with a proclamation.

Herald: It is Othello's pleasure, our noble and valiant general, that, upon certain tidings now arrived, importing the mere perdition° of the Turkish fleet, every man put himself into triumph:° some to dance, some to make bonfires, each man to what sport and revels his addiction° leads him. For, besides these beneficial news, it is the celebration of his nuptial. So much was his pleasure should be proclaimed. All offices° are open, and there is full liberty of feasting from this present hour of five till the bell have told eleven. Heaven bless the isle of Cyprus and our noble general Othello! 5

Exit.

SCENE III [CYPRUS. THE CITADEL.]

Enter Othello, Desdemona, Cassio, and attendants.

Othello: Good Michael, look you to the guard tonight.
Let's teach ourselves that honorable stop°
Not to outsport° discretion.
Cassio: Iago hath direction what to do,
But notwithstanding, with my personal eye 5
Will I look to 't.

---

276 *trace* i.e., train, or follow (?), or perhaps *trash*, a hunting term, meaning to put weights on a hunting dog in order to slow him down   277 *For* to make more eager.   *stand . . . on* respond properly when I incite him to quarrel   278 *on the hip* at my mercy, where I can throw him. (A wrestling term.)   279 *Abuse* slander. *rank garb* coarse manner, gross fashion   280 *with my nightcap* i.e., as a rival in my bed, as one who gives me cuckold's horns   283 *practicing upon* plotting against   2 *mere perdition* complete destruction   3 *triumph* public celebration   4 *addiction* inclination   6 *offices* rooms where food and drink are kept   2 *stop* restraint   3 *outsport* celebrate beyond the bounds of

Othello: Iago is most honest.
      Michael, good night. Tomorrow with your earliest°
      Let me have speech with you. [*To Desdemona.*]
                          Come, my dear love,
      The purchase made, the fruits are to ensue;
      That profit's yet to come 'tween me and you.°—   10
      Good night.

      Exit [Othello, with Desdemona and attendants].

      Enter Iago.

Cassio: Welcome, Iago. We must to the watch.
Iago: Not this hour,° Lieutenant; 'tis not yet ten o' the clock. Our general cast° us thus
      early for the love of his Desdemona; who° let us not therefore blame. He hath not
      yet made wanton the night with her, and she is sport for Jove.   15
Cassio: She's a most exquisite lady.
Iago: And, I'll warrant her, full of game.
Cassio: Indeed, she's a most fresh and delicate creature.
Iago: What an eye she has! Methinks it sounds a parley° to provocation.
Cassio: An inviting eye, and yet methinks right modest.   20
Iago: And when she speaks, is it not an alarum° to love?
Cassio: She is indeed perfection.
Iago: Well, happiness to their sheets! Come, Lieutenant, I have a stoup° of wine, and
      here without° are a brace° of Cyprus gallants that would fain have a measure° to
      the health of black Othello.   25
Cassio: Not tonight, good Iago. I have very poor and unhappy brains for drinking. I
      could well wish courtesy would invent some other custom of entertainment.
Iago: O, they are our friends. But one cup! I'll drink for you.°
Cassio: I have drunk but one cup tonight, and that was craftily qualified° too, and
      behold what innovation° it makes here.° I am unfortunate in the infirmity and   30
      dare not task my weakness with any more.
Iago: What, man? 'Tis a night of revels. The gallants desire it.
Cassio: Where are they?
Iago: Here at the door. I pray you, call them in.
Cassio: I'll do 't, but it dislikes me.°   *Exit.*   35
Iago: If I can fasten but one cup upon him,
      With that which he hath drunk tonight already,
      He'll be as full of quarrel and offense°
      As my young mistress' dog. Now, my sick fool Roderigo,
      Whom love hath turned almost the wrong side out,   40
      To Desdemona hath tonight caroused°

---

7 *with your earliest* at your earliest convenience 9–10 *The purchase . . . you* i.e., though married, we
haven't yet consummated our love 13 *Not this hour* not for an hour yet. *cast* dismissed 14 *who* i.e.,
Othello 19 *sounds a parley* calls for a conference, issues an invitation 21 *alarum* signal calling men to
arms (continuing the military metaphor of *parley,* line 19) 23 *stoup* measure of liquor, two quarts 24 *without*
outside. *brace* pair. *fain have a measure* gladly drink a toast 28 *for you* in your place. (Iago will do the
steady drinking to keep the gallants company while Cassio has only one cup.) 29 *qualified* diluted
30 *innovation* disturbance, insurrection. *here* i.e., in my head 35 *it dislikes me* i.e., I'm reluctant 38
offense readiness to take offense 41 *caroused* drunk off

Potations pottle-deep;° and he's to watch.°
Three lads of Cyprus—noble swelling° spirits,
That hold their honors in a wary distance,°
The very elements° of this warlike isle—   45
Have I tonight flustered with flowing cups,
And they watch° too. Now, 'mongst this flock of drunkards
Am I to put our Cassio in some action
That may offend the isle.—But here they come.

Enter Cassio, Montano, and gentlemen; [servants following with wine].

If consequence do but approve my dream,°   50
My boat sails freely both with wind and stream.°
Cassio: 'Fore God, they have given me a rouse° already.
Montano: Good faith, a little one; not past a pint, as I am a soldier.
Iago: Some wine, ho! [*He sings.*]
              "And let me the cannikin° clink, clink,   55
              And let me the cannikin clink.
              A soldier's a man,
              O, man's life's but a span;°
              Why, then, let a soldier drink."
      Some wine, boys!   60
Cassio: 'Fore God, an excellent song.
Iago: I learned it in England, where indeed they are most potent in potting.° Your
     Dane, your German, and your swag-bellied Hollander—drink, ho!—are nothing
     to your English.
Cassio: Is your Englishman so exquisite in his drinking?   65
Iago: Why, he drinks you,° with facility, your Dane° dead drunk; he sweats not° to
     overthrow your Almain;° he gives your Hollander a vomit ere the next pottle
     can be filled.
Cassio: To the health of our general!
Montano: I am for it, Lieutenant, and I'll do you justice.°   70
Iago: O sweet England! [*He sings.*]
              "King Stephen was and-a worthy peer,
              His breeches cost him but a crown;
              He held them sixpence all too dear,
              With that he called the tailor lown.°   75

              He was a wight of high renown,
              And thou art but of low degree.
              'Tis pride° that pulls the country down;
              Then take thy auld° cloak about thee."
      Some wine, ho!   80

42 *pottle-deep* to the bottom of the tankard. *watch* stand watch 43 *swelling* proud 44 *hold . . . distance*
i.e., are extremely sensitive of their honor 45 *very elements* typical sort 47 *watch* are members of the
guard 50 *If . . . dream* if subsequent events will only substantiate my scheme 51 *stream* current
52 *rouse* full draft of liquor 55 *cannikin* small drinking vessel 58 *span* brief span of time. (Compare
Psalm 39:6 as rendered in the 1928 Book of Common Prayer: "Thou hast made my days as it were a span
long.") 62 *potting* drinking 66 *drinks you* drinks. *your Dane* your typical Dane. *sweats not* i.e., need
not exert himself 67 *Almain* German 70 *I'll . . . justice* i.e., I'll drink as much as you 75 *lown* lout, rascal
78 *pride* i.e., extravagance in dress 79 *auld* old

Cassio: 'Fore God, this is a more exquisite song than the other.

Iago: Will you hear 't again?

Cassio: No, for I hold him to be unworthy of his place that does those things. Well, God's above all; and there be souls must be saved, and there be souls must not be saved.   85

Iago: It's true, good Lieutenant.

Cassio: For mine own part—no offense to the General, nor any man of quality°—I hope to be saved.

Iago: And so do I too, Lieutenant.

Cassio: Ay, but, by your leave, not before me; the lieutenant is to be saved before the   90
ancient. Let's have no more of this; let's to our affairs.—God forgive us our sins!—Gentlemen, let's look to our business. Do not think, gentlemen, I am drunk. This is my ancient; this is my right hand, and this is my left. I am not drunk now. I can stand well enough, and speak well enough.

Gentlemen: Excellent well.   95

Cassio: Why, very well then; you must not think then that I am drunk.   *Exit.*

Montano: To th' platform, masters. Come, let's set the watch.°

    [*Exeunt Gentlemen.*]

Iago: You see this fellow that is gone before.
    He's a soldier fit to stand by Caesar
    And give direction; and do but see his vice.   100
    'Tis to his virtue a just equinox,°
    The one as long as th' other. 'Tis pity of him.
    I fear the trust Othello puts him in,
    On some odd time of his infirmity,
    Will shake this island.

Montano: But is he often thus?   105

Iago: 'Tis evermore the prologue to his sleep.
    He'll watch the horologe a double set,°
    If drink rock not his cradle.

Montano: It were well
    The General were put in mind of it.
    Perhaps he sees it not, or his good nature   110
    Prizes the virtue that appears in Cassio
    And looks not on his evils. Is not this true?

    Enter Roderigo.

Iago [*aside to him*]: How now, Roderigo?
    I pray you, after the Lieutenant; go.   [*Exit Roderigo.*]

Montano: And 'tis great pity that the noble Moor   115
    Should hazard such a place as his own second
    With° one of an engraffed° infirmity.

---

87 *quality* rank   97 *set the watch* mount the guard   101 *just equinox* exact counterpart. (*Equinox* is an equal length of days and nights.)   107 *watch . . . set* stay awake twice around the clock or *horologe*   116–117 *hazard . . . With* risk giving such an important position as his second in command to   117 *engraffed* engrafted, inveterate

Cassio, encouraged to drink by Iago, starts a fight with Montano (II, iii, 130).

It were an honest action to say so
To the Moor.
Iago: Not I, for this fair island.
I do love Cassio well and would do much   120
To cure him of this evil.   [*Cry within: "Help! Help!"*]
                    But, hark! What noise?

Enter Cassio, pursuing° Roderigo.

Cassio: Zounds, you rogue! You rascal!
Montano: What's the matter, Lieutenant?
Cassio: A knave teach me my duty?
    I'll beat the knave into a twiggen° bottle.

121 s.d. *pursuing* (The Quarto text reads, "driving in.")   124 *twiggen* wicker-covered (Cassio vows to assail Roderigo until his skin resembles wickerwork or until he has driven Roderigo through the holes in a wickerwork.)

Roderigo: Beat me? 125
Cassio: Dost thou prate, rogue? [*He strikes Roderigo.*]
Montano: Nay, good Lieutenant. [*Restraining him.*] I pray you, sir, hold your hand.
Cassio: Let me go, sir, or I'll knock you o'er the mazard.°
Montano: Come, come, you're drunk.
Cassio: Drunk? [*They fight.*] 130
Iago [*aside to Roderigo*]: Away, I say. Go out and cry a mutiny.°

[*Exit Roderigo.*]

Nay, good Lieutenant—God's will, gentlemen—
Help, ho!—Lieutenant—sir—Montano—sir—
Help, masters!°—Here's a goodly watch indeed!

[*A bell rings.*]°

Who's that which rings the bell?—Diablo,° ho! 135
The town will rise.° God's will, Lieutenant, hold!
You'll be ashamed forever.

Enter Othello and attendants [*with weapons*].

Othello: What is the matter here?
Montano: Zounds, I bleed still.
I am hurt to th' death. He dies! [*He thrusts at Cassio.*]
Othello: Hold, for your lives!
Iago: Hold, ho! Lieutenant—sir—Montano—gentlemen— 140
Have you forgot all sense of place and duty?
Hold! The General speaks to you. Hold, for shame!
Othello: Why, how now, ho! From whence ariseth this?
Are we turned Turks, and to ourselves do that
Which heaven hath forbid the Ottomites?° 145
For Christian shame, put by this barbarous brawl!
He that stirs next to carve for° his own rage
Holds his soul light;° he dies upon his motion.°
Silence that dreadful bell. It frights the isle
From her propriety.° What is the matter, masters? 150
Honest Iago, that looks dead with grieving,
Speak. Who began this? On thy love, I charge thee.
Iago: I do not know. Friends all but now, even now,
In quarter° and in terms° like bride and groom
Devesting them° for bed; and then, but now— 155
As if some planet had unwitted men—

---

128 *mazard* i.e., head. (Literally, a drinking vessel.)   131 *mutiny* riot   134 *masters* sirs.   s.d. *A bell rings* (This direction is from the Quarto, as are *Exit Roderigo* at line 114, *They fight* at line 130, and *with weapons* at line 137.)   135 *Diablo* the devil   136 *rise* grow riotous   144–145 *to ourselves . . . Ottomites* inflict on ourselves the harm that heaven has prevented the Turks from doing (by destroying their fleet)   147 *carve for* i.e., indulge, satisfy with his sword   148 *Holds . . . light* i.e., places little value on his life.   *upon his motion* if he moves   150 *propriety* proper state or condition   154 *In quarter* in friendly conduct, within bounds.   *in terms* on good terms   155 *Devesting them* undressing themselves

Swords out, and tilting one at others' breasts
In opposition bloody. I cannot speak°
Any beginning to this peevish odds;°
And would in action glorious I had lost
Those legs that brought me to a part of it!　　　　　　160

Othello: How comes it, Michael, you are thus forgot?°

Cassio: I pray you, pardon me. I cannot speak.

Othello: Worthy Montano, you were wont be° civil;
The gravity and stillness° of your youth　　　　　　165
The world hath noted, and your name is great
In mouths of wisest censure.° What's the matter
That you unlace° your reputation thus
And spend your rich opinion° for the name
Of a night-brawler? Give me answer to it.　　　　　　170

Montano: Worthy Othello, I am hurt to danger.
Your officer, Iago, can inform you—
While I spare speech, which something° now offends° me—
Of all that I do know; nor know I aught
By me that's said or done amiss this night,　　　　　　175
Unless self-charity be sometimes a vice,
And to defend ourselves it be a sin
When violence assails us.

Othello:　　　　　　Now, by heaven,
My blood° begins my safer guides° to rule,
And passion, having my best judgment collied,°　　　　　　180
Essays° to lead the way. Zounds, if I stir,
Or do but lift this arm, the best of you
Shall sink in my rebuke. Give me to know
How this foul rout° began, who set it on;
And he that is approved in° this offense,　　　　　　185
Though he had twinned with me, both at a birth,
Shall lose me. What? In a town of° war
Yet wild, the people's hearts brim full of fear,
To manage° private and domestic quarrel?
In night, and on the court and guard of safety?°　　　　　　190
'Tis monstrous. Iago, who began 't?

Montano [*to Iago*]: If partially affined,° or leagued in office,°
Thou dost deliver more or less than truth,
Thou art no soldier.

Iago:　　　　　　Touch me not so near.
I had rather have this tongue cut from my mouth　　　　　　195

---

158 *speak* explain　159 *peevish odds* childish quarrel　162 *are thus forgot* have forgotten yourself thus
164 *wont be* accustomed to be　165 *stillness* sobriety　167 *censure* judgment　168 *unlace* undo, lay open
(as one might loose the strings of a purse containing reputation)　169 *opinion* reputation　173 *something*
somewhat.　*offends* pains　179 *blood* passion (of anger).　*guides* i.e., reason　180 *collied* darkened　181
Essays undertakes　184 *rout* riot　185 *approved in* found guilty of　187 *town of* town garrisoned for
189 *manage* undertake　190 *on . . . safety* at the main guardhouse or headquarters and on watch　192
partially affined made partial by some personal relationship.　*leagued in office* in league as fellow officers

Than it should do offense to Michael Cassio;
Yet, I persuade myself, to speak the truth
Shall nothing wrong him. Thus it is, General.
Montano and myself being in speech,
There comes a fellow crying out for help,   200
And Cassio following him with determined sword
To execute° upon him. Sir, this gentleman

[*indicating Montano*]

Steps in to Cassio and entreats his pause.°
Myself the crying fellow did pursue,
Lest by his clamor—as it so fell out—   205
The town might fall in fright. He, swift of foot,
Outran my purpose, and I returned, the rather°
For that I heard the clink and fall of swords
And Cassio high in oath, which till tonight
I ne'er might say before. When I came back—   210
For this was brief—I found them close together
At blow and thrust, even as again they were
When you yourself did part them.
More of this matter cannot I report.
But men are men; the best sometimes forget.°   215
Though Cassio did some little wrong to him,
As men in rage strike those that wish them best,°
Yet surely Cassio, I believe, received
From him that fled some strange indignity,
Which patience could not pass.°
Othello: I know, Iago,   220
Thy honesty and love doth mince this matter,
Making it light to Cassio. Cassio, I love thee,
But nevermore be officer of mine.

    Enter Desdemona, attended.

Look if my gentle love be not raised up.
I'll make thee an example.   225
Desdemona: What is the matter, dear?
Othello: All's well now, sweeting;
Come away to bed. [*To Montano.*] Sir, for your hurts,
Myself will be your surgeon.°—Lead him off.

    [*Montano is led off.*]

Iago, look with care about the town
And silence those whom this vile brawl distracted.   230

---

202 *execute* give effect to (his anger)   203 *his pause* him to stop   207 *rather* sooner   215 *forget* forget
themselves   217 *those . . . best* i.e., even those who are well disposed   220 *pass* pass over, overlook   228
be your surgeon i.e., make sure you receive medical attention

Iago advises Cassio to ask Desdemona to plead his cause with Othello (II, iii, 233–286).

Come, Desdemona. 'Tis the soldiers' life
To have their balmy slumbers waked with strife.

Exit [with all but Iago and Cassio].

Iago: What, are you hurt, Lieutenant?
Cassio: Ay, past all surgery.
Iago: Marry, God forbid!   235
Cassio: Reputation, reputation, reputation! O, I have lost my reputation! I have lost
   the immortal part of myself, and what remains is bestial. My reputation, Iago, my
   reputation!
Iago: As I am an honest man, I thought you had received some bodily wound; there
   is more sense in that than in reputation. Reputation is an idle and most false   240
   imposition,° oft got without merit and lost without deserving. You have lost no
   reputation at all, unless you repute yourself such a loser. What, man, there are
   more ways to recover° the General again. You are but now cast in his mood°—a
   punishment more in policy° than in malice, even so as one would beat his
   offenseless dog to affright an imperious lion.° Sue° to him again and he's yours.   245

240–241 *false imposition* thing artificially imposed and of no real value   243 *recover* regain favor with.
cast in his mood dismissed in a moment of anger   244 *in policy* done for expediency's sake and as a public
gesture   244–245 *would . . . lion* i.e., would make an example of a minor offender in order to deter more
important and dangerous offenders   245 *Sue* petition

Cassio: I will rather sue to be despised than to deceive so good a commander with so slight,° so drunken, and so indiscreet an officer. Drunk? And speak parrot?° And squabble? Swagger? Swear? And discourse fustian with one's own shadow? O thou invisible spirit of wine, if thou hast no name to be known by, let us call thee devil! 250

Iago: What was he that you followed with your sword? What had he done to you?

Cassio: I know not.

Iago: Is 't possible?

Cassio: I remember a mass of things, but nothing distinctly; a quarrel, but nothing wherefore.° O God, that men should put an enemy in their mouths to steal away 255 their brains! That we should, with joy, pleasance, revel, and applause° transform ourselves into beasts!

Iago: Why, but you are now well enough. How came you thus recovered?

Cassio: It hath pleased the devil drunkenness to give place to the devil wrath. One unperfectness shows me another, to make me frankly despise myself. 260

Iago: Come, you are too severe a moraler.° As the time, the place, and the condition of this country stands, I could heartily wish this had not befallen; but since it is as it is, mend it for your own good.

Cassio: I will ask him for my place again; he shall tell me I am a drunkard. Had I as many mouths as Hydra,° such an answer would stop them all. To be now a sensible 265 man, by and by a fool, and presently a beast! O, strange! Every inordinate cup is unblessed, and the ingredient is a devil.

Iago: Come, come, good wine is a good familiar creature, if it be well used. Exclaim no more against it. And, good Lieutenant, I think you think I love you.

Cassio: I have well approved° it, sir. I drunk! 270

Iago: You or any man living may be drunk at a time,° man. I'll tell you what you shall do. Our general's wife is now the general—I may say so in this respect, for that° he hath devoted and given up himself to the contemplation, mark, and denotement° of her parts° and graces. Confess yourself freely to her; importune her help to put you in your place again. She is of so free,° so kind, so apt, so blessed a dis- 275 position, she holds it a vice in her goodness not to do more than she is requested. This broken joint between you and her husband entreat her to splinter;° and, my fortunes against any lay° worth naming, this crack of your love shall grow stronger than it was before.

Cassio: You advise me well. 280

Iago: I protest,° in the sincerity of love and honest kindness.

Cassio: I think it freely;° and betimes in the morning I will beseech the virtuous Desdemona to undertake for me. I am desperate of my fortunes if they check° me here.

Iago: You are in the right. Good night, Lieutenant. I must to the watch. 285

---

247 *slight* worthless.   247–48 *speak parrot* talk nonsense, rant   255 *wherefore* why   256 *applause* desire for applause   261 *moraler* moralizer   265 *Hydra* the Lernaean Hydra, a monster with many heads and the ability to grow two heads when one was cut off, slain by Hercules as the second of his twelve labors   270 *approved* proved   271 *at a time* at one time or another   272 *in . . . that* in view of this fact, that   273–274 *mark, and denotement* (Both words mean "observation.")   274 *parts* qualities   275 *free* generous   277 *splinter* bind with splints.   278 *lay* stake, wager   281 *protest* insist, declare   282 *freely* unreservedly   283 *check* repulse

Cassio: Good night, honest Iago.   *Exit Cassio.*

Iago: And what's he then that says I play the villain,
    When this advice is free° I give, and honest,
    Probal° to thinking, and indeed the course
    To win the Moor again? For 'tis most easy   290
    Th' inclining° Desdemona to subdue°
    In any honest suit; she's framed as fruitful°
    As the free elements.° And then for her
    To win the Moor—were 't to renounce his baptism,
    All seals and symbols of redeemèd sin—   295
    His soul is so enfettered to her love
    That she may make, unmake, do what she list,
    Even as her appetite° shall play the god
    With his weak function.° How am I then a villain,
    To counsel Cassio to this parallel° course   300
    Directly to his good? Divinity of hell!°
    When devils will the blackest sins put on,°
    They do suggest° at first with heavenly shows,
    As I do now. For whiles this honest fool
    Plies Desdemona to repair his fortune,   305
    And she for him pleads strongly to the Moor,
    I'll pour this pestilence into his ear,
    That she repeals him° for her body's lust;
    And by how much she strives to do him good,
    She shall undo her credit with the Moor.   310
    So will I turn her virtue into pitch,°
    And out of her own goodness make the net
    That shall enmesh them all.

    Enter Roderigo.

                    How now, Roderigo?

Roderigo: I do follow here in the chase, not like a hound that hunts, but one that
    fills up the cry.° My money is almost spent; I have been tonight exceedingly   315
    well cudgeled; and I think the issue will be I shall have so much° experience
    for my pains, and so, with no money at all and a little more wit, return again
    to Venice.

Iago: How poor are they that have not patience!
    What wound did ever heal but by degrees?   320
    Thou know'st we work by wit, and not by witchcraft,
    And wit depends on dilatory time.

---

288 *free* (1) free from guile (2) freely given   289 *Probal* probable, reasonable   291 *inclining* favorably disposed.   *subdue* persuade   292 *framed as fruitful* created as generous   293 *free elements* i.e., earth, air, fire, and water, unrestrained and spontaneous   298 *her appetite* her desire, or, perhaps, his desire for her   299 *function* exercise of faculties (weakened by his fondness for her)   300 *parallel* corresponding to these facts and to his best interests   301 *Divinity of hell* inverted theology of hell (which seduces the soul to its damnation)   302 *put on* further, instigate   303 *suggest* tempt   308 *repeals him* attempts to get him restored   311 *pitch* i.e., (1) foul blackness (2) a snaring substance   315 *fills up the cry* merely takes part as one of the pack   316 *so much* just so much and no more

Does 't not go well? Cassio hath beaten thee,
And thou, by that small hurt, hast cashiered° Cassio.
Though other things grow fair against the sun,   325
Yet fruits that blossom first will first be ripe.°
Content thyself awhile. By the Mass, 'tis morning!
Pleasure and action make the hours seem short.
Retire thee; go where thou art billeted.
Away, I say! Thou shalt know more hereafter.   330
Nay, get thee gone.   *Exit Roderigo.*
                    Two things are to be done.
My wife must move° for Cassio to her mistress;
I'll set her on;
Myself the while to draw the Moor apart
And bring him jump° when he may Cassio find   335
Soliciting his wife. Ay, that's the way.
Dull not device° by coldness° and delay.   *Exit.*

ACT III

SCENE I [BEFORE THE CHAMBER OF OTHELLO AND DESDEMONA.]

Enter Cassio [and] Musicians.

Cassio: Masters, play here—I will content your pains°—
    Something that's brief, and bid "Good morrow, General."   [*They play.*]

[*Enter*] *Clown.*

Clown: Why, masters, have your instruments been in Naples, that they speak i' the
    nose° thus?
A Musician: How, sir, how?   5
Clown: Are these, I pray you, wind instruments?
A Musician: Ay, marry, are they, sir.
Clown: O, thereby hangs a tail.
A Musician: Whereby hangs a tale, sir?
Clown: Marry, sir, by many a wind instrument° that I know. But, masters, here's   10
    money for you. [*He gives money.*] And the General so likes your music that he
    desires you, for love's sake,° to make no more noise with it.
A Musician: Well, sir, we will not.
Clown: If you have any music that may not° be heard, to 't again; but, as they say, to
    hear music the General does not greatly care.   15

---

324 *cashiered* dismissed from service   325–326 *Though . . . ripe* i.e., plans that are well prepared and set
expeditiously in motion will soonest ripen into success   332 *move* plead   335 *jump* precisely   337 *device*
plot. *coldness* lack of zeal   1 *content your pains* reward your efforts   3–4 *speak i' the nose* (1) sound nasal
(2) sound like one whose nose has been attacked by syphilis. (Naples was popularly supposed to have a
high incidence of venereal disease.)   10 *wind instrument* (With a joke on flatulence. The *tail*, line 8, that
hangs nearby the *wind instrument* suggests the penis.)   12 *for love's sake* (1) out of friendship and affection
(2) for the sake of lovemaking in Othello's marriage   14 *may not* cannot

A Musician: We have none such, sir.

Clown: Then put up your pipes in your bag, for I'll away.° Go, vanish into air, away!

                                                        Exeunt Musicians.

Cassio: Dost thou hear, mine honest friend?

Clown: No, I hear not your honest friend; I hear you.   20

Cassio: Prithee, keep up° thy quillets.° There's a poor piece of gold for thee. [*He gives money.*] If the gentle-woman that attends the General's wife be stirring, tell her there's one Cassio entreats her a little favor of speech.° Wilt thou do this?

Clown: She is stirring, sir. If she will stir° hither, I shall seem° to notify unto her.

Cassio: Do, good my friend.   *Exit Clown.*

    Enter Iago.

                        In happy time,° Iago.   25

Iago: You have not been abed, then?

Cassio: Why, no. The day had broke
    Before we parted. I have made bold, Iago,
    To send in to your wife. My suit to her
    Is that she will to virtuous Desdemona   30
    Procure me some access.

Iago: I'll send her to you presently;
    And I'll devise a means to draw the Moor
    Out of the way, that your converse and business
    May be more free.   35

Cassio: I humbly thank you for 't.   *Exit [Iago].*
                     I never knew
    A Florentine° more kind and honest.

    Enter Emilia.

Emilia: Good morrow, good Lieutenant. I am sorry
    For your displeasure;° but all will sure be well.
    The General and his wife are talking of it,   40
    And she speaks for you stoutly.° The Moor replies
    That he you hurt is of great fame° in Cyprus
    And great affinity,° and that in wholesome wisdom
    He might not but refuse you; but he protests° he loves you
    And needs no other suitor but his likings   45
    To take the safest occasion by the front°
    To bring you in again.

Cassio: Yet I beseech you,
    If you think fit, or that it may be done,
    Give me advantage of some brief discourse
    With Desdemona alone.

---

17 *I'll away* (Possibly a misprint, or a snatch of song?)   21 *keep up* do not bring out, do not use.   *quillets* quibbles, puns   23 *a little . . . speech* the favor of a brief talk   24 *stir* bestir herself (with a play on *stirring,* "rousing herself from rest").   *seem* deem it good, think fit   25 *In happy time* i.e., well met   37 *Florentine* i.e., even a fellow Florentine. (Iago is a Venetian; Cassio is a Florentine.)   39 *displeasure* fall from favor   41 *stoutly* spiritedly   42 *fame* reputation, importance   43 *affinity* kindred, family connection   44 *protests* insists   46 *occasion . . . front* opportunity by the forelock

Emilia: Pray you, come in.   50
   I will bestow you where you shall have time
   To speak your bosom° freely.
Cassio: I am much bound to you.   [*Exeunt.*]

SCENE II [THE CITADEL.]

   Enter Othello, Iago, and Gentlemen.

Othello [*giving letters*]: These letters give, Iago, to the pilot,
   And by him do my duties° to the Senate.
   That done, I will be walking on the works;°
   Repair° there to me.
Iago: Well, my good lord, I'll do 't.
Othello: This fortification, gentlemen, shall we see 't?   5
Gentlemen: We'll wait upon° your lordship.   *Exeunt.*

SCENE III [THE GARDEN OF THE CITADEL.]

   Enter Desdemona, Cassio, and Emilia.

Desdemona: Be thou assured, good Cassio, I will do
   All my abilities in thy behalf.
Emilia: Good madam, do. I warrant it grieves my husband
   As if the cause were his.
Desdemona: O, that's an honest fellow. Do not doubt, Cassio,   5
   But I will have my lord and you again
   As friendly as you were.
Cassio: Bounteous madam,
   Whatever shall become of Michael Cassio,
   He's never anything but your true servant.
Desdemona: I know 't. I thank you. You do love my lord;   10
   You have known him long, and be you well assured
   He shall in strangeness° stand no farther off
   Than in a politic° distance.
Cassio: Ay, but, lady,
   That policy may either last so long,
   Or feed upon such nice and waterish diet,°   15
   Or breed itself so out of circumstance,°
   That, I being absent and my place supplied,°
   My general will forget my love and service.
Desdemona: Do not doubt° that. Before Emilia here
   I give thee warrant° of thy place. Assure thee,   20

---

52 *bosom* inmost thoughts   2 *do my duties* convey my respects   3 *works* breastworks, fortifications
4 *Repair* return, come   6 *wait upon* attend   12 *strangeness* aloofness   13 *politic* required by wise policy
15 *Or . . . diet* or sustain itself at length upon such trivial and meager technicalities   16 *breed . . . circum-*
stance continually renew itself so out of chance events, or yield so few chances for my being pardoned
17 *supplied* filled by another person   19 *doubt* fear   20 *warrant* guarantee

If I do vow a friendship I'll perform it
To the last article. My lord shall never rest.
I'll watch him tame° and talk him out of patience;°
His bed shall seem a school, his board° a shrift;°
I'll intermingle everything he does   25
With Cassio's suit. Therefore be merry, Cassio,
For thy solicitor° shall rather die
Than give thy cause away.°

Enter Othello and Iago [at a distance].

Emilia: Madam, here comes my lord.
Cassio: Madam, I'll take my leave.   30
Desdemona: Why, stay, and hear me speak.
Cassio: Madam, not now. I am very ill at ease,
      Unfit for mine own purposes.
Desdemona: Well, do your discretion.°   *Exit Cassio.*
Iago: Ha? I like not that.   35
Othello: What dost thou say?
Iago: Nothing, my lord; or if—I know not what.
Othello: Was not that Cassio parted from my wife?
Iago: Cassio, my lord? No, sure, I cannot think it,
      That he would steal away so guiltylike,   40
      Seeing you coming.
Othello: I do believe 'twas he.
Desdemona: How now, my lord?
      I have been talking with a suitor here,
      A man that languishes in your displeasure.   45
Othello: Who is 't you mean?
Desdemona: Why, your lieutenant, Cassio. Good my lord,
      If I have any grace or power to move you,
      His present reconciliation take;°
      For if he be not one that truly loves you,   50
      That errs in ignorance and not in cunning,°
      I have no judgment in an honest face.
      I prithee, call him back.
Othello: Went he hence now?
Desdemona: Yes, faith, so humbled   55
      That he hath left part of his grief with me
      To suffer with him. Good love, call him back.
Othello: Not now, sweet Desdemon. Some other time.
Desdemona: But shall 't be shortly?
Othello: The sooner, sweet, for you.   60
Desdemona: Shall 't be tonight at supper?

---

23 *watch him tame* tame him by keeping him from sleeping. (A term from falconry.)   *out of patience* past
his endurance   24 *board* dining table.   *shrift* confessional   27 *solicitor* advocate   28 *away* up   34 *do
your discretion* act according to your own discretion   49 *His . . . take* let him be reconciled to you right
away   51 *in cunning* wittingly

Othello: No, not tonight.

Desdemona: Tomorrow dinner,° then?

Othello: I shall not dine at home.
    I meet the captains at the citadel.   65

Desdemona: Why, then, tomorrow night, or Tuesday morn,
    On Tuesday noon, or night, on Wednesday morn.
    I prithee, name the time, but let it not
    Exceed three days. In faith, he's penitent;
    And yet his trespass, in our common reason°—   70
    Save that, they say, the wars must make example
    Out of her best°—is not almost° a fault
    T' incur a private check.° When shall he come?
    Tell me, Othello. I wonder in my soul
    What you would ask me that I should deny,   75
    Or stand so mammering on.° What? Michael Cassio,
    That came a-wooing with you, and so many a time,
    When I have spoke of you dispraisingly,
    Hath ta'en your part—to have so much to do
    To bring him in!° By 'r Lady, I could do much—   80

Othello: Prithee, no more. Let him come when he will;
    I will deny thee nothing.

Desdemona: Why, this is not a boon.
    'Tis as I should entreat you wear your gloves,
    Or feed on nourishing dishes, or keep you warm,   85
    Or sue to you to do a peculiar° profit
    To your own person. Nay, when I have a suit
    Wherein I mean to touch° your love indeed,
    It shall be full of poise° and difficult weight,
    And fearful to be granted.   90

Othello: I will deny thee nothing.
    Whereon,° I do beseech thee, grant me this,
    To leave me but a little to myself.

Desdemona: Shall I deny you? No. Farewell, my lord.

Othello: Farewell, my Desdemona. I'll come to thee straight.°   95

Desdemona: Emilia, come.—Be as your fancies° teach you;
    Whate'er you be, I am obedient.   *Exit [with Emilia]*

Othello: Excellent wretch!° Perdition catch my soul
    But I do love thee! And when I love thee not,
    Chaos is come again.°   100

Iago: My noble lord—

---

63 *dinner* (The noontime meal.)   70 *common reason* everyday judgments   71–72 *Save . . . best* were it
not that, as the saying goes, military discipline requires making an example of the very best men. (He
refers to *wars* as a singular concept.)   72 *not almost* scarcely   73 *private check* even a private reprimand
76 *mammering on* wavering about   80 *bring him in* restore him to favor   86 *peculiar* particular, personal
88 *touch* test   89 *poise* weight, heaviness; or equipoise, delicate balance involving hard choice
92 *Whereon* in return for which   95 *straight* straightway   96 *fancies* inclinations   98 *wretch* (A term of affectionate endearment.)   99–100 *And . . . again* i.e., my love for you will last forever, until the end of
time when chaos will return. (But with an unconscious, ironic suggestion that, if anything should induce
Othello to cease loving Desdemona, the result would be chaos.)

Othello: What dost thou say, Iago?
Iago: Did Michael Cassio, when you wooed my lady,
    Know of your love?
Othello: He did, from first to last. Why dost thou ask?   105
Iago: But for a satisfaction of my thought;
    No further harm.
Othello: Why of thy thought, Iago?
Iago: I did not think he had been acquainted with her.
Othello: O, yes, and went between us very oft.
Iago: Indeed?   110
Othello: Indeed? Ay, indeed. Discern'st thou aught in that?
    Is he not honest?
Iago: Honest, my lord?
Othello: Honest. Ay, honest.
Iago: My lord, for aught I know.   115
Othello: What dost thou think?
Iago: Think, my lord?
Othello: "Think, my lord?" By heaven, thou echo'st me,
    As if there were some monster in thy thought
    Too hideous to be shown. Thou dost mean something.   120
    I heard thee say even now, thou lik'st not that,
    When Cassio left my wife. What didst not like?
    And when I told thee he was of my counsel°
    In my whole course of wooing, thou criedst "Indeed?"
    And didst contract and purse° thy brow together   125
    As if thou then hadst shut up in thy brain
    Some horrible conceit.° If thou dost love me,
    Show me thy thought.
Iago: My lord, you know I love you.
Othello: I think thou dost;   130
    And, for° I know thou'rt full of love and honesty,
    And weigh'st thy words before thou giv'st them breath,
    Therefore these stops° of thine fright me the more;
    For such things in a false disloyal knave
    Are tricks of custom,° but in a man that's just   135
    They're close dilations,° working from the heart
    That passion cannot rule.°
Iago: For° Michael Cassio,
    I dare be sworn I think that he is honest.
Othello: I think so too.
Iago: Men should be what they seem;
    Or those that be not, would they might seem none!°   140
Othello: Certain, men should be what they seem.

---

123 *of my counsel* in my confidence   125 *purse* knit   127 *conceit* fancy   131 *for* because   133 *stops* pauses 135 *of custom* customary   136 *close dilations* secret or involuntary expressions or delays   137 *That passion cannot rule* i.e., that are too passionately strong to be restrained (referring to the workings), or that cannot rule its own passions (referring to the heart).   *For* as for   140 *none* i.e., not to be men, or not seem to be honest

Iago: Why, then, I think Cassio's an honest man.

Othello: Nay, yet there's more in this.
 I prithee, speak to me as to thy thinkings,
 As thou dost ruminate, and give thy worst of thoughts   145
 The worst of words.

Iago: Good my lord, pardon me.
 Though I am bound to every act of duty,
 I am not bound to that° all slaves are free to.°
 Utter my thoughts? Why, say they are vile and false,
 As where's the palace whereinto foul things   150
 Sometimes intrude not? Who has that breast so pure
 But some uncleanly apprehensions
 Keep leets and law days,° and in sessions sit
 With° meditations lawful?°

Othello: Thou dost conspire against thy friend,° Iago,   155
 If thou but think'st him wronged and mak'st his ear
 A stranger to thy thoughts.

Iago: I do beseech you,
 Though I perchance am vicious° in my guess—
 As I confess it is my nature's plague
 To spy into abuses, and oft my jealousy°   160
 Shapes faults that are not—that your wisdom then,°
 From one° that so imperfectly conceits,°
 Would take no notice, nor build yourself a trouble
 Out of his scattering° and unsure observance.
 It were not for your quiet nor your good,   165
 Nor for my manhood, honesty, and wisdom,
 To let you know my thoughts.

Othello: What dost thou mean?

Iago: Good name in man and woman, dear my lord,
 Is the immediate° jewel of their souls.
 Who steals my purse steals trash; 'tis something, nothing;   170
 'Twas mine, 'tis his, and has been slave to thousands;
 But he that filches from me my good name
 Robs me of that which not enriches him
 And makes me poor indeed.

Othello: By heaven, I'll know thy thoughts.   175

Iago: You cannot, if° my heart were in your hand,
 Nor shall not, whilst 'tis in my custody.

Othello: Ha?

Iago: O, beware, my lord, of jealousy.
 It is the green-eyed monster which doth mock
 The meat it feeds on.° That cuckold lives in bliss   180

---

148 *that* that which. *free to* free with respect to   153 *Keep leets and law days* i.e., hold court, set up their authority in one's heart. (*Leets* are a kind of manor court; *law days* are the days courts sit in session, or those sessions.)   154 *With* along with. *lawful* innocent   155 *thy friend* i.e., Othello   158 *vicious* wrong   160 *jealousy* suspicious nature   161 *then* on that account   162 *one* i.e., myself, Iago. *conceits* judges, conjectures   164 *scattering* random   169 *immediate* essential, most precious   176 *if* even if   179–180 *doth mock . . . on* mocks and torments the heart of its victim, the man who suffers jealousy

Iago plants doubts about Desdemona in Othello's mind (III, iii, 101–295).

Who, certain of his fate, loves not his wronger;°
But O, what damnèd minutes tells° he o'er
Who dotes, yet doubts, suspects, yet fondly loves!
Othello: O misery!
Iago: Poor and content is rich, and rich enough,°   185
But riches fineless° is as poor as winter
To him that ever fears he shall be poor.
Good God, the souls of all my tribe defend
From jealousy!
Othello: Why, why is this?   190
Think'st thou I'd make a life of jealousy,
To follow still the changes of the moon
With fresh suspicions?° No! To be once in doubt
Is once° to be resolved.° Exchange me for a goat

181 *his wronger* i.e., his faithless wife. (The unsuspecting cuckold is spared the misery of loving his wife
only to discover she is cheating on him.)   182 *tells* counts   185 *Poor . . . enough* to be content with
what little one has is the greatest wealth of all. (Proverbial.)   186 *fineless* boundless   192–193 *To follow
. . . suspicions* to be constantly imagining new causes for suspicion, changing incessantly like the moon
194 *once* once and for all.   *resolved* free of doubt, having settled the matter

When I shall turn the business of my soul   195
To such exsufflicate and blown° surmises
Matching thy inference.° 'Tis not to make me jealous
To say my wife is fair, feeds well, loves company,
Is free of speech, sings, plays, and dances well;
Where virtue is, these are more virtuous.   200
Nor from mine own weak merits will I draw
The smallest fear or doubt of her revolt,°
For she had eyes, and chose me. No, Iago,
I'll see before I doubt; when I doubt, prove;
And on the proof, there is no more but this—   205
Away at once with love or jealousy.

Iago: I am glad of this, for now I shall have reason
To show the love and duty that I bear you
With franker spirit. Therefore, as I am bound,
Receive it from me. I speak not yet of proof.   210
Look to your wife; observe her well with Cassio.
Wear your eyes thus, not° jealous nor secure.°
I would not have your free and noble nature,
Out of self-bounty,° be abused.° Look to 't.
I know our country disposition well;   215
In Venice they do let God see the pranks
They dare not show their husbands; their best conscience
Is not to leave 't undone, but keep 't unknown.

Othello: Dost thou say so?

Iago: She did deceive her father, marrying you;   220
And when she seemed to shake and fear your looks,
She loved them most.

Othello: And so she did.

Iago: Why, go to,° then!
She that, so young, could give out such a seeming,°
To seel° her father's eyes up close as oak,°
He thought 'twas witchcraft! But I am much to blame.   225
I humbly do beseech you of your pardon
For too much loving you.

Othello: I am bound° to thee forever.

Iago: I see this hath a little dashed your spirits.

Othello: Not a jot, not a jot.

Iago: I' faith, I fear it has.   230
I hope you will consider what is spoke
Comes from my love. But I do see you're moved.
I am to pray you not to strain my speech

---

196 *exsufflicate and blown* inflated and blown up, rumored about, or, spat out and flyblown, hence, loathsome, disgusting   197 *inference* description or allegation   202 *doubt . . . revolt* fear of her unfaithfulness   212 *not* neither.   *secure* free from uncertainty   214 *self-bounty* inherent or natural goodness and generosity.   *abused* deceived   222 *go to* (An expression of impatience.)   223 *seeming* false appearance   224 *seel* blind. (A term from falconry.)   *oak* (A close-grained wood.)   228 *bound* indebted (but perhaps with ironic sense of "tied")

To grosser issues° nor to larger reach°
Than to suspicion.   235
Othello: I will not.
Iago: Should you do so, my lord,
My speech should fall into such vile success°
Which my thoughts aimed not. Cassio's my worthy friend.
My lord, I see you're moved.
Othello: No, not much moved.   240
I do not think but Desdemona's honest.°
Iago: Long live she so! And long live you to think so!
Othello: And yet, how nature erring from itself—
Iago: Ay, there's the point! As—to be bold with you—
Not to affect° many proposèd matches   245
Of her own clime, complexion, and degree,°
Whereto we see in all things nature tends—
Foh! One may smell in such a will° most rank,
Foul disproportion,° thoughts unnatural.
But pardon me. I do not in position°   250
Distinctly speak of her, though I may fear
Her will, recoiling° to her better° judgment,
May fall to match you with her country forms°
And happily repent.°
Othello: Farewell, farewell!
If more thou dost perceive, let me know more.   255
Set on thy wife to observe. Leave me, Iago.
Iago [going]: My lord, I take my leave.
Othello: Why did I marry? This honest creature doubtless
Sees and knows more, much more, than he unfolds.
Iago [returning]: My Lord, I would I might entreat your honor   260
To scan° this thing no farther. Leave it to time.
Although 'tis fit that Cassio have his place—
For, sure, he fills it up with great ability—
Yet, if you please to hold him off awhile,
You shall by that perceive him and his means.°   265
Note if your lady strain his entertainment°
With any strong or vehement importunity;
Much will be seen in that. In the meantime,
Let me be thought too busy° in my fears—
As worthy cause I have to fear I am—   270
And hold her free,° I do beseech your honor.
Othello: Fear not my government.°
Iago: I once more take my leave.   *Exit.*

---

234 *issues* significances. *reach* meaning, scope   238 *success* effect, result   241 *honest* chaste   245 *affect* prefer, desire   246 *clime . . . degree* country, color, and social position   248 *will* sensuality, appetite   249 *disproportion* abnormality   250 *position* argument, proposition   252 *recoiling* reverting. *better* i.e., more natural and reconsidered   253 *fall . . . forms* undertake to compare you with Venetian norms of handsomeness   254 *happily repent* happily repent her marriage   261 *scan* scrutinize   265 *his means* the method he uses (to regain his post)   266 *strain his entertainment* urge his reinstatement   269 *busy* interfering   271 *hold her free* regard her as innocent   272 *government* self-control, conduct

Othello: This fellow's of exceeding honesty,
And knows all qualities,° with a learnèd spirit, 275
Of human dealings. If I do prove her haggard,°
Though that her jesses° were my dear heartstrings,
I'd whistle her off and let her down the wind°
To prey at fortune.° Haply, for° I am black
And have not those soft parts of conversation° 280
That chamberers° have, or for I am declined
Into the vale of years—yet that's not much—
She's gone. I am abused,° and my relief
Must be to loathe her. O curse of marriage,
That we can call these delicate creatures ours 285
And not their appetites! I had rather be a toad
And live upon the vapor of a dungeon
Than keep a corner in the thing I love
For others' uses. Yet, 'tis the plague of great ones;
Prerogatived° are they less than the base.° 290
'Tis destiny unshunnable, like death.
Even then this forkèd° plague is fated to us
When we do quicken.° Look where she comes.

Enter Desdemona and Emilia.

If she be false, O, then heaven mocks itself!
I'll not believe 't.
Desdemona: How now, my dear Othello? 295
Your dinner, and the generous° islanders
By you invited, do attend° your presence.
Othello: I am to blame.
Desdemona: Why do you speak so faintly?
Are you not well?
Othello: I have a pain upon my forehead here. 300
Desdemona: Faith, that's with watching.° 'Twill away again.

[*She offers her handkerchief.*]

Let me but bind it hard, within this hour
It will be well.
Othello: Your napkin° is too little.
Let it alone.° Come, I'll go in with you.

[*He puts the handkerchief from him, and it drops.*]

---

275 *qualities* natures, types   276 *haggard* wild (like a wild female hawk)   277 *jesses* straps fastened around
the legs of a trained hawk   278 *I'd . . . wind* i.e., I'd let her go forever. (To release a hawk downwind was
to invite it not to return.)   279 *prey at fortune* fend for herself in the wild.   *Haply, for* perhaps because
280 *soft . . . conversation* pleasing graces of social behavior   281 *chamberers* gallants   283 *abused* deceived
290 *Prerogatived* privileged (to have honest wives).   *the base* ordinary citizens. (Socially prominent men
are especially prone to the unavoidable destiny of being cuckolded and to the public shame that goes with
it.)   292 *forkèd* (An allusion to the horns of the cuckold.)   293 *quicken* receive life. (Quicken may also
mean to swarm with maggots as the body festers, as in IV, ii, 69, in which case lines 292–293 suggest that
even then, in death, we are cuckolded by *forkèd* worms.)   296 *generous* noble   297 *attend* await   301
watching too little sleep   303 *napkin* handkerchief   304 *Let it alone* i.e., never mind

Desdemona: I am very sorry that you are not well.   305

> *Exit [with Othello].*

Emilia [picking up the handkerchief]: I am glad I have found this napkin.
This was her first remembrance from the Moor.
My wayward° husband hath a hundred times
Wooed me to steal it, but she so loves the token—
For he conjured her she should ever keep it—   310
That she reserves it evermore about her
To kiss and talk to. I'll have the work' ta'en out,°
And give 't Iago. What he will do with it
Heaven knows, not I;
I nothing but to please his fantasy.°   315

> *Enter Iago.*

Iago: How now? What do you here alone?
Emilia: Do not you chide. I have a thing for you.
Iago: You have a thing for me? It is a common thing°—
Emilia: Ha?
Iago: To have a foolish wife.   320
Emilia: O, is that all? What will you give me now
For that same handkerchief?
Iago: What handkerchief?
Emilia: What handkerchief?
Why, that the Moor first gave to Desdemona;   325
That which so often you did bid me steal.
Iago: Hast stolen it from her?
Emilia: No, faith. She let it drop by negligence,
And to th' advantage° I, being here, took 't up.
Look, here 'tis.
Iago: A good wench! Give it me.   330
Emilia: What will you do with 't, that you have been so earnest
To have me filch it?
Iago [snatching it]:   Why, what is that to you?
Emilia: If it be not for some purpose of import,
Give 't me again. Poor lady, she'll run mad
When she shall lack° it.
Iago: Be not acknown on 't.°   335
I have use for it. Go, leave me.   *Exit Emilia.*
I will in Cassio's lodging lose° this napkin
And let him find it. Trifles light as air
Are to the jealous confirmations strong
As proofs of Holy Writ. This may do something.   340

---

308 *wayward* capricious   312 *work ta'en out* design of the embroidery copied   315 *fantasy* whim
318 *common thing* (With bawdy suggestion; *common* suggests coarseness and availability to all comers, and
thing is a slang term for the pudendum.)   329 *to th' advantage* taking the opportunity   335 *lack* miss. *Be
. . . on 't* do not confess knowledge of it   337 *lose* (The Folio spelling, *loose*, is a normal spelling for "lose,"
but it may also contain the idea of "let go," "release.")

Iago: "I have use for it. Go, leave me. / I will in Cassio's lodging lose this napkin" (III, iii, 336–337).

The Moor already changes with my poison.
Dangerous conceits° are in their natures poisons,
Which at the first are scarce found to distaste,°
But with a little act° upon the blood
Burn like the mines of sulfur.

Enter Othello.

                I did say so.   345
Look where he comes! Not poppy nor mandragora°
Nor all the drowsy syrups of the world

342 *conceits* fancies, ideas   343 *distaste* be distasteful   344 *act* action, working   346 *mandragora* an opiate made of the mandrake root

Shall ever medicine thee to that sweet sleep
Which thou owedst° yesterday.

Othello: Ha, ha, false to me?

Iago: Why, how now, General? No more of that.   350

Othello: Avaunt! Begone! Thou hast set me on the rack.
I swear 'tis better to be much abused
Than but to know 't a little.

Iago: How now, my lord?

Othello: What sense had I of her stolen hours of lust?
I saw 't not, thought it not, it harmed not me.   355
I slept the next night well, fed well, was free° and merry;
I found not Cassio's kisses on her lips.
He that is robbed, not wanting° what is stolen,
Let him not know 't and he's not robbed at all.

Iago: I am sorry to hear this.   360

Othello: I had been happy if the general camp,
Pioners° and all, had tasted her sweet body,
So° I had nothing known. O, now, forever
Farewell the tranquil mind! Farewell content!
Farewell the plumèd troops and the big° wars   365
That makes ambition virtue! O, farewell!
Farewell the neighing steed and the shrill trump,
The spirit-stirring drum, th' ear-piercing fife,
The royal banner, and all quality,°
Pride,° pomp, and circumstance° of glorious war!   370
And O, you mortal engines,° whose rude throats
Th' immortal Jove's dread clamors° counterfeit,
Farewell! Othello's occupation's gone.

Iago: Is 't possible, my lord?

Othello: Villain, be sure thou prove my love a whore!   375
Be sure of it. Give me the ocular proof,
Or, by the worth of mine eternal soul,
Thou hadst been better have been born a dog
Than answer my waked wrath!

Iago: Is 't come to this?

Othello: Make me to see 't, or at the least so prove it   380
That the probation° bear no hinge nor loop
To hang a doubt on, or woe upon thy life!

Iago: My noble lord—

Othello: If thou dost slander her and torture me,
Never pray more; abandon all remorse;°   385
On horror's head horrors accumulate;°
Do deeds to make heaven weep, all earth amazed;°

---

349 *thou owedst* you did own   356 *free* carefree   358 *wanting* missing   362 *Pioners* diggers of mines, the lowest grade of soldiers   363 *So* provided   365 *big* stately   369 *quality* character, essential nature 370 *Pride* rich display. *circumstance* pageantry   371 *mortal engines* i.e., cannon. (*Mortal* means "deadly.") 372 *Jove's dread clamors* i.e., thunder   381 *probation* proof   385 *remorse* pity, penitent hope for salvation   386 *horrors accumulate* add still more horrors   387 *amazed* confounded with horror

For nothing canst thou to damnation add
Greater than that.

Iago: O grace! O heaven forgive me!
Are you a man? Have you a soul or sense?   390
God b' wi' you; take mine office. O wretched fool,°
That lov'st to make thine honesty a vice!°
O monstrous world! Take note, take note, O world,
To be direct and honest is not safe.
I thank you for this profit,° and from hence°   395
I'll love no friend, sith° love breeds such offense.°

Othello: Nay, stay. Thou shouldst be° honest.

Iago: I should be wise, for honesty's a fool
And loses that° it works for.

Othello: By the world,
I think my wife be honest and think she is not;   400
I think that thou art just and think thou art not.
I'll have some proof. My name, that was as fresh
As Dian's° visage, is now begrimed and black
As mine own face. If there be cords, or knives,
Poison, or fire, or suffocating streams,   405
I'll not endure it. Would I were satisfied!

Iago: I see, sir, you are eaten up with passion.
I do repent me that I put it to you.
You would be satisfied?

Othello: Would? Nay, and I will.

Iago: And may; but how? How satisfied, my lord?   410
Would you, the supervisor,° grossly gape on?
Behold her topped?

Othello: Death and damnation! O!

Iago: It were a tedious difficulty, I think,
To bring them to that prospect. Damn them then,°
If ever mortal eyes do see them bolster°   415
More° than their own.° What then? How then?
What shall I say? Where's satisfaction?
It is impossible you should see this,
Were they as prime° as goats, as hot as monkeys,
As salt° as wolves in pride,° and fools as gross   420
As ignorance made drunk. But yet I say,
If imputation and strong circumstances°
Which lead directly to the door of truth
Will give you satisfaction, you might have 't.

---

391 *O wretched fool* (Iago addresses himself as a fool for having carried honesty too far.)   392 *vice* failing, something overdone   395 *profit* profitable instruction.   *hence* henceforth   396 *sith* since.   *offense* i.e., harm to the one who offers help and friendship   397 *Thou shouldst be* it appears that you are. (But Iago replies in the sense of "ought to be.")   399 *that* what   403 *Dian* Diana, goddess of the moon and of chastity   411 *supervisor* onlooker   414 *Damn them then* i.e., they would have to be really incorrigible   415 *bolster* go to bed together, share a bolster   416 *More* other.   *own* own eyes   419 *prime* lustful   420 *salt* wanton, sensual.   *pride* heat   422 *imputation . . . circumstances* strong circumstantial evidence

Othello: Give me a living reason she's disloyal.   425
Iago: I do not like the office.
    But sith° I am entered in this cause so far,
    Pricked° to 't by foolish honesty and love,
    I will go on. I lay with Cassio lately,
    And being troubled with a raging tooth   430
    I could not sleep. There are a kind of men
    So loose of soul that in their sleeps will mutter
    Their affairs. One of this kind is Cassio.
    In sleep I heard him say, "Sweet Desdemona,
    Let us be wary, let us hide our loves!"   435
    And then, sir, would he grip and wring my hand,
    Cry "O sweet creature!" and then kiss me hard,
    As if he plucked up kisses by the roots
    That grew upon my lips; then laid his leg
    Over my thigh, and sighed, and kissed, and then   440
    Cried, "Cursèd fate that gave thee to the Moor!"
Othello: O monstrous! Monstrous!
Iago: Nay, this was but his dream.
Othello: But this denoted a foregone conclusion.°
    'Tis a shrewd doubt,° though it be but a dream.
Iago: And this may help to thicken other proofs   445
    That do demonstrate thinly.
Othello: I'll tear her all to pieces.
Iago: Nay, but be wise. Yet we see nothing done;
    She may be honest yet. Tell me but this:
    Have you not sometimes seen a handkerchief
    Spotted with strawberries° in your wife's hand?   450
Othello: I gave her such a one. 'Twas my first gift.
Iago: I know not that; but such a handkerchief—
    I am sure it was your wife's—did I today
    See Cassio wipe his beard with.
Othello: If it be that—
Iago: If it be that, or any that was hers,   455
    It speaks against her with the other proofs.
Othello: O, that the slave° had forty thousand lives!
    One is too poor, too weak for my revenge.
    Now do I see 'tis true. Look here, Iago,
    All my fond° love thus do I blow to heaven.   460
    'Tis gone.
    Arise, black vengeance, from the hollow hell!
    Yield up, O love, thy crown and hearted° throne
    To tyrannous hate! Swell, bosom, with thy freight,°
    For 'tis of aspics'° tongues!   465

---

427 *sith* since   428 *Pricked* spurred   443 *foregone conclusion* concluded experience or action   444 *shrewd doubt* suspicious circumstance   450 *Spotted with strawberries* embroidered with a strawberry pattern   457 *the slave* i.e., Cassio   460 *fond* foolish (but also suggesting "affectionate")   463 *hearted* fixed in the heart   464 *freight* burden   465 *aspics'* venomous serpents'

Iago: Yet be content.°
Othello: O, blood, blood, blood!
Iago: Patience, I say. Your mind perhaps may change.
Othello: Never, Iago. Like to the Pontic Sea,°
    Whose icy current and compulsive course   470
    Ne'er feels retiring ebb, but keeps due on
    To the Propontic° and the Hellespont,°
    Even so my bloody thoughts with violent pace
    Shall ne'er look back, ne'er ebb to humble love,
    Till that a capable° and wide revenge   475
    Swallow them up. Now, by yond marble° heaven,
    [*Kneeling*] In the due reverence of a sacred vow
    I here engage my words.
Iago: Do not rise yet.
    [*He kneels.*°] Witness, you ever-burning lights above,
    You elements that clip° us round about,   480
    Witness that here Iago doth give up
    The execution° of his wit,° hands, heart,
    To wronged Othello's service. Let him command,
    And to obey shall be in me remorse,°
    What bloody business ever.°   [*They rise.*]
Othello: I greet thy love,   485
    Not with vain thanks, but with acceptance bounteous,
    And will upon the instant put thee to 't.°
    Within these three days let me hear thee say
    That Cassio's not alive.
Iago: My friend is dead;
    'Tis done at your request. But let her live.   490
Othello: Damn her, lewd minx!° O, damn her, damn her!
    Come, go with me apart. I will withdraw
    To furnish me with some swift means of death
    For the fair devil. Now art thou my lieutenant.
Iago: I am your own forever.   *Exeunt.* 495

SCENE IV [BEFORE THE CITADEL.]

    Enter Desdemona, Emilia, and Clown.

Desdemona: Do you know, sirrah,° where Lieutenant Cassio lies?°
Clown: I dare not say he lies anywhere.
Desdemona: Why, man?
Clown: He's a soldier, and for me to say a soldier lies, 'tis stabbing.

---

466 *content* calm   469 *Pontic Sea* Black Sea   472 *Propontic* Sea of Marmara, between the Black Sea and the Aegean. *Hellespont* Dardanelles, straits where the Sea of Marmara joins with the Aegean   475 *capable* ample, comprehensive   476 *marble* i.e., gleaming like marble and unrelenting   479 s.d. *He kneels* (In the Quarto text, Iago kneels here after Othello has knelt at line 477.)   480 *clip* encompass 482 *execution* exercise, action. *wit* mind 484 *remorse* pity (for Othello's wrongs) 485 *ever* soever 487 *to 't* to the proof 491 *minx* wanton 1 *sirrah* (A form of address to an inferior.) *lies* lodges. (But the Clown makes the obvious pun.)

Desdemona: Go to. Where lodges he?　　　　　　　　　　　　　　　5
Clown: To tell you where he lodges is to tell you where I lie.
Desdemona: Can anything be made of this?
Clown: I know not where he lodges, and for me to devise a lodging and say he lies
　　here, or he lies there, were to lie in mine own throat.°
Desdemona: Can you inquire him out, and be edified by report?　　　　10
Clown: I will catechize the world for him; that is, make questions, and by them
　　answer.
Desdemona: Seek him, bid him come hither. Tell him I have moved° my lord on his
　　behalf and hope all will be well.
Clown: To do this is within the compass of man's wit, and therefore I will attempt　15
　　the doing it.　　　　　　　　　　　　　　　　　　*Exit Clown.*
Desdemona: Where should I lose that handkerchief, Emilia?
Emilia: I know not, madam.
Desdemona: Believe me, I had rather have lost my purse
　　Full of crusadoes;° and but my noble Moor　　　　　　　　20
　　Is true of mind and made of no such baseness
　　As jealous creatures are, it were enough
　　To put him to ill thinking.
Emilia:　　　　　　　　　Is he not jealous?
Desdemona: Who, he? I think the sun where he was born
　　Drew all such humors° from him.
Emilia:　　　　　　　　　Look where he comes.　　　　　25

　　　Enter Othello.

Desdemona: I will not leave him now till Cassio
　　Be called to him.—How is 't with you, my lord?
Othello: Well, my good lady. [*Aside.*] O, hardness to dissemble!—
　　How do you, Desdemona?
Desdemona:　　　　　　　　Well, my good lord.
Othello: Give me your hand. [*She gives her hand.*] This hand is moist, my lady.　　30
Desdemona: It yet hath felt no age nor known no sorrow.
Othello: This argues° fruitfulness° and liberal° heart.
　　Hot, hot, and moist. This hand of yours requires
　　A sequester° from liberty, fasting and prayer,
　　Much castigation,° exercise devout;°　　　　　　　　35
　　For here's a young and sweating devil here
　　That commonly rebels. 'Tis a good hand,
　　A frank° one.
Desdemona:　　　　You may indeed say so,
　　For 'twas that hand that gave away my heart.
Othello: A liberal hand. The hearts of old gave hands,°　　　　　40

---

9 *lie … throat* (1) lie egregiously and deliberately (2) use the windpipe to speak a lie　13 *moved* petitioned
20 *crusadoes* Portuguese gold coins　25 *humors* (Refers to the four bodily fluids thought to determine temperament.)　32 *argues* gives evidence of. *fruitfulness* generosity, amorousness, and fecundity. *liberal*
generous and sexually free　34 *sequester* separation, sequestration　35 *castigation* corrective discipline.
exercise devout i.e., prayer, religious meditation, etc.　38 *frank* generous, open (with sexual suggestion)
40 *The hearts . . . hands* i.e., in former times, people would give their hearts when they gave their hands to
something

"She offers a handkerchief" (III, iv, 47 s.d.).

But our new heraldry is hands, not hearts.°
Desdemona: I cannot speak of this. Come now, your promise.
Othello: What promise, chuck?°
Desdemona: I have sent to bid Cassio come speak with you.
Othello: I have a salt and sorry rheum° offends me;   45
    Lend me thy handkerchief.
Desdemona: Here, my lord.   [*She offers a handkerchief.*]
Othello: That which I gave you.
Desdemona: I have it not about me.
Othello: Not?
Desdemona: No, faith, my lord.   50
Othello: That's a fault. That handkerchief
    Did an Egyptian to my mother give.
    She was a charmer,° and could almost read
    The thoughts of people. She told her, while she kept it
    'Twould make her amiable° and subdue my father   55
    Entirely to her love, but if she lost it
    Or made a gift of it, my father's eye
    Should hold her loathèd and his spirits should hunt

41 *But . . . hearts* i.e., in our decadent times, the joining of hands is no longer a badge to signify the giving of hearts   43 *chuck* (A term of endearment.)   45 *salt . . . rheum* distressful head cold or watering of the eyes   53 *charmer* sorceress   55 *amiable* desirable

After new fancies.° She, dying, gave it me,
And bid me, when my fate would have me wived,   60
To give it her.° I did so; and take heed on 't;
Make it a darling like your precious eye.
To lose 't or give 't away were such perdition°
As nothing else could match.
Desdemona: Is 't possible?
Othello: 'Tis true. There's magic in the web° of it.   65
    A sibyl, that had numbered in the world
    The sun to course two hundred compasses,°
    In her prophetic fury° sewed the work;°
    The worms were hallowed that did breed the silk,
    And it was dyed in mummy° which the skillful   70
    Conserved of° maidens' hearts.
Desdemona: I' faith! Is 't true?
Othello: Most veritable. Therefore look to 't well.
Desdemona: Then would to God that I had never seen 't!
Othello: Ha? Wherefore?
Desdemona: Why do you speak so startingly and rash?°   75
Othello: Is 't lost? Is 't gone? Speak, is 't out o' the way?°
Desdemona: Heaven bless us!
Othello: Say you?
Desdemona: It is not lost; but what an if° it were?
Othello: How?   80
Desdemona: I say it is not lost.
Othello: Fetch 't, let me see 't.
Desdemona: Why, so I can, sir, but I will not now.
    This is a trick to put me from my suit.
    Pray you, let Cassio be received again.
Othello: Fetch me the handkerchief! My mind misgives.   85
Desdemona: Come, come,
    You'll never meet a more sufficient° man.
Othello: The handkerchief!
Desdemona: I pray, talk° me of Cassio.
Othello: The handkerchief!
Desdemona: A man that all his time°
    Hath founded his good fortunes on your love,   90
    Shared dangers with you—
Othello: The handkerchief!
Desdemona: I' faith, you are to blame.
Othello: Zounds!   *Exit Othello.*
Emilia: Is not this man jealous?   95

59 *fancies* loves   61 *her* i.e., to my wife   63 *perdition* loss   65 *web* fabric, weaving   67 *compasses* annual circlings. (The *sibyl*, or prophetess, was two hundred years old.)   68 *prophetic fury* frenzy of prophetic inspiration.   *work* embroidered pattern   70 *mummy* medicinal or magical preparation drained from mummified bodies   71 *Conserved of* prepared or preserved out of   75 *startingly and rash* disjointedly and impetuously, excitedly   76 *out o' the way* lost, misplaced   79 *an if* if   87 *sufficient* able, complete   88 *talk* talk to   89 *all his time* throughout his career

Desdemona: I ne'er saw this before.
    Sure, there's some wonder in this handkerchief.
    I am most unhappy in the loss of it.
Emilia: 'Tis not a year or two shows us a man.°
    They are all but stomachs, and we all but° food;   100
    They eat us hungerly,° and when they are full
    They belch us.

    Enter Iago and Cassio.

                Look you, Cassio and my husband.
Iago [*to Cassio*]: There is no other way; 'tis she must do 't.
    And, lo, the happiness!° Go and importune her.
Desdemona: How now, good Cassio? What's the news with you?   105
Cassio: Madam, my former suit. I do beseech you
    That by your virtuous° means I may again
    Exist and be a member of his love
    Whom I, with all the office° of my heart,
    Entirely honor. I would not be delayed.   110
    If my offense be of such mortal° kind
    That nor my service past, nor° present sorrows,
    Nor purposed merit in futurity
    Can ransom me into his love again,
    But to know so must be my benefit;°   115
    So shall I clothe me in a forced content,
    And shut myself up in° some other course,
    To fortune's alms.°
Desdemona: Alas, thrice-gentle Cassio,
    My advocation° is not now in tune.
    My lord is not my lord; nor should I know him,   120
    Were he in favor° as in humor° altered.
    So help me every spirit sanctified
    As I have spoken for you all my best
    And stood within the blank° of his displeasure
    For my free speech! You must awhile be patient.   125
    What I can do I will, and more I will
    Than for myself I dare. Let that suffice you.
Iago: Is my lord angry?
Emilia: He went hence but now,
    And certainly in strange unquietness.
Iago: Can he be angry? I have seen the cannon   130
    When it hath blown his ranks into the air,

---

99 *'Tis . . . man* i.e., you can't really know a man even in a year or two of experience (?), or, real men come along seldom (?)   100 *but* nothing but   101 *hungerly* hungrily   104 *the happiness* in happy time, fortunately met   107 *virtuous* efficacious   109 *office* loyal service   111 *mortal* fatal   112 *nor . . . nor* neither . . . nor   115 *But . . . benefit* merely to know that my case is hopeless will have to content me (and will be better than uncertainty)   117 *shut . . . in* confine myself to   118 *To fortune's alms* throwing myself on the mercy of fortune   119 *advocation* advocacy   121 *favor* appearance. *humor* mood   124 *within the blank* within point-blank range. (The *blank* is the center of the target.)

And like the devil from his very arm
Puffed his own brother—and is he angry?
Something of moment° then. I will go meet him.
There's matter in 't indeed, if he be angry.   135

Desdemona: I prithee, do so.   *Exit [Iago].*
                         Something, sure, of state,°
Either from Venice, or some unhatched practice°
Made demonstrable here in Cyprus to him,
Hath puddled° his clear spirit; and in such cases
Men's natures wrangle with inferior things,   140
Though great ones are their object. 'Tis even so;
For let our finger ache, and it indues°
Our other, healthful members even to a sense
Of pain. Nay, we must think men are not gods,
Nor of them look for such observancy°   145
As fits the bridal.° Beshrew me° much, Emilia,
I was, unhandsome° warrior as I am,
Arraigning his unkindness with° my soul;
But now I find I had suborned the witness,°
And he's indicted falsely.

Emilia: Pray heaven it be   150
State matters, as you think, and no conception
Nor no jealous toy° concerning you.

Desdemona: Alas the day! I never gave him cause.

Emilia: But jealous souls will not be answered so;
They are not ever jealous for the cause,   155
But jealous for° they're jealous. It is a monster
Begot upon itself,° born on itself.

Desdemona: Heaven keep that monster from Othello's mind!

Emilia: Lady, amen.

Desdemona: I will go seek him. Cassio, walk hereabout.   160
If I do find him fit, I'll move your suit
And seek to effect it to my uttermost.

Cassio: I humbly thank your ladyship.

    Exit [Desdemona with Emilia].

    Enter Bianca.

Bianca: Save° you, friend Cassio!

Cassio: What make° you from home?
How is 't with you, my most fair Bianca?   165
I' faith, sweet love, I was coming to your house.

---

134 *of moment* of immediate importance, momentous   136 *of state* concerning state affairs   137
unhatched practice as yet unexecuted or undiscovered plot   139 *puddled* muddied   142 *indues* brings to
the same condition   145 *observancy* attentiveness   146 *bridal* wedding (when a bridegroom is newly
attentive to his bride).   *Beshrew me* (A mild oath.)   147 *unhandsome* insufficient, unskillful   148 *with*
before the bar of   149 *suborned the witness* induced the witness to give false testimony   152 *toy* fancy
156 *for* because   157 *Begot upon itself* generated solely from itself   164 *Save* God save.   *make* do

Cassio explains to Bianca that he does not know how the handkerchief appeared in his room (III, iv, 175–186).

Bianca: And I was going to your lodging, Cassio.
What, keep a week away? Seven days and nights?
Eightscore-eight° hours? And lovers' absent hours
More tedious than the dial° eightscore times?   170
O weary reckoning!
Cassio: Pardon me, Bianca.
I have this while with leaden thoughts been pressed;
But I shall, in a more continuate° time,
Strike off this score° of absence. Sweet Bianca,

169 *Eightscore-eight* one hundred sixty-eight, the number of hours in a week   170 *the dial* a complete revolution of the clock   173 *continuate* uninterrupted   174 *Strike . . . score* settle this account

[giving her Desdemona's handkerchief]

Take me this work out.°

Bianca: O Cassio, whence came this?   175
This is some token from a newer friend.°
To the felt absence now I feel a cause.
Is 't come to this? Well, well.

Cassio: Go to, woman!
Throw your vile guesses in the devil's teeth,
From whence you have them. You are jealous now   180
That this is from some mistress, some remembrance.
No, by my faith, Bianca.

Bianca: Why, whose is it?

Cassio: I know not, neither. I found it in my chamber.
I like the work well. Ere it be demanded°—
As like° enough it will—I would have it copied.   185
Take it and do 't, and leave me for this time.

Bianca: Leave you? Wherefore?

Cassio: I do attend here on the General,
And think it no addition,° nor my wish,
To have him see me womaned.   190

Bianca: Why, I pray you?

Cassio: Not that I love you not.

Bianca: But that you do not love me.
I pray you, bring° me on the way a little,
And say if I shall see you soon at night.   195

Cassio: 'Tis but a little way that I can bring you,
For I attend here; but I'll see you soon.

Bianca: 'Tis very good. I must be circumstanced.°

Exeunt omnes.

ACT IV

SCENE I [BEFORE THE CITADEL.]

Enter Othello and Iago.

Iago: Will you think so?

Othello: Think so, Iago?

Iago: What,
To kiss in private?

Othello: An unauthorized kiss!

Iago: Or to be naked with her friend in bed
An hour or more, not meaning any harm?

Othello: Naked in bed, Iago, and not mean harm?   5
It is hypocrisy against the devil.

---

175 *Take ... out* copy this embroidery for me   176 *friend* mistress   184 *demanded* inquired for   185 *like* likely   189 *addition* i.e., addition to my reputation   194 *bring* accompany   198 *be circumstanced* be governed by circumstance, yield to your conditions

They that mean virtuously and yet do so,
The devil their virtue tempts, and they tempt heaven.
Iago: If they do nothing, 'tis a venial° slip.
But if I give my wife a handkerchief—   10
Othello: What then?
Iago: Why then, 'tis hers, my lord, and being hers,
She may, I think, bestow 't on any man.
Othello: She is protectress of her honor too.
May she give that?   15
Iago: Her honor is an essence that's not seen;
They have it° very oft that have it not.
But, for the handkerchief—
Othello: By heaven, I would most gladly have forgot it.
Thou saidst—O, it comes o'er my memory   20
As doth the raven o'er the infectious house,°
Boding to all—he had my handkerchief.
Iago: Ay, what of that?
Othello: That's not so good now.
Iago: What
If I had said I had seen him do you wrong?
Or heard him say—as knaves be such abroad,°   25
Who having, by their own importunate suit,
Or voluntary dotage° of some mistress,
Convincèd or supplied° them, cannot choose
But they must blab—
Othello: Hath he said anything?
Iago: He hath, my lord; but, be you well assured,   30
No more than he'll unswear.
Othello: What hath he said?
Iago: Faith, that he did—I know not what he did.
Othello: What? What?
Iago: Lie—
Othello: With her?
Iago: With her, on her; what you will.
Othello: Lie with her? Lie on her? We say "lie on her" when they belie° her. Lie   35
with her? Zounds, that's fulsome.°—Handkerchief—confessions—handker-
chief!—To confess and be hanged for his labor—first to be hanged and then
to confess.°—I tremble at it. Nature would not invest herself in such shad-
owing passion without some instruction.° It is not words° that shakes me

---

9 *venial* pardonable   17 *They have it* i.e., they enjoy a reputation for it   21 *raven . . . house* (Allusion to the
belief that the raven hovered over a house of sickness or infection, such as one visited by the plague.)
25 *abroad* around about   27 *voluntary dotage* willing infatuation   28 *Convincèd or supplied* seduced or sexually
gratified   35 *belie* slander   36 *fulsome* foul   37–38 *first . . . to confess* (Othello reverses the proverbial
confess and be hanged; Cassio is to be given no time to confess before he dies.)   38–39 *Nature . . . instruction*
i.e., without some foundation in fact, nature would not have dressed herself in such an overwhelming passion that comes over me now and fills my mind with images, or in such a lifelike fantasy as Cassio had in his
dream of lying with Desdemona   39 *words* mere words

Iago lies to Cassio that Othello has "fall'n into an epilepsy" (IV, i, 48).

thus. Pish! Noses, ears, and lips.—Is 't possible?—Confess—handkerchief!— 40
O devil!

Falls in a trance.

Iago: Work on,
    My medicine, work! Thus credulous fools are caught,
    And many worthy and chaste dames even thus,
    All guiltless, meet reproach.—What, ho! My lord! 45
    My lord, I say! Othello!

    Enter Cassio.

                        How now, Cassio?
Cassio: What's the matter?
Iago: My lord is fall'n into an epilepsy.
    This is his second fit. He had one yesterday.

Cassio: Rub him about the temples.

Iago: No, forbear.   50
 The lethargy° must have his° quiet course.
 If not, he foams at mouth, and by and by
 Breaks out to savage madness. Look, he stirs.
 Do you withdraw yourself a little while.
 He will recover straight. When he is gone,   55
 I would on great occasion° speak with you.

 [*Exit Cassio.*]

 How is it, General? Have you not hurt your head?
Othello: Dost thou mock me?°
Iago: I mock you not, by heaven.
 Would you would bear your fortune like a man!
Othello: A hornèd man's a monster and a beast.   60
Iago: There's many a beast then in a populous city,
 And many a civil° monster.
Othello: Did he confess it?
Iago: Good sir, be a man.
 Think every bearded fellow that's but yoked°   65
 May draw with you.° There's millions now alive
 That nightly lie in those unproper° beds
 Which they dare swear peculiar.° Your case is better.°
 O, 'tis the spite of hell, the fiend's arch-mock,
 To lip° a wanton in a secure° couch   70
 And to suppose her chaste! No, let me know,
 And knowing what I am,° I know what she shall be.°
Othello: O, thou art wise. 'Tis certain.
Iago: Stand you awhile apart;
 Confine yourself but in a patient list.°   75
 Whilst you were here o'erwhelmèd with your grief—
 A passion most unsuiting such a man—
 Cassio came hither. I shifted him away,°
 And laid good 'scuse upon your ecstasy,°
 Bade him anon return and here speak with me,   80
 The which he promised. Do but encave° yourself
 And mark the fleers,° the gibes, and notable° scorns
 That dwell in every region of his face;
 For I will make him tell the tale anew,
 Where, how, how oft, how long ago, and when   85
 He hath and is again to cope° your wife.

---

51 *lethargy* coma. *his* its 56 *on great occasion* on a matter of great importance 58 *mock me* (Othello takes Iago's question about hurting his head to be a mocking reference to the cuckold's horns.) 62 *civil* i.e., dwelling in a city 65 *yoked* (1) married (2) put into the yoke of infamy and cuckoldry 66 *draw with you* pull as you do, like oxen who are yoked, i.e., share your fate as cuckold 67 *unproper* not exclusively their own 68 *peculiar* private, their own. *better* i.e., because you know the truth 70 *lip* kiss. *secure* free from suspicion 72 *what I am* i.e., a cuckold. *she shall be* will happen to her 75 *in . . . list* within the bounds of patience 78 *shifted him away* used a dodge to get rid of him 79 *ecstasy* trance 81 *encave* conceal 82 *fleers* sneers. *notable* obvious 86 *cope* encounter with, have sex with

I say, but mark his gesture. Marry, patience!
Or I shall say you're all-in-all in spleen,°
And nothing of a man.

Othello: Dost thou hear, Iago?
I will be found most cunning in my patience;   90
But—dost thou hear?—most bloody.

Iago: That's not amiss;
But yet keep time° in all. Will you withdraw?

[*Othello stands apart.*]

Now will I question Cassio of Bianca,
A huswife° that by selling her desires
Buys herself bread and clothes. It is a creature   95
That dotes on Cassio—as 'tis the strumpet's plague
To beguile many and be beguiled by one.
He, when he hears of her, cannot restrain°
From the excess of laughter. Here he comes.

Enter Cassio.

As he shall smile, Othello shall go mad;   100
And his unbookish° jealousy must conster°
Poor Cassio's smiles, gestures, and light behaviors
Quite in the wrong.—How do you now, Lieutenant?

Cassio: The worser that you give me the addition°
Whose want° even kills me.   105

Iago: Ply Desdemona well and you are sure on 't.
[*Speaking lower.*] Now, if this suit lay in Bianca's power,
How quickly should you speed!

Cassio [*laughing*]: Alas, poor caitiff!°

Othello [*aside*]: Look how he laughs already!   110

Iago: I never knew a woman love man so.

Cassio: Alas, poor rogue! I think, i' faith, she loves me.

Othello: Now he denies it faintly, and laughs it out.

Iago: Do you hear, Cassio?

Othello: Now he importunes him
To tell it o'er. Go to!° Well said,° well said.   115

Iago: She gives it out that you shall marry her.
Do you intend it?

Cassio: Ha, ha, ha!

Othello: Do you triumph, Roman?° Do you triumph?

Cassio: I marry her? What? A customer?° Prithee, bear some charity to my wit;° 120
do not think it so unwholesome. Ha, ha, ha!

88 *all-in-all in spleen* utterly governed by passionate impulses   92 *keep time* keep yourself steady (as in music)   94 *huswife* hussy   98 *restrain* refrain   101 *unbookish* uninstructed.   *conster* construe   104 *addition* title   105 *Whose want* the lack of which   109 *caitiff* wretch   115 *Go to* (An expression of remonstrance.) *Well said* well done   119 *Roman* (The Romans were noted for their *triumphs* or triumphal processions.) 120 *customer* i.e., prostitute.   *bear . . . wit* be more charitable to my judgment

Othello: So, so, so, so! They laugh that win.°

Iago: Faith, the cry° goes that you shall marry her.

Cassio: Prithee, say true.

Iago: I am a very villain else.°   125

Othello: Have you scored me?° Well.

Cassio: This is the monkey's own giving out. She is persuaded I will marry her out of her own love and flattery,° not out of my promise.

Othello: Iago beckons me.° Now he begins the story.

Cassio: She was here even now; she haunts me in every place. I was the other day   130 talking on the seabank° with certain Venetians, and thither comes the bauble,° and, by this hand,° she falls me thus about my neck—

[He embraces Iago.]

Othello: Crying, "O dear Cassio!" as it were; his gesture imports it.

Cassio: So hangs and lolls and weeps upon me, so shakes and pulls me. Ha, ha, ha!

Othello: Now he tells how she plucked him to my chamber. O, I see that nose of   135 yours, but not that dog I shall throw it to.°

Cassio: Well, I must leave her company.

Iago: Before me,° look where she comes.

Enter Bianca [with Othello's handkerchief].

Cassio: 'Tis such another fitchew!° Marry, a perfumed one.—What do you mean by this haunting of me?   140

Bianca: Let the devil and his dam° haunt you! What did you mean by that same handkerchief you gave me even now? I was a fine fool to take it. I must take out the work? A likely piece of work,° that you should find it in your chamber and know not who left it there! This is some minx's token, and I must take out the work? There; give it your hobbyhorse.° *[She gives him the handkerchief.]* Wheresoever   145 you had it, I'll take out no work on 't.

Cassio: How now, my sweet Bianca? How now? How now?

Othello: By heaven, that should be° my handkerchief!

Bianca: If you'll come to supper tonight, you may; if you will not, come when you are next prepared for.°   *Exit.*   150

Iago: After her, after her.

Cassio: Faith, I must. She'll rail in the streets else.

Iago: Will you sup there?

Cassio: Faith, I intend so.

Iago: Well, I may chance to see you, for I would very fain speak with you.   155

Cassio: Prithee, come. Will you?

Iago: Go to.° Say no more.   *[Exit Cassio.]*

---

122 *They . . . win* i.e., they that laugh last laugh best   123 *cry* rumor   125 *I . . . else* call me a complete rogue if I'm not telling the truth   126 *scored me* scored off me, beaten me, made up my reckoning, branded me   128 *flattery* self-flattery, self-deception   129 *beckons* signals   131 *seabank* seashore. *bauble* plaything   132 *by this hand* I make my vow   136 *not . . . to* (Othello imagines himself cutting off Cassio's nose and throwing it to a dog.)   138 *Before me* i.e., on my soul   139 *'Tis . . . fitchew* what a polecat she is! Just like all the others. (Polecats were often compared with prostitutes because of their rank smell and presumed lechery.)   141 *dam* mother   143 *A likely . . . work* a fine story   145 *hobbyhorse* harlot   148 *should be* must be   149–150 *when . . . for* when I'm ready for you (i.e., never)   157 *Go to* (An expression of remonstrance.)

Othello [*advancing*]: How shall I murder him, Iago?

Iago: Did you perceive how he laughed at his vice?

Othello: O, Iago!   160

Iago: And did you see the handkerchief?

Othello: Was that mine?

Iago: Yours, by this hand. And to see how he prizes the foolish woman your wife! She gave it him, and he hath given it his whore.

Othello: I would have him nine years a-killing. A fine woman! A fair woman! A   165 sweet woman!

Iago: Nay, you must forget that.

Othello: Ay, let her rot and perish, and be damned tonight, for she shall not live. No, my heart is turned to stone; I strike it, and it hurts my hand. O, the world hath not a sweeter creature! She might lie by an emperor's side and command him   170 tasks.

Iago: Nay, that's not your way.°

Othello: Hang her! I do but say what she is. So delicate with her needle! An admirable musician! O, she will sing the savageness out of a bear. Of so high and plenteous wit and invention!°   175

Iago: She's the worse for all this.

Othello: O, a thousand, a thousand times! And then, of so gentle a condition!°

Iago: Ay, too gentle.°

Othello: Nay, that's certain. But yet the pity of it, Iago! O, Iago, the pity of it, Iago!

Iago: If you are so fond° over her iniquity, give her patent° to offend, for if it touch   180 not you it comes near nobody.

Othello: I will chop her into messes.° Cuckold me?

Iago: O, 'tis foul in her.

Othello: With mine officer?

Iago: That's fouler.   185

Othello: Get me some poison, Iago, this night. I'll not expostulate with her, lest her body and beauty unprovide° my mind again. This night, Iago.

Iago: Do it not with poison. Strangle her in her bed, even the bed she hath contaminated.

Othello: Good, good! The justice of it pleases. Very good.   190

Iago: And for Cassio, let me be his undertaker.° You shall hear more by midnight.

Othello: Excellent good. [*A trumpet within.*] What trumpet is that same?

Iago: I warrant, something from Venice.

Enter Lodovico, Desdemona, and attendants.

'Tis Lodovico. This comes from the Duke.
See, your wife's with him.   195

Lodovico: God save you, worthy General!

Othello: With all my heart,° sir.

Lodovico [*giving him a letter*]: The Duke and the senators of Venice greet you.

Othello: I kiss the instrument of their pleasures.

---

172 *your way* i.e., the way you should think of her   175 *invention* imagination   177 *gentle a condition* wellborn and well-bred   178 *gentle* generous, yielding (to other men)   180 *fond* foolish.   *patent* license   182 *messes* portions of meat, i.e., bits   187 *unprovide* weaken, render unfit   191 *be his undertaker* undertake to dispatch him   196 *With all my heart* i.e., I thank you most heartily

[*He opens the letter, and reads.*]

Desdemona: And what's the news, good cousin Lodovico?
Iago: I am very glad to see you, signor.   200
　　Welcome to Cyprus.
Lodovico: I thank you. How does Lieutenant Cassio?
Iago: Lives, sir.
Desdemona: Cousin, there's fall'n between him and my lord
　　An unkind° breach; but you shall make all well.   205
Othello: Are you sure of that?
Desdemona: My lord?
Othello [*reads*]: "This fail you not to do, as you will—"
Lodovico: He did not call; he's busy in the paper.
　　Is there division twixt my lord and Cassio?   210
Desdemona: A most unhappy one. I would do much
　　T' atone° them, for the love I bear to Cassio.
Othello: Fire and brimstone!
Desdemona: My lord?
Othello: Are you wise?   215
Desdemona: What, is he angry?
Lodovico:　　　　　　　　　Maybe the letter moved him;
　　For, as I think, they do command him home,
　　Deputing Cassio in his government.°
Desdemona: By my troth, I am glad on 't.°
Othello: Indeed?   220
Desdemona: My lord?
Othello: I am glad to see you mad.°
Desdemona: Why, sweet Othello—
Othello [*striking her*]: Devil!
Desdemona: I have not deserved this.   225
Lodovico: My lord, this would not be believed in Venice,
　　Though I should swear I saw 't. 'Tis very much.°
　　Make her amends; she weeps.
Othello:　　　　　　　　　O devil, devil!
　　If that the earth could teem° with woman's tears,
　　Each drop she falls would prove a crocodile.°   230
　　Out of my sight!
Desdemona:　　　　　I will not stay to offend you. [*Going.*]
Lodovico: Truly, an obedient lady.
　　I do beseech your lordship, call her back.
Othello: Mistress!
Desdemona [*returning*]: My lord?   235
Othello: What would you with her, sir?°

---

205 *unkind* unnatural, contrary to their natures; hurtful 212 *atone* reconcile 218 *government* office
219 *on 't* of it 222 *I am . . . mad* i.e., I am glad to see that you are insane enough to rejoice in Cassio's
promotion (?) (Othello bitterly plays on Desdemona's *I am glad.*) 227 *very much* too much, outrageous
229 *teem* breed, be impregnated 230 *falls . . . crocodile* (Crocodiles were supposed to weep hypocritical
tears for their victims.) 236 *What . . . sir* (Othello implies that Desdemona is pliant and will do a *turn*,
lines 238–240, for any man.)

Lodovico: Who, I, my lord?
Othello: Ay, you did wish that I would make her turn.
    Sir, she can turn, and turn, and yet go on
    And turn again; and she can weep, sir, weep;   240
    And she's obedient,° as you say, obedient,
    Very obedient.—Proceed you in your tears.—
    Concerning this, sir—O well-painted passion!°—
    I am commanded home.—Get you away;
    I'll send for you anon.—Sir, I obey the mandate   245
    And will return to Venice.—Hence, avaunt!

    [*Exit Desdemona.*]

    Cassio shall have my place. And, sir, tonight
    I do entreat that we may sup together.
    You are welcome, sir, to Cyprus.—Goats and monkeys!°   *Exit.*
Lodovico: Is this the noble Moor whom our full Senate   250
    Call all in all sufficient? Is this the nature
    Whom passion could not shake? Whose solid virtue
    The shot of accident nor dart of chance
    Could neither graze nor pierce?
Iago: He is much changed.
Lodovico: Are his wits safe? Is he not light of brain?   255
Iago: He's that he is. I may not breathe my censure
    What he might be. If what he might he is not,
    I would to heaven he were!°
Lodovico: What, strike his wife?
Iago: Faith, that was not so well; yet would I knew
    That stroke would prove the worst!
Lodovico: Is it his use?°   260
    Or did the letters work upon his blood°
    And new-create his fault?
Iago: Alas, alas!
    It is not honesty in me to speak
    What I have seen and known. You shall observe him,
    And his own courses will denote° him so   265
    That I may save my speech. Do but go after,
    And mark how he continues.
Lodovico: I am sorry that I am deceived in him.   *Exeunt.*

SCENE II [THE CITADEL.]

    Enter Othello and Emilia.

Othello: You have seen nothing then?
Emilia: Nor ever heard, nor ever did suspect.

---

241 *obedient* (With much the same sexual connotation as *turn* in lines 238–240.)   243 *passion* i.e., grief
249 *Goats and monkeys* (See III, iii, 419.)   256–258 *I may . . . were* i.e., I dare not venture an opinion as
to whether he's of unsound mind, as you suggest, but, if he isn't, then it might be better to wish he were in
fact insane, since only that could excuse his wild behavior   260 *use* custom   261 *blood* passions   265
courses will denote actions will reveal

Othello: Yes, you have seen Cassio and she together.
Emilia: But then I saw no harm, and then I heard
　　Each syllable that breath made up between them.　　　5
Othello: What, did they never whisper?
Emilia: Never, my lord.
Othello: Nor send you out o' the way?
Emilia: Never.
Othello: To fetch her fan, her gloves, her mask, nor nothing?　10
Emilia: Never, my lord.
Othello: That's strange.
Emilia: I durst, my lord, to wager she is honest,
　　Lay down my soul at stake.° If you think other,
　　Remove your thought; it doth abuse your bosom.°　　15
　　If any wretch have put this in your head,
　　Let heaven requite it with the serpent's curse!°
　　For if she be not honest, chaste, and true,
　　There's no man happy; the purest of their wives
　　Is foul as slander.
Othello: 　　　　　　Bid her come hither. Go.　　　20

　　Exit Emilia.

She says enough; yet she's a simple bawd
That cannot say as much.° This° is a subtle whore,
A closet lock and key° of villainous secrets.
And yet she'll kneel and pray; I have seen her do 't.

　　Enter Desdemona and Emilia.

Desdemona: My lord, what is your will?　　　　　25
Othello: Pray you, chuck, come hither.
Desdemona: What is your pleasure?
Othello: 　　　　　　　　Let me see your eyes.
　　Look in my face.
Desdemona: 　　　　What horrible fancy's this?
Othello [to Emilia]: Some of your function,° mistress.
　　Leave procreants° alone and shut the door;　　30
　　Cough or cry "hem" if anybody come.
　　Your mystery, your mystery!° Nay, dispatch.

　　Exit Emilia.

Desdemona [kneeling]: Upon my knees, what doth your speech import?
　　I understand a fury in your words,
　　But not the words.　　　　　　　　　35
Othello: Why, what art thou?

14 *at stake* as the wager   15 *abuse your bosom* deceive you   17 *the serpent's curse* the curse pronounced by God on the serpent for deceiving Eve, just as some man has done to Othello and Desdemona. (See Genesis 3:14.)   21–22 *she's . . . much* i.e., any procuress or go-between who couldn't make up as plausible a story as Emilia's would have to be pretty stupid   22 *This* i.e., Desdemona   23 *closet lock and key* i.e., concealer   29 *Some . . . function* i.e., practice your chosen profession, that of bawd (by guarding the door)   30 *procreants* mating couples   32 *mystery* trade, occupation

"Ah, Desdemon! Away, away, away!" (IV, ii, 43).

Desdemona: Your wife, my lord, your true
   And loyal wife.
Othello: Come, swear it, damn thyself,
   Lest, being like one of heaven,° the devils themselves
   Should fear to seize thee. Therefore be double damned:
   Swear thou art honest.
Desdemona: Heaven doth truly know it.   40
Othello: Heaven truly knows that thou art false as hell.
Desdemona: To whom, my lord? With whom? How am I false?
Othello [weeping]: Ah, Desdemon! Away, away, away!
Desdemona: Alas the heavy day! Why do you weep?
   Am I the motive° of these tears, my lord?   45

38 being . . . heaven looking like an angel   45 motive cause

If haply you my father do suspect
An instrument of this your calling back,
Lay not your blame on me. If you have lost him,
I have lost him too.
Othello: Had it pleased heaven
  To try me with affliction, had they° rained   50
  All kinds of sores and shames on my bare head,
  Steeped me in poverty to the very lips,
  Given to captivity me and my utmost hopes,
  I should have found in some place of my soul
  A drop of patience. But, alas, to make me   55
  A fixèd figure for the time of scorn°
  To point his° slow and moving finger° at!
  Yet could I bear that too, well, very well.
  But there where I have garnered° up my heart,
  Where either I must live or bear no life,   60
  The fountain° from the which my current runs
  Or else dries up—to be discarded thence!
  Or keep it as a cistern° for foul toads
  To knot° and gender° in! Turn thy complexion there,°
  Patience, thou young and rose-lipped cherubin—   65
  Ay, there look grim as hell!°
Desdemona: I hope my noble lord esteems me honest.°
Othello: O, ay, as summer flies are in the shambles,°
  That quicken° even with blowing.° O thou weed,
  Who art so lovely fair and smell'st so sweet   70
  That the sense aches at thee, would thou hadst ne'er been born!
Desdemona: Alas, what ignorant° sin have I committed?
Othello: Was this fair paper, this most goodly book,
  Made to write "whore" upon? What committed?
  Committed? O thou public commoner!°   75
  I should make very forges of my cheeks,
  That would to cinders burn up modesty,
  Did I but speak thy deeds. What committed?
  Heaven stops the nose at it and the moon winks;°
  The bawdy° wind, that kisses all it meets,   80
  Is hushed within the hollow mine° of earth
  And will not hear 't. What committed?
  Impudent strumpet!

---

50 *they* i.e., heavenly powers   56 *time of scorn* i.e., scornful world   57 *his* its *slow and moving finger* i.e., hour hand of the clock, moving so slowly it seems hardly to move at all. (Othello envisages himself as being eternally pointed at by the scornful world as the numbers on a clock are pointed at by the hour hand.)   59 *garnered* stored   61 *fountain* spring   63 *cistern* cesspool   64 *knot* couple.   *gender* engender.   *Turn . . . there* change your color, grow pale, at such a sight   65–66 *Patience . . . hell* (Even Patience, that rose-lipped cherub, will look grim and pale at this spectacle.)   67 *honest* chaste 68 *shambles* slaughterhouse   69 *quicken* come to life.   *with blowing* i.e., with the puffing up of something rotten in which maggots are breeding   72 *ignorant* sin sin in ignorance   75 *commoner* prostitute 79 *winks* closes her eyes. (The moon symbolizes chastity.)   80 *bawdy* kissing one and all   81 *mine* cave (where the winds were thought to dwell)

Othello berates Desdemona as a "strumpet" and "cunning whore" (IV, ii, 73–98).

Desdemona: By heaven, you do me wrong.
Othello: Are not you a strumpet?
Desdemona: No, as I am a Christian.   85
    If to preserve this vessel° for my lord
    From any other foul unlawful touch
    Be not to be a strumpet, I am none.
Othello: What, not a whore?
Desdemona: No, as I shall be saved.   90
Othello: Is 't possible?
Desdemona: O, heaven forgive us!
Othello: I cry you mercy,° then.
    I took you for that cunning whore of Venice
    That married with Othello. [*Calling out.*] You, mistress,
    That have the office opposite to Saint Peter   95
    And keep the gate of hell!

    Enter Emilia.

                              You, you, ay, you!
    We have done our course.° There's money for your pains.   [*He gives money.*]
    I pray you, turn the key and keep our counsel.

                                                                                            Exit.

86 *vessel* body   92 *cry you mercy* beg your pardon   97 *course* business (with an indecent suggestion of
"trick," turn at sex)

Emilia: Alas, what does this gentleman conceive?°

How do you, madam? How do you, my good lady?   100

Desdemona: Faith, half asleep.°

Emilia: Good madam, what's the matter with my lord?

Desdemona: With who?

Emilia: Why, with my lord, madam.

Desdemona: Who is thy lord?

Emilia: He that is yours, sweet lady.   105

Desdemona: I have none. Do not talk to me, Emilia.

    I cannot weep, nor answers have I none

    But what should go by water.° Prithee, tonight

    Lay on my bed my wedding sheets, remember;

    And call thy husband hither.   110

Emilia: Here's a change indeed!   *Exit.*

Desdemona: 'Tis meet I should be used so, very meet.°

    How have I been behaved, that he might stick°

    The small'st opinion° on my least misuse?°

    Enter Iago.

Iago: What is your pleasure, madam? How is 't with you?   115

Desdemona: I cannot tell. Those that do teach young babes

    Do it with gentle means and easy tasks.

    He might have chid me so, for, in good faith,

    I am a child to chiding.

Iago: What is the matter, lady?   120

Emilia: Alas, Iago, my lord hath so bewhored her,

    Thrown such despite and heavy terms upon her,

    That true hearts cannot bear it.

Desdemona: Am I that name, Iago?

Iago: What name, fair lady?   125

Desdemona: Such as she said my lord did say I was.

Emilia: He called her whore. A beggar in his drink

    Could not have laid such terms upon his callet.°

Iago: Why did he so?

Desdemona [*weeping*]: I do not know. I am sure I am none such.   130

Iago: Do not weep, do not weep. Alas the day!

Emilia: Hath she forsook so many noble matches,

    Her father and her country and her friends,

    To be called whore? Would it not make one weep?

Desdemona: It is my wretched fortune.

Iago: Beshrew° him for 't!   135

    How comes this trick° upon him?

Desdemona: Nay, heaven doth know.

Emilia: I will be hanged if some eternal° villain,

---

99 *conceive* suppose, think   101 *half asleep* i.e., dazed   108 *go by water* be expressed by tears   112 *meet* fitting   113 *stick* attach   114 *opinion* censure. *least misuse* slightest misconduct   128 *callet* whore   135 *Beshrew* curse   136 *trick* strange behavior, delusion   137 *eternal* inveterate

Iago comforts Desdemona regarding Othello's accusations (IV, ii, 115–179).

> Some busy and insinuating° rogue,
> Some cogging,° cozening° slave, to get some office,
> Have not devised this slander. I will be hanged else.   140
> *Iago:* Fie, there is no such man. It is impossible.
> *Desdemona:* If any such there be, heaven pardon him!
> *Emilia:* A halter° pardon him! And hell gnaw his bones!
> Why should he call her whore? Who keeps her company?
> What place? What time? What form?° What likelihood?   145
> The Moor's abused by some most villainous knave,
> Some base notorious knave, some scurvy fellow.
> O heaven, that° such companions° thou'dst unfold,°
> And put in every honest hand a whip
> To lash the rascals naked through the world   150
> Even from the east to th' west!
> *Iago:*   Speak within door.°
> *Emilia:* O, fie upon them! Some such squire° he was
> That turned your wit the seamy side without°
> And made you to suspect me with the Moor.
> *Iago:* You are a fool. Go to.°
> *Desdemona:*   Alas, Iago,   155
> What shall I do to win my lord again?

---

138 *insinuating* ingratiating, fawning, wheedling   139 *cogging* cheating.   *cozening* defrauding   143 *halter* hangman's noose   145 *form* appearance, circumstance   148 *that* would that.   *companions* fellows. *unfold* expose   151 *within door* i.e., not so loud   152 *squire* fellow   153 *seamy side without* wrong side out 155 *Go to* i.e., that's enough

Good friend, go to him; for, by this light of heaven,
I know not how I lost him. Here I kneel. [*She kneels.*]
If e'er my will did trespass 'gainst his love,
Either in discourse of thought° or actual deed,   160
Or that° mine eyes, mine ears, or any sense
Delighted them° in any other form;
Or that I do not yet,° and ever did,
And ever will—though he do shake me off
To beggarly divorcement—love him dearly,   165
Comfort forswear° me! Unkindness may do much,
And his unkindness may defeat° my life,
But never taint my love. I cannot say "whore."
It does abhor° me now I speak the word;
To do the act that might the addition° earn   170
Not the world's mass of vanity° could make me.

[*She rises.*]

Iago: I pray you, be content. 'Tis but his humor.°
   The business of the state does him offense,
   And he does chide with you.
Desdemona: If 'twere no other—   175
Iago: It is but so, I warrant.   [*Trumpets within.*]
   Hark, how these instruments summon you to supper!
   The messengers of Venice stays the meat.°
   Go in, and weep not. All things shall be well.

Exeunt Desdemona and Emilia.

Enter Roderigo.

How now, Roderigo?   180
Roderigo: I do not find that thou deal'st justly with me.
Iago: What in the contrary?
Roderigo: Every day thou daff'st me° with some device,° Iago, and rather, as it seems
   to me now, keep'st from me all conveniency° than suppliest me with the least
   advantage° of hope. I will indeed no longer endure it, nor am I yet persuaded to   185
   put up° in peace what already I have foolishly suffered.
Iago: Will you hear me, Roderigo?
Roderigo: Faith, I have heard too much, for your words and performances are no kin
   together.
Iago: You charge me most unjustly.   190
Roderigo: With naught but truth. I have wasted myself out of my means. The jewels
   you have had from me to deliver° Desdemona would half have corrupted a

---

160 *discourse of thought* process of thinking   161 *that* if. (Also in line 163.)   162 *Delighted them* took
delight   163 *yet* still   166 *Comfort forswear* may heavenly comfort forsake   167 *defeat* destroy   169
abhor (1) fill me with abhorrence (2) make me whorelike   170 *addition* title   171 *vanity* showy splendor
172 *humor* mood   178 *stays the meat* are waiting to dine   183 *thou daff'st me* you put me off.   *device*
excuse, trick   184 *conveniency* advantage, opportunity   185 *advantage* increase   186 *put up* submit to,
tolerate   192 *deliver* deliver to

votarist.° You have told me she hath received them and returned me expectations and comforts of sudden respect° and acquaintance, but I find none.

Iago: Well, go to, very well.   195

Roderigo: "Very well"! "Go to"! I cannot go to,° man, nor 'tis not very well. By this hand, I think it is scurvy, and begin to find myself fopped° in it.

Iago: Very well.

Roderigo: I tell you 'tis not very well.° I will make myself known to Desdemona. If she will return me my jewels, I will give over my suit and repent my unlawful   200 solicitation; if not, assure yourself I will seek satisfaction° of you.

Iago: You have said now?°

Roderigo: Ay, and said nothing but what I protest intendment° of doing.

Iago: Why, now I see there's mettle in thee, and even from this instant do build on thee a better opinion than ever before. Give me thy hand, Roderigo. Thou hast   205 taken against me a most just exception; but yet I protest I have dealt most directly in thy affair.

Roderigo: It hath not appeared.

Iago: I grant indeed it hath not appeared, and your suspicion is not without wit and judgment. But, Roderigo, if thou hast that in thee indeed which I have greater   210 reason to believe now than ever—I mean purpose, courage, and valor—this night show it. If thou the next night following enjoy not Desdemona, take me from this world with treachery and devise engines for° my life.

Roderigo: Well, what is it? Is it within reason and compass?

Iago: Sir, there is especial commission come from Venice to depute Cassio in Othello's   215 place.

Roderigo: Is that true? Why, then Othello and Desdemona return again to Venice.

Iago: O, no; he goes into Mauritania and takes away with him the fair Desdemona, unless his abode be lingered here by some accident; wherein none can be so determinate° as the removing of Cassio.   220

Roderigo: How do you mean, removing of him?

Iago: Why, by making him uncapable of Othello's place—knocking out his brains.

Roderigo: And that you would have me to do?

Iago: Ay, if you dare do yourself a profit and a right. He sups tonight with a harlotry,° and thither will I go to him. He knows not yet of his honorable fortune. If you   225 will watch his going thence, which I will fashion to fall out° between twelve and one, you may take him at your pleasure. I will be near to second your attempt, and he shall fall between us. Come, stand not amazed at it, but go along with me. I will show you such a necessity in his death that you shall think yourself bound to put it on him. It is now high° suppertime, and the night grows to waste.°   230 About it.

Roderigo: I will hear further reason for this.

Iago: And you shall be satisfied.   *Exeunt.*

---

193 *votarist* nun   194 *sudden respect* immediate consideration   196 *I cannot go to* (Roderigo changes Iago's *go to*, an expression urging patience, to *I cannot go to,* "I have no opportunity for success in wooing.")
197 *fopped* fooled, duped   199 *not very well* (Roderigo changes Iago's *very well,* "all right, then," to *not very well,* "not at all good.")   201 *satisfaction* repayment. (The term normally means settling of accounts in a duel.)   202 *You . . . . now* have you finished?   203 *intendment* intention   213 *engines for* plots against   220 *determinate* conclusive   224 *harlotry* slut   226 *fall out* occur   230 *high* fully. *grows to waste* wastes away

SCENE III [THE CITADEL.]

Enter Othello, Lodovico, Desdemona, Emilia, and attendants.

Lodovico: I do beseech you, sir, trouble yourself no further.
Othello: O, pardon me; 'twill do me good to walk.
Lodovico: Madam, good night. I humbly thank your ladyship.
Desdemona: Your honor is most welcome.
Othello: Will you walk, sir?
    O, Desdemona!   5
Desdemona: My lord?
Othello: Get you to bed on th' instant. I will be returned
    forthwith. Dismiss your attendant there.
    Look 't be done.
Desdemona: I will, my lord.   10

    Exit [Othello, with Lodovico and attendants].

Emilia: How goes it now? He looks gentler than he did.
Desdemona: He says he will return incontinent,°
    And hath commanded me to go to bed,
    And bid me to dismiss you.
Emilia: Dismiss me?   15
Desdemona: It was his bidding. Therefore, good Emilia,
    Give me my nightly wearing, and adieu.
    We must not now displease him.
Emilia: I would you had never seen him!
Desdemona: So would not I. My love doth so approve him   20
    That even his stubbornness,° his checks,° his frowns—
    Prithee, unpin me—have grace and favor in them.

    [*Emilia prepares Desdemona for bed.*]

Emilia: I have laid those sheets you bade me on the bed.
Desdemona: All's one.° Good faith, how foolish are our minds!
    If I do die before thee, prithee shroud me   25
    In one of these same sheets.
Emilia: Come, come, you talk.°
Desdemona: My mother had a maid called Barbary.
    She was in love, and he she loved proved mad°
    And did forsake her. She had a song of "Willow."
    An old thing 'twas, but it expressed her fortune,   30
    And she died singing it. That song tonight
    Will not go from my mind; I have much to do
    But to go hang° my head all at one side
    And sing it like poor Barbary. Prithee, dispatch.
Emilia: Shall I go fetch your nightgown?°   35

---

12 *incontinent* immediately   21 *stubbornness* roughness.   *checks* rebukes   24 *All's one* all right. It doesn't
really matter   26 *talk* i.e., prattle   28 *mad* wild, i.e., faithless   32–33 *I . . . hang* I can scarcely keep myself from hanging   35 *nightgown* dressing gown

Desdemona: No, unpin me here.
 This Lodovico is a proper° man.
Emilia: A very handsome man.
Desdemona: He speaks well.
Emilia: I know a lady in Venice would have walked barefoot to Palestine for a touch   40
 of his nether lip.
Desdemona [*singing*]:
          "The poor soul sat sighing by a sycamore tree,
          Sing all a green willow;°
          Her hand on her bosom, her head on her knee,
          Sing willow, willow, willow.   45
          The fresh streams ran by her and murmured her moans;
          Sing willow, willow, willow;
          Her salt tears fell from her, and softened the stones—"
 Lay by these.
          [*Singing.*] "Sing willow, willow, willow—"   50
 Prithee, hie thee.° He'll come anon.°
          [*Singing.*] "Sing all a green willow must be my garland.
          Let nobody blame him; his scorn I approve—"
 Nay, that's not next.—Hark! Who is 't that knocks?
Emilia: It's the wind.   55
Desdemona [*singing*]:
          "I called my love false love; but what said he then?
          Sing willow, willow, willow;
          If I court more women, you'll couch with more men."

 So, get thee gone. Good night. Mine eyes do itch;
 Doth that bode weeping?
Emilia: 'Tis neither here nor there.   60
Desdemona: I have heard it said so. O, these men, these men!
 Dost thou in conscience think—tell me, Emilia—
 That there be women do abuse° their husbands
 In such gross kind?
Emilia: There be some such, no question.
Desdemona: Wouldst thou do such a deed for all the world?   65
Emilia: Why, would not you?
Desdemona: No, by this heavenly light!
Emilia: Nor I neither by this heavenly light;
 I might do 't as well i' the dark.
Desdemona: Wouldst thou do such a deed for all the world?
Emilia: The world's a huge thing. It is a great price   70
 For a small vice.
Desdemona: Good troth, I think thou wouldst not.
Emilia: By my troth, I think I should, and undo 't when I had done. Marry, I would
 not do such a thing for a joint ring,° nor for measures of lawn,° nor for gowns,
 petticoats, nor caps, nor any petty exhibition.° But for all the whole world! Uds°   75

---

37 *proper* handsome   43 *willow* (A conventional emblem of disappointed love.)   51 *hie thee* hurry.   *anon* right away   63 *abuse* deceive   74 *joint ring* a ring made in separate halves.   *lawn* fine linen   75 *exhibition* gift.   *Uds* God's

pity, who would not make her husband a cuckold to make him a monarch? I
should venture purgatory for 't.

Desdemona: Beshrew me if I would do such a wrong
For the whole world.

Emilia: Why, the wrong is but a wrong i' the world, and having the world for your   80
labor, 'tis a wrong in your own world, and you might quickly make it right.

Desdemona: I do not think there is any such woman.

Emilia: Yes, a dozen, and as many
To th' vantage° as would store° the world they played° for.
But I do think it is their husbands' faults   85
If wives do fall. Say that they slack their duties°
And pour our treasures into foreign laps,°
Or else break out in peevish jealousies,
Throwing restraint upon us?° Or say they strike us,
Or scant our former having in despite?°   90
Why, we have galls,° and though we have some grace,
Yet have we some revenge. Let husbands know
Their wives have sense° like them. They see, and smell,
And have their palates both for sweet and sour,
As husbands have. What is it that they do   95
When they change us for others? Is it sport?°
I think it is. And doth affection° breed it?
I think it doth. Is 't frailty that thus errs?
It is so, too. And have not we affections,
Desires for sport, and frailty, as men have?   100
Then let them use us well; else let them know,
The ills we do, their ills instruct us so.

Desdemona: Good night, good night. God me such uses° send
Not to pick bad from bad, but by bad mend!°

Exeunt.

ACT V

SCENE I [A STREET IN CYPRUS.]

Enter Iago and Roderigo.

Iago: Here stand behind this bulk.° Straight will he come.
Wear thy good rapier bare,° and put it home.
Quick, quick! Fear nothing. I'll be at thy elbow.
It makes us or it mars us. Think on that,
And fix most firm thy resolution.   5

Roderigo: Be near at hand. I may miscarry in 't.

---

84 *To th' vantage* in addition, to boot.   *store* populate.   *played* (1) gambled (2) sported sexually   86 *duties*
marital duties   87 *pour . . . laps* i.e., are unfaithful, give what is rightfully ours (semen) to other women
89 *Throwing . . . us* i.e., jealously restricting our freedom to see other men   90 *scant . . . despite* reduce
our allowance to spite us   91 *have galls* i.e., are capable of resenting injury and insult   93 *sense* physical
sense   96 *sport* sexual pastime   97 *affection* passion   103 *uses* habit, practice   104 *Not . . . mend* i.e.,
not to learn bad conduct from others' badness (as Emilia has suggested women learn from men), but to
mend my ways by perceiving what badness is, making spiritual benefit out of evil and adversity   1 *bulk*
framework projecting from the front of a shop   2 *bare* unsheathed

Iago: Here, at thy hand. Be bold, and take thy stand.

[*Iago stands aside. Roderigo conceals himself.*]

Roderigo: I have no great devotion to the deed;
And yet he hath given me satisfying reasons.
'Tis but a man gone. Forth, my sword! He dies.   10

[*He draws.*]

Iago: I have rubbed this young quat° almost to the sense,°
And he grows angry. Now, whether he kill Cassio
Or Cassio him, or each do kill the other,
Every way makes my gain. Live Roderigo,°
He calls me to a restitution large   15
Of gold and jewels that I bobbed° from him
As gifts to Desdemona.
It must not be. If Cassio do remain,
He hath a daily beauty in his life
That makes me ugly; and besides, the Moor   20
May unfold° me to him; there stand I in much peril.
No, he must die. Be 't so. I hear him coming.

Enter Cassio.

Roderigo [*coming forth*]: I know his gait, 'tis he.—Villain, thou diest!

[*He attacks Cassio.*]

Cassio: That thrust had been mine enemy indeed,
But that my coat° is better than thou know'st.   25
I will make proof° of thine.

[*He draws, and wounds Roderigo.*]

Roderigo: O, I am slain!   [*He falls.*]

[*Iago, from behind, wounds Cassio in the leg, and exits.*]

Cassio: I am maimed forever. Help, ho! Murder! Murder!

Enter Othello.

Othello: The voice of Cassio! Iago keeps his word.
Roderigo: O, villain that I am!
Othello: It is even so.   30
Cassio: O, help, ho! Light! A surgeon!
Othello: 'Tis he. O brave Iago, honest and just,
That hast such noble sense of thy friend's wrong!
Thou teachest me. Minion,° your dear lies dead,

---

11 *quat* pimple, pustule. *to the sense* to the quick   14 *Live Roderigo* if Roderigo lives   16 *bobbed* swindled
21 *unfold* expose   25 *coat* (Possibly a garment of mail under the outer clothing, or simply a tougher coat
than Roderigo expected.)   26 *proof* a test   34 *Minion* hussy (i.e., Desdemona)

And your unblest fate hies.° Strumpet, I come.   35
Forth of° my heart those charms, thine eyes, are blotted;
Thy bed, lust-stained, shall with lust's blood be spotted.   *Exit Othello.*

Enter Lodovico and Gratiano.

Cassio: What ho! No watch? No passage?° Murder! Murder!
Gratiano: 'Tis some mischance. The voice is very direful.
Cassio: O, help!   40
Lodovico: Hark!
Roderigo: O wretched villain!
Lodovico: Two or three groan. 'Tis heavy° night;
      These may be counterfeits. Let's think 't unsafe
      To come in to° the cry without more help.   45

[*They remain near the entrance.*]

Roderigo: Nobody come? Then shall I bleed to death.

Enter Iago [in his shirtsleeves, with a light].

Lodovico: Hark!
Gratiano: Here's one comes in his shirt, with light and weapons.
Iago: Who's there? Whose noise is this that cries on° murder?
Lodovico: We do not know.
Iago: Did not you hear a cry?   50
Cassio: Here, here! For heaven's sake, help me!
Iago: What's the matter?

[*He moves toward Cassio.*]

Gratiano [to Lodovico]: This is Othello's ancient, as I take it.
Lodovico [to Gratiano]: The same indeed, a very valiant fellow.
Iago [to Cassio]: What° are you here that cry so grievously?
Cassio: Iago? O, I am spoiled,° undone by villains!   55
      Give me some help.
Iago: O me, Lieutenant! What villains have done this?
Cassio: I think that one of them is hereabout,
      And cannot make° away.
Iago: O treacherous villains!

[*To Lodovico and Gratiano.*]

      What are you there? Come in, and give some help.   [*They advance.*] 60
Roderigo: O, help me there!
Cassio: That's one of them.
Iago: O murderous slave! O villain!

[*He stabs Roderigo.*]

---

35 *hies* hastens on   36 *Forth of* from out   38 *passage* people passing by   43 *heavy* thick, dark   45 *come in to* approach   49 *cries on* cries out   54 *What* who (also at lines 60 and 66)   55 *spoiled* ruined, done for   59 *make* get

Roderigo: O damned Iago! O inhuman dog!
Iago: Kill men i' the dark?—Where be these bloody thieves?—
    How silent is this town!—Ho! Murder, murder!—   65
    [*To Lodovico and Gratiano.*] What may you be? Are you of good or evil?
Lodovico: As you shall prove us, praise° us.
Iago: Signor Lodovico?
Lodovico: He, sir.
Iago: I cry you mercy.° Here's Cassio hurt by villains.   70
Gratiano: Cassio?
Iago: How is 't, brother?
Cassio: My leg is cut in two.
Iago: Marry, heaven forbid!
    Light, gentlemen! I'll bind it with my shirt.   75

[*He hands them the light, and tends to Cassio's wound.*]

Enter Bianca.

Bianca: What is the matter, ho? Who is 't that cried?
Iago: Who is 't that cried?
Bianca: O my dear Cassio!
    My sweet Cassio! O Cassio, Cassio, Cassio!
Iago: O notable strumpet! Cassio, may you suspect
    Who they should be that have thus mangled you?   80
Cassio: No.
Gratiano: I am sorry to find you thus. I have been to seek you.
Iago: Lend me a garter. [*He applies a tourniquet.*] So.—O, for a chair,°
    To bear him easily hence!
Bianca: Alas, he faints! O Cassio, Cassio, Cassio!   85
Iago: Gentlemen all, I do suspect this trash
    To be a party in this injury.—
    Patience awhile, good Cassio.—Come, come;
    Lend me a light.   [*He shines the light on Roderigo.*]
              Know we this face or no?
    Alas, my friend and my dear countryman   90
    Roderigo! No.—Yes, sure.—O heaven! Roderigo!
Gratiano: What, of Venice?
Iago: Even he, sir. Did you know him?
Gratiano: Know him? Ay.
Iago: Signor Gratiano? I cry your gentle° pardon.   95
    These bloody accidents° must excuse my manners
    That so neglected you.
Gratiano: I am glad to see you.
Iago: How do you, Cassio? O, a chair, a chair!
Gratiano: Roderigo!
Iago: He, he, 'tis he. [*A litter is brought in.*] O, that's well said;° the chair.   100
    Some good man bear him carefully from hence;

---

67 *praise* appraise   70 *I cry you mercy* I beg your pardon   83 *chair* litter   95 *gentle* noble   96 *accidents* sudden events   100 *well said* well done

I'll fetch the General's surgeon. [*To Bianca.*] For you, mistress,
Save you your labor.°—He that lies slain here, Cassio,
Was my dear friend. What malice° was between you?
Cassio: None in the world, nor do I know the man.   105
Iago [*to Bianca*]: What, look you pale?—O, bear him out o' th' air.°

[*Cassio and Roderigo are borne off.*]

Stay you,° good gentlemen.—Look you pale, mistress?—
Do you perceive the gastness° of her eye?—
Nay, if you stare,° we shall hear more anon.—
Behold her well; I pray you, look upon her.   110
Do you see, gentlemen? Nay, guiltiness
Will speak, though tongues were out of use.

[*Enter Emilia.*]

Emilia: 'Las, what's the matter? What's the matter, husband?
Iago: Cassio hath here been set on in the dark
By Roderigo and fellows that are scaped.   115
He's almost slain, and Roderigo dead.
Emilia: Alas, good gentleman! Alas, good Cassio!
Iago: This is the fruits of whoring. Prithee, Emilia,
Go know° of Cassio where he supped tonight.
[*To Bianca.*] What, do you shake at that?   120
Bianca: He supped at my house, but I therefore shake not.
Iago: O, did he so? I charge you go with me.
Emilia: O, fie upon thee, strumpet!
Bianca: I am no strumpet, but of life as honest°
As you that thus abuse me.   125
Emilia: As I? Faugh! Fie upon thee!
Iago: Kind gentlemen, let's go see poor Cassio dressed.°—
Come, mistress, you must tell's another tale.
Emilia, run you to the citadel
And tell my lord and lady what hath happed.—   130
Will you go on afore? [*Aside.*] This is the night
That either makes me or fordoes° me quite.   *Exeunt.*

SCENE II [A BEDCHAMBER IN THE CITADEL.]

Enter Othello [*with a light*], *and Desdemona in her bed.*°

Othello: It is the cause,° it is the cause, my soul.
Let me not name it to you, you chaste stars!
It is the cause. Yet I'll not shed her blood,

103 *Save . . . labor* i.e., never you mind tending Cassio   104 *malice* enmity   106 *bear . . . air* (Fresh air was thought to be dangerous for a wound.)   107 *Stay you* (Lodovico and Gratiano are evidently about to leave.)   108 *gastness* terror   109 *stare* (Iago pretends to interpret Bianca's wild looks as an involuntary confession of guilt.)   119 *know* learn   124 *honest* chaste   127 *Cassio dressed* Cassio's wounds dressed 132 *fordoes* undoes, ruins s.d. *in her bed* (Either the curtains are drawn back to reveal the bed in a recessed area backstage, or the bed is "thrust out" onstage as the scene begins.)   1 *cause* i.e., cause of justice, the offense itself, which Othello must correct as an agent of justice

"Enter Othello, and Desdemona in her bed" (V, ii, s.d.).

Nor scar that whiter skin of hers than snow,
And smooth as monumental° alabaster. 5
Yet she must die, else she'll betray more men.
Put out the light, and then put out the light.°
If I quench thee, thou flaming minister,°
I can again thy former light restore,
Should I repent me;° but once put out thy light, 10
Thou cunning'st pattern° of excelling nature,
I know not where is that Promethean heat°
That can thy light relume.° When I have plucked thy rose,
I cannot give it vital growth again;
It needs must wither. I'll smell thee on the tree. 15

[*He kisses her.*]

O balmy breath, that dost almost persuade
Justice to break her sword! One more, one more.
Be thus when thou art dead, and I will kill thee,
And love thee after. One more, and that's the last.

[*He kisses her.*]

5 *monumental* i.e., used in making tombs and funeral monuments;   7 *the light . . . light* the torch or lamp . . .
Desdemona's life   8 *flaming minister* torch or lamp that serves me   10 *repent me* change my mind   11 *Thou
. . . pattern* you skillfully wrought perfect example   12 *Promethean heat* divine fire. (Alluding to the theft of
fire from heaven by Prometheus.)   13 *relume* rekindle

So sweet was ne'er so fatal. I must weep,   20
But they are cruel° tears. This sorrow's heavenly;
It strikes where it doth love.° She wakes.
Desdemona: Who's there? Othello?
Othello: Ay, Desdemona.
Desdemona: Will you come to bed, my lord?   25
Othello: Have you prayed tonight, Desdemon?
Desdemona: Ay, my lord.
Othello: If you bethink yourself of any crime°
  Unreconciled as yet to heaven and grace,
  Solicit° for it straight.°   30
Desdemona: Alack, my lord, what may you mean by that?
Othello: Well, do it, and be brief. I will walk by.
  I would not kill thy unprepared spirit.
  No, heaven forfend!° I would not kill thy soul.
Desdemona: Talk you of killing?
Othello: Ay, I do.
Desdemona: Then heaven   35
  Have mercy on me!
Othello: Amen, with all my heart!
Desdemona: If you say so, I hope you will not kill me.
Othello: Humh!
Desdemona: And yet I fear you; for you're fatal then
  When your eyes roll so. Why I should fear I know not,   40
  Since guiltiness I know not; but yet I feel I fear.
Othello: Think on thy sins.
Desdemona: They are loves I bear to you.°
Othello: Ay, and for that thou diest.
Desdemona: That death's unnatural that kills for loving.
  Alas, why gnaw you so your nether lip?   45
  Some bloody passion shakes your very frame.
  These are portents; but yet I hope, I hope,
  They do not point on° me.
Othello: Peace, and be still!
Desdemona: I will so. What's the matter?   50
Othello: That handkerchief which I so loved and gave thee
  Thou gav'st to Cassio.
Desdemona: No, by my life and soul!
  Send for the man and ask him.
Othello: Sweet soul, take heed, take heed of perjury.
  Thou art on thy deathbed.   55
Desdemona: Ay, but not yet to die.
Othello: Yes, presently.°

---

21 *cruel* unrelenting 22 *It . . . love* (Compare Hebrews 12:6: "For whom the Lord loveth he chas-
teneth.") 28 *crime* sin 30 *Solicit* petition, pray. *straight* immediately 34 *forfend* forbid 42 *They
are . . . you* i.e., if I sinned, it was in loving you more than my father or more than God 48 *point on* point
at, predict what is to happen to 56 *presently* immediately

Therefore confess thee freely of thy sin;
For to deny each article with oath
Cannot remove nor choke the strong conception°
That I do groan withal.° Thou art to die.   60

Desdemona: Then Lord have mercy on me!
Othello: I say, amen.
Desdemona: And have you mercy too! I never did
   Offend° you in my life; never loved Cassio
   But with such general warranty° of heaven
   As I might love. I never gave him token.   65
Othello: By heaven, I saw my handkerchief in 's hand.
   O perjured woman! Thou dost stone° my heart,
   And makes me call what I intend to do
   A murder, which I thought a sacrifice.
   I saw the handkerchief.
Desdemona: He found it, then.   70
   I never gave it him. Send for him hither;
   Let him confess a truth.
Othello: He hath confessed.
Desdemona: What, my lord?
Othello: That he hath used thee.
Desdemona: How? Unlawfully?
Othello: Ay.
Desdemona: He will not say so.
Othello: No, his mouth is stopped;   75
   Honest Iago hath ta'en order° for 't.
Desdemona: O, my fear interprets. What, is he dead?
Othello: Had all his hairs been lives, my great revenge
   Had stomach for them all.
Desdemona: Alas, he is betrayed and I undone!   [*She weeps.*]   80
Othello: Out, strumpet! Weep'st thou for him to my face?
Desdemona: O, banish me, my lord, but kill me not!
Othello: Down, strumpet!
Desdemona: Kill me tomorrow; let me live tonight!
Othello: Nay, if you strive—   85
Desdemona: But half an hour!
Othello: Being done,° there is no pause.
Desdemona: But while I say one prayer!
Othello: It is too late.

   Smothers her.

Emilia [*at the door*]: My lord, my lord! What, ho! My lord, my lord!
Othello: What noise is this? Not dead? Not yet quite dead?
   I that am cruel am yet merciful;   90
   I would not have thee linger in thy pain.

---

59 *conception* (1) belief in your guilt (2) plan in my mind   60 *groan withal* (1) groan at in sorrow (2) as in giving birth   63 *Offend* wrong   64 *warranty* sanction   67 *stone* turn to stone, harden   76 *ta'en order* taken measures   86 *Being done* i.e., since justice has begun its relentless course

Othello smothers Desdemona, (V, ii, 87–91).

[*He dispatches her.*]

So, so.

Emilia [*within*]: What, ho! My lord, my lord!

Othello: Who's there?

Emilia [*within*]: O, good my lord, I would speak a word with you!

Othello: Yes, 'tis Emilia.—By and by.—She's dead.

'Tis like° she comes to speak of Cassio's death.—   95

The noise was here.° Ha! No more moving?

Still as the grave. Shall she come in? Were 't good?—

I think she stirs again. No. What's best to do?

If she come in, she'll sure speak to my wife.

My wife! My wife! What wife? I have no wife.   100

O, insupportable! O heavy hour!

Methinks it should be now a huge eclipse

Of sun and moon, and that th' affrighted globe

Should yawn° at alteration.°

Emilia [*within*]:   I do beseech you

That I may speak with you, O, good my lord!   105

Othello: I had forgot thee. O, come in, Emilia.—

Soft,° by and by. Let me the curtains draw.—

---

95 *like* likely that   96 *here* (The Folio's *high* is possible, suggesting that the commotion of the attack on Cassio was loud.)   104 *yawn* gape in amazement, i.e., move in an earthquake. (According to Pliny, earthquakes often happen during eclipses.)   *at alteration* at these cataclysmic events in nature, well suited to express the horror of Desdemona's death   107 *Soft* wait a minute

[He closes the bed-curtains and opens the door.]

Where art thou?

Enter Emilia.

	What's the matter with thee now?	
Emilia:	O, my good lord, yonder's foul murders done!	
Othello:	What, now?	110
Emilia:	But now, my lord.	
Othello:	It is the very error° of the moon;	

Othello: It is the very error° of the moon;
    She comes more nearer earth than she was wont,
    And makes men mad.
Emilia: Cassio, my lord, hath killed a young Venetian 115
    Called Roderigo.
Othello: Roderigo killed?
    And Cassio killed?
Emilia: No, Cassio is not killed.
Othello: Not Cassio killed? Then murder's out of tune,
    And sweet revenge grows harsh.
Desdemona: O, falsely, falsely murdered! 120
Emilia: O Lord, what cry is that?
Othello: That? What?
Emilia: Out° and alas, that was my lady's voice.

[She opens the bed-curtains.]

    Help, help, ho, help! O lady, speak again!
    Sweet Desdemona! O sweet mistress, speak! 125
Desdemona: A guiltless death I die.
Emilia: O, who hath done this deed?
Desdemona: Nobody; I myself. Farewell.
    Commend me to my kind lord. O, farewell!   *[She dies.]*
Othello: Why, how should she be murdered?
Emilia: Alas, who knows? 130
Othello: You heard her say herself it was not I.
Emilia: She said so. I must needs report the truth.
Othello: She's like a liar gone to burning hell!
    'Twas I that killed her.
Emilia: O, the more angel she,
    And you the blacker devil! 135
Othello: She turned to folly,° and she was a whore.
Emilia: Thou dost belie° her, and thou art a devil.
Othello: She was false as water.
Emilia: Thou art rash as fire to say
    That she was false. O, she was heavenly true! 140
Othello: Cassio did top her. Ask thy husband else.°

---

112 *error* aberration, irregularity   123 *Out* (A cry of dismay, intensifying *alas.*)   136 *folly* i.e., wantonness, fleshly sin   137 *belie* slander   141 *else* i.e., if you don't believe me

Emilia declares Desdemona's innocence (V, ii, 134–164).

O, I were damned beneath all depth in hell
But that I did proceed upon just grounds
To this extremity. Thy husband knew it all.

Emilia: My husband?   145

Othello: Thy husband.

Emilia: That she was false to wedlock?

Othello: Ay, with Cassio. Nay, had she been true,
    If heaven would make me such another world
    Of one entire and perfect chrysolite,°   150
    I'd not have sold her for it.

Emilia: My husband?

Othello: Ay, 'twas he that told me on her first.
    An honest man he is, and hates the slime
    That sticks on filthy deeds.   155

Emilia: My husband?

Othello: What needs this iterance,° woman? I say thy husband.

Emilia: O mistress, villainy hath made mocks with° love!
    My husband say that she was false?

Othello: He, woman;

150 *chrysolite* precious topaz   157 *iterance* iteration, repetition   158 *made mocks with* derided, made sport of

I say thy husband. Dost understand the word?   160
My friend, thy husband, honest, honest Iago.
Emilia: If he say so, may his pernicious soul
Rot half a grain a day! He lies to th' heart.
She was too fond of her most filthy bargain.
Othello: Ha?   [*He draws.*]   165
Emilia: Do thy worst!
This deed of thine is no more worthy heaven
Than thou wast worthy her.
Othello: Peace, you were best.°
Emilia: Thou hast not half that power to do me harm
As I have to be hurt.° O gull!° O dolt!   170
As ignorant as dirt! Thou hast done a deed—
I care not for thy sword; I'll make thee known,
Though I lost twenty lives.—Help! Help, ho, help!
The Moor hath killed my mistress! Murder, murder!

Enter Montano, Gratiano, and Iago.

Montano: What is the matter? How now, General?   175
Emilia: O, are you come, Iago? You have done well,
That men must lay their murders on your neck.
Gratiano: What is the matter?
Emilia [*to Iago*]: Disprove this villain, if thou be'st a man.
He says thou toldst him that his wife was false.   180
I know thou didst not; thou'rt not such a villain.
Speak, for my heart is full.
Iago: I told him what I thought, and told no more
Than what he found himself was apt° and true.
Emilia: But did you ever tell him she was false?   185
Iago: I did.
Emilia: You told a lie, an odious, damnèd lie!
Upon my soul, a lie, a wicked lie.
She false with Cassio? Did you say with Cassio?
Iago: With Cassio, mistress. Go to, charm° your tongue.   190
Emilia: I will not charm my tongue; I am bound to speak.
My mistress here lies murdered in her bed—
All: O heavens forfend!
Emilia: And your reports have set the murder on.
Othello: Nay, stare not, masters. It is true indeed.   195
Gratiano: 'Tis a strange truth.
Montano: O monstrous act!
Emilia: Villainy, villainy, villainy!
I think upon 't—I think I smell 't! O villainy!
I thought so then°—I'll kill myself for grief—
O villainy, villainy!   200

---

168 *you were best* it would be best for you   170 *to be hurt* i.e., to endure hurt.   *gull* dupe   184 *apt* plausible
190 *charm* keep silent (as though by a magic spell)   199 *then* (Perhaps at III, iii, 331–332 and IV, ii,
137–154.)

Iago: What, are you mad? I charge you, get you home.

Emilia: Good gentlemen, let me have leave to speak.

    'Tis proper I obey him, but not now.

    Perchance, Iago, I will ne'er go home.

Othello: O! O! O!   *[Othello falls on the bed.°]*

Emilia: Nay, lay thee down and roar,   205

    For thou hast killed the sweetest innocent

    That e'er did lift up eye.°

Othello [rising]:   O, she was foul!

    I scarce did know you, uncle. There lies your niece,

    Whose breath indeed these hands have newly stopped.

    I know this act shows° horrible and grim.   210

Gratiano: Poor Desdemon! I am glad thy father's dead.

    Thy match was mortal to him, and pure grief

    Shore his old thread° in twain. Did he live now,

    This sight would make him do a desperate turn,°

    Yea, curse his better angel from his side,   215

    And fall to reprobance.°

Othello: 'Tis pitiful. But yet Iago knows

    That she with Cassio hath the act of shame

    A thousand times committed. Cassio confessed it;

    And she did gratify° his amorous works   220

    With that recognizance° and pledge of love

    Which I first gave her. I saw it in his hand;

    It was a handkerchief, an antique token

    My father gave my mother.

Emilia: O God! O heavenly God!   225

Iago: Zounds, hold your peace.

Emilia: 'Twill out, 'twill out! I peace?

    No, I will speak as liberal as the north.°

    Let heaven and men and devils, let them all,

    All, all, cry shame against me, yet I'll speak.

Iago: Be wise, and get you home.

Emilia: I will not.

    [Iago threatens Emilia.]

Gratiano: Fie!   230

    Your sword upon a woman?

Emilia: O thou dull Moor! That handkerchief thou speak'st of

    I found by fortune and did give my husband;

    For often, with a solemn earnestness,

    More than indeed belonged° to such a trifle,   235

    He begged of me to steal 't.

---

205 s.d. *Othello . . . bed* (This direction is from the Quarto, as also *He kisses her* at line 19 and *She dies* at line 129.) 207 *lift up eye* i.e., lift her eyes to heaven 210 *shows* looks 213 *Shore . . . thread* sheared the thread of his old age (as Atropos, one of the three Fates, was thought to do) 214 *turn* deed 216 *reprobance* damnation, i.e., suicide 220 *gratify* reward 221 *recognizance* token 227 *liberal as the north* freely as the north wind (blows) 235 *belonged* was appropriate

Iago: Villainous whore!

Emilia: She give it Cassio? No, alas! I found it,
    And I did give 't my husband.

Iago: Filth, thou liest!

Emilia: By heaven, I do not, I do not, gentlemen.
    O murderous coxcomb!° What should such a fool   240
    Do with so good a wife?

Othello: Are there no stones° in heaven
    But what serves for the thunder?—Precious° villain!

[*He runs at Iago; Montano disarms Othello. Iago, from behind, stabs Emilia.*°]

Gratiano: The woman falls! Sure he hath killed his wife.

Emilia: Ay, ay. O, lay me by my mistress' side.   245

    Exit [Iago.]

Gratiano: He's gone, but his wife's killed.

Montano: 'Tis a notorious villain. Take you this weapon,
    Which I have here recovered from the Moor.
    Come, guard the door without. Let him not pass,
    But kill him rather. I'll after that same villain,   250
    For 'tis a damnèd slave.

    Exit [with all but Othello and Emilia, who has been laid by Desdemona's side].

Othello: I am not valiant neither,
    But every puny whipster° gets my sword.
    But why should honor° outlive honesty?°
    Let it go all.

Emilia: What did thy song bode, lady?   255
    Hark, canst thou hear me? I will play the swan,
    And die in music. [*She sings.*] "Willow, willow, willow."
    Moor, she was chaste. She loved thee, cruel Moor.
    So come my soul to bliss as I speak true.
    So speaking as I think, alas, I die.   [*She dies.*] 260

Othello: I have another weapon in this chamber;
    It was a sword of Spain, the ice-brook's temper°—
    O, here it is. [*He finds a sword.*] Uncle, I must come forth.

Gratiano [within]: If thou attempt it, it will cost thee dear.
    Thou hast no weapon, and perforce must suffer.   265

Othello: Look in upon me then and speak with me,
    Or, naked° as I am, I will assault thee.

    [*Enter Gratiano.*]

---

240 *coxcomb* fool. (Addressed to Othello.)   242 *stones* bolts, such as those used for thunderbolts   243
Precious i.e., arrant, utter. s.d. *He . . . Emilia* (The Quarto text reads, "The Moor runs at Iago. Iago kills
his wife." The Quarto also specifies the exit of Iago at line 245 and the death of Emilia at line 260.)   253
whipster contemptible fellow (one who is always ready to whip out his sword)   254 *honor* i.e., the bravery
for which one enjoys a soldier's reputation. *honesty* true integrity   262 *the ice-brook's temper* tempered in
ice-cold water   267 *naked* unarmed

Gratiano: What is the matter?
Othello: Behold, I have a weapon;
    A better never did itself sustain
    Upon a soldier's thigh. I have seen the day   270
    That, with this little arm and this good sword,
    I have made my way through more impediments
    Than twenty times your stop.° But O, vain boast!
    Who can control his fate? 'Tis not so now.
    Be not afraid, though you do see me weaponed;   275
    Here is my journey's end, here is my butt°
    And very seamark° of my utmost sail.

    [*Gratiano steps back.*]

    Do you go back dismayed? 'Tis a lost° fear;
    Man but a rush° against Othello's breast
    And he retires. Where should Othello go?   280

    [*He turns to Desdemona.*]

    Now, how dost thou look now? O ill-starred wench!
    Pale as thy smock! When we shall meet at compt,°
    This look of thine will hurl my soul from heaven,
    And fiends will snatch at it. Cold, cold, my girl?
    Even like thy chastity. O cursèd, cursèd slave!°   285
    Whip me, ye devils,
    From the possession of this heavenly sight!
    Blow me about in winds! Roast me in sulfur!
    Wash me in steep-down gulfs of liquid fire!
    O Desdemon! Dead, Desdemon! Dead! O! O!   290

    *Enter Lodovico, Cassio [carried in a litter°], Montano, and Iago [prisoner], with
    officers.*

Lodovico: Where is this rash and most unfortunate man?
Othello: That's he that was Othello. Here I am.
Lodovico: Where is that viper? Bring the villain forth.

    [*Iago is led forward.*]

Othello: I look down towards his feet;° but that's a fable.
    If that thou be'st a devil, I cannot kill thee.   295

    [*He wounds Iago.*]

Lodovico: Wrench his sword from him.   [*Othello is disarmed.*]
Iago: I bleed, sir, but not killed.

---

273 *stop* power (to stop)   276 *butt* goal, limit. (An archery term.)   277 *seamark* beacon (marking his destina-
tion or limit)   278 *lost* wasted, unneeded   279 *Man . . . rush* wield no more than a reed   282 *compt* account,
judgment day   285 *slave* i.e., Othello himself   290 s.d. *in a litter* (The Quarto specifies that Cassio is "in a
chair.")   294 *towards his feet* i.e., to see if they are cloven, as the devil's are fabled to be

Lodovico confronts the prisoner Iago; Desdemona and Emilia lie dead in the background (V, ii, 296–314).

Othello: I am not sorry neither. I'd have thee live,
    For in my sense° 'tis happiness to die.
Lodovico: O thou Othello, that was once so good,
    Fall'n in the practice° of a cursèd slave,°   300
    What shall be said to thee?
Othello: Why, anything.
    An honorable murderer, if you will,
    For naught I did in hate, but all in honor.
Lodovico: This wretch hath part confessed his villainy.
    Did you and he consent° in Cassio's death?   305
Othello: Ay.
Cassio: Dear General, I never gave you cause.
Othello: I do believe it, and I ask your pardon.
    Will you, I pray, demand that demi-devil
    Why he hath thus ensnared my soul and body?   310
Iago: Demand me nothing. What you know, you know.
    From this time forth I never will speak word.
Lodovico: What, not to pray?
Gratiano: Torments° will ope your lips.
Othello: Well, thou dost best.   315
Lodovico: Sir, you shall understand what hath befall'n,

298 *in my sense* to one who feels as I do   300 *in the practice* through the plotting, into the snare.   *slave* villain   305 *consent* agree   314 *Torments* torture

Which, as I think, you know not. Here is a letter
Found in the pocket of the slain Roderigo;
And here another. [*He produces letters.*] The one of them imports
The death of Cassio, to be undertook   320
By Roderigo.
Othello: O villain!
Cassio: Most heathenish and most gross!°
Lodovico [*showing another paper*]: Now here's another discontented° paper
Found in his pocket too. And this, it seems,
Roderigo meant t' have sent this damnèd villain;   325
But that belike° Iago in the interim
Came in and satisfied him.°
Othello: O thou pernicious caitiff!—
How came you, Cassio, by that handkerchief
That was my wife's?
Cassio: I found it in my chamber;   330
And he himself confessed but even now
That there he dropped it for a special purpose
Which wrought to his desire.°
Othello: O fool, fool, fool!
Cassio: There is besides in Roderigo's letter
How he upbraids Iago, that he made him   335
Brave° me upon the watch, whereon it came°
That I was cast;° and even but now he spake,
After long seeming dead, Iago hurt him,
Iago set him on.
Lodovico [*to Othello*]: You must forsake this room and go with us.   340
Your power and your command is taken off,°
And Cassio rules in Cyprus. For this slave,
If there be any cunning cruelty
That can torment him much and hold him long,°
It shall be his. You shall close prisoner rest°   345
Till that the nature of your fault be known
To the Venetian state.—Come, bring away.
Othello: Soft you;° a word or two before you go.
I have done the state some service, and they know 't.
No more of that. I pray you, in your letters,   350
When you shall these unlucky° deeds relate,
Speak of me as I am; nothing extenuate,
Nor set down aught in malice. Then must you speak
Of one that loved not wisely but too well;
Of one not easily jealous but, being wrought,°   355

---

322 *gross* monstrous   323 *discontented* full of discontent   326 *belike* most likely   327 *Came . . . him* interposed and gave him satisfactory explanation   333 *wrought . . . desire* worked out as he wished, fitted in with his plan   336 *Brave* defy. *whereon it came* whereof it came about   337 *cast* dismissed   341 *taken off* taken away   344 *hold him long* keep him alive a long time (during his torture)   345 *rest* remain   348 *Soft you* one moment   351 *unlucky* unfortunate   355 *wrought* worked upon, worked into a frenzy

Perplexed° in the extreme; of one whose hand,
Like the base Indian,° threw a pearl away
Richer than all his tribe; of one whose subdued° eyes,
Albeit unusèd to the melting mood,
Drop tears as fast as the Arabian trees   360
Their medicinable gum.° Set you down this;
And say besides that in Aleppo once,
Where a malignant and a turbaned Turk
Beat a Venetian and traduced the state,
I took by th' throat the circumcisèd dog   365
And smote him, thus.   [He stabs himself.°]
Lodovico: O bloody period!°
Gratiano: All that is spoke is marred.
Othello: I kissed thee ere I killed thee. No way but this,
    Killing myself, to die upon a kiss.   370

    [*He kisses Desdemona and dies.*]

Cassio: This did I fear, but thought he had no weapon;
    For he was great of heart.
Lodovico [*to Iago*]:   O Spartan dog,°
    More fell° than anguish, hunger, or the sea!
    Look on the tragic loading of this bed.
    This is thy work. The object poisons sight;   375
    Let it be hid.° Gratiano, keep° the house,

    [*The bed curtains are drawn*]

    And seize upon° the fortunes of the Moor,
    For they succeed on° you. [*To Cassio.*] To you, Lord Governor,
    Remains the censure° of this hellish villain,
    The time, the place, the torture. O, enforce it!   380
    Myself will straight aboard, and to the state
    This heavy act with heavy heart relate.   *Exeunt.*

Questions

ACT I

1. What is Othello's position in society? How is he regarded by those who know him? By his own words, when we first meet him in Scene ii, what traits of character does he manifest?

2. How do you account for Brabantio's dismay on learning of his daughter's marriage, despite the fact that Desdemona has married a man so generally honored and admired?

3. What is Iago's view of human nature? In his fondness for likening men to animals (as in I, i, 49–50; I, i, 90–91; and I, iii, 378–379), what does he tell us about himself?

4. What reasons does Iago give for his hatred of Othello?

---

356 *Perplexed* distraught   357 *Indian* (This reading from the Quarto pictures an ignorant savage who cannot recognize the value of a precious jewel. The Folio reading, *Iudean* or *Judean*, i.e., infidel or disbeliever, may refer to Herod, who slew Miriamne in a fit of jealousy, or to Judas Iscariot, the betrayer of Christ.) 358 *subdued* i.e., overcome by grief   361 *gum* i.e., myrr   366 s.d. *He stabs himself* (This direction is in the Quarto text.)   367 *period* termination, conclusion   372 *Spartan dog* (Spartan dogs were noted for their savagery and silence.)   373 *fell* cruel   376 *Let it be hid* i.e., draw the bed curtains. (No stage direction specifies that the dead are to be carried offstage at the end of the play.)   *keep* remain in   377 *seize upon* take legal possession of   378 *succeed on* pass as though by inheritance to   379 *censure* sentencing

5. In Othello's defense before the senators (Scene iii), how does he explain Desdemona's gradual falling in love with him?
6. Is Brabantio's warning to Othello (I, iii, 293–294) an accurate or an inaccurate prophecy?
7. By what strategy does Iago enlist Roderigo in his plot against the Moor? In what lines do we learn Iago's true feelings toward Roderigo?

ACT II

1. What do the Cypriots think of Othello? Do their words (in Scene i) make him seem to us a lesser man or a larger one?
2. What cruelty does Iago display toward Emilia? How well founded is his distrust of his wife's fidelity?
3. In II, iii, 221, Othello speaks of Iago's "honesty and love." How do you account for Othello's being so totally deceived?
4. For what major events does the merrymaking (proclaimed in Scene ii) give opportunity?

ACT III

1. Trace the steps by which Iago rouses Othello to suspicion. Is there anything in Othello's character or circumstances that renders him particularly susceptible to Iago's wiles?
2. In III, iv, 49–98, Emilia knows of Desdemona's distress over the lost handkerchief. At this moment, how do you explain her failure to relieve Desdemona's mind? Is Emilia aware of her husband's villainy?

ACT IV

1. In this act, what circumstantial evidence is added to Othello's case against Desdemona?
2. How plausible do you find Bianca's flinging the handkerchief at Cassio just when Othello is looking on? How important is the handkerchief in this play? What does it represent? What suggestions or hints do you find in it?
3. What prevents Othello from being moved by Desdemona's appeal (IV, ii, 33–92)?
4. When Roderigo grows impatient with Iago (IV, ii, 181–201), how does Iago make use of his fellow plotter's discontent?
5. What does the conversation between Emilia and Desdemona (Scene iii) tell us about the nature of each?
6. In this act, what scenes (or speeches) contain memorable dramatic irony?

ACT V

1. Summarize the events that lead to Iago's unmasking.
2. How does Othello's mistaken belief that Cassio is slain (V, i, 27–34) affect the outcome of the play?
3. What is Iago's motive in stabbing Roderigo?
4. In your interpretation of the play, exactly what impels Othello to kill Desdemona? Jealousy? Desire for revenge? Excess idealism? A wish to be a public avenger who punishes, "else she'll betray more men"?
5. What do you understand by Othello's calling himself "one that loved not wisely but too well" (V, ii, 354)?
6. In your view, does Othello's long speech in V, ii, 348–366 succeed in restoring his original dignity and nobility? Do you agree with Cassio (V, ii, 372) that Othello was "great of heart"?

General Questions

1. What motivates Iago to carry out his schemes? Do you find him a devil incarnate, a madman, or a rational human being?

2. Whom besides Othello does Iago deceive? What is Desdemona's opinion of him? Emilia's? Cassio's (before Iago is found out)? To what do you attribute Iago's success as a deceiver?

3. How essential to the play is the fact that Othello is a black man, a Moor, and not a native of Venice?

4. In the introduction to his edition of the play in *The Complete Signet Classic Shakespeare*, Alvin Kernan remarks:

   > *Othello* is probably the most neatly, the most formally constructed of Shakespeare's plays. Every character is, for example, balanced by another similar or contrasting character. Desdemona is balanced by her opposite, Iago; love and concern for others at one end of the scale, hatred and concern for self at the other.

   Besides Desdemona and Iago, what other pairs of characters strike balances?

5. Consider any passage of the play in which there is a shift from verse to prose, or from prose to verse. What is the effect of this shift?

6. Indicate a passage that you consider memorable for its poetry. Does the passage seem introduced for its own sake? Does it in any way advance the action of the play, express theme, or demonstrate character?

7. Does the play contain any tragic *recognition*—as discussed on page 1204 a moment of terrible enlightenment, a "realization of the unthinkable"?

8. Does the downfall of Othello proceed from any flaw in his nature, or is his downfall entirely the work of Iago?

THE BACKGROUND OF *HAMLET*

William Shakespeare wrote *Hamlet* around 1600. The Hamlet story first appears in the *Danish History* of the twelfth-century writer Saxo Grammaticus, but the tale is probably even older than that. Saxo's version recounts the murder of the king of Denmark by his wicked brother and the brother's marriage to the widowed queen; then Prince Amlethus, the dead king's son, feigns madness, escapes a plot on his life, and eventually gains revenge. There was an earlier English play, also called *Hamlet*, based on this tale. Written in the 1580s, probably by Thomas Kyd, it is now lost. It is believed that Shakespeare based his own play on it. Although he borrowed his story (as he did the basic plot of *Othello*), Shakespeare made it entirely his own and populated it with some of the most memorable characters in English drama. It is usually assumed that *Hamlet* was the earliest of Shakespeare's four great mature tragedies (being written just before *Othello*, *King Lear*, and *Macbeth*). If this speculative dating is true, Hamlet represented something extraordinarily innovative in world drama, especially in respect to the title character—a deeply intelligent and reflective man compelled by justice and filial duty to avenge his father's murder but simultaneously riddled with self-doubt and moral conscience. In the brooding figure of Hamlet, Shakespeare presented both the prince's inner and exterior life with startling immediacy and mysterious depth. For centuries critics have considered *Hamlet* Shakespeare's most philosophical play, yet it does not lack action. *Hamlet* contains a vengeful ghost, two sorts of madness (one tragically genuine, the other comically feigned), a suicide, sword fights, poisonings, incest, and multiple murders. The play provides both the compelling entertainment beloved by Elizabethan audiences and a tragic meditation on human existence that has haunted readers of every subsequent age.

Kenneth Branagh as Hamlet with Kate Winslet as Ophelia.

PICTURING *Hamlet*

▲ The king's ghost, *page 1399*

▲ Hamlet returns home, *page 1405*

▲ Hamlet and the gravedigger, *page 1488*

▼ Hamlet considers killing Claudius, *page 1460*

▲ "Alas, poor Yorick," *page 1491*

▼ Hamlet with his father's ghost, *page 1417*

▲ Ophelia and Hamlet, *page 1444*

▲ *The Murder of Gonzago, page 1453*

▲ Queen Gertrude mourns Ophelia, *page 1493*

▲ Swordplay turns deadly, *page 1503*

Hamlet, Prince of Denmark   about 1600

Edited by David Bevington

[DRAMATIS PERSONAE

Ghost of Hamlet, the former King of Denmark
Claudius, King of Denmark, the former King's brother
Gertrude, Queen of Denmark, widow of the former King and now wife of Claudius
Hamlet, Prince of Denmark, son of the late King and of Gertrude
Polonius, councillor to the King
Laertes, his son
Ophelia, his daughter
Reynaldo, his servant
Horatio, Hamlet's friend and fellow student

Voltimand,
Cornelius,
Rosencrantz,
Guildenstern, } members of the Danish court
Osric,
A Gentleman,
A Lord,

Bernardo,
Francisco, } officers and soldiers on watch
Marcellus,

Fortinbras, Prince of Norway
Captain in his army
Three or Four *Players*, taking the roles of *Prologue, Player King, Player Queen,* and *Lucianus*
Two Messengers
First Sailor
Two Clowns, a gravedigger and his companion
Priest
First Ambassador from England
Lords, Soldiers, Attendants, Guards, other Players, Followers of Laertes, other Sailors,
     another Ambassador or Ambassadors from England

SCENE. *Denmark*]

ACT I

SCENE I [ELSINORE CASTLE. A GUARD PLATFORM.]

Enter Bernardo and Francisco, two sentinels, [meeting].

NOTE ON THE TEXT: This text of *Hamlet* is based primarily on the Second Quarto of 1604–1605. For the reader's convenience, some material has been added by the editor, David Bevington (some indications of scenes and some stage directions). Such additions are enclosed in brackets. Mr. Bevington's text and notes were prepared for his book *The Complete Works of Shakespeare*, Updated 4th ed. (New York: Longman, 1997).

PRODUCTION PHOTOS: The photos included are from the 2003 production of *Hamlet* by the Alley Theatre of Houston, with Ty Mayberry (Hamlet), Elizabeth Heflin (Gertrude), James Black (Claudius, ghost of Hamlet's father), Philip Lehl (Horatio), Daniel Magill (Laertes), John Tyson (Polonius), Jennifer Cherry (Ophelia), and Charles Krohn (gravedigger).

Bernardo: Who's there?

Francisco: Nay, answer me.° Stand and unfold yourself.°

Bernardo: Long live the King!

Francisco: Bernardo?

Bernardo: He.   5

Francisco: You come most carefully upon your hour.

Bernardo: 'Tis now struck twelve. Get thee to bed, Francisco.

Francisco: For this relief much thanks. 'Tis bitter cold,
>And I am sick at heart.

Bernardo: Have you had quiet guard?   10

Francisco: Not a mouse stirring.

Bernardo: Well, good night.
>If you do meet Horatio and Marcellus,
>The rivals° of my watch, bid them make haste.

>*Enter Horatio and Marcellus.*

Francisco: I think I hear them.—Stand, ho! Who is there?   15

Horatio: Friends to this ground.°

Marcellus: And liegemen to the Dane.°

Francisco: Give° you good night.

Marcellus: O, farewell, honest soldier. Who hath relieved you?

Francisco: Bernardo hath my place. Give you good night.   20

>>>*Exit Francisco.*

Marcellus: Holla! Bernardo!

Bernardo: Say, what, is Horatio there?

Horatio: A piece of him.

Bernardo: Welcome, Horatio. Welcome, good Marcellus.

Horatio: What, has this thing appeared again tonight?   25

Bernardo: I have seen nothing.

Marcellus: Horatio says 'tis but our fantasy,°
>And will not let belief take hold of him
>Touching this dreaded sight twice seen of us.
>Therefore I have entreated him along°   30
>With us to watch° the minutes of this night,
>That if again this apparition come
>He may approve° our eyes and speak to it.

Horatio: Tush, tush, 'twill not appear.

Bernardo: Sit down awhile,
>And let us once again assail your ears,   35
>That are so fortified against our story,
>What° we have two nights seen.

Horatio: Well, sit we down,
>And let us hear Bernardo speak of this.

Bernardo: Last night of all,°

---

2 *me* (Francisco emphasizes that *he* is the sentry currently on watch.) *unfold yourself* reveal your identity
14 *rivals* partners 16 *ground* country, land 17 *liegemen to the Dane* men sworn to serve the Danish king
18 *Give* i.e., may God give 27 *fantasy* imagination 30 *along* to come along 31 *watch* keep watch during
33 *approve* corroborate 37 *What* with what 39 *Last . . . all* i.e., this *very* last night (Emphatic.)

When yond same star that's westward from the pole°   40
Had made his° course t' illume° that part of heaven
Where now it burns, Marcellus and myself,
The bell then beating one—

Enter Ghost.

Marcellus: Peace, break thee off! Look where it comes again!
Bernardo: In the same figure like the King that's dead.   45
Marcellus: Thou art a scholar.° Speak to it, Horatio.
Bernardo: Looks 'a° not like the King? Mark it, Horatio.
Horatio: Most like. It harrows me with fear and wonder.
Bernardo: It would be spoke to.°
Marcellus: Speak to it, Horatio.
Horatio: What are thou that usurp'st° this time of night,   50
Together with that fair and warlike form
In which the majesty of buried Denmark°
Did sometime° march? By heaven, I charge thee, speak!
Marcellus: It is offended.
Bernardo: See, it stalks away.
Horatio: Stay! Speak, speak! I charge thee, speak!   *Exit Ghost.*   55
Marcellus: 'Tis gone and will not answer.
Bernardo: How now, Horatio? You tremble and look pale.
Is not this something more than fantasy?
What think you on 't?°
Horatio: Before my God, I might not this believe   60
Without the sensible and true avouch°
Of mine own eyes.
Marcellus: Is it not like the King?
Horatio: As thou art to thyself.
Such was the very armor he had on
When he the ambitious Norway° combated.   65
So frowned he once when, in an angry parle,°
He smote the sledded° Polacks° on the ice.
'Tis strange.
Marcellus: Thus twice before, and jump° at this dead hour,
With martial stalk° hath he gone by our watch.   70
Horatio: In what particular thought to work° I know not,
But in the gross and scope° of mine opinion
This bodes some strange eruption to our state.
Marcellus: Good now,° sit down, and tell me, he that knows,
Why this same strict and most observant watch   75

40 *pole* polestar, north star   41 *his* its.   *illume* illuminate   46 *scholar* one learned enough to know how to question a ghost properly   47 *'a* he   49 *It . . . to* (It was commonly believed that a ghost could not speak until spoken to.)   50 *usurp'st* wrongfully takes over   52 *buried Denmark* the buried King of Denmark   53 *sometime* formerly   59 *on 't* of it   61 *sensible* confirmed by the senses.   *avouch* warrant, evidence   65 *Norway* King of Norway   66 *parle* parley   67 *sledded* traveling on sleds.   *Polacks* Poles   69 *jump* exactly   70 *stalk* stride   71 *to work* i.e., to collect my thoughts and try to understand this   72 *gross and scope* general drift   74 *Good now* (An expression denoting entreaty or expostulation.)

The ghost of the king appears to the watch.

So nightly toils° the subject° of the land,
And why such daily cast° of brazen cannon
And foreign mart° for implements of war,
Why such impress° of shipwrights, whose sore task
Does not divide the Sunday from the week.   80
What might be toward,° that this sweaty haste
Doth make the night joint-laborer with the day?
Who is 't that can inform me?
Horatio: That can I;
At least, the whisper goes so. Our last king,
Whose image even but now appeared to us,   85

76 *toils* causes to toil. *subject* subjects 77 *cast* casting 78 *mart* buying and selling 79 *impress* impressment, conscription 81 *toward* in preparation

Was, as you know, by Fortinbras of Norway,
Thereto° pricked on° by a most emulate° pride,
Dared to the combat; in which our valiant Hamlet—
For so this side of our known world° esteemed him—
Did slay this Fortinbras; who by a sealed° compact   90
Well ratified by law and heraldry
Did forfeit, with his life, all those his lands
Which he stood seized° of, to the conqueror;
Against the° which a moiety competent°
Was gagèd° by our king, which had returned°   95
To the inheritance° of Fortinbras
Had he been vanquisher, as, by the same cov'nant°
And carriage of the article designed,°
His fell to Hamlet. Now, sir, young Fortinbras,
Of unimprovèd mettle° hot and full,   100
Hath in the skirts° of Norway here and there
Sharked up° a list° of lawless resolutes°
For food and diet° to some enterprise
That hath a stomach° in 't, which is no other—
As it doth well appear unto our state—   105
But to recover of us, by strong hand
And terms compulsatory, those foresaid lands
So by his father lost. And this, I take it,
Is the main motive of our preparations,
The source of this our watch, and the chief head°   110
Of this posthaste and rummage° in the land.
Bernardo: I think it be no other but e'en so.
Well may it sort° that this portentous figure
Comes armèd through our watch so like the King
That was and is the question° of these wars.   115
Horatio: A mote° it is to trouble the mind's eye.
In the most high and palmy° state of Rome,
A little ere the mightiest Julius fell,
The graves stood tenantless, and the sheeted° dead
Did squeak and gibber in the Roman streets;   120
As° stars with trains° of fire and dews of blood,
Disasters° in the sun; and the moist star°

---

87 *Thereto . . . pride* (Refers to old Fortinbras, not the Danish King.) *pricked on* incited. *emulate* emulous, ambitious 89 *this . . . world* i.e., all Europe, the Western world 90 *sealed* certified, confirmed 93 *seized* possessed 94 *Against the* in return for. *moiety competent* corresponding portion 95 *gagèd* engaged, pledged. *had returned* would have passed 96 *inheritance* possession 97 *cov'nant* i.e., the *sealed compact* of line 90 98 *carriage . . . designed* carrying out of the article or clause drawn up to cover the point 100 *unimprovèd mettle* untried, undisciplined spirits 101 *skirts* outlying regions, outskirts 102 *Sharked up* gathered up, as a shark takes fish. *list* i.e., troop. *resolutes* desperadoes 103 *For food and diet* i.e., they are to serve as *food*, or "means," *to some enterprise*; also they serve in return for the rations they get 104 *stomach* (1) a spirit of daring (2) an appetite that is fed by the *lawless resolutes* 110 *head* source 111 *rummage* bustle, commotion 113 *sort* suit 115 *question* focus of contention 116 *mote* speck of dust 117 *palmy* flourishing 119 *sheeted* shrouded 121 *As* (This abrupt transition suggests that matter is possibly omitted between lines 120 and 121.) *trains* trails 122 *Disasters* unfavorable signs or aspects. *moist star* i.e., moon, governing tides

Upon whose influence Neptune's° empire stands°
Was sick almost to doomsday° with eclipse.
And even the like precurse° of feared events,   125
As harbingers° preceding still° the fates
And prologue to the omen° coming on,
Have heaven and earth together demonstrated
Unto our climatures° and countrymen.

Enter Ghost.

But soft,° behold! Lo, where it comes again!   130
I'll cross° it, though it blast° me. (*It spreads his° arms.*) Stay, illusion!
If thou hast any sound or use of voice,
Speak to me!
If there be any good thing to be done
That may to thee do ease and grace to me,   135
Speak to me!
If thou art privy to° thy country's fate,
Which, happily,° foreknowing may avoid,
O, speak!
Or if thou hast uphoarded in thy life   140
Extorted treasure in the womb of earth,
For which, they say, you spirits oft walk in death,
Speak of it! (*The cock crows.*) Stay and speak!—Stop it, Marcellus.
Marcellus: Shall I strike at it with my partisan?°
Horatio: Do, if it will not stand.   [*They strike at it.*] 145
Bernardo: 'Tis here!
Horatio: 'Tis here!   [*Exit Ghost.*]
Marcellus: 'Tis gone.
　　We do it wrong, being so majestical,
　　To offer it the show of violence,   150
　　For it is as the air invulnerable,
　　And our vain blows malicious mockery.
Bernardo: It was about to speak when the cock crew.
Horatio: And then it started like a guilty thing
　　Upon a fearful summons. I have heard   155
　　The cock, that is the trumpet° to the morn,
　　Doth with his lofty and shrill-sounding throat
　　Awake the god of day, and at his warning,
　　Whether in sea or fire, in earth or air,
　　Th' extravagant and erring° spirit hies°   160
　　To his confine; and of the truth herein
　　This present object made probation.°

---

123 *Neptune* god of the sea.　*stands* depends　124 *sick . . . doomsday* (See Matthew 24:29 and Revelation 6:12.)　125 *precurse* heralding, foreshadowing　126 *harbingers* forerunners.　*still* continually　127 *omen* calamitous event　129 *climatures* regions　130 *soft* i.e., enough, break off　131 *cross* stand in its path, confront.　*blast* wither, strike with a curse.　*s.d. his* its　137 *privy to* in on the secret of　138 *happily* haply, perchance　144 *partisan* long-handled spear　156 *trumpet* trumpeter　160 *extravagant and erring* wandering beyond bounds. (The words have similar meaning.)　*hies* hastens　162 *probation* proof

Marcellus: It faded on the crowing of the cock.
    Some say that ever 'gainst° that season comes
    Wherein our Savior's birth is celebrated,   165
    This bird of dawning singeth all night long,
    And then, they say, no spirit dare stir abroad;
    The nights are wholesome, then no planets strike,°
    No fairy takes,° nor witch hath power to charm,
    So hallowed and so gracious° is that time.   170
Horatio: So have I heard and do in part believe it.
    But, look, the morn in russet mantle clad
    Walks o'er the dew of yon high eastward hill.
    Break we our watch up, and by my advice
    Let us impart what we have seen tonight   175
    Unto young Hamlet; for upon my life,
    This spirit, dumb to us, will speak to him.
    Do you consent we shall acquaint him with it,
    As needful in our loves, fitting our duty?
Marcellus: Let's do 't, I pray, and I this morning know   180
    Where we shall find him most conveniently.   *Exeunt.*

SCENE II [THE CASTLE.]

*Flourish. Enter Claudius, King of Denmark, Gertrude the Queen, [the] Council, as°
Polonius and his son Laertes, Hamlet, cum aliis° [including Voltimand and Cornelius].*

King: Though yet of Hamlet our° dear brother's death
    The memory be green, and that it us befitted
    To bear our hearts in grief and our whole kingdom
    To be contracted in one brow of woe,
    Yet so far hath discretion fought with nature   5
    That we with wisest sorrow think on him
    Together with remembrance of ourselves.
    Therefore our sometime° sister, now our queen,
    Th' imperial jointress° to this warlike state,
    Have we, as 'twere with a defeated joy—   10
    With an auspicious and a dropping eye,°
    With mirth in funeral and with dirge in marriage,
    In equal scale weighing delight and dole°—
    Taken to wife. Nor have we herein barred
    Your better wisdoms, which have freely gone   15
    With this affair along. For all, our thanks.
    Now follows that you know° young Fortinbras,
    Holding a weak supposal° of our worth,
    Or thinking by our late dear brother's death

164 *'gainst* just before   168 *strike* destroy by evil influence   169 *takes* bewitches   170 *gracious* full of grace
s.d. *as* i.e., such as, including.   *cum aliis* with others   1 *our* my. (The royal "we"; also in the following
lines.)   8 *sometime* former   9 *jointress* woman possessing property with her husband   11 *With . . . eye*
with one eye smiling and the other weeping   13 *dole* grief   17 *that you know* what you know already, that;
or, that you be informed as follows   18 *weak supposal* low estimate

Our state to be disjoint and out of frame,   20
Co-leaguèd with° this dream of his advantage,°
He hath not failed to pester us with message
Importing° the surrender of those lands
Lost by his father, with all bonds° of law,
To our most valiant brother. So much for him.   25
Now for ourself and for this time of meeting.
Thus much the business is: we have here writ
To Norway, uncle of young Fortinbras—
Who, impotent° and bed-rid, scarcely hears
Of this his nephew's purpose—to suppress   30
His° further gait° herein, in that the levies,
The lists, and full proportions are all made
Out of his subject;° and we here dispatch
You, good Cornelius, and you, Voltimand,
For bearers of this greeting to old Norway,   35
Giving to you no further personal power
To business with the King more than the scope
Of these dilated° articles allow.   [*He gives a paper.*]
Farewell, and let your haste commend your duty.°

Cornelius, Voltimand:
  In that, and all things, will we show our duty.   40
King: We doubt it nothing.° Heartily farewell.

                  [*Exeunt Voltimand and Cornelius.*]
And now, Laertes, what's the news with you?
You told us of some suit; what is 't, Laertes?
You cannot speak of reason to the Dane°
And lose your voice.° What wouldst thou beg, Laertes, 45
That shall not be my offer, not thy asking?
The head is not more native° to the heart,
The hand more instrumental° to the mouth,
Than is the throne of Denmark to thy father.
What wouldst thou have, Laertes?

Laertes: My dread lord,   50
Your leave and favor° to return to France,
From whence though willingly I came to Denmark
To show my duty in your coronation,
Yet now I must confess, that duty done,
My thoughts and wishes bend again toward France   55
And bow them to your gracious leave and pardon.°

---

21 *Co-leaguèd with* joined to, allied with. *dream . . . advantage* illusory hope of having the advantage.
(His only ally is this hope.) 23 *Importing* pertaining to 24 *bonds* contracts 29 *impotent* helpless 31
His i.e., Fortinbras'. *gait* proceeding 31–33 *in that . . . subject* since the levying of troops and supplies is
drawn entirely from the King of Norway's own subjects 38 *dilated* set out at length 39 *let . . . duty* let
your swift obeying of orders, rather than mere words, express your dutifulness 41 *nothing* not at all 44
the Dane the Danish king 45 *lose your voice* waste your speech 47 *native* closely connected, related 48
instrumental serviceable 51 *leave and favor* kind permission 56 *bow . . . pardon* entreatingly make a deep
bow, asking your permission to depart

King: Have you your father's leave? What says Polonius?
Polonius: H'ath,° my lord, wrung from me my slow leave
    By laborsome petition, and at last
    Upon his will I sealed° my hard° consent.   60
    I do beseech you, give him leave to go.
King: Take thy fair hour,° Laertes. Time be thine,
    And thy best graces spend it at thy will!°
    But now, my cousin° Hamlet, and my son—
Hamlet: A little more than kin, and less than kind.°   65
King: How is it that the clouds still hang on you?
Hamlet: Not so, my lord. I am too much in the sun.°
Queen: Good Hamlet, cast thy nighted color° off,
    And let thine eye look like a friend on Denmark.°
    Do not forever with thy vailèd lids°   70
    Seek for thy noble father in the dust.
    Thou know'st 'tis common,° all that lives must die,
    Passing through nature to eternity.
Hamlet: Ay, madam, it is common.
Queen: If it be,
    Why seems it so particular° with thee?   75
Hamlet: Seems, madam? Nay, it is. I know not "seems."
    'Tis not alone my inky cloak, good Mother,
    Nor customary° suits of solemn black,
    Nor windy suspiration° of forced breath,
    No, nor the fruitful° river in the eye,   80
    Nor the dejected havior° of the visage,
    Together with all forms, moods,° shapes of grief,
    That can denote me truly. These indeed seem,
    For they are actions that a man might play.
    But I have that within which passes show;   85
    These but the trappings and the suits of woe.
King: 'Tis sweet and commendable in your nature, Hamlet,
    To give these mourning duties to your father.
    But you must know your father lost a father,
    That father lost, lost his, and the survivor bound   90
    In filial obligation for some term
    To do obsequious° sorrow. But to persever°
    In obstinate condolement° is a course

---

58 *H'ath* he has   60 *sealed* (as if sealing a legal document).   *hard* reluctant   62 *Take thy fair hour* enjoy your time of youth   63 *And . . . will* and may your finest qualities guide the way you choose to spend your time   64 *cousin* any kin not of the immediate family   65 A *little . . . kind* i.e., closer than an ordinary nephew (since I am stepson), and yet more separated in natural feeling (with pun on *kind* meaning "affectionate" and "natural," "lawful." This line is often read as an aside, but it need not be. The King chooses perhaps not to respond to Hamlet's cryptic and bitter remark.)   67 *the sun* i.e., the sunshine of the King's royal favor (with pun on *son*)   68 *nighted color* (1) mourning garments of black (2) dark melancholy   69 *Denmark* the King of Denmark   70 *vailèd lids* lowered eyes   72 *common* of universal occurrence. (But Hamlet plays on the sense of "vulgar" in line 74.)   75 *particular* personal   78 *customary* (1) socially conventional (2) habitual with me   79 *suspiration* sighing   80 *fruitful* abundant   81 *havior* expression   82 *moods* outward expression of feeling   92 *obsequious* suited to obsequies or funerals.   *persever* persevere   93 *condolement* sorrowing

Prince Hamlet returns to Denmark to discover his widowed mother remarried to his uncle, the new king.

Of impious stubbornness. 'Tis unmanly grief.
It shows a will most incorrect to heaven,   95
A heart unfortified,° a mind impatient,
An understanding simple° and unschooled.
For what we know must be and is as common
As any the most vulgar thing to sense,°
Why should we in our peevish opposition   100
Take it to heart? Fie, 'tis a fault to heaven,
A fault against the dead, a fault to nature,
To reason most absurd, whose common theme
Is death of fathers, and who still° hath cried,
From the first corpse° till he that died today,   105
"This must be so." We pray you, throw to earth
This unprevailing° woe and think of us
As of a father; for let the world take note,

96 *unfortified* i.e., against adversity   97 *simple* ignorant   99 *As . . . sense* as the most ordinary experience
104 *still* always   105 *the first corpse* (Abel's)   107 *unprevailing* unavailing, useless

You are the most immediate° to our throne,
And with no less nobility of love   110
Than that which dearest father bears his son
Do I impart toward° you. For° your intent
In going back to school° in Wittenberg,°
It is most retrograde° to our desire,
And we beseech you bend you° to remain   115
Here in the cheer and comfort of our eye,
Our chiefest courtier, cousin, and our son.
Queen: Let not thy mother lose her prayers, Hamlet.
   I pray thee, stay with us, go not to Wittenberg.
Hamlet: I shall in all my best° obey you, madam.   120
King: Why, 'tis a loving and a fair reply.
   Be as ourself in Denmark. Madam, come.
   This gentle and unforced accord of Hamlet
   Sits smiling to° my heart, in grace° whereof
   No jocund° health that Denmark drinks today   125
   But the great cannon to the clouds shall tell,
   And the King's rouse° the heaven shall bruit again,°
   Respeaking earthly thunder.° Come away.

                                        Flourish. Exeunt all but Hamlet.

Hamlet: O, that this too too sullied° flesh would melt,
   Thaw, and resolve itself into a dew!   130
   Or that the Everlasting had not fixed
   His canon° 'gainst self-slaughter! O God, God,
   How weary, stale, flat, and unprofitable
   Seem to me all the uses° of this world!
   Fie on 't, ah fie! 'Tis an unweeded garden   135
   That grows to seed. Things rank and gross in nature
   Possess it merely.° That it should come to this!
   But two months dead—nay, not so much, not two.
   So excellent a king, that was to° this
   Hyperion° to a satyr,° so loving to my mother   140
   That he might not beteem° the winds of heaven
   Visit her face too roughly. Heaven and earth,
   Must I remember? Why, she would hang on him
   As if increase of appetite had grown
   By what it fed on, and yet within a month—   145
   Let me not think on 't; frailty, thy name is woman!—

---

109 *most immediate* next in succession   112 *impart toward* i.e., bestow my affection on.   *For* as for   113 *to school* i.e., to your studies.   *Wittenberg* famous German university founded in 1502   114 *retrograde* contrary   115 *bend you* incline yourself   120 *in all my best* to the best of my ability   124 *to* i.e., at.   *grace* thanksgiving   125 *jocund* merry   127 *rouse* drinking of a draft of liquor.   *bruit again* loudly echo   128 *thunder* i.e., of trumpet and kettledrum, sounded when the King drinks; see I, iv, 8–12   129 *sullied* defiled. (The early quartos read *sallied*; the Folio, *solid.*)   132 *canon* law   134 *all the uses* the whole routine   137 *merely* completely   139 *to* in comparison to   140 *Hyperion* Titan sun-god, father of Helios.   *satyr* a lecherous creature of classical mythology, half-human but with a goat's legs, tail, ears, and horns   141 *beteem* allow

A little month, or ere° those shoes were old
With which she followed my poor father's body,
Like Niobe,° all tears, why she, even she—
O God, a beast, that wants discourse of reason,°   150
Would have mourned longer—married with my uncle,
My father's brother, but no more like my father
Than I to Hercules. Within a month,
Ere yet the salt of most unrighteous tears
Had left the flushing in her gallèd° eyes,   155
She married. O, most wicked speed, to post°
With such dexterity to incestuous° sheets!
It is not, nor it cannot come to good.
But break, my heart, for I must hold my tongue.

Enter Horatio, Marcellus, and Bernardo.

Horatio: Hail to your lordship!
Hamlet: I am glad to see you well.   160
       Horatio!—or I do forget myself.
Horatio: The same, my lord, and your poor servant ever.
Hamlet: Sir, my good friend; I'll change that name° with you.
       And what make you from° Wittenberg, Horatio?
       Marcellus?   165
Marcellus: My good lord.
Hamlet: I am very glad to see you. [*To Bernardo.*] Good even, sir.—
       But what in faith make you from Wittenberg?
Horatio: A truant disposition, good my lord.
Hamlet: I would not hear your enemy say so,   170
       Nor shall you do my ear that violence
       To make it truster of your own report
       Against yourself. I know you are no truant.
       But what is your affair in Elsinore?
       We'll teach you to drink deep ere you depart.   175
Horatio: My lord, I came to see your father's funeral.
Hamlet: I prithee, do not mock me, fellow student;
       I think it was to see my mother's wedding.
Horatio: Indeed, my lord, it followed hard° upon.
Hamlet: Thrift, thrift, Horatio! The funeral baked meats°   180
       Did coldly° furnish forth the marriage tables.
       Would I had met my dearest° foe in heaven
       Or ever° I had seen that day, Horatio!
       My father!—Methinks I see my father.

---

147 *or ere* even before   149 *Niobe* Tantalus' daughter, Queen of Thebes, who boasted that she had more
sons and daughters than Leto; for this, Apollo and Artemis, children of Leto, slew her fourteen children.
She was turned by Zeus into a stone that continually dropped tears.   150 *wants ... reason* lacks the faculty
of reason   155 *gallèd* irritated, inflamed   156 *post* hasten   157 *incestuous* (In Shakespeare's day, the marriage of a man like Claudius to his deceased brother's wife was considered incestuous.)   163 *change that
name* i.e., give and receive reciprocally the name of "friend" (rather than talk of "servant")   164 *make you
from* are you doing away from   179 *hard* close   180 *baked meats* meat pies   181 *coldly* i.e., as cold left-
overs   182 *dearest* closest (and therefore deadliest)   183 *Or ever* before

Horatio: Where, my lord?

Hamlet: In my mind's eye, Horatio.   185

Horatio: I saw him once. 'A° was a goodly king.

Hamlet: 'A was a man. Take him for all in all,
I shall not look upon his like again.

Horatio: My lord, I think I saw him yesternight.

Hamlet: Saw? Who?   190

Horatio: My lord, the King your father.

Hamlet: The King my father?

Horatio: Season your admiration° for a while
With an attent° ear till I may deliver,
Upon the witness of these gentlemen,   195
This marvel to you.

Hamlet: For God's love, let me hear!

Horatio: Two nights together had these gentlemen,
Marcellus and Bernardo, on their watch,
In the dead waste° and middle of the night,
Been thus encountered. A figure like your father,   200
Armèd at point° exactly, cap-à-pie,°
Appears before them, and with solemn march
Goes slow and stately by them. Thrice he walked
By their oppressed and fear-surprisèd eyes
Within his truncheon's° length, whilst they, distilled°   205
Almost to jelly with the act° of fear,
Stand dumb and speak not to him. This to me
In dreadful° secrecy impart they did,
And I with them the third night kept the watch,
Where, as they had delivered, both in time,   210
Form of the thing, each word made true and good,
The apparition comes. I knew your father;
These hands are not more like.

Hamlet: But where was this?

Marcellus: My lord, upon the platform where we watch.

Hamlet: Did you not speak to it?

Horatio: My lord, I did,   215
But answer made it none. Yet once methought
It lifted up its head and did address
Itself to motion, like as it would speak;°
But even then° the morning cock crew loud,
And at the sound it shrunk in haste away   220
And vanished from our sight.

Hamlet: 'Tis very strange.

Horatio: As I do live, my honored lord, 'tis true,

---

186 '*A* he   193 *Season your admiration* restrain your astonishment   194 *attent* attentive   199 *dead waste* desolate stillness   201 *at point* correctly in every detail.   *cap-à-pie* from head to foot   205 *truncheon* officer's staff.   *distilled* dissolved   206 *act* action, operation   208 *dreadful* full of dread   217–218 *did . . . speak* began to move as though it were about to speak   219 *even then* at that very instant

And we did think it writ down in our duty
　To let you know of it.
Hamlet:　Indeed, indeed, sirs. But this troubles me.　　　　　　225
　Hold you the watch tonight?
All:　　　　　　　　　　　　We do, my lord.
Hamlet:　Armed, say you?
All:　Armed, my lord.
Hamlet:　From top to toe?
All:　My lord, from head to foot.　　　　　　　　　　　230
Hamlet:　Then saw you not his face?
Horatio:　O, yes, my lord, he wore his beaver° up.
Hamlet:　What° looked he, frowningly?
Horatio:　A countenance more in sorrow than in anger.
Hamlet:　Pale or red?　　　　　　　　　　　　　235
Horatio:　Nay, very pale.
Hamlet:　And fixed his eyes upon you?
Horatio:　Most constantly.
Hamlet:　I would I had been there.
Horatio:　It would have much amazed you.　　　　　　240
Hamlet:　Very like, very like. Stayed it long?
Horatio:　While one with moderate haste might tell° a hundred.
Marcellus, Bernardo:　Longer, longer.
Horatio:　Not when I saw 't.
Hamlet:　His beard was grizzled°—no?　　　　　　245
Horatio:　It was, as I have seen it in his life,
　A sable silvered.°
Hamlet:　　　　　　I will watch tonight.
　Perchance 'twill walk again.
Horatio:　　　　　　　　　I warrant° it will.
Hamlet:　If it assume my noble father's person,
　I'll speak to it though hell itself should gape　　　　　250
　And bid me hold my peace. I pray you all,
　If you have hitherto concealed this sight,
　Let it be tenable° in your silence still,
　And whatsoever else shall hap tonight,
　Give it an understanding but no tongue.　　　　　255
　I will requite your loves. So, fare you well.
　Upon the platform 'twixt eleven and twelve
　I'll visit you.
All:　　　　　　Our duty to your honor.
Hamlet:　Your loves, as mine to you. Farewell.

　　　　　　　　　　　　Exeunt [all but Hamlet].

　My father's spirit in arms! All is not well.　　　　　　260
　I doubt° some foul play. Would the night were come!
　Till then sit still, my soul. Foul deeds will rise,
　Though all the earth o'erwhelm them, to men's eyes.

　　　　　　　　　　　　　　　　Exit.

232 *beaver* visor on the helmet　233 *What* how　242 *tell* count　245 *grizzled* gray　247 *sable silvered* black mixed with white　248 *warrant* assure you　253 *tenable* held　261 *doubt* suspect

SCENE III [POLONIUS' CHAMBERS.]

Enter Laertes and Ophelia, his sister.

Laertes: My necessaries are embarked. Farewell.
  And, sister, as the winds give benefit
  And convoy is assistant,° do not sleep
  But let me hear from you.
Ophelia: Do you doubt that?
Laertes: For Hamlet, and the trifling of his favor,   5
  Hold it a fashion and a toy in blood,°
  A violet in the youth of primy° nature,
  Forward,° not permanent, sweet, not lasting,
  The perfume and suppliance° of a minute—
  No more.
Ophelia: No more but so?
Laertes: Think it no more.   10
  For nature crescent° does not grow alone
  In thews° and bulk, but as this temple° waxes
  The inward service of the mind and soul
  Grows wide withal.° Perhaps he loves you now,
  And now no soil° nor cautel° doth besmirch   15
  The virtue of his will;° but you must fear,
  His greatness weighed,° his will is not his own.
  For he himself is subject to his birth.
  He may not, as unvalued persons do,
  Carve° for himself, for on his choice depends   20
  The safety and health of this whole state,
  And therefore must his choice be circumscribed
  Unto the voice and yielding° of that body
  Whereof he is the head. Then if he says he loves you,
  It fits your wisdom so far to believe it   25
  As he in his particular act and place°
  May give his saying deed, which is no further
  Than the main voice° of Denmark goes withal.°
  Then weigh what loss your honor may sustain
  If with too credent° ear you list° his songs,   30
  Or lose your heart, or your chaste treasure open
  To his unmastered importunity.
  Fear it, Ophelia, fear it, my dear sister,
  And keep you in the rear of your affection,°
  Out of the shot and danger of desire.   35
  The chariest° maid is prodigal enough

---

3 *convoy is assistant* means of conveyance are available   6 *toy in blood* passing amorous fancy   7 *primy* in its prime, springtime   8 *Forward* precocious   9 *suppliance* supply, filler   11 *crescent* growing, waxing   12 *thews* bodily strength.   *temple* i.e., body   14 *Grows wide withal* grows along with it   15 *soil* blemish. *cautel* deceit   16 *will* desire   17 *His greatness weighed* if you take into account his high position   20 *Carve* i.e., choose   23 *voice and yielding* assent, approval   26 *in . . . place* in his particular restricted circumstances   28 *main voice* general assent. *withal* along with   30 *credent* credulous. *list* listen to   34 *keep . . . affection* don't advance as far as your affection might lead you. (A military metaphor.)   36 *chariest* most scrupulously modest

If she unmask° her beauty to the moon.°
Virtue itself scapes not calumnious strokes.
The canker galls° the infants of the spring
Too oft before their buttons° be disclosed,° 40
And in the morn and liquid dew° of youth
Contagious blastments° are most imminent.
Be wary then; best safety lies in fear.
Youth to itself rebels,° though none else near.

Ophelia: I shall the effect of this good lesson keep 45
As watchman to my heart. But, good my brother,
Do not, as some ungracious° pastors do,
Show me the steep and thorny way to heaven,
Whiles like a puffed° and reckless libertine
Himself the primrose path of dalliance treads, 50
And recks° not his own rede.°

Enter Polonius.

Laertes: O, fear me not.°
I stay too long. But here my father comes.
A double° blessing is a double grace;
Occasion smiles upon a second leave.°

Polonius: Yet here, Laertes? Aboard, aboard, for shame! 55
The wind sits in the shoulder of your sail,
And you are stayed for. There—my blessing with thee!
And these few precepts in thy memory
Look° thou character.° Give thy thoughts no tongue,
Nor any unproportioned° thought his° act. 60
Be thou familiar,° but by no means vulgar.°
Those friends thou hast, and their adoption tried,°
Grapple them unto thy soul with hoops of steel,
But do not dull thy palm° with entertainment
Of each new-hatched, unfledged courage.° Beware 65
Of entrance to a quarrel, but being in,
Bear 't that° th' opposèd may beware of thee.
Give every man thy ear, but few thy voice;
Take each man's censure,° but reserve thy judgment.
Costly thy habit° as thy purse can buy, 70
But not expressed in fancy;° rich, not gaudy,
For the apparel oft proclaims the man,
And they in France of the best rank and station

---

37 *If she unmask* if she does no more than show her beauty. *moon* (Symbol of chastity.) 39 *canker galls* cankerworm destroys 40 *buttons* buds. *disclosed* opened 41 *liquid dew* i.e., time when dew is fresh and bright 42 *blastments* blights 44 *Youth . . . rebels* youth is inherently rebellious 47 *ungracious* ungodly 49 *puffed* bloated, or swollen with pride 51 *recks* heeds. *rede* counsel. 51 *fear me not* don't worry on my account 53 *double* (Laertes has already bid his father good-bye.) 54 *Occasion . . . leave* happy is the circumstance that provides a second leave-taking. The goddess Occasion, or Opportunity, smiles. 59 *Look* be sure that. *character* inscribe 60 *unproportioned* badly calculated, intemperate. *his* its 61 *familiar* sociable. *vulgar* common 62 *and their adoption tried* and also their suitability for adoption as friends having been tested 64 *dull thy palm* i.e., shake hands so often as to make the gesture meaningless 65 *courage* young man of spirit 67 *Bear 't that* manage it so that 69 *censure* opinion, judgment 70 *habit* clothing 71 *fancy* excessive ornament, decadent fashion

Are of a most select and generous chief in that.°
Neither a borrower nor a lender be,   75
For loan oft loses both itself and friend,
And borrowing dulleth edge of husbandry.°
This above all: to thine own self be true,
And it must follow, as the night the day,
Thou canst not then be false to any man.   80
Farewell. My blessing season° this in thee!
Laertes: Most humbly do I take my leave, my lord.
Polonius: The time invests° you. Go, your servants tend.°
Laertes: Farewell, Ophelia, and remember well
What I have said to you.   85
Ophelia: 'Tis in my memory locked,
And you yourself shall keep the key of it.
Laertes: Farewell.   *Exit Laertes.*
Polonius: What is 't, Ophelia, he hath said to you?
Ophelia: So please you, something touching the Lord Hamlet.   90
Polonius: Marry,° well bethought.
'Tis told me he hath very oft of late
Given private time to you, and you yourself
Have of your audience been most free and bounteous.
If it be so—as so 'tis put on° me,   95
And that in way of caution—I must tell you
You do not understand yourself so clearly
As it behooves° my daughter and your honor.
What is between you? Give me up the truth.
Ophelia: He hath, my lord, of late made many tenders°   100
Of his affection to me.
Polonius: Affection? Pooh! You speak like a green girl,
Unsifted° in such perilous circumstance.
Do you believe his tenders, as you call them?
Ophelia: I do not know, my lord, what I should think.   105
Polonius: Marry, I will teach you. Think yourself a baby
That you have ta'en these tenders for true pay
Which are not sterling.° Tender° yourself more dearly,
Or—not to crack the wind° of the poor phrase,
Running it thus—you'll tender me a fool.°   110
Ophelia: My lord, he hath importuned me with love
In honorable fashion.
Polonius: Ay, fashion° you may call it. Go to,° go to.
Ophelia: And hath given countenance° to his speech, my lord,
With almost all the holy vows of heaven.   115

---

74 *Are . . . that* are of a most refined and well-bred preeminence in choosing what to wear   77 *husbandry*
thrift   81 *season* mature   83 *invests* besieges, presses upon.   *tend* attend, wait   91 *Marry* i.e., by the Virgin
Mary. (A mild oath.)   95 *put on* impressed on, told to   98 *behooves* befits   100 *tenders* offers   103 *Unsifted*
i.e., untried   108 *sterling* legal currency.   *Tender* hold, look after, offer   109 *crack the wind* i.e., run it until it
is broken-winded   110 *tender me a fool* (1) show yourself to me as a fool (2) show me up as a fool (3) present
me with a grandchild. (*Fool* was a term of endearment for a child.)   113 *fashion* mere form, pretense.   *Go to*
(An expression of impatience.)   114 *countenance* credit, confirmation

Polonius: Ay, springes° to catch woodcocks.° I do know,
When the blood burns, how prodigal° the soul
Lends the tongue vows. These blazes, daughter,
Giving more light than heat, extinct in both
Even in their promise as it° is a-making,   120
You must not take for fire. From this time
Be something° scanter of your maiden presence.
Set your entreatments° at a higher rate
Than a command to parle.° For Lord Hamlet,
Believe so much in him° that he is young,   125
And with a larger tether may he walk
Than may be given you. In few,° Ophelia,
Do not believe his vows, for they are brokers,°
Not of that dye° which their investments° show,
But mere implorators° of unholy suits,   130
Breathing° like sanctified and pious bawds,
The better to beguile. This is for all:°
I would not, in plain terms, from this time forth
Have you so slander° any moment° leisure
As to give words or talk with the Lord Hamlet.   135
Look to 't, I charge you. Come your ways.°
Ophelia: I shall obey, my lord.   *Exeunt.*

SCENE IV [THE GUARD PLATFORM.]

Enter Hamlet, Horatio, and Marcellus.

Hamlet: The air bites shrewdly;° it is very cold.
Horatio: It is a nipping and an eager° air.
Hamlet: What hour now?
Horatio: I think it lacks of° twelve.
Marcellus: No, it is struck.
Horatio: Indeed? I heard it not.
It then draws near the season°   5
Wherein the spirit held his wont° to walk.

A flourish of trumpets, and two pieces° go off [within].

What does this mean, my lord?
Hamlet: The King doth wake° tonight and takes his rouse,°
Keeps wassail,° and the swaggering upspring° reels;°

116 *springes* snares. *woodcocks* birds easily caught; here used to connote gullibility. 117 *prodigal* prodigally 120 *it* i.e., the promise 122 *something* somewhat 123 *entreatments* negotiations for surrender. (A military term.) 124 *parle* discuss terms with the enemy. (Polonius urges his daughter, in the metaphor of military language, not to meet with Hamlet and consider giving in to him merely because he requests an interview.) 125 *so . . . him* this much concerning him 127 *In few* briefly 128 *brokers* go-between, procurers 129 *dye* color or sort. *investments* clothes. (The vows are not what they seem.) 130 *mere implorators* out and out solicitors 131 *Breathing* speaking 132 *for all* once for all, in sum 134 *slander* abuse, misuse. *moment* moment's 136 *Come your ways* come along 1 *shrewdly* keenly, sharply 2 *eager* biting 3 *lacks of* is just short of 5 *season* time 6 *held his wont* was accustomed. s.d. *pieces* i.e., of ordnance, cannon 8 *wake* stay awake and hold revel. *takes his rouse* carouses 9 *wassail* carousal. *upspring* wild German dance. *reels* dances

And as he drains his drafts of Rhenish° down,   10
The kettledrum and trumpet thus bray out
The triumph of his pledge.°
Horatio: Is it a custom?
Hamlet: Ay, marry, is 't,
But to my mind, though I am native here
And to the manner° born, it is a custom   15
More honored in the breach than the observance.°
This heavy-headed revel east and west°
Makes us traduced and taxed of° other nations.
They clepe° us drunkards, and with swinish phrase°
Soil our addition;° and indeed it takes   20
From our achievements, though performed at height,°
The pith and marrow of our attribute.°
So, oft it chances in particular men,
That for° some vicious mole of nature° in them,
As in their birth—wherein they are not guilty,   25
Since nature cannot choose his° origin—
By their o'ergrowth of some complexion,°
Oft breaking down the pales° and forts of reason,
Or by some habit that too much o'erleavens°
The form of plausive° manners, that these men,   30
Carrying, I say, the stamp of one defect,
Being nature's livery° or fortune's star,°
His virtues else,° be they as pure as grace,
As infinite as man may undergo,°
Shall in the general censure° take corruption   35
From that particular fault. The dram of evil
Doth all the noble substance often dout
To his own scandal.°

Enter Ghost.

Horatio: Look, my lord, it comes!
Hamlet: Angels and ministers of grace° defend us!
Be thou° a spirit of health° or goblin damned,   40
Bring° with thee airs from heaven or blasts from hell,
Be thy intents° wicked or charitable,

10 *Rhenish* Rhine wine   12 *The triumph . . . pledge* i.e., his feat in draining the wine in a single draft   15 *manner* custom (of drinking)   16 *More . . . observance* better neglected than followed   17 *east and west* i.e., everywhere   18 *taxed of* censured by   19 *clepe* call. *with swinish phrase* i.e., by calling us swine   20 *addition* reputation   21 *at height* outstandingly   22 *The pith . . . attribute* the essence of the reputation that others attribute to us   24 *for* on account of. *mole of nature* natural blemish in one's constitution   26 *his* its   27 *their o'ergrowth . . . complexion* the excessive growth in individuals of some natural trait   28 *pales* palings, fences (as of a fortification)   29 *o'erleavens* induces a change throughout (as yeast works in dough)   30 *plausive* pleasing   32 *nature's livery* sign of one's servitude to nature. *fortune's star* the destiny that chance brings   33 *His virtues else* i.e., the other qualities of *these men* (line 30)   34 *may undergo* can sustain   35 *general censure* general opinion that people have of him   36–38 *The dram . . . scandal* i.e., the small drop of evil blots out or works against the noble substance of the whole and brings it into disrepute. To *dout* is to blot out. (A famous crux.)   39 *ministers of grace* messengers of God   40 *Be thou* whether you are. *spirit of health* good angel   41 *Bring* whether you bring   42 *Be thy intents* whether your intentions are

Thou com'st in such a questionable° shape
That I will speak to thee. I'll call thee Hamlet,
King, father, royal Dane. O, answer me! 45
Let me not burst in ignorance, but tell
Why thy canonized° bones, hearsèd° in death,
Have burst their cerements;° why the sepulcher
Wherein we saw thee quietly inurned°
Hath oped his ponderous and marble jaws 50
To cast thee up again. What may this mean,
That thou, dead corpse, again in complete steel,°
Revisits thus the glimpses of the moon,°
Making night hideous, and we fools of nature°
So horridly to shake our disposition° 55
With thoughts beyond the reaches of our souls?
Say, why is this? Wherefore? What should we do?

                      [The Ghost] beckons [Hamlet].

Horatio: It beckons you to go away with it,
  As if it some impartment° did desire
  To you alone.
Marcellus: Look with what courteous action 60
  It wafts you to a more removèd ground.
  But do not go with it.
Horatio: No, by no means.
Hamlet: It will not speak. Then I will follow it.
Horatio: Do not, my lord!
Hamlet: Why, what should be the fear?
  I do not set my life at a pin's fee,° 65
  And for my soul, what can it do to that,
  Being a thing immortal as itself?
  It waves me forth again. I'll follow it.
Horatio: What if it tempt you toward the flood,° my lord,
  Or to the dreadful summit of the cliff 70
  That beetles o'er° his base into the sea,
  And there assume some other horrible form
  Which might deprive your sovereignty of reason°
  And draw you into madness? Think of it.
  The very place puts toys of desperation,° 75
  Without more motive, into every brain
  That looks so many fathoms to the sea
  And hears it roar beneath.
Hamlet: It wafts me still.—Go on, I'll follow thee.
Marcellus: You shall not go, my lord.   *[They try to stop him.]*

---

43 *questionable* inviting question   47 *canonized* buried according to the canons of the church. *hearsèd* coffined   48 *cerements* grave clothes   49 *inurned* entombed   52 *complete steel* full armor   53 *glimpses of the moon* pale and uncertain moonlight   54 *fools of nature* mere men, limited to natural knowledge and subject to nature   55 *So . . . disposition* to distress our mental composure so violently   59 *impartment* communication   65 *fee* value   69 *flood* sea   71 *beetles o'er* overhangs threateningly (like bushy eyebrows.)   73 *deprive . . . reason* take away the rule of reason over your mind   75 *toys of desperation* fancies of desperate acts, i.e., suicide

Hamlet:	Hold off your hands!	80
Horatio: Be ruled. You shall not go.	
Hamlet:	My fate cries out,°

    And makes each petty° artery° in this body
    As hardy as the Nemean lion's° nerve.°
    Still am I called. Unhand me, gentlemen.
    By heaven, I'll make a ghost of him that lets° me!   85
    I say, away!—Go on, I'll follow thee.

    Exeunt Ghost and Hamlet.

Horatio: He waxes desperate with imagination.
Marcellus: Let's follow. 'Tis not fit thus to obey him.
Horatio: Have after.° To what issue° will this come?
Marcellus: Something is rotten in the state of Denmark.   90
Horatio: Heaven will direct it.°
Marcellus: Nay, let's follow him.   *Exeunt.*

SCENE V [THE BATTLEMENTS OF THE CASTLE.]

    Enter Ghost and Hamlet.

Hamlet: Whither wilt thou lead me? Speak. I'll go no further.
Ghost: Mark me.
Hamlet: I will.
Ghost: My hour is almost come,
    When I to sulfurous and tormenting flames
    Must render up myself.
Hamlet: Alas, poor ghost!
Ghost: Pity me not, but lend thy serious hearing   5
    To what I shall unfold.
Hamlet: Speak. I am bound° to hear.
Ghost: So art thou to revenge, when thou shalt hear.
Hamlet: What?
Ghost: I am thy father's spirit,   10
    Doomed for a certain term to walk the night,
    And for the day confined to fast° in fires,
    Till the foul crimes° done in my days of nature°
    Are burnt and purged away. But that° I am forbid
    To tell the secrets of my prison house,
    I could a tale unfold whose lightest word   15
    Would harrow up° thy soul, freeze thy young blood,
    Make thy two eyes like stars start from their spheres,°

---

81 *My fate cries out* my destiny summons me   82 *petty* weak.   *artery* (through which the vital spirits were thought to have been conveyed)   83 *Nemean lion's* one of the monsters slain by Hercules in his twelve labors.   *nerve* sinew   85 *lets* hinders   89 *Have after* let's go after him.   *issue* outcome   91 *it* i.e., the outcome   7 *bound* (1) ready (2) obligated by duty and fate. (The Ghost, in line 8, answers in the second sense.)   12 *fast* do penance by fasting   13 *crimes* sins.   *of nature* as a mortal   14 *But that* were it not that   17 *harrow up* lacerate, tear   18 *spheres* i.e., eye-sockets, here compared to the orbits or transparent revolving spheres in which, according to Ptolemaic astronomy, the heavenly bodies were fixed

Hamlet with his father's ghost.

Thy knotted and combinèd locks° to part,
And each particular hair to stand on end   20
Like quills upon the fretful porcupine.
But this eternal blazon° must not be
To ears of flesh and blood. List, list, O, list!
If thou didst ever thy dear father love—
Hamlet: O God!   25
Ghost: Revenge his foul and most unnatural murder.
Hamlet: Murder?
Ghost: Murder most foul, as in the best° it is,
    But this most foul, strange, and unnatural.

---

19 *knotted . . . locks* hair neatly arranged and confined   22 *eternal blazon* revelation of the secrets of eternity   28 *in the best* even at best

Hamlet: Haste me to know 't, that I, with wings as swift   30
As meditation or the thoughts of love,
May sweep to my revenge.
Ghost: I find thee apt;°
And duller shouldst thou be° than the fat° weed
That roots itself in ease on Lethe° wharf,
Wouldst thou not stir in this. Now, Hamlet, hear.   35
'Tis given out that, sleeping in my orchard,°
A serpent stung me. So the whole ear of Denmark
Is by a forgèd process° of my death
Rankly abused.° But know, thou noble youth,
The serpent that did sting thy father's life   40
Now wears his crown.
Hamlet: O, my prophetic soul! My uncle!
Ghost: Ay, that incestuous, that adulterate° beast,
With witchcraft of his wit, with traitorous gifts°—
O wicked wit and gifts, that have the power   45
So to seduce!—won to his shameful lust
The will of my most seeming-virtuous queen.
O Hamlet, what a falling off was there!
From me, whose love was of that dignity
That it went hand in hand even with the vow°   50
I made to her in marriage, and to decline
Upon a wretch whose natural gifts were poor
To° those of mine!
But virtue, as it° never will be moved,
Though lewdness court it in a shape of heaven,°   55
So lust, though to a radiant angel linked,
Will sate itself in a celestial bed°
And prey on garbage.
But soft, methinks I scent the morning air.
Brief let me be. Sleeping within my orchard,   60
My custom always of the afternoon,
Upon my secure° hour thy uncle stole,
With juice of cursèd hebona° in a vial,
And in the porches of my ears° did pour
The leperous distillment,° whose effect   65
Holds such an enmity with blood of man
That swift as quicksilver it courses through
The natural gates and alleys of the body,
And with a sudden vigor it doth posset°

33 *shouldst thou be* you would have to be. *fat* torpid, lethargic 34 *Lethe* the river of forgetfulness in Hades 36 *orchard* garden 38 *forgèd process* falsified account 39 *abused* deceived 43 *adulterate* adulterous 44 *gifts* (1) talents (2) presents 50 *even with the vow* with the very vow 53 *To* compared to 54 *virtue, as it* as virtue 55 *shape of heaven* heavenly form 57 *sate . . . bed* cease to find sexual pleasure in a virtuously lawful marriage 62 *secure* confident, unsuspicious 63 *hebona* a poison. (The word seems to be a form of *ebony*, though it is thought perhaps to be related to *henbane*, a poison, or to *ebenus*, "yew.") 64 *porches of my ears* ears as a porch or entrance of the body 65 *leperous distillment* distillation causing leprosylike disfigurement 69 *posset* coagulate, curdle

And curd, like eager° droppings into milk, 70
The thin and wholesome blood. So did it mine,
And a most instant tetter° barked° about,
Most lazar-like,° with vile and loathsome crust,
All my smooth body.
Thus was I, sleeping, by a brother's hand 75
Of life, of crown, of queen at once dispatched,°
Cut off even in the blossom of my sin,
Unhouseled,° disappointed,° unaneled,°
No reckoning° made, but sent to my account
With all my imperfections on my head. 80
O, horrible! O, horrible, most horrible!
If thou hast nature° in thee, bear it not.
Let not the royal bed of Denmark be
A couch for luxury° and damnèd incest.
But, howsoever thou pursuest this act, 85
Taint not thy mind nor let thy soul contrive
Against thy mother aught. Leave her to heaven
And to those thorns that in her bosom lodge,
To prick and sting her. Fare thee well at once.
The glowworm shows the matin° to be near, 90
And 'gins to pale his° uneffectual fire.
Adieu, adieu, adieu! Remember me.   [*Exit.*]
Hamlet: O all you host of heaven! O earth! What else?
And shall I couple° hell? O, fie! Hold,° hold, my heart,
And you, my sinews, grow not instant° old, 95
But bear me stiffly up. Remember thee?
Ay, thou poor ghost, whiles memory holds a seat
In this distracted globe.° Remember thee?
Yea, from the table° of my memory
I'll wipe away all trivial fond° records, 100
All saws° of books, all forms,° all pressures° past
That youth and observation copied there,
And thy commandment all alone shall live
Within the book and volume of my brain,
Unmixed with baser matter. Yes, by heaven! 105
O most pernicious woman!
O villain, villain, smiling, damnèd villain!
My tables°—meet it is° I set it down
That one may smile, and smile, and be a villain.
At least I am sure it may be so in Denmark.   [*Writing.*] 110

---

70 *eager* sour, acid   72 *tetter* eruption of scabs.   *barked* covered with a rough covering, like bark of a tree
73 *lazar-like* leperlike   76 *dispatched* suddenly deprived   78 *Unhouseled* without having received the
Sacrament.   *disappointed* unready (spiritually) for the last journey.   *unaneled* without having received
extreme unction   79 *reckoning* settling of accounts   82 *nature* i.e., the promptings of a son   84 *luxury*
lechery   90 *matin* morning   91 *his* its   94 *couple* add.   *Hold* hold together   95 *instant* instantly   98
globe (1) head (2) world   99 *table* tablet, slate   100 *fond* foolish   101 *saws* wise sayings.   *forms* shapes or
images copied onto the slate; general ideas.   *pressures* impressions stamped   108 *tables* writing tablets.
meet it is it is fitting

So, uncle, there you are.° Now to my word:
It is "Adieu, adieu! Remember me."
I have sworn 't.

Enter Horatio and Marcellus.

Horatio: My lord, my lord!
Marcellus: Lord Hamlet!
Horatio: Heavens secure him!°   115
Hamlet: So be it.
Marcellus: Hillo, ho, ho, my lord!
Hamlet: Hillo, ho, ho, boy! Come, bird, come.°
Marcellus: How is 't, my noble lord?   120
Horatio: What news, my lord?
Hamlet: O, wonderful!
Horatio: Good my lord, tell it.
Hamlet: No, you will reveal it.
Horatio: Not I, my lord, by heaven.   125
Marcellus: Nor I, my lord.
Hamlet: How say you, then, would heart of man once° think it?
 But you'll be secret?
Horatio, Marcellus: Ay, by heaven, my lord.
Hamlet: There's never a villain dwelling in all Denmark
 But he's an arrant° knave.   130
Horatio: There needs no ghost, my lord, come from the grave
 To tell us this.
Hamlet: Why, right, you are in the right.
 And so, without more circumstance° at all,
 I hold it fit that we shake hands and part,
 You as your business and desire shall point you—   135
 For every man hath business and desire,
 Such as it is—and for my own poor part,
 Look you, I'll go pray.
Horatio: These are but wild and whirling words, my lord.
Hamlet: I am sorry they offend you, heartily;   140
 Yes, faith, heartily.
Horatio: There's no offense, my lord.
Hamlet: Yes, by Saint Patrick,° but there is, Horatio,
 And much offense° too. Touching this vision here,
 It is an honest ghost,° that let me tell you.
 For your desire to know what is between us,   145
 O'ermaster 't as you may. And now, good friends,
 As you are friends, scholars, and soldiers,
 Give me one poor request.

---

111 *there you are* i.e., there, I've written that down against you 116 *secure him* keep him safe 119 *Hillo . . . come* (A falconer's call to a hawk in air. Hamlet mocks the hallooing as though it were a part of hawking.) 127 *once* thoroughgoing 130 *arrant* thoroughgoing 133 *circumstance* ceremony, elaboration 142 *Saint Patrick* (The keeper of Purgatory and patron saint of all blunders and confusion.) 143 *offense* (Hamlet deliberately changes Horatio's "no offense taken" to "an offense against all decency.") 144 *an honest ghost* i.e., a real ghost and not an evil spirit

Horatio: What is 't, my lord? We will.
Hamlet: Never make known what you have seen tonight.   150
Horatio, Marcellus: My lord, we will not.
Hamlet: Nay, but swear 't.
Horatio: In faith, my lord, not I.°
Marcellus: Nor I, my lord, in faith.
Hamlet: Upon my sword.°   [*He holds out his sword.*] 155
Marcellus: We have sworn, my lord, already.°
Hamlet: Indeed, upon my sword, indeed.
Ghost (cries under the stage): Swear.
Hamlet: Ha, ha, boy, sayst thou so? Art thou there, truepenny?°
    Come on, you hear this fellow in the cellarage.   160
    Consent to swear.
Horatio: Propose the oath, my lord.
Hamlet: Never to speak of this that you have seen,
    Swear by my sword.
Ghost [beneath]: Swear.   [*They swear.*]°
Hamlet: Hic et ubique?° Then we'll shift our ground.   165

                    [*He moves to another spot.*]

    Come hither, gentlemen,
    And lay your hands again upon my sword.
    Swear by my sword
    Never to speak of this that you have heard.
Ghost [beneath]: Swear by his sword.   [*They swear.*] 170
Hamlet: Well said, old mole. Canst work i' th' earth so fast?
    A worthy pioner!°——Once more remove, good friends.

                    [*He moves again.*]

Horatio: O day and night, but this is wondrous strange!
Hamlet: And therefore as a stranger° give it welcome.
    There are more things in heaven and earth, Horatio,   175
    Than are dreamt of in your philosophy.°
    But come;
    Here, as before, never, so help you mercy,°
    How strange or odd soe'er I bear myself—
    As I perchance hereafter shall think meet   180
    To put an antic° disposition on—
    That you, at such times seeing me, never shall,
    With arms encumbered° thus, or this headshake,
    Or by pronouncing of some doubtful phrase
    As "Well, we know," or "We could, an if° we would,"   185

---

153 *In faith . . . I* i.e., I swear not to tell what I have seen. (Horatio is not refusing to swear.)   155 *sword* i.e., the hilt in the form of a cross   156 *We . . . already* i.e., we swore in faith   159 *truepenny* honest old fellow   164 s.d. *They swear* (Seemingly they swear here, and at lines 170 and 190, as they lay their hands on Hamlet's sword. Triple oaths would have particular force; these three oaths deal with what they have seen, what they have heard, and what they promise about Hamlet's antic disposition.   165 *Hic et ubique* here and everywhere. (Latin.)   172 *pioner* foot soldier assigned to dig tunnels and excavations   174 *as a stranger* i.e., needing your hospitality   176 *your philosophy* this subject called "natural philosophy" or "science" that people talk about   178 *so help you mercy* as you hope for God's mercy when you are judged   181 *antic* fantastic   183 *encumbered* folded   185 *an if* if

Or "If we list° to speak," or "There be, an if they might,"°
Or such ambiguous giving out,° to note°
That you know aught° of me—this do swear,
So grace and mercy at your most need help you.

Ghost [*beneath*]: Swear.   [*They swear.*]   190

Hamlet: Rest, rest, perturbèd spirit! So, gentlemen,
With all my love I do commend me to you;°
And what so poor a man as Hamlet is
May do t' express his love and friending° to you,
God willing, shall not lack.° Let us go in together,   195
And still° your fingers on your lips, I pray.
The time° is out of joint. O cursèd spite°
That ever I was born to set it right!

                                    [*They wait for him to leave first.*]
Nay, come, let's go together.°   *Exeunt.*

ACT II

SCENE I [POLONIUS' CHAMBERS.]

Enter Old Polonius with his man [Reynaldo].

Polonius: Give him this money and these notes, Reynaldo.

                                    [*He gives money and papers.*]

Reynaldo: I will, my lord.

Polonius: You shall do marvelous° wisely, good Reynaldo,
Before you visit him, to make inquire°
Of his behavior.

Reynaldo: My lord, I did intend it.   5

Polonius: Marry, well said, very well said. Look you, sir,
Inquire me first what Danskers° are in Paris,
And how, and who, what means,° and where they keep,°
What company, at what expense; and finding
By this encompassment° and drift° of question   10
That they do know my son, come you more nearer
Than your particular demands will touch it.°
Take you,° as 'twere, some distant knowledge of him,
As thus, "I know his father and his friends,
And in part him." Do you mark this, Reynaldo?   15

Reynaldo: Ay, very well, my lord.

Polonius: "And in part him, but," you may say, "not well.
But if 't be he I mean, he's very wild,

---

186 *list* wished. *There . . . might* i.e., there are people here (we, in fact) who could tell news if we were at liberty to do so 187 *giving out* intimation. *note* draw attention to the fact 192 *do . . . you* entrust myself to you 188 *aught* i.e., something secret 194 *friending* friendliness 195 *lack* be lacking 196 *still* always 197 *The time* the state of affairs. *spite* i.e., the spite of Fortune 199 *let's go together* (Probably they wait for him to leave first, but he refuses this ceremoniousness.) 3 *marvelous* marvelously 4 *inquire* inquiry 7 *Danskers* Danes 8 *what means* what wealth (they have). *keep* dwell 10 *encompassment* roundabout talking. *drift* gradual approach or course 11–12 *come . . . it* you will find out more this way than by asking pointed questions (*particular demands*) 13 *Take you* assume, pretend

Addicted so and so," and there put on° him
What forgeries° you please—marry, none so rank° 20
As may dishonor him, take heed of that,
But, sir, such wanton,° wild, and usual slips
As are companions noted and most known
To youth and liberty.
Reynaldo: As gaming, my lord. 25
Polonius: Ay, or drinking, fencing, swearing,
   Quarreling, drabbing°—you may go so far.
Reynaldo: My lord, that would dishonor him.
Polonius: Faith, no, as you may season° it in the charge.
   You must not put another scandal on him 30
   That he is open to incontinency;°
   That's not my meaning. But breathe his faults so quaintly°
   That they may seem the taints of liberty,°
   The flash and outbreak of a fiery mind,
   A savageness in unreclaimèd blood, 35
   Of general assault.°
Reynaldo: But, my good lord—
Polonius: Wherefore should you do this?
Reynaldo: Ay, my lord, I would know that.
Polonius: Marry, sir, here's my drift, 40
   And I believe it is a fetch of warrant.°
   You laying these slight sullies on my son,
   As 'twere a thing a little soiled wi' the working,°
   Mark you,
   Your party in converse,° him you would sound,° 45
   Having ever° seen in the prenominate crimes°
   The youth you breathe° of guilty, be assured
   He closes with you in this consequence:°
   "Good sir," or so, or "friend," or "gentleman,"
   According to the phrase or the addition° 50
   Of man and country.
Reynaldo: Very good, my lord.
Polonius: And then, sir, does 'a this—'a does—
   What was I about to say? By the Mass, I was about to say something. Where did
   I leave?
Reynaldo: At "closes in the consequence." 55
Polonius: At "closes in the consequence," ay, marry.
   He closes thus: "I know the gentleman,
   I saw him yesterday," or "th' other day,"
   Or then, or then, with such or such, "and as you say,

---

19 *put on* impute to   20 *forgeries* invented tales.   *rank* gross   22 *wanton* sportive, unrestrained   27 *drabbing* whoring   29 *season* temper, soften   31 *incontinency* habitual sexual excess   32 *quaintly* artfully, subtly   33 *taints of liberty* faults resulting from free living   35–36 *A savageness . . . assault* a wildness in untamed youth that assails all indiscriminately   41 *fetch of warrant* legitimate trick   43 *soiled wi' the working* soiled by handling while it is being made, i.e., by involvement in the ways of the world   45 *converse* conversation.   *sound* i.e., sound out   46 *Having ever* if he has ever.   *prenominate crimes* before-mentioned offenses   47 *breathe* speak   48 *closes . . . consequence* takes you into his confidence in some fashion, as follows   50 *addition* title

There was 'a gaming," "there o'ertook in 's rouse,"°   60
"There falling out° at tennis," or perchance
"I saw him enter such a house of sale,"
Videlicet° a brothel, or so forth. See you now,
Your bait of falsehood takes this carp° of truth;
And thus do we of wisdom and of reach,°   65
With windlasses° and with assays of bias,°
By indirections find directions° out.
So by my former lecture and advice
Shall you my son. You have° me, have you not?
Reynaldo: My lord, I have.
Polonius: God b' wi'° ye; fare ye well.   70
Reynaldo: Good my lord.
Polonius: Observe his inclination in yourself.°
Reynaldo: I shall, my lord.
Polonius: And let him ply his music.
Reynaldo: Well, my lord.   75
Polonius: Farewell.   *Exit Reynaldo.*

Enter Ophelia.

                    How now, Ophelia, what's the matter?
Ophelia: O my lord, my lord, I have been so affrighted!
Polonius: With what, i' the name of God?
Ophelia: My lord, as I was sewing in my closet,°
     Lord Hamlet, with his doublet° all unbraced,°   80
     No hat upon his head, his stockings fouled,
     Ungartered, and down-gyvèd° to his ankle,
     Pale as his shirt, his knees knocking each other,
     And with a look so piteous in purport°
     As if he had been loosèd out of hell   85
     To speak of horrors—he comes before me.
Polonius: Mad for thy love?
Ophelia: My lord, I do not know,
     But truly I do fear it.
Polonius: What said he?
Ophelia: He took me by the wrist and held me hard.
     Then goes he to the length of all his arm,   90
     And, with his other hand thus o'er his brow
     He falls to such perusal of my face
     As° 'a would draw it. Long stayed he so.
     At last, a little shaking of mine arm
     And thrice his head thus waving up and down,   95

---

60 *o'ertook in 's rouse* overcome by drink   61 *falling out* quarreling   63 *Videlicet* namely   64 *carp* a fish
65 *reach* capacity, ability   66 *windlasses* i.e., circuitous paths. (Literally, circuits made to head off the game
in hunting.)   *assays of bias* attempts through indirection (like the curving path of the bowling ball, which
is biased or weighted to one side)   67 *directions* i.e., the way things really are   69 *have* understand   70
b'wi' be with   72 *in yourself* in your own person (as well as by asking questions)   79 *closet* private chamber
80 *doublet* close-fitting jacket.   *unbraced* unfastened.   82 *down-gyvèd* fallen to the ankles (like gyves or
fetters)   84 *in purport* in what it expressed   93 *As* as if (also in line 97)

He raised a sigh so piteous and profound
As it did seem to shatter all his bulk°
And end his being. That done, he lets me go,
And with his head over his shoulder turned
He seemed to find his way without his eyes,   100
For out o' doors he went without their helps,
And to the last bended their light on me.
Polonius: Come, go with me. I will go seek the King.
This is the very ecstasy° of love,
Whose violent property° fordoes° itself   105
And leads the will to desperate undertakings
As oft as any passion under heaven
That does afflict our natures. I am sorry.
What, have you given him any hard words of late?
Ophelia: No, my good lord, but as you did command   110
I did repel his letters and denied
His access to me.
Polonius: That hath made him mad.
I am sorry that with better heed and judgment
I had not quoted° him. I feared he did but trifle
And meant to wrack° thee. But beshrew my jealousy!°   115
By heaven, it is as proper to our age°
To cast beyond° ourselves in our opinions
As it is common for the younger sort
To lack discretion. Come, go we to the King.
This must be known,° which, being kept close,° might move   120
More grief to hide than hate to utter love.°
Come.   *Exeunt.*

SCENE II [THE CASTLE.]

Flourish. Enter King and Queen, Rosencrantz, and Guildenstern [with others].

King: Welcome, dear Rosencrantz and Guildenstern.
Moreover that° we much did long to see you,
The need we have to use you did provoke
Our hasty sending. Something have you heard
Of Hamlet's transformation—so call it,   5
Sith nor° th' exterior nor the inward man
Resembles that° it was. What it should be,
More than his father's death, that thus hath put him
So much from th' understanding of himself,
I cannot dream of. I entreat you both   10

97 *bulk* body 104 *ecstasy* madness 105 *property* nature. *fordoes* destroys 114 *quoted* observed 115
wrack ruin, seduce. *beshrew my jealousy* a plague upon my suspicious nature 116 *proper . . . age* characteristic of us (old) men 117 *cast beyond* overshoot, miscalculate. (A metaphor from hunting.) 120 *known*
made known (to the King). *close* secret 120–121 *might . . . love* i.e., might cause more grief (because of
what Hamlet might do) by hiding the knowledge of Hamlet's strange behavior to Ophelia than unpleasantness by telling it 2 *Moreover that* besides the fact that 6 *Sith nor* since neither 7 *that* what

King Claudius and Queen Gertrude.

That, being of so young days° brought up with him,
And sith so neighbored to° his youth and havior,°
That you vouchsafe your rest° here in our court
Some little time, so by your companies
To draw him on to pleasures, and to gather   15
So much as from occasion° you may glean,
Whether aught to us unknown afflicts him thus
That, opened,° lies within our remedy.
Queen: Good gentlemen, he hath much talked of you,
And sure I am two men there is not living   20
To whom he more adheres. If it will please you

11 *of . . . days* from such early youth   12 *And sith so neighbored to* and since you are (or, and since that time you are) intimately acquainted with.   *havior* demeanor   13 *vouchsafe your rest* please to stay   16 *occasion* opportunity   18 *opened* being revealed

To show us so much gentry° and good will
As to expend your time with us awhile
For the supply and profit of our hope,°
Your visitation shall receive such thanks   25
As fits a king's remembrance.°

Rosencrantz: Both Your Majesties
Might, by the sovereign power you have of° us,
Put your dread° pleasures more into command
Than to entreaty.

Guildenstern: But we both obey,
And here give up ourselves in the full bent°   30
To lay our service freely at your feet,
To be commanded.

King: Thanks, Rosencrantz and gentle Guildenstern.

Queen: Thanks, Guildenstern and gentle Rosencrantz.
And I beseech you instantly to visit   35
My too much changèd son. Go, some of you,
And bring these gentlemen where Hamlet is.

Guildenstern: Heavens make our presence and our practices°
Pleasant and helpful to him!

Queen: Ay, amen!

Exeunt Rosencrantz and Guildenstern [with some attendants]

Enter Polonius.

Polonius: Th' ambassadors from Norway, my good lord,   40
Are joyfully returned.

King: Thou still° hast been the father of good news.

Polonius: Have I, my lord? I assure my good liege
I hold° my duty, as° I hold my soul,
Both to my God and to my gracious king;   45
And I do think, or else this brain of mine
Hunts not the trail of policy° so sure
As it hath used to do, that I have found
The very cause of Hamlet's lunacy.

King: O, speak of that! That do I long to hear.   50

Polonius: Give first admittance to th' ambassadors.
My news shall be the fruit° to that great feast.

King: Thyself do grace° to them and bring them in.

[Exit Polonius.]

He tells me, my dear Gertrude, he hath found
The head and source of all your son's distemper.   55

Queen: I doubt° it is no other but the main,°
His father's death and our o'erhasty marriage.

---

22 *gentry* courtesy   24 *supply . . . hope* aid and furtherance of what we hope for   26 *As fits . . . . remembrance* as would be a fitting gift of a king who rewards true service   27 *of* over   28 *dread* inspiring awe   30 *in . . . bent* to the utmost degree of our capacity. (An archery metaphor.)   38 *practices* doings   42 *still* always   44 *hold* maintain.   *as* as firmly as   47 *policy* sagacity   52 *fruit* dessert   53 *grace* honor (punning on *grace* said before a *feast*, line 52)   56 *doubt* fear, suspect.   *main* chief point, principal concern

Enter Ambassadors [Voltimand and Cornelius, with Polonius].

King: Well, we shall sift him.°—Welcome, my good friends!
    Say, Voltimand, what from our brother° Norway?
Voltimand: Most fair return of greetings and desires.°   60
    Upon our first,° he sent out to suppress
    His nephew's levies, which to him appeared
    To be a preparation 'gainst the Polack,
    But, better looked into, he truly found
    It was against Your Highness. Whereat grieved   65
    That so his sickness, age, and impotence°
    Was falsely borne in hand,° sends out arrests°
    On Fortinbras, which he, in brief, obeys,
    Receives rebuke from Norway, and in fine°
    Makes vow before his uncle never more   70
    To give th' assay° of arms against Your Majesty.
    Whereon old Norway, overcome with joy,
    Gives him three thousand crowns in annual fee
    And his commission to employ those soldiers,
    So levied as before, against the Polack,   75
    With an entreaty, herein further shown,

                                          [giving a paper]

    That it might please you to give quiet pass
    Through your dominions for this enterprise
    On such regards of safety and allowance°
    As therein are set down.
King: It likes° us well,   80
    And at our more considered° time we'll read,
    Answer, and think upon this business.
    Meantime we thank you for your well-took labor.
    Go to your rest; at night we'll feast together.
    Most welcome home!   *Exeunt Ambassadors.*
Polonius: This business is well ended.   85
    My liege, and madam, to expostulate°
    What majesty should be, what duty is,
    Why day is day, night night, and time is time,
    Were nothing but to waste night, day, and time.
    Therefore, since brevity is the soul of wit,°   90
    And tediousness the limbs and outward flourishes,
    I will be brief. Your noble son is mad.
    Mad call I it, for, to define true madness,
    What is 't but to be nothing else but mad?
    But let that go.

---

58 *sift him* question Polonius closely   59 *brother* fellow king   60 *desires* good wishes   61 *Upon our first* at our first words on the business   66 *impotence* helplessness   67 *borne in hand* deluded, taken advantage of. *arrests* orders to desist   69 *in fine* in conclusion   71 *give th' assay* make trial of strength, challenge   79 *On … allowance* i.e., with such considerations for the safety of Denmark and permission for Fortinbras   80 *likes* pleases   81 *considered* suitable for deliberation   86 *expostulate* expound, inquire into   90 *wit* sense or judgment

Queen: More matter, with less art. 95
Polonius: Madam, I swear I use no art at all.
    That he's mad, 'tis true; 'tis true 'tis pity,
    And pity 'tis 'tis true—a foolish figure,°
    But farewell it, for I will use no art.
    Mad let us grant him, then, and now remains 100
    That we find out the cause of this effect,
    Or rather say, the cause of this defect,
    For this effect defective comes by cause.°
    Thus it remains, and the remainder thus.
    Perpend.° 105
    I have a daughter—have while she is mine—
    Who, in her duty and obedience, mark,
    Hath given me this. Now gather and surmise.°
    [*He reads the letter.*] "To the celestial and my soul's idol, the most beautified
Ophelia"—That's an ill phrase, a vile phrase; "beautified" is a vile phrase. 110
But you shall hear. Thus:

                                            [*He reads.*]

    "In her excellent white bosom,° these,° etc."
Queen: Came this from Hamlet to her?
Polonius: Good madam, stay° awhile, I will be faithful.°

                                            [*He reads.*]

      "Doubt° thou the stars are fire, 115
        Doubt that the sun doth move,
      Doubt truth to be a liar,
        But never doubt I love.

    O dear Ophelia, I am ill at these numbers.° I have not art to reckon° my groans.
But that I love thee best, O most best, believe it. Adieu. Thine evermore, most 120
dear lady, whilst this machine° is to him, Hamlet."

    This in obedience hath my daughter shown me,
    And, more above,° hath his solicitings,
    As they fell out° by° time, by means, and place,
    All given to mine ear.°
King: But how hath she 125
    Received his love?
Polonius: What do you think of me?
King: As of a man faithful and honorable.
Polonius: I would fain° prove so. But what might you think,
    When I had seen this hot love on the wing—
    As I perceived it, I must tell you that, 130
    Before my daughter told me—what might you,
    Or my dear Majesty your queen here, think,

---

98 *figure* figure of speech 103 *For . . . cause* i.e., for this defective behavior, this madness, has a cause
105 *Perpend* consider 108 *gather and surmise* draw your own conclusions 112 *In . . . bosom* (The letter is
poetically addressed to her heart.) *these* i.e., the letter 114 *stay* wait. *faithful* i.e., in reading the letter
accurately 115 *Doubt* suspect 119 *ill . . . numbers* unskilled at writing verses. *reckon* (1) count (2)
number metrically, scan 121 *machine* i.e., body 123 *more above* moreover 124 *fell out* occurred. *by*
according to 125 *given . . . ear* i.e., told me about 128 *fain* gladly

If I had played the desk or table book,°
Or given my heart a winking,° mute and dumb,
Or looked upon this love with idle sight?°   135
What might you think? No, I went round° to work,
And my young mistress thus I did bespeak:°
"Lord Hamlet is a prince out of thy star;°
This must not be." And then I prescripts° gave her,
That she should lock herself from his resort,°   140
Admit no messengers, receive no tokens.
Which done, she took the fruits of my advice;
And he, repellèd—a short tale to make—
Fell into a sadness, then into a fast,
Thence to a watch,° thence into a weakness,   145
Thence to a lightness,° and by this declension°
Into the madness wherein now he raves,
And all we° mourn for.
King [to the Queen]:   Do you think 'tis this?
Queen: It may be, very like.
Polonius: Hath there been such a time—I would fain know that—   150
    That I have positively said "'Tis so,"
    When it proved otherwise?
King: Not that I know.
Polonius: Take this from this,° if this be otherwise.
    If circumstances lead me, I will find
    Where truth is hid, though it were hid indeed   155
    Within the center.°
King: How may we try° it further?
Polonius: You know sometimes he walks four hours together
    Here in the lobby.
Queen: So he does indeed.
Polonius: At such a time I'll loose° my daughter to him.
    Be you and I behind an arras° then.   160
    Mark the encounter. If he love her not
    And be not from his reason fall'n thereon,°
    Let me be no assistant for a state,
    But keep a farm and carters.°
King: We will try it.

    Enter Hamlet [reading on a book].

Queen: But look where sadly° the poor wretch comes reading.   165

133 played . . . table book i.e., remained shut up, concealing the information   134 given . . . winking closed the eyes of my heart to this   135 with idle sight complacently or uncomprehendingly   136 round roundly, plainly   137 bespeak address   138 out of thy star above your sphere, position   139 prescripts orders   140 his resort his visits   145 watch state of sleeplessness   146 lightness lightheadedness.   declension decline, deterioration (with a pun on the grammatical sense)   148 all we all of us, or, into everything that we   153 Take this from this (The actor probably gestures, indicating that he means his head from his shoulders, or his staff of office or chain from his hands or neck, or something similar.)   156 center middle point of the earth (which is also the center of the Ptolemaic universe).   try test, judge   159 loose (as one might release an animal that is being mated)   160 arras hanging, tapestry   162 thereon on that account   164 carters wagon drivers   165 sadly seriously

Polonius: Away, I do beseech you both, away.
   I'll board° him presently.° O, give me leave.°

                              Exeunt King and Queen [with attendants].

   How does my good Lord Hamlet?
Hamlet: Well, God-a-mercy.°
Polonius: Do you know me, my lord?   170
Hamlet: Excellent well. You are a fishmonger.°
Polonius: Not I, my lord.
Hamlet: Then I would you were so honest a man.
Polonius: Honest, my lord?
Hamlet: Ay, sir. To be honest, as this world goes, is to be one man picked out of ten   175
   thousand.
Polonius: That's very true, my lord.
Hamlet: For if the sun breed maggots in a dead dog, being a good kissing carrion°—
   Have you a daughter?
Polonius: I have, my lord.   180
Hamlet: Let her not walk i' the sun.° Conception° is a blessing, but as your daughter
   may conceive, friend, look to 't.
Polonius [aside]: How say you by that? Still harping on my daughter. Yet he knew me
   not at first; 'a° said I was a fishmonger. 'A is far gone. And truly in my youth I
   suffered much extremity for love, very near this. I'll speak to him again.—What   185
   do you read, my lord?
Hamlet: Words, words, words.
Polonius: What is the matter,° my lord?
Hamlet: Between who?
Polonius: I mean, the matter that you read, my lord.   190
Hamlet: Slanders, sir; for the satirical rogue says here that old men have gray beards,
   that their faces are wrinkled, their eyes purging° thick amber° and plum-tree
   gum, and that they have a plentiful lack of wit,° together with most weak hams.
   All which, sir, though I most powerfully and potently believe, yet I hold it not
   honesty° to have it thus set down, for yourself, sir, shall grow old° as I am, if like a   195
   crab you could go backward.
Polonius [aside]: Though this be madness, yet there is method in 't.—Will you walk
   out of the air,° my lord?
Hamlet: Into my grave.
Polonius: Indeed, that's out of the air. [*Aside.*] How pregnant° sometimes his replies   200
   are! A happiness° that often madness hits on, which reason and sanity could not
   so prosperously° be delivered of. I will leave him and suddenly° contrive the
   means of meeting between him and my daughter.—My honorable lord, I will
   most humbly take my leave of you.

---

167 *board* accost. *presently* at once. *give me leave* i.e., excuse me, leave me alone. (Said to those he hurries offstage, including the King and Queen.) 169 *God-a-mercy* God have mercy, i.e., thank you 171
fishmonger fish merchant 178 *a good kissing carrion* i.e., a good piece of flesh for kissing, or for the sun to
kiss 181 *i' the sun* in public (with additional implication of the sunshine of princely favors). *Conception*
(1) understanding (2) pregnancy 184 *'a* he 188 *matter* substance. (But Hamlet plays on the sense of
"basis for a dispute.") 192 *purging* discharging. *amber* i.e., resin, like the resinous *plum-tree gum* 193
wit understanding 195 *honesty* decency, decorum. *old* as old 198 *out of the air* (The open air was considered dangerous for sick people.) 200 *pregnant* quick-witted, full of meaning 201 *happiness* felicity of
expression 202 *prosperously* successfully. *suddenly* immediately

Hamlet: You cannot, sir, take from me anything that I will more willingly part 205
    withal°—except my life, except my life, except my life.

    Enter Guildenstern and Rosencrantz.

Polonius: Fare you well, my lord.
Hamlet: These tedious old fools!°
Polonius: You go to seek the Lord Hamlet. There he is.
Rosencrantz [to Polonius]: God save you, sir! 210

                                                        [Exit Polonius.]

Guildenstern: My honored lord!
Rosencrantz: My most dear lord!
Hamlet: My excellent good friends! How dost thou, Guildenstern? Ah, Rosencrantz!
    Good lads, how do you both?
Rosencrantz: As the indifferent° children of the earth. 215
Guildenstern: Happy in that we are not overhappy.
    On Fortune's cap we are not the very button.
Hamlet: Nor the soles of her shoe?
Rosencrantz: Neither, my lord.
Hamlet: Then you live about her waist, or in the middle of her favors?° 220
Guildenstern: Faith, her privates we.°
Hamlet: In the secret parts of Fortune? O, most true, she is a strumpet.° What news?
Rosencrantz: None, my lord, but the world's grown honest.
Hamlet: Then is doomsday near. But your news is not true. Let me question more in
    particular. What have you, my good friends, deserved at the hands of fortune 225
    that she sends you to prison hither?
Guildenstern: Prison, my lord?
Hamlet: Denmark's a prison.
Rosencrantz: Then is the world one.
Hamlet: A goodly one, in which there are many confines,° wards,° and dungeons, 230
    Denmark being one o' the worst.
Rosencrantz: We think not so, my lord.
Hamlet: Why then 'tis none to you, for there is nothing either good or bad but
    thinking makes it so. To me it is a prison.
Rosencrantz: Why then, your ambition makes it one. 'Tis too narrow for your mind. 235
Hamlet: O God, I could be bounded in a nutshell and count myself a king of infinite
    space, were it not that I have bad dreams.
Guildenstern: Which dreams indeed are ambition, for the very substance of the am-
    bitious° is merely the shadow of a dream.
Hamlet: A dream itself is but a shadow. 240
Rosencrantz: Truly, and I hold ambition of so airy and light a quality that it is but a
    shadow's shadow.

---

206 *withal* with   208 *old fools* i.e., old men like Polonius   215 *indifferent* ordinary, at neither extreme of
fortune or misfortune   220 *favors* i.e., sexual favors   221 *her privates we* i.e., (1) we are sexually intimate
with Fortune, the fickle goddess who bestows her favors indiscriminately (2) we are her private citizens
222 *strumpet* prostitute. (A common epithet for indiscriminate Fortune; see line 426.)   230 *confines* places
of confinement.   *wards* cells   238–239 *the very . . . ambitious* that seemingly very substantial thing that
the ambitious pursue

Hamlet: Then are our beggars bodies,° and our monarchs and outstretched° heroes the beggars' shadows. Shall we to the court? For, by my fay,° I cannot reason.

Rosencrantz, Guildenstern: We'll wait upon° you.   245

Hamlet: No such matter. I will not sort° you with the rest of my servants, for, to speak to you like an honest man, I am most dreadfully attended.° But, in the beaten way° of friendship, what make° you at Elsinore?

Rosencrantz: To visit you, my lord, no other occasion.

Hamlet: Beggar that I am, I am even poor in thanks; but I thank you, and sure, dear   250
friends, my thanks are too dear a halfpenny.° Were you not sent for? Is it your own inclining? Is it a free° visitation? Come, come, deal justly with me. Come, come. Nay, speak.

Guildenstern: What should we say, my lord?

Hamlet: Anything but to the purpose.° You were sent for, and there is a kind of con-   255
fession in your looks which your modesties° have not craft enough to color.° I know the good King and Queen have sent for you.

Rosencrantz: To what end, my lord?

Hamlet: That you must teach me. But let me conjure° you, by the rights of our fel-lowship, by the consonancy of our youth,° by the obligation of our ever-preserved   260
love, and by what more dear a better° prosper could charge° you withal, be even°
and direct with me whether you were sent for or no.

Rosencrantz [aside to Guildenstern]: What say you?

Hamlet [aside]: Nay, then, I have an eye of° you.—If you love me, hold not off.°

Guildenstern: My lord, we were sent for.   265

Hamlet: I will tell you why; so shall my anticipation prevent your discovery,° and your secrecy to the King and Queen molt no feather.° I have of late—but where-fore I know not—lost all my mirth, forgone all custom of exercises; and indeed it goes so heavily with my disposition that this goodly frame, the earth, seems to me a sterile promontory; this most excellent canopy, the air, look you, this   270
brave° o'erhanging firmament, this majestical roof fretted° with golden fire, why, it appeareth nothing to me but a foul and pestilent congregation° of vapors.
What a piece of work° is a man! How noble in reason, how infinite in faculties, in form and moving how express° and admirable, in action how like an angel, in apprehension° how like a god! The beauty of the world, the paragon of animals!   275
And yet, to me, what is this quintessence° of dust? Man delights not me—no, nor woman neither, though by your smiling you seem to say so.

---

243 *bodies* i.e., solid substances rather than shadows (since beggars are not ambitious). *outstretched* (1) far-reaching in their ambition (2) elongated as shadows   244 *fay* faith   245 *wait upon* accompany, at-tend. (But Hamlet uses the phrase in the sense of providing menial service.)   246 *sort* class, categorize   247 *dreadfully attended* waited upon in slovenly fashion   248 *beaten way* familiar path, tried-and-true course.   *make* do   251 *too dear a halfpenny* (1) too expensive at even a halfpenny, i.e., of little worth (2) too expensive *by* a halfpenny in return for worthless kindness   252 *free* voluntary   255 *Anything but to the purpose* anything except a straightforward answer. (Said ironically.)   256 *modesties* sense of shame.   *color* disguise   259 *conjure* adjure, entreat   260 *the consonancy of our youth* our closeness in our younger days   261 *better* more skillful.   *charge* urge.   *even* straight, honest   264 *of* on.   *hold not off* don't hold back   266 *so . . . discovery* in that way my saying it first will spare you from revealing the truth   267 *molt no feather* i.e., not diminish in the least   271 *brave* splendid.   *fretted* adorned (with fretwork, as in a vaulted ceiling)   272 *congregation* mass   273 *piece of work* masterpiece   274 *express* well-framed, exact, expressive   275 *apprehension* power of comprehending   276 *quintessence* the fifth essence of ancient philosophy, be-yond earth, water, air, and fire, supposed to be the substance of the heavenly bodies and to be latent in all things

Rosencrantz: My lord, there was no such stuff in my thoughts.

Hamlet: Why did you laugh, then, when I said man delights not me?

Rosencrantz: To think, my lord, if you delight not in man, what Lenten entertain-   280
ment° the players shall receive from you. We coted° them on the way, and
hither are they coming to offer you service.

Hamlet: He that plays the king shall be welcome; His Majesty shall have tribute°
of° me. The adventurous knight shall use his foil and target,° the lover shall
not sighgratis,° the humorous man° shall end his part in peace,° the clown   285
shall make those laugh whose lungs are tickle o' the sear,° and the lady
shall say her mind freely, or the blank verse shall halt° for 't. What players are
they?

Rosencrantz: Even those you were wont to take such delight in, the tragedians° of
the city.   290

Hamlet: How chances it they travel? Their residence,° both in reputation and profit,
was better both ways.

Rosencrantz: I think their inhibition° comes by the means of the late° innovation.°

Hamlet: Do they hold the same estimation they did when I was in the city? Are they
so followed?   295

Rosencrantz: No, indeed are they not.

Hamlet: How° comes it? Do they grow rusty?

Rosencrantz: Nay, their endeavor keeps° in the wonted° pace. But there is, sir, an
aerie° of children, little eyases,° that cry out on the top of question° and are most
tyrannically° clapped for 't. These are now the fashion, and so berattle° the   300
common stages°—so they call them—that many wearing rapiers° are afraid of
goose quills° and dare scarce come thither.

Hamlet: What, are they children? Who maintains 'em? How are they escoted?°
Will they pursue the quality° no longer than they can sing?° Will they not say
afterwards, if they should grow themselves to common° players—as it is most like,°   305
if their means are no better°—their writers do them wrong to make them exclaim
against their own succession?°

Rosencrantz: Faith, there has been much to-do° on both sides, and the nation holds it
no sin to tar° them to controversy. There was for a while no money bid for argument
unless the poet and the player went to cuffs in the question.°   310

280–281 *Lenten entertainment* meager reception (appropriate to Lent)   280 *coted* overtook and passed
by   283 *tribute* (1) applause (2) homage paid in money   284 *of* from.   *foil and target* sword and shield
285 *gratis* for nothing.   *humorous man* eccentric character, dominated by one trait or "humor."   *in
peace* i.e., with full license   286 *tickle o' the sear* easy on the trigger, ready to laugh easily. (A *sear* is part
of a gunlock.)   287 *halt* limp   289 *tragedians* actors   291 *residence* remaining in their usual place, i.e.,
in the city   293 *inhibition* formal prohibition (from acting plays in the city).   *late* recent.   *innovation*
i.e., the new fashion in satirical plays performed by boy actors in the "private" theaters; or possibly a political uprising; or the strict limitations set on the theaters in London in 1600   297–314 *How . . . load
too* (The passage, omitted from the early quartos, alludes to the so-called War of the Theaters,
1599–1602, the rivalry between the children's companies and the adult actors.)   298 *keeps* continues.
wonted usual   299 *aerie* nest.   *eyases* young hawks.   *cry . . . question* speak shrilly, dominating the
controversy (in decrying the public theaters)   300 *tyrannically* outrageously.   *berattle* berate, clamor
against   301 *common stages* public theaters.   *many wearing rapiers* i.e., many men of fashion, afraid to
patronize the common players for fear of being satirized by the poets writing for the boy actors   302
goose quills i.e., pens of satirists   303 *escoted* maintained   304 *quality* (acting) profession.   *no longer . . .
sing* i.e., only until their voices change   305 *common* regular, adult.   *like* likely.   306 *if . . . better* if
they find no better way to support themselves   307 *succession* i.e., future careers   308 *to-do* ado   309
tar set on (as dogs)   309–310 *There . . . question* i.e., for a while, no money was offered by the acting
companies to playwrights for the plot to a play unless the satirical poets who wrote for the boys and the
adult actors came to blows in the play itself

Hamlet: Is 't possible?

Guildenstern: O, there has been much throwing about of brains.

Hamlet: Do the boys carry it away?°

Rosencrantz: Ay, that they do, my lord—Hercules and his load° too.

Hamlet: It is not very strange; for my uncle is King of Denmark, and those that   315
would make mouths° at him while my father lived give twenty, forty, fifty, a hundred ducats° apiece for his picture in little.° Sblood,° there is something in this
more than natural, if philosophy° could find it out.

A flourish [of trumpets within].

Guildenstern: There are the players.

Hamlet [to Rosenkrantz and Guildenstern]: Gentlemen, you are welcome to Elsinore.   320
Your hands, come then. Th' appurtenance° of welcome is fashion and ceremony.
Let me comply° with you in this garb,° lest my extent° to the players, which, I
tell you, must show fairly outwards,° should more appear like entertainment°
than yours. You are welcome. But my uncle-father and aunt-mother are
deceived.   325

Guildenstern: In what, my dear lord?

Hamlet: I am but mad north-north-west.° When the wind is southerly I know a
hawk° from a handsaw.°

Enter Polonius.

Polonius: Well be with you, gentlemen!

Hamlet: Hark you, Guildenstern, and you too; at each ear a hearer. That great baby   330
you see there is not yet out of his swaddling clouts.°

Rosencrantz: Haply° he is the second time come to them, for they say an old man is
twice a child.

Hamlet: I will prophesy, he comes to tell me of the players. Mark it.—You say right,
sir, o' Monday morning, 'twas then indeed.   335

Polonius: My lord, I have news to tell you.

Hamlet: My lord, I have news to tell you. When Roscius° was an actor in Rome—

Polonius: The actors are come hither, my lord.

Hamlet: Buzz,° buzz!

Polonius: Upon my honor—

Hamlet: Then came each actor on his ass.   340

Polonius: The best actors in the world, either for tragedy, comedy, history, pastoral,
pastoral-comical, historical-pastoral, tragical-historical, tragical-comical-historical-
pastoral, scene individable,° or poem unlimited.° Seneca° cannot be too

313 *carry it away* i.e., win the day   314 *Hercules . . . load* (Thought to be an allusion to the sign of the
Globe Theatre, which was Hercules bearing the world on his shoulders.)   316 *mouths* faces   317 *ducats*
gold coins.   *in little* in miniature.   '*Sblood* by God's (Christ's) blood   318 *philosophy* i.e., scientific inquiry   321 *appurtenance* proper accompaniment   322 *comply* observe the formalities of courtesy.   *garb*
i.e., manner.   *my extent* that which I extend, i.e., my polite behavior   323 *show fairly outwards* show
every evidence of cordiality.   *entertainment* a (warm) reception   327 *north-north-west* just off true north,
only partly   328 *hawk, handsaw* i.e., two very different things, though also perhaps meaning a mattock
(or *hack*) and a carpenter's cutting tool, respectively; also birds, with a play on *hernshaw*, or heron   331
swaddling clouts cloths in which to wrap a newborn baby   332 *Haply* perhaps   337 *Roscius* a famous Roman actor who died in 62 B.C.   339 *Buzz* (An interjection used to denote stale news.)   344 *scene individable*
a play observing the unity of place; or perhaps one that is unclassifiable, or performed without intermis-
sion.   *poem unlimited* a play disregarding the unities of time and place; one that is all-inclusive.   *Seneca*
writer of Latin tragedies

heavy, nor Plautus° too light. For the law of writ and the liberty,° these° are 345
the only men.
Hamlet: O Jephthah, judge of Israel,° what a treasure hadst thou!
Polonius: What a treasure had he, my lord?
Hamlet: Why,

"One fair daughter, and no more, 350
The which he lovèd passing° well."

Polonius [aside]: Still on my daughter.
Hamlet: Am I not i' the right, old Jephthah?
Polonius: If you call me Jephthah, my lord, I have a daughter that I love passing
well. 355
Hamlet: Nay, that follows not.
Polonius: What follows then, my lord?
Hamlet: Why,

"As by lot,° God wot,"°

and then, you know, 360

"It came to pass, as most like° it was"—

the first row° of the pious chanson° will show you more, for look where my
abridgement° comes.

Enter the Players.

You are welcome, masters; welcome, all. I am glad to see thee well. Welcome, good friends. O, old friend! Why, thy face is valanced° since I saw thee 365
last. Com'st thou to beard° me in Denmark? What, my young lady° and
mistress! By 'r Lady,° your ladyship is nearer to heaven than when I saw you last,
by the altitude of a chopine.° Pray God your voice, like a piece of uncurrent°
gold, be not cracked within the ring.° Masters, you are all welcome. We'll e'en to
't° like French falconers, fly at anything we see. We'll have a speech straight.° 370
Come, give us a taste of your quality.° Come, a passionate speech.
First Player: What speech, my good lord?
Hamlet: I heard thee speak me a speech once, but it was never acted, or if it was,
not above once, for the play, I remember, pleased not the million; 'twas caviar to
the general.° But it was—as I received it, and others, whose judgments 375
in such matters cried in the top of° mine—an excellent play, well digested°
in the scenes, setdown with as much modesty° as cunning.° I remember one said
there were no sallets° in the lines to make the matter savory, nor no matter in
the phrase that might indict° the author of affectation, but called it an honest

---

345 *Plautus* writer of Latin comedy. *law . . . liberty* dramatic composition both according to the rules
and disregarding the rules. *these* i.e., the actors 347 *Jephthah . . . Israel* (Jephthah had to sacrifice his
daughter; see Judges 11. Hamlet goes on to quote from a ballad on the theme.) 351 *passing* surpassingly
359 *lot* chance. *wot* knows 361 *like* likely, probable 362 *row* stanza. *chanson* ballad, song
362–363 *my abridgment* something that cuts short my conversation; also, a diversion 365 *valanced*
fringed (with a beard) 366 *beard* confront, challenge (with obvious pun). *young lady* i.e., boy playing
women's parts 367 *By 'r Lady* by Our Lady 368 *chopine* thick-soled shoe of Italian fashion. *uncurrent*
not passable as lawful coinage 369 *cracked . . . ring* i.e., changed from adolescent to male voice, no
longer suitable for women's roles. (Coins featured rings enclosing the sovereign's head; if the coin was
cracked within this ring, it was unfit for currency.) 369–370 *e'en to 't* go at it 370 *straight* at once 371
quality professional skill 374–375 *caviar to the general* caviar to the multitude, i.e., a choice dish too
elegant for coarse tastes 376 *cried in the top of* i.e., spoke with greater authority than. *digested*
arranged, ordered 377 *modesty* moderation, restraint. *cunning* skill 378 *sallets* i.e., something savory,
spicy improprieties 379 *indict* convict

method, as wholesome as sweet, and by very much more handsome° than fine.° 380
One speech in 't I chiefly loved: 'twas Aeneas' tale to Dido, and thereabout of it
especially when he speaks of Priam's slaughter.° If it live in your memory, begin at
this line: let me see, let me see—
"The rugged Pyrrhus,° like th' Hyrcanian beast"°—
'Tis not so. It begins with Pyrrhus: 385
"The rugged° Pyrrhus, he whose sable° arms,
Black as his purpose, did the night resemble
When he lay couchèd° in the ominous horse,°
Hath now this dread and black complexion smeared
With heraldry more dismal.° Head to foot 390
Now is he total gules,° horridly tricked°
With blood of fathers, mothers, daughters, sons,
Baked and impasted° with the parching streets,°
That lend a tyrannous° and a damnèd light
To their lord's° murder. Roasted in wrath and fire, 395
And thus o'ersizèd° with coagulate gore,
With eyes like carbuncles,° the hellish Pyrrhus
Old grandsire Priam seeks."
So proceed you.

Polonius: 'Fore God, my lord, well spoken, with good accent and good discretion. 400
First Player: "Anon he finds him
    Striking too short at Greeks. His antique° sword,
Rebellious to his arm, lies where it falls,
Repugnant° to command. Unequal matched,
Pyrrhus at Priam drives, in rage strikes wide, 405
But with the whiff and wind of his fell° sword
Th' unnervèd° father falls. Then senseless Ilium,°
Seeming to feel this blow, with flaming top
Stoops to his° base, and with a hideous crash
Takes prisoner Pyrrhus' ear. For, lo! His sword, 410
Which was declining° on the milky° head
Of reverend Priam, seemed i' th' air to stick.
So as a painted° tyrant Pyrrhus stood,
And, like a neutral to his will and matter,°
    Did nothing. 415
But as we often see against° some storm

---

380 *handsome* well-proportioned. *fine* elaborately ornamented, showy 382 *Priam's slaughter* the slaying of
the ruler of Troy, when the Greeks finally took the city 384 *Pyrrhus* a Greek hero in the Trojan War, also
known as Neoptolemus, son of Achilles—another avenging son. *Hyrcanian beast* i.e., tiger. (On the death
of Priam, see Virgil, Aeneid, 2.506 ff.; compare the whole speech with Marlowe's *Dido, Queen of Carthage,*
2.1.214 ff. On the Hyrcanian tiger, see *Aeneid,* 4.366–367. Hyrcania is on the Caspian Sea.) 386 *rugged*
shaggy, savage. *sable* black (for reasons of camouflage during the episode of the Trojan horse) 388 *couchèd*
concealed. *ominous horse* fateful Trojan horse, by which the Greeks gained access to Troy 390 *dismal* ill-
omened 391 *total gules* entirely red. (A heraldic term.) *tricked* spotted and smeared. (Heraldic.) 393
impasted crusted, like a thick paste. *with . . . streets* by the parching heat of the streets (because of the fires
everywhere) 394 *tyrannous* cruel 395 *their lord's* i.e., Priam's 396 *o'ersizèd* covered as with size or glue
397 *carbuncles* large fiery-red precious stones thought to emit their own light 402 *antique* ancient, long-used
404 *Repugnant* disobedient, resistant 406 *fell* cruel 407 *unnervèd* strengthless. *senseless Ilium* inanimate
citadel of Troy 409 *his* its 411 *declining* descending. *milky* white-haired 413 *painted* i.e., painted in a
picture 414 *like . . . matter* i.e., as though suspended between his intention and its fulfillment 416 *against*
just before

A silence in the heavens, the rack° stand still,
The bold winds speechless, and the orb° below
As hush as death, anon the dreadful thunder
Doth rend the region,° so, after Pyrrhus' pause, 420
A rousèd vengeance sets him new a-work,
And never did the Cyclops'° hammers fall
On Mars's armor forged for proof eterne°
With less remorse° than Pyrrhus' bleeding sword
Now falls on Priam. 425
Out, out, thou strumpet Fortune! All you gods
In general synod° take away her power!
Break all the spokes and fellies° from her wheel,
And bowl the round nave° down the hill of heaven°
As low as to the fiends!" 430

Polonius: This is too long.

Hamlet: It shall to the barber's with your beard.—Prithee, say on. He's for a jig° or a
tale of bawdry, or he sleeps. Say on; come to Hecuba.°

First Player: "But who, ah woe! had° seen the moblèd° queen"—

Hamlet: "The moblèd queen"? 435

Polonius: That's good. "Moblèd queen" is good.

First Player: "Run barefoot up and down, threat'ning the flames°
With bisson rheum,° a clout° upon that head
Where late° the diadem stood, and, for a robe,
About her lank and all o'erteemèd° loins 440
A blanket, in the alarm of fear caught up—
Who this had seen, with tongue in venom steeped,
'Gainst Fortune's state° would treason have pronounced.°
But if the gods themselves did see her then
When she saw Pyrrhus make malicious sport 445
In mincing with his sword her husband's limbs,
The instant burst of clamor that she made,
Unless things mortal move them not at all,
Would have made milch° the burning eyes of heaven,°
And passion° in the gods." 450

Polonius: Look whe'er° he has not turned his color and has tears in 's eyes. Prithee,
no more.

Hamlet: 'Tis well; I'll have thee speak out the rest of this soon.—Good my lord, will
you see the players well bestowed?° Do you hear, let them be well used, for they
are the abstract° and brief chronicles of the time. After your death you were better 455
have a bad epitaph than their ill report while you live.

---

417 *rack* mass of clouds   418 *orb* globe, earth   420 *region* sky   422 *Cyclops* giant armor makers in the
smithy of Vulcan   423 *proof eterne* eternal resistance to assault   424 *remorse* pity   427 *synod* assembly
428 *fellies* pieces of wood forming the rim of a wheel   429 *nave* hub.   *hill of heaven* Mount Olympus   432
jig comic song and dance often given at the end of a play   433 *Hecuba* wife of Priam   434 *who . . . had*
anyone who had (also in line 442).   *moblèd* muffled   437 *threat'ning the flames* i.e., weeping hard enough
to dampen the flames   438 *bisson rheum* blinding tears.   *clout* cloth   439 *late* lately   440 *all o'erteemèd*
utterly worn out with bearing children   443 *state* rule, managing.   *pronounced* proclaimed   449 *milch*
milky, moist with tears.   *burning eyes of heaven* i.e., heavenly bodies   450 *passion* overpowering emotion
451 *whe'er* whether   454 *bestowed* lodged   455 *abstract* summary account

Polonius: My lord, I will use them according to their desert.

Hamlet: God's bodikin,° man, much better. Use every man after° his desert, and who
    shall scape whipping? Use them after your own honor and dignity. The less they
    deserve, the more merit is in your bounty. Take them in.   460

Polonius: Come, sirs.   *[Exit.]*

Hamlet: Follow him, friends. We'll hear a play tomorrow. *[As they start to leave,*
    Hamlet detains the First Player.] Dost thou hear me, old friend? Can you play *The*
    Murder of Gonzago?

First Player: Ay, my lord.   465

Hamlet: We'll ha 't° tomorrow night. You could, for a need, study° a speech of some
    dozen or sixteen lines which I would set down and insert in 't, could you not?

First Player: Ay, my lord.

Hamlet: Very well. Follow that lord, and look you mock him not.

                                         (Exeunt Players.)

    My good friends, I'll leave you till night. You are welcome to Elsinore.   470

Rosencrantz: Good my lord!

                          Exeunt [Rosencrantz and Guildenstern].

Hamlet: Ay, so, goodbye to you.—Now I am alone.
    O, what a rogue and peasant slave am I!
    Is it not monstrous that this player here,
    But° in a fiction, in a dream of passion,   475
    Could force his soul so to his own conceit°
    That from her working° all his visage wanned,°
    Tears in his eyes, distraction in his aspect,°
    A broken voice, and his whole function suiting
    With forms to his conceit?° And all for nothing!   480
    For Hecuba!
    What's Hecuba to him, or he to Hecuba,
    That he should weep for her? What would he do
    Had he the motive and the cue for passion
    That I have? He would drown the stage with tears   485
    And cleave the general ear° with horrid° speech,
    Make mad the guilty and appall° the free,°
    Confound the ignorant,° and amaze° indeed
    The very faculties of eyes and ears. Yet I,
    A dull and muddy-mettled° rascal, peak°   490
    Like John-a-dreams,° unpregnant° of my cause,
    And can say nothing—no, not for a king

---

458 *God's bodikin* by God's (Christ's) little body, *bodykin*. (Not to be confused with *bodkin,* "dagger."). *after* according to   466 *ha 't* have it. *study* memorize   475 *But* merely   476 *force . . . conceit* bring his innermost being so entirely into accord with his conception (of the role)   477 *from her working* as a result of, or in response to, his soul's activity. *wanned* grew pale   478 *aspect* look, glance   479–480 *his whole . . . conceit* all his bodily powers responding with actions to suit his thought   486 *the general ear* everyone's ear. *horrid* horrible   487 *appall* (Literally, make pale.) *free* innocent   488 *Confound the ignorant* i.e., dumbfound those who know nothing of the crime that has been committed. *amaze* stun   490 *muddy-mettled* dull-spirited. *peak* mope, pine   491 *John-a-dreams* a sleepy, dreaming idler. *unpregnant of* not quickened by

Upon whose property° and most dear life
A damned defeat° was made. Am I a coward?
Who calls me villain? Breaks my pate° across?   495
Plucks off my beard and blows it in my face?
Tweaks me by the nose? Gives me the lie i' the throat°
As deep as to the lungs? Who does me this?
Ha, 'swounds,° I should take it; for it cannot be
But I am pigeon-livered° and lack gall   500
To make oppression bitter,° or ere this
I should ha' fatted all the region kites°
With this slave's offal.° Bloody, bawdy villain!
Remorseless,° treacherous, lecherous, kindless° villain!
O, vengeance!   505
Why, what an ass am I! This is most brave,°
That I, the son of a dear father murdered,
Prompted to my revenge by heaven and hell,
Must like a whore unpack my heart with words
And fall a-cursing, like a very drab,°   510
A scullion!° Fie upon 't, foh! About,° my brains!
Hum, I have heard
That guilty creatures sitting at a play
Have by the very cunning° of the scene°
Been struck so to the soul that presently°   515
They have proclaimed their malefactions;
For murder, though it have no tongue, will speak
With most miraculous organ. I'll have these players
Play something like the murder of my father
Before mine uncle. I'll observe his looks;   520
I'll tent° him to the quick.° If 'a do blench,°
I know my course. The spirit that I have seen
May be the devil, and the devil hath power
T' assume a pleasing shape; yea, and perhaps,
Out of my weakness and my melancholy,   525
As he is very potent with such spirits,°
Abuses° me to damn me. I'll have grounds
More relative° than this. The play's the thing
Wherein I'll catch the conscience of the King.

                                                                    Exit.

---

493 *property* i.e., the crown; also character, quality   494 *damned defeat* damnable act of destruction   495
pate head   497 *Gives . . . throat* calls me an out-and-out liar   499 *'swounds* by his (Christ's) wounds
500 *pigeon-livered* (The pigeon or dove was popularly supposed to be mild because it secreted no gall.)
501 *bitter* i.e., bitter to me   502 *region kites* kites (birds of prey) of the air   503 *offal* entrails   504
Remorseless pitiless.   *kindless* unnatural   506 *brave* fine, admirable. (Said ironically.)   510 *drab* whore
511 *scullion* menial kitchen servant (apt to be foul-mouthed).   *About* about it, to work   514 *cunning* art,
skill.   *scene* dramatic presentation   515 *presently* at once   521 *tent* probe.   *the quick* the tender part of a
wound, the core.   *blench* quail, flinch   526 *spirits* humors (of melancholy)   527 *Abuses* deludes   528
relative cogent, pertinent

ACT III

SCENE I [THE CASTLE.]

Enter King, Queen, Polonius, Ophelia, Rosencrantz, Guildenstern, lords.

King: And can you by no drift of conference°
　　　　Get from him why he puts on this confusion,
　　　　Grating so harshly all his days of quiet
　　　　With turbulent and dangerous lunacy?
Rosencrantz: He does confess he feels himself distracted,　　　　5
　　　　But from what cause 'a will by no means speak.
Guildenstern: Nor do we find him forward° to be sounded,°
　　　　But with a crafty madness keeps aloof
　　　　When we would bring him on to some confession
　　　　Of his true state.
Queen:　　　　　　　Did he receive you well?　　　　　10
Rosencrantz: Most like a gentleman.
Guildenstern: But with much forcing of his disposition.°
Rosencrantz: Niggard° of question,° but of our demands
　　　　Most free in his reply.
Queen:　　　　　　　Did you assay° him
　　　　To any pastime?　　　　　　　　　　　　　15
Rosencrantz: Madam, it so fell out that certain players
　　　　We o'erraught° on the way. Of these we told him,
　　　　And there did seem in him a kind of joy
　　　　To hear of it. They are here about the court,
　　　　And, as I think, they have already order　　　　20
　　　　This night to play before him.
Polonius:　　　　　　　　　　'Tis most true,
　　　　And he beseeched me to entreat Your Majesties
　　　　To hear and see the matter.
King: With all my heart, and it doth much content me
　　　　To hear him so inclined.　　　　　　　　25
　　　　Good gentlemen, give him a further edge°
　　　　And drive his purpose into these delights.
Rosencrantz: We shall, my lord.

　　　　　　　　　　Exeunt Rosencrantz and Guildenstern.

King:　　　　　　Sweet Gertrude, leave us too,
　　　　For we have closely° sent for Hamlet hither,
　　　　That he, as 'twere by accident, may here　　　　30
　　　　Affront° Ophelia.
　　　　Her father and myself, lawful espials,°
　　　　Will so bestow ourselves that seeing, unseen,
　　　　We may of their encounter frankly judge,
　　　　And gather by him, as he is behaved,　　　　35

---

1 *drift of conference* directing of conversation 7 *forward* willing. *sounded* questioned 12 *disposition* inclination 13 *Niggard* stingy. *question* conversation 14 *assay* try to win 17 *o'erraught* overtook 26 *edge* incitement 29 *closely* privately 31 *Affront* confront, meet 32 *espials* spies

      If 't be th' affliction of his love or no
      That thus he suffers for.
Queen: I shall obey you.
      And for your part, Ophelia, I do wish
      That your good beauties be the happy cause
      Of Hamlet's wildness. So shall I hope your virtues   40
      Will bring him to his wonted° way again,
      To both your honors.
Ophelia: Madam, I wish it may.

                                              [Exit Queen.]

Polonius: Ophelia, walk you here.—Gracious,° so please you,
      We will bestow° ourselves. *[To Ophelia.]* Read on this book, *[giving her a book]*
      That show of such an exercise° may color°   45
      Your loneliness.° We are oft to blame in this—
      'Tis too much proved°—that with devotion's visage
      And pious action we do sugar o'er
      The devil himself.
King [aside]: O, 'tis too true!   50
      How smart a lash that speech doth give my conscience!
      The harlot's cheek, beautied with plastering art,
      Is not more ugly to° the thing° that helps it
      Than is my deed to my most painted word.
      O heavy burden!   55
Polonius: I hear him coming. Let's withdraw, my lord.

                          [The King and Polonius withdraw.°]

Enter Hamlet. [Ophelia pretends to read a book.]

Hamlet: To be, or not to be, that is the question:
      Whether 'tis nobler in the mind to suffer
      The slings° and arrows of outrageous fortune,
      Or to take arms against a sea of troubles   60
      And by opposing end them. To die, to sleep—
      No more—and by a sleep to say we end
      The heartache and the thousand natural shocks
      That flesh is heir to. 'Tis a consummation
      Devoutly to be wished. To die, to sleep;   65
      To sleep, perchance to dream. Ay, there's the rub,°
      For in that sleep of death what dreams may come,
      When we have shuffled° off this mortal coil,°
      Must give us pause. There's the respect°
      That makes calamity of so long life.°   70

---

41 *wonted* accustomed   43 *Gracious* Your Grace (i.e., the King)   44 *bestow* conceal   45 *exercise* religious exercise. (The book she reads is one of devotion.)   *color* give a plausible appearance to   46 *loneliness* being alone   47 *too much proved* too often shown to be true, too often practiced   53 *to* compared to.   *the thing* i.e., the cosmetic   56 s.d. *withdraw* (The King and Polonius may retire behind an arras. The stage directions specify that they "enter" again near the end of the scene.)   59 *slings* missiles   66 *rub* (Literally, an obstacle in the game of bowls.)   68 *shuffled* sloughed, cast.   *coil* turmoil   69 *respect* consideration   70 *of . . . life* so long-lived, something we willingly endure for so long (also suggesting that long life is itself a calamity)

For who would bear the whips and scorns of time,
Th' oppressor's wrong, the proud man's contumely,°
The pangs of disprized° love, the law's delay,
The insolence of office,° and the spurns°
That patient merit of th' unworthy takes,°   75
When he himself might his quietus° make
With a bare bodkin?° Who would fardels° bear,
To grunt and sweat under a weary life,
But that the dread of something after death,
The undiscovered country from whose bourn°   80
No traveler returns, puzzles the will,
And makes us rather bear those ills we have
Than fly to others that we know not of?
Thus conscience does make cowards of us all;
And thus the native hue° of resolution   85
Is sicklied o'er with the pale cast° of thought,
And enterprises of great pitch° and moment°
With this regard° their currents° turn awry
And lose the name of action.—Soft you° now,
The fair Ophelia. Nymph, in thy orisons°   90
Be all my sins remembered.
Ophelia: Good my lord,
How does your honor for this many a day?
Hamlet: I humbly thank you; well, well, well.
Ophelia: My lord, I have remembrances of yours,
That I have longèd long to redeliver.   95
I pray you, now receive them.   [*She offers tokens.*]
Hamlet: No, not I, I never gave you aught.
Ophelia: My honored lord, you know right well you did,
And with them words of so sweet breath composed
As made the things more rich. Their perfume lost, 100
Take these again, for to the noble mind
Rich gifts wax poor when givers prove unkind.
There, my lord.   [*She gives tokens.*]
Hamlet: Ha, ha! Are you honest?°
Ophelia: My lord?   105
Hamlet: Are you fair?°
Ophelia: What means your lordship?
Hamlet: That if you be honest and fair, your honesty° should admit no discourse to°
your beauty.
Ophelia: Could beauty, my lord, have better commerce° than with honesty?   110

---

72 *contumely* insolent abuse   73 *disprized* unvalued   74 *office* officialdom.   *spurns* insults   75 *of . . . takes* receives from unworthy persons   76 *quietus* acquitance; here, death   77 *a bare bodkin* a mere dagger, unsheathed.   *fardels* burdens   80 *bourn* frontier, boundary   85 *native hue* natural color, complexion   86 *cast* tinge, shade of color   87 *pitch* height (as of a falcon's flight).   *moment* importance   88 *regard* respect, consideration.   *currents* courses   89 *Soft you* i.e., wait a minute, gently   90 *orisons* prayers   104 *honest* (1) truthful (2) chaste   106 *fair* (1) beautiful (2) just, honorable   108 *your honesty* your chastity. *discourse to* familiar dealings with   110 *commerce* dealings, intercourse

Ophelia and Hamlet.

Hamlet: Ay, truly, for the power of beauty will sooner transform honesty from what
it is to a bawd than the force of honesty can translate beauty into his ° likeness.
This was sometime° a paradox,° but now the time° gives it proof. I did love you
once.

Ophelia: Indeed, my lord, you made me believe so.   115

Hamlet: You should not have believed me, for virtue cannot so inoculate° our old
stock but we shall relish of it.° I loved you not.

Ophelia: I was the more deceived.

Hamlet: Get thee to a nunnery.° Why wouldst thou be a breeder of sinners? I am myself
indifferent honest,° but yet I could accuse me of such things that it were better   120

112 *his* its   113 *sometime* formerly.   *a paradox* a view opposite to commonly held opinion.   *the time* the
present age   116 *inoculate* graft, be engrafted to   117 *but . . . it* that we do not still have about us a taste
of the old stock, i.e., retain our sinfulness   119 *nunnery* convent (with possibly an awareness that the
word was also used derisively to denote a brothel)   120 *indifferent honest* reasonably virtuous

my mother had not borne me: I am very proud, revengeful, ambitious, with more offenses at my beck° than I have thoughts to put them in, imagination to give them shape, or time to act them in. What should such fellows as I do crawling between earth and heaven? We are arrant knaves all; believe none of us. Go thy ways to a nunnery. Where's your father?   125

Ophelia: At home, my lord.

Hamlet: Let the doors be shut upon him, that he may play the fool nowhere but in 's own house. Farewell.

Ophelia: O, help him, you sweet heavens!

Hamlet: If thou dost marry, I'll give thee this plague for thy dowry: be thou as chaste   130
as ice, as pure as snow, thou shalt not escape calumny. Get thee to a nunnery, farewell. Or, if thou wilt needs marry, marry a fool, for wise men know well enough what monsters° you° make of them. To a nunnery, go, and quickly too. Farewell.

Ophelia: Heavenly powers, restore him!   135

Hamlet: I have heard of your paintings too, well enough. God hath given you one face, and you make yourselves another. You jig,° you amble,° and you lisp, you nickname God's creatures,° and make your wantonness your ignorance.° Go to, I'll no more on 't;° it hath made me mad. I say we will have no more marriage. Those that are married already—all but one—shall live. The rest shall keep as   140
they are. To a nunnery, go.   *Exit.*

Ophelia: O, what a noble mind is here o'erthrown!
  The courtier's, soldier's, scholar's, eye, tongue, sword,
  Th' expectancy° and rose° of the fair state,
  The glass of fashion and the mold of form,°   145
  Th' observed of all observers,° quite, quite down!
  And I, of ladies most deject and wretched,
  That sucked the honey of his music° vows,
  Now see that noble and most sovereign reason
  Like sweet bells jangled out of tune and harsh,   150
  That unmatched form and feature of blown° youth
  Blasted° with ecstasy.° O, woe is me,
  T' have seen what I have seen, see what I see!

Enter King and Polonius.

King: Love? His affections° do not that way tend;
  Nor what he spake, though it lacked form a little,   155
  Was not like madness. There's something in his soul
  O'er which his melancholy sits on brood,°
  And I do doubt° the hatch and the disclose°
  Will be some danger; which for to prevent,

122 *beck* command   133 *monsters* (An allusion to the horns of a cuckold.)   *you* i.e., you women   137 *jig* dance.   *amble* move coyly   137–138 *you nickname . . . creatures* i.e., you give trendy names to things in place of their God-given names.   *make . . . ignorance* i.e., excuse your affectation on the grounds of pretended ignorance   139 *on 't* of it   144 *expectancy* hope.   *rose* ornament   145 *The glass . . . form* the mirror of true self-fashioning and the pattern of courtly behavior   146 *Th' observed . . . observers* i.e., the center of attention and honor in the court   148 *music* musical, sweetly uttered   151 *blown* blooming   152 *Blasted* withered.   *ecstasy* madness   154 *affections* emotions, feelings   157 *sits on brood* sits like a bird on a nest, about to *hatch* mischief (line 158)   158 *doubt* fear.   *disclose* disclosure, hatching

> I have in quick determination   160
> Thus set it down:° he shall with speed to England
> For the demand of° our neglected tribute.
> Haply the seas and countries different
> With variable objects° shall expel
> This something-settled matter in his heart,°   165
> Whereon his brains still° beating puts him thus
> From fashion of himself.° What think you on 't?
>
> *Polonius:* It shall do well. But yet do I believe
> The origin and commencement of his grief
> Sprung from neglected love.—How now, Ophelia?   170
> You need not tell us what Lord Hamlet said;
> We heard it all.—My lord, do as you please,
> But, if you hold it fit, after the play
> Let his queen-mother° all alone entreat him
> To show his grief. Let her be round° with him;   175
> And I'll be placed, so please you, in the ear
> Of all their conference. If she find him not,°
> To England send him, or confine him where
> Your wisdom best shall think.
>
> *King:*   It shall be so.
> Madness in great ones must not unwatched go.   180
>
> *Exeunt.*

SCENE II [THE CASTLE.]

Enter Hamlet and three of the Players.

Hamlet: Speak the speech, I pray you, as I pronounced it to you, trippingly on the tongue. But if you mouth it, as many of our players° do, I had as lief° the town crier spoke my lines. Nor do not saw the air too much with your hand, thus, but use all gently; for in the very torrent, tempest, and, as I may say, whirlwind of your passion, you must acquire and beget a temperance that may give it smooth-   5
ness. O, it offends me to the soul to hear a robustious° periwig-pated° fellow tear a passion to tatters, to very rags, to split the ears of the groundlings,° who for the most part are capable of° nothing but inexplicable dumb shows° and noise. I would have such a fellow whipped for o'erdoing Termagant.° It out-Herods Herod.° Pray you, avoid it.   10

First Player: I warrant your honor.

Hamlet: Be not too tame neither, but let your own discretion be your tutor. Suit the action to the word, the word to the action, with this special observance, that

---

161 *set it down* resolved   162 *For . . . of* to demand   164 *variable objects* various sights and surroundings to divert him   165 *This something . . . heart* the strange matter settled in his heart   166 *still* continually 167 *From . . . himself* out of his natural manner   174 *queen-mother* queen and mother   175 *round* blunt 177 *find him not* fails to discover what is troubling him   2 *our players* players nowadays.   *I had as lief* I would just as soon   6 *robustious* violent, boisterous.   *periwig-pated* wearing a wig   7 *groundlings* spectators who paid least and stood in the yard of the theater   8 *capable of* able to understand.   *dumb shows* mimed performances, often used before Shakespeare's time to precede a play or each act   9 *Termagant* a supposed deity of the Mohammedans, not found in any English medieval play but elsewhere portrayed as violent and blustering   10 *Herod* Herod of Jewry. (A character in *The Slaughter of the Innocents* and other cycle plays. The part was played with great noise and fury.)

you o'erstep not the modesty° of nature. For anything so o'erdone is from°
the purpose of playing, whose end, both at the first and now, was and is to hold   15
as 't were the mirror up to nature, to show virtue her feature, scorn° her own image, and the very age and body of the time° his° form and pressure.° Now this
overdone or come tardy off,° though it makes the unskillful° laugh, cannot but
make the judicious grieve, the censure of the which one° must in your
allowance° o'erweigh a whole theater of others. O, there be players that I have   20
seen play, and heard others praise, and that highly, not to speak it profanely,°
that, neither having th' accent of Christians° nor the gait of Christian, pagan,
nor man,° have so strutted and bellowed that I have thought some of nature's
journeymen° had made men and not made them well, they imitated humanity so
abominably.°   25

First Player: I hope we have reformed that indifferently° with us, sir.

Hamlet: O, reform it altogether. And let those that play your clowns speak no more
than is set down for them; for there be of them° that will themselves laugh, to set
on some quantity of barren° spectators to laugh too, though in the meantime
some necessary question of the play be then to be considered. That's   30
villainous, and shows a most pitiful ambition in the fool that uses it. Go make
you ready.   [*Exeunt Players.*]

Enter Polonius, Guildenstern, and Rosencrantz.
How now, my lord, will the King hear this piece of work?

Polonius: And the Queen too, and that presently.°

Hamlet: Bid the players make haste.   [*Exit Polonius.*]   35
Will you two help to hasten them?

Rosencrantz: Ay, my lord.   Exeunt they two.

Hamlet: What ho, Horatio!

Enter Horatio.

Horatio: Here, sweet lord, at your service.

Hamlet: Horatio, thou art e'en as just a man
As e'er my conversation coped withal.°   40

Horatio: O, my dear lord—

Hamlet: Nay, do not think I flatter,
For what advancement may I hope from thee
That no revenue hast but thy good spirits
To feed and clothe thee? Why should the poor be flattered?
No, let the candied° tongue lick absurd pomp,   45
And crook the pregnant° hinges of the knee

---

14 *modesty* restraint, moderation. *from* contrary to   16 *scorn* i.e., something foolish and deserving of
scorn   17 *the very . . . time* i.e., the present state of affairs *his* its. *pressure* stamp, impressed character.
18 *come tardy off* inadequately done. *the unskillful* those lacking in judgment   19 *the censure . . . one* the
judgment of even one of whom   19–20 *your allowance* your scale of values   21 *not . . . profanely* (Hamlet
anticipates his idea in lines 23–25 that some men were not made by God at all.)   22 *Christians* i.e., ordinary decent folk   23 *nor man* i.e., nor any human being at all   24 *journeymen* laborers who are not yet
masters in their trade   25 *abominably* (Shakespeare's usual spelling, abhominably, suggests a literal though
etymologically incorrect meaning, "removed from human nature.")   26 *indifferently* tolerably   28 *of them*
some among them   29 *barren* i.e., of wit   34 *presently* at once   29 *barren* i.e., of wit   40 *my . . . withal*
my dealings encountered   45 *candied* sugared, flattering   46 *pregnant* compliant

Where thrift° may follow fawning. Dost thou hear?
Since my dear soul was mistress of her choice
And could of men distinguish her election,°
Sh' hath sealed thee° for herself, for thou hast been   50
As one, in suffering all, that suffers nothing,
A man that Fortune's buffets and rewards
Hast ta'en with equal thanks; and blest are those
Whose blood° and judgment are so well commeddled°
That they are not a pipe for Fortune's finger   55
To sound what stop° she please. Give me that man
That is not passion's slave, and I will wear him
In my heart's core, ay, in my heart of heart,
As I do thee.—Something too much of this.—
There is a play tonight before the King.   60
One scene of it comes near the circumstance
Which I have told thee of my father's death.
I prithee, when thou seest that act afoot,
Even with the very comment of thy soul°
Observe my uncle. If his occulted° guilt   65
Do not itself unkennel° in one speech,
It is a damnèd° ghost that we have seen,
And my imaginations are as foul
As Vulcan's stithy.° Give him heedful note,
For I mine eyes will rivet to his face,   70
And after we will both our judgments join
In censure of his seeming.°
Horatio: Well, my lord.
If 'a steal aught° the whilst this play is playing
And scape detecting, I will pay the theft.

[*Flourish.*] *Enter trumpets and kettledrums, King, Queen, Polonius, Ophelia,*
[*Rosencrantz, Guildenstern, and other lords, with guards carrying torches*].

Hamlet: They are coming to the play. I must be idle.° Get you a place.   75

[*The King, Queen, and courtiers sit.*]

King: How fares our cousin° Hamlet?
Hamlet: Excellent, i' faith, of the chameleon's dish:° I eat the air, promise-crammed.
    You cannot feed capons° so.

---

47 *thrift* profit   49 *could . . . election* could make distinguishing choices among persons   50 *sealed thee*
(Literally, as one would seal a legal document to mark possession.)   54 *blood* passion.   *commeddled* com-
mingled   56 *stop* hole in a wind instrument for controlling the sound   64 *very . . . soul* your most penetrating observation and consideration   65 *occulted* hidden   66 *unkennel* (As one would say of a fox driven
from its lair.)   67 *damnèd* in league with Satan   69 *stithy* smithy, place of stiths (anvils)   72 *censure of his
seeming* judgment of his appearance or behavior   73 *If 'a steal aught* if he gets away with anything   75 *idle*
(1) unoccupied (2) mad   76 *cousin* i.e., close relative   77 *chameleon's dish* (Chameleons were supposed to
feed on air. Hamlet deliberately misinterprets the King's *fares* as "feeds." By his phrase *eat the air*, he also
plays on the idea of feeding himself with the promise of succession, of being the *heir*.)   78 *capons* roosters
castrated and *crammed* with feed to make them succulent

King: I have nothing with° this answer, Hamlet. These words are not mine.°

Hamlet: No, nor mine now.° [*To Polonius.*] My lord, you played once i' th' univer- 80
sity, you say?

Polonius: That did I, my lord, and was accounted a good actor.

Hamlet: What did you enact?

Polonius: I did enact Julius Caesar. I was killed i' the Capitol; Brutus killed me.

Hamlet: It was a brute° part° of him to kill so capital a calf° there.—Be the players 85
ready?

Rosencrantz: Ay, my lord. They stay upon° your patience.

Queen: Come hither, my dear Hamlet, sit by me.

Hamlet: No, good Mother, here's metal° more attractive.

Polonius [*to the King*]: O, ho, do you mark that? 90

Hamlet: Lady, shall I lie in your lap?

[*Lying down at Ophelia's feet.*]

Ophelia: No, my lord.

Hamlet: I mean, my head upon your lap?

Ophelia: Ay, my lord.

Hamlet: Do you think I meant country matters?° 95

Ophelia: I think nothing, my lord.

Hamlet: That's a fair thought to lie between maids' legs.

Ophelia: What is, my lord?

Hamlet: Nothing.°

Ophelia: You are merry, my lord. 100

Hamlet: Who, I?

Ophelia: Ay, my lord.

Hamlet: O God, your only jig maker.° What should a man do but be merry?
For look you how cheerfully my mother looks, and my father died within 's° two
hours. 105

Ophelia: Nay, 'tis twice two months, my lord.

Hamlet: So long? Nay then, let the devil wear black, for I'll have a suit of sables.° O
heavens! Die two months ago, and not forgotten yet? Then there's hope a great man's
memory may outlive his life half a year. But, by'r Lady, 'a must build churches, then,
or else shall 'a suffer not thinking on,° with the hobbyhorse, whose epitaph is 110
"For O, for O, the hobbyhorse is forgot.°

---

79 *have . . . with* make nothing of, or gain nothing from. *are not mine* do not respond to what I asked
80 *nor mine now* (Once spoken, words are proverbially no longer the speaker's own—and hence should be
uttered warily.) 85 *brute* (The Latin meaning of *brutus,* "stupid," was often used punningly with the
name Brutus.) *part* (1) deed (2) role. *calf* fool 87 *stay upon* await 89 *metal* substance that is
attractive, i.e., magnetic, but with suggestion also of *mettle,* "disposition" 95 *country matters* sexual intercourse (making a bawdy pun on the first syllable of *country*) 99 *Nothing* the figure zero or naught, suggesting the female sexual anatomy. (*Thing* not infrequently has a bawdy connotation of male or female
anatomy, and the reference here could be male.) 103 *only jig maker* very best composer of jigs, i.e., pointless merriment. (Hamlet replies sardonically to Ophelia's observation that he is merry by saying, "If you're
looking for someone who is really merry, you've come to the right person.") 104 *within 's* within this (i.e.,
these) 107 *suit of sables* garments trimmed with the fur of the sable and hence suited for a wealthy person,
not a mourner (but with a pun on *sable,* "black," ironically suggesting mourning once again) 110 *suffer . . .
on* undergo oblivion 111 *For . . . forgot* (Verse of a song occurring also in *Love's Labor's Lost,* III, i,
27–28. The hobbyhorse was a character made up to resemble a horse and rider, appearing in the morris
dance and such May-game sports. This song laments the disappearance of such customs under pressure
from the Puritans.)

The trumpets sound. Dumb show follows.

Enter a King and a Queen [very lovingly]; the Queen embracing him, and he her. [She kneels, and makes show of protestation unto him.] He takes her up, and declines his head upon her neck. He lies him down upon a bank of flowers. She, seeing him asleep, leaves him. Anon comes in another man, takes off his crown, kisses it, pours poison in the sleeper's ears, and leaves him. The Queen returns, finds the King dead, makes passionate action. The Poisoner with some three or four come in again, seem to condole with her. The dead body is carried away. The Poisoner woos the Queen with gifts; she seems harsh awhile, but in the end accepts love.

[Exeunt players.]

Ophelia: What means this, my lord?
Hamlet: Marry, this' miching mallico;° it means mischief.
Ophelia: Belike° this show imports the argument° of the play.

Enter Prologue.

Hamlet: We shall know by this fellow. The players cannot keep counsel;° they'll   115
tell all.
Ophelia: Will 'a tell us what this show meant?
Hamlet: Ay, or any show that you will show him. Be not you° ashamed to show, he'll
not shame to tell you what it means.
Ophelia: You are naught, you are naught.° I'll mark the play.   120
Prologue: For us, and for our tragedy,
    Here stooping° to your clemency,
    We beg your hearing patiently.   *[Exit.]*
Hamlet: Is this a prologue, or the posy of a ring?°
Ophelia: 'Tis brief, my lord.   125
Hamlet: As woman's love.

Enter [two Players as] King and Queen.

Player King: Full thirty times hath Phoebus' cart° gone round
    Neptune's salt wash° and Tellus'° orbèd ground,
    And thirty dozen moons with borrowed° sheen
    About the world have times twelve thirties been,   130
    Since love our hearts and Hymen° did our hands
    Unite commutual° in most sacred bands.°
Player Queen: So many journeys may the sun and moon
    Make us again count o'er ere love be done!
    But, woe is me, you are so sick of late,   135
    So far from cheer and from your former state,
    That I distrust° you. Yet, though I distrust,
    Discomfort° you, my lord, it nothing° must.
    For women's fear and love hold quantity;°

---

113 *this' miching mallico* this is sneaking mischief   114 *Belike* probably.   *argument* plot   115 *counsel* secret
118 *Be not you* provided you are not   120 *naught* indecent. (Ophelia is reacting to Hamlet's pointed remarks about not being ashamed to show all.)   122 *stooping* bowing   124 *posy . . . ring* brief motto in verse inscribed in a ring   127 *Phoebus' cart* the sun-god's chariot, making its yearly cycle   128 *salt wash* the sea.   *Tellus* goddess of the earth, of the *orbèd ground*   129 *borrowed* i.e., reflected   131 *Hymen* god of matrimony   132 *commutual* mutually.   *bands* bonds   137 *distrust* am anxious about   138 *Discomfort* distress.   *nothing* not at all   139 *hold quantity* keep proportion with one another

In neither aught, or in extremity.°   140
Now, what my love is, proof° hath made you know,
And as my love is sized,° my fear is so.
Where love is great, the littlest doubts are fear;
Where little fears grow great, great love grows there.
Player King: Faith, I must leave thee, love, and shortly too; 145
My operant powers° their functions leave to do.°
And thou shalt live in this fair world behind,°
Honored, beloved; and haply one as kind
For husband shalt thou—
Player Queen: O, confound the rest!
Such love must needs be treason in my breast.   150
In second husband let me be accurst!
None° wed the second but who° killed the first.
Hamlet: Wormwood,° wormwood.
Player Queen: The instances° that second marriage move°
Are base respects of thrift,° but none of love.   155
A second time I kill my husband dead
When second husband kisses me in bed.
Player King: I do believe you think what now you speak,
But what we do determine oft we break.
Purpose is but the slave to memory,°   160
Of violent birth, but poor validity,°
Which° now, like fruit unripe, sticks on the tree,
But fall unshaken when they mellow be.
Most necessary 'tis that we forget
To pay ourselves what to ourselves is debt.°   165
What to ourselves in passion we purpose,
The passion ending, doth the purpose lose.
The violence of either grief or joy
Their own enactures° with themselves destroy.
Where joy most revels, grief doth most lament;   170
Grief joys, joy grieves, on slender accident.°
This world is not for aye,° nor 'tis not strange
That even our loves should with our fortunes change;
For 'tis a question left us yet to prove,
Whether love lead fortune, or else fortune love.   175
The great man down,° you mark his favorite flies;
The poor advanced makes friends of enemies.°

---

140 *In . . . extremity* i.e., women fear and love either too little or too much, but the two, fear and love, are equal in either case 141 *proof* experience 142 *sized* in size 146 *operant powers* vital functions. *leave to do* cease to perform 147 *behind* after I have gone 152 *None* i.e., let no woman. *but who* except the one who 153 *Wormwood* i.e., how bitter. (Literally, a bitter-tasting plant.) 154 *instances* motives. *move* motivate 155 *base . . . thrift* ignoble considerations of material prosperity 160 *Purpose . . . memory* our good intentions are subject to forgetfulness 161 *validity* strength, durability 162 *Which* i.e., purpose 164–165 *Most . . . debt* it's inevitable that in time we forget the obligations we have imposed on ourselves 169 *enactures* fulfillments 170–171 *Where . . . accident* the capacity for extreme joy and grief go together, and often one extreme is instantly changed into its opposite on the slightest provocation 172 *aye* ever 176 *down* fallen in fortune 177 *The poor . . . enemies* when one of humble station is promoted, you see his enemies suddenly becoming his friends

And hitherto° doth love on fortune tend;°
For who not needs° shall never lack a friend,
And who in want° a hollow friend doth try°   180
Directly seasons him° his enemy.
But, orderly to end where I begun,
Our wills and fates do so contrary run°
That our devices still° are overthrown;
Our thoughts are ours, their ends° none of our own.   185
So think thou wilt no second husband wed,
But die thy thoughts when thy first lord is dead.

Player Queen: Nor° earth to me give food, nor heaven light,
Sport and repose lock from me day and night,°
To desperation turn my trust and hope,   190
An anchor's cheer° in prison be my scope!°
Each° opposite that blanks° the face of joy
Meet what I would have well and it destroy!
Both here and hence° pursue me lasting strife
If, once a widow, ever I be wife!   195

Hamlet: If she should break it now!

Player King: 'Tis deeply sworn. Sweet, leave me here awhile;
My spirits° grow dull, and fain I would beguile
The tedious day with sleep.

Player Queen: Sleep rock thy brain,
And never come mischance between us twain!   200

                                                                     [*He sleeps.*] *Exit* [*Player Queen*].

Hamlet: Madam, how like you this play?

Queen: The lady doth protest too much,° methinks.

Hamlet: O, but she'll keep her word.

King: Have you heard the argument?° Is there no offense° in 't?

Hamlet: No, no, they do but jest,° poison in jest. No offense i' the world.   205

King: What do you call the play?

Hamlet: *The Mousetrap.* Marry, how? Tropically.° This play is the image of a murder
done in Vienna. Gonzago is the Duke's° name, his wife, Baptista. You shall see
anon. 'Tis a knavish piece of work, but what of that? Your Majesty, and we that
have free° souls, it touches us not. Let the galled jade° wince, our withers° are   210
unwrung.°

---

178 *hitherto* up to this point in the argument, or, to this extent. *tend* attend   179 *who not needs* he who
is not in need (of wealth)   180 *who in want* he who, being in need. *try* test (his generosity)   181
seasons him ripens him into   183 *Our . . . run* what we want and what we get go so contrarily   184
devices still intentions continually   185 *ends* results   188 *Nor* let neither   189 *Sport . . . night* may day
deny me its pastimes and night its repose   191 *anchor's cheer* anchorite's or hermit's fare. *my scope* the
extent of my happiness   192–193 *Each . . . destroy* may every adverse thing that causes the face of joy to
turn pale meet and destroy everything that I desire to see prosper.   192 *blanks* causes to blanch or grow
pale   194 *hence* in the life hereafter   198 *spirits* vital spirits   202 *doth . . . much* makes too many
promises and protestations   204 *argument* plot   204–205 *offense . . . offense* cause for objection . . . . actual injury, crime   205 *jest* make believe   207 *Tropically* figuratively. (The First Quarto reading,
trapically, suggests a pun on *trap* in *Mousetrap.*)   208 *Duke's* i.e., King's. (A slip that may be due to
Shakespeare's possible source, the alleged murder of the Duke of Urbino by Luigi Gonzaga in 1538.)
210 *free* guiltless. *galled jade* horse whose hide is rubbed by saddle or harness. *withers* the part between
the horse's shoulder blades   211 *unwrung* not rubbed sore

The players perform *The Murder of Gonzago* for Queen Gertrude and King Claudius (III, ii, 125–229).

Enter Lucianus.

This is one Lucianus, nephew to the King.
Ophelia: You are as good as a chorus,° my lord.
Hamlet: I could interpret° between you and your love, if I could see the puppets dallying.°
Ophelia: You are keen, my lord, you are keen.°
Hamlet: It would cost you a groaning to take off mine edge.

215

213 *chorus* (In many Elizabethan plays, the forthcoming action was explained by an actor known as the "chorus"; at a puppet show, the actor who spoke the dialogue was known as an "interpreter," as indicated by the lines following.)   214 *interpret* (1) ventriloquize the dialogue, as in puppet show (2) act as pander 214–215 *puppets dallying* (With suggestion of sexual play, continued in lines 216–217: *keen,* "sexually aroused," *groaning,* "moaning in pregnancy," and *edge,* "sexual desire" or "impetuosity.")   216 *keen* sharp, bitter

Ophelia: Still better, and worse.°

Hamlet: So° you mis-take° your husbands. Begin, murderer; leave thy damnable faces
and begin. Come, the croaking raven doth bellow for revenge.   220

Lucianus: Thoughts black, hands apt, drugs fit, and time agreeing,
    Confederate season,° else° no creature seeing,°
    Thou mixture rank, of midnight weeds collected,
    With Hecate's ban° thrice blasted, thrice infected,
    Thy natural magic and dire property°   225
    On wholesome life usurp immediately.

                              [He pours the poison into the sleeper's ear.]

Hamlet: 'A poisons him i' the garden for his estate.° His° name's Gonzago. The
story is extant, and written in very choice Italian. You shall see anon how the
murderer gets the love of Gonzago's wife.

                                            [Claudius rises.]

Ophelia: The King rises.   230

Hamlet: What, frighted with false fire?°

Queen: How fares my lord?

Polonius: Give o'er the play.

King: Give me some light. Away!

Polonius: Lights, lights, lights!   235

                          Exeunt all but Hamlet and Horatio.

Hamlet:

    "Why,° let the strucken deer go weep,
    The hart ungallèd° play.
    For some must watch,° while some must sleep;
    Thus runs the world away."°

Would not this,° sir, and a forest of feathers°—if the rest of my fortunes turn Turk 240
with° me—with two Provincial roses° on my razed° shoes, get me a fellowship°
in a cry° of players?

Horatio: Half a share.

Hamlet: A whole one, I.

    "For thou dost know, O Damon° dear,   245
    This° realm dismantled° was
    Of Jove himself, and now reigns here
    A very, very—pajock."

---

218 *Still . . . worse* more keen, always *bettering* what other people say with witty wordplay, but at the same
time more offensive   219 *So* even thus (in marriage).   *mis-take* take falseheartedly and cheat on. (The
marriage vows say "for better, for worse.")   222 *Confederate season* the time and occasion conspiring (to assist the murderer).   *else* otherwise.   *seeing* seeing me   224 *Hecate's ban* the curse of Hecate, the goddess of
witchcraft   225 *dire property* baleful quality   227 *estate* i.e., the kingship.   *His* i.e., the King's   231 *false
fire* the blank discharge of a gun loaded with powder but no shot   236–239 *Why . . . away* (Probably from
an old ballad, with allusion to the popular belief that a wounded deer retires to weep and die; compare with
As You Like It, II, i, 33–66.)   237 *ungallèd* unafflicted   238 *watch* remain awake   239 *Thus . . . away* thus
the world goes   240 *this* i.e., the play.   *feathers* (Allusion to the plumes that Elizabethan actors were fond
of wearing.)   240–241 *turn Turk with* turn renegade against, go back on   241 *Provincial roses* rosettes of
ribbon, named for roses grown in a part of France.   *razed* with ornamental slashing.   *fellowship . . . players*
partnership in a theatrical company.   242 *cry* pack (of hounds)   245 *Damon* the friend of Pythias, as Horatio is friend of Hamlet; or, a traditional pastoral name   246–248 *This realm . . . pajock* i.e., Jove, representing divine authority and justice, has abandoned this realm to its own devices, leaving in his stead only a
peacock or vain pretender to virtue (though the rhyme-word expected in place of *pajock* or "peacock" suggests that the realm is now ruled over by an "ass").   246 *dismantled* stripped, divested

Horatio: You might have rhymed.

Hamlet: O good Horatio, I'll take the ghost's word for a thousand pound. Didst 250
perceive?

Horatio: Very well, my lord.

Hamlet: Upon the talk of the poisoning?

Horatio: I did very well note him.

Enter Rosencrantz and Guildenstern.

Hamlet: Aha! Come, some music! Come, the recorders.° 255
"For if the King like not the comedy,
Why then, belike, he likes it not, perdy."°
Come, some music.

Guildenstern: Good my lord, vouchsafe me a word with you.

Hamlet: Sir, a whole history. 260

Guildenstern: The King, sir—

Hamlet: Ay, sir, what of him?

Guildenstern: Is in his retirement° marvelous distempered.°

Hamlet: With drink, sir?

Guildenstern: No, my lord, with choler. 265

Hamlet: Your wisdom should show itself more richer to signify this to the doctor, for
for me to put him to his purgation° would perhaps plunge him into more choler.°

Guildenstern: Good my lord, put your discourse into some frame° and start° not so
wildly from my affair.

Hamlet: I am tame, sir. Pronounce. 270

Guildenstern: The Queen, your mother, in most great affliction of spirit, hath sent
me to you.

Hamlet: You are welcome.

Guildenstern: Nay, good my lord, this courtesy is not of the right breed.° If it shall
please you to make me a wholesome answer, I will do your mother's command- 275
ment; if not, your pardon° and my return shall be the end of my business.

Hamlet: Sir, I cannot.

Rosencrantz: What, my lord?

Hamlet: Make you a wholesome answer; my wit's diseased. But, sir, such answer as
I can make, you shall command, or rather, as you say, my mother. Therefore no 280
more, but to the matter. My mother, you say—

Rosencrantz: Then thus she says: your behavior hath struck her into amazement and
admiration.°

Hamlet: O wonderful son, that can so stonish a mother! But is there no sequel at the
heels of this mother's admiration? Impart. 285

Rosencrantz: She desires to speak with you in her closet° ere you go to bed.

Hamlet: We shall obey, were she ten times our mother. Have you any further trade
with us?

255 *recorders* wind instruments of the flute kind   257 *perdy* (A corruption of the French *par dieu,* "by God.")
263 *retirement* withdrawal to his chambers.   *distempered* out of humor. (But Hamlet deliberately plays on the
wider application to any illness of mind or body, especially to drunkenness.)   267 *purgation* (Hamlet hints at
something going beyond medical treatment to blood-letting and the extraction of confession.).   *choler*
anger. (But Hamlet takes the word in its more basic humoral sense of "bilious disorder.")   268 *frame* order.
start shy or jump away (like a horse; the opposite of *tame* in line 270)   274 *breed* (1) kind (2) breeding, manners   276 *pardon* permission to depart   283 *admiration* bewilderment   286 *closet* private chamber

Rosencrantz: My lord, you once did love me.

Hamlet: And do still, by these pickers and stealers.° 290

Rosencrantz: Good my lord, what is your cause of distemper? You do surely bar the door upon your own liberty° if you deny° your griefs to your friend.

Hamlet: Sir, I lack advancement.

Rosencrantz: How can that be, when you have the voice of the King himself for your succession in Denmark? 295

Hamlet: Ay, sir, but "While the grass grows"°—the proverb is something° musty.

Enter the Players° with recorders.

O, the recorders. Let me see one. [*He takes a recorder.*] To withdraw° with you: why do you go about to recover the wind° of me, as if you would drive me into a toil?°

Guildenstern: O, my lord, if my duty be too bold, my love is too unmannerly.° 300

Hamlet: I do not well understand that.° Will you play upon this pipe?

Guildenstern: My lord, I cannot.

Hamlet: I pray you.

Guildenstern: Believe me, I cannot.

Hamlet: I do beseech you. 305

Guildenstern: I know no touch of it, my lord.

Hamlet: It is as easy as lying. Govern these ventages° with your fingers and thumb, give it breath with your mouth, and it will discourse most eloquent music. Look you, these are the stops.

Guildenstern: But these cannot I command to any utterance of harmony. I have not 310 the skill.

Hamlet: Why, look you now, how unworthy a thing you make of me! You would play upon me, you would seem to know my stops, you would pluck out the heart of my mystery, you would sound° me from my lowest note to the top of my compass,° and there is much music, excellent voice, in this little organ,° yet cannot you 315 make it speak. 'Sblood, do you think I am easier to be played on than a pipe? Call me what instrument you will, though you can fret° me, you cannot play upon me.

Enter Polonius.

God bless you, sir!

Polonius: My lord, the Queen would speak with you, and presently.° 320

Hamlet: Do you see yonder cloud that's almost in shape of a camel?

Polonius: By the Mass and 'tis, like a camel indeed.

Hamlet: Methinks it is like a weasel.

---

290 *pickers and stealers* i.e., hands. (So called from the catechism, "to keep my hands from picking and stealing.") 292 *liberty* i.e., being freed from *distemper*, line 291; but perhaps with a veiled threat as well. *deny* refuse to share 296 *While . . . grows* (The rest of the proverb is "the silly horse starves"; Hamlet may not live long enough to succeed to the kingdom.) *something* somewhat. s.d. *Players* actors 297 *withdraw* speak privately 298 *recover the wind* get to the windward side (thus driving the game into the *toil*, or "net") 299 *toil* snare 300 *if . . . unmannerly* if I am using an unmannerly boldness, it is my love that occasions it 301 *I . . . that* i.e., I don't understand how genuine love can be unmannerly 307 *ventages* finger-holes or *stops* (line 313) of the recorder 314 *sound* (1) fathom (2) produce sound in. *compass* range (of voice) 315 *organ* musical instrument 317 *fret* irritate (with a quibble on *fret*, meaning the piece of wood, gut, or metal that regulates the fingering on an instrument) 320 *presently* at once

Polonius: It is backed like a weasel.

Hamlet: Or like a whale.   325

Polonius: Very like a whale.

Hamlet: Then I will come to my mother by and by.° [*Aside.*] They fool me° to the top
of my bent.°—I will come by and by.

Polonius: I will say so.   [*Exit.*]

Hamlet: "By and by" is easily said. Leave me, friends.   330

[*Exeunt all but Hamlet.*]

'Tis now the very witching time° of night,
When churchyards yawn and hell itself breathes out
Contagion to this world. Now could I drink hot blood
And do such bitter business as the day
Would quake to look on. Soft, now to my mother.   335
O heart, lose not thy nature!° Let not ever
The soul of Nero° enter this firm bosom.
Let me be cruel, not unnatural;
I will speak daggers to her, but use none.
My tongue and soul in this be hypocrites: 340
How in my words soever° she be shent,°
To give them seals° never my soul consent!   *Exit.*

SCENE III [THE CASTLE.]

Enter King, Rosencrantz, and Guildenstern.

King: I like him° not, nor stands it safe with us
To let his madness range. Therefore prepare you.
I your commission will forthwith dispatch,°
And he to England shall along with you.
The terms of our estate° may not endure   5
Hazard so near us as doth hourly grow
Out of his brows.°

Guildenstern: We will ourselves provide.
Most holy and religious fear° it is
To keep those many many bodies safe
That live and feed upon Your Majesty.   10

Rosencrantz: The single and peculiar° life is bound
With all the strength and armor of the mind
To keep itself from noyance,° but much more
That spirit upon whose weal depends and rests
The lives of many. The cess° of majesty   15
Dies not alone, but like a gulf° doth draw

---

327 *by and by* quite soon.   *fool me* trifle with me, humor my fooling   327–328 *top of my bent* limit of my
ability or endurance. (Literally, the extent to which a bow may be bent.)   331 *witching time* time when
spells are cast and evil is abroad   336 *nature* natural feeling   337 *Nero* murderer of his mother, Agrippina
341 *How . . . soever* however much by my words.   *shent* rebuked   342 *give them seals* i.e., confirm them
with deeds   1 *him* i.e., his behavior   3 *dispatch* prepare, cause to be drawn up   5 *terms of our estate* circumstances of my royal position   7 *Out of his brows* i.e., from his brain, in the form of plots and threats   8
religious fear sacred concern   11 *single and peculiar* individual and private   13 *noyance* harm   15 *cess*
decrease, cessation   16 *gulf* whirlpool

What's near it with it; or it is a massy° wheel
Fixed on the summit of the highest mount,
To whose huge spokes ten thousand lesser things
Are mortised° and adjoined, which, when it falls,°   20
Each small annexment, petty consequence,°
Attends° the boisterous ruin. Never alone
Did the King sigh, but with a general groan.

King: Arm° you, I pray you, to this speedy voyage,
For we will fetters put about this fear,   25
Which now goes too free-footed.

Rosencrantz: We will haste us.

                           Exeunt gentlemen [Rosencrantz and Guildenstern].

Enter Polonius.

Polonius: My lord, he's going to his mother's closet.
Behind the arras° I'll convey myself
To hear the process.° I'll warrant she'll tax him home,°
And, as you said—and wisely was it said—   30
'Tis meet° that some more audience than a mother,
Since nature makes them partial, should o'erhear
The speech, of vantage.° Fare you well, my liege.
I'll call upon you ere you go to bed
And tell you what I know.

King: Thanks, dear my lord.   35

                                   Exit [Polonius].

O, my offense is rank! It smells to heaven.
It hath the primal eldest curse° upon 't,
A brother's murder. Pray can I not,
Though inclination be as sharp as will;°
My stronger guilt defeats my strong intent,   40
And like a man to double business bound°
I stand in pause where I shall first begin,
And both neglect. What if this cursèd hand
Were thicker than itself with brother's blood,
Is there not rain enough in the sweet heavens   45
To wash it white as snow? Whereto serves mercy
But to confront the visage of offense?°
And what's in prayer but this twofold force,
To be forestallèd° ere we come to fall,

---

17 *massy* massive   20 *mortised* fastened (as with a fitted joint).   *when it falls* i.e., when it descends, like
the wheel of Fortune, bringing a king down with it   21 *Each . . . consequence* i.e., every hanger-on and
unimportant person or thing connected with the King   22 *Attends* participates in   24 *Arm* prepare   28
arras screen of tapestry placed around the walls of household apartments. (On the Elizabethan stage, the
arras was presumably over a door or discovery space in the tiring-house facade.)   29 *process* proceedings.
tax him home reprove him severely   31 *meet* fitting   33 *of vantage* from an advantageous place, or, in addition   37 *the primal eldest curse* the curse of Cain, the first murderer; he killed his brother Abel   39 *Though
. . . will* though my desire is as strong as my determination   41 *bound* (1) destined (2) obliged. (The King
wants to repent and still enjoy what he has gained.)   46–47 *Whereto . . . offense* what function does
mercy serve other than to meet sin face to face?   49 *forestallèd* prevented (from sinning)

Or pardoned being down? Then I'll look up. 50
My fault is past. But O, what form of prayer
Can serve my turn? "Forgive me my foul murder"?
That cannot be, since I am still possessed
Of those effects for which I did the murder:
My crown, mine own ambition, and my queen. 55
May one be pardoned and retain th' offense?°
In the corrupted currents° of this world
Offense's gilded hand° may shove° by justice,
And oft 'tis seen the wicked prize° itself
Buys out the law. But 'tis not so above. 60
There° is no shuffling,° there the action lies°
In his° true nature, and we ourselves compelled,
Even to the teeth and forehead° of our faults,
To give in° evidence. What then? What rests?°
Try what repentance can. What can it not? 65
Yet what can it, when one cannot repent?
O wretched state, O bosom black as death,
O limèd° soul that, struggling to be free,
Art more engaged!° Help, angels! Make assay.°
Bow, stubborn knees, and heart with strings of steel, 70
Be soft as sinews of the newborn babe!
All may be well.   [*He kneels.*]

Enter Hamlet.

Hamlet: Now might I do it pat,° now 'a is a-praying;
And now I'll do 't. [*He draws his sword.*] And so 'a goes to heaven,
And so am I revenged. That would be scanned:° 75
A villain kills my father, and for that,
I, his sole son, do this same villain send
To heaven.
Why, this is hire and salary, not revenge.
'A took my father grossly, full of bread,° 80
With all his crimes broad blown,° as flush° as May;
And how his audit° stands who knows save° heaven?
But in our circumstance and course of thought°
'Tis heavy with him. And am I then revenged,
To take him in the purging of his soul, 85
When he is fit and seasoned° for his passage?

---

56 *th' offense* the thing for which one offended   57 *currents* courses   58 *gilded hand* hand offering gold as a bribe.   *shove by* thrust aside   59 *wicked prize* prize won by wickedness   61 *There* i.e., in heaven.   *shuffling* escape by trickery.   *the action lies* the accusation is made manifest. (A legal metaphor.)   62 *his* its   63 *to the teeth and forehead* face to face, concealing nothing   64 *give in* provide.   *rests* remains   68 *limèd* caught as with birdlime, a sticky substance used to ensnare birds   69 *engaged* entangled.   *assay* trial. (Said to himself.)   73 *pat* opportunely   75 *would be scanned* needs to be looked into, or, would be interpreted as follows   80 *grossly, full of bread* i.e., enjoying his worldly pleasures rather than fasting. (See Ezekiel 16:49.)   81 *crimes broad blown* sins in full bloom.   *flush* vigorous   82 *audit* account.   *save* except for   83 *in . . . thought* as we see it from our mortal perspective   86 *seasoned* matured, readied

Hamlet stops himself from killing Claudius during his prayers (III, iii, 73–96).

No!
Up, sword, and know° thou a more horrid hent.°

[*He puts up his sword.*]

When he is drunk asleep, or in his rage,°
Or in th' incestuous pleasure of his bed,   90
At game,° a-swearing, or about some act
That has no relish° of salvation in 't—
Then trip him, that his heels may kick at heaven,
And that his soul may be as damned and black
As hell, whereto it goes. My mother stays.°   95
This physic° but prolongs thy sickly days.   *Exit.*

88 *know . . . hent* await to be grasped by me on a more horrid occasion.   *hent* act of seizing   89 *drunk . . . rage* dead drunk, or in a fit of sexual passion   91 *game* gambling   92 *relish* trace, savor   95 *stays* awaits (me)   96 *physic* purging (by prayer), or, Hamlet's postponement of the killing

King: My words fly up, my thoughts remain below.
　　Words without thoughts never to heaven go.　　　　　　　　　　　　　*Exit.*

SCENE IV [THE QUEEN'S PRIVATE CHAMBER.]

　　Enter [Queen] Gertrude and Polonius.

Polonius: 'A will come straight. Look you lay home° to him.
　　Tell him his pranks have been too broad° to bear with,
　　And that Your Grace hath screened and stood between
　　Much heat° and him. I'll shroud° me even here.
　　Pray you, be round° with him.　　　　　　　　　　　　　　　　　　　　　5
Hamlet (within): Mother, Mother, Mother!
Queen: I'll warrant you, fear me not.
　　Withdraw, I hear him coming.

　　　　　　　　　　　　　　　　　　　　　　[*Polonius hides behind the arras.*]

　　Enter Hamlet.

Hamlet: Now, Mother, what's the matter?
Queen: Hamlet, thou hast thy father° much offended.　　　　　　　　　　10
Hamlet: Mother, you have my father much offended.
Queen: Come, come, you answer with an idle° tongue.
Hamlet: Go, go, you question with a wicked tongue.
Queen: Why, how now, Hamlet?
Hamlet:　　　　　　　　　　　What's the matter now?
Queen: Have you forgot me?°
Hamlet:　　　　　　　　　　　No, by the rood,° not so:　　　　　　　　　15
　　You are the Queen, your husband's brother's wife,
　　And—would it were not so!—you are my mother.
Queen: Nay, then, I'll set those to you that can speak.°
Hamlet: Come, come, and sit you down; you shall not budge.
　　You go not till I set you up a glass　　　　　　　　　　　　　　　　　20
　　Where you may see the inmost part of you.
Queen: What wilt thou do? Thou wilt not murder me?
　　Help, ho!
Polonius [*behind the arras*]: What ho! Help!
Hamlet [*drawing*]: How now? A rat? Dead for a ducat,° dead!　　　　25
　　　　　　　　　　　　　　　　[*He thrusts his rapier through the arras.*]
Polonius [*behind the arras*]: O, I am slain!　　　　　　　　[*He falls and dies.*]
Queen:　　　　　　　　　　　O me, what has thou done?
Hamlet: Nay, I know not. Is it the King?
Queen: O, what a rash and bloody deed is this!
Hamlet: A bloody deed—almost as bad, good Mother,
　　As kill a king, and marry with his brother.　　　　　　　　　　　　30

---

1 *lay home* thrust to the heart, reprove him soundly　2 *broad* unrestrained　4 *Much heat* i.e., the King's anger.
shroud conceal (with ironic fitness to Polonius' imminent death. The word is only in the First Quarto; the Second Quarto and the Folio read "silence.")　5 *round* blunt　10 *thy father* i.e., your stepfather, Claudius　12 *idle*
foolish　15 *forgot me* i.e., forgotten that I am your mother.　*rood* cross of Christ　18 *speak* i.e., to someone so
rude　25 *Dead for a ducat* i.e., I bet a ducat he's dead; or, a ducat is his life's fee

Queen: As kill a king!

Hamlet: Ay, lady, it was my word.

> [*He parts the arras and discovers Polonius.*]

Thou wretched, rash, intruding fool, farewell!
I took thee for thy better. Take thy fortune.
Thou find'st to be too busy° is some danger.—
Leave wringing of your hands. Peace, sit you down,   35
And let me wring your heart, for so I shall,
If it be made of penetrable stuff,
If damnèd custom° have not brazed° it so
That it be proof° and bulwark against sense.°

Queen: What have I done, that thou dar'st wag thy tongue   40
In noise so rude against me?

Hamlet: Such an act
That blurs the grace and blush of modesty,
Calls virtue hypocrite, takes off the rose
From the fair forehead of an innocent love
And sets a blister° there, makes marriage vows   45
As false as dicers' oaths. O, such a deed
As from the body of contraction° plucks
The very soul, and sweet religion makes°
A rhapsody° of words. Heaven's face does glow
O'er this solidity and compound mass   50
With tristful visage, as against the doom,
Is thought-sick at the act.°

Queen: Ay me, what act,
That roars so loud and thunders in the index?°

Hamlet [*showing her two likenesses*]: Look here upon this picture, and on this,
The counterfeit presentment° of two brothers.   55
See what a grace was seated on this brow:
Hyperion's° curls, the front° of Jove himself,
An eye like Mars° to threaten and command,
A station° like the herald Mercury°
New-lighted° on a heaven-kissing hill—   60
A combination and a form indeed
Where every god did seem to set his seal°
To give the world assurance of a man.
This was your husband. Look you now what follows:
Here is your husband, like a mildewed ear,°   65
Blasting° his wholesome brother. Have you eyes?

---

34 *busy* nosey   38 *damnèd custom* habitual wickedness. *brazed* brazened, hardened   39 *proof* armor. *sense* feeling   45 *sets a blister* i.e., brands as a harlot   47 *contraction* the marriage contract   48 *sweet religion makes* i.e., makes marriage vows   49 *rhapsody* senseless string   49–52 *Heaven's . . . act* heaven's face blushes at this solid world compounded of the various elements, with sorrowful face as though the day of doom were near, and is sick with horror at the deed (i.e., Gertrude's marriage)   53 *index* table of contents, prelude or preface   55 *counterfeit presentment* portrayed representation   57 *Hyperion's* the sun-god's. *front* brow   58 *Mars* god of war   59 *station* manner of standing. *Mercury* winged messenger of the gods   60 *New-lighted* newly alighted   62 *set his seal* i.e., affix his approval   65 *ear* i.e., of grain   66 *Blasting* blighting

Could you on this fair mountain leave° to feed
And batten° on this moor?° Ha, have you eyes?
You cannot call it love, for at your age
The heyday° in the blood° is tame, it's humble,   70
And waits upon the judgment, and what judgment
Would step from this to this? Sense,° sure, you have,
Else could you not have motion, but sure that sense
Is apoplexed,° for madness would not err,°
Nor sense to ecstasy was ne'er so thralled,   75
But° it reserved some quantity of choice
To serve in such a difference.° What devil was 't
That thus hath cozened° you at hoodman-blind?°
Eyes without feeling, feeling without sight,
Ears without hands or eyes, smelling sans° all,   80
Or but a sickly part of one true sense
Could not so mope.° O shame, where is thy blush?
Rebellious hell,
If thou canst mutine° in a matron's bones,
To flaming youth let virtue be as wax   85
And melt in her own fire.° Proclaim no shame
When the compulsive ardor gives the charge,
Since frost itself as actively doth burn,
And reason panders will.°
Queen: O Hamlet, speak no more!   90
Thou turn'st mine eyes into my very soul,
And there I see such black and grainèd° spots
As will not leave their tinct.°
Hamlet: Nay, but to live
In the rank sweat of an enseamèd° bed,
Stewed° in corruption, honeying and making love   95
Over the nasty sty!
Queen: O, speak to me no more!
These words like daggers enter in my ears.
No more, sweet Hamlet!
Hamlet: A murderer and a villain,
A slave that is not twentieth part the tithe°   100

67 *leave* cease 68 *batten* gorge. *moor* barren or marshy ground (suggesting also "dark-skinned") 70 *heyday* state of excitement. *blood* passion 72 *Sense* perception through the five senses (the functions of the middle or sensible soul) 74 *apoplexed* paralyzed. (Hamlet goes on to explain that, without such a paralysis of will, mere madness would not so err, nor would the five senses so enthrall themselves to *ecstasy* or lunacy; even such deranged states of mind would be able to make the obvious choice between Hamlet Senior and Claudius.) *err* so err 76 *But* but that 77 *To . . . difference* to help in making a choice between two such men 78 *cozened* cheated. *hoodman-blind* blindman's buff. (In this game, says Hamlet, the devil must have pushed Claudius toward Gertrude while she was blindfolded.) 80 *sans* without 82 *mope* be dazed, act aimlessly 84 *mutine* incite mutiny 85–86 *be as wax . . . fire* melt like a candle or stick of sealing wax held over the candle flame 86–89 *Proclaim . . . will* call it no shameful business when the compelling ardor of youth delivers the attack, i.e., commits lechery, since the *frost* of advanced age burns with as active a fire of lust and reason perverts itself by fomenting lust rather than restraining it 92 *grainèd* dyed in grain, indelible 93 *leave their tinct* surrender their color 94 *enseamèd* saturated in the grease and filth of passionate lovemaking 95 *Stewed* soaked, bathed (with a suggestion of "stew," brothel) 100 *tithe* tenth part

Of your precedent lord,° a vice° of kings,
A cutpurse of the empire and the rule,
That from a shelf the precious diadem stole
And put it in his pocket!

Queen: No more!   105

Enter Ghost.

Hamlet: A king of shreds and patches°—
Save me, and hover o'er me with your wings,
You heavenly guards! What would your gracious figure?

Queen: Alas, he's mad!

Hamlet: Do you not come your tardy son to chide,   110
That, lapsed° in time and passion, lets go by
Th' important° acting of your dread command?
O, say!

Ghost: Do not forget. This visitation
Is but to whet thy almost blunted purpose.   115
But look, amazement° on thy mother sits.
O, step between her and her fighting soul!
Conceit° in weakest bodies strongest works.
Speak to her, Hamlet.

Hamlet: How is it with you, lady?

Queen: Alas, how is 't with you,   120
That you do bend your eye on vacancy,
And with th' incorporal° air do hold discourse?
Forth at your eyes your spirits wildly peep,
And, as the sleeping soldiers in th' alarm,°
Your bedded° hairs, like life in excrements,°   125
Start up and stand on end. O gentle son,
Upon the heat and flame of thy distemper°
Sprinkle cool patience. Whereon do you look?

Hamlet: On him, on him! Look you how pale he glares!
His form and cause conjoined,° preaching to stones,   130
Would make them capable.°—Do not look upon me,
Lest with this piteous action you convert
My stern effects.° Then what I have to do
Will want true color—tears perchance for blood.°

Queen: To whom do you speak this?   135

Hamlet: Do you see nothing there?

Queen: Nothing at all, yet all that is I see.

---

101 *precedent lord* former husband. *vice* buffoon. (A reference to the Vice of the morality plays.)
106 *shreds and patches* i.e., motley, the traditional costume of the clown or fool 111 *lapsed* delaying
112 *important* importunate, urgent 116 *amazement* distraction 118 *Conceit* imagination 122 *incorporal*
immaterial 124 *as . . . alarm* like soldiers called out of sleep by an alarm 125 *bedded* laid flat. *like life
in excrements* i.e., as though hair, an outgrowth of the body, had a life of its own. (Hair was thought to be
lifeless because it lacks sensation, and so its standing on end would be unnatural and ominous.) 127
distemper disorder 130 *His . . . conjoined* his appearance joined to his cause for speaking 131 *capable*
receptive 132–133 *convert . . . effects* divert me from my stern duty 134 *want . . . blood* lack plausibil-
ity so that (with a play on the normal sense of *color*) I shall shed colorless tears instead of blood

Hamlet: Nor did you nothing hear?

Queen: No, nothing but ourselves.

Hamlet: Why, look you there, look how it steals away!   140
 My father, in his habit° as° he lived!
 Look where he goes even now out at the portal!

                                                       Exit Ghost.

Queen: This is the very° coinage of your brain.
 This bodiless creation ecstasy
 Is very cunning in.°   145

Hamlet: Ecstasy?
 My pulse as yours doth temperately keep time,
 And makes as healthful music. It is not madness
 That I have uttered. Bring me to the test,
 And I the matter will reword,° which madness   150
 Would gambol° from. Mother, for love of grace,
 Lay not that flattering unction° to your soul
 That not your trespass but my madness speaks.
 It will but skin° and film the ulcerous place,
 Whiles rank corruption, mining° all within,   155
 Infects unseen. Confess yourself to heaven,
 Repent what's past, avoid what is to come,
 And do not spread the compost° on the weeds
 To make them ranker. Forgive me this my virtue;°
 For in the fatness° of these pursy° times   160
 Virtue itself of vice must pardon beg,
 Yea, curb° and woo for leave° to do him good.

Queen: O Hamlet, thou hast cleft my heart in twain.

Hamlet: O, throw away the worser part of it,
 And live the purer with the other half.   165
 Good night. But go not to my uncle's bed;
 Assume a virtue, if you have it not.
 That monster, custom, who all sense doth eat,°
 Of habits devil,° is angel yet in this,
 That to the use of actions fair and good   170
 He likewise gives a frock or livery°
 That aptly° is put on. Refrain tonight,
 And that shall lend a kind of easiness
 To the next abstinence; the next more easy;
 For use° almost can change the stamp of nature,°   175
 And either° . . . the devil, or throw him out

---

141 *habit* clothes. *as* as when   143 *very* mere   144–145 *This . . . in* madness is skillful in creating this kind of hallucination   150 *reword* repeat word for word   151 *gambol* skip away   152 *unction* ointment   154 *skin* grow a skin for   155 *mining* working under the surface   158 *compost* manure   159 *this my virtue* my virtuous talk in reproving you   160 *fatness* grossness. *pursy* flabby, out of shape   162 *curb* bow, bend the knee. *leave* permission   168 *who . . . eat* which consumes all proper or natural feeling, all sensibility   169 *Of habits devil* devillike in prompting evil habits   171 *livery* an outer appearance, a customary garb (and hence a predisposition easily assumed in time of stress)   172 *aptly* readily   175 *use* habit. *the stamp of nature* our inborn traits   176 *And either* (A defective line, usually emended by inserting the word *master* after *either*, following the Fourth Quarto and early editors.)

With wondrous potency. Once more, good night;
And when you are desirous to be blest,
I'll blessing beg of you.° For this same lord,

[*pointing to Polonius*]

I do repent; but heaven hath pleased it so   180
To punish me with this, and this with me,
That I must be their scourge and minister.°
I will bestow° him, and will answer° well
The death I gave him. So, again, good night.
I must be cruel only to be kind.   185
This° bad begins, and worse remains behind.°
One word more, good lady.
Queen: What shall I do?
Hamlet: Not this by no means that I bid you do:
Let the bloat° king tempt you again to bed,
Pinch wanton° on your cheek, call you his mouse,   190
And let him, for a pair of reechy° kisses,
Or paddling° in your neck with his damned fingers,
Make you to ravel all this matter out°
That I essentially am not in madness,
But mad in craft.° 'Twere good° you let him know,   195
For who that's but a queen, fair, sober, wise,
Would from a paddock,° from a bat, a gib,°
Such dear concernings° hide? Who would do so?
No, in despite of sense and secrecy,°
Unpeg the basket° on the house's top,   200
Let the birds fly, and like the famous ape,°
To try conclusions,° in the basket creep
And break your own neck down.°
Queen: Be thou assured, if words be made of breath,
And breath of life, I have no life to breathe   205
What thou hast said to me.
Hamlet: I must to England. You know that?
Queen: Alack,
I had forgot. 'Tis so concluded on.
Hamlet: There's letters sealed, and my two schoolfellows,
Whom I will trust as I will adders fanged,   210
They bear the mandate; they must sweep my way

178–179 *when . . . you* i.e., when you are ready to be penitent and seek God's blessing, I will ask your blessing as a dutiful son should 182 *their scourge and minister* i.e., agent of heavenly retribution. (By *scourge*, Hamlet also suggests that he himself will eventually suffer punishment in the process of fulfilling heaven's will.) 183 *bestow* stow, dispose of. *answer* account or pay for 186 *This* i.e., the killing of Polonius. *behind* to come 189 *bloat* bloated 190 *Pinch wanton* i.e., leave his love pinches on your cheeks, branding you as wanton 191 *reechy* dirty, filthy 192 *paddling* fingering amorously 193 *ravel . . . out* unravel, disclose 195 *in craft* by cunning. *good* (Said sarcastically; also the following eight lines.) 197 *paddock* toad. *gib* tomcat 198 *dear concernings* important affairs 199 *sense and secrecy* secrecy that common sense requires 200 *Unpeg the basket* open the cage, i.e., let out the secret 201 *famous ape* (In a story now lost.) 202 *try conclusions* test the outcome (in which the ape apparently enters a cage from which birds have been released and then tries to fly out of the cage as they have done, falling to its death) 203 *down* in the fall: utterly

And marshal me to knavery.° Let it work.°
For 'tis the sport to have the engineer°
Hoist with° his own petard,° and 't shall go hard
But I will° delve one yard below their mines° 215
And blow them at the moon. O, 'tis most sweet
When in one line° two crafts° directly meet.
This man shall set me packing.°
I'll lug the guts into the neighbor room.
Mother, good night indeed. This counselor 220
Is now most still, most secret, and most grave,
Who was in life a foolish prating knave.—
Come, sir, to draw toward an end° with you.—
Good night, Mother.

Exeunt [separately, Hamlet dragging in Polonius].

ACT IV

SCENE I [THE CASTLE.]

Enter King and Queen,° with Rosencrantz and Guildenstern.

King: There's matter° in these sighs, these profound heaves.°
You must translate; 'tis fit we understand them.
Where is your son?
Queen: Bestow this place on us a little while.

[Exeunt Rosencrantz and Guildenstern.]
Ah, mine own lord, what have I seen tonight! 5
King: What, Gertrude? How does Hamlet?
Queen: Mad as the sea and wind when both contend
Which is the mightier. In his lawless fit,
Behind the arras hearing something stir,
Whips out his rapier, cries, "A rat, a rat!"
And in this brainish apprehension° kills 10
The unseen good old man.
King: O heavy° deed!
It had been so with us,° had we been there.
His liberty is full of threats to all—

211–212 *sweep . . . knavery* sweep a path before me and conduct me to some *knavery* or treachery prepared for me 212 *work* proceed 213 *enginer* maker of military contrivances 214 *Hoist with* blown up by. *petard* an explosive used to blow in a door or make a breach 214–215 *'t shall . . . will* unless luck is against me, I will 215 *mines* tunnels used in warfare to undermine the enemy's emplacements: Hamlet will countermine by going under their mines 217 *in one line* i.e., mines and countermines on a collision course, or the countermines directly below the mines. *crafts* acts of guile, plots 218 *set me packing* set me to making schemes, and set me to lugging (him), and, also, send me off in a hurry 223 *draw . . . end* finish up (with a pun on *draw*, "pull") s.d. *Enter . . . Queen* (Some editors argue that Gertrude never exits in Act III, Scene iv, and that the scene is continuous here, as suggested in the Folio, but the Second Quarto marks an entrance for her and at line 35 Claudius speaks of Gertrude's *closet* as though it were elsewhere. A short time has elapsed, during which the King has become aware of her highly wrought emotional state.) 1 *matter* significance. *heaves* heavy sighs 11 *brainish apprehension* headstrong conception 12 *heavy* grievous 13 *us* i.e., me. (The royal "we"; also in line 15.)

To you yourself, to us, to everyone.   15
Alas, how shall this bloody deed be answered?°
It will be laid to us, whose providence°
Should have kept short,° restrained, and out of haunt°
This mad young man. But so much was our love,
We would not understand what was most fit,   20
But, like the owner of a foul disease,
To keep it from divulging,° let it feed
Even on the pith of life. Where is he gone?
Queen: To draw apart the body he hath killed,
O'er whom his very madness, like some ore°   25
Among a mineral° of metals base,
Shows itself pure: 'a weeps for what is done.
King: O Gertrude, come away!
The sun no sooner shall the mountains touch
But we will ship him hence, and this vile deed   30
We must with all our majesty and skill
Both countenance° and excuse.—Ho, Guildenstern!

Enter Rosencrantz and Guildenstern.

Friends both, go join you with some further aid.
Hamlet in madness hath Polonius slain,
And from his mother's closet hath he dragged him.   35
Go seek him out, speak fair, and bring the body
Into the chapel. I pray you, haste in this.

                    [Exeunt Rosencrantz and Guildenstern.]

Come, Gertrude, we'll call up our wisest friends
And let them know both what we mean to do
And what's untimely done . . . .°   40
Whose whisper o'er the world's diameter,°
As level° as the cannon to his blank,°
Transports his poisoned shot, may miss our name
And hit the woundless° air. O, come away!
My soul is full of discord and dismay.   *Exeunt.*   45

SCENE II [THE CASTLE.]

Enter Hamlet.

Hamlet: Safely stowed.
Rosencrantz, Guildenstern (within): Hamlet! Lord Hamlet!
Hamlet: But soft, what noise? Who calls on Hamlet? O, here they come.

Enter Rosencrantz and Guildenstern.

---

16 *answered* explained   17 *providence* foresight   18 *short* i.e., on a short tether.   *out of haunt* secluded
22 *divulging* becoming evident   25 *ore* vein of gold   26 *mineral* mine   32 *countenance* put the best face on
40 *And . . . done* (A defective line: conjectures as to the missing words include *So, haply, slander* [Capell
and others]; *For, haply, slander* [Theobald and others]; and *So envious slander* [Jenkins].)   41 *diameter* extent from side to side   42 *As level* with as direct aim.   *his blank* its target at point-blank range   44
woundless invulnerable

Rosencrantz: What have you done, my lord, with the dead body?

Hamlet: Compounded it with dust, whereto 'tis kin. 5

Rosencrantz: Tell us where 'tis, that we may take it thence
 And bear it to the chapel.

Hamlet: Do not believe it.

Rosencrantz: Believe what?

Hamlet: That I can keep your counsel and not mine own.° Besides, to be demanded 10
of° a sponge, what replication° should be made by the son of a king?

Rosencrantz: Take you me for a sponge, my lord?

Hamlet: Ay, sir, that soaks up the King's countenance,° his rewards, his authorities.°
But such officers do the King best service in the end. He keeps them, like an ape,
an apple, in the corner of his jaw, first mouthed to be last swallowed. When he 15
needs what you have gleaned, it is but squeezing you, and, sponge, you shall be
dry again.

Rosencrantz: I understand you not, my lord.

Hamlet: I am glad of it. A knavish speech sleeps in° a foolish ear.

Rosencrantz: My lord, you must tell us where the body is and go with us to the King. 20

Hamlet: The body is with the King, but the King is not with the body.° The King is a
thing—

Guildenstern: A thing, my lord?

Hamlet: Of nothing.° Bring me to him. Hide fox, and all after!°

Exeunt [running].

SCENE III [THE CASTLE.]

Enter King, and two or three.

King: I have sent to seek him, and to find the body.
 How dangerous is it that this man goes loose!
 Yet must not we put the strong law on him.
 He's loved of° the distracted° multitude,
 Who like not in their judgment, but their eyes,° 5
 And where 'tis so, th' offender's scourge° is weighed,°
 But never the offense. To bear all smooth and even,°
 This sudden sending him away must seem
 Deliberate pause.° Diseases desperate grown
 By desperate appliance° are relieved, 10
 Or not at all.

---

10 *That . . . own* i.e., that I can follow your advice (by telling where the body is) and still keep my own secret 10–11 *demanded of* questioned by 11 *replication* reply 13 *countenance* favor. *authorities* delegated power, influence 19 *sleeps in* has no meaning to 21 *The . . . body* (Perhaps alludes to the legal commonplace of "the king's two bodies," which drew a distinction between the sacred office of kingship and the particular mortal who possessed it at any given time. Hence, although Claudius' body is necessarily a part of him, true kingship is not contained in it. Similarly, Claudius will have Polonius' body when it is found, but there is no kingship in this business either.) 24 *Of nothing* (1) of no account (2) lacking the essence of kingship, as in line 21 and note. *Hide . . . after* (An old signal cry in the game of hide-and-seek, suggesting that Hamlet now runs away from them.) 4 *of* by. *distracted* fickle, unstable 5 *Who . . . eyes* who choose not by judgment but by appearance 6 *scourge* punishment. (Literally, blow with a whip.) *weighed* sympathetically considered 7 *To . . . even* to manage the business in an unprovocative way 9 *Deliberate pause* carefully considered action 10 *appliance* remedies

Enter Rosencrantz, [Guildenstern,] and all the rest.

How now, what hath befall'n?

Rosencrantz: Where the dead body is bestowed, my lord,
 We cannot get from him.

King: But where is he?

Rosencrantz: Without, my lord; guarded, to know your pleasure.

King: Bring him before us.

Rosencrantz: Ho! Bring in the lord.   15

They enter [with Hamlet].

King: Now, Hamlet, where's Polonius?

Hamlet: At supper.

King: At supper? Where?

Hamlet: Not where he eats, but where 'a is eaten. A certain convocation of politic
 worms° are e'en° at him. Your worm° is your only emperor for diet.° We fat all 20
 creatures else to fat us, and we fat ourselves for maggots. Your fat king and your
 lean beggar is but variable service°—two dishes, but to one table. That's the end.

King: Alas, alas!

Hamlet: A man may fish with the worm that hath eat° of a king, and eat of the fish
 that hath fed of that worm.   25

King: What dost thou mean by this?

Hamlet: Nothing but to show you how a king may go a progress° through the guts of
 a beggar.

King: Where is Polonius?

Hamlet: In heaven. Send thither to see. If your messenger find him not there, seek 30
 him i' th' other place yourself. But if indeed you find him not within this month,
 you shall nose him as you go up the stairs into the lobby.

King [to some attendants]: Go seek him there.

Hamlet: 'A will stay till you come.   *[Exeunt attendants.]*

King: Hamlet, this deed, for thine especial safety—   35
 Which we do tender,° as we dearly° grieve
 For that which thou hast done—must send thee hence
 With fiery quickness. Therefore prepare thyself.
 The bark° is ready, and the wind at help,
 Th' associates tend,° and everything is bent°   40
 For England.

Hamlet: For England!

King: Ay, Hamlet.

Hamlet: Good.

King: So is it, if thou knew'st our purposes.   45

Hamlet: I see a cherub° that sees them. But come, for England! Farewell, dear
 mother.

19–20 *politic worms* crafty worms (suited to a master spy like Polonius) 20 *e'en* even now. *Your worm* your
average worm (Compare *your fat king* and *your lean beggar* in lines 21–22) *diet* food, eating (with a punning
reference to the Diet of Worms, a famous *convocation* held in 1521) 22 *variable service* different courses of
a single meal 24 *eat* eaten. (Pronounced *et*.) 27 *progress* royal journey of state 36 *tender* regard, hold
dear. *dearly* intensely 39 *bark* sailing vessel 40 *tend* wait. *bent* in readiness 46 *cherub* (Cherubim are
angels of knowledge. Hamlet hints that both he and heaven are onto Claudius' tricks.)

King: Thy loving father, Hamlet.
Hamlet: My mother. Father and mother is man and wife, man and wife is one flesh,
    and so, my mother. Come, for England!   50

Exit.

King: Follow him at foot;° tempt him with speed aboard.
    Delay it not. I'll have him hence tonight.
    Away! For everything is sealed and done
    That else leans on° th' affair. Pray you, make haste.

[Exeunt all but the King.]

    And, England,° if my love thou hold'st at aught°—   55
    As my great power thereof may give thee sense,°
    Since yet thy cicatrice° looks raw and red
    After the Danish sword, and thy free awe°
    Pays homage to us—thou mayst not coldly set°
    Our sovereign process,° which imports at full,°   60
    By letters congruing° to that effect,
    The present° death of Hamlet. Do it, England,
    For like the hectic° in my blood he rages,
    And thou must cure me. Till I know 'tis done,
    Howe'er my haps,° my joys were ne'er begun.   65

Exit.

SCENE IV [THE COAST OF DENMARK.]

Enter Fortinbras with his army over the stage.

Fortinbras: Go, Captain, from me greet the Danish king.
    Tell him that by his license° Fortinbras
    Craves the conveyance of° a promised march
    Over his kingdom. You know the rendezvous.
    If that His Majesty would aught with us,   5
    We shall express our duty° in his eye;°
    And let him know so.
Captain: I will do 't, my lord.
Fortinbras: Go softly° on.   *[Exeunt all but the Captain.]*

Enter Hamlet, Rosencrantz, [Guildenstern,] etc.

Hamlet: Good sir, whose powers° are these?   10
Captain: They are of Norway, sir.
Hamlet: How purposed, sir, I pray you?
Captain: Against some part of Poland.
Hamlet: Who commands them, sir?
Captain: The nephew to old Norway, Fortinbras.   15

---

51 *at foot* close behind, at heel   54 *leans on* bears upon, is related to   55 *England* i.e., King of England.   *at aught* at any value   56 *As . . . sense* for so my great power may give you a just appreciation of the importance of valuing my love   57 *cicatrice* scar   58 *free awe* voluntary show of respect   59 *coldly set* regard with indifference   60 *process* command.   *imports at full* conveys specific directions for   61 *congruing* agreeing   62 *present* immediate   63 *hectic* persistent fever   65 *haps* fortunes   2 *license* permission   3 *the conveyance of* escort during   6 *duty* respect.   *eye* presence   9 *softly* slowly, circumspectly   10 *powers* forces

Hamlet: Goes it against the main° of Poland, sir,
    Or for some frontier?
Captain: Truly to speak, and with no addition,°
    We go to gain a little patch of ground
    That hath in it no profit but the name.   20
    To pay° five ducats, five, I would not farm it;°
    Nor will it yield to Norway or the Pole
    A ranker° rate, should it be sold in fee.°
Hamlet: Why, then the Polack never will defend it.
Captain: Yes, it is already garrisoned.   25
Hamlet: Two thousand souls and twenty thousand ducats
    Will not debate the question of this straw.°
    This is th' impostume° of much wealth and peace,
    That inward breaks, and shows no cause without
    Why the man dies. I humbly thank you, sir.   30
Captain: God b' wi' you, sir.

    [*Exit.*]

Rosencrantz: Will 't please you go, my lord?
Hamlet: I'll be with you straight. Go a little before.

                    [*Exeunt all except Hamlet.*]

    How all occasions do inform against° me
    And spur my dull revenge! What is a man,
    If his chief good and market of° his time   35
    Be but to sleep and feed? A beast, no more.
    Sure he that made us with such large discourse,°
    Looking before and after,° gave us not
    That capability and godlike reason
    To fust° in us unused. Now, whether it be   40
    Bestial oblivion,° or some craven° scruple
    Of thinking too precisely° on th' event°—
    A thought which, quartered, hath but one part wisdom
    And ever three parts coward—I do not know
    Why yet I live to say "This thing's to do,"   45
    Sith° I have cause, and will, and strength, and means
    To do 't. Examples gross° as earth exhort me:
    Witness this army of such mass and charge,°
    Led by a delicate and tender° prince,
    Whose spirit with divine ambition puffed   50
    Makes mouths° at the invisible event,°
    Exposing what is mortal and unsure

---

16 *main* main part   18 *addition* exaggeration   21 *To pay* i.e., for a yearly rental of. *farm it* take a lease of
it   23 *ranker* higher. *in fee* fee simple, outright   27 *debate . . . straw* settle this trifling matter   28
impostume abscess   33 *inform against* denounce, betray: take shape against   35 *market of* profit of, compensation for   37 *discourse* power of reasoning   38 *Looking before and after* able to review past events and
anticipate the future   40 *fust* grow moldy   41 *oblivion* forgetfulness. *craven* cowardly   42 *precisely*
scrupulously. *event* outcome   46 *Sith* since   47 *gross* obvious   48 *charge* expense   49 *delicate and tender*
of fine and youthful qualities   51 *Makes mouths* makes scornful faces. *invisible event* unforeseeable outcome

To all that fortune, death, and danger dare,°
Even for an eggshell. Rightly to be great
Is not to stir without great argument,
But greatly to find quarrel in a straw   55
When honor's at the stake.° How stand I, then,
That have a father killed, a mother stained,
Excitements of° my reason and my blood,
And let all sleep, while to my shame I see   60
The imminent death of twenty thousand men
That for a fantasy° and trick° of fame
Go to their graves like beds, fight for a plot°
Whereon the numbers cannot try the cause,°
Which is not tomb enough and continent°   65
To hide the slain? O, from this time forth
My thoughts be bloody or be nothing worth!   *Exit.*

SCENE V [THE CASTLE.]

Enter Horatio, [Queen] Gertrude, and a Gentleman.

Queen: I will not speak with her.
Gentleman: She is importunate,
    Indeed distract.° Her mood will needs be pitied.
Queen: What would she have?
Gentleman: She speaks much of her father, says she hears
    There's tricks° i' the world, and hems,° and beats her heart,°   5
    Spurns enviously at straws,° speaks things in doubt°
    That carry but half sense. Her speech is nothing,
    Yet the unshapèd use° of it doth move
    The hearers to collection;° they yawn° at it,
    And botch° the words up fit to their own thoughts,   10
    Which,° as her winks and nods and gestures yield° them,
    Indeed would make one think there might be thought,°
    Though nothing sure, yet much unhappily.°
Horatio: 'Twere good she were spoken with, for she may strew
    Dangerous conjectures in ill-breeding° minds.   15
Queen: Let her come in.   [*Exit Gentleman.*]
    [*Aside.*] To my sick soul, as sin's true nature is,
    Each toy° seems prologue to some great amiss.°

---

53 *dare* could do (to him)   54–57 *Rightly . . . stake* true greatness does not normally consist of rushing into action over some trivial provocation: however, when one's honor is involved, even a trifling insult requires that one respond greatly (?)   57 *at the stake* (A metaphor from gambling or bear-baiting.)   59 *Excitements of* promptings by   62 *fantasy* fanciful caprice, illusion.   *trick* trifle, deceit   63 *plot* plot of ground   64 *Whereon . . . cause* on which there is insufficient room for the soldiers needed to engage in a military contest   65 *continent* receptacle, container   2 *distract* distracted   5 *tricks* deceptions.   *hems* makes "hmm" sounds.   *heart* i.e., breast   6 *Spurns . . . straws* kicks spitefully, takes offense at trifles.   *in doubt* obscurely   8 *unshapèd use* incoherent manner   9 *collection* inference, a guess at some sort of meaning.   *yawn* gape, wonder; grasp. (The Folio reading, *aim*, is possible.)   10 *botch* patch   11 *Which* which words.   *yield* deliver, represent   12 *thought* intended   13 *unhappily* unpleasantly near the truth, shrewdly   15 *ill-breeding* prone to suspect the worst and to make mischief   18 *toy* trifle.   *amiss* calamity

So full of artless jealousy is guilt,
It spills itself in fearing to be spilt.°   20

Enter Ophelia° [distracted].

Ophelia: Where is the beauteous majesty of Denmark?
Queen: How now, Ophelia?
Ophelia (she sings):

> "How should I your true love know
> From another one?
> By his cockle hat° and staff,   25
> And his sandal shoon.°"

Queen: Alas, sweet lady, what imports this song?
Ophelia: Say you? Nay, pray you, mark.

> "He is dead and gone, lady,   *(Song.)*
> He is dead and gone;   30
> At his head a grass-green turf,
> At his heels a stone."

    O, ho!
Queen: Nay, but Ophelia—
Ophelia: Pray you, mark. [*Sings.*]   35

> "White his shroud as the mountain snow"—

Enter King.

Queen: Alas, look here, my lord.
Ophelia:

> "Larded° with sweet flowers;   *(Song.)*
> Which bewept to the ground did not go
> With true-love showers.°"   40

King: How do you, pretty lady?
Ophelia: Well, God 'ild° you! They say the owl° was a baker's daughter. Lord, we
    know what we are, but know not what we may be. God be at your table!
King: Conceit° upon her father.
Ophelia: Pray let's have no words of this; but when they ask you what it means, say   45
    you this:

> "Tomorrow is Saint Valentine's day,   *(Song.)*
> All in the morning betime,°
> And I a maid at your window,
> To be your Valentine.   50
> Then up he rose, and donned his clothes,
> And dupped° the chamber door,
> Let in the maid, that out a maid
> Never departed more."

19–20 *So . . . split* guilt is so full of suspicion that it unskillfully betrays itself in fearing betrayal   20 *s.d*
Enter Ophelia (In the First Quarto, Ophelia enters, "playing on a lute, and her hair down, singing.")   25
cockle hat hat with cockleshell stuck in it as a sign that the wearer had been a pilgrim to the shrine of Saint
James of Compostella in Spain   26 *shoon* shoes   38 *Larded* decorated   40 *showers* i.e., tears   42 *God 'ild*
God yield or reward.   *owl* (Refers to a legend about a baker's daughter who was turned into an owl for being ungenerous when Jesus begged a loaf of bread.)   44 *Conceit* brooding   48 *betime* early   52 *dupped* did
up, opened

King: Pretty Ophelia—   55
Ophelia: Indeed, la, without an oath, I'll make an end on 't:
>   "By Gis° and by Saint Charity,
>   Alack, and he for shame!
>   Young men will do 't, if they come to 't;
>   By Cock,° they are to blame.   60
>   Quoth she, 'Before you tumbled me,
>   You promised me to wed.'"

He answers:

>   "'So would I ha' done, by yonder sun,
>   An° thou hadst not come to my bed.'"   65

King: How long hath she been thus?
Ophelia: I hope all will be well. We must be patient, but I cannot choose but weep to
think they would lay him i' the cold ground. My brother shall know of it. And so
I thank you for your good counsel. Come, my coach! Good night, ladies, good
night, sweet ladies, good night, good night.   *[Exit.]* 70
King [to Horatio]: Follow her close. Give her good watch, I pray you.

[Exit Horatio.]

O, this is the poison of deep grief; it springs
All from her father's death—and now behold!
O Gertrude, Gertrude,
When sorrows come, they come not single spies,°   75
But in battalions. First, her father slain;
Next, your son gone, and he most violent author
Of his own just remove;° the people muddied,°
Thick and unwholesome in their thoughts and whispers
For good Polonius' death—and we have done but greenly,°   80
In hugger-mugger° to inter him; poor Ophelia
Divided from herself and her fair judgment,
Without the which we are pictures or mere beasts;
Last, and as much containing° as all these,
Her brother is in secret come from France,   85
Feeds on this wonder, keeps himself in clouds,°
And wants° not buzzers° to infect his ear
With pestilent speeches of his father's death,
Wherein necessity,° of matter beggared,°
Will nothing stick our person to arraign   90
In ear and ear.° O my dear Gertrude, this,
Like to a murdering piece,° in many places
Gives me superfluous death.°   *A noise within.*
Queen: Alack, what noise is this?

---

57 *Gis* Jesus 60 *Cock* (A perversion of "God" in oaths; here also with a quibble on the slang word for penis.) 65 *An* if 75 *spies* scouts sent in advance of the main force 78 *remove* removal. *muddied* stirred
up, confused 80 *greenly* in an inexperienced way, foolishly 81 *hugger-mugger* secret haste 84 *as much
containing* as full of serious matter 86 *Feeds . . . clouds* feeds his resentment or shocked grievance, holds
himself inscrutable and aloof amid all this rumor 87 *wants* lacks. *buzzers* gossipers, informers 89
necessity i.e., the need to invent some plausible explanation. *of matter beggared* unprovided with facts
90–91 *Will . . . ear* will not hesitate to accuse my (royal) person in everybody's ears 92 *murdering piece*
cannon loaded so as to scatter its shot 93 *Gives . . . death* kills me over and over

King: Attend!°   95
    Where is my Switzers?° Let them guard the door.

    Enter a Messenger.

    What is the matter?
Messenger: Save yourself, my lord!
    The ocean, overpeering of his list,°
    Eats not the flats° with more impetuous° haste
    Than young Laertes, in a riotous head,°   100
    O'erbears your officers. The rabble call him lord,
    And, as° the world were now but to begin,
    Antiquity forgot, custom not known,
    The ratifiers and props of every word,°
    They cry, "Choose we! Laertes shall be king!"   105
    Caps,° hands, and tongues applaud it to the clouds,
    "Laertes shall be king, Laertes king!"
Queen: How cheerfully on the false trail they cry!   *A noise within.*
    O, this is counter,° you false Danish dogs!

    Enter Laertes with others.

King: The doors are broke.   110
Laertes: Where is this King?—Sirs, stand you all without.
All: No, let's come in.
Laertes: I pray you, give me leave.
All: We will, we will.
Laertes: I thank you. Keep the door.
                                                                    [*Exeunt followers.*]
                        O thou vile king, Give me my father!   115
Queen [*restraining him*]: Calmly, good Laertes.
Laertes: That drop of blood that's calm proclaims me bastard,
    Cries cuckold to my father, brands the harlot
    Even here, between° the chaste unsmirchèd brow
    Of my true mother.
King: What is the cause, Laertes,   120
    That thy rebellion looks so giantlike?
    Let him go, Gertrude. Do not fear our° person.
    There's such divinity doth hedge° a king
    That treason can but peep to what it would,°
    Acts little of his will.° Tell me, Laertes,   125
    Why thou art thus incensed. Let him go, Gertrude.
    Speak, man.

---

95 *Attend* i.e., guard me   96 *Switzers* Swiss guards, mercenaries   98 *overpeering of his list* overflowing its shore, boundary   99 *flats* i.e., flatlands near shore.   *impetuous* violent (perhaps also with the meaning of impiteous [*impitious*, Second Quarto], "pitiless")   100 *head* insurrection   102 *as* as if   104 *The ratifiers . . . word* i.e., *antiquity* (or tradition) and *custom* ought to confirm (*ratify*) and underprop our every word or promise   106 *Caps* (The caps are thrown in the air.)   109 *counter* (A hunting term, meaning to follow the trail in a direction opposite to that which the game has taken.)   119 *between* in the middle of   122 *fear our* fear for my   123 *hedge* protect, as with a surrounding barrier   124 *can . . . would* can only peep furtively, as through a barrier at what it would intend   125 *Acts . . . will* (but) performs little of what it intends

Laertes: Where is my father?

King: Dead.

Queen: But not by him.

King: Let him demand his fill.

Laertes: How came he dead? I'll not be juggled with.°

    To hell, allegiance! Vows, to the blackest devil!   130

    Conscience and grace, to the profoundest pit!

    I dare damnation. To this point I stand,°

    That both the worlds I give to negligence,°

    Let come what comes, only I'll be revenged

    Most throughly° for my father.   135

King: Who shall stay you?

Laertes: My will, not all the world's.°

    And for° my means, I'll husband them so well

    They shall go far with little.

King: Good Laertes,

    If you desire to know the certainty

    Of your dear father, is 't writ in your revenge   140

    That, swoopstake,° you will draw both friend and foe,

    Winner and loser?

Laertes: None but his enemies.

King: Will you know them, then?

Laertes: To his good friends thus wide I'll ope my arms,   145

    And like the kind life-rendering pelican°

    Repast° them with my blood.

King: Why, now you speak

    Like a good child and a true gentleman.

    That I am guiltless of your father's death,   150

    And am most sensibly° in grief for it,

    It shall as level° to your judgment 'pear

    As day does to your eye.   *A noise within.*

Laertes: How now, what noise is that?

    Enter Ophelia.

King: Let her come in.

Laertes: O heat, dry up my brains! Tears seven times salt   155

    Burn out the sense and virtue° of mine eye!

    By heaven, thy madness shall be paid with weight°

    Till our scale turn the beam.° O rose of May!

    Dear maid, kind sister, sweet Ophelia!

    O heavens, is 't possible a young maid's wits   160

---

129 *juggled with* cheated, deceived   132 *To . . . stand* I am resolved in this   133 *both . . . negligence* i.e.,
both this world and the next are of no consequence to me   135 *throughly* thoroughly   137 *My will . . .
world's* I'll stop (*stay*) when my will is accomplished, not for anyone else's.   138 *for* as for   142
swoopstake i.e., indiscriminately. (Literally taking all stakes on the gambling table at once. *Draw* is also a
gambling term meaning "take from.")   147 *pelican* (Refers to the belief that the female pelican fed its
young with its own blood.)   148 *Repast* feed   151 *sensibly* feelingly   152 *level* plain   156 *virtue* faculty,
power   157 *paid with weight* repaid, avenged equally or more   158 *beam* crossbar of a balance

    Should be as mortal as an old man's life?
    Nature is fine in° love, and where 'tis fine
    It sends some precious instance° of itself
    After the thing it loves.°

Ophelia:

        "They bore him barefaced on the bier,   (Song.)   165
        Hey non nonny, nonny, hey nonny,
        And in his grave rained many a tear—"

    Fare you well, my dove!

Laertes: Hadst thou thy wits and didst persuade° revenge,
    It could not move thus.   170

Ophelia: You must sing "A-down a-down," and you "call him a-down-a."° O, how
    the wheel° becomes it! It is the false steward° that stole his master's daughter.

Laertes: This nothing's more than matter.°

Ophelia: There's rosemary,° that's for remembrance; pray you, love, remember.
    And there is pansies;° that's for thoughts.   175

Laertes: A document° in madness, thoughts and remembrance fitted.

Ophelia: There's fennel° for you, and columbines.° There's rue° for you, and here's
    some for me; we may call it herb of grace o' Sundays. You must wear your rue
    with a difference.° There's a daisy.° I would give you some violets,° but they withered
    all when my father died. They say 'a made a good end—   180
    [*Sings.*]

        "For bonny sweet Robin is all my joy."

Laertes: Thought° and affliction, passion,° hell itself,
    She turns to favor° and to prettiness.

Ophelia:

        "And will 'a not come again?   (Song.)
        And will 'a not come again?   185
        No, no, he is dead.
        Go to thy deathbed,
        He never will come again."
        "His beard was as white as snow,
        All flaxen was his poll.°   190
        He is gone, he is gone,
        And we cast away moan.
        God ha' mercy on his soul!"

    And of all Christian souls, I pray God. God b' wi' you.

                                      [*Exit, followed by Gertrude.*]

Laertes: Do you see this, O God?   195

162 *fine in* refined by   163 *instance* token   164 *After . . . loves* i.e., into the grave, along with Polonius   169 *persuade* argue cogently for   171 *You . . . a-down a* (Ophelia assigns the singing of refrains, like her own "Hey non nonny," to others present.)   172 *wheel* spinning wheel as accompaniment to the song, or refrain. *false steward* (The story is unknown.)   173 *This . . . matter* this seeming nonsense is more eloquent than sane utterance   174 *rosemary* (Used as a symbol of remembrance both at weddings and at funerals.)   175 *pansies* (Emblems of love and courtship; perhaps from French *pensées,* "thoughts.")   176 *document* instruction, lesson   177 *fennel* (Emblem of flattery.)   *columbines* (Emblems of unchastity or ingratitude.)   *rue* (Emblem of repentance—a signification that is evident in its popular name, *herb of grace.*)   179 *with a difference* (A device used in heraldry to distinguish one family from another on the coat of arms, here suggesting that Ophelia and the others have different causes of sorrow and repentance; perhaps with a play on *rue* in the sense of "ruth," "pity.")   *daisy* (Emblem of dissembling, faithlessness.)   *violets* (Emblems of faithfulness.)   182 *Thought* melancholy.   *passion* suffering   183 *favor* grace, beauty   190 *poll* head

King: Laertes, I must commune with your grief,
    Or you deny me right. Go but apart,
    Make choice of whom° your wisest friends you will,
    And they shall hear and judge twixt you and me.
    If by direct or by collateral hand°   200
    They find us touched,° we will our kingdom give,
    Our crown, our life, and all that we call ours
    To you in satisfaction; but if not,
    Be you content to lend your patience to us,
    And we shall jointly labor with your soul   205
    To give it due content.
Laertes: Let this be so.
    His means of death, his obscure funeral—
    No trophy,° sword, nor hatchment° o'er his bones,
    No noble rite, nor formal ostentation°—
    Cry to be heard, as 'twere from heaven to earth,   210
    That° I must call 't in question.°
King: So you shall,
    And where th' offense is, let the great ax fall.
    I pray you, go with me.   *Exeunt.*

SCENE VI [THE CASTLE.]

    Enter Horatio and others.

Horatio: What are they that would speak with me?
Gentleman: Seafaring men, sir. They say they have letters for you.
Horatio: Let them come in.   *[Exit Gentleman.]*
    I do not know from what part of the world
    I should be greeted, if not from Lord Hamlet.   5

    Enter Sailors.

First Sailor: God bless you, sir.
Horatio: Let him bless thee too.
First Sailor: 'A shall, sir, an 't° please him. There's a letter for you, sir—it came from
    th' ambassador° that was bound for England—if your name be Horatio, as I am
    let to know it is.   *[He gives a letter.]*   10
Horatio [*reads*]: "Horatio, when thou shalt have overlooked° this, give these fellows
    some means° to the King; they have letters for him. Ere we were two days old at
    sea, a pirate of very warlike appointment° gave us chase. Finding ourselves too
    slow of sail, we put on a compelled valor, and in the grapple I boarded them.
    On the instant they got clear of our ship, so I alone became their prisoner. They   15
    have dealt with me like thieves of mercy,° but they knew what they did: I am to

---

198 *whom* whichever of   200 *collateral hand* indirect agency   201 *us touched* be implicated   208 *trophy* memorial.   *hatchment* tablet displaying the armorial bearings of a deceased person   209 *ostentation* ceremony   211 *That* so that.   *call 't in question* demand an explanation   8 *an 't* if it   9 *th' ambassador* (Evidently Hamlet. The sailor is being circumspect.)   11 *overlooked* looked over   12 *means* means of access   13 *appointment* equipage   16 *thieves of mercy* merciful thieves

do a good turn for them. Let the King have the letters I have sent, and repair°
thou to me with as much speed as thou wouldest fly death. I have words to speak
in thine ear will make thee dumb, yet are they much too light for the bore° of
the matter. These good fellows will bring thee where I am. Rosencrantz and   20
Guildenstern hold their course for England. Of them I have much to tell thee.
Farewell.

He that thou knowest thine, Hamlet."

Come, I will give you way° for these your letters,
And do 't the speedier that you may direct me   25
To him from whom you brought them.   *Exeunt.*

SCENE VII [THE CASTLE.]

Enter King and Laertes.

King: Now must your conscience my acquittance seal,°
    And you must put me in your heart for friend,
    Sith° you have heard, and with a knowing ear,
    That he which hath your noble father slain
    Pursued my life.
Laertes: It well appears. But tell me   5
    Why you proceeded not against these feats°
    So crimeful and so capital° in nature,
    As by your safety, greatness, wisdom, all things else,
    You mainly° were stirred up.
King: O, for two special reasons,   10
    Which may to you perhaps seem much unsinewed,°
    But yet to me they're strong. The Queen his mother
    Lives almost by his looks, and for myself—
    My virtue or my plague, be it either which—
    She is so conjunctive° to my life and soul   15
    That, as the star moves not but in his° sphere,°
    I could not but by her. The other motive
    Why to a public count° I might not go
    Is the great love the general gender° bear him,
    Who, dipping all his faults in their affection,   20
    Work° like the spring° that turneth wood to stone,
    Convert his gyves° to graces, so that my arrows,
    Too slightly timbered° for so loud° a wind,
    Would have reverted° to my bow again
    But not where I had aimed them.   25

---

17 *repair* come   19 *bore* caliber, i.e., importance   24 *way* means of access   1 *my acquittance seal* confirm or
acknowledge my innocence   3 *Sith* since   6 *feats* acts   7 *capital* punishable by death   9 *mainly* greatly
11 *unsinewed* weak   15 *conjunctive* closely united. (An astronomical metaphor.)   16 *his* its.   *sphere* one of
the hollow spheres in which, according to Ptolemaic astronomy, the planets were supposed to move
18 *count* account, reckoning, indictment   19 *general gender* common people   21 *Work* operate, act.
spring i.e., a spring with such a concentration of lime that it coats a piece of wood with limestone, in effect
gilding and petrifying it   22 *gyves* fetters (which, gilded by the people's praise, would look like badges of
honor)   23 *slightly timbered* light.   *loud* (suggesting public outcry on Hamlet's behalf)   24 *reverted* returned

Laertes: And so have I a noble father lost,
    A sister driven into desperate terms,°
    Whose worth, if praises may go back° again,
    Stood challenger on mount° of all the age
    For her perfections. But my revenge will come.   30
King: Break not your sleeps for that. You must not think
    That we are made of stuff so flat and dull
    That we can let our beard be shook with danger
    And think it pastime. You shortly shall hear more.
    I loved your father, and we love ourself;   35
    And that, I hope, will teach you to imagine—

Enter a Messenger with letters.

    How now? What news?
Messenger: Letters, my lord, from Hamlet:
    This to Your Majesty, this to the Queen.

                               [He gives letters.]

King: From Hamlet? Who brought them?
Messenger: Sailors, my lord, they say. I saw them not.   40
    They were given me by Claudio. He received them
    Of him that brought them.
King: Laertes, you shall hear them.——
    Leave us.   *[Exit Messenger.]*
    [He reads.] "High and mighty, you shall know I am set naked° on your kingdom.
    Tomorrow shall I beg leave to see your kingly eyes, when I shall, first asking your   45
    pardon,° thereunto recount the occasion of my sudden and more strange return.
    Hamlet."
    What should this mean? Are all the rest come back? Or is it some abuse,° and no
    such thing?°
Laertes: Know you the hand?
King: 'Tis Hamlet's character.° "Naked!"   50
    And in a postscript here he says "alone."
    Can you devise° me?
Laertes: I am lost in it, my lord. But let him come.
    It warms the very sickness in my heart
    That I shall live and tell him to his teeth,   55
    "Thus didst thou."°
King: If it be so, Laertes—
    As how should it be so? How otherwise?°—
    Will you be ruled by me?
Laertes: Ay, my lord,
    So° you will not o'errule me to a peace.

---

27 *terms* state, condition   28 *go back* i.e., recall what she was   29 *on mount* set up on high   44 *naked* destitute, unarmed, without following   46 *pardon* permission   48 *abuse* deceit   49 *no such thing* not what it appears   50 *character* handwriting   52 *devise* explain to   56 *Thus didst thou* i.e., here's for what you did to my father   57 *As ... otherwise* how can this (Hamlet's return) be true? Yet how otherwise than true (since we have the evidence of his letter)?   59 *So* provided that

King: To thine own peace. If he be now returned,   60
   As checking at° his voyage, and that° he means
   No more to undertake it, I will work him
   To an exploit, now ripe in my device,°
   Under the which he shall not choose but fall;
   And for his death no wind of blame shall breathe,   65
   But even his mother shall uncharge the practice°
   And call it accident.
Laertes: My lord, I will be ruled,
   The rather if you could devise it so
   That I might be the organ.°
King: It falls right.
   You have been talked of since your travel much,   70
   And that in Hamlet's hearing, for a quality
   Wherein they say you shine. Your sum of parts°
   Did not together pluck such envy from him
   As did that one, and that, in my regard,
   Of the unworthiest siege.°   75
Laertes: What part is that, my lord?
King: A very ribbon in the cap of youth,
   Yet needful too, for youth no less becomes°
   The light and careless livery that it wears
   Than settled age his sables° and his weeds°   80
   Importing health and graveness.° Two months since
   Here was a gentleman of Normandy.
   I have seen myself, and served against, the French,
   And they can well° on horseback, but this gallant
   Had witchcraft in 't; he grew unto his seat,   85
   And to such wondrous doing brought his horse
   As had he been incorpsed and demi-natured°
   With the brave beast. So far he topped° my thought
   That I in forgery° of shapes and tricks
   Come short of what he did.
Laertes: A Norman was 't?   90
King: A Norman.
Laertes: Upon my life, Lamord.
King: The very same.
Laertes: I know him well. He is the brooch° indeed
   And gem of all the nation.
King: He made confession° of you.   95
   And gave you such a masterly report

---

61 *checking at* i.e., turning aside from (like a falcon leaving the quarry to fly at a chance bird).   *that if*
63 *device* devising, invention   66 *uncharge the practice* acquit the strategem of being a plot   69 *organ*
agent, instrument   72 *Your . . . parts* i.e., all your other virtues   75 *unworthiest siege* least important rank
78 *no less becomes* is no less suited by   80 *his sables* its rich robes furred with sable.   *weeds* garments
81 *Importing . . . graveness* signifying a concern for health and dignified prosperity; also, giving an impression
of comfortable prosperity   84 *can well* are skilled   87 *As . . . demi-natured* as if he had been of one body
and nearly of one nature (like the centaur)   88 *topped* surpassed   89 *forgery* imagining   93 *brooch* ornament
95 *confession* testimonial, admission of superiority

For art and exercise in your defense,°
And for your rapier most especial,
That he cried out 'twould be a sight indeed
If one could match you. Th' escrimers° of their nation,   100
He swore, had neither motion, guard, nor eye
If you opposed them. Sir, this report of his
Did Hamlet so envenom with his envy
That he could nothing do but wish and beg
Your sudden° coming o'er, to play° with you.   105
Now, out of this—
Laertes: What out of this, my lord?
King: Laertes, was your father dear to you?
Or are you like the painting of a sorrow,
A face without a heart?
Laertes: Why ask you this?
King: Not that I think you did not love your father,   110
But that I know love is begun by time,°
And that I see, in passages of proof,°
Time qualifies° the spark and fire of it.
There lives within the very flame of love
A kind of wick or snuff° that will abate it,   115
And nothing° is at a like goodness still,
For goodness, growing to a pleurisy,°
Dies in his own too much.° That° we would do,
We should do when we would; for this "would" changes
And hath abatements° and delays as many   120
As there are tongues, are hands, are accidents,°
And then this "should" is like a spendthrift sigh,°
That hurts by easing.° But, to the quick o' th' ulcer:°
Hamlet comes back. What would you undertake
To show yourself in deed your father's son   125
More than in words?
Laertes: To cut his throat i' the church.
King: No place, indeed, should murder sanctuarize;°
Revenge should have no bounds. But good Laertes,
Will you do this,° keep close within your chamber.
Hamlet returned shall know you are come home.   130
We'll put on those shall° praise your excellence

---

97 *For . . . defense* with respect to your skill and practice with your weapon   100 *escrimers* fencers
105 *sudden* immediate.   *play* fence   111 *begun by time* i.e., created by the right circumstance and hence
subject to change   112 *passages of proof* actual instances that prove it   113 *qualifies* weakens, moderates
115 *snuff* the charred part of a candlewick   116 *nothing . . . still* nothing remains at a constant level of
perfection   117 *pleurisy* excess, plethora. (Literally, a chest inflammation.)   118 *in . . . much* of its own
excess.   *That* that which   120 *abatements* diminutions   121 *As . . . accidents* as there are tongues to
dissuade, hands to prevent, and chance events to intervene   122 *spendthrift sigh* (An allusion to the belief that sighs draw blood from the heart.)   123 *hurts by easing* i.e., costs the heart blood and wastes precious opportunity even while it affords emotional relief.   *quick o' th' ulcer* i.e., heart of the matter   127
sanctuarize protect from punishment. (Alludes to the right of sanctuary with which certain religious
places were invested.)   129 *Will you do this* if you wish to do this   131 *put on those shall* arrange for some to

And set a double varnish on the fame
The Frenchman gave you, bring you in fine° together,
And wager on your heads. He, being remiss,°
Most generous,° and free from all contriving,   135
Will not peruse the foils, so that with ease,
Or with a little shuffling, you may choose
A sword unbated,° and in a pass of practice°
Requite him for your father.

Laertes: I will do 't,
And for that purpose I'll anoint my sword.   140
I bought an unction° of a mountebank°
So mortal that, but dip a knife in it,
Where it draws blood no cataplasm° so rare,
Collected from all simples° that have virtue°
Under the moon,° can save the thing from death   145
That is but scratched withal. I'll touch my point
With this contagion, that if I gall° him slightly,
It may be death.

King: Let's further think of this,
Weigh what convenience both of time and means
May fit us to our shape.° If this should fail,   150
And that our drift look through our bad performance,°
'Twere better not assayed. Therefore this project
Should have a back or second, that might hold
If this did blast in proof.° Soft, let me see.
We'll make a solemn wager on your cunnings°—   155
I ha 't!
When in your motion you are hot and dry—
As° make your bouts more violent to that end—
And that he calls for drink, I'll have prepared him
A chalice for the nonce,° whereon but sipping,   160
If he by chance escape your venomed stuck,°
Our purpose may hold there. [*A cry within.*] But stay, what noise?

Enter Queen.

Queen: One woe doth tread upon another's heel,
So fast they follow. Your sister's drowned, Laertes.
Laertes: Drowned! O, where?   165
Queen: There is a willow grows askant° the brook,
That shows his hoar leaves° in the glassy stream;
Therewith fantastic garlands did she make

---

133 *in fine* finally   134 *remiss* negligently unsuspicious   135 *generous* noble-minded   138 *unbated* not blunted, having no button. *pass of practice* treacherous thrust   141 *unction* ointment. *mountebank* quack doctor   143 *cataplasm* plaster or poultice   144 *simples* herbs. *virtue* potency   145 *Under the moon* i.e., anywhere (with reference perhaps to the belief that herbs gathered at night had a special power) 147 *gall* graze, wound   150 *shape* part we propose to act   151 *drift . . . performance* intention should be made visible by our bungling   154 *blast in proof* burst in the test (like a cannon)   155 *cunnings* respective skills   158 *As* i.e., and you should   160 *nonce* occasion   161 *stuck* thrust. (From *stoccado;* a fencing term.)   166 *askant* aslant   167 *hoar leaves* white or gray undersides of the leaves

John Everett Millais's painting, *Ophelia* **(1852).**

Of crowflowers, nettles, daisies, and long purples,°
That liberal° shepherds give a grosser name,°   170
But our cold° maids do dead men's fingers call them.
There on the pendent° boughs her crownet° weeds
Clamb'ring to hang, an envious sliver° broke,
When down her weedy° trophies and herself
Fell in the weeping brook. Her clothes spread wide,   175
And mermaidlike awhile they bore her up,
Which time she chanted snatches of old lauds,°
As one incapable of° her own distress,
Or like a creature native and endued°
Unto that element. But long it could not be   180
Till that her garments, heavy with their drink,
Pulled the poor wretch from her melodious lay
To muddy death.
Laertes: Alas, then she is drowned?
Queen: Drowned, drowned.
Laertes: Too much of water hast thou, poor Ophelia,   185
And therefore I forbid my tears. But yet
It is our trick;° nature her custom holds.

---

169 *long purples* early purple orchids   170 *liberal* free-spoken.   *a grosser name* (The testicle-resembling tubers of the orchid, which also in some cases resemble *dead men's fingers*, have earned various slang names like "dogstones" and "cullions.")   171 *cold* chaste   172 *pendent* overhanging.   *crownet* made into a chaplet or coronet   173 *envious sliver* malicious branch   174 *weedy* i.e., of plants   177 *lauds* hymns   178 *incapable of* lacking capacity to apprehend   179 *endued* adapted by nature   187 *It is our trick* i.e., weeping is our natural way (when sad)

Let shame say what it will. [*He weeps.*] When these are gone,
The woman will be out.° Adieu, my lord.
I have a speech of fire that fain would blaze,   190
But that this folly douts° it.   Exit.

King: Let's follow, Gertrude.
How much I had to do to calm his rage!
Now fear I this will give it start again;
Therefore let's follow.   *Exeunt.*

ACT V

SCENE I [A CHURCHYARD.]

Enter two Clowns° [with spades and mattocks].

First Clown: Is she to be buried in Christian burial, when she willfully seeks her own
   salvation?°
Second Clown: I tell thee she is; therefore make her grave straight.° The crowner°
   hath sat on her,° and finds it° Christian burial.
First Clown: How can that be, unless she drowned herself in her own defense?   5
Second Clown: Why, 'tis found so.°
First Clown: It must be *se offendendo,*° it cannot be else. For here lies the point: if I
   drown myself wittingly, it argues an act, and an act hath three branches—it is to
   act, to do, and to perform. Argal,° she drowned herself wittingly.
Second Clown: Nay, but hear you, goodman° delver—   10
First Clown: Give me leave. Here lies the water; good. Here stands the man; good. If
   the man go to this water and drown himself, it is, will he, nill he,° he goes, mark
   you that. But if the water come to him and drown him, he drowns not himself.
   Argal, he that is not guilty of his own death shortens not his own life.
Second Clown: But is this law?   15
First Clown: Ay, marry, is 't—crowner's quest law.
Second Clown: Will you ha' the truth on 't? If this had not been a gentlewoman, she
   should have been buried out o' Christian burial.
First Clown: Why, there thou sayst.° And the more pity that great folk should have
   countenance° in this world to drown or hang themselves, more than their even-   20
   Christian.° Come, my spade. There is no ancient° gentlemen but gardeners,
   ditchers, and grave makers. They hold up° Adam's profession.
Second Clown: Was he a gentleman?
First Clown: 'A was the first that ever bore arms.°

188–189 *When . . . out* when my tears are all shed, the woman in me will be expended, satisfied   191
douts extinguishes. (The Second Quarto reads "drowns.")   s.d. *Clowns* rustics   2 *salvation* (A blunder for
"damnation," or perhaps a suggestion that Ophelia was taking her own shortcut to heaven.)   3 *straight*
straightway, immediately. (But with a pun on *strait,* "narrow.").   *crowner* coroner   4 *sat on her* conducted
an inquest on her case.   *finds it* gives his official verdict that her means of death was consistent with   6
found so determined so in the coroner's verdict   7 *se offendendo* (A comic mistake for *se defendendo,* a term
used in verdicts of justifiable homicide.)   9 *Argal* (Corruption of *ergo,* "therefore.")   10 *goodman* (An
honorific title often used with the name of a profession or craft.)   12 *will he, nill he* whether he will or no,
willy-nilly   19 *there thou sayst,* i.e., that's right   20 *countenance* privilege   20–21 *even-Christian* fellow
Christians   21 *ancient* going back to ancient times   22 *hold up* maintain   24 *bore arms* (To be entitled to
bear a coat of arms would make Adam a gentleman, but as one who bore a spade, our common ancestor
was an ordinary delver in the earth.)

Second Clown: Why, he had none.   25

First Clown: What, art a heathen? How dost thou understand the Scripture? The
   Scripture says Adam digged. Could he dig without arms?° I'll put another
   question to thee. If thou answerest me not to the purpose, confess thyself°—

Second Clown: Go to.

First Clown: What is he that builds stronger than either the mason, the shipwright,   30
   or the carpenter?

Second Clown: The gallows maker, for that frame° outlives a thousand tenants.

First Clown: I like thy wit well, in good faith. The gallows does well.° But how does it
   well? It does well to those that do ill. Now thou dost ill to say the gallows is built
   stronger than the church. Argal, the gallows may do well to thee. To 't again,   35
   come.

Second Clown: "Who builds stronger than a mason, a shipwright, or a carpenter?"

First Clown: Ay, tell me that, and unyoke.°

Second Clown: Marry, now I can tell.

First Clown: To 't.   40

Second Clown: Mass,° I cannot tell.

Enter Hamlet and Horatio [at a distance].

First Clown: Cudgel thy brains no more about it, for your dull ass will not mend his
   pace with beating; and when you are asked this question next, say "a grave
   maker." The houses he makes last till doomsday. Go get thee in and fetch me a
   stoup° of liquor.   45

> *[Exit Second Clown. First Clown digs.]*
>   *Song.*

> "In youth, when I did love, did love,°
> Methought it was very sweet,
> To contract—O—the time for—a—my behove,°
> O, methought there—a—was nothing—a—meet."°

Hamlet: Has this fellow no feeling of his business, 'a° sings in grave-making?   50

Horatio: Custom hath made it in him a property of easiness.°

Hamlet: 'Tis e'en so. The hand of little employment hath the daintier sense.°

First Clown: *Song.*

> "But age with his stealing steps
> Hath clawed me in his clutch,
> And hath shipped me into the land,°   55
> As if I had never been such."

>   *[He throws up a skull.]*

---

27 *arms* i.e., the arms of the body   28 *confess thyself* (The saying continues, "and be hanged.")   32 *frame*
(1) gallows (2) structure   33 *does well* (1) is an apt answer (2) does a good turn   38 *unyoke* i.e., after this
great effort, you may unharness the team of your wits   41 *Mass* by the Mass   45 *stoup* two-quart measure
46 *In . . . love* (This and the two following stanzas, with nonsensical variations, are from a poem attributed to Lord Vaux and printed in *Tottel's Miscellany*, 1557. The *O* and *a* [for "ah"] seemingly are the grunts
of the digger.)   48 *To contract . . . behove* i.e., to shorten the time for my own advantage. (Perhaps he
means to *prolong* it.)   49 *meet* suitable, i.e., more suitable   50 *'a* that he   51 *property of easiness* something he can do easily and indifferently   52 *daintier sense* more delicate sense of feeling   55 *into the land*
i.e., toward my grave (?) (But note the lack of rhyme in *steps, land*.)

Hamlet and the gravedigger.

Hamlet: That skull had a tongue in it and could sing once. How the knave jowls° it
to the ground, as if 'twere Cain's jawbone, that did the first murder! This might be
the pate of a politician,° which this ass now o'erreaches,° one that would circumvent
God, might it not?   60
Horatio: It might, my lord.
Hamlet: Or of a courtier, which could say, "Good morrow, sweet lord! How dost
thou, sweet lord?" This might be my Lord Such-a-one, that praised my Lord
Such-a-one's horse when 'a meant to beg it, might it not?
Horatio: Ay, my lord.   65
Hamlet: Why, e'en so, and now my Lady Worm's, chapless,° and knocked about the
mazard° with a sexton's spade. Here's fine revolution,° an° we had the trick to see° 't.

57 *jowls* dashes (with a pun on *jowl,* "jawbone")   59 *politician* schemer, plotter.   *o'erreaches* circumvents,
gets the better of (with a quibble on the literal sense) 66 *chapless* having no lower jaw.   67 *mazard* i.e.,
head. (Literally, a drinking vessel.)   *revolution* turn of Fortune's wheel, change.   *an* if.   *trick to see* knack
of seeing

Did these bones cost no more the breeding but° to play at loggets° with them?
Mine ache to think on 't.

First Clown: *Song.*

    "A pickax and a spade, a spade,   70
    For and° a shrouding sheet;
    O, a pit of clay for to be made
    For such a guest is meet."

                [He throws up another skull.]

Hamlet: There's another. Why may not that be the skull of a lawyer? Where be his
quiddities° now, his quillities,° his cases, his tenures,° and his tricks? Why does 75
he suffer this mad knave now to knock him about the sconce° with a dirty
shovel, and will not tell him of his action of battery?° Hum, this fellow might be
in 's time a great buyer of land, with his statutes, his recognizances,° his fines,°
his double° vouchers° his recoveries.° Is this the fine of his fines and the recovery
of his recoveries, to have his fine pate full of fine dirt?° Will his vouchers vouch 80
him no more of his purchases, and double ones too, than the length and breadth
of a pair of indentures?° The very conveyances° of his lands will scarcely lie in
this box,° and must th' inheritor° himself have no more, ha?

Horatio: Not a jot more, my lord.

Hamlet: Is not parchment made of sheepskins?   85

Horatio: Ay, my lord, and of calves' skins too.

Hamlet: They are sheep and calves which seek out assurance in that.° I will speak to
this fellow.—Whose grave's this, sirrah?°

First Clown: Mine, sir. *[Sings.]*

    "O, pit of clay for to be made   90
    For such a guest is meet."

Hamlet: I think it be thine, indeed, for thou liest in 't.

First Clown: You lie out on 't, sir, and therefore 'tis not yours. For my part, I do not
lie in 't, yet it is mine.

Hamlet: Thou dost lie in 't, to be in 't and say it is thine. 'Tis for the dead, not for the 95
quick;° therefore thou liest.

First Clown: 'Tis a quick lie, sir; 'twill away again from me to you.

Hamlet: What man dost thou dig it for?

First Clown: For no man, sir.

Hamlet: What woman, then?   100

---

68 *cost . . . but* involve so little expense and care in upbringing that we may. *loggets* a game in which
pieces of hard wood shaped like Indian clubs or bowling pins are thrown to lie as near as possible to a
stake 71 *For and* and moreover 75 *quiddities* subtleties, quibbles. (From Latin *quid,* "a thing.")
quillities verbal niceties, subtle distinctions. (Variation of *quiddities.*) *tenures* the holding of a piece of
property or office, or the conditions or period of such holding 76 *sconce* head 77 *action of battery* law-
suit about physical assault 78 *statutes, his recognizances* legal documents guaranteeing a debt by attach-
ing land and property. *fines, recoveries* ways of converting entailed estates into "fee simple" or freehold
79 *double* signed by two signatories. *vouchers* guarantees of the legality of a title to real estate 79–80
fine of his fines . . . fine pate . . . fine dirt end of his legal maneuvers . . . elegant head . . . minutely sifted
dirt 82 *pair of indentures* legal document drawn up in duplicate on a single sheet and then cut apart on a
zigzag line so that each pair was uniquely matched. (Hamlet may refer to two rows of teeth or dentures.).
conveyances deeds 83 *box* (1) deed box (2) coffin. ("Skull" has been suggested.) *inheritor* possessor,
owner 87 *assurance in that* safety in legal parchments 88 *sirrah* (A term of address to inferiors.) 96
quick living

First Clown: For none, neither.

Hamlet: Who is to be buried in 't?

First Clown: One that was a woman, sir, but, rest her soul, she's dead.

Hamlet: How absolute° the knave is! We must speak by the card,° or equivocation°
will undo us. By the Lord, Horatio, this three years I have took° note of it: the 105
age is grown so picked° that the toe of the peasant comes so near the heel of the
courtier, he galls his kibe.°—How long hast thou been grave maker?

First Clown: Of all the days i' the year, I came to 't that day that our last king Hamlet
overcame Fortinbras.

Hamlet: How long is that since? 110

First Clown: Cannot you tell that? Every fool can tell that. It was that very day that
young Hamlet was born—he that is mad and sent into England.

Hamlet: Ay, marry, why was he sent into England?

First Clown: Why, because 'a was mad. 'A shall recover his wits there, or if 'a do not,
'tis no great matter there. 115

Hamlet: Why?

First Clown: 'Twill not be seen in him there. There the men are as mad as he.

Hamlet: How came he mad?

First Clown: Very strangely, they say.

Hamlet: How strangely? 120

First Clown: Faith, e'en with losing his wits.

Hamlet: Upon what ground?°

First Clown: Why, here in Denmark. I have been sexton here, man and boy, thirty
years.

Hamlet: How long will a man lie i' th' earth ere he rot? 125

First Clown: Faith, if 'a be not rotten before 'a die—as we have many pocky° corpses
nowadays, that will scarce hold the laying in°—'a will last you° some eight year
or nine year. A tanner will last you nine year.

Hamlet: Why he more than another?

First Clown: Why, sir, his hide is so tanned with his trade that 'a will keep out water 130
a great while, and your water is a sore° decaver° of your whoreson° dead body. [*He
picks up a skull.*] Here's a skull now hath lien you° i' th' earth three-and-twenty
years.

Hamlet: Whose was it?

First Clown: A whoreson mad fellow's it was. Whose do you think it was? 135

Hamlet: Nay, I know not.

First Clown: A pestilence on him for a mad rogue! 'A poured a flagon of Rhenish° on
my head once. This same skull, sir, was, sir, Yorick's skull, the King's jester.

Hamlet: This?

First Clown: E'en that. 140

---

104 *absolute* strict, precise. *by the card* i.e., with precision. (Literally, by the mariner's compass-card, on
which the points of the compass were marked.). *equivocation* ambiguity in the use of terms 105 *took*
taken 106 *picked* refined, fastidious 107 *galls his kibe* chafes the courtier's chilblain 122 *ground* cause.
(But, in the next line, the gravedigger takes the word in the sense of "land," "country.") 126 *pocky* rotten, diseased. (Literally, with the pox, or syphilis.) 127 *hold the laying in* hold together long enough to be
interred. *last you* last. (You is used colloquially here and in the following lines.) 131 *sore* i.e., terrible,
great. *whoreson* i.e., vile, scurvy 132 *lien you* lain. (See the note at line 127.) 137 *Rhenish* Rhine wine

"Alas, poor Yorick! I knew him, Horatio . . ." (V, i, 141–149).

Hamlet: Let me see. [*He takes the skull.*] Alas, poor Yorick! I knew him, Horatio, a
fellow of infinite jest, of most excellent fancy. He hath bore° me on his back a
thousand times, and now how abhorred in my imagination it is! My gorge rises°
at it. Here hung those lips that I have kissed I know not how oft. Where be your
gibes now? Your gambols, your songs, your flashes of merriment that were   145
wont° to set the table on a roar? Not one now, to mock your own grinning?°
Quite chopfallen?° Now get you to my lady's chamber and tell her, let her
paint an inch thick, to this favor° she must come. Make her laugh at that.
Prithee, Horatio, tell me one thing.

142 *bore* borne   143 *My gorge rises* i.e., I feel nauseated   145 *were wont* used   146 *mock your own grinning*
mock at the way your skull seems to be grinning (just as you used to mock at yourself and those who
grinned at you)   147 *chopfallen* (1) lacking the lower jaw (2) dejected   148 *favor* aspect, appearance

Horatio: What's that, my lord?   150

Hamlet: Dost thou think Alexander looked o' this fashion i' th' earth?

Horatio: E'en so.

Hamlet: And smelt so? Pah! [*He throws down the skull.*]

Horatio: E'en so, my lord.

Hamlet: To what base uses we may return, Horatio! Why may not imagination trace   155
  the noble dust of Alexander till 'a find it stopping a bunghole?°

Horatio: 'Twere to consider too curiously° to consider so.

Hamlet: No, faith, not a jot, but to follow him thither with modesty° enough, and
  likelihood to lead it. As thus: Alexander died, Alexander was buried, Alexander
  returneth to dust, the dust is earth, of earth we make loam,° and why of that   160
  loam whereto he was converted might they not stop a beer barrel?
Imperious° Caesar, dead and turned to clay,
Might stop a hole to keep the wind away.
O, that that earth which kept the world in awe
Should patch a wall t' expel the winter's flaw!°   165

*Enter King, Queen, Laertes, and the corpse [of Ophelia, in procession, with Priest,
lords, etc.].*

But soft,° but soft awhile! Here comes the King,
The Queen, the courtiers. Who is this they follow?
And with such maimèd° rites? This doth betoken
The corpse they follow did with desperate hand
Fordo° its own life. 'Twas of some estate.°   170
Couch we° awhile and mark.

  [*He and Horatio conceal themselves. Ophelia's body is taken to the grave.*]

Laertes: What ceremony else?

Hamlet [to Horatio]: That is Laertes, a very noble youth. Mark.

Laertes: What ceremony else?

Priest: Her obsequies have been as far enlarged   175
  As we have warranty.° Her death was doubtful,
  And but that great command o'ersways the order°
  She should in ground unsanctified been lodged°
  Till the last trumpet. For° charitable prayers,
  Shards,° flints, and pebbles should be thrown on her.   180
  Yet here she is allowed her virgin crants,°
  Her maiden strewments,° and the bringing home
  Of bell and burial.°

Laertes: Must there no more be done?

Priest: No more be done.

---

156 *bunghole* hole for filling or emptying a cask   157 *curiously* minutely   158 *modesty* plausible moderation   160 *loam* mortar consisting chiefly of moistened clay and straw   162 *Imperious* imperial   165 *flaw*
gust of wind   166 *soft* i.e., wait, be careful   168 *maimèd* mutilated, incomplete   170 *Fordo* destroy.
estate rank   171 *Couch we* let's hide, lie low   176 *warranty* i.e., ecclesiastical authority   177 *great . . .
order* orders from on high overrule the prescribed procedures   178 *She should . . . lodged* she should have
been buried in unsanctified ground   179 *For* in place of   180 *Shards* broken bits of pottery   181 *crants*
garlands betokening maidenhood   182 *strewments* flowers strewn on a coffin   182–183 *bringing . . .
burial* laying the body to rest, to the sound of the bell

The Queen mourns at Ophelia's funeral (V, i, 192–195).

We should profane the service of the dead   185
To sing a requiem and such rest° to her
As to peace-parted souls.°
Laertes: Lay her i' th' earth,
And from her fair and unpolluted flesh
May violets spring! I tell thee, churlish priest,
A ministering angel shall my sister be   190
When thou liest howling.°
Hamlet [to Horatio]:   What, the fair Ophelia!
Queen [scattering flowers]: Sweets to the sweet! Farewell.
I hoped thou shouldst have been my Hamlet's wife.

186 *such rest* i.e., to pray for such rest   187 *peace-parted souls* those who have died at peace with God
191 *howling* i.e., in hell

I thought thy bride-bed to have decked, sweet maid,
And not t' have strewed thy grave.
Laertes: O, treble woe   195
Fall ten times treble on that cursèd head
Whose wicked deed thy most ingenious sense°
Deprived thee of! Hold off the earth awhile,
Till I have caught her once more in mine arms.
                              [*He leaps into the grave and embraces Ophelia.*]
Now pile your dust upon the quick and dead,   200
Till of this flat a mountain you have made
T' o'ertop old Pelion or the skyish head
Of blue Olympus.°
Hamlet [*coming forward*]: What is he whose grief
Bears such an emphasis,° whose phrase of sorrow   205
Conjures the wandering stars° and makes them stand
Like wonder-wounded° hearers? This is I,
Hamlet the Dane.°
Laertes [*grappling with him*°]: The devil take thy soul!
Hamlet: Thou pray'st not well.   210
I prithee, take thy fingers from my throat,
For though I am not splenitive° and rash,
Yet have I in me something dangerous,
Which let thy wisdom fear. Hold off thy hand.
King: Pluck them asunder.   215
Queen: Hamlet, Hamlet!
All: Gentlemen!
Horatio: Good my lord, be quiet.   [*Hamlet and Laertes are parted.*]
Hamlet: Why, I will fight with him upon this theme
Until my eyelids will no longer wag.°   220
Queen: O my son, what theme?
Hamlet: I loved Ophelia. Forty thousand brothers
Could not with all their quantity of love
Make up my sum. What wilt thou do for her?
King: O, he is mad, Laertes.   225
Queen: For love of God, forbear him.°
Hamlet: 'Swounds,° show me what thou'lt do.
Woo't° weep? Woo't fight? Woo't fast? Woo't tear thyself?
Woo't drink up° eisel?° Eat a crocodile?°

---

197 *ingenious sense* a mind that is quick, alert, of fine qualities   202–203 *Pelion . . . Olympus* sacred mountains in the north of Thessaly   205 *emphasis* i.e., rhetorical and florid emphasis. (*Phrase* has a similar
rhetorical connotation.)   206 *wandering stars* planets   207 *wonder-wounded* struck with amazement   208
the Dane (This title normally signifies the King; see I, i, 17 and note.)   209 s.d. *grappling with him* The testimony of the First Quarto that "*Hamlet leaps in after Laertes*" and the "Elegy on Burbage" ("Oft have I seen
him leap into the grave") seem to indicate one way in which this fight was staged; however, the difficulty
of fitting two contenders and Ophelia's body into a confined space (probably the trapdoor) suggests to
many editors the alternative, that Laertes jumps out of the grave to attack Hamlet.)   212 *splenitive* quick-
tempered   220 *wag* move. (A fluttering eyelid is a conventional sign that life has not yet gone.   226
forbear him leave him alone   227 '*Swounds* by His (Christ's) wounds   228 *Woo't* wilt thou   229 *drink up*
drink deeply.   *eisel* vinegar.   *crocodile* (Crocodiles were tough and dangerous, and were supposed to shed
hypocritical tears.)

I'll do 't. Dost come here to whine?   230
To outface me with leaping in her grave?
Be buried quick° with her, and so will I.
And if thou prate of mountains, let them throw
Millions of acres on us, till our ground,
Singeing his pate° against the burning zone,°   235
Make Ossa° like a wart! Nay, an° thou'lt mouth,°
I'll rant as well as thou.
Queen: This is mere° madness,
And thus awhile the fit will work on him;
Anon, as patient as the female dove
When that her golden couplets° are disclosed,°   240
His silence will sit drooping.
Hamlet: Hear you, sir.
What is the reason that you use me thus?
I loved you ever. But it is no matter.
Let Hercules himself do what he may,
The cat will mew, and dog will have his day.°   245
                                                            Exit Hamlet.
King: I pray thee, good Horatio, wait upon him.
                                                            [Exit] Horatio.
[*To Laertes.*] Strengthen your patience in° our last night's speech;
We'll put the matter to the present push.°—
Good Gertrude, set some watch over your son.—
This grave shall have a living° monument.   250
An hour of quiet° shortly shall we see;
Till then, in patience our proceeding be.   *Exeunt.*

SCENE II [THE CASTLE.]

Enter Hamlet and Horatio.

Hamlet: So much for this, sir; now shall you see the other.°
     You do remember all the circumstance?
Horatio: Remember it, my lord!
Hamlet: Sir, in my heart there was a kind of fighting
     That would not let me sleep. Methought I lay   5
     Worse than the mutines° in the bilboes.° Rashly,°
     And praised be rashness for it—let us know°
     Our indiscretion° sometimes serves us well

232 *quick* alive   235 *his pate* its head, i.e., top.   *burning zone* zone in the celestial sphere containing the sun's orbit, between the tropics of Cancer and Capricorn   236 *Ossa* another mountain in Thessaly. (In their war against the Olympian gods, the giants attempted to heap Ossa on Pelion to scale Olympus.)   *an* if.   *mouth* i.e., rant   237 *mere* utter   240 *golden couplets* two baby pigeons, covered with yellow down.   *disclosed* hatched   244–245 *Let . . . day* i.e., (1) even Hercules couldn't stop Laertes' theatrical rant (2) I, too, will have my turn; i.e., despite any blustering attempts at interference, every person will sooner or later do what he or she must do   247 *in* i.e., by recalling   248 *present push* immediate test   250 *living* lasting. (For Laertes' private understanding, Claudius also hints that Hamlet's death will serve as such a monument.)   251 *hour of quiet* time free of conflict   1 *see the other* hear the other news   6 *mutines* mutineers. *bilboes* shackles.   *Rashly* on impulse. (This adverb goes with lines 12 ff.)   7 *know* acknowledge   8 *indiscretion* lack of foresight and judgment (not an indiscreet act)

When our deep plots do pall,° and that should learn° us
There's a divinity that shapes our ends,   10
Rough-hew° them how we will—

Horatio: That is most certain.

Hamlet: Up from my cabin,
My sea-gown° scarfed° about me, in the dark
Groped I to find out them,° had my desire,
Fingered° their packet, and in fine° withdrew   15
To mine own room again, making so bold,
My fears forgetting manners, to unseal
Their grand commission; where I found, Horatio—
Ah, royal knavery!—an exact command,
Larded° with many several° sorts of reasons   20
Importing° Denmark's health and England's too,
With, ho! such bugs° and goblins in my life,°
That on the supervise,° no leisure bated,°
No, not to stay° the grinding of the ax,
My head should be struck off.

Horatio: Is 't possible?   25

Hamlet [giving a document]: Here's the commission. Read it at more leisure.
But wilt thou hear now how I did proceed?

Horatio: I beseech you.

Hamlet: Being thus benetted round with villainies—
Ere I could make a prologue to my brains,   30
They had begun the play°—I sat me down,
Devised a new commission, wrote it fair.°
I once did hold it, as our statists° do,
A baseness° to write fair, and labored much
How to forget that learning, but, sir, now   35
It did me yeoman's° service. Wilt thou know
Th' effect° of what I wrote?

Horatio: Ay, good my lord.

Hamlet: An earnest conjuration° from the King,
As England was his faithful tributary,
As love between them like the palm° might flourish,
As peace should still° her wheaten garland° wear   40
And stand a comma° 'tween their amities,
And many suchlike "as"es° of great charge,°
That on the view and knowing of these contents,

---

9 *pall* fail, falter, go stale. *learn* teach   11 *Rough-hew* shape roughly   13 *sea-gown* seaman's coat.
scarfed loosely wrapped   14 *them* i.e., Rosencrantz and Guildenstern   15 *Fingered* pilfered, pinched. *in
fine* finally, in conclusion   20 *Larded* garnished. *several* different   21 *Importing* relating to   22 *bugs* bug-
bears, hobgoblins. *in my life* i.e., to be feared if I were allowed to live   23 *supervise* reading. *leisure bated*
delay allowed   24 *stay* await   30–31 *Ere . . . play* before I could consciously turn my brain to the matter,
it had started working on a plan   32 *fair* in a clear hand   33 *statists* statesmen   34 *baseness* i.e., lower-
class trait   36 *yeoman's* i.e., substantial, faithful, loyal   37 *effect* purport   38 *conjuration* entreaty   40
palm (An image of health; see Psalm 92:12.)   41 *still* always. *wheaten garland* (Symbolic of fruitful agri-
culture, of peace and plenty.)   42 *comma* (Indicating continuity, link.)   43 "*as*"*es* (1) the "whereases" of
a formal document (2) asses. *charge* (1) import (2) burden (appropriate to asses)

Without debatement further more or less,   45
He should those bearers put to sudden death,
Not shriving time° allowed.
Horatio: How was this sealed?
Hamlet: Why, even in that was heaven ordinant.°
   I had my father's signet° in my purse,
   Which was the model° of that Danish seal;   50
   Folded the writ° up in the form of th' other,
   Subscribed° it, gave 't th' impression,° placed it safely,
   The changeling° never known. Now, the next day
   Was our sea fight, and what to this was sequent°
   Thou knowest already.   55
Horatio: So Guildenstern and Rosencrantz go to 't.
Hamlet: Why, man, they did make love to this employment.
   They are not near my conscience. Their defeat°
   Does by their own insinuation° grow.
   'Tis dangerous when the baser° nature comes   60
   Between the pass° and fell° incensed points
   Of mighty opposites.°
Horatio: Why, what a king is this!
Hamlet: Does it not, think thee, stand me now upon°—
   He that hath killed my king and whored my mother.
   Popped in between th' election° and my hopes,   65
   Thrown out his angle° for my proper° life,
   And with such cozenage°—is 't not perfect conscience
   To quit° him with this arm? And is 't not to be damned
   To let this canker° of our nature come
   In° further evil?   70
Horatio: It must be shortly known to him from England
   What is the issue of the business there.
Hamlet: It will be short. The interim is mine.
   And a man's life's no more than to say "one."°
   But I am very sorry, good Horatio,   75
   That to Laertes I forgot myself.
   For by the image of my cause I see
   The portraiture of his. I'll court his favors.
   But, sure, the bravery° of his grief did put me
   Into a tow'ring passion.
Horatio: Peace, who comes here?   80

   Enter a Courtier [Osric].

---

47 *shriving time* time for confession and absolution   48 *ordinant* directing   49 *signet* small seal   50 *model*
replica   51 *writ* writing   52 *Subscribed* signed (with forged signature).   *impression* i.e., with a wax seal
53 *changeling* i.e., substituted letter. (Literally, a fairy child substituted for a human one.)   54 *was sequent*
followed   58 *defeat* destruction   59 *insinuation* intrusive intervention, sticking their noses in my business
60 *baser* of lower social station   61 *pass* thrust.   *fell* fierce   62 *opposites* antagonists   63 *stand me now*
upon become incumbent on me now   65 *election* (The Danish monarch was "elected" by a small number
of high-ranking electors.)   66 *angle* fishhook.   *proper* very   67 *cozenage* trickery   68 *quit* requite, pay
back   69 *canker* ulcer   69–70 *come in* grow into   74 *a man's . . . "one"* one's whole life occupies such a
short time, only as long as it takes to count to 1   79 *bravery* bravado

Osric: Your lordship is right welcome back to Denmark.

Hamlet: I humbly thank you, sir. [*To Horatio.*] Dost know this water fly?

Horatio: No, my good lord.

Hamlet: Thy state is the more gracious, for 'tis a vice to know him. He hath much, land and fertile. Let a beast be lord of beasts, and his crib° shall stand at the   85
King's mess.° 'Tis a chuff,° but, as I say, spacious in the possession of dirt.

Osric: Sweet lord, if your lordship were at leisure, I should impart a thing to you from His Majesty.

Hamlet: I will receive it, sir, with all diligence of spirit. Put your bonnet° to his°
right use; 'tis for the head.   90

Osric: I thank your lordship, it is very hot.

Hamlet: No, believe me, 'tis very cold. The wind is northerly.

Osric: It is indifferent° cold, my lord, indeed.

Hamlet: But yet methinks it is very sultry and hot for my complexion.°

Osric: Exceedingly, my lord. It is very sultry, as 'twere—I cannot tell how. My lord,   95
His Majesty bade me signify to you that 'a has laid a great wager on your head.
Sir, this is the matter—

Hamlet: I beseech you, remember.

[*Hamlet moves him to put on his hat.*]

Osric: Nay, good my lord; for my ease,° in good faith. Sir, here is newly come to court
Laertes—believe me, an absolute° gentleman, full of most excellent differences,°   100
of very soft society° and great showing.° Indeed, to speak feelingly° of him, he is
the card° or calendar° of gentry,° for you shall find in him the continent of what
part a gentleman would see.°

Hamlet: Sir, his definement° suffers no perdition° in you,° though I know to divide
him inventorially° would dozy° th' arithmetic of memory, and yet but yaw°   105
neither° in respect of° his quick sail. But, in the verity of extolment,° I take him
to be a soul of great article,° and his infusion° of such dearth and rareness° as, to
make true diction° of him, his semblable° is his mirror and who else would trace°
him his umbrage,° nothing more.

Osric: Your lordship speaks most infallibly of him.   110

Hamlet: The concernancy,° sir? Why do we wrap the gentleman in our more rawer
breath?°

Osric: Sir?

---

85 *crib* manger   85–86 *Let . . . mess* i.e., if a man, no matter how beastlike, is as rich in livestock and possessions as Osric, he may eat at the King's table   86 *chuff* boor, churl. (The Second Quarto spelling, *chough*, is a variant spelling that also suggests the meaning here of "chattering jackdaw.")   89 *bonnet* any kind of cap or hat.   *his* its   93 *indifferent* somewhat   94 *complexion* temperament   99 *for my ease* (A conventional reply declining the invitation to put his hat back on.)   100 *absolute* perfect.   *differences* special qualities   101 *soft society* agreeable manners.   *great showing* distinguished appearance.   *feelingly* with just perception   102 *card* chart, map.   *calendar* guide.   *gentry* good breeding   102–103 *the continent . . . see* one who contains in him all the qualities a gentleman would like to see. (A *continent* is that which contains.)   104 *definement* definition. (Hamlet proceeds to mock Osric by throwing his lofty diction back at him.)   *perdition* loss, diminution.   *you* your description   104–105 *divide him inventorially* enumerate his graces   105 *dozy* dizzy.   *yaw* swing unsteadily off course. (Said of a ship.)   106 *neither* for all that.   *in respect of* in comparison with.   *in . . . extolment* in true praise (of him)   107 *of great article* one with many articles in his inventory.   *infusion* essence, character infused into him by nature.   *dearth and rareness* rarity   108 *make true diction* speak truly.   *semblable* only true likeness.   *who . . . trace* any other person who would wish to follow   109 *umbrage* shadow   111 *concernancy* import, relevance   111–112 *rawer breath* unrefined speech that can only come short in praising him

Horatio: Is 't not possible to understand in another tongue?° You will do 't,° sir,
    really. 115
Hamlet: What imports the nomination of this gentleman?
Osric: Of Laertes?
Horatio [*to Hamlet*]: His purse is empty already; all 's golden words are spent.
Hamlet: Of him, sir.
Osric: I know you are not ignorant— 120
Hamlet: I would you did, sir. Yet in faith if you did, it would not much approve° me.
    Well, sir?
Osric: You are not ignorant of what excellence Laertes is—
Hamlet: I dare not confess that, lest I should compare with him in excellence.
    But to know a man well were to know himself.° 125
Osric: I mean, sir, for° his weapon; but in the imputation laid on him by them,° in
    his meed° he's unfellowed.°
Hamlet: What's his weapon?
Osric: Rapier and dagger.
Hamlet: That's two of his weapons—but well.° 130
Osric: The King, sir, hath wagered with him six Barbary horses, against the which
    he° has impawned,° as I take it, six French rapiers and poniards,° with their
    assigns,° as girdle, hangers,° and so.° Three of the carriages,° in faith, are very
    dear to fancy,° very responsive° to the hilts, most delicate° carriages, and of very
    liberal conceit.° 135
Hamlet: What call you the carriages?
Horatio [*to Hamlet*]: I knew you must be edified by the margent° ere you had done.
Osric: The carriages, sir, are the hangers.
Hamlet: The phrase would be more germane to the matter if we could carry a cannon
    by our sides; I would it might be hangers till then. But, on: six Barbary horses 140
    against six French swords, their assigns, and three liberal—conceited carriages;
    that's the French bet against the Danish. Why is this impawned, as you call it?
Osric: The King, sir, hath laid,° sir, that in a dozen passes° between yourself and him,
    he shall not exceed you three hits. He hath laid on twelve for nine, and it would
    come to immediate trial, if your lordship would vouchsafe the answer.° 145
Hamlet: How if I answer no?
Osric: I mean, my lord, the opposition of your person in trial.

---

114 *to understand . . . tongue* i.e., for you, Osric, to understand when someone else speaks your language.
(Horatio twits Osric for not being able to understand the kind of flowery speech he himself uses, when
Hamlet speaks in such a vein. Alternatively, all this could be said to Hamlet.) *You will do 't* i.e., you can
if you try, or, you may well have to try (to speak plainly) 121 *approve* commend 124–125 *I dare . . . .*
himself I dare not boast of knowing Laertes' excellence lest I seem to imply a comparable excellence in myself. Certainly to know another person well, one must know oneself 126 *for* i.e., with. *imputation . . .*
them reputation given him by others 127 *meed* merit. *unfellowed* unmatched 130 *but well* but never
mind 132 *he* i.e., Laertes. *impawned* staked, wagered. *poniards* daggers 133 *assigns* appurtenances.
hangers straps on the sword belt (*girdle*), from which the sword hung. *and so* and so on. *carriages* (An affected way of saying *hangers*; literally, gun carriages.) 134 *dear to fancy* delightful to the fancy.
responsive corresponding closely, matching or well-adjusted. *delicate* (i.e., in workmanship) 135 *liberal*
conceit elaborate design 137 *margent* margin of a book, place for explanatory notes 143 *laid* wagered.
passes bouts. (The odds of the betting are hard to explain. Possibly the King bets that Hamlet will win at
least five out of twelve, at which point Laertes raises the odds against himself by betting he will win nine.)
145 *vouchsafe the answer* be so good as to accept the challenge. (Hamlet deliberately takes the phrase in its
literal sense of replying.)

Hamlet: Sir, I will walk here in the hall. If it please His Majesty, it is the breathing time° of day with me. Let° the foils be brought, the gentleman willing, and the King hold his purpose, I will win for him an I can; if not, I will gain nothing but   150
my shame and the odd hits.

Osric: Shall I deliver you° so?

Hamlet: To this effect, sir—after what flourish your nature will.

Osric: I commend° my duty to your lordship.

Hamlet: Yours, yours. [*Exit Osric.*] 'A does well to commend it himself; there are no   155
tongues else for 's turn.°

Horatio: This lapwing° runs away with the shell on his head.

Hamlet: 'A did comply with his dug° before 'a sucked it. Thus has he—and many more of the same breed that I know the drossy° age dotes on—only got the tune° of the time and, out of an habit of encounter,° a kind of yeasty° collection,°   160
which carries them through and through the most fanned and winnowed opinions;° and do° but blow them to their trial, the bubbles are out.°

Enter a Lord.

Lord: My lord, His Majesty commended him to you by young Osric, who brings back to him that you attend him in the hall. He sends to know if your pleasure hold to play with Laertes, or that you will take longer time.   165

Hamlet: I am constant to my purposes; they follow the King's pleasure. If his fitness speaks, mine is ready;° now or whensoever, provided I be so able as now.

Lord: The King and Queen and all are coming down.

Hamlet: In happy time.°

Lord: The Queen desires you to use some gentle entertainment° to Laertes before   170
you fall to play.

Hamlet: She well instructs me.   [*Exit Lord.*]

Horatio: You will lose, my lord.

Hamlet: I do not think so. Since he went into France, I have been in continual practice; I shall win at the odds. But thou wouldst not think how ill all's here about my   175
heart; but it is no matter.

Horatio: Nay, good my lord—

Hamlet: It is but foolery, but it is such a kind of gaingiving° as would perhaps trouble a woman.

Horatio: If your mind dislike anything, obey it. I will forestall their repair° hither and   180
say you are not fit.

148–149 *breathing time* exercise period   149 *Let* i.e., if   152 *deliver you* report what you say   154 *commend* commit to your favor. (A conventional salutation, but Hamlet wryly uses a more literal meaning, "recommend," "praise," in line 155.)   156 *for 's turn* for his purposes, i.e., to do it for him   157 *lapwing* (A proverbial type of youthful forwardness. Also, a bird that draws intruders away from its nest and was thought to run about with its head in the shell when newly hatched; a seeming reference to Osric's hat.)   158 *comply . . . dug* observe ceremonious formality toward his nurse's or mother's teat   159 *drossy* laden with scum and impurities, frivolous.   *tune* temper, mood, manner of speech   160 *an habit of encounter* a demeanor in conversing (with courtiers of his own kind).   *yeasty* frothy.   *collection* i.e., of current phrases   161–162 *carries . . . opinions* sustains them right through the scrutiny of persons whose opinions are select and refined. (Literally, like grain separated from its chaff. Osric is both the chaff and the bubbly froth on the surface of the liquor that is soon blown away.)   162 *and do* yet do.   *blow . . . out* test them by merely blowing on them, and their bubbles burst   166–167 *If . . . ready* if he declares his readiness, my convenience waits on his   169 *In happy time* (A phrase of courtesy indicating that the time is convenient.)   170 *entertainment* greeting   178 *gaingiving* misgiving   180 *repair* coming

Hamlet: Not a whit, we defy augury. There is special providence in the fall of a sparrow.
    If it be now, 'tis not to come; if it be not to come, it will be now; if it be not now,
    yet it will come. The readiness is all. Since no man of aught he leaves knows, what
    is 't to leave betimes? Let be.°   185

A table prepared. [Enter] *trumpets, drums, and officers with cushions; King, Queen,*
[*Osric,*] *and all the state; foils, daggers,* [*and wine borne in;*] *and Laertes.*

King: Come, Hamlet, come and take this hand from me.
                        [*The King puts Laertes' hand into Hamlet's.*]
Hamlet [*to Laertes*]: Give me your pardon, sir. I have done you wrong,
    But pardon 't as you are a gentleman.
    This presence° knows,
    And you must needs have heard, how I am punished°   190
    With a sore distraction. What I have done
    That might your nature, honor, and exception°
    Roughly awake, I here proclaim was madness.
    Was 't Hamlet wronged Laertes? Never Hamlet.
    If Hamlet from himself be ta'en away,   195
    And when he's not himself does wrong Laertes,
    Then Hamlet does it not, Hamlet denies it.
    Who does it, then? His madness. If 't be so,
    Hamlet is of the faction° that is wronged;
    His madness is poor Hamlet's enemy.   200
    Sir, in this audience
    Let my disclaiming from a purposed evil
    Free me so far in your most generous thoughts
    That I have° shot my arrow o'er the house
    And hurt my brother.
Laertes: I am satisfied in nature,°   205
    Whose motive° in this case should stir me most
    To my revenge. But in my terms of honor
    I stand aloof, and will no reconcilement
    Till by some elder masters of known honor
    I have a voice° and precedent of peace°   210
    To keep my name ungored.° But till that time
    I do receive your offered love like love,
    And will not wrong it.
Hamlet: I embrace it freely,
    And will this brother's wager frankly° play.—
    Give us the foils. Come on.
Laertes: Come, one for me.   215
Hamlet: I'll be your foil,° Laertes. In mine ignorance

184–185 *Since . . . Let be* since no one has knowledge of what he is leaving behind, what does an early
death matter after all? Enough; don't struggle against it.   189 *presence* royal assembly   190 *punished* af-
flicted   192 *exception* disapproval   199 *faction* party   204 *That I have* as if I had   205 *in nature* i.e., as to
my personal feelings   206 *motive* prompting   210 *voice* authoritative pronouncement.   *of peace* for reconciliation   211 *name ungored* reputation unwounded   214 *frankly* without ill feeling or the burden of rancor
216 *foil* thin metal background that sets a jewel off (with pun on the blunted rapier for fencing)

Your skill shall, like a star i' the darkest night,
    Stick fiery off° indeed.

Laertes: You mock me, sir.

Hamlet: No, by this hand.

King: Give them the foils, young Osric. Cousin Hamlet,   220
    You know the wager?

Hamlet: Very well, my lord.
    Your Grace has laid the odds o'° the weaker side.

King: I do not fear it; I have seen you both.
    But since he is bettered,° we have therefore odds.

Laertes: This is too heavy. Let me see another.   225

                    [He exchanges his foil for another.]

Hamlet: This likes me° well. These foils have all a length?

                          [They prepare to play.]

Osric: Ay, my good lord.

King: Set me the stoups of wine upon that table.
    If Hamlet give the first or second hit,
    Or quit in answer of the third exchange,°   230
    Let all the battlements their ordnance fire.
    The King shall drink to Hamlet's better breath,°
    And in the cup an union° shall he throw
    Richer than that which four successive kings
    In Denmark's crown have worn. Give me the cups,   235
    And let the kettle° to the trumpet speak,
    The trumpet to the cannoneer without,
    The cannons to the heavens, the heaven to earth,
    "Now the King drinks to Hamlet." Come, begin.

                        Trumpets the while.

    And you, the judges, bear a wary eye.   240

Hamlet: Come on, sir.

Laertes: Come, my lord. *[They play. Hamlet scores a hit.]*

Hamlet: One.

Laertes: No.

Hamlet: Judgment.

Osric: A hit, a very palpable hit.   245

             Drum, trumpets, and shot. Flourish.
                    A piece goes off.

Laertes: Well, again.

King: Stay, give me drink. Hamlet, this pearl is thine.

             [He drinks, and throws a pearl in Hamlet's cup.]

    Here's to thy health. Give him the cup.

Hamlet: I'll play this bout first. Set it by awhile.
    Come. *[They play.]* Another hit; what say you?   250

---

218 *Stick fiery off* stand out brilliantly   222 *laid the odds o'* bet on, backed   224 *is bettered* has improved; is the odds-on favorite. (Laertes' handicap is the "three hits" specified in line 144.)   226 *likes me* pleases me 230 *Or . . . . exchange* i.e., or requites Laertes in the third bout for having won the first two   232 *better breath* improved vigor   233 *union* pearl. (So called, according to Pliny's *Natural History*, 9, because pearls are *unique*, never identical.)   236 *kettle* kettledrum

Deadly swordplay between Laertes and Hamlet (V, ii, 241–269).

Laertes: A touch, a touch, I do confess 't.

King: Our son shall win.

Queen: He's fat° and scant of breath.
    Here, Hamlet, take my napkin,° rub thy brows.
    The Queen carouses° to thy fortune, Hamlet.

Hamlet: Good madam!   255

King: Gertrude, do not drink.

Queen: I will, my lord, I pray you pardon me.   [*She drinks.*]

King [*aside*]: It is the poisoned cup. It is too late.

Hamlet: I dare not drink yet, madam; by and by.

Queen: Come, let me wipe thy face.   260

Laertes [*to King*]: My lord, I'll hit him now.

King: I do not think 't.

Laertes [*aside*]: And yet it is almost against my conscience.

Hamlet: Come, for the third, Laertes. You do but dally.
    I pray you, pass° with your best violence;   265
    I am afeard you make a wanton of me.°

Laertes: Say you so? Come on.   [*They play.*]

Osric: Nothing neither way.

Laertes: Have at you now!

252 *fat* not physically fit, out of training   253 *napkin* handkerchief   254 *carouses* drinks a toast
265 *pass* thrust   266 *make . . . me* i.e., treat me like a spoiled child, trifle with me

[*Laertes wounds Hamlet; then, in scuffling, they change rapiers,° and Hamlet wounds Laertes.*]

King: Part them! They are incensed.

Hamlet: Nay, come, again.   [*The Queen falls.*]

Osric: Look to the Queen there, ho!   270

Horatio: They bleed on both sides. How is it, my lord?

Osric: How is 't, Laertes?

Laertes: Why, as a woodcock° to mine own springe,° Osric;
    I am justly killed with mine own treachery.

Hamlet: How does the Queen?

King: She swoons to see them bleed.   275

Queen: No, no, the drink, the drink—O my dear Hamlet—
    The drink, the drink! I am poisoned.   [*She dies.*]

Hamlet: O villainy! Ho, let the door be locked!
    Treachery! Seek it out.   [*Laertes falls. Exit Osric.*]

Laertes: It is here, Hamlet. Hamlet, thou art slain.   280
    No med'cine in the world can do thee good;
    In thee there is not half an hour's life.
    The treacherous instrument is in thy hand,
    Unbated° and envenomed. The foul practice°
    Hath turned itself on me. Lo, here I lie,   285
    Never to rise again. Thy mother's poisoned.
    I can no more. The King, the King's to blame.

Hamlet: The point envenomed too? Then, venom, to thy work.

                            [*He stabs the King.*]

All: Treason! Treason!

King: O, yet defend me, friends! I am but hurt.   290

Hamlet [*forcing the King to drink*]: Here, thou incestuous, murderous, damnèd Dane,
    Drink off this potion. Is thy union° here?
    Follow my mother.   [*The King dies.*]

Laertes: He is justly served.
    It is a poison tempered° by himself.
    Exchange forgiveness with me, noble Hamlet.   295
    Mine and my father's death come not upon thee,
    Nor thine on me!   [*He dies.*]

Hamlet: Heaven make thee free of it! I follow thee.
    I am dead, Horatio. Wretched Queen, adieu!
    You that look pale and tremble at this chance,°   300
    That are but mutes° or audience to this act,
    Had I but time—as this fell° sergeant,° Death,
    Is strict° in his arrest°—O, I could tell you—

---

269 s.d. *in scuffling, they change rapiers* (This stage direction occurs in the Folio. According to a widespread stage tradition, Hamlet receives a scratch, realizes that Laertes' sword is unbated, and accordingly forces an exchange.) 273 *woodcock* a bird, a type of stupidity or as a decoy. *springe* trap, snare 284 *Unbated* not blunted with a button. *practice* plot 292 *union* pearl. (See line 233; with grim puns on the word's other meanings: marriage, shared death.) 294 *tempered* mixed 300 *chance* mischance 301 *mutes* silent observers. (Literally, actors with nonspeaking parts.) 302 *fell* cruel. *sergeant* sheriff's officer 303 *strict* (1) severely just (2) unavoidable. *arrest* (1) taking into custody (2) stopping my speech

But let it be. Horatio, I am dead;
Thou livest. Report me and my cause aright   305
To the unsatisfied.

Horatio: Never believe it.
I am more an antique Roman° than a Dane.
Here's yet some liquor left.

[*He attempts to drink from the poisoned cup. Hamlet prevents him.*]

Hamlet: As thou'rt a man,
Give me the cup! Let go! By heaven, I'll ha 't.
O God, Horatio, what a wounded name,   310
Things standing thus unknown, shall I leave behind me!
If thou didst ever hold me in thy heart,
Absent thee from felicity awhile,
And in this harsh world draw thy breath in pain
To tell my story.   *A march afar off [and a volley within].*
What warlike noise is this?   315

Enter Osric.

Osric: Young Fortinbras, with conquest come from Poland,
To th' ambassadors of England gives
This warlike volley.

Hamlet: O, I die, Horatio!
The potent poison quite o'ercrows° my spirit.
I cannot live to hear the news from England,   320
But I do prophesy th' election lights
On Fortinbras. He has my dying voice.°
So tell him, with th' occurrents° more and less
Which have solicited°—the rest is silence.   [*He dies.*]

Horatio: Now cracks a noble heart. Good night, sweet prince,   325
And flights of angels sing thee to thy rest!

[*March within.*]

Why does the drum come hither?

Enter Fortinbras, with the [English] Ambassadors [with drum, colors, and attendants].

Fortinbras: Where is this sight?

Horatio: What is it you would see?
If aught of woe or wonder, cease your search.

Fortinbras: This quarry° cries on havoc.° O proud Death,   330
What feast° is toward° in thine eternal cell,
That thou so many princes at a shot
So bloodily hast struck?

---

307 *Roman* (Suicide was an honorable choice for many Romans as an alternative to a dishonorable life.)
319 *o'ercrows* triumphs over (like the winner in a cockfight)   322 *voice* vote   323 *occurrents* events, incidents   324 *solicited* moved, urged. (Hamlet doesn't finish saying what the events have prompted—
presumably, his acts of vengeance, or his reporting of those events to Fortinbras.)   330 *quarry* heap of
dead. *cries on havoc* proclaims a general slaughter   331 *feast* i.e., Death feasting on those who have
fallen. *toward* in preparation

First Ambassador: The sight is dismal,
   And our affairs from England come too late.
   The ears are senseless that should give us hearing,   335
   To tell him his commandment is fulfilled,
   That Rosencrantz and Guildenstern are dead.
   Where should we have our thanks?
Horatio: Not from his° mouth,
   Had it th' ability of life to thank you.
   He never gave commandment for their death.   340
   But since, so jump° upon this bloody question,°
   You from the Polack wars, and you from England,
   Are here arrived, give order that these bodies
   High on a stage° be placèd to the view,
   And let me speak to th' yet unknowing world   345
   How these things came about. So shall you hear
   Of carnal, bloody, and unnatural acts,
   Of accidental judgments,° casual° slaughters,
   Of deaths put on° by cunning and forced cause,°
   And, in this upshot, purposes mistook   350
   Fall'n on th' inventors' heads. All this can I
   Truly deliver.
Fortinbras: Let us haste to hear it,
   And call the noblest to the audience.
   For me, with sorrow I embrace my fortune.
   I have some rights of memory° in this kingdom,   355
   Which now to claim my vantage° doth invite me.
Horatio: Of that I shall have also cause to speak,
   And from his mouth whose voice will draw on more.°
   But let this same be presently° performed,
   Even while men's minds are wild, lest more mischance   360
   On° plots and errors happen.
Fortinbras: Let four captains
   Bear Hamlet, like a soldier, to the stage,
   For he was likely, had he been put on,°
   To have proved most royal; and for his passage,°
   The soldiers' music and the rite of war   365
   Speak° loudly for him.
   Take up the bodies. Such a sight as this
   Becomes the field,° but here shows much amiss.
   Go bid the soldiers shoot.

Exeunt [marching, bearing off the dead bodies; a peal of ordnance is shot off].

---

338 *his* i.e., Claudius'   341 *jump* precisely, immediately.   *question* dispute, affair   344 *stage* platform
348 *judgments* retributions.   *casual* occurring by chance   349 *put on* instigated.   *forced cause* contrivance
355 *of memory* traditional, remembered, unforgotten   356 *vantage* favorable opportunity   358 *voice . . . more* vote will influence still others   359 *presently* immediately   361 *On* on the basis of; on top of   363 *put on* i.e., invested in royal office and so put to the test   364 *passage* i.e., from life to death   366 *Speak* (let them) speak   368 *Becomes the field* suits the field of battle

Questions

ACT I

1. By what means does Shakespeare build suspense before the Ghost's appearances? What disturbing political events occur in the background of the first act?

2. Why is Hamlet so unwilling to trust what the Ghost tells him? What precisely does the Ghost instruct him to do? (What does the Ghost command him not to do?) Why does Hamlet not immediately obey the Ghost's orders?

3. What is Hamlet's relationship to Horatio at the beginning of the play (ii, 160–188)? How does their relationship change in the course of the play?

4. How does Claudius appear in his first scene (ii, 1–128)? Does he betray evidence of guilt?

5. Hamlet's first soliloquy (ii, 129–159) occurs before Horatio reports the Ghost's appearance. What does it reveal about the Prince's state of mind? What things trouble him?

6. Is the advice Polonius offers Laertes trustworthy? Polonius sometimes appears bumbling and self-deluded. Does his opening speech (iii, 55–81) offer good or bad advice?

7. What does Polonius tell Ophelia about Hamlet's declarations of affection (iii, 102–136)? What do his remarks reveal about his opinion of Ophelia?

ACT II

1. How does Polonius's conversation with Reynaldo change our opinion of the old counselor? What verbal mannerisms does Shakespeare give to Polonius that now make him appear comic? What precisely does Polonius ask Reynaldo to do in Paris?

2. When Ophelia tells her father about Hamlet's frightening visit to her room (i, 77–102), how does Polonius interpret the event? What does the audience know that might lead them to analyze the Prince's visit differently?

3. When Polonius announces his theory of Hamlet's madness to the King, the counselor indulges in wordplay and metaphor (ii, 86–91). What does his performance suggest about his personality?

4. Is Polonius entirely foolish? Is he capable of genuine insight? Give specific examples of wise and deluded judgments by Polonius.

5. Polonius observes "there is method" in Hamlet's madness (ii, 197). Give an example of something important that Hamlet utters under the guise of madness that he probably would not say openly in a more rational way.

6. What does Hamlet imply about Polonius in his remark "That great baby you see there is not yet out of his swaddling clouts" (ii, 330–331)? Does Rosencrantz understand the Prince's joke (332–333)?

7. What does Hamlet's request to hear a recitation from the players about Pyrrhus's bloody slaughter at Troy suggest about the Prince's state of mind? What specific actions by Pyrrhus are the most suggestive of Hamlet's own plans?

ACT III

1. In his most famous soliloquy (i, 57–91), what course of action does Hamlet contemplate? How does he resolve his internal argument?

2. How guilty is Gertrude? With what offenses does Hamlet charge her (Scene iv)? Is our attitude toward her the same as Hamlet's or different? Does our sympathy for her grow or diminish as the play continues?

3. What is odd about the Ghost's appearance to Hamlet in the Queen's bedroom (iv, 106–142)?

4. From the play-within-a-play (Scene ii) and from Hamlet's remarks on acting, what do we learn about the Elizabethan theater? How do Hamlet's remarks serve to advance the story?

5. Discuss Hamlet's treatment of Ophelia (see especially Scene i). Does his behavior seem cruel, in conflict with his supposed nobility and sensitivity?

ACT IV

1. When Claudius demands that the Queen explain her son's behavior, Gertrude claims that the Prince is insane (i, 1–27). Does she truly believe Hamlet is mad, or is she trying to protect him from Claudius?

2. What causes Ophelia to go mad? Cite lines or events in the play for your interpretation.

3. Discuss how Shakespeare differently portrays Hamlet's feigned madness and Ophelia's real madness. State some specific differences in Shakespeare's presentation.

4. When Laertes returns to avenge his father's death, does he appear heroic or confused? How does his behavior compare with Hamlet's strategy for revenge?

ACT V

1. The final act of *Hamlet* begins with a long comic scene featuring two gravediggers. This episode has little direct bearing on the plot, and the two gravediggers never reappear. What does this comic interlude add to the tragedy? Would the play be more focused and forceful without this humorous scene?

2. *Hamlet* ends with the arrival of Fortinbras. If someone suggested that Fortinbras be cut from the play, what reasons would you offer for his inclusion?

General Questions

1. What is the play's major dramatic question? (For a discussion of this term, see page 1166.) At what point is the question formulated? Does this play have a crisis, or turning point?

2. How early in the play, and from what passages, do you perceive that Claudius is a villain?

3. What comic elements does the play contain—what scenes, what characters, what exchanges of dialogue? What is their value to a play that, as a whole, is a tragedy?

4. A familiar kind of behavior is showing one face to the world and another to oneself. What characters in *Hamlet* do so? Is their deception ever justified?

5. Is Laertes a villain like Claudius, or is there reason to feel that his contrived duel with Hamlet is justified?

6. How is Hamlet shown to be a noble and extraordinary person, not merely by birth, but by nature? See Ophelia's praise of Hamlet as "The glass of fashion, and the mold of form" (III, i, 142–153). Are we to take Ophelia's speech as the prejudiced view of a lover, or does Shakespeare demonstrate that her opinion of Hamlet is trustworthy?

7. If the characters of Rosencrantz and Guildenstern are cut from the play, as is the case in some productions, what is lost?

THE BACKGROUND OF *A MIDSUMMER NIGHT'S DREAM*

The theme in *A Midsummer Night's Dream* of love being best fulfilled in marital union suggests that the play may have originally been written for performance at an aristocratic wedding. The work is certainly Shakespeare's most lyrical and romantic comedy, full of reflections on fantasy, dreaming, and desire, set mostly amid festive palaces and moonlit woods filled with fairies.

In the Renaissance there were two major varieties of comedy—both borrowed from Greek and Roman drama. The first was satiric comedy, which usually poked bitter fun at human folly. Shakespeare generally avoided this mode, which was very well practiced by his friend Ben Jonson. Instead, Shakespeare preferred the second type, romantic comedy, which he had discovered as a schoolboy reading the Latin plays of Terence and Plautus. Romantic comedy is less concerned with correcting misdeeds and folly than with following the delightful and embarrassing behavior of imperfect but mostly likeable characters. Always ending in the happy marriage (or marriages) of young lovers who have overcome considerable obstacles to unite, romantic comedy also encourages the viewer to accept and forgive human faults and frailties.

Kevin Kline as Bottom and Michelle Pfeiffer as Titania in a 1999 film adaptation of *A Midsummer Night's Dream.*

A Midsummer Night's Dream also demonstrates Shakespeare's particular genius for plotting, a necessary skill for comic theater. Although Shakespeare often borrowed (and usually greatly improved) the stories of his plays from various sources, the plot of *A Midsummer Night's Dream* appears to be original, though he took individual characters like Theseus and Titania from classical mythology. The comedy has a delightfully complex structure combining four different plots—all romantic in different ways, from young love to marital reconciliation.

The play presents five different sets of lovers. The general action is framed around the wedding of the first set of lovers, King Theseus and the Amazon Queen Hippolyta, whom he has conquered in war and taken as his wife. Both a personal and public union, their marriage will end the enmity between their nations. More complicated are the love affairs of the second group, the young aristocrats—Helena, Lysander, Hermia, and Demetrius. The adventures of these two passionately mismatched couples, who ultimately find happy marriages, form the main plot of the comedy. The third set of lovers is a supernatural couple, Oberon and Titania, the king and queen of the fairy realm, who are in the midst of a bitter marital dispute. Then, there is a group of rustic workmen dominated by Nick Bottom, a weaver with theatrical aspirations. While this group does not initially seem to contain any lovers, Bottom eventually becomes entangled in a series of enchantments that transforms him into Titania's ass-eared darling for a single night. Finally, at the play's end the rustics perform a burlesque of tragic love that presents a fifth, imaginary set of lovers, Pyramus and Thisbe. Their tale of "tragical mirth" subtly comments on the consequences of doomed romance. No other comedy by Shakespeare focuses so single-mindedly or happily on sexual love and marriage. No wonder *A Midsummer Night's Dream* has been popular for centuries, not only in English-speaking countries but around the world.

PICTURING *A Midsummer*

▲ Hippolyta and Theseus, *page 1514*

▲ Lysander and Hermia, *page 1517*

◄ Bottom as ass, *page 1540*

▼ Oberon enchants Titania, *page 1534*

► "You thief of love," *page 1551*

Night's Dream

▲ Demetrius to Helena:
"Let me go!"
page 1531

▲ The rustics plan their play,
page 1521

▲ Oberon directs Puck, *page 1528*

▼ Puck's closing soliloquy,
page 1575

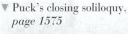

▲ The fairies tend to Bottom,
page 1557

► The performance of
Pyramus and Thisbe,
page 1569

A Midsummer Night's Dream

Edited By David Bevington

[DRAMATIS PERSONAE

Theseus, Duke of Athens
Hippolyta, Queen of the Amazons, betrothed to Theseus
Philostrate, Master of the Revels
Egeus, father of Hermia
Hermia, daughter of Egeus, in love with Lysander
Lysander, in love with Hermia
Demetrius, in love with Hermia and favored by Egeus
Helena, in love with Demetrius

Oberon, King of the Fairies
Titania, Queen of the Fairies
Puck, or Robin Goodfellow
Peaseblossom,
Cobweb,
Mote, ⎬ fairies attending Titania
Mustardseed,
Other fairies attending

Peter Quince, a carpenter,		*Prologue*
Nick Bottom, a weaver,		*Pyramus*
Francis Flute, a bellows mender,	representing	*Thisbe*
Tom Snout, a tinker,		*Wall*
Snug, a joiner,		*Lion*
Robin Starveling, a tailor,		*Moonshine*

Lords and Attendants on Theseus and Hippolyta

SCENE. *Athens, and a wood near it*]

ACT I

SCENE I [ATHENS. THESEUS' COURT.]

Enter Theseus, Hippolyta, [and Philostrate,] with others.

Theseus: Now, fair Hippolyta, our nuptial hour
Draws on apace. Four happy days bring in
Another moon; but, O, methinks, how slow

NOTE ON THE TEXT: This text of A *Midsummer Night's Dream* is taken from the First Quarto of 1600. For the reader's convenience, some material has been added by the editor, David Bevington (some indications of scenes and some stage directions). Such additions are enclosed in brackets. Mr. Bevington's text and notes were prepared for his book *The Complete Works of Shakespeare*, Updated 4th ed. (New York: Longman, 1997).

PRODUCTION PHOTOS: The photos included are from the 2005 production of A *Midsummer Night's Dream* by the Utah Shakespearean Festival, with Anne Newhall (Hippolyta and Titania), Michael Sharon (Theseus and Oberon), Christine Williams (Hermia), Michael Brusasco (Lysander), Tiffany Scott (Helena), Ashley Smith (Demetrius), Corliss Preston (Puck), John Tilhotson (Bottom) Aaron Galligan-Stierle (Flute), Peter Sham (Quince), Kevin Kiler (Snout), and Martin Swoverland (Snug).

This old moon wanes! She lingers° my desires,
Like to a stepdame° or a dowager°   5
Long withering out° a young man's revenue.
Hippolyta: Four days will quickly steep themselves° in night;
Four nights will quickly dream away the time;
And then the moon, like to a silver bow
New bent in heaven, shall behold the night   10
Of our solemnities.°
Theseus: Go, Philostrate,
Stir up the Athenian youth to merriments.
Awake the pert and nimble spirit of mirth.
Turn melancholy forth to funerals;
The pale companion° is not for our pomp.°   [*Exit Philostrate.*]   15
Hippolyta, I wooed thee with my sword°
And won thy love doing thee injuries;
But I will wed thee in another key,
With pomp, with triumph,° and with reveling.

Enter Egeus and his daughter Hermia, and Lysander, and Demetrius.

Egeus: Happy be Theseus, our renownèd duke!   20
Theseus: Thanks, good Egeus. What's the news with thee?
Egeus: Full of vexation come I, with complaint
Against my child, my daughter Hermia.—
Stand forth, Demetrius.—My noble lord,
This man hath my consent to marry her.—   25
Stand forth, Lysander.—And, my gracious Duke,
This man hath bewitched the bosom of my child.
Thou, thou Lysander, thou hast given her rhymes
And interchanged love tokens with my child.
Thou hast by moonlight at her window sung   30
With feigning° voice verses of feigning° love,
And stol'n the impression of her fantasy°
With bracelets of thy hair, rings, gauds,° conceits,°
Knacks,° trifles, nosegays, sweetmeats—messengers
Of strong prevailment in° unhardened youth.   35
With cunning hast thou filched my daughter's heart,
Turned her obedience, which is due to me,
To stubborn harshness. And, my gracious Duke,
Be it so° she will not here before Your Grace
Consent to marry with Demetrius,   40

---

4 *lingers* postpones, delays the fulfillment of   5 *stepdame* stepmother.   *a dowager* i.e., a widow (whose right of inheritance from her dead husband is eating into her son's estate)   6 *withering out* causing to dwindle   7 *steep themselves* saturate themselves, be absorbed in   11 *solemnities* festive ceremonies of marriage   15 *companion* fellow.   *pomp* ceremonial magnificence   16 *with my sword* i.e., in a military engagement against the Amazons, when Hippolyta was taken captive   19 *triumph* public festivity   31 *feigning* (1) counterfeiting (2) faining, desirous   32 *And . . . fantasy* and made her fall in love with you (imprinting your image on her imagination) by stealthy and dishonest means   33 *gauds* playthings.   *conceits* fanciful trifles   34 *Knacks* knickknacks   35 *prevailment in* influence on   39 *Be it so* if

Hippolyta, Queen of the Amazons, and her betrothed, Theseus, Duke of Athens.

I beg the ancient privilege of Athens:
As she is mine, I may dispose of her,
Which shall be either to this gentleman
Or to her death, according to our law
Immediately° provided in that case.   45
Theseus: What say you, Hermia? Be advised, fair maid.
To you your father should be as a god—
One that composed your beauties, yea, and one
To whom you are but as a form in wax
By him imprinted, and within his power   50
To leave° the figure or disfigure° it.
Demetrius is a worthy gentleman.
Hermia: So is Lysander.
Theseus: In himself he is;
But in this kind,° wanting° your father's voice,°
The other must be held the worthier.   55

45 *Immediately* directly, with nothing intervening   51 *leave* i.e., leave unaltered.   *disfigure* obliterate
54 *kind* respect.   *wanting* lacking.   *voice* approval

Hermia: I would my father looked but with my eyes.
Theseus: Rather your eyes must with his judgment look.
Hermia: I do entreat Your Grace to pardon me.
   I know not by what power I am made bold,
   Nor how it may concern° my modesty   60
   In such a presence here to plead my thoughts;
   But I beseech Your Grace that I may know
   The worst that may befall me in this case
   If I refuse to wed Demetrius.
Theseus: Either to die the death° or to abjure   65
   Forever the society of men.
   Therefore, fair Hermia, question your desires,
   Know of your youth, examine well your blood,°
   Whether, if you yield not to your father's choice,
   You can endure the livery° of a nun,   70
   For aye° to be in shady cloister mewed,°
   To live a barren sister all your life,
   Chanting faint hymns to the cold fruitless moon.
   Thrice blessèd they that master so their blood
   To undergo such maiden pilgrimage;   75
   But earthlier happy° is the rose distilled°
   Than that which, withering on the virgin thorn,
   Grows, lives, and dies in single blessedness.
Hermia: So will I grow, so live, so die, my lord,
   Ere I will yield my virgin patent° up   80
   Unto his lordship, whose unwishèd yoke
   My soul consents not to give sovereignty.
Theseus: Take time to pause, and by the next new moon—
   The sealing day betwixt my love and me
   For everlasting bond of fellowship—   85
   Upon that day either prepare to die
   For disobedience to your father's will,
   Or° else to wed Demetrius, as he would,
   Or on Diana's altar to protest°
   For aye austerity and single life.   90
Demetrius: Relent, sweet Hermia, and, Lysander, yield
   Thy crazèd° title to my certain right.
Lysander: You have her father's love, Demetrius;
   Let me have Hermia's. Do you marry him.
Egeus: Scornful Lysander! True, he hath my love,   95
   And what is mine my love shall render him.
   And she is mine, and all my right of her
   I do estate unto° Demetrius:

---

60 *concern* befit   65 *die the death* be executed by legal process   68 *blood* passions   70 *livery* habit, costume
71 *aye* ever. *mewed* shut in. (Said of a hawk, poultry, etc.)   76 *earthlier happy* happier as respects this
world. *distilled* i.e., to make perfume   80 *patent* privilege   88 *Or* either   89 *protest* vow   92 *crazèd*
cracked, unsound   98 *estate unto* settle or bestow upon

Lysander: I am, my lord, as well derived° as he,
    As well possessed;° my love is more than his;   100
    My fortunes every way as fairly° ranked,
    If not with vantage,° as Demetrius';
    And, which is more than all these boasts can be,
    I am beloved of beauteous Hermia.
    Why should not I then prosecute my right?   105
    Demetrius, I'll avouch it to his head,°
    Made love to Nedar's daughter, Helena,
    And won her soul; and she, sweet lady, dotes,
    Devoutly dotes, dotes in idolatry
    Upon this spotted° and inconstant man.   110
Theseus: I must confess that I have heard so much,
    And with Demetrius thought to have spoke thereof;
    But, being overfull of self-affairs,°
    My mind did lose it. But, Demetrius, come,
    And come, Egeus, you shall go with me;   115
    I have some private schooling° for you both.
    For you, fair Hermia, look you arm° yourself
    To fit your fancies° to your father's will,
    Or else the law of Athens yields you up—
    Which by no means we may extenuate°—   120
    To death or to a vow of single life.
    Come, my Hippolyta. What cheer, my love?
    Demetrius and Egeus, go° along.
    I must employ you in some business
    Against° our nuptial, and confer with you   125
    Of something nearly that° concerns yourselves.
Egeus: With duty and desire we follow you.

                          Exeunt [all but Lysander and Hermia].
Lysander: How now, my love, why is your cheek so pale?
    How chance the roses there do fade so fast?
Hermia: Belike° for want of rain, which I could well   130
    Beteem° them from the tempest of my eyes.
Lysander: Ay me! For aught that I could ever read,
    Could ever hear by tale or history,
    The course of true love never did run smooth;
    But either it was different in blood°—   135
Hermia: O cross!° Too high to be enthralled to low.
Lysander: Or else misgrafted° in respect of years—
Hermia: O spite! Too old to be engaged to young.
Lysander: Or else it stood upon the choice of friends°—

---

99 *as well derived* as well born and descended   100 *possessed* endowed with wealth   101 *fairly* handsomely
102 *vantage* superiority   106 *head* i.e., face   110 *spotted* i.e., morally stained   113 *self-affairs* my own concerns   116 *schooling* admonition   117 *look you arm* take care you prepare   118 *fancies* likings, thoughts of
love   120 *extenuate* mitigate, relax   123 *go* i.e., come   125 *Against* in preparation for   126 *nearly that*
that closely   130 *Belike* very likely   131 *Beteem* grant, afford   135 *blood* hereditary station   136 *cross*
vexation   137 *misgrafted* ill grafted, badly matched   139 *friends* relatives

The young lovers Lysander and Hermia.

Hermia: O hell, to choose love by another's eyes!   140
Lysander: Or if there were a sympathy° in choice,
     War, death, or sickness did lay siege to it,
     Making it momentany° as a sound,
     Swift as a shadow, short as any dream,
     Brief as the lightning in the collied° night   145
     That in a spleen° unfolds° both heaven and earth,
     And ere a man hath power to say "Behold!"
     The jaws of darkness do devour it up.
     So quick° bright things come to confusion.°

141 *sympathy* agreement   143 *momentany* lasting but a moment   145 *collied* blackened (as with coal
dust), darkened   146 *in a spleen* in a swift impulse, in a violent flash.   *unfolds* reveals   149 *quick* quickly;
also, living, alive.   *confusion* ruin

Hermia: If then true lovers have been ever crossed,° 150
　　It stands as an edict in destiny.
　　Then let us teach our trial patience,°
　　Because it is a customary cross,
　　As due to love as thoughts, and dreams, and sighs,
　　Wishes, and tears, poor fancy's° followers. 155
Lysander: A good persuasion.° Therefore, hear me, Hermia:
　　I have a widow aunt, a dowager
　　Of great revenue, and she hath no child.
　　From Athens is her house remote seven leagues;
　　And she respects° me as her only son. 160
　　There, gentle Hermia, may I marry thee,
　　And to that place the sharp Athenian law
　　Cannot pursue us. If thou lovest me, then,
　　Steal forth thy father's house tomorrow night;
　　And in the wood, a league without° the town, 165
　　Where I did meet thee once with Helena
　　To do observance to a morn of May,°
　　There will I stay for thee.
Hermia: 　　　　　　　　My good Lysander!
　　I swear to thee by Cupid's strongest bow,
　　By his best arrow° with the golden head, 170
　　By the simplicity° of Venus' doves,°
　　By that which knitteth souls and prospers loves,
　　And by that fire which burned the Carthage queen°
　　When the false Trojan° under sail was seen,
　　By all the vows that ever men have broke, 175
　　In number more than ever women spoke,
　　In that same place thou hast appointed me
　　Tomorrow truly will I meet with thee.
Lysander: Keep promise, love. Look, here comes Helena.

　　Enter Helena.

Hermia: God speed, fair° Helena! Whither away? 180
Helena: Call you me fair? That "fair" again unsay.
　　Demetrius loves your fair.° O happy fair!°
　　Your eyes are lodestars,° and your tongue's sweet air°
　　More tunable° than lark to shepherd's ear
　　When wheat is green, when hawthorn buds appear. 185
　　Sickness is catching. O, were favor° so,

150 *ever crossed* always thwarted　　152 *teach . . . patience* i.e., teach ourselves patience in this trial　　155 *fancy's* amorous passion's　　156 *persuasion* doctrine　　160 *respects* regards　　165 *without* outside　　167 *do . . . May* perform the ceremonies of May Day　　170 *best arrow* (Cupid's best gold-pointed arrows were supposed to induce love; his blunt leaden arrows, aversion.)　　171 *simplicity* innocence.　*doves* i.e., those that drew Venus' chariot　　173, 174 *Carthage queen, false Trojan* (Dido, Queen of Carthage, immolated herself on a funeral pyre after having been deserted by the Trojan hero Aeneas.)　　180 *fair* fair-complexioned (generally regarded by the Elizabethans as more beautiful than a dark complexion)　　182 *your fair* your beauty (even though Hermia is dark-complexioned).　*happy fair* lucky fair one　　183 *lodestars* guiding stars.　*air* music　　184 *tunable* tuneful, melodious　　186 *favor* appearance, looks

Yours would I catch, fair Hermia, ere I go;
My ear should catch your voice, my eye your eye,
My tongue should catch your tongue's sweet melody.
Were the world mine, Demetrius being bated,° 190
The rest I'd give to be to you translated.°
O, teach me how you look and with what art
You sway° the motion° of Demetrius' heart.
Hermia: I frown upon him, yet he loves me still.
Helena: O, that your frowns would teach my smiles such skill! 195
Hermia: I give him curses, yet he gives me love.
Helena: O, that my prayers could such affection° move!°
Hermia: The more I hate, the more he follows me.
Helena: The more I love, the more he hateth me.
Hermia: His folly, Helena, is no fault of mine. 200
Helena: None, but your beauty. Would that fault were mine!
Hermia: Take comfort. He no more shall see my face.
　Lysander and myself will fly this place.
　Before the time I did Lysander see
　Seemed Athens as a paradise to me.° 205
　O, then, what graces in my love do dwell,
　That he hath turned a heaven unto a hell?
Lysander: Helen, to you our minds we will unfold.
　Tomorrow night, when Phoebe° doth behold
　Her silver visage in the watery glass,° 210
　Decking with liquid pearl the bladed grass,
　A time that lovers' flights doth still° conceal,
　Through Athens' gates have we devised to steal.
Hermia: And in the wood, where often you and I
　Upon faint° primrose beds were wont to lie, 215
　Emptying our bosoms of their counsel° sweet,
　There my Lysander and myself shall meet,
　And thence from Athens turn away our eyes
　To seek new friends and stranger companies.°
　Farewell, sweet playfellow. Pray thou for us, 220
　And good luck grant thee thy Demetrius!
　Keep word, Lysander: We must starve our sight
　From lovers' food till morrow deep midnight.
Lysander: I will, my Hermia. *(Exit Hermia.)* Helena, adieu.
　As you on him, Demetrius dote on you! 225

　　　　　　　　　　　　　　　　　　Exit Lysander.

Helena: How happy some o'er other some can be!°
　Through Athens I am thought as fair as she.
　But what of that? Demetrius thinks not so;

---

190 *bated* excepted　191 *translated* transformed　193 *sway* control. *motion* impulse　197 *affection* passion. *move* arouse　204–205 *Before . . . to me* (Hermia seemingly means that love has led to complications and jealousies, making Athens hell for her.)　209 *Phoebe* Diana, the moon　210 *glass* mirror　212 *still* always　215 *faint* pale　216 *counsel* secret thought　219 *stranger companies* the company of strangers　226 *o'er . . . can be* can be in comparison to some others

He will not know what all but he do know.
And as he errs, doting on Hermia's eyes,   230
So I, admiring of° his qualities.
Things base and vile, holding no quantity,°
Love can transpose to form and dignity.
Love looks not with the eyes, but with the mind,
And therefore is winged Cupid painted blind.   235
Nor hath Love's mind of any judgment taste;°
Wings and no eyes figure° unheedy haste.
And therefore is Love said to be a child,
Because in choice° he is so oft beguiled.°
As waggish° boys in game° themselves forswear,   240
So the boy Love is perjured everywhere.
For ere Demetrius looked on Hermia's eyne,°
He hailed down oaths that he was only mine;
And when this hail some heat from Hermia felt,
So he dissolved, and showers of oaths did melt.   245
I will go tell him of fair Hermia's flight.
Then to the wood will he tomorrow night
Pursue her; and for this intelligence°
If I have thanks, it is a dear expense.°
But herein mean I to enrich my pain,   250
To have his sight thither and back again.

                                                                    Exit.

SCENE II [ATHENS.]

Enter Quince the carpenter, and Snug the joiner, and Bottom the weaver, and Flute the bellows mender, and Snout the tinker, and Starveling the tailor.

Quince: Is all our company here?

Bottom: You were best to call them generally,° man by man, according to the scrip.°

Quince: Here is the scroll of every man's name which is thought fit, through all Athens, to play in our interlude° before the Duke and the Duchess on his wedding day at night.   5

Bottom: First, good Peter Quince, say what the play treats on, then read the names of the actors, and so grow to° a point.

Quince: Marry,° our play is "The most lamentable comedy and most cruel death of Pyramus and Thisbe."

Bottom: A very good piece of work, I assure you, and a merry. Now, good Peter   10
Quince, call forth your actors by the scroll. Masters, spread yourselves.

Quince: Answer as I call you. Nick Bottom,° the weaver.

---

231 *admiring of* wondering at   232 *holding no quantity* i.e., unsubstantial, unshapely   236 *Nor . . . taste* i.e., nor has Love, which dwells in the fancy or imagination, any *taste* or least bit of judgment or reason   237 *figure* are a symbol of   239 *in choice* in choosing.   *beguiled* self-deluded, making unaccountable choices   240 *waggish* playful, mischievous.   *game* sport, jest   242 *eyne* eyes. (Old form of plural.)   248 *intelligence* information   249 *a dear expense* i.e., a trouble worth taking on my part, or a begrudging effort on his part.   *dear* costly   2 *generally* (Bottom's blunder for "individually.").   *scrip* scrap (Bottom's error for "script.")   4 *interlude* play   7 *grow to* come to   8 *Marry* (A mild oath; originally the name of the Virgin Mary.)   12 *Bottom* (As a weaver's term, a *bottom* was an object around which thread was wound.)

The workers meet to plan their play, and Quince hands out the parts.

Bottom: Ready. Name what part I am for, and proceed.

Quince: You, Nick Bottom, are set down for Pyramus.

Bottom: What is Pyramus? A lover or a tyrant? 15

Quince: A lover, that kills himself most gallant for love.

Bottom: That will ask some tears in the true performing of it. If I do it, let the audience look to their eyes. I will move storms; I will condole° in some measure. To
the rest—yet my chief humor° is for a tyrant. I could play Ercles° rarely, or a part
to tear a cat° in, to make all split.° 20

> "The raging rocks
> And shivering shocks
> Shall break the locks

---

18 *condole* lament, arouse pity   19 *humor* inclination, whim.   *Ercles* Hercules (The tradition of ranting
came from Seneca's *Hercules Furens.*)   20 *tear a cat* i.e., rant.   *make all split* i.e., cause a stir, bring the
house down

> Of prison gates;
> And Phibbus' car°   25
> Shall shine from far
> And make and mar
> The foolish Fates."

This was lofty! Now name the rest of the players. This is Ercles' vein, a tyrant's vein. A lover is more condoling.   30

Quince: Francis Flute, the bellows mender.

Flute: Here, Peter Quince.

Quince: Flute, you must take Thisbe on you.

Flute: What is Thisbe? A wandering knight?

Quince: It is the lady that Pyramus must love.   35

Flute: Nay, faith, let not me play a woman. I have a beard coming.

Quince: That's all one.° You shall play it in a mask, and you may speak as small° as you will.

Bottom: An° I may hide my face, let me play Thisbe too. I'll speak in a monstrous little voice, "Thisne, Thisne!" "Ah Pyramus, my lover dear! Thy Thisbe dear,   40 and lady dear!"

Quince: No, no, you must play Pyramus, and Flute, you Thisbe.

Bottom: Well, proceed.

Quince: Robin Starveling, the tailor.

Starveling: Here, Peter Quince.   45

Quince: Robin Starveling, you must play Thisbe's mother. Tom Snout, the tinker.

Snout: Here, Peter Quince.

Quince: You, Pyramus' father; myself, Thisbe's father; Snug, the joiner, you, the lion's part, and I hope here is a play fitted.

Snug: Have you the lion's part written? Pray you, if it be, give it me, for I am slow of   50 study.

Quince: You may do it extempore, for it is nothing but roaring.

Bottom: Let me play the lion too. I will roar that I will do any man's heart good to hear me. I will roar that I will make the Duke say, "Let him roar again, let him roar again."   55

Quince: An you should do it too terribly, you would fright the Duchess and the ladies, that they would shriek; and that were enough to hang us all.

All: That would hang us, every mother's son.

Bottom: I grant you, friends, if you should fright the ladies out of their wits, they would have no more discretion but to hang us; but I will aggravate° my voice so   60 that I will roar you° as gently as any sucking dove;° I will roar you an 'twere° any nightingale.

Quince: You can play no part but Pyramus; for Pyramus is a sweet-faced man, a proper° man as one shall see in a summer's day, a most lovely gentlemanlike man. Therefore you must needs play Pyramus.   65

Bottom: Well, I will undertake it. What beard were I best to play it in?

Quince: Why, what you will.

---

25 *Phibbus' car* Phoebus', the sun god's, chariot   37 *That's all one* it makes no difference.   *small* high-pitched   39 *An* if (also at line 56)   60 *aggravate* (Bottom's blunder for "moderate.")   61 *roar you* i.e., roar for you.   *sucking dove* (Bottom conflates *sitting dove* and *sucking lamb*, two proverbial images of innocence.).   *an 'twere* as if it were   64 *proper* handsome

Bottom: I will discharge° it in either your° straw-color beard, your orange-tawny beard, your purple-in-grain° beard, or your French-crown-color° beard, your perfect yellow. 70

Quince: Some of your French crowns° have no hair at all, and then you will play barefaced. But, masters, here are your parts. [*He distributes parts.*] And I am to entreat you, request you, and desire you to con° them by tomorrow night, and meet me in the palace wood, a mile without the town, by moonlight. There will we rehearse; for if we meet in the city, we shall be dogged with company, and our 75 devices° known. In the meantime I will draw a bill° of properties, such as our play wants. I pray you, fail me not.

Bottom: We will meet, and there we may rehearse most obscenely° and courageously. Take pains, be perfect.° Adieu.

Quince: At the Duke's oak we meet. 80

Bottom: Enough. Hold, or cut bowstrings.° *Exeunt.*

ACT II

SCENE I [A WOOD NEAR ATHENS.]

Enter a Fairy at one door, and Robin Goodfellow [Puck] at another.

Puck: How now, spirit, whither wander you?

Fairy:

> Over hill, over dale,
> Thorough° bush, thorough brier,
> Over park, over pale,°
> Thorough flood, thorough fire, 5
> I do wander everywhere,
> Swifter than the moon's sphere;°
> And I serve the Fairy Queen,
> To dew° her orbs° upon the green.
> The cowslips tall her pensioners° be. 10
> In their gold coats spots you see;
> Those be rubies, fairy favors;°
> In those freckles live their savors.°

I must go seek some dewdrops here
And hang a pearl in every cowslip's ear. 15
Farewell, thou lob° of spirits; I'll be gone.
Our Queen and all her elves come here anon.°

Puck: The King doth keep his revels here tonight.
Take heed the Queen come not within his sight.

---

68 *discharge* perform. *your* i.e., you know the kind I mean 69 *purple-in-grain* dyed a very deep red. (From *grain*, the name applied to the dried insect used to make the dye.) *French-crown-color* i.e., color of a French crown, a gold coin 71 *crowns* heads bald from syphilis, the "French disease" 73 *con* learn by heart 76 *devices* plans. *draw a bill* draw up a list 78 *obscenely* (An unintentionally funny blunder, whatever Bottom meant to say.) 79 *perfect* i.e., letter-perfect in memorizing your parts 81 *Hold . . . bowstrings* (An archer's expression, not definitely explained, but probably meaning here "keep your promises, or give up the play.") 3 *Thorough* through 4 *pale* enclosure 7 *sphere* orbit 9 *dew* sprinkle with dew. *orbs* circles, i.e., fairy rings (circular bands of grass, darker than the surrounding area, caused by fungi enriching the soil) 10 *pensioners* retainers, members of the royal bodyguard 12 *favors* love tokens 13 *savors* sweet smells 16 *lob* country bumpkin 17 *anon* at once

For Oberon is passing fell° and wrath,°   20
Because that she as her attendant hath
A lovely boy, stolen from an Indian king;
She never had so sweet a changeling.°
And jealous Oberon would have the child
Knight of his train, to trace° the forests wild.   25
But she perforce° withholds the lovèd boy,
Crowns him with flowers, and makes him all her joy.
And now they never meet in grove or green,
By fountain° clear, or spangled starlight sheen,°
But they do square,° that all their elves for fear   30
Creep into acorn cups and hide them there.

Fairy: Either I mistake your shape and making quite,
Or else you are that shrewd° and knavish sprite°
Called Robin Goodfellow. Are not you he
That frights the maidens of the villagery,°   35
Skim milk,° and sometimes labor in the quern,°
And bootless° make the breathless huswife° churn,
And sometimes make the drink to bear no barm,°
Mislead night wanderers,° laughing at their harm?
Those that "Hobgoblin" call you, and "Sweet Puck,"°   40
You do their work, and they shall have good luck.
Are you not he?

Puck: Thou speakest aright;
I am that merry wanderer of the night.
I jest to Oberon and make him smile
When I a fat and bean-fed° horse beguile,   45
Neighing in likeness of a filly foal;
And sometimes lurk I in a gossip's° bowl
In very likeness of a roasted crab,°
And when she drinks, against her lips I bob
And on her withered dewlap° pour the ale.   50
The wisest aunt,° telling the saddest° tale,
Sometimes for three-foot stool mistaketh me;
Then slip I from her bum, down topples she,
And "Tailor"° cries, and falls into a cough;
And then the whole choir° hold their hips and laugh,   55
And waxen° in their mirth, and neeze,° and swear

---

20 *passing fell* exceedingly angry. *wrath* wrathful 23 *changeling* child exchanged for another by the fairies 25 *trace* range through 26 *perforce* forcibly 29 *fountain* spring. *starlight sheen* shining starlight 30 *square* quarrel 33 *shrewd* mischievous. *sprite* spirit 35 *villagery* village population 36 *Skim milk* i.e., steal the cream. *quern* hand mill (where Puck presumably hampers the grinding of grain) 37 *bootless* in vain (Puck prevents the cream from turning to butter.) *huswife* housewife 38 *barm* head on the ale (Puck prevents the barm or yeast from producing fermentation.) 39 *Mislead night wanderers* i.e., mislead with false fire those who walk abroad at night (hence earning Puck his other names of Jack o' Lantern and Will o' the Wisp) 40 *Those . . . Puck* i.e., those who call you by the names you favor rather than those denoting the mischief you do. 45 *bean-fed* well fed on field beans 47 *gossip's* old woman's 48 *crab* crab apple 50 *dewlap* loose skin on neck 51 *aunt* old woman. *saddest* most serious 54 *Tailor* (possibly because she ends up sitting cross-legged on the floor, looking like a tailor, or else referring to the *tail* or buttocks.) 55 *choir* company 56 *waxen* increase. *neeze* sneeze

A merrier hour was never wasted° there.
But, room,° fairy! Here comes Oberon.
Fairy: And here my mistress. Would that he were gone!

Enter [Oberon] the King of Fairies at one door, with his train, and [Titania] the Queen at another, with hers.

Oberon: Ill met by moonlight, proud Titania.   60
Titania: What, jealous Oberon? Fairies, skip hence.
I have forsworn his bed and company.
Oberon: Tarry, rash wanton.° Am not I thy lord?
Titania: Then I must be thy lady; but I know
When thou hast stolen away from Fairyland   65
And in the shape of Corin° sat all day,
Playing on pipes of corn° and versing love
To amorous Phillida.° Why art thou here
Come from the farthest step° of India,
But that, forsooth, the bouncing Amazon,   70
Your buskined° mistress and your warrior love,
To Theseus must be wedded, and you come
To give their bed joy and prosperity.
Oberon: How canst thou thus for shame, Titania,
Glance at my credit with Hippolyta,°   75
Knowing I know thy love to Theseus?
Didst not thou lead him through the glimmering night
From Perigenia,° whom he ravishèd?
And make him with fair Aegles° break his faith,
With Ariadne° and Antiopa?°   80
Titania: These are the forgeries of jealousy;
And never, since the middle summer's spring,°
Met we on hill, in dale, forest, or mead,°
By pavèd° fountain or by rushy° brook,
Or in° the beachèd margent° of the sea,   85
To dance our ringlets° to° the whistling wind,
But with thy brawls thou hast disturbed our sport.
Therefore the winds, piping to us in vain,
As in revenge, have sucked up from the sea
Contagious° fogs which, falling in the land,   90
Hath every pelting° river made so proud

---

57 *wasted* spent   58 *room* stand aside, make room   63 *wanton* headstrong creature   66, 68 *Corin, Phillida* (Conventional names of pastoral lovers.)   67 *corn* (Here, oat stalks.)   69 *step* farthest limit of travel, or, perhaps, *steep,* "mountain range"   71 *buskined* wearing half-boots called buskins   75 *Glance . . . Hippolyta* make insinuations about my favored relationship with Hippolyta   78 *Perigenia* i.e., Perigouna, one of Theseus's conquests. (This and the following women are named in Thomas North's translation of Plutarch's "Life of Theseus.")   79 *Aegles* i.e., Aegle, for whom Theseus deserted Ariadne according to some accounts   80 *Ariadne* the daughter of Minos, King of Crete, who helped Theseus to escape the labyrinth after killing the Minotaur; later she was abandoned by Theseus.   *Antiopa* Queen of the Amazons and wife of Theseus; elsewhere identified with Hippolyta, but here thought of as a separate woman   82 *middle summer's spring* beginning of midsummer   83 *mead* meadow   84 *pavèd* with pebbled bottom. *rushy* bordered with rushes   85 *in* on.   *margent* edge, border   86 *ringlets* dances in a ring. (See *orbs* in line 9.)   *to* to the sound of   90 *Contagious* noxious   91 *pelting* paltry

Titania and Oberon.

That they have overborne their continents.°
The ox hath therefore stretched his yoke° in vain,
The plowman lost his sweat, and the green corn°
Hath rotted ere his youth attained a beard;
The fold° stands empty in the drownèd field,   95
And crows are fatted with the murrain° flock;
The nine-men's morris° is filled up with mud,
And the quaint mazes° in the wanton° green
For lack of tread are undistinguishable.   100

92 *continents* banks that contain them   93 *stretched his yoke* i.e., pulled at his yoke in plowing   94 *corn* grain of any kind   96 *fold* pen for sheep or cattle   97 *murrain* having died of the plague   98 *nine-men's morris* i.e., portion of the village green marked out in a square for a game played with nine pebbles or pegs   99 *quaint mazes* i.e., intricate paths marked out on the village green to be followed rapidly on foot as a kind of contest.   *wanton* luxuriant

The human mortals want° their winter° here;
No night is now with hymn or carol blessed.
Therefore° the moon, the governess of floods,
Pale in her anger, washes° all the air,
That rheumatic diseases° do abound.   105
And thorough this distemperature° we see
The seasons alter: hoary-headed frosts
Fall in the fresh lap of the crimson rose,
And on old Hiems'° thin and icy crown
An odorous chaplet of sweet summer buds   110
Is, as in mockery, set. The spring, the summer,
The childing° autumn, angry winter, change
Their wonted liveries,° and the mazèd° world
By their increase° now knows not which is which.
And this same progeny of evils comes   115
From our debate,° from our dissension.
We are their parents and original.°
Oberon: Do you amend it, then. It lies in you.
Why should Titania cross her Oberon?
I do but beg a little changeling boy   120
To be my henchman.°
Titania: Set your heart at rest.
The fairy land buys not the child of me.
His mother was a vot'ress of my order,°
And in the spicèd Indian air by night
Full often hath she gossiped by my side   125
And sat with me on Neptune's yellow sands,
Marking th' embarkèd traders° on the flood,°
When we have laughed to see the sails conceive
And grow big-bellied with the wanton° wind;
Which she, with pretty and with swimming° gait,   130
Following—her womb then rich with my young squire—
Would imitate, and sail upon the land
To fetch me trifles, and return again
As from a voyage, rich with merchandise.
But she, being mortal, of that boy did die;   135
And for her sake do I rear up her boy,
And for her sake I will not part with him.
Oberon: How long within this wood intend you stay?
Titania: Perchance till after Theseus' wedding day.
If you will patiently dance in our round°   140

101 *want* lack. *winter* i.e., regular winter season; or, proper observances of winter, such as the *hymn or carol* in the next line (?) 103 *Therefore* i.e., as a result of our quarrel 104 *washes* saturates with moisture 105 *rheumatic diseases* colds, flu, and other respiratory infections 106 *distemperature* disturbance in nature 109 *Hiems'* the winter god's 112 *childing* fruitful, pregnant 113 *wonted liveries* usual apparel. *mazèd* bewildered 114 *their increase* their yield, what they produce 116 *debate* quarrel 117 *original* origin 121 *henchman* attendant, page 123 *was . . . order* had taken a vow to serve me 127 *traders* trading vessels. *flood* flood tide 129 *wanton* (1) playful (2) amorous 130 *swimming* smooth, gliding 140 *round* circular dance

Oberon directs Puck to fetch the magic flower.

> And see our moonlight revels, go with us;
> If not, shun me, and I will spare° your haunts.
> *Oberon:* Give me that boy, and I will go with thee.
> *Titania:* Not for thy fairy kingdom. Fairies, away!
> We shall chide downright, if I longer stay.   145
>
> *Exeunt [Titania with her train].*
>
> *Oberon:* Well, go thy way. Thou shalt not from° this grove
> Till I torment thee for this injury.
> My gentle Puck, come hither. Thou rememb'rest
> Since° once I sat upon a promontory,
> And heard a mermaid on a dolphin's back   150
> Uttering such dulcet° and harmonious breath°

142 *spare* shun   146 *from* go from   142 *spare* shun   149 *Since* when   151 *dulcet* sweet.   *breath* voice, song

That the rude° sea grew civil at her song,
And certain stars shot madly from their spheres
To hear the sea-maid's music?
Puck: I remember.
Oberon: That very time I saw, but thou couldst not,   155
    Flying between the cold moon and the earth
    Cupid, all° armed. A certain° aim he took
    At a fair vestal° thronèd by° the west,
    And loosed° his love shaft smartly from his bow
    As° it should pierce a hundred thousand hearts;   160
    But I might° see young Cupid's fiery shaft
    Quenched in the chaste beams of the watery moon,
    And the imperial vot'ress passèd on,
    In maiden meditation, fancy-free.°
    Yet marked I where the bolt° of Cupid fell: 165
    It fell upon a little western flower,
    Before milk-white, now purple with love's wound,
    And maidens call it love-in-idleness.°
    Fetch me that flower; the herb I showed thee once.
    The juice of it on sleeping eyelids laid   170
    Will make or man or° woman madly dote
    Upon the next live creature that it sees.
    Fetch me this herb, and be thou here again
    Ere the leviathan° can swim a league.
Puck: I'll put a girdle round about the earth   175
    In forty° minutes.   [*Exit.*]
Oberon: Having once this juice,
    I'll watch Titania when she is asleep
    And drop the liquor of it in her eyes.
    The next thing then she waking looks upon,
    Be it on lion, bear, or wolf, or bull,   180
    On meddling monkey, or on busy ape,
    She shall pursue it with the soul of love.
    And ere I take this charm from off her sight,
    As I can take it with another herb,
    I'll make her render up her page to me.   185
    But who comes here? I am invisible,
    And I will overhear their conference.

    Enter Demetrius, Helena following him.

Demetrius: I love thee not; therefore pursue me not.
    Where is Lysander and fair Hermia?
    The one I'll slay; the other slayeth me.   190

---

152 *rude* rough 157 *all* fully. *certain* sure 158 *vestal* vestal virgin. (Contains a complimentary allusion
to Queen Elizabeth as a votaress of Diana and probably refers to an actual entertainment in her honor at
Elvetham in 1591.) *by* in the region of 159 *loosed* released 160 *As* as if 161 *might* could 164 *fancy-
free* free of love's spell 165 *bolt* arrow 168 *love-in-idleness* pansy, heartsease 171 *or . . . or* either . . . or
174 *leviathan* sea monster, whale 176 *forty* (Used indefinitely.)

Thou toldst me they were stol'n unto this wood;
And here am I, and wood° within this wood
Because I cannot meet my Hermia.
Hence, get thee gone, and follow me no more.

Helena: You draw me, you hardhearted adamant!° 195
But yet you draw not iron, for my heart
Is true as steel. Leave you° your power to draw,
And I shall have no power to follow you.

Demetrius: Do I entice you? Do I speak you fair?°
Or rather do I not in plainest truth 200
Tell you I do not nor I cannot love you?

Helena: And even for that do I love you the more.
I am your spaniel; and, Demetrius,
The more you beat me I will fawn on you.
Use me but as your spaniel, spurn me, strike me, 205
Neglect me, lose me; only give me leave,
Unworthy as I am, to follow you.
What worser place can I beg in your love—
And yet a place of high respect with me—
Than to be usèd as you use your dog? 210

Demetrius: Tempt not too much the hatred of my spirit,
For I am sick when I do look on thee.

Helena: And I am sick when I look not on you.

Demetrius: You do impeach° your modesty too much
To leave° the city and commit yourself 215
Into the hands of one that loves you not,
To trust the opportunity of night
And the ill counsel of a desert° place
With the rich worth of your virginity.

Helena: Your virtue° is my privilege.° For that° 220
It is not night when I do see your face,
Therefore I think I am not in the night;
Nor doth this wood lack worlds of company,
For you, in my respect,° are all the world.
Then how can it be said I am alone 225
When all the world is here to look on me?

Demetrius: I'll run from thee and hide me in the brakes,°
And leave thee to the mercy of wild beasts.

Helena: The wildest hath not such a heart as you.
Run when you will. The story shall be changed: 230
Apollo flies and Daphne holds the chase,°

---

192 *and wood* and mad, frantic (with an obvious word play on *wood,* meaning "woods") 195 *adamant* lodestone, magnet (with pun on *hardhearted,* since adamant was also thought to be the hardest of all stones and was confused with the diamond) 197 *Leave you* give up 199 *speak you fair* speak courteously to you 214 *impeach* call into question 215 *To leave* by leaving 218 *desert* deserted 220 *virtue* goodness or power to attract. *privilege* safeguard, warrant. *For that* because 224 *in my respect* as far as I am concerned, in my esteem 227 *brakes* thickets 231 *Apollo . . . chase* (In the ancient myth, Daphne fled from Apollo and was saved from rape by being transformed into a laurel tree; here it is the female who *holds the chase,* or pursues, instead of the male.)

"Let me go!" Demetrius tells Helena after she follows him into the woods (II, i, 235).

The dove pursues the griffin,° the mild hind°
Makes speed to catch the tiger—bootless° speed,
When cowardice pursues and valor flies!
Demetrius: I will not stay° thy questions.° Let me go!   235
    Or if thou follow me, do not believe
    But I shall do thee mischief in the wood.
Helena: Ay, in the temple, in the town, the field,
    You do me mischief. Fie, Demetrius!
    Your wrongs do set a scandal on my sex.°   240

---

232 *griffin* a fabulous monster with the head and wings of an eagle and the body of a lion. *hind* female deer   233 *bootless* fruitless 235 *stay* wait for, put up with. *questions* talk or argument 240 *Your . . . sex* i.e., the wrongs that you do me cause me to act in a manner that disgraces my sex

We cannot fight for love, as men may do;
We should be wooed and were not made to woo.

                                                          [*Exit Demetrius.*]

I'll follow thee and make a heaven of hell,
To die upon° the hand I love so well.   [*Exit.*]
Oberon: Fare thee well, nymph. Ere he do leave this grove,   245
Thou shalt fly him, and he shall seek thy love.

Enter Puck.

Hast thou the flower there? Welcome, wanderer.
Puck: Ay, there it is.   [*He offers the flower.*]
Oberon: I pray thee, give it me.
I know a bank where the wild thyme blows,°
Where oxlips° and the nodding violet grows,   250
Quite overcanopied with luscious woodbine,°
With sweet muskroses° and with eglantine.°
There sleeps Titania sometimes of° the night,
Lulled in these flowers with dances and delight;
And there the snake throws° her enameled skin,   255
Weed° wide enough to wrap a fairy in.
And with the juice of this I'll streak° her eyes
And make her full of hateful fantasies.
Take thou some of it, and seek through this grove.

                                                   [*He gives some love juice.*]

A sweet Athenian lady is in love   260
With a disdainful youth. Anoint his eyes,
But do it when the next thing he espies
May be the lady. Thou shalt know the man
By the Athenian garments he hath on.
Effect it with some care, that he may prove   265
More fond on° her than she upon her love;
And look thou meet me ere the first cock crow.
Puck: Fear not, my lord, your servant shall do so.

                                                   Exeunt [*separately*].

SCENE II [THE WOOD.]

Enter Titania, Queen of Fairies, with her train.

Titania: Come, now a roundel° and a fairy song;
Then, for the third part of a minute,° hence—
Some to kill cankers° in the muskrose buds,
Some war with reremice° for their leathern wings

---

244 *upon* by   249 *blows* blooms   250 *oxlips* flowers resembling cowslip and primrose   251 *woodbine* honeysuckle   252 *muskroses* a kind of large, sweet-scented rose.   *eglantine* sweetbrier, another kind of rose
253 *sometimes of* for part of   255 *throws* sloughs off, sheds   256 *Weed* garment   257 *streak* anoint, touch
gently   266 *fond on* doting on   1 *roundel* dance in a ring   2 *the third . . . minute* (Indicative of the fairies'
quickness.)   3 *cankers* cankerworms (i.e., caterpillars or grubs)   4 *reremice* bats

To make my small elves coats, and some keep back   5
The clamorous owl, that nightly hoots and wonders
At our quaint° spirits. Sing me now asleep.
Then to your offices, and let me rest.

Fairies sing.

First Fairy: You spotted snakes with double° tongue,
            Thorny hedgehogs, be not seen;   10
    Newts° and blindworms, do no wrong;
            Come not near our Fairy Queen.
Chorus [*dancing*]:   Philomel,° with melody
            Sing in our sweet lullaby;
    Lulla, lulla, lullaby, lulla, lulla, lullaby.   15
            Never harm
            Nor spell nor charm
    Come our lovely lady nigh.
    So good night, with lullaby.
First Fairy: Weaving spiders, come not here;   20
            Hence, you long-legged spinners, hence!
    Beetles black, approach not near;
            Worm nor snail, do no offense.°
Chorus [*dancing.*]:   Philomel, with melody
            Sing in our sweet lullaby;   25
    Lulla, lulla, lullaby, lulla, lulla, lullaby.
            Never harm
             Nor spell nor charm
    Come our lovely lady nigh.
    So good night, with lullaby.   30

                    [*Titania sleeps.*]

Second Fairy: Hence, away! Now all is well.
    One aloof stand sentinel.°

           [*Exeunt Fairies, leaving one sentinel.*]

Enter Oberon [and squeezes the flower on Titania's eyelids].

Oberon: What thou seest when thou dost wake,
    Do it for thy true love take;
    Love and languish for his sake.   35
    Be it ounce,° or cat, or bear,
    Pard,° or boar with bristled hair,
    In thy eye that shall appear
    When thou wak'st, it is thy dear.
    Wake when some vile thing is near.   [*Exit.*]   40

---

7 *quaint* dainty   9 *double* forked   11 *Newts* water lizards (considered poisonous, as were *blindworms*—small snakes with tiny eyes—and spiders)   13 *Philomel* the nightingale. (Philomela, daughter of King Pandion, was transformed into a nightingale, according to Ovid's *Metamorphoses* 6, after she had been raped by her sister Procne's husband, Tereus.)   23 *offense* harm   32 *sentinel* (Presumably Oberon is able to outwit or intimidate this guard.)   36 *ounce* lynx   37 *Pard* leopard

Oberon squeezes the magic flower's juice onto Titania's eyelids.

Enter Lysander and Hermia.

Lysander: Fair love, you faint with wandering in the wood;
  And to speak truth, I have forgot our way.
  We'll rest us, Hermia, if you think it good,
  And tarry for the comfort of the day.
Hermia: Be it so, Lysander. Find you out a bed,   45
  For I upon this bank will rest my head.
Lysander: One turf shall serve as pillow for us both;
  One heart, one bed, two bosoms, and one troth.°
Hermia: Nay, good Lysander, for my sake, my dear,
  Lie further off yet. Do not lie so near.   50

48 *troth* faith, trothplight

Lysander: O, take the sense, sweet, of my innocence!°
    Love takes the meaning in love's conference.°
    I mean that my heart unto yours is knit,
    So that but one heart we can make of it;
    Two bosoms interchainèd with an oath—   55
    So then two bosoms and a single troth.
    Then by your side no bed-room me deny,
    For lying so, Hermia, I do not lie.°
Hermia: Lysander riddles very prettily.
    Now much beshrew° my manners and my pride   60
    If Hermia meant to say Lysander lied.
    But, gentle friend, for love and courtesy
    Lie further off, in human° modesty.
    Such separation as may well be said
    Becomes a virtuous bachelor and a maid,   65
    So far be distant; and good night, sweet friend.
    Thy love ne'er alter till thy sweet life end!
Lysander: Amen, amen, to that fair prayer, say I,
    And then end life when I end loyalty!
    Here is my bed. Sleep give thee all his rest!   70
Hermia: With half that wish the wisher's eyes be pressed!°

                           [They sleep, separated by a short distance.]

    Enter Puck.

Puck: Through the forest have I gone,
            But Athenian found I none
            On whose eyes I might approve°
            This flower's force in stirring love.   75
            Night and silence.—Who is here?
            Weeds of Athens he doth wear.
            This is he, my master said,
            Despisèd the Athenian maid;
            And here the maiden, sleeping sound,   80
            On the dank and dirty ground.
            Pretty soul, she durst not lie
            Near this lack-love, this kill-courtesy.
            Churl, upon thy eyes I throw
            All the power this charm doth owe.°   85

                           [He applies the love juice.]

            When thou wak'st, let love forbid
            Sleep his seat on thy eyelid.
            So awake when I am gone,
            For I must now to Oberon.   *Exit.*

---

51 *take . . . innocence* i.e., interpret my intention as innocent   52 *Love . . . conference* i.e., when lovers confer, love teaches each lover to interpret the other's meaning lovingly   58 *lie* tell a falsehood (with a riddling pun on *lie*, "recline")   60 *beshrew* curse. (But mildly meant.)   63 *human* courteous (and perhaps suggesting "humane," the Quarto spelling)   71 *With . . . pressed* i.e., may we share your wish, so that your eyes too are *pressed*, closed, in sleep   74 *approve* test   85 *owe* own

Enter Demetrius and Helena, running.

Helena: Stay, though thou kill me, sweet Demetrius! 90
Demetrius: I charge thee, hence, and do not haunt me thus.
Helena: O, wilt thou darkling° leave me? Do not so.
Demetrius: Stay, on thy peril!° I alone will go.   [*Exit.*]
Helena: O, I am out of breath in this fond° chase!
    The more my prayer, the lesser is my grace.° 95
    Happy is Hermia, wheresoe'er she lies,°
    For she hath blessèd and attractive eyes.
    How came her eyes so bright? Not with salt tears;
    If so, my eyes are oftener washed than hers.
    No, no, I am as ugly as a bear, 100
    For beasts that meet me run away for fear.
    Therefore no marvel though Demetrius
    Do, as a monster, fly my presence thus.°
    What wicked and dissembling glass of mine
    Made me compare° with Hermia's sphery eyne?° 105
    But who is here? Lysander, on the ground?
    Dead, or asleep? I see no blood, no wound.
    Lysander, if you live, good sir, awake.
Lysander [awaking]: And run through fire I will for thy sweet sake.
    Transparent° Helena! Nature shows art,° 110
    That through thy bosom makes me see thy heart.
    Where is Demetrius? O, how fit a word
    Is that vile name to perish on my sword!
Helena: Do not say so, Lysander, say not so.
    What though he love your Hermia? Lord, what though? 115
    Yet Hermia still loves you. Then be content.
Lysander: Content with Hermia? No! I do repent
    The tedious minutes I with her have spent.
    Not Hermia but Helena I love.
    Who will not change a raven for a dove? 120
    The will° of man is by his reason swayed,
    And reason says you are the worthier maid.
    Things growing are not ripe until their season;
    So I, being young, till now ripe not° to reason.
    And, touching° now the point° of human skill,° 125
    Reason becomes the marshal to my will
    And leads me to your eyes, where I o'erlook°
    Love's stories written in love's richest book.
Helena: Wherefore° was I to this keen mockery born?
    When at your hands did I deserve this scorn? 130

92 *darkling* in the dark   93 *on thy peril* i.e., on pain of danger to you if you don't obey me and stay   94 *fond* doting   95 *my grace* the favor I obtain   96 *lies* dwells   102–103 *no marvel . . . thus* i.e., no wonder that Demetrius flies from me as from a monster   105 *compare* vie.   *sphery eyne* eyes as bright as stars in their spheres   110 *Transparent* (1) radiant (2) able to be seen through, lacking in deceit.   *art* skill, magic power   121 *will* desire   124 *ripe not* (am) not ripened   125 *touching* reaching.   *point* summit.   *skill* judgment   127 *o'erlook* read   129 *Wherefore* why

Is 't not enough, is 't not enough, young man,
That I did never—no, nor never can—
Deserve a sweet look from Demetrius' eye,
But you must flout my insufficiency?
Good troth, you do me wrong, good sooth,° you do,   135
In such disdainful manner me to woo.
But fare you well. Perforce I must confess
I thought you lord of° more true gentleness.°
O, that a lady, of° one man refused,
Should of another therefore be abused!°   *Exit.* 140
Lysander: She sees not Hermia. Hermia, sleep thou there,
And never mayst thou come Lysander near!
For as a surfeit of the sweetest things
The deepest loathing to the stomach brings,
Or as the heresies that men do leave   145
Are hated most of those they did deceive,°
So thou, my surfeit and my heresy,
Of all be hated, but the most of° me!
And, all my powers, address° your love and might
To honor Helen and to be her knight!   *Exit.* 150
Hermia [awaking]: Help me, Lysander, help me! Do thy best
To pluck this crawling serpent from my breast!
Ay me, for pity! What a dream was here!
Lysander, look how I do quake with fear.
Methought a serpent ate my heart away,   155
And you sat smiling at his cruel prey.°
Lysander! What, removed? Lysander! Lord!
What, out of hearing? Gone? No sound, no word?
Alack, where are you? Speak, an if° you hear;
Speak, of all loves!° I swoon almost with fear.   160
No? Then I well perceive you are not nigh.
Either death, or you, I'll find immediately.

                 Exit. [The sleeping Titania remains.]

ACT III

SCENE I [THE ACTION IS CONTINUOUS.]

Enter the clowns° [Quince, Snug, Bottom, Flute, Snout, and Starveling].

Bottom: Are we all met?
Quince: Pat,° pat; and here's a marvelous convenient place for our rehearsal. This
    green plot shall be our stage, this hawthorn brake° our tiring-house,° and we will
    do it in action as we will do it before the Duke.

---

135 *Good troth, good sooth* i.e., indeed, truly   138 *lord of* i.e., possessor of. *gentleness* courtesy   139 *of* by
140 *abused* ill treated   145–146 *as . . . deceive* as renounced heresies are hated most by those persons who
formerly were deceived by them   148 *Of . . . of* by . . . by   149 *address* direct, apply   156 *prey* act of
preying   159 *an if* if   160 *of all loves* for all love's sake *s.d. clowns* rustics   2 *Pat* on the dot, punctually
3 *brake* thicket. *tiring-house* attiring area, hence backstage

Bottom: Peter Quince?   5

Quince: What sayest thou, bully° Bottom?

Bottom: There are things in this comedy of Pyramus and Thisbe that will never
please. First, Pyramus must draw a sword to kill himself, which the ladies cannot
abide. How answer you that?

Snout: By 'r lakin,° a parlous° fear.   10

Starveling: I believe we must leave the killing out, when all is done.°

Bottom: Not a whit. I have a device to make all well. Write me° a prologue, and let
the prologue seem to say, we will do no harm with our swords, and that Pyramus
is not killed indeed; and for the more better assurance, tell them that I, Pyramus,
am not Pyramus but Bottom the weaver. This will put them out of fear.   15

Quince: Well, we will have such a prologue, and it shall be written in eight and six.°

Bottom: No, make it two more: let it be written in eight and eight.

Snout: Will not the ladies be afeard of the lion?

Starveling: I fear it, I promise you.

Bottom: Masters, you ought to consider with yourself, to bring in—God shield us!—   20
a lion among ladies° is a most dreadful thing. For there is not a more fearful°
wildfowl than your lion living, and we ought to look to 't.

Snout: Therefore another prologue must tell he is not a lion.

Bottom: Nay, you must name his name, and half his face must be seen through the
lion's neck, and he himself must speak through, saying thus or to the same   25
defect:° "Ladies," or "Fair ladies, I would wish you," or "I would request you," or
"I would entreat you, not to fear, not to tremble; my life for yours.° If you think
I come hither as a lion, it were pity of my life.° No, I am no such thing; I am a
man as other men are." And there indeed let him name his name, and tell them
plainly he is Snug the joiner.   30

Quince: Well, it shall be so. But there is two hard things: that is, to bring the moonlight into a chamber; for, you know, Pyramus and Thisbe meet by moonlight.

Snout: Doth the moon shine that night we play our play?

Bottom: A calendar, a calendar! Look in the almanac. Find out moonshine, find out
moonshine.   35

> [*They consult an almanac.*]

Quince: Yes, it doth shine that night.

Bottom: Why then may you leave a casement of the great chamber window where we
play open, and the moon may shine in at the casement.

Quine: Ay; or else one must come in with a bush of thorns° and a lantern and say he
comes to disfigure,° or to present,° the person of Moonshine. Then there is an-   40
other thing: we must have a wall in the great chamber; for Pyramus and Thisbe,
says the story, did talk through the chink of a wall.

---

6 *bully* i.e., worthy, jolly, fine fellow   10 *By 'r lakin* by our ladykin, i.e., the Virgin Mary. *parlous* perilous,
alarming   11 *when all is done* i.e., when all is said and done   12 *Write me* i.e., write at my suggestion (Me
is used colloquially.)   16 *eight and six* alternate lines of eight and six syllables, a common ballad measure
21 *lion among ladies* (A contemporary pamphlet tells how, at the christening in 1594 of Prince Henry, eldest son of King James VI of Scotland, later James I of England, a "blackamoor" instead of a lion drew the
triumphal chariot, since the lion's presence might have "brought some fear to the nearest."). *fearful* fear-
inspiring   26 *defect* (Bottom's blunder for "effect.")   27 *my life for yours* i.e., I pledge my life to make your
lives safe   28 *it were . . . life* i.e., I should be sorry, by my life; or, my life would be endangered   39 *bush of
thorns* bundle of thornbush faggots (part of the accoutrements of the man in the moon, according to the
popular notions of the time, along with his lantern and his dog)   40 *disfigure* (Quince's blunder for "figure.") *present* represent

Snout: You can never bring in a wall. What say you, Bottom?

Bottom: Some man or other must present Wall. And let him have some plaster, or
    some loam, or some roughcast° about him, to signify wall; or let him hold his fin-   45
    gers thus, and through that cranny shall Pyramus and Thisbe whisper.

Quince: If that may be, then all is well. Come, sit down, every mother's son, and
    rehearse your parts. Pyramus, you begin. When you have spoken your speech,
    enter into that brake, and so everyone according to his cue.

    Enter Robin [Puck].

Puck [aside]: What hempen homespuns° have we swaggering here   50
    So near the cradle° of the Fairy Queen?
    What, a play toward?° I'll be an auditor;
    An actor, too, perhaps, if I see cause.

Quince: Speak, Pyramus. Thisbe, stand forth.

Bottom [as Pyramus]: "Thisbe, the flowers of odious savors sweet—"   55

Quince: Odors, odors.

Bottom: "—Odors savors sweet;
    So hath thy breath, my dearest Thisbe dear.
    But hark, a voice! Stay thou but here awhile,
    And by and by I will to thee appear."   *Exit.* 60

Puck: A stranger Pyramus than e'er played here.°   *[Exit.]*

Flute: Must I speak now?

Quince: Ay, marry, must you; for you must understand he goes but to see a noise that
    he heard, and is to come again.

Flute [as Thisbe]: "Most radiant Pyramus, most lily-white of hue,   65
    Of color like the red rose on triumphant° brier,
    Most brisky juvenal° and eke° most lovely Jew,°
    As true as truest horse that yet would never tire.
    I'll meet thee, Pyramus, at Ninny's tomb."

Quince: "Ninus'° tomb," man. Why, you must not speak that yet. That you answer 70
    to Pyramus: You speak all your part° at once, cues and all. Pyramus, enter. Your
    cue is past; it is "never tire."

Flute: O—"As true as truest horse, that yet would never tire."

    [Enter Puck, and Bottom as Pyramus with the ass head.°]

Bottom: "If I were fair,° Thisbe, I were° only thine."

Quince: O, monstrous! O, strange! We are haunted. Pray, masters! Fly, masters! 75
    Help!

                  [Exeunt Quince, Snug, Flute, Snout, and Starveling.]

---

45 *roughcast* a mixture of lime and gravel used to plaster the outside of buildings   50 *hempen homespuns*
i.e., rustics dressed in clothes woven of coarse, homespun fabric made from hemp   51 *cradle* i.e., Titania's
bower   52 *toward* about to take place   61 *A stranger . . . here* (Either Puck refers to an earlier dramatic
version played in the same theater, or he has conceived of a plan to present a "stranger" Pyramus than ever
seen before.)   66 *triumphant* magnificent   67 *brisky juvenal* lively youth. *eke* also. *Jew* (An absurd repetition of the first syllable of *juvenal*, and an indication of how desperately Quince searches for his
rhymes.)   70 *Ninus* mythical founder of Nineveh (whose wife, Semiramis, was supposed to have built the
walls of Babylon where the story of Pyramus and Thisbe takes place)   71 *part* (An actor's *part* was a script
consisting only of his speeches and their cues.)   s.d. *with the ass head* (This stage direction, taken from the
Folio, presumably refers to a standard stage property.)   74 *fair* handsome. *were* would be

Bottom is transformed into an ass.

Puck: I'll follow you, I'll lead you about a round,°
    Thorough bog, thorough bush, thorough brake, thorough brier.
    Sometimes a horse I'll be, sometimes a hound,
    A hog, a headless bear, sometimes a fire;°   80
    And neigh, and bark, and grunt, and roar, and burn,
    Like horse, hound, hog, bear, fire, at every turn.   *Exit.*
Bottom: Why do they run away? This is a knavery of them to make me afeard.

    Enter Snout.

Snout: O Bottom, thou art changed! What do I see on thee?
Bottom: What do you see? You see an ass head of your own, do you?   85
                                                    [Exit Snout.]

77 *about a round* roundabout   80 *fire* will-o'-the-wisp

Enter Quince.

Quince: Bless thee, Bottom, bless thee! Thou art translated.° *Exit.*

Bottom: I see their knavery. This is to make an ass of me, to fright me, if they could. But I will not stir from this place, do what they can. I will walk up and down here, and will sing, that they shall hear I am not afraid.

[*He sings.*]

      The ouzel cock° so black of hue,   90
         With orange-tawny bill,
      The throstle° with his note so true,
         The wren with little quill°—

Titania [*awaking*]: What angel wakes me from my flowery bed?

Bottom [*sings*]:

      The finch, the sparrow, and the lark,   95
         The plainsong° cuckoo gray,
      Whose note full many a man doth mark,
         And dares not answer nay°—

For, indeed, who would set his wit to° so foolish a bird? Who would give a bird the lie,° though he cry "cuckoo" never so?°   100

Titania: I pray thee, gentle mortal, sing again.
Mine ear is much enamored of thy note;
So is mine eye enthrallèd to thy shape;
And thy fair virtue's force° perforce doth move me
On the first view to say, to swear, I love thee.   105

Bottom: Methinks, mistress, you should have little reason for that. And yet, to say the truth, reason and love keep little company together nowadays—the more the pity that some honest neighbors will not make them friends. Nay, I can gleek° upon occasion.

Titania: Thou art as wise as thou art beautiful.   110

Bottom: Not so, neither. But if I had wit enough to get out of this wood, I have enough to serve mine own turn.°

Titania: Out of this wood do not desire to go.
Thou shalt remain here, whether thou wilt or no.
I am a spirit of no common rate.°   115
The summer still doth tend upon my state,°
And I do love thee. Therefore go with me.
I'll give thee fairies to attend on thee,
And they shall fetch thee jewels from the deep,
And sing while thou on pressèd flowers dost sleep.   120
And I will purge thy mortal grossness° so
That thou shalt like an airy spirit go.
Peaseblossom, Cobweb, Mote,° and Mustardseed!

---

86 *translated* transformed   90 *ouzel cock* male blackbird   92 *throstle* song thrush   93 *quill* (Literally, a reed pipe; hence, the bird's piping song.)   96 *plainsong* singing a melody without variations   98 *dares . . . nay* i.e., cannot deny that he is a cuckold   99 *set his wit to* employ his intelligence to answer   99–100 *give . . . lie* call the bird a liar   100 *never so* ever so much   104 *thy . . . force* the power of your unblemished excellence   109 *gleek* jest   112 *serve . . . turn* answer my purpose   115 *rate* rank, value   116 *still . . . state* always waits upon me as a part of my royal retinue   121 *mortal grossness* materiality (i.e., the corporeal nature of a mortal being)   123 *Mote* i.e., speck. (The two words *moth* and *mote* were pronounced alike, and both meanings may be present.)

Enter four Fairies [Peaseblossom, Cobweb, Mote, and Mustardseed].

Peaseblossom: Ready.

Cobweb: And I.

Mote: And I.

Mustardseed: And I.

All: Where shall we go?   125

Titania: Be kind and courteous to this gentleman.
      Hop in his walks and gambol in his eyes;°
      Feed him with apricots and dewberries,°
      With purple grapes, green figs, and mulberries;
      The honey bags steal from the humble-bees,   130
      And for night tapers crop their waxen thighs
      And light them at the fiery glowworms' eyes,
      To have my love to bed and to arise;
      And pluck the wings from painted butterflies
      To fan the moonbeams from his sleeping eyes.   135
      Nod to him, elves, and do him courtesies.

Peaseblossom: Hail, mortal!

Cobweb: Hail!

Mote: Hail!

Mustardseed: Hail!   140

Bottom: I cry your worships mercy,° heartily. I beseech your worship's name.

Cobweb: Cobweb.

Bottom: I shall desire you of more acquaintance,° good Master Cobweb. If I cut my
      finger, I shall make bold with you.°—Your name, honest gentleman?

Peaseblossom: Peaseblossom.   145

Bottom: I pray you, commend me to Mistress Squash,° your mother, and to Master
      Peascod,° your father. Good Master Peaseblossom, I shall desire you of more
      acquaintance too.—Your name, I beseech you, sir?

Mustardseed: Mustardseed.

Bottom: Good Master Mustardseed, I know your patience° well. That same cowardly,   150
      giantlike ox-beef hath devoured many a gentleman of your house. I promise you,
      your kindred hath made my eyes water° ere now. I desire you of more acquain-
      tance, good Master Mustardseed.

Titania: Come wait upon him; lead him to my bower.
      The moon methinks looks with a watery eye;   155
      And when she weeps,° weeps every little flower,
      Lamenting some enforcèd° chastity.
      Tie up my lover's tongue,° bring him silently.

                                                                [*Exeunt.*]

127 *in his eyes* in his sight (i.e., before him)   128 *dewberries* blackberries   141 *I cry . . . mercy* I beg pardon of your worships (for presuming to ask a question)   143 *I . . . acquaintance* I crave to be better acquainted with you   143–144 *If . . . you* (Cobwebs were used to stanch bleeding.)   146 *Squash* unripe pea
pod   146 *Peascod* ripe pea pod   150 *your patience* what you have endured. (Mustard is eaten with beef.)
152 *water* (1) weep for sympathy (2) smart, sting   156 *she weeps* i.e., she causes dew   157 *enforcèd* forced,
violated; or, possibly, constrained (since Titania at this moment is hardly concerned about chastity)   158
Tie . . . tongue (Presumably Bottom is braying like an ass.)

SCENE II [THE WOOD.]

Enter [Oberon,] King of Fairies.

Oberon: I wonder if Titania be awaked;
    Then, what it was that next came in her eye,
    Which she must dote on in extremity.

[*Enter*] *Robin Goodfellow* [*Puck*].

    Here comes my messenger. How now, mad spirit?
    What night-rule° now about this haunted° grove?   5
Puck: My mistress with a monster is in love.
    Near to her close° and consecrated bower,
    While she was in her dull° and sleeping hour,
    A crew of patches,° rude mechanicals,°
    That work for bread upon Athenian stalls,°   10
    Were met together to rehearse a play
    Intended for great Theseus' nuptial day.
    The shallowest thickskin of that barren sort,°
    Who Pyramus presented,° in their sport
    Forsook his scene° and entered in a brake.   15
    When I did him at this advantage take,
    An ass's noll° I fixèd on his head.
    Anon his Thisbe must be answerèd,
    And forth my mimic° comes. When they him spy,
    As wild geese that the creeping fowler° eye,   20
    Or russet-pated choughs,° many in sort,°
    Rising and cawing at the gun's report,
    Sever° themselves and madly sweep the sky,
    So, at his sight, away his fellows fly;
    And, at our stamp, here o'er and o'er one falls;   25
    He "Murder!" cries and help from Athens calls.
    Their sense thus weak, lost with their fears thus strong,
    Made senseless things begin to do them wrong,
    For briers and thorns at their apparel snatch;
    Some, sleeves—some, hats; from yielders all things catch.°   30
    I led them on in this distracted fear
    And left sweet Pyramus translated there,
    When in that moment, so it came to pass,
    Titania waked and straightway loved an ass.
Oberon: This falls out better than I could devise.   35
    But hast thou yet latched° the Athenian's eyes
    With the love juice, as I did bid thee do?

---

5 *night-rule* diversion or misrule for the night. *haunted* much frequented 7 *close* secret, private 8 *dull* drowsy 9 *patches* clowns, fools. *rude mechanicals* ignorant artisans 10 *stalls* market booths 13 *barren sort* stupid company or crew 14 *presented* acted 15 *scene* playing area 17 *noll* noddle, head 19 *mimic* burlesque actor 20 *fowler* hunter of game birds 21 *russet-pated choughs* reddish brown or gray-headed jackdaws. *in sort* in a flock 23 *Sever* i.e., scatter 30 *from . . . catch* i.e., everything preys on those who yield to fear 36 *latched* fastened, snared

Puck: I took him sleeping—that is finished too—
    And the Athenian woman by his side,
    That, when he waked, of force° she must be eyed.   40

    Enter Demetrius and Hermia.

Oberon: Stand close. This is the same Athenian.
Puck: This is the woman, but not this the man.

                                    [They stand aside.]

Demetrius: O, why rebuke you him that loves you so?
    Lay breath so bitter on your bitter foe.
Hermia: Now I but chide; but I should use thee worse,   45
    For thou, I fear, hast given me cause to curse.
    If thou hast slain Lysander in his sleep,
    Being o'er shoes° in blood, plunge in the deep,
    And kill me too.
    The sun was not so true unto the day   50
    As he to me. Would he have stolen away
    From sleeping Hermia? I'll believe as soon
    This whole° earth may be bored, and that the moon
    May through the center creep, and so displease
    Her brother's° noontide with th' Antipodes.°   55
    It cannot be but thou hast murdered him;
    So should a murderer look, so dead,° so grim.
Demetrius: So should the murdered look, and so should I,
    Pierced through the heart with your stern cruelty.
    Yet you, the murderer, look as bright, as clear   60
    As yonder Venus in her glimmering sphere.
Hermia: What's this to° my Lysander? Where is he?
    Ah, good Demetrius, wilt thou give him me?
Demetrius: I had rather give his carcass to my hounds.
Hermia: Out, dog! Out, cur! Thou driv'st me past the bounds   65
    Of maiden's patience. Hast thou slain him, then?
    Henceforth be never numbered among men.
    O, once° tell true, tell true, even for my sake:
    Durst thou have looked upon him being awake?
    And hast thou killed him sleeping? O brave touch!°   70
    Could not a worm,° an adder, do so much?
    An adder did it; for with doubler° tongue
    Than thine, thou serpent, never adder stung.
Demetrius: You spend your passion° on a misprised mood.°
    I am not guilty of Lysander's blood,   75
    Nor is he dead, for aught that I can tell.
Hermia: I pray thee, tell me then that he is well.

---

40 *of force* perforce   48 *Being o'er shoes* having waded in so far   53 *whole* solid   55 *Her brother's* i.e., the sun's.   *th' Antipodes* the people on the opposite side of the earth (where the moon is imagined bringing night to noontime)   57 *dead* deadly, or deathly pale   62 *to* to do with   68 *once* once and for all   70 *brave touch!* fine stroke! (Said ironically.)   71 *worm* serpent   72 *doubler* (1) more forked (2) more deceitful 74 *passion* violent feelings. *misprised mood* anger based on misconception

Demetrius: And if I could, what should I get therefor?°
Hermia: A privilege never to see me more.
    And from thy hated presence part I so.
    See me no more, whether he be dead or no.   *Exit.*
Demetrius: There is no following her in this fierce vein.
    Here therefore for a while I will remain.
    So sorrow's heaviness doth heavier° grow
    For debt that bankrupt° sleep doth sorrow owe;
    Which now in some slight measure it will pay,
    If for his tender here I make some stay.°   *[He] lie[s] down [and sleeps].*
Oberon: What hast thou done? Thou hast mistaken quite
    And laid the love juice on some true love's sight.
    Of thy misprision° must perforce ensue
    Some true love turned, and not a false turned true.
Puck: Then fate o'errules, that, one man holding troth,°
    A million fail, confounding oath on oath.°
Oberon: About the wood go swifter than the wind,
    And Helena of Athens look° thou find.
    All fancy-sick° she is and pale of cheer°
    With sighs of love, that cost the fresh blood° dear.
    By some illusion see thou bring her here.
    I'll charm his eyes against she do appear.°
Puck: I go, I go, look how I go,
    Swifter than arrow from the Tartar's bow.°   *[Exit.]*
Oberon [applying love juice to Demetrius' eyes]:
    Flower of this purple dye,
    Hit with Cupid's archery,
    Sink in apple° of his eye.
    When his love he doth espy,
    Let her shine as gloriously
    As the Venus of the sky.
    When thou wak'st, if she be by,
    Beg of her for remedy.

    Enter Puck.

Puck: Captain of our fairy band,
          Helena is here at hand,
          And the youth, mistook by me,
          Pleading for a lover's fee.°

Line numbers: 80, 85, 90, 95, 100, 105, 110

---

78 *therefor* in return for that   84 *heavier* (1) harder to bear (2) more drowsy   85 *bankrupt* (Demetrius is saying that his sleepiness adds to the weariness caused by sorrow.)   86–87 *Which . . . stay* i.e., to a small extent, I will be able to "pay back" and hence find some relief from sorrow, if I pause here awhile (*make some stay*) while sleep "tenders" or offers itself by way of paying the debt owed to sorrow   90 *misprision* mistake   92 *that . . . troth* in that, for each man keeping true faith in love   93 *confounding . . . oath* i.e., breaking oath after oath   95 *look* i.e., be sure   96 *fancy-sick* lovesick.   *cheer* face   97 *sighs . . . blood* (An allusion to the physiological theory that each sigh costs the heart a drop of blood.)   99 *against . . . appear* in anticipation of her coming   101 *Tartar's bow* (Tartars were famed for their skill with the bow.)   104 *apple* pupil   113 *fee* privilege, reward

	Shall we their fond pageant° see?	
	Lord, what fools these mortals be!	115
Oberon:	Stand aside. The noise they make	
	Will cause Demetrius to awake.	
Puck:	Then will two at once woo one;	
	That must needs be sport alone.°	
	And those things do best please me	120
	That befall preposterously.°	

[They stand aside.]

Enter Lysander and Helena.

Lysander: Why should you think that I should woo in scorn?
Scorn and derision never come in tears.
Look when° I vow, I weep; and vows so born,
In their nativity all truth appears.° 125
How can these things in me seem scorn to you,
Bearing the badge° of faith to prove them true?
Helena: You do advance° your cunning more and more.
When truth kills truth,° O, devilish-holy fray!
These vows are Hermia's. Will you give her o'er? 130
Weigh oath with oath, and you will nothing weigh.
Your vows to her and me, put in two scales,
Will even weigh, and both as light as tales.°
Lysander: I had no judgment when to her I swore.
Helena: Nor none, in my mind, now you give her o'er. 135
Lysander: Demetrius loves her, and he loves not you.
Demetrius [*awaking*]: O Helen, goddess, nymph, perfect, divine!
To what, my love, shall I compare thine eyne?
Crystal is muddy. O, how ripe in show°
Thy lips, those kissing cherries, tempting grow! 140
That pure congealèd white, high Taurus'° snow,
Fanned with the eastern wind, turns to a crow°
When thou hold'st up thy hand. O, let me kiss
This princess of pure white, this seal° of bliss!
Helena: O spite! O hell! I see you all are bent 145
To set against° me for your merriment.
If you were civil and knew courtesy,
You would not do me thus much injury.
Can you not hate me, as I know you do,
But you must join in souls° to mock me too? 150
If you were men, as men you are in show,
You would not use a gentle lady so—

---

114 *fond pageant* foolish spectacle   119 *alone* unequaled   121 *preposterously* out of the natural order   124
Look when whenever   124–125 *vows . . . appears* i.e., vows made by one who is weeping give evidence
thereby of their sincerity   127 *badge* identifying device such as that worn on servants' livery (here, his tears)
128 *advance* carry forward, display   129 *truth kills truth* i.e., one of Lysander's vows must invalidate the other
133 *tales* lies   139 *show* appearance   141 *Taurus* a lofty mountain range in Asia Minor   142 *turns to a crow*
i.e., seems black by contrast   144 *seal* pledge   146 *set against* attack   150 *in souls* i.e., heart and soul

Helena believes the enchanted Demetrius is only pretending to love her in order to mock her.

To vow, and swear, and superpraise° my parts,°
When I am sure you hate me with your hearts.
You both are rivals, and love Hermia,   155
And now both rivals, to mock Helena.
A trim° exploit, a manly enterprise,
To conjure tears up in a poor maid's eyes
With your derision! None of noble sort°
Would so offend a virgin and extort°   160
A poor soul's patience, all to make you sport.

153 *superpraise* overpraise. *parts* qualities 157 *trim* pretty, fine (Said ironically.) 159 *sort* character, quality 160 *extort* twist, torture

Lysander: You are unkind, Demetrius. Be not so.
    For you love Hermia; this you know I know.
    And here, with all good will, with all my heart,
    In Hermia's love I yield you up my part;   165
    And yours of Helena to me bequeath,
    Whom I do love, and will do till my death.
Helena: Never did mockers waste more idle breath.
Demetrius: Lysander, keep thy Hermia; I will none.°
    If e'er I loved her, all that love is gone.   170
    My heart to her but as guestwise sojourned,°
    And now to Helen is it home returned,
    There to remain.
Lysander: Helen, it is not so.
Demetrius: Disparage not the faith thou dost not know,
    Lest, to thy peril, thou aby° it dear.   175
    Look where thy love comes; yonder is thy dear.

    Enter Hermia.

Hermia: Dark night, that from the eye his° function takes,
    The ear more quick of apprehension makes;
    Wherein it doth impair the seeing sense,
    It pays the hearing double recompense.   180
    Thou art not by mine eye, Lysander, found;
    Mine ear, I thank it, brought me to thy sound.
    But why unkindly didst thou leave me so?
Lysander: Why should he stay, whom love doth press to go?
Hermia: What love could press Lysander from my side?   185
Lysander: Lysander's love, that would not let him bide—
    Fair Helena, who more engilds° the night
    Than all yon fiery oes° and eyes of light.
    Why seek'st thou me? Could not this make thee know
    The hate I bear thee made me leave thee so?   190
Hermia: You speak not as you think. It cannot be.
Helena: Lo, she is one of this confederacy!
    Now I perceive they have conjoined all three
    To fashion this false sport in spite of me.°
    Injurious Hermia, most ungrateful maid!   195
    Have you conspired, have you with these contrived°
    To bait° me with this foul derision?
    Is all the counsel° that we two have shared—
    The sisters' vows, the hours that we have spent
    When we have chid the hasty-footed time   200
    For parting us—O, is all forgot?
    All schooldays' friendship, childhood innocence?

---

169 *will none* i.e., want no part of her   171 *to . . . sojourned* only visited with her   175 *aby* pay for   177 *his* its   187 *engilds* gilds, brightens with a golden light   188 *oes* spangles (here, stars)   194 *in spite of me* to vex me   196 *contrived* plotted   197 *bait* torment, as one sets on dogs to bait a bear   198 *counsel* confidential talk

We, Hermia, like two artificial° gods,
Have with our needles created both one flower,
Both on one sampler, sitting on one cushion,   205
Both warbling of one song, both in one key,
As if our hands, our sides, voices, and minds
Had been incorporate.° So we grew together,
Like to a double cherry, seeming parted,
But yet an union in partition,   210
Two lovely° berries molded on one stem;
So with two seeming bodies but one heart,
Two of the first, like coats in heraldry,
Due but to one and crownèd with one crest.°
And will you rend our ancient love asunder,   215
To join with men in scorning your poor friend?
It is not friendly, 'tis not maidenly.
Our sex, as well as I, may chide you for it,
Though I alone do feel the injury.
Hermia: I am amazèd at your passionate words.   220
    I scorn you not. It seems that you scorn me.
Helena: Have you not set Lysander, as in scorn,
    To follow me and praise my eyes and face?
    And made your other love, Demetrius,
    Who even but now did spurn me with his foot,   225
    To call me goddess, nymph, divine, and rare,
    Precious, celestial? Wherefore speaks he this
    To her he hates? And wherefore doth Lysander
    Deny your love, so rich within his soul,
    And tender° me, forsooth, affection,   230
    But by your setting on, by your consent?
    What though I be not so in grace° as you,
    So hung upon with love, so fortunate,
    But miserable most, to love unloved?
    This you should pity rather than despise.   235
Hermia: I understand not what you mean by this.
Helena: Ay, do! Persever, counterfeit sad° looks,
    Make mouths° upon° me when I turn my back,
    Wink each at other, hold the sweet jest up.°
    This sport, well carried,° shall be chronicled.   240
    If you have any pity, grace, or manners,
    You would not make me such an argument.°
    But fare ye well. 'Tis partly my own fault,
    Which death, or absence, soon shall remedy.
Lysander: Stay, gentle Helena; hear my excuse,   245
    My love, my life, my soul, fair Helena!

---

203 *artificial* skilled in art or creation   208 *incorporate* of one body   211 *lovely* loving   213–214 *Two . . .
crest* i.e., we have two separate bodies, just as a coat of arms in heraldry can be represented twice on a
shield but surmounted by a single crest   230 *tender* offer   232 *grace* favor   237 *sad* grave, serious   238
mouths i.e., moves, faces, grimaces.   *upon* at   239 *hold . . . up* keep up the joke   240 *carried* managed
242 *argument* subject for a jest

Helena: O excellent!

Hermia [*to Lysander*]: Sweet, do not scorn her so.

Demetrius [*to Lysander*]: If she cannot entreat,° I can compel.

Lysander: Thou canst compel no more than she entreat.

   Thy threats have no more strength than her weak prayers.   250

   Helen, I love thee, by my life I do!

   I swear by that which I will lose for thee,

   To prove him false that says I love thee not.

Demetrius [*to Helena*]:

   I say I love thee more than he can do.

Lysander: If thou say so, withdraw, and prove it too.°   255

Demetrius: Quick, come!

Hermia: Lysander, whereto tends all this?

Lysander: Away, you Ethiope!°

                              [*He tries to break away from Hermia.*]

Demetrius: No, no; he'll

   Seem to break loose; take on as° you would follow,

   But yet come not. You are a tame man. Go!

Lysander [*to Hermia*]: Hang off,° thou cat, thou burr! Vile thing, let loose,   260

   Or I will shake thee from me like a serpent!

Hermia: Why are you grown so rude? What change is this,

   Sweet love?

Lysander: Thy love? Out, tawny Tartar, out!

   Out, loathèd med'cine!° O hated potion, hence!

Hermia: Do you not jest?

Helena: Yes, sooth,° and so do you.   265

Lysander: Demetrius, I will keep my word with thee.

Demetrius: I would I had your bond, for I perceive

   A weak bond° holds you. I'll not trust your word.

Lysander: What, should I hurt her, strike her, kill her dead?

   Although I hate her, I'll not harm her so.   270

Hermia: What, can you do me greater harm than hate?

   Hate me? Wherefore? O me, what news,° my love?

   Am not I Hermia? Are not you Lysander?

   I am as fair now as I was erewhile.°

   Since night you loved me; yet since night you left me.   275

   Why, then you left me—O, the gods forbid!—

   In earnest, shall I say?

Lysander: Ay, by my life!

   And never did desire to see thee more.

   Therefore be out of hope, of question, of doubt;

   Be certain, nothing truer. 'Tis no jest   280

   That I do hate thee and love Helena.

---

248 *entreat* i.e., succeed by entreaty   255 *withdraw . . . too* i.e., withdraw with me and prove your claim in a duel. (The two gentlemen are armed.)   257 *Ethiope* (Referring to Hermia's relatively dark hair and complexion; see also *tawny Tartar* six lines later.)   258 *take on as* act as if, make a fuss as if   260 *Hang off* let go   264 *med'cine* i.e., poison   265 *sooth* truly   268 *weak bond* i.e., Hermia's arm (with a pun on *bond,* "oath," in the previous line)   272 *what news* what is the matter   274 *erewhile* just now

Hermia berates Helena, "You thief of love!" (III, ii, 283).

Hermia [to Helena]: O me! You juggler! You cankerblossom!°
    You thief of love! What, have you come by night
    And stol'n my love's heart from him?
Helena: Fine, i' faith!
    Have you no modesty, no maiden shame,   285
    No touch of bashfulness? What, will you tear
    Impatient answers from my gentle tongue?
    Fie, fie! You counterfeit, you puppet,° you!
Hermia: "Puppet"? Why, so!° Ay, that way goes the game.
    Now I perceive that she hath made compare   290
    Between our statures; she hath urged her height,
    And with her personage, her tall personage,
    Her height, forsooth, she hath prevailed with him.
    And are you grown so high in his esteem
    Because I am so dwarfish and so low?   295
    How low am I, thou painted maypole? Speak!
    How low am I? I am not yet so low
    But that my nails can reach unto thine eyes.
                       [She flails at Helena but is restrained.]

282 *cankerblossom* worm that destroys the flower bud, or wild rose   288 *puppet* (1) counterfeit (2) dwarfish woman (in reference to Hermia's smaller stature)   289 *Why, so* i.e., Oh, so that's how it is

Helena: I pray you, though you mock me, gentlemen,
  Let her not hurt me. I was never curst;°   300
  I have no gift at all in shrewishness;
  I am a right° maid for my cowardice.
  Let her not strike me. You perhaps may think,
  Because she is something° lower than myself,
  That I can match her.
Hermia: Lower? Hark, again!   305
Helena: Good Hermia, do not be so bitter with me.
  I evermore did love you, Hermia,
  Did ever keep your counsels, never wronged you,
  Save that, in love unto Demetrius,
  I told him of your stealth° unto this wood.   310
  He followed you; for love I followed him.
  But he hath chid me hence° and threatened me
  To strike me, spurn me, nay, to kill me too.
  And now, so° you will let me quiet go,
  To Athens will I bear my folly back   315
  And follow you no further. Let me go.
  You see how simple and how fond° I am.
Hermia: Why, get you gone. Who is 't that hinders you?
Helena: A foolish heart, that I leave here behind.
Hermia: What, with Lysander?
Helena: With Demetrius.
Lysander: Be not afraid; she shall not harm thee, Helena.   320
Demetrius: No, sir, she shall not, though you take her part.
Helena: O, when she is angry, she is keen° and shrewd.°
  She was a vixen when she went to school;
  And though she be but little, she is fierce.   325
Hermia: "Little" again? Nothing but "low" and "little"?
  Why will you suffer her to flout me thus?
  Let me come to her.
Lysander: Get you gone, you dwarf!
  You minimus,° of hindering knotgrass° made!
  You bead, you acorn!
Demetrius: You are too officious   330
  In her behalf that scorns your services.
  Let her alone. Speak not of Helena;
  Take not her part. For, if thou dost intend°
  Never so little show of love to her,
  Thou shalt aby° it.
Lysander: Now she holds me not.   335
  Now follow, if thou dar'st, to try whose right,
  Of thine or mine, is most in Helena.   [*Exit.*]

---

300 *curst* shrewish   302 *right* true   304 *something* somewhat   310 *stealth* stealing away   312 *chid me
hence* driven me away with his scolding   314 *so* if only   317 *fond* foolish   323 *keen* fierce, cruel.   *shrewd*
shrewish   329 *minimus* diminutive creature.   *knotgrass* a weed, an infusion of which was thought to stunt
the growth   333 *intend* give sign of   335 *aby* pay for

Demetrius: Follow? Nay, I'll go with thee, cheek by jowl.°

                                [Exit, following Lysander.]

Hermia: You, mistress, all this coil° is 'long of° you.
   Nay, go not back.°

Helena: I will not trust you, I,   340
   Nor longer stay in your curst company.
   Your hands than mine are quicker for a fray;
   My legs are longer, though, to run away.   *[Exit.]*

Hermia: I am amazed and know not what to say.   *Exit.*

   [Oberon and Puck come forward.]

Oberon: This is thy negligence. Still thou mistak'st,   345
   Or else committ'st thy knaveries willfully.

Puck: Believe me, king of shadows, I mistook.
   Did not you tell me I should know the man
   By the Athenian garments he had on?
   And so far blameless proves my enterprise   350
   That I have 'nointed an Athenian's eyes;
   And so far° am I glad it so did sort,°
   As° this their jangling I esteem a sport.

Oberon: Thou seest these lovers seek a place to fight.
   Hie° therefore, Robin, overcast the night;   355
   The starry welkin° cover thou anon
   With drooping fog as black as Acheron,°
   And lead these testy rivals so astray
   As° one come not within another's way.
   Like to Lysander sometimes frame thy tongue,   360
   Then stir Demetrius up with bitter wrong;°
   And sometimes rail thou like Demetrius.
   And from each other look thou lead them thus,
   Till o'er their brows death-counterfeiting sleep
   With leaden legs and batty° wings doth creep.   365
   Then crush this herb° into Lysander's eye,   *[giving herb.]*
   Whose liquor hath this virtuous° property,
   To take from thence all error with his° might
   And make his eyeballs roll with wonted° sight.
   When they next wake, all this derision°   370
   Shall seem a dream and fruitless vision,
   And back to Athens shall the lovers wend
   With league whose date° till death shall never end.
   Whiles I in this affair do thee employ,
   I'll to my queen and beg her Indian boy;   375

---

338 *cheek by jowl* i.e., side by side   339 *coil* turmoil, dissension. *'long of* on account of   340 *go not back* i.e., don't retreat (Hermia is again proposing a fight.)   352 *so far* at least to this extent. *sort* turn out   353 *As* that   355 *Hie* hasten   356 *welkin* sky   357 *Acheron* river of Hades (here representing Hades itself)   359 *As* that   361 *wrong* insults   365 *batty* batlike   366 *this herb* i.e., the antidote (mentioned in II, i, 184) to love-in-idleness   367 *virtuous* efficacious   368 *his* its   369 *wonted* accustomed   370 *derision* laughable business   373 *date* term of existence

And then I will her charmèd eye release
From monster's view, and all things shall be peace.
Puck: My fairy lord, this must be done with haste,
    For night's swift dragons° cut the clouds full fast,
    And yonder shines Aurora's harbinger,°   380
    At whose approach ghosts, wand'ring here and there,
    Troop home to churchyards. Damnèd spirits all,
    That in crossways and floods have burial,°
    Already to their wormy beds are gone.
    For fear lest day should look their shames upon,   385
    They willfully themselves exile from light
    And must for aye° consort with black-browed night.
Oberon: But we are spirits of another sort.
    I with the Morning's love° have oft made sport,
    And, like a forester,° the groves may tread   390
    Even till the eastern gate, all fiery red,
    Opening on Neptune with fair blessèd beams,
    Turns into yellow gold his salt green streams.
    But notwithstanding, haste, make no delay.
    We may effect this business yet ere day.   *[Exit.]* 395
Puck:

    Up and down, up and down,
    I will lead them up and down.
    I am feared in field and town.
    Goblin,° lead them up and down.
    Here comes one.   400

Enter Lysander.

Lysander: Where art thou, proud Demetrius? Speak thou now.
Puck [*mimicking Demetrius*]: Here, villain, drawn° and ready. Where art thou?
Lysander: I will be with thee straight.°
Puck: Follow me, then,
    To plainer° ground.
                               [Lysander wanders about,° following the voice.]

Enter Demetrius.
Demetrius: Lysander! Speak again!
    Thou runaway, thou coward, art thou fled?   405
    Speak! In some bush? Where dost thou hide thy head?

---

379 *dragons* (Supposed by Shakespeare to be yoked to the car of the goddess of night or the moon.)   380 *Aurora's harbinger* the morning star, precursor of dawn   383 *crossways . . . burial* (Those who had committed suicide were buried at crossways, with a stake driven through them; those who intentionally or accidentally drowned [in floods or deep water], would be condemned to wander disconsolate for lack of burial rites.)   387 *for aye* forever   389 *the Morning's love* Cephalus, a beautiful youth beloved by Aurora; or perhaps the goddess of the dawn herself   390 *forester* keeper of a royal forest   399 *Goblin* Hobgoblin. (Puck refers to himself.)   402 *drawn* with drawn sword   403 *straight* immediately   404 *plainer* more open.   s.d. *Lysander wanders about* (Lysander may exit here, but perhaps not; neither exit nor reentrance is indicated in the early texts.)

Puck [*mimicking Lysander*]:
    Thou coward, art thou bragging to the stars,
    Telling the bushes that thou look'st for wars,
    And wilt not come? Come, recreant;° come, thou child,
    I'll whip thee with a rod. He is defiled   410
    That draws a sword on thee.
Demetrius: Yea, art thou there?
Puck: Follow my voice. We'll try° no manhood here.

                                      Exeunt.

    [*Lysander returns.*]

Lysander: He goes before me and still dares me on.
    When I come where he calls, then he is gone.
    The villain is much lighter-heeled than I.   415
    I followed fast, but faster he did fly,
    That fallen am I in dark uneven way,
    And here will rest me. [*He lies down.*] Come, thou gentle day!
    For if but once thou show me thy gray light,
    I'll find Demetrius and revenge this spite.   [*He sleeps.*] 420

    [*Enter*] *Robin* [*Puck*] *and Demetrius.*

Puck: Ho, ho, ho! Coward, why com'st thou not?
Demetrius: Abide° me, if thou dar'st; for well I wot°
    Thou runn'st before me, shifting every place,
    And dar'st not stand nor look me in the face.
    Where art thou now?
Puck: Come hither. I am here.   425
Demetrius: Nay, then, thou mock'st me. Thou shalt buy° this dear,°
    If ever I thy face by daylight see.
    Now, go thy way. Faintness constraineth me
    To measure out my length on this cold bed.
    By day's approach look to be visited.   430

                          [*He lies down and sleeps.*]

    Enter Helena.

Helena: O weary night, O long and tedious night,
    Abate° thy hours! Shine comforts from the east,
    That I may back to Athens by daylight
    From these that my poor company detest;
    And sleep, that sometimes shuts up sorrow's eye,   435
    Steal me awhile from mine own company.

                          [*She lies down and*] *sleep*[*s*].

Puck: Yet but three? Come one more;
    Two of both kinds makes up four.
    Here she comes, curst° and sad.
    Cupid is a knavish lad,   440
    Thus to make poor females mad.

---

409 *recreant* cowardly wretch   412 *try* test   422 *Abide* confront, face. *wot* know   426 *buy* aby, pay for.
dear dearly   432 *Abate* lessen, shorten   439 *curst* ill-tempered

[*Enter Hermia.*]

Hermia: Never so weary, never so in woe,
 Bedabbled with the dew and torn with briers,
 I can no further crawl, no further go;
 My legs can keep no pace with my desires.   445
 Here will I rest me till the break of day.
 Heavens shield Lysander, if they mean a fray!

                 [*She lies down and sleeps.*]

Puck: On the ground
      Sleep sound.
      I'll apply   450
      To your eye,
 Gentle lover, remedy.

[*He squeezes the juice on Lysander's eyes.*]

     When thou wak'st,
     Thou tak'st
     True delight   455
     In the sight
 Of thy former lady's eye;
 And the country proverb known,
 That every man should take his own,
 In your waking shall be shown: 460
     Jack shall have Jill;°
     Naught shall go ill;
 The man shall have his mare again, and all shall be well.

         [*Exit. The four sleeping lovers remain.*]

ACT IV

SCENE I [THE ACTION IS CONTINUOUS. THE FOUR LOVERS ARE STILL ASLEEP° ONSTAGE.]

Enter [*Titania,*] *Queen of Fairies, and* [*Bottom the*] *clown, and Fairies; and* [*Oberon,*] *the King, behind them.*

Titania: Come, sit thee down upon this flowery bed,
 While I thy amiable° cheeks do coy,°
 And stick muskroses in thy sleek smooth head,
 And kiss thy fair large ears, my gentle joy.

 [*They recline.*]

Bottom: Where's Peaseblossom?   5
Peaseblossom: Ready.
Bottom: Scratch my head, Peaseblossom. Where's Monsieur Cobweb?
Cobweb: Ready.

---

461 *Jack shall have Jill* (Proverbial for "boy gets girl.")   s.d. *still asleep* (Compare with the Folio stage direction: "They sleep all the act.")   2 *amiable* lovely.   *coy* caress

The fairies tend to Bottom's wishes.

Bottom: Monsieur Cobweb, good monsieur, get you your weapons in your hand, and kill me a red-hipped humble-bee on the top of a thistle; and, good monsieur, 10
bring me the honey bag. Do not fret yourself too much in the action, monsieur; and, good monsieur, have a care the honey bag break not. I would be loath to have you overflown with a honey bag, signor. [*Exit Cobweb.*] Where's Monsieur Mustardseed?

Mustardseed: Ready. 15

Bottom: Give me your neaf,° Monsieur Mustardseed. Pray you, leave your courtesy,° good monsieur.

Mustardseed: What's your will?

Bottom: Nothing, good monsieur, but to help Cavalery° Cobweb° to scratch. I must to the barber's, monsieur, for methinks I am marvelous hairy about the face; and 20
I am such a tender ass, if my hair do but tickle me I must scratch.

Titania: What, wilt thou hear some music, my sweet love?

Bottom: I have a reasonable good ear in music. Let's have the tongs and the bones.°
[*Music: tongs, rural music.*°]

Titania: Or say, sweet love, what thou desirest to eat.

Bottom: Truly, a peck of provender.° I could munch your good dry oats. Methinks I 25
have a great desire to a bottle° of hay. Good hay, sweet hay, hath no fellow.°

---

16 *neaf* fist.   *leave your courtesy* i.e., stop bowing, or put on your hat   19 *Cavalery* cavalier. (Form of address for a gentleman.)   *Cobweb* (Seemingly an error, since Cobweb has been sent to bring honey, while Peaseblossom has been asked to scratch.)   23 *tongs . . . bones* instruments for rustic music. (The tongs were played like a triangle, whereas the bones were held between the fingers and used as clappers.)   s.d. *Music . . . music* (This stage direction is added from the Folio.)   25 *peck of provender* one-quarter bushel of grain   26 *bottle* bundle.   *fellow* equal

Titania: I have a venturous fairy that shall seek
    The squirrel's hoard, and fetch thee new nuts.
Bottom: I had rather have a handful or two of dried peas. But, I pray you, let none of
    your people stir° me. I have an exposition of° sleep come upon me.   30
Titania: Sleep thou, and I will wind thee in my arms.
    Fairies, begone, and be all ways° away.

                                                        [Exeunt Fairies.]

    So doth the woodbine° the sweet honeysuckle
    Gently entwist; the female ivy so
    Enrings the barky fingers of the elm.   35
    O, how I love thee! How I dote on thee!

                                                             [They sleep.]

    Enter Robin Goodfellow [Puck].

Oberon [coming forward]: Welcome, good Robin. Seest thou this sweet sight?
    Her dotage now I do begin to pity.
    For, meeting her of late behind the wood
    Seeking sweet favors° for this hateful fool,　　　　　　　　　　　　　40
    I did upbraid her and fall out with her.
    For she his hairy temples then had rounded
    With coronet of fresh and fragrant flowers;
    And that same dew, which sometime° on the buds
    Was wont to swell like round and orient° pearls,   45
    Stood now within the pretty flowerets' eyes
    Like tears that did their own disgrace bewail.
    When I had at my pleasure taunted her,
    And she in mild terms begged my patience,
    I then did ask of her her changeling child,   50
    Which straight she gave me, and her fairy sent
    To bear him to my bower in Fairyland.
    And, now I have the boy, I will undo
    This hateful imperfection of her eyes.
    And, gentle Puck, take this transformèd scalp   55
    From off the head of this Athenian swain,
    That he, awaking when the other° do,
    May all to Athens back again repair,°
    And think no more of this night's accidents
    But as the fierce vexation of a dream.   60
    But first I will release the Fairy Queen.

                           [He squeezes an herb on her eyes.]

    Be as thou wast wont to be;
    See as thou wast wont to see.
    Dian's bud° o'er Cupid's flower
    Hath such force and blessèd power.   65

---

30 *stir* disturb. *exposition of* (Bottom's phrase for "disposition to.")   32 *all ways* in all directions   33
woodbine bindweed, a climbing plant that twines in the opposite direction from that of honeysuckle   40
favors i.e., gifts of flowers   44 *sometime* formerly   45 *orient pearls* i.e., the most beautiful of all pearls, those
coming from the Orient   57 *other* others   58 *repair* return   64 *Dian's bud* (Perhaps the flower of the
agnus castus or chaste-tree, supposed to preserve chastity; or perhaps referring simply to Oberon's herb by
which he can undo the effects of "Cupid's flower," the love-in-idleness of II, i, 166–168.)

Now, my Titania, wake you, my sweet queen.
Titania [waking]: My Oberon! What visions have I seen!
    Methought I was enamored of an ass.
Oberon: There lies your love.
Titania: How came these things to pass?
    O, how mine eyes do loathe his visage now!   70
Oberon: Silence awhile. Robin, take off this head.
    Titania, music call, and strike more dead
    Than common sleep of all these five° the sense.
Titania: Music, ho! Music, such as charmeth° sleep!   [*Music.*]
Puck [removing the ass head]:
    Now, when thou wak'st, with thine own fool's eyes peep.   75
Oberon: Sound, music! Come, my queen, take hands with me,
    And rock the ground whereon these sleepers be.   [*They dance.*]
    Now thou and I are new in amity,
    And will tomorrow midnight solemnly°
    Dance in Duke Theseus' house triumphantly,   80
    And bless it to all fair prosperity.
    There shall the pairs of faithful lovers be
    Wedded, with Theseus, all in jollity.

Puck: Fairy King, attend, and mark:
            I do hear the morning lark.   85
Oberon: Then, my queen, in silence sad,°
            Trip we after night's shade.
            We the globe can compass soon,
            Swifter than the wandering moon.
Titania: Come, my lord, and in our flight   90
            Tell me how it came this night
            That I sleeping here was found
            With these mortals on the ground.
                           Exeunt. [Oberon, Titania, and Puck].
                                       Wind horn [within].

Enter Theseus and all his train; [Hippolyta, Egeus].

Theseus: Go, one of you, find out the forester,
    For now our observation° is performed;   95
    And since we have the vaward° of the day,
    My love shall hear the music of my hounds.
    Uncouple° in the western valley; let them go.
    Dispatch, I say, and find the forester.   [*Exit an Attendant.*]
    We will, fair queen, up to the mountain's top   100
    And mark the musical confusion
    Of hounds and echo in conjunction.

---

73 *these five* i.e., the four lovers and Bottom   74 *charmeth* brings about, as though by a charm   79 *solemnly* ceremoniously   86 *sad* sober   95 *observation* i.e., observance to a morn of May (I, i, 167)   96 *vaward* vanguard, i.e., earliest part   98 *Uncouple* set free for the hunt

Hippolyta: I was with Hercules and Cadmus° once,
      When in a wood of Crete they bayed° the bear
      With hounds of Sparta.° Never did I hear   105
      Such gallant chiding;° for, besides the groves,
      The skies, the fountains, every region near
      Seemed all one mutual cry. I never heard
      So musical a discord, such sweet thunder.
Theseus: My hounds are bred out of the Spartan kind,°   110
      So flewed,° so sanded;° and their heads are hung
      With ears that sweep away the morning dew;
      Crook-kneed, and dewlapped° like Thessalian bulls;
      Slow in pursuit, but matched in mouth like bells,
      Each under each.° A cry° more tunable°   115
      Was never holloed to nor cheered° with horn
      In Crete, in Sparta, nor in Thessaly.
      Judge when you hear.   [*He sees the sleepers.*]
            But soft!° What nymphs are these?
Egeus: My lord, this is my daughter here asleep,
      And this Lysander; this Demetrius is;   120
      This Helena, old Nedar's Helena.
      I wonder of° their being here together.
Theseus: No doubt they rose up early to observe
      The rite of May, and hearing our intent,
      Came here in grace of our solemnity.°   125
      But speak, Egeus. Is not this the day
      That Hermia should give answer of her choice?
Egeus: It is, my lord.
Theseus: Go, bid the huntsmen wake them with their horns.

                                                          [*Exit an Attendant.*]

      Shout within. Wind horns. They all start up.

      Good morrow, friends. Saint Valentine° is past.   130
      Begin these woodbirds but to couple now?
Lysander: Pardon, my lord.   [*They kneel.*]
Theseus: I pray you all, stand up.   [*They stand.*]
      I know you two are rival enemies;
      How comes this gentle concord in the world,
      That hatred is so far from jealousy°   135
      To sleep by hate and fear no enmity?

---

103 *Cadmus* mythical founder of Thebes. (This story about him is unknown.)   104 *bayed* brought to bay
105 *hounds of Sparta* (A breed famous in antiquity for their hunting skill.)   106 *chiding* i.e., yelping   110
kind strain, breed   111 *So flewed* similarly having large hanging chaps or fleshy covering of the jaw.
sanded of sandy color   113 *dewlapped* having pendulous folds of skin under the neck   114–115 *matched . . .
each* i.e., harmoniously matched in their various cries like a set of bells, from treble down to bass   115 *cry*
pack of hounds. *tunable* well tuned, melodious   116 *cheered* encouraged   118 *soft* i.e., gently, wait a
minute   122 *wonder of* wonder at   125 *in . . . solemnity* in honor of our wedding ceremony   130 *Saint
Valentine* (Birds were supposed to choose their mates on Saint Valentine's Day.)   135 *jealousy* suspicion

Lysander: My lord, I shall reply amazedly,
    Half sleep, half waking; but as yet, I swear,
    I cannot truly say how I came here.
    But, as I think—for truly would I speak,   140
    And now I do bethink me, so it is—
    I came with Hermia hither. Our intent
    Was to be gone from Athens, where° we might,
    Without° the peril of the Athenian law—
Egeus: Enough, enough, my lord; you have enough.   145
    I beg the law, the law, upon his head.
    They would have stol'n away; they would, Demetrius,
    Thereby to have defeated° you and me,
    You of your wife and me of my consent,
    Of my consent that she should be your wife.   150
Demetrius: My lord, fair Helen told me of their stealth,
    Of this their purpose hither° to this wood,
    And I in fury hither followed them,
    Fair Helena in fancy° following me.
    But, my good lord, I wot not by what power—   155
    But by some power it is—my love to Hermia,
    Melted as the snow, seems to me now
    As the remembrance of an idle gaud°
    Which in my childhood I did dote upon;
    And all the faith, the virtue of my heart,   160
    The object and the pleasure of mine eye,
    Is only Helena. To her, my lord,
    Was I betrothed ere I saw Hermia,
    But like a sickness did I loathe this food;
    But, as in health, come to my natural taste,   165
    Now I do wish it, love it, long for it,
    And will forevermore be true to it.
Theseus: Fair lovers, you are fortunately met.
    Of this discourse we more will hear anon.
    Egeus, I will overbear your will;   170
    For in the temple, by and by, with us
    These couples shall eternally be knit.
    And, for° the morning now is something° worn,
    Our purposed hunting shall be set aside.
    Away with us to Athens. Three and three,   175
    We'll hold a feast in great solemnity.°
    Come, Hippolyta.
                        [Exeunt Theseus, Hippolyta, Egeus, and train.]
Demetrius: These things seem small and undistinguishable,
    Like far-off mountains turnèd into clouds.

---

143 *where* wherever; or, to where   144 *Without* outside of, beyond   148 *defeated* defrauded   152 *hither* in coming hither   154 *in fancy* driven by love   158 *idle gaud* worthless trinket   173 *for* since. *something* somewhat   176 *in great solemnity* with great ceremony

Hermia: Methinks I see these things with parted° eye,　　　　　　　　　 180
　　When everything seems double.
Helena:　　　　　　　　　　　So methinks;
　　And I have found Demetrius like a jewel,
　　Mine own, and not mine own.°
Demetrius:　　　　　　　　　　Are you sure
　　That we are awake? It seems to me
　　That yet we sleep, we dream. Do not you think　　　　　　　　　　 185
　　The Duke was here, and bid us follow him?
Hermia: Yea, and my father.
Helena:　　　　　　　　And Hippolyta.
Lysander: And he did bid us follow to the temple.
Demetrius: Why, then, we are awake. Let's follow him,
　　And by the way let us recount our dreams.　　　　 [*Exeunt the lovers.*] 190
Bottom [awaking]: When my cue comes, call me, and I will answer. My next is, "Most
　　fair Pyramus." Heigh—ho! Peter Quince! Flute, the bellows mender! Snout, the
　　tinker! Starveling! God's° my life, stolen hence and left me asleep! I have had a
　　most rare vision. I have had a dream, past the wit of man to say what dream it
　　was. Man is but an ass if he go about° to expound this dream. Methought I was— 195
　　there is no man can tell what. Methought I was—and methought I had—
　　but man is but a patched° fool if he will offer° to say what methought I had.
　　The eye of man hath not heard, the ear of man hath not seen, man's hand is not
　　able to taste, his tongue to conceive, nor his heart to report,° what my dream
　　was. I will get Peter Quince to write a ballad° of this dream. It shall be called 200
　　"Bottom's Dream," because it hath no bottom;° and I will sing it in the latter end
　　of a play, before the Duke. Peradventure, to make it the more gracious, I shall
　　sing it at her° death.
　　　　　　　　　　　　　　　　　　　　　　　　　　　　　　[*Exit.*]

SCENE II [ATHENS.]

　　Enter Quince, Flute, [Snout, and Starveling].

Quince: Have you sent to Bottom's house? Is he come home yet?
Starveling: He cannot be heard of. Out of doubt he is transported.°
Flute: If he come not, then the play is marred. It goes not forward. Doth it?
Quince: It is not possible. You have not a man in all Athens able to discharge°
　　Pyramus but he.
Flute: No, he hath simply the best wit° of any handicraft man in Athens.　　　　 5
Quince: Yea, and the best person° too, and he is a very paramour for a sweet voice.
Flute: You must say "paragon." A paramour is, God bless us, a thing of naught.°

　　Enter Snug the joiner.

---

180 *parted* i.e., improperly focused　　182–183 *like . . . mine own* i.e., like a jewel that one finds by chance
and therefore possesses but cannot certainly consider one's own property　193 *God's* may God save　195
go about attempt　197 *patched* wearing motley, i.e., a dress of various colors.　*offer* venture　198–199 *The
eye . . . report* (Bottom garbles the terms of 1 Corinthians 2:9)　200 *ballad* (The proper medium for relating sensational stories and preposterous events.)　201 *hath no bottom* is unfathomable　203 *her* Thisbe's
(?)　2 *transported* carried off by fairies; or, possibly, transformed　4 *discharge* perform　6 *wit* intellect　7
person appearance　8 *a . . . naught* a shameful thing

The workers celebrate the return of Bottom and prepare to put on their play.

Snug: Masters, the Duke is coming from the temple, and there is two or three lords
and ladies more married. If our sport had gone forward, we had all been made   10
men.°

Flute: O sweet bully Bottom! Thus hath he lost sixpence a day° during his life; he
could not have scaped sixpence a day. An the Duke had not given him sixpence
a day for playing Pyramus, I'll be hanged. He would have deserved it. Sixpence a
day in Pyramus, or nothing.   15

    Enter Bottom.

Bottom: Where are these lads? Where are these hearts?°

Quince: Bottom! O most courageous day! O most happy hour!

Bottom: Masters, I am to discourse wonders.° But ask me not what; for if I tell you, I
am no true Athenian. I will tell you everything, right as it fell out.

Quince: Let us hear, sweet Bottom.   20

Bottom: Not a word of° me. All that I will tell you is that the Duke hath dined. Get
your apparel together, good strings° to your beards, new ribbons to your pumps;°
meet presently° at the palace; every man look o'er his part; for the short and the
long is, our play is preferred.° In any case, let Thisbe have clean linen; and let
not him that plays the lion pare his nails, for they shall hang out for the lion's   25

10–11 *we . . . men* i.e., we would have had our fortunes made   12 *sixpence a day* i.e., as a royal pension   16
hearts good fellows   18 *am . . . wonders* have wonders to relate   21 *of* out of   22 *strings* (to attach the
beards).   *pumps* light shoes or slippers   23 *presently* immediately   24 *preferred* selected for consideration

claws. And, most dear actors, eat no onions nor garlic, for we are to utter sweet breath; and I do not doubt but to hear them say it is a sweet comedy. No more words. Away! Go, away!

[*Exeunt.*]

ACT V

SCENE I [ATHENS. THE PALACE OF THESEUS.]

Enter Theseus, Hippolyta, and Philostrate, [lords, and attendants].

Hippolyta: 'Tis strange, my Theseus, that° these lovers speak of.	
Theseus: More strange than true. I never may° believe	
These antique° fables nor these fairy toys.°	
Lovers and madmen have such seething brains,	
Such shaping fantasies,° that apprehend°	5
More than cool reason ever comprehends.°	
The lunatic, the lover, and the poet	
Are of imagination all compact.°	
One sees more devils than vast hell can hold;	
That is the madman. The lover, all as frantic,	10
Sees Helen's° beauty in a brow of Egypt.°	
The poet's eye, in a fine frenzy rolling,	
Doth glance from heaven to earth, from earth to heaven;	
And as imagination bodies forth	
The forms of things unknown, the poet's pen	15
Turns them to shapes and gives to airy nothing	
A local habitation and a name.	
Such tricks hath strong imagination	
That, if it would but apprehend some joy,	
It comprehends some bringer° of that joy;	20
Or in the night, imagining some fear,°	
How easy is a bush supposed a bear!	
Hippolyta: But all the story of the night told over,	
And all their minds transfigured so together,	
More witnesseth than fancy's images°	25
And grows to something of great constancy;°	
But, howsoever,° strange and admirable.°	

Enter lovers: Lysander, Demetrius, Hermia, and Helena.

Theseus: Here come the lovers, full of joy and mirth.	
Joy, gentle friends! Joy and fresh days of love	
Accompany your hearts!	
Lysander: More than to us	30

1 *that* that which   2 *may* can   3 *antique* old-fashioned (punning too on "*antic*," "strange," "grotesque"). *fairy toys* trifling stories about fairies   5 *fantasies* imaginations. *apprehend* conceive, imagine   6 *comprehends* understands   8 *compact* formed, composed   11 *Helen's* i.e., of Helen of Troy, pattern of beauty. *brow of Egypt* i.e., face of a gypsy   20 *bringer* i.e., source   21 *fear* object of fear   25 *More . . . images* testifies to something more substantial than mere imaginings   26 *constancy* certainty   27 *howsoever* in any case. *admirable* a source of wonder

Wait in your royal walks, your board, your bed!
Theseus: Come now, what masques,° what dances shall we have,
To wear away this long age of three hours
Between our after-supper and bedtime?
Where is our usual manager of mirth?   35
What revels are in hand? Is there no play
To ease the anguish of a torturing hour?
Call Philostrate.
Philostrate: Here, mighty Theseus.
Theseus: Say, what abridgment° have you for this evening?
What masque? What music? How shall we beguile   40
The lazy time, if not with some delight?
Philostrate [giving him a paper]: There is a brief° how many sports are ripe.
Make choice of which Your Highness will see first.
Theseus [He reads]: "The battle with the Centaurs,° to be sung
By an Athenian eunuch to the harp"?   45
We'll none of that. That have I told my love,
In glory of my kinsman° Hercules.
[*He reads.*] "The riot of the tipsy Bacchanals,
Tearing the Thracian singer in their rage"?°
That is an old device;° and it was played   50
When I from Thebes came last a conqueror.
[*He reads.*] "The thrice three Muses mourning for the death
Of Learning, late deceased in beggary"?°
That is some satire, keen and critical,
Not sorting with° a nuptial ceremony.   55
[*He reads.*] "A tedious brief scene of young Pyramus
And his love Thisbe; very tragical mirth"?
Merry and tragical? Tedious and brief?
That is, hot ice and wondrous strange° snow.
How shall we find the concord of this discord?   60
Philostrate: A play there is, my lord, some ten words long,
Which is as brief as I have known a play;
But by ten words, my lord, it is too long,
Which makes it tedious. For in all the play
There is not one word apt, one player fitted.   65
And tragical, my noble lord, it is,
For Pyramus therein doth kill himself.

---

32 *masques* courtly entertainments   39 *abridgment* pastime (to abridge or shorten the evening)   42 *brief* short written statement, summary   44 *battle . . . Centaurs* (Probably refers to the battle of the Centaurs and the Lapithae, when the Centaurs attempted to carry off Hippodamia, bride of Theseus' friend Pirothous. The story is told in Ovid's *Metamorphoses* 12.)   47 *kinsman* (Plutarch's "Life of Theseus" states that Hercules and Theseus were near kinsmen. Theseus is referring to a version of the battle of the Centaurs in which Hercules was said to be present.)   48–49 *The riot . . . rage* (This was the story of the death of Orpheus, as told in *Metamorphoses* 11.)   50 *device* show, performance   52–53 *The thrice . . . beggary* (Possibly an allusion to Spenser's *Teares of the Muses*, 1591, though "satires" deploring the neglect of learning and the creative arts were commonplace.)   55 *sorting with* befitting   59 *strange* (Sometimes emended to an adjective that would contrast with *snow*, just as *hot* contrasts with *ice*.)

Which, when I saw rehearsed, I must confess,
Made mine eyes water; but more merry tears
The passion of loud laughter never shed. 70
Theseus: What are they that do play it?
Philostrate: Hardhanded men that work in Athens here,
Which never labored in their minds till now,
And now have toiled° their unbreathed° memories
With this same play, against° your nuptial. 75
Theseus: And we will hear it.
Philostrate: No, my noble lord,
It is not for you. I have heard it over,
And it is nothing, nothing in the world;
Unless you can find sport in their intents,
Extremely stretched° and conned° with cruel pain 80
To do you service.
Theseus: I will hear that play;
For never anything can be amiss
When simpleness° and duty tender it.
Go, bring them in; and take your places, ladies.

[*Philostrate goes to summon the players.*]

Hippolyta: I love not to see wretchedness o'ercharged,° 85
And duty in his service° perishing.
Theseus: Why, gentle sweet, you shall see no such thing.
Hippolyta: He says they can do nothing in this kind.°
Theseus: The kinder we, to give them thanks for nothing.
Our sport shall be to take what they mistake; 90
And what poor duty cannot do, noble respect°
Takes it in might, not merit.°
Where I have come, great clerks° have purposèd
To greet me with premeditated welcomes;
Where I have seen them shiver and look pale, 95
Make periods in the midst of sentences,
Throttle their practiced accent° in their fears,
And in conclusion dumbly have broke off,
Not paying me a welcome. Trust me, sweet,
Out of this silence yet I picked a welcome; 100
And in the modesty of fearful duty
I read as much as from the rattling tongue
Of saucy and audacious eloquence.
Love, therefore, and tongue-tied simplicity
In least° speak most, to my capacity.° 105

[*Philostrate returns.*]

---

74 *toiled* taxed. *unbreathed* unexercised 75 *against* in preparation for 80 *stretched* strained. *conned* memorized 83 *simpleness* simplicity 85 *wretchedness o'ercharged* social or intellectual inferiors overburdened 86 *his service* its attempt to serve 88 *kind* kind of thing 91 *respect* evaluation, consideration 92 *Takes . . . merit* values it for the effort made rather than for the excellence achieved 93 *clerks* learned men 97 *practiced accent* i.e., rehearsed speech; or, usual way of speaking 105 *least* i.e., saying least. *to my capacity* in my judgment and understanding

Philostrate: So please Your Grace, the Prologue° is addressed.°
Theseus: Let him approach.   [*A flourish of trumpets.*]

    Enter the Prologue [Quince].

Prologue: If we offend, it is with our good will.
    That you should think, we come not to offend,
    But with good will. To show our simple skill,   110
    That is the true beginning of our end.
    Consider, then, we come but in despite.
    We do not come, as minding° to content you,
    Our true intent is. All for your delight
    We are not here. That you should here repent you,   115
    The actors are at hand; and, by their show,
    You shall know all that you are like to know.
Theseus: This fellow doth not stand upon points.°
Lysander: He hath rid° his prologue like a rough° colt; he knows not the stop.°
    A good moral, my lord: it is not enough to speak, but to speak true.   120
Hippolyta: Indeed, he hath played on his prologue like a child on a recorder;°
    a sound, but not in government.°
Theseus: His speech was like a tangled chain: nothing° impaired, but all disordered.
    Who is next?

    *Enter Pyramus [Bottom], and Thisbe [Flute], and Wall [Snout], and Moonshine
    [Starveling], and Lion [Snug].*

Prologue:
    Gentles, perchance you wonder at this show;   125
    But wonder on, till truth makes all things plain.
    This man is Pyramus, if you would know;
    This beauteous lady Thisbe is, certain.
    This man with lime and roughcast doth present
    Wall, that vile wall which did these lovers sunder;   130
    And through Wall's chink, poor souls, they are content
    To whisper. At the which let no man wonder.
    This man, with lantern, dog, and bush of thorn,
    Presenteth Moonshine; for, if you will know,
    By moonshine did these lovers think no scorn°   135
    To meet at Ninus' tomb, there, there to woo.
    This grisly beast, which Lion hight° by name,
    The trusty Thisbe coming first by night
    Did scare away, or rather did affright;
    And as she fled, her mantle she did fall,°   140
    Which Lion vile with bloody mouth did stain.

---

106 *Prologue* speaker of the prologue. *addressed* ready   113 *minding* intending   118 *stand upon points* (1)
heed niceties or small points (2) pay attention to punctuation in his reading. (The humor of Quince's
speech is in the blunders of its punctuation.)   119 *rid* ridden. *rough* unbroken. *stop* (1) the stopping of
a colt by reining it in (2) punctuation mark   121 *recorder* a wind instrument like a flute   122 *government*
control   123 *nothing* not at all   135 *think no scorn* think it no disgraceful matter   137 *hight* is called   140
fall let fall

Anon comes Pyramus, sweet youth and tall,°
And finds his trusty Thisbe's mantle slain;
Whereat, with blade, with bloody, blameful blade,
He bravely broached° his boiling bloody breast.   145
And Thisbe, tarrying in mulberry shade,
His dagger drew, and died. For all the rest,
Let Lion, Moonshine, Wall, and lovers twain
At large° discourse, while here they do remain.

                        Exeunt Lion, Thisbe, and Moonshine.

Theseus: I wonder if the lion be to speak.   150
Demetrius: No wonder, my lord. One lion may, when many asses do.
Wall: In this same interlude° it doth befall
    That I, one Snout by name, present a wall;
    And such a wall as I would have you think
    That had in it a crannied hole or chink,   155
    Through which the lovers, Pyramus and Thisbe,
    Did whisper often, very secretly.
    This loam, this roughcast, and this stone doth show
    That I am that same wall; the truth is so.
    And this the cranny is, right and sinister,°   160
    Through which the fearful lovers are to whisper.
Theseus: Would you desire lime and hair to speak better?
Demetrius: It is the wittiest partition° that ever I heard discourse, my lord.

    [*Pyramus comes forward.*]

Theseus: Pyramus draws near the wall. Silence!
Pyramus: O grim-looked° night! O night with hue so black!   165
    O night, which ever art when day is not!
    O night, O night! Alack, alack, alack,
    I fear my Thisbe's promise is forgot.
    And thou, O wall, O sweet, O lovely wall,
    That stand'st between her father's ground and mine,   170
    Thou wall, O wall, O sweet and lovely wall,
    Show me thy chink, to blink through with mine eyne.

                        [*Wall makes a chink with his fingers.*]
    Thanks, courteous wall. Jove shield thee well for this.
    But what see I? No Thisbe do I see.
    O wicked wall, through whom I see no bliss!   175
    Cursed be thy stones for thus deceiving me!
Theseus: The wall, methinks, being sensible,° should curse again.°
Pyramus: No, in truth, sir, he should not. "Deceiving me" is Thisbe's cue: she is to
    enter now, and I am to spy her through the wall. You shall see, it will fall pat° as
    I told you. Yonder she comes.   180

---

142 *tall* courageous   145 *broached* stabbed   149 *At large* in full, at length   152 *interlude* play   160 *right and sinister* i.e., the right side of it and the left; or, running from right to left, horizontally   163 *partition* (1) wall (2) section of a learned treatise or oration   165 *grim-looked* grim-looking   177 *sensible* capable of feeling.   *again* in return   179 *pat* exactly

The workers perform *Pyramus and Thisbe*.

Enter Thisbe.

Thisbe: O wall, full often hast thou heard my moans
    For parting my fair Pyramus and me.
    My cherry lips have often kissed thy stones,
    Thy stones with lime and hair knit up in thee.
Pyramus: I see a voice. Now will I to the chink,   185
    To spy an° I can hear my Thisbe's face.
    Thisbe!
Thisbe: My love! Thou art my love, I think.
Pyramus: Think what thou wilt, I am thy lover's grace,°
    And like Limander° am I trusty still.
Thisbe: And I like Helen,° till the Fates me kill.   190

186 *an* if   188 *lover's grace* i.e., gracious lover   189, 190 *Limander, Helen* (Blunders for "Leander" and "Hero.")

Pyramus: Not Shafalus° to Procrus° was so true.

Thisbe: As Shafalus to Procrus, I to you.

Pyramus: O, kiss me through the hole of this vile wall!

Thisbe: I kiss the wall's hole, not your lips at all.

Pyramus: Wilt thou at Ninny's tomb meet me straightway?   195

Thisbe: 'Tide° life, 'tide death, I come without delay.

> [*Exeunt Pyramus and Thisbe.*]

Wall: Thus have I, Wall, my part dischargèd so;

> And, being done, thus Wall away doth go.   [*Exit.*]

Theseus: Now is the mural down between the two neighbors.

Demetrius: No remedy, my lord, when walls are so willful° to hear without   200
warning.°

Hippolyta: This is the silliest stuff that ever I heard.

Theseus: The best in this kind° are but shadows;° and the worst are no worse, if
imagination amend them.

Hippolyta: It must be your imagination then, and not theirs.   205

Theseus: If we imagine no worse of them than they of themselves, they may pass for
excellent men. Here come two noble beasts in, a man and a lion.

Enter Lion and Moonshine.

Lion: You, ladies, you, whose gentle hearts do fear

> The smallest monstrous mouse that creeps on floor,

> May now perchance both quake and tremble here,   210

> When lion rough in wildest rage doth roar.

> Then know that I, as Snug the joiner, am

> A lion fell,° nor else no lion's dam;

> For, if I should as lion come in strife

> Into this place, 'twere pity on my life.   215

Theseus: A very gentle beast, and of a good conscience.

Demetrius: The very best at a beast, my lord, that e'er I saw.

Lysander: This lion is a very fox for his valor.°

Theseus: True; and a goose for his discretion.°

Demetrius: Not so, my lord; for his valor cannot carry his discretion, and the fox   220
carries the goose.

Theseus: His discretion, I am sure, cannot carry his valor; for the goose carries not
the fox. It is well. Leave it to his discretion, and let us listen to the moon.

Moon: This lanthorn° doth the hornèd moon present—

Demetrius: He should have worn the horns on his head.°   225

Theseus: He is no crescent,° and his horns are invisible within the circumference.

---

191 *Shafalus, Procrus* (Blunders for "Cephalus" and "Procris," also famous lovers.)   196 *'Tide* betide,
come   200 *willful* willing   200–201 *without warning* i.e., without warning the parents (Demetrius makes a
joke on the proverb "Walls have ears.")   203 *in this kind* of this sort.   *shadows* likenesses, representations
213 *lion fell* fierce lion (with a play on the idea of "lion skin")   218 *is . . . valor* i.e., his valor consists of
craftiness and discretion   219 *a goose . . . discretion* i.e., as discreet as a goose, that is, more foolish than
discreet   224 *lanthorn* (This original spelling, *lanthorn*, may suggest a play on the *horn* of which lanterns
were made, and also on a cuckold's horns; however, the spelling *lanthorn* is not used consistently for comic
effect in this play or elsewhere. At V, i, 133, for example, the word is *lantern* in the original.)   225 *on his
head* (as a sign of cuckoldry)   226 *crescent* a waxing moon

Moon: This lanthorn doth the hornèd moon present;
    Myself the man i' the moon do seem to be.
Theseus: This is the greatest error of all the rest. The man should be put into the
    lanthorn. How is it else the man i' the moon?   230
Demetrius: He dares not come there for° the candle, for you see it is already in snuff.°
Hippolyta: I am aweary of this moon. Would he would change!
Theseus: It appears, by his small light of discretion, that he is in the wane; but yet, in
    courtesy, in all reason, we must stay the time.
Lysander: Proceed, Moon.   235
Moon: All that I have to say is to tell you that the lanthorn is the moon, I, the man
    i' the moon, this thornbush my thornbush, and this dog my dog.
Demetrius: Why, all these should be in the lanthorn, for all these are in the moon.
    But silence! Here comes Thisbe.

    Enter Thisbe.

Thisbe: This is old Ninny's tomb. Where is my love?   240
Lion [roaring]: O!
Demetrius: Well roared, Lion.
                         [Thisbe runs off, dropping her mantle.]
Theseus: Well run, Thisbe.
Hippolyta: Well shone, Moon. Truly, the moon shines with a good grace.
                         [The Lion worries Thisbe's mantle.]
Theseus: Well moused,° Lion.   245
                         [Enter Pyramus; exit Lion.]

Demetrius: And then came Pyramus.
Lysander: And so the lion vanished.
Pyramus: Sweet Moon, I thank thee for thy sunny beams;
    I thank thee, Moon, for shining now so bright;
    For, by thy gracious, golden, glittering gleams,   250
      I trust to take of truest Thisbe sight.
          But stay, O spite!
          But mark, poor knight,
    What dreadful dole° is here?
          Eyes, do you see?   255
          How can it be?
    O dainty duck! O dear!
          Thy mantle good,
          What, stained with blood?
    Approach, ye Furies° fell!°   260
          O Fates,° come, come,
          Cut thread and thrum;°
          Quail,° crush, conclude, and quell!°

---

231 *for* because of, for fear of. *in snuff* (1) offended (2) in need of snuffing or trimming   245 *moused*
shaken, torn, bitten   254 *dole* grievous event   260 *Furies* avenging goddesses of Greek myth. *fell* fierce
261 *Fates* the three goddesses (Clotho, Lachesis, Atropos) of Greek myth who spun, drew, and cut the
thread of human life   262 *thread and thrum* i.e., everything—the good and bad alike; literally, the warp in
weaving and the loose end of the weft   263 *Quail* overpower. *quell* kill, destroy

Theseus: This passion, and the death of a dear friend, would go near to make a man
    look sad.°   265
Hippolyta: Beshrew my heart, but I pity the man.
Pyramus: O, wherefore, Nature, didst thou lions frame?
    Since lion vile hath here deflowered my dear,
    Which is—no, no, which was—the fairest dame
    That lived, that loved, that liked, that looked with cheer.°   270
          Come, tears, confound,
          Out, sword, and wound
    The pap° of Pyramus;
          Ay, that left pap,
          Where heart doth hop.   *[He stabs himself.]* 275
    Thus die I, thus, thus, thus.
          Now am I dead,
          Now am I fled;
    My soul is in the sky.
          Tongue, lose thy light;   280
          Moon, take thy flight.   *[Exit Moonshine.]*
    Now die, die, die, die, die.   *[Pyramus dies.]*
Demetrius: No die, but an ace,° for him; for he is but one.°
Lysander: Less than an ace, man; for he is dead, he is nothing.
Theseus: With the help of a surgeon he might yet recover, and yet prove an ass.°   285
Hippolyta: How chance Moonshine is gone before Thisbe comes back and finds her
    lover?
Theseus: She will find him by starlight.

    [Enter Thisbe.]

    Here she comes, and her passion ends the play.
Hippolyta: Methinks she should not use a long one for such a Pyramus. I hope she   290
    will be brief.
Demetrius: A mote° will turn the balance, which Pyramus, which° Thisbe, is the
    better: he for a man, God warrant us; she for a woman, God bless us.
Lysander: She hath spied him already with those sweet eyes.
Demetrius: And thus she means,° videlicet:°   295
Thisbe: Asleep, my love?
          What, dead, my dove?
      O Pyramus, arise!
          Speak, speak. Quite dumb?
          Dead, dead? A tomb   300
      Must cover thy sweet eyes.
          These lily lips,
          This cherry nose,

264–265 *This . . . sad* i.e., if one had other reason to grieve, one might be sad, but not from this absurd
portrayal of passion   270 *cheer* countenance   273 *pap* breast   283 *ace* the side of the die featuring the
single pip, or spot (The pun is on *die* as a singular of *dice*; Bottom's performance is not worth a whole *die*
but rather one single face of it, one small portion.).   *one* (1) an individual person (2) unique   285 *ass*
(with a pun on *ace*)   292 *mote* small particle.   *which . . . which* whether . . . or   295 *means* moans,
laments (with a pun on the meaning, "lodge a formal complaint").   *videlicet* to wit

These yellow cowslip cheeks,
    Are gone, are gone! 305
    Lovers, make moan.
His eyes were green as leeks.
    O Sisters Three,°
    Come, come to me,
With hands as pale as milk; 310
    Lay them in gore,
    Since you have shore°
With shears his thread of silk.
    Tongue, not a word.
    Come, trusty sword, 315
    Come, blade, my breast imbrue!°   *[She stabs herself.]*
    And farewell, friends.
    Thus Thisbe ends.
    Adieu, adieu, adieu.   *[She dies.]*

Theseus: Moonshine and Lion are left to bury the dead. 320

Demetrius: Ay, and Wall too.

Bottom [starting up, as Flute does also]: No, I assure you, the wall is down that parted their fathers. Will it please you to see the epilogue, or to hear a Bergomask dance° between two of our company?

[The other players enter.]

Theseus: No epilogue, I pray you; for your play needs no excuse. Never excuse; for 325 when the players are all dead, there need none to be blamed. Marry, if he that writ it had played Pyramus and hanged himself in Thisbe's garter, it would have been a fine tragedy; and so it is, truly, and very notably discharged. But, come, your Bergomask. Let your epilogue alone.   *[A dance.]*
The iron tongue° of midnight hath told° twelve. 330
Lovers, to bed, 'tis almost fairy time.
I fear we shall outsleep the coming morn
As much as we this night have overwatched.°
This palpable-gross° play hath well beguiled
The heavy° gait of night. Sweet friends, to bed. 335
A fortnight hold we this solemnity,
In nightly revels and new jollity.   *Exeunt.*

Enter Puck [carrying a broom].

Puck: Now the hungry lion roars,
    And the wolf behowls the moon,
    Whilst the heavy° plowman snores, 340
        All with weary task fordone.°
    Now the wasted brands° do glow,
        Whilst the screech owl, screeching loud,

---

308 *Sisters Three* the Fates   312 *shore* shorn   316 *imbrue* stain with blood   323–324 *Bergomask dance* a rustic dance named from Bergamo, a province in the state of Venice   330 *iron tongue* i.e., of a bell. *told* counted, struck ("tolled")   333 *overwatched* stayed up too late   334 *palpable-gross* palpably gross, obviously crude   335 *heavy* drowsy, dull   340 *heavy* tired   341 *fordone* exhausted   342 *wasted brands* burned-out logs

  Puts the wretch that lies in woe
   In remembrance of a shroud.
  Now it is the time of night   345
   That the graves, all gaping wide,
  Every one lets forth his sprite,°
   In the church-way paths to glide.
  And we fairies, that do run   350
   By the triple Hecate's° team
  From the presence of the sun,
   Following darkness like a dream,
  Now are frolic.° Not a mouse
  Shall disturb this hallowed house.   355
  I am sent with broom before,
  To sweep the dust behind° the door.

Enter [Oberon and Titania,] King and Queen of Fairies, with all their train.

Oberon: Through the house give glimmering light,
     By the dead and drowsy fire;
     Every elf and fairy sprite   360
      Hop as light as bird from brier;
     And this ditty, after me,
     Sing, and dance it trippingly.
Titania: First, rehearse° your song by rote,
     To each word a warbling note.   365
     Hand in hand, with fairy grace,
     Will we sing, and bless this place.

                   [Song and dance.]

Oberon: Now, until the break of day,
     Through this house each fairy stray.
     To the best bride-bed will we,   370
     Which by us shall blessèd be;
     And the issue there create°
     Ever shall be fortunate.
     So shall all the couples three
     Ever true in loving be;   375
     And the blots of Nature's hand
     Shall not in their issue stand;
     Never mole, harelip, nor scar,
     Nor mark prodigious,° such as are
     Despisèd in nativity,   380
     Shall upon their children be.
     With this field dew consecrate°

---

348 *Every . . . sprite* every grave lets forth its ghost 351 *triple Hecate's* (Hecate ruled in three capacities: as Luna or Cynthia in heaven, as Diana on earth, and as Proserpina in hell.) 354 *frolic* merry 357 *behind* from behind, or else like sweeping the dirt under the carpet. (Robin Goodfellow was a household spirit who helped good housemaids and punished lazy ones, but he could, of course, be mischievous.) 364 *rehearse* recite 372 *create* created 379 *prodigious* monstrous, unnatural 382 *consecrate* consecrated

"If we shadows have offended, / Think but this, and all is mended"
(V, i, 390–391).

Every fairy take his gait,°
And each several° chamber bless,
Through this palace, with sweet peace;   385
And the owner of it blest
Ever shall in safety rest.
Trip away; make no stay;
Meet me all by break of day.

Exeunt [Oberon, Titania, and train].

Puck [*to the audience*]: If we shadows have offended,   390
        Think but this, and all is mended,
        That you have but slumbered here°

383 *take his gait* go his way   384 *several* separate   392 *That . . . here* i.e., that it is a "midsummer night's
dream"

While these visions did appear.
And this weak and idle theme,
No more yielding but a dream,°   395
Gewntles, do not reprehend.
If you pardon, we will mend.°
And, as I am an honest Puck,
If we have unearnèd luck
Now to scape the serpent's tongue,°   400
We will make amends ere long;
Else the Puck a liar call.
So, good night unto you all.
Give me your hands,° if we be friends,
And Robin shall restore amends.°   405

                                                                  [*Exit.*]

Questions

1. Describe the relationship between King Theseus and Queen Hippolyta in the opening scene. How did they meet? Does their imminent marriage promise to be happy?
2. Describe the personality of each young aristocratic lover. How does Shakespeare differentiate them?
3. Characterize Nick Bottom. What aspects of his personality and behavior make him comic?
4. In what ways does Shakespeare differentiate his rustic tradesmen from the aristocrats?
5. Are the supernatural lovers, Oberon and Titania, characterized differently from their mortal counterparts? How are they similar to the aristocratic lovers and how are they different from them?
6. In what ways is Puck the unifying character of the play? How do his actions touch on every plot and subplot?
7. The main plot of *A Midsummer Night's Dream* concludes by the end of Act IV. What purpose does the final act serve in the play? Could it be omitted without significant loss?

395 *No . . . but* yielding no more than   397 *mend* improve   400 *serpent's tongue* i.e., hissing   404 *Give . . . hands* applaud   405 *restore amends* give satisfaction in return

CRITICS ON SHAKESPEARE

Oberon and Titania in the Ninagawa Company's 1996 production of *A Midsummer Night's Dream.*

Anthony Burgess (1917–1993)

An Asian Culture Looks at Shakespeare   1982

Is translation possible? I first found myself asking this question in the Far East, when I was given the task of translating T. S. Eliot's *The Waste Land* into Indonesian. The difficulties began with the first line: "April is the cruellest month . . ." This I rendered as "*Bulan Abril ia-lah bulan yang dzalim sa-kali . . .*" I had to take *dzalim* from Arabic, since Indonesian did not, at that time, seem to possess a word for *cruel.* The term was accepted, but not the notion that a month, as opposed to a person or institution, could be cruel. Moreover, even if a month could be cruel, how—in the tropics where all the months are the same and the concepts of spring and winter do not exist— can one month be crueller than another? When I came to *forgetful snow*—rendered as *thalji berlupa*—I had to borrow a highly poetical word from the Persian, acceptable as a useful descriptive device for the brown skin of the beloved but not known in terms of a climatic reality. And, again, how could this inanimate substance possess the faculty of forgetting? I gave up the task as hopeless. Evidently the imagery of *The Waste Land* does not relate to a universal experience but applies only to the northern hemisphere, with its temperate climate and tradition of spring and fertility rituals.

As a teacher in Malaysia, I had to consider with a mixed group of Malay, Chinese, Indian, and Eurasian students, seasoned with the odd Buginese, Achinese, and Japanese, a piece of representative postwar British fiction. Although the setting of the book is West Africa, I felt that its story was of universal import. It was a novel by Graham Greene called *The Heart of the Matter*—a tragic story about a police officer named Scobie who is a Catholic convert. He is in love with his wife but falls in love with another woman, discovers that he cannot repent of this adultery, makes a sacrilegious communion so that his very Catholic wife will not suspect that a love affair is in progress, then commits suicide in despair, trusting that God will thrust him into the outer darkness and be no longer agonized by the exploits of sinning Scobie. To us this is a tragic situation. To my Muslim students it was extremely funny. One girl said: "Why cannot this Mr. Scobie become a Muslim? Then he can have four wives and there is no problem."

The only author who seemed to have the quality of universal appeal in Malaysia was William Shakespeare. Despite the problems of translating him, there is always an intelligible residue. I remember seeing in a Borneo kampong the film of *Richard III* made by Laurence Olivier, and the illiterate tribe which surrounded me was most appreciative. They knew nothing here of literary history and nothing of the great world outside this jungle clearing. They took this film about medieval conspiracy and tyranny to be a kind of newsreel representation of contemporary England. They approved the medieval costumes because they resembled their own ceremonial dress. This story of the assassination of innocents, including children, Machiavellian massacre, and the eventual defeat of a tyrant was typical of their own history, even their contemporary experience, and they accepted Shakespeare as a great poet. Eliot would not have registered with them at all. Translation is not a matter of words only; it is a matter of making intelligible a whole culture. Evidently the Elizabethan culture was still primitive enough to survive transportation over much time and space.

From spoken remarks on the "Importance of Translation"

W. H. Auden (1907–1973)

Iago as a Triumphant Villain   1962

Any consideration of the *Tragedy of Othello* must be primarily occupied, not with its official hero but with its villain. I cannot think of any other play in which only one character performs personal actions—all the *deeds* are Iago's—and all the others without exception only exhibit behavior. In marrying each other, Othello and Desdemona have performed a deed, but this took place before the play begins. Nor can I think of another play in which the villain is so completely triumphant: everything Iago sets out to do, he accomplishes—(among his goals, I include his self-destruction). Even Cassio, who survives, is maimed for life.

If *Othello* is a tragedy—and one certainly cannot call it a comedy—it is tragic in a peculiar way. In most tragedies the fall of the hero from glory to misery and death is the work, either of the gods, or of his own freely chosen acts, or, more commonly, a mixture of both. But the fall of Othello is the work of another human being; nothing he says or does originates with himself. In consequence we feel pity for him but no respect; our aesthetic respect is reserved for Iago.

Iago is a wicked man. The wicked man, the stage villain, as a subject of serious dramatic interest does not, so far as I know, appear in the drama of western Europe before the Elizabethans. In the mystery plays, the wicked characters, like Satan or Herod, are treated comically, but the theme of the triumphant villain cannot be treated comically because the suffering he inflicts is real.

From "The Joker in the Pack"

Maud Bodkin (1875–1967)

Lucifer in Shakespeare's *Othello*   1934

If we attempt to define the devil in psychological terms, regarding him as an archetype, a persistent or recurrent mode of apprehension, we may say that the devil is our tendency to represent in personal form the forces within and without us that threaten our supreme values. When Othello finds those values of confident love, of honor, and pride in soldiership, that made up his purposeful life, falling into ruin, his sense of the devil in all around him becomes acute. Desdemona has become "a fair devil"; he feels "a young and sweating devil" in her hand. The cry "O devil" breaks out among his incoherent words of raving. When Iago's falsehoods are disclosed, and Othello at last, too late, wrenches himself free from the spell of Iago's power over him, his sense of the devil incarnate in Iago's shape before him becomes overwhelming. If those who tell of the devil have failed to describe Iago, they have lied:

> I look down towards his feet; but that's a fable.
> If that thou be'st a devil, I cannot kill thee.

We also, watching or reading the play, experience the archetype. Intellectually aware, as we reflect, of natural forces, within a man himself as well as in society around, that betray or shatter his ideals, we yet feel these forces aptly symbolized for the imagination by such a figure as Iago—a being though personal yet hardly human, concentrated wholly on the hunting to destruction of its destined prey, the proud figure of the hero.

From *Archetypal Patterns in Poetry*

Virginia Mason Vaughan (b. 1947)

Black and White in *Othello*   1994

> If virtue no delighted beauty lack,
> Your son-in-law is far more fair than black.
> —*Othello* (1.3.290–291)

Black/white oppositions permeate *Othello*. Throughout the play, Shakespeare exploits a discourse of racial difference that by 1604 had become ingrained in the English psyche. From Iago's initial racial epithets at Brabantio's window ("old black ram," "barbary horse") to Emilia's cries of outrage in the final scene ("ignorant as dirt"), Shakespeare shows that the union of a white Venetian maiden and a black Moorish general is from at least one perspective emphatically unnatural. The union is of course a central fact of the play, and to some commentators, the spectacle of the pale-skinned woman caught in Othello's black arms has indeed seemed monstrous. Yet that spectacle is a major source of *Othello*'s emotional power. From Shakespeare's day to the present, the sight has titillated and terrified predominantly white audiences.

The effect of *Othello* depends, in other words, on the essential fact of the hero's darkness, the visual signifier of his Otherness. To Shakespeare's original audience, this chromatic sign was probably dark black, although there were other signifiers as well. Roderigo describes the Moor as having "thick lips," a term many sixteenth-century explorers employed in their descriptions of Africans. But, as historian Winthrop Jordan notes, by the late sixteenth century, "Blackness became so generally associated with Africa that every African seemed a black man[,] . . . the terms *Moor* and *Negro* used almost interchangeably." "Moor" became, G. K. Hunter observes, "a word for 'people not like us,' so signaled by color." Richard Burbage's Othello was probably black. But in any production, whether he appears as a tawny Moor (as nineteenth-century actors preferred) or as a black man of African descent, Othello bears the visual signs of his Otherness, a difference that the play's language insists can never be eradicated.

From *Othello: A Contextual History*

A. C. Bradley (1851–1935)

Hamlet's Melancholy   1903

That Hamlet was not far from insanity is very probable. His adoption of the pretence of madness may well have been due in part to fear of the reality; to an instinct of self-preservation, a fore-feeling that the pretence would enable him to give some utterance to the load that pressed on his heart and brain, and a fear that he would be unable altogether to repress such utterance. And if the pathologist calls his state melancholia, and even proceeds to determine its species, I see nothing to object to in that; I am grateful to him for emphasizing the fact that Hamlet's melancholy was no mere common depression of spirits; and I have no doubt that many readers of the play would understand it better if they read an account of melancholia in a work on mental diseases. If we like to use the word "disease" loosely, Hamlet's condition may truly be called diseased. No exertion of will could have dispelled it. Even if he had been able at once to do the bidding of the Ghost he would doubtless have still remained for some time under the cloud. It would be absurdly unjust to call *Hamlet* a study of melancholy, but it contains such a study.

But this melancholy is something very different from insanity, in anything like the usual meaning of that word. No doubt it might develop into insanity. The longing for death might become an irresistible impulse to self-destruction; the disorder of feeling and will might extend to sense and intellect; delusions might arise; and the man might become, as we say, incapable and irresponsible. But Hamlet's melancholy is some way from this condition. It is a totally different thing from the madness which he feigns; and he never, when alone or in company with Horatio alone, exhibits the signs of that madness. Nor is the dramatic use of this melancholy, again, open to the objections which would justly be made to the portrayal of an insanity which brought the hero to a tragic end. The man who suffers as Hamlet suffers—and thousands go about their business suffering thus in greater or less degree—is considered irresponsible neither by other people nor by himself: he is only too keenly conscious of his responsibility. He is therefore, so far, quite capable of being a tragic agent, which an insane person, at any rate according to Shakespeare's practice, is not. And, finally, Hamlet's state is not one which a healthy mind is unable sufficiently to imagine. It is probably not further from average experience, nor more difficult to realize, than the great tragic passions of Othello, Antony or Macbeth.

Let me try to show now, briefly, how much this melancholy accounts for.

It accounts for the main fact, Hamlet's inaction. For the *immediate* cause of that is simply that his habitual feeling is one of disgust at life and everything in it, himself included—a disgust which varies in intensity, rising at times into a longing for death, sinking often into weary apathy, but is never dispelled for more than brief intervals. Such a state of feeling is inevitably adverse to *any* kind of decided action; the body is inert, the mind indifferent or worse; its response is, "it does not matter," "it is not worth while," "it is no good." And the action required of Hamlet is very exceptional. It is violent, dangerous, difficult to accomplish perfectly, on one side repulsive to a man of honor and sensitive feeling, on another side involved in a certain mystery (here come in thus, in their subordinate place, various causes of inaction assigned by various theories). These obstacles would not suffice to prevent Hamlet from acting, if his state were normal; and against them there operate, even in his morbid state, healthy and positive feelings, love of his father, loathing of his uncle, desire of revenge, desire to do duty. But the retarding motives acquire an unnatural strength because they have an ally in something far stronger than themselves, the melancholic disgust and apathy; while the healthy motives, emerging with difficulty from the central mass of diseased feeling, rapidly sink back into it and "lose the name of action."

From *Shakespearean Tragedy*

Rebecca West (1892–1983)

Hamlet and Ophelia   1958

There is no more bizarre aspect of the misreading of Hamlet's character than the assumption that his relations with Ophelia were innocent and that Ophelia was a correct and timid virgin of exquisite sensibilities. . . . She was not a chaste young woman. That is shown by her tolerance of Hamlet's obscene conversations, which cannot be explained as consistent with the custom of the time. If that were the reason for it, all the men and women in Shakespeare's plays, Romeo and Juliet, Beatrice and Benedick, Miranda and Ferdinand, Antony and Cleopatra, would have talked obscenely together, which is not the case. "The marriage of true minds" would hardly, even in the most candid age, have expressed itself by this ugly chatter, which Wilson Knight has so justly described as governed by "infra-sexual neurosis." The truth is that Ophelia was a disreputable young woman: not scandalously so, but still disreputable. She was foredoomed to it by her father, whom it is a mistake to regard as a simple platitudinarian. Shakespeare, like all major writers, was never afraid of a good platitude, and he would certainly never have given time to deriding a character because his only attribute was a habit of stating the obvious. Polonius is interesting because he was a cunning old intriguer who, like an iceberg, only showed one-eighth of himself above the surface. The innocuous sort of worldly wisdom that rolled off his tongue in butter balls was a very small part of what he knew. It has been insufficiently noted that Shakespeare would never have held up the action in order that Polonius should give his son advice as to how to conduct himself abroad, unless the scene helped him to develop his theme. But "This above all: to thine own self be true; / And it must follow, as the night the day, / Thou canst not then be false to any man" (1.3.78–80), has considerable contrapuntal value when it is spoken by an old gentleman who is presently going to instruct a servant to spy on his son, and to profess great anxiety about his daughter's morals, when plainly he needed to send her away into the country if he really wanted her to retain any.

There is no mistaking the disingenuousness of his dealings with his daughter. When Ophelia comes to him with her tale of how Hamlet had come to her as she was sewing in her chamber, "with his doublet all unbraced," and had looked madly on her, Polonius eagerly interprets this as "the very ecstasy of love," and asks her "What, have you given him any hard words of late?" . . . The girl is not to be kept out of harm's way. She is a card that can be played to take several sorts of tricks. She might be Hamlet's mistress; but she might be more honored for resistance. And if Hamlet was himself an enemy of the King, and an entanglement with him had ceased to be a means of winning favor, then she can give a spy's report on him to Claudius. Surely Ophelia is one of the few authentic portraits of that army of not virgin martyrs, the poor little girls who were sacrificed to family ambition in the days when a court was a cat's cradle of conspiracies. Man's persuasion that his honor depends on the chastity of his women folk has always been liable to waste away and perish within sight of a throne. Particularly where monarchy had grown from a yeasty mass of feudalism, few families found themselves able to resist the temptation to hawk any young beauty in their brood, if it seemed likely that she might catch the eye of the king or any man close to the king. Unfortunately the king's true favorite was usually not a woman but an ideology. If royal approval was withdrawn from the religious or political faith held by the family which had hawked the girl, she was as apt to suffer fatality as any of her kinsmen. The axe has never known chivalry. Shakespeare, writing this play only three reigns from Henry the Eighth, had heard of such outrages on half-grown girls from the lips of those who had seen the final bloodletting.

From The Court and the Castle

Jan Kott (1914–2001)

Producing *Hamlet* 1964

There are many subjects in *Hamlet*. There is politics, force opposed to morality; there is discussion of the divergence between theory and practice, of the ultimate purpose of life; there is tragedy of love, as well as family drama; political, eschatological and metaphysical problems are considered. There is everything you want, including deep psychological analysis, a bloody story, a duel, and general slaughter. One can select at will. But one must know what one selects, and why.

The *Hamlet* produced in Cracow a few weeks after the XXth Congress of the Soviet Communist Party lasted exactly three hours.° It was light and clear, tense and sharp, modern and consistent, limited to one issue only. It was a political drama par

---

The Hamlet *produced . . . hours:* The production of *Hamlet* Kott discusses was staged in Cracow, Poland, in 1956 at the height of Soviet repression in Eastern Europe.

excellence. "Something is rotten in the state of Denmark" was the first chord of *Hamlet*'s new meaning. And then the dead sound of the words "Denmark's a prison," three times repeated. Finally the magnificent churchyard scene, with the gravediggers' dialogue rid of metaphysics, brutal and unequivocal. Gravediggers know for whom they dig graves. "The gallows is built stronger than the church," they say.

"Watch" and "enquire" were the words most commonly heard from the stage. In this performance everybody, without exception, was being constantly watched. Polonius, minister to the royal murderer, sends a man to France even after his own son. Was Shakespeare not a genius for our time? Let us listen to the minister:

> Inquire me first what Danskers are in Paris,
> And how, and who, what means, and where they keep,
> What company, at what expense; and finding
> By this encompassment and drift of question
> That they do know my son, come you more nearer
> Than your particular demands will touch it.
>   (2.1.7–12)

At Elsinore castle someone is hidden behind every curtain. The good minister does not even trust the Queen. Let us listen to him again:

> 'Tis meet that some more audience than a mother,
> Since nature makes them partial, should o'erhear
> The speech, of vantage.
>   (3.3.31–33)

Everything at Elsinore has been corroded by fear: marriage, love and friendship. Shakespeare, indeed, must have experienced terrible things at the time of Essex's plot and execution, since he came to learn so well the working of the Grand Mechanism. Let us listen to the King talking to Hamlet's young friends:

> . . . . . I entreat you both
> That, being of so young days brought up with him,
> And since so neighbour'd to his youth and haviour,
> That you vouchsafe your rest here in our court
> Some little time; so by your companies
> To draw him on to pleasures, and to gather
> So much as from occasion you may glean,
> Whether aught to us unknown afflicts him thus
> That, open'd, lies within our remedy.
>   (2.2.10–18)

The murderous uncle keeps a constant watchful eye on Hamlet. Why does he not want him to leave Denmark? His presence at court is inconvenient, reminding everybody of what they would like to forget. Perhaps he suspects something? Would it not be better not to issue him a passport and keep him at hand? Or does the King wish to get rid of Hamlet as soon as possible, but give way to the Queen, who wants to have her son near her? And the Queen? What does she think about it all? Does she feel guilty? What does the Queen know? She has been through passion, murder and silence. She had to suppress everything inside her. One can sense a volcano under her superficial poise.

Ophelia, too, has been drawn into the big game. They listen in to her conversations, ask questions, read her letters. It is true that she gives them up herself. She is at the same time part of the Mechanism, and its victim. Politics hangs here over every feeling, and there is no getting away from it. All the characters are poisoned by it. The only subject of their conversations is politics. It is a kind of madness.

Hamlet loves Ophelia. But he knows he is being watched; moreover—he has more important matters to attend to. Love is gradually fading away. There is no room for it in this world. Hamlet's dramatic cry: "Get thee to a nunnery!" is addressed not to Ophelia alone, but also to those who are overhearing the two lovers. It is to confirm their impression of his alleged madness. But for Hamlet and for Ophelia it means that in the world where murder holds sway, there is no room for love.

From Shakespeare: Our Contemporary

Johann von Goethe (1749–1832)

Hamlet as a Hero Unfit for His Destiny 1795

Translated by Thomas Carlyle

And when the ghost has vanished, who is it that stands before us? A young hero panting for vengeance? A prince by birth, rejoicing to be called to punish the usurper of his crown? No! trouble and astonishment take hold of the solitary young man: he grows bitter against smiling villains, swears that he will not forget the spirit, and concludes with the significant ejaculation—

> The time is out of joint. O cursèd spite
> That ever I was born to set it right! (1.5.197–198)

In these words, I imagine, will be found the key to Hamlet's whole procedure. To me it is clear that Shakespeare meant, in the present case, to represent the effects of a great action laid upon a soul unfit for the performance of it. In this view the whole play seems to me to be composed. There is an oak-tree planted in a costly jar, which should have borne only pleasant flowers in its bosom: the roots expand, the jar is shivered.

A lovely, pure, noble, and most moral nature, without the strength of nerve which forms a hero, sinks beneath a burden it cannot bear and must not cast away. All duties are holy for him: the present is too hard. Impossibilities have been required of him—not in themselves impossibilities, but such for him. He winds, and turns, and torments himself; he advances and recoils; is ever put in mind, ever puts himself in mind; at last does all but lose his purpose from his thoughts; yet still without recovering his peace of mind.

From Wilhelm Meister's Apprenticeship

Edgar Allan Poe (1809–1849)

Hamlet as a Fictional Character 1845

In all commentating upon Shakespeare, there has been a radical error, never yet mentioned. It is the error of attempting to expound his characters, to account for their action, to reconcile their inconsistencies, not as if they were the coinage of a human brain, but as if they had been actual existences upon the earth. We talk of Hamlet the man, instead of Hamlet the *dramatis persona*—of Hamlet that God, in place of Hamlet that Shakespeare created. If Hamlet had really lived, and if the tragedy were an accurate record of his deeds, from this record (with some trouble) we might, it is true, reconcile his inconsistencies and settle to our satisfaction his true character. But the task becomes the purest absurdity when we deal only with a phantom. It is not (then) the inconsistencies of the acting man which we have as a subject of discussion—(although we proceed as if it were, and thus *inevitably* err)—but the whims and vacillations, the conflicting energies and indolences of the poet. It seems to us little less than a miracle that this obvious point should have been overlooked.

From a review of William Hazlitt, *Broadway Journal*

Clare Asquith (b. 1951)

Shakespeare's Language as a Hidden Political Code   2005

Shakespeare was the one sixteenth-century writer who, it appears, never fell foul of the authorities. Yet in a strangely insistent passage, the editors of the First Folio of his work, published in 1623, urge us to look beneath the surface of the great universal plays to something hidden below. Though they are sure that his wit can "no more lie hid than it could be lost," they press us to "Read him therefore, and again, and again." We must seek help from his friends if we miss his "hidden wit," and we should act as guides to others if we find it. The insistence on readers acting as guides is striking and unusual.

• • •

Whatever its impact at the time, Shakespeare's cautious artistry was so great that his hidden language remained undetectable to succeeding generations that accepted the official version of England's Reformation. Yet the subterfuge was essential if he and his work were to survive. He was writing in a climate more dangerous and oppressive than anything experienced by his predecessors. By the 1580s, the censorship laws, regularly tightened under Elizabeth, were strictly enforced. Yet he could not remain silent. He was driven to write by a different fear, to which he returns throughout his work. This was the growing concern, shared by many contemporaries, that the true history of the age would never be told. . . . Shakespeare not only needed to write; he needed to find a new method of writing, one capable of recording the whole unhappy story of the country's political and spiritual collapse against the background of a regime for whom the slightest topical reference was justification enough to imprison a playwright.

• • •

In these dramas, there would be no room for asides or explanations. Instead, Shakespeare worked out a set of simple markers, basic call-signs that would alert his audience to the entry point they needed to access the hidden story. Unlike Erasmus, Sidney and Donne, who were poets and essayists, he was a seasoned actor addressing restless spectators, so he kept his signals simple and consistent. But he was also one of a brotherhood of dissident writers, and to them his pointers would have been as readily—even wittily—recognizable as they became baffling to later readers.

The master key to the hidden level is so simple that it is easy to miss. It takes the form of twin terms that identify the polar opposites in Elizabeth's England. They are not Shakespeare's only terms, and he uses them sparingly, but with pinpoint accuracy. They are the terms "high" and "fair," which always indicate Catholicism, and "low" and "dark," which always suggest Protestantism. Shakespeare's treatment of these words is sufficiently remarkable for critics to have wondered whether he was writing for a tall blond actor and a short dark one—but the theory is untenable. Shakespeare was not a dramatist who would have deliberately created casting problems, and the references span a ten-year period.

The opposition of high and low, representing the two opposing sides of the Reformation, was commonplace at the time. The modern Christian distinction between high and low church goes back to pre-Reformation days when High Mass, high day, and high altars involved full liturgical ceremony—Low Mass and low altars were for every day.

The opposition of dark and fair was equally recognizable. The glittering, skin-deep attractions of the scarlet woman were constantly under fire from Protestant plays, sermons, and literature: the sober reformers wore plain black, and the new Prayer Book was shorn of illuminated initials and, as far as possible, red print.

• • •

His markers are morally neutral. Fair, tall characters can be corrupt, while dark, low ones are often noble—the words merely identify the religious allegiance of one or two characters, providing a key compass-bearing from which alert readers and spectators can work out the rest of the shadowed plot. In the process an enjoyable trail of punning wordplay emerges, deepening and confirming the discovery.

From *Shadowplay: The Hidden Beliefs and Coded Politics of William Shakespeare*

Germaine Greer (b. 1939)

Shakespeare's "Honest Mirth" • • • 1986

The Puritan attack on the acting of plays rested on two assumptions, the first that the imitation of human speech and actions was lying and taught dissimulation, and the second that the dressing of men as women was evil in itself. Shakespeare mocks such ethical conundra in divers ways. In *Love's Labor's Lost* and *A Midsummer Night's Dream*, he goes behind the scenes to show the mounting of theatrical presentations, and deliberately poises the simplicity of the performers against the sophistication of the audience. Theseus's master of the revels warns the noble company (in *A Midsummer Night's Dream*) that they will not enjoy the "tedious brief scene of young Pyramus / And his love Thisbe":

It is not for you. I have heard it over,
    And it is nothing, nothing in the world;
Unless you can find sport in their intents,
    Extremely stretched and conned with cruel pain
To do you service.

(5.1.77–81)

Theseus's description of the importance of the active participation of the audience in creating and maintaining the illusion is a basic tenet of the Shakespearian aesthetic, to which he was to cling despite the gibes of more arrogant poets until the end of his writing career.

The best in this kind are but shadows; and the worst are no worse, if
    imagination amend them.

(5.1.203–204)

The frantic efforts of the players to reassure their audience that there is no need to be afraid of Snug dressed up as a lion are seen in this context as ridiculous not only because the players are not so expert that they could deceive anybody, but because audiences know that what is being presented is invented. Indeed, the action is taken from a classical source that would be known to all literate people either from their school Latin or from Golding's translation, namely the *Metamorphoses* of Ovid.

From Shakespeare

Linda Bamber (b. 1945)

Female Power in *A Midsummer Night's Dream*   1982

The best example of the relationship between male dominance and the status quo comes in *A Midsummer Night's Dream*, which begins with a rebellion of the feminine against the power of masculine authority. Hermia refuses the man both Egeus and Theseus order her to marry; her refusal sends us off into the forest, beyond the power of the father and the masculine state. Once in the forest, of course, we find the social situation metaphorically repeated in this world of imagination and nature. The fairy king, Oberon, rules the forest. His rule, too, is troubled by the rebellion of the feminine. Titania has refused to give him her page, the child of a human friend who died in childbirth. But by the end of the story Titania is conquered, the child relinquished, and order restored. Even here the comic upheavals, whether we see them as May games or bad dreams, are associated with an uprising of women. David P. Young, in *Something of Great Constancy*, has pointed out how firmly this play connects order with masculine dominance and the disruption of order with the rebellion of the feminine:

> It is appropriate that Theseus, as representative of daylight and right reason, should have subdued his bride-to-be to the rule of his masculine will. That is the natural order of things. It is equally appropriate that Oberon, as king of darkness and fantasy, should have lost control of his wife, and that the corresponding natural disorder described by Titania should ensue.

The natural order, the status quo, is for men to rule women. When they fail to do so, we have the exceptional situation, the festive, disruptive, disorderly moment of comedy.

• • •

Where are we to bestow our sympathies? On the forces that make for the disruption of the status quo and therefore for the plot? Or on the force that asserts itself against the disruption and reestablishes a workable social order? Of course we cannot choose. We can only say that in comedy we owe our holiday to such forces as the tendency of the feminine to rebel, whereas to the successful reassertion of masculine power we owe our everyday order. Shakespearean comedy endorses both sides. Holiday is, of course, the subject and the analogue of each play; but the plays always end in a return to everyday life. The optimistic reading of Shakespearean comedy says that everyday life is clarified and enriched by our holiday from it; according to the pessimistic reading the temporary subversion of the social order has revealed how much that order excludes, how high a price we pay for it. But whether our return to everyday life is a comfortable one or not, the return itself is the inevitable conclusion to the journey out.

From Comic Women, Tragic Men

WRITING *effectively*

Ben Jonson on Writing (1573?–1637)

On His Friend and Rival William Shakespeare 1640

Ben Jonson

I remember the players have often mentioned it as an honor to Shakespeare, that in his writing (whatsoever he penned) he never blotted out a line. My answer hath been, "Would he had blotted a thousand," which they thought a malevolent speech. I had not told posterity this but for their ignorance who chose that circumstance to commend their friend by wherein he most faulted; and to justify mine own candor, for I loved the man, and do honor his memory on this side idolatry as much as any. He was, indeed, honest, and of an open and free nature; had an excellent phantasy, brave notions, and gentle expressions, wherein he flowed with that facility that sometimes it was necessary he should be stopped. "*Sufflaminandus erat*,"° as Augustus° said of Haterius.° His wit was in his own power; would the rule of it had been so, too! Many times he fell into those things, could not escape laughter, as when he said in the person of Caesar,° one speaking to him, "Caesar, thou dost me wrong." He replied, "Caesar did never wrong but with just cause"; and such like, which were ridiculous. But he redeemed his vices with his virtues. There was ever more in him to be praised than to be pardoned.

From *Discoveries*

UNDERSTANDING SHAKESPEARE

The basic problem a modern reader faces with Shakespeare is language. Shakespeare's English is now four hundred years old, and it differs in innumerable small ways from contemporary American English. Although Shakespeare's idiom may at first seem daunting, it is easily mastered if you make the effort. To grow comfortable with his language, you must immerse yourself in it. Fortunately, doing so isn't all that hard; you might even find it pleasurable.

Sufflaminandus erat: Latin for "He ought to have been plugged up."   *Augustus:* the first emperor of Rome (63 B.C.–14 A.D.)   *Haterius:* a very verbose orator of the Augustan age.   *Caesar:* Shakespeare's tragedy *Julius Caesar.* Jonson misremembers the quotation, which (in the First Folio) actually reads "Know, Caesar doth not wrong, nor without cause will he be satisfied." (III, i, 47)

- **Let your ears do the work.** There is no substitute for hearing Shakespeare's words in performance. After all, the plays were written to be seen, not to be read silently on the page. After reading the play, listen to or watch a recording of it. It sometimes helps to read along as you listen or watch, hitting the pause button as needed. If you can attend a live performance of any Shakespearean play, do so.
- **But read the text first.** Watching a production is never a full substitute for reading an assigned play. Many productions abridge the play, leaving passages out. Even more important, directors and actors choose a particular interpretation of a play, and their choices might skew your understanding of events and motivation if you are unfamiliar with the original itself.
- **Before you write a paper, read the play again.** The first time through an Elizabethan-era text, you will almost certainly miss many things. As you grow more familiar with Shakespeare's language, you will be able to read it with greater comprehension. If you choose to write about a particular episode or character, carefully study the speeches and dialogue in question (and pay special attention to the footnotes) so that you understand each word.
- **Enjoy yourself.** From Beijing to Berlin, Buenos Aires to Oslo, Shakespeare is almost universally acknowledged as the world's greatest playwright, a master entertainer as well as a consummate artist.

CHECKLIST: Writing About Shakespeare

- ☐ Read closely. Work through passages with difficult language.
- ☐ Pay special attention to footnotes.
- ☐ Read the play more than once if necessary.
- ☐ Watch a DVD or listen to an audio recording after reading a play. Immerse yourself in Shakespeare's language until it becomes familiar.
- ☐ As you view or listen to a play, read along, or revisit the text afterward.
- ☐ Carefully study any speeches and dialogue you choose to write about.
- ☐ Be sure you understand each word of any passage you decide to discuss or quote.

WRITING ASSIGNMENT ON TRAGEDY

Select any tragedy found in the book (*Othello, Hamlet, Oedipus the King,* or *Antigonê*), and analyze it using Aristotle's definition of the form. Does the play measure up to Aristotle's requirements for a tragedy? In what ways does it meet the definition? In what ways does it depart from it? (Be sure to state clearly the Aristotelian rules by which drama is to be judged.)

Here is a paper written in response to this assignment by Janet Housden, a student of Melinda Barth at El Camino College.

SAMPLE STUDENT PAPER

Housden 1

Janet Housden
Professor Barth
English 201
3 January 2012

Othello: Tragedy or Soap Opera?

First paragraph gives name of author and work

Key plot information avoids excessive retelling

When we hear the word "tragedy," we usually think of either a terrible real-life disaster, or a dark and serious drama filled with pain, suffering, and loss that involves the downfall of a powerful person due to some character flaw or error in judgment. William Shakespeare's *Othello* is such a drama. Set in Venice and Cyprus during the Renaissance, the play tells the story of Othello, a Moorish general in the Venetian army, who has just married Desdemona, the daughter of a Venetian nobleman. Through the plotting of a jealous villain, Iago, Othello is deceived into believing that Desdemona has been unfaithful to him. He murders her in revenge, only to discover too late how he has been tricked. Overcome by shame and grief, Othello kills himself.

Central question is raised

Thesis statement provides response

Dealing as it does with jealousy, murder, and suicide, the play is certainly dark, but is *Othello* a true tragedy? In the fourth century B.C., the Greek philosopher Aristotle proposed a formal definition of tragedy (Kennedy and Gioia 1203–4), which only partially fits *Othello*.

Topic sentence on Othello's social position

Essay systematically applies Aristotle's definition of tragedy to Othello

The first characteristic of tragedy identified by Aristotle is that the protagonist is a person of outstanding quality and high social position. While Othello is not of royal birth as are many tragic heroes and heroines, he does occupy a sufficiently high position to satisfy this part of Aristotle's definition. Although Othello is a foreigner and a soldier by trade, he has risen to the rank of general and has married into a noble family, which is quite an accomplishment for an outsider. Furthermore, Othello is generally liked and respected by those around him. He is often described by others as being "noble," "brave," and "valiant." By virtue of his high rank and the respect he commands from others, Othello would appear to possess the high stature commonly given to the tragic hero in order to make his eventual fall seem all the more tragic.

While Othello displays the nobility and high status commonly associated with the tragic hero, he also possesses another, less admirable characteristic, the flaw or character defect shared by all heroes of classical tragedy. In Othello's case, it is a stunning gullibility, combined with a violent temper that once awakened overcomes all reason. These flaws permit Othello to be easily deceived and manipulated by the villainous Iago and make him easy prey for the "green-eyed monster" (3.3.179).

It is because of this tragic flaw, according to Aristotle, that the hero is at least partially to blame for his own downfall. While Othello's "free and open nature, / That thinks men honest that but seem to be so" (1.3.376–77) is not a fault in itself, it does allow Iago to convince the Moor of his wife's infidelity without one shred of concrete evidence. Furthermore, once Othello has been convinced of Desdemona's guilt, he makes up his mind to take vengeance, and says that his "bloody thoughts with violent pace / Shall ne'er look back, ne'er ebb to humble love" (3.3.473–74). He thereby renders himself deaf to the voice of reason, and ignoring Desdemona's protestations of innocence, brutally murders her, only to discover too late that he has made a terrible mistake. Although he is goaded into his crime by Iago, who is a master at manipulating people, it is Othello's own character flaws that lead to his horrible misjudgment.

Aristotle's definition also states that the hero's misfortune is not wholly deserved, that the punishment he receives exceeds his crime. Although it is hard to sympathize with a man as cruel as Othello is to the innocent Desdemona, Othello pays an extremely high price for his sin of gullibility. Othello loses everything—his wife, his position, even his life. Even though it's partially his fault, Othello is not entirely to blame, for without Iago's interference it's highly unlikely that things would turn out as they do. Though it seems incredibly stupid on Othello's part, that a man who has travelled the world and commanded armies should be so easily deceived, there is little evidence that Othello has had much experience with civilian society, and although he is "declined / Into the vale of years" (3.3.281–82) Othello has apparently never been married before. By his own admission, "little of this great world can I speak / More than pertains to feats of broils and battle" (1.3.88–89). Furthermore, Othello has no reason to suspect that "honest Iago" is anything but his loyal friend and supporter.

While it is understandable that Othello could be fooled into believing Desdemona unfaithful, the question remains whether his fate is deserved. In

Topic sentence on Othello's tragic flaw

Quotes from play as evidence to support point

Topic sentence elaborates on idea raised in previous paragraphs

Topic sentence on Othello's misfortune

Transitional words signal argument's direction

addition to his mistake of believing Iago's lies, Othello commits a more serious error: he lets himself be blinded by anger. Worse yet, in deciding to take vengeance, he also makes up his mind not be swayed from his course, even by his love for Desdemona. In fact, he refuses to listen to her at all, "lest her body and beauty unprovide my mind again" (4.1.186–87), therefore denying her the right to defend herself. Because of his rage and unfairness, perhaps Othello deserves his fate more than Aristotle's ideal tragic hero. Othello's punishment does exceed his crime, but just barely.

According to Aristotle, the tragic hero's fall gives the protagonist deeper understanding and self-awareness. Othello departs from Aristotle's model in that Othello apparently learns nothing from his mistakes. He never realizes that he is partly at fault. He sees himself only as an innocent victim and blames his misfortune on fate rather than accepting responsibility for his actions. To be sure, he realizes he has been tricked and deeply regrets his mistake, but he seems to feel that he was justified under the circumstances, "For naught I did in hate, but all in honor" (5.2.303). Othello sees himself not as someone whose bad judgment and worse temper have resulted in the death of an innocent party, but as one who has "loved not wisely but too well" (5.2.354). This failure to grasp the true nature of his error indicates that Othello hasn't learned his lesson.

Neither accepting responsibility nor learning from his mistakes, Othello fails to fulfill yet another of Aristotle's requirements. Since the protagonist usually gains some understanding along with his defeat, classical tragedy conveys a sense of human greatness and of life's unrealized potentialities—a quality totally absent from *Othello*. Not only does Othello fail to learn from his mistakes, he never really realizes what those mistakes are, and it apparently never crosses his mind that things could have turned out any differently. "Who can control his fate?" Othello asks (5.2.274), and this defeatist attitude, combined with his failure to salvage any wisdom from his defeat, separates *Othello* from the tragedy as defined by Aristotle.

The last part of Aristotle's definition states that viewing the conclusion of a tragedy should result in catharsis for the audience, and that the audience should be left with a feeling of exaltation rather than depression. Unfortunately, the feeling we are left with after viewing *Othello* is neither catharsis nor exaltation but rather a feeling of horror, pity, and disgust at the senseless waste of human lives. The deaths of Desdemona and Othello, as well as

Topic sentence elaborates on Othello's misfortune

Topic sentence on whether Othello learns from his mistakes

Topic sentence elaborating further on whether Othello learns from his errors

Topic sentence on catharsis

Housden 4

those of Emilia and Roderigo, serve no purpose whatsoever. They die not in the service of a great cause but because of lies, treachery, jealousy, and spite. Their deaths don't even benefit Iago, who is directly or indirectly responsible for all of them. No lesson is learned, no epiphany is reached, and the audience, instead of experiencing catharsis, is left with its negative feeling unresolved.

Since *Othello* only partially fits Aristotle's definition of tragedy, it is questionable whether or not it should be classified as one. Though it does involve a great man undone by a defect in his own character, the hero gains neither insight nor understanding from his defeat, and so there can be no inspiration or catharsis for the audience, as there would be in a "true" tragedy. *Othello* is tragic only in the everyday sense of the word, the way a plane crash or fire is tragic. At least in terms of Aristotle's classic definition, *Othello* ultimately comes across as more of a melodrama or soap opera than a tragedy.

Restatement of thesis

Conclusion

Housden 5

Works Cited

Kennedy, X. J., and Dana Gioia, eds. *Literature: An Introduction to Fiction, Poetry, Drama, and Writing.* 12th ed. New York: Pearson, 2013. 1203–4. Print.

Shakespeare, William. *Othello, The Moor of Venice. Literature: An Introduction to Fiction, Poetry, Drama, and Writing.* Ed. X. J. Kennedy and Dana Gioia. 12th ed. New York: Pearson, 2013. 1290–390. Print.

MORE TOPICS FOR WRITING

1. Write a defense of Iago.
2. "Never was any play fraught, like this of *Othello*, with improbabilities," wrote Thomas Rymer in a famous attack (*A Short View of Tragedy*, 1692). Consider Rymer's objection to the play, either answering it or finding evidence to back it up.
3. Suppose yourself a casting director assigned to a film version of either *Othello* or *Hamlet*. What well-known actors would you cast in the principal roles? Write a report justifying your choices. Don't merely discuss the stars and their qualifications; discuss (with specific reference to the play) what Shakespeare appears to call for.
4. Emilia's long speech at the end of Act IV (iii, 83–102) has been called a Renaissance plea for women's rights. Do you agree? Write a brief, close analysis of this speech. How timely is it?

5. "The downfall of Oedipus is the work of the gods; the downfall of Othello is self-inflicted." Test this comment with reference to the two plays, and report your findings.

6. In what respects does *Hamlet* resemble a classical tragedy, such as *Oedipus the King*? In what ways is Shakespeare's play different? Is Hamlet, like Oedipus, driven to his death by some inexorable force (Fate, the gods, the nature of things)?

7. Write a defense of Hamlet's uncle, Claudius.

8. "Hamlet is a mentally unstable young man who is obsessed with his father's death. He is angry at his mother for remarrying so quickly. The Ghost is not real. It is only a projection of the Prince's deranged imagination." Write an essay to support or refute this argument. Use specific incidents in the play to back up your position.

9. Contrast the palace and the woods as settings in *A Midsummer Night's Dream*.

10. Explain the connection between the comic sketch presented by the rustic tradesmen on Pyramus and Thisbe and the events that occur elsewhere in the play.

38 THE MODERN THEATER

*Speak of the moderns without contempt,
and of the ancients without idolatry.*

—LORD CHESTERFIELD

REALISM

The ancient art of the drama experienced a revival in the Renaissance and went through a number of changes over the next several centuries. The Elizabethan drama was marked by strong characterization, heightened and intense language, and crowded, sometimes sprawling plots. In the neoclassical period of the seventeenth and eighteenth centuries, greater emphasis was placed upon formality, decorum, and Aristotle's unities of time, place, and action. The early nineteenth century saw the rise of melodrama, with its florid dialogue, plots that relied heavily on often absurd coincidences, and crude stereotypes of good and evil characters. Through all these developments—from kings and generals to lords and ladies of high society to pure-hearted swashbucklers and craven villains—the one thing that seemed to remain constant was an absence of **realism**—the attempt to reproduce faithfully the surface appearance of life, especially that of ordinary people in everyday situations.

By the end of the nineteenth century, however, Realism had become the drama's dominant mode. The writer most responsible for that shift was the Norwegian playwright Henrik Ibsen. From *Pillars of Society* (1877) to *Hedda Gabler* (1890), he wrote a series of prose dramas in which realistically portrayed middle-class characters face conflicts in their lives and relationships. They are often called "problem plays" because of their engagement of social issues, such as women's place in society (*A Doll's House*) and inherited venereal disease (*Ghosts*). In actuality, the social problems in these plays serve as a context for Ibsen's real concern, an examination of the complexities of human personality and psychology, especially those aspects of our natures that are hidden or repressed because of society's expectations.

The attempt to use the theater to present the real lives of real people was taken even further by the Russian dramatist Anton Chekhov. In Chekhov's mature plays, the dialogue seems at times to meander and there appears to be little or no action. *The Cherry Orchard* (1904), his last and greatest play, presents a decayed aristocratic clan unable to deal with a threatened foreclosure on the family estate, despite advice from all quarters. The play has sparked debate for over a century: Is it a comedy or a tragedy? Are its characters foolish or sympathetic? Does it lament the passing of an old way of life or greet the dawn of a new age? The answer, of course, is *All of the above*—just like life itself.

Conventions of Realism

From Italian playhouses of the sixteenth century, the theater had inherited the **picture-frame stage**: a structure that holds the action within a **proscenium arch**, a gateway standing (as the word *proscenium* indicates) "in front of the scenery." This manner of constructing a playhouse in effect divided the actors from their audience; most commercial theaters even today are so constructed. But as the nineteenth century gave way to the twentieth, actors less often declaimed their passions in oratorical style in front of backdrops painted with waterfalls and volcanoes, while stationed exactly at the center of the stage as if to sing "duets meant to bring forth applause" (as Swedish playwright August Strindberg complained).

In the theater of Realism, a room was represented by a **box set**—three walls that joined in two corners and a ceiling that tilted as if seen in perspective—replacing drapery walls that had billowed and doors that had flapped, not slammed. Instead of posing at stage center and directly facing the audience to deliver key speeches, actors were instructed to speak from wherever the dramatic situation placed them, and now and then even to turn their backs upon the audience. They were to behave as if they were in a room with the fourth wall sliced away, unaware that they had an audience.

To encourage actors further to imitate reality, the influential director Constantin Stanislavsky of the Moscow Art Theater developed his famous system to help actors feel at home inside a playwright's characters. One of Stanislavsky's exercises was to have actors search their memories for personal experiences like those of the characters in the play; another was to have them act out things a character did *not* do in the play but might do in life. The system enabled Stanislavsky to bring authenticity to his productions of Chekhov's plays and of Maxim Gorky's *The Lower Depths* (1902), a play that showed the tenants of a sordid lodging house drinking themselves to death (and hanging themselves) in surroundings of realistic squalor. Stanislavsky's techniques are still used by stage and film actors today.

NATURALISM

Gorky's play is a masterpiece of **Naturalism,** a kind of realism in fiction and drama dealing with the more brutal or unpleasant aspects of reality. As codified by French novelist and playwright Émile Zola, who influenced Ibsen, Naturalism viewed a person as a creature whose acts are determined by heredity and environment; Zola urged writers to study their characters' behavior with the detachment of zoologists studying animals.

Another masterpiece of the naturalistic tradition is *The Hairy Ape* (1922) by the American playwright Eugene O'Neill. The title character is Yank, a brutish but good-natured engine-stoker on an ocean liner. After a rich young woman calls him a "filthy beast," he grows depressed and dislocated, trying and failing to find a comfortable place for himself in society. He ends up at the zoo, where he dies in a gorilla's embrace. (The play's enduring power was affirmed by a successful New York revival in 2006.) Universally regarded as the first true genius of the American theater, O'Neill greatly influenced several generations of American playwrights, including Arthur Miller. In many of his plays, Miller portrayed working-class characters whose lives are shaped and constrained by powerful social and cultural forces. Miller was also influenced by Ibsen, whose *Enemy of the People* he adapted for the Broadway stage in 1950.

SYMBOLISM AND EXPRESSIONISM

The ascendance of Realism had liberated drama from some outworn styles and opened rich new areas of artistic exploration, but when it became the dominant tradition, some writers began to feel confined by its themes and theatrical conventions, and new forms of drama emerged. One of these was the **Symbolist movement** in the French theater, most influentially expressed by Belgian playwright Maurice Maeterlinck, whose work conjures up a spirit world we cannot directly perceive, as in his play *The Intruder* (1890), when a blind man sees the approach of Death.

In Ireland, poet William Butler Yeats wrote (among other plays) "plays for dancers" to be performed in drawing rooms, often in friends' homes, with simple costumes and props, a few masked actors, and a very few musicians. In Sweden, August Strindberg, who earlier had won fame as a Naturalist, reversed direction and in *The Dream Play* (1902) and *The Ghost Sonata* (1907) introduced characters who change their identities and, ignoring space and time, move across dreamlike landscapes.

In these plays Strindberg anticipated the movement in German theater after World War I called **Expressionism**. Delighting in bizarre sets and exaggerated make-up and costuming, Expressionist playwrights and producers sought to reflect intense states of emotion and, sometimes, to depict the world through lunatic eyes. A classic film example is *The Cabinet of Dr. Caligari*, made in Berlin in 1919 and 1920, in which a hypnotist sends forth a subject to murder people. Garbed in jet black, the killer sleepwalks through a town of lopsided houses, twisted streets, and railings that tilt at gravity-defying angles. A restless experimenter throughout his career, Eugene O'Neill employed Expressionist techniques in his 1926 play *The Great God Brown*, in which characters speak through masks and wear one another's clothes (and identities).

AMERICAN MODERNISM

If modern American drama first came of age with Eugene O'Neill, it soon found powerful new voices. Thornton Wilder wrote experimental plays such as *Our Town* (1938) and *The Skin of Our Teeth* (1942) that were so carefully constructed, witty, and evocative that they achieved enormous popular and critical success. Wilder's plays, especially *Our Town*, have become so familiar to American audiences that we hardly realize how innovative his works were in their time.

It was not until the mid-1940s that two playwrights emerged who would rival O'Neill in the depth and artistry of their work—Arthur Miller and Tennessee Williams. Miller achieved his first major success with *All My Sons* (1947), in which an idealistic young man discovers that his father was guilty of supplying defective airplane parts to the government during World War II, resulting in the deaths of American servicemen. But it was his next play, *Death of a Salesman* (1949), that established Miller's work as a permanent part of America's literary heritage. In this emotionally devastating drama, Miller once again presents a tormented young man trying to come to terms with the deeply flawed father that he loves.

Tennessee Williams had made his mark a bit earlier, with *The Glass Menagerie*, produced in Chicago in December 1944 and on Broadway the following March. From there, Williams would go on to greater triumphs, especially in *A Streetcar Named Desire* (1947) and *Cat on a Hot Tin Roof* (1955). These two plays established the qualities most associated with Williams's name—strong but driven and sometimes brutal men who dominate their families; sensitive yet ambitious women; a kind of folk poetry grounded in vigorous speech rhythms (hinted at in the evocative titles of the plays); Southern settings in which contemporary decay embodies a nostalgia for a more refined past. But *The Glass Menagerie* is extraordinary for its tender lyricism and in the high quotient of human decency among its characters; partly for these reasons, it is still one of the most popular, if not *the* most popular, of Williams's works.

Below is one of the pioneering works of realism, Henrik Ibsen's *A Doll's House*. The play derives a good deal of its power from our ability to identify with its characters and the lives they live, an identification that Ibsen achieves in part by framing the action with the details of daily existence.

Henrik Ibsen

A Doll's House   1879

Translated by R. Farquharson Sharp
Revised by Viktoria Michelsen

Henrik Ibsen (1828–1906) was born in Skien, a seaport in Norway. When he was six, his father's business losses suddenly reduced his wealthy family to poverty. After a brief attempt to study medicine, young Ibsen worked as a stage manager in provincial Bergen; then, becoming known as a playwright, he moved to Oslo as artistic director of the National Theater—practical experiences that gained him firm grounding in his craft. Discouraged when his theater failed and the king turned down his plea for a grant to enable him to write, Ibsen left Norway and for twenty-seven years lived in Italy and Germany. There, in his middle years (1879–1891), he wrote most of his famed plays about small-town life, among them A Doll's House, Ghosts, An Enemy of the People, The Wild Duck, and Hedda Gabler. Introducing social problems to the stage, these plays aroused storms of controversy. Although best known as a Realist, Ibsen early in his career wrote poetic dramas based on Norwegian history and folklore: the tragedy Brand (1866) and the powerful, wildly fantastic Peer Gynt (1867). He ended as a Symbolist in John Gabriel Borkman (1896) and When We Dead Awaken (1899), both encompassing huge mountains that heaven-assaulting heroes try to climb. Late in life Ibsen returned to Oslo, honored at last both at home and abroad.

CHARACTERS

Torvald Helmer, a lawyer
Nora, his wife
Doctor Rank
Mrs. Kristine Linde
Nils Krogstad
The Helmers' three young children
Anne Marie, their nursemaid
Helene, the maid
A Porter

The action takes place in the Helmers' apartment.

ACT I

The scene is a room furnished comfortably and tastefully, but not extravagantly. At the back wall, a door to the right leads to the entrance hall. Another to the left leads to Helmer's study. Between the doors there is a piano. In the middle of the left-hand wall is a door, and beyond it a window. Near the window are a round table, armchairs, and a small sofa. In the right-hand wall, at the farther end, is another door, and on the same side, nearer the footlights, a stove, two easy chairs and a rocking chair. Between the stove and the door there is a small table. There are engravings on the walls, a cabinet with china and other small objects, and a small bookcase with expensively bound books. The floors are carpeted, and a fire burns in the stove. It is winter.

A bell rings in the hall. A moment later, we hear the door being opened. Enter Nora, humming a tune and in high spirits. She is wearing a hat and coat and carries a number of packages, which she puts down on the table to the right. She leaves the outer door open behind her. Through the door we see a porter who is carrying a Christmas tree and a basket, which he gives to the maid, who has opened the door.

Nora: Hide the Christmas tree carefully, Helene. Make sure the children don't see it till it's decorated this evening. (*To the Porter, taking out her purse.*) How much?
Porter: Fifty ore.
Nora: Here's a krone. No, keep the change.

(*The Porter thanks her and goes out. Nora shuts the door. She is laughing to herself as she takes off her hat and coat. She takes a bag of macaroons from her pocket and eats one or two, then goes cautiously to the door of her husband's study and listens.*)

Yes, he's there. (*Still humming, she goes to the table on the right.*)

Helmer (*calls out from his study*): Is that my little lark twittering out there?
Nora (*busy opening some of the packages*): Yes, it is!
Helmer: Is it my little squirrel bustling around?
Nora: Yes!
Helmer: When did my squirrel come home?
Nora: Just now. (*Puts the bag of macaroons into her pocket and wipes her mouth.*) Come in here, Torvald, and see what I bought.
Helmer: I'm very busy right now. (*A little later, he opens the door and looks into the room, pen in hand.*) Bought, did you say? All these things? Has my little spendthrift been wasting money again?
Nora: Yes, but, Torvald, this year we really can let ourselves go a little. This is the first Christmas that we don't have to watch every penny.
Helmer: Still, you know, we can't spend money recklessly.
Nora: Yes, Torvald, but we can be a little more reckless now, can't we? Just a tiny little bit! You're going to have a big salary and you'll be making lots and lots of money.
Helmer: Yes, after the New Year. But it'll still be a whole three months before the money starts coming in.
Nora: Pooh! We can borrow till then.
Helmer: Nora! (*Goes up to her and takes her playfully by the ear.*) The same little featherbrain! Just suppose that I borrowed a thousand kroner today, and you spent it all on Christmas, and then on New Year's Eve a roof tile fell on my head and killed me, and—
Nora (*putting her hand over his mouth*): Oh! Don't say such horrible things.

The 2009 adaptation of *A Doll's House* at the Donmar Warehouse in London, starring Gillian Anderson and Toby Stephens.

Helmer: Still, suppose that happened. What then?

Nora: If that happened, I don't suppose I'd care whether I owed anyone money or not.

Helmer: Yes, but what about the people who'd lent it to us?

Nora: Them? Who'd care about them? I wouldn't even know who they were.

Helmer: That's just like a woman! But seriously, Nora, you know how I feel about that. No debt, no borrowing. There can't be any freedom or beauty in a home life that depends on borrowing and debt. We two have managed to stay on the straight road so far, and we'll go on the same way for the short time that we still have to be careful.

Nora (moving towards the stove): As you wish, Torvald.

Helmer (following her): Now, now, my little skylark mustn't let her wings droop. What's the matter? Is my little squirrel sulking? (*Taking out his purse.*) Nora, what do you think I've got here?

Nora (turning round quickly): Money!

Helmer: There you are. (*Gives her some money.*) Do you think I don't know how much you need for the house at Christmastime?

Nora (counting): Ten, twenty, thirty, forty! Thank you, thank you, Torvald. That'll keep me going for a long time.

Helmer: It's going to have to.

Nora: Yes, yes, it will. But come here and let me show you what I bought. And all so cheap! Look, here's a new suit for Ivar, and a sword. And a horse and a trumpet for Bob. And a doll and doll's bed for Emmy. They're not the best, but she'll break them soon enough anyway. And here's dress material and handkerchiefs for the maids. Old Anne Marie really should have something nicer.

Helmer: And what's in this package?

Nora (crying out): No, no! You can't see that till this evening.

The 1896 production of *A Doll's House* at the Empire Theatre in New York.

Helmer: If you say so. But now tell me, you extravagant little thing, what would you like for yourself?

Nora: For myself? Oh, I'm sure I don't want anything.

Helmer: But you must. Tell me something that you'd especially like to have—within reasonable limits.

Nora: No, I really can't think of anything. Unless, Torvald . . .

Helmer: Well?

Nora (playing with his coat buttons, and without raising her eyes to his): If you really want to give me something, you might . . . you might . . .

Helmer: Well, out with it!

Nora (speaking quickly): You might give me money, Torvald. Only just as much as you can afford. And then one of these days I'll buy something with it.

Helmer: But, Nora—

Nora: Oh, do! Dear Torvald, please, please do! Then I'll wrap it up in beautiful gold paper and hang it on the Christmas tree. Wouldn't that be fun?

Helmer: What do they call those little creatures that are always wasting money?

Nora: Spendthrifts. I know. Let's do as I suggest, Torvald, and then I'll have time to think about what I need most. That's a very sensible plan, isn't it?

Helmer (smiling): Yes, it is. That is, if you really did save some of the money I give you, and then really buy something for yourself. But if you spend it all on the housekeeping and all kinds of unnecessary things, then I just have to open my wallet all over again.

Nora: Oh, but, Torvald—

Helmer: You can't deny it, my dear little Nora. *(Puts his arm around her waist.)* She's a sweet little spendthrift, but she uses up a lot of money. One would hardly believe how expensive such little creatures are!

Nora: That's a terrible thing to say. I really do save all I can.

Helmer (*laughing*): That's true. All you can. But you can't save anything!

Nora (*smiling quietly and happily*): You have no idea how many bills skylarks and squirrels have, Torvald.

Helmer: You're an odd little soul. Just like your father. You always find some new way of wheedling money out of me, and, as soon as you've got it, it seems to melt in your hands. You never know where it's gone. Still, one has to take you as you are. It's in the blood. Because, you know, it's true that you can inherit these things, Nora.

Nora: Ah, I wish I'd inherited a lot of Papa's traits.

Helmer: And I wouldn't want you to be anything but just what you are, my sweet little skylark. But, you know, it seems to me that you look rather—how can I put it—rather uneasy today.

Nora: Do I?

Helmer: You do, really. Look straight at me.

Nora (*looks at him*): Well?

Helmer (*wagging his finger at her*): Has little Miss Sweet Tooth been breaking our rules in town today?

Nora: No, what makes you think that?

Helmer: Has she paid a visit to the bakery?

Nora: No, I assure you, Torvald—

Helmer: Not been nibbling pastries?

Nora: No, certainly not.

Helmer: Not even taken a bite of a macaroon or two?

Nora: No, Torvald, I assure you, really—

Helmer: Come on, you know I was only kidding.

Nora (*going to the table on the right*): I wouldn't dream of going against your wishes.

Helmer: No, I'm sure of that. Besides, you gave me your word. (*Going up to her.*) Keep your little Christmas secrets to yourself, my darling. They'll all be revealed tonight when the Christmas tree is lit, no doubt.

Nora: Did you remember to invite Doctor Rank?

Helmer: No. But there's no need. It goes without saying that he'll have dinner with us. All the same, I'll ask him when he comes over this morning. I've ordered some good wine. Nora, you have no idea how much I'm looking forward to this evening.

Nora: So am I! And how the children will enjoy themselves, Torvald!

Helmer: It's great to feel that you have a completely secure position and a big enough income. It's a delightful thought, isn't it?

Nora: It's wonderful!

Helmer: Do you remember last Christmas? For three whole weeks you hid yourself away every evening until long after midnight, making ornaments for the Christmas tree and all the other fine things that were going to be a surprise for us. It was the most boring three weeks I ever spent!

Nora: I wasn't bored.

Helmer (*smiling*): But there was precious little to show for it, Nora.

Nora: Oh, you're not going to tease me about that again. How could I help it that the cat went in and tore everything to pieces?

Helmer: Of course you couldn't, poor little girl. You had the best of intentions to make us all happy, and that's the main thing. But it's a good thing that our hard times are over.

Nora: Yes, it really is wonderful.

Helmer: This time I don't have to sit here and be bored all by myself, and you don't have to ruin your dear eyes and your pretty little hands—

Nora (clapping her hands): No, Torvald, I don't have to any more, do I! It's wonderfully lovely to hear you say so! (*Taking his arm.*) Now let me tell you how I've been thinking we should arrange things, Torvald. As soon as Christmas is over—(*A bell rings in the hall.*) There's the bell. (*She tidies the room a little.*) There's somebody at the door. What a nuisance!

Helmer: If someone's visiting, remember I'm not home.

Maid (in the doorway): A lady to see you, ma'am. A stranger.

Nora: Ask her to come in.

Maid (to Helmer): The doctor's here too, sir.

Helmer: Did he go straight into my study?

Maid: Yes, sir.

(*Helmer goes into his study. The maid ushers in Mrs. Linde, who is in traveling clothes, and shuts the door.*)

Mrs. Linde (in a dejected and timid voice): Hello, Nora.

Nora (doubtfully): Hello.

Mrs. Linde: You don't recognize me, I suppose.

Nora: No, I don't know . . . Yes, of course, I think so—(*Suddenly.*) Yes! Kristine! Is it really you?

Mrs. Linde: Yes, it is.

Nora: Kristine! Imagine my not recognizing you! And yet how could I—(*In a gentle voice.*) You've changed, Kristine!

Mrs. Linde: Yes, I certainly have. In nine, ten long years—

Nora: Is it that long since we've seen each other? I suppose it is. The last eight years have been a happy time for me, you know. And so now you've come to town, and you've taken this long trip in the winter. That was brave of you.

Mrs. Linde: I arrived by steamer this morning.

Nora: To have some fun at Christmastime, of course. How delightful! We'll have such fun together! But take off your things. You're not cold, I hope. (*Helps her.*) Now we'll sit down by the stove and be cozy. No, take this armchair. I'll sit here in the rocking chair. (*Takes her hands.*) Now you look like your old self again. It was only that first moment. You are a little paler, Kristine, and maybe a little thinner.

Mrs. Linde: And much, much older, Nora.

Nora: Maybe a little older. Very, very little. Surely not very much. (*Stops suddenly and speaks seriously.*) What a thoughtless thing I am, chattering away like this. My poor, dear Kristine, please forgive me.

Mrs. Linde: What do you mean, Nora?

Nora (gently): Poor Kristine, you're a widow.

Mrs. Linde: Yes. For three years now.

Nora: Yes, I knew. I saw it in the papers. I swear to you, Kristine, I kept meaning to write to you at the time, but I always put it off and something always came up.

Mrs. Linde: I understand completely, dear.

Nora: It was very bad of me, Kristine. Poor thing, how you must have suffered. And he left you nothing?

Mrs. Linde: No.

Nora: And no children?

Mrs. Linde: No.

Nora: Nothing at all, then?

Mrs. Linde: Not even any sorrow or grief to live on.

Nora (looking at her in disbelief): But, Kristine, is that possible?

Mrs. Linde (smiles sadly and strokes Nora's hair): It happens sometimes, Nora.

Nora: So you're completely alone. How terribly sad that must be. I have three beautiful children. You can't see them just now, because they're out with their nursemaid. But now you must tell me all about it.

Mrs. Linde: No, no, I want to hear about you.

Nora: No, you go first. I mustn't be selfish today. Today I should think only about you. But there is one thing I have to tell you. Do you know we've just had a fabulous piece of good luck?

Mrs. Linde: No, what is it?

Nora: Just imagine, my husband's been appointed manager of the bank!

Mrs. Linde: Your husband? That is good luck!

Nora: Yes, it's tremendous! A lawyer's life is so uncertain, especially if he won't take any cases that are the slightest bit shady, and of course Torvald has never been willing to do that, and I completely agree with him. You can imagine how delighted we are! He starts his job in the bank at New Year's, and then he'll have a big salary and lots of commissions. From now on we can live very differently. We can do just what we want. I feel so relieved and so happy, Kristine! It'll be wonderful to have heaps of money and not have to worry about anything, won't it?

Mrs. Linde: Yes. Anyway, I think it would be delightful to have what you need.

Nora: No, not only what you need, but heaps and heaps of money.

Mrs. Linde (smiling): Nora, Nora, haven't you learned any sense yet? Back in school you were a terrible spendthrift.

Nora (laughing): Yes, that's what Torvald says now. (*Wags her finger at her.*) But "Nora, Nora" isn't as silly as you think. We haven't been in a position for me to waste money. We've both had to work.

Mrs. Linde: You too?

Nora: Oh, yes, odds and ends, needlework, crocheting, embroidery, and that kind of thing. (*Dropping her voice.*) And other things too. You know Torvald left his government job when we got married? There was no chance of promotion, and he had to try to earn more money than he was making there. But in that first year he overworked himself terribly. You see, he had to make money any way he could, and he worked all hours, but he couldn't take it, and he got very sick, and the doctors said he had to go south, to a warmer climate.

Mrs. Linde: You spent a whole year in Italy, didn't you?

Nora: Yes. It wasn't easy to get away, I can tell you that. It was just after Ivar was born, but obviously we had to go. It was a wonderful, beautiful trip, and it saved Torvald's life. But it cost a tremendous amount of money, Kristine.

Mrs. Linde: I would imagine so.

Nora: It cost about four thousand, eight hundred kroner. That's a lot, isn't it?

Mrs. Linde: Yes, it is, and when you have an emergency like that it's lucky to have the money.

Nora: Well, the fact is, we got it from Papa.

Mrs. Linde: Oh, I see. It was just about that time that he died, wasn't it?

Nora: Yes, and, just think of it, I couldn't even go and take care of him. I was expecting little Ivar any day and I had my poor sick Torvald to look after. My dear, kind father. I never saw him again, Kristine. That was the worst experience I've gone through since we got married.

Mrs. Linde: I know how fond of him you were. And then you went off to Italy?

Nora: Yes. You see, we had money then, and the doctors insisted that we go, so we left a month later.

Mrs. Linde: And your husband came back completely recovered?

Nora: The picture of health!

Mrs. Linde: But . . . the doctor?

Nora: What doctor?

Mrs. Linde: Didn't your maid say that the gentleman who arrived here with me was the doctor?

Nora: Yes, that was Doctor Rank, but he doesn't come here professionally. He's our dearest friend, and he drops in at least once every day. No, Torvald hasn't been sick for an hour since then, and our children are strong and healthy, and so am I. (*Jumps up and claps her hands.*) Kristine! Kristine! It's good to be alive and happy! But how awful of me. I'm talking about nothing but myself. (*Sits on a nearby stool and rests her arms on her knees.*) Please don't be mad at me. Tell me, is it really true that you didn't love your husband? Why did you marry him?

Mrs. Linde: My mother was still alive then, and she was bedridden and helpless, and I had to provide for my two younger brothers, so I didn't think I had any right to turn him down.

Nora: No, maybe you did the right thing. So he was rich then?

Mrs. Linde: I believe he was quite well off. But his business wasn't very solid, and when he died, it all went to pieces and there was nothing left.

Nora: And then?

Mrs. Linde: Well, I had to turn my hand to anything I could find. First a small shop, then a small school, and so on. The last three years have seemed like one long workday, with no rest. Now it's over, Nora. My poor mother's gone and doesn't need me any more, and the boys don't need me, either. They've got jobs now and can manage for themselves.

Nora: What a relief it must be if—

Mrs. Linde: No, not at all. All I feel is an unbearable emptiness. No one to live for anymore. (*Gets up restlessly.*) That's why I couldn't stand it any longer in my little backwater. I hope it'll be easier to find something here that'll keep me busy and occupy my mind. If I could be lucky enough to find some regular work, office work of some kind—

Nora: But, Kristine, that's so awfully tiring, and you look tired out now. It'd be much better for you if you could get away to a resort.

Mrs. Linde (*walking to the window*): I don't have a father to give me money for a trip, Nora.

Nora (*rising*): Oh, don't be mad at me!

Mrs. Linde (going up to her): It's you who mustn't be mad at me, dear. The worst thing about a situation like mine is that it makes you so bitter. No one to work for, and yet you have to always be on the lookout for opportunities. You have to live, and so you grow selfish. When you told me about your good luck—you'll find this hard to believe—I was delighted less for you than for myself.

Nora: What do you mean? Oh, I understand. You mean that maybe Torvald could find you a job.

Mrs. Linde: Yes, that's what I was thinking.

Nora: He must, Kristine. Just leave it to me. I'll broach the subject very cleverly. I'll think of something that'll put him in a really good mood. It'll make me so happy to be of some use to you.

Mrs. Linde: How kind you are, Nora, to be so eager to help me! It's doubly kind of you, since you know so little of the burdens and troubles of life.

Nora: Me? I know so little of them?

Mrs. Linde (smiling): My dear! Small household cares and that sort of thing! You're a child, Nora.

Nora (tosses her head and crosses the stage): You shouldn't act so superior.

Mrs. Linde: No?

Nora: You're just like the others. They all think I'm incapable of anything really serious—

Mrs. Linde: Come on—

Nora: —that I haven't had to deal with any real problems in my life.

Mrs. Linde: But, my dear Nora, you've just told me all your troubles.

Nora: Pooh! That was nothing. (*Lowering her voice.*) I haven't told you the important thing.

Mrs. Linde: The important thing? What do you mean?

Nora: You really look down on me, Kristine, but you shouldn't. Aren't you proud of having worked so hard and so long for your mother?

Mrs. Linde: Believe me, I don't look down on anyone. But it's true, I'm proud and I'm glad that I had the privilege of making my mother's last days almost worry-free.

Nora: And you're proud of what you did for your brothers?

Mrs. Linde: I think I have the right to be.

Nora: I think so, too. But now, listen to this. I have something to be proud of and happy about too.

Mrs. Linde: I'm sure you do. But what do you mean?

Nora: Keep your voice down. If Torvald were to overhear! He can't find out, not under any circumstances. No one in the world must know, Kristine, except you.

Mrs. Linde: But what is it?

Nora: Come here. (*Pulls her down on the sofa beside her.*) Now I'll show you that I too have something to be proud and happy about. I'm the one who saved Torvald's life.

Mrs. Linde: Saved? How?

Nora: I told you about our trip to Italy. Torvald would never have recovered if he hadn't gone there—

Mrs. Linde: Yes, but your father gave you the money you needed.

Nora (smiling): Yes, that's what Torvald thinks, along with everybody else, but—

Mrs. Linde: But—

Nora: Papa didn't give us a penny. I was the one who raised the money.

Mrs. Linde: You? That huge amount?

Nora: That's right, four thousand, eight hundred kroner. What do you think of that?

Mrs. Linde: But, Nora, how could you possibly? Did you win the lottery?

Nora (disdainfully): The lottery? That wouldn't have been any accomplishment.

Mrs. Linde: But where did you get it from, then?

Nora (humming and smiling with an air of mystery): Hm, hm! Ha!

Mrs. Linde: Because you couldn't have borrowed it.

Nora: Couldn't I? Why not?

Mrs. Linde: No, a wife can't borrow money without her husband's consent.

Nora (tossing her head): Oh, if it's a wife with a head for business, a wife who has the
brains to be a little clever—

Mrs. Linde: I don't understand this at all, Nora.

Nora: There's no reason why you should. I never said I'd borrowed the money.
Maybe I got it some other way. (*Lies back on the sofa.*) Maybe I got it from an
admirer. When a woman's as pretty as I am—

Mrs. Linde: You're crazy.

Nora: Now, you know you're dying of curiosity, Kristine.

Mrs. Linde: Listen to me, Nora dear. Have you done something rash?

Nora (sits up straight): Is it rash to save your husband's life?

Mrs. Linde: I think it's rash, without his knowledge, to—

Nora: But it was absolutely necessary that he not know! My goodness, can't you understand that? It was necessary he have no idea how sick he was. The doctors
came to *me* and said his life was in danger and the only thing that could save him
was to live in the south. Don't you think I tried first to get him to do it as if it was
for me? I told him how much I would love to travel abroad like other young
wives. I tried tears and pleading with him. I told him he should remember the
condition I was in, and that he should be kind and indulgent to me. I even
hinted that he might take out a loan. That almost made him mad, Kristine. He
said I was thoughtless, and that it was his duty as my husband not to indulge me
in my "whims and caprices," as I believe he called them. All right, I thought, you
need to be saved. And that was how I came to think up a way out of the mess—

Mrs. Linde: And your husband never found out from your father that the money
hadn't come from him?

Nora: No, never. Papa died just then. I'd meant to let him in on the secret and beg
him never to reveal it. But he was so sick. Unfortunately, there never was any
need to tell him.

Mrs. Linde: And since then you've never told your secret to your husband?

Nora: Good heavens, no! How could you think I would? A man with such strong
opinions about these things! Besides, how painful and humiliating it would be
for Torvald, with his masculine pride, to know that he owed me anything! It
would completely upset the balance of our relationship. Our beautiful happy
home would never be the same.

Mrs. Linde: Are you never going to tell him about it?

Nora (*meditatively, and with a half smile*): Yes, someday, maybe, in many years, when I'm not as pretty as I am now. Don't laugh at me! I mean, of course, when Torvald is no longer as devoted to me as he is now, when he's grown tired of my dancing and dressing up and reciting. Then it may be a good thing to have something in reserve—(*Breaking off.*) What nonsense! That time will never come. Now, what do you think of my great secret, Kristine? Do you still think I'm useless? And the fact is, this whole situation has caused me a lot of worry. It hasn't been easy for me to make my payments on time. I can tell you that there's something in business that's called quarterly interest, and something else called installment payments, and it's always so terribly difficult to keep up with them. I've had to save a little here and there, wherever I could, you understand. I haven't been able to put much aside from my housekeeping money, because Torvald has to live well. And I couldn't let my children be shabbily dressed. I feel I have to spend everything he gives me for them, the sweet little darlings!

Mrs. Linde: So it's all had to come out of your own allowance, poor Nora?

Nora: Of course. Besides, I was the one responsible for it. Whenever Torvald has given me money for new dresses and things like that, I've never spent more than half of it. I've always bought the simplest and cheapest things. Thank heaven, any clothes look good on me, and so Torvald's never noticed anything. But it was often very hard on me, Kristine, because it is delightful to be really well dressed, isn't it?

Mrs. Linde: I suppose so.

Nora: Well, then I've found other ways of earning money. Last winter I was lucky enough to get a lot of copying to do, so I locked myself up and sat writing every evening until late into the night. A lot of the time I was desperately tired, but all the same it was a tremendous pleasure to sit there working and earning money. It was like being a man.

Mrs. Linde: How much have you been able to pay off that way?

Nora: I can't tell you exactly. You see, it's very hard to keep a strict account of a business matter like that. I only know that I've paid out every penny I could scrape together. Many a time I was at my wits' end. (*Smiles.*) Then I used to sit here and imagine that a rich old gentleman had fallen in love with me—

Mrs. Linde: What! Who was it?

Nora: Oh, be quiet! That he had died, and that when his will was opened it said, in great big letters: "The lovely Mrs. Nora Helmer is to have everything I own paid over to her immediately in cash."

Mrs. Linde: But, my dear Nora, who could the man be?

Nora: Good gracious, can't you understand? There wasn't any old gentleman. It was only something that I used to sit here and imagine, when I couldn't think of any way of getting money. But it's all right now. The tiresome old gent can stay right where he is, as far as I'm concerned. I don't care about him or his will either, because now I'm worry-free. (*Jumps up.*) My goodness, it's delightful to think of, Kristine! Worry-free! To be able to have no worries, no worries at all! To be able to play and romp with the children! To be able to keep the house beautifully and have everything just the way Torvald likes it! And, just think of it, soon the spring will come and the big blue sky! Maybe we can take a little trip. Maybe I can see the sea again! Oh, it's a wonderful thing to be alive and happy.

(*A bell rings in the hall.*)

Mrs. Linde (*rising*): There's the bell. Perhaps I should be going.

Nora: No, don't go. No one will come in here. It's sure to be for Torvald.

Servant (*at the hall door*): Excuse me, ma'am. There's a gentleman to see the master, and as the doctor is still with him—

Nora: Who is it?

Krogstad (*at the door*): It's me, Mrs. Helmer.

(*Mrs. Linde starts, trembles, and turns toward the window.*)

Nora (*takes a step toward him, and speaks in a strained, low voice*): You? What is it? What do you want to see my husband for?

Krogstad: Bank business, in a way. I have a small position in the bank, and I hear your husband is going to be our boss now—

Nora: Then it's—

Krogstad: Nothing but dry business matters, Mrs. Helmer, that's all.

Nora: Then please go into the study.

(*She bows indifferently to him and shuts the door into the hall, then comes back and makes up the fire in the stove.*)

Mrs. Linde: Nora, who was that man?

Nora: A lawyer. His name is Krogstad.

Mrs. Linde: Then it really was him.

Nora: Do you know the man?

Mrs. Linde: I used to, many years ago. At one time he was a law clerk in our town.

Nora: That's right, he was.

Mrs. Linde: How much he's changed.

Nora: He had a very unhappy marriage.

Mrs. Linde: He's a widower now, isn't he?

Nora: With several children. There, now it's really caught. (*Shuts the door of the stove and moves the rocking chair aside.*)

Mrs. Linde: They say he's mixed up in a lot of questionable business.

Nora: Really? Maybe he is. I don't know anything about it. But let's not talk about business. It's so tiresome.

Doctor Rank (*comes out of Helmer's study. Before he shuts the door he calls to Helmer*): No, my dear fellow, I won't disturb you. I'd rather go in and talk to your wife for a little while.

(*Shuts the door and sees Mrs. Linde.*)

I beg your pardon. I'm afraid I'm in the way here too.

Nora: No, not at all. (*Introducing him:*) Doctor Rank, Mrs. Linde.

Rank: I've often heard that name in this house. I think I passed you on the stairs when I arrived, Mrs. Linde?

Mrs. Linde: Yes, I take stairs very slowly. I can't manage them very well.

Rank: Oh, some small internal problem?

Mrs. Linde: No, it's just that I've been overworking myself.

Rank: Is that all? Then I suppose you've come to town to get some rest by sampling our social life.

Mrs. Linde: I've come to look for work.

Rank: Is that a good cure for overwork?

Mrs. Linde: One has to live, Doctor Rank.

Rank: Yes, that seems to be the general opinion.

Nora: Now, now, Doctor Rank, you know you want to live.

Rank: Of course I do. However miserable I may feel, I want to prolong the agony for as long as possible. All my patients are the same way. And so are those who are morally sick. In fact, one of them, and a bad case too, is at this very moment inside with Helmer—

Mrs. Linde (sadly): Ah!

Nora: Who are you talking about?

Rank: A lawyer by the name of Krogstad, a fellow you don't know at all. He's a completely worthless creature, Mrs. Helmer. But even he started out by saying, as if it were a matter of the utmost importance, that he has to live.

Nora: Did he? What did he want to talk to Torvald about?

Rank: I have no idea. All I heard was that it was something about the bank.

Nora: I didn't know this—what's his name—Krogstad had anything to do with the bank.

Rank: Yes, he has some kind of a position there. (*To Mrs. Linde*) I don't know whether you find the same thing in your part of the world, that there are certain people who go around zealously looking to sniff out moral corruption, and, as soon as they find some, they put the person involved in some cushy job where they can keep an eye on him. Meanwhile, the morally healthy ones are left out in the cold.

Mrs. Linde: Still, I think it's the sick who are most in need of being taken care of.

Rank (shrugging his shoulders): Well, there you have it. That's the attitude that's turning society into a hospital.

(*Nora, who has been absorbed in her thoughts, breaks out into smothered laughter and claps her hands.*)

Rank: Why are you laughing at that? Do you have any idea what society really is?

Nora: What do I care about your boring society? I'm laughing at something else, something very funny. Tell me, Doctor Rank, are all the people who work in the bank dependent on Torvald now?

Rank: That's what's so funny?

Nora (smiling and humming): That's my business! (*Walking around the room.*) It's just wonderful to think that we have—that Torvald has—so much power over so many people. (*Takes the bag out of her pocket.*) Doctor Rank, what do you say to a macaroon?

Rank: Macaroons? I thought they were forbidden here.

Nora: Yes, but these are some Kristine gave me.

Mrs. Linde: What! Me?

Nora: Oh, well, don't be upset! How could you know that Torvald had forbidden them? I have to tell you, he's afraid they'll ruin my teeth. But so what? Once in a while, that's all right, isn't it, Doctor Rank? With your permission! (*Puts a macaroon into his mouth.*) You have to have one too, Kristine. And I'll have one, just a little one—or no more than two. (*Walking around.*) I am tremendously happy. There's just one thing in the world now that I would dearly love to do.

Rank: Well, what is it?

Nora: It's something I would dearly love to say, if Torvald could hear me.

Rank: Well, why can't you say it?

Nora: No, I don't dare. It's too shocking.

Mrs. Linde: Shocking?

Rank: Well then, I'd advise you not to say it. Still, in front of us you might risk it. What is it you'd so much like to say if Torvald could hear you?

Nora: I would just love to say—"Well, I'll be damned!"

Rank: Are you crazy?

Mrs. Linde: Nora, dear!

Rank: Here he is. Say it!

Nora (*hiding the bag*): Shh, shh, shh!

(*Helmer comes out of his room, with his coat over his arm and his hat in his hand.*)

Nora: Well, Torvald dear, did you get rid of him?

Helmer: Yes, he just left.

Nora: Let me introduce you. This is Kristine. She's just arrived in town.

Helmer: Kristine? I'm sorry, but I don't know any—

Nora: Mrs. Linde, dear, Kristine Linde.

Helmer: Oh, of course. A school friend of my wife's, I believe?

Mrs. Linde: Yes, we knew each other back then.

Nora: And just think, she's come all this way in order to see you.

Helmer: What do you mean?

Mrs. Linde: No, really, I—

Nora: Kristine is extremely good at bookkeeping, and she's very eager to work for some talented man, so she can perfect her skills—

Helmer: Very sensible, Mrs. Linde.

Nora: And when she heard that you'd been named manager of the bank—the news was sent by telegraph, you know—she traveled here as quickly as she could. Torvald, I'm sure you'll be able to do something for Kristine, for my sake, won't you?

Helmer: Well, it's not completely out of the question. I expect that you're a widow, Mrs. Linde?

Mrs. Linde: Yes.

Helmer: And you've had some bookkeeping experience?

Mrs. Linde: Yes, a fair amount.

Helmer: Ah! Well, there's a very good chance that I'll be able to find something for you—

Nora (*clapping her hands*): What did I tell you? What did I tell you?

Helmer: You've just come at a lucky moment, Mrs. Linde.

Mrs. Linde: How can I thank you?

Helmer: There's no need. (*Puts on his coat.*) But now you must excuse me—

Rank: Wait a minute. I'll come with you. (*Brings his fur coat from the hall and warms it at the fire.*)

Nora: Don't be long, Torvald dear.

Helmer: About an hour, that's all.

Nora: Are you leaving too, Kristine?

Mrs. Linde (putting on her cloak): Yes, I have to go and look for a place to stay.

Helmer: Oh, well then, we can walk down the street together.

Nora (helping her): It's too bad we're so short of space here. I'm afraid it's impossible for us—

Mrs. Linde: Please don't even think of it! Goodbye, Nora dear, and many thanks.

Nora: Goodbye for now. Of course you'll come back this evening. And you too, Dr. Rank. What do you say? If you're feeling up to it? Oh, you have to be! Wrap yourself up warmly.

(They go to the door all talking together. Children's voices are heard on the staircase.)

Nora: There they are! There they are!

(She runs to open the door. The nursemaid comes in with the children.)

Come in! Come in! *(Stoops and kisses them.)* Oh, you sweet blessings! Look at them, Kristine! Aren't they darlings?

Rank: Let's not stand here in the draft.

Helmer: Come along, Mrs. Linde. Only a mother will be able to stand it in here now!

(Rank, Helmer, and Mrs. Linde go downstairs. The Nursemaid comes forward with the children. Nora shuts the hall door.)

Nora: How fresh and healthy you look! Cheeks as red as apples and roses. *(The children all talk at once while she speaks to them.)* Did you have a lot of fun? That's wonderful! What, you pulled Emmy and Bob on the sled? Both at once? That was really something. You *are* a clever boy, Ivar. Let me take her for a little, Anne Marie. My sweet little baby doll! *(Takes the baby from the maid and dances her up and down.)* Yes, yes, mother will dance with Bob too. What! Have you been throwing snowballs? I wish I'd been there too! No, no, I'll take their things off, Anne Marie, please let me do it, it's such fun. Go inside now, you look half frozen. There's some hot coffee for you on the stove.

(The Nursemaid goes into the room on the left. Nora takes off the children's things and throws them around, while they all talk to her at once.)

Nora: Really! Did a big dog run after you? But it didn't bite you? No, dogs don't bite nice little dolly children. You mustn't look at the packages, Ivar. What are they? Oh, I'll bet you'd like to know. No, no, it's something boring! Come on, let's play a game! What should we play? Hide and seek? Yes, we'll play hide and seek. Bob will hide first. You want me to hide? All right, I'll hide first.

(She and the children laugh and shout, and romp in and out of the room. At last Nora hides under the table. The children rush in and out looking for her, but they don't see her. They hear her smothered laughter, run to the table, lift up the cloth and find her. Shouts of laughter. She crawls forward and pretends to scare them. More laughter. Meanwhile there has been a knock at the hall door, but none of them has noticed it. The door is opened halfway and Krogstad appears. He waits for a little while. The game goes on.)

Krogstad: Excuse me, Mrs. Helmer.

Nora (with a stifled cry, turns round and gets up onto her knees): Oh! What do you want?

Krogstad: Excuse me, the outside door was open. I suppose someone forgot to shut it.

Nora (rising): My husband is out, Mr. Krogstad.

Krogstad: I know that.

Nora: What do you want here, then?

Krogstad: A word with you.

Nora: With me? (*To the children, gently.*) Go inside to Anne Marie. What? No, the strange man won't hurt Mother. When he's gone we'll play another game. (*She takes the children into the room on the left, and shuts the door after them.*) You want to speak to me?

Krogstad: Yes, I do.

Nora: Today? It isn't the first of the month yet.

Krogstad: No, it's Christmas Eve, and it's up to you what kind of Christmas you're going to have.

Nora: What do you mean? Today it's absolutely impossible for me—

Krogstad: We won't talk about that until later on. This is something else. I presume you can spare me a moment?

Nora: Yes, yes, I can. Although . . .

Krogstad: Good. I was in Olsen's restaurant and I saw your husband going down the street—

Nora: Yes?

Krogstad: With a lady.

Nora: So?

Krogstad: May I be so bold as to ask if it was a Mrs. Linde?

Nora: It was.

Krogstad: Just arrived in town?

Nora: Yes, today.

Krogstad: She's a very good friend of yours, isn't she?

Nora: She is. But I don't see—

Krogstad: I knew her too, once upon a time.

Nora: I'm aware of that.

Krogstad: Are you? So you know all about it. I thought so. Then I can ask you, without beating around the bush. Is Mrs. Linde going to work in the bank?

Nora: What right do you have to question me, Mr. Krogstad? You're one of my husband's employees. But since you ask, I'll tell you. Yes, Mrs. Linde is going to work in the bank. And I'm the one who spoke up for her, Mr. Krogstad. So now you know.

Krogstad: So I was right, then.

Nora (walking up and down the stage): Sometimes one has a tiny little bit of influence, I should hope. Just because I'm a woman, it doesn't necessarily follow that—You know, when somebody's in a subordinate position, Mr. Krogstad, they should really be careful to avoid offending anyone who—who—

Krogstad: Who has influence?

Nora: Exactly.

Krogstad (changing his tone): Mrs. Helmer, may I ask you to use *your* influence on my behalf?

Nora: What? What do you mean?

Krogstad: Will you be kind enough to see to it that I'm allowed to keep my subordinate position in the bank?

Nora: What do you mean by that? Who's threatening to take your job away from you?

Krogstad: Oh, there's no need to keep up the pretence of ignorance. I can understand that your friend isn't very anxious to expose herself to the chance of rubbing shoulders with me. And now I realize exactly who I have to thank for pushing me out.

Nora: But I swear to you—

Krogstad: Yes, yes. But, to get right to the point, there's still time to prevent it, and I would advise you to use your influence to do so.

Nora: But, Mr. Krogstad, I have no influence.

Krogstad: Oh no? Didn't you yourself just say—

Nora: Well, obviously, I didn't mean for you to take it that way. Me? What would make you think I have that kind of influence with my husband?

Krogstad: Oh, I've known your husband since our school days. I don't suppose he's any more unpersuadable than other husbands.

Nora: If you're going to talk disrespectfully about my husband, I'll have to ask you to leave my house.

Krogstad: Bold talk, Mrs. Helmer.

Nora: I'm not afraid of you anymore. When the New Year comes, I'll soon be free of the whole thing.

Krogstad (controlling himself): Listen to me, Mrs. Helmer. If I have to, I'm ready to fight for my little job in the bank as if I were fighting for my life.

Nora: So it seems.

Krogstad: It's not just for the sake of the money. In fact, that matters the least to me. There's another reason. Well, I might as well tell you. Here's my situation. I suppose, like everybody else, you know that many years ago I did something pretty foolish.

Nora: I think I heard something about it.

Krogstad: It never got as far as the courtroom, but every door seemed closed to me after that. So I got involved in the business that you know about. I had to do something, and, honestly, I think there are many worse than me. But now I have to get myself free of all that. My sons are growing up. For their sake I have to try to win back as much respect as I can in this town. The job in the bank was like the first step up for me, and now your husband is going to kick me downstairs back into the mud.

Nora: But you have to believe me, Mr. Krogstad, it's not in my power to help you at all.

Krogstad: Then it's because you don't want to. But I have ways of making you.

Nora: You don't mean you'll tell my husband I owe you money?

Krogstad: Hm! And what if I did tell him?

Nora: That would be a terrible thing for you to do. (*Sobbing.*) To think he would learn my secret, which has been my pride and joy, in such an ugly, clumsy way— that he would learn it from you! And it would put me in a horribly uncomfortable position—

Krogstad: Just uncomfortable?

Nora (impetuously): Well, go ahead and do it, then! And it'll be so much the worse for you. My husband will see for himself how vile you are, and then you'll lose your job for sure.

Krogstad: I asked you if it's just an uncomfortable situation at home that you're afraid of.

Nora: If my husband does find out about it, of course he'll immediately pay you what I still owe, and then we'll be through with you once and for all.

Krogstad (coming a step closer): Listen to me, Mrs. Helmer. Either you have a very bad memory or you don't know much about business. I can see I'm going to have to remind you of a few details.

Nora: What do you mean?

Krogstad: When your husband was sick, you came to me to borrow four thousand, eight hundred kroner.

Nora: I didn't know anyone else to go to.

Krogstad: I promised to get you that amount—

Nora: Yes, and you did so.

Krogstad: I promised to get you that amount, on certain conditions. You were so preoccupied with your husband's illness, and you were so anxious to get the money for your trip, that you seem to have paid no attention to the conditions of our bargain. So it won't be out of place for me to remind you of them. Now, I promised to get the money on the security of a note which I drew up.

Nora: Yes, and which I signed.

Krogstad: Good. But underneath your signature there were a few lines naming your father as a co-signer who guaranteed the repayment of the loan. Your father was supposed to sign that part.

Nora: Supposed to? He did sign it.

Krogstad: I had left the date blank. That was because your father was supposed to fill in the date when he signed the paper. Do you remember that?

Nora: Yes, I think I remember. . . .

Krogstad: Then I gave you the note to mail to your father. Isn't that so?

Nora: Yes.

Krogstad: And obviously you mailed it right away, because five or six days later you brought me the note with your father's signature. And then I gave you the money.

Nora: Well, haven't I been paying it back regularly?

Krogstad: Fairly regularly, yes. But, to get back to the point, that must have been a very difficult time for you, Mrs. Helmer.

Nora: Yes, it was.

Krogstad: Your father was very sick, wasn't he?

Nora: He was very near the end.

Krogstad: And he died soon after?

Nora: Yes.

Krogstad: Tell me, Mrs. Helmer, can you by any chance remember what day your father died? On what day of the month, I mean.

Nora: Papa died on the 29th of September.

Krogstad: That's right. I looked it up myself. And, since that is the case, there's something extremely peculiar (*taking a piece of paper from his pocket*) that I can't account for.

Nora: Peculiar in what way? I don't know—

Krogstad: The peculiar thing, Mrs. Helmer, is the fact that your father signed this note three days after he died.

Nora: What do you mean? I don't understand—

Krogstad: Your father died on the 29th of September. But, look here. Your father dated his signature the 2nd of October. It is mighty peculiar, isn't it? (*Nora is silent.*) Can you explain it to me? (*Nora is still silent.*) And what's just as peculiar is that the words "October 2," as well as the year, are not in your father's handwriting, but in someone else's, which I think I recognize. Well, of course it can all be explained. Your father might have forgotten to date his signature, and someone else might have filled in the date before they knew that he had died. There's no harm in that. It all depends on the signature, and that's genuine, isn't it, Mrs. Helmer? It was your father himself who signed his name here?

Nora (after a short pause, lifts her head up and looks defiantly at him): No, it wasn't. I'm the one who wrote Papa's name.

Krogstad: Are you aware that you're making a very serious confession?

Nora: How so? You'll get your money soon.

Krogstad: Let me ask you something. Why didn't you send the paper to your father?

Nora: It was out of the question. Papa was too sick. If I had asked him to sign something, I'd have had to tell him what the money was for, and when he was so sick himself I couldn't tell him that my husband's life was in danger. It was out of the question.

Krogstad: It would have been better for you if you'd given up your trip abroad.

Nora: No, that was impossible. That trip was to save my husband's life. I couldn't give that up.

Krogstad: But didn't it ever occur to you that you were committing a fraud against me?

Nora: I couldn't take that into account. I didn't trouble myself about you at all. I couldn't stand you, because you put so many heartless difficulties in my way, even though you knew how seriously ill my husband was.

Krogstad: Mrs. Helmer, you evidently don't realize clearly what you're guilty of. But, believe me, my one mistake, which cost me my whole reputation, was nothing more and nothing worse than what you did.

Nora: You? You expect me to believe that you were brave enough to take a risk to save your wife's life?

Krogstad: The law doesn't care about motives.

Nora: Then the law must be very stupid.

Krogstad: Stupid or not, it's the law that's going to judge you, if I produce this paper in court.

Nora: I don't believe it. Isn't a daughter allowed to spare her dying father anxiety and concern? Isn't a wife allowed to save her husband's life? I don't know much about the law, but I'm sure there must be provisions for things like that. Don't you know anything about such provisions? You seem like a very poor excuse for a lawyer, Mr. Krogstad.

Krogstad: That's as may be. But business, the kind of business you and I have done together—do you think I don't know about that? Fine. Do what you want. But I can assure you of this. If I lose everything all over again, this time you're going down with me. (*He bows, and goes out through the hall.*)

Nora (appears buried in thought for a short time, then tosses her head): Nonsense! He's just trying to scare me! I'm not as naive as he thinks I am. (*Begins to busy herself putting the children's things in order.*) And yet . . . ? No, it's impossible! I did it for love.

Children (in the doorway on the left): Mother, the strange man is gone. He went out through the gate.

Nora: Yes, dears, I know. But don't tell anyone about the strange man. Do you hear me? Not even Papa.

Children: No, Mother. But will you come and play with us again?

Nora: No, no, not just now.

Children: But, Mother, you promised us.

Nora: Yes, but I can't right now. Go inside. I have too much to do. Go inside, my sweet little darlings.

(*She gets them into the room bit by bit and shuts the door on them. Then she sits down on the sofa, takes up a piece of needlework and sews a few stitches, but soon stops.*)

No! (*Throws down the work, gets up, goes to the hall door and calls out.*) Helene! Bring the tree in. (*Goes to the table on the left, opens a drawer, and stops again.*) No, no! It's completely impossible!

Maid (coming in with the tree): Where should I put it, ma'am?

Nora: Here, in the middle of the floor.

Maid: Do you need anything else?

Nora: No, thank you. I have everything I want.

(*Exit Maid.*)

Nora (begins decorating the tree): A candle here, and flowers here. That horrible man! It's all nonsense, there's nothing wrong. The tree is going to be magnificent! I'll do everything I can think of to make you happy, Torvald! I'll sing for you, dance for you—

(*Helmer comes in with some papers under his arm.*)

Oh! You're back already?

Helmer: Yes. Has anyone been here?

Nora: Here? No.

Helmer: That's strange. I saw Krogstad going out the gate.

Nora: You did? Oh yes, I forgot, Krogstad was here for a moment.

Helmer: Nora, I can tell from the way you're acting that he was here begging you to put in a good word for him.

Nora: Yes, he was.

Helmer: And you were supposed to pretend it was all your idea and not tell me that he'd been here to see you. Didn't he beg you to do that too?

Nora: Yes, Torvald, but—

Helmer: Nora, Nora, to think that you'd be a party to that sort of thing! To have any kind of conversation with a man like that, and promise him anything at all? And to lie to me in the bargain?

Nora: Lie?

Helmer: Didn't you tell me no one had been here? (*Shakes his finger at her.*) My little songbird must never do that again. A songbird must have a clean beak to chirp with. No false notes! (*Puts his arm round her waist.*) That's true, isn't it? Yes, I'm sure it is. (*Lets her go.*) We won't mention this again. (*Sits down by the stove.*) How warm and cozy it is here! (*Turns over his papers.*)

Nora (*after a short pause, during which she busies herself with the Christmas tree*): Torvald!

Helmer: Yes?

Nora: I'm really looking forward to the masquerade ball at the Stenborgs' the day after tomorrow.

Helmer: And I'm really curious to see what you're going to surprise me with.

Nora: Oh, it was very silly of me to want to do that.

Helmer: What do you mean?

Nora: I can't come up with anything good. Everything I think of seems so stupid and pointless.

Helmer: So my little Nora finally admits that?

Nora (*standing behind his chair with her arms on the back of it*): Are you very busy, Torvald?

Helmer: Well . . .

Nora: What are all those papers?

Helmer: Bank business.

Nora: Already?

Helmer: I've gotten the authority from the retiring manager to reorganize the work procedures and make the necessary personnel changes. I need to take care of it during Christmas week, so as to have everything in place for the new year.

Nora: Then that was why this poor Krogstad—

Helmer: Hm!

Nora (*leans against the back of his chair and strokes his hair*): If you weren't so busy, I would have asked you for a huge favor, Torvald.

Helmer: What favor? Tell me.

Nora: No one has such good taste as you. And I really want to look nice at the fancy-dress ball. Torvald, couldn't you take me in hand and decide what I should go as and what kind of costume I should wear?

Helmer: Aha! So my obstinate little woman has to get someone to come to her rescue?

Nora: Yes, Torvald, I can't get along at all without your help.

Helmer: All right, I'll think it over. I'm sure we'll come up with something.

Nora: That's so nice of you. (*Goes to the Christmas tree. A short pause.*) How pretty the red flowers look. But, tell me, was it really something very bad that this Krogstad was guilty of?

Helmer: He forged someone's name. Do you have any idea what that means?

Nora: Isn't it possible that he was forced to do it by necessity?

Helmer: Yes. Or, the way it is in so many cases, by foolishness. I'm not so heartless that I'd absolutely condemn a man because of one mistake like that.

Nora: No, you wouldn't, would you, Torvald?

Helmer: Many a man has been able to rehabilitate himself, if he's openly admitted his guilt and taken his punishment.

Nora: Punishment?

Helmer: But Krogstad didn't do that. He wriggled out of it with lies and trickery, and that's what completely undermined his moral character.

Nora: But do you think that that would—

Helmer: Just think how a guilty man like that has to lie and act like a hypocrite with everyone, how he has to wear a mask in front of the people closest to him, even with his own wife and children. And the children. That's the most terrible part of it all, Nora.

Nora: How so?

Helmer: Because an atmosphere of lies infects and poisons the whole life of a home. Every breath the children take in a house like that is full of the germs of moral corruption.

Nora (coming closer to him): Are you sure of that?

Helmer: My dear, I've seen it many times in my legal career. Almost everyone who's gone wrong at a young age had a dishonest mother.

Nora: Why only the mother?

Helmer: It usually seems to be the mother's influence, though naturally a bad father would have the same result. Every lawyer knows this. This Krogstad, now, has been systematically poisoning his own children with lies and deceit. That's why I say he's lost all moral character. (*Holds out his hands to her.*) And that's why my sweet little Nora must promise me not to plead his cause. Give me your hand on it. Come now, what's this? Give me your hand. There, that's settled. Believe me, it would be impossible for me to work with him. It literally makes me feel physically ill to be around people like that.

Nora (takes her hand out of his and goes to the opposite side of the Christmas tree): How hot it is in here! And I have so much to do.

Helmer (getting up and putting his papers in order): Yes, and I have to try to read through some of these before dinner. And I have to think about your costume, too. And it's just possible I'll have something wrapped in gold paper to hang up on the tree. (*Puts his hand on her head.*) My precious little songbird! (*He goes into his study and closes the door behind him.*)

Nora (after a pause, whispers): No, no, it's not true. It's impossible. It has to be impossible.

(*The nursemaid opens the door on the left.*)

Nursemaid: The little ones are begging so hard to be allowed to come in to see Mama.

Nora: No, no, no! Don't let them come in to me! You stay with them, Anne Marie.

Nursemaid: Very well, ma'am. (*Shuts the door.*)

Nora (pale with terror): Corrupt my little children? Poison my home? (*A short pause. Then she tosses her head.*) It's not true. It can't possibly be true.

ACT II

The same scene. The Christmas tree is in the corner by the piano, stripped of its ornaments and with burnt-down candle-ends on its disheveled branches. Nora's coat and hat are lying on the sofa. She is alone in the room, walking around uneasily. She stops by the sofa and picks up her coat.

Nora (drops her coat): Someone's coming! (*Goes to the door and listens.*) No, there's no one there. Of course, no one will come today. It's Christmas Day. And not tomorrow either. But maybe . . . (*opens the door and looks out*) No, nothing in the mailbox. It's empty. (*Comes forward.*) What nonsense! Of course he can't be serious about it. A thing like that couldn't happen. It's impossible. I have three little children.

(*Enter the nursemaid Anne Marie from the room on the left, carrying a big cardboard box.*)

Nursemaid: I finally found the box with the costume.

Nora: Thank you. Put it on the table.

Nursemaid (doing so): But it really needs to be mended.

Nora: I'd like to tear it into a hundred thousand pieces.

Nursemaid: What an idea! It can easily be fixed up. All you need is a little patience.

Nora: Yes, I'll go get Mrs. Linde to come and help me with it.

Nursemaid: What, going out again? In this horrible weather? You'll catch cold, Miss Nora, and make yourself sick.

Nora: Well, worse things than that might happen. How are the children?

Nursemaid: The poor little ones are playing with their Christmas presents, but—

Nora: Do they ask for me much?

Nursemaid: You see, they're so used to having their Mama with them.

Nora: Yes, but, Anne Marie, I won't be able to spend as much time with them now as I did before.

Nursemaid: Oh well, young children quickly get used to anything.

Nora: Do you think so? Do you think they'd forget their mother if she went away for good?

Nursemaid: Good heavens! Went away for good?

Nora: Anne Marie, I want you to tell me something I've often wondered about. How could you have the heart to let your own child be raised by strangers?

Nursemaid: I had to, if I wanted to be little Nora's nursemaid.

Nora: Yes, but how could you agree to it?

Nursemaid: What, when I was going to get such a good situation out of it? A poor girl who's gotten herself in trouble should be glad to. Besides, that worthless man didn't do a single thing for me.

Nora: But I suppose your daughter has completely forgotten you.

Nursemaid: No, she hasn't, not at all. She wrote to me when she was confirmed, and again when she got married.

Nora (putting her arms round her neck): Dear old Anne Marie, you were such a good mother to me when I was little.

Nursemaid: Poor little Nora, you had no other mother but me.

Nora: And if my little ones had no other mother, I'm sure that you would—What nonsense I'm talking! (*Opens the box.*) Go in and see to them. Now I have to . . . You'll see how lovely I'll look tomorrow.

Nursemaid: I'm sure there'll be no one at the ball as lovely as you, Miss Nora.

(*Goes into the room on the left.*)

Nora (begins to unpack the box, but soon pushes it away from her): If only I dared to go out. If only no one would come. If only I could be sure nothing would happen here in the meantime. What nonsense! No one's going to come. I just have to stop thinking about it. This muff needs to be brushed. What beautiful, beautiful gloves! Stop thinking about it, stop thinking about it! One, two, three, four, five, six—(*Screams.*) Aaah! Somebody *is* coming—(*Makes a movement towards the door, but stands in hesitation.*)

(*Enter Mrs. Linde from the hall, where she has taken off her coat and hat.*)

Nora: Oh, it's you, Kristine. There's no one else out in the hall, is there? How good of you to come!

Mrs. Linde: I heard you came by asking for me.

Nora: Yes, I was passing by. As a matter of fact, it's something you could help me with. Let's sit down here on the sofa. Listen, tomorrow evening there's going to be a fancy-dress ball at the Stenborgs'—they live upstairs from us—and Torvald wants me to go as a Neapolitan fisher-girl and dance the tarantella. I learned it when we were at Capri.

Mrs. Linde: I see. You're going to give them the whole show.

Nora: Yes, Torvald wants me to. Look, here's the dress. Torvald had it made for me there, but now it's all so torn, and I don't have any idea—

Mrs. Linde: We can easily fix that. Some of the trim has just come loose here and there. Do you have a needle and thread? That's all we need.

Nora: This is so nice of you.

Mrs. Linde (*sewing*): So you're going to be dressed up tomorrow, Nora. I'll tell you what. I'll stop by for a moment so I can see you in your finery. Oh, meanwhile I've completely forgotten to thank you for a delightful evening last night.

Nora (*gets up, and crosses the stage*): Well, I didn't think last night was as pleasant as usual. You should have come to town a little earlier, Kristine. Torvald really knows how to make a home pleasant and attractive.

Mrs. Linde: And so do you, if you ask me. You're not your father's daughter for nothing. But tell me, is Doctor Rank always as depressed as he was yesterday?

Nora: No, yesterday it was especially noticeable. But you have to understand that he has a very serious disease. He has tuberculosis of the spine, poor creature. His father was a horrible man who always had mistresses, and that's why his son has been sickly since childhood, if you know what I mean.

Mrs. Linde (*dropping her sewing*): But, my dear Nora, how do you know anything about such things?

Nora (*walking around the room*): Pooh! When you have three children, you get visits now and then from—from married women, who know something about medical matters, and they talk about one thing and another.

Mrs. Linde (*goes on sewing. A short silence*): Does Doctor Rank come here every day?

Nora: Every day, like clockwork. He's Torvald's best friend, and a great friend of mine too. He's just like one of the family.

Mrs. Linde: But tell me, is he really sincere? I mean, isn't he the kind of man who tends to play up to people?

Nora: No, not at all. What makes you think that?

Mrs. Linde: When you introduced him to me yesterday, he told me he'd often heard my name mentioned in this house, but later I could see that your husband didn't have the slightest idea who I was. So how could Doctor Rank—?

Nora: That's true, Kristine. Torvald is so ridiculously fond of me that he wants me completely to himself, as he says. At first he used to seem almost jealous if I even mentioned any of my friends back home, so naturally I stopped talking about them to him. But I often talk about things like that with Doctor Rank, because he likes hearing about them.

Mrs. Linde: Listen to me, Nora. You're still like a child in a lot of ways, and I'm older than you and more experienced. So pay attention. You'd better stop all this with Doctor Rank.

Nora: Stop all what?

Mrs. Linde: Two things, I think. Yesterday you talked some nonsense about a rich admirer who was going to leave you his money—

Nora: An admirer who doesn't exist, unfortunately! But so what?

Mrs. Linde: Is Doctor Rank a wealthy man?

Nora: Yes, he is.

Mrs. Linde: And he has no dependents?

Nora: No, no one. But—

Mrs. Linde: And he comes here every day?

Nora: Yes, I told you he does.

Mrs. Linde: But how can such a well-bred man be so tactless?

Nora: I don't understand what you mean.

Mrs. Linde: Don't try to play dumb, Nora. Do you think I didn't guess who lent you the four thousand, eight hundred kroner?

Nora: Are you out of your mind? How can you even think that? A friend of ours, who comes here every day! Don't you realize what an incredibly awkward position that would put me in?

Mrs. Linde: Then he's really not the one?

Nora: Absolutely not. It would never have come into my head for one second. Besides, he had nothing to lend back then. He inherited his money later on.

Mrs. Linde: Well, I think that was lucky for you, my dear Nora.

Nora: No, it would never have crossed my mind to ask Doctor Rank. Although I'm sure that if I had asked him—

Mrs. Linde: But of course you won't.

Nora: Of course not. I have no reason to think I could possibly need to. But I'm absolutely certain that if I told Doctor Rank—

Mrs. Linde: Behind your husband's back?

Nora: I have to finish up with the other one, and that'll be behind his back too. I've got to wash my hands of him.

Mrs. Linde: Yes, that's what I told you yesterday, but—

Nora (walking up and down): A man can take care of these things so much more easily than a woman.

Mrs. Linde: If he's your husband, yes.

Nora: Nonsense! *(Standing still.)* When you pay off a debt you get your note back, don't you?

Mrs. Linde: Yes, of course.

Nora: And you can tear it into a hundred thousand pieces and burn up the filthy, nasty piece of paper!

Mrs. Linde (stares at her, puts down her sewing and gets up slowly): Nora, you're hiding something from me.

Nora: You can tell by looking at me?

Mrs. Linde: Something's happened to you since yesterday morning. Nora, what is it?

Nora (going nearer to her): Kristine! (*Listens.*) Shh! I hear Torvald. He's come home. Would you mind going in to the children's room for a little while? Torvald can't stand to see all this sewing going on. You can get Anne Marie to help you.

Mrs. Linde (gathering some of the things together): All right, but I'm not leaving this house until we've talked this thing through.

(*She goes into the room on the left, as Helmer comes in from the hall.*)

Nora (going up to Helmer): I've missed you so much, Torvald dear.

Helmer: Was that the seamstress?

Nora: No, it was Kristine. She's helping me fix up my dress. You'll see how nice I'm going to look.

Helmer: Wasn't that a good idea of mine, now?

Nora: Wonderful! But don't you think it's nice of me, too, to do what you said?

Helmer: Nice, because you do what your husband tells you to? Go on, you silly little thing, I am sure you didn't mean it like that. But I'll stay out of your way. I imagine you'll be trying on your dress.

Nora: I suppose you're going to do some work.

Helmer: Yes. (*Shows her a stack of papers.*) Look at that. I've just been at the bank. (*Turns to go into his room.*)

Nora: Torvald.

Helmer: Yes?

Nora: If your little squirrel were to ask you for something in a very, very charming way—

Helmer: Well?

Nora: Would you do it?

Helmer: I'd have to know what it is, first.

Nora: Your squirrel would run around and do all her tricks if you would be really nice and do what she wants.

Helmer: Speak plainly.

Nora: Your skylark would chirp her beautiful song in every room—

Helmer: Well, my skylark does that anyhow.

Nora: I'd be a little elf and dance in the moonlight for you, Torvald.

Helmer: Nora, you can't be referring to what you talked about this morning.

Nora (moving close to him): Yes, Torvald, I'm really begging you—

Helmer: You really have the nerve to bring that up again?

Nora: Yes, dear, you have to do this for me. You have to let Krogstad keep his job in the bank.

Helmer: My dear Nora, his job is the one that I'm giving to Mrs. Linde.

Nora: Yes, you've been awfully sweet about that. But you could just as easily get rid of somebody else instead of Krogstad.

Helmer: This is just unbelievable stubbornness! Because you decided to foolishly promise that you'd speak up for him, you expect me to—

Nora: That's not the reason, Torvald. It's for your own sake. This man writes for the trashiest newspapers, you've told me so yourself. He can do you an incredible amount of harm. I'm scared to death of him—

Helmer: Oh, I see, it's bad memories that are making you afraid.

Nora: What do you mean?

Helmer: Obviously you're thinking about your father.

Nora: Yes. Yes, of course. You remember what those hateful creatures wrote in the papers about Papa, and how horribly they slandered him. I believe they'd have gotten him fired if the department hadn't sent you over to look into it, and if you hadn't been so kind and helpful to him.

Helmer: My little Nora, there's an important difference between your father and me. His reputation as a public official was not above suspicion. Mine is, and I hope it will continue to be for as long as I hold my office.

Nora: You never can tell what trouble these men might cause. We could be so well off, so snug and happy here in our peaceful home, without a care in the world, you and I and the children, Torvald! That's why I'm begging you to—

Helmer: And the more you plead for him, the more you make it impossible for me to keep him. They already know at the bank that I'm going to fire Krogstad. Do you think I'm going to let them all say that the new manager has changed his mind because his wife said to—

Nora: And what if they did?

Helmer: Right! What does it matter, as long as this stubborn little creature gets her own way! Do you think I'm going to make myself look ridiculous in front of my whole staff, and let people think that I can be pushed around by all sorts of outside influence? That would soon come back to haunt me, you can be sure! And besides, there's one thing that makes it totally impossible for me to have Krogstad working in the bank as long as I'm the manager.

Nora: What's that?

Helmer: I might have been able to overlook his moral failings, if need be—

Nora: Yes, you could do that, couldn't you?

Helmer: And I hear he's a good worker, too. But I knew him when we were boys. It was one of those rash friendships that so often turn out to be a millstone around the neck later on. I might as well tell you straight out, we were very close friends at one time. But he has no tact and no self-restraint, especially when other people are around. He thinks he has the right to still call me by my first name, and every minute it's Torvald this and Torvald that. I don't mind telling you, I find it extremely annoying. He would make my position at the bank intolerable.

Nora: Torvald, I can't believe you're serious.

Helmer: Oh no? Why not?

Nora: Because it's so petty.

Helmer: What do you mean, petty? You think I'm petty?

Nora: No, just the opposite, dear, and that's why I can't—

Helmer: It's the same thing. You say my attitude's petty, so I must be petty too! Petty! Fine! Well, I'll put a stop to this once and for all. (*Goes to the hall door and calls.*) Helene!

Nora: What are you going to do?

Helmer (*looking among his papers*): Settle it.

(*Enter Maid.*)

Here, take this letter downstairs right now. Find a messenger and tell him to deliver it, and to be quick about it. The address is on it, and here's the money.

Maid: Yes, sir. (*Exits with the letter.*)

Helmer (*putting his papers together*): There, Little Pigheaded Miss.

Nora (*breathlessly*): Torvald, what was that letter?

Helmer: Krogstad's notice.

Nora: Call her back, Torvald! There's still time. Oh, Torvald, call her back! Do it for my sake—for your own sake—for the children's sake! Do you hear me, Torvald? Call her back! You don't know what that letter can do to us.

Helmer: It's too late.

Nora: Yes, it's too late.

Helmer: My dear Nora, I can forgive this anxiety of yours, even though it's insulting to me. It really is. Don't you think it's insulting to suggest that I should be afraid of retaliation from a grubby pen-pusher? But I forgive you anyway, because it's such a beautiful demonstration of how much you love me. (*Takes her in his arms.*) And that is as it should be, my own darling Nora. Come what may, you can rest assured that I'll have both courage and strength if necessary. You'll see that I'm man enough to take everything on myself.

Nora (*in a horror-stricken voice*): What do you mean by that?

Helmer: Everything, I say.

Nora (*recovering herself*): You'll never have to do that.

Helmer: That's right, we'll take it on together, Nora, as man and wife. That's just how it should be. (*Caressing her.*) Are you satisfied now? There, there! Don't look at me that way, like a frightened dove! This whole thing is just your imagination running away with you. Now you should go and run through the tarantella and practice your tambourine. I'll go into my study and shut the door so I can't hear anything. You can make all the noise you want. (*Turns back at the door.*) And when Rank comes, tell him where I am.

(*Nods to her, takes his papers and goes into his room, and shuts the door behind him.*)

Nora (*bewildered with anxiety, stands as if rooted to the spot and whispers*): He's capable of doing it. He's going to do it. He'll do it in spite of everything. No, not that! Never, never! Anything but that! Oh, for somebody to help me find some way out of this! (*The doorbell rings.*) Doctor Rank! Anything but that—anything, whatever it is!

(*She puts her hands over her face, pulls herself together, goes to the door and opens it. Rank is standing in the hall, hanging up his coat. During the following dialogue it starts to grow dark.*)

Nora: Hello, Doctor Rank. I recognized your ring. But you'd better not go in and see Torvald just now. I think he's busy with something.

Rank: And you?

Nora (*brings him in and shuts the door behind him*): Oh, you know perfectly well I always have time for you.

Rank: Thank you. I'll make use of it for as long as I can.

Nora: What does that mean, for as long as you can?

Rank: Why, does that frighten you?

Nora: It was such a strange way of putting it. Is something going to happen?

Rank: Nothing but what I've been expecting for a long time. But I never thought it would happen so soon.

Nora (gripping him by the arm): What have you found out? Doctor Rank, you must tell me.

Rank (sitting down by the stove): I'm done for. And there's nothing I can do about it.

Nora (with a sigh of relief): Oh—you're talking about yourself?

Rank: Who else? And there's no use lying to myself. I'm the sickest patient I have, Mrs. Helmer. Lately I've been adding up my internal account. Bankrupt! In a month I'll probably be rotting in the ground.

Nora: What a horrible thing to say!

Rank: The thing itself is horrible, and the worst of it is all the horrible things I'll have to go through before it's over. I'm going to examine myself just once more. When that's done, I'll be pretty sure when I'm going to start breaking down. There's something I want to say to you. Helmer's sensitive nature makes him completely unable to deal with anything ugly. I don't want him in my sickroom.

Nora: Oh, but, Doctor Rank—

Rank: I won't have him there, period. I'll lock the door to keep him out. As soon as I'm quite sure that the worst has come, I'll send you my card with a black cross on it, and that way you'll know that the final stage of the horror has started.

Nora: You're being really absurd today. And I so much wanted you to be in a good mood.

Rank: With death stalking me? Having to pay this price for another man's sins? Where's the justice in that? In every single family, in one way or another, some such unavoidable retribution is being imposed.

Nora (putting her hands over her ears): Nonsense! Can't you talk about something cheerful?

Rank: Oh, this *is* something cheerful. In fact, it's hilarious. My poor innocent spine has to suffer for my father's youthful self-indulgence.

Nora (sitting at the table on the left): Yes, he did love asparagus and *pâté de foie gras*, didn't he?

Rank: Yes, and truffles.

Nora: Truffles, yes. And oysters too, I suppose?

Rank: Oysters, of course. That goes without saying.

Nora: And oceans of port and champagne. Isn't it sad that all those delightful things should take their revenge on our bones?

Rank: Especially that they should take their revenge on the unlucky bones of people who haven't even had the satisfaction of enjoying them.

Nora: Yes, that's the saddest part of all.

Rank (with a searching look at her): Hm!

Nora (after a short pause): Why did you smile?

Rank: No, it was you who laughed.

Nora: No, it was you who smiled, Doctor Rank!

Rank (rising): You're even more of a tease than I thought you were.

Nora: I am in a crazy mood today.

Rank: Apparently so.

Nora (putting her hands on his shoulders): Dear, dear Doctor Rank, we can't let death take you away from Torvald and me.

Rank: It's a loss that you'll easily recover from. Those who are gone are soon forgotten.

Nora (looking at him anxiously): Do you really believe that?

Rank: People make new friends, and then—

Nora: Who'll make new friends?

Rank: Both you and Helmer, when I'm gone. You yourself are already well on the way to it, I think. What was that Mrs. Linde doing here last night?

Nora: Oho! You're not telling me that you're jealous of poor Kristine, are you?

Rank: Yes, I am. She'll be my successor in this house. When I'm six feet under, this woman will—

Nora: Shh! Don't talk so loud. She's in that room.

Rank: Again today. There, you see.

Nora: She's just come to sew my dress for me. Goodness, how unreasonable you are! (*Sits down on the sofa.*) Be nice now, Doctor Rank, and tomorrow you'll see how beautifully I'll dance, and you can pretend that I'm doing it just for you—and for Torvald too, of course. (*Takes various things out of the box.*) Doctor Rank, come and sit down here, and I'll show you something.

Rank (sitting down): What is it?

Nora: Just look at these!

Rank: Silk stockings.

Nora: Flesh-colored. Aren't they lovely? It's so dark here now, but tomorrow—No, no, no! You're only supposed to look at the feet. Oh well, you have my permission to look at the legs too.

Rank: Hm!

Nora: Why do you look so critical? Don't you think they'll fit me?

Rank: I have no basis for forming an opinion on that subject.

Nora (looks at him for a moment): Shame on you! (*Hits him lightly on the ear with the stockings.*) That's your punishment. (*Folds them up again.*)

Rank: And what other pretty things do I have your permission to look at?

Nora: Not one single thing. That's what you get for being so naughty. (*She looks among the things, humming to herself.*)

Rank (after a short silence): When I'm sitting here, talking to you so intimately this way, I can't imagine for a moment what would have become of me if I'd never come into this house.

Nora (smiling): I believe you really do feel completely at home with us.

Rank (in a lower voice, looking straight in front of him): And to have to leave it all—

Nora: Nonsense, you're not going to leave it.

Rank (as before): And not to be able to leave behind the slightest token of my gratitude, hardly even a fleeting regret. Nothing but an empty place to be filled by the first person who comes along.

Nora: And if I were to ask you now for a—No, never mind!

Rank: For a what?

Nora: For a great proof of your friendship—

Rank: Yes, yes!

Nora: I mean a tremendously huge favor—

Rank: Would you really make me so happy, just this once?

Nora: But you don't know what it is yet.

Rank: No, but tell me.

Nora: I really can't, Doctor Rank. It's too much to ask. It involves advice, and help, and a favor—

Rank: So much the better. I can't imagine what you mean. Tell me what it is. You do trust me, don't you?

Nora: More than anyone. I know that you're my best and truest friend, so I'll tell you what it is. Well, Doctor Rank, it's something you have to help me prevent. You know how devoted Torvald is to me, how deeply he loves me. He wouldn't hesitate for a second to give his life for me.

Rank (leaning towards her): Nora, do you think that he's the only one—

Nora (with a slight start): The only one?

Rank: Who would gladly give his life for you.

Nora (sadly): Oh, is that it?

Rank: I'd made up my mind to tell you before I—I go away, and there'll never be a better opportunity than this. Now you know it, Nora. And now you know that you can trust me more than you can trust anyone else.

Nora (rises, deliberately and quietly): Let me by.

Rank (makes room for her to pass him, but sits still): Nora!

Nora (at the hall door): Helene, bring in the lamp. (*Goes over to the stove.*) Dear Doctor Rank, that was really horrible of you.

Rank: To love you just as much as somebody else does? Is that so horrible?

Nora: No, but to go and tell me like that. There was really no need—

Rank: What do you mean? Did you know—

(*Maid enters with lamp, puts it down on the table, and goes out.*)

Nora—Mrs. Helmer—tell me, did you have any idea I felt this way?

Nora: Oh, how do I know whether I did or I didn't? I really can't answer that. How could you be so clumsy, Doctor Rank? When we were getting along so nicely.

Rank: Well, at any rate, now you know that I'm yours to command, body and soul. So won't you tell me what it is?

Nora (looking at him): After what just happened?

Rank: I beg you to let me know what it is.

Nora: I can't tell you anything now.

Rank: Yes, yes. Please don't punish me that way. Give me permission to do anything for you that a man can do.

Nora: You can't do anything for me now. Besides, I really don't need any help at all. The whole thing is just my imagination. It really is. It has to be! (*Sits down in the rocking chair, and smiles at him.*) You're a nice man, Doctor Rank. Don't you feel ashamed of yourself, now that the lamp is lit?

Rank: Not a bit. But maybe it would be better if I left—and never came back?

Nora: No, no, you can't do that. You must keep coming here just as you always did. You know very well Torvald can't do without you.

Rank: But what about you?

Nora: Oh, I'm always extremely pleased to see you.

Rank: And that's just what gave me the wrong idea. You're a puzzle to me. I've often felt that you'd almost just as soon be in my company as in Helmer's.

Nora: Yes, you see, there are the people you love the most, and then there are the people whose company you enjoy the most.

Rank: Yes, there's something to that.

Nora: When I lived at home, of course I loved Papa best. But I always thought it was great fun to sneak down to the maids' room, because they never preached at me, and I loved listening to the way they talked to each other.

Rank: I see. So I'm their replacement.

Nora (jumping up and going to him): Oh, dear, sweet Doctor Rank, I didn't mean it that way. But surely you can understand that being with Torvald is a little like being with Papa—

(Enter Maid from the hall.)

Maid: Excuse me, ma'am. *(Whispers and hands her a card.)*

Nora (glancing at the card): Oh! *(Puts it in her pocket.)*

Rank: Is something wrong?

Nora: No, no, not at all. It's just—it's my new dress—

Rank: What? Your dress is lying right there.

Nora: Oh, yes, that one. But this is another one, one that I ordered. I don't want Torvald to find out about it—

Rank: Oh! So that was the big secret.

Nora: Yes, that's it. Why don't you just go inside and see him? He's in his study. Stay with him for as long as—

Rank: Put your mind at ease. I won't let him escape. *(Goes into Helmer's study.)*

Nora (to the maid): And he's waiting in the kitchen?

Maid: Yes, ma'am. He came up the back stairs.

Nora: Didn't you tell him no one was home?

Maid: Yes, but it didn't do any good.

Nora: He won't go away?

Maid: No, he says he won't leave until he sees you, ma'am.

Nora: Well, show him in, but quietly. Helene, I don't want you to say anything about this to anyone. It's a surprise for my husband.

Maid: Yes, ma'am. I understand. *(Exit.)*

Nora: This horrible thing is really going to happen! It's going to happen in spite of me! No, no, no, it can't happen! I can't let it happen!

(She bolts the door of Helmer's study. The maid opens the hall door for Krogstad and closes it behind him. He is wearing a fur coat, high boots, and a fur cap.)

Nora (advancing towards him): Speak quietly. My husband's home.

Krogstad: What do I care about that?

Nora: What do you want from me?

Krogstad: An explanation of something.

Nora: Be quick, then. What is it?

Krogstad: I suppose you're aware that I've been let go.

Nora: I couldn't prevent it, Mr. Krogstad. I fought for you as hard as I could, but it was no use.

Krogstad: Does your husband love you so little, then? He knows what I can expose you to, and he still goes ahead and—

Nora: How can you think that he knows any such thing?

Krogstad: I didn't think so for a moment. It wouldn't be at all like dear old Torvald Helmer to show that kind of courage—

Nora: Mr. Krogstad, a little respect for my husband, please.

Krogstad: Certainly—all the respect he deserves. But since you've kept everything so carefully to yourself, may I be bold enough to assume that you see a little more clearly than you did yesterday just what it is that you've done?

Nora: More than you could ever teach me.

Krogstad: Yes, such a poor excuse for a lawyer as I am.

Nora: What is it you want from me?

Krogstad: Only to see how you're doing, Mrs. Helmer. I've been thinking about you all day. A mere bill collector, a pen-pusher, a—well, a man like me—even he has a little of what people call feelings, you know.

Nora: Why don't you show some, then? Think about my little children.

Krogstad: Have you and your husband thought about mine? But never mind about that. I just wanted to tell you not to take this business too seriously. I won't make any accusations against you. Not for now, anyway.

Nora: No, of course not. I was sure you wouldn't.

Krogstad: The whole thing can be settled amicably. There's no need for anyone to know anything about it. It'll be our little secret, just the three of us.

Nora: My husband must never know anything about it.

Krogstad: How are you going to keep him from finding out? Are you telling me that you can pay off the whole balance?

Nora: No, not just yet.

Krogstad: Or that you have some other way of raising the money soon?

Nora: No way that I plan to make use of.

Krogstad: Well, in any case, it wouldn't be any use to you now even if you did. If you stood in front of me with a stack of bills in each hand, I still wouldn't give you back your note.

Nora: What are you planning to do with it?

Krogstad: I just want to hold onto it, just keep it in my possession. No one who isn't involved in the matter will ever know anything about it. So, if you've been thinking about doing something desperate—

Nora: I have.

Krogstad: If you've been thinking about running away—

Nora: I have.

Krogstad: Or doing something even worse—

Nora: How could you know that?

Krogstad: Stop thinking about it.

Nora: How did you know I'd thought of that?

Krogstad: Most of us think about that at first. I did, too. But I didn't have the courage.

Nora (faintly): Neither do I.

Krogstad (in a tone of relief): No, that's true, isn't it? You don't have the courage either?

Nora: No, I don't. I don't.

Krogstad: Besides, it would have been an incredibly stupid thing to do. Once the first storm at home blows over . . . I have a letter for your husband in my pocket.

Nora: Telling him everything?

Krogstad: As gently as possible.

Nora (*quickly*): He can't see that letter. Tear it up. I'll find some way of getting money.

Krogstad: Excuse me, Mrs. Helmer, but didn't I just tell you—

Nora: I'm not talking about what I owe you. Tell me how much you want from my husband, and I'll get the money.

Krogstad: I don't want any money from your husband.

Nora: Then what do you want?

Krogstad: I'll tell you what I want. I want a fresh start, Mrs. Helmer, and I want to move up in the world. And your husband's going to help me do it. I've steered clear of anything questionable for the last year and a half. In all that time I've been struggling along, pinching every penny. I was content to work my way up step by step. But now I've been fired, and it's not going to be enough just to get my job back, as if you people were doing me some huge favor. I want to move up, I tell you. I want to get back into the bank again, but with a promotion. Your husband's going to have to find me a position—

Nora: He'll never do it!

Krogstad: Oh yes, he will. I know him. He won't dare object. And as soon as I'm back there with him, then you'll see! Inside of a year I'll be the manager's right-hand man. It'll be Nils Krogstad, not Torvald Helmer, who's running the bank.

Nora: That's never going to happen!

Krogstad: Do you mean that you'll—

Nora: I have enough courage for it now.

Krogstad: Oh, you can't scare me. An elegant, spoiled lady like you—

Nora: You'll see, you'll see.

Krogstad: Under the ice, maybe? Down in the cold, coal-black water? And then floating up to the surface in the spring, all horrible and unrecognizable, with your hair fallen out—

Nora: You can't scare me.

Krogstad: And you can't scare me. People don't do that kind of thing, Mrs. Helmer. Besides, what good would it do? I'd still have him completely in my power.

Nora: Even then? When I'm no longer—

Krogstad: Have you forgotten that your reputation is completely in my hands? (*Nora stands speechless, looking at him.*) Well, now I've warned you. Don't do anything foolish. I'll be expecting an answer from Helmer after he reads my letter. And remember, it's your husband himself who's forced me to act this way again. I'll never forgive him for that. Goodbye, Mrs. Helmer. (*Exits through the hall.*)

Nora (*goes to the hall door, opens it slightly and listens.*): He's leaving. He isn't putting the letter in the box. Oh no, no! He couldn't! (*Opens the door little by little.*) What? He's standing out there. He's not going downstairs. He's hesitating? Is he?

(*A letter drops into the box. Then Krogstad's footsteps are heard, until they die away as he goes downstairs. Nora utters a stifled cry, and runs across the room to the table by the sofa. A short pause.*)

Nora: In the mailbox. (*Steals across to the hall door.*) It's there! Torvald, Torvald, there's no hope for us now!

(*Mrs. Linde comes in from the room on the left, carrying the dress.*)

Mrs. Linde: There, I can't find anything more to mend. Would you like to try it on?

Nora (*in a hoarse whisper*): Kristine, come here.

Mrs. Linde (*throwing the dress down on the sofa*): What's the matter with you? You look so agitated!

Nora: Come here. Do you see that letter? There, look. You can see it through the glass in the mailbox.

Mrs. Linde: Yes, I see it.

Nora: That letter is from Krogstad.

Mrs. Linde: Nora! It was Krogstad who lent you the money!

Nora: Yes, and now Torvald will know all about it.

Mrs. Linde: Believe me, Nora, that's the best thing for both of you.

Nora: You don't know the whole story. I forged a name.

Mrs. Linde: My God!

Nora: There's something I want to say to you, Kristine. I need you to be my witness.

Mrs. Linde: Your witness? What do you mean? What am I supposed to—

Nora: If I should go out of my mind—and it could easily happen—

Mrs. Linde: Nora!

Nora: Or if anything else should happen to me—anything, for instance, that might keep me from being here—

Mrs. Linde: Nora! Nora! What's the matter with you?

Nora: And if it turned out that somebody wanted to take all the responsibility, all the blame, you understand what I mean—

Mrs. Linde: Yes, yes, but how can you imagine—

Nora: Then you must be my witness that it's not true, Kristine. I'm not out of my mind at all. I'm perfectly rational right now, and I'm telling you that no one else ever knew anything about it. I did the whole thing all by myself. Remember that.

Mrs. Linde: I will. But I don't understand all this.

Nora: How could you understand it? Or the miracle that's going to happen!

Mrs. Linde: A miracle?

Nora: Yes, a miracle! But it's so terrible, Kristine. I can't let it happen, not for the whole world.

Mrs. Linde: I'll go and see Krogstad right this minute.

Nora: No, don't. He'll do something to hurt you too.

Mrs. Linde: There was a time when he would have gladly done anything for my sake.

Nora: What?

Mrs. Linde: Where does he live?

Nora: How should I know? Yes (*feeling in her pocket*), here's his card. But the letter, the letter—

Helmer (*calls from his room, knocking at the door*): Nora!

Nora (*cries out anxiously*): What is it? What do you want?

Helmer: Don't be so afraid. We're not coming in. You've locked the door. Are you trying on your dress?

Nora: Yes, that's it. Oh, it's going to look so nice, Torvald.

Mrs. Linde (*who has read the card*): Look, he lives right around the corner.

Nora: But it's no use. It's all over. The letter's lying right there in the box.

Mrs. Linde: And your husband has the key?

Nora: Yes, always.

Mrs. Linde: Krogstad can ask for his letter back unread. He'll have to make up some reason—

Nora: But now is just about the time that Torvald usually—

Mrs. Linde: You have to prevent him. Go in and talk to him. I'll be back as soon as I can.

(*She hurries out through the hall door.*)

Nora (*goes to Helmer's door, opens it and peeps in*): Torvald!

Helmer (*from the inner room*): Well? May I finally come back into my own room? Come along, Rank, now you'll see—(*Stopping in the doorway.*) But what's this?

Nora: What's what, dear?

Helmer: Rank led me to expect an amazing transformation.

Rank (*in the doorway*): So I understood, but apparently I was mistaken.

Nora: Yes, nobody gets to admire me in my dress until tomorrow.

Helmer: But, my dear Nora, you look exhausted. Have you been practicing too much?

Nora: No, I haven't been practicing at all.

Helmer: But you'll have to—

Nora: Yes, of course I will, Torvald. But I can't get anywhere without you helping me. I've completely forgotten the whole thing.

Helmer: Oh, we'll soon get you back up to form again.

Nora: Yes, help me, Torvald. Promise that you will! I'm so nervous about it—all those people. I need you to devote yourself completely to me this evening. Not even the tiniest little bit of business. You can't even pick up a pen. Do you promise, Torvald dear?

Helmer: I promise. This evening I will be wholly and absolutely at your service, you helpless little creature. But first I'm just going to—(*Goes towards the hall door.*)

Nora: Just going to what?

Helmer: To see if there's any mail.

Nora: No, no! Don't do that, Torvald!

Helmer: Why not?

Nora: Torvald, please don't. There's nothing there.

Helmer: Well, let me look. (*Turns to go to the mailbox. Nora, at the piano, plays the first bars of the tarantella. Helmer stops in the doorway.*) Aha!

Nora: I can't dance tomorrow if I don't practice with you.

Helmer (*going up to her*): Are you really so worried about it, dear?

Nora: Yes, terribly worried about it. Let me practice right now. We have time before dinner. Sit down and play for me, Torvald dear. Criticize me and correct me, the way you always do.

Helmer: With great pleasure, if you want me to. (*Sits down at the piano.*)

Nora (*takes a tambourine and a long multicolored shawl out of the box. She hastily drapes the shawl around her. Then she bounds to the front of the stage and calls out*): Now play for me! I'm going to dance!

(*Helmer plays and Nora dances. Rank stands by the piano behind Helmer and watches.*)

Helmer (as he plays): Slower, slower!

Nora: I can't do it any other way.

Helmer: Not so violently, Nora!

Nora: This is the way.

Helmer (stops playing): No, no, that's not right at all.

Nora (laughing and swinging the tambourine): Didn't I tell you so?

Rank: Let me play for her.

Helmer (getting up): Good idea. I can correct her better that way.

> (*Rank sits down at the piano and plays. Nora dances more and more wildly. Helmer has taken up a position beside the stove, and as she dances, he gives her frequent instructions. She doesn't seem to hear him. Her hair comes undone and falls over her shoulders. She pays no attention to it, but goes on dancing. Enter Mrs. Linde.*)

Mrs. Linde (standing as if spellbound in the doorway): Oh!

Nora (as she dances): What fun, Kristine!

Helmer: My dear darling Nora, you're dancing as if your life depended on it.

Nora: It does.

Helmer: Stop, Rank. This is insane! I said stop!

> (*Rank stops playing, and Nora suddenly stands still. Helmer goes up to her.*)

I never would have believed it. You've forgotten everything I taught you.

Nora (throwing the tambourine aside): There, you see.

Helmer: You're going to need a lot of coaching.

Nora: Yes, you see how much I need it. You have to coach me right up to the last minute. Promise me you will, Torvald!

Helmer: You can depend on me.

Nora: You can't think about anything but me, today or tomorrow. Don't open a single letter. Don't even open the mailbox—

Helmer: You're still afraid of that man—

Nora: Yes, yes, I am.

Helmer: Nora, I can tell from your face that there's a letter from him in the box.

Nora: I don't know. I think there is. But you can't read anything like that now. Nothing nasty must come between us until this is all over.

Rank (whispers to Helmer): Don't contradict her.

Helmer (taking her in his arms): The child shall have her way. But tomorrow night, after you've danced—

Nora: Then you'll be free.

> (*The Maid appears in the doorway to the right.*)

Maid: Dinner is served, ma'am.

Nora: We'll have champagne, Helene.

Maid: Yes, ma'am. (*Exit.*)

Helmer: Oh, are we having a banquet?

Nora: Yes, a banquet. Champagne till dawn! (*Calls out.*) And a few macaroons, Helene. Lots of them, just this once!

Helmer: Come on, stop acting so wild and nervous. Be my own little skylark again.

Nora: Yes, dear, I will. But go inside now, and you too, Doctor Rank. Kristine, please help me do up my hair.

Rank (whispers to Helmer as they go out): There isn't anything—she's not expecting—?

Helmer: No, nothing like that. It's just this childish nervousness I was telling you about. (*They go into the right-hand room.*)

Nora: Well?

Mrs. Linde: Out of town.

Nora: I could tell from your face.

Mrs. Linde: He'll be back tomorrow evening. I wrote him a note.

Nora: You should have left it alone. Don't try to prevent anything. After all, it's exciting to be waiting for a miracle to happen.

Mrs. Linde: What is it that you're waiting for?

Nora: Oh, you wouldn't understand. Go inside with them, I'll be there in a moment.

(*Mrs. Linde goes into the dining room. Nora stands still for a little while, as if to compose herself. Then she looks at her watch.*)

Five o'clock. Seven hours till midnight, and another twenty-four hours till the next midnight. And then the tarantella will be over. Twenty-four plus seven? Thirty-one hours to live.

Helmer (from the doorway on the right): Where's my little skylark?

Nora (going to him with her arms outstretched): Here she is!

ACT III

The same scene. The table has been placed in the middle of the stage, with chairs around it. A lamp is burning on the table. The door into the hall stands open. Dance music is heard in the room above. Mrs. Linde is sitting at the table idly turning over the pages of a book. She tries to read, but she seems unable to concentrate. Every now and then she listens intently for a sound at the outer door.

Mrs. Linde (looking at her watch): Not yet—and the time's nearly up. If only he doesn't— (*Listens again.*) Ah, there he is. (*Goes into the hall and opens the outer door carefully. Light footsteps are heard on the stairs. She whispers.*) Come in. There's no one else here.

Krogstad (in the doorway): I found a note from you at home. What does this mean?

Mrs. Linde: It's absolutely necessary that I have a talk with you.

Krogstad: Really? And is it absolutely necessary that we have it here?

Mrs. Linde: It's impossible where I live. There's no private entrance to my apartment. Come in. We're all alone. The maid's asleep, and the Helmers are upstairs at a dance.

Krogstad (coming into the room): Are the Helmers really at a dance tonight?

Mrs. Linde: Yes. Why shouldn't they be?

Krogstad: Certainly—why not?

Mrs. Linde: Now, Nils, let's have a talk.

Krogstad: What can we two have to talk about?

Mrs. Linde: Quite a lot.

Krogstad: I wouldn't have thought so.

Mrs. Linde: Of course not. You've never really understood me.

Krogstad: What was there to understand, except what the whole world could see—a heartless woman drops a man when a better catch comes along?

Mrs. Linde: Do you think I'm really that heartless? And that I broke it off with you so lightly?

Krogstad: Didn't you?

Mrs. Linde: Nils, did you really think that?

Krogstad: If not, why did you write what you did to me?

Mrs. Linde: What else could I do? Since I had to break it off with you, I had an obligation to stamp out your feelings for me.

Krogstad (wringing his hands): So that was it. And all this just for the sake of money!

Mrs. Linde: Don't forget that I had an invalid mother and two little brothers. We couldn't wait for you, Nils. Success seemed a long way off for you back then.

Krogstad: That may be so, but you had no right to cast me aside for anyone else's sake.

Mrs. Linde: I don't know if I did or not. Many times I've asked myself if I had the right.

Krogstad (more gently): When I lost you, it was as if the earth crumbled under my feet. Look at me now—a shipwrecked man clinging to a bit of wreckage.

Mrs. Linde: But help may be on the way.

Krogstad: It *was* on the way, till you came along and blocked it.

Mrs. Linde: Without knowing it, Nils. It wasn't till today that I found out I'd be taking your job.

Krogstad: I believe you, if you say so. But now that you know it, are you going to step aside?

Mrs. Linde: No, because it wouldn't do you any good.

Krogstad: Good? *I* would quit whether it did any good or not.

Mrs. Linde: I've learned to be practical. Life and hard, bitter necessity have taught me that.

Krogstad: And life has taught me not to believe in fine speeches.

Mrs. Linde: Then life has taught you something very sensible. But surely you believe in actions?

Krogstad: What do you mean by that?

Mrs. Linde: You said you were like a shipwrecked man clinging to a piece of wreckage.

Krogstad: I had good reason to say so.

Mrs. Linde: Well, I'm like a shipwrecked woman clinging to a piece of wreckage, with no one to mourn for and no one to care for.

Krogstad: That was your own choice.

Mrs. Linde: I had no other choice—then.

Krogstad: Well, what about now?

Mrs. Linde: Nils, how would it be if we two shipwrecked people could reach out to each other?

Krogstad: What are you saying?

Mrs. Linde: Two people on the same piece of wreckage would stand a better chance than each one on their own.

Krogstad: Kristine, I . . .

Mrs. Linde: Why do you think I came to town?

Krogstad: You can't mean that you were thinking about me?

Mrs. Linde: Life is unendurable without work. I've worked all my life, for as long as I can remember, and it's been my greatest and my only pleasure. But now that I'm completely alone in the world, my life is so terribly empty and I feel so abandoned. There isn't the slightest pleasure in working only for yourself. Nils, give me someone and something to work for.

Krogstad: I don't trust this. It's just some romantic female impulse, a high-minded urge for self-sacrifice.

Mrs. Linde: Have you ever known me to be like that?

Krogstad: Could you really do it? Tell me, do you know all about my past?

Mrs. Linde: Yes.

Krogstad: And you know what they think of me around here?

Mrs. Linde: Didn't you imply that with me you might have been a very different person?

Krogstad: I'm sure I would have.

Mrs. Linde: Is it too late now?

Krogstad: Kristine, are you serious about all this? Yes, I'm sure you are. I can see it in your face. Do you really have the courage, then—

Mrs. Linde: I want to be a mother to someone, and your children need a mother. We two need each other. Nils, I have faith in your true nature. I can face anything together with you.

Krogstad (grasps her hands): Thank you, thank you, Kristine! Now I can find a way to clear myself in the eyes of the world. Ah, but I forgot—

Mrs. Linde (listening): Shh! The tarantella! You have to go!

Krogstad: Why? What's the matter?

Mrs. Linde: Do you hear them up there? They'll probably come home as soon as this dance is over.

Krogstad: Yes, yes, I'll go. But it won't make any difference. You don't know what I've done about my situation with the Helmers.

Mrs. Linde: Yes, I know all about that.

Krogstad: And in spite of that you still have the courage to—

Mrs. Linde: I understand completely what despair can drive a man like you to do.

Krogstad: If only I could undo it!

Mrs. Linde: You can't. Your letter's lying in the mailbox now.

Krogstad: Are you sure?

Mrs. Linde: Quite sure, but—

Krogstad (with a searching look at her): Is that what this is all about? That you want to save your friend, no matter what you have to do? Tell me the truth. Is that it?

Mrs. Linde: Nils, when a woman has sold herself for someone else's sake, she doesn't do it a second time.

Krogstad: I'll ask for my letter back.

Mrs. Linde: No, no.

Krogstad: Yes, of course I will. I'll wait here until Helmer comes home. I'll tell him he has to give me back my letter, that it's only about my being fired, that I don't want him to read it—

Mrs. Linde: No, Nils, don't ask for it back.

Krogstad: But wasn't that the reason why you asked me to meet you here?

Mrs. Linde: In my first moment of panic, it was. But twenty-four hours have gone by since then, and in the meantime I've seen some incredible things in this house. Helmer has to know all about it. This terrible secret has to come out. They have to have a complete understanding between them. It's time for all this lying and pretending to stop.

Krogstad: All right then, if you think it's worth the risk. But there's at least one thing I can do, and do right away—

Mrs. Linde (listening): You have to leave this instant! The dance is over. They could walk in here any minute.

Krogstad: I'll wait for you downstairs.

Mrs. Linde: Yes, please do. I want you to walk me home.

Krogstad: I've never been so happy in my entire life!

(Goes out through the outer door. The door between the room and the hall remains open.)

Mrs. Linde (straightening up the room and getting her hat and coat ready): How different things will be! Someone to work for and live for, a home to bring happiness into. I'm certainly going to try. I wish they'd hurry up and come home—(Listens.) Ah, here they are now. I'd better put on my things.

(Picks up her hat and coat. Helmer's and Nora's voices are heard outside. A key is turned, and Helmer brings Nora into the hall almost by force. She is in an Italian peasant costume with a large black shawl wrapped around her. He is in formal wear and a black domino—a hooded cloak with an eye-mask—which is open.)

Nora (hanging back in the doorway and struggling with him): No, no, no! Don't bring me inside. I want to go back upstairs. I don't want to leave so early.

Helmer: But, my dearest Nora—

Nora: Please, Torvald dear, please, please, only one more hour.

Helmer: Not one more minute, my sweet Nora. You know this is what we agreed on. Come inside. You'll catch cold standing out there.

(He brings her gently into the room, in spite of her resistance.)

Mrs. Linde: Good evening.

Nora: Kristine!

Helmer: What are you doing here so late, Mrs. Linde?

Mrs. Linde: You must excuse me. I was so anxious to see Nora in her dress.

Nora: Have you been sitting here waiting for me?

Mrs. Linde: Yes, unfortunately I came too late, you'd already gone upstairs. And I didn't want to go away again without seeing you.

Helmer (taking off Nora's shawl): Yes, take a good look at her. I think she's worth looking at. Isn't she charming, Mrs. Linde?

Mrs. Linde: Yes, indeed she is.

Helmer: Doesn't she look especially pretty? Everyone thought so at the dance. But this sweet little person is extremely stubborn. What are we going to do with her? Believe it or not, I almost had to drag her away by force.

Nora: Torvald, you'll be sorry you didn't let me stay, even if only for half an hour.

Helmer: Listen to her, Mrs. Linde! She danced her tarantella and it was a huge success, as it deserved to be, though maybe her performance was a tiny bit too realistic, a little more so than it might have been by strict artistic standards. But never mind about that! The main thing is, she was a success, a tremendous success. Do you think I was going to let her stay there after that, and spoil the effect? Not a chance! I took my charming little Capri girl—my capricious little Capri girl, I should say—I took her by the arm, one quick circle around the room, a curtsey to one and all, and, as they say in novels, the beautiful vision vanished. An exit should always make an effect, Mrs. Linde, but I can't make Nora understand that. Whew, this room is hot!

(*Throws his domino on a chair and opens the door to his study.*)

Why is it so dark in here? Oh, of course. Excuse me.

(*He goes in and lights some candles.*)

Nora (*in a hurried, breathless whisper*): Well?
Mrs. Linde (*in a low voice*): I talked to him.
Nora: And?
Mrs. Linde: Nora, you have to tell your husband the whole story.
Nora (*in an expressionless voice*): I knew it.
Mrs. Linde: You have nothing to fear from Krogstad, but you still have to tell him.
Nora: I'm not going to.
Mrs. Linde: Then the letter will.
Nora: Thank you, Kristine. Now I know what I have to do. Shh!
Helmer (*coming in again*): Well, Mrs. Linde, have you been admiring her?
Mrs. Linde: Yes, I have, and now I'll say goodnight.
Helmer: What, already? Is this your knitting?
Mrs. Linde (*taking it*): Yes, thank you, I'd almost forgotten it.
Helmer: So you knit?
Mrs. Linde: Yes, of course.
Helmer: You know, you ought to embroider.
Mrs. Linde: Really? Why?
Helmer: It's much more graceful-looking. Here, let me show you. You hold the embroidery this way in your left hand, and use the needle with your right, like this, with a long, easy sweep. Do you see?
Mrs. Linde: Yes, I suppose—
Helmer: But knitting, that can never be anything but awkward. Here, look. The arms close together, the knitting needles going up and down. It's sort of Chinese looking. That was really excellent champagne they gave us.
Mrs. Linde: Well, good night, Nora, and don't be stubborn anymore.
Helmer: That's right, Mrs. Linde.
Mrs. Linde: Good night, Mr. Helmer.
Helmer (*seeing her to the door*): Good night, good night. I hope you get home safely. I'd be very happy to—but you only have a short way to go. Good night, good night.

(*She goes out. He closes the door behind her, and comes in again.*)

Ah, rid of her at last! What a bore that woman is.
Nora: Aren't you tired, Torvald?
Helmer: No, not at all.
Nora: You're not sleepy?
Helmer: Not a bit. As a matter of fact, I feel very lively. And what about you? You really look tired *and* sleepy.
Nora: Yes, I am very tired. I want to go to sleep right away.
Helmer: So, you see how right I was not to let you stay there any longer.

Nora: You're always right, Torvald.

Helmer (*kissing her on the forehead*): Now my little skylark is talking sense. Did you notice what a good mood Rank was in this evening?

Nora: Really? Was he? I didn't talk to him at all.

Helmer: And I only talked to him for a little while, but it's a long time since I've seen him so cheerful. (*Looks at her for a while and then moves closer to her.*) It's delightful to be home again by ourselves, to be alone with you, you fascinating, charming little darling!

Nora: Don't look at me like that, Torvald.

Helmer: Why shouldn't I look at my dearest treasure? At all the beauty that is mine, all my very own?

Nora (*going to the other side of the table*): I wish you wouldn't talk that way to me tonight.

Helmer (*following her*): You've still got the tarantella in your blood, I see. And it makes you more captivating than ever. Listen, the guests are starting to leave now. (*In a lower voice.*) Nora, soon the whole house will be quiet.

Nora: Yes, I hope so.

Helmer: Yes, my own darling Nora. Do you know why, when we're out at a party like this, why I hardly talk to you, and keep away from you, and only steal a glance at you now and then? Do you know why I do that? It's because I'm pretending to myself that we're secretly in love, and we're secretly engaged, and no one suspects that there's anything between us.

Nora: Yes, yes, I know you're thinking about me every moment.

Helmer: And when we're leaving, and I'm putting the shawl over your beautiful young shoulders, on your lovely neck, then I imagine that you're my young bride and that we've just come from our wedding and I'm bringing you home for the first time, to be alone with you for the first time, all alone with my shy little darling! This whole night I've been longing for you alone. My blood was on fire watching you move when you danced the tarantella. I couldn't stand it any longer, and that's why I brought you home so early—

Nora: Stop it, Torvald! Let me go. I won't—

Helmer: What? You're not serious, Nora! You won't? You won't? I'm your husband—

(*There is a knock at the outer door.*)

Nora (*starting*): Did you hear—

Helmer (*going into the hall*): Who is it?

Rank (*outside*): It's me. May I come in for a moment?

Helmer (*in an irritated whisper*): What does he want now? (*Aloud.*) Wait a minute! (*Unlocks the door.*) Come in. It's good of you not to pass by our door without saying hello.

Rank: I thought I heard your voice, and I felt like dropping by. (*With a quick look around.*) Ah, yes, these dear familiar rooms. You two are very happy and cozy in here.

Helmer: You seemed to be making yourself pretty happy upstairs too.

Rank: Very much so. Why shouldn't I? Why shouldn't we enjoy everything in this world? At least as much as we can, for as long as we can. The wine was first-rate—

Helmer: Especially the champagne.

Rank: So you noticed that too? It's almost unbelievable how much of it I managed to put away!

Nora: Torvald drank a lot of champagne tonight too.

Rank: Did he?

Nora: Yes, and it always makes him so merry.

Rank: Well, why shouldn't a person have a merry evening after a well-spent day?

Helmer: Well-spent? I'm afraid I can't take credit for that.

Rank (clapping him on the back): But I can, you know!

Nora: Doctor Rank, you must have been busy with some scientific investigation today.

Rank: Exactly.

Helmer: Listen to this! Little Nora talking about scientific investigations!

Nora: And may I congratulate you on the result?

Rank: Indeed you may.

Nora: Was it favorable, then?

Rank: The best possible result, for both doctor and patient—certainty.

Nora (quickly and searchingly): Certainty?

Rank: Absolute certainty. So wasn't I entitled to make a merry evening of it after that?

Nora: Yes, you certainly were, Doctor Rank.

Helmer: I think so too, as long as you don't have to pay for it in the morning.

Rank: Oh well, you can't have anything in this life without paying for it.

Nora: Doctor Rank, are you fond of fancy-dress balls?

Rank: Yes, if there are a lot of pretty costumes.

Nora: Tell me, what should the two of us wear to the next one?

Helmer: Little featherbrain! You're thinking of the next one already?

Rank: The two of us? Yes, I can tell you. You'll go as a good-luck charm—

Helmer: Yes, but what would be the costume for that?

Rank: She just needs to dress the way she always does.

Helmer: That was very nicely put. But aren't you going to tell us what you'll be?

Rank: Yes, my dear friend, I've already made up my mind about that.

Helmer: Well?

Rank: At the next fancy-dress ball I'm going to be invisible.

Helmer: That's a good one!

Rank: There's a big black cap . . . Haven't you ever heard of the cap that makes you invisible? Once you put it on, no one can see you anymore.

Helmer (suppressing a smile): Yes, that's right.

Rank: But I'm clean forgetting what I came for. Helmer, give me a cigar. One of the dark Havanas.

Helmer: With the greatest pleasure. *(Offers him his case.)*

Rank (takes a cigar and cuts off the end): Thanks.

Nora (striking a match): Let me give you a light.

Rank: Thank you. *(She holds the match for him to light his cigar.)* And now goodbye!

Helmer: Goodbye, goodbye, my dear old friend.

Nora: Sleep well, Doctor Rank.

Rank: Thank you for that wish.

Nora: Wish me the same.

Rank: You? Well, if you want me to. Sleep well! And thanks for the light. (*He nods to them both and goes out.*)

Helmer (*in a subdued voice*): He's had too much to drink.

Nora (*absently*): Maybe.

(*Helmer takes a bunch of keys out of his pocket and goes into the hall.*)

Torvald! What are you going to do out there?

Helmer: Empty the mailbox. It's quite full. There won't be any room for the newspaper in the morning.

Nora: Are you going to work tonight?

Helmer: You know I'm not. What's this? Someone's been at the lock.

Nora: At the lock?

Helmer: Yes, it's been tampered with. What does this mean? I never would have thought the maid—Look, here's a broken hairpin. It's one of yours, Nora.

Nora (*quickly*): Then it must have been the children—

Helmer: Then you'd better break them of those habits. There, I've finally got it open.

(*Empties the mailbox and calls out to the kitchen.*)

Helene! Helene, put out the light over the front door.

(*Comes back into the room and shuts the door into the hall. He holds out his hand full of letters.*)

Look at that. Look what a pile of them there are. (*Turning them over.*) What's this?

Nora (*at the window*): The letter! No! Torvald, no!

Helmer: Two calling cards of Rank's.

Nora: Of Doctor Rank's?

Helmer (*looking at them*): Yes, Doctor Rank. They were on top. He must have put them in there when he left just now.

Nora: Is there anything written on them?

Helmer: There's a black cross over the name. Look. What a morbid thing to do! It looks as if he's announcing his own death.

Nora: That's exactly what he's doing.

Helmer: What? Do you know anything about it? Has he said anything to you?

Nora: Yes. He told me that when the cards came it would be his farewell to us. He means to close himself off and die.

Helmer: My poor old friend! Of course I knew we wouldn't have him for very long. But this soon! And he goes and hides himself away like a wounded animal.

Nora: If it has to happen, it's better that it be done without a word. Don't you think so, Torvald?

Helmer (*walking up and down*): He's become so much a part of our lives, I can't imagine him not being with us anymore. With his poor health and his loneliness, he was like a cloudy background to our sunlit happiness. Well, maybe it's all for the best. For him, anyway. (*Standing still.*) And maybe for us too, Nora. Now we have only each other to rely on. (*Puts his arms around her.*) My darling wife, I feel as though I can't possibly hold you tight enough. You know, Nora, I've often wished you were in some kind of serious danger, so that I could risk everything, even my own life, to save you.

Nora (*disengages herself from him, and says firmly and decidedly*): Now you must go and read your letters, Torvald.

Helmer: No, no, not tonight. I want to be with you, my darling wife.

Nora: With the thought of your friend's death—

Helmer: You're right, it has affected us both. Something ugly has come between us, the thought of the horrors of death. We have to try to put it out of our minds. Until we do, we'll each go to our own room.

Nora (*with her arms around his neck*): Good night, Torvald. Good night!

Helmer (*kissing her on the forehead*): Good night, my little songbird. Sleep well, Nora. Now I'll go read all my mail. (*He takes his letters and goes into his room, shutting the door behind him.*)

Nora (*gropes distractedly about, picks up Helmer's domino and wraps it around her, while she says in quick, hoarse, spasmodic whispers*): Never to see him again. Never! Never! (*Puts her shawl over her head.*) Never to see my children again either, never again. Never! Never! Oh, the icy, black water, the bottomless depths! If only it were over! He's got it now, now he's reading it. Goodbye, Torvald . . . children!

(*She is about to rush out through the hall when Helmer opens his door hurriedly and stands with an open letter in his hand.*)

Helmer: Nora!

Nora: Ah!

Helmer: What is this? Do you know what's in this letter?

Nora: Yes, I know. Let me go! Let me get out!

Helmer (*holding her back*): Where are you going?

Nora (*trying to get free*): You're not going to save me, Torvald!

Helmer (*reeling*): It's true? Is this true, what it says here? This is horrible! No, no, it can't possibly be true.

Nora: It is true. I've loved you more than anything else in the world.

Helmer: Don't start with your ridiculous excuses.

Nora (*taking a step towards him*): Torvald!

Helmer: You little fool, do you know what you've done?

Nora: Let me go. I won't let you suffer for my sake. You're not going to take it on yourself.

Helmer: Stop play-acting. (*Locks the hall door.*) You're going to stay right here and give me an explanation. Do you understand what you've done? Answer me! Do you understand what you've done?

Nora (*looks steadily at him and says with a growing look of coldness in her face*): Yes, I'm beginning to understand everything now.

Helmer (*walking around the room*): What a horrible awakening! The woman who was my pride and joy for eight years, a hypocrite, a liar, worse than that, much worse— a criminal! The unspeakable ugliness of it all! The shame of it! The shame!

(*Nora is silent and looks steadily at him. He stops in front of her.*)

I should have realized that something like this was bound to happen. I should have seen it coming. Your father's shifty nature—be quiet!—your father's shifty nature has come out in you. No religion, no morality, no sense of duty. This is my punishment for closing my eyes to what he did! I did it for your sake, and this is how you pay me back.

Nora: Yes, that's right.

Helmer: Now you've destroyed all my happiness. You've ruined my whole future. It's horrible to think about! I'm in the power of an unscrupulous man. He can do what he wants with me, ask me for anything he wants, give me any orders he wants, and I don't dare say no. And I have to sink to such miserable depths, all because of a feather-brained woman!

Nora: When I'm out of the way, you'll be free.

Helmer: Spare me the speeches. Your father had always plenty of those on hand, too. What good would it do me if you were out of the way, as you say? Not the slightest. He can tell everybody the whole story. And if he does, I could be wrongly suspected of having been in on it with you. People will probably think I was behind it all, that I put you up to it! And I have you to thank for all this, after I've cherished you the whole time we've been married. Do you understand what you've done to me?

Nora (coldly and quietly): Yes.

Helmer: It's so incredible that I can't take it all in. But we have to come to some understanding. Take off that shawl. Take it off, I said. I have to try to appease him some way or another. It has to be hushed up, no matter what it costs. And as for you and me, we have to make it look as if everything is just as it always was, but only for the sake of appearances, obviously. You'll stay here in my house, of course. But I won't let you bring up the children. I can't trust them to you. To think that I have to say these things to someone I've loved so dearly, and that I still—No, that's all over. From this moment on happiness is out of the question. All that matters now is to save the bits and pieces, to keep up the appearance—

(The front doorbell rings.)

Helmer (with a start): What's that? At this hour! Can the worst—Can he—Go and hide yourself, Nora. Say you don't feel well. (*Nora stands motionless. Helmer goes and unlocks the hall door.*)

Maid (half-dressed, comes to the door): A letter for Mrs. Helmer.

Helmer: Give it to me. (*Takes the letter, and shuts the door.*) Yes, it's from him. I'm not giving it to you. I'll read it myself.

Nora: Go ahead, read it.

Helmer (standing by the lamp): I barely have the courage to. It could mean ruin for both of us. No, I have to know. (*Tears open the letter, runs his eye over a few lines, looks at a piece of paper enclosed with it, and gives a shout of joy.*) Nora! (*She looks at him questioningly.*) Nora! No, I'd better read it again. Yes, it's true! I'm saved! Nora, I'm saved!

Nora: And what about me?

Helmer: You too, of course. We're both saved, you and I. Look, he's returned your note. He says he's sorry and he apologizes—that a happy change in his life—what difference does it make what he says! We're saved, Nora! Nobody can hurt you. Oh, Nora, Nora! No, first I have to destroy these horrible things. Let me see. . . . (*Glances at the note.*) No, no, I don't want to look at it. This whole business will be nothing but a bad dream to me.

(*Tears up the note and both letters, throws them all into the stove, and watches them burn.*)

There, now it doesn't exist anymore. He says that you've known since Christmas Eve. These must have been a horrible three days for you, Nora.

Nora: I fought a hard fight these three days.

Helmer: And suffered agonies, and saw no way out but—No, we won't dwell on any of those horrors. We'll just shout for joy and keep saying, "It's all over! It's all over!" Listen to me, Nora. You don't seem to realize that it's all over. What's this? Such a cold, hard face! My poor little Nora, I understand. You find it hard to believe that I've really forgiven you. But I swear that it's true, Nora. I forgive you for everything. I know that you did it all out of love for me.

Nora: That's true.

Helmer: You've loved me the way a wife ought to love her husband. You just didn't have the awareness to see what was wrong with the means you used. But do you think I love you any less because you don't understand how to deal with these things? No, of course not. I want you to lean on me. I'll advise you and guide you. I wouldn't be a man if this womanly helplessness didn't make you twice as attractive to me. Don't think anymore about the hard things I said when I was so upset at first, when I thought everything was going to crush me. I forgive you, Nora. I swear to you that I forgive you.

Nora: Thank you for your forgiveness. (*She goes out through the door to the right.*)

Helmer: No, don't go—(*Looks in.*) What are you doing in there?

Nora (from within): Taking off my costume.

Helmer (standing at the open door): Yes, do. Try to calm yourself, and ease your mind again, my frightened little songbird. I want you to rest and feel secure. I have wide wings for you to take shelter underneath. (*Walks up and down by the door.*) What a warm and cozy home we have, Nora: Here's a safe haven for you, and I'll protect you like a hunted dove that I've rescued from a hawk's claws. I'll calm your poor pounding heart. It will happen, little by little, Nora, believe me. In the morning you'll see it in a very different light. Soon everything will be exactly the way it was before. Before you know it, you won't need my reassurances that I've forgiven you. You'll know for certain that I have. You can't imagine that I'd ever consider rejecting you, or even blaming you? You have no idea what a man feels in his heart, Nora. A man finds it indescribably sweet and satisfying to know that he's forgiven his wife, freely and with all his heart. It's as if he's made her his own all over again. He's given her a new life, in a way, and she's become both wife and child to him. And from this moment on that's what you'll be to me, my little scared, helpless darling. Don't worry about anything, Nora. Just be honest and open with me, and I'll be your will and your conscience. What's this? You haven't gone to bed yet? Have you changed?

Nora (in everyday dress): Yes, Torvald, I've changed.

Helmer: But why—It's so late.

Nora: I'm not going to sleep tonight.

Helmer: But, my dear Nora—

Nora (looking at her watch): It's not that late. Sit down here, Torvald. You and I have a lot to talk about. (*She sits down at one side of the table.*)

Helmer: Nora, what is this? Why this cold, hard face?

Nora: Sit down. This is going to take a while. I have a lot to say to you.

Helmer (sits down at the opposite side of the table): You're making me nervous, Nora. And I don't understand you.

Nora: No, that's it exactly. You don't understand me, and I've never understood you either, until tonight. No, don't interrupt me. I want you to listen to what I have to say. Torvald, I'm settling accounts with you.

Helmer: What do you mean by that?

Nora (after a short silence): Doesn't anything strike you as odd about the way we're sitting here like this?

Helmer: No, what?

Nora: We've been married for eight years. Doesn't it occur to you that this is the first time the two of us, you and I, husband and wife, have had a serious conversation?

Helmer: What do you mean by serious?

Nora: In the whole eight years—longer than that, for the whole time we've known each other—we've never exchanged one word on any serious subject.

Helmer: Did you expect me to be constantly worrying you with problems that you weren't capable of helping me deal with?

Nora: I'm not talking about business. I mean we've never sat down together seriously to try to get to the bottom of anything.

Helmer: But, dearest Nora, what good would that have done you?

Nora: That's just it. You've never understood me. I've been treated badly, Torvald, first by Papa and then by you.

Helmer: What? The two people who've loved you more than anyone else?

Nora (shaking her head): You've never loved me. You just thought it was pleasant to be in love with me.

Helmer: Nora, what are you saying?

Nora: It's true, Torvald. When I lived at home with Papa, he gave me his opinion about everything, and so I had all the same opinions, and if I didn't, I kept my mouth shut, because he wouldn't have liked it. He used to call me his doll-child, and he played with me the way I played with my dolls. And when I came to live in your house—

Helmer: What kind of way is that to talk about our marriage?

Nora (undisturbed): I mean that I was just passed from Papa's hands to yours. You arranged everything according to your own taste, and so I had all the same tastes as you. Or else I pretended to, I'm not really sure which. Sometimes I think it's one way and sometimes the other. When I look back, it's as if I've been living here like a beggar, from hand to mouth. I've supported myself by performing tricks for you, Torvald. But that's the way you wanted it. You and Papa have committed a terrible sin against me. It's your fault that I've done nothing with my life.

Helmer: This is so unfair and ungrateful of you, Nora! Haven't you been happy here?

Nora: No, I've never really been happy. I thought I was, but it wasn't true.

Helmer: Not—not happy!

Nora: No, just cheerful. You've always been very kind to me. But our home's been nothing but a playroom. I've been your doll-wife, the same way that I was Papa's doll-child. And the children have been my dolls. I thought it was great fun when you played with me, the way they thought it was when I played with them. That's what our marriage has been, Torvald.

Helmer: There's some truth in what you're saying, even though your view of it is exaggerated and overwrought. But things will be different from now on. Playtime is over, and now it's lesson-time.

Nora: Whose lessons? Mine, or the children's?

Helmer: Both yours and the children's, my darling Nora.

Nora: I'm sorry, Torvald, but you're not the man to give me lessons on how to be a proper wife to you.

Helmer: How can you say that?

Nora: And as for me, who am I to be allowed to bring up the children?

Helmer: Nora!

Nora: Didn't you say so yourself a little while ago, that you don't dare trust them to me?

Helmer: That was in a moment of anger! Why can't you let it go?

Nora: Because you were absolutely right. I'm not fit for the job. There's another job I have to take on first. I have to try to educate myself. You're not the man to help me with that. I have to do that for myself. And that's why I'm going to leave you now.

Helmer (jumping up): What are you saying?

Nora: I have to stand completely on my own, if I'm going to understand myself and everything around me. That's why I can't stay here with you any longer.

Helmer: Nora, Nora!

Nora: I'm leaving right now. I'm sure Kristine will put me up for the night—

Helmer: You're out of your mind! I won't let you go! I forbid it!

Nora: It's no use forbidding me anything anymore. I'm taking only what belongs to me. I won't take anything from you, now or later.

Helmer: This is insanity!

Nora: Tomorrow I'm going home. Back to where I came from, I mean. It'll be easier for me to find something to do there.

Helmer: You're a blind, senseless woman!

Nora: Then I'd better try to get some sense, Torvald.

Helmer: But to desert your home, your husband, and your children! And aren't you concerned about what people will say?

Nora: I can't concern myself with that. I only know that this is what I have to do.

Helmer: This is outrageous! You're just going to walk away from your most sacred duties?

Nora: What do you consider to be my most sacred duties?

Helmer: Do you need me to tell you that? Aren't they your duties to your husband and your children?

Nora: I have other duties just as sacred.

Helmer: No, you do not. What could they be?

Nora: Duties to myself.

Helmer: First and foremost, you're a wife and a mother.

Nora: I don't believe that anymore. I believe that first and foremost I'm a human being, just as you are—or, at least, that I have to try to become one. I know very well, Torvald, that most people would agree with you, and that opinions like yours are in books, but I can't be satisfied anymore with what most people say, or with what's in books. I have to think things through for myself and come to understand them.

Helmer: Why can't you understand your place in your own home? Don't you have an infallible guide in matters like that? What about your religion?

Nora: Torvald, I'm afraid I'm not sure what religion is.

Helmer: What are you saying?

Nora: All I know is what Pastor Hansen said when I was confirmed. He told us that religion was this, that, and the other thing. When I'm away from all this and on my own, I'll look into that subject too. I'll see if what he said is true or not, or at least whether it's true for me.

Helmer: This is unheard of, coming from a young woman like you! But if religion doesn't guide you, let me appeal to your conscience. I assume you have some moral sense. Or do you have none? Answer me.

Nora: Torvald, that's not an easy question to answer. I really don't know. It's very confusing to me. I only know that you and I look at it in very different ways. I'm learning too that the law isn't at all what I thought it was, and I can't convince myself that the law is right. A woman has no right to spare her old dying father or to save her husband's life? I can't believe that.

Helmer: You talk like a child. You don't understand anything about the world you live in.

Nora: No, I don't. But I'm going to try. I'm going to see if I can figure out who's right, me or the world.

Helmer: You're sick, Nora. You're delirious. I'm half convinced that you're out of your mind.

Nora: I've never felt so clearheaded and sure of myself as I do tonight.

Helmer: Clearheaded and sure of yourself—and that's the spirit in which you forsake your husband and your children?

Nora: Yes, it is.

Helmer: Then there's only one possible explanation.

Nora: Which is?

Helmer: You don't love me anymore.

Nora: Exactly.

Helmer: Nora! How can you say that?

Nora: It's very painful for me to say it, Torvald, because you've always been so good to me, but I can't help it. I don't love you anymore.

Helmer (regaining his composure): Are you clearheaded and sure of yourself when you say that too?

Nora: Yes, totally clearheaded and sure of myself. That's why I can't stay here.

Helmer: Can you tell me what I did to make you stop loving me?

Nora: Yes, I can. It was tonight, when the miracle didn't happen. That's when I realized you're not the man I thought you were.

Helmer: Can you explain that more clearly? I don't understand you.

Nora: I've been waiting so patiently for the last eight years. Of course I knew that miracles don't happen every day. Then when I found myself in this horrible situation, I was sure that the miracle was about to happen at last. When Krogstad's letter was lying out there, never for a moment did I imagine that you would agree to his conditions. I was absolutely certain that you'd say to him: Go ahead, tell the whole world. And when he had—

Helmer: Yes, what then? After I'd exposed my wife to shame and disgrace?

Nora: When he had, I was absolutely certain you'd come forward and take the whole thing on yourself, and say: I'm the guilty one.

Helmer: Nora—!

Nora: You mean that I would never have let you make such a sacrifice for me? Of course I wouldn't. But who would have believed my word against yours? That was the miracle that I hoped for and dreaded. And it was to keep it from happening that made me want to kill myself.

Helmer: I'd gladly work night and day for you, Nora, and endure sorrow and poverty for your sake. But no man would sacrifice his honor for the one he loves.

Nora: Hundreds of thousands of women have done it.

Helmer: Oh, you think and talk like a thoughtless child.

Nora: Maybe so. But you don't think or talk like the man I want to be with for the rest of my life. As soon as your fear had passed—and it wasn't fear for what threatened me, but for what might happen to you—when the whole thing was past, as far as you were concerned it was just as if nothing at all had happened. I was still your little skylark, your doll, but now you'd handle me twice as gently and carefully as before, because I was so delicate and fragile. (*Getting up.*) Torvald, that's when it dawned on me that for eight years I'd been living here with a stranger and had borne him three children. Oh, I can't bear to think about it! I could tear myself into little pieces!

Helmer (*sadly*): I see, I see. An abyss has opened up between us. There's no denying it. But, Nora, can't we find some way to close it?

Nora: The way I am now, I'm no wife for you.

Helmer: I can find it in myself to become a different man.

Nora: Maybe so—if your doll is taken away from you.

Helmer: But to be apart!—to be apart from you! No, no, Nora, I can't conceive of it.

Nora (*going out to the right*): All the more reason why it has to be done.

(*She comes back with her coat and hat and a small suitcase which she puts on a chair by the table.*)

Helmer: Nora, Nora, not now! Wait till tomorrow.

Nora (*putting on her cloak*): I can't spend the night in a strange man's room.

Helmer: But couldn't we live here together like brother and sister?

Nora (*putting on her hat*): You know how long that would last. (*Puts the shawl around her.*) Goodbye, Torvald. I won't look in on the children. I know they're in better hands than mine. The way I am now, I'm no use to them.

Helmer: But someday, Nora, someday?

Nora: How can I tell? I have no idea what's going to become of me.

Helmer: But you're my wife, whatever becomes of you.

Nora: Listen, Torvald. I've heard that when a wife deserts her husband's house, the way I'm doing now, he's free of all legal obligations to her. In any event, I set you free from all your obligations. I don't want you to feel bound in the slightest, any more than I will. There has to be complete freedom on both sides. Look, here's your ring back. Give me mine.

Helmer: That too?

Nora: That too.

Helmer: Here it is.

Nora: Good. Now it's all over. I've left the keys here. The maids know all about how to run the house, much better than I do. Kristine will come by tomorrow after I leave her place and pack up my own things, the ones I brought with me from home. I'd like to have them sent to me.

Helmer: All over! All over! Nora, will you ever think about me again?

Nora: I know I'll often think about you, and the children, and this house.

Helmer: May I write to you, Nora?

Nora: No, never. You mustn't do that.

Helmer: But at least let me send you—

Nora: Nothing, nothing.

Helmer: Let me help you if you're in need.

Nora: No. I can't accept anything from a stranger.

Helmer: Nora . . . can't I ever be anything more than a stranger to you?

Nora (picking up her bag): Ah, Torvald, for that, the most wonderful miracle of all would have to happen.

Helmer: Tell me what that would be!

Nora: We'd both have to change so much that—Oh, Torvald, I've stopped believing in miracles.

Helmer: But I'll believe. Tell me! Change so much that . . . ?

Nora: That our life together would be a true marriage. Goodbye.

(*She goes out through the hall.*)

Helmer (sinks down into a chair at the door and buries his face in his hands): Nora! Nora! (*Looks around, and stands up.*) Empty. She's gone. (*A hope flashes across his mind.*) The most wonderful miracle of all . . . ?

(*The heavy sound of a closing door is heard from below.*)

Questions

ACT I

1. From the opening conversation between Helmer and Nora, what are your impressions of him? Of her? Of their marriage?
2. At what moment in the play do you understand why it is called *A Doll's House*?
3. In what ways does Mrs. Linde provide a contrast for Nora?
4. What in Krogstad's first appearance on stage, and in Dr. Rank's remarks about him, indicates that the bank clerk is a menace?
5. Of what illegal deed is Nora guilty? How does she justify it?
6. When the curtain falls on Act I, what problems now confront Nora?

ACT II

1. As Act II opens, what are your feelings on seeing the stripped, ragged Christmas tree? How is it suggestive?
2. What events that soon occur make Nora's situation even more difficult?
3. How does she try to save herself?
4. Why does Nora fling herself into the wild tarantella?

ACT III

1. For what possible reasons does Mrs. Linde pledge herself to Krogstad?
2. How does Dr. Rank's announcement of his impending death affect Nora and Helmer?

3. What is Helmer's reaction to learning the truth about Nora's misdeed? Why does he blame Nora's father? What is revealing (of Helmer's own character) in his remark, "From this moment on happiness is out of the question. All that matters now is to save the bits and pieces, to keep up the appearance—"?

4. When Helmer finds that Krogstad has sent back the note, what is his response? How do you feel toward him?

5. How does the character of Nora develop in this act?

6. How do you interpret her final slamming of the door?

General Questions

1. In what ways do you find Nora a victim? In what ways is she at fault?

2. Try to state the theme of the play. Does it involve women's rights? Self-fulfillment?

3. What dramatic question does the play embody? At what moment can this question first be stated?

4. What is the crisis? In what way is this moment or event a "turning point"? (In what new direction does the action turn?)

5. Eric Bentley, in an essay titled "Ibsen, Pro and Con" (*In Search of Theater* [New York: Knopf, 1953]), criticizes the character of Krogstad, calling him "a mere pawn of the plot." He then adds, "When convenient to Ibsen, he is a blackmailer. When inconvenient, he is converted." Do you agree or disagree?

6. Why is the play considered a work of realism? Is there anything in it that does not seem realistic?

7. In what respects does *A Doll's House* seem to apply to life today? Is it in any way dated? Could there be a Nora in North America today?

Henrik Ibsen on Writing

Correspondence on the Final Scene of *A Doll's House*   1880, 1891

Translated by John Nilsen Laurvik and Mary Morison

Munich, 17 February 1880

To the Editor of the *Nationaltidende*

Sir,

In No. 1360 of your esteemed paper I have read a letter from Flensburg, in which it is stated that *A Doll's House* (in German *Nora*) has been acted there, and that the conclusion of the play has been changed—the alteration having been made, it is asserted, by my orders. This last statement is untrue. Immediately after the publication of *Nora*, I received from my translator, Mr. Wilhelm Lange of Berlin, the information that he had reason to fear that an "adaptation" of the play, giving it a different ending, was about to be published, and that this would probably be chosen in preference to the original by several of the North German theaters.

Henrik Ibsen

In order to prevent such a possibility, I sent to him, for use in case of absolute necessity, a draft of an altered last scene, according to which Nora does not leave the house, but is forcibly led by Helmer to the door of the children's bedroom; a short dialogue takes place, Nora sinks down at the door, and the curtain falls.

This change, I myself, in the letter to my translator, stigmatize as "barbaric violence" done to the play. Those who make use of the altered scene do so entirely against my wish. But I trust that it will not be used at very many German theaters.

. . . When my works are threatened, I prefer, taught by experience, to commit the act of violence myself, instead of leaving them to be treated and "adapted" by less careful and less skilful hands.

Yours respectfully,

Henrik Ibsen

Dear Count Proznor, 1891

Mr. Luigi Capuana° has, I regret to see, given you a great deal of trouble by his proposal to alter the last scene of A Doll's House for performance in the Italian theaters. . . . [T]he fact is that I cannot possibly directly authorize any change whatever in the ending of the drama. I may almost say that it was for the sake of the last scene that the whole play was written.

And, besides, I believe that Mr. Capuana is mistaken in fearing that the Italian public would not be able to understand or approve of my work if it were put on the stage in its original form. The experiment, ought, at any rate, to be tried. If it turns out a failure, then let Mr. Capuana, on his own responsibility, employ your adaptation of the closing scene; for I cannot formally authorize, or approve of, such a proceeding.

I wrote to Mr. Capuana yesterday, briefly expressing my views on the subject; and I hope that he will disregard his misgivings until he has proved by experience that they are well founded.

At the time when A Doll's House was quite new, I was obliged to give my consent to an alteration of the last scene for Frau Hedwig Niemann-Raabe, who was to play the part of Nora in Berlin. At that time I had no choice. I was entirely unprotected by copyright law in Germany, and could, consequently prevent nothing. . . . With its altered ending it had only a short run. In its unchanged form it is still being played. . . .

Your sincere and obliged,

Henrik Ibsen

Luigi Capuana: Italian novelist and dramatic critic who translated *A Doll's House* into Italian. It was the famous actress Eleonora Duse who wished him to alter the last scene of the play, but she finally relented and acted it in the original form.

Tennessee Williams

The Glass Menagerie   1945

Tennessee Williams (1911–1983) was born Thomas Lanier Williams in Columbus, Mississippi, went to high school in St. Louis, and graduated from the University of Iowa. As an undergraduate, he saw a performance of Ibsen's Ghosts and decided to become a playwright himself. His family bore a close resemblance to the Wingfields in The Glass Menagerie: his mother came from a line of Southern blue bloods (Tennessee pioneers); his sister Rose suffered from incapacitating shyness; and as a young man, Williams himself, like Tom, worked at a job he disliked (in a shoe factory where his father worked), wrote poetry, sought refuge in moviegoing, and finally left home to wander and hold odd jobs. He worked as a bellhop in a New Orleans hotel; a teletype operator in Jacksonville, Florida; an usher and a waiter in New York. In 1945 The Glass Menagerie scored a success on Broadway, winning a Drama Critics Circle award. Two years later Williams received a Pulitzer Prize for A Streetcar Named Desire, a grim, powerful study of a woman's illusions and frustrations, set in New Orleans. In 1955 Williams was awarded another Pulitzer Prize for Cat on a Hot Tin Roof. Besides other plays, including Summer and Smoke (1948), Sweet Bird of Youth (1959), The Night of the Iguana (1961), Small Craft Warnings (1973), Clothes for a Summer Hotel (1980), and A House Not Meant to Stand (1981), Williams wrote two novels, poetry, essays, short stories, and Memoirs (1975).

> Nobody, not even the rain, has such small hands.
>
> —E. E. CUMMINGS

CHARACTERS

Amanda Wingfield, the mother. A little woman of great but confused vitality clinging frantically to another time and place. Her characterization must be carefully created, not copied from type. She is not paranoiac, but her life is paranoia. There is much to admire in Amanda, and as much to love and pity as there is to laugh at. Certainly she has endurance and a kind of heroism, and though her foolishness makes her unwittingly cruel at times, there is tenderness in her slight person.

Laura Wingfield, her daughter. Amanda, having failed to establish contact with reality, continues to live vitally in her illusions, but Laura's situation is even graver. A childhood illness has left her crippled, one leg slightly shorter than the other, and held in a brace. This defect need not be more than suggested on the stage. Stemming from this, Laura's separation increases till she is like a piece of her own glass collection, too exquisitely fragile to move from the shelf.

Tom Wingfield, her son. And the narrator of the play. A poet with a job in a warehouse. His nature is not remorseless, but to escape from a trap he has to act without pity.

Jim O'Connor, the gentleman caller. A nice, ordinary, young man.

SCENE. *An alley in St. Louis.*
PART I. *Preparation for a Gentleman Caller.*
PART II. *The Gentleman Calls.*
TIME. *Now and the Past.*

Five years after *The Glass Menagerie's* Broadway debut, a movie version was filmed starring Kirk Douglas, Jane Wyman, Gertrude Lawrence, and Arthur Kennedy.

SCENE I

The Wingfield apartment is in the rear of the building, one of those vast hive-like conglomerations of cellular living-units that flower as warty growths in overcrowded urban centers of lower middle-class population and are symptomatic of the impulse of this largest and fundamentally enslaved section of American society to avoid fluidity and differentiation and to exist and function as one interfused mass of automatism.

The apartment faces an alley and is entered by a fire-escape, a structure whose name is a touch of accidental poetic truth, for all of these huge buildings are always burning with the slow and implacable fires of human desperation. The fire-escape is included in the set—that is, the landing of it and steps descending from it.

The scene is memory and is therefore unrealistic. Memory takes a lot of poetic license. It omits some details; others are exaggerated, according to the emotional value of the articles it touches, for memory is seated predominantly in the heart. The interior is therefore rather dim and poetic.

At the rise of the curtain, the audience is faced with the dark, grim rear wall of the Wingfield tenement. This building, which runs parallel to the footlights, is flanked on both sides by dark, narrow alleys which run into murky canyons of tangled clotheslines, garbage cans, and the sinister latticework of neighboring fire-escapes. It is up and down these side alleys that exterior entrances and exits are made, during the play. At the end of Tom's opening commentary, the dark tenement wall slowly reveals (by means of a transparency) the interior of the ground floor Wingfield apartment.

Karen Allen and John Malkovich in a 1987 film of *The Glass Menagerie*, directed by Paul Newman.

Downstage is the living room, which also serves as a sleeping room for Laura, the sofa unfolding to make her bed. Upstage, center, and divided by a wide arch or second proscenium with transparent faded portieres (or second curtain), is the dining room. In an old-fashioned what-not in the living room are seen scores of transparent glass animals. A blown-up photograph of the father hangs on the wall of the living room, facing the audience, to the left of the archway. It is the face of a very handsome young man in a doughboy's First World War cap. He is gallantly smiling, ineluctably smiling, as if to say, "I will be smiling forever."

The audience hears and sees the opening scene in the dining room through both the transparent fourth wall of the building and the transparent gauze portieres of the dining room arch. It is during this revealing scene that the fourth wall slowly ascends, out of sight. This transparent exterior wall is not brought down again until the very end of the play, during Tom's final speech.

The narrator is an undisguised convention of the play. He takes whatever license with dramatic convention as is convenient to his purposes.

Tom enters dressed as a merchant sailor from the alley, stage left, and strolls across the front of the stage to the fire-escape. There he stops and lights a cigarette. He addresses the audience.

Tom: Yes, I have tricks in my pocket, I have things up my sleeve. But I am the opposite of a stage magician. He gives you illusion that has the appearance of truth. I give you truth in the pleasant disguise of illusion. To begin with, I turn back time. I reverse it to that quaint period, the thirties, when the huge middle class of America was matriculating in a school for the blind. Their eyes had failed them, or they had failed their eyes, and so they were having their fingers pressed forcibly down on the fiery Braille alphabet of a dissolving economy. In Spain there was revolution. Here there was only shouting and confusion. In Spain there was Guernica. Here there were disturbances of labor, sometimes pretty violent, in otherwise peaceful cities such as Chicago, Cleveland, St. Louis. . . . This is the social background of the play.

(Music.)

The play is memory. Being a memory play, it is dimly lighted, it is sentimental, it is not realistic. In memory everything seems to happen to music. That explains the fiddle in the wings. I am the narrator of the play, and also a character in it. The other characters are my mother, Amanda, my sister, Laura, and a gentleman caller who appears in the final scenes. He is the most realistic character in the play, being an emissary from a world of reality that we were somehow set apart from. But since I have a poet's weakness for symbols, I am using this character also as a symbol; he is the long delayed but always expected something that we live for. There is a fifth character in the play who doesn't appear except in this larger-than-life photograph over the mantel. This is our father who left us a long time ago. He was a telephone man who fell in love with long distances; he gave up his job with the telephone company and skipped the light fantastic out of town. . . . The last we heard of him was a picture post-card from Mazatlan, on the Pacific coast of Mexico, containing a message of two words—"Hello—Good-bye!" and an address. I think the rest of the play will explain itself. . . .

Amanda's voice becomes audible through the portieres.

(Screen Legend: "Où Sont Les Neiges.")°

He divides the portieres and enters the upstage area.

Amanda and Laura are seated at a drop-leaf table. Eating is indicated by gestures without food or utensils. Amanda faces the audience. Tom and Laura are seated in profile.

The interior has lit up softly and through the scrim we see Amanda and Laura seated at the table in the upstage area.

Amanda (calling): Tom?
Tom: Yes, Mother.
Amanda: We can't say grace until you come to the table!
Tom: Coming, Mother. (*He bows slightly and withdraws, reappearing a few moments later in his place at the table.*)
Amanda (to her son): Honey, don't *push* with your *fingers.* If you have to push with something, the thing to push with is a crust of bread. And chew—chew! Animals have sections in their stomachs which enable them to digest food without mastication, but human beings are supposed to chew their food before they swallow it

"*Où Son Les Nieges*": A slide bearing this line is to be projected on a stage wall. The phrase is part of a famous line from French poet François Villon's *Ballad of the Dead Ladies.* The full line "*Où Sont Les Neiges D'antan?,*" meaning "But, where are the snows of yester-year?" is projected on the wall later in this scene.

down. Eat food leisurely, son, and really enjoy it. A well-cooked meal has lots of delicate flavors that have to be held in the mouth for appreciation. So chew your food and give your salivary glands a chance to function!

Tom deliberately lays his imaginary fork down and pushes his chair back from the table.

Tom: I haven't enjoyed one bite of this dinner because of your constant directions on how to eat it. It's you that makes me rush through meals with your hawk-like attention to every bite I take. Sickening—spoils my appetite—all this discussion of animals' secretion—salivary glands—mastication!

Amanda (*lightly*): Temperament like a Metropolitan star!

He rises and crosses downstage.

You're not excused from the table.

Tom: I am getting a cigarette.

Amanda: You smoke too much.

Laura rises.

Laura: I'll bring in the blanc mange.

He remains standing with his cigarette by the portieres during the following.

Amanda (*rising*): No, sister, no, sister—you be the lady this time and I'll be the darky.

Laura: I'm already up.

Amanda: Resume your seat, little sister—I want you to stay fresh and pretty—for gentlemen callers!

Laura (*sitting down*): I'm not expecting any gentlemen callers.

Amanda (*crossing out to kitchenette, airily*): Sometimes they come when they are least expected! Why, I remember one Sunday afternoon in Blue Mountain—(*Enters kitchenette.*)

Tom: I know what's coming!

Laura: Yes. But let her tell it.

Tom: Again?

Laura: She loves to tell it.

Amanda returns with bowl of dessert.

Amanda: One Sunday afternoon in Blue Mountain—your mother received— seventeen!—gentlemen callers! Why, sometimes there weren't chairs enough to accommodate them all. We had to send the nigger over to bring in folding chairs from the parish house.

Tom (*remaining at portieres*): How did you entertain those gentlemen callers?

Amanda: I understood the art of conversation!

Tom: I bet you could talk.

Amanda: Girls in those days *knew* how to talk, I can tell you.

Tom: Yes?

(Image: Amanda As A Girl On A Porch Greeting Callers.)

Amanda: They knew how to entertain their gentlemen callers. It wasn't enough for a girl to be possessed of a pretty face and a graceful figure—although I wasn't slighted in either respect. She also needed to have a nimble wit and a tongue to meet all occasions.

Tom: What did you talk about?

Amanda: Things of importance going on in the world! Never anything coarse or common or vulgar. (*She addresses Tom as though he were seated in the vacant chair at the table though he remains by portieres. He plays this scene as though reading from a script.*) My callers were gentlemen—all! Among my callers were some of the most prominent young planters of the Mississippi Delta—planters and sons of planters!

Tom motions for music and a spot of light on Amanda. Her eyes lift, her face glows, her voice becomes rich and elegiac.

(Screen Legend: "Où Sont Les Neiges D'antan?")

There was young Champ Laughlin who later became vice-president of the Delta Planters Bank. Hadley Stevenson who was drowned in Moon Lake and left his widow one hundred and fifty thousand in Government bonds. There were the Cutrere brothers, Wesley and Bates. Bates was one of my bright particular beaux! He got in a quarrel with that wild Wainright boy. They shot it out on the floor of Moon Lake Casino. Bates was shot through the stomach. Died in the ambulance on his way to Memphis. His widow was also well-provided for, came into eight or ten thousand acres, that's all. She married him on the rebound—never loved her—carried my picture on him the night he died! And there was that boy that every girl in the Delta had set her cap for! That beautiful, brilliant young Fitzhugh boy from Green County!

Tom: What did he leave his widow?

Amanda: He never married! Gracious, you talk as though all of my old admirers had turned up their toes to the daisies!

Tom: Isn't this the first you mentioned that still survives?

Amanda: That Fitzhugh boy went North and made a fortune—came to be known as the Wolf of Wall Street! He had the Midas touch, whatever he touched turned to gold! And I could have been Mrs. Duncan J. Fitzhugh, mind you! But—I picked your *father!*

Laura (rising): Mother, let me clear the table.

Amanda: No dear, you go in front and study your typewriter chart. Or practice your shorthand a little. Stay fresh and pretty!—It's almost time for our gentlemen callers to start arriving. (*She flounces girlishly toward the kitchenette.*) How many do you suppose we're going to entertain this afternoon?

Tom throws down the paper and jumps up with a groan.

Laura (alone in the dining room): I don't believe we're going to receive any, Mother.

Amanda (reappearing, airily): What? No one—not one? You must be joking! (*Laura nervously echoes her laugh. She slips in a fugitive manner through the half-open portieres and draws them gently behind her. A shaft of very clear light is thrown on her face against the jaded tapestry of the curtains.*) (**Music: "The Glass Menagerie"**

Under Faintly.) (*Lightly.*) Not one gentleman caller? It can't be true! There must be a flood, there must have been a tornado!

Laura: It isn't a flood, it's not a tornado, Mother. I'm just not popular like you were in Blue Mountain. . . . (*Tom utters another groan. Laura glances at him with a faint, apologetic smile. Her voice catching a little.*) Mother's afraid I'm going to be an old maid.

(The Scene Dims Out With "Glass Menagerie" Music.)

SCENE II

"Laura, Haven't You Ever Liked Some Boy?"

On the dark stage the screen is lighted with the image of blue roses.

Gradually Laura's figure becomes apparent and the screen goes out.

The music subsides.

Laura is seated in the delicate ivory chair at the small clawfoot table.

She wears a dress of soft violet material for a kimono—her hair tied back from her forehead with a ribbon.

She is washing and polishing her collection of glass.

Amanda appears on the fire-escape steps. At the sound of her ascent, Laura catches her breath, thrusts the bowl of ornaments away and seats herself stiffly before the diagram of the typewriter keyboard as though it held her spellbound. Something has happened to Amanda. It is written in her face as she climbs to the landing: a look that is grim and hopeless and a little absurd.

She has on one of those cheap or imitation velvety-looking cloth coats with imitation fur collar. Her hat is five or six years old, one of those dreadful cloche hats that were worn in the late twenties, and she is clasping an enormous black patent-leather pocketbook with nickel clasp and initials. This is her full-dress outfit, the one she usually wears to the D.A.R.

Before entering she looks through the door.

She purses her lips, opens her eyes wide, rolls them upward and shakes her head.

Then she slowly lets herself in the door. Seeing her mother's expression Laura touches her lips with a nervous gesture.

Laura: Hello, Mother, I was—(*She makes a nervous gesture toward the chart on the wall. Amanda leans against the shut door and stares at Laura with a martyred look.*)

Amanda: Deception? Deception? (*She slowly removes her hat and gloves, continuing the sweet suffering stare. She lets the hat and gloves fall on the floor—a bit of acting.*)

Laura (*shakily*): How was the D.A.R. meeting? (*Amanda slowly opens her purse and removes a dainty white handkerchief which she shakes out delicately and delicately touches to her lips and nostrils.*) Didn't you go to the D.A.R. meeting, Mother?

Amanda (*faintly, almost inaudibly*): —No.—No. (*Then more forcibly.*) I did not have the strength—to go to the D.A.R. In fact, I did not have the courage! I wanted to find a hole in the ground and hide myself in it forever! (*She crosses slowly to the wall and removes the diagram of the typewriter keyboard. She holds it in front of her for a second, staring at it sweetly and sorrowfully—then bites her lips and tears it in two pieces.*)

Laura (*faintly*): Why did you do that, Mother? (*Amanda repeats the same procedure with the chart of the Gregg Alphabet.*) Why are you—

Amanda: Why? Why? How old are you, Laura?

Laura: Mother, you know my age.

Amanda: I thought that you were an adult; it seems that I was mistaken. (*She crosses slowly to the sofa and sinks down and stares at Laura.*)

Laura: Please don't stare at me, Mother.

Amanda closes her eyes and lowers her head. Count ten.

Amanda: What are we going to do, what is going to become of us, what is the future?

Count ten.

Laura: Has something happened, Mother? (*Amanda draws a long breath and takes out the handkerchief again. Dabbing process.*) Mother, has—something happened?

Amanda: I'll be all right in a minute. I'm just bewildered—(*count five*)—by life . . .

Laura: Mother, I wish that you would tell me what's happened.

Amanda: As you know, I was supposed to be inducted into my office at the D.A.R. this afternoon. (**Image: A Swarm of Typewriters.**) But I stopped off at Rubicam's Business College to speak to your teachers about your having a cold and ask them what progress they thought you were making down there.

Laura: Oh . . .

Amanda: I went to the typing instructor and introduced myself as your mother. She didn't know who you were. "Wingfield," she said, "We don't have any such student enrolled at the school!" I assured her she did, that you had been going to classes since early in January. "I wonder," she said, "if you could be talking about that terribly shy little girl who dropped out of school after only a few days' attendance?" "No," I said, "Laura, my daughter, has been going to school every day for the past six weeks!" "Excuse me," she said. She took the attendance book out and there was your name, unmistakably printed, and all the dates you were absent until they decided that you had dropped out of school. I still said, "No, there must have been some mistake! There must have been some mix-up in the records!" And she said, "No—I remember her perfectly now. Her hand shook so that she couldn't hit the right keys! The first time we gave a speed-test, she broke down completely—was sick at the stomach and almost had to be carried into the wash-room! After that morning she never showed up any more. We phoned the house but never got any answer"—While I was working at Famous-Barr, I suppose, demonstrating those—(*She indicates a brassiere with her hands.*) Oh! I felt so weak I could barely keep on my feet. I had to sit down while they got me a glass of water! Fifty dollars' tuition, all of our plans—my hopes and ambitions for you—just gone up the spout, just gone up the spout like that. (*Laura draws a long breath and gets awkwardly to her feet. She crosses to the victrola and winds it up.*) What are you doing?

Laura: Oh! (*She releases the handle and returns to her seat.*)

Amanda: Laura, where have you been going when you've gone out pretending that you were going to business college?

Laura: I've just been going out walking.

Amanda: That's not true.

Laura: It is. I just went walking.

Amanda: Walking? Walking? In winter? Deliberately courting pneumonia in that light coat? Where did you walk to, Laura?

Laura: All sorts of places—mostly in the park.

Amanda: Even after you'd started catching that cold?

Laura: It was the lesser of two evils, Mother. (**Image: Winter Scene In Park.**) I couldn't go back there. I—threw up—on the floor!

Amanda: From half past seven till after five every day you mean to tell me you walked around in the park, because you wanted to make me think that you were still going to Rubicam's Business College?

Laura: It wasn't as bad as it sounds. I went inside places to get warmed up.

Amanda: Inside where?

Laura: I went in the art museum and the bird-houses at the Zoo. I visited the penguins every day! Sometimes I did without lunch and went to the movies. Lately I've been spending most of my afternoons in the Jewel-box, that big glass house where they raise the tropical flowers.

Amanda: You did all this to deceive me, just for deception? (*Laura looks down.*) Why?

Laura: Mother, when you're disappointed, you get that awful suffering look on your face, like the picture of Jesus' mother in the museum!

Amanda: Hush!

Laura: I couldn't face it.

Pause. A whisper of strings.

(**Legend: "The Crust Of Humility."**)

Amanda (*hopelessly fingering the huge pocketbook*): So what are we going to do the rest of our lives? Stay home and watch the parades go by? Amuse ourselves with the glass menagerie, darling? Eternally play those worn-out phonograph records your father left as a painful reminder of him? We won't have a business career—we've given that up because it gave us nervous indigestion! (*Laughs wearily.*) What is there left but dependency all our lives? I know so well what becomes of unmarried women who aren't prepared to occupy a position. I've seen such pitiful cases in the South—barely tolerated spinsters living upon the grudging patronage of sister's husband or brother's wife!—stuck away in some little mouse-trap of a room—encouraged by one in-law to visit another—little birdlike women without any nest—eating the crust of humility all their life! Is that the future that we've mapped out for ourselves? I swear it's the only alternative I can think of! It isn't a very pleasant alternative, is it? Of course—some girls *do marry*. (*Laura twists her hands nervously.*) Haven't you ever liked some boy?

Laura: Yes. I liked one once. (*Rises.*) I came across his picture a while ago.

Amanda (*with some interest*): He gave you his picture?

Laura: No, it's in the year-book.

Amanda (*disappointed*): Oh—a high-school boy.

(Screen Image: Jim As A High-School Hero Bearing A Silver Cup.)

Laura: Yes. His name was Jim. (*Laura lifts the heavy annual from the clawfoot table.*) Here he is in *The Pirates of Penzance*.
Amanda (*absently*): The what?
Laura: The operetta the senior class put on. He had a wonderful voice and we sat across the aisle from each other Mondays, Wednesdays, and Fridays in the Aud. Here he is with the silver cup for debating! See his grin?
Amanda (*absently*): He must have had a jolly disposition.
Laura: He used to call me—Blue Roses.

(Image: Blue Roses.)

Amanda: Why did he call you such a name as that?
Laura: When I had that attack of pleurosis—he asked me what was the matter when I came back. I said pleurosis—he thought that I said Blue Roses! So that's what he always called me after that. Whenever he saw me, he'd holler, "Hello, Blue Roses!" I didn't care for the girl he went out with. Emily Meisenbach. Emily was the best-dressed girl at Soldan. She never struck me, though, as being sincere . . . It says in the Personal Section—they're engaged. That's—six years ago! They must be married by now.
Amanda: Girls that aren't cut out for business careers usually wind up married to some nice man. (*Gets up with a spark of revival.*) Sister, that's what you'll do!

Laura utters a startled, doubtful laugh. She reaches quickly for a piece of glass.

Laura: But, Mother—
Amanda: Yes? (*Crossing to photograph.*)
Laura (*in a tone of frightened apology*): I'm—crippled!

(*Image:* Screen.)

Amanda: Nonsense! Laura, I've told you never, never to use that word. Why, you're not crippled, you just have a little defect—hardly noticeable, even! When people have some slight disadvantage like that, they cultivate other things to make up for it—develop charm—and vivacity—and—*charm!* That's all you have to do! (*She turns again to the photograph.*) One thing your father had *plenty of*—was *charm!*

Tom motions to the fiddle in the wings.

(The Scene Fades Out With Music.)

SCENE III
(Legend On The Screen: "After The Fiasco—")

Tom speaks from the fire-escape landing.

Tom: After the fiasco at Rubicam's Business College, the idea of getting a gentleman caller for Laura began to play a more important part in Mother's calculations. It became an obsession. Like some archetype of the universal unconscious, the image of the gentleman caller haunted our small apartment. . . . (**Image: Young Man At Door With Flowers.**) An evening at home rarely passed without some allusion to this image, this specter, this hope. . . . Even when he wasn't mentioned, his presence hung in Mother's preoccupied look and in my sister's frightened, apologetic manner—hung like a sentence passed upon the Wingfields! Mother was a woman of action as well as words. She began to take logical steps in the planned direction. Late that winter and in the early spring—realizing that extra money would be needed to properly feather the nest and plume the bird— she conducted a vigorous campaign on the telephone, roping in subscribers to one of those magazines for matrons called *The Home-maker's Companion,* the type of journal that features the serialized sublimations of ladies of letters who think in terms of delicate cup-like breasts, slim, tapering waists, rich, creamy thighs, eyes like wood-smoke in autumn, fingers that soothe and caress like strains of music, bodies as powerful as Etruscan sculpture.

(**Screen Image: Glamor Magazine Cover.**)

Amanda enters with phone on long extension cord. She is spotted in the dim stage.

Amanda: Ida Scott? This is Amanda Wingfield! We *missed* you at the D.A.R. last Monday! I said to myself: She's probably suffering with that sinus condition! How is that sinus condition? Horrors! Heaven have mercy!—You're a Christian martyr, yes, that's what you are, a Christian martyr! Well, I just now happened to notice that your subscription to the *Companion*'s about to expire! Yes, it expires with the next issue, honey!—just when that wonderful new serial by Bessie Mae Hopper is getting off to such an exciting start. Oh, honey, it's something that you can't miss! You remember how *Gone With the Wind* took everybody by storm? You simply couldn't go out if you hadn't read it. All everybody *talked* was Scarlett O'Hara. Well, this is a book that critics already compare to *Gone With the Wind.* It's the *Gone With the Wind* of the post-World War generation!— What?—Burning?—Oh, honey, don't let them burn, go take a look in the oven and I'll hold the wire! Heavens—I think she's hung up!

(**Dim Out.**)

(**Legend On Screen: "You Think I'm In Love With Continental Shoemakers?"**)

Before the stage is lighted, the violent voices of Tom and Amanda are heard. They are quarreling behind the portieres. In front of them stands Laura with clenched hands and panicky expression.

A clear pool of light on her figure throughout this scene.

Tom: What in Christ's name am I—
Amanda (*shrilly*): Don't you use that—
Tom: —supposed to do!
Amanda: —expression! Not in my—
Tom: Ohhh!
Amanda: —presence! Have you gone out of your senses?
Tom: I have, that's true, *driven* out!
Amanda: What is the matter with you, you—big—big—IDIOT!

Tom: Look—I've got *no thing*, no single thing—
Amanda: Lower your voice!
Tom: —in my life here that I can call my OWN! Everything is—
Amanda: Stop that shouting!
Tom: Yesterday you confiscated my books! You had the nerve to—
Amanda: I took that horrible novel back to the library—yes! That hideous book by
   that insane Mr. Lawrence. (*Tom laughs wildly.*) I cannot control the output of
   diseased minds or people who cater to them—(*Tom laughs still more wildly.*) BUT I
   WON'T ALLOW SUCH FILTH BROUGHT INTO MY HOUSE! No, no, no, no, no!
Tom: House, house! Who pays rent on it, who makes a slave of himself to—
Amanda (fairly screeching): Don't you DARE to—
Tom: No, no, I mustn't say things! *I've* got to just—
Amanda: Let me tell you—
Tom: I don't want to hear any more! (*He tears the portieres open. The upstage area is lit
   with a turgid smoky red glow.*)

   *Amanda's hair is in metal curlers and she wears a very old bathrobe, much too large for
   her slight figure, a relic of the faithless Mr. Wingfield.*

   *An upright typewriter and a wild disarray of manuscripts are on the drop-leaf table.
   The quarrel was probably precipitated by Amanda's interruption of his creative labor.
   A chair lying overthrown on the floor.*

   Their gesticulating shadows are cast on the ceiling by the fiery glow.

Amanda: You *will* hear more, you—
Tom: No, I won't hear more, I'm going out!
Amanda: You come right back in—
Tom: Out, out out! Because I'm—
Amanda: Come back here, Tom Wingfield! I'm not through talking to you!
Tom: Oh, go—
Laura (desperately): Tom!
Amanda: You're going to listen, and no more insolence from you! I'm at the end of
   my patience! (*He comes back toward her.*)
Tom: What do you think I'm at? Aren't I supposed to have any patience to reach the
   end of, Mother? I know, I know. It seems unimportant to you, what I'm *doing*—
   what *I want* to do—having a little *difference* between them! You don't think
   that—
Amanda: I think you've been doing things that you're ashamed of. That's why you
   act like this. I don't believe that you go every night to the movies. Nobody goes
   to the movies night after night. Nobody in their right minds goes to the movies
   as often as you pretend to. People don't go to the movies at nearly midnight, and
   movies don't let out at two A.M. Come in stumbling. Muttering to yourself like a
   maniac! You get three hours' sleep and then go to work. Oh, I can picture the
   way you're doing down there. Moping, doping, because you're in no condition.
Tom (wildly): No, I'm in no condition!
Amanda: What right have you got to jeopardize your job? Jeopardize the security of
   us all? How do you think we'd manage if you were—

Tom: Listen! You think I'm crazy about the *warehouse*? (*He bends fiercely toward her slight figure.*) You think I'm in love with the Continental Shoemakers? You think I want to spend fifty-five *years* down there in that—*celotex interior!* with—*fluorescent—tubes!* Look! I'd rather somebody picked up a crowbar and battered out my brains—than go back mornings! I *go!* Every time you come in yelling that God-damn *"Rise and Shine!" "Rise and Shine!"* I say to myself *"How lucky dead people are!"* But I get up. I *go!* For sixty-five dollars a month I give up all that I dream of doing and being *ever!* And you say self— *self's* all I ever think of. Why, listen, if self is what I thought of, Mother, I'd be where he is—GONE! (*Pointing to father's picture.*) As far as the system of transportation reaches! (*He starts past her. She grabs his arm.*) Don't grab at me, Mother!

Amanda: Where are you going?

Tom: I'm going to the *movies!*

Amanda: I don't believe that lie!

Tom (*crouching toward her, overtowering her tiny figure. She backs away, gasping*): I'm going to opium dens! Yes, opium dens, dens of vice and criminals' hangouts, Mother. I've joined the Hogan gang, I'm a hired assassin, I carry a tommy-gun in a violin case! I run a string of cat-houses in the Valley! They call me Killer, Killer Wingfield, I'm leading a double-life, a simple, honest warehouse worker by day, by night a dynamic *czar* of the *underworld*, Mother. I go to gambling casinos, I spin away fortunes on the roulette table! I wear a patch over one eye and a false mustache, sometimes I put on green whiskers. On those occasions they call me— *El Diablo!* Oh, I could tell you things to make you sleepless! My enemies plan to dynamite this place. They're going to blow us all sky-high some night! I'll be glad, very happy, and so will you! You'll go up, up on a broomstick, over Blue Mountain with seventeen gentlemen callers! You ugly—babbling old—*witch.* . . . (*He goes through a series of violent, clumsy movements, seizing his overcoat, lunging to the door, pulling it fiercely open. The women watch him, aghast. His arm catches in the sleeve of the coat as he struggles to pull it on. For a moment he is pinioned by the bulky garment. With an outraged groan he tears the coat off again, splitting the shoulders of it, and hurls it across the room. It strikes against the shelf of Laura's glass collection, there is a tinkle of shattering glass. Laura cries out as if wounded.*)

(Music Legend: "The Glass Menagerie.")

Laura (*shrilly*): My glass!—menagerie. . . . (*She covers her face and turns away.*)

But Amanda is still stunned and stupefied by the "ugly witch" so that she barely notices this occurrence. Now she recovers her speech.

Amanda (*in an awful voice*): I won't speak to you—until you apologize! (*She crosses through portieres and draws them together behind her. Tom is left with Laura. Laura clings weakly to the mantel with her face averted. Tom stares at her stupidly for a moment. Then he crosses shelf. Drops awkwardly to his knees to collect the fallen glass, glancing at Laura as if he would speak but couldn't.*)

("The Glass Menagerie" Music Steals In As The Scene Dims Out.)

SCENE IV

The interior is dark. Faint in the alley.

A deep-voiced bell in a church is tolling the hour of five as the scene commences.

Tom appears at the top of the alley. After each solemn boom of the bell in the tower, he shakes a little noise-maker or rattle as if to express the tiny spasm of man in contrast to the sustained power and dignity of the Almighty. This and the unsteadiness of his advance make it evident that he has been drinking.

As he climbs the few steps to the fire-escape landing light steals up inside. Laura appears in night-dress, observing Tom's empty bed in the front room.

Tom fishes in his pockets for the door-key, removing a motley assortment of articles in the search, including a perfect shower of movie-ticket stubs and an empty bottle. At last he finds the key, but just as he is about to insert it, it slips from his fingers. He strikes a match and crouches below the door.

Tom (bitterly): One crack—and it falls through!

> *Laura opens the door.*

Laura: Tom! Tom, what are you doing?

Tom: Looking for a door-key.

Laura: Where have you been all this time?

Tom: I have been to the movies.

Laura: All this time at the movies?

Tom: There was a very long program. There was a Garbo picture and a Mickey Mouse and a travelogue and a newsreel and a preview of coming attractions. And there was an organ solo and a collection for the milk-fund—simultaneously—which ended up in a terrible fight between a fat lady and an usher!

Laura (innocently): Did you have to stay through everything?

Tom: Of course! And, oh, I forgot! There was a big stage show! The headliner on this stage show was Malvolio the Magician. He performed wonderful tricks, many of them, such as pouring water back and forth between pitchers. First it turned to wine and then it turned to beer and then it turned to whiskey. I know it was whiskey it finally turned into because he needed somebody to come up out of the audience to help him, and I came up—both shows! It was Kentucky Straight Bourbon. A very generous fellow, he gave souvenirs. (*He pulls from his back pocket a shimmering rainbow-colored scarf.*) He gave me this. This is his magic scarf. You can have it, Laura. You wave it over a canary cage and you get a bowl of gold-fish. You wave it over the gold-fish bowl and they fly away canaries. . . . But the wonderfullest trick of all was the coffin trick. We nailed him into a coffin and he got out of the coffin without removing one nail. (*He has come inside.*) There is a trick that would come in handy for me—get me out of this 2 by 4 situation! (*Flops onto bed and starts removing shoes.*)

Laura: Tom—shhh!

Tom: What're you shushing me for?

Laura: You'll wake up Mother.

Tom: Goody, goody! Pay 'er back for all those "Rise an' Shines." (*Lies down, groaning.*) You know it don't take much intelligence to get yourself into a nailed-up coffin, Laura. But who in hell ever got himself out of one without removing one nail?

As if in answer, the father's grinning photograph lights up.

(Scene Dims Out.)

Immediately following: The church bell is heard striking six. At the sixth stroke the alarm clock goes off in Amanda's room, and after a few moments we hear her calling: "Rise and Shine! Rise and Shine! Laura, go tell your brother to rise and shine!"

Tom (sitting up slowly): I'll rise—but I won't shine.

The light increases.

Amanda: Laura, tell your brother his coffee is ready.

Laura slips into front room.

Laura: Tom!—It's nearly seven. Don't make Mother nervous. (*He stares at her stupidly.*) (*Beseechingly*) Tom, speak to Mother this morning. Make up with her, apologize, speak to her!

Tom: She won't to me. It's her that started not speaking.

Laura: If you just say you're sorry she'll start speaking.

Tom: Her not speaking—is that such a tragedy?

Laura: Please—please!

Amanda (calling from kitchenette): Laura, are you going to do what I asked you to do, or do I have to get dressed and go out myself?

Laura: Going, going—soon as I get on my coat! (*She pulls on a shapeless felt hat with nervous, jerky movements, pleadingly glancing at Tom. Rushes awkwardly for coat. The coat is one of Amanda's inaccurately made-over, the sleeves too short for Laura.*) Butter and what else?

Amanda (entering upstage): Just butter. Tell them to charge it.

Laura: Mother, they make such faces when I do that.

Amanda: Sticks and stones may break my bones, but the expression on Mr. Garfinkel's face won't harm us! Tell your brother his coffee is getting cold.

Laura (at door): Do what I asked you, will you, will you, Tom?

He looks sullenly away.

Amanda: Laura, go now or just don't go at all!

Laura (rushing out): Going—going! (*A second later she cries out. Tom springs up and crosses to the door. Amanda rushes anxiously in. Tom opens the door.*)

Tom: Laura?

Laura: I'm all right. I slipped, but I'm all right.

Amanda (peering anxiously after her): If anyone breaks a leg on those fire-escape steps, the landlord ought to be sued for every cent he possesses! (*She shuts door. Remembers she isn't speaking and returns to other room.*)

As Tom enters listlessly for his coffee, she turns her back to him and stands rigidly facing the window on the gloomy gray vault of the areaway. Its light on her face with its aged but childish features is cruelly sharp, satirical as a Daumier print.

(Music Under: "Ave Maria.")

Tom glances sheepishly but sullenly at her averted figure and slumps at the table. The coffee is scalding hot; he sips it and gasps and spits it back in the cup. At his gasp, Amanda catches her breath and half turns. Then catches herself and turns back to window.

Tom blows on his coffee, glancing sidewise at his mother. She clears her throat. Tom clears his. He starts to rise. Sinks back down again, scratches his head, clears his throat again. Amanda coughs. Tom raises his cup in both hands to blow on it, his eyes staring over the rim of it at his mother for several moments. Then he slowly sets the cup down and awkwardly and hesitantly rises from the chair.

Tom (hoarsely): Mother. I—I apologize. Mother. (*Amanda draws a quick, shuddering breath. Her face works grotesquely. She breaks into childlike tears.*) I'm sorry for what I said, for everything that I said, I didn't mean it.

Amanda (sobbingly): My devotion has made me a witch and so I make myself hateful to my children!

Tom: No, you *don't.*

Amanda: I worry so much, don't sleep, it makes me nervous!

Tom (gently): I understand that.

Amanda: I've had to put up a solitary battle all these years. But you're my right-hand bower! Don't fall down, don't fail!

Tom (gently): I try, Mother.

Amanda (with great enthusiasm): Try and you will *succeed!* (*The notion makes her breathless.*) Why, you—you're just *full* of natural endowments! Both of my children—they're *unusual* children! Don't you think I know it? I'm so—*proud!* Happy and—feel I've—so much to be thankful for but—promise me one thing, son!

Tom: What, Mother?

Amanda: Promise, son you'll—never be a drunkard!

Tom (turns to her grinning): I will never be a drunkard, Mother.

Amanda: That's what frightened me so, that you'd be drinking! Eat a bowl of Purina!

Tom: Just coffee, Mother.

Amanda: Shredded wheat biscuit?

Tom: No. No, Mother, just coffee.

Amanda: You can't put in a day's work on an empty stomach. You've got ten minutes—don't gulp! Drinking too-hot liquids makes cancer of the stomach. . . . Put cream in.

Tom: No, thank you.

Amanda: To cool it.

Tom: No! No, thank you, I want it black.

Amanda: I know, but it's not good for you. We have to do all that we can to build ourselves up. In these trying times we live in, all that we have to cling to is— each other. . . . That's why it's so important to—Tom, I—I sent out your sister so I could discuss something with you. If you hadn't spoken I would have spoken to you. (*Sits down.*)

Tom (gently): What is it, Mother, that you want to discuss?

Amanda: Laura!

Tom puts his cup down slowly.

(**Legend On Screen: "Laura."**)

(**Music: "The Glass Menagerie."**)

Tom: —Oh.—Laura . . .

Amanda (*touching his sleeve*): You know how Laura is. So quiet but—still water runs deep! She notices things and I think she—broods about them. (*Tom looks up.*) A few days ago I came in and she was crying.

Tom: What about?

Amanda: You.

Tom: Me?

Amanda: She has an idea that you're not happy here.

Tom: What gave her that idea?

Amanda: What gives her any idea? However, you do act strangely. I—I'm not criticizing, understand *that!* I know your ambitions do not lie in the warehouse, that like everybody in the whole wide world—you've had to—make sacrifices, but— Tom—Tom—life's not easy, it calls for—Spartan endurance! There's so many things in my heart that I cannot describe to you! I've never told you but I—*loved* your father. . . .

Tom (*gently*): I know that, Mother.

Amanda: And you—when I see you taking after his ways! Staying out late—and— well, you *had* been drinking the night you were in that—terrifying condition! Laura says that you hate the apartment and that you go out nights to get away from it! Is that true, Tom?

Tom: No. You say there's so much in your heart that you can't describe to me. That's true of me, too. There's so much in my heart that I can't describe to *you!* So let's respect each other's—

Amanda: But, why—why, Tom—are you always so *restless?* Where do you go to, nights?

Tom: I—go to the movies.

Amanda: Why do you go to the movies so much, Tom?

Tom: I go to the movies because—I like adventure. Adventure is something I don't have much of at work, so I go to the movies.

Amanda: But, Tom, you go to the movies *entirely* too *much!*

Tom: I like a lot of adventure.

Amanda looks baffled, then hurt. As the familiar inquisition resumes he becomes hard and impatient again. Amanda slips back into her querulous attitude toward him.

(**Image On Screen: Sailing Vessel With Jolly Roger.**)

Amanda: Most young men find adventure in their careers.

Tom: Then most young men are not employed in a warehouse.

Amanda: The world is full of young men employed in warehouses and offices and factories.

Tom: Do all of them find adventure in their careers?

Amanda: They do or they do without it! Not everybody has a craze for adventure.

Tom: Man is by instinct a lover, a hunter, a fighter, and none of those instincts are given much play at the warehouse!

Amanda: Man is by instinct! Don't quote instinct to me! Instinct is something that people have got away from! It belongs to animals! Christian adults don't want it!

Tom: What do Christian adults want, then, Mother?

Amanda: Superior things! Things of the mind and the spirit! Only animals have to satisfy instincts! Surely your aims are somewhat higher than theirs! Than monkeys—pigs—

Tom: I reckon they're not.

Amanda: You're joking. However, that isn't what I wanted to discuss.

Tom (rising): I haven't much time.

Amanda (pushing his shoulder): Sit down.

Tom: You want me to punch in red at the warehouse, Mother?

Amanda: You have five minutes. I want to talk about Laura.

(Legend: "Plans And Provisions.")

Tom: All right! What about Laura?

Amanda: We have to be making some plans and provisions for her. She's older than you, two years, and nothing has happened. She just drifts along doing nothing. It frightens me terribly how she just drifts along.

Tom: I guess she's the type that people call home girls.

Amanda: There's no such type, and if there is, it's a pity! That is unless the home is hers, with a husband!

Tom: What?

Amanda: Oh, I can see the handwriting on the wall as plain as I see the nose in front of my face! It's terrifying! More and more you remind me of your father! He was out all hours without explanation—Then *left! Goodbye!* And me with the bag to hold. I saw that letter you got from the Merchant Marine. I know what you're dreaming of. I'm not standing here blindfolded. (*She pauses.*) Very well, then. Then *do* it! But not till there's somebody to take your place.

Tom: What do you mean?

Amanda: I mean that as soon as Laura has got somebody to take care of her, married, a home of her own, independent—why, then you'll be free to go wherever you please, on land, on sea, whichever way the wind blows! But until that time you've got to look out for your sister. I don't say me because I'm old and don't matter! I say for your sister because she's young and dependent. I put her in business college—a dismal failure! Frightened her so it made her sick to her stomach. I took her over to the Young People's League at the church. Another fiasco. She spoke to nobody, nobody spoke to her. Now all she does is fool with those pieces of glass and play those worn-out records. What kind of a life is that for a girl to lead!

Tom: What can I do about it?

Amanda: Overcome selfishness! Self, self, self is all that you ever think of! (*Tom springs up and crosses to get his coat. It is ugly and bulky. He pulls on a cap with ear-muffs.*) Where is your muffler? Put your wool muffler on! (*He snatches it angrily from the closet and tosses it around his neck and pulls both ends tight.*) Tom! I haven't said what I had in mind to ask you.

Tom: I'm too late to—

Amanda (catching his arms—very importunately. Then shyly): Down at the warehouse, aren't there some—nice young men?

Tom: No!

Amanda: There *must* be—*some* . . .

Tom: Mother—

Gesture.

Amanda: Find one that's clean-living—doesn't drink—and ask him out for sister!

Tom: What?

Amanda: For *sister!* To *meet!* Get *acquainted!*

Tom (stamping to door): Oh, my *go-osh!*

Amanda: Will you? (*He opens door. Imploringly.*) Will you? (*He starts down.*) Will you? *Will* you, dear?

Tom (calling back): Yes!

Amanda closes the door hesitantly and with a troubled but faintly hopeful expression.

(Screen Image: Glamor Magazine Cover.)

Spot Amanda at phone.

Amanda: Ella Cartwright? This is Amanda Wingfield! How are you, honey? How is that kidney condition? (*Count five.*) Horrors! (*Count five.*) You're a Christian martyr, yes, honey, that's what you are, a Christian martyr! Well, I just happened to notice in my little red book that your subscription to the *Companion* has just run out! I knew that you wouldn't want to miss out on the wonderful serial starting in this new issue. It's by Bessie Mae Hopper, the first thing she's written since *Honeymoon for Three.* Wasn't that a strange and interesting story? Well, this one is even lovelier, I believe. It has a sophisticated society background. It's all about the horsey set on Long Island!

(Fade Out.)

SCENE V

(Legend On Screen: "Annunciation.") *Fade with music.*

It is early dusk of a spring evening. Supper has just been finished in the Wingfield apartment. Amanda and Laura in light colored dresses are removing dishes from the table, in the upstage area, which is shadowy, their movements formalized almost as a dance or ritual, their moving forms as pale and silent as moths.

Tom, in white shirt and trousers, rises from the table and crosses toward the fire-escape.

Amanda (as he passes her): Son, will you do me a favor?

Tom: What?

Amanda: Comb your hair! You look so pretty when your hair is combed! (*Tom slouches on sofa with evening paper. Enormous caption "Franco Triumphs."*) There is only one respect in which I would like you to emulate your father.

Tom: What respect is that?

Amanda: The care he always took of his appearance. He never allowed himself to look untidy. (*He throws down the paper and crosses to fire-escape.*) Where are you going?

Tom: I'm going out to smoke.

Amanda: You smoke too much. A pack a day at fifteen cents a pack. How much would that amount to in a month? Thirty times fifteen is how much, Tom? Figure it out and you will be astounded at what you could save. Enough to give you a night-school course in accounting at Washington U! Just think what a wonderful thing that would be for you, son!

Tom is unmoved by the thought.

Tom: I'd rather smoke. (*He steps out on landing, letting the screen door slam.*)

Amanda (*sharply*): I know! That's the tragedy of it. . . . (*Alone, she turns to look at her husband's picture.*)

(Dance Music: "All The World Is Waiting For The Sunrise.")

Tom (*to the audience*): Across the alley from us was the Paradise Dance Hall. On evenings in spring the windows and doors were open and the music came outdoors. Sometimes the lights were turned out except for a large glass sphere that hung from the ceiling. It would turn slowly about and filter the dusk with delicate rainbow colors. Then the orchestra played a waltz or a tango, something that had a slow and sensuous rhythm. Couples would come outside, to the relative privacy of the alley. You could see them kissing behind ash-pits and telephone poles. This was the compensation for lives that passed like mine, without any change or adventure. Adventure and change were imminent in this year. They were waiting around the corner for all these kids. Suspended in the mist over Berchtesgaden, caught in the folds of Chamberlain's umbrella. In Spain there was Guernica! But here there was only hot swing music and liquor, dance halls, bars, and movies, and sex that hung in the gloom like a chandelier and flooded the world with brief, deceptive rainbows. . . . All the world was waiting for bombardments!

Amanda turns from the picture and comes outside.

Amanda (*sighing*): A fire-escape landing's a poor excuse for a porch. (*She spreads a newspaper on a step and sits down, gracefully and demurely as if she were settling into a swing on a Mississippi veranda.*) What are you looking at?

Tom: The moon.

Amanda: Is there a moon this evening?

Tom: It's rising over Garfinkel's Delicatessen.

Amanda: So it is! A little silver slipper of a moon. Have you made a wish on it yet?

Tom: Um-hum.

Amanda: What did you wish for?

Tom: That's a secret.

Amanda: A secret, huh? Well, I won't tell mine either. I will be just as mysterious as you.

Tom: I bet I can guess what yours is.

Amanda: Is my head so transparent?

Tom: You're not a sphinx.

Amanda: No, I don't have secrets. I'll tell you what I wished for on the moon. Success and happiness for my precious children! I wish for that whenever there's a moon, and when there isn't a moon, I wish for it, too.

Tom: I thought perhaps you wished for a gentleman caller.

Amanda: Why do you say that?

Tom: Don't you remember asking me to fetch one?

Amanda: I remember suggesting that it would be nice for your sister if you brought home some nice young man from the warehouse. I think I've made that suggestion more than once.

Tom: Yes, you have made it repeatedly.

Amanda: Well?

Tom: We are going to have one.

Amanda: What?

Tom: A gentleman caller!

(The Annunciation Is Celebrated With Music.)

Amanda rises.

(Image On Screen: Caller With Bouquet.)

Amanda: You mean you have asked some nice young man to come over?

Tom: Yep. I've asked him to dinner.

Amanda: You really did?

Tom: I did!

Amanda: You did, and did he—*accept?*

Tom: He did!

Amanda: Well, well—well, well! That's—lovely!

Tom: I thought that you would be pleased.

Amanda: It's definite, then?

Tom: Very definite.

Amanda: Soon?

Tom: Very soon.

Amanda: For heaven's sake, stop putting on and tell me some things, will you?

Tom: What things do you want me to tell you?

Amanda: *Naturally* I would like to know when he's *coming!*

Tom: He's coming tomorrow.

Amanda: *Tomorrow?*

Tom: Yep. Tomorrow.

Amanda: But, Tom!

Tom: Yes, Mother?

Amanda: Tomorrow gives me no time!

Tom: Time for what?

Amanda: Preparations! Why didn't you phone me at once, as soon as you asked him, the minute that he accepted? Then, don't you see, I could have been getting ready!

Tom: You don't have to make any fuss.

Amanda: Oh, Tom, Tom, Tom, of course I have to make a fuss! I want things nice, not sloppy! Not thrown together. I'll certainly have to do some fast thinking, won't I?

Tom: I don't see why you have to think at all.

Amanda: You just don't know. We can't have a gentleman caller in a pig-sty! All my wedding silver has to be polished, the monogrammed table linen ought to be laundered! The windows have to be washed and fresh curtains put up. And how about clothes? We have to *wear* something, don't we?

Tom: Mother, this boy is no one to make a fuss over!

Amanda: Do you realize he's the first young man we've introduced to your sister? It's terrible, dreadful, disgraceful that poor little sister has never received a single gentleman caller! Tom, come inside! (*She opens the screen door.*)

Tom: What for?

Amanda: I want to ask you some things.

Tom: If you're going to make such a fuss, I'll call it off, I'll tell him not to come.

Amanda: You certainly won't do anything of the kind. Nothing offends people worse than broken engagements. It simply means I'll have to work like a Turk! We won't be brilliant, but we will pass inspection. Come on inside. (*Tom follows, groaning.*) Sit down.

Tom: Any particular place you would like me to sit?

Amanda: Thank heavens I've got that new sofa! I'm also making payments on a floor lamp I'll have sent out! And put the chintz covers on, they'll brighten things up! Of course I'd hoped to have these walls re-papered. . . . What is the young man's name?

Tom: His name is O'Connor.

Amanda: That, of course, means fish—tomorrow is Friday! I'll have that salmon loaf—with Durkee's dressing! What does he do? He works at the warehouse?

Tom: Of course! How else would I—

Amanda: Tom, he—doesn't drink?

Tom: Why do you ask me that?

Amanda: Your father *did*!

Tom: Don't get started on that!

Amanda: He *does* drink, then?

Tom: Not that I know of!

Amanda: Make sure, be certain! The last thing I want for my daughter's a boy who drinks!

Tom: Aren't you being a little premature? Mr. O'Connor has not yet appeared on the scene!

Amanda: But will tomorrow. To meet your sister, and what do I know about his character? Nothing! Old maids are better off than wives of drunkards!

Tom: Oh, my God!

Amanda: Be still!

Tom (*leaning forward to whisper*): Lots of fellows meet girls whom they don't marry!

Amanda: Oh, talk sensibly, Tom—and don't be sarcastic! (*She has gotten a hairbrush.*)

Tom: What are you doing?

Amanda: I'm brushing that cow-lick down! (*She attacks his hair with the brush.*) What is this young man's position at the warehouse?

Tom (*submitting grimly to the brush and the interrogation*): This young man's position is that of a shipping clerk, Mother.

Amanda: Sounds to me like a fairly responsible job, the sort of a job *you* would be in if you just had more *get-up*. What is his salary? Have you got any idea?

Tom: I would judge it to be approximately eighty-five dollars a month.

Amanda: Well—not princely, but—

Tom: Twenty more than I make.

Amanda: Yes, how well I know! But for a family man, eighty-five dollars a month is not much more than you can just get by on. . . .

Tom: Yes, but Mr. O'Connor is not a family man.

Amanda: He might be, mightn't he? Some time in the future?

Tom: I see. Plans and provisions.

Amanda: You are the only young man that I know of who ignores the fact that the future becomes the present, the present the past, and the past turns into everlasting regret if you don't plan for it!

Tom: I will think that over and see what I can make of it!

Amanda: Don't be supercilious with your mother! Tell me some more about this— what do you call him?

Tom: James D. O'Connor. The D. is for Delaney.

Amanda: Irish on *both* sides! *Gracious!* And doesn't drink?

Tom: Shall I call him up and ask him right this minute?

Amanda: The only way to find out about those things is to make discreet inquiries at the proper moment. When I was a girl in Blue Mountain and it was suspected that a young man drank, the girl whose attentions he had been receiving, if any girl *was*, would sometimes speak to the minister of his church, or rather her father would if her father was living, and sort of feel him out on the young man's character. That is the way such things are discreetly handled to keep a young woman from making a tragic mistake!

Tom: Then how did you happen to make a tragic mistake?

Amanda: That innocent look of your father's had everyone fooled! He *smiled*—the world was *enchanted!* No girl can do worse than put herself at the mercy of a handsome appearance! I hope that Mr. O'Connor is not too good-looking.

Tom: No, he's not too good-looking. He's covered with freckles and hasn't too much of a nose.

Amanda: He's not right-down homely, though?

Tom: Not right-down homely. Just medium homely, I'd say.

Amanda: Character's what to look for in a man.

Tom: That's what I've always said, Mother.

Amanda: You've never said anything of the kind and I suspect you would never give it a thought.

Tom: Don't be suspicious of me.

Amanda: At least I hope he's the type that's up and coming.

Tom: I think he really goes in for self-improvement.

Amanda: What reason have you to think so?

Tom: He goes to night school.

Amanda (beaming): Splendid! What does he do, I mean study?

Tom: Radio engineering and public speaking!

Amanda: Then he has visions of being advanced in the world! Any young man who studies public speaking is aiming to have an executive job some day! And radio engineering? A thing for the future! Both of these facts are very illuminating. Those are the sort of things that a mother should know concerning any young man who comes to call on her daughter. Seriously or—not.

Tom: One little warning. He doesn't know about Laura. I didn't let on that we had
    dark ulterior motives. I just said, why don't you come have dinner with us? He
    said okay and that was the whole conversation.

Amanda: I bet it was! You're eloquent as an oyster. However, he'll know about Laura
    when he gets here. When he sees how lovely and sweet and pretty she is, he'll
    thank his lucky stars he was asked to dinner.

Tom: Mother, you mustn't expect too much of Laura.

Amanda: What do you mean?

Tom: Laura seems all those things to you and me because she's ours and we love her.
    We don't even notice she's crippled any more.

Amanda: Don't say crippled! You know that I never allow that word to be used!

Tom: But face facts, Mother. She is and—that not's all—

Amanda: What do you mean "not all"?

Tom: Laura is very different from other girls.

Amanda: I think the difference is all to her advantage.

Tom: Not quite all—in the eyes of others—strangers—she's terribly shy and lives in
    a world of her own and those things make her seem a little peculiar to people
    outside the house.

Amanda: Don't say peculiar.

Tom: Face the facts. She is.

**(The Dance-Hall Music Changes To A Tango That Has A Minor
And Somewhat Ominous Tone.)**

Amanda: In what way is she peculiar—may I ask?

Tom (gently): She lives in a world of her own—a world of—little glass ornaments,
    Mother. . . . (*Gets up. Amanda remains holding brush, looking at him, troubled.*)
    She plays old phonograph records and—that's about all—(*He glances at himself in
    the mirror and crosses to door.*)

Amanda (sharply): Where are you going?

Tom: I'm going to the movies. (*Out screen door.*)

Amanda: Not to the movies, every night to the movies! (*Follows quickly to screen
    door.*) I don't believe you always go to the movies! (*He is gone. Amanda looks wor-
    riedly after him for a moment. Then vitality and optimism return and she turns from the
    door. Crossing to portieres.*) Laura! Laura! (*Laura answers from kitchenette.*)

Laura: Yes, Mother.

Amanda: Let those dishes go and come in front! (*Laura appears with dish towel.
    Gaily.*) Laura, come here and make a wish on the moon!

Laura (entering): Moon—moon?

Amanda: A little silver slipper of a moon. Look over your left shoulder, Laura, and
    make a wish! (*Laura looks faintly puzzled as if called out of sleep. Amanda seizes her
    shoulders and turns her at an angle by the door.*) Now! Now, darling, wish!

Laura: What shall I wish for, Mother?

Amanda (her voice trembling and her eyes suddenly filling with tears): Happiness! Good
    fortune!

The violin rises and the stage dims out.

SCENE VI

(Image: High-School Hero.)

Tom: And so the following evening I brought him home to dinner. I had known Jim slightly in high school. In high school Jim was a hero. He had tremendous Irish good nature and vitality with the scrubbed and polished look of white chinaware. He seemed to move in a continual spotlight. He was a star in basketball, captain of the debating club, president of the senior class and the glee club and he sang the male lead in the annual light operas. He was always running or bounding, never just walking. He seemed always at the point of defeating the law of gravity. He was shooting with such velocity through his adolescence that you would logically expect him to arrive at nothing short of the White House by the time he was thirty. But Jim apparently ran into more interference after his graduation from Soldan. His speed had definitely slowed. Six years after he left high school he was holding a job that wasn't much better than mine.

(Image: Clerk.)

He was the only one at the warehouse with whom I was on friendly terms. I was valuable to him as someone who could remember his former glory, who had seen him win basketball games and the silver cup in debating. He knew of my secret practice of retiring to a cabinet of the washroom to work on my poems when business was slack in the warehouse. He called me Shakespeare. And while the other boys in the warehouse regarded me with suspicious hostility, Jim took a humorous attitude toward me. Gradually his attitude affected the others, their hostility wore off and they also began to smile at me as people smile at an oddly fashioned dog who trots across their path at some distance.

I knew that Jim and Laura had known each other at Soldan, and I had heard Laura speak admiringly of his voice. I didn't know if Jim remembered her or not. In high school Laura had been as unobtrusive as Jim had been astonishing. If he did remember Laura, it was not as my sister, for when I asked him to dinner, he grinned and said, "You know, Shakespeare, I never thought of you as having folks!"

He was about to discover that I did. . . .

(Light Up Stage.)

(Legend On Screen: "The Accent Of A Coming Foot.")

Friday evening. It is about five o'clock of a late spring evening which comes "scattering poems in the sky."

A delicate lemony light is in the Wingfield apartment.

Amanda has worked like a Turk in preparation for the gentleman caller. The results are astonishing. The new floor lamp with its rose-silk shade is in place, a colored paper lantern conceals the broken light fixture in the ceiling, new billowing white curtains are at the windows, chintz covers are on chairs and sofa, a pair of new sofa pillows make their initial appearance.

Open boxes and tissue paper are scattered on the floor.

Laura stands in the middle with lifted arms while Amanda crouches before her, adjusting the hem of the new dress, devout and ritualistic. The dress is colored and designed by memory. The arrangement of Laura's hair is changed; it is softer and more becoming. A fragile, unearthly prettiness has come out in Laura: she is like a piece of translucent glass touched by light, given a momentary radiance, not actual, not lasting.

Amanda (impatiently): Why are you trembling?

Laura: Mother, you've made me so nervous!

Amanda: How have I made you nervous?

Laura: By all this fuss! You make it seem so important!

Amanda: I don't understand you, Laura. You couldn't be satisfied with just sitting home, and yet whenever I try to arrange something for you, you seem to resist it. (*She gets up.*) Now take a look at yourself. No, wait! Wait just a moment—I have an idea!

Laura: What is it now?

Amanda produces two powder puffs which she wraps in handkerchiefs and stuffs in Laura's bosom.

Laura: Mother, what are you doing?

Amanda: They call them "Gay Deceivers"!

Laura: I won't wear them!

Amanda: You will!

Laura: Why should I?

Amanda: Because, to be painfully honest, your chest is flat.

Laura: You make it seem like we were setting a trap.

Amanda: All pretty girls are a trap, a pretty trap, and men expect them to be. (**Legend: "A Pretty Trap."**) Now look at yourself, young lady. This is the prettiest you will ever be! (*She stands back to admire Laura.*) I've got to fix myself now! You're going to be surprised by your mother's appearance! (*She crosses through the portieres, humming gaily.*)

Laura moves slowly to the long mirror and stares solemnly at herself.

A wind blows the white curtains inward in a slow, graceful motion and with a faint, sorrowful sighing.

Amanda (offstage): It isn't dark enough yet. (*She turns slowly before the mirror with a troubled look.*)

(Legend On Screen: "This Is My Sister: Celebrate Her With Strings!" Music.)

Amanda (laughing, off): I'm going to show you something. I'm going to make a spectacular appearance!

Laura: What is it, Mother?

Amanda: Possess your soul in patience—you will see! Something I've resurrected from that old trunk! Styles haven't changed so terribly much after all. . . . (*She parts the portieres.*) Now just look at your mother! (*She wears a girlish frock of yellowed voile with a blue silk sash. She carries a bunch of jonquils—the legend of her youth is nearly revived. Feverishly.*) This is the dress in which I led the cotillion. Won the cakewalk twice at Sunset Hill, wore one Spring to the Governor's Ball in Jackson! See how I sashayed around the ballroom, Laura? (*She raises her skirt and does a mincing step around the room.*) I wore it on Sundays for my gentlemen callers! I had it on the day I met your father . . . I had malaria fever all that Spring. The change of climate from East Tennessee to the Delta—weakened resistance—I had a little temperature all the time—not enough to be serious—just enough to make me restless and giddy! Invitations poured in—parties all over the Delta!—"Stay in bed," said Mother, "you have fever!"—but I just wouldn't. I took quinine but kept on going, going! Evenings, dances! Afternoons, long, long rides! Picnics—lovely!—So lovely, that country in May—all lacy with dogwood, literally flooded with jonquils! That was the spring I had the craze for jonquils. Jonquils became an absolute obsession. Mother said, "Honey, there's no more room for jonquils." And still I kept on bringing in more jonquils. Whenever, wherever I saw them, I'd say, "Stop! Stop! I see jonquils!" I made the young men help me gather the jonquils! It was a joke, Amanda and her jonquils! Finally there were no more vases to hold them, every available space was filled with jonquils. No vases to hold them? All right, I'll hold them myself! And then I—(*She stops in front of the picture.*) (**Music.**) met your father! Malaria fever and jonquils and then—this—boy. . . . (*She switches on the rose-colored lamp.*) I hope they get here before it starts to rain. (*She crosses upstage and places the jonquils in bowl on table.*) I gave your brother a little extra change so he and Mr. O'Connor could take the service car home.

Laura (*with altered look*): What did you say his name was?
Amanda: O'Connor.
Laura: What is his first name?
Amanda: I don't remember. Oh, yes, I do. It was—Jim!

Laura sways slightly and catches hold of a chair.

(**Legend On Screen. "Not Jim!"**)

Laura (*faintly*): Not—Jim!
Amanda: Yes, that was it, it was Jim! I've never known a Jim that wasn't nice!

(**Music: Ominous.**)

Laura: Are you sure his name is Jim O'Connor?
Amanda: Yes. Why?
Laura: Is he the one that Tom used to know in high school?
Amanda: He didn't say so. I think he just got to know him at the warehouse.
Laura: There was a Jim O'Connor we both knew in high school—(*Then, with effort.*) If that is the one that Tom is bringing to dinner—you'll have to excuse me, I won't come to the table.
Amanda: What sort of nonsense is this?
Laura: You asked me once if I'd ever liked a boy. Don't you remember I showed you this boy's picture?
Amanda: You mean the boy you showed me in the year-book?
Laura: Yes, that boy.
Amanda: Laura, Laura, were you in love with that boy?
Laura: I don't know, Mother. All I know is I couldn't sit at the table if it was him!

Amanda: It won't be him! It isn't the least bit likely. But whether it is or not, you will come to the table. You will not be excused.

Laura: I'll have to be, Mother.

Amanda: I don't intend to humor your silliness, Laura. I've had too much from you and your brother, both! So just sit down and compose yourself till they come. Tom has forgotten his key so you'll have to let them in, when they arrive.

Laura (panicky): Oh, Mother—*you* answer the door!

Amanda (lightly): I'll be in the kitchen—busy!

Laura: Oh, Mother, please answer the door, don't make me do it!

Amanda (crossing into kitchenette): I've got to fix the dressing for the salmon. Fuss, fuss—silliness!—over a gentleman caller!

Door swings shut. Laura is left alone.

(Legend: "Terror!")

She utters a low moan and turns off the lamp—sits stiffly on the edge of the sofa, knotting her fingers together.

(Legend On Screen: "The Opening Of A Door!")

Tom and Jim appear on the fire-escape steps and climb to landing. Hearing their approach, Laura rises with a panicky gesture. She retreats to the portieres.

The doorbell. Laura catches her breath and touches her throat. Low drums.

Amanda (calling): Laura, sweetheart! The door!

Laura stares at it without moving.

Jim: I think we just beat the rain.

Tom: Uh-huh. (*He rings again, nervously. Jim whistles and fishes for a cigarette.*)

Amanda (very, very gaily): Laura, that is your brother and Mr. O'Connor! Will you let them in, darling?

Laura crosses toward kitchenette door.

Laura (breathlessly): Mother—you go to the door!

Amanda steps out of kitchenette and stares furiously at Laura. She points imperiously at the door.

Laura: Please, please!

Amanda (in a fierce whisper): What is the matter with you, you silly thing?

Laura (desperately): Please, you answer it, *please!*

Amanda: I told you I wasn't going to humor you, Laura. Why have you chosen this moment to lose your mind?

Laura: Please, please, please, you go!

Amanda: You'll have to go to the door because I can't!

Laura (despairingly): I can't either!

Amanda: Why?

Laura: I'm sick!

Amanda: I'm sick, too—of your nonsense! Why can't you and your brother be normal people? Fantastic whims and behavior! (*Tom gives a long ring.*) Preposterous goings on! Can you give me one reason—(*Calls out lyrically.*) Coming! Just one second!—why should you be afraid to open a door? Now you answer it, Laura!

Laura: Oh, oh, oh . . . (*She returns through the portieres. Darts to the victrola and winds it frantically and turns it on.*)

Amanda: Laura Wingfield, you march right to that door!

Laura: Yes—yes, Mother!

> A faraway, scratchy rendition of "Dardanella" softens the air and gives her strength to move through it. She slips to the door and draws it cautiously open. Tom enters with the caller, Jim O'Connor.

Tom: Laura, this is Jim. Jim, this is my sister, Laura.

Jim (*stepping inside*): I didn't know that Shakespeare had a sister!

Laura (*retreating stiff and trembling from the door*): How—how do you do?

Jim (*heartily extending his hand*): Okay!

> Laura touches it hesitantly with hers.

Jim: Your hand's *cold,* Laura!

Laura: Yes, well—I've been playing the victrola. . . .

Jim: Must have been playing classical music on it! You ought to play a little hot swing music to warm you up!

Laura: Excuse me—I haven't finished playing the victrola. . . .

> She turns awkwardly and hurries into the front room. She pauses a second by the victrola. Then catches her breath and darts through the portieres like a frightened deer.

Jim (*grinning*): What was the matter?

Tom: Oh—with Laura? Laura is—terribly shy.

Jim: Shy, huh? It's unusual to meet a shy girl nowadays. I don't believe you ever mentioned you had a sister.

Tom: Well, now you know. I have one. Here is the *Post Dispatch.* You want a piece of it?

Jim: Uh-huh.

Tom: What piece? The comics?

Jim: Sports! (*Glances at it.*) Ole Dizzy Dean is on his bad behavior.

Tom (*disinterest*): Yeah? (*Lights cigarette and crosses back to fire-escape door.*)

Jim: Where are *you* going?

Tom: I'm going out on the terrace.

Jim (*goes after him*): You know, Shakespeare—I'm going to sell you a bill of goods!

Tom: What goods?

Jim: A course I'm taking.

Tom: Huh?

Jim: In public speaking! You and me, we're not the warehouse type.

Tom: Thanks—that's good news. But what has public speaking got to do with it?

Jim: It fits you for—executive positions!

Tom: Awww.

Jim: I tell you it's done a helluva lot for me.

(Image: Executive At Desk.)

Tom: In what respect?

Jim: In every! Ask yourself what is the difference between you an' me and men in the office down front? Brains?—No!—Ability?—No! Then what? Just one little thing—

Tom: What is that one little thing?

Jim: Primarily it amounts to—social poise! Being able to square up to people and hold your own on any social level!

Amanda (offstage): Tom?

Tom: Yes, Mother?

Amanda: Is that you and Mr. O'Connor?

Tom: Yes, Mother.

Amanda: Well, you just make yourselves comfortable in there.

Tom: Yes, Mother.

Amanda: Ask Mr. O'Connor if he would like to wash his hands.

Jim: Aw—no—thank you—I took care of that at the warehouse. Tom—

Tom: Yes?

Jim: Mr. Mendoza was speaking to me about you.

Tom: Favorably?

Jim: What do you think?

Tom: Well—

Jim: You're going to be out of a job if you don't wake up.

Tom: I am waking up—

Jim: You show no signs.

Tom: The signs are interior.

(Image On Screen: The Sailing Vessel With Jolly Roger Again.)

Tom: I'm planning to change. (*He leans over the rail speaking with quiet exhilaration. The incandescent marquees and signs of the first-run movie houses light his face from across the alley. He looks like a voyager.*) I'm right at the point of committing myself to a future that doesn't include the warehouse and Mr. Mendoza or even a night-school course in public speaking.

Jim: What are you gassing about?

Tom: I'm tired of the movies.

Jim: Movies!

Tom: Yes, movies! Look at them—(*A wave toward the marvels of Grand Avenue.*) All of those glamorous people—having adventures—hogging it all, gobbling the whole thing up! You know what happens? People go to the *movies* instead of *moving!* Hollywood characters are supposed to have all the adventures for everybody in America, while everybody in America sits in a dark room and watches them have them! Yes, until there's a war. That's when adventure becomes available to the masses! *Everyone's* dish, not only Gable's! Then the people in the dark room come out of the dark room to have some adventures themselves—goody, goody! It's our turn now, to go to the South Sea Island—to make a safari—to be exotic, far-off—But I'm not patient. I don't want to wait till then. I'm tired of the *movies* and I am *about to move!*

Jim (*incredulously*): Move?

Tom: Yes!

Jim: When?

Tom: Soon!

Jim: Where? Where?

Theme three music seems to answer the question, while Tom thinks it over. He searches among his pockets.

Tom: I'm starting to boil inside. I know I seem dreamy, but inside—well, I'm boiling! Whenever I pick up a shoe, I shudder a little thinking how short life is and what I am doing!—Whatever that means. I know it doesn't mean shoes—except as something to wear on a traveler's feet! (*Finds paper.*) Look—

Jim: What?

Tom: I'm a member.

Jim (*reading*): The Union of Merchant Seamen.

Tom: I paid my dues this month, instead of the light bill.

Jim: You will regret it when they turn the lights off.

Tom: I won't be here.

Jim: How about your mother?

Tom: I'm like my father. The bastard son of a bastard! Did you notice how he is grinning in his picture in there? And he's been absent going on sixteen years!

Jim: You're just talking, you drip. How does your mother feel about it?

Tom: Shhh—Here comes Mother! Mother is not acquainted with my plans!

Amanda (*enters portieres*): Where are you all?

Tom: On the terrace, Mother.

They start inside. She advances to them. Tom is distinctly shocked at her appearance. Even Jim blinks a little. He is making his first contact with girlish Southern vivacity and in spite of the night-school course in public speaking is somewhat thrown off the beam by the unexpected outlay of social charm.

Certain responses are attempted by Jim but are swept aside by Amanda's gay laughter and chatter. Tom is embarrassed but after the first shock Jim reacts very warmly. He grins and chuckles, is altogether won over.

(Image: Amanda As A Girl.)

Amanda (*coyly smiling, shaking her girlish ringlets*): Well, well, well, so this is Mr. O'Connor. Introductions entirely unnecessary. I've heard so much about you from my boy. I finally said to him, Tom—good gracious!—why don't you bring this paragon to supper? I'd like to meet this nice young man at the warehouse!— Instead of just hearing him sing your praises so much! I don't know why my son is so stand-offish—that's not Southern behavior! Let's sit down and—I think we could stand a little more air in here! Tom, leave the door open. I felt a nice fresh breeze a moment ago. Where has it gone? Mmm, so warm already! And not quite summer, even. We're going to burn up when summer really gets started. However, we're having—we're having a very light supper. I think light things are better fo' this time of year. The same as light clothes are. Light clothes an' light food are what warm weather calls fo'. You know our blood gets so thick during th' winter— it takes a while fo' us to *adjust* ou'selves!—when the season changes . . . It's come so quick this year. I wasn't prepared. All of a sudden—heavens! Already summer!— I ran to the trunk an' pulled out this light dress—Terribly old! Historical almost! But feels so good—so good an' co-ol, y' know. . . .

Tom: Mother—

Amanda: Yes, honey?

Tom: How about—supper?

Amanda: Honey, you go ask Sister if supper is ready! You know that Sister is in full charge of supper! Tell her you hungry boys are waiting for it. (*To Jim*) Have you met Laura?

Jim: She—

Amanda: Let you in? Oh, good, you've met already! It's rare for a girl as sweet an' pretty as Laura to be domestic! But Laura is, thank heavens, not only pretty but also very domestic. I'm not at all. I never was a bit. I never could make a thing but angel- food cake. Well, in the South we had so many servants. Gone, gone, gone. All ves- tige of gracious living! Gone completely! I wasn't prepared for what the future brought me. All of my gentlemen callers were sons of planters and so of course I as- sumed that I would be married to one and raise my family on a large piece of land with plenty of servants. But man proposes—and woman accepts the proposal!— To vary that old, old saying a little bit—I married no planter! I married a man who worked for the telephone company! That gallantly smiling gentleman over there! (*Points to the picture.*) A telephone man who—fell in love with long-distance! Now he travels and I don't even know where!—But what am I going on for about my—tribulations? Tell me yours—I hope you don't have any! Tom?

Tom (*returning*): Yes, Mother?

Amanda: Is supper nearly ready?

Tom: It looks to me like supper is on the table.

Amanda: Let me look—(*She rises prettily and looks through portieres.*) Oh, lovely! But where is Sister?

Tom: Laura is not feeling well and she says that she thinks she'd better not come to the table.

Amanda: What? Nonsense! Laura? Oh, Laura!

Laura (*offstage, faintly*): Yes, Mother.

Amanda: You really must come to the table. We won't be seated until you come to the table! Come in, Mr. O'Connor. You sit over there and I'll . . . Laura? Laura Wingfield! You're keeping us waiting, honey! We can't say grace until you come to the table!

The back door is pushed weakly open and Laura comes in. She is obviously quite faint, her lips trembling, her eyes wide and staring. She moves unsteadily toward the table.

(Legend: "Terror!")

Outside a summer storm is coming abruptly. The white curtains billow inward at the windows and there is a sorrowful murmur and deep blue dusk.

Laura suddenly stumbles—She catches at a chair with a faint moan.

Tom: Laura!

Amanda: Laura! (*There is a clap of thunder.*) (**Legend: "Ah!"**) (*Despairingly.*) Why, Laura, you *are* ill, darling! Tom, help your sister into the living room, dear! Sit in the living room, Laura—rest on the sofa. Well! (*To Jim as Tom helps his sister to the sofa in the living room*) Standing over the hot stove made her ill!—I told her that it was just too warm this evening, but—(*Tom comes back in. Laura is on the sofa.*) Is Laura all right now?

Tom: Yes.

Amanda: What *is* that? Rain? A nice cool rain has come up! (*She gives the gentleman caller a frightened look.*) I think we may—have grace—now . . . (*Tom looks at her stupidly.*) Tom, honey—you say grace!

Tom: Oh . . . "For these and all thy mercies—" (*They bow their heads, Amanda stealing a nervous glance at Jim. In the living room Laura, stretched on the sofa, clenches her hand to her lips, to hold back a shuddering sob.*) God's Holy Name be praised—

(The Scene Dims Out.)

SCENE VII

A Souvenir.

Half an hour later. Dinner is just being finished in the upstage area which is concealed by the drawn portieres.

As the curtain rises Laura is still huddled upon the sofa, her feet drawn under her, her head resting on a pale blue pillow, her eyes wide and mysteriously watchful. The new floor lamp with its shade of rose-colored silk gives a soft, becoming light to her face, bringing out the fragile, unearthly prettiness which usually escapes attention. There is a steady murmur of rain, but it is slackening and stops soon after the scene begins; the air outside becomes pale and luminous as the moon breaks out.

A moment after the curtain rises, the lights in both rooms flicker and go out.

Jim: Hey, there, Mr. Light Bulb!

Amanda laughs nervously.

(Legend: "Suspension Of A Public Service.")

Amanda: Where was Moses when the lights went out? Ha-ha. Do you know the answer to that one, Mr. O'Connor?

Jim: No, Ma'am, what's the answer?

Amanda: In the dark! (*Jim laughs appreciatively.*) Everybody sit still. I'll light the candles. Isn't it lucky we have them on the table? Where's a match? Which of you gentlemen can provide a match?

Jim: Here.

Amanda: Thank you, sir.

Jim: Not at all, Ma'am!

Amanda (*as she lights the candles*): I guess the fuse has burnt out. Mr. O'Connor, can you tell a burnt-out fuse? I know I can't and Tom is a total loss when it comes to mechanics. (**Sound: Getting Up: Voices Recede A Little To Kitchenette.**) Oh, be careful you don't bump into something. We don't want our gentleman caller to break his neck. Now wouldn't that be a fine howdy-do?

Jim: Ha-ha! Where is the fuse-box?

Amanda: Right here next to the stove. Can you see anything?

Jim: Just a minute.

Amanda: Isn't electricity a mysterious thing? Wasn't it Benjamin Franklin who tied a key to a kite? We live in such a mysterious universe, don't we? Some people say that science clears up all the mysteries for us. In my opinion it only creates more! Have you found it yet?

Jim: No, Ma'am. All these fuses look okay to me.

Amanda: Tom!

Tom: Yes, Mother?

Amanda: That light bill I gave you several days ago. The one I told you we got the notices about?

Tom: Oh—yeah.

   (Legend: "Ha!")

Amanda: You didn't neglect to pay it by any chance?

Tom: Why, I—

Amanda: Didn't! I might have known it!

Jim: Shakespeare probably wrote a poem on that light bill, Mrs. Wingfield.

Amanda: I might have known better than to trust him with it! There's such a high price for negligence in this world!

Jim: Maybe the poem will win a ten-dollar prize.

Amanda: We'll just have to spend the remainder of the evening in the nineteenth century, before Mr. Edison made the Mazda lamp!

Jim: Candlelight is my favorite kind of light.

Amanda: That shows you're romantic! But that's no excuse for Tom. Well, we got through dinner. Very considerate of them to let us get through dinner before they plunged us into everlasting darkness, wasn't it, Mr. O'Connor?

Jim: Ha-ha!

Amanda: Tom, as a penalty for your carelessness you can help me with the dishes.

Jim: Let me give you a hand.

Amanda: Indeed you will not!

Jim: I ought to be good for something.

Amanda: Good for something? (*Her tone is rhapsodic.*) You? Why, Mr. O'Connor, nobody, *nobody's* given me this much entertainment in years—as you have!

Jim: Aw, now, Mrs. Wingfield!

Amanda: I'm not exaggerating, not one bit! But Sister is all by her lonesome. You go keep her company in the parlor! I'll give you this lovely old candelabrum that used to be on the altar at the church of the Heavenly Rest. It was melted a little out of shape when the church burnt down. Lightning struck it one spring. Gypsy Jones was holding a revival at the time and he intimated that the church was destroyed because the Episcopalians gave card parties.

Jim: Ha-ha.

Amanda: And how about coaxing Sister to drink a little wine? I think it would be good for her! Can you carry both at once?

Jim: Sure. I'm Superman!

Amanda: Now, Thomas, get into this apron!

Jim comes into the dining room, carrying the candelabrum, its candles lighted, in one hand and a glass of wine in the other. The door of kitchenette swings closed on Amanda's gay laughter; the flickering light approaches the portieres. Laura sits up nervously as he enters. Her speech at first is low and breathless from the almost intolerable strain of being alone with a stranger.

(The Legend: "I Don't Suppose You Remember Me At All!")

In her first speeches in this scene, before Jim's warmth overcomes her paralyzing shyness, Laura's voice is thin and breathless as though she has run up a steep flight of stairs. Jim's attitude is gently humorous. While the incident is apparently unimportant, it is to Laura the climax of her secret life.

Jim: Hello, there, Laura.

Laura (faintly): Hello. (*She clears her throat.*)

Jim: How are you feeling now? Better?

Laura: Yes. Yes, thank you.

Jim: This is for you. A little dandelion wine. (*He extends it toward her with extravagant gallantry.*)

Laura: Thank you.

Jim: Drink it—but don't get drunk! (*He laughs heartily. Laura takes the glass uncertainly; laughs shyly.*) Where shall I set the candles?

Laura: Oh—oh, anywhere . . .

Jim: How about here on the floor? Any objections?

Laura: No.

Jim: I'll spread a newspaper under to catch the drippings. I like to sit on the floor. Mind if I do?

Laura: Oh, no.

Jim: Give me a pillow?

Laura: What?

Jim: A pillow!

Laura: Oh . . . (*Hands him one quickly.*)

Jim: How about you? Don't you like to sit on the floor?

Laura: Oh—yes.

Jim: Why don't you, then?

Laura: I—will.

Jim: Take a pillow! (*Laura does. Sits on the other side of the candelabrum. Jim crosses his legs and smiles engagingly at her.*) I can't hardly see you sitting way over there.

Laura: I can—see you.

Jim: I know, but that's not fair, I'm in the limelight. (*Laura moves her pillow closer.*) Good! Now I can see you! Comfortable?

Laura: Yes.

Jim: So am I. Comfortable as a cow. Will you have some gum?

Laura: No, thank you.

Jim: I think that I will indulge, with your permission. (*Musingly unwraps it and holds it up.*) Think of the fortune made by the guy that invented the first piece of chewing gum. Amazing, huh? The Wrigley Building is one of the sights of Chicago—I saw it when I went up to the Century of Progress. Did you take in the Century of Progress?

Laura: No, I didn't.

Jim: Well, it was quite a wonderful exposition. What impressed me most was the Hall of Science. Gives you an idea of what the future will be in America, even more wonderful than the present time is! (*Pause. Smiling at her.*) Your brother tells me you're shy. Is that right, Laura?

Laura: I—don't know.

Jim: I judge you to be an old-fashioned type of girl. Well, I think that's a pretty good type to be. Hope you don't think I'm being too personal—do you?

Laura (*hastily, out of embarrassment*): I believe I *will* take a piece of gum, if you—don't mind. (*Clearing her throat.*) Mr. O'Connor, have you—kept up with your singing?

Jim: Singing? Me?

Laura: Yes. I remember what a beautiful voice you had.

Jim: When did you hear me sing?

(Voice Offstage In The Pause.)

Voice (*offstage*):

> O blow, ye winds, heigh-ho,
> A-roving I will go!
> I'm off to my love
> With a boxing glove—
> Ten thousand miles away!

Jim: You say you've heard me sing?

Laura: Oh, yes! Yes, very often . . . I—don't suppose you remember me—at all?

Jim (*smiling doubtfully*): You know I have an idea I've seen you before. I had that idea soon as you opened the door. It seemed almost like I was about to remember your name. But the name that I started to call you—wasn't a name! And so I stopped myself before I said it.

Laura: Wasn't it—Blue Roses?

Jim (*springs up, grinning*): Blue Roses! My gosh, yes—Blue Roses! That's what I had on my tongue when you opened the door! Isn't it funny what tricks your memory plays? I didn't connect you with the high school somehow or other. But that's where it was; it was high school. I didn't even know you were Shakespeare's sister! Gosh, I'm sorry.

Laura: I didn't expect you to. You—barely knew me!

Jim: But we did have a speaking acquaintance, huh?

Laura: Yes, we—spoke to each other.

Jim: When did you recognize me?

Laura: Oh, right away!

Jim: Soon as I came in the door?

Laura: When I heard your name I thought it was probably you. I knew that Tom used to know you a little in high school. So when you came in the door—well, then I was—sure.

Jim: Why didn't you *say* something, then?

Laura (*breathlessly*): I didn't know what to say, I was—too surprised!

Jim: For goodness sakes! You know, this sure is funny!

Laura: Yes! Yes, isn't it, though . . .

Jim: Didn't we have a class in something together?

Laura: Yes, we did.

Jim: What class was that?

Laura: It was—singing—chorus!

Jim: Aw!

Laura: I sat across the aisle from you in the Aud.

Jim: Aw.

Laura: Mondays, Wednesdays, and Fridays.

Jim: Now I remember—you always came in late.

Laura: Yes, it was so hard for me, getting upstairs. I had that brace on my leg—it clumped so loud!

Jim: I never heard any clumping.

Laura (*wincing at the recollection*): To me it sounded like—thunder!

Jim: Well, well, well. I never even noticed.

Laura: And everybody was seated before I came in. I had to walk in front of all those people. My seat was in the back row. I had to go clumping all the way up the aisle with everyone watching!

Jim: You shouldn't have been self-conscious.

Laura: I know, but I was. It was always such a relief when the singing started.

Jim: Aw, yes, I've placed you now! I used to call you Blue Roses. How was it that I got started calling you that?

Laura: I was out of school a little while with pleurosis. When I came back you asked me what was the matter. I said I had pleurosis—you thought I said *Blue Roses*. That's what you always called me after that!

Jim: I hope you didn't mind.

Laura: Oh, no—I liked it. You see, I wasn't acquainted with many—people. . . .

Jim: As I remember you sort of stuck by yourself.

Laura: I—I—never had much luck at—making friends.

Jim: I don't see why you wouldn't.

Laura: Well, I—started out badly.

Jim: You mean being—

Laura: Yes, it sort of—stood between me—

Jim: You shouldn't have let it!

Laura: I know, but it did, and—

Jim: You were shy with people!

Laura: I tried not to be but never could—

Jim: Overcome it?

Laura: No, I—I never could!

Jim: I guess being shy is something you have to work out of kind of gradually.

Laura (*sorrowfully*): Yes—I guess it—

Jim: Takes time!

Laura: Yes—

Jim: People are not so dreadful when you know them. That's what you have to re-member! And everybody has problems, not just you, but practically everybody has got some problems. You think of yourself as having the only problems, as being the only one who is disappointed. But just look around you and you will see lots of people as disappointed as you are. For instance, I hoped when I was going to high school that I would be further along at this time, six years later, than I am now—You remember that wonderful write-up I had in *The Torch*?

Laura: Yes! (*She rises and crosses to table.*)

Jim: It said I was bound to succeed in anything I went into! (*Laura returns with the annual.*) Holy Jeez! *The Torch!* (*He accepts it reverently. They smile across it with mutual wonder. Laura crouches beside him and they begin to turn through it. Laura's shyness is dissolving in his warmth.*)

Laura: Here you are in *Pirates of Penzance!*

Jim (*wistfully*): I sang the baritone lead in that operetta.

Laura (*rapidly*): So—*beautifully!*

Jim (*protesting*): Aw—

Laura: Yes, yes—beautifully—beautifully!

Jim: You heard me?

Laura: All three times!

Jim: No!

Laura: Yes!

Jim: All three performances?

Laura (*looking down*): Yes.

Jim: Why?

Laura: I—wanted to ask you to—autograph my program.

Jim: Why didn't you ask me to?

Laura: You were always surrounded by your own friends so much that I never had a chance to.

Jim: You should have just—

Laura: Well, I—thought you might think I was—

Jim: Thought I might think you was—what?

Laura: Oh—

Jim (*with reflective relish*): I was beleaguered by females in those days.

Laura: You were terribly popular!

Jim: Yeah—

Laura: You had such a—friendly way—

Jim: I was spoiled in high school.

Laura: Everybody—liked you!

Jim: Including you?

Laura: I—yes, I—did, too—(*She gently closes the book in her lap.*)

Jim: Well, well, well!—Give me that program, Laura. (*She hands it to him. He signs it with a flourish.*) There you are—better late than never!

Laura: Oh, I—what a—surprise!

Jim: My signature isn't worth very much right now. But some day—maybe—it will increase in value! Being disappointed is one thing and being discouraged is something else. I am disappointed but I'm not discouraged. I'm twenty-three years old. How old are you?

Laura: I'll be twenty-four in June.

Jim: That's not old age!

Laura: No, but—

Jim: You finished high school?

Laura (with difficulty): I didn't go back.

Jim: You mean you dropped out?

Laura: I made bad grades in my final examinations. (*She rises and replaces the book and the program. Her voice strained.*) How is—Emily Meisenbach getting along?

Jim: Oh, that kraut-head!

Laura: Why do you call her that?

Jim: That's what she was.

Laura: You're not still—going with her?

Jim: I never see her.

Laura: It said in the Personal Section that you were—engaged!

Jim: I know, but I wasn't impressed by that—propaganda!

Laura: It wasn't—the truth?

Jim: Only in Emily's optimistic opinion!

Laura: Oh—

(Legend: "What Have You Done Since High School?")

Jim lights a cigarette and leans indolently back on his elbows smiling at Laura with a warmth and charm which light her inwardly with altar candles. She remains by the table and turns in her hands a piece of glass to cover her tumult.

Jim (after several reflective puffs on a cigarette): What have you done since high school? (*She seems not to hear him.*) Huh? (*Laura looks up.*) I said what have you done since high school, Laura?

Laura: Nothing much.

Jim: You must have been doing something these six long years.

Laura: Yes.

Jim: Well, then, such as what?

Laura: I took a business course at business college—

Jim: How did that work out?

Laura: Well, not very—well—I had to drop out, it gave me—indigestion—

Jim laughs gently.

Jim: What are you doing now?

Laura: I don't do anything—much. Oh, please don't think I sit around doing nothing! My glass collection takes up a good deal of time. Glass is something you have to take good care of.

Jim: What did you say—about glass?

Laura: Collection I said—I have one—(*She clears her throat and turns away again, acutely shy.*)

Jim (abruptly): You know what I judge to be the trouble with you? Inferiority complex! Know what that is? That's what they call it when someone low-rates himself! I understand it because I had it, too. Although my case was not so aggravated as yours seems to be. I had it until I took up public speaking, developed my voice, and learned that I had an aptitude for science. Before that time I never thought of myself as being outstanding in any way whatsoever! Now I've never made a regular study of it, but I have a friend who says I can analyze people better than doctors that make a profession of it. I don't claim that to be necessarily true, but I can sure guess a person's psychology, Laura! (*Takes out his gum.*) Excuse me, Laura. I always take it out when the flavor is gone. I'll use this scrap of paper to wrap it in. I know how it is to get it stuck on a shoe. (*He wraps the gum in paper and puts it in his pocket.*) Yep—that's what I judge to be your principal trouble. A lack of confidence in yourself as a person. You don't have the proper amount of faith in yourself. I'm basing that fact on a number of your remarks and also on certain observations I've made. For instance that clumping you thought was so awful in high school. You say that you even dreaded to walk into class. You see what you did? You dropped out of school, you gave up an education because of a clump, which as far as I know was practically non-existent! A little physical defect is what you have. Hardly noticeable even! Magnified thousands of times by imagination! You know what my strong advice to you is? Think of yourself as *superior* in some way!

Laura: In what way would I think?

Jim: Why, man alive, Laura! Just look about you a little. What do you see? A world full of common people! All of 'em born and all of 'em going to die! Which of them has one-tenth of your good points! Or mine! Or anyone else's, as far as that goes—gosh! Everybody excels in some one thing. Some in many! (*Unconsciously glances at himself in the mirror.*) All you've got to do is discover in *what!* Take me, for instance. (*He adjusts his tie at the mirror.*) My interest happens to lie in electrodynamics. I'm taking a course in radio engineering at night school, Laura, on top of a fairly responsible job at the warehouse. I'm taking that course and studying public speaking.

Laura: Ohhhh.

Jim: Because I believe in the future of television! (*Turning back to her.*) I wish to be ready to go up right along with it. Therefore I'm planning to get in on the ground floor. In fact, I've already made the right connections and all that remains is for the industry itself to get under way! Full steam—(*His eyes are starry.*) Knowledge—Zzzzzp! Money—Zzzzzp!—Power! That's the cycle democracy is built on! (*His attitude is convincingly dynamic. Laura stares at him, even her shyness eclipsed in her absolute wonder. He suddenly grins.*) I guess you think I think a lot of myself!

Laura: No—o-o-o, I—

Jim: Now how about you? Isn't there something you take more interest in than anything else?

Laura: Well, I do—as I said—have my—glass collection—

A peal of girlish laughter from the kitchen.

Jim: I'm not right sure I know what you're talking about. What kind of glass is it?

Laura: Little articles of it, they're ornaments mostly! Most of them are little animals made out of glass, the tiniest little animals in the world. Mother calls them a glass menagerie! Here's an example of one, if you'd like to see it! This one is one of the oldest. It's nearly thirteen. (*He stretches out his hand.*) (**Music: "The Glass Menagerie."**) Oh, be careful—if you breathe, it breaks!

Jim: I'd better not take it. I'm pretty clumsy with things.

Laura: Go on, I trust you with him! (*Places it in his palm.*) There now—you're holding him gently! Hold him over the light, he loves the light! You see how the
light shines through him?

Jim: It sure does shine!

Laura: I shouldn't be partial, but he is my favorite one.

Jim: What kind of a thing is this one supposed to be?

Laura: Haven't you noticed the single horn on his forehead?

Jim: A unicorn, huh?

Laura: Mmm-hmmm!

Jim: Unicorns—aren't they extinct in the modern world?

Laura: I know!

Jim: Poor little fellow, he must feel sort of lonesome.

Laura (*smiling*): Well, if he does, he doesn't complain about it. He stays on a shelf
with some horses that don't have horns and all of them seem to get along nicely
together.

Jim: How do you know?

Laura (*lightly*): I haven't heard any arguments among them!

Jim (*grinning*): No arguments, huh? Well, that's a pretty good sign! Where shall I set
him?

Laura: Put him on the table. They all like a change of scenery once in a while!

Jim: Well, well, well, well— (*He places the glass piece on the table, then raises his arms
and stretches.*) Look how big my shadow is when I stretch!

Laura: Oh, oh, yes—it stretches across the ceiling!

Jim (*crossing to door*): I think it's stopped raining. (*Opens fire-escape door.*) Where
does the music come from?

Laura: From the Paradise Dance Hall across the alley.

Jim: How about cutting the rug a little, Miss Wingfield?

Laura: Oh, I—

Jim: Or is your program filled up? Let me have a look at it. (*Grasps imaginary card.*)
Why, every dance is taken! I'll just have to scratch some out. (**Waltz Music: "La
Golondrina."**) Ahhh, a waltz! (*He executes some sweeping turns by himself, then
holds his arms toward Laura.*)

Laura (*breathlessly*): I—can't dance!

Jim: There you go, that inferiority stuff!

Laura: I've never danced in my life!

Jim: Come on, try!

Laura: Oh, but I'd step on you!

Jim: I'm not made out of glass.

Laura: How—how—how do we start?

Jim: Just leave it to me. You hold your arms out a little.

Laura: Like this?

Jim (*taking her in his arms*): A little bit higher. Right. Now don't tighten up, that's
the main thing about it—relax.

Laura (*laughing breathlessly*): It's hard not to.

Jim: Okay.

Laura: I'm afraid you can't budge me.

Jim: What do you bet I can't? (*He swings her into motion.*)

Laura: Goodness, yes, you can!

Jim: Let yourself go, now, Laura, just let yourself go.

Laura: I'm—

Jim: Come on!

Laura: —trying!

Jim: Not so stiff—easy does it!

Laura: I know but I'm—

Jim: Loosen th' backbone! There now, that's a lot better.

Laura: Am I?

Jim: Lots, lots better! (*He moves her about the room in a clumsy waltz.*)

Laura: Oh, my!

Jim: Ha-ha!

Laura: Oh, my goodness!

Jim: Ha-ha-ha! (*They suddenly bump into the table, and the glass piece on it falls to the floor. Jim stops.*) What did we hit on?

Laura: Table.

Jim: Did something fall off it? I think—

Laura: Yes. (*She stoops to pick it up.*)

Jim: I hope that it wasn't the little glass horse with the horn!

Laura: Yes. (*she stoops to pick it up.*)

Jim: Aw, aw, aw. Is it broken?

Laura: Now it is just like all the other horses.

Jim: It's lost its—

Laura: Horn! It doesn't matter. Maybe it's a blessing in disguise.

Jim: You'll never forgive me. I bet that that was your favorite piece of glass.

Laura: I don't have favorites much. It's no tragedy, Freckles. Glass breaks so easily. No matter how careful you are. The traffic jars the shelves and things fall off them.

Jim: Still I'm awfully sorry that I was the cause.

Laura (*smiling*): I'll just imagine he had an operation. The horn was removed to make him feel less—freakish! (*They both laugh.*) Now he will feel more at home with the other horses, the ones that don't have horns . . .

Jim: Ha-ha, that's very funny! (*Suddenly serious.*) I'm glad to see that you have a sense of humor. You know—you're—well—very different! Surprisingly different from anyone else I know! (*His voice becomes soft and hesitant with a genuine feeling.*) Do you mind me telling you that? (*Laura is abashed beyond speech.*) I mean it in a nice way. You make me feel sort of—I don't know how to put it! I'm usually pretty good at expressing things, but—this is something that I don't know how to say! (*Laura touches her throat and clears it—turns the broken unicorn in her hands.*) (*Even softer.*) Has anyone ever told you that you were pretty? (**Pause: Music.**) (*Laura looks up slowly, with wonder, and shakes her head.*) Well, you are! In a very different way from anyone else. And all the nicer because of the difference, too. (*His voice becomes low and husky. Laura turns away, nearly faint with the novelty of her emotions.*) I wish you were my sister. I'd teach you to have some confidence in yourself. The different people are not like other people, but being different is nothing to be ashamed of. Because other people are not such wonderful people. They're one hundred times one thousand. You're one times one!

They walk all over the earth. You just stay here. They're common as—weeds, but—you—well, you're—*Blue Roses!*

(Image On Screen: Blue Roses.)

(Music Changes.)

Laura: But blue is wrong for—roses . . .

Jim: It's right for you! You're—pretty!

Laura: In what respect am I pretty?

Jim: In all respects—believe me! Your eyes—your hair—are pretty! Your hands are pretty! (*He catches hold of her hand.*) You think I'm making this up because I'm invited to dinner and have to be nice. Oh, I could do that! I could put on an act for you, Laura, and say lots of things without being very sincere. But this time I am. I'm talking to you sincerely. I happened to notice you had this inferiority complex that keeps you from feeling comfortable with people. Somebody needs to build your confidence up and make you proud instead of shy and turning away and—blushing—Somebody ought to—ought to—*kiss you, Laura!* (*His hand slips slowly up her arm to her shoulder.*) **(Music Swells Tumultuously.)** (*He suddenly turns her about and kisses her on the lips. When he releases her Laura sinks on the sofa with a bright, dazed look. Jim backs away and fishes in his pocket for a cigarette.*) **(Legend On Screen: "Souvenir.")** Stumble-john! (*He lights the cigarette, avoiding her look. There is a peal of girlish laughter from Amanda in the kitchen. Laura slowly raises and opens her hand. It still contains the little broken glass animal. She looks at it with a tender, bewildered expression.*) Stumble-john! I shouldn't have done that—That was way off the beam. You don't smoke, do you? (*She looks up, smiling, not hearing the question. He sits beside her a little gingerly. She looks at him speechlessly—waiting. He coughs decorously and moves a little farther aside as he considers the situation and senses her feelings, dimly, with perturbation. Gently.*) Would you—care for a—mint? (*She doesn't seem to hear him but her look grows brighter even.*) Peppermint—Life Saver? My pocket's a regular drug store—wherever I go . . . (*He pops a mint in his mouth. Then gulps and decides to make a clean breast of it. He speaks slowly and gingerly.*) Laura, you know, if I had a sister like you, I'd do the same thing as Tom, I'd bring out fellows—and introduce her to them. The right type of boys—of a type to—appreciate her. Only—well—he made a mistake about me. Maybe I've got no call to be saying this. That may not have been the idea in having me over. But what if it was? There's nothing wrong about that. The only trouble is that in my case—I'm not in a situation to—do the right thing. I can't take down your number and say I'll phone. I can't call up next week and—ask for a date. I thought I had better explain the situation in case you—misunderstood it and—I hurt your feelings. . . . (*Pause. Slowly, very slowly, Laura's look changes, her eyes returning slowly from his to the ornament in her palm.*)

Amanda utters another gay laugh in the kitchen.

Laura (*faintly*): You—won't—call again?

Jim: No, Laura, I can't. (*He rises from the sofa.*) As I was just explaining, I've—got strings on me, Laura, I've—been going steady! I go out all the time with a girl named Betty. She's a home-girl like you, and Catholic, and Irish, and in a great many ways we—get along fine. I met her last summer on a moonlight boat trip up the river to Alton, on the *Majestic.* Well—right away from the start it was—love! **(Legend: Love!)** (*Laura sways slightly forward and grips the arm of the sofa. He fails to notice, now enrapt in his own comfortable being.*) Being in love has made a new man of me! (*Leaning stiffly forward, clutching the arm of the sofa, Laura struggles visibly with her storm. But Jim is oblivious, she is a long way off.*) The power of love is really pretty tremendous! Love is something that—changes the whole world, Laura! (*The storm abates a little and Laura leans back. He notices her again.*) It happened that Betty's aunt took sick, she got a wire and had to go to Centralia. So Tom—when he asked me to dinner—I naturally just accepted the invitation, not knowing that you—that he—that I—(*He stops awkwardly.*) Huh—I'm a stumble-john! (*He flops back on the sofa. The holy candles in the altar of Laura's face have been snuffed out! There is a look of almost infinite desolation. Jim glances at her uneasily.*) I wish that you would—say something. (*She bites her lip which was trembling and then bravely smiles. She opens her hand again on the broken glass ornament. Then she gently takes his hand and raises it level with her own. She carefully places the unicorn in the palm of his hand, then pushes his fingers closed upon it.*) What are you—doing that for? You want me to have him?—Laura? (*She nods.*) What for?

Laura: A—souvenir . . .

She rises unsteadily and crouches beside the victrola to wind it up.

(Legend On Screen: "Things Have A Way Of Turning Out So Badly.")

(Or Image: "Gentleman Caller Waving Good-bye! Gaily.")

At this moment Amanda rushes brightly back in the front room. She bears a pitcher of fruit punch in an old-fashioned cut-glass pitcher and a plate of macaroons. The plate has a gold border and poppies painted on it.

Amanda: Well, well, well! Isn't the air delightful after the shower? I've made you children a little liquid refreshment. (*Turns gaily to the gentleman caller.*) Jim, do you know that song about lemonade?
    "Lemonade, lemonade
    Made in the shade and stirred with a spade—
    Good enough for any old maid!"

Jim (*uneasily*): Ha-ha! No—I never heard it.
Amanda: Why, Laura! You look so serious!
Jim: We were having a serious conversation.
Amanda: Good! Now you're better acquainted!
Jim (*uncertainly*): Ha-ha! Yes.
Amanda: You modern young people are much more serious-minded than my generation. I was so gay as a girl!
Jim: You haven't changed, Mrs. Wingfield.
Amanda: Tonight I'm rejuvenated! The gaiety of the occasion, Mr. O'Connor! (*She tosses her head with a peal of laughter. Spills lemonade.*) Oooo! I'm baptizing myself!
Jim: Here—let me—
Amanda (*setting the pitcher down*): There now. I discovered we had some maraschino cherries. I dumped them in, juice and all!

Jim: You shouldn't have gone to that trouble, Mrs. Wingfield.

Amanda: Trouble, trouble? Why it was loads of fun! Didn't you hear me cutting up in the kitchen? I bet your ears were burning! I told Tom how outdone with him I was for keeping you to himself so long a time! He should have brought you over much, much sooner! Well, now that you've found your way, I want you to be a very frequent caller! Not just occasional but all the time. Oh, we're going to have a lot of gay times together! I see them coming! Mmm, just breathe that air! So fresh, and the moon's so pretty! I'll skip back out—I know where my place is when young folks are having a—serious conversation!

Jim: Oh, don't go out, Mrs. Wingfield. The fact of the matter is I've got to be going.

Amanda: Going, now? You're joking! Why, it's only the shank of the evening, Mr. O'Connor!

Jim: Well, you know how it is.

Amanda: You mean you're a young workingman and have to keep workingmen's hours. We'll let you off early tonight. But only on the condition that next time you stay later. What's the best night for you? Isn't Saturday night the best night for you workingmen?

Jim: I have a couple of time-clocks to punch, Mrs. Wingfield. One at morning, another one at night!

Amanda: My, but you *are* ambitious! You work at night, too?

Jim: No, Ma'am, not work but—Betty! (*He crosses deliberately to pick up his hat. The band at the Paradise Dance Hall goes into a tender waltz.*)

Amanda: Betty? Betty? Who's—Betty? (*There is an ominous cracking sound in the sky.*)

Jim: Oh, just a girl. The girl I go steady with! (*He smiles charmingly. The sky falls.*)

(Legend: "The Sky Falls.")

Amanda (a long-drawn exhalation): Ohhhh . . . Is it a serious romance, Mr. O'Connor?

Jim: We're going to be married the second Sunday in June.

Amanda: Ohhhh—how nice! Tom didn't mention that you were engaged to be married.

Jim: The cat's not out of the bag at the warehouse yet. You know how they are. They call you Romeo and stuff like that. (*He stops at the oval mirror to put on his hat. He carefully shapes the brim and the crown to give a discreetly dashing effect.*) It's been a wonderful evening, Mrs. Wingfield. I guess this is what they mean by Southern hospitality.

Amanda: It really wasn't anything at all.

Jim: I hope it don't seem like I'm rushing off. But I promised Betty I'd pick her up at the Wabash depot, an' by the time I get my jalopy down there her train'll be in. Some women are pretty upset if you keep 'em waiting.

Amanda: Yes, I know—The tyranny of women! (*Extends her hand.*) Goodbye, Mr. O'Connor. I wish you luck—and happiness—and success! All three of them, and so does Laura!—Don't you, Laura?

Laura: Yes!

Jim (taking her hand): Goodbye, Laura. I'm certainly going to treasure that souvenir. And don't you forget the good advice I gave you. (*Raises his voice to a cheery shout.*) So long, Shakespeare! Thanks again, ladies—Good night!

He grins and ducks jauntily out.

Still bravely grimacing, Amanda closes the door on the gentleman caller. Then she turns back to the room with a puzzled expression. She and Laura don't dare to face each other. Laura crouches beside the victrola to wind it.

Amanda (faintly): Things have a way of turning out so badly. I don't believe that I would play the victrola. Well, well—well—Our gentleman caller was engaged to be married! *(She raises her voice.)* Tom!

Tom (from back): Yes, Mother?

Amanda: Come in here a minute. I want to tell you something awfully funny.

Tom (enters with macaroon and a glass of the lemonade): Has the gentleman caller gotten away already?

Amanda: The gentleman caller has made an early departure. What a wonderful joke you played on us!

Tom: How do you mean?

Amanda: You didn't mention that he was engaged to be married.

Tom: Jim? Engaged?

Amanda: That's what he just informed us.

Tom: I'll be jiggered! I didn't know about that.

Amanda: That seems very peculiar.

Tom: What's peculiar about it?

Amanda: Didn't you call him your best friend down at the warehouse?

Tom: He is, but how did I know?

Amanda: It seems extremely peculiar that you wouldn't know your best friend was going to be married!

Tom: The warehouse is where I work, not where I know things about people!

Amanda: You don't know things anywhere! You live in a dream; you manufacture illusions! *(He crosses to door.)* Where are you going?

Tom: I'm going to the movies.

Amanda: That's right, now that you've had us make such fools of ourselves. The effort, the preparations, all the expense! The new floor lamp, the rug, the clothes for Laura! All for what? To entertain some other girl's fiancé! Go to the movies, go! Don't think about us, a mother deserted, an unmarried sister who's crippled and has no job! Don't let anything interfere with your selfish pleasure! Just go, go, go—to the movies!

Tom: All right, I will! The more you shout about my selfishness to me the quicker I'll go, and I won't go to the movies!

Amanda: Go, then! Then go to the moon—you selfish dreamer!

Tom smashes his glass on the floor. He plunges out on the fire-escape, slamming the door. Laura screams—cut by door.

Dance-hall music up. Tom goes to the rail and grips it desperately, lifting his face in the chill white moonlight penetrating the narrow abyss of the alley.

(Legend On Screen: "And So Good-bye . . .")

Tom's closing speech is timed with the interior pantomime. The interior scene is played as though viewed through sound-proof glass. Amanda appears to be making a comforting speech to Laura who is huddled upon the sofa. Now that we cannot hear the mother's speech, her silliness is gone and she has dignity and tragic beauty. Laura's dark hair hides her face until at the end of the speech she lifts it to smile at her mother. Amanda's gestures are slow and graceful, almost dancelike, as she comforts the daughter. At the end of her speech she glances a moment at the father's picture—then withdraws through the portieres. At close of Tom's speech, Laura blows out the candles, ending the play.

Tom: I didn't go to the moon, I went much further—for time is the longest distance between two places—Not long after that I was fired for writing a poem on the lid of a shoe-box. I left Saint Louis. I descended the steps of this fire-escape for a last time and followed, from then on, in my father's footsteps, attempting to find in motion what was lost in space. I traveled around a great deal. The cities swept about me like dead leaves, leaves that were brightly colored but torn away from the branches. I would have stopped, but I was pursued by something. It always came upon me unawares, taking me altogether by surprise. Perhaps it was a familiar bit of music. Perhaps it was only a piece of transparent glass. Perhaps I am walking along a street at night, in some strange city, before I have found companions. I pass the lighted window of a shop where perfume is sold. The window is filled with pieces of colored glass, tiny transparent bottles in delicate colors, like bits of a shattered rainbow. Then all at once my sister touches my shoulder. I turn around and look into her eyes. . . . Oh, Laura, Laura, I tried to leave you behind me, but I am more faithful than I intended to be! I reach for a cigarette, I cross the street, I run into the movies or a bar, I buy a drink, I speak to the nearest stranger—anything that can blow your candles out! *Laura bends over the candles.* For nowadays the world is lit by lightning! Blow out your candles, Laura—and so good-bye— .

She blows the candles out.

Questions

1. How do Amanda's dreams for her daughter contrast with the realities of the Wingfields' day-to-day existence?
2. What suggestions do you find in Laura's glass menagerie? In the glass unicorn?
3. In the cast of characters, Jim O'Connor is listed as "a nice, ordinary, young man." Why does his coming to dinner have such earthshaking implications for Amanda? For Laura?
4. Try to describe Jim's feelings toward Laura during their long conversation in Scene VII. After he kisses her, how do his feelings seem to change?
5. Near the end of the play, Amanda tells Tom, "You live in a dream; you manufacture illusions!" What is ironic about her speech? Is there any truth in it?
6. Who is the main character in *The Glass Menagerie?* Tom? Laura? Amanda? (It may be helpful to review the definition of a protagonist.)
7. Has Tom, at the conclusion of the play, successfully made his escape from home? Does he appear to have fulfilled his dream?
8. How effective is the device of accompanying the action by projecting slides on a screen, bearing titles and images? Do you think most producers of the play are wise to leave it out?

Tennessee Williams on Writing

How to Stage *The Glass Menagerie* 1945

Tennessee Williams

Being a "memory play," *The Glass Menagerie* can be presented with unusual freedom of convention. Because of its considerably delicate or tenuous material, atmospheric touches and subtleties of direction play a particularly important part. Expressionism and all other unconventional techniques in drama have only one valid aim, and that is a closer approach to truth. When a play employs unconventional techniques, it is not, or certainly shouldn't be, trying to escape its responsibility of dealing with reality, or interpreting experience, but is actually or should be attempting to find a closer approach, a more penetrating and vivid expression of things as they are. The straight realistic play with its genuine Frigidaire and authentic ice-cubes, its characters that speak exactly as its audience speaks, corresponds to the academic landscape and has the same virtue of a photographic likeness. Everyone should know nowadays the unimportance of the photographic in art: that truth, life, or reality is an organic thing which the poetic imagination can represent or suggest, in essence, only through transformation, through changing into other forms than those which were merely present in appearance.

These remarks are not meant as a preface only to this particular play. They have to do with a conception of a new, plastic theater which must take the place of the exhausted theater of realistic conventions if the theater is to resume vitality as a part of our culture.

THE SCREEN DEVICE. There is *only one important difference between the original and acting version of the play* and that is the *omission* in the latter of the device which I tentatively included in my *original* script. This device was the use of a screen on which were projected magic-lantern slides bearing images or titles. I do not regret the omission of this device from the present Broadway production. The extraordinary power of Miss Taylor's performance° made it suitable to have the utmost simplicity in the physical production. But I think it may be interesting to some readers to see how this device was conceived. So I am putting it into the published manuscript. These images and legends, projected from behind, were cast on a section of wall between the front-room and dining-room areas, which should be indistinguishable from the rest when not in use.

The purpose of this will probably be apparent. It is to give accent to certain values in each case. Each scene contains a particular point (or several) which is structurally the most important. In an episodic play, such as this, the basic structure or narrative line may be obscured from the audience; the effect may seem fragmentary

Miss Taylor's performance: In the original Broadway production of the play in 1945 the role of Amanda Wingfield, the mother, was played by veteran actress Laurette Taylor.

rather than architectural. This may not be the fault of the play so much as a lack of attention in the audience. The legend or image upon the screen will strengthen the effect of what is merely allusion in the writing and allow the primary point to be made more simply and lightly than if the entire responsibility were on the spoken lines. Aside from this structural value, I think the screen will have a definite emotional appeal, less definable but just as important. An imaginative producer or director may invent many other uses for this device than those indicated in the present script. In fact the possibilities of the device seem much larger to me than the instance of this play can possibly utilize.

THE MUSIC. Another extra-literary accent in this play is provided by the use of music. A single recurring tune, "The Glass Menagerie," is used to give emotional emphasis to suitable passages. This tune is like circus music, not when you are on the grounds or in the immediate vicinity of the parade, but when you are at some distance and very likely thinking of something else. It seems under those circumstances to continue almost interminably and it weaves in and out of your preoccupied consciousness; then it is the lightest, most delicate music in the world and perhaps the saddest. It expresses the surface vivacity of life with the underlying strain of immutable and inexpressible sorrow. When you look at a piece of delicately spun glass you think of two things: how beautiful it is and how easily it can be broken. Both of those ideas should be woven into the recurring tune, which dips in and out of the play as if it were carried on a wind that changes. It serves as a thread of connection and allusion between the narrator with his separate point in time and space and the subject of his story. Between each episode it returns as reference to the emotion, nostalgia, which is the first condition of the play. It is primarily Laura's music and therefore comes out most clearly when the play focuses upon her and the lovely fragility of glass which is her image.

THE LIGHTING. The lighting in the play is not realistic. In keeping with the atmosphere of memory, the stage is dim. Shafts of light are focused on selected areas or actors, sometimes in contradistinction to what is the apparent center. For instance, in the quarrel scene between Tom and Amanda, in which Laura has no active part, the clearest pool of light is on her figure. This is also true of the supper scene, when her silent figure on the sofa should remain the visual center. The light upon Laura should be distinct from the others, having a peculiar pristine clarity such as light used in early religious portraits of female saints or madonnas. A certain correspondence to light in religious paintings, such as El Greco's, where the figures are radiant in atmosphere that is relatively dusky, could be effectively used throughout the play. (It will also permit a more effective use of the screen.) A free, imaginative use of light can be of enormous value in giving a mobile, plastic quality to plays of a more or less static nature.

From the author's production notes for *The Glass Menagerie*

TRAGICOMEDY AND THE ABSURD

One of the more prominent developments in mid-twentieth-century drama was the rise of **tragicomedies**, plays that stir us not only to pity and fear (echoing Aristotle's description of the effect of tragedy) but also to laughter. Although tragicomedy is a kind of drama we think distinctively modern, it is by no means new. The term was used (although jokingly) by the Roman writer of comedy Plautus in about 185 B.C.

Shakespeare's darker comedies such as *Measure for Measure* and *The Merchant of Venice* deal so forcefully with such stark themes as lust, greed, racism, revenge, and cruelty that they often seem like tragedies until their happy endings. In the tragedies of Shakespeare and others, passages of clownish humor are sometimes called **comic relief**, meaning that the section of comedy introduces a sharp contrast in mood. But such passages can do more than provide relief. In *Othello* (3.4.1–16) the clown's banter with Desdemona for a moment makes the surrounding tragedy seem, by comparison, more poignant and intense.

No one doubts that *Othello* is a tragedy, but some twentieth-century plays leave us both bemused and confused: should we laugh or cry? One of the most talked-about plays after World War II, Samuel Beckett's *Waiting for Godot* (1953) portrays two clownish tramps who mark time in a wasteland, wistfully looking for a savior who never arrives. Modern drama, by the way, has often featured such **antiheroes**: ordinary people, inglorious and inarticulate, who carry on not from bravery but from inertia. We cannot help laughing, in *Godot*, at the tramps' painful situation; but, turning the idea around, we also feel deeply moved by their ridiculous plight. Perhaps a modern tragicomedy like *Godot* does not show us great souls suffering greatly—as we observe in a classical tragedy—but Beckett's play nonetheless touches mysteriously on the universal sorrows of human existence.

Straddling the fence between tragedy and comedy, the plays of some modern playwrights portray people whose suffering seems ridiculous. These plays belong to the **theater of the absurd**: a general name for a type of play first staged in Paris in the 1950s. "For the modern critical spirit, nothing can be taken entirely seriously, nor entirely lightly," said Eugène Ionesco, one of the movement's leading playwrights. Behind the literary conventions of the theater of the absurd stands a philosophical fear that human existence has no meaning. Every person, such playwrights assume, is a helpless waif alone in a universe full of ridiculous obstacles. In Ionesco's *Rhinoceros* (1958), the human race starts turning into rhinos, except for one man, who remains human and isolated. A favorite theme in the theater of the absurd is that communication between people is impossible. Language is therefore futile. Ionesco's *The Bald Soprano* (1948) accordingly pokes fun at polite social conversation in a scene whose dialogue consists entirely of illogical strings of catchphrases.

RETURN TO REALISM

Trends in drama change along with playwrights' convictions, and during the 1970s and 1980s the theater of the absurd no longer seemed the dominant influence on new drama in America. Along with other protests of the 1960s, experimental theater seemed to have spent its force. During the later period most of the critically celebrated new plays were neither absurd nor experimental. David Mamet's *American Buffalo* (1975) realistically portrays three petty thieves in a junk shop as they plot to steal a coin collection. Albert Innaurato's *Gemini* (1977) takes a realistic (and comic) view of family life and sexual awakening in one of Philadelphia's Italian neighborhoods. Beth Henley's 1979 Pulitzer Prize–winning play *Crimes of the Heart* presents an eccentric but still believable group of sisters in a small Southern town. The dialogue in all three plays shows high fidelity to ordinary speech. Meanwhile, many of the most influential plays of **feminist theater**, which explores the lives, problems, and occasional triumphs of contemporary women, were also written in a realistic style. Notable success—with both critics and the ticket-buying public—greeted plays such as Marsha Norman's *'night, Mother* (1983), Tina Howe's *Painting Churches* (1983), and Wendy Wasserstein's *The Heidi Chronicles* (1988).

Some leading critics, among them Richard Gilman, believed that the American theater had entered an era of "new naturalism." Indeed many plays of this time subjected the lives of people, especially poor and unhappy people, to a realistic, searching light, showing the forces that shaped them. Sam Shepard in *Buried Child* (1978) explores violence and desperation in a family that dwells on the edge of poverty; while August Wilson in *Joe Turner's Come and Gone* (1988) convincingly portrays life in a Pittsburgh ghetto lodging house. But if these newly established playwrights sometimes showed life as frankly as did the earlier Naturalists, many also employed rich and suggestive symbolism.

EXPERIMENTAL DRAMA

In the latter part of the twentieth century, experimental drama, greatly influenced by the traditions of earlier Symbolist, Expressionist, and absurdist theater, continued to flourish. For example, David Hwang's work combines realistic elements with ritualistic and symbolic devices drawn from Asian theater (see his one-act play, *The Sound of a Voice*, in "Plays for Further Reading"). Caryl Churchill's *Top Girls* (1982) presents a dinner party in which a contemporary woman invites legendary women from history to a dinner party in a restaurant. Tony Kushner's *Angels in America* (1992) also mixes realism and fantasy to dramatize the plight of AIDS. Shel Silverstein, popular author of children's poetry, wrote a raucous one-man play, *The Devil and Billy Markham* (1991), entirely in rime, about a series of fantastic adventures in hell featuring a hard-drinking gambler and the Prince of Darkness. Silverstein's play is simultaneously experimental in form but traditional in content with its homage to American ballads and tall tales.

Experimental theater continues to exert a strong influence on contemporary drama. The following play, Milcha Sanchez-Scott's *The Cuban Swimmer*, deftly assimilates several dramatic styles—symbolism, new naturalism, ethnic drama, theater of the absurd—to create a brilliant original work. The play is simultaneously a family drama, a Latin comedy, a religious parable, and a critique of a media-obsessed American culture.

Milcha Sanchez-Scott

The Cuban Swimmer

1984

Milcha Sanchez-Scott was born in 1955 on the island of Bali. Her father was Colombian. Her mother was Chinese, Indonesian, and Dutch. Her father's work as an agronomist required constant travel, so when the young Sanchez-Scott reached school age, she was sent to a convent boarding school near London where she first learned English. Colombia, however, remained the family's one permanent home. Every Christmas and summer vacation was spent on a ranch in San Marta, Colombia, where four generations of family lived together. When she was fourteen, Sanchez-Scott's family moved to California. After attending the University of San Diego, where she majored in literature and philosophy, she worked at the San Diego Zoo and later at an employment agency in Los Angeles. Her first play, Latina, premiered in 1980 and won seven Drama-Logue awards. Dog Lady and The Cuban Swimmer followed in 1984. Sanchez-Scott then went to New York for a year to work with playwright Irene Fornes, in whose theater workshop she developed Roosters (1988). A feature-film version of Roosters, starring Edward James Olmos, was released in

1995. Her other plays include Evening Star *(1989),* El Dorado *(1990), and* The Old Matador *(1995). Sanchez-Scott lives in Los Angeles.*

CHARACTERS

Margarita Suárez, the swimmer
Eduardo Suárez, her father, the coach
Simón Suárez, her brother
Aída Suárez, her mother
Abuela, her grandmother
Voice of Mel Munson
Voice of Mary Beth White
Voice of Radio Operator

SETTING. *The Pacific Ocean between San Pedro and Catalina Island.*

TIME. *Summer.*

Live conga drums can be used to punctuate the action of the play.

SCENE I

Pacific Ocean. Midday. On the horizon, in perspective, a small boat enters upstage left, crosses to upstage right, and exits. Pause. Lower on the horizon, the same boat, in larger perspective, enters upstage right, crosses and exits upstage left. Blackout.

SCENE II

Pacific Ocean. Midday. The swimmer, Margarita Suárez, is swimming. On the boat following behind her are her father, Eduardo Suárez, holding a megaphone, and Simón, her brother, sitting on top of the cabin with his shirt off, punk sunglasses on, binoculars hanging on his chest.

Eduardo (leaning forward, shouting in time to Margarita's swimming): Uno, dos, uno, dos. Y uno, dos° . . . keep your shoulders parallel to the water.
Simón: I'm gonna take these glasses off and look straight into the sun.
Eduardo (through megaphone): Muy bien, muy bien° . . . but punch those arms in, baby.
Simón (looking directly at the sun through binoculars): Come on, come on, zap me. Show me something. (*He looks behind at the shoreline and ahead at the sea.*) Stop! Stop, *Papi!* Stop!

    (*Aída Suárez and Abuela, the swimmer's mother and grandmother, enter running from the back of the boat.*)

Aída and Abuela: Qué? Qué es?°
Aída: Es un shark?°
Eduardo: Eh?
Abuela: Que es un shark dicen?°

    (*Eduardo blows whistle. Margarita looks up at the boat.*)

Simón: No, *Papi,* no shark, no shark. We've reached the halfway mark.

Uno, dos, uno, dos. Y uno, dos: One, two, one, two. And one, two. *Muy bien, muy bien:* Very good, very good. *Qué? Qué es?:* What? What is it? *Es un shark?:* Is it a shark? *Que es un shark dicen?:* Did they say a shark?

2005 production of *The Cuban Swimmer* at the People's Light & Theatre, Malvern, Pennsylvania.

Abuela (*looking into the water*): A dónde está?°

Aída: It's not in the water.

Abuela: Oh, no? Oh, no?

Aída: No! A poco do you think they're gonna have signs in the water to say you are halfway to Santa Catalina? No. It's done very scientific. A ver, hijo,° explain it to your grandma.

Simón: Well, you see, Abuela—(*He points behind.*) There's San Pedro. (*He points ahead.*) And there's Santa Catalina. Looks halfway to me.

(*Abuela shakes her head and is looking back and forth, trying to make the decision, when suddenly the sound of a helicopter is heard.*)

Abuela (*looking up*): Virgencita de la Caridad del Cobre. Qué es eso?°

(*Sound of helicopter gets closer. Margarita looks up.*)

A dónde está?: Where is it?   A ver, hijo: Look here, son.   Virgencita de la Caridad del Cobre. Qué es
eso?: Virgin of Charity! What is that?

Margarita: Papi, Papi!

(*A small commotion on the boat, with everybody pointing at the helicopter above. Shadows of the helicopter fall on the boat. Simón looks up at it through binoculars.*)

Papi—qué es? What is it?

Eduardo (*through megaphone*): Uh . . . uh . . . uh, *un momentico . . . mi hija.*° . . . Your *papi*'s got everything under control, understand? Uh . . . you just keep stroking. And stay . . . uh . . . close to the boat.

Simón: Wow, *Papi!* We're on TV, man! Holy Christ, we're all over the fucking U.S.A.! It's Mel Munson and Mary Beth White!

Aída: Por Dios!° Simón, don't swear. And put on your shirt.

(*Aída fluffs her hair, puts on her sunglasses and waves to the helicopter. Simón leans over the side of the boat and yells to Margarita.*)

Simón: Yo, Margo! You're on TV, man.

Eduardo: Leave your sister alone. Turn on the radio.

Margarita: Papi! Qué está pasando?°

Abuela: Que es la televisión dicen? (*She shakes her head.*) Porque como yo no puedo ver nada sin mis espejuelos.°

(*Abuela rummages through the boat, looking for her glasses. Voices of Mel Munson and Mary Beth White are heard over the boat's radio.*)

Mel's Voice: As we take a closer look at the gallant crew of *La Havana* . . . and there . . . yes, there she is . . . the little Cuban swimmer from Long Beach, California, nineteen-year-old Margarita Suárez. The unknown swimmer is our Cinderella entry . . . a bundle of tenacity, battling her way through the choppy, murky waters of the cold Pacific to reach the Island of Romance . . . Santa Catalina . . . where should she be the first to arrive, two thousand dollars and a gold cup will be waiting for her.

Aída: Doesn't even cover our expenses.

Abuela: Qué dice?

Eduardo: Shhhh!

Mary Beth's Voice: This is really a family effort, Mel, and—

Mel's Voice: Indeed it is. Her trainer, her coach, her mentor, is her father, Eduardo Suárez. Not a swimmer himself, it says here, Mr. Suárez is head usher of the Holy Name Society and the owner-operator of Suárez Treasures of the Sea and Salvage Yard. I guess it's one of those places—

Mary Beth's Voice: If I might interject a fact here, Mel, assisting in this swim is Mrs. Suárez, who is a former Miss Cuba.

Mel's Voice: And a beautiful woman in her own right. Let's try and get a closer look.

(*Helicopter sound gets louder. Margarita, frightened, looks up again.*)

Margarita: Papi!

---

un momentico . . . mi hija: Just a second, my daughter.   *Por Dios!:* For God's Sake!   *Papi! Qué está pasando?:* Dad. What's happening?   *Que es la televisión dicen? Porque como yo no puedo ver nada sin mis espejuelos:* Did they say television? Because I can't see without my glasses.

Eduardo (*through megaphone*): Mi hija, don't get nervous . . . it's the press. I'm
    handling it.

Aída: I see how you're handling it.

Eduardo (*through megaphone*): Do you hear? Everything is under control. Get back
    into your rhythm. Keep your elbows high and kick and kick and kick and kick . . .

Abuela (*finds her glasses and puts them on*): Ay sí, es la televisión . . . (*She points to heli-
    copter.*) Qué lindo mira . . . (*She fluffs her hair, gives a big wave.*) Aló América! Viva
    mi Margarita, viva todo los Cubanos en los Estados Unidos!°

Aída: Ay por Dios, Cecilia, the man didn't come all this way in his helicopter to look
    at you jumping up and down, making a fool of yourself.

Abuela: I don't care. I'm proud.

Aída: He can't understand you anyway.

Abuela: Viva . . . (*She stops.*) Simón, cómo se dice viva?°

Simón: Hurray.

Abuela: Hurray for mi Margarita y for all the Cubans living en the United States, y un
    abrazo . . . Simón, abrazo . . .

Simón: A big hug.

Abuela: Sí, a big hug to all my friends in Miami, Long Beach, Union City, except for
    my son Carlos, who lives in New York in sin! He lives . . . (*She crosses herself.*) in
    Brooklyn with a Puerto Rican woman in sin! No decente . . .

Simón: Decent.

Abuela: Carlos, no decente. This family, decente.

Aída: Cecilia, por Dios.

Mel's Voice: Look at that enthusiasm. The whole family has turned out to cheer little
    Margarita on to victory! I hope they won't be too disappointed.

Mary Beth's Voice: She seems to be making good time, Mel.

Mel's Voice: Yes, it takes all kinds to make a race. And it's a testimonial to the all-
    encompassing fairness . . . the greatness of this, the Wrigley Invitational
    Women's Swim to Catalina, where among all the professionals there is still room
    for the amateurs . . . like these, the simple people we see below us on the ragtag
    La Havana, taking their long-shot chance to victory. Vaya con Dios!°

    (*Helicopter sound fading as family, including Margarita, watch silently. Static as
    Simón turns radio off. Eduardo walks to bow of boat, looks out on the horizon.*)

Eduardo (*to himself*): Amateurs.

Aída: Eduardo, that person insulted us. Did you hear, Eduardo? That he called us a
    simple people in a ragtag boat? Did you hear . . . ?

Abuela (*clenching her fist at departing helicopter*): Mal-Rayo los parta!°

Simón (*same gesture*): Asshole!

    (*Aída follows Eduardo as he goes to side of boat and stares at Margarita.*)

Aída: This person comes in his helicopter to insult your wife, your family, your
    daughter . . .

Aló América! Viva mi Margarita, viva todo los Cubanos en los Estados Unidos!: Hello America! Hurray
for my Margarita, hurray for all the Cubans in the United States! *cómo se dice viva?:* How do you
say "viva" [in English]? *Vaya con Dios!:* Go with God. [God bless you.] *Mal-Rayo los parta!:* To
hell with you!

Margarita (*pops her head out of the water*): Papi?

Aída: Do you hear me, Eduardo? I am not simple.

Abuela: Sí.

Aída: I am complicated.

Abuela: Sí, demasiada complicada.

Aída: Me and my family are not so simple.

Simón: Mom, the guy's an asshole.

Abuela (*shaking her fist at helicopter*): Asshole!

Aída: If my daughter was simple, she would not be in that water swimming.

Margarita: Simple? Papi . . . ?

Aída: Ahora, Eduardo, this is what I want you to do. When we get to Santa Catalina, I want you to call the TV station and demand an apology.

Eduardo: Cállete mujer! Aquí mando yo.° I will decide what is to be done.

Margarita: Papi, tell me what's going on.

Eduardo: Do you understand what I am saying to you, Aída?

Simón (*leaning over side of boat, to Margarita*): Yo Margo! You know that Mel Munson guy on TV? He called you a simple amateur and said you didn't have a chance.

Abuela (*leaning directly behind Simón.*): Mi hija, insultó a la familia. Desgraciado!

Aída (*leaning in behind Abuela*): He called us peasants! And your father is not doing anything about it. He just knows how to yell at me.

Eduardo (*through megaphone*): Shut up! All of you! Do you want to break her concentration? Is that what you are after? Eh?

(*Abuela, Aída and Simón shrink back. Eduardo paces before them.*)

Swimming is rhythm and concentration. You win a race aquí. (*Pointing to his head.*) Now . . . (*To Simón.*) you, take care of the boat, Aída y Mama . . . do something. Anything. Something practical.

(*Abuela and Aída get on knees and pray in Spanish.*)

Hija, give it everything, eh? . . . por la familia. Uno . . . dos. . . . You must win.

(*Simón goes into cabin. The prayers continue as lights change to indicate bright sunlight, later in the afternoon.*)

SCENE III

Tableau for a couple of beats. Eduardo on bow with timer in one hand as he counts strokes per minute. Simón is in the cabin steering, wearing his sunglasses, baseball cap on backward. Abuela and Aída are at the side of the boat, heads down, hands folded, still muttering prayers in Spanish.

Aída and Abuela (*crossing themselves*): En el nombre del Padre, del Hijo y del Espíritu Santo amén.°

Eduardo (*through megaphone*): You're stroking seventy-two!

Simón (*singing*): Mama's stroking, Mama's stroking seventy-two. . . .

Cállete mujer! Aquí mando yo: Quiet! I'm in charge here. *En el nombre del Padre, del Hijo y del Espíritu Santo amén:* In the name of the Father, the Son, and the Holy Ghost, Amen.

Eduardo (*through megaphone*): You comfortable with it?

Simón (*singing*): Seventy-two, seventy-two, seventy-two for you.

Aída (*looking at the heavens*): Ay, Eduardo, *ven acá,*° we should be grateful that *Nuestro Señor*° gave us such a beautiful day.

Abuela (*crosses herself*): *Sí, gracias a Dios.*°

Eduardo: She's stroking seventy-two, with no problem (*He throws a kiss to the sky.*) It's a beautiful day to win.

Aída: *Qué hermoso!*° So clear and bright. Not a cloud in the sky. *Mira! Mira!*° Even rainbows on the water . . . a sign from God.

Simón (*singing.*): Rainbows on the water . . . you in my arms . . .

Abuela *and* Eduardo (*looking the wrong way*): *Dónde?*

Aída (*pointing toward Margarita*): There, dancing in front of Margarita, leading her on . . .

Eduardo: Rainbows on . . . Ay coño! It's an oil slick! You . . . you . . . (*To Simón.*) Stop the boat. (*Runs to bow, yelling.*) Margarita! Margarita!

(*On the next stroke, Margarita comes up all covered in black oil.*)

Margarita: Papi! Papi . . . !

(*Everybody goes to the side and stares at Margarita, who stares back. Eduardo freezes.*)

Aída: *Apúrate,* Eduardo, move . . . what's wrong with you . . . *no me oíste,*° get my daughter out of the water.

Eduardo (*softly*): We can't touch her. If we touch her, she's disqualified.

Aída: But I'm her mother.

Eduardo: Not even by her own mother. Especially by her own mother. . . . You always want the rules to be different for you, you always want to be the exception. (*To Simón.*) And you . . . you didn't see it, eh? You were playing again?

Simón: *Papi,* I was watching . . .

Aída (*interrupting*): *Pues,* do something Eduardo. You are the big coach, the monitor.

Simón: Mentor! Mentor!

Eduardo: How can a person think around you? (*He walks off to bow, puts head in hands.*)

Abuela (*looking over side*): *Mira como todos los* little birds are dead. (*She crosses herself*)

Aída: Their little wings are glued to their sides.

Simón: Christ, this is like the La Brea tar pits.

Aída: They can't move their little wings.

Abuela: *Esa niña tiene que moverse.*°

Simón: Yeah, Margo, you gotta move, man.

(*Abuela and Simón gesture for Margarita to move. Aída gestures for her to swim.*)

Abuela: *Anda niña, muévete.*°

---

ven acá: Look here. *Nuestro Señor:* Our Father [God]. *Sí, gracias a Dios:* Yes, thanks be to God. *Qué hermoso!:* How beautiful! *Mira!:* look. *Apúrate . . . no me oíste:* Finish this! . . . didn't you hear me? *Esa niña tiene que moverse:* That girl has to move. *Anda niña, muévete:* Come on, girl, Move!

Aída: Swim, *hija,* swim or the *aceite*° will stick to your wings.

Margarita: Papi?

Abuela (taking megaphone): Your *papi* say "move it!"

(*Margarita with difficulty starts moving.*)

Abuela, Aída and Simón (laboriously counting): Uno, dos . . . uno, dos . . . anda . . . uno, dos.

Eduardo (running to take megaphone from Abuela): Uno, dos . . .

(*Simón races into cabin and starts the engine. Abuela, Aída and Eduardo count together.*)

Simón (looking ahead): Papi, it's over there!

Eduardo: Eh?

Simón (pointing ahead and to the right): It's getting clearer over there.

Eduardo (through megaphone): Now pay attention to me. Go to the right.

(*Simón, Abuela, Aída and Eduardo all lean over side. They point ahead and to the right, except Abuela, who points to the left.*)

Family (shouting together): Para yá!° Para yá!

(*Lights go down on boat. A special light on Margarita, swimming through the oil, and on Abuela, watching her.*)

Abuela: Sangre de mi sangre,° you will be another to save us. En Bolondron, where your great-grandmother Luz Suárez was born, they say one day it rained blood. All the people, they run into their houses. They cry, they pray, *pero* your great-grandmother Luz she had *cojones* like a man. She run outside. She look straight at the sky. She shake her fist. And she say to the evil one, "Mira . . . (*Beating her chest.*) coño, Diablo, aquí estoy si me quieres."° And she open her mouth, and she drunk the blood.

BLACKOUT

SCENE IV

Lights up on boat. Aída and Eduardo are on deck watching Margarita swim. We hear the gentle, rhythmic lap, lap, lap of the water, then the sound of inhaling and exhaling as Margarita's breathing becomes louder. Then Margarita's heartbeat is heard, with the lapping of the water and the breathing under it. These sounds continue beneath the dialogue to the end of the scene.

Aída: Dios mío. Look how she moves through the water. . . .

Eduardo: You see, it's very simple. It is a matter of concentration.

Aída: The first time I put her in water she came to life, she grew before my eyes. She moved, she smiled, she loved it more than me. She didn't want my breast any longer. She wanted the water.

aceite: oil. *Para yá:* over there. *Sangre de mi sangre:* blood of my blood. *Mira . . . coño, Diablo, aquí estoy si me quieres:* Look . . . damn it Devil, here I am if you want me.

Eduardo: And of course, the rhythm. The rhythm takes away the pain and helps the concentration.

(*Pause. Aída and Eduardo watch Margarita.*)

Aída: Is that my child or a seal. . . .

Eduardo: Ah, a seal, the reason for that is that she's keeping her arms very close to her body. She cups her hands, and then she reaches and digs, reaches and digs.

Aída: To think that a daughter of mine. . . .

Eduardo: It's the training, the hours in the water. I used to tie weights around her little wrists and ankles.

Aída: A spirit, an ocean spirit, must have entered my body when I was carrying her.

Eduardo (*to Margarita*): Your stroke is slowing down.

(*Pause. We hear Margarita's heartbeat with the breathing under, faster now.*)

Aída: Eduardo, that night, the night on the boat. . . .

Eduardo: Ah, the night on the boat again . . . the moon was . . .

Aída: The moon was full. We were coming to America. . . . *Qué romantico.*

(*Heartbeat and breathing continue.*)

Eduardo: We were cold, afraid, with no money, and on top of everything, you were hysterical, yelling at me, tearing at me with your nails. (*Opens his shirt, points to the base of his neck.*) Look, I still bear the scars . . . telling me that I didn't know what I was doing . . . saying that we were going to die. . . .

Aída: You took me, you stole me from my home . . . you didn't give me a chance to prepare. You just said we have to go now, now! Now, you said. You didn't let me take anything. I left everything behind. . . . I left everything behind.

Eduardo: Saying that I wasn't good enough, that your father didn't raise you so that I could drown you in the sea.

Aída: You didn't let me say even a good-bye. You took me, you stole me, you tore me from my home.

Eduardo: I took you so we could be married.

Aída: That was in Miami. But that night on the boat, Eduardo. . . . We were not married, that night on the boat.

Eduardo: No *pasó nada!°* Once and for all get it out of your head, it was cold, you hated me, and we were afraid. . . .

Aída: Mentiroso!°

Eduardo: A man can't do it when he is afraid.

Aída: Liar! You did it very well.

Eduardo: I did?

Aída: Sí. Gentle. You were so gentle and then strong . . . my passion for you so deep. Standing next to you . . . I would ache . . . looking at your hands I would forget to breathe, you were irresistible.

Eduardo: I was?

Aída: You took me into your arms, you touched my face with your fingertips . . . you kissed my eyes . . . *la esquina de la boca y* . . .

No pasó nada!: Nothing happened.   *Mentiroso!:* Liar!

Eduardo: Sí, Sí, and then . . .

Aída: I look at your face on top of mine, and I see the lights of Havana in your eyes. That's when you seduced me.

Eduardo: Shhh, they're gonna hear you.

(*Lights go down. Special on Aída.*)

Aída: That was the night. A woman doesn't forget those things . . . and later that night was the dream . . . the dream of a big country with fields of fertile land and big, giant things growing. And there by a green, slimy pond I found a giant pea pod and when I opened it, it was full of little, tiny baby frogs.

(*Aída crosses herself as she watches Margarita. We hear louder breathing and heartbeat.*)

Margarita: Santa Teresa. Little Flower of God, pray for me. San Martín de Porres, pray for me. Santa Rosa de Lima, *Virgencita de la Caridad del Cobre*, pray for me. . . . Mother pray for me.

SCENE V

Loud howling of wind is heard, as lights change to indicate unstable weather, fog and mist. Family on deck, braced and huddled against the wind. Simón is at the helm.

Aída: Ay Dios mío, qué viento.°

Eduardo (through megaphone): Don't drift out . . . that wind is pushing you out. (*To Simón.*) You! Slow down. Can't you see your sister is drifting out?

Simón: It's the wind, *Papi.*

Aída: Baby, don't go so far. . . .

Abuela (to heaven): Ay Gran Poder de Dios, quita este maldito viento.°

Simón: Margo! Margo! Stay close to the boat.

Eduardo: Dig in. Dig in hard. . . . Reach down from your guts and dig in.

Abuela (to heaven): Ay Virgen de la Caridad del Cobre, por lo más tú quieres a pararla.

Aída (putting her hand out, reaching for Margarita): Baby, don't go far.

(*Abuela crosses herself. Action freezes. Lights get dimmer, special on Margarita. She keeps swimming, stops, starts again, stops, then, finally exhausted, stops altogether. The boat stops moving.*)

Eduardo: What's going on here? Why are we stopping?

Simón: *Papi*, she's not moving! Yo Margo!

(*The family all run to the side.*)

Eduardo: Hija! . . . Hijita! You're tired, eh?

Aída: Por supuesto she's tired. I like to see you get in the water, waving your arms and legs from San Pedro to Santa Catalina. A person isn't a machine, a person has to rest.

Simón: Yo, Mama! Cool out, it ain't fucking brain surgery.

Ay *Dios mío, qué viento*: Oh my God, what wind!   Ay *Gran Poder de Dios, quita este maldito viento*: By the great power of God, keep the cursed winds away!

Eduardo (to Simón): Shut up, you. (*Louder to Margarita.*) I guess your mother's right for once, huh? . . . I guess you had to stop, eh? . . . Give your brother, the idiot . . . a chance to catch up with you.

Simón (clowning like Mortimer Snerd): Dum dee dum dee dum ooops, ah shucks . . .

Eduardo: I don't think he's Cuban.

Simón (like Ricky Ricardo): *Oye,* Lucy! I'm home! Ba ba lu!

Eduardo (joins in clowning, grabbing Simón in a headlock): What am I gonna do with this idiot, eh? I don't understand this idiot. He's not like us, Margarita. (*Laughing.*) You think if we put him into your bathing suit with a cap on his head . . . (*He laughs hysterically.*) You think anyone would know . . . huh? Do you think anyone would know? (*Laughs.*)

Simón (vamping): Ay, *mi amor.* Anybody looking for tits would know.

(*Eduardo slaps Simón across the face, knocking him down. Aída runs to Simón's aid. Abuela holds Eduardo back.*)

Margarita: Mía culpa!° Mía culpa!

Abuela: Qué dices hija?

Margarita: Papi, it's my fault, it's all my fault. . . . I'm so cold, I can't move. . . . I put my face in the water . . . and I hear them whispering . . . laughing at me. . . .

Aída: Who is laughing at you?

Margarita: The fish are all biting me . . . they hate me . . . they whisper about me. She can't swim, they say. She can't glide. She has no grace. . . . Yellowtails, bonita, tuna, man-o'-war, snub-nose sharks, *los baracudas* . . . they all hate me . . . only the dolphins care . . . and sometimes I hear the whales crying . . . she is lost, she is dead. I'm so numb, I can't feel. *Papi! Papi!* Am I dead?

Eduardo: *Vamos,* baby, punch those arms in. Come on . . . do you hear me?

Margarita: Papi . . . Papi . . . forgive me. . . .

(*All is silent on the boat. Eduardo drops his megaphone, his head bent down in dejection. Abuela, Aída, Simón, all leaning over the side of the boat. Simón slowly walks away.*)

Aída: Mi hija, qué tienes?

Simón: Oh, Christ, don't make her say it. Please don't make her say it.

Abuela: Say what? *Qué cosa?*

Simón: She wants to quit, can't you see she's had enough?

Abuela: Mira, para eso. Esta niña is turning blue.

Aída: Oyeme, mi hija. Do you want to come out of the water?

Margarita: Papi?

Simón (to Eduardo): She won't come out until *you* tell her.

Aída: Eduardo . . . answer your daughter.

Eduardo: Le dije to concentrate . . . concentrate on your rhythm. Then the rhythm would carry her . . . ay, it's a beautiful thing, Aída. It's like yoga, like meditation, the mind over matter . . . the mind controlling the body . . . that's how the great things in the world have been done. I wish you . . . I wish my wife could understand.

Margarita: Papi?

Simón (to Margarita): Forget him.

Mía culpa!: It's my fault.

Aída (imploring): Eduardo, *por favor.*

Eduardo (walking in circles): Why didn't you let her concentrate? Don't you understand, the concentration, the rhythm is everything. But no, you wouldn't listen. (*Screaming to the ocean.*) Goddamn Cubans, why, God, why do you make us go everywhere with our families? (*He goes to back of boat.*)

Aída (opening her arms): Mi hija, ven, come to Mami. (*Rocking.*) Your *mami* knows.

(*Abuela has taken the training bottle, puts it in a net. She and Simón lower it to Margarita.*)

Simón: Take this. Drink it. (*As Margarita drinks, Abuela crosses herself.*)

Abuela: *Sangre de mi sangre.*

(*Music comes up softly. Margarita drinks, gives the bottle back, stretches out her arms, as if on a cross. Floats on her back. She begins a graceful backstroke. Lights fade on boat as special lights come up on Margarita. She stops. Slowly turns over and starts to swim, gradually picking up speed. Suddenly as if in pain she stops, tries again, then stops in pain again. She becomes disoriented and falls to the bottom of the sea. Special on Margarita at the bottom of the sea.*)

Margarita: *Ya no puedo* . . . I can't. . . . A person isn't a machine . . . *es mi culpa* . . . Father forgive me . . . *Papi! Papi!* One, two. *Uno, dos.* (*Pause.*) *Papi!* A dónde estás? (*Pause.*) One, two, one, two. *Papi!* Ay, *Papi!* Where are you . . . ? Don't leave me. . . . Why don't you answer me? (*Pause. She starts to swim, slowly.*) *Uno, dos, uno, dos.* Dig in, dig in. (*Stops swimming.*) *Por favor, Papi!* (*Starts to swim again.*) One, two, one, two. Kick from your hip, kick from your hip. (*Stops swimming. Starts to cry.*) Oh God, please. . . . (*Pause.*) Hail Mary, full of grace . . . dig in, dig in . . . the Lord is with thee. . . . (*She swims to the rhythm of her Hail Mary.*) Hail Mary, full of grace . . . dig in, dig in . . . the Lord is with thee . . . dig in, dig in. . . . Blessed art thou among women. . . . *Mami,* it hurts. You let go of my hand. I'm lost. . . . And blessed is the fruit of thy womb, now and at the hour of our death. Amen. I don't want to die, I don't want to die.

(*Margarita is still swimming. Blackout. She is gone.*)

SCENE VI

Lights up on boat, we hear radio static. There is a heavy mist. On deck we see only black outline of Abuela with shawl over her head. We hear the voices of Eduardo, Aída, and Radio Operator.

Eduardo's Voice: La Havana! Coming from San Pedro. Over.

Radio Operator's Voice: Right, DT6-6, you say you've lost a swimmer.

Aída's Voice: Our child, our only daughter . . . listen to me. Her name is Margarita Inez Suárez, she is wearing a black one-piece bathing suit cut high in the legs with a white racing stripe down the sides, a white bathing cap with goggles and her whole body covered with a . . . with a . . .

Eduardo's Voice: With lanolin and paraffin.

Aída's Voice: Sí . . . con lanolin and paraffin.

(*More radio static. Special on Simón, on the edge of the boat.*)

Simón: Margo! Yo Margo! (*Pause.*) Man don't do this. (*Pause.*) Come on. . . . Come on. . . . (*Pause.*) God, why does everything have to be so hard? (*Pause.*) Stupid. You know you're not supposed to die for this. Stupid. It's his dream and he can't even swim. (*Pause.*) Punch those arms in. Come home. Come home. I'm your little brother. Don't forget what Mama said. You're not supposed to leave me behind. *Vamos,* Margarita, take your little brother, hold his hand tight when you cross the street. He's so little. (*Pause.*) Oh Christ, give us a sign. . . . I know! I know! Margo, I'll send you a message . . . like mental telepathy. I'll hold my breath, close my eyes, and I'll bring you home. (*He takes a deep breath; a few beats.*) This time I'll beep . . . I'll send out sonar signals like a dolphin. (*He imitates dolphin sounds.*)

(*The sound of real dolphins takes over from Simón, then fades into sound of Abuela saying the Hail Mary in Spanish, as full lights come up slowly.*)

SCENE VII

Eduardo coming out of cabin, sobbing, Aída holding him. Simón anxiously scanning the horizon. Abuela looking calmly ahead.

Eduardo: Es mi culpa, sí, es mi culpa.° (*He hits his chest.*)
Aída: Ya, ya viejo.° . . . it was my sin . . . I left my home.
Eduardo: Forgive me, forgive me. I've lost our daughter, our sister, our granddaughter, *mi carne, mi sangre, mis ilusiones.*° (*To heaven.*) *Dios mío,* take me . . . take me, I say . . . Goddammit, take me!
Simón: I'm going in.
Aída and Eduardo: No!
Eduardo (grabbing and holding Simón, speaking to heaven): God, take me, not my children. They are my dreams, my illusions . . . and not this one, this one is my mystery . . . he has my secret dreams. In him are the parts of me I cannot see.

(*Eduardo embraces Simón. Radio static becomes louder.*)

Aída: I . . . I think I see her.
Simón: No, it's just a seal.
Abuela (looking out with binoculars): Mi nietacita, dónde estás? (*She feels her heart.*) I don't feel the knife in my heart . . . my little fish is not lost.

(*Radio crackles with static. As lights dim on boat, Voices of Mel and Mary Beth are heard over the radio.*)

Mel's Voice: Tragedy has marred the face of the Wrigley Invitational Women's Race to Catalina. The Cuban swimmer, little Margarita Suárez, has reportedly been lost at sea. Coast Guard and divers are looking for her as we speak. Yet in spite of this tragedy the race must go on because . . .
Mary Beth's Voice (interrupting loudly): Mel!
Mel's Voice (startled): What!

Es mi culpa, sí, es mi culpa: It's my fault, yes, it's my fault. *Ya, ya viejo:* Yes, yes, old man. *mi carne, mi sangre, mis ilusiones:* My flesh, my blood, my dreams.

Mary Beth's Voice: Ah . . . excuse me, Mel . . . we have a winner. We've just received word from Catalina that one of the swimmers is just fifty yards from the breakers . . . it's, oh, it's . . . Margarita Suárez!

(*Special on family in cabin listening to radio.*)

Mel's Voice: What? I thought she died!

(*Special on Margarita, taking off bathing cap, trophy in hand, walking on the water.*)

Mary Beth's Voice: Ahh . . . unless . . . unless this is a tragic . . . No . . . there she is, Mel. Margarita Suárez! The only one in the race wearing a black bathing suit cut high in the legs with a racing stripe down the side.

(*Family cheering, embracing.*)

Simón (*screaming*): Way to go, Margo!

Mel's Voice: This is indeed a miracle! It's a resurrection! Margarita Suárez, with a flotilla of boats to meet her, is now walking on the waters, through the breakers . . . onto the beach, with crowds of people cheering her on. What a jubilation! This is a miracle!

(*Sound of crowds cheering. Lights and cheering sounds fade.*)

BLACKOUT

Milcha Sanchez-Scott on Writing

Writing *The Cuban Swimmer*   1989

From these women [recent immigrants Sanchez-Scott met at the employment agency where she worked] I got my material for Latina, my first play. I'd never tried to write. I was just collecting stories—for instance, a woman told me her child had died two years previously, and that at the mortuary she had lifted her child and put it across her face to give it a last goodbye. For two years, she said, the whole side of her face and her lips were cold. And being with my cousin again reminded me of the way we say things in Colombia: "Do you remember the summer when all the birds flew into the bedroom?" I was just writing things down.

About this time I was hired by Susan Loewenberg of L.A. Theatre Works to act in a project at the women's prison in Chino. I saw the way Doris Baizley, the writer, had put the women's stories together. When I offered Susan my notes, hoping she could make a piece out of them, she persuaded me to write it myself.

I'd found a channel to get all sorts of things flowing out. I liked controlling my own time, and *making* things—I've always admired architects. Acting seemed very airy to me because I could never take it home and show it to anybody. I had trouble being alone for long periods, but then I would go to the airport or someplace else busy to write. Doris and I used to do things like write under blankets by flashlight, which makes you feel like a little kid with a big secret.

L.A. Theatre Works got a grant and we toured *Latina* up and down the state with ten Latin actresses who were always feuding. We had one who was illegal, and wouldn't perform any place she thought Immigration might come, so I had to go on in her place. Then Susan commissioned me to write something else, which turned out to be *Dog Lady* and *Cuban Swimmer*. I saw the long-distance swimmer Diana Nyad on TV and I saw Salazar—the Cuban runner—and started thinking. I wanted to set a play in the water. So I put a family on a boat and a swimmer in the water and said, "Now, *what?*" I happened to be in a church and saw the most beautiful Stations of the Cross. It struck me as a good outline for anybody undertaking an endeavor—there's all this tripping and falling and rising. So that's what I used.

From *On New Ground*

DOCUMENTARY DRAMA

Some playwrights combine experimental and naturalistic elements, creating documentary works that dramatize actual events. British dramatist Michael Frayn presented the European physicists who did the work preceding the atom bomb in *Copenhagen* (1998) and explored the career of director Max Reinhardt in Nazi-era Austria in *Afterlife* (2008). Actress-playwright Anna Deavere Smith created an extremely innovative version of documentary drama in which she performed *all* of the roles herself in bravura one-woman shows. Using the actual words of real people, she constructed performance pieces to explore complex social events such as the race riots in Crown Heights, Brooklyn, in 1991 and in Los Angeles in 1992.

Anna Deavere Smith

Scenes from Twilight: Los Angeles, 1992   1994

Anna Deavere Smith was born in Baltimore, Maryland, in 1950, the daughter of a businessman and an elementary school principal. She graduated from Beaver College in 1971 and earned a Master of Fine Arts degree from the American Conservatory Theater in 1977. She taught drama at Stanford University from 1990 to 2000 and is presently a professor at both the Tisch School of the Arts at New York University and the NYU School of Law. Over many years Smith has conducted more than two thousand interviews; from them she has fashioned a number of works of "documentary theater," each of which is a stage presentation in which a single performer speaks a series of monologues using the actual words of her interview subjects. The best-known of these are Fires in the Mirror *(1993), drawn from the 1991 race riots in Crown Heights, Brooklyn,* Twilight: Los Angeles, 1992 *(1994), derived from the 1992 riot in that city, and* Let Me Down Easy *(2009), which examines health care issues. Smith has frequently performed these pieces herself, winning rave reviews both for the works and for her extraordinary ability to bring to life characters of both sexes and many ages and races. In its review of* Twilight: Los Angeles, 1992, *the New York Times said: "Anna Deavere Smith is the ultimate impressionist: she does people's souls." As an actress, she has also made many appearances on stage and in films, including* Philadelphia *and* The American President, *and has been seen on television in* The West Wing *and* Nurse Jackie. *Included here are three scenes from the over fifty monologues in* Twilight: Los Angeles, 1992.

CHARACTERS

Anonymous Young Man, former gang member
Mrs. Young-Soon Han, former liquor store owner, Korean American, 40s, heavy accent
Twilight Bey, gang truce organizer, African American, early 30s/late 20s, Crips gang.

GENERAL NOTE

This play is based on interviews conducted by Anna Deavere Smith soon after the race riots in Los Angeles of 1992. All words were spoken by real people and are verbatim from those interviews.

ANONYMOUS YOUNG MAN
Former Gang Member

Broad Daylight

(*Saturday, fall, sunny. He is wearing black pants and an oversized tee shirt. He is living with his mother after having recently gotten out of jail. His mother lives in a fancy apartment building, with pool, recreation room, etc. We are in one of the lounges. He has a goatee and wears his hair pulled back in a ponytail. He is black but looks Latino.*)

They kind of respected their elders,
as far as,
not robbing them,
but then a lot of . . .
as I got older I noticed,
like the younger ones,
the lot of the
respect,
it
just like
disappeared,
'cause I . . . when I was younger it was like
if the police had
me and a couple other guys in the middle of the street
on our knees,
the older people would
come out and question.
They like . . .
"Take 'em to jail,"
because of that loss of respect,
you know,
of the elders
by the younger ones,
losing the respect of the elders.
When I went to the Valley
I felt more respect,
because when
I was in the
Valley
I was right there with rivals.

It's like I could walk right over
and it was rivals
and the way I felt was like
strong,
'cause when I moved out there
I didn't bring
all my homeboys
with me
and it's like I used to tell them,
my rivals,
I used to tell 'em, "Man,
I'm a one-man army."
I would joke about it.
I say,
"I don't need my homeboys
and everything."
Me and my brother,
we used to call ourselves the Blues Brothers,
because it was two of us
and we
would go and we either have our blue rags hanging and go right up
there in their neighborhood where there are
Bloods
and go right up in the apartments
and there could be a crowd of 'em
and we would pass by—
"What's up, cuz?"—
and keep goin'
and every now and then
they might say
something
but the majority of 'em
knew that I keep a gun on me
and every now and then
there would be broad daylight like this.
Some of 'em
would try and test me and say,
"well, he ain't fixin' ta shoot me in this broad daylight,"
you know,
and then
when they do
then you know
I either end up chasin' 'em,
shootin' at 'em or shootin'
whatever.
'Cause they thought ain't nobody that stupid
to shoot people in broad daylight.
And I was the opposite.
My theory was when you shoot somebody in broad daylight

people gonna be mostly scared,
they not gonna just sit there and look at you,
you know, to identify you.
I figure there's gonna be like
"I gotta run"
and I figure they just gonna be too scared to see who you are to
identify you.
That's where the reputation
came,
'cause they didn't know when I was comin',
broad daylight
or at night.
My favorite song?
I like oldies.
My favorite song is by Atlantic Star.
It's called
"Am I Dreamin'?"

MRS. YOUNG-SOON HAN

Former Liquor Store Owner

Swallowing the Bitterness

(*A house on Sycamore Street in Los Angeles, just south of Beverly. A tree-lined street. A quiet street. It's in an area where many Hasidic Jews live as well as yuppie types. Mrs. Young-Soon Han's living room is impeccable. Dark pink-and-apricot rug and sofa and chairs. The sofa and chairs are made of a velour. On the back of the sofa and chairs is a Korean design. A kind of circle with lines in it, a geometric design. There is a glass coffee table in front of the sofa. There is nothing on the coffee table. There is a mantel with a bookcase, and a lot of books. The mantel has about thirty trophies. These are her nephew's. They may be for soccer. On the wall behind the sofa area, a series of citations and awards. These are her ex-husband's. They are civic awards. There are a couple of pictures of her husband shaking hands with official-looking people and accepting awards. In this area is also a large painting of Jesus Christ. There is another religious painting over the archway to the dining room. There are some objects hanging on the side of the archway. Long strips and oval shapes. It is very quiet. When we first came in, the television was on, but she turned it off.*

She is sitting on the floor and leaning on the coffee table. When she hits her hand on the table, it sounds very much like a drum. I am accompanied by two Korean-American graduate students from UCLA.)

Until last year
I believed America is the best.
I still believe it.
I don't deny that now.
because I'm a victim,
but
as
the year ends in '92
and we were still in turmoil

Anna Deavere Smith as Mrs. Young-Soon Han.

and having all the financial problems
and mental problems.
Then a couple months ago
I really realized that
Korean immigrants were left out
from this
society and we were nothing.
What is our right?
Is it because we are Korean?
Is it because we have no politicians?
Is it because we don't
speak good English?
Why?
Why do we have to be left out?

    (*She is hitting her hand on the coffee table*)

We are not qualified to have medical treatment.
We are not qualified to get, uh,
food stamp

    (*She hits the table once*),

not GR

    (*Hits the table once*),

no welfare

(*Hits the table once*).

Anything.
Many Afro-Americans

(*Two quick hits*)

who never worked

(*One hit*),

they get
at least minimum amount

(*One hit*)

of money

(*One hit*)

to survive

(*One hit*).

We don't get any!

(*Large hit with full hand spread*)

Because we have a car

(*One hit*)

and we have a house.

(*Pause six seconds*)

And we are high tax taxpayers.

(*One hit*)

(*Pause fourteen seconds*)

Where do I finda [*sic*] justice?
Okay, Black people
probably
believe they won
by the trial?
Even some complains only half right?
justice was there.
But I watched the television
that Sunday morning,
early morning as they started.
I started watch it all day.
They were having party and then they celebrated,
all of South Central,
all the churches.

They finally found that justice exists
in this society.
Then where is the victims' rights?
They got their rights.
By destroying innocent Korean merchants . . .
They have a lot of respect,
as I do,
for
Dr. Martin King?
He is the only model for Black community.
I don't care Jesse Jackson.
But
he was the model
of nonviolence.
Nonviolence?
They like to have hiseh [*sic*] spirits.
What about last year?
They destroyed innocent people.

    (*Five-second pause*)

And I wonder if that is really justice

    (*And a very soft "uh" after "justice," like "justicah," but very quick*)

to get their rights
in this way.

    (*Thirteen-second pause*)

I waseh swallowing the bitternesseh,
sitting here alone
and watching them.
They became all hilarious

    (*Three-second pause*)

and, uh,
in a way I was happy for them
and I felt glad for them.
At leasteh they got something back, you know.
Just let's forget Korean victims or other victims
who are destroyed by them.
They have fought
for their rights

    (*One hit simultaneous with the word "rights"*)

over two centuries

    (*One hit simultaneous with "centuries"*)

and I have a lot of sympathy and understanding for them.
Because of their effort and sacrificing,

other minorities, like Hispanic
or Asians,
maybe we have to suffer more
by mainstream.
You know,
that's why I understand,
and then
I like to be part of their
'joyment.
But . . .
That's why I had mixed feeling
as soon as I heard the verdict.
I wish I could
live together
with eh [sic] Blacks,
but after the riots
there were too much differences.
The fire is still there—
how do you call it?—
igni . . .
igniting fire.

   (*She says a Korean phrase phonetically: "Dashi yun gi ga nuh"°*)

It's still dere.
It canuh
burst out anytime.

TWILIGHT BEY
Organizer of Gang Truce

Limbo / Twilight #2

(*In a Denny's restaurant in a shopping center on a Saturday morning, February 1993. He is a gang member. He is short, graceful, very dark skinned. He is soft-spoken and even in his delivery. He is very confident.*)

Twilight Bey,
that's my name.
When I was
twelve and thirteen,
I stayed out until, they say,
until the sun come up.
Every night, you know,
and that was my thing.
I was a
watchdog.
You know, I stayed up in the neighborhood,
make sure we wasn't being rolled on and everything,
and when people

Dashi yun gi ga nuh: In a performance script, this stage direction reads, "She says a Korean word asking for translation. In Korean, she says 'igniting fire.'")

Anna Deavere Smith as Twilight Bey.

came into light
a what I knew,
a lot a people said,
"Well, Twilight, you know,
you a lot smarter and you have a lot more wisdom than those
twice your age."
And what I did, you know,
I was
at home writing one night
and I was writing my name
and I just looked at it and it came ta me:
"twi,"
abbreviation
of the word "twice."
You take a way the "ce."
You have the last word,
"light."
"Light" is a word that symbolizes knowledge, knowing,
wisdom,
within the Koran and the Holy Bible.
Twilight.
I have twice the knowledge of those my age,

twice the understanding of those my age.
So twilight
is
that time
between day and night.
Limbo,
I call it limbo.
So a lot of times when I've brought up ideas to my homeboys,
they say,
"Twilight,
that's before your time,
that's something you can't do now."
When I talked about the truce back in 1988,
that was something they considered before its time,
yet
in 1992
we made it
realistic.
So to me it's like I'm stuck in limbo,
like the sun is stuck between night and day
in the twilight hours.
You know,
I'm in an area not many people exist.
Nighttime to me
is like a lack of sun,
and I don't affiliate
darkness with anything negative.
I affiliate
darkness with what was first,
because it was first,
and then relative to my complexion.
I am a dark individual,
and with me stuck in limbo,
I see darkness as myself.
I see the light as knowledge and the wisdom of the world and
understanding others,
and in order for me to be a, to be a true human being,
I can't forever dwell in darkness,
I can't forever dwell in the idea,
of just identifying with people like me and understanding me and mine.
So I'm up twenty-four hours, it feels like,
and, you know,
what I see at nighttime
is,
like,
little kids
between the ages of
eight and eleven
out at three in the morning.

They beatin' up a old man on the bus stop,
a homeless old man.
You know,
I see these things.
I tell 'em, "Hey, man, what ya all doin'?
Whyn't ya go on home?
What ya doin' out this time of night?"
You know,
and then when I'm in my own neighborhood, I'm driving through and I
see the living dead, as we call them,
the base heads,
the people who are so addicted on crack,
if they need a hit they be up all night doin' whatever they have to do
to make the money to get the hit.
It's like gettin' a total dose
of what goes on in the daytime creates at night.

Questions

1. What does the speech by the Anonymous Young Man reveal about the escalation of street violence in Los Angeles?
2. Do you find Mrs. Young-Soon Han to be a sympathetic character? Why or why not?
3. Does the speech by Twilight Bey, which concludes the play, seem conciliatory or confrontational? Does it explain why the play is called *Twilight*?
4. Taking these monologues together, what do you see as the mood that emerges from the text—despair? hopefulness? resignation? Explain.

Anna Deavere Smith on Writing

A Call to the Community

1994

For over ten years now I have been creating performances based on actual events in a series I have titled *On the Road: A Search for American Character.* Each *On the Road* performance evolves from interviews I conduct with individuals directly or indirectly involved in the event I intend to explore. Basing my scripts entirely on this interview material, I perform the interviews onstage using their own words. *Twilight: Los Angeles, 1992* is the product of my search for the character of Los Angeles in the wake of the initial Rodney King verdict.

Anna Deavere Smith

• • •

The story of how Los Angeles came to experience what some call the worst riots in United States history is by now familiar. In the Spring of 1991, Rodney King, a black man, was severely beaten by four white Los Angeles police officers after a high-speed chase in which King was pursued for speeding. A nearby resident videotaped the beating from the balcony of his apartment. When the videotape was broadcast on national television, there was an immediate outcry from the community. The next year, the police officers who beat King were tried and found not guilty—and the city exploded. The verdict took the city by surprise, from public officials to average citizens. Even the defense lawyers, I was told, anticipated that there would be some convictions. Three days of burning, looting, and killing scarred Los Angeles and captured the attention of the world.

• • •

The video of the Rodney King beating, which seemed to "tell all," apparently did not tell enough, and the prosecution lost, as their lead attorney told me, "the slam-dunk case of the century." The city of Los Angeles lost much more. *Twilight* is an attempt to explore the shades of that loss. It is not really an attempt to find causes or to show where responsibility was lacking. That would be the task of a commission report. While I was in Los Angeles, and when I have returned since my initial performance of *Twilight* in the summer of 1993, I have been trying to look at the shifts in attitudes of citizens toward race relations. I have been particularly interested in the opportunity the events in Los Angeles give us to take stock of how the race canvas in America has *changed* since the Watts riots. Los Angeles shows us that the story of race in America is much larger and more complex than a story of black and white. There are new players in the race drama. Whereas Jewish merchants were hit during the Watts riots, Korean merchants were hit this time. Although the media tended to focus on blacks in South-Central, the Latino population was equally involved. We tend to think of race as us and them—us or them being black or white depending on one's own color. The relationships among peoples of color and *within* racial groups are getting more and more complicated.

• • •

When I did my research in Los Angeles, I was listening with an ear that was trained to hear stories for the specific purpose of repeating them with the elements of character intact. This becomes significant because sometimes there is the expectation that inasmuch as I am doing "social dramas," I am looking for *solutions* to social problems. In fact, though, I am looking at the *processes* of the problems. Acting is a constant process of becoming something. It is not a result, it is not an answer. It is not a solution. I am first looking for the humanness inside the problems, or the crises. The spoken word is evidence of the humanness. Perhaps the solutions come somewhere further down the road.

I see the work as a call. I played *Twilight* in Los Angeles as a call to the community. I performed it at a time when the community had not yet resolved the problems. I wanted to be a part of their examination of the problems. I believe that solutions to these problems will call for the participation of large and eclectic groups of people. I also believe that we are at a stage at which we must first break the silence about race and encourage many more people to participate in the dialogue.

One of the questions I was frequently asked when I was interviewed about *Twilight* was "Did you find any one voice that could speak for the entire city?" I think there is an expectation that in this diverse city, and in this diverse nation, a unifying voice would bring increased understanding and put us on the road to solutions. This expectation surprises me. There is little in culture or education that encourages the development of a unifying voice. In order to have real unity, all voices would have to first be heard or at least represented. Many of us who work in race relations do so from the point of view of our own ethnicity. This very fact inhibits our ability to hear more voices than those that are closest to us in proximity. Few people speak a language about race that is not their own. If more of us could actually speak from another point of view, like speaking another language, we could accelerate the flow of ideas.

Introduction to *Twilight: Los Angeles, 1992*

■ WRITING *effectively*

THINKING ABOUT DRAMATIC REALISM

When critics use the word *realism* in relation to a play, are they claiming it is true to life? Not necessarily. Realism generally refers to certain dramatic conventions that emerged during the nineteenth century. A realistic play is not necessarily any truer to life than an experimental one, although the conventions of Realist drama have become so familiar to us that other kinds of drama—though no more artificial—can seem mannered and even bizarre to the casual viewer. Remember, though, that all drama—even the theater of Realism—is artifice.

■ **Notice the conventions of Realist drama.** Compare, for example, a play by Henrik Ibsen with one by Sophocles. Ibsen's characters speak in prose, not verse. His settings are drawn from contemporary life, not a legendary past. His characters are ordinary middle-class citizens, not kings, queens, and aristocrats.

■ **Be aware that the inner lives, memories, and motivations of the characters play a crucial role in the dramatic action.** Ibsen, like other Realist playwrights, seeks to portray the complexity of human psychology—especially motivation—in detailed, subtle ways. In contrast, Shakespeare appears less interested in the reason for Iago's villainy than its consequences. Did Iago have an unhappy childhood or a troubled adolescence? These questions do not greatly matter in Renaissance drama, but to Ibsen they become central. In *A Doll's House*, for example, we can infer that Nora's self-absorption and naiveté result from her father's overprotection.

■ **Remember though, Realist drama does not necessarily come any closer than other dramatic styles to getting at the truths of human existence.** *A Doll's House*, for example, does not provide a more profound picture of psychological struggle than *Oedipus the King*. But Ibsen does offer a more detailed view of his protagonist's inner life and her daily routine.

CHECKLIST: Writing About a Realist Play

☐ List every detail the play gives about the protagonist's past. How does each detail affect the character's current behavior?

☐ What is the protagonist's primary motivation? What are the origins of that motivation?

☐ Do the other characters understand the protagonist's deeper motivations?

☐ How much of the plot arises from misunderstandings among characters?

☐ Do major plot events grow from characters' interactions? Or, do they occur at random?

☐ How does the protagonist's psychology determine his or her reactions to events?

WRITING ASSIGNMENT ON REALISM

Al Capovilla of Folsom Lake Center College has developed an ingenious assignment based on Ibsen's *A Doll's House* that asks you to combine the skills of a literary critic with those of a lawyer. Here is Professor Capovilla's assignment:

> You are the family lawyer for Torvald and Nora Helmer. The couple comes to you with a request. They want you to listen to an account of their domestic problems and recommend whether they should pursue a divorce or try to reconcile.
>
> You listen to both sides of the argument. (You also know everything that is said by every character.)
>
> Now, it is your task to write a short decision. In stating your opinion, provide a clear and organized explanation of your reasoning. Show both sides of the argument. You may employ as evidence anything said or done in the play.
>
> Conclude your paper with your recommendation. What do you advise under the circumstances—divorce or an attempt at reconciliation?

Following is a paper from Professor Capovilla's course written by Carlota Llarena, a student at Folsom Lake Center College.

Llarena 1

Carlota Llarena

Professor Capovilla

English 320

19 January 2012

Helmer vs. Helmer

Introduction establishes premise of essay

In reaching a determination of whether Torvald and Nora Helmer should either get divorced or attempt reconciliation, I have carefully considered the events leading to the breakdown of their marriage in order to decide on an amicable solution to their present predicament. In my belief, marriage is a sacred institution—one that should not be taken lightly. Love and happiness in a marriage should be cultivated by the parties. Obstacles are often found throughout marriage, but in order to overcome those obstacles, a husband and wife should share responsibilities, discuss whatever problems arise, and jointly work on finding solutions to those problems. Based on this belief, I recommend

Thesis statement

that Torvald and Nora Helmer attempt a reconciliation of the marriage.

Topic sentence weighing Torvald's faults

In reviewing the testimony provided by both parties, I find it true that Torvald has treated Nora in such a manner as to make her feel she was considered a child rather than an equal partner. Torvald handled all their

Llarena 2

finances and solely resolved all their problems. Torvald never discussed any of
their household problems with Nora or attempted to seek her advice. In that
regard, I believe that Torvald treated Nora in that fashion because he felt Nora
was incapable of handling these types of situations. Nora's every need had
always been looked after by her father. She grew up with nannies, never had to
take responsibility for herself, and never had to work to earn money as money
was always given to her.

Textual evidence

I find it also true, however, that Nora has always acted like a child. She has
the tendency to sulk if matters don't go her way, is happy when rewarded with
gifts, hides treats (like macaroons) for herself when they are prohibited, and likes
to play games. These characteristics are clearly evident in Nora. There are at least
six examples of her child-like behaviors in the testimonies. First, Nora denied
nibbling on a macaroon or two (1602) as a child would deny any wrongdoing.
Second, Nora thought it would be "fun" to hang the money in pretty gold paper
on the Christmas tree (1601) as a child would enjoy bright and colorful objects.
Third, Nora considered it to be "a tremendous pleasure" to sit and work to earn
money "like being a man" (1608) as a child would pretend and play-act adult
roles. Fourth, Nora was excited when she received a gift of money from Torvald
(1600) as a child would be excited when she receives a present. Fifth, Nora
enjoyed dreaming of a rich old gentleman falling in love with her (1608) as a
child would dream of getting married to a rich man who would take complete care
of her. And, finally, Nora would "do everything I can think of . . . I'll sing for you,
dance for you" (1617) as a child would always attempt to please her parents.

Topic sentence weighing Nora's flaws

Textual evidence

Unfortunately, Torvald reinforced Nora's child-like characteristics by
calling her names such as "my little skylark" (1618), "my little squirrel"
(1600), "little Miss Sweet Tooth" (1602), and "my little Nora" (1618). These
nicknames seem more appropriate for a child than a grown woman. Torvald
has also been very protective of Nora—just as a parent would be protective
of a child. Torvald claimed that Nora had "precious eyes" and "fair little
delicate hands" which indicates his belief that Nora was a fragile person,
one who does not know how to take care of herself. Since Nora was treated
in that same manner by her father, she has never experienced life in any
other fashion other than that of a child.

More textual evidence

Topic sentence on how Torvald's character flaws encourage Nora's dependence

As a further review of the testimony presented, I opine that Torvald
is not solely to be blamed for the predicament at hand. Nora has allowed

Torvald to treat her in this manner during the eight years they were married. She never told Torvald that she wanted to be treated as an adult and as his equal or that she wanted to become more involved with family matters to help determine solutions to problems they may have. Nora was also guilty of not confiding in Torvald or discussing her problems with him. Did Nora discuss with Torvald the need for them to live in Italy for a year (1607)? Did she sit with her husband and discuss issues concerning money to make such a trip to Italy feasible and where the money actually came from (1607)? Did Nora ever tell Torvald the truth that she had borrowed the money from Krogstad, how she was repaying the loan and what she did to secure that loan (1607, 1614)? The answer to all these questions is no! Accordingly, it is quite clear that Nora and Torvald are both equally guilty of not discussing problems and issues with one another.

In summation, Nora and Torvald are equally at fault on the following issues. First, Torvald treated Nora as a child, and Nora allowed herself to be treated in that manner. Second, Torvald never confided in Nora regarding matters concerning the family or their finances. Nora, however, also did not confide in Torvald. Now that these issues and concerns are made known to the parties, the parties may work on resolving their differences, share the responsibility of handling both family and financial matters by discussing them with one another and finding amicable solutions, and cultivate the trust and judgment of one another. Accordingly, it is my ruling that Nora and Torvald attempt reconciling their marriage and forgo divorce as an immediate option. Only if the parties reach an impasse after an honest and sustained attempt at reconciliation would I suggest reconsidering the option of divorce.

Topic sentence establishing mutual guilt

Conclusion

Restatement of thesis

Work Cited

Ibsen, Henrik. *A Doll's House.* Trans. R. Farquharson Sharp. Rev. Viktoria Michelsen. *Literature: An Introduction to Fiction, Poetry, Drama, and Writing.* Ed. X. J. Kennedy and Dana Gioia. 12th ed. New York: Pearson, 2013. 1598–1650. Print.

MORE TOPICS FOR WRITING

1. How relevant is *A Doll's House* today? Do women like Nora still exist? How about men like Torvald? Build an argument, either that the concerns of *A Doll's House* are timeless and universal or that the issues addressed by the play are historical, not contemporary.

2. Placing yourself in the character of Ibsen's Torvald Helmer, write a defense of him and his attitudes as he himself might write it.

3. Who is the protagonist of *The Glass Menagerie*? Give the reasons for your choice. Is there an antagonist? If so, who is it, and why?

4. At the end of *The Glass Menagerie*, Amanda says to Tom, "You live in a dream; you manufacture illusions." Discuss the degree to which this is true of each of the characters in the play.

5. Choose a character from Milcha Sanchez-Scott's *The Cuban Swimmer* and examine his or her motivations. What makes your character act as he or she does? Present evidence from the play to back up your argument.

6. Describe some of the difficulties of staging *The Cuban Swimmer* as a play. What would be lost or gained by remaking it as a movie?

7. How effective is the technique of *Twilight: Los Angeles, 1992*? Does the lack of interplay between characters make it less dramatic, or is there sufficient drama in what the speakers say and the ways in which they present themselves?

8. Write a paper that compares and contrasts the different points of view of two characters in *Twilight: Los Angeles, 1992*.

9. Imagine you're a casting director. Choose a play from this chapter and cast it with well-known television and movie stars. Explain, in depth, what qualities in the characters you hope to emphasize by your casting choices.

▶ TERMS FOR *review*

Modern Theater Movements

Realism ▶ An attempt to reproduce faithfully on the stage the surface appearance of life, especially that of ordinary people in everyday situations. In a historical sense, Realism (usually capitalized) refers to a movement in nineteenth-century European theater. Realist drama customarily focused on the middle class (and occasionally the working class) rather than the aristocracy.

Naturalism ▶ A type of drama in which the characters are presented as products or victims of environment and heredity. Naturalism, considered an extreme form of Realism, customarily depicts the social, psychological, and economic milieu of the primary characters.

Symbolist drama ▶ A style of drama that avoids direct statement and exposition for powerful evocation and suggestion. In place of realistic stage settings and actions, Symbolist drama uses lighting, music, and dialogue to create a mystical atmosphere.

Expressionism ▶ A dramatic style developed between 1910 and 1924 in Germany in reaction against Realism's focus on surface details and external reality. Expressionist style used episodic plots, distorted lines, exaggerated shapes, abnormally intense coloring, mechanical physical movement, and telegraphic speech to create a dreamlike subjective realm.

Theater of the absurd ▶ Postwar European genre depicting the grotesquely comic plight of human beings thrown by accident into an irrational and meaningless world. The critic Martin Esslin coined the term to characterize plays by writers such as Samuel Beckett, Jean Genet, and Eugène Ionesco.

Aspects of Drama

Tragicomedy ► A type of drama that combines elements of both tragedy and comedy. Usually it creates potentially tragic situations that bring the protagonists to the brink of disaster but then ends happily.

Comic relief ► The appearance of a comic situation or character, or clownish humor in the midst of a serious action, introducing a sharp contrast in mood.

Antihero ► A protagonist who is lacking in one or more of the conventional qualities attributed to a hero. Instead of being dignified, brave, idealistic, or purposeful, for instance, the antihero may be buffoonish, cowardly, self-interested, or weak. The antihero is often considered an essentially modern form of characterization, a satiric or realistic commentary on traditional portrayals of idealized characters.

The Stage

Proscenium arch ► An architectural picture frame or gateway "standing in front of the scenery" (as the name *proscenium* indicates) that separates the auditorium from the raised stage and the world of the play.

Picture-frame stage ► A stage that holds the action within a proscenium arch, with painted scene panels (receding into the middle distance) designed to give the illusion of three-dimensional perspective. Picture-frame stages became the norm throughout Europe and England into the twentieth century.

Box set ► A stage set consisting of three walls joined in two corners and a ceiling that tilts, as if seen in perspective, to provide the illusion of scenic realism for interior rooms.

39

EVALUATING A PLAY

The critic should describe, and not prescribe.

—EUGÈNE IONESCO

To **evaluate** a play is to decide whether the play is any good or not and, if it is good, how good it is in relation to other plays of its kind. In the theater, evaluation is usually thought to be the task of the play reviewer (or, with nobler connotations, "drama critic"), ordinarily a person who sees a new play on its first night and who then tells us, in print or over the air, what the play is about, how well it is done, and whether or not we ought to go to see it. Enthroned in an excellent free seat, the drama critic apparently plies a glamorous trade. What fun it must be to whittle a nasty epigram, for example, to be able to observe, as did a critic of a faltering production of *Uncle Tom's Cabin*, that "the Siberian wolf hound was weakly supported."

The opportunities to be a drama critic today, though, are probably few and strictly limited. Much more significant, for most of us, is the task of evaluating for our own satisfaction. We see a play, a film, or a television program, and then we make up our minds about it; we often have to decide whether to recommend it to someone else.

To evaluate new drama isn't easy. (For this discussion, let us define *drama* broadly as including not only plays but also anything that actors perform in the movies or on television, for most of us see more movies and television programs than plays.) By the time we see a production of any kind, at least a part of the process of evaluation has already been accomplished for us. To produce a new play, even in an amateur theater, or to produce a new drama for the movies or for television is complicated and involves large sums of money and the efforts of many people. Sifted from a mountain of submitted scripts, already subjected to long scrutiny and evaluation, a new play or film, whether or not it is of deep interest, arrives with a built-in air of professional competence. It seldom happens that a dull play written by the producer's relative or friend finds enough financial backers to reach the stage; only on the fictitious Broadway of Mel Brooks's film and hit play *The Producers* could there be a musical comedy as awful as *Springtime for Hitler*.

And so new plays—the few that we do see—are usually, like television drama, somebody's safe investment. More often than not, our powers of evaluation confront only slick, pleasant, and efficient mediocrity. We owe it to ourselves to discriminate. Life is too short and theater tickets too expensive to spend either on the agreeably second-rate. There are too many marvelous plays we might miss.

■ WRITING *effectively*

JUDGING A PLAY

To write an informed, useful evaluation of a dramatic work, consider how the play itself asks to be judged. Does it belong to a particular type of drama? It might be a farce, a comedy of manners, or a melodrama (a piece in which suspense and physical action are the prime ingredients). Remember that theaters, such as the classic Greek theater of Sophocles, impose conventions. Do not condemn *Oedipus the King* for the reason one spectator gave: "That damned chorus keeps sticking their noses in!" Do not complain that Hamlet utters soliloquies. Do not dismiss *Sweeney Todd* on the grounds that real people don't keep suddenly bursting into song. So, you might ask, what aspects of a play are up for critique?

- ■ **Judge how well a play fulfills its own conventions.** Ask yourself whether or not it delivers on the expectations it sets up. If a tragedy wants you to feel for the protagonist while also approving the rightness of his downfall, decide whether it has achieved those goals, and if not, why not.

- ■ **Consider whether the play's main characters are fully rounded and believable.** Ask also whether or not their actions follow naturally from their personalities. In a satisfying play, the resolution arises from the nature of the characters, and not through some *deus ex machina* or nick-of-time arrival of the Marines.

- ■ **Consider the play's theme.** How readily can you apply it to the human world beyond the play? Is it trivial, or does it seem to touch a universal chord?

- ■ **Don't be afraid to state your own honest reactions.** We cannot truthfully judge a work of art without somehow involving our own reaction—simple or complicated—to the experience of it.

- ■ **Be careful to distinguish a production from the play itself.** It is important to maintain the distinction between direction, acting, setting, and other elements of production, on the one hand, and the script, on the other.

CHECKLIST: Evaluating a Play

- ☐ What type of play are you watching or reading?
- ☐ What are the conventions of that type of play?
- ☐ How well does the play fulfill those conventions?
- ☐ Are the play's main characters fully realized?
- ☐ Do their actions follow from their personalities, or do the actions seem imposed upon them?
- ☐ Do any symbols stand out? If so, do they reveal meaning?
- ☐ Is the play sentimental? Or does it evoke honest emotion in the viewer?
- ☐ What is the play's theme? Is it of universal importance?

WRITING ASSIGNMENT ON EVALUATION

Many of the plays in this book are available in performance on tape or DVD. Choose one to watch. Pretend you are a critic attending the world premiere, and write a review. Be sure to state your criteria for judgment clearly. For tips on writing a review, see page 1960 in the chapter "Writing About a Play."

MORE TOPICS FOR WRITING

1. Read and evaluate a work from "Plays for Further Reading." Begin with your own personal response to the text, but be sure to temper it with the considerations listed above.

2. Attend a performance of a play you haven't read and write a critical review of it. Be sure to consider both the play itself and the production. For advice on reviewing and a sample review, see pages 1960–62.

3. Evaluate the skill with which Arthur Miller portrays character in *Death of a Salesman*. Focus on one particular character. What telling details are presented about that person? How is he or she characterized by dialogue? Does your character change over the course of the play? How does his or her personality contribute to the plot?

4. Read a modern or contemporary play not found in this book. In an essay of 500 to 750 words, evaluate it. You might choose your subject from this list of interesting plays:

> *The Zoo Story* by Edward Albee
> *Waiting for Godot* by Samuel Beckett
> *"Master Harold" and the Boys* by Athol Fugard
> *The Madwoman of Chaillot* by Jean Giraudoux
> *Six Degrees of Separation* by John Guare
> *Crimes of the Heart* by Beth Henley
> *Hedda Gabler, The Master Builder,* or *Peer Gynt* by Henrik Ibsen
> *The Bald Soprano* or *The Chairs* by Eugène Ionesco
> *Words, Words, Words* by David Ives
> *American Buffalo* by David Mamet
> *Andre's Mother* by Terrence McNally
> *'night, Mother* by Marsha Norman
> *Long Day's Journey into Night* by Eugene O'Neill
> *Topdog/Underdog* by Suzan-Lori Parks
> *The Birthday Party* or *The Caretaker* by Harold Pinter
> *No Exit* by Jean-Paul Sartre
> *for colored girls who have considered suicide / when the rainbow is enuf*
>   by Ntozake Shange
> *Major Barbara* or *Pygmalion* by George Bernard Shaw
> *Buried Child* or *True West* by Sam Shepard
> *Rosencrantz and Guildenstern Are Dead* by Tom Stoppard
> *How I Learned to Drive* by Paula Vogel
> *The Heidi Chronicles* by Wendy Wasserstein
> *The Piano Lesson* by August Wilson

40 PLAYS FOR FURTHER READING

A play isn't a text. It's an event.
—TOM STOPPARD

David Henry Hwang

The Sound of a Voice   1983

David Henry Hwang (b. 1957) grew up in San Gabriel, California, the son of first-generation Chinese immigrants. He was born into a family of musicians: his mother was a concert pianist, his sister plays cello in a string quartet, and he studied the violin. In 1979, as a senior at Stanford University, he directed his first play, F.O.B. (an acronym for "fresh off the boat"), in a dormitory lounge. F.O.B. was later staged at the New York Shakespeare Festival

American Repertory Theater's 2003 production of *The Sound of a Voice* in Cambridge, Massachusetts.

Public Theater and won a 1981 Obie Award. The Sound of a Voice was also produced at the Public Theater as part of a double bill with another one-act play by Hwang, The House of Sleeping Beauties. Hwang enjoyed his greatest commercial and critical success with M. Butterfly *(1988), which won the Tony Award for best play. His other plays include* Face Value *(1993),* Golden Child *(1997), and* Yellowface *(2007). While some of his plays are realistic in their approach, Hwang has always been fascinated by the possibilities of symbolic drama. In* The Sound of a Voice, *he creates a timeless, placeless scene in which two characters named Man and Woman act out a story reminiscent of a folk legend or a traditional Japanese Nō drama (a type of symbolic aristocratic drama developed in the fourteenth century in which a ghost recounts the struggles of his or her life for a traveler). Hwang's interest in nonrealistic and experimental drama has also led him to explore opera. He has collaborated with composer Philip Glass on three works:* 1000 Airplanes on the Roof *(1988), a science-fiction music drama;* The Voyage *(1992), an allegorical grand opera commissioned by New York's Metropolitan Opera for the 500th anniversary of Christopher Columbus's arrival in America; and* The Sound of a Voice *(2003), a combined staging of the following play with* The House of Sleeping Beauties. *He has also written the books for the shows* Aida *(2000), with music by Elton John and lyrics by Tim Rice, and* Tarzan *(2006), with music and lyrics by Phil Collins. Hwang lives in New York City.*

CHARACTERS

Man, fifties, Japanese
Woman, fifties, Japanese

SETTING. *Woman's house, in a remote corner of the forest.*

SCENE I

Woman pours tea for Man. Man rubs himself, trying to get warm.

Man: You're very kind to take me in.
Woman: This is a remote corner of the world. Guests are rare.
Man: The tea—you pour it well.
Woman: No.
Man: The sound it makes—in the cup—very soothing.
Woman: That is the tea's skill, not mine. (*She hands the cup to him.*) May I get you
    something else? Rice, perhaps?
Man: No.
Woman: And some vegetables?
Man: No, thank you.
Woman: Fish? (*Pause.*) It is at least two days' walk to the nearest village. I saw no
    horse. You must be very hungry. You would do a great honor to dine with me.
    Guests are rare.
Man: Thank you.
Woman (*Woman gets up, leaves. Man holds the cup in his hands, using it to warm himself. He gets up, walks around the room. It is sparsely furnished, drab, except for one shelf on which stands a vase of brightly colored flowers. The flowers stand out in sharp contrast to the starkness of the room. Slowly, he reaches out towards them. He touches them. Quickly, he takes one of the flowers from the vase, hides it in his clothes. He*

returns to where he had sat previously. He waits. Woman re-enters. She carries a tray with food.): Please. Eat. It will give me great pleasure.

Man: This—this is magnificent.

Woman: Eat.

Man: Thank you. (*He motions for Woman to join him.*)

Woman: No, thank you.

Man: This is wonderful. The best I've tasted.

Woman: You are reckless in your flattery. But anything you say, I will enjoy hearing. It's not even the words. It's the sound of a voice, the way it moves through the air.

Man: How long has it been since you last had a visitor? (*Pause.*)

Woman: I don't know.

Man: Oh?

Woman: I lose track. Perhaps five months ago, perhaps ten years, perhaps yesterday. I don't consider time when there is no voice in the air. It's pointless. Time begins with the entrance of a visitor, and ends with his exit.

Man: And in between? You don't keep track of the days? You can't help but notice—

Woman: Of course I notice.

Man: Oh.

Woman: I notice, but I don't keep track. (*Pause.*) May I bring out more?

Man: More? No. No. This was wonderful.

Woman: I have more.

Man: Really—the best I've had.

Woman: You must be tired. Did you sleep in the forest last night?

Man: Yes.

Woman: Or did you not sleep at all?

Man: I slept.

Woman: Where?

Man: By a waterfall. The sound of the water put me to sleep. It rumbled like the sounds of a city. You see, I can't sleep in too much silence. It scares me. It makes me feel that I have no control over what is about to happen.

Woman: I feel the same way.

Man: But you live here—alone?

Woman: Yes.

Man: It's so quiet here. How can you sleep?

Woman: Tonight, I'll sleep. I'll lie down in the next room, and hear your breathing through the wall, and fall asleep shamelessly. There will be no silence.

Man: You're very kind to let me stay here.

Woman: This is yours. (*She unrolls a mat; there is a beautiful design of a flower on the mat. The flower looks exactly like the flowers in the vase.*)

Man: Did you make it yourself?

Woman: Yes. There is a place to wash outside.

Man: Thank you.

Woman: Goodnight.

Man: Goodnight. (*Man starts to leave.*)

Woman: May I know your name?

Man: No. I mean, I would rather not say. If I gave you a name, it would only be made-up. Why should I deceive you? You are too kind for that.

Woman: Then what should I call you? Perhaps—"Man Who Fears Silence"?

Man: How about, "Man Who Fears Women"?

Woman: That name is much too common.

Man: And you?

Woman: Yokiko.

Man: That's your name?

Woman: It's what you may call me.

Man: Goodnight, Yokiko. You are very kind.

Woman: You are very smart. Goodnight.

(*Man exits. Hanako° goes to the mat. She tidies it, brushes it off. She goes to the vase. She picks up the flowers, studies them. She carries them out of the room with her. Man re-enters. He takes off his outer clothing. He glimpses the spot where the vase used to sit. He reaches into his clothing, pulls out the stolen flower. He studies it. He puts it underneath his head as he lies down to sleep, like a pillow. He starts to fall asleep. Suddenly, a start. He picks up his head. He listens.*)

SCENE II

Dawn. Man is getting dressed. Woman enters with food.

Woman: Good morning.

Man: Good morning, Yokiko.

Woman: You weren't planning to leave?

Man: I have quite a distance to travel today.

Woman: Please. (*She offers him food.*)

Man: Thank you.

Woman: May I ask where you're travelling to?

Man: It's far.

Woman: I know this region well.

Man: Oh? Do you leave the house often?

Woman: I used to. I used to travel a great deal. I know the region from those days.

Man: You probably wouldn't know the place I'm headed.

Woman: Why not?

Man: It's new. A new village. It didn't exist in "those days." (*Pause.*)

Woman: I thought you said you wouldn't deceive me.

Man: I didn't. You don't believe me, do you?

Woman: No.

Man: Then I didn't deceive you. I'm travelling. That much is true.

Woman: Are you in such a hurry?

Man: Travelling is a matter of timing. Catching the light. (*Woman exits; Man finishes eating, puts down his bowl. Woman re-enters with the vase of flowers.*) Where did you find those? They don't grow native around these parts, do they?

Hanako: The woman.

Woman: No; they've all been brought in. They were brought in by visitors. Such as yourself. They were left here. In my custody.

Man: But—they look so fresh, so alive.

Woman: I take care of them. They remind me of the people and places outside this house.

Man: May I touch them?

Woman: Certainly.

Man: These have just blossomed.

Woman: No; they were in bloom yesterday. If you'd noticed them before, you would know that.

Man: You must have received these very recently. I would guess—within five days.

Woman: I don't know. But I wouldn't trust your estimate. It's all in the amount of care you show to them. I create a world which is outside the realm of what you know.

Man: What do you do?

Woman: I can't explain. Words are too inefficient. It takes hundreds of words to describe a single act of caring. With hundreds of acts, words become irrelevant. (*Pause.*) But perhaps you can stay.

Man: How long?

Woman: As long as you'd like.

Man: Why?

Woman: To see how I care for them.

Man: I am tired.

Woman: Rest.

Man: The light?

Woman: It will return.

SCENE III

Man is carrying chopped wood. He is stripped to the waist. Woman enters.

Woman: You're very kind to do that for me.

Man: I enjoy it, you know. Chopping wood. It's clean. No questions. You take your axe, you stand up the log, you aim—pow!—you either hit it or you don't. Success or failure.

Woman: You seem to have been very successful today.

Man: Why shouldn't I be? It's a beautiful day. I can see to those hills. The trees are cool. The sun is gentle. Ideal. If a man can't be successful on a day like this, he might as well kick the dust up into his own face. (*Man notices Woman staring at him. Man pats his belly, looks at her.*) Protection from falls.

Woman: What? (*Man pinches his belly, showing some fat.*) Oh. Don't be silly. (*Man begins slapping the fat on his belly to a rhythm.*)

Man: Listen—I can make music—see?—that wasn't always possible. But now—that I've developed this—whenever I need entertainment.

Woman: You shouldn't make fun of your body.

Man: Why not? I saw you. You were staring.

Woman: I wasn't making fun. (*Man inflates his cheeks.*) I was just—stop that!

Man: Then why were you staring?

Woman: I was—

Man: Laughing?

Woman: No.

Man: Well?

Woman: I was—Your body. It's . . . strong. (*Pause.*)

Man: People say that. But they don't know. I've heard that age brings wisdom. That's a laugh. The years don't accumulate here. They accumulate here. (*Pause; he pinches his belly.*) But today is a day to be happy, right? The woods. The sun. Blue. It's a happy day. I'm going to chop wood.

Woman: There's nothing left to chop. Look.

Man: Oh. I guess . . . that's it.

Woman: Sit. Here.

Man: But—

Woman: There's nothing left. (*Man sits; Woman stares at his belly.*) Learn to love it.

Man: Don't be ridiculous.

Woman: Touch it.

Man: It's flabby.

Woman: It's strong.

Man: It's weak.

Woman: And smooth.

Man: Do you mind if I put on my shirt?

Woman: Of course not. Shall I get it for you?

Man: No. No. Just sit there. (*Man starts to put on his shirt. He pauses, studies his body.*) You think it's cute, huh?

Woman: I think you should learn to love it. (*Man pats his belly, talks to it.*)

Man (to belly): You're okay, sir. You hang onto my body like a great horseman.

Woman: Not like that.

Man (ibid.): You're also faithful. You'll never leave me for another man.

Woman: No.

Man: What do you want me to say? (*Woman walks over to Man. She touches his belly with her hand. They look at each other.*)

SCENE IV

Night. Man is alone. Flowers are gone from stand. Mat is unrolled. Man lies on it, sleeping. Suddenly, he starts. He lifts up his head. He listens. Silence. He goes back to sleep. Another start. He lifts up his head, strains to hear. Slowly, we begin to make out the strains of a single shakuhachi° playing a haunting line. It is very soft. He strains to hear it. The instrument slowly fades out. He waits for it to return, but it does not. He takes out the stolen flower. He stares into it.

SCENE V

Day. Woman is cleaning, while Man relaxes. She is on her hands and knees, scrubbing. She is dressed in a simple outfit, for working. Her hair is tied back. Man is sweating. He has not, however, removed his shirt.

---

shakuhachi: a Japanese bamboo flute.

Man: I heard your playing last night.

Woman: My playing?

Man: Shakuhachi.

Woman: Oh.

Man: You played very softly. I had to strain to hear it. Next time, don't be afraid. Play out. Fully. Clear. It must've been very beautiful, if only I could've heard it clearly. Why don't you play for me sometime?

Woman: I'm very shy about it.

Man: Why?

Woman: I play for my own satisfaction. That's all. It's something I developed on my own. I don't know if it's at all acceptable by outside standards.

Man: Play for me. I'll tell you.

Woman: No; I'm sure you're too knowledgeable in the arts.

Man: Who? Me?

Woman: You being from the city and all.

Man: I'm ignorant, believe me.

Woman: I'd play, and you'd probably bite your cheek.

Man: Ask me a question about music. Any question. I'll answer incorrectly. I guarantee it.

Woman: Look at this.

Man: What?

Woman: A stain.

Man: Where?

Woman: Here? See? I can't get it out.

Man: Oh. I hadn't noticed it before.

Woman: I notice it every time I clean.

Man: Here. Let me try.

Woman: Thank you.

Man: Ugh. It's tough.

Woman: I know.

Man: How did it get here?

Woman: It's been there as long as I've lived here.

Man: I hardly stand a chance. (*Pause.*) But I'll try. Uh—one—two—three—four! One—two—three—four! See, you set up . . . gotta set up . . . a rhythm—two—three—four. Like fighting! Like battle! One—two—three—four! Used to practice with a rhythm . . . beat . . . battle! Yes! (*The stain starts to fade away.*) Look—it's—yes!—whoo!—there it goes—got the sides—the edges—yes!—fading quick— fading away—ooo—here we come—towards the center—to the heart—two—three—four—slow—slow death—tough—dead! (*Man rolls over in triumphant laughter.*)

Woman: Dead.

Man: I got it! I got it! Whoo! A little rhythm! All it took! Four! Four!

Woman: Thank you.

Man: I didn't think I could do it—but there—it's gone—I did it!

Woman: Yes. You did.

Man: And you—you were great.

Woman: No—I was carried away.

Man: We were a team! You and me!

Woman: I only provided encouragement.

Man: You were great! You were! (*Man grabs Woman. Pause.*)

Woman: It's gone. Thank you. Would you like to hear me play *shakuhachi?*

Man: Yes I would.

Woman: I don't usually play for visitors. It's so . . . I'm not sure. I developed it—all by myself—in times when I was alone. I heard nothing—no human voice. So I learned to play *shakuhachi.* I tried to make these sounds resemble the human voice. The *shakuhachi* became my weapon. To ward off the air. It kept me from choking on many a silent evening.

Man: I'm here. You can hear my voice.

Woman: Speak again.

Man: I will.

SCENE VI

Night. Man is sleeping. Suddenly, a start. He lifts his head up. He listens. Silence. He strains to hear. The shakuhachi melody rises up once more. This time, however, it becomes louder and more clear than before. He gets up. He cannot tell from what direction the music is coming. He walks around the room, putting his ear to different places in the wall, but he cannot locate the sound. It seems to come from all directions at once, as omnipresent as the air. Slowly, he moves towards the wall with the sliding panel through which the Woman enters and exits. He puts his ear against it, thinking the music may be coming from there. Slowly, he slides the door open just a crack, ever so carefully. He peeks through the crack. As he peeks through, the Upstage wall of the set becomes transparent, and through the scrim, we are able to see what he sees. Woman is Upstage of the scrim. She is tending a room filled with potted and vased flowers of all variety. The lushness and beauty of the room Upstage of the scrim stands out in stark contrast to the barrenness of the main set. She is also transformed. She is a young woman. She is beautiful. She wears a brightly colored kimono. Man observes this scene for a long time. He then slides the door shut. The scrim returns to opaque. The music continues. He returns to his mat. He picks up the stolen flower. It is brown and wilted, dead. He looks at it. The music slowly fades out.

SCENE VII

Morning. Man is half-dressed. He is practicing sword maneuvers. He practices with the feel of a man whose spirit is willing, but the flesh is inept. He tries to execute deft movements, but is dissatisfied with his efforts. He curses himself, and returns to basic exercises. Suddenly, he feels something buzzing around his neck—a mosquito. He slaps his neck, but misses it. He sees it flying near him. He swipes at it with his sword. He keeps missing. Finally, he thinks he's hit it. He runs over, kneels down to recover the fallen insect. He picks up two halves of a mosquito on two different fingers. Woman enters the room. She looks as she normally does. She is carrying a vase of flowers, which she places on its shelf.

Man: Look.

Woman: I'm sorry?

Man: Look.

Woman: What? (*He brings over the two halves of mosquito to show her.*)

Man: See?

Woman: Oh.

Man: I hit it—chop!

Woman: These are new forms of target practice?

Man: Huh? Well—yes—in a way.

Woman: You seem to do well at it.

Man: Thank you. For last night. I heard your *shakuhachi.* It was very loud, strong—good tone.

Woman: Did you enjoy it? I wanted you to enjoy it. If you wish, I'll play it for you every night.

Man: Every night!

Woman: If you wish.

Man: No—I don't—I don't want you to treat me like a baby.

Woman: What? I'm not.

Man: Oh, yes. Like a baby. Who you must feed in the middle of the night or he cries. Waaah! Waaah!

Woman: Stop that!

Man: You need your sleep.

Woman: I don't mind getting up for you. (*Pause.*) I would enjoy playing for you. Every night. While you sleep. It will make me feel—like I'm shaping your dreams. I go through long stretches when there is no one in my dreams. It's terrible. During those times, I avoid my bed as much as possible. I paint. I weave. I play *shakuhachi.* I sit on mats and rub powder into my face. Anything to keep from facing a bed with no dreams. It is like sleeping on ice.

Man: What do you dream of now?

Woman: Last night—I dreamt of you. I don't remember what happened. But you were very funny. Not in a mocking way. I wasn't laughing at you. But you made me laugh. And you were very warm. I remember that. (*Pause.*) What do you remember about last night?

Man: Just your playing. That's all. I got up, listened to it, and went back to sleep. (*Man gets up, resumes practicing with his sword.*)

Woman: Another mosquito bothering you?

Man: Just practicing. Ah! Weak! Too weak! I tell you, it wasn't always like this. I'm telling you, there were days when I could chop the fruit from a tree without ever taking my eyes off the ground. (*He continues practicing.*) You ever use one of these?

Woman: I've had to pick one up, yes.

Man: Oh?

Woman: You forget—I live alone—out here—there is . . . . not much to sustain me but what I manage to learn myself. It wasn't really a matter of choice.

Man: I used to be very good, you know. Perhaps I can give you some pointers.

Woman: I'd really rather not.

Man: C'mon—a woman like you—you're absolutely right. You need to know how to defend yourself.

Woman: As you wish.

Man: Do you have something to practice with?

Woman: Yes. Excuse me. (*She exits. He practices more. She re-enters with two wooden sticks. He takes one of them.*) Will these do?

Man: Nice. Now, show me what you can do.

Woman: I'm sorry?

Man: Run up and hit me.

Woman: Please.

Man: Go on—I'll block it.

Woman: I feel so . . . undignified.

Man: Go on. (*She hits him playfully with stick.*) Not like that!

Woman: I'll try to be gentle.

Man: What?

Woman: I don't want to hurt you.

Man: You won't—Hit me! (*Woman charges at Man, quickly, deftly. She scores a hit.*) Oh!

Woman: Did I hurt you?

Man: No—you were—let's try that again. (*They square off again. Woman rushes forward. She appears to attempt a strike. He blocks that apparent strike, which turns out to be a feint. She scores.*) Huh?

Woman: Did I hurt you? I'm sorry.

Man: No.

Woman: I hurt you.

Man: No.

Woman: Do you wish to hit me?

Man: No.

Woman: Do you want me to try again?

Man: No.

Woman: Thank you.

Man: Just practice there—by yourself—let me see you run through some maneuvers.

Woman: Must I?

Man: Yes! Go! (*She goes to an open area.*) My greatest strength was always as a teacher. (*Woman executes a series of deft movements. Her whole manner is transformed. Man watches with increasing amazement. Her movements end. She regains her submissive manner.*)

Woman: I'm so embarrassed. My skills—they're so—inappropriate. I look like a man.

Man: Where did you learn that?

Woman: There is much time to practice here.

Man: But you—the techniques.

Woman: I don't know what's fashionable in the outside world. (*Pause.*) Are you unhappy?

Man: No.

Woman: Really?

Man: I'm just . . . surprised.

Woman: You think it's unbecoming for a woman.

Man: No, no. Not at all.

Woman: You want to leave.

Man: No!

Woman: All visitors do. I know. I've met many. They say they'll stay. And they do. For a while. Until they see too much. Or they learn something new. There are boundaries outside of which visitors do not want to see me step. Only who knows what those boundaries are? Not I. They change with every visitor. You have to be careful not to cross them, but you never know where they are. And one day, inevitably, you step outside the lines. The visitor knows. You don't. You didn't know that you'd done anything different. You thought it was just another part of you. The visitor sneaks away. The next day, you learn that you had stepped outside his heart. I'm afraid you've seen too much.

Man: There are stories.

Woman: What?

Man: People talk.

Woman: Where? We're two days from the nearest village.

Man: Word travels.

Woman: What are you talking about?

Man: There are stories about you. I heard them. They say that your visitors never leave this house.

Woman: That's what you heard?

Man: They say you imprison them.

Woman: Then you were a fool to come here.

Man: Listen.

Woman: Me? Listen? You. Look! Where are these prisoners? Have you seen any?

Man: They told me you were very beautiful.

Woman: Then they are blind as well as ignorant.

Man: You are.

Woman: What?

Man: Beautiful.

Woman: Stop that! My skin feels like seaweed.

Man: I didn't realize it at first. I must confess—I didn't. But over these few days—your face has changed for me. The shape of it. The feel of it. The color. All changed. I look at you now, and I'm no longer sure you are the same woman who had poured tea for me just a week ago. And because of that I remembered—how little I know about a face that changes in the night. (*Pause.*) Have you heard those stories?

Woman: I don't listen to old wives' tales.

Man: But have you heard them?

Woman: Yes. I've heard them. From other visitors—young—hotblooded—or old—who came here because they were told great glory was to be had by killing the witch in the woods.

Man: I was told that no man could spend time in this house without falling in love.

Woman: Oh? So why did you come? Did you wager gold that you could come out untouched? The outside world is so flattering to me. And you—are you like the rest? Passion passing through your heart so powerfully that you can't hold onto it?

Man: No! I'm afraid!

Woman: Of what?

Man: Sometimes—when I look into the flowers, I think I hear a voice—from inside—a voice beneath the petals. A human voice.

Woman: What does it say? "Let me out"?

Man: No. Listen. It hums. It hums with the peacefulness of one who is completely imprisoned.

Woman: I understand that if you listen closely enough, you can hear the ocean.

Man: No. Wait. Look at it. See the layers? Each petal—hiding the next. Try and see where they end. You can't. Follow them down, further down, around—and as you come down—faster and faster—the breeze picks up. The breeze becomes a wail. And in that rush of air—in the silent midst of it—you can hear a voice.

Woman (grabs flower from Man): So, you believe I water and prune my lovers? How can you be so foolish? (*She snaps the flower in half, at the stem. She throws it to the ground.*) Do you come only to leave again? To take a chunk of my heart, then leave with your booty on your belt, like a prize? You say that I imprison hearts in these flowers? Well, bits of my heart are trapped with travellers across this land. I can't even keep track. So kill me. If you came here to destroy a witch, kill me now. I can't stand to have it happen again.

Man: I won't leave you.

Woman: I believe you. (*She looks at the flower that she has broken, bends to pick it up. He touches her. They embrace.*)

SCENE VIII

Day. Woman wears a simple undergarment, over which she is donning a brightly colored kimono, the same one we saw her wearing Upstage of the scrim. Man stands apart.

Woman: I can't cry. I don't have the capacity. Right from birth, I didn't cry. My mother and father were shocked. They thought they'd given birth to a ghost, a demon. Sometimes I've thought myself that. When great sadness has welled up inside me, I've prayed for a means to release the pain from my body. But my prayers went unanswered. The grief remained inside me. It would sit like water, still. (*Pause; she models her kimono.*) Do you like it?

Man: Yes, it's beautiful.

Woman: I wanted to wear something special today.

Man: It's beautiful. Excuse me. I must practice.

Woman: Shall I get you something?

Man: No.

Woman: Some tea, maybe?

Man: No. (*Man resumes swordplay.*)

Woman: Perhaps later today—perhaps we can go out—just around here. We can look for flowers.

Man: Alright.

Woman: We don't have to.

Man: No. Let's.

Woman: I just thought if—

Man: Fine. Where do you want to go?

Woman: There are very few recreational activities around here, I know.

Man: Alright. We'll go this afternoon. (*Pause.*)

Woman: Can I get you something?

Man (turning around): What?

Woman: You might be—

Man: I'm not hungry or thirsty or cold or hot.

Woman: Then what are you?

Man: Practicing. (*Man resumes practicing; Woman exits. As soon as she exits, he rests. He sits down. He examines his sword. He runs his finger along the edge of it. He takes the tip, runs it against the soft skin under his chin. He places the sword on the ground with the tip pointed directly upwards. He keeps it from falling by placing the tip under his chin. He experiments with different degrees of pressure. Woman re-enters. She sees him in this precarious position. She jerks his head upward; the sword falls.*)

Woman: Don't do that!

Man: What?

Woman: You can hurt yourself!

Man: I was practicing!

Woman: You were playing!

Man: I was practicing!

Woman: It's dangerous.

Man: What do you take me for—a child?

Woman: Sometimes wise men do childish things.

Man: I knew what I was doing!

Woman: It scares me.

Man: Don't be ridiculous. (*He reaches for the sword again.*)

Woman: Don't! Don't do that!

Man: Get back! (*He places the sword back in its previous position, suspended between the floor and his chin, upright.*)

Woman: But—

Man: Ssssh!

Woman: I wish—

Man: Listen to me! The slightest shock, you know—the slightest shock— surprise— it might make me jerk or—something—and then . . . so you must be perfectly still and quiet.

Woman: But I—

Man: Sssssh! (*Silence.*) I learned this exercise from a friend—I can't even remember his name—good swordsman—many years ago. He called it his meditation position. He said, like this, he could feel the line between this world and the others because he rested on it. If he saw something in another world that he liked better, all he would have to do is let his head drop, and he'd be there. Simple. No fuss. One day, they found him with the tip of his sword run clean out the back of his neck. He was smiling. I guess he saw something he liked. Or else he'd fallen asleep.

Woman: Stop that.

Man: Stop what?

Woman: Tormenting me.

Man: I'm not.

Woman: Take it away!

Man: You don't have to watch, you know.

Woman: Do you want to die that way—an accident?

Man: I was doing this before you came in.

Woman: If you do, all you need to do is tell me.

Man: What?

Woman: I can walk right over. Lean on the back of your head.

Man: Don't try to threaten—

Woman: Or jerk your sword up.

Man: Or scare me. You can't threaten—

Woman: I'm not. But if that's what you want.

Man: You can't threaten me. You wouldn't do it.

Woman: Oh?

Man: Then I'd be gone. You wouldn't let me leave that easily.

Woman: Yes, I would.

Man: You'd be alone.

Woman: No. I'd follow you. Forever. (*Pause.*) Now, let's stop this nonsense.

Man: No! I can do what I want! Don't come any closer!

Woman: Then release your sword.

Man: Come any closer and I'll drop my head.

Woman (*Woman slowly approaches Man. She grabs the hilt of the sword. She looks into his eyes. She pulls it out from under his chin.*): There will be no more of this. (*She exits with the sword. He starts to follow her, then stops. He touches under his chin. On his finger, he finds a drop of blood.*)

SCENE IX

Night. Man is leaving the house. He is just about out, when he hears a shakuhachi *playing. He looks around, trying to locate the sound. Woman appears in the doorway to the outside.* Shakuhachi *slowly fades out.*

Woman: It's time for you to go?

Man: Yes. I'm sorry.

Woman: You're just going to sneak out? A thief in the night? A frightened child?

Man: I care about you.

Woman: You express it strangely.

Man: I leave in shame because it is proper. (*Pause.*) I came seeking glory.

Woman: To kill me? You can say it. You'll be surprised at how little I blanch. As if you'd said, "I came for a bowl of rice," or "I came seeking love" or "I came to kill you."

Man: Weakness. All weakness. Too weak to kill you. Too weak to kill myself. Too weak to do anything but sneak away in shame. (*Woman brings out Man's sword.*)

Woman: Were you even planning to leave without this? (*He takes sword.*) Why not stay here?

Man: I can't live with someone who's defeated me.

Woman: I never thought of defeating you. I only wanted to take care of you. To make you happy. Because that made me happy and I was no longer alone.

Man: You defeated me.

Woman: Why do you think that way?

Man: I came here with a purpose. The world was clear. You changed the shape of your face, the shape of my heart—rearranged everything—created a world where I could do nothing.

Woman: I only tried to care for you.

Man: I guess that was all it took. (*Pause.*)

Woman: You still think I'm a witch. Just because old women gossip. You are so cruel. Once you arrived, there were only two possibilities: I would die or you would leave. (*Pause.*) If you believe I'm a witch, then kill me. Rid the province of one more evil.

Man: I can't—

Woman: Why not? If you believe that about me, then it's the right thing to do.

Man: You know I can't.

Woman: Then stay.

Man: Don't try and force me.

Woman: I won't force you to do anything. (*Pause.*) All I wanted was an escape—for both of us. The sound of a human voice—the simplest thing to find, and the hardest to hold onto. This house—my loneliness is etched into the walls. Kill me, but don't leave. Even in death, my spirit would rest here and be comforted by your presence.

Man: Force me to stay.

Woman: I won't. (*Man starts to leave.*) Beware.

Man: What?

Woman: The ground on which you walk is weak. It could give way at any moment. The crevice beneath is dark.

Man: Are you talking about death? I'm ready to die.

Woman: Fear for what is worse than death.

Man: What?

Woman: Falling. Falling through the darkness. Waiting to hit the ground. Picking up speed. Waiting for the ground. Falling faster. Falling alone. Waiting. Falling. Waiting. Falling.

(*Woman wails and runs out through the door to her room. Man stands, confused, not knowing what to do. He starts to follow her, then hesitates, and rushes out the door to the outside. Silence. Slowly, he re-enters from the outside. He looks for her in the main room. He goes slowly towards the panel to her room. He throws down his sword. He opens the panel. He goes inside. He comes out. He unrolls his mat. He sits on it, cross-legged. He looks out into space. He notices near him a shakuhachi. He picks it up. He begins to blow into it. He tries to make sounds. He continues trying through the end of the play. The Upstage scrim lights up. Upstage, we see the Woman. She is young. She is hanging from a rope suspended from the roof. She has hung herself. Around her are scores of vases with flowers in them whose blossoms have been blown off. Only the stems remain in the vases. Around her swirl the thousands of petals from the flowers. They fill the Upstage scrim area like a blizzard of color. Man continues to attempt to play. Lights fade to black.*)

David Henry Hwang on Writing

Multicultural Theater   1989

Interviewer: How did you begin . . . exploring your [Chinese American] heritage?

Hwang: A lot of that happened in college. I was in college in the mid-to-late 1970s, and whereas most people seem to associate collegiate life in the seventies with John

Travolta, there was at that time a third-world consciousness, a third-world power movement, in the universities, particularly among Hispanics and Asians. The blacks really started it in the late sixties and early seventies, and it took a while to trickle down into the other third-world communities. Asians probably picked it up last. . . . While I was never a very ardent Marxist, I studied the ideas and I was interested in the degree to which we all may have been affected by certain prejudices in the society without having realized it, and to what degree we had incorporated that into our persons by the time we'd reached our early twenties.

David Henry Hwang

The other thing that I think fascinated me about exploring my Chineseness at that time was consistent with my interest in play-writing. I had become very interested in Sam Shepard, particularly in the way in which Shepard likes to create a sort of American mythology. In his case it's the cowboy mythology, but nonetheless it's something that is larger than simply our present-day, fast-food existence. In my context, creating a mythology, creating a past for myself, involved going into Chinese history and Chinese American history. I think the combination of wanting to delve into those things for artistic reasons and being exposed to an active third-world-consciousness movement was what started to get me interested in my roots when I was in college.

Interviewer: I wonder if there will come a time when the expression "ethnic theater" won't have any meaning.

Hwang: I'm hopeful that there will be a time at some point, but I think it's going to be fifty years or so down the road. The whole idea of being ethnic only applies when it's clear what the dominant culture is. Once it becomes less clear and the culture is acknowledged to be more multicultural, then the idea of what's ethnic becomes irrelevant. I think even today we're starting to see that. The monoethnic theaters—that is, the Asian theaters, the black theaters, the Hispanic theaters— are really useful; they serve a purpose. But I think, if we do our jobs correctly, we will phase out our own need for existence, and the future of theaters will be in multicultural theaters, theaters that do a black play and a Jewish play and a classic and whatever . . .

There are so many people now who can't be labeled. I know a couple in which the man is Japanese and Jewish and the woman is Haitian and Filipino. They have a child, and sociologists have told them that a child of that stock probably hasn't existed before. When someone like that becomes a writer, what do we call him? Do we say he's an Asian writer, or what? As those distinctions become increasingly muddled, the whole notion of what is ethnic as opposed to what is mainstream is going to become more and more difficult to define.

From interview in *Contemporary Authors*

Edward Bok Lee

El Santo Americano
2001

Edward Bok Lee was born in Fargo, North Dakota, the son of Korean immigrants. He attended kindergarten in Seoul, South Korea, but grew up mostly in North Dakota and Minnesota. He received a B.A. in comparative literature from the University of Minnesota and an M.F.A. from Brown University. While enrolled in a graduate program in comparative literature at the University of California, Berkeley, he wrote his first full-length play, St. Petersburg: An Exodus *(2000). Lee writes plays, poetry, fiction, and memoir. A former bartender, custodian, journalist, and translator, Lee has performed his work in the United States, Europe, and Asia, as well as on public radio and on television, including MTV. His prose and poetry collection* Real Karaoke People *(2005) won the Asian American Literary Award and the PEN/Open Book Award. Lee currently teaches at Metropolitan State University.* El Santo Americano *(2001) was originally developed as part of a "ten-minute-play" project at the Guthrie Theater in Minneapolis. His other plays include* Athens County *(1997) and* History K *(2003). "Art can show you," Bok has observed, "the interior of another person's life and soul, if only just for a few minutes."*

CHARACTERS

Clay, *a man*
Evalana, *his wife*

TIME. *Present*
PLACE. *The desert at night.*

Clay *(driving at night, 80 mph)*: that's because in Mexico it's normal to wear a
    mask. almost everybody does. silk and satin and form-fitting lycra. it makes
    the whole body more aerodynamic. you ought see them flying around, doing
    triple flips in mid-air. they got these long flowing capes like colorful wings
    sprouting from their shoulders. they don't talk much, though. not the great
    ones. the silence is mysterious. it adds a kind of weight to them when they
    climb into the ring. get a guy with that much gold and glitter on him here and
    you know he'd have to talk shit. in Mexico they just wrestle. the masks come
    from thousands and thousands of years ago. fiestas. ancient rituals. slip one
    over your head and you could become a tiger or donkey, a bat or giant lizard. a
    corn spirit dancing under the clouds for rain. those were your gods if you lived
    back then. you'll like it there in Mexico. don't you think you'll like it there?
    Jesse?

(Evalana, brooding, eventually looks in the backseat then faces front again.)

Clay: he asleep back there?
    a growing boy needs his sleep.
    yes he does.
    you hungry?
Evalana: don't talk to me.
Clay: hard to fall asleep on an empty stomach.
Evalana: i can't sleep.

Clay: you ain't tried to.

(*She checks her outburst, then looks in the backseat again, perhaps adjusting their son's blanket, then faces front. they drive on for a time.*)

Clay (*looking in rearview mirror*): hey there Jesse.
you have a nice nap?
we'll be there come morning, so you just sit back.
how you like that comic book i got you?
Jesse?
what's the matter, boy? you not feeling well?
Jesse?
Evalana: sometimes he sleeps with his eyes open.
Clay: like you.
Evalana: i do not sleep with my eyes open.
Clay: how do you know?
Evalana: i know.
Clay: how?
Evalana: 'cause someone would have said something. including you.
Clay: people do all kinds of things they're not aware of.
my daddy used to wander through the house all night, buck naked,
up and down the stairs. opening and closing windows.
carrying only his briefcase chockfull of all the vending machine products he sold.
combs. candy. chicken bouillon.
my momma warned if we woke him up he'd have a heart attack.
so we just let him sleepwalk.
he didn't know.
Evalana: maybe somebody should have told him.
Clay: he didn't want to know.

(*They drive on.*)

Evalana: you talk in your sleep.
you snore.
you drool.
and you fart. all night.

(*They drive on awhile.*)

Clay: i love you, Ev.
Evalana: jesus, Clay. listen to yourself.
your whole life you been faking it.
fake husband. fake father.
fake man. that's what they ought to call you:
Fake Man.

(*Clay drives on for a little while longer through the night, then pulls the car to a stop on the side of the road and gets out. he walks a good ways away from the car, holding a flashlight in one hand and a gun in the other—not aimed at her, but clearly present, under the starlight. Evalana hesitates, then gets out, the flashlight's beam now on her.*)

Clay (*directs flashlight beam to a place in the brush*): there's a bush over there.

(*Evalana, hesitant at first, then grabs her purse and crosses past Clay.*)

Evalana (*off*): i won't run!
    i promise!

(*Clay thinks, then lowers flashlight beam and switches it off. dim moonlight. sounds of desert at night.*)

Clay: you should have seen me last week, Ev!
    Darton, he cut me a break! he didn't have to, but he did 'cause i been loyal to him all these years! you remember when we used to work at the turkey plant together! the smell on my hands when i'd come home and try to kiss you . . .
    the match was against the eleventh-ranked contender! brand new guy, from Montreal! Kid Canuck they call him! long blonde hair, tan, all bulked up in white trunks with a red maple leaf you know where! some rich producer's nephew or something! he was scheduled to wrestle the Sheik in the opening match, but the old guy had a hernia while they was warming up, so Darton, he give me a break and put me on the bill against Kid Canuck at the last minute!
    we didn't have time to choreograph much action! i think he was kind of nervous! two minutes in he starts grabbing my hair! hard! for real! trying to get the audience more into it! he wasn't telegraphing his head butts neither! soon enough my nose was a cherry caught under a dumptruck! the blood all over sure got the crowd into it boy! up till then they was pretty quiet, waiting for the main headliners to come out!
    raking my eyes, slapping my face. i told him to ease up, it don't work like that here, but he wasn't listening. dancing around. cursing at me in French. winding his right arm up, then smacking me hard with the left until both my ears are firebells going off.
    now i can take just about anything. you know me. i've been pile-drived, figure-foured, and suplexed into losses by the best of them. but on this particular night, something happened. and one pop i took in the mouth shot my adrenaline way up, my blood running all over hell now like carbolic acid, and him twisting my arm for real, not giving a flying fuck about my bad elbow, my bad back, or my five-year-old son, who don't even like to watch wrestling no more 'cause he's ashamed, 'cause his friends call his daddy a loser, and he don't know what to say or believe in, and the next thing i knew i had that pretty boy son of a bitch Kid Canuck down hard on the mat in a scorpion leg lock!!
    they had to haul him off on a stretcher!
    i was a little dazed yet, and the crowd, they didn't know what to think!
    then the referee threw my arm up under the hot lights and before i knew it all the noise in the arena was more like cheering! it was a chemical thing! at first some people in the upper bleachers stood up! and then all of them did! everywhere! stomping, and starting to chant my name! and not 'cause they hated the other guy! they didn't! they was cheering 'cause i beat the guy fair and square! he gave up out of pain, right there in the middle of the ring! i had him wrenched in that scorpion leg lock a good two minutes screaming like a baby, like a cut pig, like a man in real pain! and they knew it!

you can't fake that! they'd seen so much phony bullshit through the years, and they could tell this match was different! and they appreciated that! they appreciated being shown the truth, just once in their sorry-ass lives!

Darton threw a wet towel at my face in the locker room.

i went out on a limb for you! he says. six months of planning and promotion! tens of thousands of dollars! t-shirts! coffee mugs! now who the hell's gonna believe Kid Canuck is a contender for the federation championship when he lost his debut match to you!!

i told him i was sorry, and after a while he put his hand on my shoulder. asked me what i'd been thinking there in the ring. tell me the truth, he says. so i can go home and feel at least a little bad about firing your dumb ass.

and i wanted to say that i did it for you.

for my wife, Evalana, who i never gave nothing to believe in.

and i did it for my boy, Jesse, who only ever got to see his daddy get beat time and again. i wanted to tell him i did it 'cause my wife and child was out there in the audience. not living in some other town. i wanted to say you was both out there watching over me. 'cause where else would you be?

Ev? Evalana!

(*Clay switches on flashlight and directs its beam onto the "bush" in the desert. Evalana has run off. he directs the flashlight all around, searching in vain.*)

shit.

(*Clay turns off the flashlight and sits down on a stone. in the moonlight, he pulls out from his pocket a colorful Mexican wrestler's mask and slips it over his head. he sits there in the darkness alone for a moment. he then, as a little boy might, twirls the gun on his finger, and pretends what it'd be like to shoot himself in the head. he tries it from a couple different angles, in strange fun. eventually he places the gun in his mouth, holds it there for a second or two with his hand, then lets go. it remains stuck there in his mouth from here on out. eventually, out of the darkness of the desert, Evalana reappears.*)

Evalana: once, when i was about Jesse's age, we took a trip to California. Disneyland. we drove all the way cross country in Daddy's Ford Falcon. Ma said it was the honeymoon she never got. a lot of the highway had just been tarred, and you could feel it. i thought we was gonna sail on forever into the future. it was somewhere in Arizona that Daddy woke us all up so we could see this great big dam at night. we stood there looking down at the bright lights and roaring darkness. Ma moved off to one side and stared down, a thousand feet.
i knew she wanted to jump.
then suddenly, she pointed at something. look, Ev, she said. a rainbow!

Shane and Darlene came running over, climbing up on the guard-rail but they couldn't see nothing. neither could Daddy.

a few hours later, somewhere outside of Flagstaff i told them i saw that rainbow too. it wasn't just Ma who saw it. i saw it too. Shane and Darlene were asleep now. Ma didn't say nothing. we drove on deeper into the night. then Daddy looked at me. i could see his eyes in the rear view mirror. hovering there in the blackness. "there's no such thing as a rainbow at night," he said. "not a real rainbow anyway."

the next day at dusk we camped on high ground. from where i stood looking down, you could see all the layers of sediment carved in the side of the mountains they cleared away for the highways a long time ago. red, black, brown, white, and sometimes almost blue, like a human vein in the side of a mountain, running parallel to the horizon. i stood there a long time, watching all the layers of earthen rainbows darkening all around me. then slowly, i noticed something. in the far distance, a cluster of fallen stars. only, it wasn't a cluster of stars, but a town. far off the highway, down there in the middle of nowhere. you wouldn't even notice it by day. but at night you could see something. twinkling. i imagined i'd been born in that town, and that that was where we was all heading back to. not Disneyland. but that town shining with tiny stars that weren't really stars, surrounded by rainbows that weren't really rainbows. but erosion. as far as the eye could see. for thousands and thousands of years. both real and imaginary. like that town down there in the valley at night. just barely shimmering. like . . . Eden.

(*We hear the sound of their car start and drive off into the night. Clay in mask with gun still in mouth and Evalana slowly turn to watch the vehicle go, converging closer together as they walk and watch. "Jesse" has driven off into the night. once the sound of the car has faded into the distance, Clay in mask with gun in mouth and Evalana slowly turn to one another. after a moment, Evalana reaches up and removes the gun from Clay's mouth and slowly points it at him.*

Fade to black.)

END OF PLAY

Edward Bok Lee on Writing

On Being a Korean American Writer   2006

Interviewer: Do you think of yourself as a Korean American writer?

Lee: What I'm doing, intentionally, is trying to participate in this thing we call Asian America, this Asian American culture, which is influenced by my parents and the way that they brought me up, their philosophies and their religious beliefs, their culture—everything from the food to the song to the art form.

I believe that a given culture has a given orientation of the soul. And you can hear it in a culture's music. It's live, it's right in front of you, it's all around you. I really believe that when I hear a culture—whether it's Irish or African or English or Hawaiian—when I hear the traditional songs

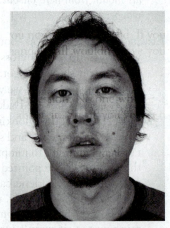

Edward Bok Lee

coming out of people, I definitely sense that there are differences of the soul. So in that way, I feel alive with some sort of Asian, and more Asian American sensibilities. I have no idea how to try and quantify those things, but I feel it.

It's sort of drenching the country when I go back to Korea—especially the countryside. It's tied to the land, it's tied to the history. It's a history, in Korea, of oppression, of colonization, and of survival. I feel, like it or not, that that ethos or whatever you want to call it, is infused in my work.

. . . I feel like a conduit between something going on in another realm. It might be something like the past, history, or something beyond memory. Voices. It's in the realm of intuition . . . and it's mysterious. And that's when I feel like I'm at my best in writing. Versus that I have things to say that I want to communicate. If that were the case, then I think I would do journalism, or write essays.

I think I'm in love with the unspeakable, the inarticulable. You're always coming up against this invisible wall, and putting a cup to it, trying to hear what's going on the other side. You're always trying to transcribe those things.

From "Thinking Souls: An Interview with Edward Bok Lee"
by Shannon Gibney

Jane Martin

Beauty   2001

The identity of Jane Martin is a closely guarded secret. No biographical details, public statements, or photographs of this Kentucky-based playwright have been published, nor has she given any interviews or made any public appearances. Often called "America's best known, unknown playwright," Martin first came to public notice in 1981 for Talking With, *a collection of monologues that received a number of productions worldwide and won a Best Foreign Play of the Year award in Germany. Of Martin's many plays, others include* What Mama Don't Know *(1988),* Cementville *(1991),* Keely and Du *(which was a finalist for the 1993 Pulitzer Prize),* Middle-Aged White Guys *(1995),* Jack and Jill *(1996),* Mr. Bundy *(1998),* Anton in Show Business *(2000),* Flaming Guns of the Purple Sage *(2001), and* Good Boys *(2002). Her most recent work is* Sez She *(2005), a monologue play for five actresses.*

CHARACTERS

Carla
Bethany

SCENE. *An apartment. Minimalist set. A young woman, Carla, on the phone.*

Carla: In love with me? You're in love with me? Could you describe yourself again? Uh-huh. Uh-huh. And you spoke to me? (*A knock at the door.*) Listen, I always hate to interrupt a marriage proposal, but . . . could you possibly hold that thought? (*Puts phone down and goes to door. Bethany, the same age as Carla and a friend, is there. She carries the sort of mid-eastern lamp we know of from Aladdin.*)
Bethany: Thank God you were home. I mean, you're not going to believe this!
Carla: Somebody on the phone. (*Goes back to it.*)
Bethany: I mean, I just had a beach urge, so I told them at work my uncle was dying . . .
Carla (*motions to Bethany for quiet*): And you were the one in the leather jacket with the tattoo? What was the tattoo? (*Carla again asks Bethany, who is gesturing wildly that she should hang up, to cool it.*) Look, a screaming eagle from shoulder to shoulder, maybe. There were a lot of people in the bar.

Bethany (gesturing and mouthing): I have to get back to work.

Carla (on phone): See, the thing is, I'm probably not going to marry someone I can't remember . . . particularly when I don't drink. Sorry. Sorry. Sorry. (*She hangs up.*) Madness.

Bethany: So I ran out to the beach . . .

Carla: This was some guy I never met who apparently offered me a beer . . .

Bethany: . . . low tide and this . . . (*The lamp*) . . . was just sitting there, lying there . . .

Carla: . . . and he tracks me down . . .

Bethany: . . . on the beach, and I lift this lid thing . . .

Carla: . . . and seriously proposes marriage.

Bethany: . . . and a genie comes out.

Carla: I mean, that's twice in a . . . what?

Bethany: A genie comes out of this thing.

Carla: A genie?

Bethany: I'm not kidding, the whole Disney kind of thing, swirling smoke, and then this twenty-foot-high, see-through guy in like an Arabian outfit.

Carla: Very funny.

Bethany: Yes, funny, but twenty feet high! I look up and down the beach, I'm alone. I don't have my pepper spray or my hand alarm. You know me, when I'm petrified I joke. I say his voice is too high for Robin Williams, and he says he's a castrati. Naturally. Who else would I meet?

Carla: What's a castrati?

Bethany: You know . . .

(*The appropriate gesture.*)

Carla: Bethany, dear one, I have three modeling calls. I am meeting Ralph Lauren!

Bethany: Okay, good. Ralph Lauren. Look, I am not kidding!

Carla: You're not kidding what?!

Bethany: There is a genie in this thingamajig.

Carla: Uh-huh. I'll be back around eight.

Bethany: And he offered me *wishes!*

Carla: Is this some elaborate practical joke because it's my birthday?

Bethany: No, happy birthday, but I'm like crazed because I'm on this deserted beach with a twenty-foot-high, see-through genie, so like sarcastically . . . you know how I need a new car . . . I said fine, gimme 25,000 dollars . . .

Carla: On the beach with the genie?

Bethany: Yeah, right, exactly, and it rains down out of the sky.

Carla: Oh sure.

Bethany (pulling a wad out of her purse): Count it, those are thousands. I lost one in the surf.

(*Carla sees the top bill. Looks at Bethany, who nods encouragement. Carla thumbs through them.*)

Carla: These look real.

Bethany: Yeah.

Carla: And they rained down out of the sky?

Bethany: Yeah.

Carla: You've been really strange lately, are you dealing?

Bethany: Dealing what, I've even given up chocolate.

Carla: Let me see the genie.

Bethany: Wait, wait.

Carla: Bethany, I don't have time to screw around. Let me see the genie or let me go on my appointments.

Bethany: Wait! So I pick up the money . . . see, there's sand on the money . . . and I'm like nuts so I say, you know, "Okay, look, ummm, big guy, my uncle is in the hospital" . . . because as you know when I said to the people at work my uncle was dying, I was on one level telling the truth although it had nothing to do with the beach, but he was in Intensive Care after the accident, and that's on my mind, so I say, okay, Genie, heal my uncle . . . which is like impossible given he was hit by two trucks, and the genie says, "Yes, Master" . . . like they're supposed to say, and he goes into this like kind of whirlwind, kicking up sand and stuff, and I'm like, "Oh my God!" and the air clears, and he bows, you know, and says, "It is done, Master," and I say, "Okay, whatever-you-are, I'm calling on my cell phone," and I get it out and I get this doctor who is like dumbstruck who says my uncle came to, walked out of Intensive Care and left the hospital! I'm not kidding, Carla.

Carla: On your mother's grave?

Bethany: On my mother's grave.

(They look at each other.)

Carla: Let me see the genie.

Bethany: No, no, look, that's the whole thing . . . I was just, like, reacting, you know, responding, and that's already two wishes . . . although I'm really pleased about my uncle, the $25,000 thing, I could have asked for $10 million, and there is only one wish left.

Carla: So ask for $10 million.

Bethany: I don't think so. I don't think so. I mean, I gotta focus in here. Do you have a sparkling water?

Carla: No. Bethany, I'm missing Ralph Lauren now. Very possibly my one chance to go from catalogue model to the very, very big time, so, if you are joking, stop joking.

Bethany: Not joking. See, see, the thing is, I know what I want. In my guts. Yes. Underneath my entire bitch of a life is this unspoken, ferocious, all-consuming urge . . .

Carla (trying to get her to move this along): Ferocious, all-consuming urge . . .

Bethany: I want to be like you.

Carla: Me?

Bethany: Yes.

Carla: Half the time you don't even like me.

Bethany: Jealous. The ogre of jealousy.

Carla: You're the one with the $40,000 job straight out of school. You're the one who has published short stories. I'm the one hanging on by her fingernails in modeling. The one who has creeps calling her on the phone. The one who had to have a nose job.

Bethany: I want to be beautiful.

Carla: You are beautiful.

Bethany: Carla, I'm not beautiful.

Carla: You have charm. You have personality. You know perfectly well you're pretty.

Bethany: "Pretty," see, that's it. Pretty is the minor leagues of beautiful. Pretty is what people discover about you after they know you. Beautiful is what knocks them out across the room. Pretty, you get called a couple of times a year; *beautiful* is 24 hours a day.

Carla: Yeah? So?

Bethany: So?! We're talking *beauty* here. Don't say "So?" Beauty is the real deal. You are the center of any moment of your life. People stare. Men flock. I've seen you get offered discounts on makeup for no reason. Parents treat beautiful children better. Studies show your income goes up. You can have sex anytime you want it. Men have to know me. That takes up to a year. I'm continually horny.

Carla: Bethany, I don't even like sex. I can't have a conversation without men coming on to me. I have no privacy. I get hassled on the street. They start pressuring me from the beginning. Half the time, it never occurs to them to start with a conversation. Smart guys like you. You've had three long-term relationships, and you're only twenty-three. I haven't had one. The good guys, the smart guys are scared to death of me. I'm surrounded by male bimbos who think a preposition is when you go to school away from home. I have no woman friends except you. I don't even want to talk about this!

Bethany: I knew you'd say something like this. See, you're "in the club" so you can say this. It's the way beauty functions as an elite. You're trying to keep it all for yourself.

Carla: I'm trying to tell you it's no picnic.

Bethany: But it's what everybody wants. It's the nasty secret at large in the world. It's the unspoken tidal desire in every room and on every street. It's the unspoken, the soundless whisper . . . millions upon millions of people longing hopelessly and forever to stop being whatever they are and be beautiful, but the difference between those ardent multitudes and me is that I have a goddamn genie and one more wish!

Carla: Well, it's not what I want. This is me, Carla. I have never read a whole book. Page 6, I can't remember page 4. The last thing I read was "The Complete Idiot's Guide to WordPerfect." I leave dinner parties right after the dessert because I'm out of conversation. You know the dumb blond joke about on the application where it says, "Sign here," she put Sagittarius? I've done that. Only beautiful guys approach me, and that's because they want to borrow my eye shadow. I barely exist outside a mirror! You don't want to *be me*.

Bethany: None of you tell the truth. That's why you have no friends. We can all see you're just trying to make us feel better because we aren't in your league. This only proves to me it should be my third wish. Money can only buy things. Beauty makes you the center of the universe.

(Bethany picks up the lamp.)

Carla: Don't do it. Bethany, don't wish it! I am telling you you'll regret it.

(Bethany lifts the lid. There is a tremendous crash, and the lights go out. Then they flicker and come back up, revealing Bethany and Carla on the floor where they have been thrown by the explosion. We don't realize it at first, but they have exchanged places.)

Carla/Bethany: Oh God.

Bethany/Carla: Oh God.

Carla/Bethany: Am I bleeding? Am I dying?

Bethany/Carla: I'm so dizzy. You're not bleeding.

Carla/Bethany: Neither are you.

Bethany/Carla: I feel so weird.

Carla/Bethany: Me too. I feel . . . *(Looking at her hands.)* Oh, my God, I'm wearing your jewelry. I'm wearing your nail polish.

Bethany/Carla: I know I'm over here, but I can see myself over there.

Carla/Bethany: I'm wearing your dress. I have your legs!!

Bethany/Carla: These aren't my shoes. I can't meet Ralph Lauren wearing these shoes!

Carla/Bethany: I wanted to be beautiful, but I didn't want to be you.

Bethany/Carla: Thanks a lot!!

Carla/Bethany: I've got to go. I want to pick someone out and get laid.

Bethany/Carla: You can't just walk out of here in my body!

Carla/Bethany: Wait a minute. Wait a minute. What's eleven eighteenths of 1,726?

Bethany/Carla: Why?

Carla/Bethany: I'm a public accountant. I want to know if you have my brain.

Bethany/Carla: One hundred thirty-two and a half.

Carla/Bethany: You have my brain.

Bethany/Carla: What shade of Rubenstein lipstick does Cindy Crawford wear with teal blue?

Carla/Bethany: Raging Storm.

Bethany/Carla: You have my brain. You poor bastard.

Carla/Bethany: I don't care. Don't you see?

Bethany/Carla: See what?

Carla/Bethany: We both have the one thing, the one and only thing everybody wants.

Bethany/Carla: What is that?

Carla/Bethany: It's better than beauty for me; it's better than brains for you.

Bethany/Carla: What? What?!

Carla/Bethany: Different problems.

BLACKOUT

Arthur Miller

Death of a Salesman   1949

Certain Private Conversations in Two Acts and a Requiem

Arthur Miller (1915–2005) was born into a lower-income Jewish family in New York City's Harlem but grew up in Brooklyn. He studied playwriting at the University of Michigan, later wrote radio scripts, and during World War II worked as a steamfitter. When the New York Drama Critics named his All My Sons *best play of 1947, Miller told an interviewer, "I don't see how you can write anything decent without using as your basis the question of right and wrong." (The play is about a guilty manufacturer of defective aircraft parts.)* Death of a Salesman *(1949, Pulitzer Prize for Drama) made Miller famous.* The Crucible *(1953), a dramatic indictment of the Salem witch trials, gained him further attention at a time when Senator Joseph McCarthy was conducting loyalty investigations; in 1996,* The Crucible *was made into a film starring Daniel Day-Lewis and Winona Ryder. For a while (1956–1961), Miller was the husband of actress Marilyn Monroe, whom the main character of his* After the Fall *(1964) resembles. Among Miller's other plays are* A View from the Bridge *(1955);* The Price *(1968);* The Creation of the World and Other Business *(1972);* Playing for Time *(1980), written for television;* Broken Glass *(1994);* Mr. Peters' Connections *(1999);* Resurrection Blues *(2002); and* Finishing the Picture *(2004). He published an*

1984 Broadway production of *Death of a Salesman* starring Dustin Hoffman as Willy Loman, with John Malkovich, Stephen Lang, and Kate Reid.

autobiography, several volumes of essays, two collections of short stories, and two novels, Focus (1945) and The Misfits (1960), drawn from his screenplay for the film starring Monroe.

A new production of Death of a Salesman, starring Brian Dennehy as Willy Loman, opened on Broadway on February 10, 1999, fifty years to the day after its original premiere. Although Miller made a number of memorable contributions to the American theater, this work is unquestionably the pinnacle of his achievement. In Willy Loman, he has given us a figure who is at once both representative and unique, whose desperate plight is conveyed through memorable dialogue and scenes of almost unbearable painfulness and intensity.

CAST

Willy Loman	Happy
Linda	Bernard
Biff	The Woman
Charley	Stanley
Uncle Ben	Miss Forsythe
Howard Wagner	Letta
Jenny	

SCENE. The action takes place in Willy Loman's house and yard and in various places he visits in the New York and Boston of today. Throughout the play, in the stage directions, left and right mean stage left and stage right.

ACT I

A melody is heard, played upon a flute. It is small and fine, telling of grass and trees and the horizon. The curtain rises.

Before us is the Salesman's house. We are aware of towering, angular shapes behind it, surrounding it on all sides. Only the blue light of the sky falls upon the house and forestage; the surrounding area shows an angry glow of orange. As more light appears, we see a solid vault

John Malkovich as Biff and Dustin Hoffman as Willy in 1984 Broadway production.

of apartment houses around the small, fragile-seeming home. An air of the dream clings to the place, a dream rising out of reality. The kitchen at center seems actual enough, for there is a kitchen table with three chairs, and a refrigerator. But no other fixtures are seen. At the back of the kitchen there is a draped entrance, which leads to the living room. To the right of the kitchen, on a level raised two feet, is a bedroom furnished only with a brass bedstead and a straight chair. On a shelf over the bed a silver athletic trophy stands. A window opens onto the apartment house at the side.

Behind the kitchen, on a level raised six and a half feet, is the boys' bedroom, at present barely visible. Two beds are dimly seen, and at the back of the room a dormer window. (This bedroom is above the unseen living room.) At the left a stairway curves up to it from the kitchen.

The entire setting is wholly or, in some places, partially transparent. The roof-line of the house is one-dimensional; under and over it we see the apartment buildings. Before the house lies an apron, curving beyond the forestage into the orchestra. This forward area serves as the backyard as well as the locale of all Willy's imaginings and of his city scenes. Whenever the action is in the present the actors observe the imaginary wall-lines, entering the house only through the door at the left. But in the scenes of the past these boundaries are broken, and characters enter or leave a room by stepping "through" a wall onto the forestage.

From the right, Willy Loman, the Salesman, enters, carrying two large sample cases. The flute plays on. He hears but is not aware of it. He is past sixty years of age, dressed quietly. Even as he crosses the stage to the doorway of the house, his exhaustion is apparent. He unlocks the door, comes into the kitchen, and thankfully lets his burden down, feeling the soreness of his palms. A word-sigh escapes his lips—it might be, "Oh, boy, oh, boy." He closes the door, then carries his cases out into the living room, through the draped kitchen doorway.

Linda, his wife, has stirred in her bed at the right. She gets out and puts on a robe, listening. Most often jovial, she has developed an iron repression of her exceptions to Willy's behavior— she more than loves him, she admires him, as though his mercurial nature, his temper, his massive dreams and little cruelties, served her only as sharp reminders of the turbulent longings within him, longings which she shares but lacks the temperament to utter and follow to their end.

Linda (hearing Willy outside the bedroom, calls with some trepidation): Willy!
Willy: It's all right. I came back.
Linda: Why? What happened? *(Slight pause.)* Did something happen, Willy?
Willy: No, nothing happened.
Linda: You didn't smash the car, did you?
Willy (with casual irritation): I said nothing happened. Didn't you hear me?
Linda: Don't you feel well?
Willy: I am tired to the death. *(The flute has faded away. He sits on the bed beside her, a little numb.)* I couldn't make it. I just couldn't make it, Linda.
Linda (very carefully, delicately): Where were you all day? You look terrible.
Willy: I got as far as a little above Yonkers. I stopped for a cup of coffee. Maybe it was the coffee.
Linda: What?
Willy (after a pause): I suddenly couldn't drive any more. The car kept going onto the shoulder, y'know?
Linda (helpfully): Oh. Maybe it was the steering again. I don't think Angelo knows the Studebaker.

Willy: No, it's me, it's me. Suddenly I realize I'm goin' sixty miles an hour and I don't remember the last five minutes. I'm—I can't seem to—keep my mind to it.

Linda: Maybe it's your glasses. You never went for your new glasses.

Willy: No, I see everything. I came back ten miles an hour. It took me nearly four hours from Yonkers.

Linda (resigned): Well, you'll just have to take a rest. Willy, you can't continue this way.

Willy: I just got back from Florida.

Linda: But you didn't rest your mind. Your mind is overactive, and the mind is what counts, dear.

Willy: I'll start out in the morning. Maybe I'll feel better in the morning. (*She is taking off his shoes.*) These goddam arch supports are killing me.

Linda: Take an aspirin. Should I get you an aspirin? It'll soothe you.

Willy (with wonder): I was driving along, you understand? And I was fine. I was even observing the scenery. You can imagine, me looking at scenery, on the road every week of my life. But it's so beautiful up there, Linda, the trees are so thick, and the sun is warm. I opened the windshield and just let the warm air bathe over me. And then all of a sudden I'm goin' off the road! I'm tellin' ya, I absolutely forgot I was driving. If I'd've gone the other way over the white line I might've killed somebody. So I went on again—and five minutes later I'm dreamin' again, and I nearly—(*He presses two fingers against his eyes.*) I have such thoughts, I have such strange thoughts.

Linda: Willy, dear. Talk to them again. There's no reason why you can't work in New York.

Willy: They don't need me in New York. I'm the New England man. I'm vital in New England.

Linda: But you're sixty years old. They can't expect you to keep traveling every week.

Willy: I'll have to send a wire to Portland. I'm supposed to see Brown and Morrison tomorrow morning at ten o'clock to show the line. Goddammit, I could sell them! (*He starts putting on his jacket.*)

Linda (taking the jacket from him): Why don't you go down to the place tomorrow and tell Howard you've simply got to work in New York? You're too accommodating, dear.

Willy: If old man Wagner was alive I'd a been in charge of New York now! That man was a prince, he was a masterful man. But that boy of his, that Howard, he don't appreciate. When I went north the first time, the Wagner Company didn't know where New England was!

Linda: Why don't you tell those things to Howard, dear?

Willy (encouraged): I will, I definitely will. Is there any cheese?

Linda: I'll make you a sandwich.

Willy: No, go to sleep. I'll take some milk. I'll be up right away. The boys in?

Linda: They're sleeping. Happy took Biff on a date tonight.

Willy (interested): That so?

Linda: It was so nice to see them shaving together, one behind the other, in the bathroom. And going out together. You notice? The whole house smells of shaving lotion.

Willy: Figure it out. Work a lifetime to pay off a house. You finally own it, and there's nobody to live in it.

Linda: Well, dear, life is a casting off. It's always that way.

Willy: No, no, some people—some people accomplish something. Did Biff say anything after I went this morning?

Linda: You shouldn't have criticized him, Willy, especially after he just got off the train. You mustn't lose your temper with him.

Willy: When the hell did I lose my temper? I simply asked him if he was making any money. Is that a criticism?

Linda: But, dear, how could he make any money?

Willy (worried and angered): There's such an undercurrent in him. He became a moody man. Did he apologize when I left this morning?

Linda: He was crestfallen, Willy. You know how he admires you. I think if he finds himself, then you'll both be happier and not fight any more.

Willy: How can he find himself on a farm? Is that a life? A farmhand? In the beginning, when he was young, I thought, well, a young man, it's good for him to tramp around, take a lot of different jobs. But it's more than ten years now and he has yet to make thirty-five dollars a week!

Linda: He's finding himself, Willy.

Willy: Not finding yourself at the age of thirty-four is a disgrace!

Linda: Shh!

Willy: The trouble is he's lazy, goddammit!

Linda: Willy, please!

Willy: Biff is a lazy bum.

Linda: They're sleeping. Get something to eat. Go on down.

Willy: Why did he come home? I would like to know what brought him home.

Linda: I don't know. I think he's still lost, Willy. I think he's very lost.

Willy: Biff Loman is lost. In the greatest country in the world a young man with such—personal attractiveness, gets lost. And such a hard worker. There's one thing about Biff—he's not lazy.

Linda: Never.

Willy (with pity and resolve): I'll see him in the morning. I'll have a nice talk with him. I'll get him a job selling. He could be big in no time. My God! Remember how they used to follow him around in high school? When he smiled at one of them their faces lit up. When he walked down the street . . . (*He loses himself in reminiscences.*)

Linda (trying to bring him out of it): Willy, dear, I got a new kind of American-type cheese today. It's whipped.

Willy: Why do you get American when I like Swiss?

Linda: I just thought you'd like a change—

Willy: I don't want a change! I want Swiss cheese. Why am I always being contradicted?

Linda (with a covering laugh): I thought it would be a surprise.

Willy: Why don't you open a window in here, for God's sake?

Linda (with infinite patience): They're all open, dear.

Willy: The way they boxed us in here. Bricks and windows, windows and bricks.

Linda: We should've bought the land next door.

Willy: The street is lined with cars. There's not a breath of fresh air in the neighborhood. The grass don't grow any more, you can't raise a carrot in the back yard. They should've had a law against apartment houses. Remember those two beautiful elm trees out there? When I and Biff hung the swing between them?

Linda: Yeah, like being a million miles from the city.

Willy: They should've arrested the builder for cutting those down. They massacred the neighborhood. (*Lost.*) More and more I think of those days, Linda. This time of year it was lilac and wisteria. And then the peonies would come out, and the daffodils. What fragrance in this room!

Linda: Well, after all, people had to move somewhere.

Willy: No, there's more people now.

Linda: I don't think there's more people. I think—

Willy: There's more people! That's what's ruining this country! Population is getting out of control. The competition is maddening! Smell the stink from that apartment house! And another on the other side . . . How can they whip cheese?

(*On Willy's last line, Biff and Happy raise themselves up in their beds, listening.*)

Linda: Go down, try it. And be quiet.

Willy (*turning to Linda, guiltily*): You're not worried about me, are you, sweetheart?

Biff: What's the matter?

Happy: Listen!

Linda: You've got too much on the ball to worry about.

Willy: You're my foundation and my support, Linda.

Linda: Just try to relax, dear. You make mountains out of molehills.

Willy: I won't fight with him any more. If he wants to go back to Texas, let him go.

Linda: He'll find his way.

Willy: Sure. Certain men just don't get started till later in life. Like Thomas Edison, I think. Or B. F. Goodrich. One of them was deaf. (*He starts for the bedroom doorway.*) I'll put my money on Biff.

Linda: And Willy—if it's warm Sunday we'll drive in the country. And we'll open the windshield, and take lunch.

Willy: No, the windshields don't open on the new cars.

Linda: But you opened it today.

Willy: Me? I didn't. (*He stops.*) Now isn't that peculiar! Isn't that a remarkable—(*He breaks off in amazement and fright as the flute is heard distantly.*)

Linda: What, darling?

Willy: That is the most remarkable thing.

Linda: What, dear?

Willy: I was thinking of the Chevvy. (*Slight pause.*) Nineteen twenty-eight . . . when I had that red Chevvy—(*Breaks off.*) That funny? I coulda sworn I was driving that Chevvy today.

Linda: Well, that's nothing. Something must've reminded you.

Willy: Remarkable. Ts. Remember those days? The way Biff used to simonize that car? The dealer refused to believe there was eighty thousand miles on it. (*He shakes his head.*) Heh! (*To Linda.*) Close your eyes, I'll be right up. (*He walks out of the bedroom.*)

Happy (*to Biff*): Jesus, maybe he smashed up the car again!

Linda (*calling after Willy*): Be careful on the stairs, dear! The cheese is on the middle shelf! (*She turns, goes over to the bed, takes his jacket, and goes out of the bedroom.*)

(*Light has risen on the boys' room. Unseen, Willy is heard talking to himself, "Eighty thousand miles," and a little laugh. Biff gets out of bed, comes downstage a bit, and stands attentively. Biff is two years older than his brother Happy, well built, but in these days bears a worn air and seems less self-assured. He has succeeded less, and his dreams are stronger and less acceptable than Happy's. Happy is tall, powerfully made. Sexuality is like a visible color on him, or a scent that many women have discovered. He, like his brother, is lost, but in a different way, for he has never allowed himself to turn his face toward defeat and is thus more confused and hardskinned, although seemingly more content.)*

Happy (getting out of bed): He's going to get his license taken away if he keeps that up. I'm getting nervous about him, y'know, Biff?

Biff: His eyes are going.

Happy: No, I've driven with him. He sees all right. He just doesn't keep his mind on it. I drove into the city with him last week. He stops at a green light and then it turns red and he goes. *(He laughs.)*

Biff: Maybe he's color-blind.

Happy: Pop? Why he's got the finest eye for color in the business. You know that.

Biff (sitting down on his bed): I'm going to sleep.

Happy: You're not still sour on Dad, are you, Biff?

Biff: He's all right, I guess.

Willy (underneath them, in the living room): Yes, sir, eighty thousand miles—eighty-two thousand!

Biff: You smoking?

Happy (holding out a pack of cigarettes): Want one?

Biff (taking a cigarette): I can never sleep when I smell it.

Willy: What a simonizing job, heh!

Happy (with deep sentiment): Funny, Biff, y'know? Us sleeping in here again? The old beds. *(He pats his bed affectionately.)* All the talk that went across those two beds, huh? Our whole lives.

Biff: Yeah. Lotta dreams and plans.

Happy (with a deep and masculine laugh): About five hundred women would like to know what was said in this room.

(They share a soft laugh.)

Biff: Remember that big Betsy something—what the hell was her name—over on Bushwick Avenue?

Happy (combing his hair): With the collie dog!

Biff: That's the one. I got you in there, remember?

Happy: Yeah, that was my first time—I think. Boy, there was a pig! *(They laugh, almost crudely.)* You taught me everything I know about women. Don't forget that.

Biff: I bet you forgot how bashful you used to be. Especially with girls.

Happy: Oh, I still am, Biff.

Biff: Oh, go on.

Happy: I just control it, that's all. I think I got less bashful and you got more so. What happened, Biff? Where's the old humor, the old confidence? *(He shakes Biff's knee. Biff gets up and moves restlessly about the room.)* What's the matter?

Biff: Why does Dad mock me all the time?

Happy: He's not mocking you, he—

Biff: Everything I say there's a twist of mockery on his face. I can't get near him.

Happy: He just wants you to make good, that's all. I wanted to talk to you about Dad for a long time, Biff. Something's—happening to him. He—talks to himself.

Biff: I noticed that this morning. But he always mumbled.

Happy: But not so noticeable. It got so embarrassing I sent him to Florida. And you know something? Most of the time he's talking to you.

Biff: What's he say about me?

Happy: I can't make it out.

Biff: What's he say about me?

Happy: I think the fact that you're not settled, that you're still kind of up in the air . . .

Biff: There's one or two other things depressing him, Happy.

Happy: What do you mean?

Biff: Never mind. Just don't lay it all on me.

Happy: But I think if you just got started—I mean—is there any future for you out there?

Biff: I tell ya, Hap, I don't know what the future is. I don't know—what I'm supposed to want.

Happy: What do you mean?

Biff: Well, I spent six or seven years after high school trying to work myself up. Shipping clerk, salesman, business of one kind or another. And it's a measly manner of existence. To get on that subway on the hot mornings in summer. To devote your whole life to keeping stock, or making phone calls, or selling or buying. To suffer fifty weeks of the year for the sake of a two-week vacation, when all you really desire is to be outdoors, with your shirt off. And always to have to get ahead of the next fella. And still—that's how you build a future.

Happy: Well, you really enjoy it on a farm? Are you content out there?

Biff (with rising agitation): Hap, I've had twenty or thirty different kinds of jobs since I left home before the war, and it always turns out the same. I just realized it lately. In Nebraska when I herded cattle, and the Dakotas, and Arizona, and now in Texas. It's why I came home now, I guess, because I realized it. This farm I work on, it's spring there now, see? And they've got about fifteen new colts. There's nothing more inspiring or—beautiful than the sight of a mare and a new colt. And it's cool there now, see? Texas is cool now, and it's spring. And whenever spring comes to where I am, I suddenly get the feeling, my God, I'm not gettin' anywhere! What the hell am I doing, playing around with horses, twenty-eight dollars a week! I'm thirty-four years old, I oughta be makin' my future. That's when I come running home. And now, I get here, and I don't know what to do with myself. (*After a pause.*) I've always made a point of not wasting my life, and everytime I come back here I know that all I've done is to waste my life.

Happy: You're a poet, you know that, Biff? You're a—you're an idealist!

Biff: No, I'm mixed up very bad. Maybe I oughta get married. Maybe I oughta get stuck into something. Maybe that's my trouble. I'm like a boy. I'm not married, I'm not in business, I just—I'm like a boy. Are you content, Hap? You're a success, aren't you? Are you content?

Happy: Hell, no!

Biff: Why? You're making money, aren't you?

Happy (moving about with energy, expressiveness): All I can do now is wait for the merchandise manager to die. And suppose I get to be merchandise manager? He's a good friend of mine, and he just built a terrific estate on Long Island. And he lived there about two months and sold it, and now he's building another one. He can't enjoy it once it's finished. And I know that's just what I would do. I don't know what the hell I'm workin' for. Sometimes I sit in my apartment—all alone. And I think of the rent I'm paying. And it's crazy. But then, it's what I always wanted. My own apartment, a car, and plenty of women. And still, goddammit, I'm lonely.

Biff (*with enthusiasm*): Listen, why don't you come out West with me?

Happy: You and I, heh?

Biff: Sure, maybe we could buy a ranch. Raise cattle, use our muscles. Men built like we are should be working out in the open.

Happy (*avidly*): The Loman Brothers, heh?

Biff (*with vast affection*): Sure, we'd be known all over the counties!

Happy (*enthralled*): That's what I dream about, Biff. Sometimes I want to just rip my clothes off in the middle of the store and outbox that goddam merchandise manager. I mean I can outbox, outrun, and outlift anybody in that store, and I have to take orders from those common, petty sons-of-bitches till I can't stand it any more.

Biff: I'm tellin' you, kid, if you were with me I'd be happy out there.

Happy (*enthused*): See, Biff, everybody around me is so false that I'm constantly lowering my ideals . . .

Biff: Baby, together we'd stand up for one another, we'd have someone to trust.

Happy: If I were around you—

Biff: Hap, the trouble is we weren't brought up to grub for money. I don't know how to do it.

Happy: Neither can I!

Biff: Then let's go!

Happy: The only thing is—what can you make out there?

Biff: But look at your friend. Builds an estate and then hasn't the peace of mind to live in it.

Happy: Yeah, but when he walks into the store the waves part in front of him. That's fifty-two thousand dollars a year coming through the revolving door, and I got more in my pinky finger than he's got in his head.

Biff: Yeah, but you just said—

Happy: I gotta show some of those pompous, self-important executives over there that Hap Loman can make the grade. I want to walk into the store the way he walks in. Then I'll go with you, Biff. We'll be together yet, I swear. But take those two we had tonight. Now weren't they gorgeous creatures?

Biff: Yeah, yeah, most gorgeous I've had in years.

Happy: I get that any time I want, Biff. Whenever I feel disgusted. The only trouble is, it gets like bowling or something. I just keep knockin' them over and it doesn't mean anything. You still run around a lot?

Biff: Naa. I'd like to find a girl—steady, somebody with substance.

Happy: That's what I long for.

Biff: Go on! You'd never come home.

Happy: I would! Somebody with character, with resistance! Like Mom, y'know? You're gonna call me a bastard when I tell you this. That girl Charlotte I was with tonight is engaged to be married in five weeks. (*He tries on his new hat.*)

Biff: No kiddin'!

Happy: Sure, the guy's in line for the vice-presidency of the store. I don't know what gets into me, maybe I just have an overdeveloped sense of competition or something, but I went and ruined her, and furthermore I can't get rid of her. And he's the third executive I've done that to. Isn't that a crummy characteristic? And to top it all, I go to their weddings! (*Indignantly, but laughing.*) Like I'm not supposed to take bribes. Manufacturers offer me a hundred-dollar bill now and then to throw an order their way. You know how honest I am, but it's like this girl, see. I hate myself for it. Because I don't want the girl, and, still, I take it and—I love it!

Biff: Let's go to sleep.

Happy: I guess we didn't settle anything, heh?

Biff: I just got one idea that I think I'm going to try.

Happy: What's that?

Biff: Remember Bill Oliver?

Happy: Sure, Oliver is very big now. You want to work for him again?

Biff: No, but when I quit he said something to me. He put his arm on my shoulder, and he said, "Biff, if you ever need anything, come to me."

Happy: I remember that. That sounds good.

Biff: I think I'll go to see him. If I could get ten thousand or even seven or eight thousand dollars I could buy a beautiful ranch.

Happy: I bet he'd back you. 'Cause he thought highly of you, Biff. I mean, they all do. You're well liked, Biff. That's why I say to come back here, and we both have the apartment. And I'm tellin' you, Biff, any babe you want . . .

Biff: No, with a ranch I could do the work I like and still be something. I just wonder though. I wonder if Oliver still thinks I stole that carton of basketballs.

Happy: Oh, he probably forgot that long ago. It's almost ten years. You're too sensitive. Anyway, he didn't really fire you.

Biff: Well, I think he was going to. I think that's why I quit. I was never sure whether he knew or not. I know he thought the world of me, though. I was the only one he'd let lock up the place.

Willy (below): You gonna wash the engine, Biff?

Happy: Shh!

(*Biff looks at Happy, who is gazing down, listening. Willy is mumbling in the parlor.*)

Happy: You hear that?

(*They listen. Willy laughs warmly.*)

Biff (growing angry): Doesn't he know Mom can hear that?

Willy: Don't get your sweater dirty, Biff!

(*A look of pain crosses Biff's face.*)

Happy: Isn't that terrible? Don't leave again, will you? You'll find a job here. You gotta stick around. I don't know what to do about him, it's getting embarrassing.

Willy: What a simonizing job!

Biff: Mom's hearing that!

Willy: No kiddin', Biff, you got a date? Wonderful!

Happy: Go on to sleep. But talk to him in the morning, will you?

Biff (reluctantly getting into bed): With her in the house. Brother!

Happy (getting into bed): I wish you'd have a good talk with him.

(*The light on their room begins to fade.*)

Biff (to himself in bed): That selfish, stupid . . .

Happy: Sh . . . Sleep, Biff.

(*Their light is out. Well before they have finished speaking, Willy's form is dimly seen below in the darkened kitchen. He opens the refrigerator, searches in there, and takes out a bottle of milk. The apartment houses are fading out, and the entire house and surroundings become covered with leaves. Music insinuates itself as the leaves appear.*)

Willy: Just wanna be careful with those girls, Biff, that's all. Don't make any promises. No promises of any kind. Because a girl, y'know, they always believe what you tell 'em, and you're very young, Biff, you're too young to be talking seriously to girls.

(*Light rises on the kitchen. Willy, talking, shuts the refrigerator door and comes downstage to the kitchen table. He pours milk into a glass. He is totally immersed in himself, smiling faintly.*)

Willy: Too young entirely, Biff. You want to watch your schooling first. Then when you're all set, there'll be plenty of girls for a boy like you. (*He smiles broadly at a kitchen chair.*) That so? The girls pay for you? (*He laughs.*) Boy, you must really be makin' a hit.

(*Willy is gradually addressing—physically—a point offstage, speaking through the wall of the kitchen, and his voice has been rising in volume to that of a normal conversation.*)

Willy: I been wondering why you polish the car so careful. Ha! Don't leave the hubcaps, boys. Get the chamois to the hubcaps. Happy, use newspaper on the windows, it's the easiest thing. Show him how to do it, Biff! You see, Happy? Pad it up, use it like a pad. That's it, that's it, good work. You're doin' all right, Hap. (*He pauses, then nods in approbation for a few seconds, then looks upward.*) Biff, first thing we gotta do when we get time is clip that big branch over the house. Afraid it's gonna fall in a storm and hit the roof. Tell you what. We get a rope and sling her around, and then we climb up there with a couple of saws and take her down. Soon as you finish the car, boys, I wanna see ya. I got a surprise for you, boys.

Biff (*offstage*): Whatta ya got, Dad?

Willy: No, you finish first. Never leave a job till you're finished—remember that. (*Looking toward the "big trees."*) Biff, up in Albany I saw a beautiful hammock. I think I'll buy it next trip, and we'll hang it right between those two elms. Wouldn't that be something? Just swingin' there under those branches. Boy, that would be . . .

(*Young Biff and Young Happy appear from the direction Willy was addressing. Happy carries rags and a pail of water. Biff, wearing a sweater with a block "S," carries a football.*)

Biff (*pointing in the direction of the car offstage*): How's that, Pop, professional?

Willy: Terrific. Terrific job, boys. Good work, Biff.

Happy: Where's the surprise, Pop?

Willy: In the back seat of the car.

Happy: Boy! (*He runs off.*)

Biff: What is it, Dad? Tell me, what'd you buy?

Willy (*laughing, cuffs him*): Never mind, something I want you to have.

Biff (*turns and starts off*): What is it, Hap?

Happy (*offstage*): It's a punching bag!

Biff: Oh, Pop!

Willy: It's got Gene Tunney's signature on it.

(*Happy runs onstage with a punching bag.*)

Biff: Gee, how'd you know we wanted a punching bag?

Willy: Well, it's the finest thing for the timing.

Happy (*lies down on his back and pedals with his feet*): I'm losing weight, you notice, Pop?

Willy (*to Happy*): Jumping rope is good too.

Biff: Did you see the new football I got?

Willy (*examining the ball*): Where'd you get a new ball?

Biff: The coach told me to practice my passing.

Willy: That so? And he gave you the ball, heh?

Biff: Well, I borrowed it from the locker room. (*He laughs confidentially.*)

Willy (*laughing with him at the theft*): I want you to return that.

Happy: I told you he wouldn't like it!

Biff (*angrily*): Well, I'm bringing it back!

Willy (*stopping the incipient argument, to Happy*): Sure, he's gotta practice with a regulation ball, doesn't he? (*To Biff.*) Coach'll probably congratulate you on your initiative.

Biff: Oh, he keeps congratulating my initiative all the time, Pop.

Willy: That's because he likes you. If somebody else took that ball there'd be an uproar. So what's the report, boys, what's the report?

Biff: Where'd you go this time, Dad? Gee we were lonesome for you.

Willy (*pleased, puts an arm around each boy and they come down to the apron*): Lonesome, heh?

Biff: Missed you every minute.

Willy: Don't say? Tell you a secret, boys. Don't breathe it to a soul. Someday I'll have my own business, and I'll never have to leave home any more.

Happy: Like Uncle Charley, heh?

Willy: Bigger than Uncle Charley! Because Charley is not—liked. He's liked, but he's not—well liked.

Biff: Where'd you go this time, Dad?

Willy: Well, I got on the road, and I went north to Providence. Met the Mayor.

Biff: The Mayor of Providence!

Willy: He was sitting in the hotel lobby.

Biff: What'd he say?

Willy: He said, "Morning!" And I said, "You've got a fine city here, Mayor." And then he had coffee with me. And then I went to Waterbury. Waterbury is a fine city. Big clock city, the famous Waterbury clock. Sold a nice bill there. And then Boston—Boston is the cradle of the Revolution. A fine city. And a couple of other towns in Mass., and on to Portland and Bangor and straight home!

Biff: Gee, I'd love to go with you sometime, Dad.

Willy: Soon as summer comes.

Happy: Promise?

Willy: You and Hap and I, and I'll show you all the towns. America is full of beautiful towns and fine, upstanding people. And they know me, boys, they know me up and down New England. The finest people. And when I bring you fellas up, there'll be open sesame for all of us, 'cause one thing, boys: I have friends. I can park my car in any street in New England, and the cops protect it like their own. This summer, heh?

Biff and Happy (together): Yeah! You bet!

Willy: We'll take our bathing suits.

Happy: We'll carry your bags, Pop!

Willy: Oh, won't that be something! Me comin' into the Boston stores with you boys carryin' my bags. What a sensation!

(*Biff is prancing around, practicing passing the ball.*)

Willy: You nervous, Biff, about the game?

Biff: Not if you're gonna be there.

Willy: What do they say about you in school, now that they made you captain?

Happy: There's a crowd of girls behind him everytime the classes change.

Biff (taking Willy's hand): This Saturday, Pop, this Saturday—just for you, I'm going to break through for a touchdown.

Happy: You're supposed to pass.

Biff: I'm takin' one play for Pop. You watch me, Pop, and when I take off my helmet, that means I'm breakin' out. Then you watch me crash through that line!

Willy (kisses Biff): Oh, wait'll I tell this in Boston!

(*Bernard enters in knickers. He is younger than Biff, earnest and loyal, a worried boy.*)

Bernard: Biff, where are you? You're supposed to study with me today.

Willy: Hey, looka Bernard. What're you lookin' so anemic about, Bernard?

Bernard: He's gotta study, Uncle Willy. He's got Regents next week.

Happy (tauntingly, spinning Bernard around): Let's box, Bernard!

Bernard: Biff! (*He gets away from Happy.*) Listen, Biff, I heard Mr. Birnbaum say that if you don't start studyin' math he's gonna flunk you, and you won't graduate. I heard him!

Willy: You better study with him, Biff. Go ahead now.

Bernard: I heard him!

Biff: Oh, Pop, you didn't see my sneakers! (*He holds up a foot for Willy to look at.*)

Willy: Hey, that's a beautiful job of printing!

Bernard (wiping his glasses): Just because he printed University of Virginia on his sneakers doesn't mean they've got to graduate him, Uncle Willy!

Willy (angrily): What're you talking about? With scholarships to three universities they're gonna flunk him?

Bernard: But I heard Mr. Birnbaum say—

Willy: Don't be a pest, Bernard! (*To his boys.*) What an anemic!

Bernard: Okay, I'm waiting for you in my house, Biff.

(*Bernard goes off. The Lomans laugh.*)

Willy: Bernard is not well liked, is he?

Biff: He's liked, but he's not well liked.

Happy: That's right, Pop.

Willy: That's just what I mean. Bernard can get the best marks in school, y'understand, but when he gets out in the business world, y'understand, you are going to be five times ahead of him. That's why I thank Almighty God you're both built like Adonises. Because the man who makes an appearance in the business world, the man who creates personal interest, is the man who gets ahead. Be liked and you will never want. You take me, for instance. I never have to wait in line to see a buyer. "Willy Loman is here!" That's all they have to know, and I go right through.

Biff: Did you knock them dead, Pop?

Willy: Knocked 'em cold in Providence, slaughtered 'em in Boston.

Happy (on his back, pedaling again): I'm losing weight, you notice, Pop?

(Linda enters, as of old, a ribbon in her hair, carrying a basket of washing.)

Linda (with youthful energy): Hello, dear!

Willy: Sweetheart!

Linda: How'd the Chevvy run?

Willy: Chevrolet, Linda, is the greatest car every built. *(To the boys.)* Since when do you let your mother carry wash up the stairs?

Biff: Grab hold there, boy!

Happy: Where to, Mom?

Linda: Hang them up on the line. And you better go down to your friends, Biff. The cellar is full of boys. They don't know what to do with themselves.

Biff: Ah, when Pop comes home they can wait!

Willy (laughs appreciatively): You better go down and tell them what to do, Biff.

Biff: I think I'll have them sweep out the furnace room.

Willy: Good work, Biff.

Biff (goes through wall-line of kitchen to doorway at back and calls down): Fellas! Everybody sweep out the furnace room! I'll be right down!

Voices: All right! Okay, Biff.

Biff: George and Sam and Frank, come out back! We're hangin' up the wash! Come on, Hap, on the double! *(He and Happy carry out the basket.)*

Linda: The way they obey him!

Willy: Well, that's training, the training. I'm tellin' you, I was sellin' thousands and thousands, but I had to come home.

Linda: Oh, the whole block'll be at that game. Did you sell anything?

Willy: I did five hundred gross in Providence and seven hundred gross in Boston.

Linda: No! Wait a minute, I've got a pencil. *(She pulls pencil and paper out of her apron pocket.)* That makes your commission . . . Two hundred—my God! Two hundred and twelve dollars!

Willy: Well, I didn't figure it yet, but . . .

Linda: How much did you do?

Willy: Well, I—I did—about a hundred and eighty gross in Providence. Well, no—it came to—roughly two hundred gross on the whole trip.

Linda (without hesitation): Two hundred gross. That's . . . *(She figures.)*

Willy: The trouble was that three of the stores were half closed for inventory in Boston. Otherwise I woulda broke records.

Linda: Well, it makes seventy dollars and some pennies. That's very good.

Willy: What do we owe?

Linda: Well, on the first there's sixteen dollars on the refrigerator—

Willy: Why sixteen?

Linda: Well, the fan belt broke, so it was a dollar eighty.

Willy: But it's brand new.

Linda: Well, the man said that's the way it is. Till they work themselves in, y'know.

(They move through the wall-line into the kitchen.)

Willy: I hope we didn't get stuck on that machine.

Linda: They got the biggest ads of any of them.

Willy: I know, it's a fine machine. What else?

Linda: Well, there's nine-sixty for the washing machine. And for the vacuum cleaner there's three and a half due on the fifteenth. Then the roof, you got twenty-one dollars remaining.

Willy: It don't leak, does it?

Linda: No, they did a wonderful job. Then you owe Frank for the carburetor.

Willy: I'm not going to pay that man! That goddam Chevrolet, they ought to prohibit the manufacture of that car!

Linda: Well, you owe him three and a half. And odds and ends, comes to around a hundred and twenty dollars by the fifteenth.

Willy: A hundred and twenty dollars! My God, if business don't pick up I don't know what I'm gonna do!

Linda: Well, next week you'll do better.

Willy: Oh, I'll knock 'em dead next week. I'll go to Hartford. I'm very well liked in Hartford. You know, the trouble is, Linda, people don't seem to take to me.

(They move on the forestage.)

Linda: Oh, don't be foolish.

Willy: I know it when I walk in. They seem to laugh at me.

Linda: Why? Why would they laugh at you? Don't talk that way, Willy.

(Willy moves to the edge of the stage. Linda goes into the kitchen and starts to darn stockings.)

Willy: I don't know the reason for it, but they just pass me by. I'm not noticed.

Linda: But you're doing wonderful, dear. You're making seventy to a hundred dollars a week.

Willy: But I gotta be at it ten, twelve hours a day. Other men—I don't know—they do it easier. I don't know why—I can't stop myself—I talk too much. A man oughta come in with a few words. One thing about Charley. He's a man of few words, and they respect him.

Linda: You don't talk too much, you're just lively.

Willy (smiling): Well, I figure, what the hell, life is short, a couple of jokes. *(To himself.)* I joke too much! *(The smile goes.)*

Linda: Why? You're—

Willy: I'm fat. I'm very—foolish to look at, Linda. I didn't tell you, but Christmas time I happened to be calling on F. H. Stewarts, and a salesman I know, as I was going in to see the buyer I heard him say something about—walrus. And I—I cracked him right across the face. I won't take that. I simply will not take that. But they do laugh at me. I know that.

Linda: Darling . . .

Willy: I gotta overcome it. I know I gotta overcome it. I'm not dressing to advantage, maybe.

Linda: Willy, darling, you're the handsomest man in the world—

Willy: Oh, no, Linda.

Linda: To me you are. (*Slight pause.*) The handsomest.

(*From the darkness is heard the laughter of a woman. Willy doesn't turn to it, but it continues through Linda's lines.*)

Linda: And the boys, Willy. Few men are idolized by their children the way you are.

(*Music is heard as behind a scrim, to the left of the house, The Woman, dimly seen, is dressing.*)

Willy (with great feeling): You're the best there is, Linda, you're a pal, you know that? On the road—on the road I want to grab you sometimes and just kiss the life outa you.

(*The laughter is loud now, and he moves into a brightening area at the left, where The Woman has come from behind the scrim and is standing, putting on her hat, looking into a "mirror" and laughing.*)

Willy: 'Cause I get so lonely—especially when business is bad and there's nobody to talk to. I get the feeling that I'll never sell anything again, that I won't make a living for you, or a business, a business for the boys. (*He talks through The Woman's subsiding laughter; The Woman primps at the "mirror."*) There's so much I want to make for—

The Woman: Me? You didn't make me, Willy. I picked you.

Willy (pleased): You picked me?

The Woman (who is quite proper-looking, Willy's age): I did. I've been sitting at that desk watching all the salesmen go by, day in, day out. But you've got such a sense of humor, and we do have such a good time together, don't we?

Willy: Sure, sure. (*He takes her in his arms.*) Why do you have to go now?

The Woman: It's two o'clock . . .

Willy: No, come on in! (*He pulls her.*)

The Woman: . . . my sisters'll be scandalized. When'll you be back?

Willy: Oh, two weeks about. Will you come up again?

The Woman: Sure thing. You do make me laugh. It's good for me. (*She squeezes his arm, kisses him.*) And I think you're a wonderful man.

Willy: You picked me, heh?

The Woman: Sure. Because you're so sweet. And such a kidder.

Willy: Well, I'll see you next time I'm in Boston.

The Woman: I'll put you right through to the buyers.

Willy (slapping her bottom): Right. Well, bottoms up!

The Woman (slaps him gently and laughs): You just kill me, Willy. (*He suddenly grabs her and kisses her roughly.*) You kill me. And thanks for the stockings. I love a lot of stockings. Well, good night.

Willy: Good night. And keep your pores open!

The Woman: Oh, Willy!

(The Woman bursts out laughing, and Linda's laughter blends in. The Woman disappears into the dark. Now the area at the kitchen table brightens. Linda is sitting where she was at the kitchen table, but now is mending a pair of silk stockings.)

Linda: You are, Willy. The handsomest man. You've got no reason to feel that—

Willy *(coming out of The Woman's dimming area and going over to Linda)*: I'll make it all up to you, Linda, I'll—

Linda: There's nothing to make up, dear. You're doing fine, better than—

Willy *(noticing her mending)*: What's that?

Linda: Just mending my stockings. They're so expensive—

Willy *(angrily, taking them from her)*: I won't have you mending stockings in this house! Now throw them out!

(Linda puts the stockings in her pocket.)

Bernard *(entering on the run)*: Where is he? If he doesn't study!

Willy *(moving to the forestage, with great agitation)*: You'll give him the answers!

Bernard: I do, but I can't on a Regents! That's a state exam! They're liable to arrest me!

Willy: Where is he? I'll whip him, I'll whip him!

Linda: And he'd better give back that football, Willy, it's not nice.

Willy: Biff! Where is he? Why is he taking everything?

Linda: He's too rough with the girls, Willy. All the mothers are afraid of him!

Willy: I'll whip him!

Bernard: He's driving the car without a license!

(The Woman's laugh is heard.)

Willy: Shut up!

Linda: All the mothers—

Willy: Shut up!

Bernard *(backing quietly away and out)*: Mr. Birnbaum says he's stuck up.

Willy: Get outa here!

Bernard: If he doesn't buckle down he'll flunk math! *(He goes off.)*

Linda: He's right, Willy, you've gotta—

Willy *(exploding at her)*: There's nothing the matter with him! You want him to be a worm like Bernard? He's got spirit, personality . . .

(As he speaks, Linda, almost in tears, exits into the living room. Willy is alone in the kitchen, wilting and staring. The leaves are gone. It is night again, and the apartment houses look down from behind.)

Willy: Loaded with it. Loaded! What is he stealing? He's giving it back, isn't he? Why is he stealing? What did I tell him? I never in my life told him anything but decent things.

(Happy in pajamas has come down the stairs; Willy suddenly becomes aware of Happy's presence.)

Happy: Let's go now, come on.

Willy *(sitting down at the kitchen table)*: Huh! Why did she have to wax the floors herself? Everytime she waxes the floors she keels over. She knows that!

Happy: Shh! Take it easy. What brought you back tonight?

Willy: I got an awful scare. Nearly hit a kid in Yonkers. God! Why didn't I go to Alaska with my brother Ben that time! Ben! That man was a genius, that man was success incarnate! What a mistake! He begged me to go.

Happy: Well, there's no use in—

Willy: You guys! There was a man started with the clothes on his back and ended up with diamond mines!

Happy: Boy, someday I'd like to know how he did it.

Willy: What's the mystery? The man knew what he wanted and went out and got it! Walked into a jungle, and comes out, the age of twenty-one, and he's rich! The world is an oyster, but you don't crack it open on a mattress!

Happy: Pop, I told you I'm gonna retire you for life.

Willy: You'll retire me for life on seventy goddam dollars a week? And your women and your car and your apartment, and you'll retire me for life! Christ's sake, I couldn't get past Yonkers today! Where are you guys, where are you? The woods are burning! I can't drive a car!

(Charley has appeared in the doorway. He is a large man, slow of speech, laconic, immovable. In all he says, despite what he says, there is pity, and, now, trepidation. He has a robe over his pajamas, slippers on his feet. He enters the kitchen.)

Charley: Everything all right?

Happy: Yeah, Charley, everything's . . .

Willy: What's the matter?

Charley: I heard some noise. I thought something happened. Can't we do something about the walls? You sneeze in here, and in my house hats blow off.

Happy: Let's go to bed, Dad. Come on.

(Charley signals to Happy to go.)

Willy: You go ahead, I'm not tired at the moment.

Happy (to Willy): Take it easy, huh? *(He exits.)*

Willy: What're you doin' up?

Charley (sitting down at the kitchen table opposite Willy): Couldn't sleep good. I had a heartburn.

Willy: Well, you don't know how to eat.

Charley: I eat with my mouth.

Willy: No, you're ignorant. You gotta know about vitamins and things like that.

Charley: Come on, let's shoot. Tire you out a little.

Willy (hesitantly): All right. You got cards?

Charley (taking a deck from his pocket): Yeah, I got them. Someplace. What is it with those vitamins?

Willy (dealing): They build up your bones. Chemistry.

Charley: Yeah, but there's no bones in a heartburn.

Willy: What are you talkin' about? Do you know the first thing about it?

Charley: Don't get insulted.

Willy: Don't talk about something you don't know anything about.

(They are playing. Pause.)

Charley: What're you doin' home?

Willy: A little trouble with the car.

Charley: Oh. (*Pause.*) I'd like to take a trip to California.

Willy: Don't say.

Charley: You want a job?

Willy: I got a job, I told you that. (*After a slight pause.*) What the hell are you offering me a job for?

Charley: Don't get insulted.

Willy: Don't insult me.

Charley: I don't see no sense in it. You don't have to go on this way.

Willy: I got a good job. (*Slight pause.*) What do you keep comin' in here for?

Charley: You want me to go?

Willy (after a pause, withering): I can't understand it. He's going back to Texas again. What the hell is that?

Charley: Let him go.

Willy: I got nothin' to give him, Charley, I'm clean, I'm clean.

Charley: He won't starve. None a them starve. Forget about him.

Willy: Then what have I got to remember?

Charley: You take it too hard. To hell with it. When a deposit bottle is broken you don't get your nickel back.

Willy: That's easy enough for you to say.

Charley: That ain't easy for me to say.

Willy: Did you see the ceiling I put up in the living room?

Charley: Yeah, that's a piece of work. To put up a ceiling is a mystery to me. How do you do it?

Willy: What's the difference?

Charley: Well, talk about it.

Willy: You gonna put up a ceiling?

Charley: How could I put up a ceiling?

Willy: Then what the hell are you bothering me for?

Charley: You're insulted again.

Willy: A man who can't handle tools is not a man. You're disgusting.

Charley: Don't call me disgusting, Willy.

> (*Uncle Ben, carrying a valise and an umbrella, enters the forestage from around the right corner of the house. He is a stolid man, in his sixties, with a mustache and an authoritative air. He is utterly certain of his destiny, and there is an aura of far places about him. He enters exactly as Willy speaks.*)

Willy: I'm getting awfully tired, Ben.

> (*Ben's music is heard. Ben looks around at everything.*)

Charley: Good, keep playing; you'll sleep better. Did you call me Ben?

> (*Ben looks at his watch.*)

Willy: That's funny. For a second there you reminded me of my brother Ben.

Ben: I have only a few minutes. (*He strolls, inspecting the place. Willy and Charley continue playing.*)

Charley: You never heard from him again, heh? Since that time?

Willy: Didn't Linda tell you? Couple of weeks ago we got a letter from his wife in Africa. He died.

Charley: That so.

Ben (chuckling): So this is Brooklyn, eh?

Charley: Maybe you're in for some of his money.

Willy: Naa, he had seven sons. There's just one opportunity I had with that man . . .

Ben: I must make a train, William. There are several properties I'm looking at in Alaska.

Willy: Sure, sure! If I'd gone with him to Alaska that time, everything would've been totally different.

Charley: Go on, you'd froze to death up there.

Willy: What're you talking about?

Ben: Opportunity is tremendous in Alaska, William. Surprised you're not up there.

Willy: Sure, tremendous.

Charley: Heh?

Willy: There was the only man I ever met who knew the answers.

Charley: Who?

Ben: How are you all?

Willy (taking a pot, smiling): Fine, fine.

Charley: Pretty sharp tonight.

Ben: Is Mother living with you?

Willy: No, she died a long time ago.

Charley: Who?

Ben: That's too bad. Fine specimen of a lady, Mother.

Willy (to Charley): Heh?

Ben: I'd hoped to see the old girl.

Charley: Who died?

Ben: Heard anything from Father, have you?

Willy (unnerved): What do you mean, who died?

Charley (taking a pot): What're you talkin' about?

Ben (looking at his watch): William, it's half-past eight!

Willy (as though to dispel his confusion he angrily stops Charley's hand): That's my build!

Charley: I put the ace—

Willy: If you don't know how to play the game I'm not gonna throw my money away on you!

Charley (rising): It was my ace, for God's sake!

Willy: I'm through, I'm through!

Ben: When did Mother die?

Willy: Long ago. Since the beginning you never knew how to play cards.

Charley (picks up the cards and goes to the door): All right! Next time I'll bring a deck with five aces.

Willy: I don't play that kind of game!

Charley (turning to him): You ought to be ashamed of yourself!

Willy: Yeah?

Charley: Yeah! *(He goes out.)*

Willy (slamming the door after him): Ignoramus!

Ben (as Willy comes toward him through the wall-line of the kitchen): So you're William.

Willy (*shaking Ben's hand*): Ben! I've been waiting for you so long! What's the answer? How did you do it?

Ben: Oh, there's a story in that.

(*Linda enters the forestage, as of old, carrying the wash basket.*)

Linda: Is this Ben?

Ben (*gallantly*): How do you do, my dear.

Linda: Where've you been all these years? Willy's always wondered why you—

Willy (*pulling Ben away from her impatiently*): Where is Dad? Didn't you follow him? How did you get started?

Ben: Well, I don't know how much you remember.

Willy: Well, I was just a baby, of course, only three or four years old—

Ben: Three years and eleven months.

Willy: What a memory, Ben!

Ben: I have many enterprises, William, and I have never kept books.

Willy: I remember I was sitting under the wagon in—was it Nebraska?

Ben: It was South Dakota, and I gave you a bunch of wild flowers.

Willy: I remember you walking away down some open road.

Ben (*laughing*): I was going to find Father in Alaska.

Willy: Where is he?

Ben: At that age I had a very faulty view of geography, William. I discovered after a few days that I was heading due south, so instead of Alaska, I ended up in Africa.

Linda: Africa!

Willy: The Gold Coast!

Ben: Principally, diamond mines.

Linda: Diamond mines!

Ben: Yes, my dear. But I've only a few minutes—

Willy: No! Boys! Boys! (*Young Biff and Happy appear.*) Listen to this. This is your Uncle Ben, a great man! Tell my boys, Ben!

Ben: Why, boys, when I was seventeen I walked into the jungle, and when I was twenty-one I walked out. (*He laughs.*) And by God I was rich.

Willy (*to the boys*): You see what I been talking about? The greatest things can happen!

Ben (*glancing at his watch*): I have an appointment in Ketchikan Tuesday week.

Willy: No, Ben! Please tell about Dad. I want my boys to hear. I want them to know the kind of stock they sprang from. All I remember is a man with a big beard, and I was in Mamma's lap, sitting around a fire, and some kind of high music.

Ben: His flute. He played the flute.

Willy: Sure, the flute, that's right!

(*New music is heard, a high, rollicking tune.*)

Ben: Father was a very great and a very wild-hearted man. We would start in Boston, and he'd toss the whole family into the wagon, and then he'd drive the team right across the country; through Ohio, and Indiana, Michigan, Illinois, and all the Western states. And we'd stop in the towns and sell the flutes that he'd made on the way. Great inventor, Father. With one gadget he made more in a week than a man like you could make in a lifetime.

Willy: That's just the way I'm bringing them up, Ben—rugged, well-liked, all-around.

Ben: Yeah? (*To Biff.*) Hit that, boy—hard as you can. (*He pounds his stomach.*)

Biff: Oh, no, sir!

Ben (*taking boxing stance*): Come on, get to me! (*He laughs.*)

Willy: Go to it, Biff! Go ahead, show him!

Biff: Okay! (*He cocks his fist and starts in.*)

Linda (*to Willy*): Why must he fight, dear?

Ben (*sparring with Biff*): Good boy! Good boy!

Willy: How's that, Ben, heh?

Happy: Give him the left, Biff!

Linda: Why are you fighting?

Ben: Good boy! (*Suddenly comes in, trips Biff, and stands over him, the point of his umbrella poised over Biff's eye.*)

Linda: Look out, Biff!

Biff: Gee!

Ben (*patting Biff's knee*): Never fight fair with a stranger, boy. You'll never get out of the jungle that way. (*Taking Linda's hand and bowing.*) It was an honor and a pleasure to meet you, Linda.

Linda (*withdrawing her hand coldly, frightened*): Have a nice—trip.

Ben (*to Willy*): And good luck with your—what do you do?

Willy: Selling.

Ben: Yes. Well . . . (*He raises his hand in farewell to all.*)

Willy: No, Ben, I don't want you to think . . . (*He takes Ben's arm to show him.*) It's Brooklyn, I know, but we hunt too.

Ben: Really, now.

Willy: Oh, sure, there's snakes and rabbits and—that's why I moved out here. Why, Biff can fell any one of these trees in no time! Boys! Go right over to where they're building the apartment house and get some sand. We're gonna rebuild the entire front stoop right now! Watch this, Ben!

Biff: Yes, sir! On the double, Hap!

Happy (*as he and Biff run off*): I lost weight, Pop, you notice?

(*Charley enters in knickers, even before the boys are gone.*)

Charley: Listen, if they steal any more from that building the watchman'll put the cops on them!

Linda (*to Willy*): Don't let Biff . . .

(*Ben laughs lustily.*)

Willy: You shoulda seen the lumber they brought home last week. At least a dozen six-by-tens worth all kinds of money.

Charley: Listen, if that watchman—

Willy: I gave them hell, understand. But I got a couple of fearless characters there.

Charley: Willy, the jails are full of fearless characters.

Ben (*clapping Willy on the back, with a laugh at Charley*): And the stock exchange, friend!

Willy (*joining in Ben's laughter*): Where are the rest of your pants?

Charley: My wife bought them.

Willy: Now all you need is a golf club and you can go upstairs and go to sleep. (*To Ben.*) Great athlete! Between him and his son Bernard they can't hammer a nail!

Bernard (rushing in): The watchman's chasing Biff!

Willy (angrily): Shut up! He's not stealing anything!

Linda (alarmed, hurrying off left): Where is he? Biff, dear! (*She exits.*)

Willy (moving toward the left, away from Ben): There's nothing wrong. What's the matter with you?

Ben: Nervy boy. Good!

Willy (laughing): Oh, nerves of iron, that Biff!

Charley: Don't know what it is. My New England man comes back and he's bleedin', they murdered him up there.

Willy: It's contacts, Charley, I got important contacts!

Charley (sarcastically): Glad to hear it, Willy. Come in later, we'll shoot a little casino. I'll take some of your Portland money. (*He laughs at Willy and exits.*)

Willy (turning to Ben): Business is bad, it's murderous. But not for me, of course.

Ben: I'll stop by on my way back to Africa.

Willy (longingly): Can't you stay a few days? You're just what I need, Ben, because I—I have a fine position, but I—well, Dad left when I was such a baby and I never had a chance to talk to him and I still feel—kind of temporary about myself.

Ben: I'll be late for my train.

(*They are at opposite ends of the stage.*)

Willy: Ben, my boys—can't we talk? They'd go into the jaws of hell for me, see, but I—

Ben: William, you're being first-rate with your boys. Outstanding, manly chaps!

Willy (hanging on to his words): Oh, Ben, that's good to hear! Because sometimes I'm afraid that I'm not teaching them the right kind of—Ben, how should I teach them?

Ben (giving great weight to each word, and with a certain vicious audacity): William, when I walked into the jungle, I was seventeen. When I walked out I was twenty-one. And, by God, I was rich! (*He goes off into darkness around the right corner of the house.*)

Willy: . . . was rich! That's just the spirit I want to imbue them with! To walk into a jungle! I was right! I was right! I was right!

(*Ben is gone, but Willy is still speaking to him as Linda, in nightgown and robe, enters the kitchen, glances around for Willy, then goes to the door of the house, looks out and sees him. Comes down to his left. He looks at her.*)

Linda: Willy, dear? Willy?

Willy: I was right!

Linda: Did you have some cheese? (*He can't answer.*) It's very late, darling. Come to bed, heh?

Willy (looking straight up): Gotta break your neck to see a star in this yard.

Linda: You coming in?

Willy: What ever happened to that diamond watch fob? Remember? When Ben came from Africa that time? Didn't he give me a watch fob with a diamond in it?

Linda: You pawned it, dear. Twelve, thirteen years ago. For Biff's radio correspondence course.

Willy: Gee, that was a beautiful thing. I'll take a walk.

Linda: But you're in your slippers.

Willy (starting to go around the house at the left): I was right! I was! (*Half to Linda, as he goes, shaking his head.*) What a man! There was a man worth talking to. I was right!

Linda (calling after Willy): But in your slippers, Willy!

(*Willy is almost gone when Biff, in his pajamas, comes down the stairs and enters the kitchen.*)

Biff: What is he doing out there?

Linda: Sh!

Biff: God Almighty, Mom, how long has he been doing this?

Linda: Don't, he'll hear you.

Biff: What the hell is the matter with him?

Linda: It'll pass by morning.

Biff: Shouldn't we do anything?

Linda: Oh, my dear, you should do a lot of things, but there's nothing to do, so go to sleep.

(*Happy comes down the stairs and sits on the steps.*)

Happy: I never heard him so loud, Mom.

Linda: Well, come around more often; you'll hear him. (*She sits down at the table and mends the lining of Willy's jacket.*)

Biff: Why didn't you ever write me about this, Mom?

Linda: How would I write to you? For over three months you had no address.

Biff: I was on the move. But you know I thought of you all the time. You know that, don't you, pal?

Linda: I know, dear, I know. But he likes to have a letter. Just to know that there's still a possibility for better things.

Biff: He's not like this all the time, is he?

Linda: It's when you come home he's always the worst.

Biff: When I come home?

Linda: When you write you're coming, he's all smiles, and talks about the future, and—he's just wonderful. And then the closer you seem to come, the more shaky he gets, and then, by the time you get here, he's arguing, and he seems angry at you. I think it's just that maybe he can't bring himself to—to open up to you. Why are you so hateful to each other? Why is that?

Biff (evasively): I'm not hateful, Mom.

Linda: But you no sooner come in the door than you're fighting!

Biff: I don't know why. I mean to change. I'm tryin', Mom, you understand?

Linda: Are you home to stay now?

Biff: I don't know. I want to look around, see what's doin'.

Linda: Biff, you can't look around all your life, can you?

Biff: I just can't take hold, Mom. I can't take hold of some kind of a life.

Linda: Biff, a man is not a bird, to come and go with the springtime.

Biff: Your hair . . . (*He touches her hair.*) Your hair got so gray.

Linda: Oh, it's been gray since you were in high school. I just stopped dyeing it, that's all.

Biff: Dye it again, will ya? I don't want my pal looking old. (*He smiles.*)

Linda: You're such a boy! You think you can go away for a year and . . . You've got to get it into your head now that one day you'll knock on this door and there'll be strange people here—

Biff: What are you talking about? You're not even sixty, Mom.

Linda: But what about your father?

Biff (*lamely*): Well, I meant him too.

Happy: He admires Pop.

Linda: Biff dear, if you don't have any feeling for him, then you can't have any feeling for me.

Biff: Sure I can, Mom.

Linda: No. You can't just come to see me, because I love him. (*With a threat, but only a threat, of tears.*) He's the dearest man in the world to me, and I won't have anyone making him feel unwanted and low and blue. You've got to make up your mind now, darling, there's no leeway any more. Either he's your father and you pay him that respect, or else you're not to come here. I know he's not easy to get along with—nobody knows that better than me—but . . .

Willy (*from the left, with a laugh*): Hey, hey, Biffo!

Biff (*starting to go out after Willy*): What the hell is the matter with him? (*Happy stops him.*)

Linda: Don't—don't go near him!

Biff: Stop making excuses for him! He always, always wiped the floor with you. Never had an ounce of respect for you.

Happy: He's always had respect for—

Biff: What the hell do you know about it?

Happy (*surlily*): Just don't call him crazy!

Biff: He's got no character—Charley wouldn't do this. Not in his own house—spewing out that vomit from his mind.

Happy: Charley never had to cope with what he's got to.

Biff: People are worse off than Willy Loman. Believe me, I've seen them!

Linda: Then make Charley your father, Biff. You can't do that, can you? I don't say he's a great man. Willy Loman never made a lot of money. His name was never in the paper. He's not the finest character that ever lived. But he's a human being, and a terrible thing is happening to him. So attention must be paid. He's not to be allowed to fall into his grave like an old dog. Attention, attention must be finally paid to such a person. You called him crazy—

Biff: I didn't mean—

Linda: No, a lot of people think he's lost his—balance. But you don't have to be very smart to know what his trouble is. The man is exhausted.

Happy: Sure!

Linda: A small man can be just as exhausted as a great man. He works for a company thirty-six years this March, opens up unheard-of territories to their trademark, and now in his old age they take his salary away.

Happy (indignantly): I didn't know that, Mom!

Linda: You never asked, my dear! Now that you get your spending money someplace else you don't trouble your mind with him.

Happy: But I gave you money last—

Linda: Christmas time, fifty dollars! To fix the hot water it cost ninety-seven fifty! For five weeks he's been on straight commission, like a beginner, an unknown!

Biff: Those ungrateful bastards!

Linda: Are they any worse than his sons? When he brought them business, when he was young, they were glad to see him. But now his old friends, the old buyers that loved him so and always found some order to hand him in a pinch—they're all dead, retired. He used to be able to make six, seven calls a day in Boston. Now he takes his valises out of the car and puts them back and takes them out again and he's exhausted. Instead of walking he talks now. He drives seven hundred miles, and when he gets there no one knows him any more, no one welcomes him. And what goes through a man's mind, driving seven hundred miles home without having earned a cent? Why shouldn't he talk to himself? Why? When he has to go to Charley and borrow fifty dollars a week and pretend to me that it's his pay? How long can that go on? How long? You see what I'm sitting here and waiting for? And you tell me he has no character? The man who never worked a day but for your benefit? When does he get the medal for that? Is this his reward—to turn around at the age of sixty-three and find his sons, who he loved better than his life, one a philandering bum—

Happy: Mom!

Linda: That's all you are, my baby! *(To Biff.)* And you! What happened to the love you had for him? You were such pals! How you used to talk to him on the phone every night! How lonely he was till he could come home to you!

Biff: All right, Mom. I'll live here in my room, and I'll get a job. I'll keep away from him, that's all.

Linda: No, Biff. You can't stay here and fight all the time.

Biff: He threw me out of this house, remember that.

Linda: Why did he do that? I never knew why.

Biff: Because I know he's a fake and he doesn't like anybody around who knows!

Linda: Why a fake? In what way? What do you mean?

Biff: Just don't lay it all at my feet. It's between me and him—that's all I have to say. I'll chip in from now on. He'll settle for half my pay check. He'll be all right. I'm going to bed. *(He starts for the stairs.)*

Linda: He won't be all right.

Biff (turning on the stairs, furiously): I hate this city and I'll stay here. Now what do you want?

Linda: He's dying, Biff.

   (Happy turns quickly to her, shocked.)

Biff (after a pause): Why is he dying?

Linda: He's been trying to kill himself.

Biff (with great horror): How?

Linda: I live from day to day.

Biff: What're you talking about?

Linda: Remember I wrote you that he smashed up the car again? In February?

Biff: Well?

Linda: The insurance inspector came. He said that they have evidence. That all these accidents in the last year—weren't—weren't—accidents.

Happy: How can they tell that? That's a lie.

Linda: It seems there's a woman . . . (*She takes a breath as—*)

Biff (sharply but contained): What woman?

Linda (simultaneously): . . . and this woman . . .

Linda: What?

Biff: Nothing. Go ahead.

Linda: What did you say?

Biff: Nothing. I just said what woman?

Happy: What about her?

Linda: Well, it seems she was walking down the road and saw his car. She says that he wasn't driving fast at all, and that he didn't skid. She says he came to that little bridge, and then deliberately smashed into the railing, and it was only the shallowness of the water that saved him.

Biff: Oh, no, he probably just fell asleep again.

Linda: I don't think he fell asleep.

Biff: Why not?

Linda: Last month . . . (*With great difficulty.*) Oh, boys, it's so hard to say a thing like this! He's just a big stupid man to you, but I tell you there's more good in him than in many other people. (*She chokes, wipes her eyes.*) I was looking for a fuse. The lights blew out, and I went down the cellar. And behind the fuse box—it happened to fall out—was a length of rubber pipe—just short.

Happy: No kidding?

Linda: There's a little attachment on the end of it. I knew right away. And sure enough, on the bottom of the water heater there's a new little nipple on the gas pipe.

Happy (angrily): That—jerk.

Biff: Did you have it taken off?

Linda: I'm—I'm ashamed to. How can I mention it to him? Every day I go down and take away that little rubber pipe. But, when he comes home, I put it back where it was. How can I insult him that way? I don't know what to do. I live from day to day, boys. I tell you, I know every thought in his mind. It sounds so old-fashioned and silly, but I tell you he put his whole life into you and you've turned your backs on him. (*She is bent over in the chair, weeping, her face in her hands.*) Biff, I swear to God! Biff, his life is in your hands!

Happy (to Biff): How do you like that damned fool!

Biff (kissing her): All right, pal, all right. It's all settled now. I've been remiss. I know that, Mom. But now I'll stay, and I swear to you, I'll apply myself. (*Kneeling in front of her, in a fever of self-reproach.*) It's just—you see, Mom, I don't fit in business. Not that I won't try. I'll try, and I'll make good.

Happy: Sure you will. The trouble with you in business was you never tried to please people.

Biff: I know, I—

Happy: Like when you worked for Harrison's. Bob Harrison said you were tops, and then you go and do some damn fool thing like whistling whole songs in the elevator like a comedian.

Biff (against Happy): So what? I like to whistle sometimes.

Happy: You don't raise a guy to a responsible job who whistles in the elevator!

Linda: Well, don't argue about it now.

Happy: Like when you'd go off and swim in the middle of the day instead of taking the line around.

Biff (his resentment rising): Well, don't you run off? You take off sometimes, don't you? On a nice summer day?

Happy: Yeah, but I cover myself!

Linda: Boys!

Happy: If I'm going to take a fade the boss can call any number where I'm supposed to be and they'll swear to him that I just left. I'll tell you something that I hate to say, Biff, but in the business world some of them think you're crazy.

Biff (angered): Screw the business world!

Happy: All right, screw it! Great, but cover yourself!

Linda: Hap! Hap!

Biff: I don't care what they think! They've laughed at Dad for years, and you know why? Because we don't belong in this nut-house of a city! We should be mixing cement on some open plain, or—or carpenters. A carpenter is allowed to whistle!

(Willy walks in from the entrance of the house, at left.)

Willy: Even your grandfather was better than a carpenter. *(Pause. They watch him.)* You never grew up. Bernard does not whistle in the elevator, I assure you.

Biff (as though to laugh Willy out of it): Yeah, but you do, Pop.

Willy: I never in my life whistled in an elevator! And who in the business world thinks I'm crazy?

Biff: I didn't mean it like that, Pop. Now don't make a whole thing out of it, will ya?

Willy: Go back to the West! Be a carpenter, a cowboy, enjoy yourself!

Linda: Willy, he was just saying—

Willy: I heard what he said!

Happy (trying to quiet Willy): Hey, Pop, come on now . . .

Willy (continuing over Happy's line): They laugh at me, heh? Go to Filene's, go to the Hub, go to Slattery's, Boston. Call out the name Willy Loman and see what happens! Big shot!

Biff: All right, Pop.

Willy: Big!

Biff: All right!

Willy: Why do you always insult me?

Biff: I didn't say a word. *(To Linda.)* Did I say a word?

Linda: He didn't say anything, Willy.

Willy (going to the doorway of the living room): All right, good night, good night.

Linda: Willy, dear, he just decided . . .

Willy (to Biff): If you get tired hanging around tomorrow, paint the ceiling I put up in the living room.

Biff: I'm leaving early tomorrow.

Happy: He's going to see Bill Oliver, Pop.

Willy (interestedly): Oliver? For what?

Biff (with reserve, but trying, trying): He always said he'd stake me. I'd like to go into business, so maybe I can take him up on it.

Linda: Isn't that wonderful?

Willy: Don't interrupt. What's wonderful about it? There's fifty men in the City of New York who'd stake him. (*To Biff.*) Sporting goods?

Biff: I guess so. I know something about it and—

Willy: He knows something about it! You know sporting goods better than Spalding, for God's sake! How much is he giving you?

Biff: I don't know, I didn't even see him yet, but—

Willy: Then what're you talkin' about?

Biff (getting angry): Well, all I said was I'm gonna see him, that's all!

Willy (turning away): Ah, you're counting your chickens again.

Biff (starting left for the stairs): Oh, Jesus, I'm going to sleep!

Willy (calling after him): Don't curse in this house!

Biff (turning): Since when did you get so clean!

Happy (trying to stop them): Wait a . . .

Willy: Don't use that language to me! I won't have it!

Happy (grabbing Biff, shouts): Wait a minute! I got an idea. I got a feasible idea. Come here, Biff, let's talk this over now, let's talk some sense here. When I was down in Florida last time, I thought of a great idea to sell sporting goods. It just came back to me. You and I, Biff—we have a line, the Loman Line. We train a couple of weeks, and put on a couple of exhibitions, see?

Willy: That's an idea!

Happy: Wait! We form two basketball teams, see? Two water-polo teams. We play each other. It's a million dollars' worth of publicity. Two brothers, see? The Loman Brothers. Displays in the Royal Palms—all the hotels. And banners over the ring and the basketball court: "Loman Brothers." Baby, we could sell sporting goods!

Willy: That is a one-million-dollar idea.

Linda: Marvelous!

Biff: I'm in great shape as far as that's concerned.

Happy: And the beauty of it is, Biff, it wouldn't be like a business. We'd be out playin' ball again . . .

Biff (enthused): Yeah, that's . . .

Willy: Million-dollar . . .

Happy: And you wouldn't get fed up with it, Biff. It'd be the family again. There'd be the old honor, and comradeship, and if you wanted to go off for a swim or somethin'—well, you'd do it! Without some smart cooky gettin' up ahead of you!

Willy: Lick the world! You guys together could absolutely lick the civilized world.

Biff: I'll see Oliver tomorrow. Hap, if we could work that out . . .

Linda: Maybe things are beginning to—

Willy (wildly enthused, to Linda): Stop interrupting! (*To Biff.*) But don't wear sport jacket and slacks when you see Oliver.

Biff: No, I'll—

Willy: A business suit, and talk as little as possible, and don't crack any jokes.

Biff: He did like me. Always liked me.

Linda: He loved you!

Willy (to Linda): Will you stop! (*To Biff.*) Walk in very serious. You are not applying for a boy's job. Money is to pass. Be quiet, fine, and serious. Everybody likes a kidder, but nobody lends him money.

Happy: I'll try to get some myself, Biff. I'm sure I can.

Willy: I can see great things for you, kids, I think your troubles are over. But remember, start big and you'll end big. Ask for fifteen. How much you gonna ask for?

Biff: Gee, I don't know—

Willy: And don't say "Gee." "Gee" is a boy's word. A man walking in for fifteen thousand dollars does not say "Gee!"

Biff: Ten, I think, would be top though.

Willy: Don't be so modest. You always started too low. Walk in with a big laugh. Don't look worried. Start off with a couple of your good stories to lighten things up. It's not what you say, it's how you say it—because personality always wins the day.

Linda: Oliver always thought the highest of him—

Willy: Will you let me talk?

Biff: Don't yell at her, Pop, will ya?

Willy (angrily): I was talking, wasn't I?

Biff: I don't like you yelling at her all the time, and I'm tellin' you, that's all.

Willy: What're you, takin' over the house?

Linda: Willy—

Willy (turning on her): Don't take his side all the time, goddammit!

Biff (furiously): Stop yelling at her!

Willy (suddenly pulling on his cheek, beaten down, guilt ridden): Give my best to Bill Oliver—he may remember me. (*He exits through the living room doorway.*)

Linda (her voice subdued): What'd you have to start that for? (*Biff turns away.*) You see how sweet he was as soon as you talked hopefully? (*She goes over to Biff.*) Come up and say good night to him. Don't let him go to bed that way.

Happy: Come on, Biff, let's buck him up.

Linda: Please, dear. Just say good night. It takes so little to make him happy. Come. (*She goes through the living room doorway, calling upstairs from within the living room.*) Your pajamas are hanging in the bathroom. Willy!

Happy (looking toward where Linda went out): What a woman! They broke the mold when they made her. You know that, Biff?

Biff: He's off salary. My God, working on commission!

Happy: Well, let's face it: he's no hot-shot selling man. Except that sometimes, you have to admit, he's a sweet personality.

Biff (deciding): Lend me ten bucks, will ya? I want to buy some new ties.

Happy: I'll take you to a place I know. Beautiful stuff. Wear one of my striped shirts tomorrow.

Biff: She got gray. Mom got awful old. Gee, I'm gonna go in to Oliver tomorrow and knock him for a—

Happy: Come on up. Tell that to Dad. Let's give him a whirl. Come on.

Biff (steamed up): You know, with ten thousand bucks, boy!

Happy (as they go into the living room): That's the talk, Biff, that's the first time I've heard the old confidence out of you! *(From within the living room, fading off.)* You're gonna live with me, kid, and any babe you want you just say the word . . . *(The last lines are hardly heard. They are mounting the stairs to their parents' bedroom.)*

Linda (entering her bedroom and addressing Willy, who is in the bathroom. She is straightening the bed for him): Can you do anything about the shower? It drips.

Willy (from the bathroom): All of a sudden everything falls to pieces! Goddam plumbing, oughta be sued, those people. I hardly finished putting it in and the thing . . . *(His words rumble off.)*

Linda: I'm just wondering if Oliver will remember him. You think he might?

Willy (coming out of the bathroom in his pajamas): Remember him? What's the matter with you, you crazy? If he'd've stayed with Oliver he'd be on top by now! Wait'll Oliver gets a look at him. You don't know the average caliber any more. The average young man today—*(he is getting into bed)*—is got a caliber of zero. Greatest thing in the world for him was to bum around.

(Biff and Happy enter the bedroom. Slight pause.)

Willy (stops short, looking at Biff): Glad to hear it, boy.

Happy: He wanted to say good night to you, sport.

Willy (to Biff): Yeah. Knock him dead, boy. What'd you want to tell me?

Biff: Just take it easy, Pop. Good night. *(He turns to go.)*

Willy (unable to resist): And if anything falls off the desk while you're talking to him—like a package or something—don't you pick it up. They have office boys for that.

Linda: I'll make a big breakfast—

Willy: Will you let me finish? *(To Biff.)* Tell him you were in the business in the West. Not farm work.

Biff: All right, Dad.

Linda: I think everything—

Willy (going right through her speech): And don't undersell yourself. No less than fifteen thousand dollars.

Biff (unable to bear him): Okay. Good night, Mom. *(He starts moving.)*

Willy: Because you got a greatness in you, Biff, remember that. You got all kinds a greatness . . . *(He lies back, exhausted. Biff walks out.)*

Linda (calling after Biff): Sleep well, darling!

Happy: I'm gonna get married, Mom. I wanted to tell you.

Linda: Go to sleep, dear.

Happy (going): I just wanted to tell you.

Willy: Keep up the good work. *(Happy exits.)* God . . . remember that Ebbets Field game? The championship of the city?

Linda: Just rest. Should I sing to you?

Willy: Yeah. Sing to me. *(Linda hums a soft lullaby.)* When that team came out—he was the tallest, remember?

Linda: Oh, yes. And in gold.

(Biff enters the darkened kitchen, takes a cigarette, and leaves the house. He comes downstage into a golden pool of light. He smokes, staring at the night.)

Willy: Like a young god. Hercules—something like that. And the sun, the sun all around him. Remember how he waved to me? Right up from the field, with the representatives of three colleges standing by? And the buyers I brought, and the cheers when he came out—Loman, Loman, Loman! God Almighty, he'll be great yet. A star like that, magnificent, can never really fade away!

(*The light on Willy is fading. The gas heater begins to glow through the kitchen wall, near the stairs, a blue flame beneath red coils.*)

Linda (*timidly*): Willy, dear, what has he got against you?
Willy: I'm so tired. Don't talk any more.

(*Biff slowly returns to the kitchen. He stops, stares toward the heater.*)

Linda: Will you ask Howard to let you work in New York?
Willy: First thing in the morning. Everything'll be all right.

(*Biff reaches behind the heater and draws out a length of rubber tubing. He is horrified and turns his head toward Willy's room, still dimly lit, from which the strains of Linda's desperate but monotonous humming rise.*)

Willy (*staring through the window into the moonlight*): Gee, look at the moon moving between the buildings!

(*Biff wraps the tubing around his hand and quickly goes up the stairs. Curtain.*)

ACT II

Music is heard, gay and bright. The curtain rises as the music fades away. Willy, in shirt sleeves, is sitting at the kitchen table, sipping coffee, his hat in his lap. Linda is filling his cup when she can.

Willy: Wonderful coffee. Meal in itself.
Linda: Can I make you some eggs?
Willy: No. Take a breath.
Linda: You look so rested, dear.
Willy: I slept like a dead one. First time in months. Imagine, sleeping till ten on a Tuesday morning. Boys left nice and early, heh?
Linda: They were out of here by eight o'clock.
Willy: Good work!
Linda: It was so thrilling to see them leaving together. I can't get over the shaving lotion in this house.
Willy (*smiling*): Mmm—
Linda: Biff was very changed this morning. His whole attitude seemed to be hopeful. He couldn't wait to get downtown to see Oliver.
Willy: He's heading for a change. There's no question, there simply are certain men that take longer to get—solidified. How did he dress?
Linda: His blue suit. He's so handsome in that suit. He could be a—anything in that suit!

(*Willy gets up from the table. Linda holds his jacket for him.*)

Willy: There's no question, no question at all. Gee, on the way home tonight I'd like to buy some seeds.

Linda (laughing): That'd be wonderful. But not enough sun gets back there. Nothing'll grow any more.

Willy: You wait, kid, before it's all over we're gonna get a little place out in the country, and I'll raise some vegetables, a couple of chickens . . .

Linda: You'll do it yet, dear.

(Willy walks out of his jacket. Linda follows him.)

Willy: And they'll get married, and come for a weekend. I'd build a little guest house. 'Cause I got so many fine tools, all I'd need would be a little lumber and some peace of mind.

Linda (joyfully): I sewed the lining . . .

Willy: I could build two guest houses, so they'd both come. Did he decide how much he's going to ask Oliver for?

Linda (getting him into the jacket): He didn't mention it, but I imagine ten or fifteen thousand. You going to talk to Howard today?

Willy: Yeah. I'll put it to him straight and simple. He'll just have to take me off the road.

Linda: And Willy, don't forget to ask for a little advance, because we've got the insurance premium. It's the grace period now.

Willy: That's a hundred . . . ?

Linda: A hundred and eight, sixty-eight. Because we're a little short again.

Willy: Why are we short?

Linda: Well, you had the motor job on the car . . .

Willy: That goddam Studebaker!

Linda: And you got one more payment on the refrigerator . . .

Willy: But it just broke again!

Linda: Well, it's old, dear.

Willy: I told you we should've bought a well-advertised machine. Charley bought a General Electric and it's twenty years old and it's still good, that son-of-a-bitch.

Linda: But, Willy—

Willy: Whoever heard of a Hastings refrigerator? Once in my life I would like to own something outright before it's broken! I'm always in a race with the junkyard! I just finished paying for the car and it's on its last legs. The refrigerator consumes belts like a goddam maniac. They time those things. They time them so when you finally paid for them, they're used up.

Linda (buttoning up his jacket as he unbuttons it): All told, about two hundred dollars would carry us, dear. But that includes the last payment on the mortgage. After this payment, Willy, the house belongs to us.

Willy: It's twenty-five years!

Linda: Biff was nine years old when we bought it.

Willy: Well, that's a great thing. To weather a twenty-five year mortgage is—

Linda: It's an accomplishment.

Willy: All the cement, the lumber, the reconstruction I put in this house! There ain't a crack to be found in it any more.

Linda: Well, it served its purpose.

Willy: What purpose? Some stranger'll come along, move in, and that's that. If only Biff would take this house, and raise a family . . . *(He starts to go.)* Good-by, I'm late.

Linda (suddenly remembering): Oh, I forgot! You're supposed to meet them for dinner.

Willy: Me?

Linda: At Frank's Chop House on Forty-eighth near Sixth Avenue.

Willy: Is that so! How about you?

Linda: No, just the three of you. They're gonna blow you to a big meal!

Willy: Don't say! Who thought of that?

Linda: Biff came to me this morning, Willy, and he said, "Tell Dad, we want to blow him to a big meal." Be there six o'clock. You and your two boys are going to have dinner.

Willy: Gee whiz! That's really somethin'. I'm gonna knock Howard for a loop, kid. I'll get an advance, and I'll come home with a New York job. Goddammit, now I'm gonna do it!

Linda: Oh, that's the spirit, Willy!

Willy: I will never get behind a wheel the rest of my life!

Linda: It's changing, Willy, I can feel it changing!

Willy: Beyond a question. G'by, I'm late. (*He starts to go again.*)

Linda (calling after him as she runs to the kitchen table for a handkerchief): You got your glasses?

Willy (feels for them, then comes back in): Yeah, yeah, got my glasses.

Linda (giving him the handkerchief): And a handkerchief.

Willy: Yeah, handkerchief.

Linda: And your saccharine?

Willy: Yeah, my saccharine.

Linda: Be careful on the subway stairs.

(*She kisses him, and a silk stocking is seen hanging from her hand. Willy notices it.*)

Willy: Will you stop mending stockings? At least while I'm in the house. It gets me nervous. I can't tell you. Please.

(*Linda hides the stocking in her hand as she follows Willy across the forestage in front of the house.*)

Linda: Remember, Frank's Chop House.

Willy (passing the apron): Maybe beets would grow out there.

Linda (laughing): But you tried so many times.

Willy: Yeah. Well, don't work hard today. (*He disappears around the right corner of the house.*)

Linda: Be careful!

(*As Willy vanishes, Linda waves to him. Suddenly the phone rings. She runs across the stage and into the kitchen and lifts it.*)

Linda: Hello? Oh, Biff! I'm so glad you called, I just . . . Yes, sure, I just told him. Yes, he'll be there for dinner at six o'clock, I didn't forget. Listen, I was just dying to tell you. You know that little rubber pipe I told you about? That he connected to the gas heater? I finally decided to go down the cellar this morning and take it away and destroy it. But it's gone! Imagine? He took it away himself, it isn't there! (*She listens.*) When? Oh, then you took it. Oh—nothing, it's just that I'd hoped he'd taken it away himself. Oh, I'm not worried, darling, because this morning he left in such high spirits, it was like the old days! I'm not afraid any more. Did Mr. Oliver see you? . . . Well, you wait there then. And make a nice impression on him, darling. Just don't perspire too much before you see him. And have a nice time with Dad. He may have big news too! . . . That's right, a New York job. And be sweet to him tonight, dear. Be loving to him. Because he's only a little boat looking for a harbor. (*She is trembling with sorrow and joy.*) Oh, that's wonderful, Biff, you'll save his life. Thanks, darling. Just put your arm around him when he comes into the restaurant. Give him a smile. That's the boy . . . Good-by, dear. . . . You got your comb? . . . That's fine. Good-by, Biff dear.

(*In the middle of her speech, Howard Wagner, thirty-six, wheels in a small typewriter table on which is a wire-recording machine and proceeds to plug it in. This is on the left forestage. Light slowly fades on Linda as it rises on Howard. Howard is intent on threading the machine and only glances over his shoulder as Willy appears.*)

Willy: Pst! Pst!

Howard: Hello, Willy, come in.

Willy: Like to have a little talk with you, Howard.

Howard: Sorry to keep you waiting. I'll be with you in a minute.

Willy: What's that, Howard?

Howard: Didn't you ever see one of these? Wire recorder.

Willy: Oh. Can we talk a minute?

Howard: Records things. Just got delivery yesterday. Been driving me crazy, the most terrific machine I ever saw in my life. I was up all night with it.

Willy: What do you do with it?

Howard: I bought it for dictation, but you can do anything with it. Listen to this. I had it home last night. Listen to what I picked up. The first one is my daughter. Get this. (*He flicks the switch and "Roll out the Barrel" is heard being whistled.*) Listen to that kid whistle.

Willy: That is lifelike, isn't it?

Howard: Seven years old. Get that tone.

Willy: Ts, ts. Like to ask a little favor if you . . .

(*The whistling breaks off, and the voice of Howard's Daughter is heard.*)

His Daughter: "Now you, Daddy."

Howard: She's crazy for me! (*Again the same song is whistled.*) That's me! Ha! (*He winks.*)

Willy: You're very good!

(*The whistling breaks off again. The machine runs silent for a moment.*)

Howard: Sh! Get this now, this is my son.

His Son: "The capital of Alabama is Montgomery; the capital of Arizona is Phoenix; the capital of Arkansas is Little Rock; the capital of California is Sacramento . . ." (*And on, and on.*)

Howard (*holding up five fingers*): Five years old, Willy!

Willy: He'll make an announcer some day!

His Son (*continuing*): "The capital . . ."

Howard: Get that—alphabetical order! (*The machine breaks off suddenly.*) Wait a minute. The maid kicked the plug out.

Willy: It certainly is a—

Howard: Sh, for God's sake!

His Son: "It's nine o'clock, Bulova watch time. So I have to go to sleep."

Willy: That really is—

Howard: Wait a minute! The next is my wife.

(*They wait.*)

Howard's Voice: "Go on, say something." (*Pause.*) "Well, you gonna talk?"

His Wife: "I can't think of anything."

Howard's Voice: "Well, talk—it's turning."

His Wife (*shyly, beaten*): "Hello." (*Silence.*) "Oh, Howard, I can't talk into this . . . "

Howard (*snapping the machine off*): That was my wife.

Willy: That is a wonderful machine. Can we—

Howard: I tell you, Willy, I'm gonna take my camera, and my bandsaw, and all my hobbies, and out they go. This is the most fascinating relaxation I ever found.

Willy: I think I'll get one myself.

Howard: Sure, they're only a hundred and a half. You can't do without it. Supposing you wanna hear Jack Benny, see? But you can't be at home at that hour. So you tell the maid to turn the radio on when Jack Benny comes on, and this automatically goes on with the radio . . .

Willy: And when you come home you . . .

Howard: You can come home twelve o'clock, one o'clock, any time you like, and you get yourself a Coke and sit yourself down, throw the switch, and there's Jack Benny's program in the middle of the night!

Willy: I'm definitely going to get one. Because lots of times I'm on the road, and I think to myself, what I must be missing on the radio!

Howard: Don't you have a radio in the car?

Willy: Well, yeah, but who ever thinks of turning it on?

Howard: Say, aren't you supposed to be in Boston?

Willy: That's what I want to talk to you about, Howard. You got a minute?

(*He draws a chair in from the wing.*)

Howard: What happened? What're you doing here?

Willy: Well . . .

Howard: You didn't crack up again, did you?

Willy: Oh, no. No . . .

Howard: Geez, you had me worried there for a minute. What's the trouble?

Willy: Well, to tell you the truth, Howard, I've come to the decision that I'd rather not travel any more.

Howard: Not travel! Well, what'll you do?

Willy: Remember, Christmas time, when you had the party here? You said you'd try to think of some spot for me here in town.

Howard: With us?

Willy: Well, sure.

Howard: Oh, yeah, yeah. I remember. Well, I couldn't think of anything for you, Willy.

Willy: I tell ya, Howard. The kids are all grown up, y'know. I don't need much any more. If I could take home—well, sixty-five dollars a week, I could swing it.

Howard: Yeah, but Willy, see I—

Willy: I tell ya why, Howard. Speaking frankly and between the two of us, y'know—I'm just a little tired.

Howard: Oh, I could understand that, Willy. But you're a road man, Willy, and we do a road business. We've only got a half-dozen salesmen on the floor here.

Willy: God knows, Howard, I never asked a favor of any man. But I was with the firm when your father used to carry you in here in his arms.

Howard: I know that, Willy, but—

Willy: Your father came to me the day you were born and asked me what I thought of the name of Howard, may he rest in peace.

Howard: I appreciate that, Willy, but there just is no spot here for you. If I had a spot I'd slam you right in, but I just don't have a single, solitary spot.

(He looks for his lighter. Willy has picked it up and gives it to him. Pause.)

Willy (with increasing anger): Howard, all I need to set my table is fifty dollars a week.

Howard: But where am I going to put you, kid?

Willy: Look, it isn't a question of whether I can sell merchandise, is it?

Howard: No, but it's a business, kid, and everybody's gotta pull his own weight.

Willy (desperately): Just let me tell you a story, Howard—

Howard: 'Cause you gotta admit, business is business.

Willy (angrily): Business is definitely business, but just listen for a minute. You don't understand this. When I was a boy—eighteen, nineteen—I was already on the road. And there was a question in my mind as to whether selling had a future for me. Because in those days I had a yearning to go to Alaska. See, there were three gold strikes in one month in Alaska, and I felt like going out. Just for the ride, you might say.

Howard (barely interested): Don't say.

Willy: Oh, yeah, my father lived many years in Alaska. He was an adventurous man. We've got quite a little streak of self-reliance in our family. I thought I'd go out with my older brother and try to locate him, and maybe settle in the North with the old man. And I was almost decided to go, when I met a salesman in the Parker House. His name was Dave Singleman. And he was eighty-four years old, and he'd drummed merchandise in thirty-one states. And old Dave, he'd go up to his room, y'understand, put on his green velvet slippers—I'll never forget—and pick up his phone and call the buyers, and without ever leaving his room, at the age of eighty-four, he made his living. And when I saw that, I realized that selling was the greatest career a man could want. 'Cause what could be more satisfying than to be able to go, at the age of eighty-four, into twenty or thirty different cities, and pick up a phone, and be remembered and loved and helped by so many different people? Do you know? When he died—and by the way he died the death of a salesman, in his green velvet slippers in the smoker of the New York, New Haven and Hartford, going into Boston—when he died, hundreds of salesmen and buyers were at his funeral. Things were sad on a lotta trains for months after that. *(He stands up. Howard has not looked at him.)* In those days there was personality in it, Howard. There was respect, and comradeship, and gratitude in it. Today, it's all cut and dried, and there's no chance for bringing friendship to bear—or personality. You see what I mean? They don't know me any more.

Howard (moving away, to the right): That's just the thing, Willy.

Willy: If I had forty dollars a week—that's all I'd need. Forty dollars, Howard.

Howard: Kid, I can't take blood from a stone, I—

Willy (*desperation is on him now*): Howard, the year Al Smith was nominated, your father came to me and—

Howard (*starting to go off*): I've got to see some people, kid.

Willy (*stopping him*): I'm talking about your father! There were promises made across this desk! You mustn't tell me you've got people to see—I put thirty-four years into this firm, Howard, and now I can't pay my insurance! You can't eat the orange and throw the peel away—a man is not a piece of fruit! (*After a pause.*) Now pay attention. Your father—in 1928 I had a big year. I averaged a hundred and seventy dollars a week in commissions.

Howard (*impatiently*): Now, Willy, you never averaged—

Willy (*banging his hand on the desk*): I averaged a hundred and seventy dollars a week in the year of 1928! And your father came to me—or rather, I was in the office here—it was right over this desk—and he put his hand on my shoulder—

Howard (*getting up*): You'll have to excuse me, Willy, I gotta see some people. Pull yourself together. (*Going out.*) I'll be back in a little while.

(*On Howard's exit, the light on his chair grows very bright and strange.*)

Willy: Pull yourself together! What the hell did I say to him? My God, I was yelling at him! How could I! (*Willy breaks off, staring at the light, which occupies the chair, animating it. He approaches this chair, standing across the desk from it.*) Frank, Frank, don't you remember what you told me that time? How you put your hand on my shoulder, and Frank . . . (*He leans on the desk and as he speaks the dead man's name he accidentally switches on the recorder, and instantly—*)

Howard's Son: ". . . of New York is Albany. The capital of Ohio is Cincinnati, the capital of Rhode Island is . . . " (*The recitation continues.*)

Willy (*leaping away with fright, shouting*): Ha! Howard! Howard! Howard!

Howard (*rushing in*): What happened?

Willy (*pointing at the machine, which continues nasally, childishly, with the capital cities*): Shut it off! Shut it off!

Howard (*pulling the plug out*): Look, Willy . . .

Willy (*pressing his hands to his eyes*): I gotta get myself some coffee. I'll get some coffee . . .

(*Willy starts to walk out. Howard stops him.*)

Howard (*rolling up the cord*): Willy, look . . .

Willy: I'll go to Boston.

Howard: Willy, you can't go to Boston for us.

Willy: Why can't I go?

Howard: I don't want you to represent us. I've been meaning to tell you for a long time now.

Willy: Howard, are you firing me?

Howard: I think you need a good long rest, Willy.

Willy: Howard—

Howard: And when you feel better, come back, and we'll see if we can work something out.

Willy: But I gotta earn money, Howard. I'm in no position—

Howard: Where are your sons? Why don't your sons give you a hand?

Willy: They're working on a very big deal.

Howard: This is no time for false pride, Willy. You go to your sons and tell them that you're tired. You've got two great boys, haven't you?

Willy: Oh, no question, no question, but in the meantime . . .

Howard: Then that's that, heh?

Willy: All right, I'll go to Boston tomorrow.

Howard: No, no.

Willy: I can't throw myself on my sons. I'm not a cripple!

Howard: Look, kid, I'm busy this morning.

Willy (grasping Howard's arm): Howard, you've got to let me go to Boston!

Howard (hard, keeping himself under control): I've got a line of people to see this morning. Sit down, take five minutes, and pull yourself together, and then go home, will ya? I need the office, Willy. (*He starts to go, turns, remembering the recorder, starts to push off the table holding the recorder.*) Oh, yeah. Whenever you can this week, stop by and drop off the samples. You'll feel better, Willy, and then come back and we'll talk. Pull yourself together, kid, there's people outside.

(*Howard exits, pushing the table off left. Willy stares into space, exhausted. Now the music is heard—Ben's music—first distantly, then closer, closer. As Willy speaks, Ben enters from the right. He carries valise and umbrella.*)

Willy: Oh, Ben, how did you do it? What is the answer? Did you wind up the Alaska deal already?

Ben: Doesn't take much time if you know what you're doing. Just a short business trip. Boarding ship in an hour. Wanted to say good-by.

Willy: Ben, I've got to talk to you.

Ben (glancing at his watch): Haven't the time, William.

Willy (crossing the apron to Ben): Ben, nothing's working out. I don't know what to do.

Ben: Now, look here, William. I've bought timberland in Alaska and I need a man to look after things for me.

Willy: God, timberland! Me and my boys in those grand outdoors!

Ben: You've a new continent at your doorstep, William. Get out of these cities, they're full of talk and time payments and courts of law. Screw on your fists and you can fight for a fortune up there.

Willy: Yes, yes! Linda! Linda!

(*Linda enters as of old, with the wash.*)

Linda: Oh, you're back?

Ben: I haven't much time.

Willy: No, wait! Linda, he's got a proposition for me in Alaska.

Linda: But you've got—(*To Ben.*) He's got a beautiful job here.

Willy: But in Alaska, kid, I could—

Linda: You're doing well enough, Willy!

Ben (to Linda): Enough for what, my dear?

Linda (*frightened of Ben and angry at him*): Don't say those things to him! Enough to be happy right here, right now. (*To Willy, while Ben laughs.*) Why must everybody conquer the world? You're well liked, and the boys love you, and someday—(*to Ben*)—why, old man Wagner told him just the other day that if he keeps it up he'll be a member of the firm, didn't he, Willy?

Willy: Sure, sure. I am building something with this firm, Ben, and if a man is building something he must be on the right track, mustn't he?

Ben: What are you building? Lay your hand on it. Where is it?

Willy (*hesitantly*): That's true, Linda, there's nothing.

Linda: Why? (*To Ben.*) There's a man eighty-four years old—

Willy: That's right, Ben, that's right. When I look at that man I say, what is there to worry about?

Ben: Bah!

Willy: It's true, Ben. All he has to do is go into any city, pick up the phone, and he's making his living and you know why?

Ben (*picking up his valise*): I've got to go.

Willy (*holding Ben back*): Look at this boy!

(*Biff, in his high school sweater, enters carrying suitcase. Happy carries Biff's shoulder guards, gold helmet, and football pants.*)

Willy: Without a penny to his name, three great universities are begging for him, and from there the sky's the limit, because it's not what you do, Ben. It's who you know and the smile on your face! It's contacts, Ben, contacts! The whole wealth of Alaska passes over the lunch table at the Commodore Hotel, and that's the wonder, the wonder of this country, that a man can end with diamonds here on the basis of being liked! (*He turns to Biff.*) And that's why when you get out on that field today it's important. Because thousands of people will be rooting for you and loving you. (*To Ben, who has again begun to leave.*) And Ben! when he walks into a business office his name will sound out like a bell and all the doors will open to him! I've seen it, Ben, I've seen it a thousand times! You can't feel it with your hand like timber, but it's there!

Ben: Good-by, William.

Willy: Ben, am I right? Don't you think I'm right? I value your advice.

Ben: There's a new continent at your doorstep, William. You could walk out rich. Rich. (*He is gone.*)

Willy: We'll do it here, Ben! You hear me? We're gonna do it here!

(*Young Bernard rushes in. The gay music of the boys is heard.*)

Bernard: Oh, gee, I was afraid you left already!

Willy: Why? What time is it?

Bernard: It's half-past one!

Willy: Well, come on, everybody! Ebbets Field next stop! Where's the pennants?
  (*He rushes through the wall-line of the kitchen and out into the living room.*)

Linda (*to Biff*): Did you pack fresh underwear?

Biff (*who has been limbering up*): I want to go!

Bernard: Biff, I'm carrying your helmet, ain't I?

Happy: No, I'm carrying the helmet.

Bernard: Oh, Biff, you promised me.

Happy: I'm carrying the helmet.

Bernard: How am I going to get in the locker room?

Linda: Let him carry the shoulder guards. (*She puts her coat and hat on in the kitchen.*)

Bernard: Can I, Biff? 'Cause I told everybody I'm going to be in the locker room.

Happy: In Ebbets Field it's the clubhouse.

Bernard: I meant the clubhouse. Biff!

Happy: Biff!

Biff (*grandly, after a slight pause*): Let him carry the shoulder guards.

Happy (*as he gives Bernard the shoulder guards*): Stay close to us now.

(*Willy rushes in with the pennants.*)

Willy (*handing them out*): Everybody wave when Biff comes out on the field. (*Happy and Bernard run off.*) You set now, boy?

(*The music has died away.*)

Biff: Ready to go, Pop. Every muscle is ready.

Willy (*at the edge of the apron*): You realize what this means?

Biff: That's right, Pop.

Willy (*feeling Biff's muscles*): You're comin' home this afternoon captain of the All-Scholastic Championship Team of the City of New York.

Biff: I got it, Pop. And remember, pal, when I take off my helmet, that touchdown is for you.

Willy: Let's go! (*He is starting out, with his arm around Biff, when Charley enters, as of old, in knickers.*) I got no room for you, Charley.

Charley: Room? For what?

Willy: In the car.

Charley: You goin' for a ride? I wanted to shoot some casino.

Willy (*furiously*): Casino! (*Incredulously.*) Don't you realize what today is?

Linda: Oh, he knows, Willy. He's just kidding you.

Willy: That's nothing to kid about!

Charley: No, Linda, what's goin' on?

Linda: He's playing in Ebbets Field.

Charley: Baseball in this weather?

Willy: Don't talk to him. Come on, come on! (*He is pushing them out.*)

Charley: Wait a minute, didn't you hear the news?

Willy: What?

Charley: Don't you listen to the radio? Ebbets Field just blew up.

Willy: You go to hell! (*Charley laughs. Pushing them out.*) Come on, come on! We're late.

Charley (*as they go*): Knock a homer, Biff, knock a homer!

Willy (*the last to leave, turning to Charley*): I don't think that was funny, Charley. This is the greatest day of his life.

Charley: Willy, when are you going to grow up?

Willy: Yeah, heh? When this game is over, Charley, you'll be laughing out of the other side of your face. They'll be calling him another Red Grange. Twenty-five thousand a year.

Charley (kidding): Is that so?

Willy: Yeah, that's so.

Charley: Well, then, I'm sorry, Willy. But tell me something.

Willy: What?

Charley: Who is Red Grange?

Willy: Put up your hands. Goddam you, put up your hands!

(*Charley, chuckling, shakes his head and walks away, around the left corner of the stage. Willy follows him. The music rises to a mocking frenzy.*)

Willy: Who the hell do you think you are, better than everybody else? You don't know everything, you big, ignorant, stupid . . . Put up your hands!

(*Light rises, on the right side of the forestage, on a small table in the reception room of Charley's office. Traffic sounds are heard. Bernard, now mature, sits whistling to himself. A pair of tennis rackets and an overnight bag are on the floor beside him.*)

Willy (offstage): What are you walking away for? Don't walk away! If you're going to say something say it to my face! I know you laugh at me behind my back. You'll laugh out of the other side of your goddam face after this game. Touchdown! Touchdown! Eighty thousand people! Touchdown! Right between the goal posts.

(*Bernard is a quiet, earnest, but self-assured young man. Willy's voice is coming from right upstage now. Bernard lowers his feet off the table and listens. Jenny, his father's secretary, enters.*)

Jenny (distressed): Say, Bernard, will you go out in the hall?

Bernard: What is that noise? Who is it?

Jenny: Mr. Loman. He just got off the elevator.

Bernard (getting up): Who's he arguing with?

Jenny: Nobody. There's nobody with him. I can't deal with him any more, and your father gets all upset everytime he comes. I've got a lot of typing to do, and your father's waiting to sign it. Will you see him?

Willy (entering): Touchdown! Touch—(*He sees Jenny.*) Jenny, Jenny, good to see you. How're ya? Workin'? Or still honest?

Jenny: Fine. How've you been feeling?

Willy: Not much any more, Jenny. Ha, ha! (*He is surprised to see the rackets.*)

Bernard: Hello, Uncle Willy.

Willy (almost shocked): Bernard! Well, look who's here! (*He comes quickly, guiltily, to Bernard and warmly shakes his hand.*)

Bernard: How are you? Good to see you.

Willy: What are you doing here?

Bernard: Oh, just stopped by to see Pop. Get off my feet till my train leaves. I'm going to Washington in a few minutes.

Willy: Is he in?

Bernard: Yes, he's in his office with the accountant. Sit down.

Willy (sitting down): What're you going to do in Washington?

Bernard: Oh, just a case I've got there, Willy.

Willy: That so? (*indicating the rackets.*) You going to play tennis there?

Bernard: I'm staying with a friend who's got a court.

Willy: Don't say. His own tennis court. Must be fine people, I bet.

Bernard: They are, very nice. Dad tells me Biff's in town.

Willy (with a big smile): Yeah, Biff's in. Working on a very big deal, Bernard.

Bernard: What's Biff doing?

Willy: Well, he's been doing very big things in the West. But he decided to establish himself here. Very big. We're having dinner. Did I hear your wife had a boy?

Bernard: That's right. Our second.

Willy: Two boys! What do you know!

Bernard: What kind of deal has Biff got?

Willy: Well, Bill Oliver—very big sporting-goods man—he wants Biff very badly. Called him in from the West. Long distance, carte blanche, special deliveries. Your friends have their own private tennis court?

Bernard: You still with the old firm, Willy?

Willy (after a pause): I'm—I'm overjoyed to see how you made the grade, Bernard, overjoyed. It's an encouraging thing to see a young man really—really—Looks very good for Biff—very—(He breaks off, then.) Bernard—(He is so full of emotion, he breaks off again.)

Bernard: What is it, Willy?

Willy (small and alone): What—what's the secret?

Bernard: What secret?

Willy: How—how did you? Why didn't he ever catch on?

Bernard: I wouldn't know that, Willy.

Willy (confidentially, desperately): You were his friend, his boyhood friend. There's something I don't understand about it. His life ended after that Ebbets Field game. From the age of seventeen nothing good ever happened to him.

Bernard: He never trained himself for anything.

Willy: But he did, he did. After high school he took so many correspondence courses. Radio mechanics; television; God knows what, and never made the slightest mark.

Bernard (taking off his glasses): Willy, do you want to talk candidly?

Willy (rising, faces Bernard): I regard you as a very brilliant man, Bernard. I value your advice.

Bernard: Oh, the hell with the advice, Willy. I couldn't advise you. There's just one thing I've always wanted to ask you. When he was supposed to graduate, and the math teacher flunked him—

Willy: Oh, that son-of-a-bitch ruined his life.

Bernard: Yeah, but, Willy, all he had to do was go to summer school and make up that subject.

Willy: That's right, that's right.

Bernard: Did you tell him not to go to summer school?

Willy: Me? I begged him to go. I ordered him to go!

Bernard: Then why wouldn't he go?

Willy: Why? Why! Bernard, that question has been trailing me like a ghost for the last fifteen years. He flunked the subject, and laid down and died like a hammer hit him!

Bernard: Take it easy, kid.

Willy: Let me talk to you—I got nobody to talk to. Bernard, Bernard, was it my fault? Y'see? It keeps going around in my mind, maybe I did something to him. I got nothing to give him.

Bernard: Don't take it so hard.

Willy: Why did he lay down? What is the story there? You were his friend!

Bernard: Willy, I remember, it was June, and our grades came out. And he'd flunked math.

Willy: That son-of-a-bitch!

Bernard: No, it wasn't right then. Biff just got very angry, I remember, and he was ready to enroll in summer school.

Willy (surprised): He was?

Bernard: He wasn't beaten by it at all. But then, Willy, he disappeared from the block for almost a month. And I got the idea that he'd gone up to New England to see you. Did he have a talk with you then?

(Willy stares in silence.)

Bernard: Willy?

Willy (with a strong edge of resentment in his voice): Yeah, he came to Boston. What about it?

Bernard: Well, just that when he came back—I'll never forget this, it always mystifies me. Because I'd thought so well of Biff, even though he'd always taken advantage of me. I loved him, Willy, y'know? And he came back after that month and took his sneakers—remember those sneakers with "University of Virginia" printed on them? He was so proud of those, wore them every day. And he took them down in the cellar, and burned them up in the furnace. We had a fist fight. It lasted at least half an hour. Just the two of us, punching each other down the cellar, and crying right through it. I've often thought of how strange it was that I knew he'd given up his life. What happened in Boston, Willy?

(Willy looks at him as at an intruder.)

Bernard: I just bring it up because you asked me.

Willy (angrily): Nothing. What do you mean, "What happened?" What's that got to do with anything?

Bernard: Well, don't get sore.

Willy: What are you trying to do, blame it on me? If a boy lays down is that my fault?

Bernard: Now, Willy, don't get—

Willy: Well, don't—don't talk to me that way! What does that mean, "What happened?"

(Charley enters. He is in his vest, and he carries a bottle of bourbon.)

Charley: Hey, you're going to miss that train. *(He waves the bottle.)*

Bernard: Yeah, I'm going. *(He takes the bottle.)* Thanks, Pop. *(He picks up his rackets and bag.)* Good-by, Willy, and don't worry about it. You know, "If at first you don't succeed . . ."

Willy: Yes, I believe in that.

Bernard: But sometimes, Willy, it's better for a man just to walk away.

Willy: Walk away?

Bernard: That's right.

Willy: But if you can't walk away?

Bernard (after a slight pause): I guess that's when it's tough. *(Extending his hand.)* Good-by, Willy.

Willy (*shaking Bernard's hand*): Good-by, boy.

Charley (*an arm on Bernard's shoulder*): How do you like this kid? Gonna argue a case in front of the Supreme Court.

Bernard (*protesting*): Pop!

Willy (*genuinely shocked, pained, and happy*): No! The Supreme Court!

Bernard: I gotta run. 'By, Dad!

Charley: Knock 'em dead, Bernard!

(*Bernard goes off.*)

Willy (*as Charley takes out his wallet*): The Supreme Court! And he didn't even mention it!

Charley (*counting out money on the desk*): He don't have to—he's gonna do it.

Willy: And you never told him what to do, did you? You never took any interest in him.

Charley: My salvation is that I never took any interest in anything. There's some money—fifty dollars. I got an accountant inside.

Willy: Charley, look . . . (*With difficulty.*) I got my insurance to pay. If you can manage it—I need a hundred and ten dollars.

(*Charley doesn't reply for a moment; merely stops moving.*)

Willy: I'd draw it from my bank but Linda would know, and I . . .

Charley: Sit down, Willy.

Willy (*moving toward the chair*): I'm keeping an account of everything, remember. I'll pay every penny back. (*He sits.*)

Charley: Now listen to me, Willy.

Willy: I want you to know I appreciate . . .

Charley (*sitting down on the table*): Willy, what're you doin'? What the hell is goin' on in your head?

Willy: Why? I'm simply . . .

Charley: I offered you a job. You can make fifty dollars a week. And I won't send you on the road.

Willy: I've got a job.

Charley: Without pay? What kind of a job is a job without pay? (*He rises.*) Now, look, kid, enough is enough. I'm no genius but I know when I'm being insulted.

Willy: Insulted!

Charley: Why don't you want to work for me?

Willy: What's the matter with you? I've got a job.

Charley: Then what're you walkin' in here every week for?

Willy (*getting up*): Well, if you don't want me to walk in here—

Charley: I am offering you a job.

Willy: I don't want your goddam job!

Charley: When the hell are you going to grow up?

Willy (*furiously*): You big ignoramus, if you say that to me again I'll rap you one! I don't care how big you are! (*He's ready to fight.*)

(*Pause.*)

Charley (*kindly, going to him*): How much do you need, Willy?

Willy: Charley, I'm strapped. I'm strapped. I don't know what to do. I was just fired.

Charley: Howard fired you?

Willy: That snotnose. Imagine that? I named him. I named him Howard.

Charley: Willy, when're you gonna realize that them things don't mean anything? You named him Howard, but you can't sell that. The only thing you got in this world is what you can sell. And the funny thing is that you're a salesman, and you don't know that.

Willy: I've always tried to think otherwise, I guess. I always felt that if a man was impressive, and well liked, that nothing—

Charley: Why must everybody like you? Who liked J. P. Morgan? Was he impressive? In a Turkish bath he'd look like a butcher. But with his pockets on he was very well liked. Now listen, Willy, I know you don't like me, and nobody can say I'm in love with you, but I'll give you a job because—just for the hell of it, put it that way. Now what do you say?

Willy: I—I just can't work for you, Charley.

Charley: What're you, jealous of me?

Willy: I can't work for you, that's all, don't ask me why.

Charley (angered, takes out more bills): You been jealous of me all your life, you damned fool! Here, pay your insurance. (*He puts the money in Willy's hand.*)

Willy: I'm keeping strict accounts.

Charley: I've got some work to do. Take care of yourself. And pay your insurance.

Willy (moving to the right): Funny, y'know? After all the highways, and the trains, and the appointments, and the years, you end up worth more dead than alive.

Charley: Willy, nobody's worth nothin' dead. (*After a slight pause.*) Did you hear what I said?

(*Willy stands still, dreaming.*)

Charley: Willy!

Willy: Apologize to Bernard for me when you see him. I didn't mean to argue with him. He's a fine boy. They're all fine boys, and they'll end up big—all of them. Someday they'll all play tennis together. Wish me luck, Charley. He saw Bill Oliver today.

Charley: Good luck.

Willy (on the verge of tears): Charley, you're the only friend I got. Isn't that a remarkable thing? (*He goes out.*)

Charley: Jesus!

(*Charley stares after him a moment and follows. All light blacks out. Suddenly raucous music is heard, and a red glow rises behind the screen at right. Stanley, a young waiter, appears, carrying a table, followed by Happy, who is carrying two chairs.*)

Stanley (putting the table down): That's all right, Mr. Loman, I can handle it myself. (*He turns and takes the chairs from Happy and places them at the table.*)

Happy (glancing around): Oh, this is better.

Stanley: Sure, in the front there you're in the middle of all kinds a noise. Whenever you got a party, Mr. Loman, you just tell me and I'll put you back here. Y'know, there's a lotta people they don't like it private, because when they go out they like to see a lotta action around them because they're sick and tired to stay in the house by theirself. But I know you, you ain't from Hackensack. You know what I mean?

Happy (sitting down): So how's it coming, Stanley?

Stanley: Ah, it's a dog's life. I only wish during the war they'd a took me in the Army. I coulda been dead by now.

Happy: My brother's back, Stanley.

Stanley: Oh, he come back, heh? From the Far West.

Happy: Yeah, big cattle man, my brother, so treat him right. And my father's coming too.

Stanley: Oh, your father too!

Happy: You got a couple of nice lobsters?

Stanley: Hundred per cent, big.

Happy: I want them with the claws.

Stanley: Don't worry, I don't give you no mice. (*Happy laughs.*) How about some wine? It'll put a head on the meal.

Happy: No. You remember, Stanley, that recipe I brought you from overseas? With the champagne in it?

Stanley: Oh, yeah, sure. I still got it tacked up yet in the kitchen. But that'll have to cost a buck apiece anyways.

Happy: That's all right.

Stanley: What'd you, hit a number or somethin'?

Happy: No, it's a little celebration. My brother is—I think he pulled off a big deal today. I think we're going into business together.

Stanley: Great! That's the best for you. Because a family business, you know what I mean?—that's the best.

Happy: That's what I think.

Stanley: 'Cause what's the difference? Somebody steals? It's in the family. Know what I mean? (*Sotto voce.*) Like this bartender here. The boss is goin' crazy what kinda leak he's got in the cash register. You put it in but it don't come out.

Happy (raising his head): Sh!

Stanley: What?

Happy: You notice I wasn't lookin' right or left, was I?

Stanley: No.

Happy: And my eyes are closed.

Stanley: So what's the—?

Happy: Strudel's comin'.

Stanley (catching on, looks around): Ah, no, there's no—

(*He breaks off as a furred, lavishly dressed Girl enters and sits at the next table. Both follow her with their eyes.*)

Stanley: Geez, how'd ya know?

Happy: I got radar or something. (*Staring directly at her profile.*) Oooooooo . . . Stanley.

Stanley: I think that's for you, Mr. Loman.

Happy: Look at that mouth. Oh, God. And the binoculars.

Stanley: Geez, you got a life, Mr. Loman.

Happy: Wait on her.

Stanley (going to The Girl's table): Would you like a menu, ma'am?

Girl: I'm expecting someone, but I'd like a—

Happy: Why don't you bring her—excuse me, miss, do you mind? I sell champagne, and I'd like you to try my brand. Bring her a champagne, Stanley.

Girl: That's awfully nice of you.

Happy: Don't mention it. It's all company money. (*He laughs.*)

Girl: That's a charming product to be selling, isn't it?

Happy: Oh, gets to be like everything else. Selling is selling, y'know.

Girl: I suppose.

Happy: You don't happen to sell, do you?

Girl: No, I don't sell.

Happy: Would you object to a compliment from a stranger? You ought to be on a magazine cover.

Girl (looking at him a little archly): I have been.

(*Stanley comes in with a glass of champagne.*)

Happy: What'd I say before, Stanley? You see? She's a cover girl.

Stanley: Oh, I could see, I could see.

Happy (to The Girl): What magazine?

Girl: Oh, a lot of them. (*She takes the drink.*) Thank you.

Happy: You know what they say in France, don't you? "Champagne is the drink of the complexion"—Hya, Biff!

(*Biff has entered and sits with Happy.*)

Biff: Hello, kid. Sorry I'm late.

Happy: I just got here. Uh, Miss—?

Girl: Forsythe.

Happy: Miss Forsythe, this is my brother.

Biff: Is Dad here?

Happy: His name is Biff. You might've heard of him. Great football player.

Girl: Really? What team?

Happy: Are you familiar with football?

Girl: No, I'm afraid I'm not.

Happy: Biff is quarterback with the New York Giants.

Girl: Well, that is nice, isn't it? (*She drinks.*)

Happy: Good health.

Girl: I'm happy to meet you.

Happy: That's my name. Hap. It's really Harold, but at West Point they called me Happy.

Girl (now really impressed): Oh, I see. How do you do? (*She turns her profile.*)

Biff: Isn't Dad coming?

Happy: You want her?

Biff: Oh, I could never make that.

Happy: I remember the time that idea would never come into your head. Where's the old confidence, Biff?

Biff: I just saw Oliver—

Happy: Wait a minute. I've got to see that old confidence again. Do you want her? She's on call.

Biff: Oh, no. (*He turns to look at The Girl.*)

Happy: I'm telling you. Watch this. (*Turning to The Girl.*) Honey? (*She turns to him.*) Are you busy?

Girl: Well, I am . . . but I could make a phone call.

Happy: Do that, will you, honey? And see if you can get a friend. We'll be here for a while. Biff is one of the greatest football players in the country.

Girl (standing up): Well, I'm certainly happy to meet you.

Happy: Come back soon.

Girl: I'll try.

Happy: Don't try, honey, try hard.

(*The Girl exits. Stanley follows, shaking his head in bewildered admiration.*)

Happy: Isn't that a shame now? A beautiful girl like that? That's why I can't get married. There's not a good woman in a thousand. New York is loaded with them, kid!

Biff: Hap, look—

Happy: I told you she was on call!

Biff (strangely unnerved): Cut it out, will ya? I want to say something to you.

Happy: Did you see Oliver?

Biff: I saw him all right. Now look, I want to tell Dad a couple of things and I want you to help me.

Happy: What? Is he going to back you?

Biff: Are you crazy? You're out of your goddam head, you know that?

Happy: Why? What happened?

Biff (breathlessly): I did a terrible thing today, Hap. It's been the strangest day I ever went through. I'm all numb, I swear.

Happy: You mean he wouldn't see you?

Biff: Well, I waited six hours for him, see? All day. Kept sending my name in. Even tried to date his secretary so she'd get me to him, but no soap.

Happy: Because you're not showin' the old confidence, Biff. He remembered you, didn't he?

Biff (stopping Happy with a gesture): Finally, about five o'clock, he comes out. Didn't remember who I was or anything. I felt like such an idiot, Hap.

Happy: Did you tell him my Florida idea?

Biff: He walked away. I saw him for one minute. I got so mad I could've torn the walls down! How the hell did I ever get the idea I was a salesman there? I even believed myself that I'd been a salesman for him! And then he gave me one look and—I realized what a ridiculous lie my whole life has been! We've been talking in a dream for fifteen years. I was a shipping clerk.

Happy: What'd you do?

Biff (with great tension and wonder): Well, he left, see. And the secretary went out. I was all alone in the waiting-room. I don't know what came over me, Hap. The next thing I know I'm in his office—paneled walls, everything. I can't explain it. I—Hap, I took his fountain pen.

Happy: Geez, did he catch you?

Biff: I ran out. I ran down all eleven flights. I ran and ran and ran.

Happy: That was an awful dumb—what'd you do that for?

Biff (*agonized*): I don't know, I just—wanted to take something, I don't know. You gotta help me, Hap. I'm gonna tell Pop.

Happy: You crazy? What for?

Biff: Hap, he's got to understand that I'm not the man somebody lends that kind of money to. He thinks I've been spiting him all these years and it's eating him up.

Happy: That's just it. You tell him something nice.

Biff: I can't.

Happy: Say you got a lunch date with Oliver tomorrow.

Biff: So what do I do tomorrow?

Happy: You leave the house tomorrow and come back at night and say Oliver is thinking it over. And he thinks it over for a couple of weeks, and gradually it fades away and nobody's the worse.

Biff: But it'll go on forever!

Happy: Dad is never so happy as when he's looking forward to something!

(*Willy enters.*)

Happy: Hello, scout!

Willy: Gee, I haven't been here in years!

(*Stanley has followed Willy in and sets a chair for him. Stanley starts off but Happy stops him.*)

Happy: Stanley!

(*Stanley stands by, waiting for an order.*)

Biff (*going to Willy with guilt, as to an invalid*): Sit down, Pop. You want a drink?

Willy: Sure, I don't mind.

Biff: Let's get a load on.

Willy: You look worried.

Biff: N-no. (*To Stanley.*) Scotch all around. Make it doubles.

Stanley: Doubles, right. (*He goes.*)

Willy: You had a couple already, didn't you?

Biff: Just a couple, yeah.

Willy: Well, what happened, boy? (*Nodding affirmatively, with a smile.*) Everything go all right?

Biff (*takes a breath, then reaches out and grasps Willy's hand*): Pal . . . (*He is smiling bravely, and Willy is smiling too.*) I had an experience today.

Happy: Terrific, Pop.

Willy: That so? What happened?

Biff (*high, slightly alcoholic, above the earth*): I'm going to tell you everything from first to last. It's been a strange day. (*Silence. He looks around, composes himself as best he can, but his breath keeps breaking the rhythm of his voice.*) I had to wait quite a while for him, and—

Willy: Oliver?

Biff: Yeah, Oliver. All day, as a matter of cold fact. And a lot of—instances—facts, Pop, facts about my life came back to me. Who was it, Pop? Who ever said I was a salesman with Oliver?

Willy: Well, you were.

Biff: No, Dad, I was a shipping clerk.

Willy: But you were practically—

Biff (with determination): Dad, I don't know who said it first, but I was never a salesman for Bill Oliver.

Willy: What're you talking about?

Biff: Let's hold on to the facts tonight, Pop. We're not going to get anywhere bullin' around. I was a shipping clerk.

Willy (angrily): All right, now listen to me—

Biff: Why don't you let me finish?

Willy: I'm not interested in stories about the past or any crap of that kind because the woods are burning, boys, you understand? There's a big blaze going on all around. I was fired today.

Biff (shocked): How could you be?

Willy: I was fired, and I'm looking for a little good news to tell your mother, because the woman has waited and the woman has suffered. The gist of it is that I haven't got a story left in my head, Biff. So don't give me a lecture about facts and aspects. I am not interested. Now what've you got to say to me?

(Stanley enters with three drinks. They wait until he leaves.)

Willy: Did you see Oliver?

Biff: Jesus, Dad!

Willy: You mean you didn't go up there?

Happy: Sure he went up there.

Biff: I did. I—saw him. How could they fire you?

Willy (on the edge of his chair): What kind of a welcome did he give you?

Biff: He won't even let you work on commission?

Willy: I'm out! (*Driving.*) So tell me, he gave you a warm welcome?

Happy: Sure, Pop, sure!

Biff (driven): Well, it was kind of—

Willy: I was wondering if he'd remember you. (*To Happy.*) Imagine, man doesn't see him for ten, twelve years and gives him that kind of welcome!

Happy: Damn right!

Biff (trying to return to the offensive): Pop, look—

Willy: You know why he remembered you, don't you? Because you impressed him in those days.

Biff: Let's talk quietly and get this down to the facts, huh?

Willy (as though Biff had been interrupting): Well, what happened? It's great news, Biff. Did he take you into his office or'd you talk in the waiting-room?

Biff: Well, he came in, see, and—

Willy (with a big smile): What'd he say? Betcha he threw his arm around you.

Biff: Well, he kinda—

Willy: He's a fine man. (*To Happy.*) Very hard man to see, y'know.

Happy (agreeing): Oh, I know.

Willy (to Biff): Is that where you had the drinks?

Biff: Yeah, he gave me a couple of—no, no!

Happy (cutting in): He told him my Florida idea.

Willy: Don't interrupt. (*To Biff.*) How'd he react to the Florida idea?

Biff: Dad, will you give me a minute to explain?

Willy: I've been waiting for you to explain since I sat down here! What happened? He took you into his office and what?

Biff: Well—I talked. And—and he listened, see.

Willy: Famous for the way he listens, y'know. What was his answer?

Biff: His answer was—(*He breaks off, suddenly angry.*) Dad, you're not letting me tell you what I want to tell you!

Willy (*accusing, angered*): You didn't see him, did you?

Biff: I did see him!

Willy: What'd you insult him or something? You insulted him, didn't you?

Biff: Listen, will you let me out of it, will you just let me out of it!

Happy: What the hell!

Willy: Tell me what happened!

Biff (*to Happy*): I can't talk to him!

(*A single trumpet note jars the ear. The light of green leaves stains the house, which holds the air of night and a dream. Young Bernard enters and knocks on the door of the house.*)

Young Bernard (*frantically*): Mrs. Loman, Mrs. Loman!

Happy: Tell him what happened!

Biff (*to Happy*): Shut up and leave me alone!

Willy: No, no! You had to go and flunk math!

Biff: What math? What're you talking about?

Young Bernard: Mrs. Loman, Mrs. Loman!

(*Linda appears in the house, as of old.*)

Willy (*wildly*): Math, math, math!

Biff: Take it easy, Pop.

Young Bernard: Mrs. Loman!

Willy (*furiously*): If you hadn't flunked you'd've been set by now!

Biff: Now, look, I'm gonna tell you what happened, and you're going to listen to me.

Young Bernard: Mrs. Loman!

Biff: I waited six hours—

Happy: What the hell are you saying?

Biff: I kept sending in my name but he wouldn't see me. So finally he . . . (*He continues unheard as light fades low on the restaurant.*)

Young Bernard: Biff flunked math!

Linda: No!

Young Bernard: Birnbaum flunked him! They won't graduate him!

Linda: But they have to. He's gotta go to the university. Where is he? Biff! Biff!

Young Bernard: No, he left. He went to Grand Central.

Linda: Grand—You mean he went to Boston?

Young Bernard: Is Uncle Willy in Boston?

Linda: Oh, maybe Willy can talk to the teacher. Oh, the poor, poor boy!

(*Light on house area snaps out.*)

Biff (*at the table, now audible, holding up a gold fountain pen*): . . . so I'm washed up with Oliver, you understand? Are you listening to me?

Willy (at a loss): Yeah, sure. If you hadn't flunked—

Biff: Flunked what? What're you talking about?

Willy: Don't blame everything on me! I didn't flunk math—you did! What pen?

Happy: That was awful dumb, Biff, a pen like that is worth—

Willy (seeing the pen for the first time): You took Oliver's pen?

Biff (weakening): Dad, I just explained it to you.

Willy: You stole Bill Oliver's fountain pen!

Biff: I didn't exactly steal it! That's just what I've been explaining to you!

Happy: He had it in his hand and just then Oliver walked in, so he got nervous and stuck it in his pocket!

Willy: My God, Biff!

Biff: I never intended to do it, Dad!

Operator's voice: Standish Arms, good evening!

Willy (shouting): I'm not in my room!

Biff (frightened): Dad, what's the matter? (*He and Happy stand up.*)

Operator: Ringing Mr. Loman for you!

Willy: I'm not there, stop it!

Biff (horrified, gets down on one knee before Willy): Dad, I'll make good, I'll make good. (*Willy tries to get to his feet. Biff holds him down.*) Sit down now.

Willy: No, you're no good, you're no good for anything.

Biff: I am, Dad, I'll find something else, you understand? Now don't worry about anything. (*He holds up Willy's face.*) Talk to me, Dad.

Operator: Mr. Loman does not answer. Shall I page him?

Willy (attempting to stand, as though to rush and silence the Operator): No, no, no!

Happy: He'll strike something, Pop.

Willy: No, no . . .

Biff (desperately, standing over Willy): Pop, listen! Listen to me! I'm telling you something good. Oliver talked to his partner about the Florida idea. You listening? He—he talked to his partner, and he came to me . . . I'm to be all right, you hear? Dad, listen to me, he said it was just a question of the amount!

Willy: Then you . . . got it?

Happy: He's gonna be terrific, Pop!

Willy (trying to stand): Then you got it, haven't you? You got it! You got it!

Biff (agonized, holds Willy down): No, no. Look, Pop. I'm supposed to have lunch with them tomorrow. I'm just telling you this so you'll know that I can still make an impression, Pop. And I'll make good somewhere, but I can't go tomorrow, see?

Willy: Why not? You simply—

Biff: But the pen, Pop!

Willy: You give it to him and tell him it was an oversight!

Happy: Sure, have lunch tomorrow!

Biff: I can't say that—

Willy: You were doing a crossword puzzle and accidentally used his pen!

Biff: Listen, kid, I took those balls years ago, now I walk in with his fountain pen? That clinches it, don't you see? I can't face him like that! I'll try elsewhere.

Page's voice: Paging Mr. Loman!

Willy: Don't you want to be anything?

Biff: Pop, how can I go back?

Willy: You don't want to be anything, is that what's behind it?

Biff (now angry at Willy for not crediting his sympathy): Don't take it that way! You think it was easy walking into that office after what I'd done to him? A team of horses couldn't have dragged me back to Bill Oliver!

Willy: Then why'd you go?

Biff: Why did I go? Why did I go? Look at you! Look at what's become of you!

(*Off left, The Woman laughs.*)

Willy: Biff, you're going to go to that lunch tomorrow, or—

Biff: I can't go. I've got no appointment!

Happy: Biff, for . . . !

Willy: Are you spiting me?

Biff: Don't take it that way! Goddammit!

Willy (strikes Biff and falters away from the table): You rotten little louse! Are you spiting me?

The Woman: Someone's at the door, Willy!

Biff: I'm no good, can't you see what I am?

Happy (separating them): Hey, you're in a restaurant! Now cut it out, both of you! (*The Girls enter.*) Hello, girls, sit down.

(*The Woman laughs, off left.*)

Miss Forsythe: I guess we might as well. This is Letta.

The Woman: Willy, are you going to wake up?

Biff (ignoring Willy): How're ya, miss, sit down. What do you drink?

Miss Forsythe: Letta might not be able to stay long.

Letta: I gotta get up very early tomorrow. I got jury duty. I'm so excited! Were you fellows ever on a jury?

Biff: No, but I been in front of them! (*The Girls laugh.*) This is my father.

Letta: Isn't he cute? Sit down with us, Pop.

Happy: Sit him down, Biff!

Biff (going to him): Come on, slugger, drink us under the table. To hell with it! Come on, sit down, pal.

(*On Biff's last insistence, Willy is about to sit.*)

The Woman (now urgently): Willy, are you going to answer the door!

(*The Woman's call pulls Willy back. He starts right, befuddled.*)

Biff: Hey, where are you going?

Willy: Open the door.

Biff: The door?

Willy: The washroom . . . the door . . . where's the door?

Biff (leading Willy to the left): Just go straight down.

(*Willy moves left.*)

The Woman: Willy, Willy, are you going to get up, get up, get up, get up?

(*Willy exits left.*)

Letta: I think it's sweet you bring your daddy along.

Miss Forsythe: Oh, he isn't really your father!

Biff (*at left, turning to her resentfully*): Miss Forsythe, you've just seen a prince walk by. A fine, troubled prince. A hard-working, unappreciated prince. A pal, you understand? A good companion. Always for his boys.

Letta: That's so sweet.

Happy: Well, girls, what's the program? We're wasting time. Come on, Biff. Gather round. Where would you like to go?

Biff: Why don't you do something for him?

Happy: Me!

Biff: Don't you give a damn for him, Hap?

Happy: What're you talking about? I'm the one who—

Biff: I sense it, you don't give a good goddam about him. (*He takes the rolled-up hose from his pocket and puts it on the table in front of Happy.*) Look what I found in the cellar, for Christ's sake. How can you bear to let it go on?

Happy: Me? Who goes away? Who runs off and—

Biff: Yeah, but he doesn't mean anything to you. You could help him—I can't! Don't you understand what I'm talking about? He's going to kill himself, don't you know that?

Happy: Don't I know it! Me!

Biff: Hap, help him! Jesus . . . Help him . . . Help me, help me, I can't bear to look at his face! (*Ready to weep, he hurries out, up right.*)

Happy (*starting after him*): Where are you going?

Miss Forsythe: What's he so mad about?

Happy: Come on, girls, we'll catch up with him.

Miss Forsythe (*as Happy pushes her out*): Say, I don't like that temper of his!

Happy: He's just a little overstrung, he'll be all right!

Willy (*off left, as The Woman laughs*): Don't answer! Don't answer!

Letta: Don't you want to tell your father—

Happy: No, that's not my father. He's just a guy. Come on, we'll catch Biff, and, honey, we're going to paint this town! Stanley, where's the check? Hey, Stanley!

(*They exit. Stanley looks toward left.*)

Stanley (*calling to Happy indignantly*): Mr. Loman! Mr. Loman!

(*Stanley picks up a chair and follows them off. Knocking is heard off left. The Woman enters, laughing. Willy follows her. She is in a black slip; he is buttoning his shirt. Raw, sensuous music accompanies their speech.*)

Willy: Will you stop laughing? Will you stop?

The Woman: Aren't you going to answer the door? He'll wake the whole hotel.

Willy: I'm not expecting anybody.

The Woman: Whyn't you have another drink, honey, and stop being so damn self-centered?

Willy: I'm so lonely.

The Woman: You know you ruined me, Willy? From now on, whenever you come to the office, I'll see that you go right through to the buyers. No waiting at my desk any more, Willy. You ruined me.

Willy: That's nice of you to say that.

The Woman: Gee, you are self-centered! Why so sad? You are the saddest self-centeredest soul I ever did see-saw. (*She laughs. He kisses her.*) Come on inside, drummer boy. It's silly to be dressing in the middle of the night. (*As knocking is heard.*) Aren't you going to answer the door?

Willy: They're knocking on the wrong door.

The Woman: But I felt the knocking. And he heard us talking in here. Maybe the hotel's on fire!

Willy (*his terror rising*): It's a mistake.

The Woman: Then tell him to go away!

Willy: There's nobody there.

The Woman: It's getting on my nerves, Willy. There's somebody standing out there and it's getting on my nerves!

Willy (*pushing her away from him*): All right, stay in the bathroom here, and don't come out. I think there's a law in Massachusetts about it, so don't come out. It may be that new room clerk. He looked very mean. So don't come out. It's a mistake, there's no fire.

(*The knocking is heard again. He takes a few steps away from her, and she vanishes into the wing. The light follows him, and now he is facing Young Biff, who carries a suitcase. Biff steps toward him. The music is gone.*)

Biff: Why didn't you answer?

Willy: Biff! What are you doing in Boston?

Biff: Why didn't you answer? I've been knocking for five minutes, I called you on the phone—

Willy: I just heard you. I was in the bathroom and had the door shut. Did anything happen at home?

Biff: Dad—I let you down.

Willy: What do you mean?

Biff: Dad . . .

Willy: Biffo, what's this about? (*Putting his arm around Biff.*) Come on, let's go downstairs and get you a malted.

Biff: Dad, I flunked math.

Willy: Not for the term?

Biff: The term. I haven't got enough credits to graduate.

Willy: You mean to say Bernard wouldn't give you the answers?

Biff: He did, he tried, but I only got a sixty-one.

Willy: And they wouldn't give you four points?

Biff: Birnbaum refused absolutely. I begged him, Pop, but he won't give me those points. You gotta talk to him before they close the school. Because if he saw the kind of man you are, and you just talked to him in your way, I'm sure he'd come through for me. The class came right before practice, see, and I didn't go enough. Would you talk to him? He'd like you, Pop. You know the way you could talk.

Willy: You're on. We'll drive right back.

Biff: Oh, Dad, good work! I'm sure he'll change it for you!

Willy: Go downstairs and tell the clerk I'm checkin' out. Go right down.

Biff: Yes, Sir! See, the reason he hates me, Pop—one day he was late for class so I got up at the blackboard and imitated him. I crossed my eyes and talked with a lithp.

Willy (laughing): You did? The kids like it?

Biff: They nearly died laughing!

Willy: Yeah? What'd you do?

Biff: The thquare root of thixthy twee is . . . (*Willy bursts out laughing; Biff joins him.*) And in the middle of it he walked in!

(*Willy laughs and The Woman joins in offstage.*)

Willy (without hesitating): Hurry downstairs and—

Biff: Somebody in there?

Willy: No, that was next door.

(*The Woman laughs offstage.*)

Biff: Somebody got in your bathroom!

Willy: No, it's the next room, there's a party—

The Woman (enters, laughing. She lisps this): Can I come in? There's something in the bathtub, Willy, and it's moving!

(*Willy looks at Biff, who is staring open-mouthed and horrified at The Woman.*)

Willy: Ah—you better go back to your room. They must be finished painting by now. They're painting her room so I let her take a shower here. Go back, go back . . . (*He pushes her.*)

The Woman (resisting): But I've got to get dressed, Willy, I can't—

Willy: Get out of here! Go back, go back . . . (*Suddenly striving for the ordinary.*) This is Miss Francis, Biff, she's a buyer. They're painting her room. Go back, Miss Francis, go back . . .

The Woman: But my clothes, I can't go out naked in the hall!

Willy (pushing her offstage): Get outa here! Go back, go back!

(*Biff slowly sits down on his suitcase as the argument continues offstage.*)

The Woman: Where's my stockings? You promised me stockings, Willy!

Willy: I have no stockings here!

The Woman: You had two boxes of size nine sheers for me, and I want them!

Willy: Here, for God's sake, will you get outa here!

The Woman (enters holding a box of stockings): I just hope there's nobody in the hall. That's all I hope. (*To Biff.*) Are you football or baseball?

Biff: Football.

The Woman (angry, humiliated): That's me too. G'night. (*She snatches her clothes from Willy, and walks out.*)

Willy (after a pause): Well, better get going. I want to get to the school first thing in the morning. Get my suits out of the closet. I'll get my valise. (*Biff doesn't move.*) What's the matter? (*Biff remains motionless, tears falling.*) She's a buyer. Buys for J. H. Simmons. She lives down the hall—they're painting. You don't imagine— (*He breaks off. After a pause.*) Now listen, pal, she's just a buyer. She sees merchandise in her room and they have to keep it looking just so . . . (*Pause. Assuming command.*) All right, get my suits. (*Biff doesn't move.*) Now stop crying and do as I say. I gave you an order. Biff, I gave you an order! Is that what you do when I give you an order? How dare you cry! (*Putting his arm around Biff.*) Now look, Biff, when you grow up you'll understand about these things. You mustn't— you mustn't overemphasize a thing like this. I'll see Birnbaum first thing in the morning.

Biff: Never mind.

Willy (getting down beside Biff): Never mind! He's going to give you those points. I'll see to it.

Biff: He wouldn't listen to you.

Willy: He certainly will listen to me. You need those points for the U. of Virginia.

Biff: I'm not going there.

Willy: Heh? If I can't get him to change that mark you'll make it up in summer school. You've got all summer to—

Biff (his weeping breaking from him): Dad . . .

Willy (infected by it): Oh, my boy . . .

Biff: Dad . . .

Willy: She's nothing to me, Biff. I was lonely, I was terribly lonely.

Biff: You—you gave her Mama's stockings! (*His tears break through and he rises to go.*)

Willy (grabbing for Biff): I gave you an order!

Biff: Don't touch me, you—liar!

Willy: Apologize for that!

Biff: You fake! You phony little fake! (*Overcome, he turns quickly and weeping fully goes out with his suitcase. Willy is left on the floor on his knees.*)

Willy: I gave you an order! Biff, come back here or I'll beat you! Come back here! I'll whip you!

(*Stanley comes quickly in from the right and stands in front of Willy.*)

Willy (shouts at Stanley): I gave you an order . . .

Stanley: Hey, let's pick it up, pick it up, Mr. Loman. (*He helps Willy to his feet.*) Your boys left with the chippies. They said they'll see you at home.

(*A second waiter watches some distance away.*)

Willy: But we were supposed to have dinner together.

(*Music is heard, Willy's theme.*)

Stanley: Can you make it?

Willy: I'll—sure, I can make it. (*Suddenly concerned about his clothes.*) Do I—I look all right?

Stanley: Sure, you look all right. (*He flicks a speck off Willy's lapel.*)

Willy: Here—here's a dollar.

Stanley: Oh, your son paid me. It's all right.

Willy (putting it in Stanley's hand): No, take it. You're a good boy.

Stanley: Oh, no, you don't have to . . .

Willy: Here—here's some more, I don't need it any more. (*After a slight pause.*) Tell me—is there a seed store in the neighborhood?

Stanley: Seeds? You mean like to plant?

(As Willy turns, Stanley slips the money back into his jacket pocket.)

Willy: Yes. Carrots, peas . . .

Stanley: Well, there's hardware stores on Sixth Avenue, but it may be too late now.

Willy (anxiously): Oh, I'd better hurry. I've got to get some seeds. (*He starts off to the right.*) I've got to get some seeds, right away. Nothing's planted. I don't have a thing in the ground.

(Willy hurries out as the light goes down. Stanley moves over to the right after him, watches him off. The other waiter has been staring at Willy.)

Stanley (to the waiter): Well, whatta you looking at?

(The waiter picks up the chairs and moves off right. Stanley takes the table and follows him. The light fades on this area. There is a long pause, the sound of the flute coming over. The light gradually rises on the kitchen, which is empty. Happy appears at the door of the house, followed by Biff. Happy is carrying a large bunch of long-stemmed roses. He enters the kitchen, looks around for Linda. Not seeing her, he turns to Biff, who is just outside the house door, and makes a gesture with his hands, indicating "Not here, I guess." He looks into the living room and freezes. Inside, Linda, unseen, is seated, Willy's coat on her lap. She rises ominously and quietly and moves toward Happy, who backs up into the kitchen, afraid.)

Happy: Hey, what're you doing up? (*Linda says nothing but moves toward him implacably.*) Where's Pop? (*He keeps backing to the right, and now Linda is in full view in the doorway to the living room.*) Is he sleeping?

Linda: Where were you?

Happy (trying to laugh it off): We met two girls, Mom, very fine types. Here, we brought you some flowers. (*Offering them to her.*) Put them in your room, Ma.

(She knocks them to the floor at Biff's feet. He has now come inside and closed the door behind him. She stares at Biff, silent.)

Happy: Now what'd you do that for? Mom, I want you to have some flowers—

Linda (cutting Happy off, violently to Biff): Don't you care whether he lives or dies?

Happy (going to the stairs): Come upstairs, Biff.

Biff (with a flare of disgust, to Happy): Go away from me! (*To Linda.*) What do you mean, lives or dies? Nobody's dying around here, pal.

Linda: Get out of my sight! Get out of here!

Biff: I wanna see the boss.

Linda: You're not going near him!

Biff: Where is he? (*He moves into the living room and Linda follows.*)

Linda (shouting after Biff): You invite him for dinner. He looks forward to it all day— (*Biff appears in his parents' bedroom, looks around, and exits*)—and then you desert him there. There's no stranger you'd do that to!

Happy: Why? He had a swell time with us. Listen, when I—(*Linda comes back into the kitchen*)—desert him I hope I don't outlive the day!

Linda: Get out of here!

Happy: Now look, Mom . . .

Linda: Did you have to go to women tonight? You and your lousy rotten whores!

(*Biff re-enters the kitchen.*)

Happy: Mom, all we did was follow Biff around trying to cheer him up! (*To Biff.*) Boy, what a night you gave me!

Linda: Get out of here, both of you, and don't come back! I don't want you torment- ing him anymore. Go on now, get your things together! (*To Biff.*) You can sleep in his apartment. (*She starts to pick up the flowers and stops herself.*) Pick up this stuff, I'm not your maid any more. Pick it up, you bum, you!

(*Happy turns his back to her in refusal. Biff slowly moves over and gets down on his knees, picking up the flowers.*)

Linda: You're a pair of animals! Not one, not another living soul would have had the cruelty to walk out on that man in a restaurant!

Biff (*not looking at her*): Is that what he said?

Linda: He didn't have to say anything. He was so humiliated he nearly limped when he came in.

Happy: But, Mom, he had a great time with us—

Biff (*cutting him off violently*): Shut up!

(*Without another word, Happy goes upstairs.*)

Linda: You! You didn't even go in to see if he was all right!

Biff (*still on the floor in front of Linda, the flowers in his hand; with self-loathing*): No. Didn't. Didn't do a damned thing. How do you like that, heh? Left him babbling in a toilet.

Linda: You louse. You . . .

Biff: Now you hit it on the nose! (*He gets up, throws the flowers in the wastebasket.*) The scum of the earth, and you're looking at him!

Linda: Get out of here!

Biff: I gotta talk to the boss, Mom. Where is he?

Linda: You're not going near him. Get out of this house!

Biff (*with absolute assurance, determination*): No. We're gonna have an abrupt conver- sation, him and me.

Linda: You're not talking to him!

(*Hammering is heard from outside the house, off right. Biff turns toward the noise.*)

Linda (*suddenly pleading*): Will you please leave him alone?

Biff: What's he doing out there?

Linda: He's planting the garden!

Biff (*quietly*): Now? Oh, my God!

(*Biff moves outside, Linda following. The light dies down on them and comes up on the center of the apron as Willy walks into it. He is carrying a flashlight, a hoe and a hand- ful of seed packets. He raps the top of the hoe sharply to fix it firmly, and then moves to the left, measuring off the distance with his foot. He holds the flashlight to look at the seed packets, reading off the instructions. He is in the blue of night.*)

Willy: Carrots . . . quarter-inch apart. Rows . . . one-foot rows. (*He measures it off.*) One foot. (*He puts down a package and measures off.*) Beets. (*He puts down another package and measures again.*) Lettuce. (*He reads the package, puts it down.*) One foot—(*He breaks off as Ben appears at the right and moves slowly down to him.*) What a proposition, ts, ts. Terrific, terrific. 'Cause she's suffered, Ben, the woman has suffered. You understand me? A man can't go out the way he came in, Ben, a man has got to add up to something. You can't, you can't—(*Ben moves toward him as though to interrupt.*) You gotta consider, now. Don't answer so quick. Remember, it's a guaranteed twenty-thousand-dollar proposition. Now look, Ben, I want you to go through the ins and outs of this thing with me. I've got nobody to talk to, Ben, and the woman has suffered, you hear me?

Ben (*standing still, considering*): What's the proposition?

Willy: It's twenty thousand dollars on the barrelhead. Guaranteed, gilt-edged, you understand?

Ben: You don't want to make a fool of yourself. They might not honor the policy.

Willy: How can they dare refuse? Didn't I work like a coolie to meet every premium on the nose? And now they don't pay off? Impossible!

Ben: It's called a cowardly thing, William.

Willy: Why? Does it take more guts to stand here the rest of my life ringing up a zero?

Ben (*yielding*): That's a point, William. (*He moves, thinking, turns.*) And twenty thousand—that is something one can feel with the hand, it is there.

Willy (*now assured, with rising power*): Oh, Ben, that's the whole beauty of it! I see it like a diamond, shining in the dark, hard and rough, that I can pick up and touch in my hand. Not like—like an appointment! This would not be another damned-fool appointment, Ben, and it changes all the aspects. Because he thinks I'm nothing, see, and so he spites me. But the funeral—(*Straightening up.*) Ben, that funeral will be massive! They'll come from Maine, Massachusetts, Vermont, New Hampshire! All the old-timers with the strange license plates—that boy will be thunder-struck, Ben, because he never realized—I am known! Rhode Island, New York, New Jersey—I am known, Ben, and he'll see it with his eyes once and for all. He'll see what I am, Ben! He's in for a shock, that boy!

Ben (*coming down to the edge of the garden*): He'll call you a coward.

Willy (*suddenly fearful*): No, that would be terrible.

Ben: Yes. And a damned fool.

Willy: No, no, he mustn't, I won't have that! (*He is broken and desperate.*)

Ben: He'll hate you, William.

(*The gay music of the boys is heard.*)

Willy: Oh, Ben, how do we get back to all the great times? Used to be so full of light, and comradeship, the sleigh-riding in winter, and the ruddiness on his cheeks. And always some kind of good news coming up, always something nice coming up ahead. And never even let me carry the valises in the house, and simonizing, simonizing that little red car! Why, why can't I give him something and not have him hate me?

Ben: Let me think about it. (*He glances at his watch.*) I still have a little time. Remarkable proposition, but you've got to be sure you're not making a fool of yourself.

(*Ben drifts off upstage and goes out of sight. Biff comes down from the left.*)

Willy (*suddenly conscious of Biff, turns and looks up at him, then begins picking up the packages of seeds in confusion*): Where the hell is that seed? (*Indignantly.*) You can't see nothing out here! They boxed in the whole goddam neighborhood!

Biff: There are people all around here. Don't you realize that?

Willy: I'm busy. Don't bother me.

Biff (taking the hoe from Willy): I'm saying good-by to you, Pop. (*Willy looks at him, silent, unable to move.*) I'm not coming back any more.

Willy: You're not going to see Oliver tomorrow?

Biff: I've got no appointment, Dad.

Willy: He put his arm around you, and you've got no appointment?

Biff: Pop, get this now, will you? Everytime I've left it's been a fight that sent me out of here. Today I realized something about myself and I tried to explain it to you and I—I think I'm just not smart enough to make any sense out of it for you. To hell with whose fault it is or anything like that. (*He takes Willy's arm.*) Let's just wrap it up, heh? Come on in, we'll tell Mom. (*He gently tries to pull Willy to the left.*)

Willy (frozen, immobile, with guilt in his voice): No, I don't want to see her.

Biff: Come on! (*He pulls again, and Willy tries to pull away.*)

Willy (highly nervous): No, no, I don't want to see her.

Biff (tries to look into Willy's face, as if to find the answer there): Why don't you want to see her?

Willy (more harshly now): Don't bother me, will you?

Biff: What do you mean, you don't want to see her? You don't want them calling you yellow, do you? This isn't your fault; it's me, I'm a bum. Now come inside! (*Willy strains to get away.*) Did you hear what I said to you?

(*Willy pulls away and quickly goes by himself into the house. Biff follows.*)

Linda (to Willy): Did you plant, dear?

Biff (at the door, to Linda): All right, we had it out. I'm going and I'm not writing any more.

Linda (going to Willy in the kitchen): I think that's the best way, dear. 'Cause there's no use drawing it out, you'll just never get along.

(*Willy doesn't respond.*)

Biff: People ask where I am and what I'm doing, you don't know, and you don't care. That way it'll be off your mind and you can start brightening up again. All right? That clears it, doesn't it? (*Willy is silent, and Biff goes to him.*) You gonna wish me luck, scout? (*He extends his hand.*) What do you say?

Linda: Shake his hand, Willy.

Willy (turning to her, seething with hurt): There's no necessity to mention the pen at all, y'know.

Biff (gently): I've got no appointment, Dad.

Willy (erupting fiercely): He put his arm around . . . ?

Biff: Dad, you're never going to see what I am, so what's the use of arguing? If I strike oil I'll send you a check. Meantime forget I'm alive.

Willy (to Linda): Spite, see?

Biff: Shake hands, Dad.

Willy: Not my hand.

Biff: I was hoping not to go this way.

Willy: Well, this is the way you're going. Good-by.

(*Biff looks at him a moment, then turns sharply and goes to the stairs.*)

Willy (*stops him with*): May you rot in hell if you leave this house!

Biff (*turning*): Exactly what is it that you want from me?

Willy: I want you to know, on the train, in the mountains, in the valleys, wherever you go, that you cut down your life for spite!

Biff: No, no.

Willy: Spite, spite, is the word of your undoing! And when you're down and out, remember what did it. When you're rotting somewhere beside the railroad tracks, remember, and don't you dare blame it on me!

Biff: I'm not blaming it on you!

Willy: I won't take the rap for this, you hear?

(*Happy comes down the stairs and stands on the bottom step, watching.*)

Biff: That's just what I'm telling you!

Willy (*sinking into a chair at the table, with full accusation*): You're trying to put a knife in me—don't think I don't know what you're doing!

Biff: All right, phony! Then let's lay it on the line. (*He whips the rubber tube out of his pocket and puts it on the table.*)

Happy: You crazy—

Linda: Biff! (*She moves to grab the hose, but Biff holds it down with his hand.*)

Biff: Leave it there! Don't move it!

Willy (*not looking at it*): What is that?

Biff: You know goddam well what that is.

Willy (*caged, wanting to escape*): I never saw that.

Biff: You saw it. The mice didn't bring it into the cellar! What is this supposed to do, make a hero out of you? This supposed to make me sorry for you?

Willy: Never heard of it.

Biff: There'll be no pity for you, you hear? No pity!

Willy (*to Linda*): You hear the spite!

Biff: No, you're going to hear the truth—what you are and what I am!

Linda: Stop it!

Willy: Spite!

Happy (*coming down toward Biff*): You cut it now!

Biff (*to Happy*): The man don't know who we are! The man is gonna know! (*To Willy.*) We never told the truth for ten minutes in this house!

Happy: We always told the truth!

Biff (*turning on him*): You big blow, are you the assistant buyer? You're one of the two assistants to the assistant, aren't you?

Happy: Well, I'm practically—

Biff: You're practically full of it! We all are! And I'm through with it. (*To Willy.*) Now hear this, Willy, this is me.

Willy: I know you!

Biff: You know why I had no address for three months? I stole a suit in Kansas City and I was in jail. (*To Linda, who is sobbing.*) Stop crying. I'm through with it.

(*Linda turns away from them, her hands covering her face.*)

Willy: I suppose that's my fault!

Biff: I stole myself out of every good job since high school!

Willy: And whose fault is that?

Biff: And I never got anywhere because you blew me so full of hot air I could never stand taking orders from anybody! That's whose fault it is!

Willy: I hear that!

Linda: Don't, Biff!

Biff: It's goddam time you heard that! I had to be boss big shot in two weeks, and I'm through with it!

Willy: Then hang yourself! For spite, hang yourself!

Biff: No! Nobody's hanging himself, Willy! I ran down eleven flights with a pen in my hand today. And suddenly I stopped, you hear me? And in the middle of that office building, do you hear this? I stopped in the middle of that building and I saw—the sky. I saw the things that I love in this world. The work and the food and time to sit and smoke. And I looked at the pen and said to myself, what the hell am I grabbing this for? Why am I trying to become what I don't want to be? What am I doing in an office, making a contemptuous, begging fool of myself, when all I want is out there, waiting for me the minute I say I know who I am! Why can't I say that, Willy? (*He tries to make Willy face him, but Willy pulls away and moves to the left.*)

Willy (*with hatred, threateningly*): The door of your life is wide open!

Biff: Pop! I'm a dime a dozen, and so are you!

Willy (*turning on him now in an uncontrolled outburst*): I am not a dime a dozen! I am Willy Loman, and you are Biff Loman!

(*Biff starts for Willy, but is blocked by Happy. In his fury, Biff seems on the verge of attacking his father.*)

Biff: I am not a leader of men, Willy, and neither are you. You were never anything but a hard-working drummer who landed in the ash can like all the rest of them! I'm one dollar an hour, Willy! I tried seven states and couldn't raise it. A buck an hour! Do you gather my meaning? I'm not bringing home any prizes any more, and you're going to stop waiting for me to bring them home!

Willy (*directly to Biff*): You vengeful, spiteful mutt!

(*Biff breaks from Happy. Willy, in fright, starts up the stairs. Biff grabs him.*)

Biff (*at the peak of his fury*): Pop, I'm nothing! I'm nothing, Pop. Can't you understand that? There's no spite in it any more. I'm just what I am, that's all.

(*Biff's fury has spent itself, and he breaks down, sobbing, holding on to Willy, who dumbly fumbles for Biff's face.*)

Willy (*astonished*): What're you doing? What're you doing? (*To Linda.*) Why is he crying?

Biff (*crying, broken*): Will you let me go, for Christ sake? Will you take that phony dream and burn it before something happens? (*Struggling to contain himself, he pulls away and moves to the stairs.*) I'll go in the morning. Put him—put him to bed. (*Exhausted, Biff moves up the stairs to his room.*)

Willy (*after a long pause, astonished, elevated*): Isn't that remarkable? Biff—he likes me!

Linda: He loves you, Willy!

Happy (deeply moved): Always did, Pop.

Willy: Oh, Biff! (*Staring wildly.*) He cried! Cried to me. (*He is choking with his love, and now cries out his promise.*) That boy—that boy is going to be magnificent!

(*Ben appears in the light just outside the kitchen.*)

Ben: Yes, outstanding, with twenty thousand behind him.

Linda (sensing the racing of his mind, fearfully, carefully): Now come to bed, Willy. It's all settled now.

Willy (finding it difficult not to rush out of the house): Yes, we'll sleep. Come on. Go to sleep, Hap.

Ben: And it does take a great kind of man to crack the jungle.

(*In accents of dread, Ben's idyllic music starts up.*)

Happy (his arm around Linda): I'm getting married, Pop, don't forget it. I'm changing everything. I'm gonna run that department before the year is up. You'll see, Mom. (*He kisses her.*)

Ben: The jungle is dark but full of diamonds, Willy.

(*Willy turns, moves, listening to Ben.*)

Linda: Be good. You're both good boys, just act that way, that's all.

Happy: 'Night, Pop. (*He goes upstairs.*)

Linda (to Willy): Come, dear.

Ben (with greater force): One must go in to fetch a diamond out.

Willy (to Linda, as he moves slowly along the edge of the kitchen, toward the door): I just want to get settled down, Linda. Let me sit alone for a little.

Linda (almost uttering her fear): I want you upstairs.

Willy (taking her in his arms): In a few minutes, Linda. I couldn't sleep right now. Go on, you look awful tired. (*He kisses her.*)

Ben: Not like an appointment at all. A diamond is rough and hard to the touch.

Willy: Go on now, I'll be right up.

Linda: I think this is the only way, Willy.

Willy: Sure, it's the best thing.

Ben: Best thing!

Willy: The only way. Everything is gonna be—go on, kid, get to bed. You look so tired.

Linda: Come right up.

Willy: Two minutes.

(*Linda goes into the living room, then reappears in her bedroom. Willy moves just outside the kitchen door.*)

Willy: Loves me. (*Wonderingly.*) Always loved me. Isn't that a remarkable thing? Ben, he'll worship me for it!

Ben (with promise): It's dark there, but full of diamonds.

Willy: Can you imagine that magnificence with twenty thousand dollars in his pocket?

Linda (calling from her room): Willy! Come up!

Willy (calling from the kitchen): Yes! Yes! Coming! It's very smart, you realize that, don't you, sweetheart? Even Ben sees it. I gotta go, baby. 'By! 'By! (*Going over to Ben, almost dancing.*) Imagine? When the mail comes he'll be ahead of Bernard again!

Ben: A perfect proposition all around.

Willy: Did you see how he cried to me? Oh, if I could kiss him, Ben!

Ben: Time, William, time!

Willy: Oh, Ben, I always knew one way or another we were gonna make it, Biff and I!

Ben (*looking at his watch*): The boat. We'll be late. (*He moves slowly off into the darkness.*)

Willy (*elegiacally, turning to the house*): Now when you kick off, boy, I want a seventy-yard boot, and get right down the field under the ball, and when you hit, hit low and hit hard, because it's important, boy. (*He swings around and faces the audience.*) There's all kinds of important people in the stands, and the first thing you know . . . (*Suddenly realizing he is alone.*) Ben! Ben, where do I . . . ? (*He makes a sudden movement of search.*) Ben, how do I . . . ?

Linda (*calling*): Willy, you coming up?

Willy (*uttering a gasp of fear, whirling about as if to quiet her*): Sh! (*He turns around as if to find his way; sounds, faces, voices, seem to be swarming in upon him and he flicks at them, crying.*) Sh! Sh! (*Suddenly music, faint and high, stops him. It rises in intensity, almost to an unbearable scream. He goes up and down on his toes, and rushes off around the house.*) Shhh!

Linda: Willy?

(*There is no answer. Linda waits. Biff gets up off his bed. He is still in his clothes. Happy sits up. Biff stands listening.*)

Linda (*with real fear*): Willy, answer me! Willy!

(*There is the sound of a car starting and moving away at full speed.*)

Linda: No!

Biff (*rushing down the stairs*): Pop!

As the car speeds off, the music crashes down in a frenzy of sound, which becomes the soft pulsation of a single cello string. Biff slowly returns to his bedroom. He and Happy gravely don their jackets. Linda slowly walks out of her room. The music has developed into a dead march. The leaves of day are appearing over everything. Charley and Bernard, somberly dressed, appear and knock on the kitchen door. Biff and Happy slowly descend the stairs to the kitchen as Charley and Bernard enter. All stop a moment when Linda, in clothes of mourning, bearing a little bunch of roses, comes through the draped doorway into the kitchen. She goes to Charley and takes his arm. Now all move toward the audience, through the wall-line of the kitchen. At the limit of the apron, Linda lays down the flowers, kneels, and sits back on her heels. All stare down at the grave.

REQUIEM

Charley: It's getting dark, Linda.

(*Linda doesn't react. She stares at the grave.*)

Biff: How about it, Mom? Better get some rest, heh? They'll be closing the gate soon.

(*Linda makes no move. Pause.*)

Happy (*deeply angered*): He had no right to do that! There was no necessity for it. We would've helped him.

Charley (*grunting*): Hmmm.

Biff: Come along, Mom.

Linda: Why didn't anybody come?

Charley: It was a very nice funeral.

Linda: But where are all the people he knew? Maybe they blame him.

Charley: Naa. It's a rough world, Linda. They wouldn't blame him.

Linda: I can't understand it. At this time especially. First time in thirty-five years we were just about free and clear. He only needed a little salary. He was even finished with the dentist.

Charley: No man only needs a little salary.

Linda: I can't understand it.

Biff: There were a lot of nice days. When he'd come home from a trip; or on Sundays, making the stoop; finishing the cellar; putting on the new porch; when he built the extra bathroom; and put up the garage. You know something, Charley, there's more of him in that front stoop than in all the sales he ever made.

Charley: Yeah. He was a happy man with a batch of cement.

Linda: He was so wonderful with his hands.

Biff: He had the wrong dreams. All, all, wrong.

Happy (almost ready to fight Biff): Don't say that!

Biff: He never knew who he was.

Charley (stopping Happy's movement and reply. To Biff): Nobody dast blame this man. You don't understand: Willy was a salesman. And for a salesman, there is no rock bottom to the life. He don't put a bolt to a nut, he don't tell you the law or give you medicine. He's a man out there in the blue, riding on a smile and a shoeshine. And when they start not smiling back—that's an earthquake. And then you get yourself a couple of spots on your hat, and you're finished. Nobody dast blame this man. A salesman is got to dream, boy. It comes with the territory.

Biff: Charley, the man didn't know who he was.

Happy (infuriated): Don't say that!

Biff: Why don't you come with me, Happy?

Happy: I'm not licked that easily. I'm staying right in this city, and I'm gonna beat this racket! (*He looks at Biff, his chin set.*) The Loman Brothers!

Biff: I know who I am, kid.

Happy: All right, boy. I'm gonna show you and everybody else that Willy Loman did not die in vain. He had a good dream. It's the only dream you can have—to come out number-one man. He fought it out here, and this is where I'm gonna win it for him.

Biff (with a hopeless glance at Happy, bends toward his mother): Let's go, Mom.

Linda: I'll be with you in a minute. Go on, Charley. (*He hesitates.*) I want to, just for a minute. I never had a chance to say good-by.

(*Charley moves away, followed by Happy. Biff remains a slight distance up and left of Linda. She sits there, summoning herself. The flute begins, not far away, playing behind her speech.*)

Linda: Forgive me, dear. I can't cry. I don't know what it is, but I can't cry. I don't understand it. Why did you ever do that? Help me, Willy, I can't cry. It seems to me that you're just on another trip. I keep expecting you. Willy, dear, I can't cry. Why did you do it? I search and search and search, and I can't understand it, Willy. I made the last payment on the house today. Today, dear. And there'll be nobody home. (*A sob rises in her throat.*) We're free and clear. (*Sobbing more fully, released.*) We're free. (*Biff comes slowly toward her.*) We're free ... We're free ...

Biff lifts her to her feet and moves out up right with her in his arms. Linda sobs quietly. Bernard and Charley come together and follow them, followed by Happy. Only the music of the flute is left on the darkening stage as over the house the hard towers of the apartment buildings rise into sharp focus, and—

THE CURTAIN FALLS

Arthur Miller on Writing

Tragedy and the Common Man[1]

1949

In this age few tragedies are written. It has often been held that the lack is due to a paucity of heroes among us, or else that modern man has had the blood drawn out of his organs of belief by the skepticism of science, and the heroic attack on life cannot feed on an attitude of reserve and circumspection. For one reason or another, we are often held to be below tragedy—or tragedy above us. The inevitable conclusion is, of course, that the tragic mode is archaic, fit only for the very highly placed, the kings or the kingly, and where this admission is not made in so many words it is most often implied.

Arthur Miller

I believe that the common man is as apt a subject for tragedy in its highest sense as kings were. On the face of it this ought to be obvious in the light of modern psychiatry, which bases its analysis upon classific formulations, such as the Oedipus and Orestes complexes, for instance, which were enacted by royal beings, but which apply to everyone in similar emotional situations.

More simply, when the question of tragedy in art is not at issue, we never hesitate to attribute to the well-placed and the exalted the very same mental processes as the lowly. And finally, if the exaltation of tragic action were truly a property of the high-bred character alone, it is inconceivable that the mass of mankind should cherish tragedy above all other forms, let alone be capable of understanding it.

As a general rule, to which there may be exceptions unknown to me, I think the tragic feeling is evoked in us when we are in the presence of a character who is ready to lay down his life, if need be, to secure one thing—his sense of personal dignity. From Orestes to Hamlet, Medea to Macbeth, the underlying struggle is that of the individual attempting to gain his "rightful" position in his society.

Sometimes he is one who has been displaced from it, sometimes one who seeks to attain it for the first time, but the fateful wound from which the inevitable events spiral is the wound of indignity, and its dominant force is indignation. Tragedy, then, is the consequence of a man's total compulsion to evaluate himself justly.

[1]This essay was originally published in the *New York Times*, February 27, 1949.

In the sense of having been initiated by the hero himself, the tale always reveals what has been called his "tragic flaw," a failing that is not peculiar to grand or elevated characters. Nor is it necessarily a weakness. The flaw, or crack in the character, is really nothing—and need be nothing—but his inherent unwillingness to remain passive in the face of what he conceives to be a challenge to his dignity, his image of his rightful status. Only the passive, only those who accept their lot without active retaliation, are "flawless." Most of us are in that category.

But there are among us today, as there always have been, those who act against the scheme of things that degrades them, and in the process of action, everything we have accepted out of fear or insensitivity or ignorance is shaken before us and examined, and from this total onslaught by an individual against the seemingly stable cosmos surrounding us—from this total examination of the "unchangeable" environment— comes the terror and the fear that is classically associated with tragedy.

More important, from this total questioning of what has been previously unquestioned, we learn. And such a process is not beyond the common man. In revolutions around the world, these past thirty years, he has demonstrated again and again this inner dynamic of all tragedy.

Insistence upon the rank of the tragic hero, or the so-called nobility of his character, is really but a clinging to the outward forms of tragedy. If rank or nobility of character was indispensable, then it would follow that the problems of those with rank were the particular problems of tragedy. But surely the right of one monarch to capture the domain from another no longer raises our passions, nor are our concepts of justice what they were to the mind of an Elizabethan king.

The quality in such plays that does shake us, however, derives from the underlying fear of being displaced, the disaster inherent in being torn away from our chosen image of what and who we are in this world. Among us today this fear is as strong, and perhaps stronger, than it ever was. In fact, it is the common man who knows this fear best.

Now, if it is true that tragedy is the consequence of a man's total compulsion to evaluate himself justly, his destruction in the attempt posits a wrong or an evil in his environment. And this is precisely the morality of tragedy and its lesson. The discovery of the moral law, which is what the enlightenment of tragedy consists of, is not the discovery of some abstract or metaphysical quantity.

The tragic right is a condition of life, a condition in which the human personality is able to flower and realize itself. The wrong is the condition which suppresses man, perverts the flowing out of his love and creative instinct. Tragedy enlightens— and it must, in that it points the heroic finger at the enemy of man's freedom. The thrust for freedom is the quality in tragedy which exalts. The revolutionary questioning of the stable environment is what terrifies. In no way is the common man debarred from such thoughts or such actions.

Seen in this light, our lack of tragedy may be partially accounted for by the turn which modern literature has taken toward the purely psychiatric view of life, or the purely sociological. If all our miseries, our indignities, are born and bred within our minds, then all action, let alone the heroic action, is obviously impossible.

And if society alone is responsible for the cramping of our lives, then the protagonist must needs be so pure and faultless as to force us to deny his validity as a character. From neither of these views can tragedy derive, simply because neither represents a balanced concept of life. Above all else, tragedy requires the finest appreciation by the writer of cause and effect.

No tragedy can therefore come about when its author fears to question absolutely everything, when he regards any institution, habit or custom as being either everlasting, immutable or inevitable. In the tragic view the need of man to wholly realize himself is the only fixed star, and whatever it is that hedges his nature and lowers it is ripe for attack and examination. Which is not to say that tragedy must preach revolution.

The Greeks could probe the very heavenly origin of their ways and return to confirm the rightness of laws. And Job could face God in anger, demanding his right, and end in submission. But for a moment everything is in suspension, nothing is accepted, and in this stretching and tearing apart of the cosmos, in the very action of so doing, the character gains "size," the tragic stature which is spuriously attached to the royal or the high born in our minds. The commonest of men may take on that stature to the extent of his willingness to throw all he has into the contest, the battle to secure his rightful place in his world.

There is a misconception of tragedy with which I have been struck in review after review, and in many conversations with writers and readers alike. It is the idea that tragedy is of necessity allied to pessimism. Even the dictionary says nothing more about the word than that it means a story with a sad or unhappy ending. This impression is so firmly fixed that I almost hesitate to claim that in truth tragedy implies more optimism in its author than does comedy, and that its final result ought to be the reinforcement of the onlooker's brightest opinions of the human animal.

For, if it is true to say that in essence the tragic hero is intent upon claiming his whole due as a personality, and if this struggle must be total and without reservation, then it automatically demonstrates the indestructible will of man to achieve his humanity.

The possibility of victory must be there in tragedy. Where pathos rules, where pathos is finally derived, a character has fought a battle he could not possibly have won. The pathetic is achieved when the protagonist is, by virtue of his witlessness, his insensitivity, or the very air he gives off, incapable of grappling with a much superior force.

Pathos truly is the mode for the pessimist. But tragedy requires a nicer balance between what is possible and what is impossible. And it is curious, although edifying, that the plays we revere, century after century, are the tragedies. In them, and in them alone, lies the belief—optimistic, if you will—in the perfectibility of man.

It is time, I think, that we who are without kings took up this bright thread of our history and followed it to the only place it can possibly lead in our time—the heart and spirit of the average man.

From *The Theater Essays of Arthur Miller*

August Wilson

Fences   1985

August Wilson (1945–2005) was born in Pittsburgh, one of six children of a German American father and an African American mother. His parents separated early, and the young Wilson was raised on the Hill, a Pittsburgh ghetto neighborhood. Although he quit school in the ninth grade when a teacher wrongly accused him of submitting a ghost-written paper, Wilson continued his education in local libraries, supporting himself by working as a cook and stock clerk. In 1968 he co-founded a community troupe, the Black Horizons Theater, staging plays by LeRoi Jones and other militants; later he moved from Pittsburgh to Saint Paul, Minnesota,

Viola Davis and Denzel Washington in 2010 Broadway production of *Fences*.

where at last he saw a play of his own performed. Jitney, his first important work, won him entry to a 1982 playwrights' conference at the Eugene O'Neill Theater Center. There, Lloyd Richards, dean of Yale University School of Drama, took an interest in Wilson's work and offered to produce his plays at Yale. Ma Rainey's Black Bottom was the first to reach Broadway (in 1985), where it ran for ten months and received an award from the New York Drama Critics Circle. In 1987 Fences, starring Mary Alice and James Earl Jones, won another Critics Circle Award, as well as a Tony Award and the Pulitzer Prize for best American play of its year. It set a box office record for a Broadway nonmusical. Joe Turner's Come and Gone (1988) also received high acclaim, and The Piano Lesson (1990) won Wilson a second Pulitzer Prize. His subsequent plays were Two Trains Running (1992), Seven Guitars (1995), King Hedley II (2000), Gem of the Ocean (2003), and Radio Golf (2005).

Wilson's ten plays, each one set in a different decade of the 1900s, constitute his "Century Cycle" that traces the black experience in America throughout the twentieth century. Seamlessly interweaving realistic and mythic approaches, filled with vivid characters, pungent dialogue, and strong dramatic scenes, it is one of the most ambitious projects in the history of the American theater and an epic achievement in our literature. Wilson died of liver cancer in October 2005, a few months after completing the final play in his cycle. Two weeks after his death the Virginia Theater on Broadway was renamed the August Wilson Theater in his honor. A published poet as well as a dramatist, Wilson once told an interviewer, "After writing poetry for twenty-one years, I approach a play the same way. The mental process is poetic: you use metaphor and condense."

Mary Alice, Ray Aranha, and James Earl Jones in Yale Repertory Theatre's 1985 world premiere of *Fences*.

For Lloyd Richards, Who Adds to Whatever He Touches

> When the sins of our fathers visit us
> We do not have to play host.
> We can banish them with forgiveness
> As God, in His Largeness and Laws.

> —AUGUST WILSON

LIST OF CHARACTERS

Troy Maxson
Jim Bono, Troy's friend
Rose, Troy's wife
Lyons, Troy's oldest son by previous marriage
Gabriel, Troy's brother
Cory, Troy and Rose's son
Raynell, Troy's daughter

SETTING. *The setting is the yard which fronts the only entrance to the Maxson household, an ancient two-story brick house set back off a small alley in a big-city neighborhood. The entrance to the house is gained by two or three steps leading to a wooden porch badly in need of paint.*

A relatively recent addition to the house and running its full width, the porch lacks congruence. It is a sturdy porch with a flat roof. One or two chairs of dubious value sit at one end where the kitchen window opens onto the porch. An old-fashioned icebox stands silent guard at the opposite end.

The yard is a small dirt yard, partially fenced, except for the last scene, with a wooden saw horse, a pile of lumber, and other fence-building equipment set off to the side. Opposite is a tree from which hangs a ball made of rags. A baseball bat leans against the tree. Two oil drums serve as garbage receptacles and sit near the house at right to complete the setting.

THE PLAY. *Near the turn of the century, the destitute of Europe sprang on the city with tenacious claws and an honest and solid dream. The city devoured them. They swelled its belly until it burst into a thousand furnaces and sewing machines, a thousand butcher shops and bakers' ovens, a thousand churches and hospitals and funeral parlors and money-lenders. The city grew. It nourished itself and offered each man a partnership limited only by his talent, his guile, and his willingness and capacity for hard work. For the immigrants of Europe, a dream dared and won true.*

The descendants of African slaves were offered no such welcome or participation. They came from places called the Carolinas and the Virginias, Georgia, Alabama, Mississippi, and Tennessee. They came strong, eager, searching. The city rejected them and they fled and settled along the riverbanks and under bridges in shallow, ramshackle houses made of sticks and tarpaper. They collected rags and wood. They sold the use of their muscles and their bodies. They cleaned houses and washed clothes, they shined shoes, and in quiet desperation and vengeful pride, they stole, and lived in pursuit of their own dream. That they could breathe free, finally, and stand to meet life with the force of dignity and whatever eloquence the heart could call upon.

By 1957, the hard-won victories of the European immigrants had solidified the industrial might of America. War had been confronted and won with new energies that used loyalty and patriotism as its fuel. Life was rich, full, and flourishing. The Milwaukee Braves won the World Series, and the hot winds of change that would make the sixties a turbulent, racing, dangerous, and provocative decade had not yet begun to blow full.

ACT I

SCENE I

It is 1957. Troy and Bono enter the yard, engaged in conversation. Troy is fifty-three years old, a large man with thick, heavy hands; it is this largeness that he strives to fill out and make an accommodation with. Together with his blackness, his largeness informs his sensibilities and the choices he has made in his life.

Of the two men, Bono is obviously the follower. His commitment to their friendship of thirty-odd years is rooted in his admiration of Troy's honesty, capacity for hard work, and his strength, which Bono seeks to emulate.

It is Friday night, payday, and the one night of the week the two men engage in a ritual of talk and drink. Troy is usually the most talkative and at times he can be crude and almost vulgar, though he is capable of rising to profound heights of expression. The men carry lunch buckets and wear or carry burlap aprons and are dressed in clothes suitable to their jobs as garbage collectors.

Bono: Troy, you ought to stop that lying!

Troy: I ain't lying! The nigger had a watermelon this big. (*He indicates with his hands.*) Talking about . . . "What watermelon, Mr. Rand?" I liked to fell out! "What watermelon, Mr. Rand?" . . . And it sitting there big as life.

Bono: What did Mr. Rand say?

Troy: Ain't said nothing. Figure if the nigger too dumb to know he carrying a watermelon, he wasn't gonna get much sense out of him. Trying to hide that great big old watermelon under his coat. Afraid to let the white man see him carry it home.

Bono: I'm like you . . . I ain't got no time for them kind of people.

Troy: Now what he look like getting mad cause he see the man from the union talking to Mr. Rand?

Bono: He come to me talking about . . . "Maxson gonna get us fired." I told him to get away from me with that. He walked away from me calling you a troublemaker. What Mr. Rand say?

Troy: Ain't said nothing. He told me to go down the Commissioner's office next Friday. They called me down there to see them.

Bono: Well, as long as you got your complaint filed, they can't fire you. That's what one of them white fellows tell me.

Troy: I ain't worried about them firing me. They gonna fire me cause I asked a question? That's all I did. I went to Mr. Rand and asked him, "Why? Why you got the white mens driving and the colored lifting?" Told him, "what's the matter, don't I count? You think only white fellows got sense enough to drive a truck. That ain't no paper job! Hell, anybody can drive a truck. How come you got all whites driving and the colored lifting?" He told me "take it to the union." Well, hell, that's what I done! Now they wanna come up with this pack of lies.

Bono: I told Brownie if the man come and ask him any questions . . . just tell the truth! It ain't nothing but something they done trumped up on you cause you filed a complaint on them.

Troy: Brownie don't understand nothing. All I want them to do is change the job description. Give everybody a chance to drive the truck. Brownie can't see that. He ain't got that much sense.

Bono: How you figure he be making out with that gal be up at Taylors' all the time . . . that Alberta gal?

Troy: Same as you and me. Getting just as much as we is. Which is to say nothing.

Bono: It is, huh? I figure you doing a little better than me . . . and I ain't saying what I'm doing.

Troy: Aw, nigger, look here . . . I know you. If you had got anywhere near that gal, twenty minutes later you be looking to tell somebody. And the first one you gonna tell . . . that you gonna want to brag to . . . is gonna be me.

Bono: I ain't saying that. I see where you be eyeing her.

Troy: I eye all the women. I don't miss nothing. Don't never let nobody tell you Troy Maxson don't eye the women.

Bono: You been doing more than eyeing her. You done bought her a drink or two.

Troy: Hell yeah, I bought her a drink! What that mean? I bought you one, too. What that mean cause I buy her a drink? I'm just being polite.

Bono: It's alright to buy her one drink. That's what you call being polite. But when you wanna be buying two or three . . . that's what you call eyeing her.

Troy: Look here, as long as you known me . . . you ever known me to chase after women?

Bono: Hell yeah! Long as I done known you. You forgetting I knew you when.

Troy: Naw, I'm talking about since I been married to Rose?

Bono: Oh, not since you been married to Rose. Now, that's the truth, there. I can say that.

Troy: Alright then! Case closed.

Bono: I see you be walking up around Alberta's house. You supposed to be at Taylors' and you be walking up around there.

Troy: What you watching where I'm walking for? I ain't watching after you.

Bono: I seen you walking around there more than once.

Troy: Hell, you liable to see me walking anywhere! That don't mean nothing cause you see me walking around there.

Bono: Where she come from anyway? She just kinda showed up one day.

Troy: Tallahassee. You can look at her and tell she one of them Florida gals. They got some big healthy women down there. Grow them right up out the ground. Got a little bit of Indian in her. Most of them niggers down in Florida got some Indian in them.

Bono: I don't know about that Indian part. But she damn sure big and healthy. Woman wear some big stockings. Got them great big old legs and hips as wide as the Mississippi River.

Troy: Legs don't mean nothing. You don't do nothing but push them out of the way. But them hips cushion the ride!

Bono: Troy, you ain't got no sense.

Troy: It's the truth! Like you riding on Goodyears!

(*Rose enters from the house. She is ten years younger than Troy, her devotion to him stems from her recognition of the possibilities of her life without him: a succession of abusive men and their babies, a life of partying and running the streets, the Church, or aloneness with its attendant pain and frustration. She recognizes Troy's spirit as a fine and illuminating one and she either ignores or forgives his faults, only some of which she recognizes. Though she doesn't drink, her presence is an integral part of the Friday night rituals. She alternates between the porch and the kitchen, where supper preparations are under way.*)

Rose: What you all out here getting into?

Troy: What you worried about what we getting into for? This is men talk, woman.

Rose: What I care what you all talking about? Bono, you gonna stay for supper?

Bono: No, I thank you, Rose. But Lucille say she cooking up a pot of pigfeet.

Troy: Pigfeet! Hell, I'm going home with you! Might even stay the night if you got some pigfeet. You got something in there to top them pigfeet, Rose?

Rose: I'm cooking up some chicken. I got some chicken and collard greens.

Troy: Well, go on back in the house and let me and Bono finish what we was talking about. This is men talk. I got some talk for you later. You know what kind of talk I mean. You go on and powder it up.

Rose: Troy Maxson, don't you start that now!

Troy (*puts his arm around her*): Aw, woman . . . come here. Look here, Bono . . . . when I met this woman . . . I got out that place, say, "Hitch up my pony, saddle up my mare . . . there's a woman out there for me somewhere. I looked here. Looked there. Saw Rose and latched on to her." I latched on to her and told her—I'm gonna tell you the truth—I told her, "Baby, I don't wanna marry, I just wanna be your man." Rose told me . . . tell him what you told me, Rose.

Rose: I told him if he wasn't the marrying kind, then move out the way so the marrying kind could find me.

Troy: That's what she told me. "Nigger, you in my way. You blocking the view! Move out the way so I can find me a husband." I thought it over two or three days. Come back—

Rose: Ain't no two or three days nothing. You was back the same night.

Troy: Come back, told her . . . "Okay, baby . . . but I'm gonna buy me a banty rooster and put him out there in the backyard . . . and when he see a stranger come, he'll flap his wings and crow . . ." Look here, Bono, I could watch the front door by myself . . . it was that back door I was worried about.

Rose: Troy, you ought not talk like that. Troy ain't doing nothing but telling a lie.

Troy: Only thing is . . . when we first got married . . . forget the rooster . . . we ain't had no yard!

Bono: I hear you tell it. Me and Lucille was staying down there on Logan Street. Had two rooms with the outhouse in the back. I ain't mind the outhouse none. But when that goddamn wind blow through there in the winter . . . that's what I'm talking about! To this day I wonder why in the hell I ever stayed down there for six long years. But see, I didn't know I could do no better. I thought only white folks had inside toilets and things.

Rose: There's a lot of people don't know they can do no better than they doing now. That's just something you got to learn. A lot of folks still shop at Bella's.

Troy: Ain't nothing wrong with shopping at Bella's. She got fresh food.

Rose: I ain't said nothing about if she got fresh food. I'm talking about what she charge. She charge ten cents more than the A&P.

Troy: The A&P ain't never done nothing for me. I spends my money where I'm treated right. I go down to Bella, say, "I need a loaf of bread, I'll pay you Friday." She give it to me. What sense that make when I got money to go and spend it somewhere else and ignore the person who done right by me? That ain't in the Bible.

Rose: We ain't talking about what's in the Bible. What sense it make to shop there when she overcharge?

Troy: You shop where you want to. I'll do my shopping where the people been good to me.

Rose: Well, I don't think it's right for her to overcharge. That's all I was saying.

Bono: Look here . . . I got to get on. Lucille going be raising all kind of hell.

Troy: Where you going, nigger? We ain't finished this pint. Come here, finish this pint.

Bono: Well, hell, I am . . . if you ever turn the bottle loose.

Troy (*hands him the bottle*): The only thing I say about the A&P is I'm glad Cory got that job down there. Help him take care of his school clothes and things. Gabe done moved out and things getting tight around here. He got that job . . . He can start to look out for himself.

Rose: Cory done went and got recruited by a college football team.

Troy: I told that boy about that football stuff. The white man ain't gonna let him get nowhere with that football. I told him when he first come to me with it. Now you come telling me he done went and got more tied up in it. He ought to go and get recruited in how to fix cars or something where he can make a living.

Rose: He ain't talking about making no living playing football. It's just something the boys in school do. They gonna send a recruiter by to talk to you. He'll tell you he ain't talking about making no living playing football. It's a honor to be recruited.

Troy: It ain't gonna get him nowhere. Bono'll tell you that.

Bono: If he be like you in the sports . . . he's gonna be alright. Ain't but two men ever played baseball as good as you. That's Babe Ruth and Josh Gibson.° Them's the only two men ever hit more home runs than you.

Troy: What it ever get me? Ain't got a pot to piss in or a window to throw it out of.

Rose: Times have changed since you was playing baseball, Troy. That was before the war. Times have changed a lot since then.

Troy: How in hell they done changed?

Rose: They got lots of colored boys playing ball now. Baseball and football.

Bono: You right about that, Rose. Times have changed, Troy. You just come along too early.

Troy: There ought not never have been no time called too early! Now you take that fellow . . . what's that fellow they had playing right field for the Yankees back then? You know who I'm talking about, Bono. Used to play right field for the Yankees.

Rose: Selkirk?°

Troy: Selkirk! That's it! Man batting .269, understand? .269. What kind of sense that make? I was hitting .432 with thirty-seven home runs! Man batting .269 and playing right field for the Yankees! I saw Josh Gibson's daughter yesterday. She walking around with raggedy shoes on her feet. Now I bet you Selkirk's daughter ain't walking around with raggedy shoes on her feet! I bet you that!

Rose: They got a lot of colored baseball players now. Jackie Robinson° was the first. Folks had to wait for Jackie Robinson.

Troy: I done seen a hundred niggers play baseball better than Jackie Robinson. Hell, I know some teams Jackie Robinson couldn't even make! What you talking about Jackie Robinson. Jackie Robinson wasn't nobody. I'm talking about if you could play ball then they ought to have let you play. Don't care what color you were. Come telling me I come along too early. If you could play . . . then they ought to have let you play.

(Troy takes a long drink from the bottle.)

Rose: You gonna drink yourself to death. You don't need to be drinking like that.

Josh Gibson: legendary catcher in the Negro Leagues whose batting average and home-run totals far outstripped Major League records; he died of a stroke at age 35 in January 1947, three months before Jackie Robinson's debut with the Brooklyn Dodgers.   *Selkirk:* Andy Selkirk, Yankee outfielder who hit .269 in 118 games in 1940.   *Jackie Robinson:* the first African American to play in major league baseball, joined the Brooklyn Dodgers in 1947.

Troy: Death ain't nothing. I done seen him. Done wrassled with him. You can't tell me nothing about death. Death ain't nothing but a fastball on the outside corner. And you know what I'll do to that! Lookee here, Bono . . . am I lying? You get one of them fastballs, about waist high, over the outside corner of the plate where you can get the meat of the bat on it . . . and good god! You can kiss it goodbye. Now, am I lying?

Bono: Naw, you telling the truth there. I seen you do it.

Troy: If I'm lying . . . that 450 feet worth of lying! (*Pause.*) That's all death is to me. A fastball on the outside corner.

Rose: I don't know why you want to get on talking about death.

Troy: Ain't nothing wrong with talking about death. That's part of life. Everybody gonna die. You gonna die, I'm gonna die. Bono's gonna die. Hell, we all gonna die.

Rose: But you ain't got to talk about it. I don't like to talk about it.

Troy: You the one brought it up. Me and Bono was talking about baseball . . . you tell me I'm gonna drink myself to death. Ain't that right, Bono? You know I don't drink this but one night out of the week. That's Friday night. I'm gonna drink just enough to where I can handle it. Then I cuts it loose. I leave it alone. So don't you worry about me drinking myself to death. 'Cause I ain't worried about Death. I done seen him. I done wrestled with him.

Look here, Bono . . . I looked up one day and Death was marching straight at me. Like Soldiers on Parade! The Army of Death was marching straight at me. The middle of July, 1941. It got real cold just like it be winter. It seem like Death himself reached out and touched me on the shoulder. He touch me just like I touch you. I got cold as ice and Death standing there grinning at me.

Rose: Troy, why don't you hush that talk.

Troy: I say . . . what you want, Mr. Death? You be wanting me? You done brought your army to be getting me? I looked him dead in the eye. I wasn't fearing nothing. I was ready to tangle. Just like I'm ready to tangle now. The Bible say be ever vigilant. That's why I don't get but so drunk. I got to keep watch.

Rose: Troy was right down there in Mercy Hospital. You remember he had pneumonia? Laying there with a fever talking plumb out of his head.

Troy: Death standing there staring at me . . . carrying that sickle in his hand. Finally he say, "You want bound over for another year?" See, just like that . . . "You want bound over for another year?" I told him, "Bound over hell! Let's settle this now!"

It seem like he kinda fell back when I said that, and all the cold went out of me. I reached down and grabbed that sickle and threw it just as far as I could throw it . . . and me and him commenced to wrestling.

We wrestled for three days and three nights. I can't say where I found the strength from. Everytime it seemed like he was gonna get the best of me, I'd reach way down deep inside myself and find the strength to do him one better.

Rose: Every time Troy tell that story he find different ways to tell it. Different things to make up about it.

Troy: I ain't making up nothing. I'm telling you the facts of what happened. I wrestled with Death for three days and three nights and I'm standing here to tell you about it. (*Pause.*) Alright. At the end of the third night we done weakened each other to where we can't hardly move. Death stood up, throwed on his robe

. . . had him a white robe with a hood on it. He threwed on that robe and went off to look for his sickle. Say, "I'll be back." Just like that. "I'll be back." I told him, say, "Yeah, but . . . you gonna have to find me!" I wasn't no fool. I wasn't going looking for him. Death ain't nothing to play with. And I know he's gonna get me. I know I got to join his army . . . his camp followers. But as long as I keep my strength and see him coming . . . as long as I keep up my vigilance . . . he's gonna have to fight to get me. I ain't going easy.

Bono: Well, look here, since you got to keep up your vigilance . . . let me have the bottle.

Troy: Aw hell, I shouldn't have told you that part. I should have left out that part.

Rose: Troy be talking that stuff and half the time don't even know what he be talking about.

Troy: Bono know me better than that.

Bono: That's right. I know you. I know you got some Uncle Remus in your blood. You got more stories than the devil got sinners.

Troy: Aw hell, I done seen him too! Done talked with the devil.

Rose: Troy, don't nobody wanna be hearing all that stuff.

(*Lyons enters the yard from the street. Thirty-four years old, Troy's son by a previous marriage, he sports a neatly trimmed goatee, sport coat, white shirt, tieless and buttoned at the collar. Though he fancies himself a musician, he is more caught up in the rituals and "idea" of being a musician than in the actual practice of the music. He has come to borrow money from Troy, and while he knows he will be successful, he is uncertain as to what extent his lifestyle will be held up to scrutiny and ridicule.*)

Lyons: Hey, Pop.

Troy: What you come "Hey, Popping" me for?

Lyons: How you doing, Rose? (*He kisses her.*) Mr. Bono. How you doing?

Bono: Hey, Lyons . . . how you been?

Troy: He must have been doing alright. I ain't seen him around here last week.

Rose: Troy, leave your boy alone. He come by to see you and you wanna start all that nonsense.

Troy: I ain't bothering Lyons. (*Offers him the bottle.*) Here . . . get you a drink. We got an understanding. I know why he come by to see me and he know I know.

Lyons: Come on, Pop . . . I just stopped by to say hi . . . see how you was doing.

Troy: You ain't stopped by yesterday.

Rose: You gonna stay for supper, Lyons? I got some chicken cooking in the oven.

Lyons: No, Rose . . . thanks. I was just in the neighborhood and thought I'd stop by for a minute.

Troy: You was in the neighborhood alright, nigger. You telling the truth there. You was in the neighborhood cause it's my payday.

Lyons: Well, hell, since you mentioned it . . . let me have ten dollars.

Troy: I'll be damned! I'll die and go to hell and play blackjack with the devil before I give you ten dollars.

Bono: That's what I wanna know about . . . that devil you done seen.

Lyons: What . . . Pop done seen the devil? You too much, Pops.

Troy: Yeah, I done seen him. Talked to him too!

Rose: You ain't seen no devil. I done told you that man ain't had nothing to do with the devil. Anything you can't understand, you want to call it the devil.

Troy: Look here, Bono . . . I went down to see Hertzberger about some furniture. Got three rooms for two-ninety-eight. That what it say on the radio. "Three rooms . . . two-ninety-eight." Even made up a little song about it. Go down there . . . man tell me I can't get no credit. I'm working every day and can't get no credit. What to do? I got an empty house with some raggedy furniture in it. Cory ain't got no bed. He's sleeping on a pile of rags on the floor. Working every day and can't get no credit. Come back here—Rose'll tell you—madder than hell. Sit down . . . try to figure what I'm gonna do. Come a knock on the door. Ain't been living here but three days. Who know I'm here? Open the door . . . devil standing there bigger than life. White fellow . . . got on good clothes and everything. Standing there with a clipboard in his hand. I ain't had to say nothing. First words come out of his mouth was . . . "I understand you need some furniture and can't get no credit." I liked to fell over. He say "I'll give you all the credit you want, but you got to pay the interest on it." I told him, "Give me three rooms worth and charge whatever you want." Next day a truck pulled up here and two men unloaded them three rooms. Man what drove the truck give me a book. Say send ten dollars, first of every month to the address in the book and every thing will be alright. Say if I miss a payment the devil was coming back and it'll be hell to pay. That was fifteen years ago. To this day . . . the first of the month I send my ten dollars, Rose'll tell you.

Rose: Troy lying.

Troy: I ain't never seen that man since. Now you tell me who else that could have been but the devil? I ain't sold my soul or nothing like that, you understand. Naw, I wouldn't have truck with the devil about nothing like that. I got my furniture and pays my ten dollars the first of the month just like clockwork.

Bono: How long you say you been paying this ten dollars a month?

Troy: Fifteen years!

Bono: Hell, ain't you finished paying for it yet? How much the man done charged you?

Troy: Aw hell, I done paid for it. I done paid for it ten times over! The fact is I'm scared to stop paying it.

Rose: Troy lying. We got that furniture from Mr. Glickman. He ain't paying no ten dollars a month to nobody.

Troy: Aw hell, woman. Bono know I ain't that big a fool.

Lyons: I was just getting ready to say . . . I know where there's a bridge for sale.

Troy: Look here, I'll tell you this . . . it don't matter to me if he was the devil. It don't matter if the devil give credit. Somebody has got to give it.

Rose: It ought to matter. You going around talking about having truck with the devil . . . God's the one you gonna have to answer to. He's the one gonna be at the Judgment.

Lyons: Yeah, well, look here, Pop . . . Let me have that ten dollars. I'll give it back to you. Bonnie got a job working at the hospital.

Troy: What I tell you, Bono? The only time I see this nigger is when he wants something. That's the only time I see him.

Lyons: Come on, Pop, Mr. Bono don't want to hear all that. Let me have the ten dollars. I told you Bonnie working.

Troy: What that mean to me? "Bonnie working." I don't care if she working. Go ask her for the ten dollars if she working. Talking about "Bonnie working." Why ain't you working?

Lyons: Aw, Pop, you know I can't find no decent job. Where am I gonna get a job at? You know I can't get no job.

Troy: I told you I know some people down there. I can get you on the rubbish if you want to work. I told you that the last time you came by here asking me for something.

Lyons: Naw, Pop . . . thanks. That ain't for me. I don't wanna be carrying nobody's rubbish. I don't wanna be punching nobody's time clock.

Troy: What's the matter, you too good to carry people's rubbish? Where you think that ten dollars you talking about come from? I'm just supposed to haul people's rubbish and give my money to you cause you too lazy to work. You too lazy to work and wanna know why you ain't got what I got.

Rose: What hospital Bonnie working at? Mercy?

Lyons: She's down at Passavant working in the laundry.

Troy: I ain't got nothing as it is. I give you that ten dollars and I got to eat beans the rest of the week. Naw . . . you ain't getting no ten dollars here.

Lyons: You ain't got to be eating no beans. I don't know why you wanna say that.

Troy: I ain't got no extra money. Gabe done moved over to Miss Pearl's paying her the rent and things done got tight around here. I can't afford to be giving you every payday.

Lyons: I ain't asked you to give me nothing. I asked you to loan me ten dollars. I know you got ten dollars.

Troy: Yeah, I got it. You know why I got it? Cause I don't throw my money away out there in the streets. You living the fast life . . . wanna be a musician . . . running around in them clubs and things . . . then, you learn to take care of yourself. You ain't gonna find me going and asking nobody for nothing. I done spent too many years without.

Lyons: You and me is two different people, Pop.

Troy: I done learned my mistake and learned to do what's right by it. You still trying to get something for nothing. Life don't owe you nothing. You owe it to yourself. Ask Bono. He'll tell you I'm right.

Lyons: You got your way of dealing with the world . . . I got mine. The only thing that matters to me is the music.

Troy: Yeah, I can see that! It don't matter how you gonna eat . . . where your next dollar is coming from. You telling the truth there.

Lyons: I know I got to eat. But I got to live too. I need something that gonna help me to get out of the bed in the morning. Make me feel like I belong in the world. I don't bother nobody. I just stay with my music cause that's the only way I can find to live in the world. Otherwise there ain't no telling what I might do. Now I don't come criticizing you and how you live. I just come by to ask you for ten dollars. I don't wanna hear all that about how I live.

Troy: Boy, your mama did a hell of a job raising you.

Lyons: You can't change me, Pop. I'm thirty-four years old. If you wanted to change me, you should have been there when I was growing up. I come by to see you . . . ask for ten dollars and you want to talk about how I was raised. You don't know nothing about how I was raised.

Rose: Let the boy have ten dollars, Troy.

Troy (to Lyons): What the hell you looking at me for? I ain't got no ten dollars. You know what I do with my money. (*To Rose.*) Give him ten dollars if you want him to have it.

Rose: I will. Just as soon as you turn it loose.

Troy (handing Rose the money): There it is. Seventy-six dollars and forty-two cents. You see this, Bono? Now, I ain't gonna get but six of that back.

Rose: You ought to stop telling that lie. Here, Lyons. (*She hands him the money.*)

Lyons: Thanks, Rose. Look . . . I got to run . . . I'll see you later.

Troy: Wait a minute. You gonna say, "thanks, Rose" and ain't gonna look to see where she got that ten dollars from? See how they do me, Bono?

Lyons: I know she got it from you, Pop. Thanks. I'll give it back to you.

Troy: There he go telling another lie. Time I see that ten dollars . . . he'll be owing me thirty more.

Lyons: See you, Mr. Bono.

Bono: Take care, Lyons!

Lyons: Thanks, Pop. I'll see you again.

(*Lyons exits the yard.*)

Troy: I don't know why he don't go and get him a decent job and take care of that woman he got.

Bono: He'll be alright, Troy. The boy is still young.

Troy: The *boy* is thirty-four years old.

Rose: Let's not get off into all that.

Bono: Look here . . . I got to be going. I got to be getting on. Lucille gonna be waiting.

Troy (puts his arm around Rose): See this woman, Bono? I love this woman. I love this woman so much it hurts. I love her so much . . . I done run out of ways of loving her. So I got to go back to basics. Don't you come by my house Monday morning talking about time to go to work . . . 'cause I'm still gonna be stroking!

Rose: Troy! Stop it now!

Bono: I ain't paying him no mind, Rose. That ain't nothing but gin-talk. Go on, Troy. I'll see you Monday.

Troy: Don't you come by my house, nigger! I done told you what I'm gonna be doing.

(*The lights go down to black.*)

SCENE II

The lights come up on Rose hanging up clothes. She hums and sings softly to herself. It is the following morning.

Rose (sings):

> Jesus, be a fence all around me every day
> Jesus, I want you to protect me as I travel on my way.
> Jesus, be a fence all around me every day.

(*Troy enters from the house.*)

> Jesus, I want you to protect me
> As I travel on my way.

(*To Troy.*) 'Morning. You ready for breakfast? I can fix it soon as I finish hanging up these clothes.

Troy: I got the coffee on. That'll be alright. I'll just drink some of that this morning.

Rose: That 651 hit yesterday. That's the second time this month. Miss Pearl hit for a dollar . . . seem like those that need the least always get lucky. Poor folks can't get nothing.

Troy: Them numbers don't know nobody. I don't know why you fool with them. You and Lyons both.

Rose: It's something to do.

Troy: You ain't doing nothing but throwing your money away.

Rose: Troy, you know I don't play foolishly. I just play a nickel here and a nickel there.

Troy: That's two nickels you done thrown away.

Rose: Now I hit sometimes . . . that makes up for it. It always comes in handy when I do hit. I don't hear you complaining then.

Troy: I ain't complaining now. I just say it's foolish. Trying to guess out of six hundred ways which way the number gonna come. If I had all the money niggers, these Negroes, throw away on numbers for one week—just one week—I'd be a rich man.

Rose: Well, you wishing and calling it foolish ain't gonna stop folks from playing numbers. That's one thing for sure. Besides . . . some good things come from playing numbers. Look where Pope done bought him that restaurant off of numbers.

Troy: I can't stand niggers like that. Man ain't had two dimes to rub together. He walking around with his shoes all run over bumming money for cigarettes. Alright. Got lucky there and hit the numbers . . .

Rose: Troy, I know all about it.

Troy: Had good sense, I'll say that for him. He ain't throwed his money away. I seen niggers hit the numbers and go through two thousand dollars in four days. Man bought him that restaurant down there . . . fixed it up real nice . . . . . . and then didn't want nobody to come in it! A Negro go in there and can't get no kind of service. I seen a white fellow come in there and order a bowl of stew. Pope picked all the meat out of the pot for him. Man ain't had nothing but a bowl of meat! Negro come behind him and ain't got nothing but the potatoes and carrots. Talking about what numbers do for people, you picked a wrong example. Ain't done nothing but make a worser fool out of him than he was before.

Rose: Troy, you ought to stop worrying about what happened at work yesterday.

Troy: I ain't worried. Just told me to be down there at the Commissioner's office on Friday. Everybody think they gonna fire me. I ain't worried about them firing me. You ain't got to worry about that. (*Pause.*) Where's Cory? Cory in the house? (*Calls.*) Cory?

Rose: He gone out.

Troy: Out, huh? He gone out 'cause he know I want him to help me with this fence. I know how he is. That boy scared of work.

(*Gabriel enters. He comes halfway down the alley and, hearing Troy's voice, stops.*)

Troy (*continues*): He ain't done a lick of work in his life.

Rose: He had to go to football practice. Coach wanted them to get in a little extra practice before the season start.

Troy: I got his practice . . . running out of here before he get his chores done.

Rose: Troy, what is wrong with you this morning? Don't nothing set right with you. Go on back in there and go to bed . . . get up on the other side.

Troy: Why something got to be wrong with me? I ain't said nothing wrong with me.

Rose: You got something to say about everything. First it's the numbers . . . then it's the way the man runs his restaurant . . . then you done got on Cory. What's it gonna be next? Take a look up there and see if the weather suits you . . . or is it gonna be how you gonna put up the fence with the clothes hanging in the yard?

Troy: You hit the nail on the head then.

Rose: I know you like I know the back of my hand. Go on in there and get you some coffee . . . see if that straighten you up. 'Cause you ain't right this morning.

(*Troy starts into the house and sees Gabriel. Gabriel starts singing. Troy's brother, he is seven years younger than Troy. Injured in World War II, he has a metal plate in his head. He carries an old trumpet tied around his waist and believes with every fiber of his being that he is the Archangel Gabriel. He carries a chipped basket with an assortment of discarded fruits and vegetables he has picked up in the Strip District and which he attempts to sell.*)

Gabriel (*singing*):

> Yes, ma'am, I got plums
> You ask me how I sell them
> Oh ten cents apiece
> Three for a quarter
> Come and buy now
> 'Cause I'm here today
> And tomorrow I'll be gone

(*Gabriel enters.*)

> Hey, Rose!

Rose: How you doing, Gabe?

Gabriel: There's Troy . . . Hey, Troy!

Troy: Hey, Gabe.

(*Exit into kitchen.*)

Rose (*to Gabriel*): What you got there?

Gabriel: You know what I got, Rose. I got fruits and vegetables.

Rose (*looking in basket*): Where's all these plums you talking about?

Gabriel: I ain't got no plums today, Rose. I was just singing that. Have some tomorrow. Put me in a big order for plums. Have enough plums tomorrow for St. Peter and everybody.

(*Troy reenters from kitchen, crosses to steps.*)

(*To Rose.*) Troy's mad at me.

Troy: I ain't mad at you. What I got to be mad at you about? You ain't done nothing to me.

Gabriel: I just moved over to Miss Pearl's to keep out from in your way. I ain't mean no harm by it.

Troy: Who said anything about that? I ain't said anything about that.

Gabriel: You ain't mad at me, is you?

Troy: Naw . . . I ain't mad at you, Gabe. If I was mad at you I'd tell you about it.

Gabriel: Got me two rooms. In the basement. Got my own door too. Wanna see my key? (*He holds up a key.*) That's my own key! Ain't nobody else got a key like that. That's my key! My two rooms!

Troy: Well, that's good, Gabe. You got your own key . . . that's good.

Rose: You hungry, Gabe? I was just fixing to cook Troy his breakfast.

Gabriel: I'll take some biscuits. You got some biscuits? Did you know when I was in heaven . . . every morning me and St. Peter would sit down by the gate and eat some big fat biscuits? Oh, yeah! We had us a good time. We'd sit there and eat us them biscuits and then St. Peter would go off to sleep and tell me to wake him up when it's time to open the gates for the judgment.

Rose: Well, come on . . . I'll make up a batch of biscuits.

(*Rose exits into the house.*)

Gabriel: Troy . . . St. Peter got your name in the book. I seen it. It say . . . Troy Maxson. I say . . . I know him! He got the same name like what I got. That's my brother!

Troy: How many times you gonna tell me that, Gabe?

Gabriel: Ain't got my name in the book. Don't have to have my name. I done died and went to heaven. He got your name though. One morning St. Peter was looking at his book . . . marking it up for the judgment . . . and he let me see your name. Got it in there under M. Got Rose's name . . . I ain't seen it like I seen yours . . . but I know it's in there. He got a great big book. Got everybody's name what was ever been born. That's what he told me. But I seen your name. Seen it with my own eyes.

Troy: Go on in the house there. Rose going to fix you something to eat.

Gabriel: Oh, I ain't hungry. I done had breakfast with Aunt Jemimah. She come by and cooked me up a whole mess of flapjacks. Remember how we used to eat them flapjacks?

Troy: Go on in the house and get you something to eat now.

Gabriel: I got to sell my plums. I done sold some tomatoes. Got me two quarters. Wanna see? (*He shows Troy his quarters.*) I'm gonna save them and buy me a new horn so St. Peter can hear me when it's time to open the gates. (*Gabriel stops suddenly. Listens.*) Hear that? That's the hellhounds. I got to chase them out of here. Go on get out of here! Get out!

(*Gabriel exits singing.*)

> Better get ready for the judgment
> Better get ready for the judgment
> My Lord is coming down

(*Rose enters from the house.*)

Troy: He gone off somewhere.

Gabriel (*offstage*):
>   Better get ready for the judgment
>   Better get ready for the judgment morning
>   Better get ready for the judgment
>   My God is coming down

Rose: He ain't eating right. Miss Pearl say she can't get him to eat nothing.

Troy: What you want me to do about it, Rose? I done did everything I can for the man. I can't make him get well. Man got half his head blown away . . . what you expect?

Rose: Seem like something ought to be done to help him.

Troy: Man don't bother nobody. He just mixed up from that metal plate he got in his head. Ain't no sense for him to go back into the hospital.

Rose: Least he be eating right. They can help him take care of himself.

Troy: Don't nobody wanna be locked up, Rose. What you wanna lock him up for? Man go over there and fight the war . . . messin' around with them Japs, get half his head blown off . . . and they give him a lousy three thousand dollars. And I had to swoop down on that.

Rose: Is you fixing to go into that again?

Troy: That's the only way I got a roof over my head . . . cause of that metal plate.

Rose: Ain't no sense you blaming yourself for nothing. Gabe wasn't in no condition to manage that money. You done what was right by him. Can't nobody say you ain't done what was right by him. Look how long you took care of him . . . till he wanted to have his own place and moved over there with Miss Pearl.

Troy: That ain't what I'm saying, woman! I'm just stating the facts. If my brother didn't have that metal plate in his head . . . I wouldn't have a pot to piss in or a window to throw it out of. And I'm fifty-three years old. Now see if you can understand that!

(*Troy gets up from the porch and starts to exit the yard.*)

Rose: Where you going off to? You been running out of here every Saturday for weeks. I thought you was gonna work on this fence?

Troy: I'm gonna walk down to Taylors'. Listen to the ball game. I'll be back in a bit. I'll work on it when I get back.

(*He exits the yard. The lights go to black.*)

SCENE III

The lights come up on the yard. It is four hours later. Rose is taking down the clothes from the line. Cory enters carrying his football equipment.

Rose: Your daddy like to had a fit with you running out of here this morning without doing your chores.

Cory: I told you I had to go to practice.

Rose: He say you were supposed to help him with this fence.

Cory: He been saying that the last four or five Saturdays, and then he don't never do nothing, but go down to Taylors'. Did you tell him about the recruiter?

Rose: Yeah, I told him.

Cory: What he say?

Rose: He ain't said nothing too much. You get in there and get started on your chores before he gets back. Go on and scrub down them steps before he gets back here hollering and carrying on.

Cory: I'm hungry. What you got to eat, Mama?

Rose: Go on and get started on your chores. I got some meat loaf in there. Go on and make you a sandwich . . . and don't leave no mess in there.

(Cory exits into the house. Rose continues to take down the clothes. Troy enters the yard and sneaks up and grabs her from behind.)

Troy: Troy! Go on, now. You liked to scared me to death. What was the score of the game? Lucille had me on the phone and I couldn't keep up with it.

Troy: What I care about the game? Come here, woman. *(He tries to kiss her.)*

Rose: I thought you went down Taylors' to listen to the game. Go on, Troy! You supposed to be putting up this fence.

Troy (attempting to kiss her again): I'll put it up when I finish with what is at hand.

Rose: Go on, Troy. I ain't studying you.

Troy (chasing after her): I'm studying you . . . fixing to do my homework!

Rose: Troy, you better leave me alone.

Troy: Where's Cory? That boy brought his butt home yet?

Rose: He's in the house doing his chores.

Troy (calling): Cory! Get your butt out here, boy!

(Rose exits into the house with the laundry. Troy goes over to the pile of wood, picks up a board, and starts sawing. Cory enters from the house.)

Troy: You just now coming in here from leaving this morning?

Cory: Yeah, I had to go to football practice.

Troy: Yeah, what?

Cory: Yessir.

Troy: I ain't but two seconds off you noway. The garbage sitting in there overflowing . . . you ain't done none of your chores . . . and you come in here talking about "Yeah."

Cory: I was just getting ready to do my chores now, Pop . . .

Troy: Your first chore is to help me with this fence on Saturday. Everything else come after that. Now get that saw and cut them boards.

(Cory takes the saw and begins cutting the boards. Troy continues working. There is a long pause.)

Cory: Hey, Pop . . . why don't you buy a TV?

Troy: What I want with a TV? What I want one of them for?

Cory: Everybody got one. Earl, Ba Bra . . . Jesse!

Troy: I ain't asked you who had one. I say what I want with one?

Cory: So you can watch it. They got lots of things on TV. Baseball games and everything. We could watch the World Series.

Troy: Yeah . . . and how much this TV cost?

Cory: I don't know. They got them on sale for around two hundred dollars.

Troy: Two hundred dollars, huh?

Cory: That ain't that much, Pop.

Troy: Naw, it's just two hundred dollars. See that roof you got over your head at
night? Let me tell you something about that roof. It's been over ten years since
that roof was last tarred. See now . . . the snow come this winter and sit up there
on that roof like it is . . . and it's gonna seep inside. It's just gonna be a little bit . . .
ain't gonna hardly notice it. Then the next thing you know, it's gonna be leak-
ing all over the house. Then the wood rot from all that water and you gonna
need a whole new roof. Now, how much you think it cost to get that roof tarred?

Cory: I don't know.

Troy: Two hundred and sixty-four dollars . . . . cash money. While you thinking
about a TV, I got to be thinking about the roof . . . and whatever else go wrong
here. Now if you had two hundred dollars, what would you do . . . fix the roof or
buy a TV?

Cory: I'd buy a TV. Then when the roof started to leak . . . when it needed fixing . . .
I'd fix it.

Troy: Where you gonna get the money from? You done spent it for a TV. You gonna
sit up and watch the water run all over your brand new TV.

Cory: Aw, Pop. You got money. I know you do.

Troy: Where I got it at, huh?

Cory: You got it in the bank.

Troy: You wanna see my bankbook? You wanna see that seventy-three dollars and
twenty-two cents I got sitting up in there?

Cory: You ain't got to pay for it all at one time. You can put a down payment on it
and carry it on home with you.

Troy: Not me. I ain't gonna owe nobody nothing if I can help it. Miss a payment and
they come and snatch it right out of your house. Then what you got? Now, soon
as I get two hundred dollars clear, then I'll buy a TV. Right now, as soon as I get
two hundred and sixty-four dollars, I'm gonna have this roof tarred.

Cory: Aw . . . . Pop!

Troy: You go on and get you two hundred dollars and buy one if ya want it. I got
better things to do with my money.

Cory: I can't get no two hundred dollars. I ain't never seen two hundred dollars.

Troy: I'll tell you what . . . . you get you a hundred dollars and I'll put the other
hundred with it.

Cory: Alright, I'm gonna show you.

Troy: You gonna show me how you can cut them boards right now.

> (*Cory begins to cut the boards. There is a long pause.*)

Cory: The Pirates won today. That makes five in a row.

Troy: I ain't thinking about the Pirates. Got an all-white team. Got that boy . . .
that Puerto Rican boy . . . Clemente.° Don't even half-play him. That boy could
be something if they give him a chance. Play him one day and sit him on the
bench the next.

Cory: He gets a lot of chances to play.

Clemente: Hall of Fame outfielder Roberto Clemente, a dark-skinned Puerto Rican, played 17 seasons with
the Pittsburgh Pirates.

Troy: I'm talking about playing regular. Playing every day so you can get your timing. That's what I'm talking about.

Cory: They got some white guys on the team that don't play every day. You can't play everybody at the same time.

Troy: If they got a white fellow sitting on the bench . . . you can bet your last dollar he can't play! The colored guy got to be twice as good before he get on the team. That's why I don't want you to get all tied up in them sports. Man on the team and what it get him? They got colored on the team and don't use them. Same as not having them. All them teams the same.

Cory: The Braves got Hank Aaron and Wes Covington. Hank Aaron hit two home runs today. That makes forty-three.

Troy: Hank Aaron ain't nobody. That's what you supposed to do. That's how you supposed to play the game. Ain't nothing to it. It's just a matter of timing . . . getting the right follow-through. Hell, I can hit forty-three home runs right now!

Cory: Not off no major-league pitching, you couldn't.

Troy: We had better pitching in the Negro leagues. I hit seven home runs off of Satchel Paige.° You can't get no better than that!

Cory: Sandy Koufax.° He's leading the league in strikeouts.

Troy: I ain't thinking of no Sandy Koufax.

Cory: You got Warren Spahn° and Lew Burdette.° I bet you couldn't hit no home runs off of Warren Spahn.

Troy: I'm through with it now. You go on and cut them boards. (*Pause.*) Your mama tell me you done got recruited by a college football team? Is that right?

Cory: Yeah. Coach Zellman say the recruiter gonna be coming by to talk to you. Get you to sign the permission papers.

Troy: I thought you supposed to be working down there at the A&P. Ain't you suppose to be working down there after school?

Cory: Mr. Stawicki say he gonna hold my job for me until after the football season. Say starting next week I can work weekends.

Troy: I thought we had an understanding about this football stuff? You suppose to keep up with your chores and hold that job down at the A&P. Ain't been around here all day on a Saturday. Ain't none of your chores done . . . and now you telling me you done quit your job.

Cory: I'm going to be working weekends.

Troy: You damn right you are! And ain't no need for nobody coming around here to talk to me about signing nothing.

Cory: Hey, Pop . . . you can't do that. He's coming all the way from North Carolina.

Troy: I don't care where he coming from. The white man ain't gonna let you get nowhere with that football noway. You go on and get your book-learning so you can work yourself up in that A&P or learn how to fix cars or build houses or something, get you a trade. That way you have something can't nobody take

---

Satchel Paige . . . Sandy Koufax . . . Warren Spahn . . . Lew Burdette: The great Satchel Paige pitched many years in the Negro Leagues; beginning in 1948, when he was in his forties and long past his prime, he appeared in nearly 200 games in the American League. Star pitchers Sandy Koufax of the Dodgers and Warren Spahn and Lew Burdette of the Braves were all white.

away from you. You go on and learn how to put your hands to some good use. Besides hauling people's garbage.

Cory: I get good grades, Pop. That's why the recruiter wants to talk with you. You got to keep up your grades to get recruited. This way I'll be going to college. I'll get a chance . . .

Troy: First you gonna get your butt down there to the A&P and get your job back.

Cory: Mr. Stawicki done already hired somebody else 'cause I told him I was playing football.

Troy: You a bigger fool than I thought . . . to let somebody take away your job so you can play some football. Where you gonna get your money to take out your girlfriend and whatnot? What kind of foolishness is that to let somebody take away your job?

Cory: I'm still gonna be working weekends.

Troy: Naw . . . naw. You getting your butt out of here and finding you another job.

Cory: Come on, Pop! I got to practice. I can't work after school and play football too. The team needs me. That's what Coach Zellman say . . .

Troy: I don't care what nobody else say. I'm the boss . . . you understand? I'm the boss around here. I do the only saying what counts.

Cory: Come on, Pop!

Troy: I asked you . . . did you understand?

Cory: Yeah . . .

Troy: What?!

Cory: Yessir.

Troy: You go on down there to that A&P and see if you can get your job back. If you can't do both . . . then you quit the football team. You've got to take the crookeds with the straights.

Cory: Yessir. (*Pause.*) Can I ask you a question?

Troy: What the hell you wanna ask me? Mr. Stawicki the one you got the questions for.

Cory: How come you ain't never liked me?

Troy: Liked you? Who the hell say I got to like you? What law is there say I got to like you? Wanna stand up in my face and ask a damn fool-ass question like that. Talking about liking somebody. Come here, boy, when I talk to you.

(*Cory comes over to where Troy is working. He stands slouched over and Troy shoves him on his shoulder.*)

Straighten up, goddammit! I asked you a question . . . what law is there say I got to like you?

Cory: None.

Troy: Well, alright then! Don't you eat every day? (*Pause.*) Answer me when I talk to you! Don't you eat every day?

Cory: Yeah.

Troy: Nigger, as long as you in my house, you put that sir on the end of it when you talk to me.

Cory: Yes . . . sir.

Troy: You eat every day.

Cory: Yessir!

Troy: Got a roof over your head.

Cory: Yessir!

Troy: Got clothes on your back.

Cory: Yessir.

Troy: Why you think that is?

Cory: Cause of you.

Troy: Aw, hell I know it's cause of me . . . but why do you think that is?

Cory (hesitant): 'Cause you like me.

Troy: Like you? I go out of here every morning . . . bust my butt . . . putting up with them crackers every day . . . cause I like you? You about the biggest fool I ever saw. (*Pause.*) It's my job. It's my responsibility! You understand that? A man got to take care of his family. You live in my house . . . sleep you behind on my bed-clothes . . . fill you belly up with my food . . . cause you my son. You my flesh and blood. Not cause I like you! Cause it's my duty to take care of you. I owe a responsibility to you!

   Let's get this straight right here . . . before it go along any further . . . I ain't got to like you. Mr. Rand don't give me my money come payday cause he likes me. He gives me cause he owe me. I done give you everything I had to give you. I gave you your life! Me and your mama worked that out between us. And liking your black ass wasn't part of the bargain. Don't you try and go through life worrying about if somebody like you or not. You best be making sure they doing right by you. You understand what I'm saying, boy?

Cory: Yessir.

Troy: Then get the hell out of my face, and get on down to that A&P.

(*Rose has been standing behind the screen door for much of the scene. She enters as Cory exits.*)

Rose: Why don't you let the boy go ahead and play football, Troy? Ain't no harm in that. He's just trying to be like you with the sports.

Troy: I don't want him to be like me! I want him to move as far away from my life as he can get. You the only decent thing that ever happened to me. I wish him that. But I don't wish him a thing else from my life. I decided seventeen years ago that boy wasn't getting involved in no sports. Not after what they did to me in the sports.

Rose: Troy, why don't you admit you was too old to play in the major leagues? For once . . . why don't you admit that?

Troy: What do you mean too old? Don't come telling me I was too old. I just wasn't the right color. Hell, I'm fifty-three years old and can do better than Selkirk's .269 right now!

Rose: How's was you gonna play ball when you were over forty? Sometimes I can't get no sense out of you.

Troy: I got good sense, woman. I got sense enough not to let my boy get hurt over playing no sports. You been mothering that boy too much. Worried about if people like him.

Rose: Everything that boy do . . . he do for you. He wants you to say "Good job, son." That's all.

Troy: Rose, I ain't got time for that. He's alive. He's healthy. He's got to make his own way. I made mine. Ain't nobody gonna hold his hand when he get out there in that world.

Rose: Times have changed from when you was young, Troy. People change. The world's changing around you and you can't even see it.

Troy (*slow, methodical*): Woman . . . I do the best I can do. I come in here every Friday. I carry a sack of potatoes and a bucket of lard. You all line up at the door with your hands out. I give you the lint from my pockets. I give you my sweat and my blood. I ain't got no tears. I done spent them. We go upstairs in that room at night . . . and I fall down on you and try to blast a hole into forever. I get up Monday morning . . . find my lunch on the table. I go out. Make my way. Find my strength to carry me through to the next Friday. (*Pause.*) That's all I got, Rose. That's all I got to give. I can't give nothing else.

(*Troy exits into the house. The lights go down to black.*)

SCENE IV

It is Friday. Two weeks later. Cory starts out of the house with his football equipment. The phone rings.

Cory (*calling*): I got it! (*He answers the phone and stands in the screen door talking.*) Hello? Hey, Jesse. Naw . . . I was just getting ready to leave now.

Rose (*calling*): Cory!

Cory: I told you, man, them spikes is all tore up. You can use them if you want, but they ain't no good. Earl got some spikes.

Rose (*calling*): Cory!

Cory (*calling to Rose*): Mam? I'm talking to Jesse. (*Into phone.*) When she say that? (*Pause.*) Aw, you lying, man. I'm gonna tell her you said that.

Rose (*calling*): Cory, don't you go nowhere!

Cory: I got to go to the game, Ma! (Into the phone.) Yeah, hey, look, I'll talk to you later. Yeah, I'll meet you over Earl's house. Later. Bye, Ma.

(*Cory exits the house and starts out the yard.*)

Rose: Cory, where you going off to? You got that stuff all pulled out and thrown all over your room.

Cory (*in the yard*): I was looking for my spikes. Jesse wanted to borrow my spikes.

Rose: Get up there and get that cleaned up before your daddy get back in here.

Cory: I got to go to the game! I'll clean it up when I get back.

(*Cory exits.*)

Rose: That's all he need to do is see that room all messed up.

(*Rose exits into the house. Troy and Bono enter the yard. Troy is dressed in clothes other than his work clothes.*)

Bono: He told him the same thing he told you. Take it to the union.

Troy: Brownie ain't got that much sense. Man wasn't thinking about nothing. He wait until I confront them on it . . . then he wanna come crying seniority. (*Calls.*) Hey, Rose!

Bono: I wish I could have seen Mr. Rand's face when he told you.

Troy: He couldn't get it out of his mouth! Liked to bit his tongue! When they called me down there to the Commissioner's office . . . he thought they was gonna fire me. Like everybody else.

Bono: I didn't think they was gonna fire you. I thought they was gonna put you on the warning paper.

Troy: Hey, Rose! (*To Bono.*) Yeah, Mr. Rand like to bit his tongue.

(*Troy breaks the seal on the bottle, takes a drink, and hands it to Bono.*)

Bono: I see you run right down to Taylors' and told that Alberta gal.

Troy (*calling*): Hey, Rose! (*To Bono.*) I told everybody. Hey, Rose! I went down there to cash my check.

Rose (*entering from the house*): Hush all that hollering, man! I know you out here. What they say down there at the Commissioner's office?

Troy: You supposed to come when I call you, woman. Bono'll tell you that. (*To Bono.*) Don't Lucille come when you call her?

Rose: Man, hush your mouth. I ain't no dog . . . talk about "come when you call me."

Troy (*puts his arm around Rose*): You hear this, Bono? I had me an old dog used to get uppity like that. You say, "C'mere, Blue!" . . . and he just lay there and look at you. End up getting a stick and chasing him away trying to make him come.

Rose: I ain't studying you and your dog. I remember you used to sing that old song.

Troy (*he sings*):

Hear it ring! Hear it ring!
I had a dog his name was Blue.

Rose: Don't nobody wanna hear you sing that old song.

Troy (*sings*):

You know Blue was mighty true.

Rose: Used to have Cory running around here singing that song.

Bono: Hell, I remember that song myself.

Troy (*sings*):

You know Blue was a good old dog.
Blue treed a possum in a hollow log.

That was my daddy's song. My daddy made up that song.

Rose: I don't care who made it up. Don't nobody wanna hear you sing it.

Troy (*makes a song like calling a dog*): Come here, woman.

Rose: You come in here carrying on, I reckon they ain't fired you. What they say down there at the Commissioner's office?

Troy: Look here, Rose . . . Mr. Rand called me into his office today when I got back from talking to them people down there . . . it come from up top . . . he called me in and told me they was making me a driver.

Rose: Troy, you kidding!

Troy: No I ain't. Ask Bono.

Rose: Well, that's great, Troy. Now you don't have to hassle them people no more.

(*Lyons enters from the street.*)

Troy: Aw hell, I wasn't looking to see you today. I thought you was in jail. Got it all over the front page of the *Courier* about them raiding Sefus's place . . . where you be hanging out with all them thugs.

Lyons: Hey, Pop . . . that ain't got nothing to do with me. I don't go down there gambling. I go down there to sit in with the band. I ain't got nothing to do with the gambling part. They got some good music down there.

Troy: They got some rogues . . . is what they got.

Lyons: How you been, Mr. Bono? Hi, Rose.

Bono: I see where you playing down at the Crawford Grill tonight.

Rose: How come you ain't brought Bonnie like I told you? You should have brought Bonnie with you, she ain't been over in a month of Sundays.

Lyons: I was just in the neighborhood . . . thought I'd stop by.

Troy: Here he come . . .

Bono: Your daddy got a promotion on the rubbish. He's gonna be the first colored driver. Ain't got to do nothing but sit up there and read the paper like them white fellows.

Lyons: Hey, Pop . . . if you knew how to read you'd be alright.

Bono: Naw . . . naw . . . you mean if the nigger knew how to *drive* he'd be alright. Been fighting with them people about driving and ain't even got a license. Mr. Rand know you ain't got no driver's license?

Troy: Driving ain't nothing. All you do is point the truck where you want it to go. Driving ain't nothing.

Bono: Do Mr. Rand know you ain't got no driver's license? That's what I'm talking about. I ain't asked if driving was easy. I asked if Mr. Rand know you ain't got no driver's license.

Troy: He ain't got to know. The man ain't got to know my business. Time he find out, I have two or three driver's licenses.

Lyons (going into his pocket): Say, look here, Pop . . .

Troy: I knew it was coming. Didn't I tell you, Bono? I know what kind of "Look here, Pop" that was. The nigger fixing to ask me for some money. It's Friday night. It's my payday. All them rogues down there on the avenue . . . the ones that ain't in jail . . . and Lyons is hopping in his shoes to get down there with them.

Lyons: See, Pop . . . if you give somebody else a chance to talk sometime, you'd see that I was fixing to pay you back your ten dollars like I told you. Here . . . I told you I'd pay you when Bonnie got paid.

Troy: Naw . . . you go ahead and keep that ten dollars. Put it in the bank. The next time you feel like you wanna come by here and ask me for something . . . you go on down there and get that.

Lyons: Here's your ten dollars, Pop. I told you I don't want you to give me nothing. I just wanted to borrow ten dollars.

Troy: Naw . . . you go on and keep that for the next time you want to ask me.

Lyons: Come on, Pop . . . here go your ten dollars.

Rose: Why don't you go on and let the boy pay you back, Troy?

Lyons: Here you go, Rose. If you don't take it I'm gonna have to hear about it for the next six months. *(He hands her the money.)*

Rose: You can hand yours over here too, Troy.

Troy: You see this, Bono. You see how they do me.

Bono: Yeah, Lucille do me the same way.

(Gabriel is heard singing offstage. He enters.)

Gabriel: Better get ready for the Judgment! Better get ready for . . . Hey! . . . Hey! . . . There's Troy's boy!

Lyons: How are you doing, Uncle Gabe?

Gabriel: Lyons . . . The King of the Jungle! Rose . . . hey, Rose. Got a flower for you. *(He takes a rose from his pocket.)* Picked it myself. That's the same rose like you is!

Rose: That's right nice of you, Gabe.

Lyons: What you been doing, Uncle Gabe?

Gabriel: Oh, I been chasing hellhounds and waiting on the time to tell St. Peter to open the gates.

Lyons: You been chasing hellhounds, huh? Well . . . you doing the right thing, Uncle Gabe. Somebody got to chase them.

Gabriel: Oh, yeah . . . I know it. The devil's strong. The devil ain't no pushover. Hellhounds snipping at everybody's heels. But I got my trumpet waiting on the judgment time.

Lyons: Waiting on the Battle of Armageddon, huh?

Gabriel: Ain't gonna be too much of a battle when God get to waving that Judgment sword. But the people's gonna have a hell of a time trying to get into heaven if them gates ain't open.

Lyons (putting his arm around Gabriel): You hear this, Pop. Uncle Gabe, you alright!

Gabriel (laughing with Lyons): Lyons! King of the Jungle.

Rose: You gonna stay for supper, Gabe? Want me to fix you a plate?

Gabriel: I'll take a sandwich, Rose. Don't want no plate. Just wanna eat with my hands. I'll take a sandwich.

Rose: How about you, Lyons? You staying? Got some short ribs cooking.

Lyons: Naw, I won't eat nothing till after we finished playing. *(Pause.)* You ought to come down and listen to me play, Pop.

Troy: I don't like that Chinese music. All that noise.

Rose: Go on in the house and wash up, Gabe . . . I'll fix you a sandwich.

Gabriel (to Lyons, as he exits): Troy's mad at me.

Lyons: What you mad at Uncle Gabe for, Pop?

Rose: He thinks Troy's mad at him cause he moved over to Miss Pearl's.

Troy: I ain't mad at the man. He can live where he want to live at.

Lyons: What he move over there for? Miss Pearl don't like nobody.

Rose: She don't mind him none. She treats him real nice. She just don't allow all that singing.

Troy: She don't mind that rent he be paying . . . that's what she don't mind.

Rose: Troy, I ain't going through that with you no more. He's over there cause he want to have his own place. He can come and go as he please.

Troy: Hell, he could come and go as he please here. I wasn't stopping him. I ain't put no rules on him.

Rose: It ain't the same thing, Troy. And you know it.

(Gabriel comes to the door.)

Now, that's the last I wanna hear about that. I don't wanna hear nothing else about Gabe and Miss Pearl. And next week . . .

Gabriel: I'm ready for my sandwich, Rose.

Rose: And next week . . . when that recruiter come from that school . . . I want you to sign that paper and go on and let Cory play football. Then that'll be the last I have to hear about that.

Troy (to Rose as she exits into the house): I ain't thinking about Cory nothing.

Lyons: What . . . Cory got recruited? What school he going to?

Troy: That boy walking around here smelling his piss . . . thinking he's grown. Thinking he's gonna do what he want, irrespective of what I say. Look here, Bono . . . I left the Commissioner's office and went down to the A&P . . . that boy ain't working down there. He lying to me. Telling me he got his job back . . . telling me he working weekends . . . telling me he working after school . . . Mr. Stawicki tell me he ain't working down there at all!

Lyons: Cory just growing up. He's just busting at the seams trying to fill out your shoes.

Troy: I don't care what he's doing. When he get to the point where he wanna disobey me . . . then it's time for him to move on. Bono'll tell you that. I bet he ain't never disobeyed his daddy without paying the consequences.

Bono: I ain't never had a chance. My daddy came on through . . . but I ain't never knew him to see him . . . or what he had on his mind or where he went. Just moving on through. Searching out the New Land. That's what the old folks used to call it. See a fellow moving around from place to place . . . woman to woman . . . called it searching out the New Land. I can't say if he ever found it. I come along, didn't want no kids. Didn't know if I was gonna be in one place long enough to fix on them right as their daddy. I figured I was going searching too. As it turned out I been hooked up with Lucille near about as long as your daddy been with Rose. Going on sixteen years.

Troy: Sometimes I wish I hadn't known my daddy. He ain't cared nothing about no kids. A kid to him wasn't nothing. All he wanted was for you to learn how to walk so he could start you to working. When it come time for eating . . . he ate first. If there was anything left over, that's what you got. Man would sit down and eat two chickens and give you the wing.

Lyons: You ought to stop that, Pop. Everybody feed their kids. No matter how hard times is . . . everybody care about their kids. Make sure they have something to eat.

Troy: The only thing my daddy cared about was getting them bales of cotton in to Mr. Lubin. That's the only thing that mattered to him. Sometimes I used to wonder why he was living. Wonder why the devil hadn't come and got him. "Get them bales of cotton in to Mr. Lubin" and find out he owe him money . . .

Lyons: He should have just went on and left when he saw he couldn't get nowhere. That's what I would have done.

Troy: How he gonna leave with eleven kids? And where he gonna go? He ain't knew how to do nothing but farm. No, he was trapped and I think he knew it. But I'll say this for him . . . he felt a responsibility toward us. Maybe he ain't treated us the way I felt he should have . . . but without that responsibility he could have walked off and left us . . . made his own way.

Bono: A lot of them did. Back in those days what you talking about . . . they walk out their front door and just take on down one road or another and keep on walking.

Lyons: There you go! That's what I'm talking about.

Bono: Just keep on walking till you come to something else. Ain't you never heard of nobody having the walking blues? Well, that's what you call it when you just take off like that.

Troy: My daddy ain't had them walking blues! What you talking about? He stayed right there with his family. But he was just as evil as he could be. My mama couldn't stand him. Couldn't stand that evilness. She run off when I was about eight. She sneaked off one night after he had gone to sleep. Told me she was coming back for me. I ain't never seen her no more. All his women run off and left him. He wasn't good for nobody.

When my turn come to head out, I was fourteen and got to sniffing around Joe Canewell's daughter. Had us an old mule we called Greyboy. My daddy sent me out to do some plowing and I tied up Greyboy and went to fooling around with Joe Canewell's daughter. We done found us a nice little spot, got real cozy with each other. She about thirteen and we done figured we was grown anyway . . . so we down there enjoying ourselves . . . ain't thinking about nothing. We didn't know Greyboy had got loose and wandered back to the house and my daddy was looking for me. We down there by the creek enjoying ourselves when my daddy come up on us. Surprised us. He had them leather straps off the mule and commenced to whupping me like there was no tomorrow. I jumped up, mad and embarrassed. I was scared of my daddy. When he commenced to whupping on me . . . quite naturally I run to get out of the way. (*Pause.*) Now I thought he was mad cause I ain't done my work. But I see where he was chasing me off so he could have the gal for himself. When I see what the matter of it was, I lost all fear of my daddy. Right there is where I become a man . . . at fourteen years of age. (*Pause.*) Now it was my turn to run him off. I picked up them same reins that he had used on me. I picked up them reins and commenced to whupping on him. The gal jumped up and run off . . . and when my daddy turned to face me, I could see why the devil had never come to get him . . . cause he was the devil himself. I don't know what happened. When I woke up, I was laying right there by the creek, and Blue . . . this old dog we had . . . was licking my face. I thought I was blind. I couldn't see nothing. Both my eyes were swollen shut. I layed there and cried. I didn't know what I was gonna do. The only thing I knew was the time had come for me to leave my daddy's house. And right there the world suddenly got big. And it was a long time before I could cut it down to where I could handle it.

Part of that cutting down was when I got to the place where I could feel him kicking in my blood and knew that the only thing that separated us was the matter of a few years.

(*Gabriel enters from the house with a sandwich.*)

Lyons: What you got there, Uncle Gabe?

Gabriel: Got me a ham sandwich. Rose gave me a ham sandwich.

Troy: I don't know what happened to him. I done lost touch with everybody except Gabriel. But I hope he's dead. I hope he found some peace.

Lyons: That's a heavy story, Pop. I didn't know you left home when you was fourteen.

Troy: And didn't know nothing. The only part of the world I knew was the forty-two acres of Mr. Lubin's land. That's all I knew about life.

Lyons: Fourteen's kinda young to be out on your own. (*Phone rings.*) I don't even think I was ready to be out on my own at fourteen. I don't know what I would have done.

Troy: I got up from the creek and walked on down to Mobile. I was through with farming. Figured I could do better in the city. So I walked the two hundred miles to Mobile.

Lyons: Wait a minute . . . you ain't walked no two hundred miles, Pop. Ain't nobody gonna walk no two hundred miles. You talking about some walking there.

Bono: That's the only way you got anywhere back in them days.

Lyons: Shhh. Damn if I wouldn't have hitched a ride with somebody!

Troy: Who you gonna hitch it with? They ain't had no cars and things like they got now. We talking about 1918.

Rose (entering): What you all out here getting into?

Troy (to Rose): I'm telling Lyons how good he got it. He don't know nothing about this I'm talking.

Rose: Lyons, that was Bonnie on the phone. She say you supposed to pick her up.

Lyons: Yeah, okay, Rose.

Troy: I walked on down to Mobile and hitched up with some of them fellows that was heading this way. Got up here and found out . . . not only couldn't you get a job . . . you couldn't find no place to live. I thought I was in freedom. Shhh. Colored folks living down there on the riverbanks in whatever kind of shelter they could find for themselves. Right down there under the Brady Street Bridge. Living in shacks made of sticks and tarpaper. Messed around there and went from bad to worse. Started stealing. First it was food. Then I figured, hell, if I steal money I can buy me some food. Buy me some shoes too! One thing led to another. Met your mama. I was young and anxious to be a man. Met your mama and had you. What I do that for? Now I got to worry about feeding you and her. Got to steal three times as much. Went out one day looking for somebody to rob . . . that's what I was, a robber. I'll tell you the truth. I'm ashamed of it today. But it's the truth. Went to rob this fellow . . . pulled out my knife . . . and he pulled out a gun. Shot me in the chest. It felt just like somebody had taken a hot branding iron and laid it on me. When he shot me I jumped at him with my knife. They told me I killed him and they put me in the penitentiary and locked me up for fifteen years. That's where I met Bono. That's where I learned how to play baseball. Got out that place and your mama had taken you and went on to make life without me. Fifteen years was a long time for her to wait. But that fifteen years cured me of that robbing stuff. Rose'll tell you. She asked me when I met her if I had gotten all that foolishness out of my system. And I told her, "Baby, it's you and baseball all what count with me." You hear me, Bono? I meant it too. She say, "Which one comes first?" I told her, "Baby, ain't no doubt it's baseball . . . but you stick and get old with me and we'll both outlive this baseball." Am I right, Rose? And it's true.

Rose: Man, hush your mouth. You ain't said no such thing. Talking about, "Baby you know you'll always be number one with me." That's what you was talking.

Troy: You hear that, Bono. That's why I love her.

Bono: Rose'll keep you straight. You get off the track, she'll straighten you up.

Rose: Lyons, you better get on up and get Bonnie. She waiting on you.

Lyons (gets up to go): Hey, Pop, why don't you come on down to the Grill and hear me play?

Troy: I ain't going down there. I'm too old to be sitting around in them clubs.

Bono: You got to be good to play down at the Grill.

Lyons: Come on, Pop . . .

Troy: I got to get up in the morning.

Lyons: You ain't got to stay long.

Troy: Naw, I'm gonna get my supper and go on to bed.

Lyons: Well, I got to go. I'll see you again.

Troy: Don't you come around my house on my payday.

Rose: Pick up the phone and let somebody know you coming. And bring Bonnie with you. You know I'm always glad to see her.

Lyons: Yeah, I'll do that, Rose. You take care now. See you, Pop. See you, Mr. Bono. See you, Uncle Gabe.

Gabriel: Lyons! King of the Jungle!

(*Lyons exits.*)

Troy: Is supper ready, woman? Me and you got some business to take care of. I'm gonna tear it up too.

Rose: Troy, I done told you now!

Troy (*puts his arm around Bono*): Aw hell, woman . . . this is Bono. Bono like family. I done known this nigger since . . . how long I done know you?

Bono: It's been a long time.

Troy: I done know this nigger since Skippy was a pup. Me and him done been through some times.

Bono: You sure right about that.

Troy: Hell, I done know him longer than I known you. And we still standing shoulder to shoulder. Hey, look here, Bono . . . a man can't ask for no more than that. (*Drinks to him.*) I love you, nigger.

Bono: Hell, I love you too . . . but I got to get home see my woman. You got yours in hand. I got to go get mine.

(*Bono starts to exit as Cory enters the yard, dressed in his football uniform. He gives Troy a hard, uncompromising look.*)

Cory: What you do that for, Pop?

(*He throws his helmet down in the direction of Troy.*)

Rose: What's the matter? Cory . . . what's the matter?

Cory: Papa done went up to the school and told Coach Zellman I can't play football no more. Wouldn't even let me play the game. Told him to tell the recruiter not to come.

Rose: Troy . . .

Troy: What you Troying me for. Yeah, I did it. And the boy know why I did it.

Cory: Why you wanna do that to me? That was the one chance I had.

Rose: Ain't nothing wrong with Cory playing football, Troy.

Troy: The boy lied to me. I told the nigger if he wanna play football . . . to keep up his chores and hold down that job at the A&P. That was the conditions. Stopped down there to see Mr. Stawicki . . .

Cory: I can't work after school during the football season, Pop! I tried to tell you that Mr. Stawicki's holding my job for me. You don't never want to listen to nobody. And then you wanna go and do this to me!

Troy: I ain't done nothing to you. You done it to yourself.

Cory: Just cause you didn't have a chance! You just scared I'm gonna be better than you, that's all.

Troy: Come here.

Rose: Troy . . .

(*Cory reluctantly crosses over to Troy.*)

Troy: Alright! See. You done made a mistake.

Cory: I didn't even do nothing!

Troy: I'm gonna tell you what your mistake was. See . . . you swung at the ball and didn't hit it. That's strike one. See, you in the batter's box now. You swung and you missed. That's strike one. Don't you strike out!

(*Lights fade to black.*)

ACT II

SCENE I

The following morning. Cory is at the tree hitting the ball with the bat. He tries to mimic Troy, but his swing is awkward, less sure. Rose enters from the house.

Rose: Cory, I want you to help me with this cupboard.

Cory: I ain't quitting the team. I don't care what Poppa say.

Rose: I'll talk to him when he gets back. He had to go see about your Uncle Gabe. The police done arrested him. Say he was disturbing the peace. He'll be back directly. Come on in here and help me clean out the top of this cupboard.

(*Cory exits into the house. Rose sees Troy and Bono coming down the alley.*)

Troy . . . what they say down there?

Troy: Ain't said nothing. I give them fifty dollars and they let him go. I'll talk to you about it. Where's Cory?

Rose: He's in there helping me clean out these cupboards.

Troy: Tell him to get his butt out here.

(*Troy and Bono go over to the pile of wood. Bono picks up the saw and begins sawing.*)

Troy (to Bono): All they want is the money. That makes six or seven times I done went down there and got him. See me coming they stick out their *hands.*

Bono: Yeah. I know what you mean. That's all they care about . . . that money. They don't care about what's right. (*Pause.*) Nigger, why you got to go and get some hard wood? You ain't doing nothing but building a little old fence. Get you some soft pine wood. That's all you need.

Troy: I know what I'm doing. This is outside wood. You put pine wood inside the house. Pine wood is inside wood. This here is outside wood. Now you tell me where the fence is gonna be?

Bono: You don't need this wood. You can put it up with pine wood and it'll stand as long as you gonna be here looking at it.

Troy: How you know how long I'm gonna be here, nigger? Hell, I might just live forever. Live longer than old man Horsely.

Bono: That's what Magee used to say.

Troy: Magee's a damn fool. Now you tell me who you ever heard of gonna pull their own teeth with a pair of rusty pliers.

Bono: The old folks . . . my granddaddy used to pull his teeth with pliers. They ain't had no dentists for the colored folks back then.

Troy: Get clean pliers! You understand? Clean pliers! Sterilize them! Besides we ain't living back then. All Magee had to do was walk over to Doc Goldblum's.

Bono: I see where you and that Tallahassee gal . . . that Alberta . . . I see where you all done got tight.

Troy: What you mean "got tight"?

Bono: I see where you be laughing and joking with her all the time.

Troy: I laughs and jokes with all of them, Bono. You know me.

Bono: That ain't the kind of laughing and joking I'm talking about.

(*Cory enters from the house.*)

Cory: How you doing, Mr. Bono?

Troy: Cory? Get that saw from Bono and cut some wood. He talking about the wood's too hard to cut. Stand back there, Jim, and let that young boy show you how it's done.

Bono: He's sure welcome to it.

(*Cory takes the saw and begins to cut the wood.*)

Whew-e-e! Look at that. Big old strong boy. Look like Joe Louis. Hell, must be getting old the way I'm watching that boy whip through that wood.

Cory: I don't see why Mama want a fence around the yard noways.

Troy: Damn if I know either. What the hell she keeping out with it? She ain't got nothing nobody want.

Bono: Some people build fences to keep people out . . . and other people build fences to keep people in. Rose wants to hold on to you all. She loves you.

Troy: Hell, nigger, I don't need nobody to tell me my wife loves me. Cory . . . go on in the house and see if you can find that other saw.

Cory: Where's it at?

Troy: I said find it! Look for it till you find it!

(*Cory exits into the house.*)

What's that supposed to mean? Wanna keep us in?

Bono: Troy . . . I done known you seem like damn near my whole life. You and Rose both. I done know both of you all for a long time. I remember when you met Rose. When you was hitting them baseball out the park. A lot of them old gals was after you then. You had the pick of the litter. When you picked Rose, I was happy for you. That was the first time I knew you had any sense. I said . . . My man Troy knows what he's doing . . . I'm gonna follow this nigger . . . he might take me somewhere. I been following you too. I done learned a whole heap of things about life watching you. I done learned how to tell where the shit lies. How to tell it from the alfalfa. You done learned me a lot of things. You showed

me how to not make the same mistakes . . . to take life as it comes along and
keep putting one foot in front of the other. (*Pause.*) Rose a good woman, Troy.

Troy: Hell, nigger, I know she a good woman. I been married to her for eighteen
years. What you got on your mind, Bono?

Bono: I just say she a good woman. Just like I say anything. I ain't got to have
nothing on my mind.

Troy: You just gonna say she a good woman and leave it hanging out there like that?
Why you telling me she a good woman?

Bono: She loves you, Troy. Rose loves you.

Troy: You saying I don't measure up. That's what you trying to say. I don't measure
up cause I'm seeing this other gal. I know what you trying to say.

Bono: I know what Rose means to you, Troy. I'm just trying to say I don't want to see
you mess up.

Troy: Yeah, I appreciate that, Bono. If you was messing around on Lucille I'd be
telling you the same thing.

Bono: Well, that's all I got to say. I just say that because I love you both.

Troy: Hell, you know me . . . I wasn't out there looking for nothing. You can't find a
better woman than Rose. I know that. But seems like this woman just stuck onto
me where I can't shake her loose. I done wrestled with it, tried to throw her off
me . . . but she just stuck on tighter. Now she's stuck on for good.

Bono: You's in control . . . that's what you tell me all the time. You responsible for
what you do.

Troy: I ain't ducking the responsibility of it. As long as it sets right in my heart . . .
then I'm okay. Cause that's all I listen to. It'll tell me right from wrong every
time. And I ain't talking about doing Rose no bad turn. I love Rose. She done
carried me a long ways and I love and respect her for that.

Bono: I know you do. That's why I don't want to see you hurt her. But what you
gonna do when she find out? What you got then? If you try and juggle both of
them . . . sooner or later you gonna drop one of them. That's common sense.

Troy: Yeah, I hear what you saying, Bono. I been trying to figure a way to work it
out.

Bono: Work it out right, Troy. I don't want to be getting all up between you and
Rose's business . . . but work it so it come out right.

Troy: Aw hell, I get all up between you and Lucille's business. When you gonna get
that woman that refrigerator she been wanting? Don't tell me you ain't got no
money now. I know who your banker is. Mellon° don't need that money bad as
Lucille want that refrigerator. I'll tell you that.

Bono: Tell you what I'll do . . . when you finish building this fence for Rose . . . I'll
buy Lucille that refrigerator.

Troy: You done stuck your foot in your mouth now!

(*Troy grabs up a board and begins to saw. Bono starts to walk out the yard.*)

Hey, nigger . . . where you going?

Mellon: banker and industrialist Andrew Mellon (1855–1937), U.S. Treasury Secretary 1921–32, was
active in philanthropic enterprises, especially in his native Pittsburgh.

Bono: I'm going home. I know you don't expect me to help you now. I'm protecting my money. I wanna see you put that fence up by yourself. That's what I want to see. You'll be here another six months without me.

Troy: Nigger, you ain't right.

Bono: When it comes to my money . . . I'm right as fireworks on the Fourth of July.

Troy: Alright, we gonna see now. You better get out your bankbook.

(Bono exits, and Troy continues to work. Rose enters from the house.)

Rose: What they say down there? What's happening with Gabe?

Troy: I went down there and got him out. Cost me fifty dollars. Say he was disturbing the peace. Judge set up a hearing for him in three weeks. Say to show cause why he shouldn't be re-committed.

Rose: What was he doing that cause them to arrest him?

Troy: Some kids was teasing him and he run them off home. Say he was howling and carrying on. Some folks seen him and called the police. That's all it was.

Rose: Well, what's you say? What'd you tell the judge?

Troy: Told him I'd look after him. It didn't make no sense to recommit the man. He stuck out his big greasy palm and told me to give him fifty dollars and take him on home.

Rose: Where's he at now? Where'd he go off to?

Troy: He's gone on about his business. He don't need nobody to hold his hand.

Rose: Well, I don't know. Seem like that would be the best place for him if they did put him into the hospital. I know what you're gonna say. But that's what I think would be best.

Troy: The man done had his life ruined fighting for what? And they wanna take and lock him up. Let him be free. He don't bother nobody.

Rose: Well, everybody got their own way of looking at it I guess. Come on and get your lunch. I got a bowl of lima beans and some cornbread in the oven. Come on get something to eat. Ain't no sense you fretting over Gabe.

(Rose turns to go into the house.)

Troy: Rose . . . got something to tell you.

Rose: Well, come on . . . wait till I get this food on the table.

Troy: Rose!

(She stops and turns around.)

I don't know how to say this. *(Pause.)* I can't explain it none. It just sort of grows on you till it gets out of hand. It starts out like a little bush . . . and the next thing you know it's a whole forest.

Rose: Troy . . . what is you talking about?

Troy: I'm talking, woman, let me talk. I'm trying to find a way to tell you . . . I'm gonna be a daddy. I'm gonna be somebody's daddy.

Rose: Troy . . . you're not telling me this? You're gonna be . . . what?

Troy: Rose . . . now . . . see . . .

Rose: You telling me you gonna be somebody's daddy? You telling your *wife* this?

(Gabriel enters from the street. He carries a rose in his hand.)

Gabriel: Hey, Troy! Hey, Rose!

Rose: I have to wait eighteen years to hear something like this.

Gabriel: Hey, Rose . . . I got a flower for you. (*He hands it to her.*) That's a rose. Same rose like you is.

Rose: Thanks, Gabe.

Gabriel: Troy, you ain't mad at me is you? Them bad mens come and put me away. You ain't mad at me is you?

Troy: Naw, Gabe, I ain't mad at you.

Rose: Eighteen years and you wanna come with this.

Gabriel (*takes a quarter out of his pocket*): See what I got? Got a brand new quarter.

Troy: Rose . . . it's just . . .

Rose: Ain't nothing you can say, Troy. Ain't no way of explaining that.

Gabriel: Fellow that give me this quarter had a whole mess of them. I'm gonna keep this quarter till it stop shining.

Rose: Gabe, go on in the house there. I got some watermelon in the Frigidaire. Go on and get you a piece.

Gabriel: Say, Rose . . . you know I was chasing hellhounds and them bad mens come and get me and take me away. Troy helped me. He come down there and told them they better let me go before he beat them up. Yeah, he did!

Rose: You go on and get you a piece of watermelon, Gabe. Them bad mens is gone now.

Gabriel: Okay, Rose . . . gonna get me some watermelon. The kind with the stripes on it.

(*Gabriel exits into the house.*)

Rose: Why, Troy? Why? After all these years to come dragging this in to me now. It don't make no sense at your age. I could have expected this ten or fifteen years ago, but not now.

Troy: Age ain't got nothing to do with it, Rose.

Rose: I done tried to be everything a wife should be. Everything a wife could be. Been married eighteen years and I got to live to see the day you tell me you been seeing another woman and done fathered a child by her. And you know I ain't never wanted no half nothing in my family. My whole family is half. Everybody got different fathers and mothers . . . my two sisters and my brother. Can't hardly tell who's who. Can't never sit down and talk about Papa and Mama. It's your papa and your mama and my papa and my mama . . .

Troy: Rose . . . stop it now.

Rose: I ain't never wanted that for none of my children. And now you wanna drag your behind in here and tell me something like this.

Troy: You ought to know. It's time for you to know.

Rose: Well, I don't want to know, goddamn it!

Troy: I can't just make it go away. It's done now. I can't wish the circumstance of the thing away.

Rose: And you don't want to either. Maybe you want to wish me and my boy away. Maybe that's what you want? Well, you can't wish us away. I've got eighteen years of my life invested in you. You ought to have stayed upstairs in my bed where you belong.

Troy: Rose . . . now listen to me . . . we can get a handle on this thing. We can talk this out . . . come to an understanding.

Rose: All of a sudden it's "we." Where was "we" at when you was down there rolling around with some godforsaken woman? "We" should have come to an understanding before you started making a damn fool of yourself. You're a day late and a dollar short when it comes to an understanding with me.

Troy: It's just . . . She gives me a different idea . . . a different understanding about myself. I can step out of this house and get away from the pressures and problems . . . be a different man. I ain't got to wonder how I'm gonna pay the bills or get the roof fixed. I can just be a part of myself that I ain't never been.

Rose: What I want to know . . . is do you plan to continue seeing her. That's all you can say to me.

Troy: I can sit up in her house and laugh. Do you understand what I'm saying. I can laugh out loud . . . and it feels good. It reaches all the way down to the bottom of my shoes. (*Pause.*) Rose, I can't give that up.

Rose: Maybe you ought to go on and stay down there with her . . . if she's a better woman than me.

Troy: It ain't about nobody being a better woman or nothing. Rose, you ain't the blame. A man couldn't ask for no woman to be a better wife than you've been. I'm responsible for it. I done locked myself into a pattern trying to take care of you all that I forgot about myself.

Rose: What the hell was I there for? That was my job, not somebody else's.

Troy: Rose, I done tried all my life to live decent . . . to live a clean . . . hard . . . useful life. I tried to be a good husband to you. In every way I knew how. Maybe I come into the world backwards, I don't know. But . . . you born with two strikes on you before you come to the plate. You got to guard it closely . . . always looking for the curve-ball on the inside corner. You can't afford to let none get past you. You can't afford a call strike. If you going down . . . you going down swinging. Everything lined up against you. What you gonna do. I fooled them, Rose. I bunted. When I found you and Cory and a halfway decent job . . . I was safe. Couldn't nothing touch me. I wasn't gonna strike out no more. I wasn't going back to the penitentiary. I wasn't gonna lay in the streets with a bottle of wine. I was safe. I had me a family. A job. I wasn't gonna get that last strike. I was on first looking for one of them boys to knock me in. To get me home.

Rose: You should have stayed in my bed, Troy.

Troy: Then when I saw that gal . . . she firmed up my backbone. And I got to thinking that if I tried . . . I just might be able to steal second. Do you understand after eighteen years I wanted to steal second.

Rose: You should have held me tight. You should have grabbed me and held on.

Troy: I stood on first base for eighteen years and I thought . . . well, goddamn it . . . go on for it!

Rose: We're not talking about baseball! We're talking about you going off to lay in bed with another woman . . . and then bring it home to me. That's what we're talking about. We ain't talking about no baseball.

Troy: Rose, you're not listening to me. I'm trying the best I can to explain it to you. It's not easy for me to admit that I been standing in the same place for eighteen years.

Rose: I been standing with you! I been right here with you, Troy. I got a life too. I gave eighteen years of my life to stand in the same spot with you. Don't you think I ever wanted other things? Don't you think I had dreams and hopes? What about my life? What about me. Don't you think it ever crossed my mind to want to know other men? That I wanted to lay up somewhere and forget about my responsibilities? That I wanted someone to make me laugh so I could feel good? You not the only one who's got wants and needs. But I held on to you, Troy. I took all my feelings, my wants and needs, my dreams . . . and I buried them inside you. I planted a seed and watched and prayed over it. I planted myself inside you and waited to bloom. And it didn't take me no eighteen years to find out the soil was hard and rocky and it wasn't never gonna bloom.

But I held on to you, Troy. I held you tighter. You was my husband. I owed you everything I had. Every part of me I could find to give you. And upstairs in that room . . . with the darkness falling in on me . . . I gave everything I had to try and erase the doubt that you wasn't the finest man in the world. And wherever you was going . . . I wanted to be there with you. Cause you was my husband. Cause that's the only way I was gonna survive as your wife. You always talking about what you give . . . and what you don't have to give. But you take too. You take . . . and don't even know nobody's giving!

(*Rose turns to exit into the house; Troy grabs her arm.*)

Troy: You say I take and don't give!

Rose: Troy! You're hurting me!

Troy: You say I take and don't give.

Rose: Troy . . . you're hurting my arm! Let go!

Troy: I done give you everything I got. Don't you tell that lie on me.

Rose: Troy!

Troy: Don't you tell that lie on me!

(*Cory enters from the house.*)

Cory: Mama!

Rose: Troy. You're hurting me.

Troy: Don't you tell me about no taking and giving.

(*Cory comes up behind Troy and grabs him. Troy, surprised, is thrown off balance just as Cory throws a glancing blow that catches him on the chest and knocks him down. Troy is stunned, as is Cory.*)

Rose: Troy. Troy. No!

(*Troy gets to his feet and starts at Cory.*)

Troy . . . no. Please! Troy!

(*Rose pulls on Troy to hold him back. Troy stops himself.*)

Troy (to Cory): Alright. That's strike two. You stay away from around me, boy. Don't you strike out. You living with a full count. Don't you strike out.

(*Troy exits out the yard as the lights go down.*)

SCENE II

It is six months later, early afternoon. Troy enters from the house and starts to exit the yard. Rose enters from the house.

Rose: Troy, I want to talk to you.

Troy: All of a sudden, after all this time, you want to talk to me, huh? You ain't wanted to talk to me for months. You ain't wanted to talk to me last night. You ain't wanted no part of me then. What you wanna talk to me about now?

Rose: Tomorrow's Friday.

Troy: I know what day tomorrow is. You think I don't know tomorrow's Friday? My whole life I ain't done nothing but look to see Friday coming and you got to tell me it's Friday.

Rose: I want to know if you're coming home.

Troy: I always come home, Rose. You know that. There ain't never been a night I ain't come home.

Rose: That ain't what I mean . . . and you know it. I want to know if you're coming straight home after work.

Troy: I figure I'd cash my check . . . hang out at Taylors' with the boys . . . maybe play a game of checkers . . .

Rose: Troy, I can't live like this. I won't live like this. You livin' on borrowed time with me. It's been going on six months now you ain't been coming home.

Troy: I be here every night. Every night of the year. That's 365 days.

Rose: I want you to come home tomorrow after work.

Troy: Rose . . . I don't mess up my pay. You know that now. I take my pay and I give it to you. I don't have no money but what you give me back. I just want to have a little time to myself . . . a little time to enjoy life.

Rose: What about me? When's my time to enjoy life?

Troy: I don't know what to tell you, Rose. I'm doing the best I can.

Rose: You ain't been home from work but time enough to change your clothes and run out . . . and you wanna call that the best you can do?

Troy: I'm going over to the hospital to see Alberta. She went into the hospital this afternoon. Look like she might have the baby early. I won't be gone long.

Rose: Well, you ought to know. They went over to Miss Pearl's and got Gabe today. She said you told them to go ahead and lock him up.

Troy: I ain't said no such thing. Whoever told you that is telling a lie. Pearl ain't doing nothing but telling a big fat lie.

Rose: She ain't had to tell me. I read it on the papers.

Troy: I ain't told them nothing of the kind.

Rose: I saw it right there on the papers.

Troy: What it say, huh?

Rose: It said you told them to take him.

Troy: Then they screwed that up, just the way they screw up everything. I ain't worried about what they got on the paper.

Rose: Say the government send part of his check to the hospital and the other part to you.

Troy: I ain't got nothing to do with that if that's the way it works. I ain't made up the rules about how it work.

Rose: You did Gabe just like you did Cory. You wouldn't sign the paper for Cory . . . but you signed for Gabe. You signed that paper.

(The telephone is heard ringing inside the house.)

Troy: I told you I ain't signed nothing, woman! The only thing I signed was the release form. Hell, I can't read, I don't know what they had on that paper! I ain't signed nothing about sending Gabe away.

Rose: I said send him to the hospital . . . you said let him be free . . . now you done went down there and signed him to the hospital for half his money. You went back on yourself, Troy. You gonna have to answer for that.

Troy: See now . . . you been over there talking to Miss Pearl. She done got mad cause she ain't getting Gabe's rent money. That's all it is. She's liable to say anything.

Rose: Troy, I seen where you signed the paper.

Troy: You ain't seen nothing I signed. What she doing got papers on my brother anyway? Miss Pearl telling a big fat lie. And I'm gonna tell her about it too! You ain't seen nothing I signed. Say . . . you ain't seen nothing I signed.

(Rose exits into the house to answer the telephone. Presently she returns.)

Rose: Troy . . . that was the hospital. Alberta had the baby.

Troy: What she have? What is it?

Rose: It's a girl.

Troy: I better get on down to the hospital to see her.

Rose: Troy . . .

Troy: Rose . . . I got to go see her now. That's only right . . . what's the matter . . . the baby's alright, ain't it?

Rose: Alberta died having the baby.

Troy: Died . . . you say she's dead? Alberta's dead?

Rose: They said they done all they could. They couldn't do nothing for her.

Troy: The baby? How's the baby?

Rose: They say it's healthy. I wonder who's gonna bury her.

Troy: She had family, Rose. She wasn't living in the world by herself.

Rose: I know she wasn't living in the world by herself.

Troy: Next thing you gonna want to know if she had any insurance.

Rose: Troy, you ain't got to talk like that.

Troy: That's the first thing that jumped out your mouth. "Who's gonna bury her?" Like I'm fixing to take on that task for myself.

Rose: I am your wife. Don't push me away.

Troy: I ain't pushing nobody away. Just give me some space. That's all. Just give me some room to breathe.

(Rose exits into the house. Troy walks about the yard.)

Troy (with a quiet rage that threatens to consume him): Alright . . . Mr. Death. See now . . . I'm gonna tell you what I'm gonna do. I'm gonna take and build me a fence around this yard. See? I'm gonna build me a fence around what belongs to me. And then I want you to stay on the other side. See? You stay over there until you're ready for me. Then you come on. Bring your army. Bring your sickle. Bring your wrestling clothes. I ain't gonna fall down on my vigilance this time.

You ain't gonna sneak up on me no more. When you ready for me . . . when the top of your list say Troy Maxson . . . that's when you come around here. You come up and knock on the front door. Ain't nobody else got nothing to do with this. This is between you and me. Man to man. You stay on the other side of that fence until you ready for me. Then you come up and knock on the front door. Anytime you want. I'll be ready for you.

(*The lights go down to black.*)

SCENE III

The lights come up on the porch. It is late evening three days later. Rose sits listening to the ball game waiting for Troy. The final out of the game is made and Rose switches off the radio. Troy enters the yard carrying an infant wrapped in blankets. He stands back from the house and calls.

Rose enters and stands on the porch. There is a long, awkward silence, the weight of which grows heavier with each passing second.

Troy: Rose . . . I'm standing here with my daughter in my arms. She ain't but a wee bittie little old thing. She don't know nothing about grownups' business. She innocent . . . and she ain't got no mama.

Rose: What you telling me for, Troy?

(*She turns and exits into the house.*)

Troy: Well . . . I guess we'll just sit out here on the porch.

(*He sits down on the porch. There is an awkward indelicateness about the way he handles the baby. His largeness engulfs and seems to swallow it. He speaks loud enough for Rose to hear.*)

A man's got to do what's right for him. I ain't sorry for nothing I done. It felt right in my heart. (*To the baby.*) What you smiling at? Your daddy's a big man. Got these great big old hands. But sometimes he's scared. And right now your daddy's scared cause we sitting out here and ain't got no home. Oh, I been homeless before. I ain't had no little baby with me. But I been homeless. You just be out on the road by your lonesome and you see one of them trains coming and you just kinda go like this . . .

(*He sings as a lullaby.*)

　　Please, Mr. Engineer let a man ride the line
　　Please, Mr. Engineer let a man ride the line
　　I ain't got no ticket please let me ride the blinds

(*Rose enters from the house. Troy, hearing her steps behind him, stands and faces her.*)

She's my daughter, Rose. My own flesh and blood. I can't deny her no more than I can deny them boys. (*Pause.*) You and them boys is my family. You and them and this child is all I got in the world. So I guess what I'm saying is . . . I'd appreciate it if you'd help me take care of her.

Rose: Okay, Troy . . . you're right. I'll take care of your baby for you . . . cause . . . like you say . . . she's innocent . . . and you can't visit the sins of the father upon the child. A motherless child has got a hard time. (*She takes the baby from him.*) From right now . . . this child got a mother. But you a womanless man.

(*Rose turns and exits into the house with the baby. Lights go down to black.*)

SCENE IV

It is two months later. Lyons enters the street. He knocks on the door and calls.

Lyons: Hey, Rose! (*Pause.*) Rose!

Rose (*from inside the house*): Stop that yelling. You gonna wake up Raynell. I just got her to sleep.

Lyons: I just stopped by to pay Papa this twenty dollars I owe him. Where's Papa at?

Rose: He should be here in a minute. I'm getting ready to go down to the church. Sit down and wait on him.

Lyons: I got to go pick up Bonnie over her mother's house.

Rose: Well, sit it down there on the table. He'll get it.

Lyons (*enters the house and sets the money on the table*): Tell Papa I said thanks. I'll see you again.

Rose: Alright, Lyons. We'll see you.

(*Lyons starts to exit as Cory enters.*)

Cory: Hey, Lyons.

Lyons: What's happening, Cory? Say man, I'm sorry I missed your graduation. You know I had a gig and couldn't get away. Otherwise, I would have been there, man. So what you doing?

Cory: I'm trying to find a job.

Lyons: Yeah I know how that go, man. It's rough out here. Jobs are scarce.

Cory: Yeah, I know.

Lyons: Look here, I got to run. Talk to Papa . . . he know some people. He'll be able to help get you a job. Talk to him . . . see what he say.

Cory: Yeah . . . alright, Lyons.

Lyons: You take care. I'll talk to you soon. We'll find some time to talk.

(*Lyons exits the yard. Cory wanders over to the tree, picks up the bat, and assumes a batting stance. He studies an imaginary pitcher and swings. Dissatisfied with the result, he tries again. Troy enters. They eye each other for a beat. Cory puts the bat down and exits the yard. Troy starts into the house as Rose exits with Raynell. She is carrying a cake.*)

Troy: I'm coming in and everybody's going out.

Rose: I'm taking this cake down to the church for the bake sale. Lyons was by to see you. He stopped by to pay you your twenty dollars. It's laying in there on the table.

Troy (*going into his pocket*): Well . . . here go this money.

Rose: Put it in there on the table, Troy. I'll get it.

Troy: What time you coming back?

Rose: Ain't no use in you studying me. It don't matter what time I come back.

Troy: I just asked you a question, woman. What's the matter . . . can't I ask you a question?

Rose: Troy, I don't want to go into it. Your dinner's in there on the stove. All you got to do is heat it up. And don't you be eating the rest of them cakes in there. I'm coming back for them. We having a bake sale at the church tomorrow.

(*Rose exits the yard. Troy sits down on the steps, takes a pint bottle from his pocket, opens it and drinks. He begins to sing.*)

Troy:

Hear it ring! Hear it ring!
Had an old dog his name was Blue
You know Blue was mighty true
You know Blue was a good old dog
Blue trees a possum in a hollow log
You know from that he was a good old dog

(*Bono enters the yard.*)

Bono: Hey, Troy.

Troy: Hey, what's happening, Bono?

Bono: I just thought I'd stop by to see you.

Troy: What you stop by and see me for? You ain't stopped by in a month of Sundays. Hell, I must owe you money or something.

Bono: Since you got your promotion I can't keep up with you. Used to see you every day. Now I don't even know what route you working.

Troy: They keep switching me around. Got me out in Greentree now . . . hauling white folks' garbage.

Bono: Greentree, huh? You lucky, at least you ain't got to be lifting them barrels. Damn if they ain't getting heavier. I'm gonna put in my two years and call it quits.

Troy: I'm thinking about retiring myself.

Bono: You got it easy. You can *drive* for another five years.

Troy: It ain't the same, Bono. It ain't like working the back of the truck. Ain't got nobody to talk to . . . feel like you working by yourself. Naw, I'm thinking about retiring. How's Lucille?

Bono: She alright. Her arthritis get to acting up on her sometime. Saw Rose on my way in. She going down to the church, huh?

Troy: Yeah, she took up going down there. All them preachers looking for somebody to fatten their pockets. (*Pause.*) Got some gin here.

Bono: Naw, thanks. I just stopped by to say hello.

Troy: Hell, nigger . . . you can take a drink. I ain't never known you to say no to a drink. You ain't got to work tomorrow.

Bono: I just stopped by. I'm fixing to go over to Skinner's. We got us a domino game going over his house every Friday.

Troy: Nigger, you can't play no dominoes. I used to whup you four games out of five.

Bono: Well, that learned me. I'm getting better.

Troy: Yeah? Well, that's alright.

Bono: Look here . . . I got to be getting on. Stop by sometime, huh?

Troy: Yeah, I'll do that, Bono. Lucille told Rose you bought her a new refrigerator.

Bono: Yeah, Rose told Lucille you had finally built your fence . . . so I figured we'd call it even.

Troy: I knew you would.

Bono: Yeah . . . okay. I'll be talking to you.

Troy: Yeah, take care, Bono. Good to see you. I'm gonna stop over.

Bono: Yeah. Okay, Troy.

(Bono exits. Troy drinks from the bottle.)

Troy:

> Old Blue died and I dug his grave
> Let him down with a golden chain
> Every night when I hear old Blue bark
> I know Blue treed a possum in Noah's Ark.
> Hear it ring! Hear it ring!

(Cory enters the yard. They eye each other for a beat. Troy is sitting in the middle of the steps. Cory walks over.)

Cory: I got to get by.

Troy: Say what? What's you say?

Cory: You in my way. I got to get by.

Troy: You got to get by where? This is my house. Bought and paid for. In full. Took me fifteen years. And if you wanna go in my house and I'm sitting on the steps . . . you say excuse me. Like your mama taught you.

Cory: Come on, Pop . . . I got to get by.

(Cory starts to maneuver his way past Troy. Troy grabs his leg and shoves him back.)

Troy: You just gonna walk over top of me?

Cory: I live here too!

Troy (advancing toward him): You just gonna walk over top of me in my own house?

Cory: I ain't scared of you.

Troy: I ain't asked if you was scared of me. I asked you if you was fixing to walk over top of me in my own house? That's the question. You ain't gonna say excuse me? You just gonna walk over top of me?

Cory: If you wanna put it like that.

Troy: How else am I gonna put it?

Cory: I was walking by you to go into the house cause you sitting on the steps drunk, singing to yourself. You can put it like that.

Troy: Without saying excuse me???

(Cory doesn't respond.)

I asked you a question. Without saying excuse me???

Cory: I ain't got to say excuse me to you. You don't count around here no more.

Troy: Oh, I see . . . I don't count around here no more. You ain't got to say excuse me to your daddy. All of a sudden you done got so grown that your daddy don't count around here no more . . . Around here in his own house and yard that he done paid for with the sweat of his brow. You done got so grown to where you gonna take over. You gonna take over my house. Is that right? You gonna wear my pants. You gonna go in there and stretch out on my bed. You ain't got to say excuse me cause I don't count around here no more. Is that right?

Cory: That's right. You always talking this dumb stuff. Now, why don't you just get out my way?

Troy: I guess you got someplace to sleep and something to put in your belly. You got that, huh? You got that? That's what you need. You got that, huh?

Cory: You don't know what I got. You ain't got to worry about what I got.

Troy: You right! You one hundred percent right! I done spent the last seventeen years worrying about what you got. Now it's your turn, see? I'll tell you what to do. You grown . . . we done established that. You a man. Now, let's see you act like one. Turn your behind around and walk out this yard. And when you get out there in the alley . . . you can forget about this house. See? Cause this is my house. You go on and be a man and get your own house. You can forget about this. Cause this is mine. You go on and get yours cause I'm through with doing for you.

Cory: You talking about what you did for me . . . what'd you ever give me?

Troy: Them feet and bones! That pumping heart, nigger! I give you more than anybody else is ever gonna give you.

Cory: You ain't never gave me nothing! You ain't never done nothing but hold me back. Afraid I was gonna be better than you. All you ever did was try and make me scared of you. I used to tremble every time you called my name. Every time I heard your footsteps in the house. Wondering all the time . . . what's Papa gonna say if I do this? . . . What's he gonna say if I do that? . . . What's Papa gonna say if I turn on the radio? And Mama, too . . . she tries . . . but she's scared of you.

Troy: You leave your mama out of this. She ain't got nothing to do with this.

Cory: I don't know how she stand you . . . after what you did to her.

Troy: I told you to leave your mama out of this!

(He advances toward Cory.)

Cory: What you gonna do . . . give me a whupping? You can't whup me no more. You're too old. You just an old man.

Troy (shoves him on his shoulder): Nigger! That's what you are. You just another nigger on the street to me!

Cory: You crazy! You know that?

Troy: Go on now! You got the devil in you. Get on away from me!

Cory: You just a crazy old man . . . talking about I got the devil in me.

Troy: Yeah, I'm crazy! If you don't get on the other side of that yard . . . I'm gonna show you how crazy I am! Go on . . . get the hell out of my yard.

Cory: It ain't your yard. You took Uncle Gabe's money he got from the army to buy this house and then you put him out.

Troy (advances on Cory): Get your black ass out of my yard!

(Troy's advance backs Cory up against the tree. Cory grabs up the bat.)

Cory: I ain't going nowhere! Come on . . . put me out! I ain't scared of you.

Troy: That's my bat!

Cory: Come on!

Troy: Put my bat down!

Cory: Come on, put me out.

(Cory swings at Troy, who backs across the yard.)

What's the matter? You so bad . . . put me out!

(*Troy advances toward Cory.*)

Cory (*backing up*): Come on! Come on!

Troy: You're gonna have to use it! You wanna draw that bat back on me . . . you're gonna have to use it.

Cory: Come on! . . . Come on!

(*Cory swings the bat at Troy a second time. He misses. Troy continues to advance toward him.*)

Troy: You're gonna have to kill me! You wanna draw that bat back on me. You're gonna have to kill me.

(*Cory, backed up against the tree, can go no farther. Troy taunts him. He sticks out his head and offers him a target.*)

Come on! Come on!

(*Cory is unable to swing the bat. Troy grabs it.*)

Troy: Then I'll show you.

(*Cory and Troy struggle over the bat. The struggle is fierce and fully engaged. Troy ultimately is the stronger, and takes the bat from Cory and stands over him ready to swing. He stops himself.*)

Go on and get away from around my house.

(*Cory, stung by his defeat, picks himself up, walks slowly out of the yard and up the alley.*)

Cory: Tell Mama I'll be back for my things.

Troy: They'll be on the other side of that fence.

(*Cory exits.*)

Troy: I can't taste nothing. Helluljah! I can't taste nothing no more. (*Troy assumes a batting posture and begins to taunt Death, the fastball on the outside corner.*) Come on! It's between you and me now! Come on! Anytime you want! Come on! I be ready for you . . . but I ain't gonna be easy.

(*The lights go down on the scene.*)

SCENE V

The time is 1965. The lights come up in the yard. It is the morning of Troy's funeral. A funeral plaque with a light hangs beside the door. There is a small garden plot off to the side. There is noise and activity in the house as Rose, Lyons, and Bono have gathered. The door opens and Raynell, seven years old, enters dressed in a flannel nightgown. She crosses to the garden and pokes around with a stick. Rose calls from the house.

Rose: Raynell!

Raynell: Mam?

Rose: What you doing out there?

Raynell: Nothing.

(*Rose comes to the door.*)

Rose: Girl, get in here and get dressed. What you doing?

Raynell: Seeing if my garden growed.

Rose: I told you it ain't gonna grow overnight. You got to wait.

Raynell: It don't look like it never gonna grow. Dag!

Rose: I told you a watched pot never boils. Get in here and get dressed.

Raynell: This ain't even no pot, Mama.

Rose: You just have to give it a chance. It'll grow. Now you come on and do what I told you. We got to be getting ready. This ain't no morning to be playing around. You hear me?

Raynell: Yes, Mam.

(*Rose exits into the house. Raynell continues to poke at her garden with a stick. Cory enters. He is dressed in a Marine corporal's uniform, and carries a duffelbag. His posture is that of a military man, and his speech has a clipped sternness.*)

Cory (*to Raynell*): Hi. (*Pause.*) I bet your name is Raynell.

Raynell: Uh huh.

Cory: Is your mama home?

(*Raynell runs up on the porch and calls through the screen door.*)

Raynell: Mama . . . there's some man out here. Mama?

(*Rose comes to the door.*)

Rose: Cory? Lord have mercy! Look here, you all!

(*Rose and Cory embrace in a tearful reunion as Bono and Lyons enter from the house dressed in funeral clothes.*)

Bono: Aw, looka here . . .

Rose: Done got all grown up!

Cory: Don't cry, Mama. What you crying about?

Rose: I'm just so glad you made it.

Cory: Hey Lyons. How you doing, Mr. Bono.

(*Lyons goes to embrace Cory.*)

Lyons: Look at you, man. Look at you. Don't he look good, Rose. Got them Corporal stripes.

Rose: What took you so long?

Cory: You know how the Marines are, Mama. They got to get all their paperwork straight before they let you do anything.

Rose: Well, I'm sure glad you made it. They let Lyons come. Your Uncle Gabe's still in the hospital. They don't know if they gonna let him out or not. I just talked to them a little while ago.

Lyons: A Corporal in the United States Marines.

Bono: Your daddy knew you had it in you. He used to tell me all the time.

Lyons: Don't he look good, Mr. Bono?

Bono: Yeah, he remind me of Troy when I first met him. (*Pause.*) Say, Rose, Lucille's down at the church with the choir. I'm gonna go down and get the pallbearers lined up. I'll be back to get you all.

Rose: Thanks, Jim.

Cory: See you, Mr. Bono.

Lyons (*with his arm around Raynell*): Cory . . . look at Raynell. Ain't she precious? She gonna break a whole lot of hearts.

Rose: Raynell, come and say hello to your brother. This is your brother, Cory. You remember Cory.

Raynell: No, Mam.

Cory: She don't remember me, Mama.

Rose: Well, we talk about you. She heard us talk about you. (*To Raynell.*) This is your brother, Cory. Come on and say hello.

Raynell: Hi.

Cory: Hi. So you're Raynell. Mama told me a lot about you.

Rose: You all come on into the house and let me fix you some breakfast. Keep up your strength.

Cory: I ain't hungry, Mama.

Lyons: You can fix me something, Rose. I'll be in there in a minute.

Rose: Cory, you sure you don't want nothing? I know they ain't feeding you right.

Cory: No, Mama . . . thanks. I don't feel like eating. I'll get something later.

Rose: Raynell . . . get on upstairs and get that dress on like I told you.

(*Rose and Raynell exit into the house.*)

Lyons: So . . . I hear you thinking about getting married.

Cory: Yeah, I done found the right one, Lyons. It's about time.

Lyons: Me and Bonnie been split up about four years now. About the time Papa retired. I guess she just got tired of all them changes I was putting her through. (*Pause.*) I always knew you was gonna make something out yourself. Your head was always in the right direction. So . . . you gonna stay in . . . make it a career . . . put in your twenty years?

Cory: I don't know. I got six already, I think that's enough.

Lyons: Stick with Uncle Sam and retire early. Ain't nothing out here. I guess Rose told you what happened with me. They got me down the workhouse. I thought I was being slick cashing other people's checks.

Cory: How much time you doing?

Lyons: They give me three years. I got that beat now. I ain't got but nine more months. It ain't so bad. You learn to deal with it like anything else. You got to take the crookeds with the straights. That's what Papa used to say. He used to say that when he struck out. I seen him strike out three times in a row . . . and the next time up he hit the ball over the grandstand. Right out there in Homestead Field. He wasn't satisfied hitting in the seats . . . he want to hit it over everything! After the game he had two hundred people standing around waiting to shake his hand. You got to take the crookeds with the straights. Yeah, Papa was something else.

Cory: You still playing?

Lyons: Cory . . . you know I'm gonna do that. There's some fellows down there we got us a band . . . we gonna try and stay together when we get out . . . but yeah, I'm still playing. It still helps me to get out of bed in the morning. As long as it do that I'm gonna be right there playing and trying to make some sense out of it.

Rose (*calling*): Lyons, I got these eggs in the pan.

Lyons: Let me go on and get these eggs, man. Get ready to go bury Papa. (*Pause.*) How you doing? You doing alright?

(Cory nods. Lyons touches him on the shoulder and they share a moment of silent grief. Lyons exits into the house. Cory wanders about the yard. Raynell enters.)

Raynell: Hi.

Cory: Hi.

Raynell: Did you used to sleep in my room?

Cory: Yeah . . . that used to be my room.

Raynell: That's what Papa call it. "Cory's room." It got your football in the closet.

(Rose comes to the door.)

Rose: Raynell, get in there and get them good shoes on.

Raynell: Mama, can't I wear these? Them other one hurt my feet.

Rose: Well, they just gonna have to hurt your feet for a while. You ain't said they hurt your feet when you went down to the store and got them.

Raynell: They didn't hurt then. My feet done got bigger.

Rose: Don't you give me no backtalk now. You get in there and get them shoes on.

(Raynell exits into the house.)

Ain't too much changed. He still got that piece of rag tied to that tree. He was out here swinging that bat. I was just ready to go back in the house. He swung that bat and then he just fell over. Seem like he swung it and stood there with this grin on his face . . . and then he just fell over. They carried him on down to the hospital, but I knew there wasn't no need . . . why don't you come on in the house?

Cory: Mama . . . I got something to tell you. I don't know how to tell you this . . . but I've got to tell you . . . I'm not going to Papa's funeral.

Rose: Boy, hush your mouth. That's your daddy you talking about. I don't want hear that kind of talk this morning. I done raised you to come to this? You standing there all healthy and grown talking about you ain't going to your daddy's funeral?

Cory: Mama . . . listen . . .

Rose: I don't want to hear it, Cory. You just get that thought out of your head.

Cory: I can't drag Papa with me everywhere I go. I've got to say no to him. One time in my life I've got to say no.

Rose: Don't nobody have to listen to nothing like that. I know you and your daddy ain't seen eye to eye, but I ain't got to listen to that kind of talk this morning. Whatever was between you and your daddy . . . the time has come to put it aside. Just take it and set it over there on the shelf and forget about it. Disrespecting your daddy ain't gonna make you a man, Cory. You got to find a way to come to that on your own. Not going to your daddy's funeral ain't gonna make you a man.

Cory: The whole time I was growing up . . . living in his house . . . Papa was like a shadow that followed you everywhere. It weighed on you and sunk into your flesh. It would wrap around you and lay there until you couldn't tell which one was you anymore. That shadow digging in your flesh. Trying to crawl in. Trying to live through you. Everywhere I looked, Troy Maxson was staring back at me . . . hiding under the bed . . . in the closet. I'm just saying I've got to find a way to get rid of that shadow, Mama.

Rose: You just like him. You got him in you good.

Cory: Don't tell me that, Mama.

Rose: You Troy Maxson all over again.

Cory: I don't want to be Troy Maxson. I want to be me.

Rose: You can't be nobody but who you are, Cory. That shadow wasn't nothing but you growing into yourself. You either got to grow into it or cut it down to fit you. But that's all you got to make life with. That's all you got to measure yourself against that world out there. Your daddy wanted you to be everything he wasn't . . . and at the same time he tried to make you into everything he was. I don't know if he was right or wrong . . . but I do know he meant to do more good than he meant to do harm. He wasn't always right. Sometimes when he touched he bruised. And sometimes when he took me in his arms he cut.

When I first met your daddy I thought . . . Here is a man I can lay down with and make a baby. That's the first thing I thought when I seen him. I was thirty years old and had done seen my share of men. But when he walked up to me and said, "I can dance a waltz that'll make you dizzy," I thought, Rose Lee, here is a man that you can open yourself up to and be filled to bursting. Here is a man that can fill all them empty spaces you been tipping around the edges of. One of them empty spaces was being somebody's mother.

I married your daddy and settled down to cooking his supper and keeping clean sheets on the bed. When your daddy walked through the house he was so big he filled it up. That was my first mistake. Not to make him leave some room for me. For my part in the matter. But at that time I wanted that. I wanted a house that I could sing in. And that's what your daddy gave me. I didn't know to keep up his strength I had to give up little pieces of mine. I did that. I took on his life as mine and mixed up the pieces so that you couldn't hardly tell which was which anymore. It was my choice. It was my life and I didn't have to live it like that. But that's what life offered me in the way of being a woman and I took it. I grabbed hold of it with both hands.

By the time Raynell came into the house, me and your daddy had done lost touch with one another. I didn't want to make my blessing off of nobody's misfortune . . . but I took on to Raynell like she was all them babies I had wanted and never had.

(The phone rings.)

Like I'd been blessed to relive a part of my life. And if the Lord see fit to keep up my strength . . . I'm gonna do her just like your daddy did you . . . I'm gonna give her the best of what's in me.

Raynell (entering, still with her old shoes): Mama . . . Reverend Tolliver on the phone.

(Rose exits into the house.)

Raynell: Hi.

Cory: Hi.

Raynell: You in the Army or the Marines?

Cory: Marines.

Raynell: Papa said it was the Army. Did you know Blue?

Cory: Blue? Who's Blue?

Raynell: Papa's dog what he sing about all the time.

Cory (singing):

> Hear it ring! Hear it ring!
> I had a dog his name was Blue

> You know Blue was mighty true
> You know Blue was a good old dog
> Blue treed a possum in a hollow log
> You know from that he was a good old dog.
> Hear it ring! Hear it ring!

(Raynell joins in singing.)

Cory and Raynell:

> Blue treed a possum out on a limb
> Blue looked at me and I looked at him
> Grabbed that possum and put him in a sack
> Blue stayed there till I came back
> Old Blue's feets was big and round
> Never allowed a possum to touch the ground.
>
> Old Blue died and I dug his grave
> I dug his grave with a silver spade
> Let him down with a golden chain
> And every night I call his name
> Go on Blue, you good dog you
> Go on Blue, you good dog you.

Raynell:

> Blue laid down and died like a man
> Blue laid down and died . . .

Both:

> Blue laid down and died like a man
> Now he's treeing possums in the Promised Land
> I'm gonna tell you this to let you know
> Blue's gone where the good dogs go
> When I hear old Blue bark
> When I hear old Blue bark
> Blue treed a possum in Noah's Ark
> Blue treed a possum in Noah's Ark.

(Rose comes to the screen door.)

Rose: Cory, we gonna be ready to go in a minute.

Cory (to Raynell): You go on in the house and change them shoes like Mama told you so we can go to Papa's funeral.

Raynell: Okay, I'll be back.

(Raynell exits into the house. Cory gets up and crosses over to the tree. Rose stands in the screen door watching him. Gabriel enters from the alley.)

Gabriel (calling): Hey, Rose!

Rose: Gabe?

Gabriel: I'm here, Rose. Hey, Rose, I'm here!

(Rose enters from the house.)

Rose: Lord . . . Look here, Lyons!

Lyons: See, I told you, Rose . . . I told you they'd let him come.

Cory: How you doing, Uncle Gabe?

Lyons: How you doing, Uncle Gabe?

Gabriel: Hey, Rose. It's time. It's time to tell St. Peter to open the gates. Troy, you ready? You ready, Troy. I'm gonna tell St. Peter to open the gates. You get ready now.

(Gabriel, with great fanfare, braces himself to blow. The trumpet is without a mouthpiece. He puts the end of it into his mouth and blows with great force, like a man who has been waiting some twenty-odd years for this single moment. No sound comes out of the trumpet. He braces himself and blows again with the same result. A third time he blows. There is a weight of impossible description that falls away and leaves him bare and exposed to a frightful realization. It is a trauma that a sane and normal mind would be unable to withstand. He begins to dance. A slow, strange dance, eerie and life-giving. A dance of atavistic signature and ritual. Lyons attempts to embrace him. Gabriel pushes Lyons away. He begins to howl in what is an attempt at song, or perhaps a song turning back into itself in an attempt at speech. He finishes his dance and the gates of heaven stand open as wide as God's closet.)

That's the way that go!

BLACKOUT

August Wilson on Writing

A Look into Black America

1999

Interviewer: Is it a concern to effect social change with your plays?

Wilson: I don't write primarily to effect social change. I believe writing can do that, but that's not why I write. I work as an artist. However, all art is political in the sense that it serves the politics of someone. Here in America whites have a particular view of blacks, and I think my plays offer them a different and new way to look at black Americans. For instance, in *Fences* they see a garbageman, a person they really don't look at, although they may see a garbageman every day. By looking at Troy's

August Wilson

life, white people find out that the content of this black garbageman's life is very similar to their own, that he is affected by the same things—love, honor, beauty, betrayal, duty. Recognizing that these things are as much a part of his life as of theirs can be revolutionary and can affect how they think about and deal with black people in their lives.

Interviewer: How would that same play, *Fences*, affect a black audience?

Wilson: Blacks see the content of their lives being elevated into art. They don't always know that it is possible, and it's important to know that.

From "Interview with August Wilson"
by Bonnie Lyons and George Plimpton

INDEX OF MAJOR THEMES

If you prefer to study by theme or want to research possible subjects for an essay, here is a listing of plays arranged into fifteen major themes.

INDEX OF AUTHORS AND TITLES

Every page number immediately following a writer's name indicates a quotation from or reference to that writer. A number in **bold** refers you to the page on which you will find the author's biography.